Portugal

John King
Julia Wilkinson

B-343 © 1988 Sudi McCollum

FROM THE
LIBRARY OF

George Washington

LONELY PLANET PUBLICATIONS
Melbourne • Oakland • London • Paris

PORTUGAL

PARQUE NACIONAL DA PENEDA-GERÊS
Portugal's first and most popular protected area, with a kaleidoscope of outdoor activities and rural accommodation

VILA NOVA DE FOZ CÔA
The world's largest outdoor gallery of Stone Age art

PARQUE NATURAL DA SERRA DA ESTRELA
Rough and ready landscape of traditional settlements, high peaks, excellent walks and winter snow

BRAGA
Portugal's religious capital, with 35 churches, a fine cathedral, and the extraordinary stairs of Bom Jesus do Monte

PORTO
The country's hard-working second city, with a Unesco-listed old town centre, and the old port lodges of Vila Nova de Gaia

COIMBRA
'Portugal's Oxford', with an ancient university, fado-singing students and the country's finest Roman ruins nearby

BATALHA & ALCOBAÇA
Superb architectural masterpieces in Gothic and Manueline styles

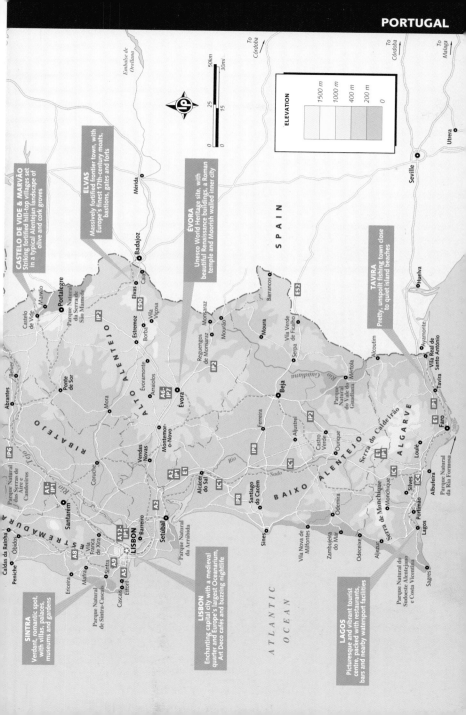

PORTUGAL

ELEVATION

	1500 m
	1000 m
	400 m
	200 m
	0

To Córdoba
To Córdoba
To Málaga

CASTELO DE VIDE & MARVÃO
Striking fortified hill-top villages set in a typical Alentejan landscape of olive and cork groves

ELVAS
Massively fortified frontier town, with Europe's finest 17th-century moats, bastions, gates and forts

ÉVORA
Unesco World Heritage site, with beautiful Renaissance buildings, a Roman temple and Moorish walled inner city

TAVIRA
Pretty, unspoilt fishing town close to quiet island beaches

SINTRA
Verdant, romantic spot, with villas, palaces, museums and gardens

LISBON
Enchanting capital city with a medieval quarter and Europe's largest Oceanarium, Art Deco cafés and buzzing nightlife

LAGOS
Picturesque and vibrant tourist centre, packed with restaurants, bars and nearby watersport facilities

SPAIN

ALTO ALENTEJO

BAIXO ALENTEJO

RIBATEJO

ESTREMADURA

ALGARVE

Serra do Caldeirão

ATLANTIC OCEAN

Embalse de Orellana

Mérida
Badajoz
Caia
Elvas
Vila Viçosa
Borba
Estremoz
Marvão
Portalegre
Castelo de Vide
Belver
Abrantes
Ponte de Sor
Mora
Arraiolos
Évoramonte
Évora
Reguengos de Monsaraz
Monsaraz
Mourão
Moura
Vila Verde de Ficalho
Serpa
Beja
Ferreira
Aljustrel
Mértola
Alcoutim
Vila Real de Santo António
Tavira
Faro
Loulé
Albufeira
Silves
Portimão
Lagos
Sagres
Monchique
Serra de Monchique
Aljezur
Odeceixe
Odemira
Zambujeira do Mar
Vila Nova de Milfontes
Sines
Santiago do Cacém
Alcácer do Sal
Setúbal
Barreiro
Vendas Novas
Montemor-o-Novo
Coruche
Santarém
Vila Franca de Xira
LISBON
Cascais
Estoril
Sintra
Mafra
Ericeira
Peniche
Óbidos
Caldas da Rainha
Castro Verde
Ourique
Alentejo

Parque Natural da Serra de São Mamede
Parque Natural das Serras de Aire e Candeeiros
Parque Natural de Sintra-Cascais
Parque Natural da Arrábida
Parque Natural do Vale do Guadiana
Parque Natural da Ria Formosa
Parque Natural do Sudoeste Alentejano e Costa Vicentina

Rio Tejo
Rio Sado
Rio Guadiana

Seville
Huelva
Ayamonte
Utrera

To Córdoba

50km
30mi

Lonely Planet

Portugal
4th edition – March 2003
First published – May 1997

Published by
Lonely Planet Publications Pty Ltd ABN 36 005 607 983
90 Maribyrnong St, Footscray, Victoria 3011, Australia

Lonely Planet Offices
Australia Locked Bag 1, Footscray, Victoria 3011
USA 150 Linden St, Oakland, CA 94607
UK 10a Spring Place, London NW5 3BH
France 1 rue du Dahomey, 75011 Paris

Photographs
Many of the images in this guide are available for licensing from
Lonely Planet Images.
w www.lonelyplanetimages.com

Front cover photograph
People sunbaking on the beach in the small seaside town of Carvoeiro,
the Algarve (Gerry Reilly, Lonely Planet Images)

ISBN 1 74059 339 1

text & maps © Lonely Planet Publications Pty Ltd 2003
photos © photographers as indicated 2003

Printed by The Bookmaker International Ltd
Printed in China

Contents – Text

Contents – Maps

MAPS

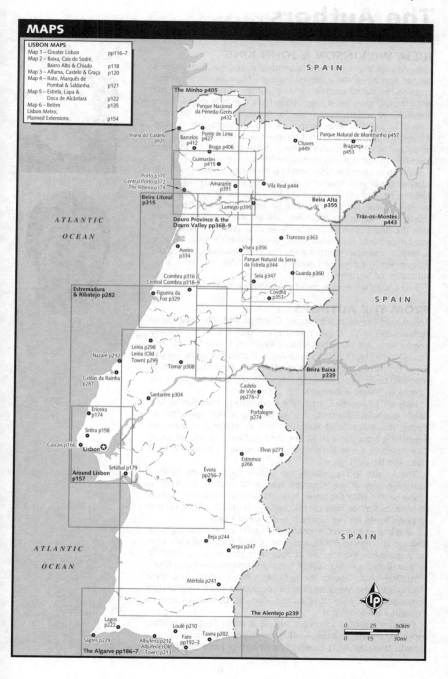

The Authors

JULIA WILKINSON & JOHN KING

Julia Wilkinson got her first taste of port and *bacalhau* over a decade ago when she explored Portugal from the mountainous north to the balmy south on a long journey of discovery for her first Portugal guidebook. She's been back regularly ever since to research and update this Lonely Planet guide as well as past editions of LP's *Lisbon, Western Europe* and *Mediterranean Europe*. A freelance journalist and photographer all her life, she's also now co-author of LP's *Southwest France*. When she's not on the road she takes to the skies, flying hot-air balloons.

John grew up in the USA, and in earlier 'incarnations' has been a university physics teacher and an environmental consultant. In 1984 he headed off for a look at China and ended up living there for half a year. During that time he and Julia crossed paths in Lhasa, the Tibetan capital. John took up travel writing in 1988 with the first edition of Lonely Planet's *Karakoram Highway*; he also co-authored early editions of Lonely Planet's *Russia, Ukraine & Belarus; Pakistan; Central Asia; Czech & Slovak Republics* and *Prague*. He is author of Lonely Planet's *Wales*, and co-author, with Julia, of *Southwest France*.

Julia and John live with their two children in southwest England.

FROM THE AUTHORS

Julia would like to thank Miguel Gonzaga and Vitor Carriço of Turismo de Lisboa. Other tourist office staff who were notably helpful were Assis Coelho (Algarve Regional Tourist Board); Ana Seixas Palma (Beja); Abílio Sousa Viegas (Faro); Felicidade Tavares (Marvão; thanks for the great tomato soup, Felicidade!); Marília Afonso (Leiria); Paula Maria Valadas (Mafra); and Luisa Maria da Conceição Neves (Estremoz).

Hats off to Fenella Grey of the Cork Information Bureau and sleuth-journalist Eduardo Goncalves for help on Portugal's cork industry. Rui Borralho of Naturlink was as efficient as ever, on everything from dams to lynxes. And António Serzedo of Opus Gay deserves a special *obrigada* for directing us to all the right clubs and bars in Lisbon.

Thanks also to Nicolette & Jon Gomes for luring me to their Salir hideaway in the Algarve's wonderful back of beyond; to Christine and Max for beers, tips and companionship in Castelo de Vide; to Senhor Teles for his generous hospitality in Évora; and to Dona Benta for her motherly welcome in Lagos.

John thanks Marco Oliveira for his fresh look at Porto nightlife and for answers to 1000 questions. Other tourist officials who have gone beyond the call of duty over the years are Anabela Pereira (Bragança), Maria-José Ferreira (Lamego) and Paula Monteiro (Trancoso). Thanks also to Susan Vieira (Aveiro), José Serra (Manteigas) and Maria do Rosário Graça (Vila Real). Helpful staff too modest to give their names were at Guimarães and at Coimbra's hill-top office.

I'm also indebted to several people in other Portugal offices, especially Dr Suzana Marques (Parque Natural do Douro Internacional), Dona Arminda Guedes (Caminhos de Ferro Portugueses in Porto) and Isabel Dantas (Adere-PG). Thanks to Robert Moura (Parque Natural do Alvão) for text review and medical compassion, and to Sofia Oliveira (Parque Natural da Serra da Estrela, Manteigas) and Parque Nacional da Peneda-Gerês researcher Gisela Moço.

Our appreciation goes to Dr António Martinho Baptista, director of the Centro Nacional de Arte Rupestre, and to Jorge Rosas and Ana Filipa Correia at the Ramos Pinto port-wine lodge, who kindly gave permission to use proprietary images.

Two friends in the UK who have always given cheerful assistance are Paul Gowen at the RAC and Charles Page of Rail Europe.

LP editor-sage Tim Ryder was sweating on this project before we even hit the road. Cheers also to London LP staffers Imogen Franks for updating the Lisbon entertainment section, and Tom Hall for ready help on the subject of European football. LP author John Noble passed along much Spain information as usual.

This Book

Julia Wilkinson and John King researched and wrote the previous three editions of *Portugal*. For this fourth edition Julia worked on the southern and central Portugal chapters and John covered the mountains and the north. Imogen Franks wrote the Lisbon Entertainment section.

FROM THE PUBLISHER

This edition of *Portugal* 4 was produced in Lonely Planet's Melbourne office. Editing was coordinated by Kyla Gillzan with assistance from Hilary Ericksen, Elizabeth Swan and Jane Thompson. Mapping was coordinated by Valentina Kremenchutskaya with assistance from Helen Rowley, Tessa Rottiers, Jarrod Needham, Jacqueline Nguyen, Laurie Mikkelsen, Mark Griffiths and Ed Pickard. Layout design and the compilation of the colour sections were undertaken by Vicki Beale. Csanád Csutoros prepared the climate charts, Quentin Frayne compiled the Language chapter and Annika Roojun designed the cover. Illustrations were created by Nicky Caven and Martin Harris. Heather Dickson was the commissioning editor and oversaw development of the title in conjunction with series publishing manager Maria Donohoe. The whole production process was run smoothly by project manager Celia Wood.

Acknowledgements

The photograph used in the boxed text 'Rock art in the Vale do Côa' was used courtesy of Dr António Martinho Baptista.

The colour pictures of the stained-glass window and the Ramos Pinto poster were used with kind permission from Jorge Rosas and Ana Filipa Correia at the Ramos Pinto port-wine lodge.

THANKS
Many thanks to the travellers who used the last edition and wrote to us with helpful hints, advice and interesting anecdotes. Your names appear in the back of this book.

Foreword

ABOUT LONELY PLANET GUIDEBOOKS

The story begins with a classic travel adventure: Tony and Maureen Wheeler's 1972 journey across Europe and Asia to Australia. There was no useful information about the overland trail then, so Tony and Maureen published the first Lonely Planet guidebook to meet a growing need.

From a kitchen table, Lonely Planet has grown to become the largest independent travel publisher in the world, with offices in Melbourne (Australia), Oakland (USA), London (UK) and Paris (France).

Today Lonely Planet guidebooks cover the globe. There is an ever-growing list of books and information in a variety of media. Some things haven't changed. The main aim is still to make it possible for adventurous travellers to get out there – to explore and better understand the world.

At Lonely Planet we believe travellers can make a positive contribution to the countries they visit – if they respect their host communities and spend their money wisely. Since 1986 a percentage of the income from each book has been donated to aid projects and human rights campaigns, and, more recently, to wildlife conservation.

> Although inclusion in a guidebook usually implies a recommendation we cannot list every good place. Exclusion does not necessarily imply criticism. In fact there are a number of reasons why we might exclude a place – sometimes it is simply inappropriate to encourage an influx of travellers.

UPDATES & READER FEEDBACK

Things change – prices go up, schedules change, good places go bad and bad places go bankrupt. Nothing stays the same. So, if you find things better or worse, recently opened or long-since closed, please tell us and help make the next edition even more accurate and useful.

Lonely Planet thoroughly updates each guidebook as often as possible – usually every two years, although for some destinations the gap can be longer. Between editions, up-to-date information is available in our free, monthly email bulletin *Comet* (**w** www.lonelyplanet.com/newsletters). You can also check out the *Thorn Tree* bulletin board and *Postcards* section of our website, which carry unverified, but fascinating, reports from travellers.

Tell us about it! We genuinely value your feedback. A well-travelled team at Lonely Planet reads and acknowledges every email and letter we receive and ensures that every morsel of information finds its way to the relevant authors, editors and cartographers.

Everyone who writes to us will find their name listed in the next edition of the appropriate guidebook. The very best contributions will be rewarded with a free guidebook.

We may edit, reproduce and incorporate your comments in Lonely Planet products such as guidebooks, websites and digital products, so let us know if you don't want your comments reproduced or your name acknowledged.

How to contact Lonely Planet:
Online: **e** talk2us@lonelyplanet.com.au, **w** www.lonelyplanet.com
Australia: Locked Bag 1, Footscray, Victoria 3011
UK: 10a Spring Place, London NW5 3BH
USA: 150 Linden St, Oakland, CA 94607

Introduction

Portugal is an extraordinarily diverse little country. Only 560km long and 220km wide, it packs in a fantastic range of attractions, from lush green valleys and high mountain ranges in the north to balmy beaches and dreamy olive groves and cork plantations in the south. Cultural gems are everywhere, including Unesco World Heritage Sites at Évora, Porto, Guimarães, Batalha and Alcobaça. Entertainment is among the hottest in Europe, with bars and clubs staying open till dawn in Lisbon, Porto, Cascais, Lagos and Albufeira. And if you're after outdoor action you can find it at championship surf spots all along the coast, at top-notch golf courses in the Algarve, or on challenging bike trails in the unspoilt hinterlands.

Best of all, none of this is hard to reach. You can take a train from Faro, the Algarve's capital in the south, to Porto, in the north, in just seven hours; or cross the waist of the country, west to east, from Lisbon to Elvas, in under four. Not that anyone likes to rush in Portugal. Savouring life slowly is a Portuguese passion. And much of the best is humble – traditional folk festivals celebrated with fervour in the tiniest village; food that is simple and honest, often drowning in olive oil; music that pulls at the heart strings, recalling past loves and glories; and markets that overflow with fish, fruit and flowers.

Only relatively recently has all this begun to be appreciated. At the southwesternmost corner of Europe, Portugal has long been considered a land apart, overlooked on Western itineraries. For centuries it was ruled by Romans and then Moors, and perennially in Spain's shadow. But in the 12th century it emerged as a nation-state, making it one of Europe's oldest countries. Two hundred years later its brave mariners ventured into the unknown, ultimately discovering a sea route to India and turning Portugal into one of the richest, most powerful kingdoms in the western hemisphere. It was an extraordinary achievement for such a tiny country and one that shaped the people's relationship to the sea forever.

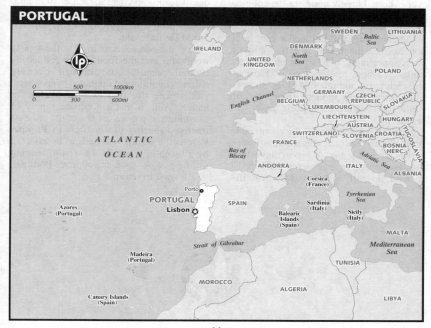

But the Golden Age couldn't last; by the 17th century Portugal had begun to slip into chaos and obscurity on Europe's forgotten hem. Political turmoil, a devastating earthquake in 1755 and complicated wars seriously weakened the nation. The modern turning point came in 1974 when an almost bloodless revolution finally brought 48 years of dictatorship under António de Oliveira Salazar to an end. Portugal's African colonies were given their independence, and a new constitution committed the country to a blend of socialism and democracy.

Thanks largely to massive European Union (EU) funding, recent changes have been fast and furious: new highways to Spain, new urban development, new enterprises and new confidence. Events such as Expo 98 encouraged major infrastructure development, transforming the capital and restoring its pride. The country steps into the limelight again in 2004 as host of the European Football Championships, providing a further boost to national prestige.

The growing affluence of the past decade has altered the lifestyles of many young Portuguese and introduced better facilities everywhere. Largely gone are the cobbled, potholed roads, donkey carts and simple guesthouses which many earlier visitors found charming. But Portugal's long isolation has left much that is extraordinarily, often appealingly, old-fashioned. Even the capital, Lisbon, remains one of Europe's most attractive and relaxing cities, successfully introducing modern improvements while rejuvenating its historic areas with sensitivity.

Much the same is true of the countryside. Although patches of Portugal's coastline (in particular along the Algarve) have been overdeveloped, there is plenty still left that is wild, unspoilt and stunningly beautiful,

protected within a network of parks and reserves that host an amazing variety of flora and fauna.

While the south, particularly the Alentejo, seems carpeted with vast farming estates (originally founded by the Romans) and yawning vistas of cork oaks and wheat, the north reflects an even older agricultural system of tiny smallholdings. Socially, too, there are obvious north-south divisions: southern Portuguese tend to be outgoing and 'Mediterranean', while northerners are more conservative and religious, taking their traditions very seriously. In remote parts of the rural north (especially Trás-os-Montes) where EU funds have yet to trickle down, life seems to have changed little in centuries.

As a traveller in this still underexplored corner of Europe you've got some enviable choices: stick to the Algarve with its lively resorts, golf courses and water sports; loiter in Lisbon with its upbeat attitude and lively nightlife (and with music from *fado* – Portugal's own soul-searing blues – to immigrant African sounds); trek into remote mountains where Portuguese themselves rarely go; or follow a cultural trail that could include immaculate hill-top villages, such as Monsanto, Monsaraz or Marvão, or the famous Alto Douro port wine region, another Unesco World Heritage site.

Accommodation is admirable, the wine is wonderful and the food, if not refined, is certainly plentiful. And although prices are rising as facilities get upgraded everywhere, you'll generally find excellent value for money. Add to this a generous supply of sunshine and you've got one of the most attractive, alluring destinations in Europe. Rare is the visitor who fails to be affected by a touch of *saudade* – a wistful longing for the past. As soon as you leave Portugal, you'll want to return.

Facts about Portugal

HISTORY
Pre-Roman & Roman Eras

The Iberian Peninsula has been inhabited for at least 500,000 years. If you want to see the earliest evidence of human habitation in Portugal, check out the Palaeolithic inscriptions near Vila Nova de Foz Côa in the Alto Douro. For Neolithic ghosts, head for the atmospheric fortified hill-top settlements, dating from 5500 BC, in the lower Tejo (Tagus) valley.

In the first millennium BC Celtic people started trickling into the Iberian Peninsula, settling in northern and western areas of Portugal around 700 BC. The resulting culture was responsible for dozens of *citânias* (fortified villages), especially in the Minho. Many, including the formidable *citânia* of Briteiros, near Braga, remained in use right up to Roman times.

Further south, Phoenician traders, followed by the Greeks and Carthaginians, founded coastal stations and mined metals inland. The Carthaginians held sway until their defeat by the Romans in the Second Punic War (218–202 BC).

When the Romans swept into southern Portugal in 210 BC, they expected an easy victory. But they hadn't reckoned on the Lusitani, a Celtic warrior tribe based between the Rio Tejo and Rio Douro, which resisted ferociously for half a century. Only when its brilliant leader, Viriato (or Viriathus), was tricked and assassinated in 139 BC did resistance collapse.

By 19 BC the Romans had eliminated all traces of Lusitanian independence. Under Decimus Junius Brutus and Julius Caesar a capital was established at Olisipo (Lisbon) in 60 BC, while other major colonies were founded at Scallabis (Santarém), Bracara Augusta (Braga), Pax Julia (Beja) and Ebora (Évora).

Around 25 BC this part of the empire was divided by Augustus into several provinces, including Lusitania (south of the Douro) and Baetica (Andalucía). In the 3rd century AD the Minho became part of a new province called Gallaecia (Galicia). It was aound this time that Christianity was established, with important bishoprics at Évora and Braga.

By the 5th century, when the Roman Empire had all but collapsed, Portugal's inhabitants had been under Roman rule for 600 years. So what did they get from it? Most usefully, roads and bridges. But also wheat, barley, olives and vines; a system of large farming estates (called *latifúndios* and still in existence in the Alentejo); a legal system; and, above all, a Latin-derived language. In fact, no other invader proved so useful.

Moors & Christians

The gap left by the Romans was filled by barbarian invaders from beyond the Pyrenees: Vandals, Alans, Visigoths and Suevi. The Germanic Suevi had the greatest impact, settling between the Rio Minho and Rio Douro and ruling from Braga and Portucale (Porto). From 469 onwards Arian Christian Visigoths had the upper hand.

Internal Visigoth disputes paved the way for Portugal's next great wave of invaders, the Moors – North African Muslim forces invited in 711 to help a Visigoth faction. Commanded by Tariq ibn Ziyad, they quickly occupied Portugal's southern coast. Egyptians settled around Beja and Faro, and Syrians between Faro and Seville, an area they called al-Gharb al-Andalus (the origin of 'Algarve'). The north – known as the county of Portucale – remained unstable, unsettled and predominantly Christian.

Under the Moors, who established a capital at Shelb (Silves), southerners enjoyed peace and productivity. The new rulers were tolerant of Jews and Christians. Christian smallholding farmers, called Mozarabs, were allowed to keep their land and were encouraged to try new irrigation methods and new crops, especially citrus and rice. Arabic words began filtering into the Portuguese language, and Arabic influences into the local cuisine – in particular an obsession with cakes and desserts of unsurpassed sweetness.

Meanwhile in the north, Christian forces were gaining strength. An early, largely symbolic kick-start to the Reconquista was a Christian victory over a small force of Moors in 718 at Covadonga in the Asturias (northern Spain). From this point the kingdom of Asturias-León expanded, ultimately absorbing Portucale (including Porto, taken in 868).

By the 11th century Portucale was an important regional power, for a time autonomous under the dynasty of Mumadona Dias. And things began to hot up for the Christians. In 1064 Coimbra fell within the Christian sphere. In 1085 Alfonso VI, king of the Christian kingdoms of León and Castile, thrashed the Moors in their Spanish heartland of Toledo; he is said to have secured Seville by winning a game of chess with its emir. But in the following year the ruthless Almoravids of Morocco, answering the emir's call for help, defeated Alfonso and drove out the Mozarabs. Worse followed with the arrival of the even more fanatical Almohads.

When Alfonso in turn called for foreign help, European crusaders were quick to rally against the 'infidels'. Among them were Henri of Burgundy and his cousin Raymond, who won not only battlefield glory but the hands of Alfonso's daughters. Henri married Teresa and became Count of Portucale, and Raymond married Urraca and became Lord of Galicia and Coimbra.

On Alfonso's death in 1109 things got messy. Urraca's son, Alfonso Raimúndez (later Alfonso VII), took control of León, while Teresa – regent for her son Afonso Henriques, after the death of her husband in 1112 – favoured a union with Galicia, thanks to a dalliance with a Galician. But she did not reckon with the nationalist ideas of her son.

In 1128 Afonso Henriques took up arms against his mother, defeating her forces near his capital, Guimarães. At first he bowed to the superior power of his cousin, Alfonso VII of León. But a few years after a dramatic victory against the Moors in 1139 at Ourique (Alentejo), Afonso Henriques began calling himself Dom – King of Portugal – a title confirmed in 1179 by the pope (after extra tribute was paid, naturally). He also retook Santarém and Lisbon from the Moors.

By the time Afonso Henriques died in 1185, the Portuguese frontier was secure to the Rio Tejo. Yet despite the ruthless help of the crusaders (notably in 1147 at Lisbon and later at Silves), it was almost another century before the Alentejo and the Algarve were wrested from the Moors.

In 1297, following disputes with neighbouring Castile, the boundaries of the Portuguese kingdom – much the same then as they are today – were recognised in the Treaty of Alcañices. The kingdom of Portugal had arrived.

The Burgundian Era

During the Reconquista, the country's 400,000 inhabitants – most of them living in the north – faced more than just war and turmoil; in the wake of Christian victories they had to cope with new rulers and new Christian settlers.

The Church and its wealthy clergy were the greediest landowners. Next in the pecking order came the nobles from the aristocratic class. Some local powers emerged during the rule of Afonso Henriques' son, Sancho I, when many *concelhos* (municipalities) were given special privileges embodied in charters. This enfranchisement extended to some Muslims, too, although enslavement of Moors persisted in some places into the 13th century. Segregated Moorish quarters – *mourarias* – were common.

Though theoretically free, most common people remained subjects of the landowning class, with few rights. In the south especially, many were recruited as foot soldiers for ongoing raids into Muslim territory. The first hint of democratic rule came with the establishment of the *cortes* (parliament). This assembly of nobles and clergy first met in 1211 at Coimbra, which was then the capital. Municipal representation – allowing commoners (mostly wealthy merchants) to attend the *cortes* – followed in 1254 under Afonso III. Six years later, the capital was moved to Lisbon.

Afonso III deserves credit for important administrative changes and for standing up to the power of the Church, but it was his son Dinis (1279–1325) who began shaking Portugal into shape. A far-sighted, cultured man, he brought the judicial system under royal control, started progressive afforestation programmes and encouraged internal trade. He suppressed the dangerously powerful military order of the Knights Templar by refounding them as the Order of Christ (see the boxed text 'The Order of the Knights Templar' under Tomar in the Estremadura & Ribatejo chapter). He cultivated music, the arts and education, founding a university in Lisbon in 1290, which was later transferred to Coimbra.

Dom Dinis' foresight was spot-on when it came to defending Portugal's borders: he built or rebuilt some 50 fortresses along the eastern frontier with Castile, and signed a pact of friendship with England in 1308, the basis for a future, long-lasting alliance.

It was none too soon. Within 60 years of Dinis' death, Portugal was at war with Castile over claims to the Portuguese throne. Fernando I, last of the Burgundian kings, had done much to provoke the clash by playing a game of alliances with both Castile and the English (represented by John of Gaunt, Duke of Lancaster). Fernando had promised his daughter Beatriz to John of Gaunt's nephew when the English arrived in 1381 to help with an invasion of Castile. In the event, Fernando made peace with the Castilians halfway through the campaign and offered Beatriz to Juan I of Castile instead, thereby throwing Portugal's future into Castilian hands.

On Fernando's death in 1383 his wife, Leonor Teles, ruled as regent. But she too was entangled with the Spanish, having long had a Galician lover. While nobles and bishops supported her, the merchant classes turned to a truly Portuguese candidate – João, Grand Master of the Order of Avis and son (albeit illegitimate) of Fernando's father, Pedro I. João assassinated Leonor's lover, Leonor fled to Castile and the Castilians duly invaded. But João had the support of the common people, who rose in revolt not only against the invaders but against Castilian nobles who had settled in Portugal.

The showdown came in 1385 when João faced an imposing force of Castilians at Aljubarrota. Even with Nuno Álvares Pereira (the Holy Constable) as his military right-hand man and with a force of English archers as support, the odds were stacked against him. João vowed to build a monastery to the Virgin if he won – and he did.

The victory sealed Portugal's independence (and João's vow produced the superb architectural legacy of Batalha's Battle Abbey). It also sealed Portugal's alliance with England; the 1386 Treaty of Windsor formalising the alliance was followed by João's marriage to John of Gaunt's daughter, Philippa of Lancaster. Peace with Castile was finally concluded in 1411. Portugal was ready to look further afield for adventure.

The Age of Discoveries

Morocco was the obvious first outlet for João's military energies, and in 1415 Ceuta fell to his forces. Although his son and successor, Duarte, failed in a first bid to capture Tangier in 1437, these advances marked the start of something very big indeed.

It was João's third son, Henry, who focused the spirit of the age – a combination of crusading zeal, love of martial glory and desire for gold and riches – into extraordinary

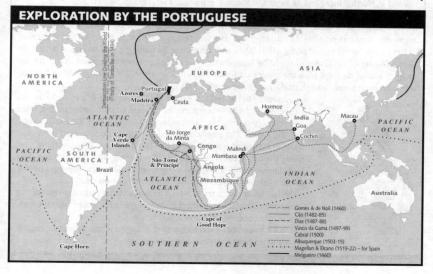

EXPLORATION BY THE PORTUGUESE

Gomes & de Noli (1460)
Cão (1482-85)
Dias (1487-88)
Vasco da Gama (1497-99)
Cabral (1500)
Albuquerque (1503-15)
Magellan & Elcano (1519-22) – for Spain
Melgueiro (1660)

explorations across the seas. These explorations were to transform the small kingdom into a great imperial power (see the boxed text 'Prince Henry the Navigator').

The biggest breakthrough came in 1497 during the reign of Manuel I (who titled himself 'Lord of the Conquest, Navigation, and Commerce of India, Ethiopia, Arabia and Persia'), when Vasco da Gama reached southern India. With gold and slaves from Africa and spices from the East, Portugal soon grew fabulously wealthy.

Spain, however, had also jumped on the exploration bandwagon and was soon disputing some of the Portuguese claims. Christopher Columbus' 1492 'discovery' of America for Spain led to a fresh outburst of jealous conflict. It was resolved by the pope in the extraordinary 1494 Treaty of Tordesillas, by which the world was divided between the two great powers along a line 370 leagues west of the Cape Verde islands. Portugal won the lands to the east of the line, including Brazil, whose existence explorers may already have confirmed (it was officially claimed for Portugal in 1500).

The rivalry spurred the first circumnavigation of the world. In 1519 the Portuguese navigator Fernão Magalhães (Ferdinand Magellan), his allegiance transferred to Spain after a tiff with Manuel I, set off around the southern tip of South America in an effort to prove that the Spice Islands (Moluccas) lay in Spanish 'territory'. He crossed the Pacific and reached the Philippines in 1521 but was killed in a skirmish there. Only one of his five ships, under the Basque navigator Juan Sebastián Elcano, reached the Moluccas, and then sailed home via the Cape of Good Hope, proving the earth was round.

As its explorers reached Timor, China and eventually Japan, Portugal consolidated its power and world trading status with garrison ports and trading and missionary posts: Goa in 1510, Melaka in 1511, Hormoz in 1515,

Prince Henry the Navigator

Henrique, Infante de Portugal (Prince of Portugal), was born in present-day Porto in 1394. By the time he died 66 years later he had almost single-handedly set Portugal on course for its Age of Discoveries, turning it into a wealthy maritime power and transforming seaborne exploration from a groping process to a near science.

At the age of 18, he and his brothers persuaded their father, João I, to invade Ceuta. The city fell with ease in 1415 and Henry was appointed its governor. He spent little time there but it stirred his interest in North Africa, and he began to sponsor exploratory voyages.

In 1419, as governor of the Algarve, Henry began assembling the best sailors, map makers, shipbuilders, instrument makers and astronomers, with the aim of getting Portuguese explorers as far across the world as possible. His strategy was as much religious as commercial – to sap the power of the Islamic world by siphoning off its trade and, ultimately, by finding a way around it by sea. As Grand Master of the Order of Christ he tapped into the order's resources to support this ambitious project, and all his ships bore the order's trademark red cross on their sails. Though Henry took no vows, he lived simply and chastely, remaining single all his life.

Madeira (1419) and the Azores (1427) were the first lands to be discovered. In 1434 Gil Eanes sailed beyond Cape Bojador on the West African coast, breaking a maritime superstition that this was the end of the world. The newly designed, highly manoeuvrable Portuguese caravel made this possible. In 1441 – just as unease was mounting over Henry's lavish spending – ships began returning with West African gold and slaves. Within a few years the slave trade was galloping, and the prince's interest turned from exploration to commerce.

The last great discovery to which he was witness was of several of the Cape Verde islands. The furthest his sailors got in his lifetime was present-day Sierra Leone, or possibly Côte d'Ivoire.

On 13 November 1460 Henry died at Sagres – heavily in debt in spite of revenues from the slave and gold trade.

NC

The Portuguese in Australia

It's believed by many historians that Portuguese explorers reached Australia in the 16th century, 250 years before its 'official' discoverer, Captain James Cook. At least one Australian historian, Kenneth McIntyre, is convinced that by 1536 the Portuguese had secretly mapped three-quarters of the island's coastline. In September 1996 a 500-year-old Portuguese coin was found by a treasure hunter on the Mornington Peninsula, on the Victorian coast, adding further weight to this interesting theory.

Macau in 1557. The monarchy, taking its 'royal fifth' of trading profits, became the richest monarchy in Europe, and the lavish Manueline style of architecture (which was named after Manuel I) symbolised the exuberance of the age.

It couldn't last, of course. By the 1570s the huge cost of expeditions and the maintenance of an overseas empire was taking its toll. The new riches went little further than the monarchy and nobility, while domestic agriculture declined and prices in Europe fell. The expulsion of many commercially minded refugee Spanish Jews in 1496 and the subsequent persecution of converted Jews – New Christians or *marranos* – during the Inquisition (see under Religion later in this chapter) only worsened the financial situation.

The final straw came in 1557 when the young idealistic prince Sebastião took the throne, determined to bring Christianity to Morocco. The next year he rallied a force of 18,000 and set off, only to be disastrously defeated at the Battle of Alcácer-Quibir. Sebastião and 8000 others were killed, including much of the Portuguese nobility. Over the next few years his aged successor, Cardinal Henrique, drained the royal coffers ransoming those captured.

On Henrique's death in 1580, Sebastião's uncle, Felipe II of Spain, claimed the throne after defeating Portuguese forces at the battle of Alcântara. The following year he was crowned Felipe I of Portugal. This marked the end of the Avis dynasty, centuries of independence, Portugal's golden age and its glorious moment on the world stage.

Spain's Rule & Portugal's Revival

The start of Spanish rule looked promising – Felipe I promised to preserve Portugal's autonomy and to pay frequent visits to the long-ignored parliament. But commoners strongly resented Spanish rule and held onto the dream that Sebastião was still alive; pretenders continued to pop up until 1600. Though Felipe was honourable, his successors were considerably less so, using Portugal to raise money and soldiers for Spain's wars overseas, and appointing Spaniards to govern Portugal.

Meanwhile, Portugal's overseas empire was slipping out of its grasp. In 1622 the English seized Hormoz, and by the 1650s the Dutch had taken Malaka, Ceylon (present-day Sri Lanka) and part of Brazil.

Portuguese resentment against the Spanish exploded in 1640, when an attempt was made to recruit Portuguese to crush a revolt in Catalonia. Encouraged by the French (who were at war with Spain at the time), a group of nationalist leaders forced the woman governor of Portugal from her office in Lisbon and drove out the Spanish garrison. The Duke of Bragança, grandson of a former claimant to the throne and head of a powerful landowning family, reluctantly stepped into the hot seat and was crowned João IV.

With a hostile Spain on the doorstep, Portugal searched for allies. In 1654 it signed a treaty with England. Another treaty in 1661 led to the marriage of Charles II of England with João's daughter, Catherine of Bragança, and the ceding of Tangier and Bombay to England. In return the English promised arms and soldiers for the war with Spain. Preoccupied elsewhere, Spain made only half-hearted attempts to recapture Portugal. After losing a series of frontier battles between 1663 and 1665, Spain recognised Portuguese independence with the 1668 Treaty of Lisbon.

Moves towards democracy, begun over 400 years earlier with municipal representation at the parliament, now stalled under João's successors. The Crown hardly bothered to call the parliament, thanks to its renewed financial independence following the discovery of gold and precious stones in Brazil at the end of the 17th century. There followed another era of profligate expenditure. The awesome baroque monastery palace in Mafra is a perfect example of this over-the-top extravagance.

The most notable event on the economic front was the 1703 Methuen Treaty, which stimulated Anglo-Portuguese trade with preferential terms for the import of English textiles and the export of Portuguese wines. But this wasn't the boon it first appeared, since it increased Portugal's dependence on Britain, hurt the local textile industry and detracted from efforts to increase wheat production.

Into the looming chaos stepped a man for the moment – the Marquês de Pombal, chief minister to the hedonistic Dom José I (the latter more interested in opera than affairs of state). Popularly described as an enlightened despot, Pombal dragged Portugal into the modern era, crushing any opposition with brutal efficiency.

Pombal reformed trade and industry by setting up state monopolies, curbing the power of British merchants and boosting agriculture and domestic industry as Brazilian gold production declined. He abolished slavery in mainland Portugal and the distinctions between traditional and New Christians. He founded royal schools and reformed the universities, eliminating the influence of the Jesuits and establishing faculties of science.

When Lisbon suffered a devastating earthquake in November 1755, Pombal acted swiftly and pragmatically to deal with the crisis and to rebuild the city. He was by then at the height of his power. In the following years he dispensed with his main enemies – the most powerful Jesuits and several noble families – by implicating them in an attempt on the king's life.

He might have continued his autocratic rule had it not been for the accession of the devout Dona Maria I in 1777. The anticlerical Pombal was promptly sacked, tried and charged with various offences, though never imprisoned. Although his religious legislation was repealed, his economic, agricultural and educational policies were largely maintained, helping the country back towards prosperity.

But turmoil was once again on the horizon, as Napoleon swept through Europe.

The Dawn of a Republic

In 1793 Portugal found itself at war again when it joined England in sending naval forces against revolutionary France. After a few years of uneasy peace, Napoleon threw Portugal an ultimatum: close your ports to British shipping or be invaded.

There was no way Portugal could turn its back on Britain, upon which it depended for half its trade (especially in cloth and wine) and for protection of its sea routes. In 1807 Portugal's royal family fled to Brazil (where it stayed for 14 years), and General Junot led Napoleon's forces right into Lisbon, sweeping Portugal into the so-called Peninsular War (France's invasion of Spain and Portugal, which lasted until 1814).

Portugal soon had the help of Sir Arthur Wellesley (later Duke of Wellington) and Viscount William Beresford, leading a force of seasoned British troops. After a series of setbacks, the joint Portuguese-British army drove the French back across the Spanish border in 1811.

Free but seriously weakened, Portugal was administered by Beresford while João VI and his court remained in Brazil. In 1810 Portugal lost a profitable intermediary role when it gave Britain the right to trade directly with Brazil. The next humiliation was João's 1815 proclamation of Brazil as a kingdom united with Portugal. With soaring debts and dismal trade, Portugal was at one of the lowest points in its history, reduced to a de facto colony of Brazil and a protectorate of Britain.

Meanwhile, resentment simmered in the army, not only over the unpopular Beresford but over lack of pay and promotion. Influenced by liberal ideas circulating in Spain, a group of rebel officers took advantage of Beresford's absence in 1820 to convene a parliament and start drawing up a new, liberal constitution. Based on Enlightenment ideals, it abolished clerical privileges and the rights of the nobility, and instituted a single-chamber parliament.

Faced with this *fait accompli*, João returned and accepted its terms – though his wife and his son Miguel, bitterly opposed to it, won widespread support in rural areas. João's elder son, Pedro, also had other ideas; left behind to govern Brazil, he snubbed the constitutionalists by declaring Brazil independent in 1822 and himself its emperor. When João died in 1826, leaving no obvious successor, the stage was set for civil war.

Offered the crown, Pedro first drew up a new, less liberal charter and then abdicated in favour of his seven-year-old daughter Maria, provided she marry her uncle Miguel, and provided Miguel accept the new constitution. In 1827 Miguel took the oath and was appointed regent, but promptly abolished Pedro's constitution and proclaimed himself king, reverting to the old monarchist system. Liberals rallied under Pedro and, encouraged by French, British and Spanish liberals, forced Miguel to surrender at Évoramonte in May 1834.

Revolutionary zeal quickly led to changes, notably the abolition of the religious orders in 1834. Pedro died the same year but his daughter Maria, now Queen of Portugal at the age of 15, kept his flame alive with her fanatical support of his 1826 charter. Radical supporters of the liberal 1822 constitution were even more vociferous. By 1846, with urban discontent exacerbated by economic recession, the prospect of civil war again loomed. The Duke of Saldanha (a supporter of the 1826 charter) sought British and Spanish intervention, and peace was restored with the 1847 Convention of Gramido.

Saldanha governed the country from 1851 to 1856, steering it into more stable waters. Pedro's 1826 charter was rendered more palatable with restricted suffrage and a rotation of power between radicals and moderates. Under Minister of Works Fontes Pereira de Melo, the country's infrastructure was modernised, with new roads, bridges, railways and ports, and an electric telegraph network.

Although these improvements helped the economy, the country remained in dire straits at the turn of the century. Industrial growth was miniscule, budgets were rarely balanced and foreign (notably British) involvement left a quarter of Portugal's trade and industry outside its control. With the development of sardine-canning and tobacco industries, rural areas were depopulated in favour of the cities, and emigration (especially to Brazil) grew in popularity among northern villagers.

Much was changing, but for many the changes weren't happening fast enough. Urban discontent was growing, and so was support for socialism and trade unions. A nationalist republican movement swept through the lower middle classes of Lisbon, Porto and the south. When Dom Carlos allowed his premier, João Franco, to rule dictatorially, resentment exploded in an attempted republican coup in 1908. It failed, but the following month the king and crown prince were assassinated while driving through the streets of Lisbon.

Carlos' younger son, Manuel II, and his ministers tried feebly to appease republicans, but it was too late. On 5 October 1910, after an uprising by military officers, a republic was declared. Manuel 'the Unfortunate' sailed into exile in Britain where he died in 1932.

The Rise & Fall of Salazar

Hopes were high among republicans after a landslide victory in the 1911 elections, but it became clear that the sentiments of the new national anthem ('Oh sea heroes, oh noble people...raise again the splendour of Portugal...!') were vain hopes. Under Afonso Augusto da Costa's leftist Democrat Party, power was maintained by a combination of patronage and a divisive anticlericalism bitterly opposed in rural areas. Particularly controversial was the disestablishment of the Roman Catholic Church and the internationally criticised persecution of Catholics.

Meanwhile, the economy was in tatters, strained by Portugal's economically disastrous decision to join the Allies in WWI. In the recessionary post-war years the chaos deepened: republican factions squabbled, workers' unions went on strike and were repressed and the military grew powerful. The new republic soon had a reputation as Europe's most unstable regime. Between 1910 and 1926 there were 45 changes of government, often the result of military intervention. Another coup in May 1926 brought another round of new names and faces, but one rose above all the others – António de Oliveira Salazar.

A renowned professor of economics at Coimbra University, Salazar was appointed finance minister by the new president, General Óscar Carmona, and given sweeping powers to bring order to Portugal's economy. This he did with such success that by 1932 he was prime minister, a post he was to hold for 36 years. In 1933 he announced a new constitution and a 'New State' – a

NC

António de Oliveira Salazar

corporatist republic that was nationalistic, Catholic, authoritarian and repressive.

All political parties were banned except the National Union. This loyalist movement provided the National Assembly (successor to the parliament) with all its elected members. Strikes were banned and workers were organised into employer-controlled national syndicates or associations. Propaganda, censorship and brute force kept society in order. The feared Polícia Internacional e de Defesa do Estado (PIDE) was the most sinister development, a secret force using both imprisonment and torture to suppress the opposition. Various attempted coups during Salazar's rule came to nothing.

The only good news was a dramatic economic turnaround. The country's debt was reduced, as was its dependence on British investment. Although agriculture stagnated from under-mechanisation, industry and infrastructure development responded well. Through the 1950s and 1960s Portugal experienced an annual industrial growth rate of 7% to 9%.

Internationally, Salazar played two hands, unofficially supporting Franco's nationalists in the Spanish Civil War, and allowing the British to use Azores airfields during WWII despite official neutrality (and illegal sales of tungsten to Germany until 1944). In 1997 it was discovered that he had authorised the transfer of Nazi-looted gold from Switzerland to Portugal –

44 tonnes according to Allied records, some allegedly transferred to a Bank of Portugal account in New York, and only a 10th of it repaid after the war.

But it was something else on the international scene that finally brought Salazar down – decolonisation. Refusing to relinquish the colonies, he was faced with increasingly costly military expeditions that were internationally deplored and domestically unpopular, even among the military. In 1961 Goa was occupied by India and in Angola local nationalists rose up. Similar guerrilla movements appeared in Portuguese Guinea and Mozambique.

In the event, Salazar didn't have to face the consequences. In 1968 he had a stroke, and he died two years later. His successor, Marcelo Caetano, made some attempt at reform, which only stirred up more unrest.

Military officers sympathetic to African freedom fighters grew reluctant to serve in colonial wars. Several hundred officers formed the Movimento das Forças Armadas (MFA). Led by General Costa Gomes, General António de Spínola and Lieutenant Colonel Otelo Saraiva de Carvalho, on 25 April 1974 they carried out a nearly bloodless coup, later nicknamed the Revolution of the Carnations (after victorious soldiers stuck carnations in the barrels of their rifles). Carnations are still a national symbol of freedom.

From Revolution to Democracy

Although the coup was generally popular, the year following it was marked by unprecedented chaos. The first major change took place where the revolution had begun –in the African colonies. Independence was granted almost immediately to newly named Guinea-Bissau. This was followed by the decolonisation of the Cape Verde islands, São Tomé e Príncipe, Mozambique and Angola.

The transition wasn't always smooth: civil war broke out in Angola, and freshly liberated East Timor was invaded by Indonesia. Within Portugal, too, the effects of the 1975 decolonisation were turbulent. Suddenly it had to cope with nearly a million refugees from the African colonies – a social upheaval that it managed remarkably well.

Politically and economically, however, the country was in a mess, with widespread strikes and a tangle of political ideas and parties. The two most powerful groups, the communists (dominating the trade unions) and a radical wing of the MFA, launched a revolutionary movement, nationalising firms and services. Peasant farmers seized some of the Alentejo's huge *latifúndio* to establish communal farms (few of which succeeded and most of which were later returned to their owners).

Conservatives in the north were led by Mário Soares and his Partido Socialista (PS; Socialist Party) while revolutionaries held sway in the south. In August 1975 a more moderate government was formed, bitterly opposed by the extreme left and the Partido Comunista Português (PCP; Communist Party). On 25 November 1975 a radical leftist coup was crushed by moderate army troops under General Ramalho Eanes. The revolution had ended.

The Rocky Road to Stability

A new constitution in April 1976 committed Portugal to a blend of socialism and democracy, with a powerful president, an assembly elected by universal suffrage and a Council of the Revolution to control the armed forces. After parliamentary elections, Mário Soares formed a minority government and General Eanes won the presidential election.

A year later Soares' government faltered and there followed a series of attempts at government by coalitions and nonparty candidates, including Portugal's first woman prime minister, Maria de Lurdes Pintassilgo. In the 1980 parliamentary elections a new political force took over the reins – the conservative Aliança Democrática (AD; Democratic Alliance), a coalition of right-leaning parties led by social democrat Francisco de Sá Carneiro.

After Carneiro's death in a plane crash that same year (of which secret evidence of foul play surfaced in 1999), Francisco Pinto Balsemão took over as prime minister and persuaded socialists in the assembly to accept constitutional changes establishing full civilian rule. The first steps were taken to join the European Community (EC), forerunner of today's European Union (EU).

It was partly to satisfy EC admission requirements and keep the International Monetary Fund (IMF) happy that a new coalition government of socialists and social democrats under Mário Soares was forced to implement a strict programme of economic modernisation. Not surprisingly, the belt-tightening wasn't popular. The most vocal critics were Soares' right-wing partners in the Partido Social Democrata (PSD; Social Democrat Party), led by the dynamic Aníbal Cavaco Silva. Communist trade unions in the industrial and transport sectors organised strikes.

Adding to the unrest was the appearance of urban terrorism, mainly by the radical left-wing Forças Populares de 25 Abril (FP-25). In June 1984 over 40 terrorist suspects were arrested, including the former revolutionary leader Otelo Saraiva de Carvalho. A new security intelligence agency was established.

By June 1985 the coalition government had collapsed over disagreements on labour and agricultural reform. In October elections the PSD emerged a narrow winner, forming a minority government led by Cavaco Silva. But this wasn't the end of Soares' political career. In the February 1986 presidential elections the veteran socialist leader became president – the country's first civilian head of state for 60 years. Another political record was set the following year when parliamentary elections returned Cavaco Silva and the PSD with the first clear majority since 1974. With a repeat performance four years later, it looked as if the country had finally reached calm waters.

In January 1986, after nine years of negotiations, Portugal was admitted to the EC. Flush with EC funds, it raced ahead of many of its equally poor neighbours, with an unprecedented 4.5% to 5% annual economic growth rate. The new prosperity gave Cavaco Silva the power to push ahead with his programme of radical economic reform and free enterprise. Privatisation continued and fundamental changes were made in agriculture, education and the media.

But there was considerable resistance among industrial workers to the proposed reform of labour laws. The 1980s saw major strikes, including one in March 1988 involving an estimated 1.5 million workers. The controversial legislation was passed in February 1989, but unrest continued.

The PSD, now also stricken by corruption scandals, suffered serious losses in municipal elections. The PS, backed by communists and greens, took control of Lisbon and other major cities. The canny Cavaco Silva fought back with a surprise cabinet reshuffle in January 1990, removing scandal-tainted ministers. Soares, who was still immensely popular, won an outright victory in the presidential elections in 1991. And, surprisingly, the PSD renewed its absolute majority in subsequent legislative elections.

The electorate may have been disgusted by scandals and worried about unemployment, inflation and shortcomings in health and education, but they were still attracted by the PSD's promises of continued growth and stability.

Portugal Today

It was soon obvious that these promises were going to be hard to fulfil. In 1992 EC trade barriers fell and Portugal suddenly faced the threat of competition. Fortunes dwindled as recession set in, and disillusionment with the PSD grew as Europe's single market revealed the backwardness of Portugal's agricultural sector. Unregulated profiteering, corruption and industrial pollution were also undermining the PSD's reputation. Tensions were rising, too, between the socialist Soares and his centre-right prime minister, with Soares frequently exercising his veto to stall or modify controversial legislation.

Throughout 1993 and 1994 there were strikes (mainly in support of wage increases), charges of corruption (including missing EU funds at the Ministry of Finance) and student demonstrations over rising fees. The government was further shaken when Amnesty International expressed concern over allegations of torture by Portuguese police and prison officers.

With waning public support for the PSD, Cavaco Silva resigned as leader in January 1995. Inevitably, the October elections were won by the PS, under the dynamic, 46-year-old António Guterres. Silva had still hoped to win the 1996 presidential elections but his socialist rival, Jorge Sampaio, won instead. It marked the end of the PSD's decade in power, and the first time since 1974 that the president and prime minister were both from the same party (SP).

The uneasy coalitions and economic instability of the 1970s and early 1980s seemed to be over. Business was reassured by Guterres'

commitment to budgetary rigour and his unexpected success in qualifying for European and Monetary Union in 1998.

Steady economic growth helped Guterres' party win a second term in October 1999, although it failed again (by one seat) to win an overall parliamentary majority. But corruption scandals, rising inflation and a seriously faltering economy spelt disaster for the PS in the 2001 local elections, in which all the major towns, echoing a European trend, swung to the centre-right. Guterres resigned and in the March 2002 general elections his party was defeated by the PSD.

Things are far from rosy for the new PSD prime minister, José Manuel Durão Barroso. Having failed to win an absolute majority he has had to form a coalition government with former foe, the more radically right-wing Popular Party (CDS-PP; Centro Democrático Social – Partido Popular). It now has the unenviable job of tackling Portugal's financial and budgetary crisis, one of the worst in the EU.

GEOGRAPHY

Together with Ireland, Portugal lies at the westernmost edge of Europe. Covering an area of 92,389 sq km and measuring only 560km north to south and 220km east to west, it's one of Europe's smallest countries.

But it's also one of the most geographically diverse. Bordered on the west and south by the Atlantic Ocean and on the east and north by Spain, it offers everything from dramatic mountain ranges in the north to undulating meadows in the south. Its 830km of coastline ranges from wicked surf-crashing Atlantic waves to balmy Mediterranean Algarve beaches perfect for paddlers.

Dividing the country roughly in half is the Rio Tejo, flowing northeast to southwest and emptying into the Atlantic at Lisbon, one of Portugal's few natural harbours. North of the Tejo are most of the mountains – largely 400m to 700m high. While fertile, heavily populated northwestern Minho is characterised by rolling plateaus and by rivers flowing through deep gorges, the adjacent provinces of Beira Alta, Douro and Trás-os-Montes are marked by high granite, schist and slate plateaus. This region, rising to 800m, is known as the *terra fria* (cold country). The southern and eastern part of the Alto Douro (in southern Trás-os-Montes)

Provinces, Districts & Tourist Regions

Traditionally, Portugal was composed of seven loosely defined provinces *(províncias)* – the Minho (named after the Rio Minho), the Douro (named after the Rio Douro), Trás-os-Montes (beyond the mountains), the Beira (border), the Estremadura (farthest from the Rio Douro), the Alentejo (beyond the Rio Tejo) and the Algarve (after the Moorish al-gharb, meaning west country).

In the 1830s these provinces were subdivided into administrative districts *(distritos)*. Later, several provinces were broken into smaller pieces (eg, the Estremadura into Estremadura and Ribatejo). Our guidebook largely corresponds to these traditional provinces.

More recently, the government and ICEP, the state tourism authority, has divided the country into five large regions for administrative and statistical purposes. ICEP's brochures and maps, and the locations of regional tourist offices, are all based on these regions (and the 19 smaller *regiões de turismo*, or tourist regions, within them), of which the borders don't correspond exactly with political borders.

PROVINCES & DISTRICTS

REGIÕES DE TURISMO

is known as *terra quente* (hot country), a landscape of sheltered valleys with dark schists that trap the heat and create the perfect microclimate – described by locals as 'nine months of winter and three months of hell' – for growing port-wine grapes.

Further south are several major mountain ranges, notably the Serra da Estrela, which tops out at the 1993m Torre, the highest peak in mainland Portugal. Dropping south, you'll reach the low-lying, often marshy Atlantic coastline of Beira Litoral and Estremadura, marked by river-mouth lagoons and salt marshes. Inland, between the Rio Tejo and the Rio Guadiana, the Alto Alentejo features a series of plateaus, a continuation of the Spanish tablelands. Further south still, in northern Baixo Alentejo, are ridges of quartz and marble, and a vast undulating landscape of wheat, and cork and olive trees.

Only the eastern Serra do Caldeirão and western Serra de Monchique break the flatness of the south, and are a natural border between the Alentejo and the Algarve. They also act as a climatic buffer for the Algarve, which basks in a Mediterranean climate.

The islands of Madeira and the Azores, originally colonised in the 15th century, are also part of Portugal, although too far away to be considered in a peninsular visit: Madeira (a popular destination in its own right) lies 900km to the southwest, off Africa's west coast; the nine-island Azores archipelago sprawls 1440km west of Lisbon.

Macau, the last remaining overseas territory under Portuguese administration, was returned to Chinese rule at the end of 1999.

CLIMATE

Portugal falls within both Atlantic and Mediterranean climatic zones. The Atlantic has the strongest influence, especially in the northwest where the weather is noticeably milder and damper than elsewhere. Bring your brolly if you're heading here: up to 2000mm of rain can fall annually (the national average is 1100mm). Intense rains in December 2000 (the wettest month in the century) even caused landslides, floods and fatalities.

You can thank the Atlantic for slightly moderating the dry Mediterranean climate of the southern coast, where top summer temperatures average a sizzling 28°C. Summer maximums in Lisbon and Porto are slightly

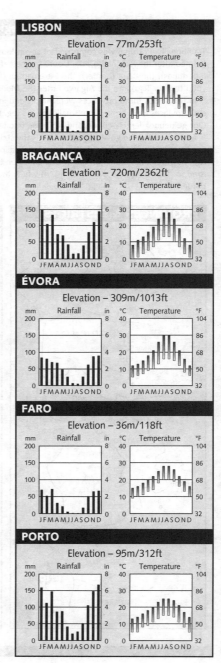

lower, and rain is rare everywhere in July and August. You can expect a lovely average of 12/six hours daily sunshine in a typical Algarve summer/winter and about 10/four hours up north. Coastal winters are mild, averaging 13°C in Lisbon, 12°C in Porto and 16°C in Faro.

Inland there's greater variation, thanks to continental winds from the interior. Summers can be painfully hot in the Alto Douro and the Alentejo (where temperatures soar as high as 40°C), with drought often lasting for a month or more. In the south, drought can last even longer. Winters can be severe in the northeast and the Serra da Estrela (where skiers are usually out on the slopes from January to March). The national winter average temperature is a deliciously mild 11°C.

ECOLOGY & ENVIRONMENT

Portugal has been slow to wake up to its environmental problems, notably soil erosion, pollution, rubbish disposal and the effects of mass tourism on fragile coastal areas. Of growing concern, too, is the spread of huge, water-thirsty eucalyptus plantations that effectively destroy regional wildlife habitat and aggravate an already serious drought problem brought on by climatic change. While such intensively cultivated plantations continue to proliferate (now accounting for over 20% of the country's forest area), Portugal's traditional, sustainable cork plantations are under serious threat (see the boxed text 'Cork or Plastic?').

For visitors, however, mass tourism is the most obvious problem, especially in the overdeveloped Algarve with its widespread hotel, villa and apartment-block complexes. Elsewhere, too, the influx of summer visitors – as many as 40,000 per year in villages with populations less than 2000 is not that uncommon – stretches the local services and infrastructure to the limit. Litter is a growing problem at popular sites (including beaches), as is widespread fouling of beaches and urban pavements by pet dogs.

But industrial development is to blame for Portugal's most polluted seasides – you'd be wise to avoid beaches near Porto and the industrial centre of Sines. Disaster struck Portugal's northwestern coast in November

Cork or Plastic?

Travel across the vast Alentejo plains and you'll see thousands of tall, round-topped evergreens with glossy, hollylike leaves and wrinkled bark that's often stripped away, leaving a strangely naked, ochre trunk.

Quercus suber, or cork oak, grows happily almost anywhere in Portugal, and is one of the country's most profitable agricultural products. Prized for its lightness, admired for its insulating and sealing qualities, more versatile than any synthetic alternative, cork is used for everything from footwear to floor-coverings, gaskets to girders. And particularly, of course, for bottlestoppers. The absence of smell, taste and toxicity make it the essential 'bung' for quality wines. Some 15 thousand million corks a year come from Portugal, accounting for most of the country's prodigious cork output – around 60% of world output.

Cork is cultivated as carefully as vintage port wine. Trees are allowed to mature for at least 25 years before the first bark is cut; indeed, there are laws against stripping cork oaks before they've reached a certain size. After that they may only be stripped every ninth year. Cork cutters work by hand, as skilfully as barbers. A properly cultivated tree will produce cork for around 100 years.

This fantastically renewable, sustainable resource is now under threat. There have long been critics of cork stoppers – some 300 million bottles of wine a year do indeed end up 'corked', contaminated by an organic compound in the cork. Now there's growing worldwide use of what is seen as the modern, reliable alternative: plastic.

Few realise what's at stake if the economic viability of the cork forests declines. These are agroforestry systems of exceptional biological diversity on which various threatened species depend, including the Iberian lynx and Bonelli's eagle. In 2001 a new law was passed to protect cork forests from developers, and an international campaign launched to promote 'real cork' and urge producers and retailers to publicise its importance. But the use of plastic stoppers, particularly in Britain, continues inexorably to grow.

The *Prestige* Oil Disaster

In November 2002, Portugal faced an environmental and ecological disaster when an outdated Greek-owned fuel tanker, the *Prestige*, broke apart and sank 80km north of Portuguese waters. Some 10% of its 77,000 tons of fuel oil immediately smothered at least 90 beaches on the Spanish Galician coast, devastating the shellfish beds and large seabird population. A fifth of Portugal's coastline faced certain risk of contamination. Hundreds of fishermen, both in Spain and northern Portugal, were banned from fishing. And teams were on standby as far south as Aveiro to try and prevent further damage.

At the time of going to press oil was still leaking from the tanker and heading for the Portuguese beaches at Caminha and Viana do Castelo. Greenpeace and the Portuguese environmental group, Quercus, have warned that the effects of the tanker's sinking will be felt 'for decades', if not 'permanently'. Politically, too, the disaster has strained Portuguese-Spanish relations, with some Portuguese politicians criticising the Spanish decision to tow the stricken tanker away from its coastline towards Portuguese waters and demanding compensation.

2002 when the oil tanker *Prestige* spilled 6000 tonnes of oil, causing one of the world's worst environmental catastrophes.

A free, regularly updated map of coastal water, *Qualidade da Água em Zonas Balneares*, is available from **Instituto da Água** (☎ *218 430 000;* e *inforag@inag.pt)*.

It's water – or rather the lack of it – that could become Portugal's worst environmental nightmare. Four years of drought in the mid-1990s, the worst dry cycle of the 20th century, followed in 1999 by the worst drought in 150 years, suggest an alarming trend. Brush and forest fires in northern and central Portugal in 2000 destroyed more than half the country's cereal crops (around 3% of Portugal's forests burn every year). Global climatic change could threaten the country's ability to sustain itself.

The biggest immediate worry concerns Spain's proposed National Hydrographic Plan, a mammoth scheme that would include diverting water from the rainy north to the dry south. Unfortunately for Portugal, three of its major rivers – the Douro, the Tejo and the Guadiana – originate in Spain. And like Spain, Portugal desperately needs this water for agriculture (which accounts for 76% of water use in Portugal), hydroelectric production and the environment generally. Despite water-sharing agreements with Portugal, Spain is increasing its withdrawals from the Guadiana and has vowed to get the controversial Hydrographic Plan moving.

Meanwhile, Portugal's own answer to this water problem is a giant dam at Alqueva, near Beja (see the boxed text 'The Alqueva Dam' in The Alentejo chapter). Finished in 2002, it's now slowly flooding the arid Alentejo, despite huge environmental concerns. Land clearing for the dam will destroy over a million oak and olive trees and the habitats of several endangered species, including Bonelli's eagle, the otter and the Iberian lynx. The planned water diversion to the Sado estuary could also endanger the dolphins there due to the water's high pollution levels. Even the supposed beneficiaries – the farmers themselves – may find the irrigation costs too high. A coalition of Portuguese and Spanish environmental organisations, called the Level 139 Movement, continue to battle for the water level to be limited to 139m (instead of the proposed 152m), thereby saving around 400,000 trees.

Environmental Organisations

Portugal's busiest environmental group is Quercus: the **Associação Nacional de Conservação da Natureza** *(National Association for the Conservation of Nature;* ☎ *217 788 474;* w *www.quercus.pt; Bairro do Calhau, Parque Florestal de Monsanto, Apartado 4333, 1503-003 Lisbon).* Founded in 1985, it has some 12,000 members, 19 branch offices and two environmental education centres. In addition to carrying out studies and publishing environmental guides to specific areas, Quercus members bring issues to public and government attention through regular campaigns. Some branches arrange field trips, though information is hard to come by.

Another activist group arranging weekend trips is **Geota** *(Grupo de Estudos de Ordenomento do Território e Ambiente or*

Environment Study Group; ☎ *213 956 120;* e *geota@mail.telepac.pt; Travessa do Moinho de Vento 17, 1200-727 Lisbon).*

Portugal's oldest conservation group is **Liga para a Proteção da Natureza-LPN** *(League for the Protection of Nature;* ☎ *217 780 097;* w *www.lpn.pt; Estrela do Calhariz de Benfica 187, 1500-124 Lisbon),* which often publicises environmental issues. Active in the Algarve is **Almargem** *(*☎ *289 412 959;* e *almargem@mail.telepac.pt; Alto de São Domingos 14, 8100-536 Loulé).*

An excellent website on Portuguese environmental or nature-related topics is w www.naturlink.pt.

FLORA & FAUNA
Flora

Like its climate, Portugal's flora is a blend of Mediterranean and Atlantic ingredients. Before the land was reshaped by humans, oaks dominated the vegetation – deciduous species in the north and evergreens in the south. Today, little natural forest remains and scrubland prairies prevail.

In the sunny, dry Algarve and Alentejo, Mediterranean flowers set the countryside ablaze in spring and early summer; especially striking are white and purple rockroses *(gum cistus).* The pretty Bermuda buttercup is an invasive and herbicide-resistant South African immigrant that turns Algarve fields brilliant yellow from November to May. Orchid lovers will find a wide variety of the plant thriving in the Algarve, especially in the limestone soil around Faro.

In rainier, more mountainous northern regions, species typical of temperate Europe take over: gorse, heather and broom cover the hillsides, while natural woodland includes sweet chestnut, Scots pine, oak, elm and poplar.

Up to a third of Portugal's species are of foreign origin. Early settlers in the south cultivated vines and planted citrus trees, while the Moors introduced almonds, carobs, figs, palms and the large white irises commonly seen along roadsides. Portuguese explorers and colonists brought back foreign plants, including the gaudy purple or yellow Hottentot fig of South Africa, which generates huge mats of succulents; and the prickly pear cactus, believed to have been introduced from the Americas by Christopher Columbus. In Sintra you'll see exotic thuja firs, enormous sequoias and araucarias, planted as fashionable novelties in the 18th and 19th centuries.

More recently, vast commercial plantations of Australian eucalyptus have transformed huge areas into dreary swaths of thirsty monoculture, now accounting for over 21% of Portugal's forest area. This quick-growing species (tall enough for felling in 10 years) is one of the most profitable trees on the market, much in demand by paper pulp companies. Two other commercially important trees that have crafted Portugal's landscape and lifestyle are the olive and the cork oak, the latter a protected, though increasingly threatened, species (see the boxed text 'Cork or Plastic?' under Ecology & Environment earlier). Since Roman times both have been grown and harvested in harmony with the environment, providing not only income but protection for many species. Although the olive prefers the sunny climate of the south, it's also taken root in the north. The cork oak, too, predominates in the south, especially the Alentejo plains.

Fauna

Portugal's fauna is typical of southern Europe, although a few North African species have found their way here. The fauna you're most likely to encounter are rabbits, hares and bats. In more remote areas you might come across fox, deer, otter or even foraging wild boar.

Two well-established North African species are the genet, a spotted, weasel-like mammal that hides during the day, and the Egyptian mongoose, which you may well encounter trotting across quieter Algarve roads. Portugal's most delightful North African settler is the Mediterranean chameleon, introduced about 70 years ago and found in the eastern coastal Algarve (see the boxed text 'Now You See Me, Now You Don't…' in The Algarve chapter).

Portugal's birdlife is a rich mix of temperate and Mediterranean species plus migrants, including Audouin's gull, black tern and pied flycatcher. Outside protected areas, birds are often hard to spot – hunting and habitat loss having taken their toll – but in reserves, such as the Reserva Natural do Sapal de Castro Marim and the Parque Natural da

Ria Formosa (see boxed texts in The Algarve chapter), you stand a good chance of seeing several wetland species, including flamingos, egrets, herons, spoonbills and many species of shore birds, gulls and terns.

You may even spot more unusual birds: lesser kestrels at Mértola, purple gallinules in the Parque Natural da Ria Formosa (see the boxed text 'Golf & Gallinules' in The Algarve chapter), bustards and sandgrouse on the Alentejo plains, and Iberian species such as the great spotted cuckoo, red-winged nightjar, rufous bushchat, spectacled warbler and azure-winged magpie. Several of these, along with the hoopoe, bee-eater and Sardinian warbler, can be seen in protected farmland and scrubland of the Parque Natural da Ria Formosa. As for birds of prey, your best chance of spotting these is probably in the Parque Natural do Douro Internacional (see the Trás-os-Montes chapter for details).

Portugal's leading ornithological society is the **Sociedade Portuguesa para o Estudo**

Portugal's Parks & Nature Reserves

Following are contact details for Portugal's national and natural parks and reserves.

1 **Paisagem Protegida do Litoral de Esposende**
(☎ 253 965 830, fax 253 965 330,
e apple@icn.pt) Rua 1 de Dezembro 6,
4740-226 Esposende (Minho)

2 **Parque Nacional da Peneda-Gerês**
(☎ 253 203 480, fax 253 613 169,
e pnpg@icn.pt) Quinta das Parretas, Avenida
António Macedo, 4700 Braga (Minho)

3 **Parque Natural de Montesinho**
(☎ 273 381 444, fax 273 381 179,
e pnm@icn.pt or cpn_montesinho@ip.pt)
Rua Cónego Albano Falcão 5, 5300 Bragança
(Trás-os-Montes)

4 **Parque Natural do Douro Internacional**
(☎ 279 340 030, fax 279 341 596,
e pndi@icn.pt) Rua de Santa Marinha 4,
5200 Mogadouro (Trás-os-Montes)

5 **Parque Natural do Alvão**
(☎ 259 302 830, fax 259 302 831,
e pnal@icn.pt) Praceta do Tronco, lote 17,
Cruz das Almas, 5000-528 Vila Real
(Trás-os-Montes)

6 **Reserva Natural das Dunas de São Jacinto**
(☎/fax 234 831 063, e mpa.santosmf@icn.pt)
Centro de Interpretação, N327, 3800-901
São Jacinto

7 **Parque Natural da Serra da Estrela**
(☎ 275 980 060, fax 275 980 069,
e pnse@icn.pt) Rua 1 de Maio 2, 6260
Manteigas (Beira Alta)

8 **Reserva Natural da Serra da Malcata**
(☎ 277 394 467, fax 277 394 580,
e rnsm@icn.pt) Rua dos Bombeiros
Voluntários, 6090 Penamacor
(Beira Baixa)

9 **Parque Natural do Tejo Internacional**
(☎ 272 321 445, fax 272 342 375) Rua Sra
da Piedade, Lt 4-A Esc 3, 6000-279 Castelo
Branco (Beira Baixa)

10 **Paisagem Protegida da Serra de Açor**
(☎ 235 741 329) Casa Grande, Mata da
Margaraça, 3305 Benfeita
Headquarters (☎ 239 499 020, fax 239 499
029, e rnpa.santosmf@icn.pt) Mata Nacional
do Choupal, 3000 Coimbra (Beira Litoral)

11 **Reserva Natural do Paúl de Arzila**
(☎ 239 980 500) Rua do Bairro 1,
3040-604 Arzila
Headquarters (☎ 239 499 020, fax 239 499
029, e rnpa.santosmf@icn.pt) Mata Nacional
do Choupal, 3000 Coimbra (Beira Litoral)

12 **Reserva Natural das Berlengas**
(☎ 262 787 910, fax 262 787 930,
e rnb@icn.pt) Av Mariano Calado 55,
2520-224 Peniche (Estremadura)

13 **Parque Natural das Serras de Aire e
Candeeiros**
(☎ 243 999 480, fax 243 999 488,
e pnsac@icn.pt) Rua Dr Augusto César Silva
Ferreira, 2040 Rio Maior (Estremadura &
Ribatejo)

14 **Reserva Natural do Paúl do Boquilobo**
(☎ 249 820 550, fax 249 820 378,
e rnpb@icn.pt) Quinta do Paúl,
Brogueira, Apartado 27, 2350-334 Torres
Novas (Ribatejo)

15 **Parque Natural da Serra de São Mamede**
(☎ 245 203 631, fax 245 207 501,
e pnssm@icn.pt) Rua General Conde Jorge
de Avilez 22, 7300-185 Portalegre (Alentejo)

de Aves *(SPEA; ☎ 213 431 847; ⓦ www.spea .pt; Rua da Vitória 53, 1100-618 Lisbon)*. Major efforts of SPEA are the Important Bird Areas (IBA) programme and the Projecto Atlas, a government-funded project, run in coordination with ICN (see National Parks later), to map the distribution of Portugal's breeding birds.

For details of UK-based Naturetrek, which runs bird-watching tours to Portugal, see Organised Tours in the Getting There & Away chapter.

Endangered Species

Among endangered mammal species in Portugal, the most at risk is the Iberian lynx, the only big cat endemic in Europe and now the world's most endangered feline. Fewer than 150 Iberian lynx are now left in Spain and Portugal, its numbers decimated by disease, poachers, habitat destruction and scarcity of rabbits (its main diet). The last remaining hide-outs of the 50 or so animals in Portugal are mostly in scattered, remote regions of the Algarve; only one lynx is believed to still

Portugal's Parks & Nature Reserves

16 **Reserva Natural do Estuário do Tejo**
(☎ 212 341 742, fax 212 341 654,
ⓔ rnet@icn.pt) Avenida dos Combatentes da Grande Guerra 1, 2890 Alcochete (Ribatejo; see Around Lisbon chapter)

17 **Parque Natural de Sintra-Cascais**
(☎ 219 247 200, fax 219 247 227,
ⓔ pnsc@icn.pt) Rua Gago Coutinho 1, 2710-566, Sintra (Estremadura; see Around Lisbon chapter)

18 **Paisagem Protegida da Arriba Fóssil da Costa da Caparica**
(☎ 212 918 270, fax 212 918 279,
ⓔ appafcc@icn.pt) Estrada Florestal Costa de Caparica, Praia da Rainha, 2825 Costa da Caparica (Estremadura)

19 **Parque Natural da Arrábida**
(☎ 265 541 140, fax 265 541 155,
ⓔ pnarr@icn.pt) Praça da República, 2900-587 Setúbal (Estremadura; see Around Lisbon chapter)

20 **Reserva Natural do Estuário do Sado**
(☎ 265 541 140, fax 265 541 155,
ⓔ rnes@icn.pt) Praça da República, 2900-587 Setúbal (Estremadura; see Around Lisbon chapter)

21 **Reserva Natural das Lagoas de Santo André e da Sancha**
(☎ 269 708 400, fax 269 752 145,
ⓔ pnsacv.vidala@icn.pt) Colectiva C4, St André, 7500 Santiago do Cacém (Alentejo)

22 **Parque Natural do Sudoeste Alentejano e Costa Vicentina**
(☎ 283 322 735, fax 283 322 830,
ⓔ pnsacv.od@icn.pt) Rua Serpa Pinto 32, 7630 Odemira (Algarve & Alentejo; see the Algarve chapter)

23 **Parque Natural do Vale do Guadiana**
(☎ 286 611 084, fax 286 611 085,
ⓔ pnvg@icn.pt) Rua Dr Afonso Costa 40, Apartado 45, 7750 Mértola (Alentejo)

24 **Reserva Natural do Sapal de Castro Marim e Vila Real de Santo António**
(☎ 281 510 680, fax 281 531 257,
ⓔ rnscm@icn.pt) Sapal de Venta Moínhos, Apartado 7, 8950 Castro Marim (Algarve)

25 **Parque Natural da Ria Formosa**
(☎ 289 704 134, fax 289 704 165,
ⓔ pnrf@icn.pt) Centro de Educação Ambiental de Marim, Quelfes, 8700 Olhão (Algarve)

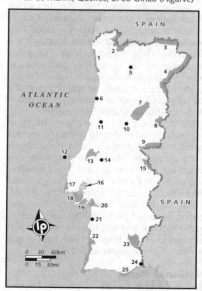

exist in Portugal's so-called lynx reserve, the Reserva Natural de Serra da Malcata. A network of protected areas, habitat corridors and captive breeding programmes are now being urgently arranged to try and save the species. For details, check the website of **SOS Lynx** (w www.soslynx.org), which has warned that if the species dies out, it will be the first feline extinction since prehistoric times.

The Iberian wolf is also in serious decline. There are thought to be less than 200 left in Portugal (out of an estimated 1500 in the Iberian Peninsula). Most live in the Parque Natural de Montesinho (Trás-os-Montes) and adjacent protected areas of Spain. Although protected by law, the wolf is illegally killed – shot, trapped or poisoned – at the rate of about 20 a year as it is blamed (often mistakenly) for attacking cattle and domestic animals. See the boxed text 'Safe Haven for Wolves' in the Around Lisbon chapter for details of a wolf sanctuary near Mafra.

Portugal's protected areas harbour several endangered birds, including the Spanish imperial eagle and the tawny owl in the Parque Nacional da Peneda-Gerês, and the purple gallinule in the Parque Natural da Ria Formosa. Ria Formosa is also home to the strictly protected Mediterranean chameleon and, at the park centre in Quinta de Marim, the bizarre Algarve water-dog, whose unique webbed feet once made it the fisherman's best friend, able to dive down to depths of 6m to retrieve broken nets. Now practically extinct (dog fanciers in the USA snapped up many in recent years) it's the subject of a special breeding programme at the Quinta de Marim headquarters.

Outside the parks you're most likely to see endangered or strictly protected species in the southern Alentejo in Mértola, which hosts the country's largest nesting colony of lesser kestrels between March and September, or in the Castro Verde region, a haunt of the great bustard, Europe's heaviest bird.

An EU habitats and species directive, giving essential protection to such endangered species, was intended to become part of member states' laws in 1994, but not one country has yet implemented it.

National Parks

Portugal has a variety of protected areas: the Parque Nacional da Peneda-Gerês is the only national park (that is, it meets certain international requirements) but there are also 12 other parks called *parques naturais* (natural parks). In addition are nine *reservas naturais* (nature reserves) and three areas of *paisagens protegidas* (protected landscape areas), with a fourth in the early stages of creation. Lesser protection is afforded several *sítios classificados* (classified sites) and *monumentos naturais* (natural monuments). These areas total some 6500 sq km – just over 7% of Portugal's land area.

The Instituto da Conservação da Natureza (ICN) is the government agency responsible for overall park management, publicity and policy. Its **Divisão de Informática** *(Information Division; ☎ 213 523 317, fax 213 542 501;* w *www.icn.pt; Rua da Lapa 29A, 1250-701 Lisbon)* has general information on the parks, but detailed maps and English-language material are surprisingly scant. Individual park offices often don't have much to offer either. Standards of maintenance and facilities vary greatly, and hopeful hikers may be disappointed: 'trails' often turn out to be roads or nothing at all; the park 'map' a glossy leaflet for motorists; and 'park accommodation' a couple of huts, which need to be booked well in advance, geared for school groups.

But the parks do feature vast areas of unspoilt mountains, forests and coastal lagoons. The reluctance of most Portuguese to go walking anywhere, let alone venture into remote areas, means you can find some incredibly quiet, isolated spots. We describe the best of the parks in the respective regional chapters.

GOVERNMENT & POLITICS

Portugal has been a sovereign republic ever since the overthrow of the monarchy in 1910. Western-style, multiparty democracy only came after the 1974 Revolution of the Carnations, which removed the authoritarian Salazar-era government.

Portugal's chief of state is the president of the republic, directly elected by universal suffrage for a maximum of two consecutive five-year terms. Presidents have wide powers, including the power to dissolve parliament and veto laws.

The prime minister is responsible both to the president and the Assembléia da República, the national legislature. This single-chamber body has 230 members, elected for four years by popular vote under a system of proportional representation. The legislative programme drawn up by the prime minister's Council of Ministers must be approved by the Assembléia.

Portugal has 25 representatives in the European Parliament (EP). The last EP elections in 1999 saw the PS winning 12 seats and the PSD winning nine, with the rest divided among other parties.

Portuguese citizens can cast their first vote when they're 18 years old. From then on men can also be called up for compulsory military service – anything from four to 18 months – although they have a right to conscientious objection.

Local tiers of government in the country's 18 *distritos* consist of 278 *concelhos* (municipalities) and 4047 *freguesias* (parishes) within those councils, each governed by an assembly elected by popular vote under a system of proportional representation. The PSD currently controls most municipal councils.

Since 1976 the archipelagos of Madeira and the Azores have been recognised as autonomous regions and have their own governments, legislatures and administrations.

Portugal's two main political parties are the ruling centre-right PSD and opposition left-of-centre PS. The PSD have formed a coalition government with the small rightwing CDS-PP. Other major opposition parties include the communist PCP and a militant coalition of radical parties, the Bloco de Esquerda (BE; Left Bloc), which includes ecologists, feminists and other like-minded groups.

The current prime minister is Durão Barroso of the PSD, which won the 2002 elections after six years in opposition (see Portugal Today under History for details). The socialist president, Jorge Sampaio, has been in office since 1996; the next presidential elections are due in 2006.

ECONOMY

Where did the good times go? Once the darling of the EU, with an impressive growth rate and low unemployment and inflation, Portugal has now plunged into economic shambles. 'The country,' announced the new prime minister in 2002, 'is in tatters.'

After joining the euro currency zone in 1999 (astonishing everyone by managing to meet the strict criteria), Portugal became one of its star performers. It boasted growing prosperity and rapid development, particularly in communications and financial services (it has more mobile phones per capita than almost anywhere else in Europe). And now? Growth rates are at a miserable 1%, inflation is above 4%, and worst of all, the budget deficit has soared to a staggering 3.9%, exceeding the EU's 3% ceiling. A lenient EU has given Portugal until 2006 to balance its books or face hefty fines.

So what went wrong? Years of overspending, for a start. The government has spent up to 44% of GDP, while personal debt is almost 100% of disposable income, both figures among the highest in the EU. But there are more deep-rooted problems. Portugal has lacked motivation and discipline, say analysts. The country's competitiveness and productivity has deteriorated. Largely to blame are lacklustre training mechanisms and deficiencies in education and technology. There's also been failure to reform services, such as the bloated civil service and the state-run health service (€1 billion in the red in 2001). And corruption has continually reared its ugly head, tainting Portugal as one of the most corrupt countries in the EU.

One of the government's biggest economic burdens is an inefficient agriculture sector. Some 10% of the workforce is still engaged in agriculture, forestry and fishing (the EU average is 5%), but this sector accounts for only 4.1% of the country's GDP. Agriculture's most important contributions are in tomato paste and cork – Portugal is the world's largest exporter of both these commodities. By contrast, the services sector (real estate, banking, financial services, wholesale and tourism) has, until recently, been thriving. Tourism alone accounts for 8% of Portugal's GDP. More than 12 million tourists visit Portugal annually, contributing valuable foreign exchange earnings.

The manufacturing sector still includes important traditional industries, such as textiles and clothing, footwear, cork, wood and paper pulp but these now face stiff competition from cheaper products from developing countries. A few bright signs are the successful manufacturing projects funded by foreign investment (such as the Volkswagen-run Autoeuropa car plant near Setúbal). EU countries (notably Germany, Spain, France and the UK) account for almost 80% of foreign direct investment, primarily in manufacturing, finance, real estate and tourism, and some 80% of Portugal's foreign trade.

But Portugal hardly looks very appealing to investors these days. The new government has acted quickly to try and put the economy back on track, but the challenges of structural reform, fiscal belt-tightening and competition from a newly enlarged EU (now numbering 25 countries) are immense. From 2006 Portugal will not be able to rely on EU funding anymore either. Indeed, from 2004 it will have to shell out financial aid to other, poorer EU countries.

POPULATION & PEOPLE

Portugal has a population of 10.3 million. Around 16% are under 15 years old and 16.4% over 65. Most Portuguese share typically Mediterranean features, such as brown eyes and dark hair. The vast majority live in rural areas, for example, the Minho, one of Portugal's poorest and most densely populated regions, and the Algarve, where the population has increased by 15.8% in the last decade. But the urban population has increased dramatically since the 1960s, from 22% of the total to around 36% (Britain's urban population, by comparison, is about 90%).

Saudade

It's been described as nostalgia for a glorious past, a fathomless yearning and a longing for home, but unless you're Portuguese you'll probably never really grasp the uniquely Portuguese passion of *saudade*. Its musical form is the aching sorrow of *fado* – a melancholic submission to the twists and turns of fate. In Portuguese and Brazilian poetry it's a mystical reverence for nature, a brooding sense of loneliness, especially popular among certain 19th- and early 20th-century poets who fostered a cult of *saudosismo*. In tangible form it's the return of thousands of emigres to their home villages every August, drawn not just by family ties but by something deeper – a longing for all that home and that Portugal represents: the heroism of the past, the sorrows of the present, and wistful hopes for the future.

One major reason for this was the arrival of nearly a million African colonial refugees *(retornados)* in 1974 and 1975. In the late 1970s African refugees from war-torn Angola and Mozambique also arrived, followed by others from Guinea-Bissau and São Tomé e Príncipe. They generally integrated well into Portuguese society, with many picking up work in the booming construction industry.

Officially, there are now 98,000 Africans in Portugal (plus many illegal immigrants, although a recent amnesty has legalised many immigrant workers). They make up Portugal's major ethnic groups (the 47,000 Cape Verdeans are the biggest group). Some 22,000 Brazilians also make up a sizable community and there's a small resident Roma (Gypsy) population. There are also increasing numbers of immigrant workers from central and Eastern Europe. Altogether, there are 225,000 foreign residents.

Portugal has one of the lowest percentages of avowed racists in the EU, but incidents of racism do occur. Gang-related tensions between Angolans and Cape Verdeans have also recently exploded in Lisbon. The slum living conditions of many immigrants is a depressing indication of the lack of government and national attention to this growing Afro-Portuguese community.

Emigres

Ever since gold and diamonds were discovered in Brazil in the 17th century, the Portuguese have sought their fortunes or a better life overseas, notably during the 18th and 19th centuries (in Brazil) and in the 1950s and 1960s in France and Germany. That second wave of emigres included young men avoiding conscription into Portuguese forces during the wars of independence in the African colonies.

Portugal's emigration rate is still one of Europe's highest and its overseas population one of the largest. It's estimated that three million Portuguese live or work abroad. Brazil, South Africa, the USA and Canada have the largest settlements, and France and Germany the largest number of temporary workers, who flock home for holidays in August or at Christmas.

[Continued on page 42]

Portugal's Architecture

Title page: Wooden coffered ceiling of Sala das Armas in the Palácio Nacional de Sintra (photograph by Bruce yuan-yue Bi)

Top Left: Cloisters of Igreja de São Vicente de Fora, in Lisbon, with 18th-century *azulejos* depicting La Fontaine's fables

Top Right: The tall columns and vaulted Manueline roof of the Mosteiro dos Jerónimos, in Lisbon's Belém district

Middle: Gothic architecture of Mosteiro de Santa Maria de Alcobaça, a Unesco World Heritage site

Bottom Left: The neo-classical Palácio Nacional de Mafra and its basilica dominate 10 hectares of Mafra

Bottom Right: Art Nouveau interior of Café Astória, a classic old coffee house in Braga

Pre-Roman

An isolated clearing in an Alentejan olive grove near Évora is the setting for one of Portugal's earliest and most memorable prehistoric sites. The Cromeleque dos Almendres, a vast oval of some 95 monoliths, is the Iberian Peninsula's finest cromlech (a circle or oval of huge boulders used for funerary purposes).

All over Portugal, especially in the Alentejo, are similar funerary and religious structures, built during the Neolithic and Megalithic eras, five to six thousand years ago. Most impressive are the dolmens: funerary chambers – rectangular, polygonal or round – reached by a corridor of stone slabs and covered with earth to create an artificial mound. Most striking is the Anta Grande do Zambujeiro (Great Dolmen of Zambujeiro), also near Évora. It's Europe's largest dolmen, with six 6m-high stones forming a huge chamber. Single monoliths, or menhirs, often carved with phallic or religious symbols, also dot the countryside like an army of stone sentinels. See the boxed text 'Dolmens, Menhirs & Other Mysteries' in the Alentejo chapter for more on these Stonehenge-like wonders.

With the arrival of the Celts (800–200 BC) came the first established hill-top settlements, called *castros*. The best-preserved example is the Citânia de Briteiros near Guimarães, where you can literally step into Portugal's past. Stone dwellings were built on a circular or elliptical plan, and the complex was surrounded with a dry-stone defensive wall. In the *citânias* (fortified villages) further south, dwellings tended to be rectangular.

Roman & Early Christian
(3rd century BC to 8th century AD)

The Romans left a wealth of architectural evidence – roads, bridges, towns complete with forums (marketplaces), villas, public baths and aqueducts. Most of Portugal's major cities are built on Roman foundations, though these foundations have mostly been covered over or destroyed. At the country's largest Roman site, at Conimbriga (near Coimbra), an entire Roman town is under excavation. Revealed so far are some splendid mosaics, along with structural or decorative columns, carved entablatures and classical ornamentation.

Portugal's most famous and photogenic Roman ruin is the so-called Temple of Diana in Évora, with its elaborately carved Corinthian columns. This is the finest temple of its kind in the Iberian Peninsula, its survival the result of having been walled up in the Middle Ages.

The various Teutonic tribes who invaded after the fall of Rome in the early 5th century left little trace other than a few churches built by the Visigoths, a fierce lot of Arian Christians. Though heavily restored over the centuries, these ancient churches still reveal a Roman basilican outline, rectangular in shape and divided by columns into a nave and two aisles. Two fine examples are the Capela de São Pedro de Balsemão (near Lamego) and the Igreja de Santa Amaro (in Beja). Most unusual is the Capela de São Frutuoso (near Braga) – Byzantine (Graeco-Asiatic) in character, laid out in the shape of a Greek cross.

The Visigoths also rebuilt the Roman town of Idanha-a-Velha, now a quiet hamlet near Castelo Branco; you can see their influence in parts of the cathedral here. Many other Visigothic churches were destroyed by the Moors after they kicked out the Visigoths in AD 711.

Moorish (8th to 12th centuries)

Unlike Spain, Portugal has no complete buildings left from the Moorish period. But there's the odd Moorish arch or wall, bits of fortresses, and the atmospheric remains of several *mourarias*, or Moorish quarters, notably in Moura, in the Alentejo. In nearby Mértola is a distinctive former mosque converted into a church.

The Moors did, however, introduce many elements that have persisted in Portuguese architecture, particularly in private homes and especially in the south: patios and horseshoe arches, wrought-iron work and whitewash, abundant ornamentation and the use of water as an interior and exterior decorative element.

BETHUNE CARMICHAEL

Left: Templo Romano with the spire of the *sé* (cathedral) in the background, Évora

Romanesque (11th to late 13th centuries)

During the Christian recapture of Portugal from the Moors, completed by 1297, virtually every Moorish mosque was replaced by a church or cathedral, often on the same site. These were in the simple, robust Romanesque style – with rounded arches, thick walls and heavy vaulting – originally introduced to Portugal by Burgundian monks. As with Coimbra's dour example, they were often heavily fortified because of the continuing military threat from the Moors and, later, the Castilians.

More delicate Romanesque touches can be found in several small, lovely churches (notably the Igreja de São Salvador at Bravães, near Ponte da Barca in the Minho), where portals often display fine animal or plant motifs in their archivolts. Only one complete example of a secular building remains from this time – Bragança's endearing, five-sided Domus Municipalis, Portugal's oldest town hall.

Gothic (12th to 15th centuries)

Gothic architecture has produced some of Portugal's most aesthetically pleasing religious monuments. The austere abbey church and cloister of the Mosteiro de Santa Maria de Alcobaça, begun in 1178, is considered one of Europe's finest examples of Cistercian architecture, with a soaring lightness and simplicity strongly influenced by the style of the French abbey at Clairvaux. Distinctive Gothic touches include pointed arches and ribbed vaults. Alcobaça's most memorable corner is the simple Cloisters of Silence, a model for later cathedral cloisters at Coimbra, Lisbon and Évora, and many other cloisters throughout the land.

Pillory Power

Portugal's *pelourinhos*, or pillories, are a distinctive feature of many towns and villages, especially in the Minho and Trás-os-Montes.

Believed to have originated in Roman times, these stone columns became prominent in Portugal around the 12th century and were in use for some 500 years. Originally devoid of decoration, they served as a public place where criminals could be handcuffed or chained as punishment. Eventually their symbolic value as reminders of municipal power became paramount, which is why most pillories are beside town halls, cathedrals or monasteries.

During the 16th-century Manueline era, pillories became elaborate works of art, often topped by Dom Manuel's motifs of an armillary sphere and the cross of the Order of Christ, while the column was carved into ropelike coils.

Some of Portugal's more unusual pillories include a 16th-century one in Elvas, covered in stone dots; a hexagonal pillory in Barcelos, topped by a graceful granite lantern; and Soajo's curiously pagan pillory, carved with a crude smiling face.

A pillory with armillary sphere

But simplicity went out the window with the construction of the Mosteiro de Santa Maria da Vitória (Mosteiro da Batalha) at the end of the 14th century. Portuguese, Irish and French architects worked on this breathtaking monument over the following two centuries and more. The combination of their skills and the changing architectural fashions of the times – from Flamboyant (late) Gothic to Gothic Renaissance to Manueline (see the following section) – makes this Portugal's most stimulating Gothic building. It revels in decorative elements (especially in its Gothic Royal Cloisters and Chapter House), while the eye-catching flying buttresses are typical of the style called English Perpendicular Gothic.

Secular architecture also enjoyed a Gothic boom, thanks to the need for fortifications against the Moors and to the castle-building fervour of the 13th-century ruler, Dom Dinis. Dozens of impressive castles (eg, at Estremoz, Óbidos and Bragança) date from this time, many featuring massive double perimeter walls and an inner square tower.

VITOR VIEIRA

Left: Gothic facade of the Mosteiro dos Jerónimos, Belém

Manueline (late 15th to mid-16th centuries)

Manueline is the term given to a specifically Portuguese variety of late-Gothic architecture. A highly decorative style, it coincided roughly with the reign of Dom Manuel I (1495–1521), although it popped up for centuries afterwards (eg, in the over-the-top neo-Manueline Palace Hotel do Buçaco in Luso, built in the early 20th century).

During Dom Manuel's reign Vasco da Gama and fellow explorers claimed new overseas lands and new wealth for Portugal. The confidence of this Age of Discoveries was expressed in sculptural creations of extraordinary inventiveness, drawing heavily on nautical themes: twisted ropes, coral and anchors in stone, topped by the ubiquitous armillary sphere (a navigational device, which became Dom Manuel's personal symbol) and the Cross of the Order of Christ (symbol of the religious military order that largely financed and inspired Portugal's explorations).

The style first emerged in Setúbal's Igreja de Jesus, designed in the 1490s by French expatriate Diogo de Boitaca, who gave it columns and ribbed vaulting reminiscent of twisted ropes. The sweeping style, as dramatic as ocean waves, soon caught on elsewhere, embellished with a plethora of decoration (aptly described by the eccentric 18th-century English novelist William Beckford as 'scollops and twistifications').

Outstanding Manueline masterpieces are the Mosteiro dos Jerónimos at Belém (Lisbon), masterminded largely by Diogo de Boitaca and João de Castilho, and the Mosteiro da Batalha's flamboyant Unfinished Chapels. Other famous creations include Belém's Torre de Belém, a Manueline-Moorish concoction by Diogo de Boitaca and his brother Francisco, and Diogo de Arruda's fantastical window in the Chapter House of Tomar's Convento de Cristo, heavy on exotic plants and maritime detail (and sadly obscured by centuries of grime).

Renaissance (16th century)

The Portuguese were slow to take up the Renaissance style, a return to Roman classical design and proportion. One of its protagonists, the Italian Andrea Sansovino, is thought to have spent time in Portugal, though he made little impression. The Quinta da Bacalhoa, a 15th-century house at Vila Nogueira de Azeitão (near Setúbal) is his only notable contribution. The French sculptor Nicolas Chanterène was the main pioneer of Renaissance ideas in Portugal. From around 1517 onwards, his influence abounds in sculpture and architectural decoration.

Among the best of Portugal's few Renaissance buildings are the Great Cloisters in Tomar's Convento de Cristo, designed by Spanish Diogo de Torralva in the late 16th century, the nearby Igreja de Nossa Senhora da Conceição, and the Convento de Bom Jesus at Valverde, outside Évora.

Mannerist (late 16th to late 17th centuries)

Sober and severe, the Mannerist style reflects the spirit of its time, coinciding with the years of Spanish rule (1580–1640) and the heavy influence of the Inquisition and the Jesuits. It persisted throughout much of the 17th century. Lisbon's Igreja de São Vicente de Fora, built between 1582 and 1627 by Felipe Terzi, is a typical example (which served as a model for many other churches) of balanced Mannerist classicism.

PORTUGAL'S ARCHITECTURE

Baroque (late 17th to late 18th centuries)

With independence from Spain re-established and the influence of the Inquisition on the wane, Portugal burst out in baroque fever – an architectural style that was exuberant, theatrical and aimed at the senses. Nothing could recapture the Manueline flourish, but for flamboyance the baroque style – named after the Portuguese word for a rough pearl, *barroco* – clearly surpassed it. At its height in the 18th century (almost a century later than in Italy), it was characterised by curvaceous forms, huge monuments and spatially complex schemes.

Financed by the 17th-century gold and diamond discoveries in Brazil, and encouraged by the extravagant Dom João V, local and foreign (particularly Italian) artists created mind-bogglingly opulent masterpieces. A hallmark of the style was the lavish use of talha dourada (gilded woodwork) in church interiors, notably Aveiro's Convento de Jesus, Lisbon's Igreja de São Roque and Porto's Igreja de São Francisco.

The baroque of central and southern Portugal was more restrained. Examples include the chancel of Évora's cathedral, and the Palácio Nacional de Mafra. Designed by the German architect João Frederico Ludovice to rival the similar palace-monastery of San Lorenzo de El Escorial (near Madrid), the Mafra version is relatively sober, but so immense it took 15,000 labourers 13 years to complete.

Meanwhile, the Tuscan painter and architect Nicolau Nasoni (who settled in Porto around 1725) introduced a more ornamental baroque style to the north. Nasoni is responsible for Porto's Torre dos Clérigos and Igreja da Misericórdia, and the whimsical Palácio de Mateus near Vila Real (internationally famous as the image on Mateus rosé wine bottles).

In the mid-18th century, a notable school of architecture evolved in Braga. Local artists such as André Soares built churches and palaces in a very decorative style, heavily influenced by Augsburg engravings from southern Germany. Soares' Casa do Raio, in Braga, and much of the monumental staircase of the nearby Bom Jesus do Monte, are typical examples of this period's ornamentation.

JOHN KING

Left: The elegant town hall of Braga is a fine example of baroque architecture

Only when the gold ran out did the baroque fad fade. At the end of the 18th century, architects flirted briefly with the rococo style (best exemplified by Mateus Vicente's Palácio de Queluz, begun in 1747) before embracing neoclassicism.

Neoclassical (mid-18th to 19th centuries)

After Lisbon's devastating 1755 earthquake, the Marquês de Pombal invited architect Eugenio dos Santos to rebuild the Baixa area in a plain style using classical elements that could be easily built and repeated. This new 'Pombaline' style featured a grid pattern marked by un-adorned houses and wide avenues. It had a knock-on effect and led to a reaction against the excesses of the baroque period in other parts of the country. In Porto, for instance, the Hospital de Santo António and the Feitoria Inglesa (Factory House), both designed by Englishmen, show a noticeable return to sober Palladian and classical designs. Lisbon's early-19th-century Palácio Nacional da Ajuda was also de-signed on neoclassical lines and served as the inspiration for the ele-gantly restrained Palácio de Brejoeira (near Monção, in the Minho).

19th Century & Modern

In the early 19th century virtually all new building of major monuments came to a halt. This was partly due to the after-effects of the Penin-sular War (1807–14) and partly because a liberal decree in 1834 dis-solved the religious orders, allowing their many buildings to be appropriated by the state. Some former monasteries are still used by the government today – notably Lisbon's Benedictine Mosteiro de São Bento, now the seat of parliament (the Palácio da Assembleia da República).

When new buildings did emerge they tended to draw on all the architectural styles of the past, from Moorish (as in Lisbon's Rossio station) to neoclassical (Porto's stock exchange, the Palácio da Bolsa). A distinctly French influence can be seen in many grand apartment blocks and office buildings built at this time.

Towards the end of the 19th century the increased use of iron and steel reflected Portugal's emergence as an industrial nation. Train sta-tions (eg, Lisbon's Alcântara station) and other grand buildings were covered in iron and glass. Gustave Eiffel built iron bridges across the rivers Minho, Lima and Douro, and his followers were responsible for several Eiffel look-alikes, including Lisbon's eye-catching Elevador de Santa Justa.

One of the most delightful movements during this period was Art Nouveau, a burst of carefree, decorative fancy that produced many beautifully decorated cafés and shops (check out Lisbon's Versailles or Braga's Café Astória).

The Salazar years produced decidedly severe, almost Soviet-style, state commissions (eg, Coimbra University's dull faculty buildings, which replaced elegant 18th-century neoclassical ones). Many ugly buildings and apartment blocks rose on city outskirts. Notable excep-tions dating from the 1960s are Lisbon's Palácio da Justiça in the Cam-polide district, and the purpose-built Museu Calouste Gulbenkian.

Azulejos

JULIA WILKINSON

A striking 18th-century azulejo, Aveiro

There's no question which decorative art is Portugal's favourite – painted tiles called *azulejos* (probably after the Arabic *al zulaycha*, meaning polished stone) cover everything from church interiors to train stations to private homes. The Portuguese can't claim to have invented the technique – they learned about it from the Moors, who picked it up from the Persians – but it has been used more widely and inventively here than anywhere else.

Portugal's earliest 16th-century tiles are Moorish, but after the Portuguese captured Ceuta (Morocco) in 1415, they began exploring the art themselves. The 16th-century Italian invention of majolica, in which colours are painted directly onto wet clay over a layer of white enamel, gave the Portuguese the impetus they needed, and the azulejo craze began.

The first truly Portuguese tiles – multicoloured and geometric – appeared in the 1580s, gracing churches such as Lisbon's Igreja de São Roque. The late 17th century saw a fashion for huge panels in churches and on houses and public buildings, depicting everything from cherubs to commerce, saints to landscapes. Quality eventually gave way to quantity, and the blue-and-white Delft tiles of the Netherlands took over the market.

In the 18th century the Portuguese masters António de Oliveira Bernardes and his son Policarpo revived the use of blue-and-white and polychrome tiles, producing brilliant panels perfectly suited to their surroundings. Rococo themes appeared, decorating fountains, stairways (notably at Lamego's Igreja de Nossa Senhora dos Remédios) and sacristies (Lisbon's Igreja de Nossa Senhora da Madre de Deus). By the end of the century, quality was again on the decline, a consequence this time of industrial-scale manufacture and the demand for tiles after the 1755 Lisbon earthquake.

Imaginative azulejos appeared in the 19th century, including panels in restaurants such as Lisbon's Cervejaria da Trindade. The Art Nouveau and Art Deco movements took azulejos further into the public domain, with fantastic facades and interiors for shops, restaurants and residential buildings – notably by Rafael Bordalo Pinheiro and Jorge Colaço. Azulejos still have a place in contemporary Portuguese life – Maria Keil and Júlio de Resende are responsible for some stunning wall mosaics and murals.

For a detailed look at the history of this uniquely Portuguese art, visit Lisbon's Museu Nacional do Azulejo.

The tendency towards urban mediocrity continued after the 1974 revolution, although architects such as Fernando Távora and Eduardo Souto Moura have produced impressive schemes. Lisbon's postmodern Amoreiras shopping complex, by Tomás Taveira, is another striking contribution.

Portugal's greatest contemporary architect is Álvaro Siza Vieira. A believer in 'clarity and simplism', his expressionist approach is reflected in projects such as the Pavilhão de Portugal (Portuguese National Pavilion) for Expo 98, Porto's splendid Museu de Arte Contemporânea and the Igreja de Santa Maria at Marco de Canavezes, south of Amarante. He has also restored central Lisbon's historic Chiado shopping district with notable sensitivity, following a major fire in 1988.

Post-1974 legislation specifies that old buildings of historical or architectural value be restored or incorporated into new schemes. A fine Lisbon example of this trend is the headquarters of the Association of Portuguese Architects, combining its original neoclassical facade with a contemporary interior.

Vernacular (Local) Architecture

A relatively unsung aspect of architecture is so-called 'vernacular architecture' – the shapes and forms in a region's common buildings that arise naturally over the centuries in response to climate, land use and other constraints. Northern Portugal, for example, is a land of granite, a hard material perfect for constructing thick-walled, two-storey houses with slate roofs that keep out winter weather. In the coastal Beiras, local limestone is used for houses that are faced with painted stucco or, occasionally, azulejo (see the boxed text).

On the coast near Aveiro, several villages are famous for their candy-striped houses built of wood from nearby pine forests. Brick houses in the Ribatejo and the Alentejo are long, single-storey structures, stuccoed and whitewashed, with a single colour (usually blue) outlining their architectural features. To keep out the summer heat these houses have few doors and windows; their huge fireplaces and chimneys provide both warmth and a place to smoke the meat and sausages typical of the region. Around Estremoz in the Alentejo you'll find a most extravagant housing material: marble. A plentiful local supply ensures its generous use in everything from palaces and town houses to kerbs and walls.

By contrast, the Algarve's clay or stone houses appear quite modest. Those with flat terraces (used for drying produce and catching rainwater), instead of the usual red tile roofs, take on a North African or Moorish appearance. Another Moorish touch very characteristic of the Algarve is the decorative pierced chimney. Typical, too, of Mediterranean houses is the Algarve's shaded porches and arcaded verandas at ground level.

A fine book on the vernacular architecture of Portugal and Spain is Norman F Carver Jr's *Iberian Villages*, published in 1988.

[Continued from page 32]

Women in Society

Despite the official reversal of many traditional attitudes towards women after the 1974 revolution and a constitution that actively promotes women's rights more than most other EU countries, Portugal remains, at least on the face of it, a man's world. There are very few women in top business posts or in politics (only 45 members of parliament and two cabinet ministers). And although 60% of women are employed they get, on average, 22% less pay than men.

But things are likely to change. Already, 56% of Portuguese university students (and two-thirds of successful graduates) are female. Women make up over half the total labour force and over 40% of the country's doctors, judges and lawyers. The only professions unlikely to see women dominating soon are engineering, architecture and theology. Even politics may be forced to admit more women. A 1997 amendment to the constitution promoted equality in access to political office. A subsequent, hotly debated law to enforce minimum quotas of women candidates in elections was defeated in 1999, but is still on the agenda.

The main state body promoting equal rights and opportunities is the Comissão para a Igualdade e para os Direitos das Mulheres (Commission for the Equality and Rights of Women; see under Women Travellers in the Facts for the Visitor chapter). Working with the government, it recently embarked on a high-profile programme publicising women's issues and training police to cope with domestic violence.

According to reports, domestic violence against women is a persistent but hidden problem. Sexual harassment in the workplace is also fairly common but is only considered a sex crime if perpetrated by a superior. In both circumstances, traditional attitudes often discourage victims from turning to the courts.

EDUCATION

The state of Portugal's education system is embarrassingly awful. Some 75% of Portugal's employees have a 'low level' of education (compared with 18% in Germany). The Salazar regime is largely to blame; for four decades it invested as little as possible in education, and only four years schooling was compulsory. Today there's free preschool education for children aged three to six, and nine years of compulsory education (from age six to 15), provided free of charge in state schools. Private schools supplement state schools. Secondary education (not compulsory) lasts for three years. Higher education is provided at the country's 18 universities and around 100 other establishments such as regional technical colleges.

According to figures, 99% of school-age children enrol in basic and secondary education, but the reality is that many of them leave early to find work. Only 35% of those aged 25 to 29 have finished secondary education (the EU average is 71%). Only half even receive preschool education. And only 10% of the relevant age group get a degree (the EU average is 21%).

An inefficient, excessively centralised system is part of the problem, plus insufficient teachers and schools. The lack of emphasis given to vocational training in specialised colleges results in many students making little practical use of what they are taught. Too many people leave school with low skills or with a second-rate education that fails to meet today's needs. All this, plus a paltry effort at promoting new technologies (only 0.4% of GDP is invested in research), seriously affect labour productivity, which is half that of the EU average.

Recent improvements offer grounds for hope. More resources and attention have been focused on the preschool population; and many more schools now have computers. But people are still waiting for the government to do its own sums and fulfil its promise of major improvements.

ARTS
Music

Fundamental to Portugal's history of musical expression is its foot-tapping folk music, which you can hear throughout the country at almost every festival. It traces its roots to the medieval troubadour, and is traditionally accompanied by a band of guitars, violins, clarinets, harmonicas and various wooden percussion instruments. In fact, the instruments are often more attractive than the singing, which could generously be described as a high-pitched repetitive wail.

Far more enigmatic is Portugal's most famous style of music, *fado* (Portuguese for 'fate'). These melancholic chants – performed as a set of three songs, each one lasting three minutes – are also said to have their roots in troubadour songs (although African slave songs have had an influence too). They're traditionally sung by one performer accompanied by a 12-string Portuguese *guitarra* (a pear-shaped guitar), and often a Spanish guitar as well. Fado emerged in the 18th century in Lisbon's working-class districts of Alfama and Mouraria and gradually moved upmarket.

There are two styles of fado music, one from Lisbon (still considered the most genuine) and the other from the university town of Coimbra. The latter is traditionally sung by men only since it praises the beauty of women. In 1996 *fadista* Manuela Bravo caused an outcry when she recorded a CD of Coimbra fados (the entire issue of CDs mysteriously disappeared almost as soon as it had appeared).

The greatest modern *fadista* was Amália Rodrigues, who brought fado international recognition. She died in 1999 aged 79, after more than 60 years of extraordinary fado performances ('I don't sing fado,' she once said, 'it sings me'). Amália's recordings are still the best – pick up a copy of her greatest hits (or the pricey double CD set *O Melhor*) to hear what fado should really sound like.

A contemporary performer with many fans is the dynamic young Mísia, considered a leading exponent of a new fado style. She has experimented with instrumentation (including piano, accordion and violin, as well as the usual guitar) and commissioned lyrics by contemporary poets. Her *Garras dos Sentidos* (Claws of the Heart) CD is particularly fine. Another young *fadista* well worth hearing is Mafalda Arnauth, often accompanied by both guitar and double bass. The men aren't outdone: one of the great young male voices in traditional fado these days is star-quality Camané.

Venues for live fado in Lisbon, Coimbra, Porto and elsewhere are recommended under Entertainment for each town. See the Lisbon chapter for details on an annual fado festival, and a museum dedicated to its history.

Both fado and traditional folk songs – and, increasingly, 'foreign' strains from Europe and Africa – have shaped Portugal's modern folk-music scene *(música popular)*. Often censored during the Salazar years, its lyrics became overtly political after 1974, with singers using performances to support various revolutionary factions. Today's *música popular* has returned to its folk roots while adding contemporary innovations, thanks to singer-songwriters such as Júlio Pereira.

The Portuguese guitar, too, has taken on a new range of expression under masters such as Carlos Paredes and António Chaínho. Well-known folk groups include the venerable Brigada Victor Jara, Trovante, Almanaque and the internationally known Madredeus. At the grass-roots level are traditional student song groups, called *tunas académicas*, who give performances all over the country during March.

A popular genre in Lisbon is contemporary African jazz and rock. Dozens of African nightclubs now resonate to the rhythms of the former colonies. Big names include Cesaria Évora from Cape Verde, Guem from Angola, Fernando Luís from Mozambique and Kaba Mane from Guinea-Bissau. Mainstream jazz artists also hitting the headlines are Jacinta, Ensemble Raum (a young group led by guitarist Paulo Duarte) and Rão Kyao, who blend Ravi Shankar styles with uniquely Portuguese jazz elements. On the rock scene, don't miss Xutos & Pontapés or The Gift, whose latest album, *Film*, has some great tracks.

Literature

Portuguese literature has been moulded by foreign influences since the 13th century, particularly the styles and standards of Spain. Nevertheless, it retains a distinct temperament and individuality. Two major styles dominate: lyric poetry and realistic fiction. The country's most outstanding literary figure is Luís Vaz de Camões (1524–80), a poet who enjoyed little fame or fortune in his lifetime. Only after his death was his genius recognised, thanks largely to an epic poem, *Os Lusiadas* (The Lusiads). It tells of Vasco da Gama's 1497 sea voyage to India, but it's also a superbly lyrical paean to the Portuguese spirit, written when Portugal was still one of the most powerful countries in the Western world. On its publication in 1572 it received few plaudits; four centuries later it's considered the national epic, its poet a national hero.

In the 19th century a tide of romanticism flooded Portuguese literature. A prominent figure in this movement was poet, playwright and romantic novelist Almeida Garrett (1799–1854), who devoted much of his life to stimulating political awareness through his writings. Among his most notable works is the novel *Viagens na Minha Terra* (Travels in My Homeland), an allegory of contemporary political events, presented as a home-grown travelogue. Despite being Portugal's most talented playwright since the 16th-century court dramatist Gil Vicente, he was exiled for his political liberalism.

Garrett's contemporary Alexandre Herculano (also exiled) was meanwhile continuing the long Portuguese tradition of historical literature (which flourished most strongly during the Age of Discoveries) with an enormous body of work, most notably his magnum opus *História de Portugal*.

Towards the end of the 19th century several other writers emerged, among them José Maria Eça de Queirós, who introduced realism to Portuguese literature with his powerful 1876 novel *O Crime do Padre Amaro* (The Sin of Father Amaro). His other works include the entertaining narratives *Os Maias* (The Maias) and a finely translated collection of short stories, *The Anarchist Banker and Other Portuguese Stories*.

Fernando Pessoa (1888–1935), author of the 1934 *Mensagem* (Message), is posthumously regarded as the most extraordinary poet of his generation; his four different poet-personalities (which he referred to as heteronyms) created four distinct strains of poetry and prose. *A Centenary Pessoa*, published in English, provides a fascinating insight into his work.

The Salazar dictatorship, spanning much of the early modern era, suppressed creativity and freedom of expression. Several writers suffered during this period, including the poet and storyteller Miguel Torga (1907–95), whose background in Trás-os-Montes brought a radical individualism to his writings (so much so that his novel *Contos de Montanha*, or Tales from the Mountain, was banned). Also affected was Maria Velho da Costa, one of the three authors of *Novas Cartas Portuguesas* (The Three Marias: New

José Saramago

When José Saramago (born in 1922 to a poor, intensely Catholic peasant family) was awarded the 1998 Nobel prize for literature, the Vatican reacted as if bitten. Why? In 1991 Saramago had published *O Evangelho segundo Jesus Cristo* (The Gospel According to Jesus Christ), a unique reinterpretation of the biblical gospels, in which Jesus is depicted as a human being of flesh and blood, complete with sexual feelings and doubts about his role. Mary Magdalene appears as a strong, intelligent and loving woman, no longer associated with licentiousness. Up above, God and Satan argue about which of them embodies true evil, a fight God easily wins.

The Roman Catholic clergy was appalled. After a furious article in the papal press, the book was removed by the Portuguese government from the list of nominations for the EU's European Literary Award. Saramago, disgusted by this act of subservience to the Church, went into self-imposed exile on Lanzarote in Spain's Canary Islands.

A common thread in Saramago's stories is the inherent goodness of human nature – although humanity itself comes in for fierce criticism. Saramago's conviction that humankind is prone to submissiveness, collaboration and abuse is the haunting theme of his apocalyptic novel *Ensaio sobre a Cegueira* (Blindness).

And yet Saramago displays an unconditional belief in the power of love. Probably his most powerful novel is *Memorial do Convento* (Memorial of the Convent), originally published in 1982. Set in the turbulent 18th century, with the construction of Mafra's giant convent as a backdrop, it's arguably one of the most empathic love stories ever written. Reprinted in Portugal 29 times and translated into 20 languages, it launched Saramago to international fame.

Hans de Clercq

Portuguese Letters), whose modern feminist interpretation of the 17th-century *Letters of a Portuguese Nun* so shocked the Salazar regime that its authors were put on trial.

One of the most notable writers who survived and often documented this repressive era was José Cardoso Pires (1925–98), a popular novelist and playwright whose finest work, *Balada da Praia dos Cães* (Ballad of Dog's Beach), is a gripping thriller based on a real political assassination in the Salazar era. Prominent poets of the time were Jorge de Sena (1919–78), a humanist thinker who also wrote much fiction and criticism; and David Mourão-Ferreira (1927–97) whose works include the novel *Un Amor Feliz* (Lucky in Love). In Portugal's former colonies (particularly Brazil), writers such as Nobel prize–winner Jorge Amado (1912–2001) have also made their mark on modern Portuguese-language literature.

Today's literary scene is largely dominated by two names: José Saramago and António Lobo Antunes. Saramago, winner of the 1998 Nobel prize for literature (see the boxed text), has won international fame with works such as *Memorial do Convento* (Memorial of the Convent), which combines realism, astute political comment and poetic fancy. Antunes (b. 1942) produces magical, fast-paced prose, often with dark undertones and vast historical sweeps. His latest novel, *O Regresso das Caravelas* (The Return of the Caravels), features a surreal time warp where 15th-century navigators meet 1970s soldiers and contemporary Lisboêtas.

Hot names on today's poetry front include Pedro Tamen, whose works have been translated into many languages; and Sophia de Mello Breyner (awarded the Camões Prize in 1999 for her contribution to Portuguese culture), who has found fame both as a poet and, more recently, as a writer of children's stories, using the sea as her great theme. Up-and-coming novelists include Ana Gusmão, whose stories are set in urban landscapes and reflect conflicts in relationships, cultures and traditions; Manuela Gonzaga, whose books are more mystical, full of imagery from South American and Asian literature; and José Riço Direitinho, whose haunting novel *Breviário das Más Inclinações* (The Book of Bad Habits) is peopled by folk memories, superstitious peasants and rural traditions.

Painting

The earliest examples of visual art in Portugal are several treasure-troves of 20,000-year-old Palaeolithic paintings and carvings; the most impressive are those along the Rio Côa near Vila Nova de Foz Côa in Beira Alta (see the boxed text 'Rock Art in the Vale do Côa' in The Douro chapter).

The cave dwellers' modern successors were heavily influenced by French, Italian and Flemish styles. The first major exception was the 15th-century primitive painter Nuno Gonçalves, whose polyptych of the *Adoration of St Vincent* (now in Lisbon's Museu Nacional de Arte Antiga) is a unique tapestry-style revelation of contemporary Portuguese society.

The 16th-century Manueline school produced some uniquely Portuguese works, remarkable for their delicacy, realism and luminous colours. The big names of this school are Vasco Fernandes (known as Grão Vasco) and Gaspar Vaz, who both worked from Viseu (their best works are in Viseu's first-rate Museu de Grão Vasco). In Lisbon, other outstanding Manueline artists were Jorge Afonso (court painter to Dom Manuel I), Cristóvão de Figueiredo and Gregório Lopes.

The Renaissance era produced more notable sculpture than painting (see the following section), but the 17th century saw artist Josefa de Óbidos make waves with her rich still lifes (see the boxed text under Óbidos in the Estremadura & Ribatejo chapter). In the late 18th century, Domingos António de Sequeira produced wonderful portraits. The 19th century saw an artistic echo of both the naturalist and romantic movements, expressed strongly in the works of Silva Porto and Marquês de Oliveira, while Sousa Pinto excelled as a pastel artist in the early 20th century.

Naturalism remained the dominant trend into the 20th century, although Amadeo de Souza Cardoso struck out on his own path of cubism and expressionism, and Maria Helena Vieria da Silva came to be considered the country's finest abstract painter (although she lived in Paris for most of her life).

Other eminent figures in contemporary art include Almada Negreiros (often called the father of Portugal's modern art movement) and Guilherme Santa-Rita. Their works and others can be seen in Lisbon's

Centro de Arte Moderna and Porto's Museu Nacional Soares dos Reis.

Among today's artists the best known is probably Paula Rego, born in Lisbon in 1935 although resident in London since 1976. Her colourful paintings and prints often use fables and fantasy to explore sexuality and the relationships between stereotypes. Her contemporary, Helena Almeida, has had a particularly strong influence on Portugal's younger artists. Her large-scale often self-reflective photographic portraits combine drawing, photography and painting, challenging the relationship between illusion and reality.

Among the younger generation, born around the time of the 1974 revolution – an event which inspired a surge of artistic development – Miguel Branco is the link between the new and old eras. His small, studiolike oil paintings of people and animals are very evocative. Eduardo Batarda produces influential works in acrylic, often adapting paintings in comic-strip style. Among today's younger stars are António Areal, Angelo de Sousa and Nadir Afonso. Alfonso specialises in oils and gouaches. Graça Morais, a figurative artist from Trás-os-Montes, paints moving scenes from her village life. Innovative video artists are also gaining increasing recognition, notably João Onofre, whose creations are often concerned with human relations, and Miguel Soares, whose futuristic, slightly unsettling works reflect Portugal's rapidly changing times. Augusto Alves da Silva, who studied in the UK, has also won international acclaim for both his videos and photographs.

Variations on tradition include the work of young collectives such as the Tone Scientists (Carlos Roque, Rui Valério and Rui Toscano), which blend visual art with classical music, and events such as the Festival Internacional de Banda Desenhada da Amadora (held every November), which showcases the talents of Portugal's comic-strip artists.

Sculpture

Sculptors have excelled in many periods of Portugal's history. Among the first memorable creations are the carved tombs of the 12th to 14th centuries, including the limestone tombs of Inês de Castro and Dom Pedro in the Mosteiro de Alcobaça, where the detailed friezes are still impressive despite vandalism by French soldiers in 1811.

During the Manueline era sculptors, including Diogo de Boitaca, went wild with Portuguese seafaring fantasies and exuberant decoration (see the special section 'Portugal's Architecture'). At the same time, foreign influences were seeping in: Flemish (thanks to resident Flemish masters Olivier de Gand and Jean d'Ypres) was followed in the 16th century by the Flamboyant Gothic and plateresque styles of Spanish Galicia and Biscay. The Biscayan artists João and Diogo de Castilho created the most outstanding work during this time, often combining native styles with Manueline (for example, the cloisters of the Mosteiro dos Jerónimos in Lisbon).

During the Renaissance period, several French artists who had settled in Coimbra, including Nicolas Chanterène and Jean de Rouen, excelled in sculpting doorways, pulpits, altarpieces and bas reliefs. The ornate pulpit in Coimbra's Igreja de Santa Cruz is regarded as Chanterène's masterpiece.

Foreign schools continued to influence Portuguese sculptors in the 18th century baroque era, when Dom João V took advantage of the assembly of foreign artists working on the Convento do Mafra to found a school of sculpture. Its first principal was the Italian Alexander Giusti, but its most famous Portuguese teacher was Joaquim Machado de Castro (the museum named after him in Coimbra contains some of Portugal's finest works). Castro's work shows influences from the classical and romantic traditions of France and Italy, especially in the terracotta figures of his baroque manger scenes.

A century later the work of António Soares dos Reis reflects similar influences, although Soares also tried to create something uniquely Portuguese (and impossibly intangible) by attempting to portray in sculpture the melancholic feeling of *saudade* (see the boxed text 'Saudade' earlier in this chapter).

At the turn of the 20th century two names were prominent: Francisco Franco and the prolific sculptor António Teixeira Lopes (a pupil of Soares dos Reis), whose most famous work is his series of children's heads. These, along with work by Soares, are on display in the Museu Nacional Soares dos Reis in Porto.

Leading lights on the contemporary scene include Noé Sendas, who creates life-size figures in thought-provoking poses and dress; Leonor Antunes, whose sculptural installations invite viewers to explore how they relate to their surroundings; and Carlos Nogueira from Mozambique, who also creates large-scale sculptural installations.

Cinema

Portugal has a distinguished history of film making, though poor foreign distribution has left the world largely ignorant of it. The only internationally famous director is Manoel de Oliveira, described by the British *Guardian* newspaper as 'the most eccentric and the most inspired of cinema's world masters'. The nonagenarian ex-racing driver has made over 20 films (all except three after he turned 60), including *The Convent*, starring Catherine Deneuve and John Malkovich, who also appear in his latest offering, *Je Rentre à la Maison* (I'm Going Home), made in French and set in Paris. Oliveira's rather theatrical, fastidious films often feature long, silent takes and can be difficult to appreciate.

Alongside other older and well-established film makers (notably João Botelho, Paulo Rocha and the maverick sexagenarian João Cesar Monteiro), a new generation of directors has now emerged, producing works that are often provocative and harrowing, exposing the darker side of Portugal. These include Pedro Costa, whose 1998 film, *Ossos*, spotlights Lisbon slum life, and Teresa Villaverde, whose 1999 film, *Os Mutantes*, is a disturbing work about unwanted youngsters. The most controversial recent film in this style is *O Fantasma* (The Phantom; 2000), by João Pedro Rodrigues, which recounts the tale of a sex-obsessed trash collector. Less dark but just as gripping is the award-winning *Tarde Demais* (Too Late; 2001) by José Nascimento, featuring the true-story adventure of four fishermen who fight for survival after their boat sinks.

The country's best-known actress is Maria de Medeiros, who turned director with her *Capitães de Abril* (April Captains; 2000), based on the 1974 Revolution of the Carnations. Significantly, this was funded by the Portuguese Film Institute (ICAM; Instituto de Cinema, Audiovisual e Multimédia), which has recently grown more daring in its approach.

Performing Arts

The theatre scene has finally cast out the demons of the Salazar years. The venerable Teatro Nacional Dona Maria II of Lisbon and Teatro Nacional de São João of Porto have now been joined by numerous private companies, boosted by events such as Expo 98 and increased funding by the Ministry of Culture and local authorities. In 1999 the ministry embarked upon an ambitious theatre restoration and construction programme, aimed at establishing more facilities beyond the cities. Portugal's biggest recent theatre success has been the musical *Amália* (about fado's greatest diva), seen by over a million people.

The Gulbenkian Foundation, one of Portugal's most generous and wide-ranging private arts sponsors, also continues to support new theatre companies, plus a wide range of other performing arts, notably dance (the Ballet Gulbenkian is one of the country's leading dance groups). Indeed, Portuguese modern dance is capturing increased international acclaim; every November contemporary dance fans flock to Lisbon's Festival Internacional de Dança Contemporânea. One of the country's leading choreographers is Vera Mantero, previously a ballerina, now an exponent of a modern dance style closely connected with speech and music.

Handicrafts & Indigenous Arts

You only have to visit the big weekly markets in Portugal to see the astounding range of handicrafts available. The Algarve, Alentejo and Minho produce some of the finest work, although nearly every area has its speciality, often for sale at *turismos* (tourist offices) and rural museums. Ceramics are perhaps the most impressive: you'll find pottery encrusted with marble chips in Estremoz (Alentejo); brightly coloured pots and cockerels in Barcelos (Minho); green and geometric wares in Coimbra (Beira Litoral) and the famous cabbage-leaf designs in Caldas da Rainha (Estremadura). The Algarve is also packed with pottery, especially huge, Roman-style amphora jugs.

Baskets of rush, willow, cane or rye straw are among the traditional rural necessities now widely sold to tourists: the tiny straw dolls in traditional costume are some of Portugal's cutest souvenirs. Less easily carried in your backpack are pieces of the fabulous painted wooden furniture of the Alentejo, and carved ox yokes from the Minho.

Hand-embroidered linen is popular and found throughout Portugal. Weaving (especially woollen blankets) is a long-established craft, particularly in the Algarve and southern Alentejo, including at Mértola, Odemira and Alté (which is also famous for crochet work).

Another speciality is lace, mainly found along the coast ('where there are nets, there is lace,' goes the saying), although Loulé and Silves in inland Algarve are also famous for it. Children are still taught the art of bobbin lace (from the age of six) at Silves, Peniche (Estremadura) and Vila do Conde (Douro). The latter also hosts a great annual crafts fair in late July and early August.

SOCIETY & CONDUCT
Traditional Culture
Thanks to a strong Catholic influence and decades of repression under Salazar, Portugal remains a traditional and conservative country. *Romarias* (religious festivals in honour of a patron saint) are taken seriously everywhere, especially in the Minho where they can last for days and include solemn religious processions or pilgrimages. Most wind up with lay festivities in a fairground atmosphere of picnics, parades and fireworks.

Much livelier are Portugal's many *folclore* (folk) festivals, featuring traditional music and dancing, mainly in spring and summer. Again, the north presents the most flamboyant versions, with groups from every village, all in brilliantly embroidered costumes, the women draped in jewellery, the children clad in junior versions of their parents' outfits.

The only modern entertainment to rival the popularity of folk festivals is football – bar and restaurant customers are glued to the TV on big match days (see Spectator Sports in the Facts for the Visitor chapter), and almost every village and town fields a team. Traditional entertainment requiring a certain amount of dedication (such as the *pauliteiros*, or stick dancers, of Miranda do Douro in Trás-os-Montes) is finding it hard to compete with this relatively new obsession.

One cultural activity impervious to changing times is men's lingering fondness for cafés and squares. As in most Mediterranean countries, men of all ages seem to spend hours gossiping over coffee or wine, or gathering in cobbled squares to watch the world go by.

Social Graces
Generally, the Portuguese share characteristics of friendliness and an unhurried approach to life – in other words, expect smiles and warmth but neither punctuality nor brisk efficiency. Though this habitual lassitude may sometimes drive you mad, displays of anger will get you nowhere.

When asked for information, Portuguese have a tendency to save face by giving an answer even if they don't know it's right. This frustrating habit sometimes extends to turismo staff. You'll rarely hear *não sei* (I don't know). Get multiple opinions if the answer is important. Speaking Portuguese – however clumsily – will earn you lots of points. Politeness is highly valued, so be sure to address people correctly (*senhor* for men, *senhora* for women, *senhora dona* followed by the Christian name for an elderly or respected woman). A handshake is the norm when you're introduced to someone, although you may well get a light peck on each cheek from a young person.

In traditionally minded rural areas (especially up north), outlandish dress may cause offence. And while beachwear (and even nudity on some beaches) is acceptable in coastal tourist resorts, shorts and skimpy tops on a visit to a church are a definite no-no (as is intruding during church services). If you're visiting the police or other authorities, you'll get more help if you're well dressed.

Treatment of Animals
Hunting The urge to shoot any wild animal within range is deep-rooted among Portuguese men. There are over 250,000 licensed hunters in the land, and many more unlicensed hunters. Migratory birds are a favourite target, as well as rabbit, quail, partridge, duck and wild boar. Indeed, almost anything from wolves to songbirds can fall prey to this passion.

Officially, there are defined hunting zones and seasons, plus many private *zonas de caça* (hunting reserves) geared to visitors or private associations. Many have been created from the Alentejo's large estates, with facilities for both game and clay-pigeon shooting. Red deer, pheasant and red-legged partridge are popular species reared for hunters in these zones, but even the protected wild boar can be culled under licence when its numbers are considered excessive.

Hunting is restricted by law to Thursday, Sunday and public holidays during open season. Landowners can forbid hunting on their land (red-and-white metal markers by the roadside indicate out-of-bounds areas), and the trapping of small birds is illegal. But policing the laws is almost impossible. Even hunting reserves aren't the simple solution they appear to be – at the very least they hinder rural development and affect grazing rights. Birds of prey, even protected species, may find they're unwelcome if they snatch the profits from a land that was once freely theirs.

Bullfighting Although bullfights are not as popular in Portugal as in Spain, they're still held by many Portuguese to be a spectacular form of 'entertainment' and a noble tradition dating back 2000 years. At least 300 *touradas* (bullfights) are held every March-to-October season (traditionally Easter Sunday to All Saints' Day), many in tourist areas such as the Algarve. To calm foreigners, posters often declare, 'The bull isn't killed!'. But the bulls do suffer and they are killed (after the show). You just don't get to see the final blow.

Supporters point out that the Portuguese *tourada* is far less brutal and bloody than the Spanish version. There's a good deal more skilled horsemanship, artistry, valour and bravado. The most obvious differences are that the bull is initially fought by a man on horseback, then by a team of young men who tackle the bull by hand, and the fight is not to the death (at least, not in public – the gory death of a nobleman, Count dos Arcos, in 1799, put a stop to that). Another difference is that the bull's horns are covered in leather or capped with metal balls.

But this hardly disguises the fact that bullfighting is cruel. If you must see for yourself, first read about the *tourada* under Spectator Sports in the Facts for the Visitor chapter. Portugal's anti-bullfighting lobby is vocal but small. Most Portuguese are either impartial or surprised at the fuss. If you feel strongly you can write to the turismo or the *câmara municipal* (town hall) of those places that promote bullfighting as tourist entertainment.

For further information and suggestions for action, contact the **Liga Portuguesa dos Direitos dos Animais** (*Portuguese League for Animal Rights, LPDA;* ☎ *214 581 818;* ⓦ *www .lpda.pt; Avenida da República 1189, 2775 Parede*); or two international organisations, the **People for the Ethical Treatment of Animals** (*PETA;* ⓦ *www.peta-online.org*) or the **World Society for the Protection of Animals** (*WSPA;* ⓦ *www.wspa-international.org*).

RELIGION

As freedom of religion is part of the constitution, there is no state religion in Portugal,

The Jews of Portugal

Communities of Jews first became prominent in Portugal in medieval times. They wielded power and influence as bankers, financiers, court doctors, tax collectors, astronomers and map makers. Although the Afonsine Ordinance of 1446 decreed that they live in segregated Jewish quarters called *judiarias*, they faced relatively little harassment. Indeed, when Spain's zealous Catholic rulers Ferdinand and Isabella expelled Jews from their country in 1492, Portugal's João II offered temporary refuge to an estimated 60,000 of them. Many settled around Guarda, Belmonte, Bragança, Tomar and Viana do Castelo.

Five years later Portugal's new king, Manuel I, was forced to show his anti-Semitic credentials as a condition for marrying the Spanish ruler's daughter, Isabella. He offered the Jews a choice: 'conversion' to Christianity (with no inquiry made into their beliefs for 20 years) or emigration. Not surprisingly, many scorned the offer and left (Holland was a popular destination). Those who remained – subsequently known as New Christians or *marranos* – faced the horrors of the Inquisition, launched by João III in 1540. Thousands were tortured, imprisoned or burnt at the stake.

Today some 2000 Jews live in Portugal, with the largest community in Belmonte (Beira Alta). Traces of *judiarias* can still be found in many towns. Castelo de Vide has the country's oldest synagogue, dating from the 13th century, while Tomar's former synagogue now serves as a Luso-Hebraic museum, displaying gifts from Jewish visitors from all over the world.

though Roman Catholicism is the dominant faith, adhered to by roughly 95% of Portuguese. Other Christian denominations include Anglicans, Evangelists, Baptists, Congregationalists, Methodists, Jehovah's Witnesses and Mormons. There are some 15,000 Muslims and 2000 Jews.

Christianity has been a major force in shaping Portugal's history. It first reached Portugal in the 1st century AD, thriving despite pagan invaders. By the 3rd century, bishoprics had been established at Braga, Lisbon, Évora and Faro. After the Moors invaded in 711, Christians (and Jews) were initially allowed freedom of worship, but with the arrival of fanatical Almoravids in the early 11th century, the Christian Reconquista picked up speed. Crusaders en route to the Holy Land frequently helped the kings of Portugal defeat the Moors.

Other Christian forces that influenced Portugal's development at this time were the Cistercians (a Benedictine order that enriched both agriculture and architecture around Alcobaça) and powerful military orders such as the Knights Templar (later reorganised as the Order of Christ). The wealth and resources of the Order of Christ largely financed Portugal's overseas explorations in the 15th century.

However, the Church has also been responsible for some of the darkest moments in Portugal's history, notably the Inquisition, started in the 1530s by João III and his staunchly Catholic Spanish wife. Thousands were tortured, imprisoned or burnt at the stake at public sentencing ceremonies known as *autos-da-fé*. The terror was only really suppressed in 1820.

Today's Catholic Church is powerful and highly respected. Sunday masses are widely attended (although decreasingly so by the young), as are the many religious festivals honouring local patron saints. Northern Portugal has always been the most religious part of the country, though certain festivals (such as the Os Santos Populares celebrations in June for St Anthony, St John and St Peter) are celebrated with fervour throughout the land. One of Europe's most important centres of pilgrimage is at Fátima (see the Estremadura & Ribatejo chapter), where up to 100,000 pilgrims congregate every 12 to 13 May and 12 to 13 October.

In the north you're also most likely to see more bizarre expressions of faith. On a hill above Ponte de Lima is a chapel dedicated to St Ovido, patron saint of ears. The walls are covered with votive offerings of wax ears, given in hopes of, or in thanks for, a cured ear affliction. Similar chapels, adorned with wax limbs of all kinds, can be found even inside churches, revealing a pragmatic sort of tolerance by the Catholic Church.

Facts for the Visitor

SUGGESTED ITINERARIES

The following itineraries get you to most of Portugal's worthwhile destinations, leaving you to dress them up with local excursions. They assume a total of one day each week in transit.

One Week

Lisbon Sampler Lisbon, Belém and Sintra (four days); Óbidos and Nazaré (two days)

Porto & the Douro Porto and Vila Nova de Gaia (three days); Guimarães, Amarante and Lamego (three days)

The Algarve Sagres and Cabo de São Vicente (two days); Lagos (two days); Tavira and Ilha de Tavira (two days)

Two Weeks

Lisbon to the Algarve Lisbon, Belém and Sintra (four days); Costa Vicentina (down the west coast of the Alentejo and Algarve to Cabo de São Vicente), Sagres and Cabo São Vicente (three days); Lagos (two days); Tavira and the Ilha de Tavira (three days); depart from Faro

Lisbon to the Spanish Border Lisbon, Belém and Sintra (five days); Évora and Monsaraz (three days); Estremoz and Elvas (two days); Castelo de Vide and Marvão (two days)

Lisbon to Porto Lisbon, Belém and Sintra (four days); Óbidos and Nazaré (two days); Coimbra and Luso (two days); Lamego (one day); Peso da Régua to Porto by train or the Rio Douro cruise boat; Porto and Vila Nova de Gaia (three days)

Porto, the Douro & the Minho Porto and Vila Nova de Gaia (three days); Viana do Castelo and Ponte de Lima (three days); Braga and Guimarães (three days); Parque Nacional da Peneda-Gerês (three days); return to Porto by train or the Rio Douro cruise boat from Peso da Régua

One Month

Central Portugal Lisbon, Belém and Sintra (six days); Évora, Estremoz and Elvas (four days); Marvão and Castelo de Vide (two days); Parque Natural da Serra da Estrela (three days); Coimbra and Luso (three days); Lamego, Amarante and Mondim de Basto (four days); Peso da Régua to Porto by train or the Rio Douro cruise boat; Porto and Vila Nova de Gaia (four days); depart from Porto

Lisbon & the South Lisbon, Belém and Sintra (six days); Óbidos, Nazaré, Batalha and Tomar (three days); Évora, Monsaraz and Elvas (four days); Beja, Serpa and Mértola (three days);

Tavira, Ilha de Tavira and Parque Natural da Ria Formosa (four days); Lagos (three days); Sagres and Cabo de São Vicente (three days); depart from Faro or Lisbon

Lisbon & the North Lisbon, Belém and Sintra (five days); Coimbra (two days); Parque Natural da Serra da Estrela (three days); Lamego, Amarante and Mondim de Basto (four days); train or Rio Douro cruise boat from Peso da Régua to Porto; Porto and Vila Nova de Gaia (four days); Braga (two days); Parque Nacional da Peneda-Gerês (three days); Bragança and Parque Natural de Montesinho (three days); return to Porto

PLANNING
When to Go

Portugal's climate is temperate and its weather is agreeable just about everywhere from April to September or October, and almost year-round in the Algarve. Spring (late March and April) and early autumn (late September and October) bring spectacular foliage. July and August are mostly dry, except in the far north, but the Algarve, the Alentejo and the upper Douro valley can get ferociously hot.

Higher areas, such as the Serra da Estrela and the ranges of Peneda-Gerês, and much of the Minho and Trás-os-Montes, are a bit showery in summer and uncomfortably cold and wet in winter. The wettest season is from November to March, and the wettest regions are the Minho and the Serra da Estrela. Snowfall is substantial only in the Serra da Estrela, where skiers will find basic facilities. The ski season lasts from January to March; and February is the best month.

For more about the weather, see Climate in the Facts about Portugal chapter.

If you're after beaches, remember that Portugal faces the blustery Atlantic, not the Mediterranean. Only in sheltered, shallow areas of the eastern Algarve, in summer, could you call the water warm.

Certain local festivals and celebrations are worth going out of your way for, particularly Carnaval (the three days leading up to Ash Wednesday) and Easter. Dates vary from year to year; see Public Holidays & Special Events later in this chapter.

If you're not a football (soccer) fanatic, several places are worth *avoiding* from 12

Highlights

Here's a list to help you find the best of everything in Portugal:

Architecture
Mosteiro dos Jerónimos, Belém (Lisbon); Batalha's Mosteiro de Santa Maria da Vitória and Mosteiro de Alcobaça (Estremadura); Convento de Cristo (Tomar); the baroque stairways of Nossa Senhora dos Remédios (Lamego) and Bom Jesus do Monte (Braga)

Hand-Painted Tiles
Museu Nacional do Azulejo (Lisbon); Igreja do Carmo, Capela das Almas and São Bento station (Porto); Igreja de São João Evangelista (Évora); Igreja de São Lourenço, Almancil (Algarve)

Beaches
Barril, Praia da Rocha and Praia de Odeceixe (Algarve); São Martinho do Porto (Estremadura); Costa da Caparica (Around Lisbon); São Jacinto (Aveiro)

Festivals
Carnaval (especially Loulé, Nazaré, Ovar and Viana do Castelo); Easter week (Braga); Queima das Fitas (Coimbra); Festa de São João (Porto); Festa de Santo António (Lisbon); Festa dos Tabuleiros (Tomar); Romaria da Nossa Senhora da Agonia (Viana do Castelo); Feiras Novas (Ponte de Lima)

Fortresses, Castles & Walled Towns
Valença do Minho; Bragança; Monsanto and Sortelha (Beiras); Óbidos (Estremadura); Marvão, Elvas, Monsaraz and Mértola (Alentejo)

Hill & Mountain Treks
Parque Nacional da Peneda-Gerês (Minho); Parque Natural da Serra da Estrela (Beiras); Sintra (near Lisbon)

Markets
Feira de Barcelos (Minho); Caldas da Rainha (Estremdura); Ponte de Lima (Minho); Feira da Ladra (Lisbon)

Museums
Museu Calouste Gulbenkian (Lisbon); Museu de Arte Moderna (Sintra); Museu de Serralves and Centro Português de Fotografia (Porto); Museu do Abade de Baçal (Bragança); Museu Martins Sarmento (Guimarães); Museu Machado de Castro (Coimbra)

Towns of Historical Interest
Évora; Guimarães; Coimbra

Pre-Roman Remains
Citânia de Briteiros (near Guimarães); standing stones (around Évora and Castelo de Vide)

Roman Ruins
Conimbriga (near Coimbra); Roman temple (Évora)

Surfing & Windsurfing
Moledo (Minho); Figueira da Foz (Beiras); Peniche and Ericeira (Estremadura); Praia do Guincho (Costa da Caparica)

Trams
The No 28 (Lisbon); Nos 1E and 18 (Porto); tram to Praia das Maçãs (Sintra)

Miscellaneous
Espigueiros (stone granaries) at Soajo and Lindoso (Minho); Iron-Age *berrões* (stone pigs) of Trás-os-Montes; *ossuaries* (bone chapels) at Évora and Faro; Europe's most southwesterly corner at Cabo de São Vicente

June to 4 July 2004, when hundreds of thousands of fans will descend on venues at Aveiro, Braga, Coimbra, Faro/Loulé, Guimarães, Leiria, Lisbon and Porto for the European Football Championships. For details on the event, see the boxed text 'Euro2004' later in this chapter.

Peak season – when *pensões* (guesthouses) and hotels charge top whack – is roughly mid-June to August or September, plus Carnaval, Easter week and Christmas/New Year. At these times, consider booking mid-range or top-end accommodation a few days or weeks ahead. Outside peak season crowds thin out, rooms are plentiful and prices may drop by as much as 50% (prices in this book are for July, though some August prices may go even higher). The exception is the Algarve, where peak season runs for much of the year, from March to November.

Maps

Road & Tourist Maps Lonely Planet publishes the well-indexed, full-colour *Portugal road atlas* at 1:400,000. *Portugal Continental Mapa de Estradas*, a 1:250,000 road atlas from the Instituto Geográfico do Exército (see under Topographical Maps, following), is precise but not always up-to-date.

Most current, though not indexed, is the 1:350,000 *Mapa das Estradas*, updated every June by the Automóvel Club de Portugal (see under Car & Motorcycle in the Getting Around chapter for addresses). More or less equivalent is Michelin's 1:400,000 *Portugal, Madeira*, No 940.

Most tourist offices have regional and/or town maps of varying utility. IGeoE publishes a detailed, 1:10,000 *Lisbon* map.

Topographic Maps Two government-mapping agencies exist: the military **Instituto Geográfico do Exército** *(IGeoE or Army Geographic Institute;* ☎ *218 520 063, fax 218 532 119;* **w** *www.igeoe.pt; Avenida Dr Alfredo Bensaúde, Lisbon)*; and the civilian **Instituto Geográfico Português** *(IGP or Portuguese Geographic Institute;* ☎ *213 819 600, fax 213 819 699;* **w** *www.ipcc.pt; Rua Artilharia Um 107, Lisbon)*.

IGeoE publishes 1:25,000 topographic sheets (€5.90) covering the entire country, plus less useful 1:50,000 and 1:250,000 series. IGP's 1:50,000 maps (€5) tend to be

more current but lack the detail and precision of the military publications; IGP also publishes 1:100,000, 1:200,000 and a new 1:10,000 series.

Both agencies sell maps from their Lisbon headquarters, though IGeoE is in the middle of nowhere. Most IGeoE 1:25,000 sheets are also available at the Livraria Porto Editora bookshop in Porto (see under that city in the Douro chapter).

National and natural park offices usually have simple park maps, though these are of little use for trekking or cycling. Other local sources for topographic maps are noted in the text.

Maps by Mail Order & the Internet

Many road and topographic maps are available by post, fax or online – but shop around as shipping costs and delivery times vary widely. The following firms offer a good range of Portugal maps:

GeoCenter ILH (☎ 0711-788 93 40, **w** www .geokatalog.de) Schockenriedstrasse 44, D-70565 Stuttgart, Germany

Maps Worldwide (☎ 01225-707004, **w** www .mapsworldwide.co.uk) Datum House, Lancaster Road, Melksham SN12 6TL, UK

Omni Resources (☎ 336-227 8300, **w** www .omnimap.com) PO Box 2096, Burlington, NC 27216-2096, USA

Stanfords (☎ 020-7836 1321, **w** www.stanfords .co.uk) 12–14 Long Acre, Covent Garden, London WC2E 9LP, UK

Instituto Geográfico Português also sells maps via its website (**w** www.ipcc.pt).

What to Bring

You can find most comforts and essentials in small-town supermarkets and big-city hypermarkets. Pharmacies stock a wide range of medicines plus tampons and *preservativos* (condoms). You needn't even worry much about clothes: weekly markets in most sizeable towns have stalls selling cheap clothing, and shoes are a bargain everywhere.

Seasoned travellers will already have a secure moneybelt. Other helpful items are a penknife, universal sink plug, sunscreen lotion, sunhat, sunglasses, torch (flashlight), compass, a few clothes pegs and a length of cord as a washing line, a small sewing kit, and electrical and modem adapters. A little bar of soap comes in handy when your cheapo guesthouse doesn't furnish any. For a suggested medical kit see the Health section later in this chapter.

The Portuguese are conservative dressers, and other than at beaches and in coastal Algarve towns, it's rare to see the Portuguese in shorts or even short sleeves. Take some modest clothes for covering up in churches and very rural areas. You might need a sweater in the Algarve as late as March, and certainly in the Serra da Estrela, even in May, but you'll hardly use it elsewhere. If you plan to spend much time outside July and August in the showery north, a collapsible umbrella is more comfortable than a raincoat.

See also Visas & Documents, later in this chapter.

RESPONSIBLE TOURISM

Mass tourism has had a huge impact on the Algarve coast (see Ecology & Environment in the Facts about Portugal chapter). Of more than 12 million visitors to Portugal each year, at least half go to the Algarve for its fine climate, beaches and facilities. Supposedly 'eco-friendly' activities such as jeep safaris are on the increase in this area, and inevitably they damage once-remote habitats.

Organised walks are a nondestructive way to see the country. You can get first-hand knowledge of environmental issues on regular walks organised by Quercus, the country's leading environmental organisation (see Ecology & Environment in the Facts about Portugal chapter). In local listings we note other organisations offering guided walks.

In many popular destinations the summer tourist influx puts a real strain on local infrastructure, ancient buildings and the environment. One way to minimise your impact, and probably enjoy yourself more, is to visit outside the high season. Spending your money in less-visited areas is another way to even out tourism's financial impact, while simultaneously broadening your view of the country; many remote park areas, such as the Parque Natural de Montesinho in Trás-os-Montes, are worth the extra effort to visit.

TOURIST OFFICES
Local Tourist Offices

Portugal's umbrella tourism organisation is **Investimentos, Comércio e Turismo de Portugal** (*ICEP;* ☎ *217 909 500, fax 217 935 028;*

[e] *informacao@icep.pt; Avenida 5 de Outubro 101, 1050-051 Lisbon).*

Locally managed *postos de turismo* (tourist offices, usually signposted *turismo*) are everywhere, offering brochures and varying degrees of help with sights and accommodation. ICEP maintains a regional office in the main town of each of its regions, or *regiões de turismo* (see the boxed text 'Provinces, Districts & Tourist Regions' under Geography in the Facts about Portugal chapter), and information desks at Lisbon, Porto and Faro airports. Lisbon, Porto, Coimbra and a few other towns have both municipal and ICEP turismos.

Multilingual staff at the toll-free tourist helpline **Linha Verde do Turista** (☎ *800 296 296; operating 9am-9pm daily)* can provide basic – though not uniformly accurate – information on accommodation, sightseeing and so on.

Tourist Offices Abroad

ICEP-affiliated trade and tourism offices abroad include the following:

Canada (☎ 416-921 7376, [e] iceptor@
  idirect.com) 60 Bloor St West, Suite 1005,
  Toronto, ON M4W 3B8
France (☎ 01 56 88 30 80, [e] icepar@
  worldnet.fr) 135 boulevard Haussmann,
  75008 Paris
Germany (☎ 069-234 094, [e] dir@icepfra.de)
  Schäfergasse 17, 60313 Frankfurt-am-Main
Ireland (☎ 01-670 9133; [e] info@icep.ie)
  54 Dawson St, Dublin 2
The Netherlands (☎ 070-326 2525,
  [e] icephaia@mail2.icep.pt) Paul Gabriëlstraat
  70, 2596 VG Den Haag
Spain (☎ 91 522 93 54, [e] acarrilho@
  mail2.icep.pt) 1st floor, Gran Via 27, 28013
  Madrid
UK (☎ 020-7494 1441, [e] iceplondt@aol.com)
  22–25a Sackville St, London W1X 1DE
USA (☎ 212-354 4403, [e] tourism@
  portugal.org) 4th floor, 590 Fifth Ave, New
  York, NY 10036-4785

VISAS & DOCUMENTS
Passport

You may have trouble getting a visa if your passport expires soon after your proposed visit, or if there are no blank pages left in it.

Police in Portugal are empowered to check your papers at any time, so always carry your passport with you.

Visas

Nationals of European Union (EU) countries need no visa for any length of stay in Portugal. Those from Canada, New Zealand, the USA and (by temporary agreement) Australia can stay for up to 90 days in any half-year without a visa. Others, including nationals of South Africa, need a visa unless they're the spouse or child of an EU citizen.

The general requirements for entry into Portugal also apply to citizens of other signatories of the 1990 Schengen Convention (Austria, Belgium, Denmark, Finland, France, Germany, Greece, Iceland, Italy, Luxembourg, the Netherlands, Norway, Spain and Sweden). A visa issued by one Schengen country is generally valid for travel in all the others, but unless you're a citizen of the UK, Ireland or a Schengen country, you should check visa regulations with the consulate of each Schengen country you plan to visit. You must apply for any Schengen visa in your country of residence.

Visa Extensions To extend a visa or 90-day period of stay after arriving in Portugal, contact the **Foreigners Registration Service** *(Serviço de Estrangeiros e Fronteiras;* ☎ *213 585 545; Rua São Sebastião da Pedreira 15, Lisbon; open 9am-3pm Mon-Fri)*; major tourist towns also have branches. As entry regulations are already liberal, you'll need convincing proof of employment or financial independence, or a pretty good story, if you're asking to stay longer.

Travel Insurance

A travel insurance policy to cover theft, loss and medical problems is strongly recommended. You should cover yourself for the worst case, eg, an accident or illness requiring hospitalisation and a flight home; if you can't afford that, you certainly can't afford to deal with a medical emergency abroad. A wide variety of policies are available; the international policies handled by youth and student travel agencies are good value.

Check the small print – some policies specifically exclude 'dangerous activities' such as scuba diving, motorcycling or even trekking. If these are on your agenda, get another policy or ask about an amendment (for an extra premium) that includes them.

You may prefer a policy that pays doctors or hospitals directly rather than one that requires you to pay upfront and claim later, though in Portugal you'll usually find immediate cash payment is expected. If you have to claim later, make sure you keep all documentation. Some policies ask you to call back (reverse charges) to a centre in your home country, where an immediate assessment of your problem is made.

Citizens of the EU are eligible for free emergency medical treatment if they have an E111 certificate; see Predeparture Planning under Health later in this chapter for details.

Driving Licence & Permits

Nationals of EU countries need only their home driving licences to operate a car or motorcycle in Portugal, although holders of the UK's old, pre-EU green licences should also carry an International Driving Permit (IDP). Portugal also accepts licences issued in Brazil, Switzerland and the USA. Others should get an IDP through an automobile licensing department or automobile club in their home country (or at some post offices in the UK).

See under Car & Motorcycle in the Getting There & Away chapter for information on paperwork and insurance.

Hostel Cards

Portugal's network of youth hostels, or *pousadas da juventude* (see Accommodation later in this chapter), is part of the Hostelling International (HI) network. An HI card from your hostelling association at home entitles you to the standard cheap rates.

Camping Card International

The Camping Card International (CCI) can be presented instead of your passport at camp sites affiliated to the Federation Internationale de Camping et de Caravanning (FICC). It guarantees third-party insurance for any damage you may cause and is sometimes good for discounts. Certain camp sites run by local camping clubs may be used by foreigners *only* if they have a CCI.

The CCI is available to members of most national automobile clubs, except those in the USA; the RAC in the UK charges members UK£4 for a card. It's also issued by FICC affiliates such as the UK's **Camping & Caravanning Club** (☎ 024-7669 4995) and the **Federação Portuguesa de Campismo**

(☎ 218 126 890; w *www.fpcampismo.pt; Avenida Coronel Eduardo Galhardo 24D, 1199-007 Lisbon).*

Other Documents

If you're cycling around Portugal on your own bike, proof of ownership and a written description and a photograph of it will help police in case it's stolen.

Copies

All important documents (passport data and visa pages, credit cards, travel-insurance policy, air/bus/train tickets, driving licence and so on) should be photocopied before you leave home. Leave one copy with someone at home and keep another with you, separate from the originals. Other copies you might want to carry include travellers-cheque numbers (plus telephone numbers for cancelling cheques and credit cards), birth certificate and any documents related to possible employment.

EMBASSIES & CONSULATES
Portuguese Embassies & Consulates

Portuguese embassies and consulates abroad include the following:

Angola
Embassy: (☎ 02-33 30 27, fax 39 03 92) Avenida de Portugal 50, Caixa Postal 1346, Luanda
Australia
Embassy: (☎ 02-6290 1733, fax 6290 1957, w www.consulportugalsydney.org.au) 23 Culgoa Circuit, O'Malley, ACT 2606
Consulate: (☎ 02-9262 2199, fax 9262 5991) Level 9, 30 Clarence St, Sydney, NSW 2000
Brazil
Embassy: (☎ 061-321 3434, fax 224 7347) Avenida das Nações, Lote 2, CEP 70402-900, Brasilia
Canada
Embassy: (☎ 613-729 0883, fax 729 4236, w www.embportugal-ottawa.org) 645 Island Park Drive, Ottawa, ON K1Y OB8
Consulate: (☎ 604-688 6514, fax 685 7042) 700 West Pender St, Vancouver, BC V6C 1G8; also in Montreal and Toronto
Cape Verde
Embassy: (☎ 62 30 32, fax 62 30 36) Achada de Santo António, Cidade da Praia CP 160
France
Embassy: (☎ 01 47 27 35 29, fax 01 44 05 94 02, w www.embaixada-portugal-fr.org) 3 rue de Noisiel, 75116 Paris

Consulate: (☎ 04 78 17 34 40, fax 04 78 17 34 50) 71 rue Crillon, 69458 Lyon; also in Bayonne, Bordeaux, Marseille, Strasbourg and Toulouse
Germany
Embassy: (☎ 030-590 06 35 00, fax 590 06 36 00) Zimmerstrasse 56, 10117 Berlin
Consulate: (☎ 0211-13 87 80, fax 32 33 57) Graf-Adolf-Strasse 16, 4000 Düsseldorf; also in Stuttgart, Frankfurt-am-Main and Hamburg
Guinea-Bissau
Embassy: (☎ 20 12 61, fax 20 12 69) Avenida Cidade de Lisboa, Apartado 76, 1021 Bissau Codex
Ireland
Embassy: (☎ 01-289 4416, fax 289 2849) Knock Sinna House, Knock Sinna, Fox Rock, Dublin 18
Morocco
Embassy: (☎ 07-756 446, fax 756 445) 5 rue Thami Lamdouar, Souissi, Rabat
Mozambique
Embassy: (☎ 01-490 316, fax 491 172) Avenida Julius Nyerere 720, CP 4696 Maputo
The Netherlands
Embassy: (☎ 070-363 02 17, fax 361 55 89, e ambportugal@wxs.nl) Bazarstraat 21, 2518 AG The Hague
Consulate: (☎ 010-411 15 40, fax 414 98 89) Willemskade 18, 3016 DL Rotterdam
New Zealand
Honorary Consulate: (☎ 09-309 1454, fax 308 9061, e daniel@silva.co.nz) PO Box 305, 33 Garfield Street, Parnell, Auckland
São Tomé e Príncipe
Embassy: (☎ 012-21130, fax 21190) Avenida Marginal 12 de Julho, CP 173 São Tomé
Spain
Embassy: (☎ 91 782 49 60, fax 91 782 49 72, e embaportugal@telefonica.net) Calle Pinar 1, 28006 Madrid
Consulate: (☎ 93 318 81 50, fax 93 318 59 12) Ronda San Pedro 7, 08010 Barcelona; also in Sevilla and Vigo
UK
Embassy: (☎ 020-7235 5331, fax 7245 1287, e london@portembassy.co.uk) 11 Belgrave Square, London SWIX 8PP
Consulate: (☎ 020-7581 8722, fax 7581 3085) 62 Brompton Rd, London SW3 1BJ
USA
Embassy: (☎ 202-328 8610, fax 462 3726, w www.portugalemb.org) 2125 Kalorama Rd NW, Washington, DC 20008
Consulate: (☎ 212-765 2980, 262 2143) Suite 801, 630 Fifth Ave, New York, NY 10111; also in Boston and San Francisco

Embassies & Consulates in Portugal

Your embassy or consulate is the best first stop in any emergency. Most can provide lists of reliable local doctors, lawyers and interpreters. If your money or documents have been stolen, they might help you get a new passport or advise you on how to have funds transferred, but a free ticket home or a loan for onward travel is unlikely. Most embassies no longer have mail-holding services, or reading rooms with home newspapers.

Foreign embassies and consulates in Portugal include:

Angola
Embassy: (☎ 217 967 041, fax 217 971 238, e emb.angola@mail.telepac.pt) Avenida República 68, 1069-213 Lisbon
Consulate: (☎ 222 058 827, fax 222 050 328, e consulado.angola@clix.pt) Rua Alexandre Herculano 352, 4000-053 Porto

Australia
Embassy: (☎ 213 101 500, fax 213 101 555, e austemb@oninet.pt) 2nd floor, Avenida da Liberdade 200, 1250-147 Lisbon

Brazil
Embassy: (☎ 217 248 510, fax 217 287 623) Estrada das Laranjeiras 144, 1949-021 Lisbon
Consulate: (☎ 225 430 655, fax 226 106 678, e cgportp@mail.telepac.pt) 1st floor, Avenida de França 20, 4050-275 Porto

Canada
Embassy: (☎ 213 164 600, fax 213 164 991, e lisbon@dfait-maeci.gc.ca) 3rd floor, Avenida da Liberdade 196, 1269-121 Lisbon
Consulate: (☎ 289 803 757) Rua Frei Lourenço de Santa Maria 1, 8000-352 Faro

Cape Verde
Embassy: (☎ 213 015 271, fax 213 015 308) Avenida do Restelo 33, 1449-025 Lisbon

France
Embassy: (☎ 213 939 100, fax 213 939 150, e ambafrance@hotmail.com) Rua de Santos-o-Velho 5, 1249-079 Lisbon
Consulate: (☎ 226 094 805, fax 226 064 205) Rua Eugénio de Castro 352, 4100-225 Porto

Germany
Embassy: (☎ 218 810 210, fax 218 853 846, e embaixada.alemanha@clix.pt) Campo dos Mártires da Pátria 38, 1169-043 Lisbon
Consulate: (☎ 226 052 810, fax 226 052 819) 6th floor, Avenida de França 20, 4050-275 Porto; also in Faro

Guinea-Bissau
Embassy: (☎ 213 929 440, fax 213 977 363) Rua da Imprensa à Estrela 1, 1200-684 Lisbon

Morocco
Embassy: (☎ 213 010 842, fax 213 020 935) Rua Alto do Duque 21, 1400-099 Lisbon

Mozambique
Embassy: (☎ 217 971 994, fax 217 932 720) Avenida de Berna 7, 1050-036 Lisbon
Consulate: (☎ 225 077 535, fax 225 103 405) Rua Santos Pousada 441, 4000-486 Porto

The Netherlands
Embassy: (☎ 213 914 900, fax 213 966 436, e nlgovlis@mail.telepac.pt) Avenida Infante Santo 43, 1399-011 Lisbon
Consulate: (☎/fax 222 080 061) Rua da Reboleira 7, 4050-492 Porto; also in Faro

São Tomé e Príncipe
Embassy: (☎ 218 461 917, fax 218 461 895, e op4369@mail.telepac.pt) Avenida Almirante Gago Coutinho 26, 1000-017 Lisbon

Spain
Embassy: (☎ 213 472 381, fax 213 472 384, e embesppt@correo.mae.es) Rua do Salitre 1, 1269-052 Lisbon
Consulate: (☎ 225 101 685, fax 225 101 914, e consulado.porto@oninet.pt) Rua de Dom João IV 341, 4000-302 Porto; also in Valença do Minho and Vila Real de Santo António

UK
Embassy: (☎ 213 924 000, fax 213 924 183, e ppa@fco.gov.uk) Rua de São Bernardo 33, 1249-082 Lisbon
Consulate: (☎ 226 184 789, fax 226 100 438, e consular@oporto.mail.fco.gov.uk) Avenida da Boavista 3072, 4100-120 Porto; also in Portimão

USA
Embassy: (☎ 217 273 300, fax 217 269 109) Avenida das Forças Armadas, 1600-081 Lisbon
Consulate: (☎ 226 172 384, fax 226 102 495) Rua Marechal Saldanha 454, 4150-652 Porto

There's no New Zealand embassy in Portugal. In emergencies, New Zealand citizens can call the **honorary consul** (☎ 213 509 690; operating 9am-1pm Mon-Fri) in Lisbon. The nearest **New Zealand embassy** (☎ 00-39-6-441 7171, fax 440 2984; e nzemb.rom@flashnet.it) is in Rome.

CUSTOMS

There's no limit on the amount of foreign currency you can bring into Portugal. Customs regulations say anyone who needs a visa must bring in at least €50 plus €10 per day, but this isn't strictly enforced.

The duty-free allowance for travellers over 17 years old from non-EU countries is 200 cigarettes or the equivalent in tobacco, and 1L of alcohol over 22% alcohol or 2L of wine or beer. Nationals of EU countries can bring in 800 cigarettes or the equivalent, plus either 10L of spirits, 20L of fortified wine, 60L of sparkling wine or a mind-boggling 90L of still wine or 110L of beer!

There's no more duty-free shopping in Portugal's airports, but see Taxes & Refunds under Money in this chapter for information on sales-tax refunds.

MONEY
Currency
On 1 January 2002 the Portuguese – along with the citizens of Austria, Belgium, Finland, France, Germany, Ireland, Italy, Luxembourg, the Netherlands and Spain – officially said hello to the euro (€), and six months later waved goodbye forever to their old currencies. Even in the remotest Portuguese villages the changeover from *escudo* to euro was trauma-free, aided perhaps by the roundness of the conversion (100 *escudos* is almost exactly half a euro), although some older folk still talk in *escudos*.

The euro is divided into 100 cents. Coins come in denominations of one, two, five, 10, 20 and 50 cents, and one and two euros; and notes in denominations of five, 10, 20, 50, 100, 200 and 500 euros. Notes are identical across the 'euro zone', but each country can decorate the reverse of its euro coins with its own designs. All euro notes and coins are legal tender in all countries of the zone.

Post-conversion market prices in Portugal are gradually being rounded up to the nearest 10 cents, and plenty of opportunists have rounded more drastically.

Exchange Rates
Approximate exchange rates at the time of printing were:

country	unit		euros
Australia	A$1	=	€0.55
Canada	C$1	=	€0.63
Japan	¥100	=	€0.80
New Zealand	NZ$1	=	€0.49
UK	UK£1	=	€1.56
USA	US$1	=	€0.99

Exchanging Money
Portuguese banks and exchange bureaus accept most foreign currencies but are free to set their own fees and rates; thus a low commission may be offset by an unfavourable exchange rate. If you're watching every penny you'll have to shop around, calculator in hand.

Travellers cheques are easily exchanged at slightly better rates than those for cash, but they're poor value in Portugal because commission is so high: banks charge around €12.50 per transaction of any size, and exchange bureaus about €5. American Express (AmEx) travellers cheques can be encashed commission-free (except, curiously, those denominated in euros, which draw a 1% fee) at Top Tours travel agencies in Lisbon, Porto, Faro and Portimão.

Fees for exchanging Eurocheques are sometimes lower than for other travellers cheques, though for these cheques and the accompanying card you must pay an annual subscription fee.

The most convenient option is a Visa, Access/MasterCard, AmEx or similar card. Nearly every town has 24-hour Multibanco automated teller machines (ATMs), where you can use your card to get a cash advance in euros; all you need is your PIN number from home. Your home bank levies a charge of about 1.5% per transaction, and rates are reasonable. Cards are also accepted by many shops and hotels, as well as by a growing number of guesthouses and restaurants.

Portuguese ATMs accept six-digit PIN numbers, though if your own PIN has fewer digits it should still work if you press the *'continuar'* button after keying in your PIN. Some travellers have solved the problem by adding zeroes at the end.

ATMs occasionally spit out cards with a message such as 'communication failure' or 'wrong PIN number'. A second try or using another ATM will in most cases work, but bear in mind that three 'wrong PIN number' messages may invalidate your card.

Foreign cash can also be changed (for a higher commission) in automatic 24-hour cash-exchange machines in a few tourist destinations, but rarely elsewhere.

Security
Keeping your money secure is largely a matter of common sense; see Crime under Dangers & Annoyances later in this chapter.

In addition to looking after your cash, be careful when you pay for something with a credit card: to be on the safe side, complete the 'total' box on the sales slip yourself, add a currency symbol before it with no space in between, and be sure the card is swiped only once, or that only one sales slip is printed.

Costs

Concentrating on less-touristed areas, travelling by public transport (about €4 to €6 per 100km), staying in camp sites (€4 to €8 for one person in a small tent) or hostels (dorm beds €8 to €15), and mostly self-catering, you could squeeze by on €25 to €30 per day.

With budget accommodation (€15 to €20 per person) and the occasional modest restaurant meal (€10 to €20), daily costs would hover around €30 to €45. Two people travelling together in the off-season can eat and sleep well for €50 to €75 per day.

Alcohol (€0.50/0.75 for a 33cL bottle of Portuguese beer from a supermarket/bar; €2 to €7 for 1L of table wine) pushes costs up. So does driving (€0.90 per 1L of 95 octane unleaded petrol; €0.70 for diesel). Most prices are likely to climb in the run-up to the Euro2004 football championships (see the boxed text under Spectator Sports later in this chapter) – and not only in the towns hosting matches.

Discounts

Numerous discounts are available to full-time students and teachers, and to travellers aged under 26 years or over 59.

The international student identity card (ISIC) and international teacher identity card (ITIC) are good for reducing air fares, museum admission and other travel costs. The Euro<26 and Go25/IYTC youth-card schemes provide more general discounts (eg, in shops and cinemas) and some accommodation and travel discounts. All are valid for a year and are available from youth-oriented travel agencies such as STA Travel, Council Travel and Travel CUTS (about UK£6) and in Portugal from Tagus and Wasteels (€6).

The websites **w** www.istc.org and **w** www.counciltravel.com have information on ISIC, ITIC and IYTC/Go25 cards; **w** www.euro26.org has information on Euro>26.

Portugal's own Euro>26 card, the widely accepted Cartão Jovem (€5.30), is available to foreign residents and Portuguese,

from youth-travel agencies, youth hostels, offices of the Instituto Português da Juventude (see Useful Organisations, later in this chapter) and elsewhere.

Senior travellers can get similar discounts and more. Domestic train travel is half-price on weekdays for anyone aged 65 or over. With the Rail Plus card those aged 60 and over get up to 25% off any rail journey that crosses an international border. To be eligible you first need a local senior citizens' railcard; in the UK this is called a Senior Railcard (UK£18) and is sold, along with the Rail Plus card (UK£12), at major stations and through rail companies such as **Connex South Eastern** (☎ 0870 001 0174). Rail Plus cards are also available from Rail Europe (see under Train in the Getting There & Away chapter).

For information on discounts for children see Travel with Children, later in this chapter.

Tipping & Bargaining

If you're satisfied with the service, a reasonable restaurant tip is 5% to 10%. The bill at an upper-end restaurant may already include a *serviço* (service charge). For a snack at a bar, cake shop or café, a bit of loose change is enough. Taxi drivers appreciate 10% of the fare and petrol station attendants €0.50 or so.

Good-humoured bargaining is acceptable in markets. For long stays or during low season, you can often bargain down the price of accommodation.

Taxes & Refunds

Imposto Sobre Valor Acrescentado (IVA) is a sales tax levied on a wide range of goods and services. In most shops it's 17%, though at the time of writing it had jumped 'temporarily' to 19% on certain goods as the government fretted over EU-imposed budget-deficit targets.

In some circumstances tourists resident outside the EU can claim an IVA refund on goods from shops belonging to Europe Tax-Free Shopping Portugal (as displayed on a sign in the window or at the till). The minimum purchase for a refund is about €60 in any one shop. The shop assistant fills in a cheque for the refund (minus an administration fee). When you leave Portugal you show your goods, cheque and passport at customs for a cash, postal-note or credit-card refund.

This service is available at Lisbon, Porto and Faro airports (postal refund at Faro only). If you're leaving overland, contact customs at your final EU border point, or call **Europe Tax-Free Shopping Portugal** (☎ *218 408 813, 218 463 025; Lisbon).*

Items *not* covered by the refund scheme include grocery-shop food, books, hotel costs and car rental.

POST & COMMUNICATIONS
Sending Mail
Correio normal (posted in red letter boxes) refers to ordinary post, including airmail, while *correio azul* ('blue post'; posted in blue letter boxes) is priority or express mail. Postcards and letters up to 20g cost €0.70 to points outside Europe, €0.54 to Europe (except to Spain, which costs €0.46) and €0.28 to destinations within Portugal. International *correio azul* costs €1.75 for a 20g letter.

Allow four to six days for delivery within Europe and eight to 10 days to the USA or Australia. Economy air (or surface airlift) costs about a third less than ordinary airmail, but usually arrives a week or so later.

A 4kg to 5kg parcel sent surface mail to the UK costs €27.26. Printed matter is cheapest to send by surface mail in batches under 2kg (a 2kg parcel to the UK costs €9).

Most post offices of any size also have a NetPost terminal or two for Internet access, though these aren't usually the cheapest option (see under Email & Internet Access, later in this chapter).

Courier Services Agencies in Portugal include **DHL** (☎ *218 100 099),* **TNT** (☎ *218 545 050)* and **FedEx** (☎ *800 244 144).* All are open during normal business hours (and DHL until noon Saturday). A 200g parcel costs €32 to London (24-hour delivery) and €49 to New York (one to two working days).

Receiving Mail
Most towns have post restante service at the central post office. Letters should be addressed: name (family name first, capitalised and underlined), c/o posta restante, central post office, town name. To collect mail you must show your passport and pay €0.35 per item. Unclaimed letters are normally returned after a month.

AmEx cardholders can have mail (and faxes) sent to them care of Top Tours travel

Addresses

Addresses in Portugal are written with the street name first, followed by the building number. A letter tagged on the number, for example, 2-A or 2A, indicates an adjacent entrance or building. Floor numbers may be included, with a degree symbol, so 15-3° means entrance No 15, 3rd floor. The further abbreviations D, dir or Dta (for *direita*, meaning right), or E, esq or Esqa (for *esquerda*, meaning left), tell you which door to go to. Floor numbering is by European convention, ie, the 1st floor is one flight up from the ground floor. R/C (*rés do chão*) means ground floor.

agency offices in Lisbon, Porto, Faro and Portimão (see those city entries).

Telephone
To call Portugal from abroad, dial the international access code of the country you're in, plus ☎ 351 (Portugal's country code), plus the full number. Aside from a few assistance numbers, all domestic numbers have nine digits. There are no area codes as such: all digits must be dialled from any location.

Home telephones aside, the easiest way to make a call is from a card-operated public telephone; these are plentiful in most towns. Coin-operated telephones are also common but can be maddeningly fickle. You can also call, at coin-phone rates, from booths in Portugal Telecom offices and post offices, where you pay over the counter after your call is finished.

Calls from public telephones are charged according to the number of *impulsos* ('beeps' or time units) used. The price per beep is fixed (€0.07 with a phonecard) but the duration of a beep depends on destination, time of day and type of call (see the following sections). Coin telephones cost 15% more than cardphones, and a metered telephone in a hotel or café will cost *three to six times* as much! It costs an additional two beeps' worth to make a domestic connection, or three to make an international connection.

All but local calls are cheaper from 9pm to 9am weekdays and all day Saturday, Sunday and holidays; international calls to certain countries are cheaper still on Saturday and Sunday.

Local, Regional & National Calls The cheapest way to call within Portugal is with a Portugal Telecom *cartão telefónico* (phonecard). These are available for €3/6/9 (50/100/150 beeps) from post and telephone offices and many newsagents; a youth or student card should get you a 10% discount.

A beep lasts three minutes for any local call. It lasts 46 seconds for a regional call (under about 50km) and 30 seconds for a national call, and lasts twice as long during the previously mentioned economy periods.

Numbers starting with 800 (*linha verde*, green line) are toll free. Those starting with 808 (*linha azul*, blue line) are charged at local rates from anywhere in the country.

Portugal's directory inquiries number is ☎ 118 (€0.38), and operators will search by address as well as by name. Two independent enquiry services, charged at local-call rates, are **Telelista** (☎ 707 222 707; w *www.telelista .iol.pt*) and **Páginas Amarelas** (*Yellow Pages*; ☎ 707 202 222; w *www.paginasamarelas.pt*).

International Calls & Cards With a Portugal Telecom (PT) phonecard, the cheapest (weekend) three-minute call costs about €8 to Spain, €9 to the UK or USA or €23 to Australia. But a number of international cards now available offer international rates that make PT's look like licensed robbery.

Lonely Planet's eKno card offers competitive rates, free messaging services, email, travel information and secure online storage of important documents. You can join online at w *www.ekno.lonelyplanet.com*, where you'll also find local-access numbers for the 24-hour customer-service centre, as well as new features. At the time of writing a three-minute call from Portugal cost about €2.70 to Spain, €1.70 to the USA, €1.80 to the UK and €2.10 to Australia.

Another good-value international card, sold at many Portugal newsagencies and lottery shops, is Onicard. Note that actual peak and off-peak periods vary according to which card you use.

For international directory inquiries, call ☎ 177 (€0.86). To make a reverse-charge (*pago no destino*) call with the help of a multilingual operator, dial ☎ 171. From Portugal, the international access code is ☎ 00.

Country-Direct Service Portuguese operators can help you make both collect or credit-card calls. For an extra charge you can dial direct to operators in certain countries, including the following:

Australia	☎ 00 800 287 7421
Canada (AT&T)	☎ 800 800 124
Canada (Stentor)	☎ 800 800 122
France	☎ 800 800 330
Germany	☎ 800 800 490
Ireland	☎ 800 800 353
The Netherlands	☎ 800 800 310
New Zealand	☎ 800 800 640
Spain	☎ 800 800 340
UK	☎ 800 800 440
USA (Ameritech)	☎ 800 800 119
USA (AT&T)	☎ 800 800 128
USA (Bellsouth)	☎ 800 800 117
USA (MCI)	☎ 800 800 123
USA (Southwestern Bell)	☎ 800 800 115
USA (Teleglobe USA)	☎ 800 800 118
USA (TRT)	☎ 800 800 188
USA (USSprint)	☎ 800 800 187

Fax

Post offices offer a domestic and international fax service called Corfax, costing €4.25 for the first page to the UK, North America or Australia. Collecting a fax at the post office costs about €1.50 per page. Guesthouses and some computer and photocopy shops charge considerably less.

Email & Internet Access

Free Internet access is rapidly becoming the norm all over Portugal – at municipal libraries, at local branches of the Instituto Português da Juventude (IPJ; see under Useful Organisations later in this chapter) and at a growing number of municipally-run *cyberespaços* – see local listings. In general you must book ahead and are limited to a half-hour slot, especially if others are waiting.

Cybercafés, common only in bigger cities and towns, charge anywhere from €0.50 to €3 or more per online hour. Most post offices now have terminals for NetPost, an Internet facility payable with a special card at €2.40 per hour. Just to confuse matters, some towns also have branches of a private stationery company called PostNet, unrelated to the post office, with some postal services and Internet access. Some newer youth hostels offer access for €2.50 per hour.

If you've got your own laptop/palmtop and modem, and your Internet service provider (ISP) at home offers global roaming (access via local telephone numbers in countries where you'll be travelling), you might succeed in logging on from your hotel room. ISPs such as CompuServe, AOL and AT&T Global have access numbers in Portugal. Calls, especially from hotels, are expensive in Portugal so get on and off quickly. Some computer-shy *pensões* may refuse to let you plug in.

With luck your room will have a telephone socket. Most sockets in Portugal are US standard (RJ-11); for those few older ones that aren't RJ-11 you'll need an adapter. Be sure the hotel doesn't have a digital telephone exchange, which can fry your modem; you can always plug safely into an analog data line such as the hotel's fax line. A line tester will ensure that the line is safe to use.

An occasional problem with ordinary lines in Portugal is the faint 'beeps' that mark units of calling time, which can interfere with modem connections. The solution is an in-line filter.

Line testers, filters, telephone and power adapters and many other accessories are available from Web-based dealers such as TeleAdapt (**w** www.teleadapt.com) and Konexx (**w** www.konexx.com).

PCMCIA card-modems may not work once you leave your home country, and you won't know for sure until you try. The safest option is to carry a reputable global modem or to buy a card-modem in Portugal if you're staying for a while.

For some handy Internet terms in Portuguese, see the boxed text 'Portuguese Cyber-Jargon'.

DIGITAL RESOURCES

The World Wide Web is a rich travel resource. You can research your trip, hunt down bargain fares, book hotels, check the weather and chat with locals and other travellers about things to do (or avoid!).

A good place to start is the Lonely Planet website (**w** www.lonelyplanet.com). Here you'll find succinct summaries on travelling to most places on earth, postcards from other travellers and the Thorn Tree bulletin board, where you can ask questions before you go or dispense advice when you get back. You can also find travel news and the subWWWay section links you to useful resources elsewhere on the Web.

Three sites with abundant links to attractions, practicalities, maps, air fares, books,

---

Portuguese Cyber-Jargon

If you surf the Web in Portugal you may have to do it in Portuguese. Following is a bit of useful Portuguese cyber-speak:

bookmark	*marcador*
close	*fechar*
copy	*copiar*
cut	*cortar*
edit	*editar*
email	*correio eletrónico*
exit	*sair*
file	*ficheiro*
help	*ajuda*
new	*novo*
open	*abrir*
paste	*colar*
print	*imprimir*
return	*regressar*
save	*guardar*
save as...	*guardar como...*
search	*procurar* or *pesquisar*

When quoting email addresses, the @ symbol is *arroba*, a dot is *punt*, a slash is *barre* and a hyphen is *trace*.

---

entertainment, personal narratives and more are A Collection of Home Pages about Portugal (**w** www.well.com/user/ideamen/por tugal.html), Portugal Virtual (**w** www.portu galvirtual.pt) and Portugal Live (**w** www .portugal-live.net).

Portugal's state tourism organisation, ICEP (see Tourist Offices earlier in this chapter), operates the sometimes-lively Portugal Insite (**w** www.portugal-insite.pt), mixing coming events, features and adventure sports with more routine tips. For links on history, politics and current events, see Political Science Resources (**w** www.psr .keele.ac.uk/area/portugal.htm).

On the more cultured side is the Camões Institute's English-language site (**w** www .instituto-camoes.pt/cvc/literaturaingles/in dex.html), with background information on Portuguese language, literature and theatre, plus potted biographies of the country's most important authors and poets.

Sapo (**w** www.sapo.pt) is a versatile search engine on Portugal topics, though it's only in Portuguese.

BOOKS

Not many shops outside Lisbon, Porto and the main Algarve towns have a decent supply of English-language books about the country, so it's worth visiting your local bookshop before you go. Check the Spain listings too, as Portugal often gets lumped in with them.

In different countries, books are generally published in different editions by different publishers. Your bookshop or library can advise you on availability and order books for you.

Lonely Planet

If you plan to journey more widely than just Portugal, consider one of Lonely Planet's multicountry guides: *Europe on a shoestring*, *Western Europe* or *Mediterranean Europe* (which covers Lisbon and the Algarve). For a short break to Lisbon there's the Lonely Planet *Lisbon* city guide.

If the way to your heart is through your stomach, don't go without Lonely Planet's *World Food Portugal*, a fine introduction to the country's rich cuisine. And how's your Portuguese? Lonely Planet can help there too, with its *Portuguese phrasebook* or *Western Europe phrasebook*.

Other Guidebooks

Bethan Davies & Ben Cole's peerless *Walking in Portugal* (2000) features routes in most of the country's national/natural parks and many reserves, with colour maps and information on flora and fauna, practicalities and rainy-day options. Less single-minded pedestrians will like Brian & Eileen Anderson's Landscapes of Portugal series, featuring both car tours and walks, in separate books on the *Algarve* (2000); *Sintra, Cascais and Estoril* (1991); and *Costa Verde, Minho and Peneda-Gerês* (1991; out of print but can be downloaded at w www .sunflowerbooks.co.uk).

One of the finest of numerous regional guidebooks is John & Madge Measures' *Southern Portugal: Its People, Traditions & Wildlife* (1995), with comprehensive coverage of the archaeology, landscapes, agriculture, flora, fauna and products of many little-visited places in the Algarve and southern Alentejo. Another nice perspective is that of Joe Staines & Lia Duarte in *Exploring Rural Portugal* (1992).

Travel

Rose Macaulay's entertaining and well-known collections *They Went to Portugal* (1946, 1988) and *They Went to Portugal, Too* (1991) follow the experiences of a variety of English visitors from medieval times until the 19th century. These are recommended 'companion' books, easy to enjoy in small doses.

Paul Hyland's *Backwards out of the Big World: A Voyage into Portugal* (1996) is the poetic account of a voyage of discovery encompassing Lisbon, Sintra and the far corners of the Alentejo.

History & Politics

Readable, portable and thorough up to its publication date is David Birmingham's *Concise History of Portugal* (1993). Also user-friendly, and augmented with a handy historical gazetteer, is *Portugal: A Companion History* (1998), by José Hermano Saraiva. Too big to tote but probably the best English-language history of the Portuguese nation is AH de Oliveira Marques' *History of Portugal* (1976).

Specific references on 'the Discoveries' include John Ure's *Prince Henry the Navigator* (1977) and CR Boxer's *The Portuguese Seaborne Empire, 1415–1825* (1969, 1991). For a look into the depressing Salazar years see António de Figueiredo's *Portugal: Fifty Years of Dictatorship* (1976). The dramatic events of 1974 are replayed in *Revolution & Counter-Revolution in Portugal* (1987), by Martin Kayman.

Portugal is just one player in Daniel J Boorstin's classic *The Discoverers* (1983), an original and panoramic look at the way humans keep discovering their world. Chapters on Portugal include the discovery of a sea route to India, Portugal's rivalry with Spain, and the slave trade.

Historical Thrillers Two recent thrillers offer fictionalised but vivid windows into the past. Cast as the translation of a long-lost manuscript about the murder of a 16th-century Jewish mystic, *The Last Kabbalist of Lisbon* (2000), by Richard Zimler, reveals much about the harrowing life of secret Jews during Portugal's Inquisition.

Robert Wilson's award-winning *A Small Death in Lisbon* (1999), cutting between 1941 and a post-1974 murder investigation, shows the impacts of WWII and the Revolution of the Carnations on Portuguese psyche.

Food & Drink

Edite Vieira's *The Taste of Portugal* (1988, 1995) is more than a cookbook; its selected regional recipes are spiced with cultural insights and anecdotes; there's also a section on wines and an appendix on vegetarian dishes, which you'll wish you could find in Portuguese restaurants. Another good cookbook is Maite Manjon's *The Home Book of Portuguese Cookery* (1974).

Richard Mayson & Hugh Johnson's *Portugal's Wines & Wine-Makers: Port, Madeira & Regional Wines* (1998) is a brisk, readable introduction to the country's favourite product. Another good introduction to the subject is *The Wines of Portugal* (1987), by Jan Read. Sarah Bradford's *The Englishman's Wine: the Story of Port* (1969, revised 1978) is the definitive history of the port-wine trade and of the British colony in Porto.

Lonely Planet's *World Food Portugal* by Lynelle Scott-Aitken is also a great read.

Music, Art & Architecture

An appealing book on the region's vernacular architecture is *Iberian Villages* (1989), by architect Norman F Carver Jr. Though it's largely Spain-oriented, close attention is paid to the Portuguese towns of Lindoso, Mértola, Monsanto, Albufeira, Calcadinha, Guarda, Loulé and Monsaraz.

One of the most handsome of many coffee-table books on Portugal's idiosyncratic architecture is *Country Manors of Portugal: A Passage Through Seven Centuries* (1988), with text by Marcus Binney and lush photos by Nicolas Sapieha & Francesco Venturi.

Paul Vernon's *A History of the Portuguese Fado* (1999) is an affectionate, comprehensively grand (but pricey) tour of Portugal's most famous brand of music.

Living & Working in Portugal

The best source of advice and practical information on lingering or settling down in Portugal is Sue Tyson-Ward's *Living and Working in Portugal* (2000), with details on everything from buying a house and starting a business to domestic life, education and health services.

Potential expatriates will be charmed and sobered by Richard Hewitt's *A Cottage in Portugal* (1996), recounting, à la Peter Mayle, an American couple's tribulations in renovating a cottage near Sintra in the face of Portuguese bureaucracy.

General

One of the finest all-round books about the Portuguese is Marion Kaplan's perceptive *The Portuguese: The Land & Its People* (1992, revised 1998). Ranging knowledgeably from literature to the Church, from agriculture to *emigrantes*, its sympathetic female perspective seems appropriate for a country whose men so often seem to be abroad.

An accessible anthropological pop-classic is *Portugal: A Book of Folk Ways* (1936, 1961), by Rodney Gallop. Malcom Jack's *Sintra: A Glorious Eden* (2002) evokes the romantic spirit of Sintra with a fascinating account at its historical and literary background.

Poetry and novels by Portuguese writers, many of which are translated into English, are noted under Arts in the Facts about Portugal chapter.

FILMS

Wim Wenders' *A Lisbon Story* had its world premiere in Lisbon in 1994, when the capital was European City of Culture. Originally conceived as a documentary, it acquired a story line as it went along: a movie soundman wanders the streets trying to salvage a film that its director has abandoned, recording the sounds of the city. In the process he falls in love, has a close call with gangsters and is followed by a pack of school children. Wenders pays tribute to many cinema greats, including Fellini, Chaplin and Portuguese director Manoel do Oliveira (see Arts in the Facts about Portugal chapter).

NEWSPAPERS & MAGAZINES
Portuguese-Language Press

Major Portuguese-language daily newspapers include *Diário de Notícias* (**w** www .dn.pt), *Público* (**w** www.publico.pt) and *Jornal de Notícias* (**w** www.jnoticias.pt), which also have online editions, and the gossip tabloid *Correio da Manhã*, which licks all of the others for circulation. Popular weeklies include *O Independente* and *Expresso*.

News-stands groan under the weight of sports publications; the best on football is *A Bola*. For entertainment listings, check local

In Portugal *azulejos* cover everything from church interiors to train stations to private homes. Wherever you turn you'll see these painted tiles in a mixture of styles, themes and colours. The technique has been used more widely and inventively here than anywhere else.

RICHARD I'ANSON

RICHARD I'ANSON

JOHN KING

RICHARD I'ANSON

RICHARD I'ANSON

Sample some cheese at the Mercado do Bolhão

Eat, drink and be merry in the Douro region

The aroma of delicious *sardinhas assadas* (grilled sardines) fills the air in Portimão, the Algarve

Porto's lively municipal market, the Mercado do Bolhão, offers a range of fresh produce

dailies; the Lisbon and Porto editions of *Público* have comprehensive listings.

Foreign-Language Press

Several English-language newspapers are published in Portugal by and for its expatriate population, especially in the Algarve. In addition to entertainment listings and information on regional attractions and events, they have adverts for long-term accommodation, cheap flights, language and other courses, and even work. Best known are *APN* (Anglo-Portuguese News), published every Thursday, and *The News* (**w** www .the-news.net), published fortnightly in regional editions. Another is the weekly *Algarve Resident* magazine (**w** www.algar veresident.com). The last two publications also have online editions.

In the biggest towns and tourist destinations it's easy to find a range of foreign papers, including the *International Herald Tribune*, *Le Monde*, *Le Figaro* and the *Guardian*. They cost around €1.50 to €3 and are usually a day or two old. At some big-city newsagents you can also find magazines such as *Paris-Match*, *Le Point*, *L'Express*, *Der Spiegel*, *Bünte* and the *Economist*.

RADIO

Domestic radio is represented by state-owned Rádiodifusão Portuguesa (RDP) stations Antena 1 on MW and FM, and Antena 2 and Antena 3 on FM; the private Rádio Comercial, Rádio Renascença, Rádio Nostalgia and RFM; and a clutch of local stations. Essentially, all broadcasts are in Portuguese. Evening programming includes helpings of music, with jazz on Antena 1 and rock on Rádio Comercial.

Frequencies vary with locale. Look out for Antena 1 at MW 666kHz, FM 95.7MHz or 99.4MHz in Lisbon; MW 1377kHz or FM 96.7MHz in Porto; or MW 720kHz, FM 88.9MHz or 97.6MHz in the Algarve. For Rádio Comercial try MW 1035kHz or alternatively FM 97.4MHz in Lisbon; MW 1170kHz or FM 97.7MHz in Porto; or MW 558kHz or FM 88.1MHz or 96.1MHz in the Algarve.

English-language broadcasts of the BBC World Service and Voice of America (VOA) can be picked up on various medium-wave and short-wave frequencies in Portugal, though BBC reception is generally poor.

TV

Portuguese TV consists of the state-run Rádio Televisão Portuguesa (RTP) channels RTP-1 (VHF) and RTP-2 (UHF), plus private channels Sociedade Independente de Communicação (SIC) and TV Independente (TVI). Portuguese and Brazilian soap operas, lightweight entertainment and subtitled foreign movies dominate TV airtime.

There are at least 15 cable-TV and satellite channels available, mostly featuring sports, music and movies. Some mid-range and many top-end hotels provide satellite TV in their rooms.

VIDEO SYSTEMS

Portugal uses the PAL system, which is compatible with systems in Australia and most of Europe. It is not compatible with the French Secam system or the North American and Japanese NTSC system.

PHOTOGRAPHY & VIDEO
Film & Equipment

Ektachrome, Fujichrome and other brands of slide film, plus print film and 8mm video cassettes, are widely available. It's best to bring camera equipment and higher-quality films such as Kodachrome with you. You can buy video accessories in major towns but take along the necessary battery charger, plugs and transformer (plus a few cartridges).

Print-film processing is as fast and cheap as anywhere in Europe. Slide and video processing are rare. Imported point-and-shoot cameras are available in franchise shops and elsewhere, at marked-up prices.

Technical Tips

Except for the occasional indoor shot with a high-speed film such as 400 ASA/ISO film, you'll rarely need anything faster than 100 ASA/ISO.

Contrast between light and shadow is harshest at high noon; try to get out in the early morning or just before sunset for the gentlest light. Consider adding Lonely Planet's *Travel Photography – A Guide to Taking Better Pictures* to your library.

Video cameras have amazingly sensitive microphones. Filming beside a busy road may produce only a deafening roar as a soundtrack. Try to film in long takes and not move the camera around too much.

Restrictions

There are no customs limits on equipment for personal use. There are no significant restrictions on what you can shoot in Portugal, though military sites aren't a very good idea. Some museums and galleries forbid flash photography.

Photographing People

Older Portuguese often become serious and frustratingly uncandid when you take their photos, but few will object to it and many will be delighted. Everybody seems to like having their children photographed! Nevertheless, the courtesy of asking beforehand is always appreciated. 'May I take a photograph?' is *Posse tirar uma fotografia, por favor?* in Portuguese.

Airport Security

Carrying unprocessed film in your checked baggage, even in a lead-lined 'filmsafe' pouch, is inviting trouble. Several international airports now use 'smart' CTX 5000 scanners for checked baggage. These scan first with a mild beam, then zero in ferociously on anything suspicious. A lead pouch would not only be ineffective but would invite further scans, and film inside is certain to be ruined.

By contrast, scanners for carry-on bags at most major airports are relatively harmless, at least for slow and medium-speed films. The moral of the tale is obvious: carry unprocessed film in your carry-on bags, and if possible get officials to hand-inspect it. Having the film in clear plastic bags (and preferably clear canisters) can help to persuade them.

TIME

Portugal, like Britain, is on GMT/UTC in winter and GMT/UTC plus one hour in summer. This puts it an hour earlier than Spain year-round. Clocks are set forward by an hour on the last Sunday in March and back on the last Sunday in October.

ELECTRICITY

Electricity is 220V, 50Hz. Plugs normally have two round pins, though some have a third, projecting, earth pin.

North American appliances will need a transformer if they don't have built-in voltage adjustment.

WEIGHTS & MEASURES

Portugal uses the metric system; see the inside back cover for conversion information. Decimals are indicated with commas, and thousands with points.

LAUNDRY

Lavandarias provide laundry services at reasonable cost everywhere, though most concentrate on dry-cleaning *(limpar/limpeza a seco)*. Those that also do wash-and-dry *(lavar e secar)* usually take at least a day or two. Some may do ironing *(passar a ferro)* too. Genuine self-service places are rare. Figure €6 to wash and dry a 6kg load. Your guesthouse proprietor may be willing to do small loads.

TOILETS

Public toilets are rare, though coin-operated street toilets (€0.10 or €0.15) are becoming increasingly evident in major cities. Most people just go to the nearest café for a drink or a pastry and use the facilities there. Look for a 'WC' sign, or 'H' *(homens,* men) or 'S' *(senhoras,* women).

HEALTH

Portugal, like the rest of Europe, presents few health risks to the sensible traveller. Your main problems are likely to be insect bites, sunburn, upset stomach or foot blisters. Some people routinely experience a day or two of 'travellers diarrhoea' upon arriving in any new country.

Predeparture Planning

Immunisations No vaccinations are required for entry into Portugal unless you're coming from an infected area and are destined for the Azores or Madeira, in which case you may be asked for proof of vaccination against yellow fever. A few routine vaccinations are recommended: polio (usually administered during childhood), diptheria and tetanus (usually administered together in childhood, with a booster every 10 years) and sometimes measles. See your physician or health service about these. Some vaccinations are contraindicated if you're pregnant.

Health Insurance Most travel insurance policies include medical cover. For important suggestions about travel insurance, see Visas & Documents earlier in this chapter.

Free or reduced-cost emergency treatment is available in Portugal to citizens of the EU member states and Iceland, Liechtenstein and Norway on presentation of an E111 form. Ask about the E111 at your local health service or travel agency at least a few weeks before you travel. Charges are likely for medication, dental work or secondary examinations, including x-rays and laboratory tests. Treatment in private hospitals is not covered.

Visitors with UK passports are entitled to free in-patient treatment in the general ward of any public hospital in Portugal.

Health Preparations If you wear glasses take a spare pair and your prescription. You can usually get new spectacles made up quickly, cheaply and competently.

If you need a particular medication, take an adequate supply, as it may not be available (though most pharmacies are remarkably well equipped). It's wise to carry a legible prescription to show that you legally use the medication. If you need more, you're better off knowing the medication's generic name than its brand name, which can vary.

Dental care is available in Portugal, but it's not a bad idea to have a routine checkup before you leave home.

Contraception Throughout Portugal the most widely available contraceptive is condoms (*preservativos*), available in all pharmacies (though you may have to ask for them in smaller towns) and sometimes in supermarkets. If you're taking a contraceptive pill, it's safest to bring a supply from home.

Basic Rules

Many health problems can be avoided simply by taking good care of yourself, eg, washing your hands often and keeping out of the sun when it's very hot. Care in what you eat and drink is also important, though the worst you can expect in Portugal is a temporary stomach upset.

Food Salads and fruit are safe anywhere in Portugal. Ice cream is OK, but beware of any that has melted and been refrozen. Take care with shellfish (eg, cooked mussels that haven't opened properly can be dangerous) and avoid undercooked meat, particularly

minced meat. Be careful with food that has been cooked and then left to go cold.

Water Tap water is almost always safe to drink in Portugal's towns and cities, though you should be wary in small villages. The Portuguese love their fresh spring water and often stop at roadside fountains to fill up – though some more remote springs may just be surface streams through populated areas or pastureland. Bottled water is widely

---

Medical Kit Check List

Following is a list of items you should consider including in your medical kit – consult your pharmacist for brands available in your country.

☐ **Aspirin or paracetamol (acetaminophen in the USA)** – for pain or fever

☐ **Antihistamine** – for allergies, eg, hay fever; to ease the itch from insect bites or stings; and to prevent motion sickness

☐ **Cold and flu tablets, throat lozenges and nasal decongestant**

☐ **Multivitamins** – consider for long trips, when dietary vitamin intake may be inadequate

☐ **Antibiotics** – consider including these if you're travelling well off the beaten track; see your doctor, as they must be prescribed, and carry the prescription with you

☐ **Loperamide or diphenoxylate** – 'blockers' for diarrhoea

☐ **Prochlorperazine or metaclopramide** – for nausea and vomiting

☐ **Rehydration mixture** – to prevent dehydration, which may occur, for example, during bouts of diarrhoea; particularly important when travelling with children

☐ **Insect repellent, sunscreen, lip balm and eye drops**

☐ **Calamine lotion, sting relief spray or aloe vera** – to ease irritation from sunburn and insect bites or stings

☐ **Antifungal cream or powder** – for fungal skin infections and thrush

☐ **Antiseptic (such as povidone-iodine)** – for cuts and grazes

☐ **Bandages, Band-Aids (plasters) and other wound dressings**

☐ **Water purification tablets or iodine**

☐ **Scissors, tweezers and a thermometer** – note that mercury thermometers are prohibited by airlines

available, though nondegradable plastic bottles bring with them a significant environmental impact.

If you're planning long hikes where you'll depend on natural water, you should be prepared to purify it. The simplest way is to boil it vigorously – five minutes should be enough at altitudes typical of Portugal. Iodine treatment, available in tablet form (such as Potable Aqua or Globaline), is very effective and safe for short-term use unless you're pregnant or have thyroid problems. A flavoured powder will disguise the taste of treated water. Chlorine tablets (such as Puritabs or Steritabs) kill many, but not all pathogens, for example, giardia and amoebic cysts. The only commercial water filters that stop all pathogens are combined charcoal and iodine-resin filters.

Nutrition If you're travelling hard and fast and therefore missing meals or not eating a balanced diet, it's a good idea to take multivitamin and mineral supplements. Fresh fruit and vegetables are also good vitamin sources.

In hot weather, don't rely on thirst to remind you to drink enough. Carry a water bottle on long trips. Excessive sweating can lead to loss of salt and result in muscle cramping; to avoid this, add a bit more salt to your food than usual.

Medical Treatment

Every sizable Portuguese town has its own *centro de saúde* (state-administered medical centre), which is typically open from 8am to 8pm daily. Big cities have full-scale hospitals and clinics with 24-hour emergency services; we include contact addresses under Information in each city. There are also numerous – and pricier – English-speaking private physicians, and in Lisbon there is even a Hospital Britânico (British Hospital).

For minor health problems you can pop into a *farmácia* (pharmacy) for advice; these are abundant in larger towns and usually very well supplied, and often have English-speaking staff. There's always one pharmacy open after hours. The address of the late-night pharmacy is usually posted in the window of the others, or you can call **general inquiries** (☎ 118) to find out which pharmacy in your area is open.

Environmental Hazards

Heat Exhaustion Dehydration or salt deficiency can cause heat exhaustion, characterised by fatigue, lethargy, headaches, giddiness and muscle cramps. Salt tablets may help, but adding extra salt to your food is much better. Vomiting or diarrhoea can also deplete your liquid and salt levels. Take time to acclimatise to high temperatures (don't do anything too physically demanding) and make sure you get sufficient liquids.

Heatstroke This serious, sometimes fatal, condition can occur if the body's heat-regulating mechanism breaks down and body temperature rises to dangerous levels. Long, continuous periods of exposure to high temperatures can leave you vulnerable to heatstroke.

Symptoms include feeling unwell, not sweating much or at all, and high body temperature (39° to 41°C, or 102° to 106°F). Where sweating has ceased, the skin becomes flushed and red. Severe, throbbing headaches and lack of coordination will also occur, and the sufferer may be confused or aggressive. Eventually the victim will become delirious or convulse. Hospitalisation is essential but, meanwhile, move victims out of the sun, remove their clothing, cover them with a wet sheet or towel and fan them continually. Give them fluids if they're conscious.

Sunburn In Portugal, especially on water or sand, you can get sunburnt surprisingly quickly, even through cloud. Wear a wide-brimmed hat and use a sunscreen or sunblock. Calamine lotion soothes mild sunburn.

Good quality sunglasses, treated to filter out ultraviolet radiation, are vital if you plan to spend much time at the beach.

Stings & Insect Bites Bee and wasp stings are usually painful rather than dangerous. Calamine lotion provides relief and ice packs will reduce pain and swelling. Mosquitoes are only a minor nuisance in Portugal, and mosquito-borne diseases are almost unknown in Europe.

Snakebites Two venomous snakes, Lataste's viper and the Montpellier snake, live in remoter areas of Portugal, although neither is deadly. Snakes are probably more afraid of humans than we are of them. To minimise your chances of being bitten, wear boots, socks and long trousers when walking through heavy undergrowth; tramp heavily to give snakes time to flee; and don't put your hands into holes or crevices. Campers should be careful when collecting firewood.

Antivenenes are usually available. Keep any snakebite victim calm and still, wrap the bitten limb tightly, as you would for a sprained ankle, and attach a splint to immobilise it. Then seek medical help, if possible with the dead snake for identification (but don't attempt to catch the snake if there is even a remote possibility of anyone being bitten again). Tourniquets and sucking out the poison are now comprehensively discredited.

There's a countrywide **emergency number** (☎ 217 950 143) for advice on poisoning and snakebites.

Jellyfish, Sea Urchins & Weever Fish

Stings from jellyfish can be painful but are not dangerous. Dousing in vinegar will deactivate any stingers that haven't 'fired'. Calamine lotion, antihistamines or analgesics may reduce the reaction and relieve the pain.

Watch for sea urchins around rocky beaches. If you get their needles embedded in your skin, immersing the limb in hot water will relieve the pain. But to avoid infection you should visit a doctor to have the needles removed.

Thankfully very rare are weever fish, found in shallow tidal zones along the Atlantic coast. They bury themselves in the sand with only their spines protruding and inject a powerful toxin if trodden upon. Soaking the foot in very hot water breaks down the poison, but you should seek medical advice as in rare cases it can cause permanent local paralysis.

Fungal Infections

These infections occur with greater frequency in hot weather and are most likely to appear on the scalp, between the toes (athlete's foot) or fingers, in the groin area and on the body (ringworm). You get ringworm – which is not a worm – from infected animals or other people.

To prevent fungal infections wear loose, comfortable clothes, avoid artificial fibres, wash frequently and dry yourself carefully.

If you get an infection, wash the infected area daily with a disinfectant or medicated soap, and rinse and dry well. Apply antifungal cream or powder, such as tolnaftate (Tinaderm). Expose the infected area to air or sunlight as much as possible, change all towels and underwear often and wash them in hot water.

Infectious Diseases

Diarrhoea You may have a mild bout of travellers' diarrhoea on arrival in a new place, but a few dashes to the toilet with no other symptoms do not suggest anything serious. Half a dozen loose movements in a day can be more of a nuisance. Dehydration is the main danger, particularly for children, and fluid replacement is the main treatment. Soda water, soft drinks allowed to go flat and diluted 50% with water, or weak black tea with a little sugar, are all good replacements. Stick to a bland diet for a few days. With any diarrhoea more severe than this, go straight to a doctor.

Lomotil or Imodium can stop you up but they don't cure the problem. Use them only when absolutely necessary; for example, if you *must* travel. They are not recommended for children under 12 years old. Do not use them if the person has a high fever or is severely dehydrated.

HIV & AIDS Infection with the human immunodeficiency virus (HIV) may lead to acquired immune deficiency syndrome (AIDS), which is a fatal disease. Any exposure to blood, blood products or body fluids may put an individual at risk. The disease is often transmitted through sexual contact or dirty needles – vaccinations, acupuncture, tattooing and body piercing can be potentially as dangerous as intravenous drug use.

The Portuguese Institute of Blood screens all blood used for transfusions.

Sexually Transmitted Infections (STIs) Gonorrhoea, herpes and syphilis are common STIs; sores, blisters or rashes around the genitals, discharges or pain when urinating are common symptoms. With some STIs, such as wart virus or chlamydia, symptoms may be less marked or not observed at all, especially in women; but chlamydia can cause infertility in men and women before any symptoms have been noticed at all. Syphilis symptoms eventually disappear completely but the disease continues and can cause severe problems in later years.

While abstinence is the only 100% effective prevention, using condoms is also effective. Gonorrhoea and syphilis are treated with antibiotics. The different sexually transmitted infections each require specific antibiotics. (See also HIV & AIDS, earlier.)

Women's Health
Antibiotic use, synthetic underwear, sweating and contraceptive pills can lead to fungal vaginal infections, characterised by a rash, itch and discharge. The usual treatment is with antifungal pessaries or cream but they can also be treated with a highly diluted vinegar or lemon-juice douche, or with yogurt. Good personal hygiene, loose-fitting clothes and cotton underwear may help prevent these infections. (See also Sexually Transmitted Infections, earlier.)

WOMEN TRAVELLERS
In rural areas an unaccompanied foreign woman is an oddity. Older villagers may ask women visitors where their husbands are, and fuss over them as if they were in need of protection. Never mind that these same areas often seem entirely populated by unaccompanied Portuguese women whose husbands are either working in the fields, gossiping in the bars, employed abroad or long dead.

Women travelling alone in Portugal report few serious problems. Portuguese machismo is more irritating than dangerous – waiters, for example, may serve every man in the place before even glancing at you. A bigger risk may be stoked-up male tourists in seaside resorts, particularly in the Algarve.

If you're travelling with a male partner, everyone will expect him to do all the talking and ordering. In some conservative pockets of the north, unmarried couples seeking accommodation may avoid hassle by saying they're married.

Women should be cautious about where they go after dark, especially in certain areas of Porto and Lisbon (see those city entries for details). Hitching is not recommended for solo women anywhere in Portugal.

There's no specific rape-crisis hotline, but the **Comissão para a Igualdade e para os Direitos das Mulheres** (Commission for the Equality & Rights of Women; ☎ 217 983 000, fax 217 983 098; Avenida da República 32, Lisbon) operates a toll-free telephone number (☎ 800 202 148) for victims of violence. The **Associação Portuguêse Apoio a Vitima** (Portuguese Association for Victims; ☎ 218 884 732) can also offer assistance.

The Commissão para a Igualdade e para os Direitos das Mulheres was founded by the government in 1976 to alter public perceptions of women's social status. It has produced and distributed materials on women's issues, and it maintains a **library** (open 10am-5pm Mon-Fri). The **Associação Portuguesa de Mulheres Empresárias** (Association of Portuguese Women Entrepreneurs; ☎ 213 872 148; e apme@mail.telepac .pt; Rua Marquês de Fronteira 4B, Lisbon) lobbies for female entrepreneurs and for the full integration of women in society. For more on the role of women in Portuguese society, see under Population & People in the Facts about Portugal chapter.

GAY & LESBIAN TRAVELLERS
Attitudes towards gay lifestyles range from a dramatically increased level of acceptance in Lisbon, Porto and the Algarve to bafflement in remoter parts of the country; lesbians appear to be more or less ignored. In this overwhelmingly Catholic country there is still little understanding of homosexuality and negligible tolerance of it within families. Although homophobic violence is relatively unknown, there's a steady stream of reported discrimination in schools and workplaces.

Lisbon has the most places for gay/lesbian socialising, including two community centres, plus restaurants, bars, discos, saunas and beaches. The annual Arraial Gay e Lésbico (Gay Pride Festival), on the Saturday closest to 28 June, is backed by the city authorities and has become a popular event. Also popular is the independent Festival de Cinema Gay e Lésbico de Lisboa (Gay & Lesbian Film Festival), held during the last two weeks of September. In October 2002 Lisbon hosted, for the first time, the annual European conference of the International Lesbian & Gay Association (ILGA).

Porto and Leiria held their own Gay Pride marches for the first time in 2001, and the Algarve has a growing number of gay-oriented meeting places, but there are few elsewhere in the country. Many gay venues still keep a very low profile. They may look closed from the outside and you'll need to ring a doorbell to get in.

Legal Matters

Homosexuality is not illegal in Portugal, though legal discrimination remains: the penal code recognises 16 as the age of consent between homosexual partners, compared with 14 for heterosexuals. Any homosexual act between an adult and an adolescent aged 14 to 16 is considered a criminal offence, and the adult is liable to a fine and/or a jail term of up to two years.

In a major step forward a Partnership Bill for both homosexual and heterosexual couples was passed in 2001, giving gay and lesbian couples that have lived together for at least two years the same civil rights (excluding adoption) as married couples.

Organisations

Associação Opus Gay (☎ 213 151 396; e anser@netcabo.pt; 2nd floor, Rua da Ilha Terceira 34, Lisbon ● ☎ 966 505 455; Apartado 10026, Porto) is an activist member organisation of ILGA and represents Portugal in ILGA's European lobby. It works with the Associação Turismo de Lisboa and the International Gay & Lesbian Travel Association developing gay and lesbian tourism in Portugal, including gay-friendly hotels (contact e opusgayturismo@hotmail.com). It has its own visitor-friendly centre in Lisbon (see the Lisbon chapter) and presents a weekly interactive gay-and-lesbian FM radio programme, Vidas Alternativas, from 9pm to 10pm every Wednesday (91.6MHz in Lisbon, 90.0MHz in Porto).

ILGA-Portugal (☎ 218 873 918; e ilga-portugal@ilga.org; Centro Comunitário Gay e Lésbico de Lisboa, Rua São Lazaro 88, Lisbon) welcomes visitors to its base at the Gay & Lesbian Community Centre, and publishes a bimonthly Portuguese newsletter, Boletim Informátivo. Another gay magazine is the quarterly Korpus.

Clube Safo (e clube_safo@hotmail.com; Apartado 95, Santarém) is Portugal's leading lesbian club, organising meetings and debates and publishing a bimonthly newsletter, Zona Livre. Another lesbian periodical is Lilás.

Grupo de Mulheres (Women's Group; ☎ 218 873 918; e gmulheres@geocities.com)

works to support isolated lesbians and promote lesbian rights, culture and pride. It organises regular social gatherings and lesbian film screenings at the Centro Comunitário Gay e Lésbico de Lisboa (see the Lisbon chapter for details).

Internet Resources

For details of the Festival de Cinema Gay e Lésbico de Lisboa, check out w www.planeta.clix.pt/festival. All of the following Internet sites have Portuguese and English versions:

Gay Motard (w www.geocities.com/westhollywood/heights/4091) For Portuguese gay and lesbian bikers, with news, events and gay-friendly accommodation
GayPt.com (w www.gaypt.com) Listings of upcoming events, news and films
ILGA-Portugal (w www.ilga-portugal.org) Listings of gay clubs, news and information
ILGA's Women's Group (w www.geocities.com/westhollywood/stonewall/9915) Good site with links to other lesbian organisations
Opus Gay (w www.opusgayassociation.com) Listings of gay clubs, news and information
Portugal Gay (w www.portugalgay.pt) Includes an English-Portuguese message board

DISABLED TRAVELLERS

Portuguese law requires public offices and agencies to provide access and facilities for disabled people but it doesn't cover private businesses, so relatively few places have facilities for disabled travellers.

Lisbon airport is wheelchair-accessible. Lisbon, Porto and Faro airports and at least the international terminals of major train stations have toilets with wheelchair access. The website w www.allgohere.com has an airline directory with information on facilities offered by various airlines.

A few special parking spaces (marked with a wheelchair symbol) are available in cities and bigger towns, although they're often used by nondisabled drivers. Car parks don't generally offer concessions. There is now a standard European parking card entitling disabled visitors to EU (and a few other) countries to the same on-street concessions given to disabled residents. In the UK these cards, issued by local social-services departments, replace the old Orange Badge scheme; for details contact the **Department for Transport** (☎ 020-7944 6800; w www.mobility-unit.dft.gov.uk).

ICEP offices abroad (see Tourist Offices earlier in this chapter) have limited information on barrier-free accommodation, most of it quite pricey. For local barrier-free hotels, camp sites and other facilities, turismos will know what's available. Wheelchair-accessible youth hostels are noted under Accommodation later in this chapter.

Organisations

The **Secretariado Nacional de Rehabilitação** (☎ 217 936 517, fax 217 942 181; Avenida Conde de Valbom 63, Lisbon) publishes the Portuguese-language *Guia de Turismo para Pessoas com Deficiências (Tourist Guide for Disabled People)*, with sections on barrier-free accommodation, transport, shops, restaurants and sights. But it's only available from its (barrier-free) offices.

Cooperativa Nacional Apoio Deficientes (CNAD; ☎/fax 218 595 332; Praça Dr Fernando Amado, Lote 566-E, 1900 Lisbon), a private organisation that can help with travel needs, has a specific department, Turintegra, devoted to holidays for disabled travellers.

Wheeling Around the Algarve (☎ 289 393 636, fax 289 397 448; W www.player.pt; Rua 5 de Outubro 181, Apartado 3421, 8135-905 Almancil) offers help with accessible accommodation, adapted transport, sport and leisure facilities, personal support and equipment in the Algarve.

A website dedicated to helping disabled travellers plan their holidays (including to Portugal) is the **Good Access Guide** (W www.goodaccessguide.co.uk).

SENIOR TRAVELLERS

Travellers aged 60 and over are entitled to various discounts; see under Money earlier in this chapter for details. Discounts at specific tourist sights are noted throughout this book. SAGA is a senior-citizens' organisation whose travel-related services – including **SAGA Holidays** (UK ☎ 0800 300 500, USA ☎ 1 800 343 0273; W www.saga.co.uk) and **SAGA Flights Service** (UK ☎ 01303-773 532) – offer some good-value airfare and holiday bargains.

TRAVEL WITH CHILDREN

Portugal is splendidly child-friendly. Following are some tips for making a trip with kids easier. For more wide-ranging suggestions, pick up Lonely Planet's *Travel with Children*.

Discounts & Children's Rates

Children under the age of eight are entitled to a 50% discount in hotels and guesthouses if they share their parents' room; budget places may charge nothing extra at all. Few restaurants object to providing child-sized portions at child-sized prices. Preschool children usually get into museums and other sights for free. Children from four to 12 years old get 50% off tickets on Portuguese railways, and those under four travel free.

Supplies

Most *minimercados*, and many pharmacies, have disposable nappies and Portuguese and imported brands of tinned baby food. Pharmacies are a good source of baby supplies, from nappies to food supplements. Big *hipermercados* stock toys and kid's clothes.

Entertainment

From a child's perspective, the best part of Portugal is probably the Algarve, with warm, calm beaches, water sports and beachside cafés; several big waterslides and theme parks; and plenty of horse riding and bike rental. Several UK-based tour operators, including **JMC** (☎ 0870-758 0203; W www.jmc.com), **Cosmos** (☎ 0870-442 8601; W www.cosmos-holidays.co.uk) and **Powder Byrne** (☎ 020-8246 5300; W www.powderbyrne.com), have kids' clubs at their Algarve resorts.

Beaches are an obvious source of fun and an outlet for energy, but beware the Atlantic's undertow, Portugal's strong midday sun and the serious pollution around Sines and Porto.

Lisbon's trams and funiculars are great fun and its breezy waterfront Parque das Nações (including the Oceanarium) is perfect for families. Several museums in Belém are very kid-friendly, and the tram ride to get there is half the fun. Sintra's horse-drawn carts, Toy Museum and nearby beaches are less than an hour away.

Portugal dos Pequenitos is a Coimbra theme park with kid-sized miniatures of architectural monuments from around the old empire. The full-sized castles of Óbidos, Marvão, Castelo de Vide, Valença and Elvas are great for letting kids' imaginations run wild (but beware many sheer-drop battlements). Lisbon and Évora have entertaining puppet theatres. Every sizable festival in the country comes complete with parades, fireworks, music, dancing and food.

For older children, see local references in this book for horse-riding centres and biking trips, especially in the Algarve, Alentejo and Parque Nacional da Peneda-Gerês. See also Activities, later in this chapter.

Childcare

Turismos can often recommend babysitters. Local Algarve and Lisbon papers advertise babysitting services, as do branches of the Instituto Português da Juventude (see Useful Organisations, following). Many resorts and larger hotels have childcare facilities staffed by trained nursery nurses.

USEFUL ORGANISATIONS

The Instituto Português da Juventude (IPJ; Portuguese Youth Institute), is a state-funded network of youth centres offering a wide range of facilities to people under 30 years of age. Its **Departamento de Informação aos Jovens** (☎ 213 522 694; e ipj .infor@mail.telepac.pt; Avenida da Liberdade 194, Lisbon), at the Lisbon headquarters, has information on courses and adventure activities, as well as notice boards advertising accommodation and things to sell and buy.

There are IPJ branches in Aveiro, Beja, Braga, Bragança, Castelo Branco, Coimbra, Évora, Faro, Guarda, Leiria, Portalegre, Porto, Santarém, Setúbal, Viana do Castelo, Vila Real and Viseu. Most have libraries (with free Internet access), cafés and study rooms, and are good places to meet students and young locals.

DANGERS & ANNOYANCES
Crime

Portugal has minimal crime by European standards but it's on the rise, fuelled by greed, open borders and smuggled handguns. A 2001 UK government study, the *International Comparison of Criminal Justice Statistics*, concluded from 1995–99 figures that violent crime was rising in Portugal by a staggering 22% per year, faster than anywhere else in the world. In mid-2002 a leaked Portuguese government report on the the country's burgeoning black-market weapons trade concluded, unsurprisingly, that this was a major factor in starkly escalating levels of gang violence.

Crime against foreigners usually involves rush-hour pickpocketing and bag-snatching, pilfering from camp sites and theft from rental cars. But there have been some armed robberies and assaults on tourists by gangs of youths, especially at beach resorts (including Estoril/Cascais and Lagos) and in parts of Lisbon and Porto.

Take the usual precautions against theft: don't carry your wallet, cash or credit cards in your back pocket or an open bag; use a moneybelt for large sums; don't leave valuables in your car, tent, hotel room or unattended backpack; and use common sense about going out at night. And if you are robbed, do not under any circumstances put up a fight.

For further peace of mind, take out travel insurance. For other useful advice see Emergencies later in this chapter.

Nightclub-Related Violence

Nightclub violence has grown in recent years. A horrific 1997 arson attack at a club in Amarante left 13 people dead. Seven were killed when pepper gas was released in Lisbon's Luanda Club in April 2000. At the Kremlin nightclub in Lisbon in March 2001, three people opened fire after being refused entry. In the same year a teenager was stabbed to death at a disco in Albufeira in the Algarve.

Common sense is your best friend: make a fast exit if things start to look ugly wherever you are.

Drugs

In July 2001 Portugal made waves across Europe by decriminalising the possession of any drug for personal use. Anyone caught with small amounts of a drug is now subject to possible fines but not to arrest, trial or imprisonment; dealing, however, remains a criminal offence. For further details see Legal Matters, later in this chapter.

But don't go lighting up in the main square. Early evidence suggests an increase in official harassment of those enjoying a spliff or popping ecstasy publicly.

Smoking

Three-quarters of the Portuguese population seems to smoke. Restaurants rarely have nonsmoking areas, and there's little you can do but move upwind, outdoors or elsewhere. Portugal has no high-profile anti-smoking lobby. All Portuguese railway trains have nonsmoking sections somewhere on board.

Portuguese Drivers

Many normally peace-loving Portuguese men and women become irascible, deranged speed-freaks behind the wheel. Tailgating at 120km/h and passing on blind curves are common. Not surprisingly, Portugal has Europe's highest per capita death rate from road accidents. Perhaps in response to such statistics, the police have initiated a zero-tolerance crackdown on several traditionally lethal routes; see under Car & Motorcycle in the Getting Around chapter for details.

Ocean z & Pollution

Atlantic Ocean currents in some coastal areas are dangerous. Beaches may be marked with coloured flags: red means the beach is closed to all bathing, yellow means swimming is prohibited but wading is fine, and green means anything goes. Be careful about swimming on beaches not identified as safe. Steer clear, too, of dangerously polluted beaches near Porto and Sines.

Hunting Season

Much of the Portuguese countryside (especially inland Algarve and the Alentejo) is open for hunting on certain days of the week – usually Thursday, Sunday and public holidays – from about August to mid-February. If you're planning any long country walks, check with the local turismo about places and days to avoid.

EMERGENCIES

The nationwide emergency telephone number for police, fire and other services is ☎ 112. Calls can be taken in English, French or Spanish, as well as in Portuguese. For medical emergencies it's probably better to contact the local hospital directly (phone numbers are provided under Information in each city entry). The countrywide number for information on snakebites and poisoning is ☎ 217 950 143 in Lisbon.

See also under Embassies & Consulates, earlier in this chapter.

Police

If you've been robbed or burgled, you should visit the local police, not just to report the crime but to get a police report, which you'll need if you hope to make an insurance claim. We identify the appropriate office under each major town. Other than in

larger cities, you won't find much English spoken (and the police report may be in Portuguese), nor will you find much sympathy.

In major towns you'll probably deal with the blue-uniformed Polícia de Segurança Pública (PSP). In rural areas and smaller towns it's more likely to be the leather-booted Guarda Nacional Republicana (GNR).

In Lisbon, Porto, Albufeira, Cascais, Praia da Rocha, Vila Nova de Milfontes and Vila Moura you'll find a new breed of earnest, multilingual 'tourist police'. In Lisbon at least, they actually walk certain beats.

LEGAL MATTERS

Foreigners in Portugal, as elsewhere, are subject to the laws of the host country. If you're charged with a crime while here, you're entitled to a lawyer to represent you, to have an interpreter present at all times and to have documents translated before being asked to sign them. But not all police or judges will recognise these rights, and appointed defence lawyers are often third-rate.

You're entitled to get in touch with your own embassy, which can provide information on local lawyers and the Portuguese legal system, follow up allegations of ill-treatment in detention and be a liaision between you and your family – but not much more.

In July 2001 Portugal decriminalised the possession and use of all narcotic drugs, with the aim to clean up festering public-health problems among drug users, and to address drug abuse as a social problem instead of a criminal one. Anyone caught with up to 10 daily doses of any drug for their own use is now brought before a special commission and is subject to possible fines and/or treatment, but not to arrest, trial or imprisonment.

Drug dealing remains a criminal offence. Anyone suspected of this or other serious crimes can be held on preliminary charges for months; the period between arrest and trial is typically six to 18 months. Bail is at the discretion of the court, although it's rarely granted for serious offences. Portugal today has more people in prison than any other EU country.

Fair Trials Abroad (FTA; in the UK ☎ 020-8332 2800, 020-8892 5403, 01223-319009; w www.fairtrialsabroad.org), a charity working to protect the rights of EU citizens wrongly charged with crimes abroad, can contact your own lawyer or seek a good local one, and monitor your case for adherence to international law. FTA doesn't charge for services but depends on donations.

For the legal situation regarding homosexuality, see Legal Matters under Gay & Lesbian Travellers.

BUSINESS HOURS

Don't plan on doing much business between noon and 3pm, when the Portuguese give serious and lingering attention to lunch.

Most shops open from 9.30am to noon or 1pm, and 3pm to 7pm; most close Saturday afternoon (except near Christmas) and Sunday. Shopping centres are usually open from 10am to at least 10pm daily. Most banks open only from 8.30am to 3pm, and most post offices from 9am to 12.30pm and 2.30pm to 6pm Monday to Friday.

Government offices typically open from 9am to noon or 12.30pm, and 2pm to 5pm or 5.30pm Monday to Friday.

Museums, almost invariably closed on Monday, open from about 10am to 12.30pm and 2pm to 5pm Tuesday to Saturday. If Monday is a holiday, they're often closed the following day too. Unless noted, turismos and tourist sights closed on Sunday are usually closed on holidays too.

In instances when a tourist attraction or turismo keeps seasonal hours and specific months are not mentioned, 'summer' usually means the months of Daylight Savings Time (see under Time in this chapter).

PUBLIC HOLIDAYS & SPECIAL EVENTS
Public Holidays

On the following public holidays in Portugal, banks, offices, department stores and some shops close, public workers get the day off and public transport thins out. Many museums and other tourist attractions also close. On New Year's Day, Easter Sunday, Labour Day and Christmas Day, even turismos close.

New Year's Day 1 January
Carnaval Tuesday February/March – day before Ash Wednesday
Good Friday March/April
Liberty Day 25 April – celebrating 1974 revolution
Labour Day 1 May
Corpus Christi May/June – ninth Thursday after Easter
Portugal Day 10 June – also known as Camões & the Communities Day

Feast of the Assumption 15 August
Republic Day 5 October – commemorating 1910 declaration of Portuguese Republic
All Saints' Day 1 November
Independence Day 1 December – commemorating 1640 restoration of independence from Spain
Feast of the Immaculate Conception 8 December
Christmas Day 25 December

Fairs & Festivals

Portugal abounds with *romarias* (religious pilgrimages), *festas* (festivals) and *feiras* (fairs), which can bring whole towns or regions to a cheerful standstill. At the core of many are religious processions. The further north you go, the more traditional and less touristy these celebrations get. Some are well worth going out of your way for, though accommodation is often tight.

Turismos can tell you what's coming up, and some regional tourist authorities (such as the Minho's) publish annual listings. Bigger turismos may have the countrywide booklet *Fairs, Festivals & Folk Pilgrimages* or the more general and descriptive *Religious Festivals*. Following are some of the big ones:

February/March
Carnaval Held during the last few days before Lent, Carnaval was traditionally an occasion for letting off steam and thumbing one's nose at public decorum, and things often got out of hand. But since the 1970s Carnaval seems to consist mainly of fairs and parades full of outlandish costumes, although it has a pagan edge in the north (see the boxed text 'Devils in Disguise' in the Trás-os-Montes chapter). The biggest celebrations are at Loulé, Nazaré, Ovar and Viana do Castelo.

March
Ovibeja The Alentejo's biggest agricultural fair, held at Beja in mid-March, features handicrafts, gastronomy and horse racing.

March/April
Senhor Ecce Homo Braga's Easter Week Festival is the grandest in Portugal, with a series of vast, colourful processions. The most famous of these is Senhor Ecce Homo on Maundy Thursday, led by barefoot, torch-bearing penitents.

May
Fátima Romarias Two annual pilgrimages to Fátima celebrate the first and last apparitions of the Virgin Mary to three shepherd children here in 1917. These are strictly religious events, with

hundreds of thousands of pilgrims from around the world visiting one of the Catholic world's most-holy sites. The pilgrimages take place over 12–13 May and 12–13 October.

Festa das Cruzes Held in early May, the Festival of the Crosses in Barcelos is noted for its processions, folk performances and regional handicrafts exhibitions.

June
Corpo de Deus Corpus Christi, the ninth Thursday after Easter, is a big time for processions and merrymaking in the north of Portugal.

Feira Nacional da Agricultura This grand farming and livestock fair, which also includes bullfighting, folk singing and dancing, is held in Santarém in the first week of June.

Festa de Santo António The Festival of St Anthony is an all-night street fair on 12–13 June in Lisbon's Alfama and Mouraria districts; the 13th is also a municipal holiday in Lisbon. Other communities also celebrate St Anthony's day.

Festa de São João Many communities celebrate St John's Festival over 23–24 June, but Porto parties for nearly a week beforehand. The night of the 23rd sees everybody out on the streets, and the 24th is a municipal holiday in Porto.

July
Festa dos Tabuleiros The Feast of Trays in Tomar, held during the week before the first Sunday in July every four years (most recently in 2003), features a procession of children bearing trays laden with huge loaves of bread (see the boxed text 'Festa dos Tabuleiros' under Tomar in the Estremadura & Ribatejo chapter).

August
Romaria e Festa da Nossa Senhora da Agonia The Pilgrimage and Festival of Our Lady of Suffering in Viana do Castelo is famed for its parades, fireworks, folk art and handicrafts fair. It takes place for three or four days around 20 August.

September
Feiras Novas Featuring a vast market on the banks of the Rio Lima, plus folk music, processions and funfair, the New Fairs of Ponte de Lima date back to the 12th century. They're held over three days in mid-September.

October
Fátima See May earlier in this list.

November
Feira de São Martinho This national horse fair, held between 3 and 11 November in Golegã (Ribatejo), features horse parades, riding competitions and bullfights, as well as a feast of roast chestnuts and young wine.

School Holidays
Bus timetables in many parts of Portugal change when school is out. Typical school holidays are: Carnaval (one week), Easter (two weeks), summer (two months), All Saints (one week) and Christmas (two weeks). Dates for Carnaval, Easter and All Saints change from year to year, and the exact dates for most of these school holidays vary across regions.

ACTIVITIES
Organised outdoor activities are a booming industry in Portugal. Following is a summary of the kaleidoscope of offerings. For overseas operators organising activity holidays to Portugal, see Organised Tours in the Getting There & Away chapter.

Walking
Despite some magnificent rambling country, walking ranks low among Portuguese passions. There are no national walking clubs and no official cross-country trails. Thus, armed with good maps (see Planning earlier in this chapter for map sources) you can have remoter parts of the country almost to yourself. Camping is usually restricted to established sites, though most trails pass close enough to villages or towns for you to find accommodation there.

The Algarve has the most enthusiastic walking clubs, with regular outings and their own network of trails. The best walks, though, are up north. Most demanding is the Serra da Estrela, which includes mainland Portugal's tallest peak, 1993m Torre; the Parque Natural da Serra da Estrela has a network of marked trails. Less taxing but more beautiful are the Parque Nacional da Peneda-Gerês in the Minho, the lovely and little-visited Parque Natural de Montesinho in Trás-os-Montes and the tiny Parque Natural do Alvão near Vila Real.

A fine resource for serious ramblers is *Routes to the Landscapes & Habitats of Portugal* (€25), a fat book published by the Instituto da Conservação da Natureza (ICN), the agency that manages Portugal's protected areas. Inside are details of walks in all the country's national and natural parks, plus flora, fauna, history and more. It's sold at park offices and bigger bookshops.

For other resources on walking in Portugal, see Books earlier in this chapter. For more on Portugal's protected areas, see Flora & Fauna in the Facts about Portugal chapter, plus local listings.

Private agencies doing local guided walks are listed throughout this guide.

Two outfits offering countrywide walks are English-run **Portugal Walks** (☎/fax 282 698 676, ☎ 965 753 033; [W] www.portugal walks.com; Vila do Bispo) and **Rotas do Vento** (☎ 213 649 852, fax 213 649 843; [e] rotas@ rotasdovento.pt; Lisbon).

Quercus (see Ecology & Environment in the Facts about Portugal chapter) organises trips to areas of environmental interest or concern.

Cycling

Mountain biking is one of Portugal's fastest-growing sports. You can rent mountain bikes (bicyclete tudo terrano, or BTT) at a growing number of outlets, especially in the Algarve and around Parque Nacional da Peneda-Gerês. Prices range from €7 to €15 per day.

For an introduction to cycling as a way of travelling around Portugal, see under Bicycle in the Getting Around chapter.

Guided biking trips are popular in Monchique and Tavira (Algarve), Sintra and Setúbal (Around Lisbon). PlanAlto runs BTT trips all round the Minho and Trás-os-Montes; see Activities under Parque Nacional da Peneda-Gerês in the Minho chapter for details.

Surfing

Portugal's 830km Atlantic coast offers some of Europe's best surfing, with 30 or 40 major reefs and beaches, the best of them around Ericeira and Peniche on the Estremadura coast. Surfing is a year-round activity here, although most professional contests take place in summer.

The Costa da Caparica and the Algarve have the highest density of surf shops and gear rental. There are summertime surf schools here and at Viana do Castelo, Porto, Aveiro, Peniche, Torres Vedras, Ericeira, the Estoril coast, Sintra and Lisbon. See under these individual towns for more details.

Generally, a full-day group course costs €15 to €30, or you can go for pricier individual lessons. You can hire out a surfboard for €15 to €25 per day.

Surf Experience Portugal (☎/fax 282 761 943; [W] www.surf-experience.com), based in Lagos, organises three-, seven- and 14-day surfing holidays in the Algarve.

Other Water Sports

Among the country's best windsurfing spots are Praia do Guincho (west of Sintra) and Lagoa de Óbidos, a sheltered venue to the north. South of Lisbon, the Costa da Caparica's Fonte da Telha is popular. In the Algarve, windy Sagres attracts the pros, while resorts around Lagos, Praia da Rocha and Quarteira cater for everyone. In the Algarve and around Lagoa de Óbidos you can also try your hand at sailing and water-skiing.

Scuba diving is popular in summer. An introductory pool session costs €30 to €60, and two- to four-day courses about €200 to €350. Experienced divers can enjoy a day's outing for €20 to €60.

Inland water sports include a limited amount of flat-water and white-water boating and canoeing and lots of motorised and nonmotorised reservoir boating.

Canyoning tackles all the challenges offered by a river canyon: trekking, swimming, abseiling and rock climbing. Hydrospeed is a solo version of white-water boating, with individual boards and helmets instead of a boat. Outfits offering programmes in these high-adrenaline sports include **Templar** (☎ 249 323 493, fax 249 321 720; Tomar), **Capitão Dureza** (☎ 233 427 772, 919 079 852, 914 929 407; [W] www.capitaodureza .com; Apartado 247, 3081-801 Figueira da Foz) and **Trilhos** (☎ 225 504 604, ☎ 967 014 277; [W] www.trilhos.pt; Porto).

Horse Riding

Portugal is the birthplace of the Lusitano thoroughbred, the world's oldest breed of saddle horse. There are many riding centres (though only a few with Lusitanos; see Courses, following), especially in the Algarve and Alentejo; some do organised treks as well. Typical high-season rates are around €15 to €20 per hour. See individual chapters for further details. ICEP publishes a booklet on horse riding destinations and holidays.

Golf

Southern Portugal is full of championship-standard golf courses. The Algarve has 26, Estremadura and Ribatejo 18. There are eight in Beira Alta and the Minho, and one in northern Alentejo. ICEP produces a

Surfing Portugal

Following is a run-down of Portugal's better surfing beaches. Each beach may consist of several surf spots of varying quality.

Venues with significant pollution are indicated by *. Four venues near Porto (Leça, Matosinhos, Miramar and Espinho) are now so badly polluted that they're no longer worth surfing. 'Localism' – violence by local surfers towards visiting surfers to protect their waves and surfing rights – can be a problem at Sagres.

region	beach	nearest town
North	Moledo	Caminha
	Afife	Viana do Castelo
	Esposende	Barcelos
	Póvoa de Varzim	Póvoa de Varzim
	Vila do Conde	Vila do Conde
Central	Praia da Barra, Costa Nova	Aveiro
	Praia de Mira	Praia de Mira
	Buarcos, Cabedelo	Figueira da Foz
	São Pedro de Muel	Marinha Grande
	Nazaré	Nazaré
	Foz do Arelho	Caldas da Rainha
	Baleal, Supertubos, Consolação	Peniche
	Areia Branca	Lourinha
	Santa Cruz	Torres Vedras
	São Lourenço, Ribeira de Ilhas, Ericeira,	
	Foz de Lisandro, São Julião	Ericeira
	Praia Grande, Praia do Guincho	Sintra
	São Pedro do Estoril*	Cascais
	Carcavelos*	Estoril
	Praia da Caparica*	Costa da Caparica
South	São Torpes, Porto Covo	Sines
	Vila Nova de Milfontes	Vila Nova de Milfontes
	Odeceixe	Odeceixe
	Carreagem, Monte Clérigo, Arrifana	Aljezur
	Praia do Amado	Carrapateira
	Tonel	Sagres
	Praia da Rocha	Portimão

More Information

For details on venues, wave types and conditions, check out *The Stormrider Guide: Europe*, an atlas of European surfing. It's sold for UK£25 by **Low Pressure** (☎/fax 01288-359867; e *mail@lowpressure.co.uk; 11 Efford Farm, Bude, Cornwall EX23 8LP*) and from the **Low Pressure shop** (☎ 020-7792 3134; 23 Kensington Park Rd, London W11 2EU).

A good website featuring breaks, forecasts, shops, schools and links is the Portuguese Surf Guide at ⓦ www.infopraias.com/guide/engvers.htm. The Federação Portuguesa de Surf has a Portuguese-language website at ⓦ www.fps.pt.

glossy booklet with loving descriptions of every one of them. See Organised Tours in the Getting There & Away chapter for information on golf tours to Portugal.

Tennis
There are tennis clubs with professional instructors all over Portugal, especially in the Algarve where most top-end hotels have courts. ICEP can provide a full list of tennis clubs and sports centres.

Jeep Tours
Numerous outfits in the south offer one-day jeep tours to the foothills and coastal regions. Shop around as some are little more than noisy off-road scrabbles. See local listings for details.

Marathon Running
Lisbon hosts the annual international Maratona de Lisboa, or Discoveries Marathon, in late November; there is also a half-marathon in early March. For information see Special Events in the Lisbon chapter, or contact the **Federação Portuguesa de Atletismo** (☎ 214 146 020; **w** www.fpatletismo.pt).

Skiing
The only place with guaranteed snow is around Torre in the Parque Natural da Serra da Estrela, though facilities are pretty basic. Penhas da Saúde is the major accommodation base. The season runs from January to March, with reliably good snow only in February. For details see under Parque Natural da Serra da Estrela in the Beiras chapter.

Hot-Air Ballooning
If you've got €125 to €150 to spare you can enjoy some of Europe's most unspoilt aerial vistas from the comfort of a wicker basket. Among operators offering commercial rides are **Hemisférios** (☎ 919 445 868; **w** www.hemisferios-balloons.com; Alcácer do Sal), near Setúbal; **Publibalão** (☎ 917 629 210; **e** publibalao@oninet.pt; Abrantes) in Ribatejo; and **Real Eólica de Almeida** (☎ 271 574 700, fax 271 947 699; **w** www.realeolica.pt; Almeida) in Beira Alta.

COURSES
Language
All of the following are group courses; be sure to check whether there's an additional enrolment fee. Most schools also offer private lessons for about €25 per hour.

Cambridge School (☎ 213 124 600, **w** www.cambridge.pt) Lisbon, Porto and Coimbra; intensive 40-hour course, €537

Centro de Línguas de Lagos (☎/fax 282 761 070, **e** cll@mail.telepac.pt) Lagos; 30-hour course, €215

Centro de Línguas e Informática da Costa do Sol (☎ 214 671 304, **e** clics@mail.telepac.pt) Estoril; intensive 42-hour courses in July and August, €225

CIAL-Centro de Línguas (☎ 217 940 448, **w** www.cial.pt) Lisbon and Faro; courses from €230 weekly

Interlingua (☎ 282 427 690, **e** interlingua@mail.telepac.pt) Portimão; two-hour fun course in Portuguese basics, €20

Ipfel (Instituto Particular de Formação e Ensino de Línguas; ☎ 213 154 116, **e** instituto@ipfel.pt) Lisbon, Porto and Leiria; intensive 40-hour course, €309

Universidade de Coimbra (☎ 239 859 943, **w** www.fl.uc.pt/cursos/cursos.htm) Coimbra; five-week summer courses at all levels, €450

Universidade de Lisboa (☎ 217 816 150, **w** www.fl.ul.pt/dlcp) Lisbon; 80-hour beginner's course in July, August or September, €530

Other Courses
Among other things you can learn while in Portugal are the following:

Dance
Chapitô (☎ 218 861 410, **e** chapito@ip.pt) Costa de Castelo 1, Lisbon; monthly evening courses in Afro-Brazilian martial dance

Casa da América Latina (☎ 963 621 515, **e** info@espassolatino.pt) Calçada do Marquês de Abrantes 115, Lisbon; two-hour Saturday afternoon workshops covering popular dances from Central America, Brazil, Cuba and the Caribbean

Pottery
Casa de Yavanna (☎ 251 839 211, **e** falkingham sue@teacher.com) Lugar da Insua, Fontoura, Valença do Minho; 10-day pottery holidays

Gastronomy
CIAL-Centro de Línguas (☎ 217 940 448, **w** www.cial.pt) Lisbon and Faro; eight-hour courses in Portuguese gastronomy

Horse Riding
Escola de Equitação de Alcainça (☎ 219 662 122, fax 218 686 117) Rua de São Miguel, Alcainça; lessons on Portugal's famous Lusitano horses, near Mafra

Skydiving
Associação de Paraquedistas do Minho (☎ 253 626 530) Aeroclube de Palmeira, Palmeira; weekend courses held near Braga

For information on US universities with exchange programmes in Portugal, check out [w] www.studyabroad.com.

WORK
Nationals of the EU can compete for any job in Portugal without a work permit. Non-EU citizens who want to work here are expected to get a Portuguese work permit before they arrive, with the help of their prospective employer.

Several organisations can help you search for a job in Portugal before you arrive, and even arrange your work permit. One of the best known is the **Council on International Educational Exchange** (☎ 212-822 2600; [w] www.ciee.org; 205 East 42nd St, New York, NY 10017-5706, USA).

You may decide after arriving that you need extra cash, though the prospects of on-the-spot work are limited unless you have a skill that's scarce. The search will be easier if you've brought your curriculum vitae, references and certified copies of relevant diplomas or certificates. The odds also improve if you speak passable Portuguese. You'll probably have to sign a work contract.

The most realistic option is English-language teaching, but only if you're prepared to stay in one place for a few months. A TEFL certificate is a big help, though not essential. See the *Páginas Amarelas (Yellow Pages)* under Escolas de Línguas for schools in your chosen area. Check the classified ads in Portugal's English-language press or, if your Portuguese is good enough, in dailies such as *Diário de Notícias* and *Público*. You can also try posting notices in student-oriented places; a reasonable rate is about €8 per hour.

English-language newspapers (see Newspapers & Magazines earlier in this chapter) may be interested in writers or reporters. There are occasional jobs in Algarve bars, and in summer you can sometimes pick up cash passing out leaflets for bars and clubs around Lagos or other Algarve towns.

Another good place to source jobs or advertise your services is the Departamento de Informação aos Jovens (Youth Information

Department) of the IPJ (see Useful Organisations earlier in this chapter).

If you plan to stay more than three months you'll also need a residence permit, from the local Foreigners Registration Service (see Visas & Documents earlier in this chapter).

ACCOMMODATION
Most turismos have lists of accommodation to suit a wide range of budgets, and can help you find and sometimes book a place, although they often overlook the 'unofficial' budget options. Most (but not all) turismos scrupulously avoid making recommendations. The government grades most accommodation with a bewildering and not very useful system of stars.

Prices in most tourist areas are seasonal; elsewhere they're fairly stable year-round. High season is typically mid-June or July to August or September, plus Carnaval and Easter week; middle season is April to the middle or end of June, plus September or October; and low season the rest of the year. High season in the Algarve runs from March to November. We list July prices.

You'll have to prebook most mid-range and top-end accommodation in high season, a few days to a few weeks ahead.

Prices are nearly always per room, not per person. Single rates are usually about two-thirds the price of a double (travel with a friend and save money!); few lower-end places even have dedicated single rooms. Some places have a range of prices (eg, for rooms with/without a view) and many give discounts for longer stays, but you must usually ask.

For a room with a double bed, ask for *um quarto de casal* or *um quarto de matrimonial*; for twin beds (nearly always more expensive) ask for *um duplo*; and for a single room, ask for *um quarto individual*.

In this book we use the following price categories for an establishment's most basic double with toilet and bathroom: budget (up to €30); mid-range (from €30 to €75); top end (over €75). Most rooms, even in budget *pensões*, now have a private bathroom and a television; we generally call attention only to those that *don't*.

Camping
Widespread and popular in Portugal, camping is easily the cheapest option. Depending

on facilities, high-season nightly prices are about €1.50 to €4 per adult, plus €1.50 to €3.50 for a small tent and €1.50 to €3.50 per car. Many camp sites close in low season.

Portugal's biggest, best equipped and best located camp sites are run by **Orbitur** (bookings ☎ 218 117 000; e info@orbitur.pt). We note Orbitur sites throughout the book.

The annual *Roteiro Campista* (€4.90), sold in larger Portuguese bookshops, is a multilingual guide with details of, and directions to, nearly every camp site in the country. It's also online, at w www.roteiro-campista.pt.

For information about the Camping Card International, see under Visas & Documents earlier in this chapter.

The **European Centre for Eco Agro Tourism** (ECEAT; ☎ 31-20-668 1030; w www .greenguideonline.co; Postbus 10899, 1001 EW Amsterdam) produces the *Green Holiday Guide Spain & Portugal* (€15 or UK£10), listing dozens of small organic or eco-friendly farms with basic camping or farmhouse accommodation in rural areas.

Hostels

Portugal has a network of 39 pousadas da juventude, all affiliated with Hostelling International (HI).

In high season dorm beds cost €9.50 to €15 (higher in more popular hostels, such as those in Lisbon and Porto). Most hostels also have a few spartan doubles that come with shower and toilet for €26.50 to €42; a few have doubles without a bathroom and others have family rooms or small apartments. Bed linen and continental breakfast are included in the price; lunch or dinner costs €5. Many hostels have kitchens where you can do your own cooking, plus TV rooms and social areas.

Advance reservations are essential in summer, especially for the doubles. Contact **Movijovem** (☎ 213 596 000; w www.pousad asjuventude.pt; Avenida Duque d'Ávila 137, Lisbon). There's a charge of €1.50 per set of bookings, although you can usually call ahead from one hostel to your next one for nothing.

If you don't already have an HI card from your national hostel association, you can get a 'guest card' which will be stamped at each of the first six hostels where you stay (for an

Portugal's Hostels

Following is a list of Portugal's pousadas da juventude (those suitable for wheelchair-users are indicated by *):

Alentejo Alcoutim*, Almograve*, Beja, Évora*, Portalegre, Sines*

Algarve Faro, Lagos*, Portimão, Vila Real de Santo António

Beiras Aveiro*, Castelo Branco, Coimbra*, Guarda*, Mira, Ovar*, Penhas da Saúde* (Covilhã), São Pedro do Sul, Vila Nova de Foz Côa*, Viseu*

Douro Porto*

Estremadura Areia Branca (Lourinha), Leiria*, São Martinho do Porto

Lisbon Area Almada*, Catalazete* (Oeiras), Lisbon*, Lisbon Parque das Nações*, Setúbal, Sintra

Minho Braga, Fóz do Cávado* (Fão), Viana do Castelo*, Vila Nova de Cerveira, Vilarinho das Furnas (Campo do Gerês)

Trás-os-Montes Bragança*, Vila Real

Ribatejo Abrantes*, Santarém*

additional €1 each time), after which you've effectively paid for your membership.

Most hostels open their doors from 8am to midnight; some (Almada, Braga, Bragança, Évora, Foz Côa, Fóz do Cávado, Lagos, Lisbon, Portimão, Porto and Viana do Castelo) stay open 24 hours a day. You can usually stash your bags and return at check-in time, typically 8am to noon and 6pm to midnight.

Private Rooms

Another cheap option – especially in coastal towns and mostly in summer – is a *quarto particular* or just *quarto* (private room), usually in a private house and with shared facilities. Owners may approach you at the bus or train station; otherwise watch for 'quartos' signs. Some turismos keep lists of private rooms.

Rooms are invariably clean, modestly priced (about €20 a double; up to €30 in popular resorts) and free from hostel-style restrictions, and the owners can be very welcoming. A more commercial variant is a *dormida* or rooming house (doubles about €25). Prices are rarely seasonal except in popular resorts.

In the smallest rural villages, if public accommodation is full or nonexistent you might find a kind of community hall called a *casa de povos* (literally, 'people's house') where you can crash with the permission of the mayor or other local bigwig. Facilities tend to be limited to a floor to sleep on and a toilet.

Guesthouses

The most common types of guesthouse – the Portuguese equivalent of a bed and breakfast (B&B) – are the *residencial* (plural *residenciais*) and *pensão* (plural *pensões*). Both are graded from one to three stars, and the best are often cheaper and better run than some lower-end hotels. Lower-standard places are often ignored by turismos, though they may be the only budget options.

High-season *pensão* rates for a double with a private bathroom range from €25 to €50; you'll pay a bit more for a *residencial*, where breakfast is often included. Regulations now allow an establishment to call itself a hotel-*residencial* or *pensão-residencial* and charge separately for breakfast. Cheaper rooms with a shared bathroom are disappearing as owners upgrade.

Pensões and *residenciais* are Portugal's most popular form of tourist accommodation and tend to fill up in summer. Try to book at least a week ahead in high season and/or in tourist areas. Low-season rates may drop by at least a third.

Some places that don't qualify for, or can't be bothered with, official approval may go by the name *residência*. While these aren't graded and guaranteed by the government, some are as good as the approved versions at the lower end of the scale.

Hospedarias and *casas de hóspedes* are cheaper boarding houses with shared toilets and showers.

Hotels

Hotels are graded from one to five stars. For a double in high season you'll pay anywhere from €60 to €200. Low-season prices can drop spectacularly, with doubles in four-star hotels going for as little as €50. Breakfast is usually included.

In the same category but more like upmarket inns are *albergarias* and the pricier *estalagens*. In some towns you may find *aparthotels* – whole blocks of self-contained apartments for rent to tourists and managed as hotels.

Prices in this book are official walk-in rates. You can often get discounted or promotional rates with some chain hotels by booking online or through a travel agent.

Turismo de Habitação

Under a government-monitored scheme called Turismo de Habitação, and smaller schemes known as Turismo Rural and Agroturismo (all often collectively referred to as Turihab), you can stay in anything from a farmhouse to a mansion as the owner's guest. Some have self-contained cottages, though owners prefer stays of at least three or four days in these.

Turihab properties include some of Portugal's finest middle and upper-range bargains – invariably welcoming, relaxing places with tactful, helpful hosts. If you have the money to spend on them, you'll rarely regret it.

For a double in high season you'll pay a minimum of €95 in a Turihab manor house but just €50 in a farmhouse. In low season prices can drop significantly and you can literally stay in a palace for the price of an average B&B elsewhere in Europe.

A hefty, multilingual book, *Turismo no Espaço Rural*, describing most of them, is available for €13 from ICEP tourist offices. But unless you plan on 'Turihabbing' every night of your trip and want to book every one, you won't need this book, as nearly all turismos have lists of local Turihab properties.

Pousadas de Portugal

These are deluxe, government-run former castles, monasteries and palaces (plus some new establishments), usually in areas of natural beauty or historical significance. Most offer professional service and a friendly welcome, though visitors describe some as aloof, disproportionately overpriced and sited purely for the grand view.

Doubles in high season cost €82 to €266 from Sunday to Thursday night and €89 to €279 Friday and Saturday. For more information contact ICEP offices abroad or **Pousadas de Portugal** (☎ 218 442 001; **w** www.pousadas.pt; *Avenida Santa Joana Princesa 10, 1749-090 Lisbon*).

FOOD

Without a shadow of doubt the Portuguese is the most refined, the most voluptuous and succulent cuisine in the world... We did acquire – thanks to the spices from the Orient, the tangy bits from Brazil and the art of using sugar from sweet-toothed countries, Turkey, India and the Moors of northern Africa – culinary skills, foods, delicacies, recipes, which turned us into a foremost gastronomic people. There is no other country that can boast such an array of national dishes...

Fialho de Almeida
Os Gatos (1893)

Olive oil, wine and friendship, the older the better.
Portuguese proverb

Don't get your hopes up: most travellers' experiences of Portuguese cuisine don't come close to Almeida's lyrical description. There's no doubt that eating and drinking get serious attention here, but traditional Portuguese cuisine is basically the honest fare of farmers and fisherfolk, and that means cheap, hearty portions, lots of fish and meat, and rice and potatoes.

The only meal that may fail to fill your stomach is *pequeno almoço* (breakfast), traditionally just coffee and a bread roll.

Almoço (lunch) is a far bigger affair, often lasting two hours or more. Like *jantar* (the evening meal), it features three courses, including a hot main dish, invariably served with potatoes and sometimes rice as well. Vegetables usually consist of a few ornamental bits of lettuce or carrot – though there are signs that Portuguese diners are starting to appreciate properly cooked vegetables with their meals. There's a trend to shorter lunch hours and smaller, cheaper meals, but even with the full-length affair it's easy to gorge yourself for under €10.

Lunch is better value than the evening meal, especially in the form of *pratos do dia* (daily specials) at around €4.50. If you're prepared to eat at the counter instead of a table it can be even cheaper; several popular lunch cafés in Lisbon are almost entirely stand-up.

Restaurantes are typically open from 12.30pm or 1pm to about 3pm for lunch. They open for dinner at about 7pm – though most locals don't eat until around 8pm – with last orders around 10pm (earlier in the countryside, later in the cities). Most restaurants close, or come nearly to a standstill, from 4pm to 7pm, though many café-bars and snack-bars serve snacks and light meals throughout the afternoon.

Another popular option, especially for lunch, is a *casa de pasto*, a casual eatery offering a few cheap, simple meals. Slightly upmarket and popular with locals for both lunch and dinner is a *tasca*, a simple tavern, often with rustic decor. A *churrasqueira*, or *churrascaria*, is actually a family-style restaurant serving good-value grilled foods, especially chicken. A *cervejaria* (literally 'beer house') serves plain food as well as drinks, while a *marisqueira* specialises in seafood and therefore tends to be expensive.

If you can't face the massive servings, ask for a *meia dose* (half-portion); the price is usually about two-thirds that of a *dose*. Westerners tend to be shy about asking for a *meia dose*, as if it were a child's portion. The Portuguese have no such hesitation when they can't face the usual huge portions. Not all restaurants offer half-portions, and they're less common for evening meals, but it's always worth asking. A few places even have *mini-doses*. Alternatively, you can always share a full-portion with your companion.

Many restaurants advertise an *ementa turística* (tourist menu), a daily set meal with a modest choice of dishes and a glass of beer or half-bottle of wine. These make ordering easy but aren't always great value.

Couvert

Bread, butter, cheese, pâté, olives and other unsolicited nibbles served at the start of your meal are a wicked temptation, especially after a Portuguese micro-breakfast. But be warned: the meal will be filling enough without them. If you eat any of them – and, quite often, even if you don't – they'll be added to your bill (usually as *couvert* or as *pão e manteiga*, bread and butter), and they can be quite pricey.

Try to think of these snacks as a service, not a plot to take your money. If you don't want them *send them back immediately*; nobody will be offended. From a restaurateur's point of view, anything that sits uneaten at your table for an hour is arguably unsuitable to offer to anyone else later and may just have to be binned.

Another poor-value item is the so-called *couvert* (see the boxed text 'Couvert').

Finally, be prepared for two common features of Portuguese restaurants: a TV blaring in the corner (especially in budget or mid-range restaurants), and widespread smoking. Few restaurants have nonsmoking sections so all nonsmokers can do is avoid the dining rush-hour.

To order the bill, ask for *a conta, se faz favor*. Cafés don't usually charge for service, but a tip of small change is acceptable. In restaurants you can add 5% to 10% of the total if you're happy with the meal and the service. The bill at an upper-end restaurant may already include a *serviço* or service charge.

See under Food in the Language chapter for a listing of useful culinary terms.

Snacks

Popular snacks include *sandes* (sandwiches), typically with *queijo* (cheese), *fiambre* (ham) or as a *tosta mista* (toasted cheese and ham sandwich); *prego no pão* (a slab of meat sandwiched in a roll, often with a fried egg); and *pastéis de bacalhau* (cod fishcakes). Prices start at about €2.

Combinados are tasty miniature portions, costing about €4, of a regular meat or fish dish, served with chips and sometimes salad.

Main Meals

Before wading into the menu *(a ementa* or *a lista)* it's usually worth asking if there's a *prato do dia* (dish of the day) or *especialidade da casa/região* (speciality of the house/region). While some tourist-geared eateries may simply suggest the pricey *arroz de marisco* – a rich seafood and rice stew, usually for a minimum of two – elsewhere you could end up with something far more exciting than the standard menu items.

Among *entradas* or starters, best value are the excellent home-made soups. Ubiquitous and popular is jade-green *caldo verde*, a warming potato and cabbage soup. Starters may also include good local cheeses or *queijo fresco* (fresh goat cheese).

Portugal has Europe's highest per capita consumption of fish, and for main meals *peixe* (fish) and seafood offer exceptional value, especially at seaside resorts – though you'll find fish on menus in every corner of the country. The variety is amazing, from

linguada and *lulas grelhado* (grilled sole and squid) and *pescada* (hake) to *bife de atúm* (tuna steak) – often served smothered in onions – and *espadarte* (swordfish, sometimes confused in translation with *peixe espada* or scabbard fish).

Cheapest are *sardinhas assadas* (grilled sardines), delicious with salad and chilled white wine or port. And you won't get far before discovering Portugal's favourite fish, *bacalhau* (salted cod), a Portuguese preoccupation for five centuries (see the boxed text 'Bacalhau – the Faithful Friend').

More exotic fish specialities include popular but expensive *arroz de marisco* (seafood paella); *caldeirada* and *açorda de marisco* (fish stews); *cataplana*, shellfish and ham cooked in a sealed pan, typical of the Algarve; and every variety of shellfish from *amêijoas* (clams) and *camarões* (shrimps) to *lagostins* (crayfish) and *chocos* (cuttlefish).

Portuguese are voracious meat-eaters but choosing a good *carne* (meat) or *aves* (poultry) dish is hit-or-miss. You may find delicious specialities such as *leitão assado* (roast suckling pig), famous around Coimbra; *rojões* (marinated pig trotters fried with black pudding and chestnuts), a Minho speciality;

Bacalhau – the Faithful Friend

The Portuguese have been obsessed with *bacalhau* since the early 16th century, when Portuguese fishing boats started to fish for cod around Newfoundland. Sailors salted and sun-dried their catch to make it last the long journey home, thereby discovering the perfect convenience food both for seafarers (who were sailing as far as India at the time) and for fish-loving but fridgeless folk back home. Indeed, so popular did *bacalhau* become that it soon became known as *fiel amigo*, the faithful friend.

Most of today's *bacalhau* is made from Norwegian cod and is fairly expensive, but seeing as *bacalhau* more than doubles in volume after soaking, keeps well and is extremely nourishing, it's still popular. There's said to be a different *bacalhau* recipe for every day of the year. *Bacalhau à Gomes de Sá*, a tastier version than most of the 364 others, features flaked cod baked with potatoes, onions, hard-boiled eggs and black olives.

famous Alentejo *borrego* (lamb); or *presunto* (smoked ham), delicious in Chaves and Lamego. *Carne de porco á alentejana* is an inspired combination of pork and clams.

But strike it unlucky and you'll get *tripas* (tripe), a Porto speciality; *migas alentejanas*, a stodge of corn bread and fatty pork; impossibly meaty *cozido á Portuguesa* stew; or a bloody, bready sludge called *papas de sarrabulho*.

Even the lowliest menu features *vitela* (veal) and *bife* (steak), and sometimes *coelho* (rabbit) and *cabrito* (kid). A *bitoque* is beef with an egg on top. Note that *bife* doesn't always mean 'beef': eg, *bife de peru* is turkey steak and *bife de porco* is pork steak. The most popular poultry by a wide margin is *frango* (chicken), widely available grilled on a spit *(frango assado)*, the perfect takeaway meal.

Vegetarian Food

If you're a vegetarian who'll eat fish, you'll have little trouble in Portugal. But strict vegetarians may have a bad time with traditional cuisine, in which vegetables figure so seldom. Many restaurants (especially in touristed areas) now offer a few token vegetarian dishes, though genuine vegetarian restaurants are rare. The best bet is top-end hotel restaurants, ready to oblige the most demanding guests. It's an enduring mystery why markets groan under the weight of fresh vegetables in season but so little ends up in restaurants, other than puréed into soups.

Mind you, these soups are delicious and grace every menu – though even the popular potato-and-cabbage soup is often topped with spicy sausage or bits of fatty pork, and there's no telling how the stock was made.

In addition to standard international vegetarian items like omelettes and salads, there are some traditional Portuguese specialities that avoid meat. Simple peasant bread-soup dishes such as *migas do Ribatejo* look awful (their main ingredient is soaked maize bread, with lots of olive oil and garlic to taste) but fit the bill when you're ravenous. Keep an eye out, too, for *arroz de tomate* (tomato rice) or *favas com azeite* (broad beans with olive oil).

If nothing on the menu looks suitable, you could just ask the waiter if they have vegetables *(tem alguma hortaliça, por favor?)*. Alternatively, you can shop for yourself: in addition to excellent fruit and vegetables, markets usually have freshly baked bread and local cheeses. Markets, normally open from early morning to about 6pm, are best on Saturday, worst on Monday and closed on Sunday.

If you can, get a Portuguese friend to write down what you can and cannot eat.

Desserts & Pastries

Sobremesas (desserts) tend to be disappointing in restaurants, though you're in for a treat if a home-cooked *doce* (sweet pudding) such as a *leite creme* (custard) or *mousse de chocolate* is available. More likely you'll be offered *pudim* (crème caramel), *arroz doce* (sweet rice) or *gelado* (ice cream, usually overpriced commercial varieties).

A variety of fresh fruit is usually available – grapes and oranges, plus seasonal apricots, figs or strawberries. There's also cheese; best and priciest is *queijo da serra*, a soft white variety made from ewe milk from the Serra da Estrela.

Pastelarias (pastry and cake shops) and *casas de chá* (teahouses) have the sweetest concoctions, full of egg yolks and sugar. Nuns of the 18th century created many of the recipes, and presumably gave them their tongue-in-cheek names, such as *papos de anjo* (angel's breasts) and *barriga de freira* (nun's belly).

Regional specialities include Aveiro's eggy *doces de ovos*, and Sintra's *queijadas* (cheesecakes) and *travesseiros* (almond pastries). Sweet *pasteis de nata* (custard tarts) are found everywhere.

DRINKS
Nonalcoholic Drinks

Many cafés serve *sumo de laranja* (fresh orange juice) or stock local bottled varieties. Portuguese *agua mineral* (mineral water) is good, and widely available, either *com gás* (carbonated) or *sem gás* (still).

Coffee drinkers are in for a high time: it's nearly always freshly brewed, even in the most humble rural café, and there are dozens of varieties (see the boxed text 'Coffee Confusion', later). *Uma bica* usually costs about €0.45, though it may depend on where you drink it: a Lisbon pastry shop might charge this much if you drink it standing by the counter, but €0.60 at the table or as much as €1 outside at a street table.

Coffee Confusion

You almost need a dictionary to order coffee in Portugal. Following are the major variations:

um café or *uma bica* – a standard small black espresso, the most popular form

um café cheio or *uma bica cheia* – small espresso cup, filled to the top with coffee

um carioca – a bica's worth of coffee, filled to the top with hot water

um café duplo – a double espresso in an ordinary coffee cup

um pingado – a bica with a few drops of milk

um garoto – a cup of coffee with milk

um café com leite – a big cup of coffee with milk

um meia de leite – equal parts milk and filter coffee

um meia de leite de máquina – equal parts milk and espresso

um galão – a glass of hot milk with a dash of coffee, popular at breakfast (*um galão bem escuro* makes it stronger)

If you want (heaven forbid!) instant decaffeinated coffee, ask for *um descaféinado*.

Chá (tea) is usually served rather weak, in the style of Catherine of Bragança – best remembered not for being the wife of Charles II but for starting England on its long love affair with tea. You can ask for it *com leite* (with milk) or *com limão* (lemon). If you ask for *um chá de limão* you'll get a glass of hot water with a lemon rind – which is actually quite refreshing.

Also available in cafés and teahouses is *um chocolate quente* (hot chocolate), or you can just get *um copo de leite*, a glass of milk. Fresh milk is found in hypermarkets and supermarkets but is rare in small grocery shops, where long-life varieties are the norm.

Alcoholic Drinks

The Portuguese like a tipple; you can pick up anything from a glass of beer or wine to a shot of *aguardente* (firewater) at cafés, restaurants and bars throughout the day and most of the night. A mix of alcoholic drinks is common, too, including the morning-only *Martini com cerveja* (Martini topped with beer). And bartenders aren't stingy; most don't even bother with spirit measures. A single brandy here often contains the equivalent of a double in the UK or USA.

In most places you pay when you're ready to leave (as in a restaurant) but some foreign-owned bars are *pronto pagamento* (pay-as-you-order).

Wines Portuguese wine offers great value in all varieties – red, white and rosé; mature and young. You can find decent *vinho da casa* (house wine) everywhere for as little as €1.50 for a 350mL bottle or jug. For less than €4 you can buy a bottle to please the most discerning taste buds. In shops and supermarkets wine is available by the bottle, box or 5L container.

Restaurant wine lists differentiate not only between *branco* (white) and *tinto* (red), but between *maduro* (mature wine) and *vinho verde* (semisparkling young wine). As there are over a dozen major regional wines (usually produced by cooperatives), with new ones coming onto the market all the time, you're spoilt for choice.

The most famous of the *maduro* wines are probably the red Dão table wines, produced just north of the Serra da Estrela. Sweet and velvety, they resemble a Burgundy. Other *maduros* worth trying are those from the Alentejo (reds from Reguengos are excellent); the reds and whites of Buçaco, near Coimbra; the dry, straw-coloured whites of Bucelas in Estremadura; and the table wines of Ribatejo, especially reds from Torres Vedras and whites from Chamusca. The expensive but venerable reds of Colares (famous since the 13th century) near Sintra are made from vines grown on sand dunes and untouched by phylloxera (a fungus that has ravaged many a European wine region over the years).

The *vinho verde* of the northern Minho and lower Douro valley is very popular. Young (hence its name) and slightly sparkling, it has a low alcoholic content and comes in red, white and rosé varieties. Whites are undoubtedly the best, and are good with shellfish. The best-known *vinho verde* label is Casal Garcia, but worth the extra cost are Alvarinho whites from Monção and Melgaço, reds from Ponte da Barca and whites from Ponte de Lima.

Portugal's most famous rosé wine is the sweet, semisparkling Mateus rosé. The

Portuguese prefer their bubbles either as *vinho verde* or *espumantes naturais* (sparkling wines). The best of these are from the Bairrada region near Coimbra (try some with the local speciality, roast suckling pig) and the Raposeira wines of Lamego.

Sweet dessert wines are rare; the *moscatel* of Setúbal and Favaíos and Carcavelos from Estremadura offer the fruitiest flavours.

Port *Vinho do Porto*, a fortified wine from grapes grown in demarcated parts of the Douro valley, can be red or white; dry, medium or sweet. See the Douro chapter for a special section about port, and for details of visits to the port-wine lodges of Vila Nova de Gaia.

Madeira *Vinho da Madeira* is one of the oldest fortified wines of all; vines were first

A Glossary of Wines & Labels

adega	winery or cellar
ano	year
branco	white
bruto	extra dry
colheita	a single-harvest vintage tawny port, aged for at least seven years
doce	sweet
engarrofado por...	bottled by...
espumante	sparkling
garrafeira	wines of an outstanding vintage: at least three years old for reds, one year for whites
generoso	fortified wine
LBV	late-bottled vintage; a vintage port aged four to six years in oak casks before bottling
licoroso	sweet fortified wine
maduro	mature wine
meio seco	medium dry
quinta	country property or wine estate
região demarcada	officially demarcated wine region
reserva	wine from a year of outstanding quality
ruby port	cheapest and sweetest port wine
seco	dry
tawny port	a sweet or semisweet port, the best of which has been aged for at least 10 years
tinto	red
velho	old
vinho da casa	house wine
vinho do Porto	port wine
vinho maduro	wine matured for more than a year
vinho regionão	a new classification for superior country wines, similar to the French *vins de pays*
vinho verde	young (literally 'green') wine, slightly sparkling and available in red, white and rosé varieties
vintage-character port	a cheap version of a vintage port, blended and aged for about four years
vintage port	the unblended product of a single harvest of outstanding or rare quality, bottled after two years and then aged in the bottle for up to two decades, sometimes more
white port	usually dry, crisp and fresh; popular as an aperitif

introduced to this Atlantic Ocean island-province soon after Portuguese explorers claimed it in 1419. The English, who called the sweet version of the wine malmsey, became particularly partial to it (the Duke of Clarence drowned in a butt of the stuff). In addition to malmsey dessert wine there's a dry aperitif version called *sercial* and a semisweet *verdelho*.

Spirits Portuguese whisky, brandy and gin are all much cheaper than elsewhere in Europe, though of lower quality. If you fancy something with a more unique taste and punch, try some of the *aguardente* firewaters: *medronho* (made from arbutus berries; see the boxed text 'Monchique's Moonshine' in the Algarve chapter), *figo* (figs), *ginjinha* (cherries) and *licor beirão* (aromatic plants) are all delicious – and safe in small doses. For some rough stuff that tries hard to destroy your throat, ask for a *bagaço* (made from grape husks).

Beer Stronger and cheaper than in the UK or USA, Portugal's *cerveja* (beer) consists largely of three fairly indistinguishable lagers: Sagres and Cristal, favoured in the south, and Super Bock, popular in the north. Take your empties back to a supermarket checkout for a refund.

You can order beer in bars by the bottle or on draught. A 20cL glass of draught beer is called *um fino* in the north and *um imperial* in Lisbon and the south, 33cL is *um príncipe* (prince), 50cL is *uma caneca* (mug) and 1L is *uma girafa* (giraffe). Bars in tourist resorts often have popular foreign brews such as bitter or stout.

ENTERTAINMENT

The Portuguese love a bit of fun and you're likely to come across some sort of daytime entertainment almost anywhere, especially in spring and summer. Every sizable town has a few bars and a disco, and in the Algarve, Lisbon, Porto and other major towns the fun goes on until at least 3am most nights. One of the liveliest scenes features African and Brazilian music (see Entertainment under Lisbon and Porto).

Among traditional entertainment, the most accessible and enjoyable include local fairs and festivals. Many are centred on saints' days, religious processions and pilgrimages, and the Minho is the richest in these. Whole towns or regions may down tools for several days and revel in music, dance, fireworks, colourful parades, handicrafts fairs or vast animal markets. The Festa de São João is one of the largest and liveliest, especially in Porto and Lisbon, and Carnaval is one of the most exuberant. Huge market fairs at Ponte de Lima, Viseu, Santarém and Beja offer a chance to see Portugal's traditions at their best. See Public Holidays & Special Events earlier in this chapter, and local listings, for details.

International music, dance and cinema festivals fill the spring and summer calendars. Two venerable classical-music festivals take place in Sintra and Estoril between June and August. In July Cascais and Estorial jointly host a jazz festival and Lisbon a rock festival; Porto jumps to Celtic music in March/April, folk music in July and rock in August. Enjoy Portuguese folk music in Viana do Castelo in May, Barcelos in July and Chaves in October. Viana also hosts festivals of jazz in August and blues in November.

If you like *fado*, the melancholy Portuguese equivalent of the blues (see Arts in the Facts about Portugal chapter), Lisbon and Coimbra will keep you busy. Coimbra celebrates its style of fado with gusto during Queima das Fitas, a week of student mayhem in May, and Lisbon and Porto host tabacarias festivals in February and October respectively.

If dance is your pleasure, an international festival of contemporary dance comes to Lisbon in November, and prestigious ballet performances get palatial settings in Sintra during August.

Cinema buffs will find international festivals in the Algarve and Viana do Castelo in May, Tróia in June and Figueira da Foz in September. Lisbon hosts a gay-and-lesbian film festival in September. In Portuguese cinemas subtitled European and American films tend to edge out local works. Cinema tickets, fairly cheap at €4 to €5, are often cheaper on one day each week (usually Monday) in an effort to lure audiences away from their video players.

For up-to-the-minute information on local events, ask the turismos (many have monthly or seasonal what's-on publications) or see the entertainment listings in local papers.

SPECTATOR SPORTS
Football

Football (soccer) is a Portuguese national obsession. Life – male life at any rate – and quite possibly the national economy come to a near standstill during any big match, with bar and restaurant TVs showing nothing else. The season lasts from September to May, and almost every village and town finds enough players to field a team. Local papers and turismos will have information on upcoming matches, and tickets are fairly cheap. Major teams and their stadiums are noted under bigger towns in this book.

The story of Portuguese football is mainly about Lisbon and Porto. The big three teams – Lisbon's Sporting Clube de Portugal and SL Benfica, and Porto's FC Porto – have among them won every national championship but two since the 1920s. Porto's upstart Boavista FC broke the spell in 2000–01, pushing the big three aside to take the championship.

Boozey post-match celebrations are a tradition in themselves, with fans ever ready to take to the streets, honking, setting off fireworks and gridlocking entire town centres until the wee hours. They had three excuses to go bonkers at the end of the 2001–02 season: when Sporting clinched the championship (their second in three years), a week later when the season ended and a

Euro2004

In October 1999 the fondest dreams of football fans and property developers across the country came true when UEFA, the governing body of European football, invited Portugal to host Euro2004, the 2004 European football championships.

Sports authorities here are counting on the tournament to provide a big shot in the arm for Portuguese football. Local clubs, with mounting debts and ageing stadiums, watch the country's star players earn a fortune abroad (for example Nuno Gomes at Fiorentina, Rui Costa at Milan and, most visibly, Luís Figo at Real Madrid) while the finances of the domestic game founder.

Tourism officials are naturally delighted at the prospect of all those extra visitors, who are expected to leave several hundred million euros behind.

Of course the 'sports-venue industry' is cheered too. Five new stadiums are being built and five others refurbished, in eight cities: Aveiro, Braga, Coimbra, Faro/Loulé, Guimarães, Leiria, Lisbon and Porto. Associated development funded by the government, local authorities, football clubs and private companies will also serve other sports. Other projects include motorways, new urban and regional railways, and the upgrading of Lisbon, Porto and Faro airports.

But it hasn't been smooth sailing. The overall cost will probably exceed €450 million, and not everybody thinks this is the way to kick-start the struggling Portuguese economy. Stadium projects in Lisbon and Porto have been dogged by political controversy. Municipal elections in December 2001 saw the centre-right Social Democrats win power in Lisbon and Porto, and dispute funding promises made by their predecessors. A nervous UEFA warned in March 2002 that Portugal could lose the right to host the championships if it didn't get its act together.

That would probably be a great relief for some police officials. Portugal has never faced a public-security task like this, with boisterous supporters – and probably troublemakers – streaming in from all over Europe. Estimates vary from a third of a million to a million extra visitors in the space of just 3½ weeks.

The qualifying competition is staged in 10 groups of five teams, with matches on 10 allocated days from September 2002 to October 2003. The winners in each group qualify for the tournament; runners-up take part in five play-off matches in November 2003, with those winners also progressing to the finals. Portugal, as the host, qualifies automatically. The tournament – 31 matches in total – kicks off on 12 June 2004 at Porto's new Estádio das Antas, with the final match on 4 July 2004 at Lisbon's Estádio da Luz (Stadium of Light).

Two useful websites for those who want to keep up with developments are: W www.uefa .com/competitions/Euro2004, the official UEFA site, and best source for scores, fixtures, qualifying tables and gossip; and W www.news.bbc.co.uk/sport1/hi/football/europe/1776367.stm, for Euro2004 news, FAQs and trivia.

week after that when Sporting came up tops in the post-championship eliminations for the Taça de Portugal (Portugal Cup).

Despite the national team's early departure from the 2002 World Cup, Portuguese fans took solace in FIFA's selection of countryman Luís Figo as world football's Best Player of 2001 – tempered only by the fact that Figo currently plays for the Spanish team Real Madrid.

The country looks certain to be consumed with football hysteria in 2004 when it hosts the UEFA European Football Championships, the biggest sports event ever staged in Portugal (see the boxed text).

Bullfighting

Bullfighting was first recorded in Portugal by the 1st-century Roman historian Strabo. He wrote that 'the peoples inhabiting the coastal regions of the Peninsula like to challenge isolated bulls, which in Hispania are very wild'.

The sport's modern version dates from the 12th, century when the *tourada* was developed as a way to maintain military fitness and prepare kings and nobles for battle on horseback. The gory death in 1799 of a Portuguese nobleman resulted in a less blatantly cruel style of fight in Portugal, in which the bulls' horns are capped and the animals are not killed publicly.

A typical *tourada* starts with a bull charging into the ring towards a *cavaleiro*, a mounted horseman dressed in 18th-century costume and plumed tricorn hat. The *cavaleiro* sizes the animal up as his team of *peões de brega* (footmen) distract and provoke the bull with capes. Then, with superb horsemanship, he gallops within inches of the bull's horns and plants several short, barbed *bandarilha* spears in the bull's neck.

The next phase, the *pega*, features a team of eight young *forcados* dressed in breeches, white stockings and short jackets, who face the weakened bull barehanded and in a single line. The leader swaggers towards the bull, provoking it to charge. Bearing the brunt of the attack, he throws himself onto the animal's head and grabs the horns while his mates rush in behind him to try to immobilise the beast, often being tossed in all directions. Their success marks the end of the contest and the bull is led out of the pen among a herd of steers.

Though the rules for Portuguese bullfighting prohibit a public kill, the hapless animal is usually dispatched in private afterwards.

Another style of performance (often the final contest in a day-long *tourada*) is similar to the Spanish version, with a *toureiro* challenging the bull – its horns uncapped – on foot with cape and *bandarilhas*. Unlike in Spain, there's no *picador* on horseback to weaken the bull with lances, and the kill is only symbolic, with a short *bandarilha* feigning the thrust of a sword.

Bullfighting is still a fiercely male domain. There is just one female Portuguese *cavaleira*, Marta Manuela. Spain's only female matador, Cristina Sanchez, who had been fighting successfully for 10 years, gave up in 1999 in the face of continual harassment and prejudice.

Bullfighting remains popular here despite opposition from local and international animal-welfare organisations. The season runs from late April or March to October. The most traditional contests take place in bull-breeding Ribatejo province, especially in Santarém during the June agricultural fair, and in Vila Franca de Xira during the town's July and October festivals. *Touradas* in the Algarve and Lisbon are more tourist-oriented.

Fights usually last two hours or more. Tickets range from €15 to €50. Cheapest are *sol* seats (in the sun). *Sol e sombra* seats provide some shade as the sun moves around, while the priciest tickets are for the always-shady *sombra* seats.

See Treatment of Animals under Society & Conduct in the Facts about Portugal chapter for more on the unpleasant side of the sport.

Athletics

Portugal has a distinguished history in track and field, especially long-distance events. Carlos Lopes won the 1984 Olympic gold medal in the men's marathon. António Pinto's winning time in the 2000 London Marathon (his third victory in the event) was at the time of writing the eighth fastest marathon time in history. In the 2002 European Championships Francis Obikwelu took silver in the 100m (setting a national record) and 200m, while Rui Silva brought home bronze in the 1500m.

Rosa Mota won the women's marathon in the European Championships of 1982,

1986 and 1990, and took Olympic gold in 1988. Manuela Machado won the same race at the 1994 and 1998 Europeans and the 1996 Olympics. In the Olympic women's 10,000m, Fernanda Ribeiro took gold in 1996 and bronze in 2000.

Tennis

Tennis draws sizable crowds in Portugal. The annual Open Clay Court Tournament at the Estoril Tennis Club attracts top-seeded international stars. Other important centres are in Porto, Coimbra, Évora and the Algarve.

SHOPPING

Shopping can be a pleasure in Portugal. Artisans still take pride in producing some fine handicrafts, prices are reasonable and the choice is wide. Particularly good buys are port wine (with plenty of choice at cheap prices, at least for lesser wines); rural handicrafts and pottery; and unique deluxe items such as Arraiolos carpets.

For information about tax-free shopping see Taxes & Refunds under Money earlier in this chapter.

Gourmet Products

Port wine, Portugal's best-known export, is readily available. To pick it up at the source, visit a few of the port-wine lodges at Vila Nova de Gaia, across the river from Porto – or pop into any supermarket, where you'll find a reasonable selection at modest prices. For something fancier, Lisbon, Porto and other major cities have specialist wine and port shops.

Other quality foodstuffs worth considering are olive oil, numerous varieties of fresh olives, and honey from all over the country.

Linen, Cotton & Lace

Hand-embroidered linen and cotton, traditional costumes (in children's sizes too) and lacework (a speciality of coastal fishing towns) are sold at modest prices all over the country, but especially in seaside resorts such as Nazaré and Viana do Castelo. Castelo Branco is renowned for embroidered bed covers. Embroidered tablecloths are a common item at the open-air markets appearing regularly on the outskirts of most Portuguese towns – but bargain hard. The home of Portuguese-style bobbin lace is

Shop Names

Many smaller shops appear to have no name, only a sign indicating their generic speciality, so it's worth learning a few terms: *artesanato* (handicrafts), *livraria* (books), *papelaria* (stationery), *sapateria* (shoes) and *joalheria* (jewellery). A *discoteca* can be either a music shop or a discotheque!

Vila do Conde, north of Porto, though quality work also comes from the eastern Algarve and from Peniche, north of Lisbon.

Azulejos & Ceramics

Azulejo (hand-painted tiles) are tempting buys, especially in Lisbon (which has several azulejo showrooms and a shop at the Museu dos Azulejos), and in Sintra and the Algarve. Souvenir tiles can be remarkably cheap, though made-to-order items get pricey. For some background on the tradition of azulejo tiles, see the boxed text in the 'Architecture' special section in the Facts about Portugal chapter.

Another uniquely Portuguese purchase is ceramics – and not just the trademark Barcelos cockerel that appears ad nauseam in every gift shop in the country. Among quality pottery are the famous black pots of Trás-os-Montes, the unique cabbage-leaf crockery of Caldas da Rainha, earthenware jugs from Estremoz and some interesting work from Barcelos itself. São Pedro do Corval, near Monsaraz in the Alentejo, is one of Portugal's largest pottery centres.

Rugs, Jewellery & Leather

Those with more money to spend should consider the hand-stitched carpets of Arraiolos (now made under contract in many parts of the country), earlier versions of which graced manor houses and castles. Traditional woollen blankets are an Alentejan speciality.

Another good-value but expensive purchase is the gold and silver filigree jewellery of the Porto area. Leather goods, especially shoes and bags, are also good value; Porto is full of leather and shoe shops, though the leatherworkers of Loulé and Almodôvar in the Algarve count themselves among the best.

Other Handicrafts

Within range for those on a budget is rush, palm and wicker basketwork, which are available throughout the country and are best tracked down in municipal markets. Trás-os-Montes is a good place for woven goods and tapestries, and, with Beira Alta and Beira Beixa, for wrought-iron work. If you're around Nazaré, look for inexpensive woollen pullovers.

The Alentejo is known for its simple hand-painted wooden furniture; there's a handicrafts centre for this and other crafts at Reguengos de Monsaraz. Cheap souvenirs of native cork are also plentiful. An eye-catching item, for adults and children alike, are the beautifully dressed porcelain dolls found everywhere and often considered a collector's item in Portugal.

Markets

Almost every town in Portugal has a *mercado municipal* (municipal market), usually open daily except Sunday, selling fruit and vegetables, freshly baked bread, fresh meat and fish, cakes and local cheeses, and sometimes handicrafts. Most sizable towns also have weekly farmers' markets, and many have big, usually monthly, open-air markets, featuring itinerant hawkers of everything from souvenirs to kitchenware. For listings check the what's-on pages of the English-language papers or the turismos' monthly events pamphlets.

Artesanatos

Finally, even if you won't be travelling widely, bear in mind that certain quality *artesanatos* (handicrafts shops), such as Santos Oficios in Lisbon and Arte Facto in Porto, display quality work from all around the country. For more on the crafts of the Algarve and Alentejo, see the excellent regional guide by John & Madge Measures, *Southern Portugal: Its People, Traditions & Wildlife*.

Getting There & Away

Buses are the cheapest way to get to Portugal from elsewhere in Europe, but not by much. Prices for the alternatives are coming down fast, thanks to the rise of 'no-frills' airlines and to the growing popularity of rail passes.

AIR

Unless otherwise noted, quoted fares are approximate return fares (including taxes) during peak air-travel season, based on advertised rates at the time of writing. None of them constitutes a recommendation for any airline.

In North America and Europe, peak season is roughly June to mid-September plus Christmas; 'shoulder' season is April to May and mid-September to October. In Australia and New Zealand, peak season is roughly December to January.

Airports & Airlines

Portugal has international airports at Lisbon, Porto and Faro. Lisbon has by far the most scheduled flights, while Faro gets heavy charter traffic from all over Europe.

Portugal's flagship international airline is TAP Air Portugal. The main domestic airline – but with a growing menu of European connections – is PGA Portugália Airlines. The boxed text 'Airlines, Airports &

Booking Contacts' lists major carriers and their coordinates in Portugal.

Buying Tickets

World aviation has never been so competitive, making air travel better value everyday – but you should research the options carefully to get the best deal. The Internet is a useful resource for comparing fares, although you'll also find short-term bargains in good old-fashioned newspaper travel ads. Full-time students and people under 26 years old have access to some great deals; you just have to prove your date of birth or show a valid international student card when buying your ticket and when boarding the plane.

In general there's little to be gained from going directly to the airlines. They release discounted tickets to selected travel agencies and discount agencies, and these are often the best deals.

One exception to this rule is the so-called 'no-frills' carriers, which mostly sell direct. At the time of writing, those with Portugal links included Go/easyJet (London, Bristol and East Midlands to Faro) and BMIbaby (East Midlands and Cardiff to Faro). The other exception to this rule is do-it-yourself Internet booking. Many airlines (both full-service and no-frills) and travel agencies offer some very cheap seats online, though they tend to be 'subject to availability' – meaning there aren't many and they sell fast, so you must book well ahead, be flexible about dates, and have a certain amount of plain good luck. The best of these are competitive with under-26/student fares.

Direct and online ticket sales work well if you're planning a simple one-way or return trip on specified dates, though superfast online fare generators are no substitute for a travel agent who knows all about special deals, has strategies for avoiding layovers and can offer advice on everything from travel insurance to vegetarian meals.

You may find some very cheap flights advertised by obscure agencies. Most are honest and solvent, but there are a few rogue outfits around. Paying by credit card generally offers protection since most card issuers provide refunds if you don't get what you paid for. Agencies that accept only cash should hand over the tickets straightaway. After you have made a booking or paid your deposit, you should call the airline and confirm that the booking was made. Established agencies such as those noted in this book offer extra security and are just about as competitive as you can get; similar protection can be obtained by buying from a bonded agency, such as those covered by the Air Travel Organiser's Licence (ATOL) scheme in the UK.

If you purchase a ticket and later want to make changes to your route or get a refund, you need to contact the original travel agent. Airlines issue refunds only to the purchaser of a ticket – usually the agency that bought the ticket on your behalf. Many travellers change their plans halfway through their trips, so think carefully before you buy a ticket that is not easily changed or refunded.

Travellers with Specific Needs

If you have special requirements – you're in a wheelchair, taking the baby, vegetarian, terrified of flying – let the airline know when you book. Restate your needs when

Airlines, Airports & Booking Contacts

Following are booking numbers and websites for major carriers serving Portugal, along with the airports they use (L = Lisbon, P = Porto, F = Faro).

Airline	Contact	Airports
Aer Lingus	(W www.aerlingus.ie)	F
Aeroflot	(Lisbon ☎ 213 467 776, W www.aeroflot.com)	L
Aero Lloyd	(Faro ☎ 289 800 749, W www.aerolloyd.de)	F
Air France	(☎ 808 202 800, W www.airfrance.fr)	L, P
Air Luxor	(Lisbon ☎ 210 026 800, W www.airluxor.com)	L, P
Alitalia	(toll-free ☎ 800 307 300, W www.alitalia.it)	L
British Airways	(☎ 808 212 125, W www.britishairways.com)	L, P, F
British Midland/BMIbaby	(☎ 952 048 301, W www.bmibaby.com)	F
Continental Airlines	(Lisbon ☎ 213 834 000, W www.flycontinental.com)	L, P
Finnair	(Lisbon ☎ 213 522 689, W www.finnair.fi)	L, F
Go/easyJet Airways	(W www.go-fly.com)	L, F
Iberia	(☎ 808 261 261, W www.iberia.com)	L, P
KLM	(☎ 808 222 747, W www.klm.nl)	L
LAM	(Linhas Aéreas de Moçambique; Lisbon ☎ 213 219 960)	L
Lufthansa	(Lisbon ☎ 214 245 155, W www.lufthansa.pt)	L, P, F
Maersk Air	(Lisbon ☎ 213 139 110, W www.maersk-air.dk)	L
Monarch Airlines	(Faro ☎ 289 889 475, W www.flymonarch.com)	F
PGA Portugália Airlines	(Lisbon ☎ 218 425 559, W www.pga.pt)	L, P, F
Regional Air Lines	(Lisbon ☎ 218 425 559, W www.regional.com)	L
Royal Air Maroc	(Lisbon ☎ 213 190 770, W www.royalairmaroc.com)	L
Spanair	(Lisbon ☎ 218 498 578, W www.spanair.com)	L
Swiss International Airlines	(☎ 808 200 487, W www.swiss.com)	L, P
TAAG	(Angola Airlines; Lisbon ☎ 213 575 899, W www.taag-airlines.com)	L
TACV	(Transportes Aéreos de Cabo Verde; Lisbon ☎ 213 230 555)	L
TAP Air Portugal	(☎ 808 205 700, W www.tap.pt)	L, P, F
Transbrasil	(Lisbon ☎ 213 139 861)	L
Transavia Airlines	(☎ 808 222 747, W www.transavia.nl)	P, F
Tunisair	(Lisbon ☎ 218 496 346, W www.tunisair.com.tn)	L
TWA	(toll-free ☎ 800 201 284, W www.twa.com)	L
Varig	(Lisbon ☎ 214 245 170, W www.varig.com.br)	L
Virgin Express	(☎ 808 208 082, W www.virgin-express.com)	L, F

you reconfirm, and again when you check in at the airport.

With advance warning most international airports can provide escorts from check-in to the plane, and most have ramps, lifts, wheelchair-accessible toilets and telephones. Major carriers can arrange wheelchairs. Aircraft toilets present problems for wheelchair users, who should discuss this early on with the airline and/or their doctor. The website at **w** www.allgohere.com has an airline directory with information on facilities for the disabled offered by various airlines.

Except on certain routes, hearing dogs and guide dogs must travel in a pressurised baggage compartment with other animals. They're subject to the same quarantine laws as any other animal entering rabies-free countries such as the UK, Portugal or Australia. Animals travelling to Portugal require an export health certificate (available in the UK from the nearest Animal Health Divisional Office). The UK's Pet Travel Scheme (PETS) enables pet cats and dogs to enter or re-enter the UK without quarantine from certain countries (including Portugal), on approved routes with approved transport companies, provided they meet certain requirements, including being blood tested, vaccinated against rabies and tagged with an ID microchip. For details contact the **PETS Helpline** (☎ 0870-241 1710; **w** www.defra.gov.uk/animalh/quarantine).

Children under two years old normally travel for around 10% of the standard fare, as long as they don't occupy a seat. They don't get a baggage allowance. Bassinets or 'skycots' can usually be provided by the airline if requested in advance. Children between two and 12 years can usually occupy a seat for half to two-thirds the full fare, and do get a baggage allowance. Pushchairs can often be taken as hand luggage.

Airport Taxes

International airport taxes, normally levied by countries of both origin and destination, are included in the price of your ticket, either scheduled or charter. Sample taxes for return flights between Lisbon and other European destinations at the time of writing were about €17 to Madrid, €24 to Paris, €29 to Brussels, €33 to London and €41 to Amsterdam.

The UK & Ireland

Thanks to the UK's long love affair with Portugal and its 'bucket-shop' tradition, bargains are plentiful. Some of the best deals are online, but don't overlook ads in the weekend national papers and, in London, in *Time Out*, the *Evening Standard* and the free *TNT* magazine.

The UK's best-known bargain-ticket agencies are **Trailfinders** (☎ 020-7937 1234; **w** www.trailfinders.co.uk), **Travel CUTS** (☎ 020-7266 2082; **w** www.travelcuts.co.uk) and **STA Travel** (☎ 0870-160 0599; **w** www.statravel.co.uk); all have branches throughout the country. Another UK option is **Flight Centre** (☎ 0870-890 8099; **w** www.flightcentre.co.uk). Reliable sources in Ireland include **usit Now** (☎ 01-602 1600; **w** www.usitnow.ie) and **Trailfinders** (☎ 01-677 7888; **w** www.trailfinders.ie).

Scheduled direct flights go daily to Lisbon from London Heathrow with **TAP Air Portugal** (☎ 0845-601 0932) and **British Airways** (BA; ☎ 0845-773 3377), from London Gatwick with TAP, and from Manchester with **PGA Portugália Airlines** (☎ 0870-755 0025). Direct Porto connections leave daily from Heathrow with TAP, once a week from Gatwick with BA, and daily from Manchester with Portugália.

There's a veritable bandwagon of direct flights to Faro: daily from Heathrow with TAP, from Gatwick with BA's franchise **GB Airways** (☎ 01293-664239; **w** www.gbairways.com), or from London Stansted, Bristol or East Midlands with **Go/easyJet** (☎ 0870-607 6543); three times weekly from London Luton or Manchester with **Monarch** (☎ 0870-040 5040); or one to three times daily from East Midlands and four times weekly from Cardiff with **BMIbaby** (☎ 0870-264 2229).

The best midsummer return fares for London–Lisbon start at about UK£130, flying nonstop with BA. The best fare for London–Porto is about UK£160 via Frankfurt with Lufthansa. Return fares to Faro at the time of writing were as low as UK£65 from BMIbaby or UK£88 from Go/easyJet (online and subject to availability); Monarch charges from UK£104 from Luton to Faro.

Charters operate from all over the UK, mostly to Faro (high-season return fares from UK£175). A reliable charter-flight clearinghouse is **Destination Portugal** (☎ 0870-744 0050; **w** www.destination-portugal.co.uk).

Continental Europe

France With its huge Portuguese immigrant population, France has abundant air links with Portugal.

Under-26/student specialist agencies with branches around the country include **OTU Voyages** (☎ *08 20 81 78 17;* w *www .otu.fr)* and **Voyages Wasteels** (☎ *08 25 88 70 70;* w *www.voyages-wasteels.fr).* Other reliable agencies are **Nouvelles Frontières** (☎ *08 25 00 07 47;* w *www.nouvelles-frontieres .fr)* and **Voyageurs du Monde** (☎ *01 42 86 17 20;* w *www.vdm.com).*

Carriers with multiple daily nonstop Paris–Lisbon and Paris–Porto connections are **TAP** (☎ *08 02 31 93 20),* mostly from Orly, and **Air France** (☎ *08 20 82 08 20)* from Charles de Gaulle. **Portugália** (☎ *08 03 08 38 18)* codeshares daily with **Air Luxor** (☎ *01 48 16 28 52)* from Paris to Porto.

Direct daily connections to Lisbon from elsewhere in France include Portugália's from Bordeaux, Nice, Lyon and Toulouse; TAP's from Nice; and Air France's from Lyon. Additional links to Porto are daily from Lyon and weekly from Nice with Portugália, and daily from Bordeaux with Air France. Currently there are no scheduled flights to Faro.

Expect to pay at least €220 return for a Paris–Lisbon or Paris–Porto flight in high season.

Spain Reliable Madrid-based airfare specialists with offices throughout Spain are **Usit Unlimited** (☎ *91-225 2575;* w *www.usi tunlimited.es),* **Barceló Viajes** (☎ *91-559 1819;* w *www.barceloviajes.es)* and **Tui Viajes** (☎ *91-547 42 00;* w *www.tuiviajes.com).*

Carriers with daily Madrid–Lisbon connections include **Portugália** (☎ *902 100 145)* and **Spanair** (☎ *971 745 020)* with fares of about €200 return, plus **TAP** (☎ *901 116 718),* **Iberia** (☎ *902 400 500)* and also **Lufthansa** (☎ *902 220 101).* Portugália, Spanair, TAP and Iberia also fly Barcelona–Lisbon. Portugália's PGA Express flies smaller aircraft direct to Lisbon from Bilbao, La Coruña, Málaga and Valencia, with fares only marginally higher than for routings via Madrid.

For Porto, Portugália and Spanair have daily direct flights from Madrid (codesharing at about €270) and Barcelona; Iberia flies from Madrid only.

Elsewhere in Continental Europe An airfare specialist with branches around Germany is **STA Travel** (*Frankfurt* ☎ *01805-456 422;* w *www.statravel.de).* In Belgium go to **Usit Connections** (*Brussels* ☎ *02-550 01 00;* w *www.connections.be)* or **Wats Reizen** (*Antwerp* ☎ *03-233 70 20, fax 232 17 64).* In the Netherlands, try Amsterdam-based **Air Fair** (☎ *020-620 5121;* w *www.airfair.nl)* or **Malibu Travel** (☎ *020-638 6059;* w *www .etn.nl/malibu/).*

The major corridors into Portugal from Germany are Frankfurt–Lisbon, Munich–Lisbon and Frankfurt–Porto; Lufthansa and TAP have daily direct flights on each route. Other direct connections are to Lisbon from Berlin, Cologne, Hamburg and Stuttgart, and to Porto from Cologne and Stuttgart (Portugália); and to Faro from Frankfurt (Lufthansa). Frankfurt–Lisbon return fares start at around €245. Germany also runs close behind the UK in the volume of charter traffic to Portugal.

From Amsterdam, KLM and TAP fly direct to Lisbon and Porto daily, and TAP travels several times weekly to Faro; expect to pay at least €250 for a return fare. Charter specialist **Transavia** (☎ *020-406 04 06)* also offers scheduled flights from Amsterdam to Porto and Faro, and from Rotterdam to Faro.

From Brussels, **Virgin Express** (☎ *070-35 36 37)* has daily flights to Lisbon and weekend connections to Faro; TAP also flies daily to Lisbon; and Portugália flies daily to Porto. Discount return fares start at around €250.

The USA & Canada

Discount travel agencies in the USA and Canada are called consolidators, and can be found through the Yellow Pages or major newspapers. **Circle The Planet** (☎ *1 800 799 8888;* w *www.circletheplanet.com)* is a leading consolidator. The *Los Angeles Times, New York Times,* San Francisco *Examiner,* Chicago *Tribune,* Toronto *Globe & Mail,* Toronto *Star,* Montreal *Gazette* and Vancouver *Sun* have weekly travel sections with ads and information.

Two big airfare specialists in the USA are **Council Travel** (☎ *1 800 226 8624;* w *www .counciltravel.com)* and **STA Travel** (☎ *1 800 781 4040;* w *www.statravel.com).* Canada's best bargain-ticket agency is **Travel CUTS/**

Voyages Campus (☎ 1 866 246 9762; W www .travelcuts.com). All three companies have offices countrywide.

The only direct air links are to Lisbon: daily from New York JFK (TWA and TAP), Newark (Continental and TAP) and Los Angeles (Continental and TWA); and twice weekly from Boston (TAP). There are no direct flights between Canada and Portugal. You can save money and fly from a wider range of cities with an indirect connection such as BA's via London.

Adult/under-26 return fares start at around US$900/850 from New York or US$1200/1050 from Los Angeles. Canadian fares start at around C$1600 from Montreal or Toronto, and C$1800 from Calgary, Edmonton or Vancouver.

Australia & New Zealand
Saturday's travel sections in the *Sydney Morning Herald*, *The Age* in Melbourne and the *New Zealand Herald* have many ads for cheap fares to Europe.

Flight Centre (*Australia* ☎ 133 133; W www .flightcentre.com.au • *New Zealand* ☎ 0800-243 544; W www.flightcentre.co.nz) and **STA Travel** (*Australia* ☎ 131 776; W www.statravel .com.au • *New Zealand* ☎ 0508-782 872; W www.statravel.co.nz) are major dealers in cheap air fares. Both have offices across Australia and New Zealand. Bargain-ticket agency **Trailfinders** (W www.trailfinders.com .au) has branches in Sydney, Melbourne, Brisbane, Cairns and Perth.

There are no direct flights from Australasia to Portugal, but dozens of indirect routes via third countries. Shop around, as airlines such as Thai Airways International, Malaysia Airlines, Garuda, Qantas and Singapore Airlines have frequent promotional fares. The only Asian carrier serving both Australasia and Portugal is Thai Airways.

At the time of writing, return fares to Lisbon started at about A$2100 from Melbourne or Sydney, or NZ$2399 from Auckland. An alternative is a bargain flight to London (eg, about A$1800 from Sydney with Garuda) plus an onward no-frills or charter flight.

Africa
All scheduled flights between mainland Africa and Portugal go to Lisbon. The cheapest (and most frequent) option from North Africa is the daily nonstop flight from

Casablanca on a Portugália/Regional codeshare (about €210).

TAP also flies to Portugal, with direct flights from several former Portuguese colonies. Flights depart on a few days each week and are usually the best high-season deals. Example of routes and fares include Angola (Luanda; about €750, codeshare with TAAG), Dakar (Senegal; €350), Guinea-Bissau (Bissau; €420), Mozambique (Maputo; €450, codeshare with LAM) and São Tomé & Príncipe (São Tomé; €620).

There are numerous carriers offering indirect Johannesburg–Lisbon flights for €350 to €400 return.

South America
Historically, Lisbon was an important stop on the air route between Europe and South America; and indeed the first-ever flight between Heathrow and South America stopped in Lisbon.

Today, TAP offers the most flights: to Lisbon daily in summer from Rio, São Paulo and Recife (Brazil), and two to three times weekly from Caracas (Venezuela). Varig flies daily from Rio to Lisbon. TAP also flies direct to Porto, daily from Rio and twice weekly from Caracas. The best high-season fares start at about €800 return for Rio–Lisbon or Rio–Porto flights, and €1030 return for Caracas–Lisbon.

BUS
Buses are slower and less comfortable than trains, but cheaper – especially if you qualify for a under-26/student or senior discount. While a long-distance bus trip from northern Europe to Portugal can be a bit tedious, you do get reclining seats, on-board toilets and sometimes air-conditioning. Buses stop frequently for meals, though you'll save money by packing your own munchies. It's a good idea to book at least a week ahead in summer.

The two major options for European long-distance bus travel are Eurolines and Busabout.

Eurolines
Eurolines (W www.eurolines.com) is a French-owned consortium of operators forming Europe's largest international coach network, linking cities all over Western and Central Europe, Scandinavia and Morocco.

Eurolines' main Portugal offices are:

Lisbon (☎ 218 957 398, fax 218 940 967)
Estação do Oriente, Avenida Dom João 1990
Porto (☎ 225 189 299, fax 225 189 310) Centro
Comercial Central Shopping, Campo 24 de
Agosto 125

For some European routes, Eurolines is affiliated with one of the three big Portuguese operators:

Intercentro (☎ 213 571 745, fax 213 570 039)
Rua Actor Taborda 25, Lisbon
Internorte (☎ 226 052 420, fax 226 099 570)
Praça da Galiza 96, Porto
Intersul (☎ 289 899 770, fax 289 899 759)
Terminal Rodoviário, Avenida da República,
Faro

Among some 200 Eurolines offices elsewhere in Europe are the following:

Amsterdam (☎ 020-560 87 88, fax 560 87 17,
W www.eurolines.nl)
Brussels (☎ 02-274 1350, fax 201 1140,
W www.eurolines.be)
Frankfurt (☎ 069-790 350, fax 790 3219,
W www.deutsche-touring.com)
London (☎ 0870-580 8080, fax 01582-400694,
W www.eurolines.co.uk)
Madrid (☎ 91-327 1381, fax 327 1329,
W www.eurolines.es)
Paris (☎ 08 36 69 52 52, fax 01 49 72 57 99,
W www.eurolines.fr)

Discounts on most Eurolines routes to Portugal are 80% for children up to age three, 15% to 50% for children aged four to 12 and 5% to 10% for travellers aged under 26 or over at least 60. Return fares are about 15% lower than two one-way fares.

If you're travelling widely in Europe by bus, the Eurolines Pass gives you unlimited travel among 31 European cities – although Madrid is currently the closest city to Portugal covered by the pass, and you must buy it prior to your arrival in Portugal. High-season prices range from €249/209 (adult/under-26 and senior) for a 15-day pass to €429/329 for a 60-day pass; low-season prices are 20% to 25% lower.

Busabout

Busabout (**W** www.busabout.com) is a hop-on hop-off network linking 66 European cities. Buses run from mid-April or mid-May to mid-September or mid-October, and travellers can move freely around the network using one of two passes available online from Busabout.

The Consecutive Pass is good for a set period from two weeks (€299) to the entire season (€1179). The Flexi-Pass lets you choose the number of travel days you want, from six days within one month (€289) to 25 days within four months (€929). Youth (under 26) and student-card holders pay about 10% less.

The bus stops are near camp sites, hostels or other budget accommodation, and buses pass by every two days. Stops in Portugal are in Lisbon and Lagos (see listings under those towns for details). Busabout also offers an add-on, return-trip London–Paris shuttle by bus and ferry. Each bus comes with a guide who can answer questions and make computerised travel and accommodation arrangements en route.

The UK

Eurolines runs several services to Portugal from Victoria coach station in London, via channel ferry and a 4½- to seven-hour stopover and change of bus in Paris. These include three a week to Viana do Castelo (UK£82 one way, 38 hours), five to Porto (UK£82, 40 hours), six via Coimbra to Lisbon (UK£82, 42 hours) and three via Évora and Faro to Lagos (UK£83, 45 hours).

Continental Europe

France Eurolines offers connections from Paris to all over Portugal, including six services per week to Porto (€88 one way, 25 hours), daily to Lisbon (€84, 26 hours) and three per week to Faro (€91, 29 hours). Hefty surcharges apply to one-way or return tickets for most departures from July to mid-August (€25) and also on Saturday year-round (€8).

Buses of the Spanish operator IASA (Interacesa SA) depart Tuesday, Thursday and Saturday on four separate routes: Paris–Viana do Castelo–Vila do Conde; Paris–Guimarães–Braga; Paris–Guarda–Porto; and Paris–Coimbra–Lisbon. One-way/return fares from Paris range from €64/110 to €78/140, with discounts of 50% for travellers aged four to 12, and 10% for those under 26 or aged at least 60. IASA offices include:

Paris (☎ 01 43 53 90 82, fax 01 43 53 49 57)
170 rue de Paris, 94220 Charenton le Pont
Porto (☎/fax 225 373 205) Centro Comercial
Central Shopping, Rua Santos Pousada 200
Lisbon (☎ 213 143 979, fax 213 143 980)
Centro Comercial Imaviz, Ave Fontes Pereira
Melo 35

Buses of both Eurolines and IASA also stop at intermediate French, Spanish and/or Portuguese cities.

Spain UK–Portugal and France–Portugal Eurolines and IASA services (see the earlier UK and France sections) cross to Portugal via northwest Spain, and can be boarded at a number of Spanish towns. Sample fares to Lisbon include €41 from Burgos, €35 from Valladolid and €30 from Salamanca.

From Madrid, Eurolines/Internorte runs daily via Guarda to Porto (€35 one way, 8½ hours) and also via Badajoz and Évora to Lisbon (€37, eight hours); twice weekly the Lisbon service starts from Barcelona (€61, 18 hours). The Spanish lines **AutoRes** (☎ 902 02 09 99; **w** www.auto-res.net) and Eurolines affiliate **Alsa** (☎ 902 42 22 42; **w** www.alsa .es) each have twice-daily Madrid–Lisbon services.

From Seville, Alsa/Eurolines goes five to six times weekly via Badajoz and Évora to Lisbon (€32, seven hours). Twice weekly the service to Lisbon starts from Granada (€32, 11 hours); there are also connections at Seville on the service from Málaga via the Costa del Sol.

The Portuguese carrier **Eva** (Lisbon ☎ 213 147 710, Faro ☎ 289 899 700; **w** www.eva-bus .com) and the Spanish line **Damas** (☎ 95 925 69 00; **w** www.damas-sa.es) operate a joint service three times weekly from Seville via Serpa and Beja to Lisbon (€29, 4½ hours); additional daily connections are possible with a change at the border town of Ficalho, though it will then take you about 10 hours.

The Spanish line **Agobe** (☎ 902 154 568; **w** www.agobe.es) runs three times weekly from Granada via Seville to Albufeira and Lisbon (€51, 14½ hours), continuing once a week to Coimbra and Porto.

Intersul (☎ 289 899 770, fax 289 899 759; Terminal Rodoviário, Avenida da República, Faro) runs from Seville through the Algarve to Lagos (€13, 5¼ hours) four to six times weekly from April to October. Eva and Damas have a joint, twice-daily service from Seville via Huelva to Faro (€10.50, four to five hours), Albufeira and Lagos (€15, 4½ hours).

Elsewhere in Continental Europe Eurolines has services to Portugal from across Europe, typically about twice a week. At the time of writing, sample one-way fares from Hamburg were €133 to Porto, €140 to Lisbon and €158 to Faro; fares from more southerly cities in Germany were up to 15% lower. Sample fares from Amsterdam or Brussels were €117 to Porto and €123 to Lisbon or Faro.

TRAIN

Trains are a popular way to get around Europe – comfortable, frequent and generally on time – and they're good places to meet other travellers. But unless you have a rail pass (see Rail Passes) or a senior rail card (see Money in the Facts for the Visitor chapter) the cost can be higher than flying.

There are two standard long-distance rail journeys into Portugal. Both take the *TGV Atlantique* from Paris to Irún (in Spain), where you must change trains. From there the *Sud-Expresso* crosses into Portugal at Vilar Formoso (Fuentes de Oñoro in Spain), continuing to Coimbra and Lisbon; change at Pampilhosa for Porto. The other journey runs from Irún to Madrid, with a change to the *Talgo Lusitânia*, crossing into Portugal at Marvão-Beirã and on to Lisbon. For trips to the south of Portugal, change at Lisbon (see Getting There & Away in the Lisbon chapter for details). To reach Portugal from elsewhere in Europe you must go via Paris.

Two other important Spain-Portugal crossings are at Valença do Minho and at Caia (Caya in Spain), near Elvas.

You'll have few problems buying long-distance tickets as little as a day or two ahead, even in summer. Paris, Amsterdam, Munich and Vienna are major Western European rail hubs.

For those intending to do a lot of European rail travel, the exhaustive *Thomas Cook European Timetable* is updated monthly and includes all you need to know about reservations and supplements. Single issues are available from **Thomas Cook Publishing** (UK ☎ 01733-416477; **w** www.thomasco oktimetables.com) costing UK£9.50 online or costing UK£11/13/14.50 by post from the UK/Europe/elsewhere.

Rail Passes

The following passes are available through Rail Europe and other travel agencies (see the following country sections for contact details). Note that even with a pass you must still pay for seat and couchette reservations and express-train supplements.

The **Inter-Rail Pass** divides Europe into zones (zone F is Spain, Portugal and Morocco). One-zone passes are good for 12 or 22 consecutive days; the 2nd-class adult/under-26 price is €248/169 for 12 days or €300/206 for 22 days. Better-value multi-zone passes, good for a month, range from €386/274 for two zones to €518/365 for all eight. The **EuroDomino Pass** is good for a number of consecutive days within a specified month, in a specified country. For 2nd-class travel in Portugal the cost is from €80/40 for three days to €110/86 for eight days. Both passes are available to anyone resident in Europe for six months before starting their travels. You cannot use either one in your home country.

The Eurail pass and the Europass (both for non-European residents) are meant to be purchased from your home country but are available at some European locations if your passport shows you've been in Europe for under six months. The **Eurail pass** is valid for unlimited travel (1st/2nd class for those over/under 26) in 17 European countries, including Portugal. It's good for 15 days (US$572/401) to up to three months (US$1606/1126); various 'flexi' versions allow a chosen number of travel days per longer period. The **Europass** provides unlimited 1st-class travel in France, Germany, Italy, Spain and Switzerland, with the option of adding other countries, for a specified number of days within a two-month period. With Portugal, it costs from US$422/296 for five days to US$772/540 for 15 days. For details on both of these passes see **w** www.eurail.com.

The **Iberic Rail Pass**, available only to non-European residents, is good for a specified period of 1st-class travel in Spain and Portugal during a two-month period, from three days (€205) to 10 days (€520). It's sold by travel agencies outside Europe, in Spain at offices of the state railway company

Renfe (**w** www.renfe.es) and at stations in Madrid, Barcelona, Valencia and Seville, but not in Portugal.

Dangers & Annoyances

International trains are a favourite target for thieves, so always carry your valuables with you, keep your bags in sight (or at least chained to the luggage rack) and make sure your compartment is securely locked at night. The occasional bent ticket collector may falsely claim your rail pass doesn't cover a transit country (moral: know what your pass covers).

The UK

The fastest and most convenient route to Portugal is with Eurostar from London Waterloo to Paris via the Channel Tunnel, and then onward by *TGV* (see under France). A 2nd-class London–Lisbon adult (Apex)/under-26 return fare is UK£227/223, including *TGV* supplements, and the journey takes about 25 hours. The overnight Irún–Lisbon section costs about UK£14 more for a couchette in a six-person sleeper. Tickets are available from travel agencies, larger main-line stations or **Rail Europe** (**☎** 08705-848848; **w** www.raileurope.co.uk; 179 Piccadilly, London).

The 'rail-sea-rail' alternative – by train from Charing Cross, across the Channel by ferry or SeaCat and on to Paris by train – will save you UK£20 but takes about six hours longer and involves a change of stations in Paris.

Continental Europe

France The daily train journey from Paris (Gare d'Austerlitz) to Lisbon takes about 20 hours. A 2nd-class adult (Apex)/under-26 ticket costs as little as €95/92 return, plus €9 for a couchette in a six-berth compartment on the overnight Irún-Lisbon section. You can book directly with **SNCF** (French Railways; **☎** 08 36 35 35 35; **w** www.sncf.com).

Spain The daily Paris–Lisbon train (see the France and UK sections) goes via Vitória, Burgos, Valladolid and Salamanca, entering Portugal at Vila Formoso. A 2nd-class one-way reserved seat from Salamanca to Lisbon costs €33.40; a couchette in a six-person sleeper costs €43.80.

The main Spain–Portugal rail route is from Madrid to Lisbon via Cáceres and the border station of Marvão-Beirã. The nightly journey on the *Talgo Lusitânia* takes 10½ hours. A 2nd-class one-way reserved seat costs €47.50; add on €67 for a berth in a four-person compartment or €86.50 in a two-person compartment.

You can get from Seville to Lisbon (€44, about 16 hours), with a change of trains and four- or five-hour night-time layover, at Cáceres.

The Badajoz–Caia–Elvas–Lisbon route (€10.20, five hours), with two regional trains a day with a change at Entroncamento, is tedious, though the scenery through the Serra de Marvão is grand. The only Seville–Badajoz connections are by bus (see the Bus section, earlier).

In the south, trains run west from Seville only as far as Huelva. For destinations in the Algarve you must then take a bus to Ayamonte and either a bus or a ferry across the border to Vila Real de Santo António, where there are frequent onward train connections to Faro and Lagos. You're better off on a long-distance bus (see Spain in the Bus section).

USA & Canada
Those who want to book a European rail journey before they leave home can do so with **Rail Europe** (*USA* ☎ *1 800 4 EURAIL, Canada* ☎ *1 800 361 RAIL;* W *www.raileurope.com*).

CAR & MOTORCYCLE
Of over 30 roads crossing the Portugal-Spain border, the best and biggest do so near Valença do Minho (E1/A3), Chaves (N532), Bragança (E82/IP4), Guarda/Vilar Formoso (E80/IP5), Elvas (E90/A6/IP7), Serpa (N260) and Vila Real de Santo António (E1/IP1). There are no longer any border controls.

Insurance & Documents
If you're driving your own car or motorcycle into Portugal, in addition to a passport and driving licence (see Visas & Documents in the Facts for the Visitor chapter) you'll need vehicle registration (proof of ownership) and insurance documents. If these are in order you should be able to keep the vehicle in Portugal for up to six months.

Any driver other than the registered owner needs written authorisation from the owner. For guidance on preparing and validating such a document, contact your national automobile licensing department or auto club, or the nearest Portuguese consular office.

Motor vehicle insurance with at least third-party cover is compulsory throughout the European Union (EU). Your home policy may or may not be extendable to Portugal, and the coverage of some comprehensive policies automatically drops to third-party-only outside the home country unless the insurer is notified. Though not a legal requirement, it's wise to carry written confirmation from your home insurer that you have the correct coverage.

Carry these documents whenever you're driving. If you hire a car, the rental firm will furnish you with registration and insurance papers, plus a rental contract.

The UK
The quickest automobile route from the UK to Portugal is by car-ferry to northern Spain with **P&O Portsmouth** (☎ *0870-242 4999;* W *www.poportsmouth.com*) from Portsmouth to Bilbao (29 to 35 hours, twice weekly mid-March to mid-December) or **Brittany Ferries** (☎ *0870-366 5333;* W *www.brittany-ferries .com*) from Plymouth to Santander (24 hours, twice weekly from April to September, once weekly October to mid-November). From Bilbao or Santander it's roughly 1000km to Lisbon, 800km to Porto or 1300km to Faro.

Fares are wildly seasonal. A standard weekday, high-season, return ticket for a car/motorcycle with driver and one passenger (with cabin accommodation) starts at about UK£700/450, but with advance planning and flexibility on dates you can beat this with special offers at all but the busiest times.

An alternative is to catch a ferry across the Channel (or Eurotunnel vehicle train beneath it) to France and motor down the coast. From France's channel ports it is approximately 1900km to Lisbon, 1800km to Porto or 2200km to Faro.

BICYCLE
Bicycles can travel by air. You can take yours to pieces and put it in a bag or box, though it's much easier to simply wheel it to the check-in desk, where it should be treated as baggage. But check this with the airline well in advance. Let much (but not all) of the air out of the tyres to prevent

Any Distinguishing Marks?

As with cars, it's a good idea to pack some sort of document showing you to be the owner of your bicycle, in the unlikely event that the police stop you. Some cyclists also carry photographs and written descriptions of their bicycles, to assist the police if their bike is stolen.

them from bursting in the low-pressure baggage hold.

If you're getting to Portugal by train, you can box your bike up and take it as accompanied baggage, or send it separately as cargo. Bikes are not allowed as baggage on either Eurolines or Busabout buses.

Before you leave home, fill your bicycle repair kit with every imaginable spare. You probably won't be able to buy that crucial widget if your machine breaks down in the back of beyond.

For information on cycling in Portugal, see the Bicycle section in the Getting Around chapter, and Activities in the Facts for the Visitor chapter.

SEA

There are no scheduled seagoing ferries to Portugal, but many to Spain. For details on those from the UK to Spain, see the earlier Car & Motorcycle section.

The closest North African ferry connections are from Morocco to Spain. **Transmediterranea** (**w** www.trasmediterranea.net) and **EuroFerrys** (**w** www.euroferrys.com) have daily ferries and hydrofoils from Tangier to Algeciras. **FerriMaroc** (**w** www.ferrimaroc.com) and **Limadet** (**w** www.limadet-ferry.com) sail daily between Nador and Almería. Additional services run via the Spanish enclaves of Ceuta and Melilla. There are also twice-weekly car-ferries from Tangier to Gibraltar.

For details on car-ferries across the Rio Guadiana from Spain, see under Vila Real de Santo António in the Algarve chapter.

ORGANISED TOURS

There are plenty of reliable tour operators offering special-interest or made-to-order tours to Portugal. A good listing of the UK's most interesting specialist operators is in the free *AITO Directory of Real Holidays*, an annual index of members of the Association of Independent Tour Operators. It's available from **AITO** (**☎** 020-8744 9280; **w** www.aito.co.uk). UK, France and other offices of ICEP, the Portuguese state tourism organisation (see Tourist Offices in the Facts for the Visitor chapter), publish their own directories of tour operators.

Locally run adventure holidays and tours are noted under Activities in the Facts for the Visitor chapter, with operators identified under individual town listings. For domestic bus and train tours, see Organised Tours in the Getting Around chapter.

Walking Tours

UK-based **ATG Oxford** (**☎** 01865-315678; **w** www.atg-oxford.co.uk) has informative, guided walking tours with vehicle support and comfortable local-style accommodation, in the Minho, Sintra area and Alentejo. **Ramblers Holidays** (**☎** 01707-331133; **w** www.ramblersholidays.co.uk) arranges walking holidays in northern Portugal, the Douro valley, Lisbon, the Alentejo and the Algarve.

For fit, map-savvy hikers **Sherpa Expeditions** (**☎** 020-8577 2717; **w** www.sherpa-walking-holidays.co.uk) has good self-guided walks in the Parque Nacional da Peneda-Gerês, complete with route notes, maps and baggage transfer. **Headwater** (**☎** 01606-813333; **w** www.headwater.com) has week-long jaunts in the Serra da Estrela in summer and the 'hidden Algarve' in winter, plus self-guided tours in the Alentejo.

Gentle rambles in the Douro valley with a wine and gourmet-dining angle are a speciality of **Winetrails** (**☎** 01306-712111; **w** www.winetrails.co.uk).

Another agency with Portugal itineraries is **Explore Worldwide** (**☎** 01252-760000; **w** www.exploreworldwide.com).

Cycling Tours

CTC (*Cyclists' Touring Club;* **☎** 0870-873 0060; **w** www.ctc.org.uk) is the UK's biggest cycling organisation. Portugal is a frequent venue for good-value, not-for-profit tours run by and for members. These, and many commercial bike-holiday outfits, are listed in CTC's *Cycle Holiday Guide* magazine. For more on CTC, see the Getting Around chapter.

Skedaddle (**☎** 0191-265 1110; **w** www.skedaddle.co.uk) has eight-day tours through amazingly isolated countryside and wilderness close to the Spanish border. **Rough Tracks** (☎ 07000 560749; w www.roughtracks .com) offers one-week mountain biking tours in the Minho and road tours from Lisbon to Faro. **Headwater** (see Walking Tours) offers independent cycling holidays in the Alentejo.

In the USA, **Easy Rider Tours** (☎ 978-463 6955, toll-free ☎ 1 800 488 8332; w www .easyridertours.com) has an impressive menu of small-group cycling and walking itineraries – each with one North American and one Portuguese guide – covering the Minho, Alentejo and southwest coast. Loosely structured guided tours by **Blue Marble Travel** (☎ 973-326 9533; w www .bluemarble.org) include a four-week Trans-Iberian tour and shorter trips around Spain and Portugal.

Other Specialist Tours

Cultural specialist **Martin Randall Travel** (☎ 020-8742 3355; w www.martinrandall .com) arranges first-rate escorted art and architecture tours.

BTCV (☎ 01491-821600; w www.btcv.org) is a charity offering volunteers the chance to participate in conservation projects around the world. A recent 'holiday' in Portugal involved 10 days of work in the Parque Natural do Alvão.

Arblaster & Clarke (☎ 01730-893344; w www.arblasterandclarke.com) and **Winetrails** (☎ 01306-712111; w www.winetrails .co.uk) offer wine tours in the Douro valley.

Naturetrek (☎ 01962-733051; w www.na turetrek.co.uk), a specialist in bird-watching and botanical tours, runs an eight-day excursion around southern Portugal. For a weeklong natural history tour of the Algarve, contact **The Travel Club of Upminster** (☎ 01708 224000; w www.travelclub.org.uk).

Is walking too slow for you? **LPG** (☎ 0800-0186101; w www.leisurepursuits.com) will take you running, with spring training or resort facilities in the Algarve, or to the Lisbon half-marathon.

For riding holidays contact **Equitour** (☎ 01865-511642; w www.equitour.com) or

Inntravel (☎ 01653-629010; w www.inntravel .co.uk).

3D Golf (☎ 0870-120 0300; w www.3dgolf .com) and **Longshot Golf Holidays** (☎ 01730-268621; w www.longshotgolf.co.uk) offer golfing packages in the Algarve and the Estoril coast. The website **Golf in Europe** (w www.ecs.net/golf/) features clubs in, and golf tours to, Portugal.

Finally, if you would like to try thalassotherapy in the Algarve, watch a Benfica football match or learn salsa dancing at Estoril, contact **Unmissable.com** (☎ 0870-442 1350; w www.unmissable.com), which specialises in unique events, activities and destinations.

Do-it-Yourself Holidays

If you prefer to assemble your own holiday, Portugal specialist **Destination Portugal** (☎ 01993-773269; w www.destination-por tugal.co.uk) will tell you all you need to know and can help with flights, car-hire and accommodation, separately or together.

Fancy chilling out in a restored castle, manor house or rural farmhouse? UK agencies who can set it up, typically as part of a fly-drive package, include **Individual Travellers Portugal** (☎ 0870-077 3773; w www .indiv-travellers.com), **Simply Portugal** (☎ 020-8541 2207; w www.simply-travel.com) and **Vintage Travel** (☎ 01954-261431; w www .vintagetravel.co.uk). For more on these options, see Accommodation in the Facts for the Visitor chapter.

There are scores more flight and accommodation packages on offer, particularly to the Algarve; outside the high season, this can actually be the cheapest way to get there. Other agencies that have Portugal experience include **Magic of Portugal** (☎ 0870-027 0480; w www.magicofportugal.co.uk), **Portuguese Affair** (☎ 020-7385 4775; w www .portugueseaffair.com) and **Travellers' Way** (☎ 01527-559000; w www.travellersway .co.uk).

For details of several tour operators that have kids' clubs at their Algarve resorts, see Travel with Children in the Facts for the Visitor chapter.

Getting Around

AIR

Domestic Air Services

Flights within mainland Portugal are expensive. For the short distances involved they're hardly worth considering, though an under-26 card will save you 5% with **PGA Portugália Airlines** *(Lisbon ☎ 218 425 559;* **w** *www.pga.pt)*, the country's main domestic carrier.

Portugália and **TAP Air Portugal** *(☎ 808 205 700;* **w** *www.tap.pt)* both have multiple daily Lisbon–Porto and Lisbon–Faro flights (taking under one hour) year-round. From July to September Portugália flies on Friday from Porto to Faro (but not directly back). A high-season one-way fare (including taxes) with Portugália costs €102 for the Lisbon–Porto or Lisbon–Faro routes, and €145 for Porto–Faro. There are no discounts on return tickets.

Domestic Departure Tax

The tax is about €6, and is invariably included in the ticket price.

BUS

A host of small private bus operators, most of them amalgamated into regional companies,

> **Timetable Gobbledegook**
>
> One thing sure to drive bus and train travellers up the wall is timetables *(horários)*. Schedules change frequently (between school term and summer holidays, between summer and winter), and may be conditional on religious celebrations. They often differ for each day of the week (workday, market day, Tuesday after a holiday, school days that aren't a Saturday etc). While non-Portuguese speakers will have little trouble with the schedules themselves, the footnotes – which reveal whether a bus actually departs when the schedule says it does – can be baffling.
>
> Following are some common footnote phrases. For the names of months and the days of the week, see the Language chapter at the back of this guide. Weekday names are based on the numbers one to seven; thus 2as. Feiras *(segundas feiras)* means Mondays, and so on.

a partir de ...	beginning on ...
aos (Sábados)	on (Saturdays)
chegada	arrival
de (segunda) a (sexta)	from (Monday) to (Friday)
diariamente, diário or *todos os dias*	daily
dias úteis	working days
efectua(m)-se or *em vigôr*	effective, in force
excepto or *exc* or *não se efectua(m)*	except
feriados nacionais/oficiais	national holidays
ligação de/para ...	connection from/to ...
no período de aulas/escolas or *nos dias escolares*	during school term (early September to late June except around Easter and Christmas)
partida	departure
se a dia fôr feriado or *se feriado*	if it is a holiday
se a dia seguinte a feriado	if it follows a holiday
se vespera de feriado	if it precedes a holiday
só	only

> Now you can work out that *de 16 Set a 30 Jun, aos Sábados (ou 6as. feiras se feriado) e 2as. feiras (ou 3as. feiras se dia seguinte a feriado)* means 'from 16 September to 30 June, on Saturday (or Friday if the Friday is a holiday) and Monday (or Tuesday if the Tuesday follows a holiday)'!
>
> Incidentally, timetables are a rare commodity in rural areas; stock up on information at turismos or bus and train stations in major towns.

Take the Slow Bus to...

If you're planning a quick trip anywhere, avoid buses marked *carreiras* (or CR for short). Never mind that *carreiras* means something like 'in a hurry' in Portuguese – these are the slowest of slow local buses, stopping everywhere.

operate a dense network of services across the country. Included among the largest companies are **Rede Expressos** *(information ☎ 707 223 344; timetables* W *rede-expressos .pt)*, **Renex** and the Algarve line **Eva** *(*W *www .eva-bus.com)*.

Bus services are of three general types: *expressos* are comfortable, fast, direct buses between major cities, *rápidas* are fast regional buses, and *carreiras* stop at every crossroad. Eva also offers a fast deluxe category called *alta qualidade*.

Expressos are generally the best cheap way to get around (particularly for long trips, where per-kilometre costs are lowest), and even in summer you'll have little problem booking a ticket for the same or next day. A Lisbon–Faro express bus takes four to five hours and costs €13.50; Lisbon–Porto takes 3½ hours for €12.50. By contrast, local services, especially up north, can thin out to almost nothing on weekends, especially in summer when school is out.

An under-26 card should get you a discount of around 20%, at least on the long-distance services. Senior travellers can often get up to 50% off.

Don't rely on *turismos* (tourist offices) for accurate timetable information. Given your origin and destination, most bus-station ticket desks will give you a little computer printout of fares and all services. If you're counting your euros, be sure to ask about cheaper local services too.

TRAIN

If you can match your itinerary and pace to a regional service, travelling with Caminhos de Ferro Portugueses (CP), the state railway company, is cheaper than going by bus, thanks in part to state subsidies. Trains are generally slower than long-distance buses, though railway lovers consider this a plus.

The 'Portugal's Railways' map shows the extent of the network. Until main-line tracks are completed to Pinhal Novo (by 2004, say optimists) there is no direct rail link from Lisbon to the south of Portugal; for that you must first take a ferry across the Rio Tejo to Barreiro (see the Lisbon chapter for details).

Train Passes

The Portuguese Railpass (US$105) gives you unlimited 1st-class travel on any four days out of 15. This is only available to travellers from outside Europe, and must be purchased before you arrive; eg, contact **Rail Europe** (W *www.raileurope.com)*. For information on other rail passes, see the Train section in the Getting There & Away chapter.

Types & Classes of Service

There are three main types of long-distance service: *regional* trains (marked R on timetables), which stop everywhere; reasonably fast *interregional* (IR) trains; and express trains, called *rápido* or *intercidade* (IC). *Alfa Pendular* is a deluxe, marginally faster and considerably pricier IC service on the Lisbon–Coimbra–Porto main line. International services are marked IN on timetables.

Lisbon and Porto have their own *suburbano* (suburban; 'soo-boor-**bah**-noo') networks, with separate price structures. Lisbon's network extends predictably to Sintra, Cascais, Setúbal and up the lower Tejo Valley. Porto's network – now undergoing major reconstruction – takes the definition of 'suburban' to new lengths, running all the way to Braga, Guimarães and Aveiro. There are also *suburbano* services

Narrow-Gauge Railways

Three of Portugal's most appealing old railway lines, on narrow-gauge track climbing out of the Douro Valley, survive in truncated form: the Linha da Tâmega from Livração to Amarante (originally to Mondim de Basto), the Linha da Corgo from Peso da Régua to Vila Real (originally to Chaves) and the beautiful Linha da Tua from Tua to Mirandela (originally to Bragança).

For details on riding these lines, see under Amarante, Peso da Régua and Tua in the Douro chapter, or Vila Real and Mirandela in the Trás-os-Montes chapter.

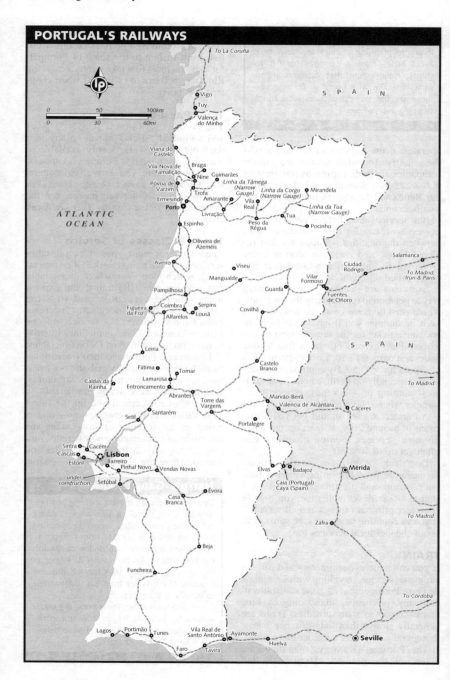

PORTUGAL'S RAILWAYS

between Coimbra and Figueira da Foz. The distinction matters where long-distance services parallel the more convenient, plentiful – and considerably cheaper – *suburbanos*.

Most trains have both 1st- and 2nd-class carriages. R, IR and IC fares go strictly by distance, from €8 per 100km for short trips to about €2.40 per 100km for the longest ones (2nd class). Return tickets for journeys over 50km one way are discounted by 10%. Sample 2nd-class one-way IC/IR fares include €14.10/11 for Lisbon–Porto and €11.30/10.20 for Lisbon–Faro.

Only the weekend Faro–Porto *Comboio Azul* and the international *Sud-Expresso* and *Talgo Lusitânia* have restaurant cars on board, though all IC and *Alfa* trains have aisle service and most have bars. There's a nonsmoking section (though probably not an entire car) somewhere on every CP train. Only Lisbon and Porto stations have left-luggage offices.

Information & Reservations
Timetable and fare information is available at all stations and from **CP** *(national ☎ 808 208 208, 7am-11pm daily; **w** www.cp.pt)*. Tickets can only be purchased from the departure station or from travel agencies; discounted and other special tickets can be purchased only at certain main-line stations.

You can book IC and *Alfa* tickets up to 30 days ahead, though you'll have little problem booking for the next or even the same day. Other services can only be booked 24 hours in advance. A seat reservation is mandatory on most IC and *Alfa* trains and the booking fee is included in the ticket price. There's no need to buy domestic tickets before you arrive in Portugal.

Serious rail-riders may want to buy the *Guia Horário Oficial* (€2.50), CP's complete domestic and international timetables, available from ticket windows at major stations.

Discounts
Children under four years travel free; those aged four to 12 go for half-price. A Euro<26 card gets you a 30% discount on R and IR services on any day, and on IC services from Monday noon to Friday noon. Travellers aged 65 and over can get 50% off any service by showing some identification with a birth date. For information on other discounts, see Money in the Facts for the Visitor chapter.

Special CP *bilhetes turísticos* (tourist tickets), valid for unlimited travel during seven/14/21 consecutive days, cost €100/170/250 (half-price for those aged under 12, or 65 and over), though they're only worthwhile if you plan to spend a great deal of time on trains. They're on sale at major stations.

CAR & MOTORCYCLE
Thanks to European Union (EU) subsidies, Portugal's modest network of *estradas* (highways) is gradually spreading across the country. Main roads are sealed and generally in good condition. Minor roads in the countryside get better every year, and often have surprisingly little traffic.

The downside is your road mates. A leading Swedish road-safety investigator was quoted as saying the Portuguese 'drive like car thieves'. The country's annual per capita death rate from road accidents is Europe's highest – twice the EU average – which means visitors need to drive defensively.

A 'zero-tolerance' police crackdown – with heavy patrols, strict speed limits and headlights-on driving – has failed to dent accident rates on several accident-prone routes: the IC2/N1 from Porto to Coimbra; the IP5 across the Beiras from the IC2 to the Spanish border; the N11 loop east of Lisbon; and the Via do Infante (N125) across the Algarve.

City driving can be nightmarish, not least in Portugal's small walled towns, where roads may taper down to donkey-cart size before you know it. Fiendish one-way systems – arguably the only way for towns to cope with cars in their narrow lanes – can force you far out of your way. Parking is often metered within city centres (€0.25 to €0.50 per hour, but free on Saturday afternoon and Sunday).

For information on what to bring in the way of documents, see Car & Motorcycle in the Getting There & Away chapter.

Highways & Toll-Roads
Top of the range are *auto-estradas* (motorways), all of them *portagens* (toll-roads), the longest of these is Lisbon–Porto (304km) and Lisbon–Algarve (235km). The present total of 1136km of toll-roads charges cars and motorcycles around €0.05 per kilometre (eg, total €15.80 for Lisbon–

Porto). At the time of writing, the government was floating the idea of converting additional motorways to toll-roads – to almost unanimous disapproval.

Nomenclature can be baffling. Motorway numbers prefixed with an E are Europewide designations. Portugal's toll-roads are prefixed with an A. Highways in the country's main network are prefixed IP *(itinerário principal)* and subsidiary ones IC *(itinerário complementar)*. Some highways have several designations, and numbers that change in mid-flow: eg, the Lisbon–Porto road is variously called E80, E1, A1 and IP1.

Numbers for the main two-lane *estradas nacionais* (national roads) have no prefix letter on some road maps (such as the one published by the Automóvel Club de Portugal), while on other maps, including the Michelin No 940; they're prefixed by N. We use the N prefix in this book.

N roads look appealing on a map but are often choked with truck traffic on weekdays. If you want to get off the big roads, consider going for the really small ones, which can be faster than some N roads and tend to be prettier and more peaceful.

Assistance

Automóvel Club de Portugal *(ACP; head office ☎ 213 180 100;* w *www.acp.pt; Rua Rosa Araújo 24, Lisbon)*, Portugal's national auto club, provides medical, legal and breakdown assistance for its members. Road information and maps are available to anyone at ACP offices, including the head office in Lisbon and branches at Aveiro, Braga, Bragança, Coimbra, Évora, Faro, Porto, Vila Real and elsewhere.

If your national auto club belongs to the Fédération Internationale de l'Automobile or the Alliance de Tourisme, you can also use ACP's emergency services and get discounts on maps and other products. Among clubs that qualify are the AA and RAC in the UK, and the Australian, New Zealand, Canadian and American Automobile Associations.

ACP emergency help numbers are ☎ 219 429 103 (Lisbon) for southern Portugal, and ☎ 228 340 001 (Porto) for northern Portugal.

Road Rules

You may not believe it after seeing what Portuguese drivers do, but there are rules. To begin with, driving is on the right, overtaking

Road Distances (km)

	Aveiro	Beja	Braga	Bragança	Castelo Branco	Coimbra	Évora	Faro	Guarda	Leiria	Lisbon	Portalegre	Porto	Santarém	Setúbal	Viana do Castelo	Vila Real	Viseu
Aveiro	---																	
Beja	383	---																
Braga	129	504	---															
Bragança	287	566	185	---														
Castelo Branco	239	271	366	299	---													
Coimbra	60	329	178	314	191	---												
Évora	305	78	426	488	191	251	---											
Faro	522	166	643	732	437	468	244	---										
Guarda	163	369	260	197	102	161	291	535	---									
Leiria	126	273	244	402	179	72	195	412	233	---								
Lisbon	256	183	372	530	264	202	138	296	402	146	---							
Portalegre	276	178	403	390	93	222	100	344	193	172	219	---						
Porto	71	446	58	216	308	123	368	585	202	189	317	339	---					
Santarém	188	195	309	464	181	134	117	346	295	78	80	147	251	---				
Setúbal	299	143	420	575	316	246	105	256	406	189	47	186	362	123	---			
Viana do Castelo	144	519	56	241	382	191	441	658	275	262	387	412	73	324	435	---		
Vila Real	169	528	94	120	261	199	450	683	159	282	412	352	98	349	460	150	---	
Viseu	86	415	185	228	177	86	366	554	75	158	288	268	127	220	331	241	113	

Need Any Help With Your Car?

A common sight in larger towns is the down-and-outers who lurk around squares and car parks, wave you into the parking space you've just found for yourself, and ask for payment for this 'service'. Polite Portuguese call them *arrumadores* (arrangers). Of course it's a racket and of course there's no need to give them anything, but the Portuguese often do, and €0.20 or €0.50 might keep your car out of trouble.

is on the left and most signs use international symbols, as in the rest of continental Europe.

An important rule to remember is that traffic from the right usually has priority. Portugal has lots of nonright-angle, ambiguously marked intersections, so this is more important than you might think.

Except when marked otherwise, speed limits for cars (without a trailer) and motorcycles (without a sidecar) are 50km/h in towns and villages, 90km/h outside such built-up areas and 120km/h on motorways. If you've held your driving licence for less than a year, you're restricted to 90km/h even on motorways and your vehicle must display a '90' disk, available from any ACP office. Oncoming drivers who flash their lights at you are probably indicating that there are police ahead, and that you'd better watch your speed.

By law, car safety belts must be worn in the front and back seats, and children under 12 years may not ride in the front. Motorcyclists and their passengers must wear helmets, and motorcycles must have their headlights on day and night.

The police can impose on-the-spot fines for speeding and parking offences (though they must issue receipts for them). Typical parking fines are about €25. The police can be unpleasant to deal with in these circumstances, so save yourself the hassle and toe the line.

Accidents

If you are involved in a minor 'fender-bender' with no injuries, the easiest way for drivers to sort things out with their insurance companies is to fill out a Constat Aimable (the English version is called a European Accident Statement). There's no risk in signing this: it's just a way to exchange the relevant information; there's usually one included in rental-car documents. Make sure it includes any details that may help you prove that the accident was not your fault.

To alert the police, dial ☎ 112.

Fuel

Fuel is expensive – about €0.90 for a litre of 95-octane *sem chumbo* (unleaded petrol) and €0.65 for *gasóleo* (diesel) at the time of writing. Unleaded petrol is readily available and there are plenty of self-service stations. Major credit cards are accepted at many, but not all, stations.

Motorail

CP, the state railway company, offers car transport by rail with certain services on the Lisbon–Porto, Lisbon–Guarda, Lisbon–Castelo Branco and Porto–Faro lines. Reduced fares apply if more than one person travels with the car, except on the Porto–Faro *Comboio Azul* train. For details contact CP (ⓦ www.cp.pt).

Rental

To rent a car in Portugal you must be at least 25 years old and have held your driving licence for over a year (some companies allow younger drivers, at higher rates).

There are dozens of firms in the country, from international outfits such as Avis, Hertz, Budget, Europcar and National/

Drinking, Driving & Dying in Portugal

In the weeks following the October 2001 passage of a law dropping the legal blood-alcohol level to just 0.2g/L – equivalent to a single glass of wine – both road deaths and wine sales are said to have fallen by 30%. But the law was suspended two months later following intense pressure from – you guessed it – Portugal's wine producers.

Even the present limit of 0.5g/L is pretty stringent. If you drink and drive and are caught, you can expect to spend the night in a lockup, and the next morning in a courtroom.

Alamo to modest local ones. The widest choice is at Lisbon, Porto and Faro airports. Competition has driven Algarve rates lower than elsewhere.

Some of the best advance-booking rates are offered by Internet-based brokers such as **Autos Abroad** (Hire for Lower; **w** www.autos abroad.com) and **Holiday Autos** (**w** www.holi dayautos.com). Other bargains come as part of 'fly-drive' packages. The worst deals tend to be those done with international firms on arrival, though their prepaid promotional rates are competitive. Book at least a few days ahead in high season. For on-the-spot rental, domestic firms such as **Auto Jardim** (☎ 800 200 613; **w** www.auto-jar dim.com) have the best rates.

Renting the smallest available car for a week in the high season costs as little as UK£130 or €200 (with tax, insurance and unlimited mileage) if booked from the UK, and a similar amount through a Portuguese firm, but can cost up to €300 from the Portuguese branch of an international firm.

For an additional fee you can get personal insurance through the rental company, unless you're covered by your home policy (see Insurance & Documents in the Car & Motorcycle section in the Getting There & Away chapter). A minimum of third-party coverage is compulsory throughout the EU.

Rental cars are especially at risk of break-ins or petty theft in larger towns, so don't leave anything of value visible in the car. If you can unscrew the radio antenna, leave it inside the car at night; and put the wheel covers (hubcaps) in the boot (trunk) for the duration of your trip. Hatchbacks are favourite targets as their boots are easy to enter through the back seat.

Motorcycles and scooters can be rented in larger cities, and all over coastal Algarve. Typical summertime charges for one/three days start at about €30/60 for a scooter or €50/100 for a motorbike.

BICYCLE

Mountain biking is amazingly popular in Portugal, although there are few dedicated bicycle paths (but see Getting Around in the Lisbon chapter about one along the Rio Tejo).

Possible itineraries are numerous, in the mountainous national/natural parks of the north, along the coast or across the Alentejo plains. Coastal trips are easiest from north

to south, with the prevailing winds. Veteran cyclists recommend Parque Nacional da Peneda-Gerês. More demanding is the Serra da Estrela (which serves as the Tour de Portugal's 'mountain run'). Another favourite is the Serra do Marão between Amarante and Vila Real.

Local bike clubs organise regular *Passeio BTT* trips; check their flyers at rental agencies, bike shops and turismos. Guided trips are often available in popular tourist destinations; we note worthy ones in local listings. For jaunts arranged from abroad, see Organised Tours in the Getting There & Away chapter.

Cobbled roads in some old-town centres may jar your teeth loose if your tyres aren't fat enough – at least 38mm in diameter.

Transporting Your Bicycle

Boxed-up or bagged-up bicycles can be taken free on all R and IR trains as accompanied baggage. They can also go, unboxed, on a few suburban services – eg, Lisbon–Sintra on weekends or for €1.50/2.50 one way/return on weekdays outside the rush hour.

Most domestic bus lines won't accept bikes, though Renex will take them, unboxed, if there's space, for an extra €15 to €20. The alternatives are to use a collapsible bike, or to send your machine on ahead as cargo.

Information

For listings of national events and bike shops, purchase a copy of the monthly Portuguese-language *Bike Magazine*, available from many larger newsagents.

For its members, the UK-based **Cyclists' Touring Club** (CTC; ☎ 01483-417217, fax 426994; **w** www.ctc.org.uk) publishes a useful, free information booklet on cycling in Portugal, plus notes for half a dozen routes around the country. CTC also offers tips on bikes, spares, insurance etc, and maps, topoguides and other publications for sale by mail order.

Other useful information on cycling is under Activities in the Facts for the Visitor chapter, and in the Bicycle and Organised Tours sections of the Getting There & Away chapter.

Rental

There are numerous places to rent bikes, especially in the Algarve and other touristy areas. Prices range from €7 to €15 per day. Rental outfits are noted in the text.

HITCHING
Hitching is never entirely safe anywhere, and we don't recommend it. Travellers who hitch should understand that they're taking a small but potentially serious risk. In any case it doesn't look like an easy way to get around Portugal. Almost nobody stops on major highways, and on smaller roads drivers tend to be going short distances. You can meet some pretty interesting characters, but you may only advance from one field to the next!

BOAT
Other than river cruises along the Rio Douro from Porto (see the Douro chapter) and along the Rio Tejo from Lisbon, Portugal's only remaining waterborne transport is cross-river ferries. The longest routes are commuter ferries across the Rio Tejo to/from Lisbon, and across the mouth of the Rio Sado between Setúbal and Tróia (see the Lisbon and Around Lisbon chapters for details).

LOCAL TRANSPORT
Bus
Except in Lisbon or Porto there's little reason to take municipal buses, as most attractions are within walking distance. Most areas have regional bus services, for better or worse (for more on these see the Bus section earlier in this chapter).

Metro
Lisbon's underground system, the metro, was considerably upgraded and expanded in time for Expo 98, and is still growing (see the metro maps in the Lisbon chapter). Porto is now building its own system.

Taxi
Taxis offer good value over short distances, especially for two or more people, and are plentiful in larger towns. Ordinary taxis are usually marked A (for *aluguer*, 'for hire') on the door, number plate or elsewhere. They use meters and are available on the street or at taxi ranks. In many towns you can book a taxi by telephone, for a surcharge of around €0.80; numbers are listed in the Getting Around sections of individual towns.

What's in a Street Name?

Throughout Portugal the same street names keep cropping up. Here's what they're about:

Rua/Avenida

1 de Dezembro	restoration of Portuguese independence following Spanish rule (1640)
5 de Outubro	overthrow of the monarchy and founding of a republic (1910)
25 de Abril	start of the Revolution of the Carnations (1974)
Afonso de Albuquerque	viceroy of India in the early 16th century, expanded Portuguese empire to include Goa, Melaka and Hormoz
Alexandre Herculano	19th-century historian
Alexandre Serpa Pinto	late-19th-century African explorer
Almeida Garrett	19th-century poet, playwright and novelist
Cândido dos Reis	distinguished rear admiral and supporter of the 1910 revolution
da Liberdade	referring to freedoms that followed the 1974 revolution
Egas Moniz	renowned physician and 1949 Nobel Laureate for the 'invention' of lobotomy
Gil Vicente	16th-century court dramatist
João de Deus	19th-century lyric poet
Luís de Camões	Portugal's most famous 16th-century poet
Manuel Cardoso	17th-century composer
Miguel Bombarda	psychiatrist and republican figure whose murder precipitated the 1910 revolution
Pedro Álvares Cabral	'discoverer' of Brazil (1500)
dos Restauradores	restorers of independence after Spanish rule

The fare on weekdays during daylight hours is about €1.80 *bandeirada* (flag fall) plus around €0.40 per kilometre, and a bit more for periods spent idling in traffic. A fare of €2.50 to €3 will usually get you across bigger towns. It's best to insist on the meter, although it's possible to negotiate a flat fare. If you have a sizable load of luggage you'll pay a further €1.50.

Rates are about 20% higher at night (10pm to 6am) and on weekends and holidays. Once a taxi leaves the city limits you also pay a surcharge or higher rate, and usually the cost of a return trip (whether you take it or not).

In larger cities, including Lisbon and Porto, meterless taxis marked T (for *turismo*) can be hired from private companies for excursions. Rates for these are higher, but standardised; drivers are honest and polite, and speak foreign languages.

Other Transport

Enthusiasts for stately progress shouldn't miss the trams of Lisbon and Porto, an endangered species. Also worth trying are the *elevadores* (funiculars and elevators) of Lisbon, Bom Jesus do Monte (Braga), Nazaré, Coimbra and elsewhere.

ORGANISED TOURS

Lisbon-based **Gray Line** (☎ 213 522 594; w www.grayline.com) organises three- to seven-day bus tours to selected regions of Portugal, usually through travel agencies or top-end tourist hotels. The Viana do Castelo bus company **AVIC** (☎ 258 800 364; w www.avic.pt) does full-day tours of the Douro, Minho and Lima valleys. A Porto agency offering Douro valley and Minho day trips is **Diana Tours** (☎ 223 771 230; w www.dianatours.com). **Mega Tur** (☎ 289 807 485; w www.megatur.pt) runs bus tours around the Algarve and further afield, eg, to Lisbon and Seville.

CP, the state railway company, organises weekend day-trips by special train and bus up the Douro valley held during almond-blossom time. For details see the boxed text 'Blossoms by Rail' in the Douro chapter.

Adventure holidays and tours – mountain biking, trekking, jeep tours and so on – are described under Activities in the Facts for the Visitor chapter; see individual towns for details of local Portuguese operators. For adventure and specialist interest tours to Portugal from abroad, see Organised Tours in the Getting There & Away chapter.

Lisbon

postcode central Lisbon 1100 • pop 564,700

Lisbon is an enticing tangle of past and present – funky and old-fashioned, unpretentious and quirky, restored and revitalised, booming with new confidence. Its position on seven low hills beside the Rio Tejo (River Tagus) was the main attraction for traders and settlers in centuries past, and it's still a stunning site. Add today's cultural diversity together with a laid-back ambience and an architectural time-warp, and you have one of Europe's most enjoyable cities. And, despite rising prices, it's still good value for money, cheap enough to remain a base as you explore beyond the city limits.

It's also small and manageable enough to explore on foot, though its muscle-busting hills can defeat the fittest in the heat. Fortunately, the hills are tamed by a bevy of *elevadors* (funiculars) and cranky old trams (don't even think about getting around by car – driving and parking is a nightmare).

At Lisbon's heart are wide, tree-lined avenues graced by Art Nouveau buildings, mosaic pavements and outdoor cafés. The Alfama district below Castelo de São Jorge is a warren of narrow streets redolent of the city's Moorish and medieval past. Seen from the river – one of the city's many great viewpoints – Lisbon appears as an impressionist picture of low-rise ochre and pastel, punctuated by church towers and domes.

But it has also undergone massive redevelopment in recent years. Although the Alfama and Chiado districts have seen some sensitive restoration projects, many fine old buildings have given way to office blocks. Once-sleepy old Lisbon is on a helter-skelter ride to modernisation, thanks to the attention it got as host to the millennium's last exposition, Expo 98, and the flurry of new hotels and infrastructure projects in the run-up to the 2004 European Football Championships. Traditionalists may disapprove, but this is a city on the move.

The resulting contrasts are arresting: in the shadow of glittering high-rises are the occasional seedy backstreets. And despite frenzied traffic, the city's squares have a caravanserai character, with lingering lottery ticket-sellers, shoe-shiners, itinerant hawkers and pavement artists.

Highlights

- Gaze upon superb Manueline architecture at the Mosteiro dos Jerónimos in Belém
- Explore the revitalised medieval district of the Alfama, topped by the Castelo São Jorge with its panoramic views
- Take tram No 28 from the Baixa, trundling east into the Alfama or west into the Bairro Alto
- Experience the nightlife of Bairro Alto, famous for great bars, restaurants and fado
- Visit the riverside restaurants and clubs of Alcântara and Doca de Santo Amaro
- View amazing cultural treasures at the Museu Calouste Gulbenkian, the Museu Nacional de Arte Antiga and the Museu Nacional do Azulejo
- Wander through the Parque das Nações, with Europe's largest Oceanarium and other family-friendly entertainment

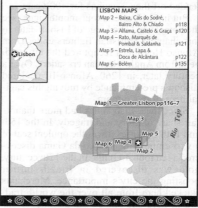

LISBON MAPS	
Map 2 – Baixa, Cais do Sodré, Bairro Alto & Chiado	p118
Map 3 – Alfama, Castelo & Graça	p120
Map 4 – Rato, Marquês de Pombal & Saldanha	p121
Map 5 – Estrela, Lapa & Doca de Alcântara	p122
Map 6 – Belém	p135

Map 1 – Greater Lisbon pp116–7

You'll find abundant history and culture, from Belém's Manueline masterpieces to the world-class Museu Calouste Gulbenkian. You'll hear the angst-filled strains of *fado* (which originated here in the Alfama) alongside African rhythms from a new generation of clubs responding to a surging demand for the music of the former African colonies.

And when you are ready for a break, there are plenty of options: day trips to the massive monastery at Mafra or the rococo palace at Queluz, seaside frolics in Costa da Caparica or Cascais, or long walks in the wooded hills of Sintra. For information on these places, and more, see the Around Lisbon chapter.

HISTORY

Legend has it that Lisbon was founded by Ulysses but it was probably the Phoenicians who first settled here 3000 years ago, attracted by the fine harbour and strategic hill of São Jorge. They called the city Alis Ubbo (Delightful Shore). Others, too, soon recognised its delightful qualities: Greeks displaced Phoenicians, and were themselves booted out by Carthaginians.

In 205 BC the Romans arrived in the city, known by then as Olisipo, and held on to it until the 5th century AD. Julius Caesar raised its rank (and changed its name to Felicitas Julia), making it the most important city in Lusitania. After the Romans, and a succession of northern tribes, the Moors arrived in 714 from North Africa. They fortified the city they called Lissabona and fended off the Christians for 400 years.

But in 1147, after a four-month siege (see the boxed text 'The Siege of Lisbon' later in this chapter), Christian fighters under Dom Afonso Henriques recaptured the city with help from Anglo-Norman crusaders. Over a century later, in 1260, Afonso III declared Lisbon's pre-eminence by moving his capital here from Coimbra.

Since then, Lisbon has had more than its fair share of glory and tragedy. In the 15th and 16th centuries it was the opulent seat of a vast empire after Vasco da Gama discovered a sea route to India. In the 17th century, gold was discovered in Brazil, further boosting the city's importance. Merchants flocked here from all over the world, trading in gold and spices, silks and precious stones. During the reign of Dom Manuel I, the extravagant style of architecture that came to be called Manueline – typified by the Mosteiro dos Jerónimos at Belém – complemented Lisbon's role as the world's most prosperous trading centre. But it was an extravagance that crumbled into rubble in the massive earthquake of 1755.

Lisbon never regained its power and prestige after the earthquake. In November 1807 Napoleon's forces occupied the city (to be driven from Portugal four years later by a joint British-Portuguese force) and Lisbon slid with the rest of the country into political chaos and insurrection.

In 1908, at the height of the turbulent republican movement, Dom Carlos and his eldest son were assassinated riding in a carriage through the streets of Lisbon. Over the next 16 years there were 45 changes of government, another high-profile assassination (President Sidónio Pais, at Rossio station in 1918), and a cloak-and-dagger period during WWII when Lisbon (which was officially neutral) developed a reputation as a nest of spies.

Two bloodless coups (in 1926 and 1974) have rocked the city, but it was the massive influx of refugees from the former African colonies in 1974–75 that had the most radical effect on Lisbon, straining its housing resources but also introducing an exciting new element.

The 1980s and 1990s saw Lisbon revitalised. After Portugal joined the European Community (EC) in 1986, massive EC funding started to boost redevelopment

---

Lisbon's Great Earthquake

It was 9.30am on All Saints' Day, 1 November 1755, when the earth lurched under Lisbon. Residents were caught inside churches, celebrating High Mass, as three major tremors hit in quick succession. In their wake came an even more devastating fire and a tidal wave that submerged the quay and destroyed the lower town.

At least 13,000 of the city's 270,000 inhabitants perished and much of the city was ruined. Dom João I's chief minister, the redoubtable Marquês de Pombal, immediately coped with the crisis (though it was actually the Marquês de Alorna who uttered the famous words 'we must bury the dead, and feed the living'), rebuilding the city in a revolutionary new style.

Lisbon recovered, but many of its glorious monuments and works of art had gone. It lost its role as Europe's leading port and finest city. Once revered by Luís de Camões as 'the princess of the world...before whom even the ocean bows', the city had finally bowed before the ocean.

(especially welcome after a major fire in 1988 destroyed the Chiado district) and put Lisbon back in the limelight, first as European City of Culture in 1994 and then as host of Expo 98. Continual sprucing-up projects and improved infrastructure have given it a go-getting new status. It's now hoping that it'll gain extra kudos as the major host city for Euro2004. Its role today may not be as glorious as in Vasco da Gama's time but it's certainly reclaiming a place on the European stage.

ORIENTATION

Lisbon nestles among seven hills on the northern side of Portugal's finest natural harbour, the wide mouth of the Rio Tejo. The hills – Estrela, Santa Catarina, São Pedro de Alcântara, São Jorge, Graça, Senhora do Monte and Penha de França – are fine places for bird's-eye views of this very photogenic city. São Jorge is topped by Lisbon's famous *castelo*, and each of the others by a church or a *miradouro* (viewpoint).

At the river's edge is the grand Praça do Comércio, the traditional gateway to the city. Behind it march the latticework streets of the Baixa (lower) district, up to the twin squares of Praça da Figueira and Praça Dom Pedro IV – the latter commonly known as Rossio.

Here the city forks along two main arteries. Lisbon's splendid main street, Avenida da Liberdade – more a long park than a boulevard – stretches 1.5km northwest from the Rossio and the adjacent Praça dos Restauradores to Praça Marquês de Pombal and the elegant Parque Eduardo VII. The other fork is the main commercial artery of Avenida Almirante Reis, running north, straight as an arrow, for almost 6km from Praça da Figueira (where it's called Rua da Palma) to the airport.

From the Baixa it's a steep climb west, through an upmarket shopping district called the Chiado, into the pastel mini-canyons of the Bairro Alto, Lisbon's traditional centre for dining and nightlife. Eastwards from the Baixa it's another climb to the Castelo de São Jorge and the ancient, maze-like Alfama district around it.

River ferries depart from Praça do Comércio and from Cais do Sodré to the west of it. Lisbon's long-haul train stations are Santa Apolónia (1.5km east of Praça do Comércio), Rossio, Cais do Sodré, and Barreiro (across the Tejo). Gare do Oriente (one of Expo 98's associated developments) is Lisbon's newest and biggest intermodal terminal, combining bus, train and metro stations on the northeastern outskirts of town.

The city has two main long-distance bus terminals: Arco do Cego, on Avenida João Crisóstomo, near Saldanha metro station; and Gare do Oriente. For more details, see Getting There & Away later in this chapter.

In addition to the metro and buses, ageing trams clank picturesquely around the hills, and smart new ones run 6km west from Praça da Figueira to the waterfront suburb of Belém.

Lisbon is connected south across the Tejo to the Costa da Caparica and Setúbal Peninsula by the immense, 70m-high Ponte 25 de Abril, Europe's longest suspension bridge, which also carries trains to the suburbs. The newer Vasco da Gama bridge – at 18km Portugal's longest river crossing – reaches across the Tejo further north, from Sacavem (near Parque das Nações) to Montijo, providing a convenient bypass for north-south traffic.

Maps

Staff at the *turismos* (tourist offices) dispense a free but microscopic city map. Decent maps for sale in bookshops include the colourful 1:13,000 Falk *Lisboa Plan*; EuroCity's 1:15,000 map; and Michelin's regularly updated 1:10,000 *Lisboa Planta*, with a separate street index. Kümmerly + Frey's 1:15,000 *Lisboa* includes bus and metro routes.

The best street index is the 230-page *Guia Urbano* city atlas (€10), which noses into every corner of the city at 1:5000 (available at the ICEP turismo office). It's not updated very often, so check before buying.

Hikers and map junkies can find excellent topographic maps from two government mapping agencies, the **Instituto Geográfico do Exército** *(Map 1)* and **Instituto Gráfico Português** *(Map 4)*. For addresses and details about the maps they sell, see Planning in the Facts for the Visitor chapter.

[Continued on page 123]

MAP 1 – GREATER LISBON

PLACES TO STAY & EAT
2 Pousada da Juventude da Lisboa Parque Nações
38 Bica do Sapato
42 Lisboa Camping – Parque Municipal
46 Café In

OTHER
1 Instituto Geográfico do Exército
3 Torre Vasco da Gama
4 Tejo Bike
5 Fil; Lisbon Exhibition Centre
6 Pavilhão Atlântico
7 Teleférico (Cable Car)
8 Pavilhão de Portugal
9 Posto de Informação
10 Bowling Internacional de Lisboa
11 Centro Vasco da Gama
12 Gare do Oriente; Eurolines Ticket Office; Ciber Oceanos
13 Pavilhão do Conhecimento
14 Oceanário
15 Pavilhão da Realidade Virtual
16 Teatro Camões
17 Buggix
18 Museu da Cidade
19 Bus Station for Ericeira, Mafra, Peniche, Torres Vedras & Malveira
20 Estádio José de Alvalade
21 Centro Comercial Colombo
22 Estádio da Luz (SL Benfica)
23 Centro Desportivo Universidade de Lisboa
24 Complexo de Piscinas do EUL

To A9 (CREL) & A8-IC1 to Torres Vedras (40km) & Caldas da Rainha (88km)

IC1

20

Campo Grande

19

18

Pontinha

Carnide

Alameda da Universidade

Avenida Marechal Teixeira Rebelo

Colégio Militar-Luz

21

Avenida General Norton de Matos

22

Av. Lusíada

Alto dos Moinhos

24

23

Cidade Universitária

26

To Queluz (5km), Almornos (20km) & Sintra (28km)

25

Laranjeiras

31

Avenida das Forças Armadas

30

IC19

Aqueduto das Águas Livres

32

Jardim Zoológico

Av. de B

Parque Florestal de Monsanto

Aqueduto

Praça de Espanha

São Sebastião

N117

Campolide

Parque

CRIL-IC17

Rua Joaquim António de Aguiar

42

das

A5-IC15

Águas

Estrada do Alvito

Av Eng Duarte Pacheco

Mãe d'Água

Marquês de Pomba

To Estoril (23km) & Cascais (26km)

Estrada do Penedo

Livres

Rato

41

Av da Ponte

Map 4 – Rato, Marquês de Pombal & Saldanha

Rua Ferreira Borges

Restelo

Av. das Descobertas

Av. da Ilha da Madeira

Av. de Ceuta

Estrela

Bai Al

Alcântara

Lapa

Rua do Alto do Duque

Av. Infante Santo

Ajuda

Calçada da Ajuda

Alcântara-Mar Train Station

3

Map 6 – Belém Map

Av. do Restelo

Belém

To Cruz Quebrada (3km), Oeiras (9km), Estoril (20km) & Cascais (23km)

Rua da Junqueira

45

Av da Índia

Doca de Alcântara

Map 5 – Estrela, Lapa & Doca de Alcântara

44

Av de Brasília

46

Ponte 25 de Abril

North South Railway Line

To Trafaria

To Porto Brandão

To Costa da Caparica (8km) & A2/A12 to Setúbal (47km)

To A1-IP1 to
Santarém (60km)
& Porto (305km)

Aeroporto
de Lisboa

To Ponte Vasco
da Gama (1.5km),
A12 to Setúbal
(45km) & A2-IP1 to
the Algarve (240km)

Av Dr Alfredo Bensaúde

Av Cidade do Porto

Av de Berlim

Avenida Marechal Craveiro Lopes

Olivais
Norte

Parque
das
Nações

Gare do
Oriente

Av de Boa Esperança

Av João II

Rua da Pimenta

Av Dom João II

Oceanos

Alameda dos Oceanos

Cabo Ruivo

Doca dos
Olivais

Av Marechal Gomes da Costa

Olivais

Avenida Infante Dom Henrique

Av do Santo Condestável

Avenida Almirante Gago Coutinho

Alvalade

Entrecampos
Train Station

Av dos Estados Unidos da América

Entrecampos

Roma

Chelas

Rua D Fuas Roupinho

Entrecampos
Poente Train
Station

Campo
Pequeno

Av da República

Saldanha

Areeiro

Olaias

Bela Vista

Estrada de Chelas

Av Almirante Reis

Alameda

Arroios

Rua Morais Soares

Anjos

Av Dom Afonso III

Av Mouzinho de Albuquerque

Xabregas

Intendente

Avenida Infante Dom Henrique

Avenida

Martim Moniz

Graça

Santa Apolónia
Train Station
(Metro Station
due to open
2003)

Rossio
Train
Station

Restauradores

Rossio

Castelo

Baixa-
Chiado

Baixa

Alfama

Cais do Sodré
Train & Metro
Station

Map 2 – Baixa, Cais
Do Sodré, Bairro
Alto & Chiado

Map 3 – Alfama,
Castelo & Graça

RIO TEJO

To Cacilhas &
Almada

To Barreiro

To Montijo
& Seixal

0   0.5   1km
0   0.5   1mi

N

LP

OTHER (continued)
25 Hospital de Santa
    Maria
26 Biblioteca Nacional
27 São Tomé e Príncipe
    Embassy
28 Cooperativa
    Necional Apoio
    Deficientes (CNAD)
29 Tagus
30 US Embassy &
    Consulate
31 Jardim Zoológico
32 Quinta dos
    Marquêses da
    Fronteira
33 Igreja de Penha de
    França
34 Federçaõs Portuguesa
    de Campismo
35 Museu Nacional do
    Azulejo
36 Museu da Água
37 Lux
39 Cerâmica Viúva
    Lamego
40 Olaria do Desterros
41 Instalações de Ténis
    de Monsanto
43 Moroccan Embassy
44 Tejo Bike
45 Parque Junqueira
    Congressos Centro

MAP 2   BAIXA, CAIS DO SODRE, BAIRRO ALTO & CHIADO

Map 4 - Rato, Marquês
de Pombal & Saldanha

Praça da
Alegría

Elevador
da Lavra

Rua da Alegria

Rua da Mãe de Água

Rua da Conceição da Glória

Rua de Santo António da Glória

Avenida da Liberdade

Rua dos Condes

Elevador
da Glória

Rua das Taipas

Rua Dom Pedro V

Rua Luísa Todi

Rua da Rosa

Rua São Boaventura

Rua da Vinha

Cç Cabra

Rua São Pedro

Tv de São Pedro

Rua do Teixeira

Rua dos Mouros

Rua da Cara

Tv da Boa Hora

Rua São Pedro Alcântara

Elevador da Glória

Rua do Diário
de Noticias

Praça dos
Restauradores

Restauradores

Rua das Portas de Santo Antão

Calçada de Santana

C.ª Nova do Colégio

Calçada de Santana

Martim
Moniz

Rua de São Lázaro

Rua do Arco do Graça

Rua da Palma

Largo
Martim
Moniz

BAIRRO ALTO

R. do Grémio Luístano

Largo de
São
Domingos

Rossio
Train
Station

Rua do Arco do Marquês do Alegrete

Rua João
das Regras

Rossio

Praça
da Figueira

Tv Nova de São
Domingos

Rua Dom Duarte

Calçada do Duque

Rua 1° de Dezembro

Praça
Dom Pedro IV
(Rossio)

Largo
Trindade
Coelho

Travessa dos Inglesinhos

Rua da Atalaia

Rua do Norte

Rua da Misericórdia

Calçada do Duque

Rua da Oliveira

Rua da Condesa

Rua do Duque

Tv da Quemada

Rua Nova da Trindade

Rua da Rosa

Rua Luz Soriano

Travessa da Espera

Travessa dos Fiéis
de Deus

Poço da Cidade

Tv de
João de Deus

Rua da Trindade

Largo
do Carmo

Rua da Betesga

Rua de Santa Justa

Rua da Prata

Rua da Madalena

Largo
Adelino Amaro
da Costa

BAIXA

Rua do Sacramento

Largo Rafael
Bordalo
Pinheiro

Travessa do Carmo

Rua Garrett

Baixa-
Chiado

Rua da Assunção

Rua da Vitória

Rua dos Sapateiros

Rua Áurea

Rua Augusta

Rua da Prata

Rua dos Correeiros

Rua dos Dourados

Rua dos Fanqueiros

Travessa das Mercês

Rua do Loreto

Rua da Salgadeiras

Praça de
Luís Camões

Largo
do Chiado

Baixa-Chiado

Rua Serpa Pinto

Rua Paiva de Andrade

Rua Garrett

Cç São Francisco

Rua Anchieta

Rua Ivens

Rua Capelo

Rua Nova do Almada

Rua de São Nicolau

Rua de Conceição

Rua São Julião

Rua do Crucifixo

Elevador da Bica

Rua da Bica
Duarte Belo

Tv do Sequeiro

Tv da Laranjeira

Iv do Português

Tv do Cabral

Rua da Horta Seca

Emenda

Flores

Largo do
Barão
de Quintela

Travessa de Guilherme Coussel

Rua das Chagas

Rua António Maria Cardoso

Largo de
São Carlos

Largo da
Academia
Nacional de
Belas Artes

Calçada do Sacramento

Rua do Alecrim

Rua dos Duques de Bragança

Rua Serpa Pinto

Largo do
Picadeiro

Rua Vítor Cordon

Calçada de São Francisco

Rua Nova do Almada

Rua de São Paulo

Tv do
Alecrim

Rua de São
Paulo

Rua Ferragial

Rua do Corpo Santo

Rua Bernardino Costa

Rua do Arsenal

Praça do
Município

Praça do
Comércio

Government Ministries

Travessa Carvalho

Rua dos Remolares

Rua dos Remolares

Avenida 24 de Julho

Praça do
Duque da
Terceira
(Cais do Sodré)

Rua Cais do Sodré

Avenida da Ribeira

das Naus

Cais do
Sodré

RIO TEJO

0   50   100m
0   50   100yd

Government
Ministri...

Map 5 - Estrela, Lapa
& Doca de Alcântara

LISBON

MAP 2 – BAIXA, CAIS DO SODRÉ, BAIRRO ALTO & CHIADO

PLACES TO STAY
2 Hotel Botânico
3 Residencial Nova
   Avenida
9 Orion Eden Lisboa
12 Pensão Imperial
14 Pensão Residencial
   Florescente
22 Pensão Residencial
   Gerês
29 Pensão Londres
32 Pensão Globo
47 Pensão Estrela de Ouro
49 Residencial Estrela do
   Mondego; Hospedaria
   Bons Dias
53 Hotel Métrópole
56 Pensão Santo Tirso
59 Pensão Praça da
   Figueira
60 Pensão Residencial
   Alcobia
61 Hotel Lisboa Tejo
63 Pensão Norte
88 New Aljubarrota
91 Residencial Duas
   Nações
94 Lisboa Regency
   Chiado
111 Pensão Prata

PLACES TO EAT
4 O Fumeiro
5 O Brinco da Glória
15 Gambrinus
16 Casa do Alentejo
33 Mastiga na Tola
37 Ali-a-Papa
38 Casa Nostra
39 A Toca
43 Hau Lon
48 Restaurante Solar do
   Duque
50 Celeiro Health-Food
   Shop
51 Pingo Doce
   Supermarket
54 Café Nicola
58 Casa Suíça
62 São Cristóvão
64 Confeitaria Nacional
69 UMA
70 Chiadomel
73 Cervejaria da
   Trindade
74 Bachus
75 Rouge
78 Pap'Açorda
80 Tasca do Manel

82 Sabor e Arte
85 Calcuta
89 Ena Pai
90 Adega Regional
   da Beira
95 Caffé Rosso
97 Café A Brasileira
99 Tendinha da Atalaia
100 Restaurante Alto
   Minho
102 La Brasserie de
   l'Entrecôte
116 Martinho da Arcada
126 Cervejaria Alemã
128 Mercado da Ribeira;
   Centro de Artesanato

BARS, CLUBS & FADO HOUSES
24 A Ginjinha
30 Melting Pop
31 O Forcado
34 Solar do Vinho do Porto
35 Fragil
36 Portas Largas
40 House of Vodka
41 Adega Mesquita
42 A Tasca
76 Tertúlia
77 Adega do Machado
79 Clube da Esquina
81 Adega do Ribatejo
83 Nono
84 Mistura Fina
86 Heróis
123 Hennessy's
124 Bar Americano
125 British Bar
127 Ó Gilins

OTHER
1 Lave Neve
6 Salão Foz (Instituto
   da Cinemateca
   Portuguesa)
7 ICEP Turismo
8 Tourist Police Post
10 Bank & ATM
11 ABEP Ticket Agency
13 Post Office
17 Coliseu dos Recreios
18 Ateneu Comercial
   Complexo de Piscinas
19 Hospital de São José
20 Gay & Lesbian
   Community Centre
21 Tram No 28 to Alfama
   or to Alfama & Graça
23 Igreja de São
   Domingos

25 Teatro Nacional de
   Dona Maria II
26 Portugal Telecom
   Office
27 Abracadabra
28 Farmácia Estácio
44 Web Café
45 Igreja de São Roque
46 Museu de São Roque
52 Cota Câmbios
55 Editorial Notícias
57 Carris Ticket Kiosk
65 Manuel Tavares
66 Livraria Diário de
   Notícias
67 Discoteca Amália
68 Arte Rústica
71 Elevador de Santa
   Justa
72 Convento do Carmo
   Ruins & Museu
   Arqueológico do Carmo
87 Valentim de Carvalho
   Megastore & Edifício
   Grandella
92 Madeira House
93 Armazens do Chiado;
   Fnac;
96 Livraria Bertrand
98 Vista Alegre
101 Brazilian Consulate
103 Fábrica Sant'Ana
104 Teatro Municipal de
   São Luís
105 Ciber Chiado & Café
   no Chiado
106 Teatro Nacional de
   São Carlos
107 Police Headquarters
108 Lisboa info kiosk
109 Banco Comércil
   Portuguesa
110 Núcleo Arqueológico
112 Santos Ofícios
113 Napoleão
114 Tram No 28 to Alfama
   or to Alfama & Graça
115 ATM & Cash Exchange
   Machine
117 Arco da Victória
118 Main Post Office
119 Lisboa Welcome Center;
   Ponto Net
120 Santos Ofícios
121 Paços do Concelho
   (Town Hall)
122 Museu do Chiado
129 Crais Do Sodré Ferry
   Terminal

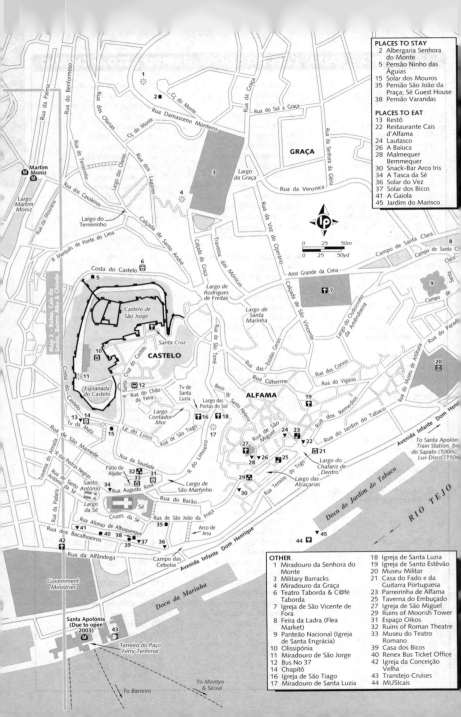

GRAÇA

Martim
Moniz

Largo
Martim
Moniz

Largo do
Terreirinho

Costa do Castelo

Castelo de
São Jorge

Santa Cruz

CASTELO

Esplanada
do Castelo

Largo de
Rodrigues
de Freitas

Largo de
Santa
Marinha

Arco Grande da Cima

Campo de Santa Clara

Largo
da Graça

Tv de
Santa
Luzia

Largo das
Portas do Sol

ALFAMA

Largo
Contador
Mor

Pátio do
Aljube

Largo de
São Martinho

Largo da Sé

Cruzes da Sé

Rua do Barão

Arco de
Jesu

Campo das
Cebolas

Government
Ministries

Santa Apolónia
(Due to open
2003)

Terreiro do Paço
Ferry Terminal

To Barreiro

To Montyo
& Seixal

Doca da Marinha

RIO TEJO

Doca do Jardim do Tabaco

To Santa Apolón
Train Station, bie
do Sapato (100m)
Lux Disco (150n

PLACES TO STAY
26 Hotel Impala
27 Residencial Marisela
28 Residencial Lisbonense
36 Lisboa Pousada da Juventude
38 Hotel Miraparque
41 Best Western Hotel Eduardo VII
50 Residência Dublin
51 Hotel Presidente
60 Hotel Britania
66 Pensão Residencial 13 da Sorte

PLACES TO EAT
16 Mãe Preta
19 Versailles
20 Bella Italia III
32 Restaurante Espiral
35 Li Yuan
55 Real Fábrica
59 Estrela de Santa Marta
65 Cervejaria Ribadouro
71 Restaurante Os Tibetanos

EMBASSIES
1 Brazilian Embassy
3 Angolan Embassy
8 Mozambican Embassy
57 Canadian Embassy; Australian Embassy
61 German Embassy
64 Spanish Embassy & Consulate

OTHER
2 Banque Nationale de Paris
4 Praça de Touros
5 Biblioteca Central
6 Culturgest
7 Barclays Bank
9 Bus Station for Costa da Caparica & Sesimbra
10 Museu Calouste Gulbenkian
11 Concert Halls (Fundação Calouste Gulbenkian)
12 Secretariado Nacional de Rehabilitação
13 Librairie Française
14 ICEP Head Office
15 Comissão para a Igualdade e para os Direitos das Mulheres
17 Arco do Cego Bus Station; Eurolines (Intercentro) Ticket Office
18 Livraria Municipal
21 Movijovem
22 Centro de Arte Moderna
23 Associação Portuguesa de Mulheres Empresárias
24 El Corte Inglés
25 Institut Franco-Portugais de Lisbonne; Alliance Française
29 Galerias Monumental
30 Atrium Saldanha
31 Associação Opus Gay
33 Eurolines (Intercentro) Ticket Office
34 Hiper Net
37 PostNet
39 Serviço de Estrangeiros e Fronteiras (Foreigners' Registration Service)
40 Mussulo
42 Estufas

43 Instituto Gráfico Português
44 Tour Bus Terminal
45 Instituto Particular de Formação e Ensino de Linguas
46 Top Tours
47 Instituto da Conservação da Natureza (ICN)
48 Hospital Dona Estefânia
49 Tagus
52 Livraria Buchholz
53 Amoreiras Shopping Centre
54 Mãe d'Água Reservoir
56 Automóvel Club de Portugal (ACP)
58 Instituto Português da Juventude (IPJ)
63 Goethe Institut
63 Hot Clube de Portugal
67 Cambridge School
68 São Jorge Cinema
69 Instituto da Cinemateca Portuguesa
70 Grupo Deutsche Bank

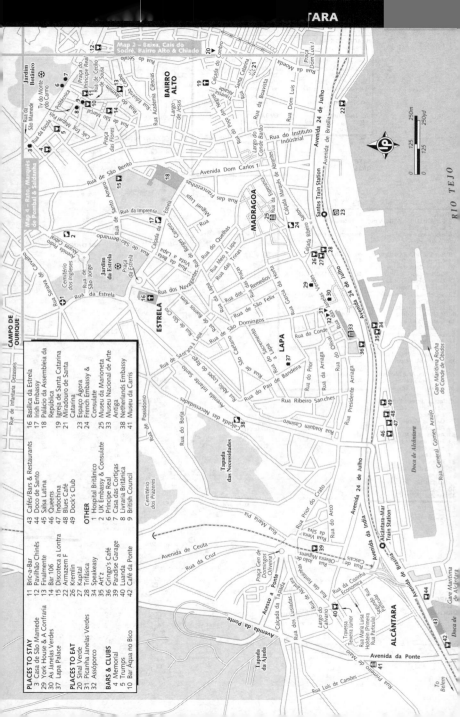

Map 2 – Baixa, Cais do
Sodré, Bairro Alto & Chiado

BAIRRO ALTO

Jardim Botânico

Tv do Monte do Carmo

RIO TEJO

Santos Train Station

MADRAGOA

Map 4 – Rato, Marquês
de Pombal & Saldanha

Jardim
da Estrela

ESTRELA

LAPA

Avenida 24 de Julho

Avenida de Brasília

Alcântara-Mar
Train Station

Doca de Alcântara

Gare Marítima Rocha
do Conde de Óbidos

Cemitério
dos Ingleses

Cemitério
dos Prazeres

Tapada
das Necessidades

CAMPO DE
OURIQUE

Avenida de Ceuta

Avenida da Ponte

Tapada
da Ajuda

ALCÂNTARA

Avenida da Ponte

Gare Marítima
de Alcântara

Doca de
Alcântara

To
Belém

PLACES TO STAY
3 Casa de São Mamede
29 York House & A Confraria
30 As Janelas Verdes
37 Lapa Palace

PLACES TO EAT
20 Sinal Verde
31 Picanha Janelas Verdes
32 Assóporco

BARS & CLUBS
4 Memorial
5 Trumps
10 Bar Áqua no Bico
11 Bric-a-Bar
12 Pavilhão Chinês
13 Finalmente
14 Bar 106
15 Discoteca a Lontra
22 Armazém F
26 Kremlin
27 Kapital
28 Trifásica
34 Speakeasy
35 Art'z
36 Gringo's Café
39 Paradise Garage
42 Café da Ponte

CAFÉS/BARS & RESTAURANTS
43 Bric-a-Bar
44 Doca de Santo
45 Salsa Latina
46 Queens
47 Indochina
48 Blues Café
49 Dock's Club

OTHER
1 Hospital Británico
2 UK Embassy & Consulate
6 Principe Real
7 Casa das Cortiças
8 Livraria Británica
9 British Council
16 Basílica da Estrela
17 Irish Embassy
18 Palácio da Assembleia da
   República
19 Igreja de Santa Catarina
21 Miradouro de Santa
   Catarina
23 Espaço Ágora
24 French Embassy &
   Consulate
25 Museu da Marioneta
33 Museu Nacional de Arte
   Antiga
38 Netherlands Embassy
41 Museu da Carris

250m
250yd

[Continued from page 115]

INFORMATION
Tourist Offices
The **Turismo de Lisboa** (☎ 210 312 700, fax 210 312 899; e atl@atl-turismolisboa.pt) has a smart new information centre, the **Lisboa Welcome Center** *(Map 2; ☎ 210 312 810; Praça do Comércio; open 9am-8pm daily)*, dealing specifically with inquiries about Lisbon. For national inquiries, try the **ICEP turismo** *(Map 2; ☎ 213 463 643, fax 213 468 772; Palácio Foz, Praça dos Restauradores; open 9am-8pm daily)*, run by the state's umbrella organisation for tourism. There's also a Turismo de Lisboa desk here.

Turismo de Lisboa also runs several **Ask Me Lisboa information kiosks** *(usually open 10am-6pm daily high season)*, with varying opening hours, most usefully at Rua Augusta (Map 2), near Rua Conceição; inside Santa Apolónia train station (Map 1; door No 47); and in Belém (Map 6).

In the airport arrivals hall you'll find two turismos: the **ICEP desk** *(☎ 218 493 689; open 6am-1am daily)*, which dispenses information and maps but little else; and the smaller **Turismo de Lisboa desk** *(☎ 218 450 660; open 6am-midnight daily)*, opposite, which can advise on taxis and other transport, and make hotel reservations.

Excellent free publications worth picking up at all these offices include *Follow Me Lisboa*, a fortnightly Portuguese/English leisure guide; *Lisboa Step by Step*, a quarterly glossy; *Lisboa City Walks*; and a *Guia*

Gay e Lésbico (Gay & Lesbian Guide to Lisbon) leaflet. Also available at all Turismo de Lisboa outlets is the Lisboa Card (see the boxed text in this section).

Keep an eye out, too, for the free, regularly updated *Your Guide: Lisboa* published by ANA, the airport authority, listing shops, restaurants, and nightlife (also available at the airport arrivals terminal); and *Tips*, an info-packed miniguide, more often available in hotels.

Money
Nearly every bank has a Multibanco ATM. You can also find 24-hour cash-exchange machines (where you can exchange foreign banknotes for euros) at the airport, Santa Apolónia train station and Rua Augusta 24 (Map 2).

Your best bet for changing cash or travellers cheques is a private-exchange bureau such as **Cota Câmbios** *(Map 2; Rossio 41; open 8.30am-10pm daily)*.

Top Tours (Map 4; see Travel Agencies later in this section) is Lisbon's American Express (AmEx) representative. Here, you can cash AmEx travellers cheques, and AmEx cards can be used for cash advances at back-home rates.

International banks include **Banque Nationale de Paris** *(Map 4; ☎ 217 910 200; Avenida 5 de Outubro 206)*; **Barclays Bank** *(Map 4; ☎ 217 911 100; Avenida da República 50)*; and **Grupo Deutsche Bank** *(Map 4; ☎ 210 001 200; Rua Castilho 20)*.

Post
The **main post office** *(Map 2; Praça do Comércio; open 8.30am-6.30pm Mon-Fri)* is the place for poste restante collection. Mail addressed to Posta Restante, Central Correios, Terreiro do Paço, 1100-148 Lisboa, will go to counter 13 or 14 here. There's a more convenient **post office** *(Map 2; ☎ 213 238 700; Praça dos Restauradores; open 8am-10pm Mon-Fri, 9am-6pm Sat & Sun)*, opposite the ICEP turismo, and a 24-hour post office at the airport.

Telephone & Fax
With a phonecard, including the Portugal Telecom card, you can make international direct dial (IDD) calls from most street telephones. At Portugal Telecom booths in post offices, and the **Portugal Telecom Office**

Lisboa Card

Holders of this card get free travel on the metro, buses, trams and lifts (plus the train to Belém); free admission to 26 museums and monuments (including some in Sintra); and discounts of up to 50% on other sights, bus and tram tours, river cruises and other admission charges. There are 24-, 48- and 72-hour versions costing €11.30/18.50/23.50 (or €4.50/6.30/9 for children from five to 11 years) – reasonable value if you plan on cramming lots of sights into a short stay. You validate the card when you want to start it.

The card is sold at all Turismo de Lisboa outlets and Carris ticket kiosks.

(Map 2; Rossio 68; open 8am-11pm daily), you can pay when you're done. Faxes can be sent from post offices.

Email & Internet Access

Among many places to log onto the Internet are:

Abracadabra (Map 2) Rossio 65 – open 7.30am to 10pm daily; €1 per 15 minutes

Ciber Chiado (Map 2; ☎ 213 225 764) Café no Chiado, 1st floor, Largo do Picadeiro 10 – open 11am to 11pm Monday to Friday, 8pm to 11pm Saturday; €1.80 per half-hour

Ciber Oceanos (Map 1; ☎ 218 951 995) 1st basement level, Gare do Oriente – open 10am to 11pm daily; €1.50 per half-hour

Espaço Ágora (Map 5; ☎ 213 940 170) Armazém 1, Avenida de Brasilia, Santos – open 9am to around 3am Monday to Saturday, 9am to 10pm Sunday; €0.50 per 15 minutes, €0.80 per half-hour

Fnac (Map 2; ☎ 213 221 800) Fnac's café, Armazéns do Chiado, Rua do Carmo 3 – open 10am to 10pm daily; €0.05 per minute plus €12.30 card deposit

Hiper Net (Map 4; ☎ 213 522 292) ground floor, Edifício Portugal Telecom, Picoas – open 9am to 7pm Monday to Friday; €1 per half-hour

Ponto Net (Map 2; ☎ 210 312 810) 1st floor, Lisboa Welcome Center, Praça do Comércio – open 9am to 8pm daily; €1.80 per 15 minutes

PostNet (Map 4; ☎ 213 511 100) Avenida António Augusto Aguiar 17B – open 8am to 8pm Monday to Friday, 9am to 1pm Saturday; €0.80 per 15 minutes

Web Café (Map 2; ☎ 213 421 181) Rua do Diário de Notícias 126 – open 4pm to 2am daily; €1.50 per 15 minutes, €2.50 per half-hour

Internet Resources

The Turismo de Lisboa's multilingual website (**w** www.atl-turismolisboa.pt) includes upcoming events, accommodation, and a visitor's guide. Similar information, with a useful search facility, is available at **w** www.lisboa-online.com. Fancy a virtual tour of the city? Check out **w** www.lisbon.cx. John Laidlar's lovingly detailed website (**w** www.luso.u-net.com/lisbon.htm) is a must for transport buffs, describing every kind of transport in and around Lisbon.

Several entertainment venues have their own websites listing current and forthcoming events, notably the Centro Cultural de Belém at **w** www.ccb.pt and the Parque das Nações at **w** www.parquedasnacoes.pt. The Gulbenkian Foundation's bilingual site at **w** www.musica.gulbenkian.pt lists the many Gulbenkian-sponsored events.

Travel Agencies

The city's leading youth-oriented travel agency, offering budget-minded hotel, bus, train and air bookings (plus ISIC, ITIC and Go25 cards) is **Tagus** *(Map 4; ☎ 213 525 986, fax 213 532 715; Rua Camilo Castelo Branco 20 ● Map 1; ☎ 218 491 531; Praça de Londres 9C; open 9am-6pm Mon-Fri, 10am-1.30pm Sat).* A similar outfit is **Wasteels** *(☎ 218 869 793, fax 218 869 797; Rua dos Caminhos do Ferro 90)* by Santa Apolónia train station (Map 1).

A good mainstream travel agency is Lisbon's AmEx representative, **Top Tours** *(Map 4; ☎ 213 108 800; **e** tourism@toptours.pt; Avenida Duque de Loulé 108, 1050-093 Lisbon; open 9.30am-1pm & 2.30pm-6.30pm Mon-Fri).* Holders of AmEx cards or travellers cheques can change money (see Money, earlier), and have mail and faxes held or forwarded here.

Bookshops

Lisbon's biggest and best bookshop is **Livraria Bertrand** *(Map 2; ☎ 213 421 941; Rua Garrett 73, Chiado).* It has several other branches, including in the Centro Comercial Colombo shopping centre (Map 1) and the Centro Cultural de Belém (Map 6). Smaller bookshops include **Livraria Diário de Notícias** *(Map 2; Rossio 11)* and **Editorial Notícias** *(Map 2; Rossio 23).*

The only shop devoted entirely to Lisbon – history, art and architecture, with a few titles in English – is the elegant **Livraria Municipal** *(Map 4; Avenida da República 21A).* Nearby is the city's only exclusively French bookshop, **Librairie Française** *(Map 4; Avenida Marquês de Tomar 38).* **Livraria Buchholz** *(Map 4; Rua Duque de Palmela 4)* has a huge collection of literature in Portuguese, English, French and German. For a wide range of exclusively English-language books visit **Livraria Britânica** *(Map 5; Rua de São Marçal 83).*

There are several second-hand bookshops on Calçada do Carmo (Map 2) behind Rossio train station and some stalls in the arcades of Praça do Comércio (Map 2), at the end of Rua Augusta.

Libraries

Lisbon's best libraries are the **Biblioteca Nacional** *(Map 1; ☎ 217 982 000; Campo Grande 83)* and **Biblioteca Central** *(Map 4; ☎ 217 971 326; Palácio Galveias, Campo Pequeno)*. For more information on libraries, see Cultural Centres later in this section.

Universities

The **Universidade de Lisboa** *(Map 1; metro Cidade Universitária)*, 5km northwest of the Rossio, has its own metro station. The most prestigious university is the private Universidade Católica, near Sete Ríos. There are nearly a dozen other private universities in Lisbon.

An easier place to meet students is the Espaço Ágora (see Email & Internet Access, earlier), with study rooms and a café (with discounts for students), plus useful notice boards. During term time it's open almost round the clock.

Cultural Centres

The **British Council** *(Map 5; ☎ 213 476 141; Rua de São Marçal 174)* has a huge **library** *(Rua Luís Fernandes 1-3; open 2pm-6pm Mon-Sat)*, with the latest English newspapers. Opening hours vary but those given here are a sure bet.

Similar centres include **Alliance Française** *(Map 4; ☎ 213 111 483; e a.f.lisbonne@clix.pt; Avenida Luís Bívar 91)* and **Institut Franco-Portugais de Lisbonne** *(Map 4; ☎ 213 111 400; e ifplisb@esoterica.pt; Avenida Luís Bívar 91)*. The latter has regular cultural (including film) events, and a library called **Mediateca** *(☎ 213 111 421; open 1pm-6pm Mon-Thur, 10am-2.30pm Fri)*. There's a **library** *(open 3pm-7pm Mon-Thur)* at the **Goethe Institut** *(Map 4; ☎ 218 824 511; Campo dos Mártires da Pátria 37)*.

Gay & Lesbian Travellers

A great place for gays and lesbians is the **Centro Comunitário Gay e Lésbico de Lisboa** *(Lisbon Gay & Lesbian Community Centre; Map 2; ☎ 218 873 918; e ilga-portugal@ilga.org; Rua de São Lazaro 88; open 4pm-8pm Mon-Sat Sept-July)*. It has a café, library, Internet facility and counselling facilities. The **Grupo de Mulheres** *(Women's Group; ☎/fax 218 873 918; e gmulheres@yahoo.com)*, part of ILGA-Portugal, organises social gatherings here from 8pm to

midnight on the second Saturday of each month, and lesbian film screenings at 6pm on the fourth Saturday.

Associação Opus Gay *(Map 4; ☎ 213 151 396, after hrs 962 400 017; e opus@opusgayassociation.com; 2nd floor, Rua da Ilha Terceira 34; open 5pm-8pm Wed-Sat)* also has a visitor-friendly centre, including Internet café.

Lisbon's Gay Pride Festival takes place in June, and its Festival de Cinema Gay e Lésbico is in late September.

Laundry

The only self-service place is **Lave Neve** *(Map 2; Rua da Alegria 37; open 10am-1pm & 3pm-7pm Mon-Fri, 9am-1pm Sat)*.

Left Luggage

The left-luggage store at the airport (by Level 2's car park) charges €1.60/2.70/5.40 per day for luggage up to 10kg/30kg/over 30kg. Arco do Cego's bus terminal charges €2.50 per day per item, but you'll only find coin-operated lockers (of various sizes) at Gare do Oriente, Rossio, Cais do Sodré and Santa Apolónia train stations. Costs for the lockers range from €0.50 to €2.50 per hour (depending on locker size) to €3.30 to €7.80 for the maximum 24 hours.

Medical Services

Farmácias (pharmacies) are plentiful in Lisbon. A competent one near the centre is **Farmácia Estácio** *(Map 2; Rossio 62)*.

The **Hospital Britânico** *(British Hospital or Hospital Inglês; Map 5; ☎ 213 955 067, 213 976 329; Rua Saraiva de Carvalho 49)* has English-speaking staff and doctors. Other large hospitals include **Hospital de São José** *(Map 2; ☎ 218 841 000; Rua José António Serrano)* and **Hospital de Santa Maria** *(Map 1; ☎ 217 805 000; Avenida Professor Egas Moniz)*. The turismo has a list of private doctors and dentists who speak English or other languages.

Emergency

There's a 24-hour **tourist police post** *(Map 2; ☎ 213 421 634; Palácio Foz, Praça dos Restauradores)* in a building signposted Foz Cultura next to the ICEP turismo; alternatively you can go to the **police headquarters** *(Map 2; ☎ 217 654 242; Rua Capelo 13)*. The countrywide emergency number is ☎ 112.

Dangers & Annoyances

Lisbon has a low crime rate by European standards, but it's on the rise. Most crime against foreigners involves car break-ins or pickpocketing and bag-snatching. Use a moneybelt and keep cameras and other tourist indicators out of sight. Park cars in guarded or locked garages.

Late at night (especially at weekends), it's unwise to wander alone through the streets of Bairro Alto, Alfama and Cais do Sodré. There have been isolated assaults by gangs of kids as young as 11 or 12 in these nightclub neighbourhoods as well as in some deserted metro stations and even in crowded streets during the day. Suspected rivalry between gangs of Cape Verdeans and Angolans has also led to a rash of attacks in African nightclubs: seven people died at the city's popular Luanda club in April 2000 when tear gas canisters were set off.

Other places in the Lisbon area with a small but growing reputation for violent crime are the Estoril-Cascais beach resorts and the Setúbal region. A tourist police post is now installed in the Cascais tourist office.

WHAT'S FREE

Many museums are free on Sunday morning, as noted in the text. The Centro Cultural de Belém (Map 6) presents free music and dance performances at its Bar Terraço from 7pm to 9pm on winter weekdays and from 10pm on Friday and Saturday during July and August in its outdoor Jardim dos Oliveiras. Everything during its day-long Festa da Primavera (Spring Festival) in late March is also free. The Museu Calouste Gulbenkian (Map 4) gives free musical recitals at noon in the library foyer on the second and fourth Sunday of the month. Fnac (Map 2; see Email & Internet Access) has a regular programme of free exhibitions, concerts and films: pick up a brochure for details. The Mercado da Ribeira (Map 2) has free live music shows on Friday and Saturday evenings.

Every weekend from July to September the BaixAnima Festival enlivens the Baixa (Rua Augusta, Rossio and Praça da Figueira) with some zany free street performances of song, dance, drama, games and circus acts from 5pm to 7pm.

BAIXA & THE RIVERFRONT (MAP 2)

Following the 1755 earthquake, one of the few people who kept his head was the autocratic Marquês de Pombal, Dom José I's chief minister. He took the opportunity to rebuild the city centre as quickly as possible, in a severe and simple, low-cost, easily managed style.

The area from the riverside to the Rossio was reborn as a grid of wide, commercial streets (with footpaths), each dedicated to a trade. The memory of these districts lives on in the Baixa's street names – Áurea (formerly called Ouro, gold), Sapateiros (shoemakers), Correeiros (saddlers), Prata (silver), Douradores (gilders) and Fanqueiros (cutlers).

This lower town remains the de facto heart of Lisbon. Down the middle runs pedestrianised Rua Augusta, the old street of the cloth merchants, now hosting cafés, shops and banks. A number of the city's bus and tramlines funnel through Praça do Comércio at the Baixa's riverside end, or Rossio and Praça da Figueira at its upper end.

Praça do Comércio to Cais do Sodré

Before the earthquake, Praça do Comércio was called Terreiro do Paço (Palace Square), after the royal Palácio da Ribeira that overlooked it until the morning of 1 November 1755. Most visitors coming by river or sea in bygone days would have arrived here. The huge square still feels like the entrance to the city, thanks to Joaquim Machado de Castro's bronze **equestrian statue** of Dom José I; the 18th-century, arcaded **ministries** along three sides; and Veríssimo da Costa's **Arco da Victória**, the arch opening onto Rua Augusta.

Just off the northwestern corner of the square is a smaller square, **Praça do Município**, dominated by Lisbon's 1874 **Paços do Concelho** (town hall) on the eastern side, the former marine arsenal on the southern side, and a finely carved, 18th-century *pelourinho* (stone pillory) at the centre.

Continuing west for another 400m along Rua do Arsenal, you arrive at Lisbon's other main riverfront plaza, the rather scruffy Praça do Duque da Terceira, better known by its riverfront name, **Cais do Sodré**, where you'll find the Transtejo car ferry and the Cais do Sodré metro and train station (for Cascais and the Estoril coast). A few short blocks west is the domed **Mercado da Ribeira**, the city's main food market, whose 1st floor has been converted into a tourists' 'cultural centre' (see the boxed text 'Markets' in the Shopping section for details).

From here, Avenida 24 de Julho runs for 3km along the river to the Port of Lisbon and the former warehouse district of Alcântara and Doca de Santo Amaro. This strip is a major axis for Lisbon's nightlife (see Entertainment later in this chapter). A pleasant way to return to Praça do Comércio is along the breezy riverfront promenade.

Central Baixa

Under the streets of the Baixa is the **Núcleo Arqueológico** (☎ 213 211 700; admission free), a web of tunnels believed to be the remnants of a Roman spa (or possibly a temple) and probably dating from the 1st century AD. You can descend into the mouldy depths – via the offices of **Banco Comércial Portuguesa** (Rua dos Correeiros 9) – on a guided tour that is run by the Museu da Cidade (see Greater Lisbon later in this chapter). Tour times are at 3pm, 4pm and 5pm Thursday, and hourly from 10am to noon and 3pm to 5pm Saturday.

Alternatively you can rise above the Baixa at a stately pace. From the Largo Martim Moniz, the **No 28 tram** clanks up into the Alfama and Graça districts. At the other end of the Baixa, the **Elevador de Santa Justa**, an incongruously huge but charming wrought-iron lift designed by Raul Mésnier du Ponsard (a follower of Gustave Eiffel) and completed in 1902, will hoist you 32m above Rua de Santa Justa to a viewing platform and café at eye level with the Convento do Carmo ruins in the Chiado district. In high season, long queues for the lift can unfortunately destroy the charm of the trip.

Rossio & Praça da Figueira

This pair of plazas forms the gritty heart of the Baixa, with lots of cafés from which to watch a cross-section of Lisbon's multicultural population and hustlers and hawkers preying cheerfully on visitors.

In the middle of the Rossio is a **statue**, allegedly of Dom Pedro IV, after whom the square is formally named. On the northern

---

Rolling Motion Square

This was the nickname given to the Rossio by early English visitors because of the undulating mosaic pattern of its footpaths. Such cobbled pavements – made of hard-cut white limestone and grey basalt cubes (and originally installed by prison labour gangs in the 19th century) – are still much in evidence everywhere, painstakingly pounded by hand into a bed of sand. To find Lisbon's best contemporary 'rolling motion' pavement art, take a look at the creations in the Parque das Nações beside the Atlantic Pavilion and Oceanarium.

---

side of the square is the restored 1846 **Teatro Nacional de Dona Maria II**, its facade topped by a statue of 16th-century playwright Gil Vicente.

In less orderly times the Rossio was the scene of animal markets, fairs and bullfights. The theatre was built on the site of a palace in which the unholiest excesses of the Portuguese Inquisition took place during the 16th to 19th centuries. In the nearby **Igreja de São Domingos** the Inquisition's judgements, or autos-da-fé, were handed down.

CHIADO & BAIRRO ALTO (MAP 2)

These two districts, lying above the Baixa to the west, make a perfect pair for day and night exploration. The Chiado, a wedge of wide streets roughly between Rua do Crucifixo and Rua da Misericórdia, is the posh place for shopping and for loitering in cafés. The Bairro Alto, a fashionable residential district in the 17th century (and still boasting some fine mansions), is now better known as the raffish heartland of Lisbon nightlife.

In the Chiado the ruins of the **Convento do Carmo,** uphill from Rua Garrett, stand as stunning testimony to the 1755 earthquake. Now regularly used as an open-air theatre, only the Gothic arches, walls and flying buttresses remain of what was once one of Lisbon's largest churches, built in 1423 under the orders of Nuno Álvares Pereira, Dom João I's military commander. Its shell now houses the **Museu Arqueológico do Carmo** (☎ 213 478 629; adult/under-26 or senior €3/1.50, 10am-2pm Sun free; open 10am-6pm Tues-Sun Apr-Sept, 10am-5pm

Oct-Mar), a sober collection of tombs, Roman and Islamic inscribed funerary stones and a spooky 3500-year-old seated mummy, clasping its knees.

By contrast, the gutted buildings that once pockmarked the Chiado since a massive fire in 1988 have now been magnificently restored by architect Álvaro de Siza Vieira, most housing elegant shopping malls. One survivor of the fire is the **Teatro Nacional de São Carlos** *(Rua Serpa Pinto)* – Lisbon's opera house and the city's largest, most handsome theatre, built in the 1790s. It stands opposite the smaller, recently renovated **Teatro Municipal de São Luís**.

Nearby, in the former Convento de São Francisco, is the **Museu do Chiado** (☎ 213 432 148; Rua Serpa Pinto 4; adult/under-26 or senior €3/1.50, 10am-2pm Sun free; open 2pm-6pm Tues, 10am-6pm Wed-Sun), with frequently changing exhibitions of contemporary art plus a permanent display of some of its own 19th- and 20th-century Portuguese art, and an excellent art bookshop. Pause for a *bica* (espresso) in the café's intimate sculpture garden.

Two funiculars – the Elevador da Glória and Elevador da Bica – provide stately entrances to the Bairro Alto. From Praça dos Restauradores, the **Elevador da Glória** climbs up to a superb viewpoint atop one of Lisbon's seven hills, **São Pedro de Alcântara**. Across the road is the **Solar do Vinho do Porto** *(Map 2)* – see the boxed text 'Sampling the Local Tipples' in the Entertainment section – where you can sample port wine. Continuing uphill you reach the venerable **Jardim Botânico** *(Rua da Escola Politécnica 58; admission €1.30; open 9am-6pm Mon-Fri, 10am-6pm Sat & Sun Oct-Apr; 9am-8pm Mon-Fri, 10am-8pm Sat & Sun May-Sept)*, a peaceful place shaded by some magnificent old trees.

It's a short walk downhill from São Pedro de Alcântara to Largo Trindade Coelho and the late-16th-century Jesuit **Igreja de São Roque** *(admission free; open 8.30am-5pm Mon-Fri, 9.30am-5pm Sat & Sun)*, whose dull facade is one of Lisbon's biggest deceptions. Inside the church are chapels stuffed with gold, marble and Florentine *azulejos* (hand-painted tiles). The *pièce de résistance* is its restrained but exquisite **Capela de São João Baptista**, to the left of the altar. Commissioned in 1742 by Portugal's most extravagant king, Dom João V, this chapel was designed and built in Rome using the most expensive materials possible, including amethyst, alabaster, agate, lapis lazuli and Carrara marble. After its consecration by Pope Benedict XIV it was dismantled and shipped to Lisbon for what was then a staggering UK£225,000.

The adjacent **Museu de São Roque** (☎ 213 235 381; admission €1, Sun free; open 10am-5pm Tues-Sun) contains rich liturgical items, and paintings from the 16th and 17th centuries.

From the southern end of the Bairro Alto (walking distance from Cais do Sodré) the **Elevador da Bica** creeps up to Rua do Loreto, a few blocks west of Praça de Luís Camões. Riding this gives you a chance to explore unsung **Santa Catarina**, a compact, maze-like district bright with fluttering laundry and alive with balcony gossip and caged songbirds. At the end of Rua Marechal Saldanha, on another of Lisbon's seven hills, is the **Miradouro de Santa Catarina** (with a popular outdoor café), offering a bird's-eye view of the river and the Ponte 25 de Abril.

ALFAMA, CASTELO & GRAÇA (MAP 3)

This area east and northeast of the Baixa is Lisbon's oldest and most historically interesting district, with a warren of medieval streets and outstanding views from three of Lisbon's seven hills – São Jorge, Graça and Senhora do Monte.

Alfama

The Alfama was inhabited by the Visigoths as far back as the 5th century, and remnants of a Visigothic town wall remain. But it was the Moors who gave the district its shape and atmosphere, as well as its name – the Arabic *alhama* means springs or bath, probably a reference to hot springs found near Largo das Alcaçarias. In Moorish times this was an upper-class residential area. After earthquakes brought down many of its mansions (and post-Moorish churches) it reverted to a working-class and fisherfolk quarter. It was one of the few districts to ride out the 1755 earthquake.

The Alfama's tangled alleys *(becos* and *travessas)* and vertiginous stairways make a sharp contrast to the Baixa's prim streets. Plunging from the castle to the river, with

Lisbon has an eclectic, ever-changing mix of bars

Doca de Santo Amaro, Lisbon

Carnaval, the last few days before Lent, consists of fairs, parades and outlandish costumes

Port-lovers should visit Lisbon's Solar do Vinho do Porto, with around 200 types of port to tempt you

PASCALE BEROUJON

Lisbon's Alfama district is a warren of narrow streets reminiscent of its Moorish and medieval past

ANDERS BLOMQVIST

Parque das Nações, Lisbon, features the modern Pavilhão de Portugal designed by Álvaro Siza Vieira

JOHN KING

Tram, Bairro Alto, Lisbon

CARLOS COSTA

Bird's-eye view of Lisbon's red rooftops

lanes often narrow enough to shake hands across, it has a village atmosphere; you can quickly feel like an intruder if you take a wrong turn into someone's back yard. By day it's a lively enclave of restaurants and tiny grocery stores; early morning is best, when women sell fresh fish from their doorways. For a real rough-and-tumble atmosphere, visit during the Festas dos Santos Populares in June (see Special Events later in this chapter).

Walking east from the Praça do Comércio, along Rua dos Bacalhoeiros, you'll come to the startling early-16th-century **Casa dos Bicos** (House of Points) – a folly with a prickly facade built by Afonso de Albuquerque, a former viceroy of India. It is now the offices for the Comemorações dos Descobrimentos organisation; in the lobby you can buy Age of Discoveries souvenirs and see bits of the old Moorish city wall and brick streets.

From here it's an easy stroll up to the **sé** (admission free; open 9am-7pm Tues-Sat, 9am-5pm Mon & Sun). This Romanesque cathedral was built in 1150, soon after the city was recaptured from the Moors by Afonso Henriques. He was wary enough to want the church built like a fortress. It's been extensively restored and is now rather

dull except for a baroque organ and an intricate baroque crib by Machado de Castro in a chapel off the northern aisle. Religious paraphernalia is on display in the **treasury** (admission €2.50; open 10am-5pm Mon-Sat). The Gothic **cloister** (admission €1; open 10am-5pm Mon, 10am-6.30pm Tues-Sat May-Sept; 10am-5pm Mon-Sat Oct-Apr) is in a dishevelled state but the deep archaeological excavation at its centre is worth a look, revealing stonework from the 6th century BC, plus bits of Roman and Islamic habitation.

Just uphill from the cathedral is the new **Museu do Teatro Romano** (☎ 217 513 200; Pátio do Aljube 5; admission free; open 10am-1pm & 2pm-6pm Tues-Sun), which has finally focused attention on the city's **ruined Roman theatre** (Map 3). Originally built during Emperor Augustus' time, the theatre was rebuilt in AD 57 to seat up to 5000 spectators and finally abandoned in the 4th century, its stones gradually used to build the city. There's not a tremendous amount left to see, in fact, but the museum's modern audiovisual displays cleverly reconstruct the scene.

Uphill from here you'll soon reach two stunning viewpoints: the **Miradouro de Santa Luzia** with an attractive little garden, and, a little further on, **Largo das Portas do Sol** (the 'sun gateway', originally one of the seven gateways into the Moorish city).

A direct route into the heart of the Alfama runs from behind the cathedral: Rua de São João da Praça leads downhill to Largo de São Rafael and a ruined **Moorish tower**, part of the Moors' original town wall. The old **Jewish Quarter** is adjacent, marked by tiny Rua da Judiaria. Along Rua de São Miguel and Rua de São Pedro, as far as Largo do Chafariz de Dentro, are shops, restaurants and cafés. In the Largo itself, don't miss the **Casa do Fado e da Guitarra Portuguesa** (☎ 218 823 470; adult/child 6-14/student or senior €2.50/0.80/1.30; open 10am-1pm & 2pm-6pm daily), an excellent audiovisual display of fado's history.

Castelo de São Jorge

A short, steep climb from Largo das Portas do Sol via Travessa de Santa Luzia (or catch bus No 37 from Rossio) brings you to the Castelo de São Jorge (admission free; open 9am-9pm daily Mar-Oct, 9am-6pm Nov-Feb).

St Anthony

Although St Vincent is Lisbon's official patron saint, Lisboêtas are fonder of St Anthony, despite the fact that he spent most of his life in France and Italy. Born in Lisbon in 1195, he joined the Augustinian and, later, Franciscan order.

Revered in Italy as St Anthony of Padua, or simply Il Santo, his humanistic preachings and concern for the poor made him internationally famous. Less than a year after his death in 1231 he was canonised. Many miracles are attributed to him but he is especially renowned for his assistance in fixing marriages; many single women still ask for his help in finding husbands, and newly wed couples leave gifts of thanks at the Igreja de Santo António. The best time to feel the city's affection for him is during the Festa de Santo António from 12 to 13 June (see Special Events later in this chapter).

The Siege of Lisbon

The reconquest of Lisbon in 1147 is one of the more unsavoury chapters in Portugal's early history. Afonso Henriques had already thrashed the Moors at Ourique in 1139 (and started calling himself King of Portugal) and his sights were now on Lisbon. Short of experienced troops, he persuaded a ruffian band of English, Flemish, French and German adventurer-crusaders on their way to Palestine to give him a hand.

In June 1147 the siege of the Castelo de São Jorge began. The Moors managed to hold out for 17 weeks, but finally the castle's defences gave way. The 'Christian' forces (described more correctly by a contemporary reporter as 'plunderers, drunkards and rapists...men not seasoned with the honey of piety') showed their true colours by pillaging their way through the city, despite assurances of leniency for the losers from Afonso himself. The only good man among them appears to have been one Gilbert of Hastings, an English priest who later became Bishop of Lisbon.

From its Visigothic beginnings in the 5th century, the castle was later fortified by the Moors in the 9th century, sacked by Christians in the 12th century and used as a royal residence from the 14th to 16th centuries – and as a prison in every century.

What remains has now been considerably restored by EBAHL (Equipamentos dos Bairros Históricos de Lisboa), which is also responsible for continuing restoration works elsewhere in the city (especially the Alfama). But the castle's best feature is unchangeable: its fantastic panoramas. Near the entrance is **Olisipónia** (☎ 218 877 244; adult/under-26 €3/1.50; open 10am-12.30pm & 2pm-5pm daily), a multimedia exhibition with multilingual headphone commentary about Lisbon's history and demography.

North of the castle is the former **Mouraria Quarter**, where the Moors lived after the Christian reconquest. It's now rather sombre, though Rua da Mouraria has been modernised and pedestrianised.

Graça

Northeast of the castle lies the Graça district. Following Rua de São Tomé up from Largo das Portas do Sol, you pass Largo de Rodrigues de Freitas and reach Calçada da Graça, which leads to a splendid viewpoint (with café), the **Miradouro da Graça**. To the right is a former Augustinian convent, which now serves as a military barracks, and about 700m beyond the convent is the area's third major viewpoint, on another of Lisbon's hills, the **Miradouro da Senhora do Monte**. This is the best point in town for views of the castle, Mouraria and city centre.

Two cultural sites lie within walking distance to the east (tram No 28 also passes close by). Dominating the scene is the huge dome of the Igreja de Santa Engrácia. When work began on this church in 1682, it was expected to be one of Lisbon's grandest. After almost three centuries of dithering and neglect, it was inaugurated in 1966 as a sombre and rather incongruous **Panteão Nacional** (National Pantheon; ☎ 218 881 529; adult/under-26 or senior €2/1, 10am-2pm Sun free; open 10am-5pm Tues-Sun). Its marble cenotaphs to historic and literary figures (among them Vasco da Gama and Henry the Navigator as well as General Humberto Delgado, the opposition leader assassinated by the secret police in 1962) are swathed in pink and grey marble. Take the lift to the rooftop for great views of the river and Alfama, or just chill out inside the fabulously cool dome.

Far more aesthetically impressive is the nearby **Igreja de São Vicente de Fora** (adult/under-26 or senior €2.50/1.30; open 10am-6pm Tues-Sun). Built by the master of the Italian Renaissance, Felipe Terzi, between 1582 and 1627, its wide nave and coffered vault are striking in their simplicity. In the two tranquil cloisters and on practically every wall are striking 18th-century azulejos – the 1st floor features a special display of 38 panels depicting La Fontaine's fables (moral tales featuring animal characters, written in the 17th century), accompanied by excellent background text in English and French. The former refectory is now a mausoleum containing the sombre marble tombs of almost the entire Bragança dynasty. The top of the monastery has more fantastic views of the river, and its café an appealing menu of salads, cakes and light lunches.

Santa Apolónia

Just west of Santa Apolónia train station, is the **Museu Militar** (Military Museum; Map 3;

☎ 218 842 569; Largo do Museu de Artil-haria; admission €2; open 10am-5pm Tues-Sun). Its main claim to fame is its artillery collection, said to be the world's biggest.

Northeast of Santa Apolónia train station perhaps Lisbon's most attractive museum, the **Museu Nacional do Azulejo** (Map 1; National Azulejos Museum; ☎ 218 147 747; Rua Madre de Deus 4; adult/under-26 or senior €2.30/1.30, 10am-2pm Sun free; open 2pm-6pm Tues, 10am-6pm Wed-Sun). A splendid array of tiles from the 15th to 20th centuries (plus displays on how they're made) is integrated into the elegant buildings of the former 16th-century convent of Igreja de Nossa Senhora da Madre de Deus. Among highlights are a 36m-long panel depicting pre-earthquake Lisbon. (For more on azulejos, see the boxed text in the Facts about Portugal chapter.) The church (with its own beautiful tiles), the Manueline cloister and stupendous baroque chapel, are highlights in their own right. There's also a relaxing restaurant here (see the boxed text 'Azulejos for Lunch?' later in the Places to Eat section).

ESTRELA, LAPA & DOCA DE ALCÂNTARA (MAP 5)
The attractions in this district west of Bairro Alto are limited, though getting here on a westbound tram No 28 from Largo Martim Moniz (Baixa) is fun (you can also take bus No 13 from Praça do Comércio).

In the Largo de São Bento is one of the area's most imposing sights, the **Palácio da Assembleia da República** (Palácio da Assembleia Nacional), Portugal's parliament, the nucleus of which is the 17th-century former convent of São Bento. The national assembly has convened here since 1833.

At the top of Calçada da Estrela are the massive dome and belfries of the **Basílica da Estrela** (admission free; open 7.30am-1pm & 3pm-8pm daily). Completed in 1790 by order of Dona Maria I (whose tomb is here) in gratitude for bearing a male heir, the church is all elegant neoclassicism outside and chilly, echoing baroque inside. Its best feature is the view across Lisbon from the dome.

Across the road is an attractive public park, the **Jardim da Estrela**, with a good children's playground. Beyond this lies a patch of heresy in this Catholic land, the Protestant **Cemitério dos Ingleses** (English Cemetery), founded in 1717. Among expats

at rest here are novelist Henry Fielding (author of Tom Jones), who died during a visit to Lisbon (ironically, for his health) in 1754. At the far corner is all that remains of Lisbon's old Jewish cemetery.

To the south of Estrela is **Lapa**, Lisbon's diplomatic quarter. The main attraction (besides the bars and nightclubs of Avenida 24 de Julho and Doca de Santo Amaro; see Entertainment later in this chapter) is the first-class **Museu Nacional de Arte Antiga** (National Museum of Ancient Art; ☎ 213 964 151; Rua das Janelas Verdes 9; adult/under-26 or senior €3/1.50, 10am-2pm Sun free; open 2pm-6pm Tues, 10am-6pm Wed-Sun). Housed in a 17th-century palace (take bus Nos 40 or 60 from Praça da Figueira or tram No 15 west from Praça do Comércio) this is the country's largest collection of works by Portuguese painters, as well as other 14th- to 20th-century European works and an extensive collection of applied art.

The most outstanding item is undoubtedly the Panels of São Vicente by Nuno Gonçalves, most brilliant of the Flemish-influenced Portuguese painters prominent in the 15th century. The six extraordinarily detailed panels show a crowd of contemporary Portuguese figures from every level of society (including the Duke of Bragança and his family) paying homage to São Vicente, Portugal's patron saint. You may recognise the frequently reproduced central panels, which include Prince Henry the Navigator in his floppy hat.

Japanese namban screens are the most interesting items in the museum's newer wing. Namban (meaning 'southern barbarians'), the Japanese name for the Portuguese who landed on Tanegaxima island in southern Japan in 1543, has come to refer to all Japanese art inspired by this encounter. The 16th-century screens show the Portuguese arrival in intriguing detail.

Lastly, don't overlook the fantastic silverware collection, with dozens of masterpieces by the French silversmith Thomas Germain and his son François-Thomas, made in the late 18th century for the Portuguese court and royal family.

A charming alternative to all this high art is the **Museu da Carris** (☎ 213 613 087; Rua 1 de Maio; adult/under-26 or senior €2.50/1.30; open 10am-4.30pm Mon-Fri, 10am-1pm & 2pm-4.30pm Sat), housed in the Carris

LISBON

headquarters, which details the fascinating history of Lisbon's transport system. Tram No 15 passes right by.

One of Lisbon's newest museums, **Museu da Marioneta** (Puppet Museum; ☎ 213 942 810; Rua da Esperança 144; adult/under-26 or senior €2.50/1.30; open 10am-1pm & 2pm-6pm Wed-Sun), in the eastern part of the district, houses a fantastic collection of puppets that had been half-forgotten in an older museum. Now they've got a splendid setting in the restored Convento das Bernardas. There's something of everything here, from Vietnamese water and elephant puppets to full-sized Portuguese creations, plus a fascinating display on how puppets were created for a film sequence.

RATO, MARQUÊS DE POMBAL & SALDANHA (MAP 4)

Northern and northwestern Lisbon have a hotchpotch of attractions, from hothouses to high culture. The one must-see is the **Museu**

Calouste Gulbenkian (☎ 217 823 000; e museu@gulbenkian.pt; Avenida de Berna 45A; metro São Sebastião; adult €3, child, student, teacher or senior free, Sun all free; combined ticket with Centro de Arte Moderna €5; open 2pm-5.45pm Tues, 10am-5.45pm Wed-Sun). Calouste Sarkis Gulbenkian, born to Armenian parents in Istanbul in 1869, was one of the 20th-century's wealthiest men and best-known philanthropists, and an astute and generous patron of the arts years before he struck it rich in Iraqi oil. His great artistic coup was the purchase of works from Leningrad's Hermitage between 1928 and 1930, when the young Soviet Union desperately needed hard currency. In his later years he adopted Portugal as his home and bequeathed to it his entire, stupendous art collection as well as a charitable foundation that has become Portugal's main cultural life force (see Special Events).

The museum is undoubtedly Portugal's finest, and one of Europe's unsung treasures.

Museu Calouste Gulbenkian Highlights

Among the classical and Oriental art collections, some of the most memorable items are in the **Egyptian Room**: an exquisite 2700-year-old alabaster bowl, small female statuettes (each with a different hairstyle), and a series of bronze cats. In the adjoining **Greek and Roman** section, note the 2400-year-old Attic vase, Roman glassware in magical colours and an absorbing collection of Hellenic coins with finely carved heads and figures.

In the **Oriental Islamic Art** collection are some 16th- and 17th-century Turkish faïence glowing with brilliant greens and blues, and 14th-century mosque lamps from Syria, with strikingly sensuous shapes. The adjoining **Armenian** collection includes illuminated manuscripts and books from the 16th to 18th centuries.

The **Chinese and Japanese** collection features a rich display of porcelain, lacquer, jade and celadon. Especially lovely are the 19th-century Japanese prints of flowers and birds by Sugakudo.

The huge **European Art** section ranges from medieval ivories and manuscripts to paintings from the 15th to 19th centuries. All the big names are here, including Rembrandt, Van Dyck and Rubens. Particularly lovely is the 15th-century Portrait of a Girl by Ghirlandaio and a white marble Diana by Houdon.

Eighteenth- and 19th-century European art is comprehensively represented with Aubusson tapestries, fabulous if often fussy furniture (including items from Versailles), Sèvres porcelain, and intricate clocks. Outstanding paintings in the collection are Gainsborough's Mrs Lowndes, two atmospheric La Tour portraits, some typically turbulent Turners and a passionate Spring Kiss by Rodin.

Finally, fans of Art Nouveau will appreciate the magical jewellery of French designer **René Lalique**: fantasies in the form of coronets and hair combs, brooches and necklaces, exhibited in their own gallery.

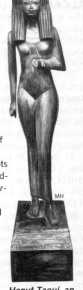

Henut Taoui, an Egyptian artefact

The collection – consisting of over 6000 pieces, although only 1500 can be permanently exhibited – spans every major epoch of Western art and much Eastern art (see the boxed text 'Museu Calouste Gulbenkian Highlights'). Recent gallery refurbishments include touch-screen bilingual information screens and a choice of two circuits: one of Oriental and classical art and one of European art. You'll need at least a full day here.

A stroll through the surrounding peaceful, landscaped gardens will bring you to the foundation's other major museum in Lisbon, the **Centro de Arte Moderna** (Modern Art Centre; ☎ 217 823 474; open 2pm-5.45pm Tues, 10am-5.45pm Wed-Sun). This boasts the country's best collection of 20th-century Portuguese art, including works by Amadeo de Souza Cardoso, José de Almada Negreiros and Maria Helena Vieira da Silva.

When you need a breather, the **Parque Eduardo VII** (Avenida da Liberdade; metro Parque) is down the road. The park (named after England's Edward VII, who visited Lisbon in 1903) provides a fine escape, especially in its gorgeous **estufas** (greenhouses; adult/child under 10 €1.10/free) – the **estufa fria** (cool greenhouse; open 9am-5pm daily Oct-Apr, 9am-6pm May-Sept) and **estufa quente** (hot greenhouse; open 9am-4.30pm daily Oct-Apr, 9am-5.30pm May-Sept) – with an exotic collection of tropical and subtropical plants. There's an **outdoor area** (open 9am-4.30pm daily Oct-Apr, 9am-5.30pm May-Sept) too, with a large pond. Access is from Rua Castilho on the western side of the park. There's a great playground nearby.

GREATER LISBON (MAP 1)

Two metro stops north of the Parque Eduardo VII is the **Jardim Zoológico** (zoo; ☎ 217 232 900; all-inclusive ticket adult/child 3-11/senior €10/7.50/8; open 10am-6pm daily Oct-Apr, 10am-8pm May-Sept). Criticised in the past for its poor conditions and management style, the zoo has introduced some improvements. There are various shows, including a dolphin show (heavy on slapstick).

More uplifting is the **Quinta dos Marquêses da Fronteira** (☎ 217 782 023; Largo de São Domingos de Benfica 1; admission palace & garden/garden only Mon-Fri €5/2, Sat €7.50/2.50; open 10.30am-noon Mon-Sat June-Sept, 11am-noon Oct-May), southwest of the zoo. This 17th-century mansion

is renowned for its azulejos and garden of box hedges. There are guided visits every half-hour during opening hours.

Further out to the north the **Museu da Cidade** (City Museum; ☎ 217 591 617; Campo Grande 245; metro Campo Grande; admission €1.90, 10am-1pm Sun free; open 10am-1pm & 2pm-6pm Tues-Sun) offers a telescopic view of Lisbon's history, with an enormous model of pre-earthquake Lisbon and azulejo panels of city scenes.

Parque das Nações

The old Expo 98 site on the northeastern riverfront is now called Parque das Nações (naz-oish; Nations Park). A largely traffic-free zone, it features some stunning modern architecture (notably the Pavilhão de Portugal by Portugal's leading architect, Álvaro Siza Vieira) as well as family-geared attractions, (pricey) restaurants and bars, and relaxing gardens. Surrounded by continuing construction work (representing Portugal's largest urban regeneration project, with 340 hectares of offices, houses and parkland planned) the 2km-long site still feels rather raw, although its entertainment venues (see Entertainment later in this chapter) and bars can pack in capacity crowds on weekend nights.

The park's major attraction is the **Oceanário** (Oceanarium; adult/child 4-12/senior €9/4.50/5; open 10am-7pm daily Apr-Oct, 10am-6pm Nov-Mar), Europe's largest, with 25,000 fish, birds and mammals in a strikingly designed, two-storey aquarium, which recreates the entire global scene.

The **Pavilhão da Realidade Virtual** (Virtual Reality Pavilion; adult/youth 6-17 or senior €7.50/3.80; open noon-5.30pm Tues-Sun) presents a show (with English and Spanish translations) on the life of Luís de Camões, Portugal's national poet.

Science nerds and schoolkids love the **Pavilhão do Conhecimento** (Knowledge Pavilion; adult/youth 7-17 or senior/child 3-6 €5/2.50/2; open 10am-6pm Tues-Fri, 11am-7pm Sat & Sun), with its interactive science and technology displays.

The 140m-high **Torre de Vasco da Gama** (adult/youth 5-14 or senior €2.50/1.30; open 10am-8pm daily) is the place to go for panoramic views.

Take the metro to Gare do Oriente (another impressive Expo 98 architectural project) and walk through the Centro Vasco da Gama shopping mall to the park's main **Posto de Informação** (☎ *218 919 333;* **w** *www .parquedasnacoes.pt; open 9am-8pm daily)*, with free maps and information on what's happening, and a free left-luggage office. The Cartão do Parque (costing €14/7 adult/senior and child four to 12 years) gives free admission to the Oceanarium and Vasco da Gama tower, as well as discounts on other attractions.

The most exciting way to get from one end of the park to the other is on the riverside **Teleférico** *(cable car; adult/youth 5-14 or senior €3/1.50; operating 11am-7pm Mon-Fri, 10am-8pm Sat & Sun)*.

There is an outlet of **Tejo Bike** (☎ *917 201 749; open 10am-8pm daily)* at the northern end of the park, which rents bikes (€3/4/7 per hour for a junior/adult/tandem bike) for use within the park.

For details about the park's bowling centre, see Activities later in this chapter.

The Aqueduct of Free Waters

The extraordinary Aqueduto das Águas Livres is one of the city's most imposing but least-acclaimed sights. Its 109 grey stone arches lope across the hills into Lisbon from Caneças, over 18km away. They're most impressive at Campolide, where the tallest arch is about 65m high (take any train from Rossio station to the first stop). The aqueduct was built between 1728 and 1835, by order of Dom João V, to bring the city its first clean drinking water.

The king laid the aqueduct's final stone at **Mãe d'Água** *(Mother of Water; Map 4; Praça das Amoreiras; adult/student or senior €2/1; open 10am-6pm Mon-Sat)*, the city's massive, 5500-cu-metre main reservoir. The reservoir's cool, echoing chamber (from where you can see the start of the narrow aqueduct passage), completed in 1834, now hosts art exhibitions.

The aqueduct and reservoir are two of the four parts of the Museu da Água run by Empresa Portuguesa das Águas Livres (EPAL), the municipal water company. The **main museum** *(Map 1; ☎ 218 135 522; Rua do Alviela 12; adult/student or senior €2/1; open 10am-6pm Mon-Sat)* is located in a restored 19th-century pump station near Santa Apolónia train station.

BELÉM (MAP 6)

The district of Belém, 6km west of the Rossio, was one of the main launch pads for Portugal's Age of Discoveries. Most famously, this was the place from which the great explorer Vasco da Gama set sail on 8 July 1497 for the two-year voyage on which he discovered a sea route to India, setting in motion a fundamental shift in the world's balance of power.

Upon Vasco da Gama's safe return, Dom Manuel I ordered the construction of a monastery on the site of the riverside chapel (founded by Henry the Navigator) in which da Gama and his officers had kept an all-night vigil before departing on their historic voyage.

The Mosteiro dos Jerónimos, like its predecessor, was dedicated to the Virgin Mary, St Mary of Bethlehem (Belém) – hence the district's name.

The monastery and an offshore watchtower also commissioned by Manuel I (both of them Unesco World Heritage sites) are essential viewing for every Lisbon visitor. They are among the finest remaining examples of the exuberant Portuguese brand of Renaissance-Gothic architecture called Manueline (see the special section 'Portugal's Architecture' in the Facts about Portugal chapter).

This peaceful suburb, which also boasts several other historical monuments and a clutch of worthwhile museums, makes a good full-day outing from central Lisbon – but don't go on a Monday, when nearly everything is closed.

The most interesting way to get here is on the modern No 15 tram from Praça da Figueira or Praça do Comércio; alternatively you can take bus No 14 from the Rossio or Praça da Figueira. Trains from Cais do Sodré station to Oeiras stop at Belém (€0.70, three to five per hour, fewer at weekends).

Mosteiro dos Jerónimos

Manuel I ordered this monastery built in memory of Vasco da Gama's discovery of a sea route to India and, while he was at it, arranged that its church be made a pantheon for himself and his royal descendants (many of whom are now entombed in its chancel and side chapels). Huge sums were funnelled into the project, including the so-called 'pepper money', a 5% tax levied on all income

MAP 6 – BELÉM

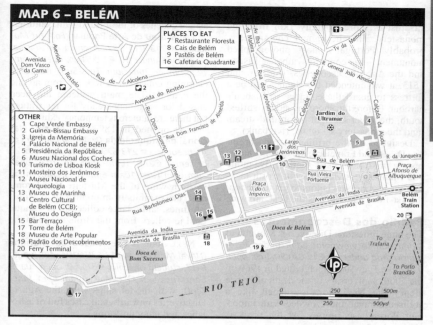

PLACES TO EAT
7 Restaurante Floresta
8 Cais de Belém
9 Pastéis de Belém
16 Cafetaria Quadrante

OTHER
1 Cape Verde Embassy
2 Guinea-Bissau Embassy
3 Igreja da Memória
4 Palácio Nacional de Belém
5 Presidência da República
6 Museu Nacional dos Coches
10 Turismo de Lisboa Kiosk
11 Mosteiro dos Jerónimos
12 Museu Nacional de Arqueologia
13 Museu de Marinha
14 Centro Cultural de Belém (CCB); Museu do Design
15 Bar Terraço
17 Torre de Belém
18 Museu de Arte Popular
19 Padrão dos Descobrimentos
20 Ferry Terminal

from the spice trade with Portugal's expanding African and Far Eastern colonies.

Work began in about 1502, following a Gothic design by architect Diogo de Boitaca, considered one of the originators of the Manueline style. After his death in 1517, building resumed with a Renaissance flavour under Spaniard João de Castilho and, later, with classical overtones under Diogo de Torralva and Jérome de Rouen (Jerónimo de Ruão). The monastery was only completed towards the end of the 16th century. The huge neo-Manueline western wing and the domed bell tower, which date from the 19th century, seem out of keeping with the rest.

The monastery was populated with monks of the Order of St Jerome, whose spiritual job was to give comfort and guidance to sailors – and of course to pray for the king's soul. When the order was dissolved in 1833 the monastery was used as a school and orphanage until about 1940.

The façade of the church is dominated by João de Castilho's fantastic southern portal, dense with religious and secular carvings. You enter the **church** (*admission free; open 10am-6.30pm Tues-Sun May-Sept, 10am-5pm Oct-Apr, last admission 30min before closing*) through the western portal, designed by the French sculptor Nicholas Chanterène and now obscured by a modern connecting passage. In contrast to the extravagant exterior, the interior is sparsely adorned, spacious and lofty beneath an unsupported baroque transept vault 25m high. Vasco da Gama is interred in the lower chancel, in a place of honour opposite the revered 16th-century poet Luís de Camões.

The central courtyard of the monastery's **cloisters** (*adult/under-26 or senior €3/1.50, 10am-2pm Sun free*) is magically peaceful even when it's crowded. Its recently restored stonework reveals every amazing Manueline detail. In the refectory off the western side of the cloisters, an azulejo panel depicts the Biblical story of Joseph. The sarcophagus in the echoing chapterhouse on the northeastern corner belongs to the 19th-century Portuguese historian Alexandre Herculano.

Torre de Belém

The Tower of Belém (*admission free; open 10am-6.30pm Tues-Sun May-Sept, 10am-5pm*

Oct-Apr, last admission 30min before closing) sits just offshore, roughly 1km from the monastery. This hexagonal chesspiece – probably Portugal's most photographed monument – has come to symbolise Lisbon and the Age of Discoveries. Built around 1515, it was intended by Manuel I to be a fortress to guard the entrance to Lisbon's harbour. Before the shoreline slowly shifted south, the tower sat right out in mid-stream (and the monastery sat on the riverbank).

Designed by the brilliant Arruda brothers, Diogo and Francisco, the tower is an arresting mixture of early Gothic, Byzantine and Manueline styles. It's not worth tackling the log-jam of visitors to get to the top; the 1st-floor panorama is the best, anyway.

Padrão dos Descobrimentos

The huge limestone Discoveries Monument *(admission to viewpoint adult/under-26 or senior/child under 12 €1.80/0.90/free; open 9am-5pm Tues-Sun)*, inaugurated in 1960 on the 500th anniversary of the death of Prince Henry the Navigator, is shaped like a stylised caravel and crowded with important Portuguese figures. At the prow is Henry the Navigator; behind him are explorers Vasco da Gama, Diogo Cão and Fernão de Magalhães, poet Luís de Camões, painter Nuno Gonçalves and 27 others. Inside are exhibition rooms, and a lift and stairs to the top, which offers a bird's-eye view of the monastery and the river.

Centro Cultural de Belém & Museu do Design

The huge Centro Cultural de Belém *(CCB; ☎ 213 612 400; Praça do Império)* is one of Lisbon's busiest and most important cultural venues. Inside is the brilliant Museu do Design *(☎ 213 612 934; adult/youth 13-15 or senior/child under 12 €3/1.50/0.80; open 11am-8pm daily, last admission 7.15pm)*, with a fabulous collection of 20th-century furnishing and design items from the collection of Francisco Capelo. Other halls feature changing modern art exhibitions.

Other Museums

The Museu Nacional dos Coches *(National Coach Museum; ☎ 213 610 850; Praça Afonso de Albuquerque; adult/student €3/1.50; open 10am-5.30pm Tues-Sun)*, in the former royal riding school, has one of the world's finest collections of royal, aristocratic and ecclesiastical coaches of the 17th to 19th centuries.

The Museu de Arte Popular *(Folk Art Museum; ☎ 213 011 282; Avenida de Brasília; adult/child under 12 €1.80/free; open 10am-12.30pm & 2pm-5pm Tues-Sun)* houses a charming collection of folk art from around the country. The main museum has been closed for years, apparently for renovation, but there are numerous temporary exhibitions.

First opened in 1893, the Museu Nacional de Arqueologia *(National Museum of Archaeology; ☎ 213 620 000; adult/under-26 or senior €2/1, 10am-2pm Sun free; open 2pm-6pm Tues, 10am-6pm Wed-Sun)*, in the western wing of the Mosteiro dos Jerónimos, has exhibits from prehistory to Moorish times, and a large collection of antique gold jewellery from the Bronze Age to the Roman era.

Next door is the Museu de Marinha *(Naval Museum; ☎ 213 620 019; adult/youth 6-17, student or senior €3/1.50; open 10am-5pm Tues-Sun Oct-May, 10am-6pm June-Sept)*, with model ships from the Age of Discoveries onwards, and cases full of astrolabes and navy uniforms.

ACTIVITIES

The handiest **swimming** pool is the small rooftop **Ateneu Comercial Complexo de Piscinas** *(Map 2; ☎ 213 430 947; Rua das Portas de Santo Antão 102; admission Mon-Fri €3.30, Sat €3.50; open 9am-noon, 1.30pm-4.30pm & 9pm-10pm Mon, Wed & Fri, 7.30am-10am, 1.30pm-4.30pm & 9pm-10pm Tues & Thur, 3.30pm-7pm Sat)*. The professional-standard **Complexo de Piscinas do EUL** *(Map 1; ☎ 217 994 970; Avenida Professor Gama Pinto; admission €7.50; open 6.45am-10pm Mon-Fri, 6.45am-7pm Sat)* is part of the university's sports complex (head north for about 400m from the Cidade-Universitária metro stop).

Also at this complex are the university's **tennis courts** *(☎ 217 932 895)*. More quality courts are at the **Instalações de Ténis de Monsanto** *(Map 1; ☎ 213 648 741)* in the Parque Florestal de Monsanto; to get there take bus No 24 from Alcântara or 29 from Belém. You'll need to book ahead at both places.

Golfers are spoilt for choice. There are six major **golf** courses in the area (see the boxed text 'Golf on the Estoril Coast' in the

Around Lisbon chapter), plus the **Lisbon Sports Club** (☎ 214 310 077; *Casal da Carregueira, Belas*), just north of Queluz.

Bowling Internacional de Lisboa (*Map 1*; ☎ 218 922 521; *Parque das Nações*; open noon-2am Mon-Thur, noon-4am Fri, 11am-4am Sat, 11am-2am Sun*) is Portugal's biggest **bowling** centre. It costs €3.50/4 before/after 8pm (€3.50/4.80 Friday, €4.80/4.80 weekends), with reductions for children under 12 and seniors.

Lisbon hosts an international **marathon**, the **Maratona de Lisboa** (☎ 214 412 182; W *www.pgsite.com/memotur*) every late November, attracting some 5000 athletes. In late March or early April a half-marathon, the **Meia Maratona Cidade de Lisboa**, starts from Almada with approximately 30,000 runners crossing the Ponte 25 de Abril into Lisbon, finishing in Belém; contact the **Federação Portuguese de Atletismo** (☎ 214 146 020; W *www.fpatletismo.pt/index0.htm*) for details. Both events include a 7km minimarathon for kids.

ORGANISED TOURS
Bus & Tram Tours
Carris (☎ 213 582 334; e *carristur@carris.pt*), the municipal transport company, runs 1½-hour tram tours (€16/8 adult/child): the Hills Tramcar tour of the hills around the Baixa and Alfama three to four times daily; and the Discoveries Tour, which continues to Belém, three to six times daily. Carris also runs frequent open-top bus tours (€13/8) from Praça do Comércio: the Tagus Tour of the city and Belém; and the Orient Tour of northeast Lisbon, including Parque das Nações.

Cityrama (☎ 213 191 091; W *www.cityrama.pt*), **Portugal Tours** (☎ 213 522 902) and **Gray Line** (☎ 213 522 594) run practically identical sightseeing bus tours of Lisbon and the surrounding region, including a 5½-hour city tour (€27.50); Lisbon by Night (€54.90, four hours) with a restaurant meal; and Lisbon plus Sintra and the Estoril coast (€69.90, full day with lunch). All depart from Marquês de Pombal (Map 4; you can hop aboard these without prebooking if there's space), picking up passengers at selected hotels.

Cityline (☎ 213 191 090) and **Lisboa Vision** (☎ 214 788 792) operate more casual 'hop-on-hop-off' open-bus tours via all the major sights (including to Belém) for €12.50/6.30 per adult/child aged five to 15 (children under five are free). Their circular routes have numerous city centre pick-up points; the turismo has details. **Art Shuttle** (☎ 213 959 818, toll-free ☎ 800 250 251) also runs 'hop-on-hop-off' minibus tours to the most important museums, galleries and cultural sites from 10am to 7pm daily between April and September for €6/12 per half/full day (tickets available on board or at Turismo de Lisboa outlets).

Walking Tours
The **Centro Nacional de Cultura** (☎ 213 466 722; *Rua António Maria Cardoso 68*) organises three-hour themed walks (€25 per person, minimum five people); advance booking is essential. Contact the turismo for further information.

Papa-Léguas (☎ 218 452 689; *Rua Conde de Sabugosa 3F*) offers occasional nature walks (eg, to the Parque Florestal de Monsanto) for around €13 per person.

River Cruises
Transtejo (*Map 3*; ☎ 218 820 348) runs 2½-hour, multilingual Rio Tejo cruises (€15/8 adult/child) at 11am and 3pm daily (3pm only in winter) from April to October, from the eastern end of the Terreiro do Paço terminal.

Transtróia (☎ 265 235 101; *Rua Padre Silvestre Serrão 6, Setúbal*) offers river trips with a nature angle, including a 2½-hour tour (€47.50/25) to see the flamingos of the Tagus Estuary (plus the southern-bank town of Alcochete) five times on Monday and Tuesday from Cais do Sodré.

SPECIAL EVENTS
The following is a selection of Lisbon's abundant festivals.

Religious Festivals
In June, in common with many Portuguese towns, the city enjoys the Festas dos Santos Populares (Festivals of the Popular Saints), Christianised versions of traditional summer solstice celebrations. These include the Festa de São João (St John; 23–24 June) and the Festa de São Pedro (St Peter; 28–29 June), but it's during the Festa de Santo António (St Anthony; 12–13 June; see the boxed text 'St Anthony' earlier in this chapter) that Lisbon really lets its hair down. This is the climax of

three weeks of partying known as the Festas de Lisboa, celebrated with particular gusto in the historical quarters of Alfama and Madragoa, with some 50 *arraiais* (street parties) brimming with music and dancing, plus lots of wine and grilled sardines, and masses of floral decoration. The highlight is the Marchas Populares on the evening of 12 June when dozens of communities march along Avenida da Liberdade. The same night witnesses the ultimate *arraial* in the Alfama.

Theme Festivals

The Festival dos Oceanos (Oceans Festival), held for two weeks from mid-August, has expanded its nautical theme (regattas, nautical-paraphernalia markets and water sports contests) to encompass big shows and parades, musical performances and a gastronomic fair.

The Festival do Vinho (first fortnight in November) features a wine fair plus folk dancing and handicrafts.

Music, Dance & Film Festivals

The Festival das Músicas e dos Portos (Harbour and Music Festival), held during 10 days in early February, features fado and sea-inspired music from another port city (Athens and New Orleans were previous participants) and with a diverse programme of fado as well as concerts, films, drama and dance.

Lisbon shares its biggest rock event with Porto: Super Bock Super Rock, a fortnight of 18 concerts in both cities in March.

The **Fundação Calouste Gulbenkian** (☎ 217 935 131) organises several annual international music festivals, including Encontros de Música Contemporânea (Contemporary Music Encounters) in May and Jazz em Agosto (Jazz in August) in early August. Check details at **w** www.musica .gulbenkian.pt.

The south-bank town of Seixal hosts the unusual Festival Cantigas do Maio (Songs of May) in late May, with traditional music from around the world. Nearby Cascais, Estoril and Sintra also have their own major music festivals; see these sections in the Around Lisbon chapter for details.

Increasingly popular is Lisbon's two-week Festival de Cinema Gay e Lésbico (Gay and Lesbian Film Festival), which is held in late September. More mainstream is

the long-established Festival Internacional de Cinema de Tróia in early June. Every November, contemporary dance fans flock to Centro Cultural de Belém's Festival Internacional de Dança Contemporânea, billed as a 'deliberately alternative event'.

PLACES TO STAY

Although at least 16 new hotels have gone up in the last few years, advance bookings are still strongly recommended during high season for mid-range to upmarket city centre hotels. Prices listed here are for doubles in July (August is higher). Some places may offer discounts for long stays. Most budget accommodation is in the Baixa and Rossio areas, while many mid-range and top-end hotels are in the Saldanha, Marquês de Pombal and Avenida da Liberdade districts.

PLACES TO STAY – BUDGET
Camping

Lisboa Camping – Parque Municipal (*Map 1*; ☎ *217 623 100, fax 217 623 106; adult/tent/car €4.70/4.70/3*), in the Parque Florestal de Monsanto, 6km west of the Rossio, is big and well-equipped, with a pool and tennis court. Bungalows for two to six people are also available. To get there, take bus No 43 from Cais do Sodré, No 14 from Praça da Figueira or No 50 from Gare do Oriente.

Clube de Campismo de Lisboa (☎ *219 623 960, fax 219 623 144; adult/tent/car €4.40/4.70/4.40*), open to Camping Card International (CCI) card-holders only, is 20km northwest of Lisbon at Almornos.

There are other camp sites at Costa de Caparica, Sintra, Praia Grande and Praia do Guincho (see the Around Lisbon chapter).

Hostels

The central **Pousada da Juventude de Lisboa** (*Map 4*; ☎ *213 532 696*; **e** *lisboa@movi jovem.pt; Rua Andrade Corvo 46; metro Picoas, bus No 46 or 90 from Santa Apolónia or Rossio, or AeroBus from airport; dorm beds/doubles €15/42; open 24hr*) has double beds with private shower and toilet; there are no cooking facilities.

The newer **Pousada da Juventude de Lisboa Parque Nações** (*Map 1*; ☎ *218 920 890*; **e** *lisboaparque@movijovem.pt; Via de Moscavide; dorm beds/doubles €12.50/35; reception open 8am-midnight daily*) is near Parque das Nações, 1km north of Gare do

Oriente. It has a restaurant, plus cooking and laundry facilities.

There are other **pousadas da juventude** across the Tejo at Almada (☎ 212 943 491; e almada@movijovem.pt; Quinta do Bucelinho, Pragal) and near the beach at Catalazete (☎ 214 430 638; e catalazete@movi jovem.pt; Estrada Marginal, Oeiras), 12km west of Lisbon, accessible by frequent trains from Cais do Sodré station. Reservations are essential – at least a month ahead in summer.

There's also a hostel in Sintra, 45 minutes by train from Rossio station (see the Around Lisbon chapter).

Pensões & Residenciais
Rossio, Praça dos Restauradores, Baixa & Bairro Alto Many cheap places in the Baixa are on upper floors of old residential flats, with grotty stairwells and thin-walled rooms. All of the following are on Map 2.

Pensão Norte (☎ 218 878 941, fax 218 868 462; 2nd-4th floors, Rua dos Douradores 159; doubles with shower/bathroom €30/40) has a warren of small, plain doubles with telephone and TV.

Pensão Prata (☎ 213 468 908; 4th floor, Rua da Prata 71; doubles with/without shower €30/25) has basic facilities but provides a friendly welcome.

Pensão Santo Tirso (☎ 213 470 428; Rossio 18; doubles with/without bathroom €30/20) comes as a pleasant surprise after climbing three floors up a grimy stairwell: the folk are friendly and the pricier rooms fairly decent.

Pensão Imperial (☎ 213 420 166; 4th floor, Praça dos Restauradores 78; doubles with/without shower €35/30) is a cheery place with an irresistible location (but no lift); some rooms overlook the *praça*.

There's a clutch of places near Rossio station, better inside than the seedy entrances suggest: **Hospedaria Bons Dias** (☎ 213 471 918; 5th floor, Calçada do Carmo 25; doubles €30-40) has brightly decorated rooms (with shared bathroom), some with a small balcony, and a lift.

Residencial Estrela do Mondego (☎ 213 240 840; 2nd floor, Calçada do Carmo 25; doubles with/without bathroom from €35/30) is homely and popular, with spacious rooms (some with fridge, all with air-con and telephone). It also has flats for rent.

Residência Nova Avenida (☎/fax 213 423 689; Rua de Santo António da Glória 87; doubles with/without shower €30/25, triples with shower €40), an old house in the Bairro Alto boasting high ceilings and fancy chandeliers, has a variety of simple rooms.

Pensão Estrela de Ouro (☎ 213 465 110; 3rd floor, Largo Trindade Coelho 6; doubles €25-30) offers bright, clean rooms (without bathroom) in a fairly quiet location.

Pensão Globo (☎/fax 213 462 279; Rua do Teixeira 37; doubles with/without bathroom from €30/25, triples without bathroom €50) is the most tempting choice among several in this price bracket, a popular, well-run place close to the nightlife district.

Alfama The best among several waterfront cheapies here is cheerful **Pensão Varandas** (Map 3; ☎ 218 870 519; Rua Afonso de Albuquerque 7 • 2nd floor, Rua dos Bacalhoeiros 8; doubles €35-40). The best rooms (with a shower cubicle) have tiny balconies overlooking Campo das Cebolas.

Pensão São João da Praça (Map 3; ☎ 218 862 591, fax 218 880 415; 2nd floor, Rua São João da Praça 97; doubles with/without bathroom from €33/28) is a rather dour place but the location is great.

PLACES TO STAY – MID-RANGE
Rossio, Praça dos Restauradores & Baixa
All of the following are on Map 2.

Pensão Praça da Figueira (☎/fax 213 424 323; e rrcoelho@clix.pt; 3rd floor, Travessa Nova de São Domingos 9; doubles with/without shower €42.50/40, triples without bathroom €45) is a brilliant place with a range of bright, well-kept rooms, plus communal 'mini-kitchens', Internet access and laundry service. Some of the rooms overlook the *praça*.

New Aljubarrota (☎/fax 213 460 112; e p_aljubarrota@hotmail.com; 4th floor, Rua da Assunção 53; doubles per 1/3 days with shower €47.50/42.50, without €40/ 35, triples with shower €66.50/60, without shower €61.50/54) is a friendly, family-run establishment in the pedestrian area, with big, clean rooms. Rates include breakfast.

Pensão Residencial Florescente (☎ 213 463 517, fax 213 427 733; Rua das Portas de Santo Antão 99; doubles with/without bathroom €45/35) is less homely than New

Aljubarrota, but has a huge range of rooms that quickly get booked up.

Pensão Residencial Gerês (☎ 218 810 497, fax 218 882 006; Calçada do Garcia 6; doubles with/without bathroom €55/45) is a small, security-conscious guesthouse, with attractive rooms.

Residencial Duas Nações (☎ 213 460 710, fax 213 470 206; Rua da Vitória 41; doubles with/without bathroom €50/25), in the Baixa's pedestrianised district, is very popular; book ahead.

Pensão Residencial Alcobia (☎ 218 865 171, fax 218 865 174; Poço do Borratém 15; doubles with/without bathroom €43/40) is a rambling, fraying establishment with antiquarian facilities (bathrooms especially) but it's down-to-earth and friendly. Choose between streetside rooms with castle views, or quieter back rooms; rates include breakfast.

Bairro Alto & Rato

Pensão Londres (Map 2; ☎ 213 462 203; e pensaolondres@mail.telepac.pt; Rua Dom Pedro V 53; doubles with/without bathroom from €62/40) has a huge range of rooms, some with fancy stucco decoration. Avoid the claustrophobic, noisy rooms facing the lift shaft. Rates include breakfast. Book well ahead in summer.

Casa de São Mamede (Map 5; ☎ 213 963 166, fax 213 951 896; Rua da Escola Politécnica 159; doubles with breakfast €75) is a small traditional hotel in an elegant townhouse. Doubles include safe and telephone.

Alfama

Pensão Ninho das Águias (Map 3; ☎ 218 854 070; Costa do Castelo 74; doubles/triples with bathroom €43/50, without bathroom €40/45), just below the castle and a steep climb up from the Baixa, has stunning views, elegant rooms and a garden. Without a reservation you'll be lucky if anyone even answers the door.

Sé Guest House (Map 3; ☎/fax 218 864 400; 1st floor, Rua São João da Praça 97; doubles with breakfast €60-80) is a friendly, cosy place full of knick-knacks. Rooms have shared bathroom.

Saldanha & Avenida da Liberdade

Residencial Lisbonense (Map 4; ☎ 213 544 628, fax 213 544 899; Rua Pinheiro Chagas 1; doubles with breakfast €40), a small, modest

establishment, has bright rooms on four upper storeys.

Residencial Marisela (Map 4; ☎/fax 213 160 423; e rsid.marisela@oninet.pt; Rua Filipe Folque 1; doubles around €35) in a quiet street, offers decent doubles, including (oooh!) one with a water bed for €45.

Hotel Impala (Map 4; ☎ 213 148 914, fax 213 575 362; Rua Filipe Folque 49; doubles €45, apartments €80) has reasonable rooms plus apartments for one to four people.

Pensão Residencial 13 da Sorte (Map 4; ☎ 213 539 746, fax 213 531 851; Rua do Salitre 13; doubles/triples €52.50/60) is justifiably popular, thanks to attractive, spacious rooms (with telephone) and good management.

Residência Dublin (Map 4; ☎ 213 555 489, fax 213 543 365; Rua de Santa Marta 45; doubles €42.50) is a friendly establishment, with excellent breakfasts and helpful staff.

PLACES TO STAY – TOP END

Unless stated otherwise, the following prices include breakfast.

Rossio & Praça dos Restauradores

Hotel Lisboa Tejo (Map 2; ☎ 218 866 182; e hotellisboatejo.reservas@evidenciagrupo .com; Poço do Borratém 4; doubles €97), in a fine old building, has 51 nicely decorated doubles; the ancient poço (well) is near the hotel entrance.

Hotel Metrópole (Map 2; ☎ 213 219 030; e metropole@almeidahotels.com; Rossio 30; doubles €145) is a small, low-key hotel with spacious, renovated but wonderfully old-fashioned rooms with 1950s furnishings.

Orion Eden Lisboa (Map 2; ☎ 213 216 600, fax 213 216 666; Praça dos Restauradores 24; studio flats €125, apartments €180) has studios for one or two people and apartments for up to four (all with kitchen, satellite TV and telephone). Three apartments have wheelchair access.

Lisboa Regency Chiado (Map 2; ☎ 213 256 100; e regencychiado@madeiraregency .pt; Rua Nova do Almada 114; doubles Mon-Fri €150-195, Sat & Sun €140-185) is a discreet venue featuring Oriental furnishings and plush rooms (some with castle, cathedral and river views all in one).

Graça & Alfama

Albergaria Senhora do Monte (Map 3; ☎ 218 866 002, fax 218 877 783; Calçada do Monte

39; doubles €112), near the Miradouro da Senhora do Monte, has comfortable rooms, some with spectacular views. Free car parking is available on the quiet street, and tram No 28 runs close by.

Solar dos Mouros (Map 3; ☎ 218 854 940; e mouroslisboa@hotmail.com; Rua do Milagre de Santo António 4; doubles €175) is an incredible seven-room establishment, designed and adorned by painter Luís Lemos. The rooms are a visual delight, huge and bright, with views of the river.or up to the castle.

Marquês de Pombal & Avenida da Liberdade

Hotel Miraparque (Map 4; ☎ 213 524 286; e miraparque@esoterica.pt; Avenida Sidónio Pais 12; doubles €84), a traditional hotel in a quiet location overlooking the park, retains a personal touch and relaxing ambience despite its tour groups.

Hotel Presidente (Map 4; ☎ 213 173 570; e hpresidente@mail.telepac.pt; Rua Alexandre Herculano 13; doubles €97) is a three-star establishment that provides great breakfasts, and rooms with air-con and minibar.

Hotel Botânico (Map 2; ☎ 213 420 392; e hotelbotanico@mail.telepac.pt; Rua Mãe d'Água 16; doubles with air-con & minibar €95) is quieter but blander than Hotel Presidente. There are a few free parking spaces.

Best Western Hotel Eduardo VII (Map 4; ☎ 213 568 800, reservations toll-free ☎ 800 839 361; e sales@hoteleduardovii.pt; Avenida Fontes Pereira de Melo 5; doubles €101) is a long-established, classic hotel with a panoramic rooftop restaurant, business centre, snooker room, and rooms with fridge and safe. Nonsmoking rooms are available.

Hotel Britania (Map 4; ☎ 213 155 016; e britania.hotel@heritage.pt; Rua Rodrigues Sampaio 17; doubles €140-168), designed by Portuguese modernist architect Cassiano Branco in the 1940s, has masses of charm. Its 30 rooms (with marble bathrooms) are huge but intimate. Breakfast costs €12.

Lapa

Two exquisite hotels here are **York House** (Map 5; ☎ 213 962 435; e yorkhouseJohn /Julia:hlcmm.pt; Rua das Janelas Verdes 32; doubles €190), a former 17th-century convent with antique-furnished rooms; and **As Janelas Verdes** (Map 5; ☎ 213 968 143; e jverdes@heritage.pt; Rua das Janelas Verdes

47; doubles €175-215). The website at w www .heritage.pt features other historic properties in the latter's exclusive chain.

Lapa Palace (Map 5; ☎ 213 950 005; e reservas@lapa-palace.com; doubles €300-2000), a 19th-century mansion stuffed with luxurious trappings, is the place for an outrageous splurge.

PLACES TO EAT

Lisbon has hundreds of restaurants, many offering great value for money, especially at lunch time when daily specials cost as little as €4.50. Many places close on Sunday night, and popular Bairro Alto restaurants can fill by 8.30pm.

Turismo de Lisboa's Restaurant Card offers discounts of 10% to 15% in over 40 restaurants. Valid for 72 hours and available at turismos and some hotels, the cost per person/couple/family (ie, two adults and two children under 14) is €5.80/7.80/10.30.

Rossio, Praça dos Restauradores & Baixa

All of the following are on Map 2.

Budget Rua da Glória has several locally popular budget places, including **O Brinco da Glória** (☎ 213 468 635; Rua da Glória 23; half-portions €4.50), where the food is nothing great but portions are generous.

Restaurante Solar do Duque (☎ 213 426 901; Rua do Duque 67; dishes €6-8) is the most appealing of several restaurants with fado-muzak and outdoor seating at the top of Calçada do Duque.

Rua dos Correeiros has lots of good-value places, catering to Portuguese at lunch time and tourists at night. **Ena Pai** (☎ 213 421 759; Rua dos Correeiros 182; dishes €6-8) is typical, a no-frills venue with a rapid turnover of customers for its good-value fare (which even includes vegetables).

Adega Regional da Beira (☎ 213 467 014; Rua dos Correeiros 132; half-portions €5), is a pleasantly simple spot, offering filling half-portions.

Mid-Range The restaurant **UMA** (☎ 213 427 425; Rua dos Sapateiros 177; dishes €7-8) boasts an award-winning arroz de marisco (rice and seafood stew; €19.50 for two), described by one reader as 'a terrific mix of spices with rice'.

Casa do Alentejo (☎ 213 469 231; Rua das Portas de Santo Antão 58; dishes €8.50) has so-so food but an extraordinary setting: a 19th-century melange of Franco-Arabic decor, with a gloriously faded ballroom and two azulejo-adorned dining rooms. The menu features Alentejan cuisine (eg, carne de porco à Alentejana, a pork and clam dish, for €9) and lots of Alentejan wines.

Along this same street, Rua das Portas de Santo Antão, are loads of more touristy cafés and restaurants, many with outdoor seating.

O Fumeiro (☎ 213 474 203; Rua da Conceição da Glória 25), nicely down-to-earth, is devoted to the cuisine of the mountainous Beira Alta and Serra da Estrela region; even the pictures on the walls are of sausages.

Cervejaria Ribadouro (☎ 213 549 411; Rua do Salitre 2; dishes €8) is a traditional (though modernised) beer hall, popular with locals, offering hearty fare such as the house special, beefsteak (€10.40).

Top End A top-notch restaurant is **Gambrinus** (☎ 213 421 466; Rua das Portas de Santo Antão 23; dishes €20-30), serving treats such as caviar, truffles and partridge with mushroom (€34).

Bachus (☎ 213 421 260; Largo da Trindade 8; dishes from €15), famous for its wildfowl dishes, offers a refined ambience on the doorstep of the raffish Bairro Alto.

Bairro Alto & Chiado

All of the following are on Map 2 unless otherwise stated.

Budget Hau Lon (☎ 213 420 683; Rua do Norte 100; dishes from €4) has all the familiar, bargain noodle and rice dishes. Its tourist menu (€22 for two) offers more variety.

Restaurante Alto Minho (☎ 213 468 133; Rua da Bica Duarte Belo 61; dishes €4.90), next to the Elevador da Bica line, does cheap, filling fare (eg, chips and rice with everything).

A Toca (☎ 213 467 160; Rua da Atalaia 85; dishes €6-8; open Mon-Sat) is dead basic; just the place to fuel up on stodge before hitting the Bairro Alto bars.

Mid-Range The small and unpretentious **Sabor e Arte** (☎ 213 471 846; Travessa da Espera 29; dishes €6-8) offers cheaper fare than most in the neighbourhood, including four vegetarian options.

Tasca do Manel (☎ 346 38 13; Rua da Barroca 24; dishes from €7) serves reasonably priced standards, including a tasty leitão assado a bairrada (roast suckling pig; €7).

Mastiga na Tola (☎ 213 477 195; Travessa da Cara 20; dishes from €8; open dinner Tues-Sat), a homely venue named after a contemporary bandit (though he doesn't know it), offers classical music, smiles, and home-cooked fare.

Ali-a-Papa (☎ 213 472 116; Rua da Atalaia 95) specialises in Moroccan cuisine such as delicious couscous (€8.90).

Casa Nostra (☎ 213 425 931; Travessa do Poço da Cidade 60; dishes €7-8; closed Mon, lunch Sat) is a chic, bright Italian restaurant.

Sinal Verde (Map 5; ☎ 213 421 601; Calçada do Combro 42; dishes €7-9), on the western edge of the district, specialises in hearty fare from northeastern Portugal.

Tendinha da Atalaia (☎ 213 461 844; Rua da Atalaia 4; dishes €7-10) is a tiny, traditional place serving delicious no carvão (fish grilled over coals).

Cervejaria da Trindade (☎ 213 423 506; Rua Nova da Trindade 20C; dishes from €6.90, daily specials €4.60), in a former convent building, has a robust, busy atmosphere and azulejo-adorned walls; its beef and seafood dishes are particularly popular.

Top End A stylish novelty is **Rouge** (☎ 213 426 372; Travessa dos Freis de Deus 28; dishes €12-15), specialising in Thai and Mediterranean fare; outdoor tables on the cobbled steps are a bonus.

Pap'Açorda (☎ 213 464 811; Rua da Atalaia 57; dishes €13-50; closed evening Sat, Sun) features a striking minimalist decor and excellent açorda (a bread and shellfish mush served in a clay pot; €13). The chocolate mousse, served from a huge tureen, is legendary.

La Brasserie de l'Entrecôte (☎ 213 428 344; Rua do Alecrim 117) is a modernist venue, high on style and ambience. It offers a simple French menu – rib steak, salad and chips (€13), cooked to perfection, with superb herb and nut sauces.

Marquês de Pombal, Saldanha & Rato

Budget Bright and cheerful **Bella Italia III** (Map 4; ☎ 213 528 636; Avenida Duque d'Ávila 40C) is a pastry-shop-cum-restaurant near the youth hostel, serving pizzas and pastas (€4.80), and other fare.

East of Avenida da Liberdade, Rua de Santa Marta is a good hunting ground for unpretentious restaurants. **Restaurante Estrela de Santa Marta** (Map 4; ☎ 213 548 400; Rua de Santa Marta 14A; dishes €5-9) is typical of these, and is crammed with Portuguese at lunch time.

Mid-Range Popular **Li Yuan** (Map 4; ☎ 213 577 740; Rua Viriato 23; dishes €5.90-6.50) offers delectable Chinese dishes.

Real Fábrica (Map 4; ☎ 213 852 090; Rua da Escola Politécnica 275; dishes €9-12, lunch specials €4-6.30), one of the Rato's artiest eateries, is both bar and restaurant. This converted 19th-century silk factory serves surprisingly low-cost lunch-time specials plus a buffet ao peso (buffet by weight) at €1.50 per 100g. There's an outdoor terrace, and occasional live music or dancing at night.

Mãe Preta (Map 4; ☎ 217 968 116; 1st floor, Avenida António José de Almeida 5D; dishes €10-15; closed Sun, evening Mon), in the Centro Comercial São João de Deus, is an upmarket African restaurant where you can sample fare such as Angolan muzongué (fish broth with sweet potatoes; €9).

Alfama

All of the following are on Map 3 unless otherwise stated.

Budget With its outdoor tables, **Solar do Vez** (☎ 218 870 794; Campo das Cebolas 48; dishes €6-7, daily specials €4.50) is very appealing, offering bargain pratos do dia.

Snack-Bar Arco Iris (☎ 218 864 536; Rua de São João da Praça 17; dishes €6-7, daily specials €4) is a tiny place with a few outdoor tables and live (free) fado from 7.30pm Saturday.

A Gaiola (☎ 218 870 843; Rua dos Bacalhoeiros 24F; dishes €6-7, lunch specials under €5) is one of several eateries along this road, offering cheap and cheerful lunch-time specials.

Restaurante Cais d'Alfama (☎ 218 873 274; Largo do Chafariz de Dentro 24; dishes €5.50-6.50) attracts the locals, with its cheerful atmosphere and extensive menu, including fresh sardines that are often grilled outdoors.

A Tasca da Sé (☎ 218 875 551; Rua Augusto Rosa 62; dishes €6.50), small and welcoming, offers delicious home-cooked fare.

São Cristóvão (Map 2; ☎ 218 885 578; Rua de São Cristóvão 30) is a no-frills, family-run restaurant famous for its Cape Verdean dishes and other African fare; try moamba de Galinha (Angolan chicken stew; €4.90).

Mid-Range The Alfama's waterfront restaurants may be touristy but the outdoor seating is irresistible.

Solar dos Bicos (☎ 218 869 447; Rua dos Bacalhoeiros 8; dishes €7-9) has bargain dishes at lunch time; it's pricier at night.

Malmequer Bemmequer (☎ 218 876 535; Rua de São Miguel 23; dishes €7.40-9.90) is a very attractive restaurant, with an extensive menu of excellent dishes.

A Baiuca (☎ 218 867 284; Rua de São Miguel 20; dishes €9-11), opposite Malmequer Bemmequer, is a small, jovial tavern with great ambience.

Lautasco (☎ 218 860 173; Beco do Azinhal 7; dishes €9-11) has a wonderfully romantic location, tucked away in a shaded courtyard.

Restô (☎ 218 878 225; Costa do Castelo 7; tapas €4-5, restaurant dishes €10-14; open 7.30pm-2am Tues-Sun), part of the Chapitô arts cooperative, has an open-air terrace with wicked views, an arty tapas bar and an eccentric upstairs restaurant. Barbecue lunches (€9) are sometimes on offer.

Top End Vast minimalist dockside venue **Bica do Sapato** (Map 1; ☎ 218 810 320; Cais da Pedra, Avenida Infante Dom Henrique; dishes from €15), part-owned by actor John Malkovich, is the place to see (courtesy of floor-to-ceiling windows) and be seen.

Nearby, the revitalised riverside Doca do Jardim do Tabaco complex boasts several

---

Azulejos for Lunch?

A fine setting for a light lunch is the restaurant in the Museu Nacional do Azulejo, in the old convent of Igreja de Nossa Senhora da Madre de Deus (see Santa Apolónia earlier in this chapter). Choose from a small menu of salads, crepes, and meat and fish dishes, and eat in the bright, traditional kitchen (tiled with azulejos, of course) or the plant-filled garden.

worthy restaurants, including the airy, open-plan **Jardim do Marisco** (*☎ 218 824 242; seafood platter €30*), where you can feast on lobsters, crab and other seafood delicacies. Steaks (from €11) are the other speciality here.

Alcântara & Lapa

Mid-Range In the elegant Lapa district, **Assóporco** (*Map 5; ☎ 213 951 800; Rua das Janelas Verdes 98; set-price dish €7.90*) has a set-price, one-dish deal: *entrecosta grelhado*, grilled pork ribs marinated in honey and served with vegetables and rice.

Picanha Janelas Verdes (*Map 5; ☎ 213 975 401; Rua das Janelas Verdes 96; set-price dish €13.50*), next door to Assóporco, has a similar arrangement, serving *picanha*, a popular Brazilian beef dish.

Top End The upmarket restaurant at York House (see Places to Stay), **A Confraria** (*Map 5; ☎ 213 962 435; dishes €20-50*) serves French delicacies such as *magret* and *foie gras*, lobster or sautéed rack of roe-deer. Sit outside in the lovely garden courtyard.

Cais do Sodré & Belém

Mid-Range If you are yearning for bratwurst, head for **Cervejaria Alemã** (*Map 2; ☎ 213 422 916, Rua do Alecrim 23; dishes €11*), an upmarket place specialising in German cuisine.

Chic & Open-Air

Doca de Santo Amaro, in the Alcântara area of western Lisbon, is the most popular of the recently revamped waterfront areas, with a dozen restaurants-cum-bars. Overlooking the yachts in the marina, and beneath the massive Ponte de 25 Abril, it's a great place for open-air dining and late-night boozing. Restaurants range from pizzerias to fancy fish restaurants, all open until at least 1am (3am on the weekend). Check the Entertainment section in this chapter for some recommended night-out venues. Take the train from Cais do Sodré to Alcântara Mar station and follow *maritima* signs, turning right to Doca de Santo Amaro; or catch tram No 15 from Praça da Figueira, alighting at Dock's Club.

Belém's most tempting restaurants are on Rua Vieira Portuense, all with outdoor seating overlooking the park. **Restaurante Floresta** (*Map 6; Rua Vieira Portuense 2; dishes €5-6*) is the most reasonably priced, while **Cais de Belém** (*Map 6; ☎ 213 621 537; Rua Vieira Portuense 64; dishes €7-9*) is considerably posher.

For snacks with a panoramic view, try the rooftop **Cafétaria Quadrante** (*Map 6*) at the Centro Cultural de Belém.

Café In (*Map 1; ☎ 213 626 249; Avenida de Brasilia, Pavilhão Nascente; dishes around €10*), a short walk eastwards along the riverfront promenade (opposite the Parque Junqueira congress centre) is very chic. A coffee alone will cost you €1, but the setting is unbeatable.

Vegetarian

In a country that loves its meat, the capital fortunately has some good, modestly priced vegetarian places.

Restaurante Os Tibetanos (*Map 4; ☎ 213 142 038; Rua do Salitre 117; open Mon-Fri*), part of a school of Tibetan Buddhism in an old house topped with prayer flags, offers a small selection of quiches (€4), salads (€2 to €4) and other fare.

Restaurante Espiral (*Map 4; ☎ 213 573 585; Praça da Ilha do Faial 14A; open Mon-Sat*) is a trim little place with a pleasant artificial 'garden'. Go early at lunch time to get a seat.

Celeiro (*Map 2; ☎ 213 422 463; Rua 1 de Dezembro 65*) is a health-food shop with a downstairs self-service **macrobiotic restaurant** (*☎ 213 422 463; dishes €4; open 9am-7pm Mon-Fri*) serving tofu stew, soya burgers and other honest vegie food.

Calcuta (*Map 2; ☎ 213 428 295; Rua do Norte 17; vegetarian dishes €5, other dishes €6-8; open Tues-Sun*) is a conveniently located Indian tandoori restaurant, with a decent selection of bargain vegetarian dishes.

C@fé Taborda (*Map 3; ☎ 218 879 484; Costa do Castelo 75; set menus €14-16*), up near Castelo de São Jorge, has an appealing vegetarian and fish restaurant with panoramic views.

While visiting the Museu Calouste Gulbenkian and Centro de Arte Moderna (both Map 4), pop into their great **self-service canteens** (*open lunch Tues-Sun*), both offering terrific fruit salads.

Pastelarias, Cafés & Confeitarias

Lisbon has enough pastry shops and coffee-shops to keep you buzzing all day. Many serve cheap meals at lunch time. Note that you'll pay more to have your coffee or snack outside.

Plain but well-located cafés are **Chiado-mel** (Map 2; ☎ 213 474 401; Rua de Santa Justa 105) right by the Elevador Santa Justa; and gay-friendly **Caffé Rosso** (Map 2; ☎ 213 471 524; Rua Garrett 19; dishes from €6), in its own quiet courtyard, with pastas, pizzas and other fare, plus an eclectic choice of coffees.

The classiest and best-known cafés are in the city centre, many with outdoor seating. **Café Nicola** (Map 2; ☎ 213 460 579; Rossio 24) is the grande dame of Lisbon's cafés with some cool Art Deco features. **Casa Suíça** (Map 2; ☎ 213 214 090; 2 entrances – Rossio 96-101 & Praça da Figueira) is a long-established favourite doing a brisk trade with tourists outside and sedate elderly locals inside.

Confeitaria Nacional (Map 2; ☎ 213 461 720; Praça da Figueira 18) is a 170-year-old café with a dizzying array of pastries and sweets.

Café A Brasileira (Map 2; ☎ 213 469 547; Rua Garrett 120) has strong literary associations – the bronze statue sitting outside is of the poet and writer Fernando Pessoa, a frequent habitué of the café in his day. Come here for artistic elegance and public attention.

Martinho da Arcada (Map 2; ☎ 218 879 259; Praça do Comércio 3; lunch specials €4, dinner dishes €10-15), in business since 1782, was another haunt of Pessoa and other literary notables. Its cheap lunch-time fare now attracts office workers; evening fare is pricier.

Versailles (Map 4; ☎ 213 546 340; Avenida da República 15A) is one of Lisbon's grandest pastelarias, with splendidly over-the-top chandeliers and marble columns. As well as masses of cakes and desserts it also serves reasonably priced meals.

For the best traditional pastéis de Belém custard tarts, make a beeline for **Pastéis de Belém** (Map 6; Rua de Belém 88), where they are both made and consumed in vast quantities.

Many of Lisbon's famous viewpoints have café-kiosks – top billing goes to those at Largo das Portas do Sol (Map 3) and Miradouro de Santa Catarina (Map 5).

Self-Catering

There are supermarkets and **minimercados** (grocery shops) everywhere. A well-stocked **Pingo Doce supermarket** (Map 2), near Rossio train station, even stocks foreign cereal, chocolate and other luxuries. The big shopping complexes such as **Amoreiras** (Map 2), **Colombo** (Map 1) and **Vasco da Gama** (Map 1) also have supermarkets.

ENTERTAINMENT

As befits a capital city, Lisbon caters to all tastes – whether you're a theatre buff, a night owl bent on a bar crawl, or a fado aficionado after a blast of the Portuguese blues.

Information & Tickets

For details of events during your stay, grab a copy of the monthly Follow Me Lisboa (free) from any of the Turismo de Lisboa outlets or, if your Portuguese is up to it, call the **What's On** (☎ 217 901 062) hotline. The monthly Agenda Cultural Lisboa (€0.50; w www.lisboacultural.com) includes details of performances and screenings; cinema listings can also be found in the daily Diário de Notícias (€0.60).

Tickets are available from the following outlets:

ABEP Ticket Agency (Map 2; ☎ 213 475 824) Praça dos Restauradores
Fnac (Map 1; ☎ 217 114 237) Centro Comercial Colombo
(Map 2; ☎ 213 221 800) Armazéns do Chiado, Rua do Carmo 3
NetParque (☎ 218 917 600; w www.netpar que.pt)
Ticket Line (☎ 217 120 300)

Fado

In time-old tradition, Lisbon's most famous form of entertainment is also the most exploited. The Bairro Alto abounds with restaurants where you can listen to fado while eating what is probably an overpriced meal. These fado houses do their best to create the appropriate melancholy atmosphere for their fadista (fado singer), ie, low lighting, no talking during performances and so on, but be aware that this is not the most authentic of experiences.

The following list is a brief smattering of fado venues available. Reservations are advisable at all these places and most require you to spend a minimum amount, which will include the cost of the fado. For more information on fado, see Music in the Facts about Portugal chapter.

Adega do Ribatejo (Map 2; ☎ 213 468 343) Rua Diario de Noticias 23, Bairro Alto – open 8.30pm to 12.30am Monday to Saturday; minimum spend €10

Adega Machado (Map 2; ☎ 213 224 640) Rua do Norte 91, Bairro Alto – open 8.30pm to 3am Tuesday to Sunday; minimum spend €15

Adega Mesquita (Map 2; ☎ 213 219 280, ⓦ www.adegamesquita.com) Rua Diario de Noticias 107, Bairro Alto – open 8pm to 1am daily; minimum spend €15

Nono (Map 2; ☎ 213 429 989) Rua do Norte 47-49, Bairro Alto – open 9pm to 2.30am Monday to Saturday; minimum spend €10

O Forcado (Map 2; ☎ 213 468 579, fax 213 474 887) Rua da Rosa 221, Bairro Alto – open 8pm to 2am Thursday to Tuesday; minimum spend €15, tourist menu €25

Parreirinha de Alfama (Map 3; ☎ 218 868 209; Beco do Espírito Santo 1, Alfama) open 8pm to 3am daily; minimum spend €15

Taverna do Embuçado (Map 3; ☎ 218 865 088) Beco dos Cortumes 10, Alfama – open 9pm to 2.30am Monday to Saturday; minimum spend €10, tourist menu €35

The Portuguese blues are not everyone's cup of tea, however, and rather than subject yourself to an entire night of it, you may prefer to wander the streets of the Bairro Alto or Alfama district until you find an impromptu fado session – you can usually join in as well, if the mood takes you.

Bars

Stylish gay bars, finely tuned jazz joints and unique drinking dens you will fall in love with – Lisbon's bars are an eclectic, ever-changing mix. The best way to find your favourite is to explore the different districts as they come alive at night and see what catches your eye. To point you in the right direction, the following are a small selection of all that Lisbon has to offer in the bar department. Most are open from around 10pm until the early hours of the morning (normally around 3am), do not charge for admission, and operate a fairly relaxed dress code.

Sampling the Local Tipples

Kickstart the night with a shot – or bottle if you prefer – of *ginjinha*, the cherry liquor fashioned by a certain Espinheira (who remains vigilant above the entrance) in 1840, from **A Ginjinha** *(Map 2; Largo de São Domingos 8; open 9am-10.30pm daily; small glass €0.60, bottle €9).*

Port lovers should prioritise a visit to **Solar do Vinho do Porto** *(Map 2; ☎ 213 475 707; Rua de São Pedro de Alcântara 45; open 11am-midnight Mon-Sat; glass from €7)* for a taste of around 200 varieties of port in cosy surroundings. Local connoisseurs will make recommendations but, unless you're feeling flush, be careful what you chose as prices reach €160 – and that's per glass.

Bairro Alto & Chiado You will have no problem locating a watering hole or two here, but Rua da Barroca is a good starting point. All of the following are on Map 2.

Clube de Esquina *(Rua da Barroca 30)* has minimal decor, a DJ playing funky jazz and a slightly pretentious bunch jostling at the bar.

Melting Pop *(Rua do Rosa 225)*, all deep reds and wooden floors, is a real chill-out zone earlier in the evening.

A Tasca *(Travessa da Queimada 13-15)* is small, lively, bright and loud. Take on the tequila.

Portas Largas *(Rua da Atalaia 105)* is well worn and well loved – and everyone gets a warm welcome, particularly the gay crowd.

Mistura Fina *(Rua de Gáveas 15)* is a predominantly gay 'retro' bar, with funky furniture and a dub-techno sound.

Tertúlia *(Rua Diário de Notícias 60)* has low lighting and carefully positioned tables, and is a great place to hear live jazz.

Heróis *(Calçada do Sacramento)* boasts retro furnishings, a cool crowd and very groovy beats.

Príncipe Real Known primarily for gay and lesbian bars, this area is also home to a unique drinking den and is a stone's throw away from Portugal's most famous jazz club.

Pavilhão Chines *(Map 5; Rua Dom Pedro V 89-91)* is crammed with international bric-a-brac; choose a cocktail from the comic-book menu, sit back in a chair straight out of your granny's living room, and let your eyes wander.

Hot Clube de Portugal (Map 4; w www .jazzportugal.net/clubes/hot/; Praça da Algeria 39; open 10pm-2am Tues-Sat) will have the masters play you jazz in a small, smoky setting, just the way it should be.

If it's the gay and lesbian scene you're after, check out **Bar Água No Bico** (Map 5; w www.agua-no-bico.com; Rua de São Marçal 170), **Bric-a-Bar** (Map 5; Rua Cecilio de Sousa 82-84) and **Bar 106** (Map 5; Rua de São Marçal 106). All are popular places with friendly faces and disco tunes. While no longer in the closet, gay and lesbian venues remain discreet to the outside world; a doorbell system operates at all these places.

Cais do Sodré If you're a pub person, head to Cais do Sodré, where you can choose from two Irish pubs – need we say more? – **Ó Gilíns** (Map 2; Rua dos Remolares 8-10) and **Hennessy's** (Map 2; Rua Cais do Sodré 32-38) plus a couple of others with an international flavour to their names, if not their set-up. Both **British Bar** (Map 2; Rua Bernardino Costa 52) and **Bar Americano** (Map 2; Rua Bernardino Costa 35) are low-key, relaxed bars serving a mature, local clientele – perfect for a late-afternoon drink after a hard day's sightseeing.

Avenida 24 de Julho & Around A rather desolate stretch on first impressions, this area is definitely worth investigating for drinks after dark.

Gringo's Café (Map 5; Avenida 24 de Julho 116-118) has a Wild-West theme to its dark interior. Too many drinks and you'll think that moose is coming off the wall and after you...

Trifásica (Map 5; Avenida 24 de Julho 66), light, spacey and minimal, fills up with cool clubbers as the DJ notches up the house beats.

Speakeasy (Map 5; w www.speakeasy-bar .com; Armazém 115, Cais das Oficinas), on the other side of the tracks, is worth a detour if you're after live music. Reggae, rock and Portuguese covers are played in this cosy converted warehouse but jazz rules the day.

Doca do Santo Amaro This small dock, with its breezy views over the water and up to the Ponte 25 de Abril, is lined with bars and restaurants-cum-bars, all of which are pretty mainstream in their approach, attitude and music. A couple of favourites are **Café da Ponte** (Map 5), where you can sing your heart out to karaoke on a Saturday, and **Doca de Santo** (Map 5; w www.docadesanto.pt) for leisurely cocktails at the start of the night.

Parque das Nações If you've enjoyed wandering around this park by day, chances are you'll enjoy an evening in one (or more) of the many restaurants-cum-bars along **Rua da Pimenta** (Map 1). None of them particularly stand out, but they all do a roaring trade at the weekends – perfect if you're up for a laugh and a bit of bustling boozing.

Discos & Clubs

Whether you want to bop to pop, strut your stuff to funk or play it super-cool to house, there's dancing for everyone. For a fun, disco-infused night, head to the Docas. More discerning dancers may prefer the jazz or funk alternatives of the bohemian Barrio Alto and, if you are serious about clubbing, the converted warehouses along the waterfront will keep you going until the sun starts to shine. Gay and lesbian groovers will not be disappointed with the variety of venues available at the ring of a doorbell and if it's African or Latin American beats that tickle your fancy, Portugal's colonial history ensures there's a strong international flavour to the club scene. Unless you're after the kind of dancing that involves laps, avoid Rua Nova do Carvalho, the sleazy back street of Cais do Sodre.

Most clubs have an admission fee (anything from €5 to €20, often including one or more drinks) and many operate a card-stamping system to ensure that you spend a minimum amount while you're inside. Note that for the bigger clubs, this minimum consumption can be as much as €150 (€250 in the case of Kapital; see later), intended to deter the 'wrong' sort of people.

Opening hours vary but it's unusual to find a club that is even remotely getting going before midnight; the music dies when the punters leave, which can be anytime between 4am and 10am.

Whereas bars tend to clutter together, Lisbon's clubs are often in unusual locations so the following suggestions are listed alphabetically rather than by area.

Armazém F *(Map 5; Armazém 65, Avenida de Brasilia)*, an upmarket bar, restaurant and club rolled into one, is home to varied rhythms from salsa to techno, and often hosts live music acts.

Art'z *(Map 5; Armazém 113, Cais da Rocha Conde de Obidos)*, off Avenida de Brasilia, has a large dance floor to shake your stuff on once the music has stopped at nearby Speakeasy (see Bars, earlier).

Blues Cafe *(Map 5; Rua Cintura do Porto)*, more like a gentleman's club than a dance club with its plush decor and sophisticated look, attracts a more mature clientele after some gentle grooving.

Buggix *(Map 1; Rua D Fuas Roupinho, Parque das Nações)* has live music most nights and is popular with out-of-towners; a natural conclusion to a night begun on the Rua da Pimenta.

Discoteca a Lontra *(Map 5; Rua de São Bento 155)*, near Barrio Alto, hosts an eclectic clientele bumping and grinding to popular African beats long into the night.

Dock's Club *(Map 5; Rua Cintura do Porto)* is one of Lisbon's better dance clubs and deservedly popular as a result.

Finalmente *(Map 5; Rua da Palmeira 38)*, a short walk from Praça do Príncipe Real, offers a tiny dance floor and drag shows nightly, and lots and lots of people.

Fragil *(Map 2; Rua da Atalaia 126, Bairro Alto)* is home to a small dance floor, a relaxed and predominantly gay crowd, and house beats.

House of Vodka *(Map 2; Rua da Barroca 111-113, Bairro Alto)* blends a cave-like interior with funky tunes, making it perfect for intimate grooving.

Indochina *(Map 5; Rua Cintura do Porto)* brings the Far East to Lisbon's docks and then introduces dance music resulting in an unusual mix.

Kapital *(Map 5; Avenida 24 de Julho 68)* is, for young, wealthy Lisboêtas, the place to be and be seen. Expect chrome, black-and-white decor, people so cool they're almost frozen, and music to match.

Kremlin *(Map 5; Escadinhas da Praia 5)*, as eccentric as Kapital is exclusive, plays on its location in what used to be a monastery. No doubt the house beats have the previous inhabitants turning in their graves, but acid and techno certainly seem to do the trick for the regulars.

Luanda *(Map 5; Travessa Teixeira Júnior 6, Alcântara)* is another energetic and addictive African club, with beats that leave their European counterparts dead in their tracks.

Lux *(Map 1; Avenida Infante Dom Henrique)*, near Santa Apolónia train station is Lisbon's first 'super club'. It is housed in a huge warehouse on the waterfront, and plays house and garage to a knowing crowd.

Memorial *(Map 5; Rua Gustavo de Matos Sequeira 42A)* is supposedly a lesbian-only stop for pop tunes after hours; you may see a few men nosing around though.

MUSIcais *(Map 3; Avenida Infante Dom Henrique, Pavilion A/B, Doca do Jardim do Tabaco, Alfama)* is a good place to go if you're after a bop to live music and cheesy tunes.

Mussulo *(Map 4; Rua Sousa Martins 5D, Estefânia)* keeps faithful to its Angolan roots with a mixture of soft rhythms and Afro-techno for when things really get going, and they do…into the small hours.

Queens *(Map 5; Avenida de Brasilia 226)* isn't quite as camp as the name suggests, but is still the place for disco divas and dancing monarchs on this stretch.

Salsa Latina *(Map 5; Gare Maritima de Alcântara, Doca de Santo Amaro)* will feed all your Latin needs with salsa, merengue and Latino tunes at the weekend; lessons are available during the week.

Trumps *(Map 5; Rua da Imprensa Nacional 104B)* kicks up the gay beat with a variety of tunes playing in two bars (one particularly intimate) and a sizeable dance floor.

Theatres & Cinemas

Lording over the Rossio, you can't fail to see the attractive **Teatro Nacional Dona Maria II** *(Map 2; ☎ 213 472 246; Rossio)*, Portugal's national theatre with a somewhat unpredictable schedule.

Both the **Teatro Nacional de São Carlos** *(Map 2; ☎ 213 465 914; Rua Serpa Pinto 9)* and the nearby **Teatro Municipal de São Luis** *(Map 2; ☎ 213 225 140; Rua Antonio Maria Cardoso 38)* offer opera, ballet and theatre seasons.

Teatro Camões *(Map 1; ☎ 213 474 049; Parque das Nações)* is home to the Portuguese Symphony Orchestra (Orquestra Sinfónica Portuguesa) and the National Ballet Company (Companhia Nacional de Bailado); there are regular performances here by both.

Slightly more off-beat, **Teatro Taborda** *(Map 3; ☎ 218 879 484; Costa del Castelo 75)* hosts dance shows and youth theatre, and **Chapitô** *(☎ 218 878 225; W www.chapito .org; Costa do Castelo 1-7)* has original physical theatre performances. Both places boast spectacular views and quirky restaurants.

Classical music concerts (often organised by the Fundação Calouste Gulbenkian) are held at the foundation's three **concert halls** *(Map 4; ☎ 217 935 131; W www.musica.gul benkian.pt; Avenida de Berna)* or the **Centre Cultural de Belém** *(CCB; Map 6; ☎ 213 612 444; W www.ccb.pt; Praça do Imperío, Belém)* and the **Coliseu dos Recreios** *(Map 2; ☎ 213 240 580; Rua das Portas de Santo Antão 92)*. The CCB and the Coliseu dos Recreios also host popular music or dance events.

Popular international acts such as Oasis and Moby usually play at the **Pavilhão Atlântico** *(Map 1; ☎ 218 918 409; W www .atlantico-multiusos.pt; Parque das Nações)*, Portugal's largest indoor arena. Another popular venue is **Paradise Garage** *(Map 5; ☎ 213 243 400; W www.paradisegarage.com; Rua João Oliveira Miguens 38-48)*, which hosts rock and pop concerts, festivals and club nights.

A versatile exhibition venue is **Culturgest** *(Map 4; ☎ 217 905 155; Rua Arco do Cego)*, where you can do anything from watch a ballet and listen to opera to attend conferences.

For the latest movie blockbusters (usually in the original language with Portuguese subtitles), try the multiplexes in the **Amoreiras** *(Map 4; ☎ 213 878 752)* and **Centro Comercial Colombo** *(Map 1; ☎ 217 113 222)* shopping centres. More traditional cinemas are **São Jorge** *(Map 4; ☎ 213 579 144; Avenida da Liberdade 175)* and the **Instituto da Cinemateca Portuguesa** *(Map 4; ☎ 213 546 279; Rua Barata Salgueiro 39)*, just around the corner. An average ticket costs around €5. The Instituto sometimes shows films at the **Salão Foz** *(Praça dos Restauradores)*.

For details on where to get information and buy tickets for plays, concerts and films, see 'Information & Tickets' at the beginning of this section.

SPECTATOR SPORTS
Football
Of Portugal's 'big three' clubs, two – SL Benfica (Sport Lisboa e Benfica) and Sporting

(Sporting Club de Portugal) – are based in Lisbon. They've been rivals ever since Sporting beat Benfica 2-1 in 1907.

The season runs from September to mid-June, with most league matches on Sunday; check the papers (especially *Bola*, the daily football paper) or ask at the turismo. Tickets cost €10 to €70 and are sold at the stadium on match day or, for slightly inflated prices, at the **ABEP ticket agency** *(Map 2; Praça dos Restauradores)*.

SL Benfica plays at the recently upgraded, 65,000-seat **Estádio da Luz** *(Map 1; ☎ 217 219 540; W www.slbenfica.pt; metro Colégio Militar-Luz)* in the northwestern Benfica district. Euro2004 is slated to kick off here.

Sporting plays at the **Estádio José de Alvalade** *(Map 1; ☎ 217 514 069; metro Campo Grande, bus No 1 or 36 from Rossio)*, just north of the university. A new 54,000-seat stadium here will also host some Euro2004 matches.

The **Estádio Nacional** *(☎ 214 197 212; Cruz Quebrada; train from Cais do Sodré)* hosts the national Taça de Portugal (Portugal Cup) each May.

Other major sporting events are held at the **Pavilhão Atlântico** *(Map 1)* in Parque das Nações.

Bullfighting
Lisbon's **Praça de Touros** *(bullring; Map 4; ☎ 217 932 442; Avenida da República)*, near the Campo Pequeno metro station, is normally where bullfights are staged but at the time of writing the ancient, Moorish-style venue was closed for long-term restoration. The season runs from May to October, with fights usually on Thursday or Sunday. Tickets, on sale outside the bullring, range from €15 to €60 depending on where you sit. You can also buy slightly pricier tickets from the **ABEP ticket agency** *(Map 2; Praça dos Restauradores)*.

See under Spectator Sports in the Facts for the Visitor chapter for more about bullfights, and Society & Conduct in the Facts about Portugal chapter for a look at the treatment of the bulls.

SHOPPING
Lisbon is a tempting place to shop if only because street life moves slowly enough to make browsing a pleasure. Delightful to

look at are the Art Deco speciality shops of the kind your grandmother would recognise, dealing exclusively in shirts, hats or gloves.

Shopaholics may like to take advantage of the Lisboa Shopping Card, which offers discounts of up to 20% in over 200 selected stores. It costs €3/5 for 24-/72-hour versions, and is available at all Turismo de Lisboa outlets.

Most city centre shops are open 9am to 1pm and 3pm to 7pm Monday to Saturday (but often until 10pm or 11pm in the shopping centres).

Azulejos & Ceramics

Fábrica Sant'Ana (Map 2; ☎ 213 638 292; Rua do Alecrim 95) is one of Lisbon's finest (and priciest) azulejo factories and showrooms.

Cerâmica Viúva Lamego (Map 1; ☎ 218 852 408; Largo do Intendente Pina Manique 25) is another good showroom for azulejos (including made-to-order items) and other ceramic ware.

Olaria do Desterros (Map 1; ☎ 218 850 329; Rua Nova do Desterro 14) is a venerable, family-run pottery factory, a few blocks west of Cerâmica Viúva Lamego in a neighbourhood of warehouses and hospitals. The factory (there's no obvious showroom) is at entry F in an alley, seemingly within the grounds of the Hospital do Desterro.

The attractive **Museu Nacional do Azulejo** (Map 1; see Santa Apolónia earlier in this chapter) also sells a few azulejo souvenirs.

Vista Alegre (Map 2; ☎ 213 461 401; Largo do Chiado 20) is the most famous name in ceramics. Its finely crafted products can be found at a number of stores in Lisbon.

Arte Rústica (Map 2; ☎ 213 421 127; Rua d'Aurea 246) has an excellent range of more rustic ceramics.

Wine

Portuguese wine of any variety is very good value. In most supermarkets you can buy something to please all but the snobbiest taste buds for as little as €4 a bottle.

If it's port wine you want, have a taste at the **Solar do Vinho do Porto** (Map 2) – see the boxed text 'Sampling the Local Tipples' in the Entertainment section – and then head for the supermarket, or a wine speciality shop such as **Napoleão** (Map 2;

☎ 218 861 108; Rua dos Fanqueiros 70) or **Manuel Tavares** (Map 2; ☎ 213 424 209; Rua da Betesga 1A). Staff here can also offer recommendations.

See Drinks in the Facts for the Visitor chapter for more about Portuguese wines, and also the special section on port wine in the Douro chapter.

Handicrafts & Textiles

Santos Ofícios (Map 2; ☎ 218 872 031; Rua da Madalena 87) and its big new **showroom** (Map 2; ☎ 210 312 820; Rua do Arsenal 15; open 10am-8pm daily) is a fascinating artesanato (handicrafts shop), stocking an eclectic range of folk art from all around Portugal.

Príncipe Real (Map 5; ☎ 213 465 945; Rua da Escola Politécnica 12) sells beautiful embroidered linen and cotton as well as lace from Peniche.

Casa das Cortiças (Map 5; ☎ 213 425 858; Rua da Escola Politécnica 4), a dusty, derelict store specialising in cork items, has some bargain souvenirs plus useful cork mats.

Madeira House (Map 2; ☎ 213 426 813; Rua Augusta 131) is where hand-embroidered linen from its most famous source, Madeira, can be found.

Centro de Artesanato (Map 2; ☎ 213 225 126; Mercado da Ribeira, Cais do Sodré; open 9am-8pm Mon-Thur, 10am-10pm Fri & Sat, 7.30am-2pm Sun) on the revamped 1st floor of the old market, sells fancy, high-quality handicrafts from the Tejo region.

Music

Valentim de Carvalho is Lisbon's longest established music store. It has a huge **Megastore** (Map 2; ☎ 213 241 570; Rua do Carmo) in Edifício Grandella.

Fnac (Map 2; ☎ 213 221 800; Rua Nova do Almada 110), near Valentim de Carvalho in Armazéns do Chiado, also sells a vast array of music and audiovisual gear.

Discoteca Amália (Map 2; ☎ 213 421 485; Rua de Áurea 272) specialises in fado and cheap classical CDs.

Shopping Centres

The trend in booming Lisbon is for huge indoor shopping centres. The colossal **Centro Comercial Colombo** (Map 1; Avenida Colégio Militar) ranks as the biggest, though the modernist **Complexo das Amoreiras** (Map 4;

Markets

For something decidedly downmarket, but good entertainment, browse the sprawling **Feira da Ladra** *(Map 3)*, or Thieves Market, which materialises every Tuesday morning and all day Saturday at Campo de Santa Clara, beside the Igreja de São Vincent de Fora. In addition to cheap clothes and shoes you'll find a motley array of intriguing junk and a clutch of antique shops and stalls.

The renovated **Mercado da Ribeira** *(Map 2)*, near Cais do Sodré, becomes a flower market every afternoon and is also the venue for a 'collector's market' every Sunday morning.

Sunday themed markets also take place at the **Parque das Nações** *(Map 1)*, near Gare do Oriente: the first Sunday of the month features books, stamps and coins; the second is for Portuguese handicrafts; the third is antiques; and the fourth is arts and decorative items.

Avenida Engenheiro Duarte Pacheco; bus No 11 from Praça do Comércio) is still popular.

Newer additions include the swanky **Atrium Saldanha** *(Map 4; Praça Duque de Saldanha)* and its neighbour, the **Galerias Monumental** *(Map 4; Praça Duque de Saldanha)*; **Centro Vasco da Gama** *(Map 1)* between Gare do Oriente and Parque das Nações; and the massive Spanish **El Corte Inglés** *(Map 4; Avenida António Augusto de Aguiar 31)*.

GETTING THERE & AWAY
Air
Aeroporto de Lisboa *(Map 1; Aeroporto da Portela; flight information ☎ 218 413 700)* is about 4km northeast of the city centre. A new international airport is due to open at Ota, 48km north of the city, in 2010.

Portugália and TAP both have multiple daily flights to Lisbon from Porto and Faro, and over 20 carriers operate scheduled international services. For details, including sample fares and airline telephone numbers, see the Getting There & Away and Getting Around chapters.

Bus
The major long-distance bus terminal is **Arco do Cego** *(Map 4; ☎ 213 545 439; Avenida João Crisóstomo)*. From here the big

carriers, **Rede Expressos** *(24hr ☎ 707 223 344)* and **Eva/Mundial Turismo** *(☎ 213 147 710)*, run frequent services to almost every major destination in the country. Destinations with 10 or more services a day include Coimbra (€9, 2½ hours), Évora (€9.20, 1¾ hours), Porto (€12.50, 3½ to four hours), and Faro (€14, 4½ to five hours).

The other major terminal is at **Gare do Oriente** *(Map 1)*, which concentrates on services to the north and to Spain. On the 1st floor of this fantastic-looking (but miserably signposted) stunner are bus company ticket booths, most open from 9am to 5.30pm Monday to Saturday (to 7pm or 7.30pm Friday) except lunch time – although smaller operators only open when there's a bus about to arrive or depart. On weekends you may have to buy your ticket on the bus (though it's wise to phone ahead for a seat reservation). The biggest companies operating from here are **AVIC** *(☎ 218 940 238)*, **Renex** *(☎ 218 874 871, 218 882 829)* and the Spanish operator **Auto-Res** *(☎ 968 056 080)*.

At the time of writing, many Renex buses still took on passengers 20 minutes early at Campo das Cebolas in the Alfama district, before heading for their scheduled departure from Gare do Oriente.

Several regional companies with destinations in the north, including Mafrense (for Ericeira and Mafra), Barraqueiro Oeste (for Malveira and Torres Vedras) and Rodoviária do Tejo (for Peniche), operate from outside Campo Grande metro station.

Buses to Sesimbra and Costa da Caparica still go from a scruffy **terminal** *(Map 4)* at Praça de Espanha.

Eurolines *(Map 4; ☎ 218 957 398; Loja 203, Gare do Oriente; open 9.30am-1pm & 2pm-6.30pm Mon-Fri, 9am-1pm & 2pm-4pm Sat)* runs coaches to destinations all over Europe (see the Getting There & Away chapter), with all coaches serving both Arco do Cego and Gare do Oriente. You can also go to many European cities from Arco do Cego with Eurolines affiliate **Intercentro** *(Map 4; ☎ 213 571 745; Rua Actor Taborda 25; open Mon-Fri)*, which has an additional ticket office in the **Arco do Cego bus station** *(☎ 213 159 277; Arco do Cego; open 8am-12.30pm & 1.30pm-5pm Mon-Fri, 8am-1pm Sat)*.

Lisbon's Busabout stop (see the Getting There & Away chapter) is at the Parque Municipal de Campismo de Monsanto.

Information and tickets for international departures are scarce on weekends, so avoid that last-minute Sunday dash out of Portugal.

Train

Lisbon is linked by train to all major cities in Portugal. See the Getting Around chapter for details on domestic services, and the Getting There & Away chapter on international services. Some sample 2nd-class direct journeys to/from Lisbon (Faro times include ferry connection) are:

destination	service	duration (hrs)	cost (€)	services per day
Coimbra	Alfa	2	14	six
	IC/IN	2¼	10.30	seven
	IR	2½	8.10	three
Faro	IC	4¾	11.30	two
	IR	5¼	10.20	two
Porto	Alfa	3¼	19	seven
	IC	3½	14.10	four
	IR	4½	11	three

Lisbon has four major stations plus some smaller ones. **Santa Apolónia** (Map 1) is the terminal for trains from northern and central Portugal, and for all international services. It has a helpful **information desk** (☎ 808 208 208; open 7.30am-9pm daily) at door No 8. The international section at door No 47 includes an international ticket desk, bank, ATM and cash-exchange machine, snack bar, car-rental agencies and a **Turismo de Lisboa desk** (usually open 10am-6pm daily). Left-luggage lockers are nearby.

All of Santa Apolónia's services also stop at the increasingly important **Gare do Oriente station** (Map 1). Ticket booths are on the 1st floor here (platforms on the 2nd) and car rental offices, banks and shops on the street level. A few left-luggage lockers are on the basement metro level.

Barreiro (Map 3) is the terminal for *suburbano* services to Setúbal and for all long-distance services to the south of Lisbon; connecting ferries leave frequently from the pier at Terreiro do Paço where travellers buy two tickets: a €1 ferry ticket to Barreiro plus their onward train ticket. Barreiro will become redundant once the North-South Railway Line (which currently reaches to the Setúbal Peninsula suburbs via the Ponte 25 de Abril) is extended to the main line south.

Rossio station (Map 2; ☎ 800 200 904) serves Queluz-Belas, Cacém (connections to Estremadura) and Sintra. **Cais do Sodré station** (Map 2) is the station for Cascais and Estoril.

The modernised **Entrecampos station** (Map 4; Avenida 5 de Outubro) serves the northern suburbs as well as Fertagus trains across the Ponte 25 de Abril. **Entrecampos Poente station** (Map 4), 200m east of Entrecampos, serves the suburban line to Cacém.

Car & Motorcycle

Local operators with reasonable multiday rates include **Sixt** (218 311 133, fax 218 408 748) and **Rentauto** (☎ 218 462 294, fax 218 462 295). International firms include **Avis** (toll-free ☎ 800 201 002, fax 217 547 852), **Europcar** (toll-free ☎ 808 204 050, fax 218 473 130) and **Hertz** (toll-free ☎ 800 238 238, fax 219 400 490). For details on rates, see the Getting Around chapter.

The nearest place to rent a motorbike is Cascais (see the Around Lisbon chapter).

Boat

The Transtejo ferry line has several riverfront terminals. From the eastern end of the **Terreiro do Paço terminal** (Map 3), swanky catamarans ferry passengers do the run across the Tejo to Montijo (€1.60, 30 minutes) and Seixal (€1.20, 30 minutes) every hour or so (every 15 minutes during rush hour; fewer at weekends). From the main part of the terminal, called Estação do Sul e Sueste, Soflusa ferries run to Barreiro (€1, 30 minutes, every 30 to 60 minutes), from where you can pick up rail connections to the Alentejo and Algarve. From Cais da Alfândega, passenger ferries go to Cacilhas (€0.60, 10 minutes, every 10 minutes all day); at the time of writing, these had been transferred temporarily to the pier at Cais do Sodré due to metro works. Car (and bicycle) ferries also go from Cais do Sodré to Cacilhas.

From Belém, ferries depart every 30 to 60 minutes for Trafaria and Porto Brandão (€0.60), about 3.5km and 5km respectively from Costa da Caparica town.

GETTING AROUND
To/From the Airport

The AeroBus departs from outside the arrivals hall roughly every 20 minutes from 7.45am to 9pm. It takes around 30 to 45 minutes (depending on traffic) to get to Cais do Sodré station, with a stop near the turismo on Praça do Comércio. The €2.30 fare gets you a Bilhete Turístico, which you can use on all city buses, trams and funiculars for the rest of the day. TAP Air Portugal passengers who show their boarding pass (not just the airline ticket) get one free.

Local bus Nos 8, 44, 45 and 83 also run between the airport and the centre but they're a nightmare in rush hour if you have baggage. There's also a direct bus service to/from Cascais (see the Around Lisbon chapter).

If you're arriving in Lisbon by train just to get to the airport, the most convenient option is bus No 44 from Gare do Oriente (with Vasco da Gama shopping centre behind you, the stop is under the station's arches to the left).

Taxi rip-offs are common on the airport-to-city route. You can buy a prepaid Táxi Voucher from the Turismo de Lisboa desk in the arrivals terminal at set prices for specific destinations (eg, most of central Lisbon about €14/16 per day/night and weekends). Only taxis involved in the scheme – marked

with a colour sticker – will accept the vouchers. With nonvoucher cowboys, expect to pay about €8 to the city centre, plus €1.50 if your luggage needs to go in the boot. Avoid long queues by flagging down a taxi at the departures terminal.

Bus, Tram & Funicular
Companhia Carris de Ferro de Lisboa (*Carris;* ☎ 213 613 000; ⩊ *www.carris.pt*) operates all transport except the metro. Its buses and trams run from about 5am or 6am to 1am daily; there are some night bus and tram services.

You can get a transport map, *Planta dos Transportes Públicas da Carris* (including a map of night-time services) from turismos or from **Carris kiosks** (*open 8am-8pm daily*). The Carris website has timetables and route details.

Individual tickets cost €0.90 on board or half that price if you buy a BUC (Bilhete Único de Coroa, a one-zone ticket for the city centre) beforehand. These prepaid tickets are sold at Carris kiosks – most conveniently at Praça da Figueira, at the foot of the Elevador de Santa Justa, and at Santa Apolónia and Cais do Sodré train stations.

The Carris kiosks also sell a one-/three-day (€2.30/5.50) Bilhete Turístico, valid for all buses, trams and funiculars. Carris kiosks and metro stations sell the Passe Turístico (€9.30/13.10 for four/seven days), valid for buses (except the AeroBus), trams, funiculars *and* the metro; you must show your passport to get the (nontransferable) Passe Turístico.

Note that these passes aren't great bargains unless you're planning a lot of travel far from the centre. A better deal is the Lisboa Card (see the boxed text earlier in this chapter), which is good for most tourist sights as well as bus, tram, funicular and metro travel.

Trams The clattering, antediluvian *eléctricos* (trams) are an endearing component of Lisbon. Don't leave the city without riding the No 28 from Largo Martim Moniz or No 12 from Praça da Figueira through the narrow streets of the Alfama.

Two other useful lines are the No 15 from Praça da Figueira and Praça do Comércio via Alcântara to Belém, and the No 18 from Praça do Comércio via Alcântara to Ajuda.

Funicular Fun

The city has three funiculars (*elevadores* or *ascensors*), which labour up and down some of the city centre's steepest hills, plus the extraordinary **Elevador de Santa Justa** *(Map 2)*, a huge wrought-iron lift that raises you from the Baixa straight up to eye level with the Convento do Carmo ruins.

Santa Justa is the most popular with tourists (though the queues can quickly sap enthusiasm), but the most charming ride is on the **Elevador da Bica** *(Map 2)* through the Santa Catarina district, at the southwestern corner of Bairro Alto. The other two funiculars are the **Elevador da Glória** *(Map 2)*, from Praça dos Restauradores up to the São Pedro de Alcântara viewpoint, and the **Elevador do Lavra** *(Map 2)* from Largo de Anunciada, on the eastern side of Restauradores.

The Elevador de Santa Justa operates daily from 7am to 11.45pm (Sunday and holidays from 9am to 10.45pm); the Elevadors da Bica and do Lavra from 7am to 10.45pm; and the Elevador da Glória from 7am to 12.55am daily. They're not for anyone in a hurry!

LISBON

The No 15 line features space-age articulated trams with on-board machines for buying tickets and passes. Tram stops are marked by a small yellow *paragem* (stop) sign hanging from a lamppost or the overhead wires.

Metro

The rapidly expanding *metropolitano* (underground) system, which currently has 28km of track and 40 stations, is useful not only for short hops across the city but also to reach the Gare do Oriente and nearby Parque das Nações. By late 2003 or early 2004, when a Santa Apolónia link from Baixa-Chiado is expected to be completed, there will be 47km of track and 60 stations.

Tickets cost €0.60/1.10 one-way/return, and a *caderneta* (booklet) of 10 tickets costs €4.50. Tickets can be purchased from windows or automatic dispensers in metro stations. A one-day metro pass costs €1.40 (€4.80 for seven days). Both the Passe Turístico and the Lisboa Card are also valid on the metro.

The system operates from 6.30am to 1am daily. Entrances are marked by a big red M. Useful signs include *correspondência* (transfer between lines) and *saída* (exit to the street).

Pickpockets can be a nuisance in rush-hour crowds. And computer diskettes can be at risk – wrap them in foil to avoid harmful

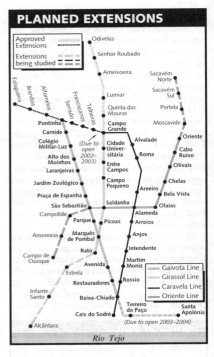

magnetic interference. The metro's website is at **w** www.metrolisboa.pt.

Car & Motorcycle

Lisbon is no fun for drivers, thanks to heavy traffic, metro roadworks and manic drivers. There are two ring roads, both useful for staying out of the centre: the inner Cintura Regional Interna de Lisboa (CRIL) and the outer Cintura Regional Externa de Lisboa (CREL).

If you do venture into the city centre you'll find parking spaces scarce and the rates at central car parks extortionate. Up-market hotels usually have their own garages. Alternatively, park in cheaper (or free) car parks near Parque das Nações (metro Gare do Oriente) or Belém (then catch a bus or tram to the centre). Always lock up and don't leave any valuables inside, as theft from cars is common.

Taxi

Compared with the rest of Europe, Lisbon's *táxis* are reasonably cheap and plentiful. Hailing one can be difficult but ranks are

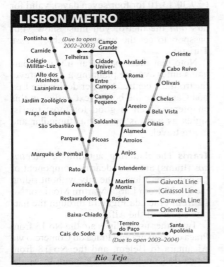

numerous, including at the Rossio, Praça dos Restauradores, near all train and bus stations and ferry terminals, and at top-end hotels. To call one, try **Rádio Táxis de Lisboa** (☎ *218 119 000*) or **Autocoope** (☎ *217 932 756*).

All taxis have meters, but rip-offs do happen, in particular with some taxis that haunt the airport (see To/From the Airport, earlier). If you think you've been cheated, get a receipt from the driver (and note the car's registration number and your time of departure and arrival) and make a claim with **Antral** (*Associação dos Transportadores Rodoviários em Automóveis Ligeiros;* ☎ *213 563 831/835*). The police or turismos should also be able to help.

For more about taxis and taxi fares, see under Local Transport in the Getting Around chapter.

Bicycle

Lisbon traffic is a nightmare for cyclists. You're better off stashing your bike with the left-luggage office at the bus station or airport and seeing the city by public transport. Better hotels and *pensões* may have a storage room. On the Lisbon–Sintra train you can take it for free on weekends or for €2.50 return on weekdays (only outside the rush hour). For more information on transporting your bike between cities, see Bicycle in the Getting Around chapter.

The only pleasant places to ride a bike in Lisbon are Parque das Nações (see this section earlier in this chapter) and a 5km stretch along the Rio Tejo from 1km west of Doca de Santo Amaro to Belém and Praia d'Algés. **Tejo Bike** (☎ *218 871 976*) has a **bike-rental stall** (*Map 1; open 10am-8pm daily June-Sept, 10am-7pm Sat & Sun Oct-May*) on this riverfront promenade just west of Café In; charges are €4 per hour (€25 for 10 hours). Tandems and child bikes are also available.

The nearest place to rent a mountain bike or motorbike is Transrent in Cascais (see the Around Lisbon chapter).

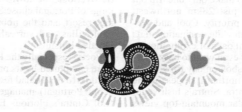

Around Lisbon

AROUND LISBON

The area around Lisbon, including the Setúbal Peninsula, is part of a 234-sq-km region called Lisboa e Vale do Tejo. Inhabited by 3.4 million people (some 564,700 of them in Lisbon city), it has the highest population density in the country.

But beyond the crowded suburbs, just an hour or so from Lisbon, you'll find some fantastic destinations, several of which are worth considering for more than just a day trip. Top of the list is Sintra, a verdant cultural spot within the Parque Natural de Sintra-Cascais and a favourite of royals and romantics in times past. There are several good beaches nearby, including Praia do Guincho, famous for its crashing surf. Just 23km further north, near popular, pretty Ericeira, you'll find even more brilliant surfing spots.

The coastline west of Lisbon, Costa do Estoril, hosts the lively seaside resort of Cascais – with a bopping weekend and summertime nightlife scene – and elegant Estoril, home of Europe's biggest casino.

Further afield, and best considered for an overnight stay, is Setúbal, the largest and liveliest town on the Setúbal Peninsula. In addition to its great seafood, it makes an excellent base for exploring the Parque Natural da Arrábida (see Setúbal later in this chapter for details of organised biking, walking and dolphin-watching trips).

Several fine beaches run west along the coast from Setúbal, notably Sesimbra, a popular city getaway. Even closer to Lisbon is the surfing and sunbathing haven of Costa da Caparica, an 8km stretch of beach on the peninsula's west coast.

SINTRA
postcode 2710 • pop 20,600
• elevation 280m

If you're planning to make only one trip out of Lisbon, Sintra, just 28km northwest, should receive top priority. Cool and verdant, it's also a worthwhile destination in its own right for several days of exploration or relaxation. You may even want to base yourself here and see Lisbon on day trips.

Situated on the northern slopes of the craggy Serra de Sintra, Sintra's lush vegetation and spectacular mountain-top views

Highlights

- Explore the enchanting Unesco World Heritage site of Sintra, with its palaces, museums and fabulous parks
- Bar hop in Cascais, the liveliest seaside resort on the Costa do Estoril
- Sunbathe on the sandy beaches of Costa da Caparica, a brilliant 8km-long stretch of coastline
- Take on crashing surf at Praia do Guincho, Praia Grande, Ericeira and Costa da Caparica
- Spot dolphins in the Sado Estuary, or take a jeep or bike trip through the Parque Natural da Arrábida

have lured admirers since the times of the early Iberians; they found the ridge so mystical they called it the Mountain of the Moon and made it a centre of cult worship. The Romans and the Moors were equally captivated – the remains of a Moorish castle overlook the town. For 500 years the kings of Portugal chose Sintra as their summer resort, and the nobility built extravagant villas and surrealist palaces on its wooded hillsides.

Poets – especially the Romantic English – were enraptured by its natural beauty. Even Lord Byron (who had few nice things to say about Portugal) managed to be charmed: 'Lo! Cintra's glorious Eden intervenes, in variegated maze of mount and glen,' he wrote in his famous travel epic, *Childe Harold*.

Despite hordes of tourists, Sintra still has a bewitching atmosphere and offers some fantastic walks and day trips – the Parque Natural de Sintra-Cascais encompasses both the Serra de Sintra and nearby coastal attractions (including Cabo da Roca, Europe's most westerly point). Try to avoid weekends and public holidays when the place is packed, and Monday when almost everything is closed.

Designated a Unesco World Heritage site in 1995, Sintra is linked in tourist promotions with Cascais, Estoril and Mafra but inevitably takes the limelight. Among its forthcoming projects is a big, new theme park, but its final ambition is to become 'the cultural capital of Portugal'.

Orientation

There are four parts to Sintra: the historic centre (Centro Histórico), called Sintra-Vila (or Vila Velha, 'old town'); the new-town district of Estefânia, 1.5km northeast, where the Lisbon–Sintra railway terminates and where most of the cheap accommodation is located; this new town's extension, Portela de Sintra, 1km further east, where you'll find Sintra's new bus station called Portela Interface (beside the Portela de Sintra train station); and the district of São Pedro de Penaferrim, 2km southeast of Sintra-Vila. São Pedro hosts antique shops and restaurants and an excellent fortnightly

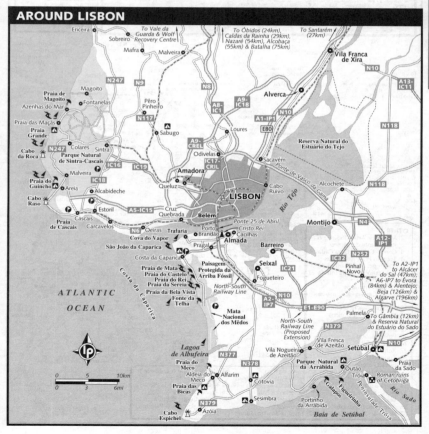

AROUND LISBON

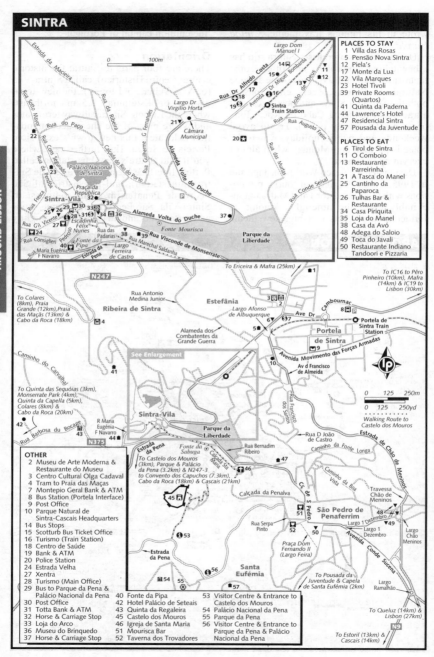

SINTRA

PLACES TO STAY
1 Villa das Rosas
5 Pensão Nova Sintra
12 Piela's
17 Monte da Lua
22 Vila Marques
23 Hotel Tivoli
39 Private Rooms (Quartos)
41 Quinta da Paderna
44 Lawrence's Hotel
47 Residencial Sintra
57 Pousada da Juventude

PLACES TO EAT
6 Tirol de Sintra
11 O Comboio
13 Restaurante Parreirinha
21 A Tasca do Manel
25 Cantinho da Paparoca
26 Tulhas Bar & Restaurante
34 Casa Piriquita
35 Loja do Manel
38 Casa da Avó
42 Adega do Saloio
49 Toca do Javali
50 Restaurante Indiano Tandoori e Pizzaria

OTHER
2 Museu de Arte Moderna & Restaurante do Museu
3 Centro Cultural Olga Cadaval
4 Tram to Praia das Maçãs
7 Montepio Geral Bank & ATM
8 Bus Station (Portela Interface)
9 Post Office
10 Parque Natural de Sintra-Cascais Headquarters
14 Bus Stops
15 Scotturb Bus Ticket Office
16 Turismo (Train Station)
18 Centro de Saúde
19 Bank & ATM
20 Police Station
24 Estrada Velha
27 Xentra
28 Turismo (Main Office)
29 Bus to Parque da Pena & Palácio Nacional da Pena
30 Post Office
31 Totta Bank & ATM
32 Horse & Carriage Stop
33 Loja do Arco
36 Museu do Brinquedo
37 Horse & Carriage Stop
40 Fonte da Pipa
42 Hotel Palácio de Seteais
45 Quinta da Regaleira
45 Castelo dos Mouros
46 Igreja de Santa Maria
51 Mourisca Bar
52 Taverna dos Trovadores
53 Visitor Centre & Entrance to Castelo dos Mouros
54 Palácio Nacional da Pena
55 Parque da Pena
56 Visitor Centre & Entrance to Parque da Pena & Palácio Nacional da Pena

market, the Feira de São Pedro, held on the second and fourth Sunday of the month.

There's a cunning one-way system to deter cars from the historic centre (where parking is severely restricted and metered). For details about buses to the main sights, see the Getting Around section.

Information

Tourist Offices There are two **turismos** (tourist offices), one at the train station (☎ 219 241 623; open 9am-7pm daily Oct-May, 9am-8pm June-Sept), and the main office (☎ 219 231 157, fax 219 235 176; e dtur@cm-sintra.pt; 23 Praça da República; open 9am-7pm daily Oct-May, 9am-8pm June-Sept), in Sintra-Vila. Both provide a free map, packed with information, as well as help with accommodation.

Most of the major parks and gardens, now managed by **Parques de Sintra – Monte da Lua** (☎ 219 237 300; e info@parquesdesintra.pt), feature smart-looking visitor centres where you can pick up multilingual brochures.

Money Banks with ATMs include **Totta** (Rua das Padarias 2) in Sintra-Vila and several others in Estefânia, including **Montepio Geral** (Avenida Heliodoro Salgado 42).

Post & Communications There are **post offices** (open 9.30am-12.30pm & 2.30pm-6pm Mon-Fri), both in Sintra-Vila and Estefânia (the latter has NetPost). You can connect to the Internet (€2.50 per half-hour) at **Loja do Arco** (Rua Arco do Teixeira 2; open 11am-7.30pm daily), which also stocks a wide range of Portuguese literature, music and tasteful crafts. **Hotel Tivoli** (☎ 219 233 505; e htsintra@mail.telepac.pt; Praça da República) has a credit-card fax and Internet facility available to all.

Medical Services & Emergency The **centro de saúde** (medical centre; ☎ 219 106 685; Rua Dr Alfredo Costa 34) and **police station** (☎ 219 230 761; Rua João de Deus 6) are both in Estefânia.

Palácio Nacional de Sintra

The Sintra National Palace (Paço Real or Palácio da Vila; adult/under-26 or senior €3/1.50; open 10am-5.30pm Thur-Tues, last admission 5pm) dominates the town with its

two huge white conical chimneys. Of Moorish origins, the palace was greatly enlarged by João I in the early 15th century, adorned with Manueline additions by Manuel I in the following century, and repeatedly restored and redecorated right up to the present day.

It's connected with a treasury of notable occasions: João I planned his 1415 Ceuta campaign here; the three-year-old Sebastião was crowned king in the palace in 1557; and Afonso VI, who was effectively imprisoned here by his brother Pedro II for six years, died of apoplexy in 1683 while listening to Mass in the chapel gallery.

Highlights inside include an unrivalled display of 15th- and 16th-century azulejos (hand-painted tiles; especially in the Sala dos Árabes or Arab Room), which are some of the oldest in Portugal; the Sala das Armas (Armoury Room, also called the Sala dos Brasões or Coat of Arms Room), with the heraldic shields of 74 leading 16th-century families on its wooden coffered ceiling; and the delightful Sala dos Cisnes (Swan Room), with a polychrome ceiling adorned with 27 gold-collared swans.

Most memorable of all is the ground floor Sala das Pêgas (Magpie Room), its ceiling thick with painted magpies, each holding in its beak a scroll with the words por bem (in honour). The story goes that João I commissioned the cheeky decoration to represent the court gossip about his advances towards one of the ladies-in-waiting. Caught red-handed by his queen, 'por bem' was the king's allegedly innocent response.

On weekends and public holidays the palace is crammed with tour groups.

Castelo dos Mouros

The battlements of this ruined castle (adult/student 6-17 or senior €3/2; open 9am-8pm daily mid-June–mid-Sept, 9am-7pm May–mid-June & mid-Sept–Oct, 9.30am-6pm Nov-May, last admission 1hr before closing) snake over the craggy mountainside above Sintra-Vila. First built by the Moors, the castle was captured by Christian forces under Afonso Henriques in 1147. Much restored in the 19th century, the castle offers some wonderful panoramas. The best walking route here from Sintra-Vila is not along the main road (a very steep and car-busy 3km) but the quicker, partly off-road route via Rua Marechal Saldanha (see map).

Parque da Pena

A further 200m up the road from the entrance to Castelo dos Mouros is the enchanting Parque da Pena (adult/student 6-17 or senior €3/2, combination ticket with Palácio Nacional da Pena €5/3.50; open 9am-8pm daily mid-June–mid-Sept, 9am-7pm May–mid-June & mid-Sept–Oct, 9.30am-6pm Nov-May, last admission 1hr before closing). It's redolent with lakes and exotic plants, huge redwoods and fern trees, camellias and rhododendrons. The free leaflet that comes with your ticket has a suggested walking route (1½ hours).

Palácio Nacional da Pena

The Pena National Palace (adult/student 6-17 or senior €3/2, combination ticket with Parque da Pena €5/3.50; open 10am-6.30pm Tues-Sun, 10am-5pm Nov-May, last admission 1hr before closing) is Sintra's most bizarre building. This extraordinary architectural confection, which rivals the best Disneyland castle, was cooked up in the fertile imagination of Ferdinand of Saxe Coburg-Gotha (artist-husband of Queen Maria II) and Prussian architect Ludwig von Eschwege. Commissioned in 1840 to build a 'romantic' or 'Gothick' baronial castle from the ruins of a 16th-century Jeronimite monastery that stood on the site, Eschwege delivered a Bavarian-Manueline fantasy of embellishment, turrets and battlements (and added a statue of himself in armour, overlooking the palace from a nearby peak).

The interior is just as mind-boggling – the rooms have been left practically as they were when the royal family fled on the eve of the revolution in 1910. There's Eiffel-designed furniture, Ferdinand-designed china, and a wall of cavorting nudes painted by Dom Carlos I. More serious works of art include a 16th-century carved alabaster altarpiece by Nicolas Chanterène in the original monastery chapel. Every room is crammed with fascinating treasures, from Messein lampstands to trompe l'oeil walls, chandeliers of crystal leaves to intricate stucco work, statues of candle-bearing Turks to a teak-furnished tearoom. Dom Carlos' bathroom features a magnificent bathtub; his queen's bedroom a fabulous carved mahogany four-poster. Despite the opulence, there's an air of lived-in homeliness.

Since the only entrance to the palace is via Parque da Pena, it's cheaper to buy the combination ticket. If you can't face the 10-minute climb up, there's a shuttle bus directly from the park entrance to the palace for €1.50 return.

Buses to the park entrance leave from Sintra train station and near the turismo (see Getting Around later in this section).

Convento dos Capuchos

If the Palácio Nacional da Pena leaves you aghast at its extravagance, try this atmospheric **Capuchin monastery** (adult/student 6-17 or senior €3/2; open 9am-8pm daily June-Oct, 9am-6pm Nov-May, last admission 1hr before closing) for the greatest contrast imaginable.

A tiny troglodyte hermitage, buttressed by huge boulders and darkened by surrounding trees, the monastery was built in 1560 to house 12 monks. Their child-sized cells (some little more than hollows in the rock) are lined with cork, hence the monastery's popular name, Cork Convent. Visiting here is an Alice-in-Wonderland experience as you squeeze through low, narrow doorways to explore the warren of cells, chapels, kitchen, and cavern where one recluse, Honorius, spent an astonishing but obviously healthy 36 years (he was 95

Parque Natural de Sintra-Cascais

The Sintra-Cascais Natural Park is one of the most delightful areas in Portugal. Its terrain ranges from the verdant lushness of Sintra itself to the crashing coastline of Praia do Guincho (a champion site for surfers), and the wild and rugged Cabo da Roca, Europe's most westerly point. Sintra's mountains experience exceptional climatic conditions enjoyed by dozens of plant and tree species; a large number of exotic species were also introduced to Pena Park and Monserrate Park during the 18th and 19th centuries. For details of jeep, walking and biking tours in the park, see Activities later in this section.

The park's **headquarters** (☎ 219 247 200; Rua Gago Coutinho 1; open 9am-midday & 2pm-5pm Mon-Fri) offers scant information.

For sea views with your wine, visit the Esplanada Rainha overlooking Praia do Rainha, Cascais

The architectural confection of Palácio Nacional da Pena, Sintra

Praia do Guincho, near Sintra

The Moorish-looking *quinta* at the heart of rambling and romantic Monserrate Park, near Sintra-Vila

Praia de Beliche, a secluded beach near Sagres, with isolated Cabo de São Vicente in the distance

The historic town of Estói

Colourful fishing boats lined up on the beach, the Algarve

It's all sand and sun at Praia da Falésia, with a string of other beaches close by

when he died in 1596). Hermits hid away here right up until 1834 when the monastery was finally abandoned.

Think twice before walking here: the monastery is 7.3km away from Sintra-Vila (5.1km from the turn-off to Parque da Pena) along a remote, wooded road. There's no bus connection (taxis charge around €25 return, including waiting time). Entry is by guided visit only (lasting 45 minutes), usually every 15 to 30 minutes.

Monserrate Park

Just over 3km west of Sintra-Vila (beware of traffic on the narrow road if you set out to walk here) is Monserrate Park, previously known as Monserrate Gardens (adult/student 6-17 or senior €3/2; open 9am-8pm daily mid-June–mid-Sept, 9am-7pm May–mid-June & mid-Sept–Oct, 9.30am-6pm daily Nov-May, last admission 1hr before closing). Rambling and romantic, they cover 30 hectares of wooded hillside and feature flora ranging from roses and conifers to tropical tree ferns, eucalyptus, Himalayan rhododendrons and at least 24 species of palms.

The gardens, first created in the 18th century by Gerard de Visme, a wealthy English merchant, were enlarged in the 1850s by the painter William Stockdale (with help from London's Kew Gardens), who imported many plants from Australasia and Mexico. Neglected for many years (the site was sold to the Portuguese government in 1949 and practically forgotten), the garden is now being trimmed up by Parques de Sintra but there's still an appealing aura of wild abandon.

At the heart of the gardens is a bizarre Moorish-looking quinta (mansion) constructed in the late 1850s by James Knowles for another wealthy Englishman, Sir Francis Cook. Its previous incarnation was as a Gothic-style villa rented by the rich and infamous British writer William Beckford in 1794 after he fled Britain in the wake of a homosexual scandal. The quinta is in the process off being restored, possibly to become a museum.

Museu do Brinquedo

Sintra has several art museums of rather specialist interest, but this toy museum (adult/child or student €3/1.50; open 10am-6pm Tues-Sun), found in a spacious modern building, is a delightful international collection of clockwork trains, lead soldiers, Dinky toys, porcelain dolls and much more, from 3000-year-old Egyptian stone toys to a couple of computers on which visitors can play games. João Arbués Moreira, an engineer by profession, began this collection (now over 20,000 pieces) more than 50 years ago when he was 14. Often to be found in the museum, the wheelchair-bound João is still fascinated by the toys and the history they represent, and the collection continues to grow.

The museum (wheelchair-accessible, of course) also has a café and a small shop.

Museu de Arte Moderna

Sintra put itself on the international art map when this museum (☎ 219 248 170; adult/student €3/1.50, under-18 or senior Thur free; open 10am-6pm Tues-Sun) opened in 1997 in Sintra's neoclassical former casino in Estefânia. Some of the world's best postwar art (including a particularly strong selection of pop art) was collected by business tycoon José Berardo and his associate Francisco Capelo. Among the 350 or so pieces displayed are works by Warhol, Lichtenstein, Pollock and Kossoff.

Quinta da Regaleira

This fairy-tale villa (☎ 219 106 650; adult/under-26 or senior €10/5; open 10am-6pm daily June-Sept, 10am-4pm Mar-May, Oct & Nov, 11am-3.30pm Dec-Feb) is a collection of pseudo-Manueline buildings created in the early 20th century by the stage designer, Luigi Manini (who also designed the stunning Palace Hotel do Buçaco in the Beiras) for António Carvalho Monteiro, a Brazilian mining millionaire. Now belonging to the town council and finally open to the public, the quinta's showpiece is the Palácio dos Milhões (so called because it cost so many millions to build). Also in the extensive grounds are a chapel, the Capela da Santíssima Trindade, and an initiation well, the Poço Iniciáto, which spirals down 30m to a labyrinth of underground galleries. The quinta is open daily for guided, pre-booked visits only (reservations are only taken from Monday to Friday), lasting 2½ hours. On weekends, if you haven't booked, you can try turning up at the gate (check the tour times with the turismo).

Activities

The Sintra region is increasingly popular for **mountain biking** and **walking**. A favourite walking trail is from Sintra-Vila to Castelo dos Mouros, a relatively easy 50-minute hike. The energetic can continue to Palácio Nacional da Pena (another 20 minutes) and up to the Serra de Sintra's highest point, the 529m Cruz Alta, which offers spectacular views.

With a few days' notice **Wild Side Tours/ Active Outdoors** (☎ 938 608 797; e wild -side@clix.pt) can organise day-long walking trips for around €30 per person (minimum three people). It also offers mountain biking in the Peninha region of Sintra, Cabo da Roca or Praia do Guincho, as well as **rock-climbing** and **kayaking** along the Estoril coast.

Ozono Mais (☎ 219 243 673; e ozonoma is@ip.pt; Rua General Alves Roçades 10) offers a day's **jeep tour** costing around €48 per person, including lunch and a visit to a wine cellar.

Special Events

Sintra's big cultural event is the classical Festival de Música, held from mid-June to mid-July in palaces and other posh venues here, Estoril and Cascais. It's followed by the equally international Noites de Bailado, a classical and contemporary dance festival continuing until the end of August and held in the gardens of the luxurious Hotel Palácio de Seteais; contact the turismo for details. Sintra's newest cultural venue is the Centro Cultural Olga Cadaval in Estefânia, beautifully converted from an old cinema.

Places to Stay – Budget

The nearest camp site is **Camping Praia Grande** (see West of Sintra later in this chapter), on the coast 12km from Sintra.

The **pousada da juventude** (youth hostel; ☎ 219 241 210; e sintra@movijovem.pt; dorm beds €9.50, doubles with/without bathroom €22.90/21) is in Santa Eufémia, 4km from Sintra-Vila and 2km uphill from São Pedro. Take the bus to Parque da Pena, walk 100m downhill and follow the rough forest path (by the ruined 'Casa da Lapa').

Some of the cheapest accommodation in Sintra itself is in the 80 or so *quartos* (private rooms); doubles usually cost about €35/25 with/without bathroom. The cheapest – and dampest – are probably those of **Senhora Deolinda Silva** (☎ 219 233 463; Rua Visconde de Monserrate 60). The turismo also has details of private apartments with kitchens costing from €40.

Piela's (☎ 219 241 691, 966 237 682; Rua João de Deus 70; singles/doubles €25/35), long popular, has comfy, spacious doubles (with shared bathroom) and a genial owner.

Places to Stay – Mid-Range & Top End

Monte da Lua (☎/fax 219 241 029; Avenida Miguel Bombarda 51; doubles €50) offers tastefully decorated rooms, the best overlooking the wooded valley at the back. Credit cards are not accepted here.

Vila Marques (☎ 219 230 027, fax 219 241 155; Rua Sotto Mayor 1; doubles with/ without bathroom €60/54) is a handsome house in central Sintra-Vila, with a relaxing terrace.

Quinta da Paderna (☎ 219 235 053, 919 461 261; Rua da Paderna 4; doubles €65) is an eclectic (if somewhat musty) private home, with fantastic views.

Residencial Sintra (☎ 219 230 738; e pen sao.residencial.sintra@clix.pt; Travessa dos Avelares 12; doubles/triples €80/100, online bookings €5 cheaper), in an enviably picturesque position on the high road between Sintra-Vila and São Pedro, is a big old mansion featuring 10 spacious rooms, with high ceilings. It's perfect for families, with a rambling garden, outdoor patio and swimming pool.

Villa das Rosas (☎/fax 219 234 216; Rua António Cunha 2-4; doubles €100), among several Turihab properties in the area, is a 19th-century house boasting some splendid decor (including azulejos in the hall and dining room) and a swimming pool in the fragrant garden.

Pensão Nova Sintra (☎/fax 219 230 220; Largo Afonso de Albuquerque 25; doubles €70) is a renovated mansion above the main road, offering deluxe doubles and big outdoor patio.

Hotel Tivoli (☎ 219 233 505; e htsintra@ mail.telepac.pt; Praça da República; doubles €119) is a modern, very central choice (right by the Palácio da Vila), with parking provided.

Lawrence's Hotel (☎ 219 105 500, fax 219 105 505; e lawrences_hotel@iol.pt; Rua

Consigliéri Pedroso 38; singles/doubles €182/ 236) was the former hostelry of Lord Byron. Restored in exquisite taste by a Dutch couple, many of its fabulous rooms overlook the wooded valley.

Rural alternatives nearby include **Quinta das Sequóias** (☎ 219 243 821; |e| candigon zalez@hotmail.com; doubles €135), a superb five-bedroom manor house adorned with art and flowers, en route to Monserrate Park; and a 16th-century former farmhouse, **Quinta da Capella** (☎ 219 290 170, fax 219 293 425; doubles €150) set in a secluded wooded valley nearby.

Places to Eat
Estefânia Big and busy **Tirol de Sintra** (Largo Afonso de Albuquerque 9; dishes €6-7) is the place to head for cheap pizzas and lunch-time meals.

Rua João de Deus, by the train station, has several nontouristy budget choices, including the humble **O Comboio** (☎ 219 241 187; Rua João de Deus 84; dishes under €5), with huge servings (and check out the jovial owner's vast pen collection!).

Restaurante Parreirinha (☎ 219 231 207; Rua João de Deus 41; dishes €6-7; open Mon-Sat) is smarter and justifiably popular; it serves grilled fish cooked on coals outside, plus fresh vegetables (rare joy!).

A Tasca do Manel (☎ 219 230 215; Largo Dr Virgílio Horta 5), another unpretentious place, offers decent fare for an appetising €5.

Restaurante do Museu (☎ 219 107 000; dishes €9-10; open Tues-Sun), in the basement of the Museu de Arte Moderna, has a more refined ambience. Come here for arty fare such as bife Picasso (€9.50) in an ultra-cool, yellow-cushioned setting.

Sintra-Vila Places here are inevitably pricey and packed with tourists, but there are still a few decent choices.

Casa da Avó (☎ 219 231 280; Rua Visconde de Monserrate 46; dishes €5-9) is a plain café-restaurant, offering cheap, simple fare.

Tulhas Bar & Restaurante (☎ 219 232 378; Rua Gil Vicente 4; dishes €7; open Thur-Tues) is a converted grain warehouse with a relaxing ambience and reasonably priced dishes (eg, veal steaks with Madeira for €6.90).

Cantinho da Paparoca (☎ 968 316 465; Rua da Biquinha 5; dishes €6-8, half-portions €4.50) is a fab new addition to the Sintra

food scene, with a few outdoor tables and a homely feel.

Casa Piriquita (Rua das Padarias 1-5) is where everyone likes to sample Sintra's famous queijadas (sweet cheese cakes) and travesseiros (almond pastries).

Loja do Manel (Rua do Arco do Teixeira), a grocery store nearby, can provide picnic supplies.

São Pedro Carnivores can get their teeth into a chunk of javali (wild boar; €14.20) or other churrasco (charcoal-grilled) dishes at **Toca do Javali** (☎ 219 233 503; Rua 1 de Dezembro 12; open Thur-Tues); go early to grab an outdoor table.

Adega do Saloio (☎ 219 231 422; Travessa Chão de Meninos; dishes €9-15, half-portions €6; open Wed-Mon) has two outlets nearby, both specialising in grills.

Restaurante Indiano Tandoori e Pizzaria (☎ 219 244 667; Praça Dom Fernando 11; dishes €6-9) offers some refreshingly different dishes at reasonable prices.

Entertainment
Fonte da Pipa (☎ 219 234 437; Rua Fonte da Pipa 11-13; open from around 9pm daily) is a cosy bar, with snacks and inexpensive drinks.

Estrada Velha (☎ 219 234 355; Rua Consiglieri Pedroso 16) is another popular bar.

Xentra (☎ 219 240 759; Rua Consiglieri Pedroso 2A) attracts a youthful gang, thanks to high-decibel music.

Taverna dos Trovadores (☎ 219 233 548), in São Pedro, is an upmarket tavern which also has live Portuguese music Friday and Saturday nights.

Mourisca Bar (☎ 219 235 253; Calçada de São Pedro 56) is a casual dive usually jam-packed with locals, where you can play snooker, darts or chess.

Getting There & Away
Buses run by **Scotturb** (formerly Stagecoach; ☎ 214 699 100) or **Mafrense** (☎ 219 230 971) leave regularly for Cascais (€2.30/ 2.70 direct/via Cabo da Roca, 45/60 minutes), Estoril (€2.30, 40 minutes), Mafra (€2.10, 45 minutes) and Ericeira (€2.10, 45 minutes). Most services leave from Sintra train station (estação on timetables) via the new Portela Interface terminal, in Portela de Sintra. For a useful bus service to

AROUND LISBON

AROUND LISBON

the airport, see Getting There & Away in the Cascais section later in this chapter.

Train services (€1.10, 45 minutes) run every 15 minutes between Sintra and Lisbon (Rossio or Entrecampos train stations). Bikes travel for free at weekends and holidays (€2.50 return on weekdays, only outside rush hour, which is between 8am and 10am, and 4pm and 6pm).

Getting Around

Bus The bus No 433 runs regularly from Portela Interface to São Pedro (*Largo 1 Dez* on timetables; €0.60, 15 minutes) via Estefânia and Sintra-Vila. To get to the Palácio Nacional da Pena (€3.20, 15 minutes), catch bus No 434. It starts from Sintra train station and goes via the turismo in Sintra-Vila daily every 40 minutes (20 minutes in summer) from 10.20am to 5.15pm.

For €7 you can buy a Day Rover Ticket, which is valid on all Scotturb bus routes, including the Pena service. A one-day Train & Bus Travelcard (€9) is valid on Lisbon–Cascais/Sintra trains and all Scotturb buses. There are ticket kiosks at Portela Interface (near the car park) and opposite Sintra train station.

Taxi & Car Taxis are available at the train station or opposite the post office in Sintra-Vila. They aren't metered, so check the fares first with the turismo. Figure on about €7 one-way to Palácio Nacional da Pena, or €25 return to Convento dos Capuchos (including one hour waiting time). There's a 20% supplement on weekends and holidays.

There's a free car park below Sintra-Vila (follow the signs by the *câmara municipal*, town hall, in Estefânia). Alternatively, park at the Portela Interface car park (€1) and take the bus.

Diller (☎ 219 271 225, fax 219 271 122), based in nearby Pêro Pinheiro, will deliver rental cars to Sintra for no extra charge.

Horse & Carriage Getting around by horse and carriage is the most romantic option. They clip-clop all over the place, even as far as Monserrate (€50 one way). The turismo has a full list of prices. The carriages wait by the entrance to the Parque da Liberdade (on Alameda Volta do Duche) or by the *pelourinho* (stone pillory) immediately below the Palácio Nacional de Sintra.

WEST OF SINTRA

The most alluring destinations for day trips from Sintra are the beaches of Praia Grande and Praia das Maçãs, about 12km to the west. **Praia Grande**, as its name suggests, is a big sandy beach with ripping breakers, which hosts heats of the European Surfing Championships. It also boasts a 102m-long ocean-water **swimming pool** (*adult/child Mon-Fri €6/3, Sat & Sun €7/4; open June-Oct*), reputedly the largest in Europe. **Praia das Maçãs** has a smaller and cosier beach and a trio of popular discos in the village. **Azenhas do Mar**, 2km further, has an even smaller beach, with a spectacular cliff-top location for its village.

En route to the beaches, 8km west of Sintra, is the ancient village of **Colares** atop a ridge (not to be confused with traffic-clogged Várzea de Colares on the main road below). It's a laid-back spot with spectacular views. It has been famous for its wines since the 13th century, made from the only vines in Europe to survive the 19th-century phylloxera plague, thanks to their deep roots and the local sandy soil. Call in advance to arrange a visit to the **Adega Regional de Colares** (☎ 219 291 210) and taste some of its velvety reds.

Attracting all of the tour buses, however, is **Cabo da Roca** (Rock Cape), about 18km west of Sintra. This sheer cliff, rising 150m above the roaring sea, is Europe's westernmost point. It's a wild and rugged spot, and surprisingly uncommercialised, perhaps because it feels too uncomfortably remote; there are only a couple of stalls, a café, and a tourist office where you can buy a certificate to show you've been here.

Places to Stay & Eat

Camping Praia Grande (☎ 219 290 581; e *wondertur@ip.pt; Avenida Maestro Frederico de Freitas 28; adult/tent/car €2.90/2.70/2.10*), Praia Grande's often crowded site, is 600m from the beach. It also has bungalows and luxury *quartos* available.

Senhora Maria Pereira (☎/fax 219 290 319; *Avenida Maestro Frederico de Freitas 19; doubles/triples with breakfast €45/55, apartments €60*), 1km before Praia Grande beach, has delightful *quartos* that overlook a large rambling garden (with barbecue facilities). Three self-catering apartments are also available.

Hotel Miramonte (☎ 219 288 200; e ho telmiramonte@viphotels.com; Avenida do Atlântico 155, Pinhal da Nazaré; doubles with breakfast Sept–mid-July €85, mid-July–Aug €92) is an endearingly old-fashioned place on the Sintra–Praia das Maçãs road, 400m before the turn-off to Praia Grande.

Hotel Arribas (☎ 219 292 145; e hotel .arribas@mail.telepac.pt; Avenida Alfredo Coelho, Praia Grande; doubles €100) is a deluxe choice, overlooking Praia Grande; residents have free use of the huge ocean-water pool.

Residencial Real (☎ 219 292 002; Rua Fernão Magalhães, Praia das Maças; doubles with breakfast around €50), an old, spacious place in Praia das Maças, was undergoing a face-lift at the time of writing. It's at the northern end of the village, and has expansive ocean views.

Residencial Oceano (☎ 219 292 399, fax 219 292 123; e pensaoceano@iol.pt; Avenida Eugénio Levy 52; doubles with breakfast €70) located right by the tram terminal in Praia das Maças, has neat, modern rooms on offer.

Restaurante Pôr do Sol (☎ 219 291 740; Rua António Brandão de Vasconcelos 25; open daily July & Aug, Wed-Mon Sept-June) is a fantastically situated restaurant in Azenhas do Mar, right at the top of the village, with good pratos do dia (daily specials; €6.30) and live music nightly. Its staff can also recommend quartos.

There are plenty of cafés and restaurants at both Praia Grande and Praia das Maças.

Entertainment
Three popular nightclubs at Praia das Maças are Concha (☎ 219 292 067), on the left by the Galp station; Casino Monumental (☎ 219 292 024) in the centre; and Quivuvi (☎ 219 291 217) further along on the right in a modern shopping mall, going strong until at least 4am on weekends.

Getting There & Away
Bus No 441 from Portela Interface goes frequently via Colares to Praia das Maças (€1.80, 25 minutes) and on to Azenhas do Mar (€1.80, 30 minutes), stopping at Praia Grande (€1.80, 25 minutes) three times daily (more in summer). Bus No 440 (€2.30, 35 minutes) is another service that travels from Sintra to Azenhas do Mar.

The century-old tram service that was established to connect Sintra with the bathing resort of Praia das Maças was recently revived, but at the time of writing its service was in some doubt. It should run from Ribeira de Sintra (1.5km from Sintra-Vila; take bus No 441 or 403) three to four times daily except Monday and Tuesday (€2.50). Check with the turismo in Sintra.

Bus No 403 to Cascais runs regularly via Cabo da Roca (€2.30, 45 minutes) from outside Sintra station.

CASCAIS
postcode 2750 • pop 33,000 (municipality)
The former fishing village of Cascais (kuhsh-kaish) has been tuned in to tourism from as early as 1870, when the royal court first came here for the summer, bringing a train of nobility in its wake. It is now the liveliest beach resort on the Estoril coast, attracting a young and international crowd. If you like your home comforts (Britishstyle pubs etc), you'll be happy in the touristy pedestrianised centre, but there is also a surprisingly unspoilt old town area which provides a pleasant afternoon's meander, plus a new marina with hip bars and restaurants.

Orientation & Information
The train station and nearby bus station are about 250m north of the main pedestrianised Rua Frederico Arouca.

The turismo (☎ 214 868 204, fax 214 672 280; Rua Visconde da Luz 14; open 9am-7pm Mon-Fri Sept-June, 9am-8pm Mon-Fri July-Aug; 10am-6pm Sat & Sun year-round) can help with accommodation.

Money Among the many banks in town with ATMs are Banco Espirito Santo (Largo Luís Camões 40) and Banco Comercial Português (Largo da Estação). A private-exchange bureau, Empório (Rua Frederico Arouca 45; open 9am-7.30pm Mon-Fri, 10am-6.30pm Sat & Sun), operates from the basement of a shopping centre.

Post & Communications The post office (Avenida Marginal; open 8.30am-6pm Mon-Fri) also has NetPost.

Smartprint (☎ 214 866 776; Rua Frederico Arouca 45, Loja 13; open 10am-6pm Mon-Fri), in the basement of a shopping mall, charges €0.70 per five minutes for Internet access. **Ciber Forum** *(☎ 214 868 311; Rua da Bela Vista 126; open 10am-8pm Sun-Thur, 10am-11pm Fri & Sat)*, also with an outdoor café, charges €0.50 per 10 minutes.

Medical Services & Emergency For medical help, contact the **Cascais Hospital** *(☎ 214 827 700; Rua Padre Loureiro)*; for other emergencies call the **main police station** *(☎ 214 861 217; Rua Afonso Sanches)*.

Cascais has a small but growing reputation for violent crime, some of it directed at tourists. There is a special **tourist police post** *(☎ 214 863 929; e psp.cascais@mail .telepac.pt; open 10am-8pm daily Sept-June, 10am-10pm July & Aug)* located next to the turismo.

Old Cascais

For a hint of Cascais' former life as a fishing village, head for the **fish market**, between Praia da Ribeira and Praia da Rainha, where an auctioneer sells off the day's catch in unintelligible rapid-fire lingo at about 6pm Monday to Saturday.

The atmospheric back lanes and alleys to the west of the *câmara municipal* are also worth exploring. In a shady square southwest of the *câmara municipal* is the **Igreja de Nossa Senhora da Assunção**, decorated with azulejos predating the 1755 earthquake that destroyed most of the town.

Museums

The large and leafy Parque Municipal da Gandarinha is great for kids, with aviaries,

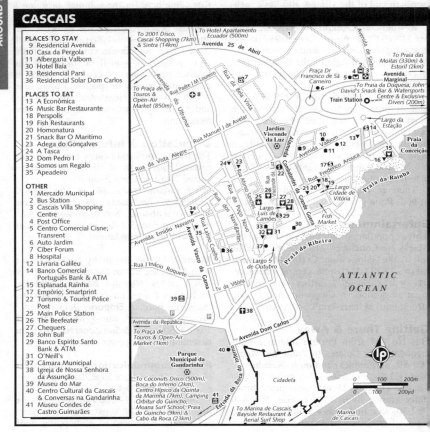

CASCAIS

PLACES TO STAY
9   Residencial Avenida
10 Casa da Pergola
11 Albergaria Valbom
30 Hotel Baía
33 Residencial Parsi
36 Residencial Solar Dom Carlos

PLACES TO EAT
13 A Económica
16 Music Bar Restaurante
18 Perspolis
19 Fish Restaurants
20 Homonatura
21 Snack Bar O Marítimo
23 Adega do Gonçalves
24 A Tasca
32 Dom Pedro I
34 Somos um Regalo
35 Apeadeiro

OTHER
1   Mercado Municipal
2   Bus Station
3   Cascais Villa Shopping Centre
4   Post Office
5   Centro Comercial Cisne; Transrent
6   Auto Jardim
7   Ciber Forum
8   Hospital
12 Livraria Galileu
14 Banco Comercial Português Bank & ATM
15 Esplanada Rainha
17 Empório; Smartprint
22 Turismo & Tourist Police Post
25 Main Police Station
26 The Beefeater
27 Chequers
28 John Bull
29 Banco Espirito Santo Bank & ATM
31 O'Neill's
37 Câmara Municipal
38 Igreja de Nossa Senhora da Assunção
39 Museu do Mar
40 Centro Cultural da Cascais & Conversas na Gandarinha
41 Museu Condes de Castro Guimarães

duck ponds and playground. It also contains the delightful **Museu Condes de Castro Guimarães** (☎ *214 825 407; admission €1.30; open 10am-5pm Tues-Sun*). The late-19th-century mansion of the Counts of Castro Guimarães displays the family's furnishings and *objets d'art* from the 17th and 18th centuries, including a number of striking Indo-Portuguese furniture as well as Oriental silk tapestries; its walls are liberally adorned with early azulejos. Downstairs is a small display of archaeological finds from the area. Admission is with guided tours only, every half-hour. A bilingual booklet (€2.50) is available at the entrance.

The admirable **Museu do Mar** (☎ *214 825 400; admission €1.30, Sun free; open 10am-5pm Tues-Sun*), in Jardim da Parada, has a small but excellent display of model boats, fish, dolphins and whales, traditional fisherfolk's clothing, and other marine artefacts.

Near the Museu Condes de Castro Guimarães, the colourful new **Centro Cultural de Cascais** (☎ *214 848 900; Avenida Rei Humberto II de Itália; admission free; open 10.30am-6.30pm Tues-Sun*) hosts changing exhibitions and other cultural events.

Beaches
Cascais has three sandy bits of beach – **Praia da Ribeira** is the largest and closest – tucked into little bays just a few minutes' walk south of the main drag. They're nothing to write home about (nor is the water quality) but they make pleasant suntraps if you can find an empty patch.

Far more exciting waves break at **Praia do Guincho**, 9km northwest of Cascais. This long, wild beach is a surfer's and windsurfer's paradise (the site of previous World Surfing Championships) with its massive crashing rollers. The strong undertow can be dangerous for swimmers and novice surfers.

Boca do Inferno
Cascais' most famous tourist attraction, 2km west, is Boca do Inferno (Mouth of Hell), where the sea roars into an abyss in the coast. Taxis charge about €4 return. Don't expect anything dramatic unless there's a storm raging.

Activities
There are **horse-riding** facilities (around €20 per hour) at the **Centro Hípico da**

Quinta da Marinha (☎ *214 869 433*), 2km inland from Praia do Guincho.

John David's Snack Bar & Watersports Centre (☎ *214 830 455*) at Praia da Duquesa, midway between Cascais and Estoril, has sailboards for rent (€20 per hour), and organises **water-skiing** jaunts (€25 per 15 minutes) and **banana-boat rides** (€4 per person). Also based at this beach is **Exclusive Divers** (☎ *937 654 322;* e *info@exclusive-divers.com*), which can take you **scuba-diving** around the Cascais coastline and beyond for €40 per dive.

Moana Surf School (☎ *964 449 436;* e *surfmoana@hotmail.com*), based at Praia do Guincho, offers various **surfing** courses, including an introductory 90-minute lesson for €27 or five 90-minute classes for €90.

Surfboards can be rented from **Aerial** (☎ *214 836 745; Loja 129*), at the Marina de Cascais, for €23 per day.

Special Events
Summertime musical events include the Estoril Festival de Jazz and the Festival de Música da Costa do Estoril, held in both Cascais and Estoril during July. Between July and mid-September, there's a programme of free outdoor entertainment (eg, live bands) at around 10.30pm nightly, usually at Estoril's Praia de Tamariz and/or Cascais' Praia de Moitas (en route to Estoril). During this same period firework displays take place at midnight every Saturday, usually over Praia de Tamariz.

The Festas do Mar (end of June) is the most traditional event, celebrating Cascais' marine ties and honouring the patron saint of its fisherfolk, the Senhora dos Navegantes, with a day-long procession through the streets plus a parade of fishing boats.

Places to Stay
Advance reservations are essential for summer. The prices listed here are for July (August is higher).

Camping Orbitur do Guincho (☎ *214 870 450, fax 214 872 167; adult/tent/car €4.40/ 3.70/4*) is in Areia, about 1km inland from Praia do Guincho and 9km from Cascais. Buses run regularly to Guincho from Cascais.

Quartos cost €30 to €35 a double. The turismo doesn't officially keep a list but staff may know of some available. Otherwise, ask at Adega do Gonçalves (see Places to Eat).

Residencial Avenida (☎ 214 864 417; Rua da Palmeira 14; doubles €30), so long-established its sign is practically invisible, has just four prettily decorated doubles with shared bathroom.

Residencial Parsi (☎ 214 845 744, fax 214 837 150; Rua Afonso Sanches 8; doubles with/without bathroom €45/35) is a crumbling old building near the waterfront.

Rates at all the following places include breakfast.

Casa da Pergola (☎ 214 840 040, fax 214 834 791; e pergolahouse@netc.pt; Avenida Valbom 13; doubles with/without balcony €102/92) is a very pretty Turihab establishment with an ornate facade and a gorgeous garden.

Albergaria Valbom (☎ 214 865 801; e al bergariavalbom@mail.telepac.pt; Avenida Valbom 14; doubles €63-68) has more modern and less inspired accommodation than Casa da Pergola.

Residencial Solar Dom Carlos (☎ 214 828 115; e solardecarlos@mail.telepac.pt; Rua Latino Coelho 8; doubles €60-70) is a 16th-century former royal residence featuring a chapel where Dom Carlos used to pray. It's a welcoming, old-fashioned place in a quiet location.

Hotel Baía (☎ 214 831 033; e hotelbaia@mail.telepac.pt; Avenida dos Combatentes da Grande Guerra; doubles €110) is a big, brash hotel with a prime sea-view spot and stylish facilities.

Hotel Apartamento Ecuador (☎ 214 826 500, fax 214 840 703; e hotelequador@mail.telepac.pt; Alto da Pampilheira; 2-person apartments with kitchen early-mid-July €71.50-93), a high-rise on the northern outskirts of town offers some of the most reasonably priced apartments.

Places to Eat

A Económica (☎ 214 833 524; Rua Sebastião J C Melo 11; dishes €6), true to its name, is a casa de pasto (casual eatery) serving economically priced standard fare (though watch for overpriced couvert extras).

A Tasca (Rua Afonso Sanches 61; dishes €6) is another good-value place, with bargain grilled fish for €6.30.

Adega do Gonçalves (☎ 214 830 287; Rua Afonso Sanches 54; dishes €9), near A Tasca, is a popular haunt, providing hearty servings of the usual fare.

A cluster of appealing venues with outdoor seating is in the cobbled Largo Cidade de Vitória, including the low-key **Snack Bar O Maritímo** (☎ 214 843 988; dishes €7; open lunch Mon-Sat). Behind the nearby fish market is a string of upmarket fish restaurants.

Dom Pedro I (☎ 214 833 734; Beco dos Invalides 5; dishes €5-8; open Mon-Sat) is a tucked-away gem, serving great-value fare. Early arrivals may strike lucky and get one of the few outdoor tables on the cobbled steps. Credit cards are not accepted here.

Apeadeiro (☎ 214 832 731; Avenida Vasco da Gama 32; dishes €6-8; open Tues-Sat, lunch Sun) is renowned locally for its grilled fish.

Somos um Regalo (☎ 214 865 487; Avenida Vasco da Gama 36; dishes €7-9; open lunch Tues-Sun) does yummy grilled chicken (half-portion €4.30) and has a takeaway service.

Need a taste of something different? **Perspolis** (☎ 214 831 285; Rua das Flores 11A; dishes €9; open Tues-Sun) specialises in Persian fare – plus English breakfasts!

Conversas na Gandarinha (☎ 214 866 402; dishes €6-7), in the new Centro Cultural de Cascais (see Museums), is a fantastic airy, arty space where you can nibble cakes or enjoy a light lunch.

Music Bar Restaurante (☎ 214 820 848; Largo Praia da Rainha 121; dishes €13) is another bright, classy venue, overlooking the sea.

The Marina de Cascais has even more breezy seaview restaurants, including **Bayside** (☎ 214 861 318; Loja 54; dishes from €9), which offers Brazilian fare as well as fish dishes.

Homonatura (☎ 214 837 382; 2 entrances – Largo Cidade de Vitória 32 & 1st floor, Rua Frederico Arouca 24) is a vegetarian restaurant (rare in Portugal), which also offers Hatha yoga and alternative medicine courses.

Many of Cascais' bars (see Entertainment) also offer food.

Entertainment

There's no lack of bars to keep the nights buzzing, especially in Largo Luís de Camões, where the bars triple as cafés, restaurants and live music venues.

John Bull (☎ 214 483 319; Largo Luís de Camões 4) is stuffed with comfy chairs and English ambience.

Chequers (☎ 214 830 926; Largo Luís de Camões) dishes up traditional Sunday grub (eg, roast beef and apple pie, €9).

The Beefeater (☎ 214 840 696; Rua Visconde da Luz 1) serves all your favourite brews.

O'Neill's (☎ 214 868 230; Largo 5 de Outubro) provides Irish stews, a wicked St Patrick's Day celebration and frequent live music.

For a sea view with your drinks, head for outdoor **Esplanada Rainha**, overlooking Praia da Rainha, or to the marina, with several neat bars and cafés.

Coconuts (☎ 214 844 109; Avenida Rei Humberto II de Itália 7; open 11pm-4am daily), Cascais' most popular nightclub, has seven bars, two dance floors and an esplanade by the sea. Wednesday is Ladies' Night, featuring a male stripper.

2001 (☎ 214 690 550), a long-established rock-music disco, is located around 7km north of town.

Shopping

Livraria Galileu (Avenida Valbom 24A) is a good source of second-hand books in English, Spanish, Italian, French and German.

Serious shoppers should head for **CascaiShopping**, a massive shopping complex en route to Sintra. Bus No 417 passes by regularly. Cascais also has the new **Cascais Villa shopping centre** (Avenida Marginal) by the bus station.

The **mercado municipal** (municipal market), on the northern outskirts of town, is best on Wednesday and Saturday morning, while an **open-air market** fills the area next to the former bullring, 1km west of town, on the first and third Sunday of the month.

Getting There & Away

Buses go frequently to Sintra from both Estoril and Cascais (quickest route €2.30, 40 minutes) and to Cabo da Roca (€2.70, 30 minutes), and seven times daily from Cascais to Praia do Guincho (€1.80, 20 minutes). Tickets cost less at the bus station kiosk than on board the bus.

There's a direct hourly bus service to Lisbon's airport (€7, 45 minutes) via Estoril train station and Lisbon's Centro Comercial Colombo. On weekends some services continue to Lisbon's Parque das Nações. Since the ticket is equivalent to a Day Rover Ticket you could sightsee en route if you're lightly laden.

Trains from Lisbon's Cais do Sodré station run regularly to Cascais via Estoril (€1.10, 30 minutes). Bikes travel for free on this line on weekends.

Getting Around

Since car parking is such a nightmare (you could try near Museu do Mar), the best option is to park on the outskirts (eg, at the Praça de Touros) and take the busCas minibus service (€1.20 return) into town: it does a circular route via the centre every seven minutes from 7.30am to 9.20pm (10.20pm in summer).

At the time of writing, free bikes were available from 8am to 5pm daily at various points around town, including the train station and Hotel Baía. Or you can rent them from **Transrent** (☎ 214 864 566), in the basement of Centro Comercial Cisne, for €7.50 per day. Transrent also rents scooters and motorbikes (from €16.50 and €30 per day, respectively). A cycle path from Cascais to Guincho was due to open at the time of writing; ask at the turismo for details.

Often waiting at the Jardim Visconde da Luz are a couple of horse carriages, which do half-hour trips to Boca do Inferno for about €20 return.

Among the reliable car-rental agencies is **Auto Jardim** (☎ 214 831 073). For a taxi call ☎ 214 660 101.

ESTORIL

postcode 2765 • pop 40,000 (municipality)
Long a favoured haunt of the rich and famous (and a well-known nest of spies during WWII), the genteel resort of Estoril (shtoereel) is nowadays very much in the shadow of its livelier neighbour, Cascais. Its unique attraction is Europe's biggest casino. It also has a pleasant beach and several nearby golf courses.

Orientation & Information

The bus and adjacent train stations are on Avenida Marginal, opposite shady Parque do Estoril, at the top of which is the casino. The **turismo** (☎ 214 663 813; e estorilcoast@ mail.telepac.pt; open 9am-7pm Mon-Sat Sept-June, 9am-8pm Mon-Sat July-Aug; 10am-6pm Sun year-round) is almost opposite the train station.

Casino

The casino (☎ 214 667 700; open 3pm-3am daily) has an admission charge of €5 (passport required) for the gaming room (everything from roulette to baccarat, French bank and blackjack), though it's free to play the slot machines and bingo. The vast **restaurant** (☎ 214 684 521; floor show tickets with/without dinner €50/25) attached to the casino puts on an international floor show nightly at 11pm.

Beach

Estoril's small but pleasant Praia de Tamariz has showers, cafés and beachside bars as well as an ocean **swimming pool** (adult/child 4-9 Mon-Fri €10/7.50, Sat & Sun €15/10; open 10am-7pm daily mid-June–mid-Sept). A pedestrian underpass links the beach with the park.

Special Events

A **feira do artesanato** (handicrafts fair; open 6pm-midnight daily July & Aug) takes place beside the casino. Every early October, the art gallery on the 1st floor of the casino hosts an International Naïve Painting Salon,

---

Golf on the Estoril Coast

If you're a gambler and a golfer (and preferably wealthy) you'll be in seventh heaven in Estoril. This elegant beach resort has not only Europe's biggest casino, but also a dozen spectacular golf courses within 25km.

The closest is just 2km to the north – **Golf do Estoril** is one of the best-known courses in Portugal, having hosted the Portuguese Open Championship several times. **Quinta da Marinha**, 9km to the west, was designed by Robert Trent Jones to give both high handicappers and scratch golfers a challenge, with the course rolling over wind-blown dunes and rocky outcrops.

Some 10km to the northwest is the **Penha Longa Club**, a well-equipped Trent Jones Jr creation with superb views of the Serra de Sintra. Nearby are **Estoril-Sol**, with one of the country's best practice areas; and **Quinta da Beloura**, designed by Rocky Roquemore, also responsible for Belas Clube de Campo, 22km northeast of Estoril in the Carregueira hills.

Estoril's turismo has full details of all courses.

---

acknowledged as the biggest and best such exhibition in Iberia.

The Autodromo do Estoril, 9km north of Estoril, is the venue for various go-karting and car races and may host Formula 1 races again after recent management and track improvements.

For details about shared summer-music festivals, see Special Events in the Cascais section earlier in this chapter.

Places to Stay & Eat

Pensão Costa (☎ 214 681 699; Rua de Olivença 2; doubles with/without bathroom €25/20) is a dead basic cheapo near the train station.

Pensão Residencial Smart (☎ 214 682 164; e residencial.smart@clix.pt; Rua José Viana 3; doubles €60-70), in a quiet residential area about 700m northeast of the station, features super-snazzy rooms plus a swimming pool.

Comfort Hotel São Mamede (☎ 214 659 110; e reservas@hotelsmamede.com; Avenida Marginal 7105; doubles €63), with some rooms boasting seaviews, is among more run-of-the-mill hotels lining this busy road, about 200m uphill from the station.

Hôtel Inglaterra (☎ 214 684 461; e hotelinglaterra@mail.telepac.pt; Rua do Porto 1; doubles €110) is an eye-catching place that fits the bill for old-world looks, though as a Best Western franchise it tends to attract tour groups.

Praia de Tamariz (☎ 214 681 010; Praia de Tamariz; dishes €12), a beachfront venue with specials such as Spanish paella (€21 for two), is the most tempting dining choice.

Garrett do Estoril (☎ 214 680 365; Avenida de Nice 54), a fabulous old-fashioned pastelaria (pastry or cake shop) and tea salon on the eastern side of the park.

Getting There & Away

Bus 412 goes frequently to Cascais (€1.20). For details of other train and bus services, see under Cascais earlier in this chapter.

QUELUZ

The only reason to stop at otherwise dull Queluz (keh-**loozh**), 5km northwest of Lisbon, is to see the pink-hued **Palácio de Queluz** (adult/under-26 or senior €3/1.50; open 10am-5pm Wed-Mon, last admission 4.30pm), converted in the late 18th century from a hunting lodge to a summer residence for the royal family. It's the finest example of rococo architecture in Portugal, a miniature Versailles with feminine charm and formal gardens of whimsical fancy. One wing of the palace is often used to accommodate state guests and an annexe is now a deluxe *pousada* (upmarket inn), but the rest is open to the public.

The palace was designed by the Portuguese architect Mateus Vicente de Oliveira and French artist Jean-Baptiste Robillon for Prince Dom Pedro in the 1750s. It was Pedro's niece and wife, Queen Maria I, who inspired the most scintillating gossip about the place – she lived here for most of her reign, going increasingly mad. Her fierce, scheming Spanish daughter-in-law, Carlota Joaquina, supplied even more bizarre material for the equally eccentric British visitor William Beckford to write about – most famously, an occasion when she insisted that Beckford run a race with her maid in the garden and then dance a bolero (which he did, he related, 'in a delirium of romantic delight').

Interior highlights are a mirror-lined Throne Room, the Ambassador's Room, with a floor of chequered marble and a painted ceiling, and Pedro IV's bedroom, with scenes from *Don Quixote* on the walls, and a circular ceiling. The palace's vast kitchens have been converted into an expensive restaurant, **Cozinha Velha** (☎ 214 350 740).

The garden, a medley of box hedges, fountains and statues, features an azulejo-lined canal where the royal family went boating.

Getting There & Away

Frequent trains from Lisbon's Rossio station stop at Queluz-Belas (€0.70, 20 minutes).

MAFRA

postcode 2640 • pop 10,000
• elevation 250m

This low-key town, 39km northwest of Lisbon, is famous for the massive Palácio Nacional de Mafra, the most awesome of many extravagant monuments created during the 18th-century reign of Dom João V, when money was no problem. The former royal park, Tapada de Mafra, is an additional attraction. Mafra doesn't have much

accommodation but it's an easy day trip from Lisbon, Sintra or Ericeira.

Orientation

You can't miss the palace – its massive, restored facade dominates the town. Opposite is a pleasant little square, Largo da República, where you can find cafés and restaurants. Mafra's **bus terminal** (☎ 261 816 152) is 1.5km northwest of town but buses also stop in front of the palace (called 'convent' on timetables). A Mafrense bus **ticket office** (*Avenida Movimento Forças Armadas 22*) is near the square.

Information

The **turismo** (☎ 261 812 023; e turismo@cm-mafra.pt; *Terreiro Dom João V; open 9am-7pm Mon-Fri, 9.30am-1pm & 2.30pm-6pm Sat & Sun*) is in part of the palace. It has a picturesque (though outdated) map of the Mafra area and a bilingual *Mafra Real* booklet describing the palace and park.

Palácio Nacional de Mafra

The Mafra National Palace (*adult/youth 14-25 or senior/child under 14 €3/1.50/free, morning Sun free; open 10am-5pm Wed-Mon, closed Tues & public holidays, last admission 4.30pm*) is a combination of palace, monastery and basilica, a huge baroque and neoclassical monument covering 10 hectares.

It was begun in 1717, six years after Dom João V promised to build a monastery if he received an heir: a daughter, Dona Maria, was fortuitously born the same year. As the king's coffers filled with newly discovered gold from Brazil, the initial design – meant for 13 monks – was expanded to house 280 monks and 140 novices and to incorporate two royal wings. No expense was spared to build its 880 halls and rooms, 5200 doorways, 2500 windows and two bell towers with the world's largest collection of bells (57 in each). Indeed when the Flemish bell-founders queried the extravagant order for a carillon of bells, Dom João is said to have doubled the order and to have sent the money in advance.

If you have read *Memorial do Convento*, the magical novel by Nobel Laureate José Saramago (translated into English as *Baltasar & Blimunda*), which is centred on the building of the palace, you'll appreciate the incredible effort involved in its construction (for more on Saramago, see the boxed text in the Facts about Portugal chapter).

Under the supervision of the German architect Friedrich Ludwig, up to 20,000 artisans (including Italian carpenters and masons) worked on the monument – and a mind-boggling 45,000 in the last two years of construction, all of them kept in order by 7000 soldiers. The presence of so many outstanding artists spurred João V to establish a school of sculpture in the palace; open from 1753 to 1770, it employed many of Portugal's most important sculptors. Though the building may have been an artistic coup, the expense of its construction and the use of such a large workforce helped destroy the country's economy.

It was only briefly used as a palace. In 1799, as the French prepared to invade Portugal, Dom João VI and the royal family fled to Brazil, taking most of Mafra's furniture with them. In 1807 General Junot billeted his troops in the monastery, followed by Wellington and his men. From then on the palace became a favourite military haven. Even today, most of it is used as a military academy.

On the one-hour visit, escorted by a guard, it's easy to get dazed by the 230m corridors and interminable salons and apartments, but a few things stand out: amusing 18th-century pinball machines in the games room, grotesque hunting decor in the dining room, and the monastery's infirmary where insane monks were locked away. Most impressive is the 88m-long, barrel-vaulted baroque library,

housing nearly 40,000 books dating from the 15th to 18th centuries.

The central basilica, with its two bell towers, is wonderfully restrained by comparison, featuring multihued marble floors and panelling and Carrara marble statues.

Guided English-language tours usually set off at 11am and 2.30pm. A multilingual leaflet (€4) is useful for the non-English, escorted visits.

If you're here on a Sunday, linger until 4pm to hear one of the **Concertos de Carrilhão**, a concert of the basilica's famous bells (preceded by a free guided tour of the bell tower). The palace's **Jardim do Cerco** *(Enclosed Garden; admission free; open 9am-5pm daily)* at the northern end of the palace, where the queen once picked her flowers, makes an agreeable place to wait.

Tapada Nacional de Mafra

The palace's 819-hectare park and hunting ground, Tapada Nacional de Mafra *(☎ 261 817 050, fax 261 814 984 Mon-Fri, ☎/fax 261 814 240 Sat & Sun; walker/cyclist/horse-rider €4/7.50/20)*, was created in 1747 and is still partly enclosed by its original 21km perimeter wall. Since it's full of wild boar and deer, visits are limited. There are 90-minute tours by minibus or electric tourist-train at 10.15am and 3pm on Saturday and Sunday (€8.50/4.50/6.50 per adult/child under 10/senior), which take in the park's wildlife and a falcon-recuperation centre. Weekday visits (at 10am and 2pm daily) are reserved for school groups, but you may be

---

Safe Haven for Wolves

Some 10km northeast of Mafra is the **Centro de Recuperaçáo de Lobo Ibérico** *(Iberian Wolf Recovery Centre; ☎ 261 785 037; admission free; open 4pm-8pm Sat, Sun & holidays May-Sept, 2.30pm-6pm Oct-Apr)*, established in 1989 to provide a home for wolves trapped, snared or kept in dire conditions and no longer able to function in the wild. The centre's 17 hectares of secluded woodland provide a refuge for some 26 animals, all from the north of the country where Portugal's last Iberian wolves roam. (See Endangered Species under Flora & Fauna in the Facts about Portugal chapter for more on the Iberian wolf.)

The best time to visit is around 5pm when the wolves emerge in the cool of dusk, though even then sightings are never guaranteed.

The centre isn't signposted. From Mafra head east to Malveira, then take the Torres Vedras road for 3km and turn off to Picão just after Vale da Guarda. At the end of the village there's a steep cobbled track to the left (opposite Picão's only café). The last part of this 1km-long track is badly potholed. Those without wheels can catch one of the frequent buses from Mafra to Malveira (€1.10, 20 minutes) and change to a Torres Vedras bus to Vale da Guarda; the centre is 2km from the Picão turn-off.

able to join them if there's room: call ☎ 261 817 050 to check.

If you fancy walking, there's a 7.5km trail to follow; bikers and horse-riders have 15km. Horses (at €30 per hour) are available for experienced riders only; bikers have to bring their own bikes. The park opens its gates only at 10am and 2pm daily for these visits; you can stay until 5pm.

The Tapada is about 6km north of Mafra, along the road to Gradil. From Mafra, taxis charge around €3 one way.

Sobreiro

At the village of Sobreiro, 4km northwest of Mafra (take any Ericeira-bound bus), sculptor José Franco has created an enchanting craft village (admission free; open 9.30am–around 7.30pm daily) of miniature windmills, watermills and traditional shops. José Franco himself can often be seen crafting clay figures at the entrance. Kids love it here; so do adults, especially when they discover the rustic adega (winery) serving good red wine, snacks and meals.

Places to Stay & Eat

Hotel Castelão (☎ 261 816 050, fax 261 816 059; Avenida 25 de Abril; doubles €61), the town's only hotel, is 100m north of the turismo; rates include breakfast.

Among several café-restaurants around Largo da República is the smartish Restaurante Snack Bar Paris (☎ 261 815 797; dishes €6-8), which offers decent local fare.

Getting There & Around

There are regular buses to/from Ericeira (€1.30, 20 minutes), Sintra (€2.10, 45 minutes) and Lisbon's Campo Grande terminal (€2.80, 75 minutes). Mafra's train station is 6km away with infrequent bus connections (taxis charge around €7.50); go to Malveira station instead for easier bus connections (€1.10, 20 minutes).

Taxis (☎ 261 815 512) are available in Praça da República.

ERICEIRA

postcode 2655 • pop 6000

This pretty but rapidly developing seaside town, located 10km west of Mafra, is a firm summertime favourite with the young Lisbon and European crowd thanks to its fabulous surf and beaches, reasonably priced accommodation, lively bars, and restaurants. On weekends, especially, it has an appealing family atmosphere (many Lisboêtas have holiday homes here), with the pedestrianised streets perfect for kids.

Orientation

The town sits high above the sea, its old centre clustered around Praça da República, with a newer district to the south. There are three beaches within walking distance of the praça: Praia do Sul (also called Praia da Baleia), Praia do Norte (also called Praia do Algodio) and Praia de São Sebastião to the north. Some 5km north is unspoilt Praia de São Lourenço, while Praia Foz do Lizandro is 3km south.

The bus station is 800m north of the Praça de República, off the N247 highway, but there's a bus stop at the top of town on the N247.

Information

The turismo (☎ 261 863 122; ⓦ www.ericeira .net; Rua Dr Eduardo Burnay 46; open 9.30am–midnight daily July–mid-Sept; 9.30am-7pm Mon-Fri & Sun, 9.30am-10pm Sat mid-Sept–June) has telephones for public use and a computer for searching its website.

Bank with ATMs include Nova Rede (Praça da República).

Café Morais (☎ 261 862 472; Rua Dr Miguel Bombarda 1; usually open 9am-midnight Thur-Tues) has a coin-operated Internet facility (€0.50 per 12 minutes). Near Praia de São Sebastião, Café A Perola (☎ 261 863 433; Rua Arrabalde 5; usually open 7am-10pm Thur-Tues) charges €1.40 per half-hour. The Clube de Video (☎ 261 865 743; Praça da República; open 11am-11pm daily) charges €0.80 per 15 minutes.

Emergency services include a centro de saúde (medical centre; ☎ 261 864 100; Rua Prudéncio Franco da Trindade) and the police station (☎ 261 863 533; Rua 5 de Outubro).

Activities

Ericeira's big attraction is surfing. Praia da Ribeira de Ilhas, a World Championship site, is just a few kilometres north, though the waves at the nearer Praia de São Sebastião are challenging enough for most amateurs. For more on surfing generally, see the boxed text 'Surfing Portugal' in the Facts for the Visitor chapter.

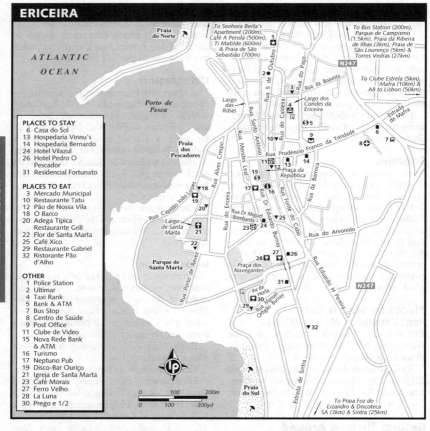

ERICEIRA

PLACES TO STAY
6 Casa do Sol
13 Hospedaria Vinnu's
14 Hospedaria Bernardo
24 Hotel Vilazul
26 Hotel Pedro O Pescador
31 Residencial Fortunato

PLACES TO EAT
3 Mercado Municipal
10 Restaurante Tatu
12 Pão de Nossa Vila
18 O Barco
20 Adega Típica Restaurante Grill
22 Flor de Santa Marta
25 Café Xico
29 Restaurante Gabriel
32 Ristorante Pão d'Alho

OTHER
1 Police Station
2 Ultimar
4 Taxi Rank
5 Bank & ATM
7 Bus Stop
8 Centro de Saúde
9 Post Office
11 Clube de Video
15 Nova Rede Bank & ATM
16 Turismo
17 Neptuno Pub
19 Disco-Bar Ouriço
21 Igreja de Santa Marta
23 Café Morais
27 Ferro Velho
28 La Luna
30 Prego e 1/2

Ultimar (☎ 261 862 371; Rua 5 de Outubro 37A; open 9.30am-1pm & 3pm-7.30pm Mon-Fri, 3pm-7.30pm Sat) rents surfboards for €15 per day.

Places to Stay
Camping The **Parque de Campismo Municipal de Mil Regos** (☎ 261 862 706; adult/tent/car €1.50/1.30/0.50), which is found close to the N247, is a big, smart facility that is 800m north of Praia de São Sebastião. There's a municipal swimming pool next door.

Clube Estrela (☎ 261 815 525, fax 261 813 333; adult/tent/car €2.80/2.10/1.80) at Sobreiro, 5km east of Ericeira, is open to visitors that have a Camping Card International (CCI).

Private Rooms & Apartments There are plenty of *quartos* and *apartamentos* costing around €30/40 per *quarto/apartmento* in summer (cheaper the longer you stay). Ask at the turismo or look for signs displayed in shops, *pensões* (guesthouses) or private homes along Rua de Baixo or Rua de Norte. Readers have recommended the apartment (with sea views) that belongs to **Senhora Berta Fontão Alberto** (☎ 261 862 213; Rua de Baixo 51).

Pensões & Residenciais You need to book well ahead in summer (prices escalate in August).

Hospedaria Bernardo (☎/fax 261 862 378; Rua Prudéncio Franco da Trindade 11; doubles €35-40, apartments €50) is a friendly place with homely, spacious doubles and two rather plain apartments (one located in the south of town).

Residencial Vinnu's (*☎/fax 261 863 830; Rua Prudéncio Franco da Trindade 19; doubles €45-50*) has bright, modern rooms, including triples with fridge.

Casa do Sol (*☎ 261 862 665, fax 261 864 402; Rua Prudéncio Franco da Trindade 1; doubles €45*), a Turihab place, is an old family house with spacious, carpeted rooms (some with adjoining lounge) and loads of ornate furnishings. Despite its main road location, it's surprisingly quiet inside.

Residencial Fortunato (*☎/fax 261 862 829; Rua Prudéncio Franco da Trindade 7; doubles with breakfast €40-45*) offers good-value doubles (the pricier ones upstairs are brighter) as well as relatively easy car parking, nearby.

Hotel Pedro O Pescador (*☎ 261 869 121; e hotelpedropescador@oninet.pt; Rua Dr Eduardo Burnay 22; doubles with breakfast €60*) is a more modern choice, with attractively furnished rooms.

Hotel Vilazul (*☎ 261 860 000; e vilazul@ mail.pt; Calçada da Baleia 10; doubles €67-69*) is a smart establishment offering rooms with air-con.

Places to Eat
Not surprisingly, considering its clientele of wealthy Lisbon weekenders, Ericeira has few bargain restaurants. Café-restaurants are your best bet, including bright and busy **Café Xico** (*☎ 261 864 151; Rua Dr Eduardo Burnay 35; dishes €6-8*).

Ti Matilde (*☎ 261 862 734; Rua Dr Manuel Arraiga; dishes €6-7; open Tues-Sun*), in the teeth of the wind from Praia de São Sebastião (but with indoor seating for the timid), has a simple, decent menu.

Fabulous grilled fish is found everywhere. **Restaurante Gabriel** (*☎ 261 863 349; Avenida da Horta; dishes from €6.50*), is low-key and reasonably priced, serving generous portions. **Restaurante Tatu** (*☎ 261 864 705; Rua Fonte do Cabo 58; grills €7.50-9, daily specials €8*) is another relatively modest place. **Ristorante Pão d'Alho** (*☎ 261 863 762; Estrada de Sintra 2; pizzas or pastas from €6, salads from €3.80; open Thur-Tues*) is the best of several pizzerias in town.

How about squid cooked in beer? **Flor de Santa Marta** (*☎ 261 862 368; Largo de Santa Marta 4A; dishes €6-7*) can come up with the goods, for €7.

Adega Típica Restaurante Grill (*☎ 261 862 149; Rua Alves Crespo; open Thur-Tues*) has an extensive menu, including *picanha* (grilled beef; €11.50), which is a popular Brazilian dish.

O Barco (*☎ 261 862 759; Rua Capitão João Lopes; dishes from €13; open Fri-Wed*) fits the (pricey) bill for a classier venue, and provides some of the town's finest seafood.

Self-caterers can find every kind of bread at **Pão de Nossa Vila** (*Praça da República*), and other supplies at the **mercado municipal** (*Largo Conde da Ericeira*).

Entertainment
Of Ericeira's 18-odd bars and nightclubs the biggest is **Discoteca SA – Sociedade Anonima** (*☎ 261 862 325; open Fri & Sat*), in a former *adega* just off the N247, 3km south of town above Praia Foz do Lizandro. On the beach itself are a couple of bars, including **Limipicos** (*☎ 261 864 121*).

Neptuno Pub (*☎ 261 862 017; Rua Mendes Leal 12*) is a friendly English-style option in the town centre, with live music most Friday nights. There's also a clutch of café-bars in Praça dos Navegantes, with great outdoor seating, notably **La Luna** (*☎ 261 865 704*), in the corner of the upper esplanade. On the street level, **Prego e 1/2** (*☎ 261 863 514*) is another lively dive.

Late-night clubs include the **Disco-Bar Ouriço** (*☎ 261 862 138; Rua Caminho Novo 9*) and the seedier **Ferro Velho** (*☎ 261 865 893; Rua Dr Eduardo Burnay*), which has live music from 10.30pm on Friday.

Getting There & Away
Express buses to/from Lisbon's Campo Grande station (€3.80, 80 minutes) via Mafra (€1.30, 20 minutes) run every 30 to 60 minutes. Services to/from Sintra (€2.10, 45 minutes) depart every hour. The turismo has timetables, or call Ericeira's **bus station** (*☎ 261 862 717*).

Getting Around
Regular local buses to Torres Vedras go past the Parque de Campismo and Praia da Ribeira de Ilhas (€0.70). For Praia Foz do Lizandro (€0.70), take any Sintra-bound bus to a stop on the N247 above the beach.

The turismo rents bikes for €7.50 per day (March to September only). **Taxis** (☎ 261 865 567) wait in Largo Conde da Ericeira.

Setúbal Peninsula

Easily accessible from Lisbon, the Setúbal Peninsula is the northern spur of the region the tourist board calls the Costa Azul. You can laze on the vast beaches of the Costa da Caparica, join hip Lisboêtas at the resort of Sesimbra further south or eat great seafood in Setúbal, where express bus connections make it a convenient stopover if you're heading south or east. Activities in the region – which also includes two fine nature reserves, the Reserva Natural do Estuário do Sado and the Parque Natural da Arrábida – include surfing, dolphin-watching, mountain biking and walking trips.

CACILHAS

Above this suburb across the Rio Tejo from Lisbon, and visible from almost everywhere in Lisbon, is the **Cristo Rei** (☎ 212 751 000), a 28m-high statue of Christ with outstretched hands, imitating the one in Rio de Janeiro. Built in 1959, it was partly paid for by Portuguese women grateful for the country having been spared the horrors of WWII. A lift (€2; operating 9.30am to 7pm daily summer) takes you right to the top, to gasp at the panoramic views.

Cacilhas is also famous for its seafood restaurants: **Marisqueria Cabrinha** (☎ 212 764 732; fish dishes €7-9), near the ferry terminal, is a good place to try. Buzzing with locals, it serves especially tasty shrimps, garlicky clams, and crab.

Getting There & Away

Ferries to Cacilhas (€0.60, 10 minutes) run frequently from Lisbon's Cais da Alfândega terminal (at the time of writing, temporarily from Cais do Sodré). A car-ferry service runs every 20 minutes (from 4.30am to 2.30am) from Cais do Sodré (and back from Cacilhas from 4.30am to 2am), or you can take bus No 101 from the bus station beside the Cacilhas terminal.

COSTA DA CAPARICA

This 8km beach on the western coast of the peninsula is Lisbon's favourite weekend escape. Surfing and windsurfing is big here, especially along the northern part of the coastline. During the summer a narrow-gauge railway runs the entire length of the beach from Costa da Caparica town (which confusingly shares the same name as the coastline itself), and you can jump off at any one of 20 stops.

Continuing along the coast all the way to Lagoa de Albufeira is the Paisagem Protegida da Arriba Fóssil, a protected fossilised cliff of geological importance backed by the Mata Nacional dos Mêdos (also called Pinhal do Rei), a 600-hectare pine forest originally planted by Dom João V to stop the encroaching sand dunes.

Orientation & Information

Praça da Liberdade is the focus of scruffy Costa da Caparica town (home to an abundance of dogs). Immediately west of the *praça*, pedestrianised Rua dos Pescadores, hosting hotels and restaurants, leads directly to the seaside. The main beach (called Praia do CDS, or Centro Desportivo de Surf), with cafés, bars and surfing clubs along its promenade, is a short walk north of here. The **bus terminal** (Avenida General Humberto Delgado) is 400m northwest of the Praça da Liberdade; additional stops are by the *praça*.

The **turismo** (☎ 212 900 071, fax 212 900 210; Avenida da República 18; open 9.30am-1pm & 2pm-5.30pm Mon-Fri year-round; 9.30am-1pm & 2pm-5.30pm Sat June-Sept, 9.30am-1pm Sat Oct-May) is located just off the *praça*.

Activities

The long coastline has its distinctive 'neighbourhoods': the northern beaches, including **Praia do Norte** and **Praia do São Sebastião**, attracts families, while **Praia do Castelo** (stop No 11 on the train) and **Praia da Bela Vista** (No 17) are gay and nudist havens.

Among the hottest spots for **surfing** are São João da Caparica, Praia da Mata and Praia da Sereia. Fonte da Telha (where the train terminates) is best for **windsurfing**. Check the handy *Tabela de Marés* booklet (available at the turismo), which lists tide times, surf shops and clubs.

Escola de Surf e Bodyboard (☎ 212 919 078; e caparicasurfingclube@clix.pt; Praia do CDS) is the main surfing school: a one-day individual/group course costs €20/12.50. To rent a surfboard/bodyboard/wetsuit costs €20/20/12.50 per day. Other operators include **Escola Oficial de Surf** (☎ 212 913 141, fax 212 906 064; Rua dos Pescadores 17), and **Bulldog Surfshop** (☎ 212 912 036; e nuno_matta@ip.pt; Rua João Inácio de Alfama 22B) near Rua dos Pescadores, which also rents boards and runs courses. Weekend prices tend to be higher.

For more on surfing generally, see the boxed text 'Surfing Portugal' in the Facts for the Visitor chapter.

Places to Stay

Costa da Caparica (☎ 212 903 894, fax 212 900 661; adult/tent/car €4.40/3.70/4), Orbitur's camp site 1km north of town, has excellent facilities.

Residencial Mar e Sol (☎ 212 900 017, fax 212 913 429; Rua dos Pescadores 42; doubles €40) is probably the best choice among several cheap pensões along this street.

Hotel Maia (☎ 212 904 948, fax 212 901 276; Avenida Dr Aresta Branco 22; doubles €80), 200m south of Praça de Liberdade, has rooms with minibar, telephone and air-con.

Hotel Costa de Caparica (☎ 212 910 310; e hcc.comercial@mail.telepac.pt; Avenida General Humberto Delgado 47; doubles €120-130) is a stylish seafront hotel popular with golfers.

Residencial Lareira (☎ 212 978 230, fax 212 978 239; Avenida do Mar, Lote 204, Aroeira; doubles with breakfast €55), 1km above Fonte da Telha beach (opposite the turning to Golf da Aroeira), is a bright-white Moorish-style place with crisp-clean rooms (some with balconies) and a pool.

Places to Eat & Drink

In Costa da Caparica town, pricey seafood and other touristy restaurants line Rua dos Pescadores.

Carolina do Aires (☎ 212 900 124; Avenida General Humberto Delgado; dishes €9-10; closed Wed Nov-Mar), on the beach, has a good reputation.

Restaurante O Primoroso (☎ 212 914 383; Avenida 1 de Maio; open Sat-Thur), the first of many eateries along Praia do CDS, is similarly priced to Carolina do Aires and popular.

Manuel dos Frangos (☎ 212 961 819; fish dishes €8-12), in Fonte da Telha, is a friendly

venue with a relaxed atmosphere and, naturally, great fish dishes.

One of several bars popular with surfers is **Bar Waikiki** (☎ 212 962 129; Praia da Sereia); it's stop No 15 on the train. **Kontiki** (Praia de São João) is also worth checking out.

Getting There & Away

Transportes Sul do Tejo (TST; ☎ 217 262 740) runs regular buses (€1.80, 20 to 60 minutes) to Costa da Caparica from Lisbon's Praça de Espanha. During July and August Carris bus No 75 does a weekend-only Costa da Caparica run (€2.70 return, every 15 minutes) from Campo Grande metro station; the ticket gives you one-day use of all Carris transport.

Alternatively, take a ferry to Cacilhas from Lisbon's Cais d'Alfândega (or to Trafaria from Belém), where bus No 135 (€1.80, 30 to 45 minutes, every 30 to 60 minutes) runs to Costa da Caparica town. (At the time of writing, this ferry service was departing temporarily from Cais do Sodré terminal.) There are also connections from Cacilhas to Fonte da Telha (€2.30). During July and August buses run about hourly from Trafaria to Fonte da Telha (€1.80) via Costa da Caparica; in winter the service stops at Pinhal do Rei (near Praia do Rei).

Another option to avoid the worst of the traffic is the Fertagus air-conditioned train across the Ponte 25 de Abril, between Entrecampos and Fogueteiro via Sete Rios and Campolide. At Pragal (€1.50, 17 minutes from Entrecampos), the stop nearest Costa da Caparica, buses run to town (€1.80, 25 minutes, every 20 minutes). Services are reduced on weekends.

Getting Around

The train along the beach operates daily during summer (weekends only from Easter until about May) and costs €3.40 return to Fonte da Telha.

SETÚBAL

postcode 2900 • pop 90,000

Once an important Roman settlement, Setúbal (**shtoo**-bahl) is now the largest town on the Setúbal Peninsula and Portugal's third-largest port (after Lisbon and Porto). Situated on the northern bank of the Sado Estuary 50km south of Lisbon, it's got a lot going for it: an easy-going, untouristy atmosphere,

AROUND LISBON

Parque Natural da Arrábida

The Arrábida Natural Park stretches along the southeastern coast of the Setúbal Peninsula from Setúbal to Sesimbra. Covering the 35km-long Serra da Arrábida mountain ridge, this is an area rich in Mediterranean thickets and plants, butterflies, beetles and birds, especially birds of prey. Even seaweed comes in 70 different varieties.

The variety of flora makes for great local honey, especially in the gardens of the **Convento da Arrábida** (☎ 212 180 520), a 16th-century former convent overlooking the sea just north of Portinho (best days to visit are Tuesday or Thursday, but call ahead). Another famous product is Azeitão ewe's cheese, whose characteristic flavour owes much to lush Arrábida pastures and a variety of thistle used in the curdling process.

Public transport through the middle of the park is nonexistent. Your best option is to rent a car or motorcycle, or take an organised trip (see Activities in the Setúbal section).

Headquarters for both this park and the **Reserva Natural do Estuário do Sado** (☎ 265 541 140, fax 265 541 155) are on Praça da República, Setúbal. Its only English-language publication is the *Guide of Protected Areas of Lisbon* (€3). A multilingual guide to all the region's nature reserves is available at the turismo.

✿ ◉ ◯ ✿ ◉ ◯ ✿ ◉ ◯ ✿ ◉ ◯ ✿

nearby beaches, and fantastic fish restaurants. It's also the base for a number of adventure activities, notably trips to see the estuary's famous dolphins, and explorations of the Parque Natural da Arrábida and the Reserva Natural do Estuário do Sado.

Orientation

The extensively pedestrianised centre focuses on Praça de Bocage and Largo da Misericórdia, with most places of interest within easy walking distance. The bus station is about 150m from the municipal turismo. The main train station is 700m north of the centre, and there's a local station (serving only Praia da Sado, by the Rio Sado) at the eastern end of Avenida 5 de Outubro. Ferries shuttle across the Sado Estuary to the Tróia Peninsula from terminals around Doca do Comércio.

Drivers should save themselves headaches (and meter charges) by heading for the free car parking in Largo José Afonso (follow signs to the 'Albergaria' nearby).

Information

Tourist Offices The best of the two turismos is the **municipal turismo** (☎/fax 265 534 402; Praça do Quebedo; open 9am-7pm daily). The Costa Azul **regional turismo** (☎ 265 539 120; ᴡ www.costa-azul.rts.pt; Travessa Frei Gaspar 10; open 9.30am-12.30pm & 3pm-7pm Mon & Sat, 9.30am-7pm Tues-Fri, 9.30am-12.30pm Sun May-Sept; to 6pm Mon-Fri, closed Sun Oct-Apr) has a startling glass floor revealing the remains of a Roman fish-condiment factory. The office has stacks of free publications, including a comprehensive *Artesãos e Artesanato* (Craftsmen and Handicrafts) booklet. Worth buying is the *Costa Azul* map (€1) and the multilingual *Parques e Reservas Naturais* (€1.50).

Money Among banks with ATMs along Avenida Luísa Todi is **Caixa Geral de Dépositos** (Avenida Luísa Todi 210).

Post & Communications Purchase your stamps at the **main post office** (Avenida Mariano de Carvalho; open 9am-12.30pm & 2.30pm-6pm Mon-Fri, 9am-12.30pm Sat) or the **branch post office** (Praça de Bocage; open 9am-12.30pm & 2.30pm-6pm Mon-Fri).

Free Internet access is available at the **Instituto Português da Juventude** (IPJ; ☎ 265 532 707; Largo José Afonso) between 9.30am and 7pm Monday to Friday (maximum 30 minutes).

Café Com Estória (☎ 265 525 633; Avenida 5 de Outubro 35; open 9am-8pm Mon-Thur, 10am-2am Fri & Sat), a cool Internet café in Edifício Arrábida (unsignposted at the time of writing – look for the communist flag!), charges €0.50 per 10 minutes. At **Sobicome Cybercafe** (1st floor, Avenida Luísa Todi 333; open 11am-4am Mon-Sat, 1pm-4am Sun) rates are €1.30 per 15 minutes.

Medical Services & Emergency The **police station** (☎ 265 522 022; Avenida Luísa Todi 350) is centrally located. The **hospital** (☎ 265 522 133) is near the Praça de Touros (bullring), off Avenida Dom João II.

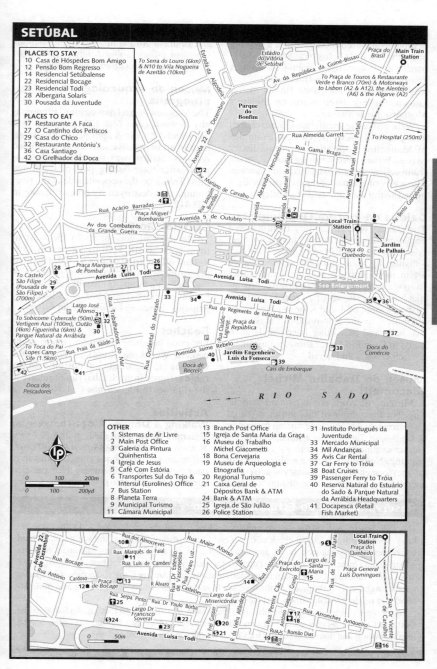

SETÚBAL

PLACES TO STAY
10 Casa de Hóspedes Bom Amigo
12 Pensão Bom Regresso
14 Residencial Setúbalense
22 Residencial Bocage
23 Residencial Todi
28 Albergaria Solaris
30 Pousada da Juventude

PLACES TO EAT
17 Restaurante A Faca
27 O Cantinho dos Petiscos
29 Casa do Chico
32 Restaurante Antóniu's
36 Casa Santiago
42 O Grelhador da Doca

OTHER
1 Sistemas de Ar Livre
2 Main Post Office
3 Galeria da Pintura Quinhentista
4 Igreja de Jesus
5 Café Com Estória
6 Transportes Sul do Tejo & Intersul (Eurolines) Office
7 Bus Station
8 Planeta Terra
9 Municipal Turismo
11 Câmara Municipal
13 Branch Post Office
15 Igreja de Santa Maria da Graça
16 Museu do Trabalho Michel Giacometti
18 Bona Cervejaria
19 Museu de Arqueologia e Etnografia
20 Regional Turismo
21 Caixa Geral de Dépositos Bank & ATM
24 Bank & ATM
25 Igreja de São Julião
26 Police Station
31 Instituto Português da Juventude
33 Mercado Municipal
34 Mil Andanças
35 Avis Car Rental
37 Car Ferry to Tróia
38 Boat Cruises
39 Passenger Ferry to Tróia
40 Reserva Natural do Estuário do Sado & Parque Natural da Arrábida Headquarters
41 Docapesca (Retail Fish Market)

AROUND LISBON

Igreja de Jesus

Setúbal's only architectural site is a striking one – the Igreja de Jesus *(Praça Miguel Bombarda; admission free; open 9am-1pm & 2pm-5pm Tues-Sat)*. Constructed in 1491, it was designed by Diogo de Boitac, better known for his later work on Belém's Mosteiro dos Jerónimos.

Walk inside the small, late-Gothic church and you will view the earliest examples of Manueline decoration – extraordinary twisted pillars, like writhing snakes, made from delicately coloured Arrábida marble. The walls of the nave and chancel are decorated with fine 18th-century azulejos.

Galeria da Pintura Quinhentista

The Gallery of 16th-Century Painting *(Rua do Balneário Paula Borba; admission free; open 9am-noon & 1.30pm-5.30pm Tues-Sat)* – displaying some of the finest Renaissance art in the country – is around the corner from the Igreja de Jesus in a bizarre, prison-like building. The set of 14 panels from the Lisbon school of Jorge Afonso (sometimes attributed to the anonymous 'Master of Setúbal') and four other later panels attributed to Gregório Lopes show extraordinarily rich colours and detail.

Museu do Trabalho Michel Giacometti

A Museum of Work doesn't sound enthralling, but the setting of this museum *(Largo Defensores da República; admission free; open 9.30am-6pm Tues-Sat)* – a huge, cavernous former sardine-canning factory – is itself intriguing. Not only is there a realistic display of the former canning factory's activities, there's also an upper-floor display of rural crafts and professions, collected in northern and central Portugal in 1975 by the famous Corsican ethnographer Michel Giacometti with the help of a hundred youngsters.

Museu de Arqueologia e Etnografia

The Museum of Archaeology and Ethnography *(Avenida Luísa Todi 162; admission free; open 9am-12.30pm & 2pm-5.30pm Tues-Sat)* houses an impressive collection of Roman remains. Setúbal was founded by the Romans after their fishing port of Cetobriga (now Tróia), on the opposite side of the river mouth, was destroyed by an earthquake in AD 412.

Castelo São Filipe

Worth the half-hour stroll to the west of town is this castle built by Filipe I in 1590 to fend off an English attack on the invincible Armada. Converted into a *pousada* in the 1960s, its ramparts are still huge and impressive and its chapel boasts 18th-century azulejos depicting the life of São Filipe.

Beaches

For good beaches, head west (ignoring the cement works en route) to **Figueirinha**, **Galapos** or, best of the lot, **Portinho da Arrábida**. Buses from Setúbal run regularly in the summer to Figueirinha (€1.10).

Activities

Walking & Donkey Rides The company **Sistemas de Ar Livre** *(SAL; ☎ 265 227 685; ⓦ www.sal.pt; Avenida Manuel Maria Portela 40)* organises three-hour guided walks in or near Setúbal every Saturday (€5 per person) and Sunday (€6).

Reserva Natural do Estuário do Sado

The Sado Estuary Natural Reserve encompasses a vast coastal area around the Sado River and Estuary, stretching from Setúbal at the northern end to near Alcácer do Sal at the southeast. Its mud banks and marshes, lagoons, dunes and former salt pans are a vital habitat for mammals, molluscs and migrating birds. The mammal that attracts the most attention is the Bottlenose Dolphin, about 30 of which survive in the increasingly polluted coastal waters. Among some 100 notable bird species are flamingos (over a thousand of them regularly winter here), white storks (spring and summertime) and resident marsh harriers and little egrets.

The reserve's headquarters in Setúbal (see the boxed text 'Parque Natural da Arrábida' in the Costa da Caparica section, earlier) has limited information, but a few local operators offer several great canoeing and dolphin-watching trips (see Activities in the Setúbal section).

Biosani (☎ 212 333 019; e info@biosani .com; Casal de Santo Isidro, Serra do Louro) arranges two-hour guided donkey rides in the Parque Natural da Arrábida for €27.50 per donkey.

Hot-Air Balloon Trips If you have a head for heights, **Hemisférios** (☎ 919 445 868; w www.hemisferios-balloons.com; Alcácer do Sal) will fly you over the beautiful landscape of nearby Alcácer do Sal (€125 per person), inland Ourique (€149) or the Algarve (€174). The charges include an after-flight celebration with champagne, Alentejan bread and sausage.

Jeep Tours Two-hour 4WD tours in the park are offered by **Mil Andanças** (☎ 265 532 996; e milandancas@mail.telepac.pt; Avenida Luísa Todi 121) for €12.50 per person.

Ozono Mais (☎ 219 243 673; e ozono mais@ip.pt; Rua General Alves Roçades 10) does a 'guided adventure' of the Parque Natural da Arrábida, including lunch and a visit to a wine cellar, for around €48.

Cruises, Canoeing & Dolphin-Watching Another way to experience the area is aboard a traditional salt galleon, which sails along the Sado Estuary on two-hour trips (€12.50 per person); for details contact **Troiacruze** (☎ 265 228 482). **Nautur** (☎ 265 532 914) offers cuises on a modern boat (€12.50 for a two-hour mini-cruise).

Vertigem Azul (☎ 265 238 000; w www .vertigemazul.com; Avenida Luísa Todi 375) offers two- to three-hour dolphin-watching tours in the Sado Estuary (with a stop for snorkelling) for €28/15 per adult/child; half-day canoeing trips in the estuary (€28/15); or a full-day's dolphin-watching and jeep tour for €58/30, including lunch.

All these cruises leave from Doca do Comércio.

Wine Tours Wine buffs may be interested in the free wine-cellar tours of the **José Maria da Fonseca adega and museum** (☎ 212 198 940; e info@jmf.pt; Rua José Augusto Coelho 11; open 9am-noon & 2.30pm-4pm Mon-Fri) in nearby Vila Nogueira de Azeitão, where Setúbal's famous moscatel wine is made. From Setúbal, buses leave frequently to Vila Nogueira de Azeitão (€1.30, 20 minutes).

Places to Stay

Camping & Hostels An adequate municipal camp site **Toca do Pai Lopes** (☎ 265 522 475; Rua Praia da Saúde; adult/tent/car €1.60/1.40/1.40) is 1.5km west of town near the shipyards. There's another **parque de campismo** (☎ 265 238 318; Outão; adult/tent/car €2.60/3.20/1.80) 3km further along the coast, accessible by regular bus (€1.10, 25 minutes).

The **pousada da juventude** (☎ 265 534 431; e setubal@movijovem.pt; dorm beds €9.50, doubles with shower & toilet €26.50) is attached to the IPJ (see Post & Communications, earlier).

Pensões & Residenciais Fraying, dowdy but friendly **Residencial Todi** (☎ 265 220 592; Avenida Luísa Todi 244; doubles with/without bathroom from €20/15, triples with bathroom €25) has an easy-going atmosphere.

Casa de Hóspedes Bom Amigo (☎ 265 526 290; 2nd floor, Rua do Concelho 7; doubles with/without shower €35/30) is a homely, thin-walled place, with clean, neat rooms.

Pensão Bom Regresso (☎ 265 229 812, 966 423 324; Praça de Bocage; doubles with shared bathroom €40) has scruffy, overpriced rooms, but its location is unbeatable, overlooking the attractive praça.

Residencial Bocage (☎ 265 543 080; e residencia.bocage@clix.pt; Rua São Cristovão 14; doubles with breakfast €37.40), in the old town centre, is an upmarket choice, accommodating mostly business folk.

Residencial Setúbalense (☎ 265 525 790, fax 265 525 789; Rua Major Afonso Pala 17; doubles with breakfast €47) is a notch smarter, with room service and its own bar.

Albergaria Solaris (☎ 265 541 770; e al bergaria.solaris@netc.pt; Praça Marquês de Pombal 12; doubles €55) is efficient, and convenient for drivers (free parking is available nearby).

Pousada de São Filipe (☎ 265 523 844, fax 265 532 538; doubles Mon-Fri €159, Sat & Sun €176) is the most luxurious option of all, located right within the town's hill-top castle.

Places to Eat

For the town's best budget fare, delve into the lanes east of the regional turismo. **Restaurante A Faca** (☎ 265 523 937; Rua Arronches Junqueiro 71; daily specials €4.30;

open Sun-Fri) is typically simple, offering bargain *pratos do dia*.

Setúbal is packed with fish restaurants (nearly all with outdoor seating), especially along the western end of Avenida Luísa Todi. The fish prices are typically per kilogram, according to the day's catch; expect to pay around €8 for a fresh *dourada* (bream), grilled on the street outside and served with potatoes and salad.

Casa do Chico (☎ 265 239 502; *Avenida Luísa Todi 490; dishes €7-8; open Tues-Sun)* is small, friendly and modest.

O Cantinho dos Petiscos (☎ 265 233 280; *Avenida Luísa Todi 374; dishes €8-10)* is a more upmarket choice.

Casa Santiago (☎ 265 221 688; *Avenida Luísa Todi 92; dishes €9-11)* specialises in *chôco frito* (deep-fried cuttlefish; grab a cuttlefish sandwich for just €1.90), but the menu also has loads of other fish fare. Go early for a lunch-time space.

Opposite the Doca dos Pescadores (where fish is auctioned off at the Docapesca fish market), savour the freshest fish possible at places such as **O Grelhador da Doca** (☎ 265 526 656; *Rua Praia da Saúde 36; dishes €9-11)*.

Restaurante Antóniu's (☎ 265 523 706; *Rua Trabalhadores do Mar 31; open Thur-Tues)*, a long-popular, more old-fashioned venue, serves a fantastic *arroz de marisco* (rice and seafood stew; €20 for two) or fish kebabs for €5.50.

Restaurante Verde e Branco (☎ 265 526 546; *Rua Maria Batista 33)*, beside the Praça de Touros, is famous for miles around. Very traditional and only open at lunch time (you'll be lucky to get a seat before 2pm), it serves only grilled fish: simple and superb.

Entertainment

Café-bars staying open until around 4am are plentiful along the western end of Avenida Luísa Todi.

Sobicome Cybercafe (*1st floor, Avenida Luísa Todi 333; open 11am-4am Mon-Sat,* *1pm-4am Sun)* has a disco downstairs; with karaoke on Thursday evening.

Bona Cervejaria (☎ 967 717 505; *Rua Dr Antóniu Joaquim Granjo 32)*, a German-run option, is fancier and has live *fado* on Wednesday evening.

Getting There & Away

Bus Frequent buses run between Setúbal and Lisbon's Praça de Espanha (€2.90, 45 to 60 minutes) – or from Cacilhas (€2.60, 45 minutes), a quick ferry-hop from Cais de Alfândega. There are also express services to Évora (€8, 1¾ hours) and Faro (€12.50, 3¾ hours) around six times daily, and four daily runs to Santarém (€5, three hours).

You can buy Eurolines (Intersul) tickets at the **Transportes Sul do Tejo office** (☎ 265 233 808) by the bus station.

Train From Lisbon's Terreiro do Paço terminal you can take the ferry to Barreiro station, from where there are hourly *suburbano* trains to Setúbal (€1.10, 45 minutes), plus both *interregional* (IR) and *intercidade* (IC) trains.

Boat Ferries to Tróia (€1/4.30 per person/car) depart every 30 to 45 minutes daily. Note that car ferries, cruises and passenger ferries all have different departure points.

Getting Around

You can rent bikes for €7.50/15 per one/three days from **Planeta Terra** (☎ 919 471 871; *Praça General Luís Domingues 9)*.

Car-rental agencies include **Avis** (☎ 265 538 710; *Avenida Luísa Todi 96)* and **Alucar** (☎ 265 538 320; *Avenida Combatentes da Grande Guerra 60)*.

SESIMBRA

postcode 2970 • pop 8100 • elevation 60m
This former fishing village, 30km southwest of Setúbal, shelters under the Serra da Arrábida at the western edge of the Parque

---

Reserva Natural do Estuário do Tejo

For birdlife on a grand scale, book a visit to the Tejo Estuary Natural Reserve, upriver from Lisbon. A vitally important wetland area, it hosts around 40,000 migrant wading birds during the winter, including avocets and teals.

The reserve's **headquarters** (☎ 212 341 742; *Avenida dos Combatentes da Grande Guerra 1, Alcochete)* are accessible from Montijo (a ferry ride from Lisbon's Terreiro do Paço).

Natural da Arrábida. It's long been a favourite getaway with Lisboêtas and is now rapidly developing into a major resort. On weekends and in high season the place buzzes. Cruises, guided walks and scuba-diving activities are also on offer, including trips to Cabo Espichel where dinosaurs once roamed.

Orientation & Information

The **bus station** (*Avenida da Liberdade*) is about 250m north of the seafront. Turn right when you reach the bottom of the avenida and pass the small 17th-century Forte de Santiago (now a police station) to the **turismo** (☎ *212 288 540; Largo do Marinho; open 9am-8pm daily June-Sept, 9am-12.30pm & 2pm-5.30pm Oct-May*), in an arcade off the seafront Avenida dos Náufragos.

Castelo

The ruined but imposing Moorish castle (*admission free; open 7am-8pm Mon-Wed, Fri & Sat, 7am-7pm Sun & Thur*), perched 200m above Sesimbra, was taken by Dom Afonso Henriques in the 12th century, re-taken by the Moors, and finally snatched back by Christians under Dom Sancho I in the following century.

There are great coastal panoramas but little inside except for the Igreja Santa Maria do Castelo and its cemetery. A recent addition is the small **Centro de Documentação** (*admission free; open 9am-12.30pm & 2pm-5.30pm Mon & Tues, 9am-12.30pm & 1pm-7pm Wed & Fri, 10am-1pm & 2pm-6pm Sat & Sun*) detailing the castle's history (and offering free Internet access); there's also a café next door. The shady castle grounds are great for picnics.

Porto de Abrigo

Porto de Abrigo, 1km west of town, is a busy fishing centre and the summertime base for several tourist cruises and activities. Early morning and late afternoon, when fishermen auction their catch, is still a good time to catch a more traditional fishing atmosphere.

Activities

Clube Naval de Sesimbra (☎ *212 233 451, fax 212 281 668; Porto de Abrigo*) runs three-hour **coastal cruises** (€15 per person) at 9.30am Tuesday, and six-hour coastal **fishing trips** (€40) at 7am Saturday.

Lisbon-based **Nautilus-Sub** (☎ *212 551 969;* W *www.nautilus-sub.com*) is a five-star IDC PADI Dive Centre offering courses (including some for kids) and dives in the Sesimbra area. **Sersub** (☎ *212 280 604, 962 375 309; Porto de Abrigo*) also runs **diving** courses; a day's outing for experienced divers costs about €60, including equipment.

Setúbal-based **SAL** (see Activities in the Setúbal section) organises short **nature tours** from here (€5 per person); the turismo has details.

If you're into **caving** and **climbing**, contact **Núcleo de Espeleologia da Costa Azul** (☎ *966 201 276*) about its activities and courses, or ask at the turismo.

Places to Stay

The municipal **Forte do Cavalo** (☎ *212 233 694; adult/tent/car €1.30/2/0.70*) is a fairly basic camp site, 1km west of town.

Parque de Campismo de Valbom (☎ *212 687 545; adult/tent/car €2.90/2.50/2.50*), in Cotovia, is a well-equipped facility 5km north of Sesimbra (to get here just take any Lisbon-bound bus).

In Sesimbra your best budget bets are *quartos* from €25 to €35 a double; ask at the turismo for details. The well-advertised central ones of **Senhora Garcia** (☎ *212 233 227; Travessa Xavier da Silva 1; doubles €35*) are plain and functional.

Residencial Nautico (☎ *212 233 233; Bairro Infante Dom Henrique 3; doubles with breakfast €40-60*), about 500m uphill from the waterfront, has comfortable doubles (pricier ones have air-con and terrace).

Sana Park (☎ *212 289 000;* e *sanapark .sesimbra@sanahotels.com; Avenida 25 de Abril; doubles with breakfast €123-143*) is Sesimbra's smartest four-star, a seaside property with swimming pools, health club and deluxe rooms.

Quinta do Rio (☎ *212 189 343, fax 212 185 442; doubles with breakfast €35-40*) in Alto das Vinhas, 7km towards Setúbal, is an attractive converted *quinta* set among orange groves. Also available are horse rides (€15 per hour), a swimming pool and tennis court.

Places to Eat & Drink

Fish restaurants abound on the waterfront: east of the fort try unpretentious **Toca do Ratinho** (☎ *212 232 572; Rua Plínio Mesquita 17; dishes €8-9*), where you can get a great grilled *dourada* for €8.80. More spacious is **Pedra Alta** (☎ 212 231 791; Largo de Bombaldes 13; dishes €12-14), with lots of outdoor seating.

O Farol (☎ 212 2233 356; Largo da Marinha 4/5; dishes €10-14; open Wed-Mon), just behind the turismo, serves a wicked fish kebab for €11.50.

For cheaper fare head for Rua da Liberdade or Largo do Município (near the market): **Restaurante A Sesimbrense** (☎ 212 230 148; Rua Jorge Nunes 19; dishes €6-7), just off the *largo*, has all the usual items and a local clientele.

For evening snacks and late-night drinks, trawl Avenida dos Náufragos. **Sereia** (☎ 223 20 90; Avenida dos Náufragos 20) and stylish **Café Bar Aquárius** (Avenida dos Náufragos 16) are located along here among the most popular venues.

Getting There & Away

Buses depart from Lisbon's Praça de Espanha three or four times daily (€3, 60 to 90 minutes), at least nine times daily from Setúbal (€2.30, 45 minutes) and hourly from Cacilhas (€2.40, around 50 minutes). There are twice-daily runs to Cabo Espichel (€1.70) and more frequent runs to the village of Azóia (€1.60), about 3km before the cape.

AROUND SESIMBRA
Aldeia do Meco

This tiny village 12km northwest of Sesimbra has become famous for its abundance of restaurants – around 16 here and in adjacent Alfarim – most specialising in seafood, of course.

Campimeco (☎ 212 683 393; adult/tent/car €2.90/2.50/2.50) is a big, shady camp site 3km away above Praia das Bicas.

Country House (☎/fax 212 685 001; Rua Alto da Carona, Alfarim; doubles €45, 2-/4-person apartments €60/75), a fancy house 1.4km north in a wooded setting, has four immaculate, spacious rooms (with coffeemakers and fridge) and three apartments, most with balconies. Breakfast costs €8.

Acácio (☎ 212 683 901; Rua do Comércio) has reasonable prices (eg, *feijoada de marisco*, seafood stew; €20 for two) although fish prices generally depend on the daily catch.

Getting There & Away

Buses run six to eight times daily from Sesimbra (€1.30, 30 minutes).

The Algarve

The Algarve has been the country's major tourist resort area since Faro airport opened in the 1960s, leading to a flood of package tours from the UK and, increasingly, Germany and France. The big attraction? Almost year-round sun, great beaches and plentiful tourist facilities.

Those are still the Algarve's major selling points, though rampant development during the late 1970s between Lagos and Faro destroyed much of the coastline's picturesque quality. In recent years tourism has gone upmarket, with more environmentally conscious developers and luxurious villa resorts complete with designer golf courses and marinas.

The biggest and liveliest summertime resorts along the 270km coastline are Albufeira and Lagos. But you don't need to go far to find quieter villages and beaches – between Lagos and Sagres are several low-key coves. North of Sagres stretches the rugged, wild coastline of the Parque Natural do Sudoeste Alentejano e Costa Vicentina. And east of Faro is a string of sandy offshore islands that make up the Parque Natural da Ria Formosa, a favourite haunt for birds and other wildlife.

And then there are the wonderful inland attractions: the forested slopes of the Serra de Monchique and wild Serra do Caldeirão; the ancient Moorish fortified town of Silves and market town of Loulé; and the remote-feeling frontier with Spain, curving northwards beside the lugubrious Rio Guadiana.

History
The Algarve's sunny disposition and long, warm coastline has attracted foreigners since the time of the Phoenicians some 3000 years ago. The Phoenicians, who made their mark by establishing trading posts along the coast, were followed by the Carthaginians, who founded several major entrepots, including Portus Hannibalis (Portimão) in 550 BC.

But their influence was overshadowed by that of the Romans. During their 400-year presence the Romans spread the cultivation of wheat, barley and grapes and built roads and luxurious palaces (check the remains at Milreu, near Faro).

Highlights

- Enjoy the lively seaside resorts of Lagos and Albufeira
- Explore unspoilt off-shore islands in the bird-rich Parque Natural da Ria Formosa
- Visit the attractive and historic towns of Tavira and Silves
- Survey wild, unspoilt coastline and sample the surfing hot spots between Sagres and Odeceixe
- Choose from a superb range of challenging golf courses

In the wake of the Romans came the Visigoths, and then in 711 the first wave of Moors from North Africa. The Algarve was to remain their stronghold for 500 years. Silves (called Xelb by the Moors) became their opulent capital.

The Moors of the Algarve were a mixed ethnic bunch: around Faro they were mostly Egyptians but elsewhere they included Persians, Syrians and Berbers from Morocco. It was the Syrian Moors who gave the Algarve its present name, calling the region in which they settled (east of Faro to Seville) al-Gharb al-Andalus (western Andalucía). By the mid-9th century the prosperous Algarve had become quite independent of the larger Muslim emirate to the east, which was centred around what is now Seville and Córdoba in Spain.

As the Christian Reconquista got under way in the early 12th century, the Algarve became the ultimate goal for a succession of crusaders and kings. Though Dom Sancho I captured Silves and territories to the west in 1189, the Moors staged a comeback. It was not until the first half of the 13th century that the Portuguese finally reclaimed the area for good.

Two centuries later came the Algarve's age of importance, when Prince Henry the Navigator chose windswept Sagres as the base (or at any rate as a point of inspiration) for his school of navigation. He had ships built and staffed in Lagos for the daring expeditions that soon followed to Africa and Asia, raising Portugal to the status of a major imperial power. (See also the boxed text 'Prince Henry the Navigator' under History in the Facts about Portugal chapter.)

Today, the Algarve serves a rather more modest role as a premier sun-and-surf destination and expat haven.

Geography

The Algarve divides neatly into five regions: the leeward coast (or Sotavento), from Vila Real de Santo António to Faro, largely fronted by a chain of sandy offshore *ilhas* (islands); the central coast, from Faro to Portimão, featuring the heaviest resort development; the increasingly rocky windward coast (or Barlavento), from Lagos to Sagres, culminating in the wind-scoured grandeur of the Cabo de São Vicente, Europe's southwestern corner; the Costa Vicentina, facing

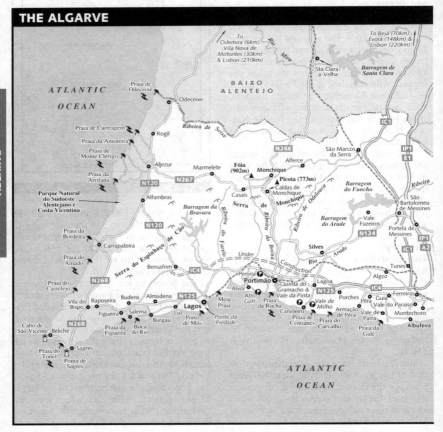

west into the teeth of Atlantic gales; and the surprisingly hilly and verdant interior, which rises to two high mountain ranges, the Serra de Monchique and less-visited Serra do Caldeirão.

The Algarve's capital and largest town is Faro. Its easternmost town, Vila Real de Santo António, is linked to Spain by the nearby E1 motorway bridge and by a car ferry across the Rio Guadiana to Ayamonte.

Information

Tourist Offices At the *turismos* (tourist offices) you can get free leaflets, town maps and information, and decent regional maps of the Algarve (€1.30). Keep an eye out, too, for the monthly *Agenda Cultural* publications in each major town, the quarterly

newspaper-format *Welcome to the Algarve*, and a glossy info-booklet called *Algarve Tips. Your Guide Algarve*, produced by the airport authority, ANA, is particularly good on bar, club and hotel listings. There are also privately produced *Free Maps* of popular resorts (often available at bars and shops, too), which are free and great for up-to-date tips on entertainment spots.

The Algarve tourist board's website is at w www.rtalgarve.pt.

Newspapers, Magazines & Maps In addition to the English-language newspapers *APN* and *The News*, there are several Algarve-specific magazines in English or German, including *Algarve Resident* and *Entdecken Sie Algarve*. One of the clearest

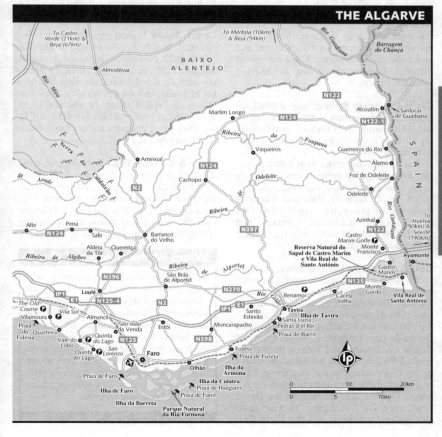

THE ALGARVE

ALGARVE

maps of the Algarve, including six small-town maps, is published by Freytag & Berndt (1:150,000).

Dangers & Annoyances The Algarve has one of Portugal's higher levels of petty crime, mainly theft. Paranoia is unwarranted, but don't leave anything of value in your vehicle or unattended on the beach. More worrying are occasional, unprovoked attacks on young tourists at popular resorts such as Lagos.

Swimmers should beware of dangerous ocean currents, especially on the west coast. Beaches are marked by coloured flags: red means that the beach is closed to all bathing, yellow means that swimming is prohibited but wading is fine; and green means that anything goes.

Activities

For contact details of operators running activities mentioned in this section, see under the relevant towns. The Faro tourist office has a complete list of 'Active Tourism' operators.

Cycling & Horse Riding Several small operators offer bike trips from Tavira, Lagos, and Monchique. Zebra Safari in Albufeira organises adventure trips with canoes as well as mountain bikes.

The Algarve has more than a dozen *centros hípicos* (riding centres) and *centros de equitação* (equestrian centres), concentrated mainly between Faro and Albufeira (turismos can give you a complete list). One of the longest-established is **Paraíso dos Cavalos** (☎ 289 394 189; *Almancil*). Expect to pay around €20 per hour.

Golf & Tennis At last count there were 26 golf courses in the Algarve, mostly between Faro and Albufeira although the three newest are near Tavira and Castro Marim, east of Faro. The Algarve boasts seven of Europe's top 100 courses, including San Lorenzo and Quinta do Lago (Almancil), Vila Sol and Old Course (Vilamoura) and Vale da Pinta (Carvoeiro). Full details are published in ICEP's glossy *Golf* publication and in *Algarve, Land of Golf* available at tourist offices in the Algarve. Golfing schools include the David Leadbetter Golf Academy in Carvoeiro (see under Carvoeiro) and the **Vigia Golf**

Academy (☎ 282 690 054; |e| *golf@vigiasa .com*), near Salema.

Most top-end resort hotels in the Algarve have tennis courts, and there are nearly 20 professionally equipped clubs, including **Vilamouraténis Center** (☎ 289 312 369, fax 289 310 169; Vilamoura).

Jeep Tours Several companies run one-day jeep trips into the hills or along the west coast, notably **Riosul** (☎ 281 510 200; Monte Gordo). One of the more environmentally conscious operators is **Horizonte** (☎/fax 282 695 920), which specialises in the Parque Natural do Sudoeste Alentejano e Costa Vicentina (see also see the Salema section). Prices for one-day trips range from €36 to €41 per person and include lunch; there are various pick-up points (eg, Albufeira, Tavira and Monte Gordo for the Riosul safaris).

Coach Tours Typical regional coach trips, operated largely by Faro-based **Mega Tur** (☎ 289 807 648) include the inland 'Unspoilt Algarve'; Silves and the Serra de Monchique; Lagos and Sagres; the Saturday market at Loulé; and the Wednesday market at Quarteira. Typical prices are around €18.50 for a half-day tour, and between €33 to €44 for a full day. Brochures are available at hotels, turismos and travel agencies.

River & Coastal Trips You can cruise the Rio Arade between Portimão and Silves (see Portimão later in this chapter for details), or the Rio Guadiana between Vila Real de Santo António and Foz de Odeleite (see the boxed text 'Cruising & Biking Along the Guadiana', later in this chapter).

Wines of the Algarve

The Algarve has long been an important wine-making area: the Mediterranean climate, rich soil and high-quality vines produce full-bodied wines with low acidity and a high alcohol content. The whites are traditionally very dry, the reds light and young. Although modern development has erased many vineyards, there are still about 40,000 acres of them in the Lagoa area, producing the Algarve's best-known wines. Smaller wine-producing areas are Lagos, Tavira, and Portimão.

Faro-based **Animaris** (☎ *917 811 856*) arranges trips through the Ria Formosa to Ilha Deserta.

Walking The **Os Caminheiros do Algarve/ Walkers** (☎ *289 360 270;* **e** *ebor@mail .telepac.pt*) is an informal club that convenes every third Saturday of the month between September and May for a gentle trek, mainly in eastern Algarve. Visitors are welcome (€2.50 per person). The club also arranges Discovery trips to places further afield (around €25 per person, including lunch).

Almargem (☎ *289 412 959*) is a Loulé-based environmental group that welcomes visitors on its frequent walks of 10km or so. The **Liga para a Proteção da Natureza** (*League for the Protection of Nature;* ☎ *282 968 380*) also organises short walks to areas of natural interest on the first Saturday of the month (except January and August).

For club meeting times, check listings in the *Algarve Resident* magazine. For details of other guided walks, see the Monchique and Tavira sections later in this chapter. See also the boxed text 'Via Algarviana' in this section.

Several guidebooks can help you on your way, including the locally published *Algarve: Let's Walk* by Julie Statham, describing 20 easy walks in the region, and two *Discovery Walking Guides* to areas around Loulé and Silves, featuring 1:25,000 map sections. These latter titles can be ordered online at **w** www.walking.demon.co.uk.

Julie Statham's **Portugal Walks** (☎ *282 698 676*) has a weekly programme of half-day guided walks in the Algarve for €12 per person, plus longer walking holidays (see Activities in the Facts for the Visitor chapter).

Water & Animal Parks One of the biggest Algarve attractions is the **Zoomarine** (☎ *289 560 300*) aquatic park near Albufeira (see that town for details). There are also four huge water-slide parks along or near the N125 – **Slide & Splash** (☎ *282 341 685; adult/child 5-10 €12.50/10*) west of Lagoa, **The Big One** (☎ *282 322 827; adult/child 5-10 €13/10.50*) near Albufeira, **Atlântico Parque** (☎ *289 397 282; adult/child 5-10 €11/9*) between Almancil and Loulé, and **Aqua Show** (☎ *289 388 874; adult/child 5-10 €13/10*) in Vilamoura.

Via Algarviana

Thanks largely to two walking clubs in the Algarve – Loulé-based Almargem and Silves-based Os Caminheiros do Algarve/Walkers (OCDAW) – a 243km trail has been pioneered right across the Algarve, from Alcoutim to Cabo de São Vicente. Tested by both walkers and horse riders, the Via Algarviana is now largely way marked.

By creating an 80km spur from Alcoutim to Val Verde del Camino in Spain and then to the Caminho do Portugal to Seville, the enthusiastic club members and their Spanish counterparts aim to link the Via Algarviana with the network of Europe-wide long-distance footpaths known as Euro Routes.

For more details, contact the two clubs directly (see Walking earlier), or the **Federação Portuguesa de Campismo Caravanismo** (☎ *218 126 890;* **e** *info@fpcampismo.pt; Avenida Coronel Eduardo Galhardo 24D, 1100-007 Lisbon*).

Krazy World (☎ *282 574 134; open 10am-7.30pm daily June-Sept, 10am-6pm Nov-Mar*), near São Bartolomeu de Messines, is an animal and crocodile park with minigolf and quad-bike courses.

Water Sports Fancy going down-under? Head to Lagos, Sagres or Carvoeiro for some recommended scuba-diving centres. Water-skiing, windsurfing or bodyboarding can be easily arranged through resorts or with operators in Lagos or Sagres.

Sailors can check out Dynamic Vela Sailing School in Praia da Rocha. Deep-sea fishing fans have plenty of options in Sagres, Lagos, Portimão and Praia da Rocha.

As for surfing, you'll find some of the most wicked surfing spots in Portugal along the wild coast north of Sagres (for more details see the boxed text 'Surfing Portugal' under Activities in the Facts for the Visitor chapter).

Special Events

The Algarve's most important religious festival, the Romaria da Nossa Senhora da Piedade, takes place at Loulé on the second Sunday after Easter. One of Portugal's biggest Carnaval celebrations is also held

ALGARVE

here in late February/early March (see Loulé later in this chapter for details). Several religious fairs take place in October throughout the region.

Cultural highlights, featuring performances in various Algarve towns, include the Festival Internacional de Música do Algarve from May to July; and the Festival Nacional de Folclore (Folk Music and Dance Festival) in September, culminating with a big show at Praia da Rocha. An open-air programme of Animação de Rua (Street Entertainment) lasts from July to September in Portimão, Faro and Albufeira.

Shopping

The region's main handicrafts centre is Loulé. Look out for locally produced woollens and Moorish-influenced ceramics. For more on the crafts of the Algarve, see the excellent guide by John & Madge Measures, *Southern Portugal: Its People, Traditions & Wildlife*, available in local bookshops.

Local markets offer some of the best shopping experiences. The following are some of the biggest and best:

Every Saturday – Loulé, Olhão, São Brás de Alportel, Tavira
Every Wednesday – Quarteira
1st Saturday of the month – Lagos
1st Sunday – Almancil, Azinhal (Castro Marim)
1st Monday – Portimão
1st Tuesday – Albufeira
2nd Tuesday – Alvor
2nd Friday – Monchique
3rd Monday – Aljezur, Silves, Tavira
3rd Tuesday – Albufeira

Faro & the Leeward Coast

FARO
postcode 8000 • pop 42,000
Faro (**Fah-roo**) is the Algarve's capital and main transport hub. It's also a thriving commercial centre – but surprisingly pleasant for all that. The main sights of historical interest are within the compact old town centre.

History
Once a trading post used by both Phoenicians and Carthaginians, Faro became a major port under the Romans who named it Ossonoba. Under the Moors, it became the cultured capital of a short-lived 11th-century principality founded by Mohammed ben Said ben Hárun, from whose name 'Faro' is said to have evolved. Afonso III took the town in 1249 (it was the last major Portuguese town to be recaptured from the Moors), and walled it.

The first works produced on a printing press in Portugal came from Faro in 1487 – books in Hebrew made by a Jewish printer named Samuel Gacon.

A brief golden age – heralded by an episcopal seat transferred from Silves in 1577 – was brought to an abrupt end in 1596, during the period of Spanish rule. Troops under the Earl of Essex, en route to England from Cádiz in Spain, plundered the city, burned most of it to the ground and carried off hundreds of volumes of priceless theological works from the bishop's palace.

A rebuilt Faro was shattered by an earthquake in 1722 and, except for its sturdy old centre, flattened by the big one in 1755. Its present form dates largely from post-quake rebuilding.

Orientation
The town's hub, Praça Dr Francisco Gomes, features a marina and a little garden called Jardim Manuel Bívar (or just Jardim). The bus and train stations, both on Avenida da República, are a short walk away. The airport is about 6km west of the centre, off the N125 highway.

Offshore is the widest stretch of the Parque Natural da Ria Formosa. While many of the near-shore sandbars along here simply disappear at high tide, two of the bigger sea-facing islands – Ilha de Faro to the southwest and Ilha da Culatra to the southeast – have small summer settlements and good beaches.

Information
Tourist Offices The municipal turismo (☎ 289 803 604; Rua da Misericórdia 8; open 9.30am-7pm daily May-Oct; 9.30am-12.30pm & 2pm-5.30pm Fri-Mon, 9.30am-5.30pm Tues-Thur Nov-Apr) is beside Arco da Vila, the gate to the old town. There's an **ICEP turismo** (open 8am-11.30pm daily) at the airport.

The **regional turismo administrative office** (☎ 289 800 400; [e] rtalgarve@rtalgarve .pt; Avenida 5 de Outubro 18) also has an

information desk *(open 9am-6pm Mon-Fri)* but it's of minimal use.

Money In addition to several banks and ATMs in the town centre, there's also a private-exchange bureau, **Cota Câmbios** *(Rua Dr Francisco Gomes 26; open 8.30am-6.30pm Mon-Fri, 10am-2pm Sat)*. You can change American Express (AmEx) travellers cheques at **Top Tours** (see Travel Agencies later in this section).

Post & Communications Send your sun-and-sand postcards from the **main post office** *(Largo do Carmo; open 9am-6.30pm Mon-Fri, 9am-noon Sat)*.

Free Internet access is available at the **Instituto Português da Juventude** *(IPJ; open 9am-7pm Mon-Fri)* – see Places to Stay – for up to 30 minutes; and at the Mediatéca room in the **Centro Ciência Viva** (Science Alive Centre; see later), although you must pay an admission fee here. **EQInformática** *(☎ 289 873 731; Rua da Trindade 1A; open 9.30am-1.30pm & 2.30pm-7.30pm Mon-Sat)* charges €1.50 per half-hour.

Travel Agencies The best student-oriented agency is **Tagus** *(☎ 289 805 483, fax 289 805 134; Avenida 5 de Outubro 26C)*. Another option is **Abreu Tours** *(☎ 289 870 900; e faro@abreu.pt; Avenida da República 124)*, a major national agency that can arrange both local and overseas trips. **Top Tours** *(☎ 289 895 340; e faro@toptours.pt; Rua da Comunidade Lusiada; open Mon-Fri)* is the local AmEx representative.

Bookshops Faro's main bookshop is **Livraria Bertrand** *(☎ 289 828 147; Rua Dr Francisco Gomes 27)*, although souvenir shops or newsagents (eg, inside Café Aliança; see Places to Eat) stock more local maps and guides.

Laundry The **Lavandaria Sólimpa** *(☎ 289 822 891; Rua Batista Lopes 30; open 9am-1pm & 3pm-7pm Mon-Fri, 9am-1pm Sat)* calls itself self-service but isn't, though it does have a one-day wash-and-dry service for €1.70 per kg (minimum 4kg).

Left Luggage There are left-luggage facilities at both the **train station newsagent kiosk** *(open 7am-midnight daily)*, which charges €1/3.60 per item per two/24 hours, and the **bus station** *(open 9am-1pm & 3pm-7pm Mon-Fri)*, with rates from €1.50 per item per 24 hours.

Medical Services & Emergency The **Faro district hospital** *(☎ 289 891 100; Rua Leão Penedo)* is over 2km northeast of the centre. For other emergencies go to the **main police station** *(☎ 289 822 022; Rua da Polícia de Segurança Pública 32)*.

Cidade Velha
Within the medieval walls of the small Cidade Velha (Old Town) is what little of Faro survived the Earl of Essex era and the two big earthquakes, most of it renovated in a jumble of styles. Nevertheless, it has a pleasant, lived-in feel.

You enter through the Renaissance-style **Arco da Vila**, built by order of Bishop Francisco Gomes, Faro's answer to the Marquês de Pombal, who saw to the city's brisk reconstruction after the 1755 earthquake. At the top of the street is **Largo da Sé**, adorned with orange trees, with the **câmara municipal** (town hall) on the left and the ancient **sé** (cathedral) in front of you.

The cathedral was completed in 1251, on what was probably the site of a Moorish mosque, an earlier Visigoth cathedral and, before that, a Roman temple. After being badly damaged in 1755, the building's original Romanesque-Gothic exterior has been submerged in subsequent Gothic renovations and extensions, except for its tower gate and two chapels. It's been closed for years, supposedly for restoration. To the right of the cathedral is the 18th-century **Bishop's Palace**, finished in multicoloured *azulejos* (hand-painted tiles). At the southern end of the square is a little 15th-century town gate, the **Arco da Porta Nova** leading to the ferry pier.

Around to the left of the cathedral, in a small square, is the 16th-century **Convento de Nossa Senhora da Assunção**, which now houses the town's Museu Municipal (see later in this section).

From here you can leave the old town through the medieval **Arco de Repouso**, or Gate of Rest (named after the story that Afonso III, after taking Faro from the Moors, rested and heard Mass in a nearby chapel). Around the gateway are some of

ALGARVE

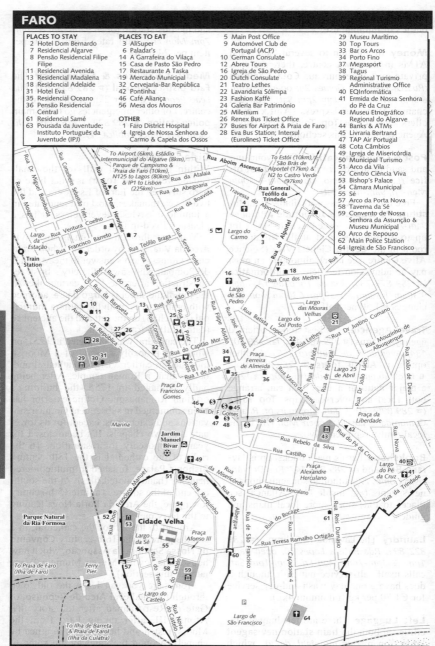

FARO

PLACES TO STAY
- 2 Hotel Dom Bernardo
- 7 Residencial Algarve
- 8 Pensão Residencial Filipe Filipe
- 11 Residencial Avenida
- 13 Residencial Madalena
- 18 Residencial Adelaide
- 31 Hotel Eva
- 35 Residencial Oceano
- 36 Pensão Residencial Central
- 61 Residencial Samé
- 63 Pousada da Juventude; Instituto Português da Juventude (IPJ)

PLACES TO EAT
- 3 AliSuper
- 6 Paladar's
- 14 A Garrafeira do Vilaça
- 15 Casa de Pasto São Pedro
- 17 Restaurante A Taska
- 19 Mercado Municipal
- 32 Cervejaria-Bar República
- 42 Pontinha
- 46 Café Aliança
- 56 Mesa dos Mouros

OTHER
- 1 Faro District Hospital
- 4 Igreja de Nossa Senhora do Carmo & Capela dos Ossos
- 5 Main Post Office
- 9 Automóvel Club de Portugal (ACP)
- 10 German Consulate
- 12 Abreu Tours
- 16 Igreja de São Pedro
- 20 Dutch Consulate
- 21 Teatro Lethes
- 22 Lavandaria Sólimpa
- 23 Fashion Kaffé
- 24 Galeria Bar Património
- 25 Milenium
- 26 Renex Bus Ticket Office
- 27 Buses for Airport & Praia de Faro
- 28 Eva Bus Station; Intersul (Eurolines) Ticket Office
- 29 Museu Marítimo
- 30 Top Tours
- 33 Bar os Arcos
- 34 Porto Fino
- 37 Megasport
- 38 Tagus
- 39 Regional Turismo Administrative Office
- 40 EQInformática
- 41 Ermida de Nossa Senhora do Pé da Cruz
- 43 Museu Etnográfico Regional do Algarve
- 44 Banks & ATMs
- 45 Livraria Bertrand
- 47 TAP Air Portugal
- 48 Cota Câmbios
- 49 Igreja de Misericórdia
- 50 Municipal Turismo
- 51 Arco da Vila
- 52 Centro Ciência Viva
- 53 Bishop's Palace
- 54 Câmara Municipal
- 55 Sé
- 57 Arco da Porta Nova
- 58 Taverna da Sé
- 59 Convento de Nossa Senhora da Assunção & Museu Municipal
- 60 Arco de Repouso
- 62 Main Police Station
- 64 Igreja de São Francisco

ALGARVE

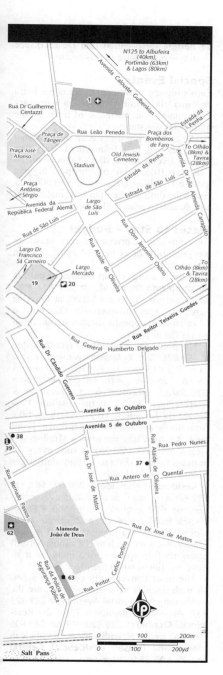

the oldest sections of the town walls, Afonso III's improvements on the Moorish defences.

A free leaflet, *The Inward Village, Route 1*, available from the Museu Municipal, provides a good historical summary for a walking tour of the old town.

Igreja de Nossa Senhora do Carmo

The twin-towered, vanilla-and-butterscotch Church of Our Lady of Carmel *(open 10am-1pm & 3pm-5pm Mon-Fri Oct-Apr, until 6pm Mon-Fri May-Sept; 10am-1pm Sat year-round)* was completed in 1719 under João V and paid for (and spectacularly gilded inside) with Brazilian gold. Many visitors overlook this in favour of a more ghoulish attraction in the pretty little cemetery behind the church – the **Capela dos Ossos** *(admission €0.80)*. This 19th-century chapel was built from the bones and skulls of more than a thousand monks as a pointed reminder of earthly impermanence. The distinctly lively voices from a kindergarten right next door are a poignant contrast.

Other Churches

If you haven't seen enough gilded woodwork yet, have a look at the dazzling 18th-century baroque interior of the **Igreja de São Francisco**, which also includes azulejo panels depicting the life of St Francis. Its old cloisters now serve as barracks for the Faro Infantry. It has no fixed opening hours, but mass is at 6.30pm daily.

The main attraction of the 16th-century **Igreja de Misericórdia**, across the road from the Arco da Vila, is its striking Manueline portico, the only part of an earlier chapel that withstood the 1755 earthquake. It also has no fixed opening hours; mass is at 9am daily.

At the southern end of Largo do Carmo is the 16th-century **Igreja de São Pedro** *(open 9am-1pm & 3pm-7pm Mon-Fri)*. Its interior is filled with 18th-century azulejos and carved woodwork.

Museu Municipal

The Museu Municipal *(Museu Arqueológico; ☎ 289 897 400; Largo Dom Afonso III; adult/student €2/1; open 2.30pm-6pm Mon & Sat, 10am-6pm Tues-Fri Apr-Sept; 2pm-5.30pm Mon & Sat, 9.30am-5.30pm Tues-Fri Oct-Mar)*, in the splendid Convento de Nossa

Senhora da Assunção in the Cidade Velha, was being reorganised at the time of writing but its highlight – a huge Roman mosaic (known as the 'Mosaic of the Ocean') found in 1976 on a Faro building site – bags pride of place downstairs. Upstairs are temporary exhibitions, plus works by a notable Faro painter, Carlos Filipe Porfírio (1895–1970).

Other Museums

In the left entrance of the district assembly building is the **Museu Etnográfico Regional do Algarve** (*Algarve Regional Museum; Praça da Liberdade; admission €1.50; open 9am-12.30pm & 2pm-5.30pm Mon-Fri*). On display are ceramics, fabrics, lots of baskets, straw mats, photos and little dioramas of 20th-century home life – with not a word, in any language, about what, when or who. It's a poor bargain.

In the harbourmaster's building at the northern end of the marina is the modest **Museu da Marítimo** (*Maritime Museum; admission €1; open 2.30pm-4.30pm Mon-Fri*), full of maps, model ships, fish, and nautical gear.

Centro Ciência Viva

The Science Alive Center (☎ 289 890 920; *Rua Comandante Francisco Manuel; adult/youth 13-17/child €2/1/0.50, Wed half-price; open 10am-5pm Tues-Fri, 3pm-7pm Sat & Sun mid-Sept–June; 4pm-11pm Tues-Sun July–mid-Sept*) is a modern interactive educational display on the sun and its influences. There are lots of great computer links and hands-on displays, but it's all in Portuguese. Free Internet access is available in the upstairs Mediatéca room.

Teatro Lethes

This little Italianate theatre (*Rua Lethes*) is Faro's most charming cultural venue, hosting drama, music and dance programmes. Built in 1874, it was once the Jesuit Colégio de Santiago Maior and is now the property of the Portuguese Cruz Vermelha (Red Cross).

Beaches

The town's beach, **Praia de Faro**, with miles of sand, windsurfing operators and half a dozen cafés, is on the nearby Ilha de Faro. Take bus No 16 from opposite the bus station (departures every half-hour in summer, via the airport; €0.90). There are ferries out

to **Praia de Farol** (Ilha da Culatra) and **Ilha da Barreta** (also called Ilha Deserta); see Getting Around later in this section.

Special Events

Faro's biggest traditional event is the Feira de Santa Iria, in mid-October at a temporary fairground in the northeast of town by the municipal fire station.

The cultural highlight is an international music festival, held from May to July (see Special Events at the start of this chapter).

Rallye Biker, one of Europe's biggest motorbike rallies, attracts some 30,000 bikers on the third weekend in July, making accommodation practically impossible.

Places to Stay – Budget

Accommodation prices are very seasonal; we give July rates here (August is even higher still).

There is a big, cheap municipal **parque de campismo** (*camp site; ☎ 289 817 876; adult/tent/car €0.40/0.30/0.20*) at Praia de Faro, with a restaurant on site. Take bus No 14 or 16 from opposite the bus station (both go via the airport).

The **pousada da juventude** (*youth hostel; ☎ 289 826 521; e faro@movijovem.pt; Rua da Polícia de Segurança Pública 1; dorm beds €9.50, doubles with/without bathroom €26.50/23; reception open 8am-noon & 6pm-midnight daily*), at the Instituto Português da Juventude (IPJ), is a long hike from the centre and rather run-down. From the bus station take the town's Minibus service, Circuito 2 (€0.50); it runs every 15 minutes from 7.35am to 8.10pm daily (less frequently at weekends).

Residencial Adelaide (*☎ 289 802 383, fax 289 826 870; Rua Cruz dos Mestres 7; rooftop sleeping €7.50, quads per person €11.30, singles/doubles €14/23, with private bathroom €20/26*) is a popular budget *pensão* (guesthouse) with a homely atmosphere. It offers rooftop space (price includes mattress and linen) when the place is full.

The most conveniently central *pensões*, all with doubles from around €50, are the welcoming **Residencial Avenida** (*☎ 289 823 347; Avenida da República 150*); the **Residencial Oceano** (*☎ 289 823 349, fax 289 805 590; Rua Ivens 21*), with very plain but clean rooms; and **Pensão Residencial Central** (*☎ 289 807 291; Praça Ferreira de Almeida*

12), with cool, tiled, spacious rooms (the ones at the back are quieter).

Residencial Madalena (☎ 289 805 806, fax 289 805 807; Rua Conselheiro de Bívar 109; doubles with/without bathroom €50/40) is efficiently run but has rather small rooms. Breakfast is available for €3.50.

Pensão Residencial Filipe (☎/fax 289 824 182; Rua Infante Dom Henrique 55; doubles with/without bathroom €50/40) is less pretentious and cosily old-fashioned.

Places to Stay – Mid-Range & Top End

Residencial Samé (☎ 289 824 375, fax 289 804 166; Rua do Bocage 66; singles/doubles from €32/52), in a quiet spot, offers bland but good-value modern rooms with air-con and TV.

Residencial Algarve (☎ 289 895 700, fax 289 895 703; e reservas@residencialalgarve .com; Rua Infante Dom Henrique 52; singles/ doubles with breakfast €52.50/65) is a newish place in traditional style, offering bright, cheerful rooms with air-con, telephone and TV.

Hotel Dom Bernardo (☎ 289 889 800; e hdb@net.sapo.pt; Rua General Teófilo da Trindade 20; singles/doubles with breakfast €83/100) is a mainstream three-star hotel.

Hotel Eva (☎ 289 803 354, fax 289 802 304; Avenida da República; singles/doubles €112/130), Faro's best hotel, is a smart four-star place overlooking the marina and the sea beyond. It also boasts a rooftop swimming pool.

Places to Eat

Paladar's (☎ 916 707 048; Rua Infante Dom Henrique 110; dishes from €5; open Mon-Sat) is a neat choice if you're counting the euros; it serves simple fare in a plain, bright setting.

Pontinha (☎ 289 820 649; Rua do Pé da Cruz 5; dishes from €7.50; open Mon-Sat) is one of several bargain restaurants in this street, offering regional fare, including a cataplana especial – shellfish and ham cooked in a sealed pan, an Algarve standard – at €21.20 for two.

Casa de Pasto São Pedro (☎ 289 826 743; Rua de São Pedro 55; dishes around €7) is another no-frills place whose chef prides himself on his grilled fish and meat dishes.

A Garrafeira do Vilaça (☎ 289 802 150; Rua de São Pedro 33; dishes €7-9; open Wed-Mon), slightly more upmarket than Casa de Pasto, is popular with locals.

Restaurante A Taska (☎ 289 824 739; Rua do Alportel 38; dishes €8-10; open Mon-Sat) is a popular, trattoria-style venue, serving great regional food.

Cervejaria-Bar República (☎ 289 807 312; Avenida da República 40; dishes around €9; closed lunch Sat & Sun), a favourite with expats, is small and homely, with an impressively large menu of steaks and grilled fish dishes.

Mesa dos Mouros (☎ 289 878 873; Largo da Sé 10; dishes from €12.50), right next to the cathedral, is one of the nicest upmarket spots, and has splendid outdoor seating. Choose from loads of seafood and shellfish or more unusual dishes such as rabbit with chestnuts (€17.50) or Andalucían black pig loin (€12.50).

For coffees, snacks and people-watching, head for the run-down, old-fashioned **Café Aliança** (Rua Dr Francisco Gomes).

Self-Catering Faro's big mercado municipal (municipal market) is in Largo Mercado. As well as several minimercados (grocery shops) around town, there's the larger **AliSuper** (Largo do Carmo; open 9am-8pm Mon-Sat, 9am-1pm Sun).

Entertainment

Rua do Prior and its surrounding scruffy alleys are a den of bar-clubs, which are liveliest at weekends. Options include **Milenium** (☎ 289 823 628; Rua do Prior 23), **Fashion Kaffé** (☎ 289 812 310; Rua do Prior 38) and buzzing **Bar os Arcos** (Travessa dos Arcos 8).

Galeria Bar Património (Rua do Prior 19) is a laid-back venue. **Porto Fino** (☎ 289 825 088; Rua 1 de Maio 21), nearby, attracts more of the suit-and-tie kind of clientele.

Taverna da Sé (Praça Afonso III 26) is a relaxing little place in the old town, serving snacks as well as drinks.

Spectator Sports

The 30,000-seat Estádio Intermunicipal do Algarve is a brand-new stadium built for the 2004 European Football Championships at São João da Venda, 8km northwest of Faro en route to Loulé. Here you can also watch Faro's own team, SC Farense, and Loulé's Louletano.

ALGARVE

Getting There & Away

Air Portugália and TAP each have multiple daily Lisbon–Faro flights (year-round) and both have frequent onward connections from Lisbon to Porto. From July to September Portugália flies on Friday from Porto to Faro (but not directly back). For details of international services, see the Getting There & Away chapter.

For flight inquiries call the **airport** (☎ 289 800 801/617). **TAP** has a booking office (☎ 808 205 700; Rua Dr Francisco Gomes; open 9am-5.30pm Mon-Fri) located in the town centre.

Bus From the main **Eva bus station** (☎ 289 899 760; Avenida da República 5) express coaches run at least a dozen times daily to Lisbon (€13.50, four to five hours) including a night run; some services involve changing at Vale do Paraíso, near the IP1 motorway north of Albufeira. Opposite the bus station is a ticket office called **Caima** (☎ 289 812 980), where you can buy tickets for the Renex Lisbon express bus (€13, four to six times daily).

There are nine buses daily to Vila Real de Santo António (€3.30, 1¾ hours), via Tavira (€2.20, one hour); 14 runs to Albufeira (€3, 1¼ hours); and seven daily transrápido (express) services to Lagos (€3.60, 1¾ hours) via Portimão. Services are reduced at weekends. For Sagres, change at Lagos.

There are twice-daily Eva services between Faro and Seville (€10.50, five hours) via Huelva (€4.70, 3½ hours). For further details, see the Getting There & Away chapter.

Busing Around the Algarve

Two big bus companies, **Eva** (☎ 289 899 740) and **Rede Expressos** (☎ 289 899 760), operate frequent services between the Algarve's major towns and elsewhere in Portugal (Eva's long-distance routes are marketed under the name Eva Mundial Turismo). Smaller lines include Caima, Renex and Frota Azul. If you plan to bus around the Algarve, consider buying the Passe Turístico (€15.50/21.50), good for three/seven days of unlimited travel on most main routes between Lagos and Loulé. It's available from major bus stations.

Train From Lisbon there are five trains daily to Faro: one snail's-pace regional service, two interregional (IR) services (€9.90, 5¼ hours, including Tejo ferry crossing to Barreiro) and two intercidade (IC) services (€11.90, 4¼ to 5¼ hours, including ferry crossing).

The once-weekly Comboio Azul train links Faro directly to Porto (€15.90, seven hours) via Beja, Évora and Coimbra, departing Faro on Friday afternoon and Porto on Sunday evening.

From Faro there are eight fast trains daily to Albufeira (€1.60, 30 minutes), six to Vila Real de Santo António (€2.70, 65 minutes), and five to Lagos (€3.90, 1¾ hours). Additional services to Lagos involve a change at Tunes junction.

There's an **information kiosk** (open 9am-1pm & 2pm-6pm daily) at the train station.

Car The most direct route from Lisbon to Faro takes about five hours. The final stretch of the A2-IP1 Lisbon–Algarve motorway via São Bartolomeu de Messines was finally completed in 2002. Due to be finished in 2003 is the western extension of the IP1-IC4 Via do Infante motorway linking Faro with Vila Real de Santo António to the east and Lagos to the west. A nonmotorway alternative is the often traffic-clogged N125.

Most major car-rental agencies are represented at the airport. Good local ones include **Auto Jardim do Algarve** (☎ 289 580 500, fax 289 587 780), **Rentauto** (☎ 289 310 100, fax 289 315 626) and **City Car** (☎ 289 589 999, fax 289 588 429).

Portugal's national auto club, **Automóvel Club de Portugal** (ACP), has a branch office (☎ 289 898 950; Rua Francisco Barreto 26A; open 9am-12.45pm & 2pm-4.30pm Mon-Fri).

The easiest parking in Faro is in Largo de São Francisco.

Getting Around

To/From the Airport From June to October an AeroBus shuttle runs into town via the bus station, Jardim and Hotel Dom Bernardo, hourly from 9am to 8pm; it's free to airline ticket holders.

Bus Nos 14 and 16 make the trip (€0.90, 18 minutes) between the airport and Jardim roughly every half-hour (No 16 is more frequent) daily until about 9pm in summer. Note that in winter they only go every hour or two. Both routes also go, via the airport, to the camp site.

The handiest bus stop in town is opposite the bus station (timetables are posted).

A taxi into town costs about €7.60 (€8.70 after 10pm and at weekends).

Bus Eva offers a one-day Tour Pass for €2.50 (valid from 7am to 10pm daily), which you can use on the city bus routes, including out to Praia de Faro and the IPJ. It's on sale at the bus terminal.

Taxi To call a taxi, ring ☎ 289 895 795, or find one at the eastern end of Jardim Manuel Bívar.

Bicycle You can rent bikes (including tandems and bikes for kids) from **Megasport** (☎/fax 289 802 136; e megasport@mail .telepac.pt; Rua Ataíde de Oliveira 39C; open Mon-Fri, morning Sat) for €10 per day. Bikes can be taken on the train to Vila Real de Santo António (but not back) for €2.

Boat From April to September, **Tavares e Guerreiro** (☎ 289 702 121) operates ferries from the pier next to Arco da Porta Nova to Ilha de Farol and Ilha da Barreta (also known as Ilha Deserta). For current times and prices check with the turismo or ask at the pier.

Also from this pier, **Animaris** (☎ 917 811 856) runs 1½-hour trips (€6) four times daily between June and September to Ilha da Barreta through the canals of the Ria Formosa.

SÃO BRÁS DE ALPORTEL
postcode 8150 • pop 10,000
• elevation 210m

Few visitors think of staying overnight in this friendly town 17km north of Faro. However, it makes a pleasantly untouristy base for visiting the so-called Barrocal region, a fertile limestone belt between the mountains and the sea, which stretches all the way from Cabo de São Vicente. It is characterised by an abundance of olive, carob, fig and almond trees.

Orientation & Information
Buses stop in the central Largo de São Sebastião. At the time of writing, there were plans to open a turismo in the Largo.

Top Algarve Beaches

Fancy surfing the breaks? Lazing about with sandcastles? Take your pick from the following beach suggestions (for details see individual town listings). Note that during August almost nowhere is quiet, while in winter, crowds and facilities fade away.

Bars and Water Sports: Meia Praia (Lagos); Praia da Luz (5km west of Lagos); Ilha de Faro (Faro) and Ilha de Tavira (Tavira); Praia de Galé (6km west of Albufeira)

Surfing: Praia da Arrifana (10km southwest of Aljezur); Praia de Monte Clérigo (8km northwest of Aljezur); Praia do Amado (Carrapateira); Praia do Tonel (Sagres)

Spectacular Setting: Praia de Dona Ana (Lagos); Praia da Rocha (Portimão); Praia de Centianes (Carvoeiro); Praia de Odeceixe (Odeceixe)

Peace and Quiet: Praia do Barril (Ilha da Culatra, 4km west of Tavira); Praia da Figueira and Boca do Rio (Salema, 17km west of Lagos); Armona (Ilha da Armona, near Olhão)

Museu Etnográfico do Trajo Algarvio
This unexpectedly delightful museum (☎ 289 842 618; Rua Dr José Dias Sancho 61; admission €0.80; open 10am-noon & 2pm-5pm Mon-Fri, 2pm-5pm Sat, Sun & holidays) is 200m east of the Largo (along the Tavira road). A rambling collection of local costumes, handicrafts, agricultural implements and household goods (with occasional special exhibitions) is displayed in an old mansion with lots of dark and musty corners.

Old Town
Another surprise is the peaceful old town area. Follow Rua Gago Coutinho southwards from the Largo to the 16th-century **igreja matriz**, with breezy views of orange groves from its doorstep. Nearby, below what used to be a bishop's palace (now a nursery school), is a nicely landscaped **municipal swimming pool** (open 10am-7pm daily May-Sept) and children's play area.

Places to Stay & Eat
Estalagem Sequeira (☎ 289 843 444, fax 289 843 792; Rua Dr Evaristo Gago 9; singles/

doubles/triples €23/40/55) is dull-looking but actually a good bargain: all rooms have bathroom, TV and telephone, and prices include breakfast.

Residencial São Brás (☎/fax 289 842 213; Rua Luís Bívar 27; singles/doubles €25/42), around the corner (along the busy Loulé road), is delightfully old-fashioned and plentifully adorned with plants and azulejos. Rooms are musty but spacious (more modern ones are in a back annexe). Rates include breakfast.

There are several rural guesthouses in the vicinity, including English-run **Santo António** (☎/fax 289 843 996; e st.antonio@ mail.telepac.pt; Poco dos Ferreiros; doubles per day/week €62.50/405), 1.5km north off the N2 Lisbon road. It has four large doubles and a small swimming pool. Be prepared for a lavish, exotic breakfast (included in the price), described as 'quite an event'.

Pousada de São Brás (☎ 289 842 305, fax 289 841 726; doubles Mon-Fri €126, Sat & Sun €132) is situated on a panoramic hilltop site 500m further on from Santo António. The renovated 1950s building offers deluxe rooms.

Churrasqueira Afonso (☎ 289 842 635; Estrada de Tavira 134; dishes from €5; open Fri-Wed), 500m east of the Largo (beyond the museum), does great grilled dishes.

Casa de Pasto Lena (☎ 289 842 494; open Mon-Sat) is 1.5km along the Loulé road. This unpretentious casa típica (typical restaurant), is a popular lunch-time stop with locals.

Getting There & Away
Ten buses daily (fewer at weekends) run to São Brás de Alportel from Faro (€2.30 via Estói, 35 minutes) and four daily from Loulé (€1.80, 25 minutes).

ESTÓI
A rewarding day trip from Faro is to the enchantingly derelict palace at Estói, 10km north of Faro, and the nearby Roman ruins at Milreu.

Palácio do Visconde de Estói
This 18th-century palace is a short walk from Estói's village square, where the bus from Faro stops. Down a palm-shaded avenue, past abandoned stables and outhouses, are the palace's delightfully unkempt gardens

(admission free; open 9am-12.30pm & 2pm-5.30pm Tues-Sat), adorned with busts of poets, 19th-century azulejos depicting naked mythological ladies and an ornamental pool with equally voluptuous statues. The actual palace (closed to the public), a pink Rococo affair reminiscent of Queluz palace near Lisbon, is slated to become a pousada (up-market inn).

Milreu
Some 800m down the main road from Estói's square (the bus from Faro passes it en route to Estói) are the ruins of Milreu (adult/under-25 €1.30/0.60; open 9.30am-12.30pm & 2pm-6pm Tues-Sun Apr-Sept, to 5pm Oct-Mar), a Roman equivalent of the Estói palace. Dating from the 1st century AD, the ruins show the characteristic form of a peristyle villa, with a gallery of columns around a courtyard. In the surrounding rooms geometric motifs and friezes of fish were found, although these have now been removed for restoration. The most tantalising glimpses left of the villa's former glory are the **fish mosaics** in the suite of bathing chambers to the west of the villa's courtyard.

The remains of the bathing rooms include the **apodyterium**, or changing-room (note the arched niches and benches for clothes and post-bath massage), and the **frigidarium**, which had a marble basin to hold cold water for cooling off after the bath. Other luxuries were underground heating and marble sculptures (now in the museums of Faro and Lagos).

To the right of the entrance is the most interesting aspect of the site – its **nymphaerium**, or water sanctuary, a temple devoted to the cult of water. The interior was once decorated with polychrome marble slabs and its exterior with fish mosaics (some are still visible). In the 3rd century the Visigoths converted it into a church, adding a baptismal font and a small mausoleum.

You can pick up an information sheet (in English, Spanish or German; €1) at the entrance.

Getting There & Away
During the week, 11 buses daily make the 20-minute run from Faro to Estói (continuing on to São Brás de Alportel). The last bus back to Faro is at 7pm.

Golf & Gallinules

The purple gallinule (also known as the purple swamp-hen or, far more exotically, as the sultan chicken) is one of Europe's most rare and elusive birds. It's an extraordinary violet-blue water bird the size of a large domestic fowl and has a massive red bill and red legs. In Portugal, its only confirmed nesting place is in an isolated fragment of wetland, which is partly in the grounds of the exclusive Quinta do Lago villa estate, at the western end of the Parque Natural da Ria Formosa, about 12km west of Faro.

Not so long ago, the bird was facing local extinction with just two pairs recorded. But when the estate built a freshwater lake to help irrigate its new São Lourenço golf course, the gallinule's fortunes dramatically improved. The normally shy birds – now numbering about 60 – often strut around the fairways before the first golfers arrive.

You can get a good look at the sultan from an elevated public hide overlooking the lake, about 1km along the estate's São Lourenço Nature Trail. To reach the start of the trail, at a wooden bridge crossing the lagoon, head for roundabout 6 from the estate's entrance.

Clive Viney

OLHÃO

postcode 8700 • pop 24,900

Olhão (ol-**yowng**), the Algarve's biggest fishing port, is a clamorous, sprawling town beside a vast precinct of docks, canning factories and the Sopursal salt works. But buried at the historical centre is an appealing little kernel of town, surprisingly well preserved and untouristy.

Not surprisingly, there's also loads of good seafood restaurants. Saturday is the biggest and best day for the colourful **market** (Avenida 5 de Outubro), a sumptuous affair even on weekdays.

Offshore are the numerous sandy islands of the Parque Natural da Ria Formosa. There are great beaches on Ilha da Culatra and Ilha da Armona, both of which can be reached by boat.

Orientation

From the small **Eva bus terminal** (Rua General Humberto Delgado), turn right (or from the train station, turn left; east) and it's one block to the inner town's main avenue, Avenida da República. Turn right and 300m down the Avenida you'll reach the parish church, at the edge of the central, pedestrianised shopping zone.

At the far side of this zone, Avenida 5 de Outubro runs along the waterfront. Here are the twin-domed brick buildings of the market and just to the left (east) is the town park, Jardim Patrão Joaquim Lopes.

Information

Olhão's **turismo** (☎ 289 713 936; Largo Sebastião Martins Mestre; open 9.30am-noon & 1pm-5.30pm Mon-Fri Oct-Apr, 9.30am-7pm May-Sept) is in the centre of the pedestrian zone (from the bus station bear right at the prominent fork beside the parish church).

The **post office** (Avenida da República) is a block north of the parish church, opposite a bank with an ATM. Useful numbers include the **police** (☎ 289 702 144) and the local **centro de saúde** (medical centre; ☎ 289 704 648).

Bairro dos Pescadores

Just back from the fish market and park is the so-called Fishermen's Quarter, a compact knot of whitewashed, cubical houses, often with tiled fronts. The *bairro* (neighbourhood) is threaded by lanes too narrow for cars and is all (so far) mercifully ungentrified. From a distance it looks charmingly North African, although the Moors left in the 13th century and none of these houses is more than a few hundred years old. Nobody seems to have a good explanation for this style, found elsewhere in the Algarve only at Fuzeta (10km east).

Beaches

Good beaches nearby include **Praia de Farol** (the best of the lot) and **Praia de Angares** on Ilha da Culatra, and **Praia de Armona** and **Praia de Fuzeta** on Ilha da Armona. There are ferries to both islands from the pier just east of Jardim Patrão Joaquim Lopes (see Getting Around later in this section).

Special Events

Olhão's best-known festival is the Festival do Marisco, a seafood festival featuring food stalls and folk music, held in the Jardim Patrão Joaquim Lopes during the second week of August.

ALGARVE

Places to Stay
Camping The well-equipped 800-site **Camping Olhão** (☎ 289 700 300; e sbsicamp ing@mail.telepac.pt; adult/tent/car €3.30/ 2.40/2.80, family bungalows €45.40) is 2km east of Olhão and 800m off the N125. During summer, a bus goes there departing from beside Jardim Patrão Joaquim Lopes every hour or two weekdays and Saturday morning.

Parque de Campismo de Fuzeta (☎ 289 793 459, fax 289 794 034; adult/tent/car €2.30/2/3.10) is a small, plain municipal site right on the waterfront at the end of the main street in tiny Fuzeta, about 10km east of Olhão.

Pensões & Hotels There are fewer places to stay here than you would expect, and they quickly fill up in summer.

Alojamentos Vasco da Gama (☎ 289 703 146; Rua Vasco da Gama; singles/doubles €15/25) is an old-fashioned house offering plain rooms with shared bathroom.

Pensão Bicuar (☎ 289 703 146; Rua Vasco da Gama 5; doubles €25.50), opposite Alojamentos Vasco da Gama, is several notches up, offering trim rooms with bathroom. Rua Vasco da Gama is to the left (east) of the parish church.

Pensão Bela Vista (☎ 289 702 538; Rua Teófilo Braga 65; doubles with/without bathroom €40/30), a short walk west of the turismo, is friendly and efficiently run, and the best choice among the pensões.

Hotel Residencial Armona (☎ 289 700 680, fax 289 700 681; singles/doubles €45/55) is on the N125 at the western edge of town (opposite the BP station). This motel-style hotel (bizarrely, on the 3rd floor of a furniture showroom) is convenient for car drivers. Rooms are attractive and modern with air-con, bathroom and free breakfast. Visa and MasterCard are not accepted.

Places to Eat
Avenida 5 de Outubro is lined with seafood restaurants.

Restaurante Isidro (☎ 289 714 124; Avenida 5 de Outubro 68; fish dishes from €8) is one of the most popular, offering more unusual fare than most (eg, prawn stroganoff for €13 or eel stew for €11).

Casa de Pasto Algarve (☎ 289 704 270; Praça Patrão Joaquim Lopes; dishes from €6), almost opposite the market, offers more modest fare than Isidro.

Getting There & Away
Bus Eva express buses run five times daily to Lisbon (€13.50, four to five hours). Renex also has a service (€13, four to five hours) seven times daily on weekdays (less frequently at weekends). There's a **Renex ticket office** (Avenida da República 101) in town.

Buses run between Faro and Olhão (€1.10, 20 minutes) roughly every 15 minutes on weekdays. Some weekday buses continue from Olhão bus station to the waterfront at Bairro dos Pescadores. Services to Tavira (€1.40, 40 minutes) run almost hourly.

Train Olhão is 10 to 15 minutes from Faro (€0.80), with trains coming through every two hours or so. Fuzeta (€0.80) is the same distance eastwards and Tavira (€1.70) 30 minutes away.

Getting Around
Ferries run out to the *ilhas* from the pier at the eastern end of Jardim Patrão Joaquim Lopes. There are boats to Ilha da Armona (€1.90 return, 15 minutes) nine times daily (starting at 7.40am) in June and September (with more at weekends), and hourly during July and August; the last trip back from Armona from 1 July to 31 August leaves at 8.30pm. In winter boats run just four times daily.

For Ilha da Culatra (€2, 35 minutes) and Farol (€2.50, 45 minutes), boats go six to seven times daily in June and September (seven times in July and August) and four times daily in winter; the last boat back in summer leaves Culatra at 8pm and Farol at 8.20pm.

TAVIRA
postcode 8800 • pop 10,600
This picturesque town straddling the Rio Gilão 3km from the coast is still remarkably unspoilt, though its popularity booms to bursting in summer. Elegant 18th-century houses border the river, castle ruins overlook at least 37 churches in a tangle of old streets, 16th-century mansions with Manueline window-flourishes line the back streets, and fishing boats bob at the quay. Recent restoration projects – including converting the former riverside market into a restaurant and shopping venue – have spruced up the town

Parque Natural da Ria Formosa

The Ria Formosa Natural Park is primarily a lagoon system stretching for 60km along the Algarve coastline from just west of Faro to Cacela Velha. It encloses a vast area of marsh *(sapal)*, salt pans *(salinas)*, creeks and dune islands. Near the western boundary of the park there are also two fresh-water lakes, at Ludo and Quinta do Lago, which constitute a vital habitat for migrating and nesting birds. A huge variety of wetland birds can be seen in the park, as well as ducks, shorebirds, gulls and terns. This is the favoured nesting place of the little tern and rare purple gallinule (see the boxed text 'Golf & Gallinules' earlier in this chapter).

You'll also find some of the Algarve's quietest, biggest beaches on the sandbank *ilhas* of Faro, Culatra, Armona and Tavira (see the Faro, Olhão and Tavira sections).

The **park headquarters** (☎ 289 704 134, fax 289 704 165; [e] pnrf@icn.pt; Quinta de Marim) is 3km east of Olhão and has an excellent **visitor centre** *(open 9am-5.30pm daily)*. Try the 2.4km nature trail across the dunes (admission €1.50).

To get to Quinta de Marim take any Tavira-bound bus from Olhão, get off at the Cepsa petrol station, and walk seaward for 1km (the visitor centre is 200m beyond Camping Olhão). Alternatively, a bus goes to the camp site every hour or two on weekdays and Saturday morning, from beside Jardim Patrão Joaquim Lopes in Olhão.

even further. Two new golf courses in the area may also change the tenor of the place.

There are bars aplenty for those who want them and bikes to rent for exploring further afield. There's also a superb beach (with camp site) on the nearby Ilha de Tavira (though it gets swamped in summer). If you're looking for a relaxing base in an attractive setting, Tavira is hard to beat.

History

Tavira's origins are vague. It's likely that the area was inhabited in Neolithic times, and later by Phoenicians, Greeks and Carthaginians. The Romans left more traces – their settlement of Balsa was just down the road, near Santa Luzia (3km west). The seven-arched bridge the Romans built at Tavira (then called Tabira) was an important link in the route between Baesuris (Castro Marim) and Ossonoba (Faro).

In the 8th century, Tavira was occupied by the Moors. They built the castle (probably on the site of a Roman fortress) and two mosques. Their downfall came in 1242 when Dom Paio Peres Correia reconquered the town. Those Moors who remained were segregated into the *mouraria* (Moorish quarter) outside the town walls. Excavations have discovered some important Phoenician and Moorish remains, including a unique 11th-century marriage vase.

Tavira's importance was established in the Age of Discoveries: as the port closest to

the Moroccan coast it was the base for Portuguese expeditions to North Africa, supplying provisions (especially salt, wine and dried fish) and providing a hospital for sick soldiers. Its maritime trade also expanded, with exports of salted fish, almonds, figs and wine to northern Europe. In 1520, by then the most populated settlement in the Algarve and rich in churches and the houses of Portuguese nobles, it was raised to the rank of city.

Decline set in during the early 17th century when the North African campaign was abandoned and the Rio Gilão became so silted up that large boats couldn't enter the port. In 1645 came the devastating effects of the plague, followed by the 1755 earthquake.

After a brief spell producing carpets in the late 18th century, Tavira found a more stable income in its tuna fishing and canning industry, although this, too, declined in the 1950s when the tuna shoals moved elsewhere. Today, it relies increasingly on tourism.

Orientation

The train station is on the southern edge of town, 1km from the centre. The bus terminal is a 200m walk west of central Praça da República. Most of the town's shops and facilities are on the southern side of the river.

Information

Tourist offices The turismo (☎ 281 322 511; Rua da Galeria 9; open 9.30am-1pm & 2pm-5.30pm Mon-Fri Oct-Apr; 9.30am-

ALGARVE

TAVIRA

PLACES TO STAY
6   Pensão Residencial Almirante
11 Pensão Residencial Lagõas
14 Residencial Princesa do Gilão
17 Residencial Bela Fria
24 Pensão Residencial Castelo
32 Residencial Imperial
33 Mare's Residencial

PLACES TO EAT
1   Cantinho do Emigrante
7   Snack-Bar Petisqueira-Belmar
8   Churrasqueira O Manel
9   Aquasul
10 Restaurante Bica
13 Pingo Doce Supermarket
15 Pastelaria Anazu
31 Pastelaria Tavirense
34 Casa de Pasto A Barquinha
39 Restaurante Avenida
43 Mercado Municipal
44 Snack Bar A Velha 2

OTHER
2   Balsa
3   UBI
4   Exploratio (Rent a Bike)
5   Arco Bar
12 Bar O Talabriga
16 Bus Station
18 Palácio da Galeria
19 Igreja da Misericórdia
20 Turismo
21 Lorisrent
22 Bank & ATM
23 Câmara Municipal
25 Castelo
26 Igreja de Santa Maria do Castelo

27 Convento da Nossa Senhora da Graça
28 Igreja de Santiago
29 Post Office
30 Cota Câmbios
35 Taxi Rank
36 Cinema
37 PostNet
38 Clinica Medica
40 Centro de Saúde
41 Mudarent
42 Lavandaria Lavitt
45 Capela de São Sebastião
46 Police Station

Rua Prof. Egas Moniz

Rua dos Namarrais

Rua dos Limpinhos

Rua Fumeiros Detrás

R Fumeiros de Diante

Rua João Vaz Corte Real

Rua dos Limpinhos

Praça Dr Padinha

Largo de Santana

Calçada de Sant'Ana

Rua de Sant'Ana

Largo de São Braz

Rio Séqua

Rua Borda d'Água da Asseça

Largo do Carmo

Rua Feixinho de Vides

To Hotel Vila Galé Albocora (4km)

Rua 1º Dezembro

Rua 1º Dezembro

Rua Álvaro de Campos

Rua Álvares Botelho

Rua Almirante Cândido dos Reis

Rua do Forno

Rua do Salto

Rua da Oliveira

Largo do Trem

Rua Almirante Cândido dos Reis

Rua Poeta Emiliano da Costa

Rua José Joaquim Jara

To Casa do Rio (450m)

Ponte Romana (pedestrian only)

Rua dos Pelames

Rua Jaques Pessoa

Largo da Caracolinha

Rua Borda d'Água de Aguiar

Rua Comandante Henrique Brito

Salt Pans

Rua Detrás dos Muros

Calçada D Ana

Calçada R da Galeria

Praça da República

Ponte das Forças Armadas

Rua do Cais

Rio Gilão

Largo José Joaquim Jara

Rua Dr José Pires Padinha

Mercado da Ribeira

Ponte dos Descobrimentos

Rua D Paio Peres Correia

Largo da Porta do Postigo

Porta de Dom Manuel

Rua da Liberdade

Rua Dr Parreira

To Quinta da Lua (4km), IP1 to Faro (29km) & Vila Real de Santó António (23km)

To Quinta do Caracol (100m), Faro & N125

Rua Marcelino Franco

Rua Dr Augusto Carlos Palma

Rua Guilherme Gomes Fernandes

Rua 1º de Maio

Rua da Silva

To Quatro Águas & Ilha de Tavira (2km)

Rua Dr Miguel Bombarda

Rua Dr Silvestre Falcão

Rua Montalvão

Rua Poço do Bispo

Rua 31 de Janeiro

Rua 4 de Outubro

Rua das Salinas

Salt Pans

To Train Station (250m)

Rua 25 de Abril

Rua Tenente Couto

Praça Zacarias Guerreiro

Av Dr Teixeira de Azevedo

Rua do Poeta Isidoro Pires

Tv de São Sebastião

Largo de Atalaia

Tv do Poço

Rua João Arias

Salt Pans

Quartel (Military Quartel)

Campo dos Mártires da Pátria

Rua 9 de Abril

Rua Dr Fausto Cansado

Rua da Atalaia Pequena

Rua da Atalaia

Rua de Santo António

Rua dos Mártires da República

Rua Francisco Sá Carneiro

To Santa Luzia (4km), Pedras d'el Rei & Praia do Barril (6km)

0   50   100m
0   50   100yd

ALGARVE

12.30pm & 2pm-6pm Fri-Mon, 9.30am-7pm Tues-Thur May-Sept) can provide local and regional information, and help with accommodation. The municipal website **w** www .cm-tavira.pt is also useful.

Money There are several banks with ATMs around Praça da República and along Rua da Liberdade. There's also the private-exchange bureau **Cota Câmbios** *(Rua Estácio da Veiga 21; open 8.30am-6.30pm Mon-Fri, 10am-2pm Sat).*

Email & Internet Access Internet access is offered at **Residencial Bela Fria** *(see Places to Stay)* for €1 per 15 minutes from 9am to 11pm Monday to Saturday. **PostNet** *(☎ 281 320 910; Rua Dr Silvestre Falcão, Lote 6; open 9am-8pm Mon-Fri, 9am-1.30pm Sat)* and **Pastelaria Anazu** *(Rua Jaques Pessoa; open 8.30am-around midnight Mon-Sat)* both charge €1.30 per 15 minutes.

Laundry The **Lavandaria Lavitt** *(☎ 281 326 776; Rua das Salinas 6; open 9am-1pm & 3pm-7pm Mon-Sat, 9am-1pm Sun)* charges €3 per 6kg (plus €3 for tumble-dry).

Medical Services & Emergency For medical emergencies, go to the **centro de saúde** *(medical centre; ☎ 281 329 000; Rua Tenente Couto)*. A 24-hour private clinic, **Clinica Medica** *(☎ 281 321 750; Avenida Dr Teixeira de Azevêdo 5)*, provides speedier (and pricier) treatment.

The **police station** *(☎ 281 322 022; Campo dos Mártires da Pátria)* is at the southern edge of town.

Igreja da Misericórdia
Built in the 1540s, this church *(Rua da Galeria; admission free; open 9am-noon & 2pm-5pm Mon-Fri)* is considered the Algarve's most important Renaissance monument, thanks largely to its finely carved, arched doorway (recently restored), topped by statues of Nossa Senhora da Misericórdia, São Pedro and São Paulo.

Igreja de Santa Maria do Castelo
This 13th-century church *(admission free)*, beside the castle, was built on the site of a Moorish mosque (its clock tower still has some Arabic-style windows). Inside, you'll find a plaque marking the tomb of Dom Paio

Peres Correia (see History earlier in this section) as well as those of the seven Christian knights whose murder by the Moors precipitated the final attack on Tavira.

Castelo
Now more a prim garden than a defensive bulwark, the castle *(admission free; open 8am-5pm Mon-Fri, 9am-5.30pm Sat & Sun)* does feature a restored octagonal tower that is a great place to look out over Tavira's attractive tiled rooftops – they probably owe their wave-like Oriental style to ideas brought back by 15th-century explorers.

Other Old Town Attractions
The main entrance to the old town these days is through the town gate, **Porta de Dom Manuel** (by the turismo), built in 1520 when Dom Manuel I made Tavira a city. Around the back, along Calçada da Galeria, the elegant **Palácio da Galeria** has been converted into an **exhibition gallery** *(admission free; open 10am-12.30pm & 2pm-6pm Tues-Fri, 2pm-6pm Sat)*.

Just south of the castle is the white-washed **Igreja de Santiago**, built in the 17th century where a small mosque probably once stood. The area beside it was formerly the Praça da Vila, the old town square.

On the other side of the square is the former **Convento da Nossa Senhora da Graça**. Founded in 1568 on the site of the former Jewish quarter, this convent was largely rebuilt at the end of the 18th century and is now destined to become a *pousada*.

Downhill from here is the **Largo da Porta do Postigo**, at the site of another old town gate and the town's Moorish quarter.

Ponte Romana
This Roman bridge near the Praça da República owes its present design to a 17th-century restoration. The latest touch-up job was in 1989, after floods knocked down one of its pillars.

Quatro Águas
More energetic visitors can walk 2km east along the river, past the salt pans (see the boxed text 'Salt of the South' in this section) to Quatro Águas. As well as being the jumping-off point for Ilha de Tavira (see Around Tavira later in this chapter), this seaside hub has a couple of seafood restaurants

ALGARVE

(see Places to Eat) and a recently rehabilitated tuna-canning factory (now a hotel; see Places to Stay), across the river.

For information on buses to Quatro Águas, see under Ilha de Tavira.

Organised Tours

Two-hour guided walking historical tours are offered twice daily in summer for around €2.50 per person. Call ☎ 281 321 946 for reservations and details.

Two bike rental places organise bike tours: **Rent a Bike** *(Exploratio; ☎/fax 281 321 973, ☎ 919 338 226; e exploratio@netc.pt; Rua do Forno 33)* offers four-hour trips for €10 per person in and around Tavira and the Parque Natural da Ria Formosa. **Balsa** *(☎ 281 322 882; Rua Álvares Botelho 51)* offers similar trips for €7.50. With advance notice, Rent a Bike can also arrange half-day walking tours from €12.50 to €25 per person (depending on numbers).

Safari Boat *(☎ 933 683 237, 917 286 382; e safariboat@clix.pt; Cais de Santa Luzia)* offers various summertime 'nature tours' from nearby Santa Luzia (4km west of Tavira), including a full-day outing for €15 per person.

Riosul *(☎ 281 510 201; Monte Gordo)* has a pick-up point in Tavira for its jeep tours and Rio Guadiana cruises.

Special Events

Tavira's biggest festival is the Festa de Cidade held 24–25 June. Myrtle and paper flowers decorate streets throughout the entire town, free sardines are provided by the municipal authorities, and dancing and frolicking in the street continue until the wee hours.

Places to Stay – Budget

Ilha de Tavira *(☎ 281 324 455; sites per person/2 people plus tent Mon-Fri €7.50/10, Sat & Sun €14/19; open mid-Apr–mid-Oct)*, the nearest camp site, is ideally located on Ilha de Tavira (see Around Tavira), a step away from the island's huge beach, though readers complain that it gets noisy and crowded in summer. There's no car access.

The turismo can recommend available *quartos* (private rooms) – a good bet in high season, they cost from €25 to €35 a double. It also has details of self-catering alternatives within 10km of town.

Pensão Residencial Lagôas *(☎ 281 322 252; Rua Almirante Cândido dos Reis 24; doubles with/without bathroom €35/25)* is a long-standing favourite across the river, near restaurants and bars.

Pensão Residencial Almirante *(☎ 281 322 163; Rua Almirante Cândido dos Reis 51; doubles without bathroom €25)*, not far from Residencial Lagôas, is a dark but cosy family house full of clutter, with just six rooms.

Residencial Princesa do Gilão *(☎/fax 281 325 171; Rua Borda d'Água de Aguiar 10; doubles €50)* is an eye-catching riverside place with rather thin-walled rooms.

Residencial Imperial *(☎ 282 322 234; Rua Dr José Pires Padinha 24; doubles with bathroom & breakfast €40)* is bang in the centre (nearby parking is tricky).

Places to Stay – Mid-Range & Top End

Residencial Bela Fria *(☎/fax 281 325 375; e belafria@hotmail.com; Rua dos Pelames 1; doubles with breakfast €69.80)* is a soulless, modern place opposite the bus station. It has functional rooms (some with small balconies at the back) and bargain off-season rates. Beware of the Friday and Saturday karaoke nights here!

Mare's Residencial *(☎ 281 325 815; e maresresidencial@mail.telepac.pt; Rua Dr José Pires Padinha 134; doubles with breakfast €65)* is an attractive riverside establishment.

Pensão Residencial Castelo *(☎ 281 320 790, fax 281 320 799; Rua da Liberdade 22; doubles with breakfast €70, apartments with breakfast €100)* has been completely revamped and now boasts smart new rooms with air-con, plus eight spacious, modern apartments. It has wheelchair access.

Casa do Rio *(☎/fax 281 326 578, 917 356 623; e mail@tavira-inn.com; Rua Chefe António Afonso 39; doubles €55-90)* is a charming riverside spot with eclectic decor, a small salt-water swimming pool and a funky jazz bar.

Quinta do Caracol *(☎ 281 322 475; e quintadocaracol@netc.pt; São Pedro; singles/doubles €93/110)* is a 17th-century farmhouse with a large garden. Its seven rooms have been converted into separate quarters with typical Algarve furnishings (all but one with a kitchenette).

Quinta da Lua *(☎/fax 281 961 070; e quintalua@oninet.pt; Bernardinheiro, Sto Estevão;*

doubles/suites with breakfast €70/ 90) is set among orange groves 4km northwest of Tavira. It has eight rooms, each of which is uniquely and tastefully furnished, and a large salt-water swimming pool. No smoking, no TVs (but CD players in the rooms) and no animals!

Hotel Vila Galé Albacora (☎ 281 380 800; e reserv.albacora@vilagale.pt; Quatro Águas; doubles €162) is 4km east of town overlooking Ilha de Tavira. The first of a new rash of four-star hotels, this 162-room establishment, partly converted from the former tuna-canning factory and fisherfolk's houses, is low-rise and luxurious, boasting a health club and two pools. Rates drop dramatically off-season.

Places to Eat

Budget With walls adorned with Benfica football team paraphernalia, **Snack Bar A Velha 2** (☎ 281 323 661; Campo Martires da Pátria 1; dishes €4-6; open Mon-Wed, Fri & Sat) is popular with locals for its bargain fare. Go early at lunch time to get a seat.

Along Rua Almirante Cândido dos Reis are several more budget choices, including **Restaurante Bica** (☎ 281 323 843; Rua Almirante Cândido dos Reis 24), where you can eat fabulously well for under €6.50 and down cheap bottles of decent Borba wine; and **Snack-Bar Petisqueira-Belmar** (☎ 281 324 995; Rua Almirante Cândido dos Reis 16; dishes from €5; open Tues-Sun), which has rustic decor.

Churrasqueira O Manel (☎ 281 323 343; Rua Dr António Cabreira 39; dishes from €5) has great frango no churrasco (grilled chicken) and other dishes, plus a takeaway service.

Cantinho do Emigrante (☎ 281 323 696; Praça Dr Padinha 27; mains €5-7, daily specials €5) is a modest, recently spruced-up venue with tasty, good-value food.

Cafés in town include the popular hangout **Pastelaria Anazu** (Rua Jaques Pessoa; open 8.30am-around midnight Mon-Sat), with an irresistible riverside location, and **Pastelaria Tavirense** (☎ 281 323 451; Rua Dr Marcelino Franco 17), which serves the town's scrummiest pastries.

There's a huge modern **market** (most stalls open mornings only) on the eastern edge of town, and a **Pingo Doce Supermarket** across the river.

Mid-Range & Top-End The delightfully low-key **Casa de Pasto A Barquinha** (☎ 281 322 843; Rua Dr José Pires Padinha 142; dishes €6-7) has reasonable prices and friendly service. The salads are great, too.

Restaurante Avenida (☎ 281 321 113; Avenida Dr Teixeira de Azevêdo; dishes €6-10; open Wed-Mon) is less scenic but a local favourite with a generously long menu of both fish and meat dishes.

Aquasul (☎ 32 51 66; Rua Dr Augusto da Silva Carvalho 11) is the best around for great French fare.

Kudissanga (☎ 281 321 670; Dr Augusto da Silva 6) offers a change, with its menu of African and vegetarian dishes.

For seafood splurges, head to Quatro Águas where you'll find **Quatro Águas** (☎ 281 325 329; open Thur-Tues), serving delicious fare such as octopus salad (€4.70) or prawn kebabs (€11.70); or, next door, the slightly cheaper **Porto do Mar** (281 321 255; dishes €6-14); try this tasty shrimp curry (€7.20).

Fancy new restaurants can also be found inside the **Mercado da Ribeira**, the converted former market.

Entertainment

Most bars are clustered along Rua Almirante Cândido dos Reis and Rua Poeta Emiliano da Costa.

Arco Bar (Rua Almirante Cândido dos Reis 67; open Tues-Sun) has a laid-back atmosphere and multicultural clientele, while **Bar O Talabriga** (Rua Poeta Emiliano da Costa 3) is a bit smarter.

UBI (☎ 281 324 577; Rua Almirante Cândido dos Reis; open until 5am daily May-Oct, Sat & Sun Nov-Apr) is the only huge nightclub in town, with an open-air bar and music until 5am.

Getting There & Around

There are 15 trains daily between Faro and Tavira (€1.60, 35 to 50 minutes) and 11 to Vila Real de Santo António (€1.20, 35 minutes). Frequent buses, including six express runs, go to Faro (€2.20, 30 minutes) and Vila Real de Santo António (€2.10, 40 minutes). There are a dozen runs, including five alta qualidade (fast deluxe) services, to Lisbon (€14, five hours). You can get to Huelva (Spain) twice-daily for €4.10 (2 hours) with onward connections to Seville (€9.80, 3 hours).

ALGARVE

Bike rental is offered by **Lorisrent** (☎ 281 325 203, 964 079 233; Rua da Galeria 9A; open summer); **Rent a Bike** and **Balsa** (see Organised Tours, earlier). Cheap local car-rental agencies include **Mudarent** (☎ 281 326 815; Rua da Silva 18D).

Taxis (☎ 281 321 544, 917 220 456) line up near the cinema on Rua Dr Marcelino Franco.

AROUND TAVIRA
Ilha de Tavira
Part of the Parque Natural da Ria Formosa, this is one of a string of sandy islands stretching along the coast from Cacela Velha to just west of Faro. The huge beach at this island's eastern end, opposite Tavira, has a camp site as well as a string of café-restaurants, and water sports facilities in summer. During off-season, it feels incredibly remote and empty. Don't forget the sunscreen – the low dunes offer no shade.

Further west along the island is **Praia do Barril**, accessible by a miniature train that trundles over the mud flats from **Pedras d'el Rei**, a classy chalet resort 4km from Tavira. There are a couple of eateries where the

shuttle train stops, but the rest is just sand, sand, sand as far as the eye can see.

Getting There & Away Ferries make the five-minute hop to the *ilha* (€0.90 return) from Quatro Águas, 2km southeast of Tavira. Between June and mid-September they run daily from around 9am, leaving every 15 minutes (five times daily other times). The last boat back leaves at about 7pm in April, May and September, 9pm or later in July and August – check with the ferryman!

In addition, **Áqua-Taxis** (☎ 964 515 073) operates 24 hours daily from July to mid-September; until midnight May to June. The fare from Quatro Águas/Tavira to the island is €1/2 return between 8am and 9pm, and €1.80/2.50 from 9pm to 8am.

A bus goes nine times daily to Quatro Águas from the Tavira bus terminal between July and mid-September. A taxi to Quatro Águas costs about €3. For Praia do Barril, take a bus from Tavira to Pedras d'el Rei (€1.20, 10 minutes), from where the little train runs regularly to the beach from March to September. In off-season the timetable is subject to the whims of the driver.

Cacela Velha
This tiny hamlet 12km east of Tavira is still remarkably untouched by the 20th century. All you'll find here are a clutch of cottages next to gardens, olive and orange groves, a church, an old fort, a café-restaurant and a splendid view of the sea. Magically, there's nothing to do here but follow a path down the scrubby hillside to the beach, or sit on the church walls, listen to the surf and watch pigeons wheel above the olive trees.

Getting There & Away There's no direct bus service from Tavira, but Cacela Velha is only 1km south of the N125 (2km before Vila Nova de Cacela; €1.20), which is the Faro–Vila Real de Santo António bus route. Coming from Faro, there are two sign-posted turn-offs to Cacela Velha; the second is the more direct.

VILA REAL DE SANTO ANTÓNIO
postcode 8900 • pop 10,500
Vila Real de Santo António is no longer a vital frontier post and ferry-crossing point for Spain – the highway bridge over the Rio Guadiana 4km north of town allows buses

---

Salt of the South

Take plenty of sea water. Add weeks of hot sun. Let the water evaporate in specially enclosed areas. Add more water, let it evaporate and hey presto, you've got salt! This is the process, more or less, that has been followed in Portugal and elsewhere for thousands of years in order to make salt.

The Algarve's long coastline, vast salt marshes and long, hot summers make it ideal for salt production. Near Olhão, the huge Sopursal factory uses modern mechanical methods to produce some 10,000 tonnes of salt a year (about half of Portugal's entire consumption). The best quality is reserved for table salt; the rest is used to produce everything from bleach to baking soda to glass.

Just outside Tavira, en route to Quatro Águas, you can see extensive salt pans (salinas) and enormous heaps of salt piled up by tractors and left to dry; salt collection usually starts around the end of August. Many salt pans are now being transformed into fish farms to cultivate lucrative species such as sole and bream for export to northern Europe.

to whizz on to other destinations. But it's still a popular shopping destination, mainly for its cheap linen, towels and booze. It's also the base for boat or biking trips along the Rio Guadiana (see the boxed text 'Cruising & Biking Along the Guadiana').

The town itself is architecturally impressive, thanks to the Marquês de Pombal who, in a few brisk months in 1774, stamped the town with his hallmark grid pattern of streets (just like Lisbon's Baixa district) after the original town was destroyed by floods.

Orientation & Information

The seafront Avenida da República is one of the town's two main shopping and eating thoroughfares; the other is the pedestrianised Rua Teofílio de Braga, which leads straight up from the seafront and past the main square, Praça Marquês de Pombal.

The **bus station** (Avenida da República) is just beyond the ferry terminal, 100m east of Rua Teofílio de Braga. The train station is about 400m northeast of the centre.

The **turismo** (☎ 281 542 100; Rua Teofílio de Braga; open 9.30am-1pm & 2pm-5.30pm Mon-Fri, sometimes later summer) is housed in the attractive Centro Cultural António Aleixo, a former market hall.

Places to Stay & Eat

There's a municipal **parque de campismo** (☎ 281 542 588; adult/tent/car €4.20/1.80/ 2.90) in Monte Gordo – 6km west, with frequent bus connections.

The **pousada da juventude** (☎ 281 544 565; e vrsantonio@movijovem.pt; Rua Dr Sousa Martins 40; dorm beds €9.50, doubles with shared bathroom €27) is small and simple, though it does have kitchen facilities.

Residência Matos Pereira (☎ 281 543 325; Rua Dr Sousa Martins 57; doubles with bathroom €35-40), near the turismo, is friendly, and has tidy doubles.

Residência Baixa Mar (☎ 281 543 511; Rua Teofílio de Braga 3; doubles around €45) has decent rooms, though it's less homely than Residência Matos Pereira.

Among the town's tempting restaurants (most with outdoor seating) along Avenida da República is **Caves do Guadiana** (☎ 281 544 498; Avenida da República 90; dishes €6-9.50; open Fri-Wed). **Snack Bar 2000** (Rua Dr Sousa Martins 80; dishes under €6), near the turismo, is a decent, cheap option.

Getting There & Away

Bus There are at least eight buses daily to Tavira (€2.10, 40 minutes) and Faro (€3.30, one hour 40 minutes), and regular buses to Monte Gordo (€1.80, eight minutes). Four *alta qualidade* buses run to Lisbon (€14, five hours). Buses to Huelva (Spain) run twice daily (€3.50, 2½ hours), with connections on to Seville (from Vila Real de Santo António €9 total, 3½ hours).

Cruising & Biking Along the Guadiana

A great way to see Portugal and Spain at the same time is on a boat up the Rio Guadiana (which serves as the border for some 50km). The main operator is **Riosul** (☎ 281 510 200; Monte Gordo), which runs trips from Vila Real de Santo António to Foz de Odeleite at least four times weekly in summer and twice-weekly year-round. The trips cost €37.50/18 per adult/child, including lunch.

Turismar (☎ 281 513 504, 968 201 810) cruises further, to Alcoutim, three times weekly between April and October. Book a day ahead; tickets (€48/24 adult/child aged 3 to 10, including lunch) are available at its kiosk by the ferry pier in Vila Real de Santo António.

The quiet back road that hugs the river for 14km from Foz de Odeleite to Alcoutim (see the last section in this chapter) is also popular with bikers. Along this scenic route are several villages worth visiting, including Álamo, with its Roman dam, and Guerreiros do Rio, which has a small **Museu do Rio** (River Museum; ☎ 281 547 380; admission €1; open 9am-12.30pm & 1.30pm-5pm Tues-Sat), a one-room ethnological display (with English text available) of traditional river life.

Rural accommodation is available at **Umbria das Casas Velhas** (☎/fax 281 547 443; Álamo; doubles with breakfast €32).

You can rent bikes in Alcoutim or Monte Gordo (see Information in the Vila Real de Santo António section), 26km from Foz de Odeleite. Contact the boat operators in advance if you want to take your bike on the boat.

Train Eight trains daily connect the town with Lagos (€5.20, 3½ hours), all requiring changes at Faro and/or Tunes. A dozen trains run daily to Faro (€3.10, 70 minutes).

Ferry Every 40 minutes from 8.20am to 7pm daily, ferries cross the river border to white-washed Ayamonte; fares are €1/3.50/0.50 per person/car/bike.

Getting Around
The nearest place to rent bikes is in Monte Gordo, from **Riosul** (☎ 281 510 201). Bikes can be delivered if you call in advance.

CASTRO MARIM
postcode 8950 • pop 6600
This village 5km north of Vila Real de Santo António is entirely dominated by its huge castle. The battlements provide a ring-side seat for gazing out over the fens and marshes of the **Reserva Natural do Sapal** (see the boxed text), the bridge to Spain, and the pretty village.

There are few facilities in the village but it makes a pleasant stopover en route north or as a day trip from Vila Real, and is especially rewarding if you're a bird-watcher – the nature reserve is famous for its flamingos.

Orientation & Information
The **turismo** (☎ 281 531 232; Praça 1 de Maio 2-4; open 9.30am-12.30pm & 2pm-5.30pm Mon-Fri, 9am-noon Sat May-Sept; closed Sat & Sun Oct-Apr) is right below the castle in the centre of the village.

Inside the castle are the offices of **Odiana** (☎/fax 281 531 171; e odiana@mail.telepac .pt), an organisation promoting the Baixo (lower) Guadiana region. It sells an attractive brochure (€5; also available at the turismo) detailing the culture and history of the region, with six suggested day trips in the area.

Castelo
Castro Marim's castle (admission free; open 9am-5pm daily Nov-Mar, 9am-7pm Apr-Oct) was built by Dom Afonso III in the 13th century on the site of Roman and Moorish fortifications. In 1319 it became the first headquarters of the religious military order known as the Order of Christ, a revamped version of the Knights Templar (see the boxed text 'The Order of the Knights Templar' under Tomar in the Estremadura & Ribatejo chapter). Until they moved their base to Tomar in 1334, the soldiers of the Order of Christ used this castle to keep watch over the estuary of the Rio Guadiana and the frontier with Spain – where the Moors were still in power.

The ruins you see today, however, date from the 17th century, when Dom João IV ordered the addition of vast ramparts. At the same time a smaller fort, the **Castelo de São Sebastião**, was built on a nearby hill top (plans are afoot to restore this ruin). Much in the area was destroyed in the 1755 earthquake, but the hill-top ruins of the main fort are still pretty awesome.

Inside the wonderfully derelict castle walls is a small **Museu Arqueológico** (admission free; open 10am-1pm & 3pm-6pm daily May-Sept, 10am-1pm & 2pm-5pm Oct-Apr). There's also a 14th-century church, the **Igreja de Santiago**, where Henry the Navigator, who was also Grand Master of the Order of Christ, is said to have prayed.

Now You See Me, Now You Don't...

The Mediterranean chameleon (Chamaeleo chamaeleon) is a bizarre 25cm-long reptile with independently moving eyes, a tongue that's longer than its body and a skin that changes colour according to its environment (from bright yellow to jet black). It only started creeping around southern Portugal about 75 years ago, probably introduced from North Africa. Strictly protected, it is the only type of chameleon found in Europe, with a habitat limited to Crete and the Iberian Peninsula. Its only home in Portugal is in the leeward Algarve, where it hides out in pine groves and coastal shrublands.

Your best chance of seeing this shy creature is in the Quinta de Marim area of the Parque Natural da Ria Formosa or in Monte Gordo's conifer woods, now a protected habitat for the species. Hibernating from December to March (the only other time it comes down to ground level is in October to lay its eggs), the chameleon is most commonly seen on spring mornings, slowly clambering along branches.

Reserva Natural do Sapal de Castro Marim e Vila Real de Santo António

Established in 1975, this nature reserve is the oldest in Portugal, covering some 20 sq km of marshland and commercial salt pans bordering the Rio Guadiana north of Vila Real. Among its most important winter visitors are greater flamingos, spoonbills, avocets and Caspian terns. In spring you can see dozens of white storks.

The park's **administrative office** (☎ 281 510 680, fax 281 531 257; Sapal de Venta Moínhos; open 9am-12.30pm & 2pm-5.30pm Mon-Fri) is 2km from Monte Francisco (a five-minute bus ride north of Castro Marim); get directions from the turismo at Castro Marim as there are no signs.

There's some accommodation in the park but it's popular with botanists and bird-watching groups, so you need to book ahead. Another rewarding area for spotting the park's birdlife is around Cerro do Bufo, 2km southwest of Castro Marim. Staff at the park office and at Castro Marim's turismo can provide details.

The best time to see the castle is during the Feira Mediéval, which takes place for three days in early September.

Places to Stay & Eat

There's no accommodation in the village. If you're keen to study the flora or fauna of the park, your best bet is the quiet **Vila do Sol** (☎ 281 531 597; villas €60), self-catering villas in Vista Real, a few kilometres northwest of Castro Marim. Ask at the turismo for details. There are several reasonable restaurants on Rua de São Sebastião, just west of the turismo.

Getting There & Away

Buses from Vila Real de Santo António make the run to Castro Marim (€1.80, eight minutes) and on to Monte Francisco, a short distance north, around seven times daily on weekdays.

The Central Coast

LOULÉ

postcode 8100 • pop 12,100
• elevation 160m

Loulé (lo-leh), 16km northwest of Faro, is a former Roman and Moorish settlement with an attractive old quarter and castle ruins. One of the Algarve's largest inland towns, it's become a popular destination for tour groups every Saturday, thanks to its big weekly open-air market and its reputation as a centre for handicrafts. Its laid-back atmosphere and great selection of restaurants make it a pretty decent overnight stay.

Orientation

The bus station is about 250m north of the centre. The train station is 5km southwest (take any Quarteira-bound bus). If you're coming by car on market day (Saturday), get there early or you'll have nightmarish parking problems.

Information

The **turismo** (☎ 289 463 900; open 9.30am-1.30pm & 2pm-5.30pm Mon-Fri Sept-June; 9.30am-7pm Mon-Fri, 9.30am-3.30pm Sat July-Aug) is inside the converted ruins of the castle.

You can connect to the Internet at **Ciber Espaço** (☎ 289 415 860; Casa da Cultura, Praça da República 36; open noon-9pm Mon-Fri) for €1 per half-hour.

Castelo

The restored castle ruins house the **Museu Municipal de Arqueológica** (admission €1; open 9am-5.30pm Mon-Fri, 10am-2pm Sat), beside the turismo, which contains fine fragments of Bronze Age and Roman ceramics. The admission fee includes entry to a stretch of the castle walls and the **Cozinha Tradicional Algarvia** (open 9am-5.30pm Mon-Fri, 10am-2pm Sat), a traditional Algarve kitchen display up the steps from the museum.

Activities

Crazy Horse Ranch (☎ 289 415 051, 962 685 293; Vale do Telheiro), a few kilometres north, offers outings ranging from a two-hour cross-country 'safari trek' (€30) to a two-day, all-inclusive trip to Rocha da Pena, including an overnight camp below the cliffs (€170).

ALGARVE

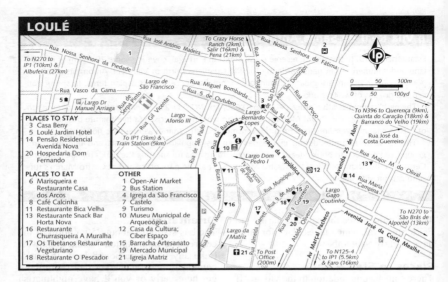

LOULÉ

PLACES TO STAY
3 Casa Beny
5 Loulé Jardim Hotel
14 Pensão Residencial
Avenida Nova
20 Hospedaria Dom
Fernando

PLACES TO EAT
6 Marisqueira e
Restaurante Casa
dos Arcos
8 Café Calcinha
11 Restaurante Bica Velha
13 Restaurante Snack Bar
Horta Nova
16 Restaurante
Churrasqueira A Muralha
17 Os Tibetanos Restaurante
Vegetariano
18 Restaurante O Pescador

OTHER
1 Open-Air Market
2 Bus Station
4 Igreja da São Francisco
7 Castelo
9 Turismo
10 Museu Municipal de
Arqueoógica
12 Casa da Cultura;
Ciber Espaço
15 Barracha Artesanato
19 Mercado Municipal
21 Igreja Matriz

Special Events

On weekdays and outside high season, Loulé is a pretty dozy place. But come Carnaval time (late February or early March) it's livelier than almost anywhere else in the Algarve, with parades and tractor-drawn floats, and lots of dancing and singing.

Another major but far more sombre event is the *romaria* (religious festival) of Nossa Senhora da Piedade. Linked to ancient maternity rites, it's probably the Algarve's most important religious festival. On Easter Sunday a 16th-century image of Our Lady of Pity (or Piety) is carried down from its hill-top chapel, 2km north of town, to the parish church. Two weeks later, a much larger procession of devotees lines the steep route to the chapel to witness and accompany the return of the image to its home. The eye-catching modern Igreja de Nossa Senhora da Piedade, next to this old chapel, was completed in 1995 and now dominates the skyline.

Places to Stay

Hospedaria Dom Fernando (☎ 289 415 553, fax 289 463 781; Travessa do Mercado 1; singles/doubles €25/38), a characterless place has small, modern doubles with air-con. If no-one answers the door, ask at the nearby Restaurante O Pescador (see Places to Eat).

Pensão Residencial Avenida Nova (☎ 289 415 097, 289 416 406; Rua Maria Campina 1; doubles/triples/quads without bathroom €25/35/40, double with private shower €30) is rambling and old-fashioned, with big, squeaky-floored rooms. It's great value, especially for families.

Casa Beny (☎ 289 417 702; Rua São Domingos 13; doubles around €50) is a new Spanish-run addition, with seven tastefully decorated rooms with air-con in a finely restored old house. The rooftop view of the castle and sea beyond are fantastic.

Loulé Jardim Hotel (☎ 289 413 094, fax 289 463 177; Largo Dr Manuel Arriaga; singles/doubles €49/63), a late-19th-century building with comfortable, modernised rooms, has the quietest location (plus a small swimming pool).

Quinta do Coração (☎/fax 289 489 959; e info@algarveparadise.com; Carrasqueiro; doubles €49, studio €55, apartment €59; minimum stay 2 nights) is a fantastic choice if you're into quiet, dramatic wilderness. A converted old farmhouse 18km north of Loulé, 7km east of Salir and 1.8km off the road (down a very potholed track!), it's surrounded by hills of olive groves. Accommodation is simple and rural; the surroundings majestic. Rates include a chic breakfast.

Places to Eat

Restaurante O Pescador (☎ 289 462 821; Rua José F Guerreiro; dishes €6-12) is the place for a good family hubbub (especially on market days), big helpings and reasonable prices.

Os Tibetanos Restaurante Vegetariano (☎ 289 462 067; Rua Almeida Garrett 6; set menu €7.50; open Mon-Sat) has a small selection of vegie delights (tofu curry, goat cheese rissoles, salads); check the set menu.

Restaurante Snack Bar Horta Nova (☎ 289 462 429; Rua Major Manuel do Olival; dishes €3.50-10; open Mon-Sat) offers open-air dining in a walled garden and specialises in home-made pizzas (€3.50 to €6.50), and charcoal-grilled meat and fish (€4 to €10).

Marisqueira e Restaurante Casa dos Arcos (☎ 289 416 713; Rua Sá de Miranda 23-25; dishes €5-10; open Mon-Sat) is a deceptively unpretentious place, with an impressive menu, including everything from lobster to crab, and swordfish steak to filet mignon.

Restaurante Churrasqueira A Muralha (☎ 289 412 629; Rua Martim Moniz 41; dishes €7-12; open Tues-Sat, dinner Mon), in the shadow of the old town walls, is a popular venue with a wide range of regional favourites and an attractive little garden.

Restaurante Bica Velha (☎ 289 463 376; Rua Martim Moniz 17; open lunch & dinner daily by prior reservation), near Churrasqueira A Muralha, is the place for a splurge. It has the best reputation in town for typical Algarve specialities such as *cataplanas*.

Café Calcinha (☎ 289 415 763; Praça da República 67) is a rare example of a traditional 1950s-style café, complete with ceiling fans, wooden chairs and marble-topped tables.

Shopping
Many of Loulé's excellent arts and crafts – especially leather goods, brass and copperware, wooden and cane furniture – are made and sold in craft shops along Rua da Barbaca (behind the castle). Loulé's biggest copperware shop, **Barracha Artesanato**, is right by the **mercado municipal**, which also has several traditional craft stalls.

On Saturday morning head for the tourist-geared open-air market west of town, where you'll find loads of cheap clothes, shoes, toys and souvenirs.

Getting There & Away
Both Faro and Lagos-bound trains stop at Loulé station (5km out of town) at least

---

Where Eagle Owls Fly

In the foothills of the Serra do Caldeirão, 21km northwest of Loulé, is the Rocha da Pena, a 479m-high limestone outcrop marked as a classified site because of its rich flora and fauna. Orchids, narcissi and native cistus cover the slopes, where red foxes and Egyptian mongooses are common. Among many bird species seen here are the huge eagle owl, Bonelli's eagle and the buzzard.

A *centro ambiental* (environmental centre) has been established in the village of Pena, and there's a 4.7km circular walking trail starting from Rocha, 1km from Pena.

---

eight times daily. More conveniently, there are frequent bus connections from Faro (€1.80, 40 minutes, every half-hour), about seven buses daily from Albufeira (€2.60, 40 minutes) and three departing from Portimão (€3.60, one hour 40 minutes). Four *alta qualidade* services run daily to Lisbon (€13.50, 4¾ hours); change at Albufeira.

ALBUFEIRA
postcode 8200 • pop 13,700
This once-pretty fishing village now epitomises the success of Algarve mass-market tourism, catering almost entirely for tourists. Its narrow streets are chock-a-block with souvenir shops, bars and restaurants, while towers of apartment hotels and holiday flats cover the surrounding hillsides. Albufeira's modern extension is Montechoro, located 3km to the east, where 'The Strip', which leads up from Praia da Oura and crosses the resort area of Areias de São João, is jam-packed with even more shops, bars and restaurants.

The extensive beaches are still a big attraction, however, and there is a picturesque quality to the old town's steep, narrow back streets and its small fishing harbour. During the summer it has a great resort atmosphere, with buskers and artisan stalls in the street by day and plenty of entertainment at night.

If you want to forget you're in Portugal (you'll hear more English and German than Portuguese), Albufeira may be just the ticket for a hassle-free holiday with all-day bargain breakfasts, shopping galore, beer on tap and football on TV.

ALGARVE

Orientation

Albufeira's 'historic centre' lies below the busy N526 (Avenida dos Descobrimentos). Its focal point is Largo Engenheiro Duarte Pacheco, where most of the cafés, bars and restaurants are clustered. But sprawled to the north and east of this old town is modern-day Albufeira: the market, new bus station and main police station are almost 2km north and new shopping centres are 2km east. The train station is 6km north at Ferreiras, connected to the bus station by shuttle bus.

Information

Tourist Offices The turismo (☎ 289 585 279; Rua 5 de Outubro; open 9.30am-7pm Mon-Fri May-Sept, 9.30am-12.30pm & 1.30pm-5.30pm Oct-Apr) is by a tunnel that leads to the beach.

Money Along and near Avenida 25 de Abril are several banks with ATMs, including **Banco Português do Atlântico** (Largo Engenheiro Duarte Pacheco 23), and no-commission private exchange bureaus.

Post & Communications The **post office** (Rua 5 de Outubro; open 9am-12.30pm & 2pm-6pm Mon-Fri) also has NetPost.

Windcafe.com (☎ 289 586 451; 2nd floor, Centro Comercial California, Rua Cândido dos Reis 12; open 10am-10pm daily May-Sept,

10.30am-7pm Oct-Apr), next to Hotel California, is a tiny Internet café where you can also have a coffee or browse the second-hand books on sale. Internet access costs €1.30 per 15 minutes.

H@ppynet NetKafé (☎ 967 964 953; Rua 5 de Outubro 87B; open 10am-midnight daily Sept-June, 9am-1am July & Aug) charges €2.50 per hour and also has a relaxing lounge-bar.

Bookshops For second-hand books of everything from English to Swahili, check **Centro de Livros do Algarve** (☎ 289 513 773; Rua da Igreja Nova 6). The kiosks around Largo Engenheiro Duarte Pacheco stock a wide range of international newspapers and magazines.

Medical Services & Emergency The **centro de saúde** (medical centre; ☎ 289 587 550; open 24hr) is 2km north of the old town. There's a private **Clioura Clinic** (☎ 289 587 000; open 24hr) in Montechoro.

The **GNR police station** (☎ 289 587 809; Estrada Vale de Pedras) is north of town, near the mercado municipal. There's a more central **GNR police post** (☎ 289 513 203; Avenida 25 de Abril 22; open 9am-noon & 2pm-5pm daily), which also serves as a Gabinete de Apoio à Vítima (office to help victims) next to Hotel Baltum.

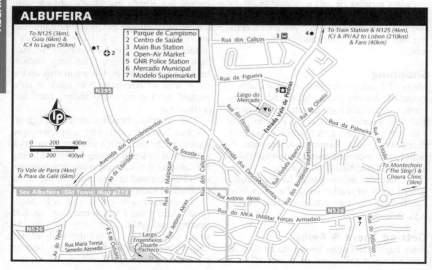

ALBUFEIRA

1 Parque de Campismo
2 Centro de Saúde
3 Main Bus Station
4 Open-Air Market
5 GNR Police Station
6 Mercado Municipal
7 Modelo Supermarket

To N125 (3km),
Guia (6km) &
IC4 to Lagos (50km)

Rua dos Caliços

To Train Station & N125 (4km),
ICI & IPI/A2 to Lisbon (210km)
& Faro (40km)

Rua da Figueira

Largo do
Mercado

N395

Rua das Escolas

Rua da Oliveira

Estrada Vale de Pedras

Rua da Palmeira

0   200   400m
0   200   400yd

Avenida dos Descobrimentos

Rua da Encosta

Avenida dos Descobrimentos

Av da Liberdade

To Vale de Parra (4km)
& Praia da Galé (6km)

Rua da Malpique

Rua dos Caliços

Rua Florbela Espanca

Rua dos Bombeiros Voluntários

To Montechoro
('The Strip') &
Clioura Clinic
(3km)

See Albufeira (Old Town) Map p213

Rua António Aleixo

Rua do MFA (Militar Forças Armadas)

N526

N526

Av do Ténis

R5 de Outubro

Rua Maria Teresa
Semedo Azevedo

Largo
Engenheiro
Duarte
Pacheco

Rua do Estádio

Rua do Atlântico

ALGARVE

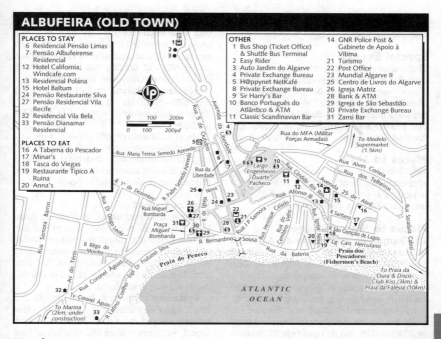

ALBUFEIRA (OLD TOWN)

PLACES TO STAY
6 Residencial Pensão Limas
7 Pensão Albufeirense Residencial
12 Hotel California; Windcafe.com
13 Residencial Polana
15 Hotel Baltum
24 Pensão Restaurante Silva
27 Pensão Residencial Vila Recife
32 Residencial Vila Bela
33 Pensão Dianamar Residencial

PLACES TO EAT
16 A Taberna do Pescador
17 Minar's
18 Tasca do Viegas
19 Restaurante Tipico A Ruína
20 Anna's

OTHER
1 Bus Shop (Ticket Office) & Shuttle Bus Terminal
2 Easy Rider
3 Auto Jardim do Algarve
4 Private Exchange Bureau
5 H@ppynet NetKafé
8 Private Exchange Bureau
9 Sir Harry's Bar
10 Banco Português do Atlântico & ATM
11 Classic Scandinavian Bar
14 GNR Police Post & Gabinete de Apoio à Vítima
21 Turismo
22 Post Office
23 Mundial Algarve II
25 Centro de Livros do Algarve
26 Igreja Matriz
28 Bank & ATM
29 Igreja de São Sebastião
30 Private Exchange Bureau
31 Zansi Bar

ATLANTIC OCEAN

Beaches

Albufeira's entire seafront is now pedestrianised, making seaside strolls very attractive. The town's beach, **Praia do Peneco**, through the tunnel near the turismo, is pleasant but often packed. For a bit of local flavour, head 400m east to **Praia dos Pescadores** (Fishermen's Beach, also called Praia dos Barcos), where there's still a hint of Albufeira's fishing past, with fishermen mending their nets beside their high-prowed and brightly painted boats.

Further afield – both east and west of the town – there are numerous beautifully rugged coves and bays, though the nearest are heavily developed and often crowded. The easiest to reach is **Praia da Oura**, 3km to the east (roughly 30 minutes on foot; follow Avenida 25 de Abril and climb the steps at the end to reach the road to the beach).

Between Praia da Oura and **Praia da Falésia**, 10km to the east, is a string of less crowded beaches, including **Balaia** and **Olhos de Água**. There's over a dozen buses every weekday to Olhos de Água (€1.20, 10 minutes), all but three of which continue to Praia da Falésia (€1.80, 20 minutes).

One of the best beaches to the west, **Praia da Galé**, about 6km away, is a centre for jet-skiing and water-skiing. There's no direct bus service to this beach or the others en route, though local buses to Portimão do run along the main road about 2km above the beaches (get off at Vale de Parra).

Activities

Zebra Safari (☎ 289 583 300; e zebrasafari@ mail.telepac.pt) organises full-day jeep safaris (€49 per person) as well as a Zebra Adventure Day (€60 per person, available from May to October only) including mountain biking, canoeing, hiking and abseiling. **Riosul** (☎ 281 510 201; Monte Gordo) can whizz you off for its one-day Super Safari (€49), including a cruise up the Rio Guadiana.

Zoomarine (☎ 289 560 300; adult/child 5-10 €14.50/9.50; open 10am-7.30pm daily July-Sept, 10am-6pm Apr-June & Sept-Oct, 10am-5pm Jan-Mar & Nov-Dec) at Guia, 8km northwest, has huge swimming pools and slides plus dolphin, seal and parrot 'performances'.

You can book any of these, and more, at **Mundial Algarve II** (☎ 289 510 480; Rua

ALGARVE

Joaquim Mendonça Gouveia 14), which is near the turismo.

Special Events
The major local festival is the Festa da Ourada on 14 August, honouring the fishermen's patron saint, Nossa Senhora da Ourada (Our Lady of the Oracle), with a procession from the parish church along the seaside promenade, culminating in a midnight fireworks display over Praia dos Pescadores.

Places to Stay
You'll need to book well ahead to bag accommodation in the high season. Off-season, many places close. The following prices are for July (August is higher).

Places to Stay – Budget
The **Parque de Campismo de Albufeira** *(☎ 289 587 629, fax 289 587 633; adult/tent/car €4.70/4.70/4.20)*, near Alpouvar, 2km north of town, is well equipped.

There are dozens of *quartos* (the turismo has a list), most costing around €30 a double.

Recommended budget *residenciais* include the central **Residencial Pensão Limas** *(☎ 289 514 025; Rua da Liberdade 25; doubles around €50)* and **Pensão Albufeirense Residencial** *(☎ 289 512 079; Rua da Liberdade 18; doubles around €50)*.

Pensão Restaurante Silva *(☎ 289 512 669; Travessa 5 de Outubro 21; full board €75)* also has cheap rooms but only accepts full board in high season (July and August).

Places to Stay – Mid-Range & Top End
A stroll westwards along the seafront to the picturesque old fishing quarter brings you to several quieter *residenciais*, including the charming, Scandinavian-run **Pensão Dianamar Residencial** *(☎ 289 587 801; e info@dianamar.com; Rua Latino Coelho 36; doubles €40-50)*, which sports a sun terrace, bar and Internet facility. Half the rooms have sea views and most have a private balcony. Credit cards are not accepted.

Residencial Vila Bela *(☎ 289 515 535, fax 289 512 101; Rua Coronel Águas 32; doubles around €70)* is very pretty and popular. Most of the rooms have balconies, and there's a swimming pool.

In the same price bracket (but often block-booked by tour groups) is the more

central and cute-looking **Pensão Residencial Vila Recife** *(☎/fax 289 587 182; Rua Miguel Bombarda 12; doubles with breakfast around €70)* and mainstream **Hotel Baltum** *(☎ 289 589 102, fax 289 586 146; Avenida 25 de Abril 26; doubles with breakfast €52)*.

Residencial Polana *(☎ 289 583 400, fax 289 583 450; Rua Cândido dos Reis 32; doubles with breakfast €102)* is in the thick of the bar area.

Hotel California *(☎ 289 583 400; e hotelcalifornia@mail.telepac.pt; Rua Cândido dos Reis 12; doubles with breakfast €107)* is under the same management as Residencial Polana, but is slightly more posh.

Places to Eat
You can find just about everything here, from all-day €4 breakfasts, pizzas and pub grub to seafood splurges and Indian, Italian and Irish cuisine. One of the neatest dining areas is Largo Cais Herculano, an irresistible suntrap of outdoor tables overlooking Praia dos Pescadores.

Restaurante Tipico A Ruína *(☎ 289 512 094; Largo Cais Herculano; dishes €10-15)* is the priciest and most traditional place, with superb sea views from the rooftop terrace (or a pleasantly rustic setting inside).

Tasca do Viegas *(☎ 289 514 087; dishes €9-10)* is more laid-back than Tipico A Ruína, with an extensive menu of everything from prawns to steaks.

Anna's *(☎ 289 513 558; Rua Nova 7; dishes €9-12)*, in a quieter setting, offers more unusual fare: how about Caribbean curried prawns (€12) or cajun popcorn (€6.50)?

Minar's *(☎ 289 513 196; Rua Diogo Cão; dishes from €4.50)*, a big, smartish venue, offers good Indian fare, including vegetarian options.

A Taberna do Pescador *(☎ 289 589 196; Travessa Cais Herculano; grills from €5.50)* is a fun, cavernous place specialising in grilled fish.

There is a **Modelo supermarket** *(Rua do Militar Forças Armadas)* northeast of town.

Entertainment
Summertime events include tourist-oriented bullfights every Saturday from Easter to September in the Praia da Oura bullring, and live dance or music shows Tuesday, Friday and Saturday nights in Largo Engenheiro Duarte Pacheco.

ALGARVE

Bars are a dime a dozen around Largo Engenheiro Duarte Pacheco and nearby Rua Cândido dos Reis. Nearly all offer happy hours (at various times of the day) and stay open until at least 4am in summer.

Classic Scandinavian Bar *(Rua Cândido dos Reis 10)* has great music and vibes (plus rudely named, zany cocktails).

Zansi Bar *(Rua Miguel Bombarda)* has darts, snooker and satellite TV (including sports channels), as well as pizzas, hamburgers and other grub.

Sir Harry's Bar *(Largo Engenheiro Duarte Pacheco 37)* is one of the older (and pricier) British-style pubs, with the best of British brews on tap.

Disco-Club Kiss (☎ 289 515 639), one of the Algarve's most famous clubs, is at Praia da Oura. Thursday night (around 1am) gives the gals male striptease shows.

Shopping

An open-air market – mostly clothes and shoes – is held on the first and third Tuesday of the month near the new bus station, 2km north of the old town.

Getting There & Away

The bad news is that the **main bus station** (☎ 289 589 755) is now 2km north of town, on Rua dos Caliços. The good news? There's a helpful **Bus Shop** (☎ 289 588 122; *Avenida da Liberdade; open 6.30am-8pm Mon-Sat, 8am-7.30pm Sun)* where you can buy your tickets. Shuttle buses leave from outside the Bus Shop every 15 minutes between 7am and 8pm to the main terminal (free, on presentation of onward bus tickets; otherwise €0.50). The only buses still coming to Avenida da República are expresses to Lisbon. The following services all leave from the new terminal.

To Lagos, there are six daily Linha Litoral services (€4.30, 75 minutes) and six *transrápido* express services (€3.30, 65 minutes), both via Portimão. Around a dozen buses go to Faro daily, including six *transrápidos* (€3, 40 minutes). Eight services run to Silves daily and six to Loulé (both €2.60, 40 minutes). All services are reduced at weekends.

Services to Lisbon (some requiring a change of bus at Vale do Paraíso) include four *alta qualidade* services (€13.50, 3½ hours) and six Renex *expressos* daily (€13,

3¾ hours). There are four runs daily to Évora (€9.50, 4½ hours) and two to Huelva in Spain (€7.70, 4¼ hours, via Faro), with onward connections to Seville.

Trains include three daily IR services to Lagos (€2.70) and seven IR or IC services a day to Faro (€1.60) – beware of the tedious local services. There are six trains daily to nearby Tunes, from where you can pick up connecting services to Lisbon.

Getting Around

To reach the train station, take the *estação* (station) shuttle bus (€1.20, 10 minutes), which leaves once or twice an hour (less at weekends) between 6.45am and 8pm from the new bus terminal.

A major car rental agency is **Auto Jardim do Algarve** (☎ 289 580 500, fax 289 587 780; *Avenida da Liberdade)* in the Edifício Brisa. **Easy Rider** (☎ 289 501 102; *Avenida da Liberdade 115)* rents mountain bikes for €10 per day and scooters from €19 per day.

CARVOEIRO

Flanked by cliffs, backed by hills and surrounded by an ever-expanding collection of shops, bars and restaurants, this small seaside resort 5km south of Lagoa has grown in 20 years from a little-known fishing village to one of the Algarve's most popular self-catering holiday areas, with estates of foreign-owned villas sprawled across the hillsides. The town itself is a laid-back spot compared to resorts such as Albufeira, though the summertime tourist invasion tends to suffocate the place.

Orientation & Information

Buses from Lagoa stop right by the beach, beside a small **turismo** (☎ 282 357 728; *open 9.30am-1pm & 2pm-5.30pm Mon-Sat, later summer)*. The post office and several banks are on Rua dos Pescadores (the one-way road in from Lagoa).

Beaches

The town's little beach, **Praia do Carvoeiro**, bordered by several cafés, is set in a picturesque cove. About 1km east on the coastal road is the bay of **Algar Seco**, a favourite stop on the tour-bus itinerary thanks to its dramatic rock formations.

If you're looking for a stunning swimming spot, it's worth continuing several kilometres

ALGARVE

east along the main road, Estrada do Farol, to **Praia de Centianes**, where the secluded cliff-wrapped beach is almost as dramatic as Algar Seco. Buses heading for **Praia do Carvalho** (nine a day from Lagoa, via Carvoeiro) pass nearby – ask for Colina Sol Aparthotel, the massive Moorish-style clifftop hotel.

Activities
The nearest water park is **Slide & Splash** *(open 10am-7pm daily)*, 2km west of Lagoa.

Golfers have a choice of three nearby courses: nine-hole **Gramacho** and neighbouring 18-hole **Pinta** *(both at Pestana Golf Resort;* ☎ *282 340 900, fax 282 340 901)*; and the challenging nine-hole **Vale de Milho** *(☎ 282 358 502;* e *gericonstroi@mail.telepac .pt)* near Praia de Centianes, east of town, with some of the Algarve's best-value play (€19/30 for nine/18 holes). The **David Leadbetter Golf Academy** *(☎ 282 340 900;* e *sales@pestanagolf.com)*, in the heart of the Pinta course, can arrange golfing packages.

Divers Cove *(☎ 282 356 594;* e *info@ diverscove.de; Quinta do Paraíso)* is a family-run diving centre offering a three-hour introductory pool course (€44.90), or two-/four-day PADI courses (€194.60/344.30).

Places to Stay
Among the most attractive *quartos* and studios are those belonging to a Canadian woman, **Brigitte Lemieux** *(☎/fax 282 356 318; Rampa da Nossa Senhora da Encarnação 4; doubles per day/week €45/300, studio €55/375, apartment €60/400)* – facing the sea take the steep road up to the left from the beach. A double comes with sea view, fridge and toaster.

Casa von Baselli *(☎ 282 357 159; Rua da Escola; doubles with breakfast €35-40)* is a cosy five-room place around the corner from Brigitte Lemieux. Rooms have shared bathroom.

Hotel Carvoeiro Sol *(☎ 282 357 301;* e *car voeirosol@mail.telepac.pt; doubles €109-164)*, right by the beach, boasts all-frills rooms with satellite TV and air-con, and a pool. Rates drop by half in winter.

Places to Eat
There are loads of restaurants in the main part of town and along Estrada do Farol.

Curva do Casino *(☎ 282 357 596; Rua do Casino 36; dishes around €9; open Tues-Sat)*,

up the hill from the post office, is friendly and low-key, with a select menu of imaginative sauce-adorned dishes.

Mitch's Restaurant & Bar *(☎ 282 356 379, Rua dos Pescadores 104; dishes €10-14; open Wed-Sun)* has great jazz music and a terrace; there's tapas and sushi at the bar, a daily fresh vegetarian dish (€10) and richer fare such as fillet steak with truffle sauce (€14).

Getting There & Around
Buses run almost every 20 minutes on weekdays from Portimão to Lagoa (€1.20, 20 minutes) from where there are over a dozen connections daily to Carvoeiro (€0.60, 10 minutes).

There's a taxi rank at the bottom of Estrada do Farol. You can rent bicycles, scooters and motorbikes from **Motorent** *(☎ 282 356 551; Rua do Barranco)* on the road back to Lagoa. Several car-rental agencies are also along this road.

SILVES
postcode 8300 • pop 5900
It's hard to believe now, but this small town beside the silted-up Rio Arade, 15km northeast of Portimão, was once the Moorish capital of the Algarve. Its imposing red stone castle towers above the rapidly developing town, a powerful reminder of the past.

Geometric patterns in ornate white-washed chimney pots like this show Moorish influence

These days, Silves is embracing tourism with enthusiasm, its cobbled pedestrianised streets sporting an increasing number of restaurants and souvenir shops.

Silves has recently launched major redevelopment schemes (due to end in 2005), including a riverside promenade, new bus terminal, car park, and general tarting-up of the castle and old town.

History

From the mid-11th to mid-13th centuries, Shelb (or Xelb) as it was then known, rivalled Lisbon in prosperity and influence: according to the 12th-century Arab geographer Idrisi, it had a population of 30,000, a port and shipyards, and 'attractive buildings and well-furnished bazaars'.

Its downfall began in June 1189 when Dom Sancho I laid siege to it, supported by a horde of (mostly English) hooligan crusaders who had been persuaded (with the promise of loot) to pause in their journey to Jerusalem and give Sancho a hand. The Moors holed up inside their impregnable castle, but after three hot months of harassment they finally ran out of water and were forced to surrender. Sancho was all for mercy and honour, but the crusaders would have none of it – they stripped the Moors of their possessions as they left (including the clothes on their backs), tortured those remaining and wrecked the town.

Two years later the Moors exacted their revenge by recapturing the place. It wasn't until 1249 that Christians gained control once and for all. But by then Silves was a shadow of its former self.

Orientation & Information

The centre of Silves is 2km north of the train station, a mostly downhill walk on a busy highway. Buses stop on the riverfront road at the bottom of town, crossing the Rio Arade on a modern bridge slightly upriver from a picturesque 13th-century version (now for pedestrians only).

It's a steep but short climb from here to the **turismo** (☎ 282 442 255; Rua 25 de Abril; usually open 9.30am-1pm & 2pm-5.30pm Mon-Fri).

Things to See

The **castelo** (castle; adult/child under 12 €1.30/free; open 9am-7pm daily May-Sept,

9am-5.30pm Oct-Apr) is the town's highlight, with great views over the town and surrounding countryside. Restored in 1835, its chunky red sandstone walls enclose a dull garden and some archaeological digs that reveal a bit more of the site's Roman and pre-Roman past. The Moorish occupation is recalled by a deep well and a vast pink, vaulted water cistern (still in use today).

Just below the castle is the **sé** (cathedral; admission free; open 8.30am-6.30pm daily), built in 1189 on the site of an earlier mosque, rebuilt after the 1249 Reconquista and subsequently restored several times. The stark, fortress-like building has only a few of its original Gothic touches left, including the nave and aisles. Apart from several fine tombs (probably of 13th-century crusaders) there's little of interest inside.

Just below the cathedral, the impressive **Museu de Arqueologia** (Archaeological Museum; Rua das Portas de Loulé; adult/student €1.50/free; open 9am-6pm Mon-Sat) offers some intriguing glimpses into Silves' illustrious history. Its centrepiece is an original, 10m-deep Moorish well.

The award-winning **Museu da Cortiça** (Cork Museum; adult/child 7-12 €1.50/1; open 9.30am-12.45pm & 2pm-6.15pm daily) is housed inside the Fábrica do Inglês (English Factory; see Entertainment). The museum has excellent bilingual displays on the process and history of cork production, a major industry in Silves for 150 years until the factory's closure in the mid-1990s, largely due to the silting-up of the Rio Arade.

Activities

For information on river cruises up the Rio Arade to Silves, see Portimão later in this chapter. At **Quinta Penedo** (☎ 282 332 466; Vale Fuzeiros), 13km to the northeast, you can ride horses through lovely fruit farm countryside (€15 for one hour).

Special Events

For 10 days in late June the Festival da Cerveja (Beer Festival) is held at the Fábrica do Inglês accompanied by music, folk dance and other entertainment.

Places to Stay

Residencial Sousa (☎ 282 442 502; Rua Samoura Barros 17; singles/doubles around €15/30), in the heart of the old town, is a

ALGARVE

run-down, old-fashioned place, sometimes plagued by street noise. Rooms have shared bathroom.

Residencial Restaurante Ponte Romana (☎ 282 443 275; singles/doubles €15/30) is far more appealing, set beside the old bridge. Its rooms have private bathroom – choose one of the riverside rooms with fantastic castle views. Renovation plans may increase rates.

Vila Sodre (☎/fax 282 443 441; Estrada de Messines; singles/doubles with breakfast €25/60) is a pretty blue-and-white villa 1.4km east of the new bridge. Rather brash and impersonal, it does boast a swimming pool and rooms with air-con.

If you're after rural tranquillity, head 5km northeast (en route to São Bartolomeu de Messines) to Sítio São Estevão, where you'll find the charming **Quinta do Rio** (☎/fax 282 445 528; doubles with breakfast €50), a restored farmhouse set among orange groves.

Places to Eat

There are plenty of café-restaurants in the pedestrianised streets leading up to the castle or down by the river where you'll also find a reasonable market (just west of the old pedestrian bridge).

Ú Monchiqueiro (☎ 282 442 142; dishes €6-8), by the river, is geared largely for groups but serves a very decent piri-piri chicken (see the boxed text 'Piri-Piri' later in this chapter) for just €3.80.

Suzie's Bar (☎ 282 442 107; dishes €3-7; open Fri-Wed) is a cosy expat-run bar-cum-restaurant, also by the river. It serves home-made burgers, pastas, vegetarian fare and cakes, plus an evening bistro menu.

Tasca do Béné (☎ 282 444 767; Rua Policarpo Dias; dishes €4-7, daily specials €4.80; open Mon-Sat), up the pedestrianised street from the river, is a casual, bench-style tasca (tavern) serving honest, no-frills food. Hungry locals like the hearty fare at **Restaurante Ponte Romana** (dishes €3.50-7, daily specials €5.50) and at the similarly priced **Restaurante Ladeiro** (☎ 282 442 870) on the nearby main road (the N124-1).

Café Inglês (☎ 282 442 585; open Sun-Fri), just below the castle entrance, is a great place to indulge in home-made soups, fruit juices and cakes. Its outdoor terrace is a big attraction.

Restaurante Rui (☎ 282 442 682; Rua Comendador Vilarinho 27; fish dishes €22-40; open Wed-Mon), in the old town, is the finest seafood restaurant around: savour everything here from cockles, clams and crabs to sea snails, stone bass and grouper.

Entertainment

Fábrica do Inglês (English Factory; ☎ 282 440 440; Rua Gregório Mascarenhas) is a converted 19th-century English cork factory 300m northeast of the new bridge, hosting restaurants, bars and a nightly multimedia show (adult/child 4-12 €20/10; open July–mid-Sept) with dancers, clowns and singers, lasers and 'cybernetic fountains'. The ticket price also includes dinner and admission to the Museu da Cortiça (see earlier). Reservations are advised. Off-season, there's usually a theme evening once a week; check at the museum's reception.

Getting There & Away

Six buses daily (four at weekends) shuttle between Silves and its train station (€0.50), timed to meet the trains from Lagos (€1.40, 35 minutes) and Faro (€2.70, one hour, with a change at Tunes). There are six daily buses to Albufeira (€2.60, 40 minutes); around 10 to Lagoa (€1.20, 15 minutes) and nine to Portimão (€1.80, 35 minutes). All buses leave from the riverfront; the ticket office is on the western side of the market.

PORTIMÃO

postcode 8500 • pop 33,000

This sprawling fishing port and sardine canning centre, 16km east of Lagos, hogs the western bank of the Rio de Arade 3km inland from Praia da Rocha.

Portimão's past sounds rather more glorious than its present: inhabited by successive settlers – Phoenicians, Greeks and Carthaginians (Hannibal himself is said to have set foot here) – it was called Portos Magnus by the Romans and fought over by Moors and Christians. In 1189 crusaders under Dom Sancho I sailed up the Rio Arade from here to besiege Silves. The 1755 earthquake practically flattened the place.

Today, it's the Algarve's second most important fishing port (after Olhão) and a major shopping destination and transport hub. The only other reasons to come here are to take a boat trip or to enjoy a slap-up sardine lunch; overnight accommodation, tourist facilities and nightlife are far better in the nearby resort of Praia da Rocha.

Orientation

The town's focal point is the revamped Praça Manuel Teixeira Gomes, next to a smart-looking new riverside promenade. There's no bus station, but buses stop at various points along riverside Avenida Guanaré (look for the Shell petrol station) and parallel Avenida Afonso Henriques (look for the Agip station). The train station is a 15-minute walk (1.1km) north of the centre – follow pedestrianised Rua do Comércio and its continuation, Rua Vasco da Gama. The easiest car parking is a free riverside lot by the Shell station. An underground car park was being built in the town centre at the time of writing.

Information

The **municipal turismo** (☎ 282 470 717; e turismo@cm-portimao.pt; Avenida Zeca Afonso; open 9am-6pm Mon-Fri, 9am-1pm Sat June-Aug; 9am-12.30pm & 2pm-5.30pm Mon-Fri Sept-May) is opposite the football stadium, around 600m west of the river.

There are several banks with ATMs around the riverside Praça Manuel Teixeira Gomes. Change your AmEx travellers cheques at **Top Tours** (☎ 282 417 552; Rua Judice Biker 25), which is around the corner from Praça Manuel Teixeira.

Things to See

The town's parish church, the **igreja matriz** (admission free), stands on high ground to the north of the town centre and features a 14th-century Gothic portal – all that remains of the original structure after the 1755 earthquake. More interesting echoes of the past can be found in the narrow streets of the **old fishing quarter** around Largo da Barca, just before the old highway bridge.

Activities

Several operators along the riverside promenade offer boat trips: **Arade Mar** (☎ 965 140 400) runs 3½-hour trips in traditional painted boats upriver to Silves (€17.50 per person), during which you should watch for flamingos, herons and other birdlife; or to the nearby coastal grottoes (€16). Arade Mar also offers five- to six-hour fishing trips (anglers/spectators €37.50/30, including

lunch), and dolphin-spotting cruises (10-person boat charter €200).

The nearest place to go for a gallop is at **Centro Hípico Vale de Ferro** (☎ 282 968 444), near Mexilhoeira Grande (4.2km west of Portimão), where the hourly rate is around €20.

Places to Stay & Eat

The **pousada da juventude** (☎ 282 491 804; e portimao@movijovem.pt; Lugar do Coca Maravilhas; dorm beds €9.50, doubles with bathroom €29) is a well-equipped place with restaurant and swimming pool. It's about 3km north of town, with infrequent bus connections. A **taxi** (☎ 282 423 645) will cost around €4.

For a great outdoor sardine lunch, head for the strip of restaurants by the bridge, where you can buy charcoal-grilled sardines for a bargain €3 or so per half-dozen.

Dona Barca (☎ 282 484 189; fish dishes €6-10), among more upmarket seafood restaurants in nearby Largo da Barca (under the arches of the bridge), is famous for its Algarve seafood specialities.

Casa Inglesa (☎ 282 416 290; Praça Manuel Teixeira Gomes) is a cool, minimalist café popular for snacks and people-watching.

Shopping

Trawl Rua do Comércio, Rua Vasco da Gama and adjacent Rua Direita for quality handicrafts (especially ceramics, crystal and copper goods), shoes and cotton items. A big open-air market is held on the first Monday of every month behind the train station. A flea market also takes place on the first and third Sunday of the month (mornings only) along Avenida São João de Deus (west of Rua do Comércio).

Getting There & Away

Portimão has excellent bus connections, including seven transrápidos daily to Albufeira (€3.50, 45 minutes); a dozen services to Faro (€3.30, 1½ hours); around eight services daily to Silves (€1.80, 45 minutes) and Monchique (€2.10, 30 minutes), and twice-hourly services to Lagos (€1.90, 20 minutes). There are at least a dozen expresses daily to Lisbon (€13.50, four hours). Information and tickets for Eva and Intersul (Eurolines) services are available at the **Eva office** (☎ 282 418 120; Largo do Duque 3) by the riverside.

ALGARVE

Trains connect Portimão with Tunes (via Silves) and Lagos six times daily. Change at Tunes for services to Lisbon.

PRAIA DA ROCHA

This vast stretch of sand backed by towering ochre-red cliffs and scattered with bizarre rocky outcrops was one of the first beaches in the Algarve to be patronised by overseas tourists in the 1950s and 1960s. Although ranks of hotels, shops and bars have long since destroyed its charm and tranquillity, it still has a few old mansions and guesthouses (some dating from the 19th century) that give it a touch of class. And the beach itself is still one of the most impressive in the Algarve.

Orientation

Set high above the beach, the esplanade, Avenida Tomás Cabreira, is the resort's main drag, with shops, hotels and restaurants. At the eastern end is the shell of the **Fortaleza da Santa Catarina**, built in the 16th century to stop pirates and invaders sailing up the Rio Arade to Portimão. Down below is the new Marina de Portimão, sporting more restaurants and bars.

Information

Right in the centre of the esplanade, opposite Hotel Júpiter, is the **turismo** (☎ 282 419 132; open 9.30am-1pm & 2pm-5.30pm Mon-Fri Sept-June, 9.30am-7pm daily July & Aug). A helpful **police post** (open 9am-12.30pm & 2pm-5pm Mon-Fri) is next door.

The **post office** is near the turismo. You can access the Internet at **Polotur** (see Activities), which charges €2.60 per 30 minutes, or at various bars, including **Classics Bar** (Edifício Vista Mar, Avenida Tomás Cabreira; open 11am-2am daily), across from Pensão Residencial Penguin (see Places to Stay), with a half-hourly rate of €2.50.

Activities

Various tours and excursions are available from travel agencies, notably **Polotur** (☎ 282 485 037; e polotur@clix.pt; open 9.30am-6.30pm Mon-Fri, 9.30am-1pm Sat; later summer), near the turismo, which offers jeep tours (€31) and fishing trips (€62).

Sailing courses are available from **Dynamic Vela Sailing School** (☎ 963 900 322), at the new marina, with three-hour/12-day courses for €60/400.

Places to Stay

Pensão and hotel accommodation is almost impossible to find in high season without prior reservation, though it's worth asking at the turismo about quartos. The following prices are for July.

Pensão Residencial Penguin (☎ 282 424 308; e residencial.penguin@mail.telepac.pt; Rua António Feu; singles with bathroom €35, doubles €50) is an old villa set back from the esplanade. Run by the same Englishwoman for over 30 years, it has seen better days (the 'pulsating monster' of the adjacent Discoteca Katedral has also ruined its peace), but the musty atmosphere and decor are redolent of Praia da Rocha's sedate early days. Some rooms come with sea views.

More modern options include **Residencial Tursol** (☎ 282 424 046; Rua António Feu; singles/doubles around €35/45) and the nearby **Residencial São José** (☎ 282 424 035; Rua Engenheiro Francisco Bívar; singles/doubles around €30/40).

In the upper price bracket there are two century-old gems. **Albergaria Vila Lido** (☎ 282 424 127, fax 282 424 246; Avenida Tomás Cabreira; singles/doubles €67/75; closed Nov-Mar), near the fort, is a delightful 19th-century mansion.

Hotel Bela Vista (☎ 282 450 480; e inf.reservas@hotelbelavista.net; singles/doubles €110/125.50) bags the best beach view from the middle of the esplanade. It's a whimsical late-19th century creation, with marvellously worked wooden ceilings and original azulejos. Only two of the 14 rooms lack a sea view. Rates drop dramatically in winter.

Places to Eat

Lena's Croissanteria, on the esplanade nearly opposite Hotel Bela Vista, is a pleasant spot for breakfast, vegetarian dishes, ice cream and crepes, though **Gelateria Bella Italia** rivals all other ice-cream spots for its brilliant sea views and historic location, right inside the fort.

Safari Restaurante (☎ 282 423 540; dishes €8-10), behind Discoteca Katedral, has an interior adorned with hunting trophies and a beach-view terrace. Its roast duck (€9.80) is yummy.

Cervejaria e Marisqueira (☎ 282 416 541; dishes €6-10, daily specials €4.70; open Mon-Sat), across from the casino, is popular and low-key, offering decently priced Portuguese fare.

Fancy a complete change? Try **Chang Thai** (☎ 967 018 328; Edifício Rio-A-Vista, Rua António Feu; dishes €5-6), where you can savour some tasty Oriental flavours.

At the time of writing, the marina had its first new dining and drinking spots, including **Dockside** (☎ 282 417 268; lunch specials €5.50, fish dishes €10-45), a bright, classy spot with sea views. If you're out to impress, go for the cataplana de tamboril, ameijoas e gambas (monkfish, clams and prawn cataplana; €32.50 for two).

Entertainment

You won't have any trouble finding a decent bar with entertainment on tap. Commonly run by Irish or English expats, they cater for all age groups and offer everything from darts and quiz nights to satellite TV and live music.

Check **The Celt Bar** (Rua António Feu) and adjacent **Twiins** (Rua António Feu) for Irish atmosphere and brews, or **Kerri's Bar** (☎ 282 483 195; Rua Jerónimo Buisel), just before the fort, for Finnish liqueurs (and no TV!). **Discoteca Katedral** (Rua António Feu), in front of Pensão Residencial Penguin, keeps the beat going from 11pm to 6am nightly during summer.

The classy **casino** (☎ 282 402 000; Av Tomás Cabreira), in Hotel Algarve, midway along the esplanade, has slot machines (admission free; open 4pm to 3am daily), gambling room (admission €4, plus passport and respectable attire; open 7.30pm to 3am) and nightly dinner show (8.30pm dinner, 10.30pm show) for €35 (€10 show only).

Getting There & Around

Buses shuttle between Praia da Rocha and Portimão every 15 minutes until midnight (€1.20, or €2.50/5 for five/10 tickets prepurchased) in summer. The bus terminus in Praia da Rocha is by the fort, with another stop behind Hotel da Rocha on Rua Engenheiro José Bívar.

At **Motorent** (☎ 282 416 998, fax 282 483 495; Rua Caetano Feu), behind the Hotel da Rocha, you can hire mountain bikes (€9.50 per day), scooters (€20 per day) and motorbikes (from around €37.50 per day). Next door, **Citycar** (☎ 282 414 398, fax 282 413 915) offers good car rental deals.

The Windward Coast & Costa Vicentina

LAGOS

postcode 8600 • pop 14,700

Heaving with young people all summer, bursting with restaurants, shops and bars, and adjacent to some of the Algarve's best beaches and most dramatic coastline, cheerful Lagos (la-goosh) has acquired a reputation as a good-time town but see Dangers & Annoyances under Information at the start of this chapter.

Contrasting with this modern-day identity is its honoured history as the point of origin for most voyages of Portugal's extraordinary Age of Discoveries. Other than sturdy town walls and the layout of the steep and narrow streets, only a few fragments of this period survived the devastating 1755 earthquake.

History

Phoenicians and Greeks established themselves at this port (later called Lacobriga by the Romans) at the mouth of the muddy Rio Bensafrim. Afonso III recaptured it from the Moors in 1241, and it was from here that the Portuguese carried on harassing the Muslims of North Africa. In 1415 a giant fleet set sail from Lagos under the command of the 21-year-old Prince Henry (see the boxed text 'Prince Henry the Navigator' under History in the Facts about Portugal chapter) to seize Ceuta in Morocco – and set the stage for Portugal's groping exploration of the West African coast and the successes of its ambitious Age of Discoveries.

Lagos' shipyards built and launched Prince Henry's caravels, and Henry split his time between his own trading company here and his school of navigation at Sagres. Local boy Gil Eanes left here in command of the first ship to round West Africa's Cape Bojador in 1434. Others continued to bring back information about the African coast – along with ivory, gold and slaves. Lagos has the dubious distinction of having hosted (in 1444) the first sale of black Africans as slaves to Europeans, and it subsequently grew into a centre of the slave trade. The former customs house on a corner of Praça do Infante supposedly stands on the site of the first slave market.

ALGARVE

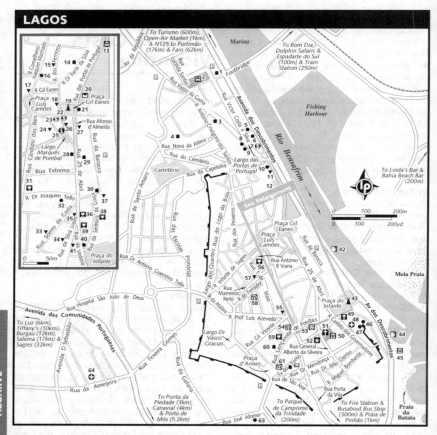

It was also from Lagos in 1578 that Dom Sebastião, along with the cream of Portuguese nobility and an army of Portuguese, Spanish, Dutch and German buccaneers, left on a disastrous crusade to Christianise North Africa, which ended in a debacle at Alcácer-Quibir in Morocco. Sir Francis Drake inflicted heavy damage on Lagos a few years later, in 1587.

Lagos was the Algarve's high-profile capital from 1576 until the 1755 earthquake, which flattened the city and brought its illustrious career to an end.

Orientation

The town's main commercial drag is the riverfront Avenida dos Descobrimentos. Drivers are strongly advised to leave their cars here – or head for one of the signposted free car parks on the outskirts – to avoid getting trapped in the inner town's web of narrow one-way lanes. Close to the centre, parking spaces are metered.

The administrative hub of Lagos is pedestrianised Praça Gil Eanes (zheel **yan**-ish), centred on a bizarre statue of Dom Sebastião looking like a teenage girl astronaut.

The bus station is roughly 500m north of Praça Gil Eanes off the Avenida dos Descobrimentos; the train station is on the other side of the river, accessible by a footbridge.

Information

Tourist Offices There are two turismos. The old **turismo** (☎ 282 763 031; open 9.30am-12.30pm & 2pm-5.30pm Mon-Fri year-round,

LAGOS

PLACES TO STAY		55	Mullen's		39	Stones
1	Albergaria Marina Rio	57	O Galeão		40	Customs House
3	Residencial Solar				42	Ferry to Meia Praia
4	Hotel Tivoli Lagos	**OTHER**			43	Statue of Henry the
14	Residencial Lagosmar	2	Bus Station			Navigator
28	Residencial Caravela	5	Auto Jardim		44	Boat Trips to Grottoes
29	Residencial Marazul	6	Lavandaria Miéle		45	Fortaleza da Ponta da
30	Residencial Rubi-Mar	7	Bank & ATM			Bandeira
60	Pousada da Juventude	8	Avis		46	Manueline window
62	Sra Benta Pereira Chaves	9	Luzcar		47	Castelo dos Governadores
	(private rooms)	10	Caima Ticket Office			(Governors Castle)
		12	Mercado Municipal		48	Hospital
PLACES TO EAT		13	Taxi Stand		49	Igreja de Santa Maria
11	Restaurante Bar Barros	16	Lavandaria Aida		50	Museu Municipal
15	Adega Tipica A Forja	19	Statue of Dom Sebastião		51	Igreja de Santo António
17	A Gamba	20	Post & Telephone Office		52	Police Station
18	Café Gil Eanes	21	Câmara Municipal		53	Centro Cultural
24	Restaurante Kalunga	22	Cota Câmbios		54	The E-m@ilbox
26	Restaurante Piri-Piri	23	Bank & ATM		56	Fools and Horses
27	O Cantinho Algarvio	25	Posto de Informação		58	Irish Rover Pub &
33	O Degrau		(turismo)			Cybercafe
34	Café Xpreitaqui Nature	31	Rosko's		59	Taverna Velha
35	Millenium Jardim	32	Loja do Livro		61	Gélibar
37	Barroca	36	Eddie's Bar		63	Motoride
41	Restaurante O João	38	Stevie Ray's Blues Jazz Bar		64	Medilagos

sometimes Sat & Sun summer) is inconveniently situated at Situo São João roundabout, 1km north of town (600m from the bus station) – follow the Avenida until you see the Galp petrol station. A new municipal **posto de informação** (☎ 282 764 111; *Largo Marquês de Pombal; open 10am-6pm Mon-Sat, sometimes longer summer)* offers excellent maps (including a suggested walking route) and historical leaflets on the town.

For entertainment information, check the listings in *The Best of Lagos & Alvor*, a privately produced, frequently updated free map available at better *residenciais*, shops and bars.

Lagos' big **open-air market** *(1st Sat of month)* takes place by the municipal stadium, just beyond the first roundabout east of the turismo.

Money Praça Gil Eanes has several banks with ATMs, as well as a private exchange bureau, **Cota Câmbios** *(open 8.30am-6.30pm Mon-Fri, 10am-2pm Sat)*.

Post & Communications A central **post and telephone office** *(open 9am-6pm Mon-Fri)* is just off Praça Gil Eanes.

There are several places to access the Internet, including the *pousada da juventude* (see Places to Stay), which charges €1.50 per 30 minutes, available 9am to 1am daily; nearby **Gélibar** (☎ *282 081 336; Rua Lançerote de Freitas; open 10am-10pm Mon-Sat, 1pm-10pm Sun)*, with similar rates; and **Irish Rover Pub & Cybercafe** (☎ *282 768 033; Rua do Ferrador; open 8pm-2am daily, 10pm-2am Oct-Apr)* at €1.30 the first 15 minutes, and €0.30 each subsequent five minutes. **Bom Dia** (☎ *282 764 670, 917 810 761;* e *bomdia_cruises@ip.pt; open 10am-4pm Mon-Fri Sept-June, 9am-9pm daily July & Aug)* charges €1.20 for 10 minutes (€3.20 for 30 minutes).

At **The E-m@ilbox** (☎ *282 768 950; Rua Cândido dos Reis 112; open 10am-6pm Mon-Fri May, June & Sept, 10am-2pm Oct-Apr, 9.30am-8.30pm July & Aug)* the rate is €1 per 10 minutes. It also offers fax, translation, United Parcel Service (UPS) and safe-box services.

Bookshops The **Loja do Livro** has a small supply of English, French and German-language paperbacks as well as some English and Portuguese-language CD-ROMs.

Laundry A self-service laundry is available at the *pousada da juventude* (see Places to Stay). **Lavandaria Aida** (☎ *282 762 191; Rua*

Conselheiro Joaquim Machado 28; open 9am-1pm & 3pm-7pm Mon-Fri, 9.30am-noon Sat) and **Lavandaria Miéle** (☎ 282 763 969; Avenida dos Descobrimentos 27; open 9am-7pm Mon-Fri, 9am-1pm Sat) both offer a one-day wash and dry service for €6.50 per 5kg.

Medical Services & Emergency The hospital (☎ 282 770 100; Rua do Castelo dos Governadores) is just off Praça do Infante. One of several private clinics is **Medilagos** (☎ 282 760 181; Amejeira de Cima, Bela Vista, Lote 2; open 24hr). There's a central **police station** (☎ 282 762 930; Rua General Alberto da Silveira).

Igreja de Santo António & Museu Municipal

A block south of Praça do Infante is Lagos' main historical attraction, the little Igreja de Santo António (Rua General Alberto da Silveira; admission €2; open 9.30am-12.30pm & 2pm-5pm Tues-Sun, closed holidays). It has an astonishing interior of gilded, carved wood – a baroque extravaganza of ripening grapes and beaming cherubs. The dome and azulejo panels were installed during repairs after the 1755 earthquake.

Enter from the adjacent **Museu Municipal** (☎ 282 762 301), a bizarre but appealing collection of azulejos, 16th-century grave markers, pickled foetuses, coins, handicrafts and church vestments plus unique archaeological items.

Igreja de Santa Maria

This church (open 9am-noon & 3pm-6pm daily) facing Praça do Infante is of interest mainly for its 16th-century entrance; most of the rest dates from the mid-19th century. Take a look at the spacey modern mural behind the altar.

Town Walls

Just south of Praça do Infante is a restored section of the stout town walls, built (atop earlier versions) during the reigns of both - Manuel I and João III in the 16th century. In fact they extend intermittently, with at least six bastions, for about 1.5km around the central town.

Following tradition, Dom Sebastião attended an open-air Mass here and spoke to the assembled nobility from a small **Manueline window** located in the **Castelo dos Governadores** (at the back of the present-day hospital), before leading them to defeat at Alcácer-Quibir.

Fortaleza da Ponta da Bandeira

This little fortress (Avenida dos Descobrimentos; admission €1.90; open 9.30am-12.30pm & 2pm-5pm Tues-Sun), at the southern end of the avenue, was built in the 17th century to protect the port. It now houses a museum on the Portuguese Discoveries.

Beaches

Meia Praia, the vast expanse of sand to the east of town, has outlets offering sailboard rental and water-skiing lessons, plus several laid-back restaurants and beach bars. South of town the beaches – Batata, Pinhão, Dona Ana, Camilo and others – are smaller and more secluded, lapped by calm waters and punctuated with amazing grottoes, coves and towers of coloured sandstone. Avoid swimming at Batata and, to the east, at Ana – their waters are officially rated 'bad' (see Ecology & Environment in the Facts about Portugal chapter for information on the Instituto da Água's regular water quality reports).

Ponta da Piedade

Aside from its beaches, Lagos' big geophysical attraction is Piety Point, a dramatic wedge of headland protruding south from Lagos. Three windswept kilometres out of town, the point is well worth a visit for its contorted, polychrome sandstone cliffs and towers, complete with lighthouse and hundreds of nesting egrets. The surrounding area is brilliant with wild orchids in spring. On a clear day you can see east to Carvoeiro and west to Sagres.

Activities

Water Sports For dive safaris, snorkelling or diving courses, contact **Blue Ocean Divers** (☎/fax 282 782 718, 964 048 002; e oceandivers@hotmail.com; Motel Ancora, Ponta da Piedade), which offers a half-day 'Snorkelling Safari' (€25), a full-day diving experience (€60) and a three-day PADI scuba course (€200). It also offers kayak safaris (€25/40 half/full day).

Surf Experience Portugal (☎/fax 282 761 943; w www.surf-experience.com) organises complete surfing holidays. Check its website for details.

Boat Trips Various operators have ticket stands at the marina or along the promenade opposite the marina.

The biggest operator is **Bom Dia** (☎ 282 764 670, 917 810 761; e bomdia_cruises@ip.pt), at the marina, which runs trips on traditional schooners, including a five-hour barbecue cruise for €35/17.50 per adult/child aged 5 to 10, or a full-day sail to Sagres, including lunch (€50/30). Two-hour grotto trips cost €15/7.50. You can also book many other activities at its office.

Espadarte do Sul (☎ 282 767 252) offers 90-minute trips to the grottoes beneath Ponta da Piedade (€25), a three-hour coastal cruise (€30) and a day-long big-game fishing jaunt for €55 (€35 spectators).

Local fishermen offering jaunts to the grottoes by motorboat trawl wait for customers along the promenade and by the Fortaleza da Ponta da Bandeira.

Dolphin Safaris Based at the marina, **Dolphin Seafaris** (☎ 282 792 586, 919 359 359; e dolphinseafaris@mail.com) offers two thrills in one: a high-speed 90-minute trip in a RIB (rigid inflatable boat) plus an 85% chance of seeing dolphins (total €30). Both these activities are available April to October only.

Parasailing Booked through Bom Dia (see Boat Trips earlier), parasailing trips cost €39.90 for 15 minutes of high-adrenaline thrills out at Ponta da Piedade.

Horse Riding About 10km west of Lagos, **Tiffany's** (☎ 282 697 395; Vale Grifo, Almádena) charges €20 an hour for horse riding and has other options, including a three-hour 'Safari' (€52.50) and a five-hour 'Adventure' (€87.50), which includes a champagne picnic. Another centre with similarly tempting activities (eg, moonlit rides for €25) is **Quinta Paraíso Alto** (☎ 282 687 596; Fronteira), 7km north of Lagos.

Bird-Watching For bird-watching **Simon Wates** (☎ 282 798 044) offers day trips to west or east Algarve or longer excursions further afield.

Cycling Full-day bike trips can be organised through **Cycle Paths** (Eddie's Bar, Rua 25 de Abril 99) for around €25 per person, including lunch. It also does excursions to

Morocco. Tickets and information are available from Eddie's Bar (see Bars under Entertainment later in this Lagos section).

Places to Stay – Budget

In addition to its *pensões* and *residenciais*, Lagos abounds in resort-style hotels, motels and rental apartment blocks. There are more places out on Meia Praia and south on Praia da Dona Ana. Most are filled to the gunwales in summer, with prices rocketing in August; we give July rates here.

Parque de Campismo da Trindade (☎ 282 763 893, fax 282 762 885; adult/tent/car €2.90/3.20/4.10) is a small site 200m south of the Lançarote gate in the town walls.

The welcoming **pousada da juventude** (☎ 282 761 970; e lagos@movijovem.pt; Rua Lançarote de Freitas 50; dorm beds €15, doubles with bathroom €42; open 24hr) is one of the best in Portugal. It has a kitchen and pleasant sitting-out area plus Internet access.

Plenty of private, unlicensed *quartos* are available in summer; if you don't get approached by owners, look for *quartos* signs in shop windows or ask at the turismo for recommendations. Figure on at least €27.50 a double (up to €50 for fancier versions).

The tidy, cosy rooms of charming **Senhora Benta Pereira Chaves** (☎ 282 760 940, 964 159 230; ask at Travessa do Forno 13A) are particularly useful for those with a car – a big (free) car park is nearby, just outside the city walls. Also recommended are the rooms and apartments, in several different locations, of **Senhora Margarida** (☎ 282 763 096, 917 628 003) and **Senhora Celeste Silva** (☎ 282 762 446). They will meet you and take you to whichever place is available.

Places to Stay – Mid-Range

Residencial Rubi-Mar (☎ 282 763 165; e rubimarlagos@yahoo.com; 2nd floor, Rua da Barocca 70; doubles with/without bathroom €45/35) is homely and welcoming – but you'll need to book at least a week ahead in summer.

Residencial Caravela (☎ 282 763 361; Rua 25 de Abril 8; doubles €35), in the central pedestrian zone, has plain doubles with shower.

Residencial Marazul (☎ 282 769 749, fax 282 769 960; Rua 25 de Abril 13; doubles €60-70) is a posher option, with comfortable rooms.

ALGARVE

Residencial Lagosmar (☎ 282 763 722; e lagosmar@clix.pt; Rua Dr Faria da Silva 13; doubles with breakfast €68) is a slick place with well-furnished rooms.

Residencial Solar (☎ 282 762 477, fax 282 761 784; Rua António Crisógono dos Santos 60; singles/doubles with breakfast from €40/50), near the bus station, is a modern establishment with big, plain rooms with bathroom and fridge.

Places to Stay – Top End

Albergaria Marina Rio (☎ 282 769 859; e marinario@ip.pt; Avenida dos Descobrimentos; doubles with breakfast €65, with harbour view & breakfast €78) is very plush boasting balcony views of the marina.

Hotel Tivoli Lagos (☎ 282 790 079; e hotel.lagos@mail.telepac.pt; Rua Nova da Aldeia; doubles with breakfast from €148) leaves no doubt it's No 1 in town.

Places to Eat

There's abundant good food in town, both Portuguese and international, though restaurants in the centre can be a little pricey. The best bargains are at lunch time when you'll often find pratos do dia (daily specials) for around €5. Many of the bars that are listed in the Entertainment section also offer food.

Café Xpreitaqui Nature (☎ 282 762 758; Rua da Silva Lopes 14; salads €2-5; open Mon-Sat) is a cool new venue, serving fab juices, smoothies, salads and 'natural' breakfasts.

Café Gil Eanes (☎ 282 762 886; Praça Gil Eanes; dishes €2-5) is an unbeatable people-watching venue, serving everything from sandwiches and salads, to cocktails.

A Gamba (Rua Conselheiro Joaquim Machado 5; dishes €5.50-6.50) provides bargain-priced fish and chips and takeaway grilled chicken.

Millenium Jardim (☎ 282 762 897; Rua 25 de Abril 72; pizzas from €5.50), an airy, two-storey affair with a fountain at the entrance, serves pizzas and other fare.

Adega Tipica A Forja (☎ 282 768 588; Rua dos Ferreiros 17; dishes €5-7, daily specials around €5), offering good value for money, is popular. It dishes up huge daily specials that are sure to fill you up.

Mullen's (Rua Cândido dos Reis 86; dishes €6.50-10), a long-established adega típica

(wine bar), serving good grilled dishes, also has a lively bar.

Restaurante Piri-Piri (☎ 282 763 803; Rua Lima Leitão 15; dishes €7-9.50) serves standard cozinha regional (regional cuisine), including cataplana dishes for one (€13.50).

O Cantinho Algarvio (☎ 282 761 289; Rua Afonso d'Almeida 17; dishes €8-9; open Mon-Sat) has a similar menu to Piri-Piri plus some unusual dishes (eg, 'wild boar in a pot', €8).

Restaurante Bar Barros (☎ 282 762 276; Rua Portas de Portugal 83; dishes €5-9, daily specials €4.90), right by the market, is a more modest, local choice with a huge fish menu and bargain pratos do dia.

Restaurante O João (☎ 282 761 067; Rua da Silva Lopes 15; dishes €8-12) is an unpretentious, cosy nook with honest prices (and candlelit tables at night), which manages to cater to both locals and tourists. Try its house special: paella (€9).

O Degrau (☎ 282 764 716; Rua Soeiro da Costa 46; dishes €8-10), an upmarket choice, has a fantastically varied menu: everything from Tuscan tomato soup (€2.50) to Thai vegetable curry (€7).

You can splash out, too, at **O Galeão** (☎ 282 763 909; Rua da Laranjeira 1; dishes €9-12). It serves Portuguese fare, including luxuries such as lobster thermidor (€74.30), from an open-view kitchen where the chefs work – as one reader described it – 'with quiet precision'.

Want a taste of somewhere else? Angolan fare is on offer at **Restaurante Kalunga** (☎ 282 760 727; Rua Marquês de Pombal 26; dishes from €6). Alternatively, chocolate-coated chicken (€7.50) can be yours at **Barroca** (☎ 282 760 162; Rua da Barroca; dishes €8-10), a Mexican restaurant and tequila bar also offering delicious fajitas (€8.50).

Entertainment

Bars Lagos is chock-a-block with bars and cafés, most of them staying open to at least 4am in summer. Among the popular places are **Taverna Velha** (Rua Lançarote de Freitas 54); **Rosko's** (☎ 282 763 905; Rua Cândido dos Reis 79), an Irish bar; and venues along Rua 25 de Abril including **Eddie's Bar** (☎ 282 768 329; Rua 25 de Abril 99) and **Stones** (Rua 25 de Abril 101).

Stevie Ray's Blues Jazz Bar (☎ 282 760 673; Rua da Senhora da Graça 9; admission

€5; open 8pm-4am) has live music (blues, jazz, oldies) every Saturday. 'Smart casual dress' is required.

Fools and Horses (☎ 282 762 970; Rua António Barbosa Viana 7), a long-established favourite, offers English breakfasts (€4.50), tea for two, or pints and pub grub.

Out at Meia Praia, **Linda's Bar** (☎ 282 761 651) has fab food and tunes, and a Friday night barbecue party. The **Bahia Beach Bar** (☎ 282 792 089) is a neat place to hang out, with rock music from 5pm every Sunday.

Concerts & Exhibitions Lagos' main venue for classical recitals and performances, as well as art exhibitions, is the **Centro Cultural** (☎ 282 770 450; Rua Lançarote de Freitas; open 10am-8pm daily). It also has a café, serving bargain *pratos do dia* in summer.

Getting There & Away
Bus From the bus station (☎ 282 762 944) there are six Linha Litoral/*transrápido* services daily to Albufeira (€4.30/3.30, 75/65 minutes). Services to Portimão run roughly every 15 minutes, including six *transrápido* services (€1.90, 20 minutes) that continue to Faro (€3.60, 1¾ hours). Connections to Sagres run every hour or two (€2.40, 45 to 65 minutes). For details of a service to Cabo de São Vicente, see Getting There & Around under Sagres later in this chapter.

Around a dozen Eva express buses run to Lisbon daily (€13.50). Renex also has a frequent express service to Lisbon (€13); tickets for these are available from the **Caima ticket office** (☎ 282 768 931; Rua das Portas de Portugal 101), which can also arrange minibus transfers to Faro airport (€55 for one to four people).

Between April and October, Intersul runs express coaches between Lagos and Seville (Spain), four to six times a week (€13, 5¼ hours). Busabout buses (see Bus in the Getting There & Away chapter) stop near the fire station.

Train Lagos is at the western end of the Algarve line, with seven direct regional services to Faro daily (€3.90, 1½ hours) and onward connections from there to Vila Real de Santo António (€5.20, 3¼ hours). There are five trains daily to Lisbon (all requiring a change at Tunes); IR services take 5½

hours (€10.90), IC trains just under five hours (€12.20).

Getting Around
Car & Taxi Several local agencies can offer competitive car rental rates; try **Auto Jardim** (☎ 282 769 486; Rua Victor Costa e Silva 18A) or **Luzcar** (☎ 282 761 016; Largo das Portas de Portugal). An international agency is **Avis** (☎ 282 763 691; Largo das Portas de Portugal), near Luzcar.

You can call for **taxis** (☎ 800 200 846, 282 764 481) or find them on Rua das Portas de Portugal.

Motorcycle & Bicycle The company **Motoride** (☎ 282 761 720; Rua José Afonso 23) rents bikes, scooters and motorcycles from just outside the town walls, or through agents in the centre (eg, the Caima ticket office at Rua das Portas de Portugal 101). Typical rates for one/three days are about €9/24 for a mountain bike, €30/61 for a scooter, or from €50/89 for a motorbike. August prices are about 7% higher.

Ferry In summer, ferries run to and fro across the estuary to the Meia Praia side from a landing just north of Praça do Infante.

LAGOS TO SAGRES
The steep, rugged shoreline west of Lagos has been the last segment of the southern coastline to fall prey to developers. Thanks to their fine beaches, the once-sleepy fishing hamlets are rapidly being 'resortified', but in the low season there's a lingering sense of isolation.

Luz
Just 6km from Lagos, Luz is well-endowed with tourist facilities, villas and day-trippers. Fronting its small sandy beach (popular with families) and attractive promenade is a row of restaurants and shops, including **Azure Seas** (☎ 282 788 304), which can organise bike and car rental and just about everything else. Buses arrive at central Praça da República.

Places to Stay & Eat The nearest camp sites are Orbitur's **Valverde Camping** (☎ 282 789 211, fax 282 789 213; adult/tent/car €4.80/3.90/4), a slick site also offering caravan rental; and the Turiscampo-run

Camping de Espiche (☎ 282 789 265; adult/tent/car €2.50/2.50/1.80). Both are about 2km from Luz.

There are lots of pubs and restaurants near Praça da República including **The Bull** (☎ 282 788 823; Rua Calheta 5; dishes €4-9), serving British grub such as sausage and chips (€4.20).

Nautilus Bar (☎ 282 789 290; Rua 1 de Maio; breakfasts €3.50) offers the cheapest breakfasts around.

Fortaleza da Luz (☎ 282 789 926; Rua da Igreja 3; daily specials €10-15) looks pretty decrepit, but inside this former 16th-century fortress is an upmarket restaurant with some unusual fare, including duck confit (€12.70) and guineafowl casserole (€14). Pity the sea-view terrace is enclosed (though the restaurant brochure does say you can 'ogle the nymphs on the rocks below').

Getting There & Away There are frequent bus connections between Lagos and Praia da Luz (€1.20, 15 minutes).

Salema

This small coastal resort, set on a wide bay 17km from Lagos, is delightful. Despite the apartment blocks rising like mushrooms around it, Salema has an easy-going atmosphere, and there are several small, secluded beaches within a few kilometres – **Praia da Salema** by the village, **Praia da Figueira** to the west and **Boca do Rio** to the east.

Salema also has a useful travel agency called **Horizonte** (☎/fax 282 695 920; e horizonte.passeios.turis@mail.telepac.pt), opposite Hotel Residencial Salema (see Places to Stay). Horizonte can help with bookings for hotel and villa accommodation (often at discounted prices), car rental, boat or coach trips, and runs ecofriendly jeep trips within the Parque Natural do Sudoeste Alentejano e Costa Vicentina (see the boxed text on this park later in this chapter).

Places to Stay & Eat

Quinta dos Carriços (☎ 282 695 201, fax 282 695 122; adult/tent/car €3.60/3.60/3.60), just 1.5km north of Salema, is definitely into peace and quiet (Music Prohibited!). It has studios and apartments and even its own secluded naturist camping area.

Private rooms are plentiful along seaside Rua dos Pescadores; expect to pay €30

upwards for a double. **Senhora Silvina Maria Pedro** (☎ 282 695 473; Rua dos Pescadores 91; double €30, apartment €45) has tiny rooms and shared bathroom, all very clean, in a dinky former fisherfolk's house right on the beach.

Estalagem Infante do Mar (☎ 282 690 100, fax 282 690 109; doubles around €63), a hotel perched high above the beach, is the choice for peace and elegance.

Hotel Residencial Salema (☎ 282 695 328, fax 282 695 329; e hotel.salema@clix.pt; doubles with breakfast €62-72) has a great location, just a few steps from the beach.

Restaurante Atlântico (☎ 282 695 742; dishes from €7.50), overlooking Praia da Salema, has an appealing range of fish dishes.

O Carapau Frances (☎ 282 695 730; pizzas from €5.30), opposite the Atlântico, is pleasantly casual.

Getting There & Away

At least six buses daily connect Lagos and Salema (€1.60, 30 minutes).

SAGRES
postcode 8650 • pop 2500

Blasted by a steady, cutting wind and huge Atlantic waves, and with sheer cliffs facing a sea horizon on three sides, the Ponta de Sagres promontory at the western end of the Algarve seems the very edge of Europe. Its position and the austere landscape surely figured in Prince Henry the Navigator's choice of this place for a new, fortified town and a semimonastic school of navigation that specialised in cartography, astronomy and ship design, and set Portugal on course for the Age of Discoveries.

At least, that is what the current mix of history and myth says. Henry was, among other things, governor of the Algarve and had a residence in its primary port town, Lagos, from where most expeditions actually set sail. He certainly did put together a kind of nautical think-tank, though how much thinking actually went on out at Sagres is not known. He had a house somewhere near Sagres, where he died in November 1460. In any case, he did have close links with the town and it's easy to see why.

In May 1587 the English privateer Sir Francis Drake, in the course of harassing supply lines to the Spanish Armada, captured and wrecked the fortifications around

Sagres. The Ponta de Sagres was refortified after the earthquake of 1755, which had left little of verifiable antiquity standing.

Paradoxically, quirky ocean currents give Sagres some of Portugal's mildest winter weather and Atlantic winds keep the summers cool.

Orientation

From Vila do Bispo, the district's administrative centre at the western end of the N125, a 9km gauntlet of villas along the N268 attests to the arrival of development even in this remote corner of the Algarve.

From a roundabout at the end of the N268, roads go west for 6km to the Cabo de São Vicente, south for 1km to the Ponta de Sagres and east for 250m to little Praça da República at the head of Sagres town (what there is of it). One kilometre east of the square, past holiday villas and restaurants, is the port, still a centre for boat building and lobster fishing, and the marina.

Information

The **turismo** (*☎ 282 624 873; Rua Comandante Matoso; open 9.30am-1pm & 2pm-5.30pm Tues-Sat*) is 100m east of Praça da República, near a triangular monument.

Turinfo (*☎ 282 620 003, fax 282 620 004; Praça da República; open 10am-1pm & 2pm-7pm daily*), a private tourist agency, offers currency exchange, regional maps and books, excursions, bicycle and car rental, and contacts for private rooms and flats. It also has an Internet facility costing €0.10 per minute.

There's a bank and ATM just beyond the turismo and a post office just beyond Pensão Navegante II (see Places to Stay).

Fortaleza de Sagres

The Sagres fortress (*adult/youth 15-25/child €3/1.50/free; open 10am-6.30pm daily, 10am-8.30pm May-Sept*) is more impressive from outside than inside, consisting only of a massive front wall and two bastions. Apparently there were once short lateral walls inside as well – the flat promontory's sheer cliffs were protection enough around the rest. In its present form it dates from 1793.

Just inside the gate is a stone **rosa dos ventos** (wind rose, for measuring the direction of the wind), 43m in diameter. Excavated

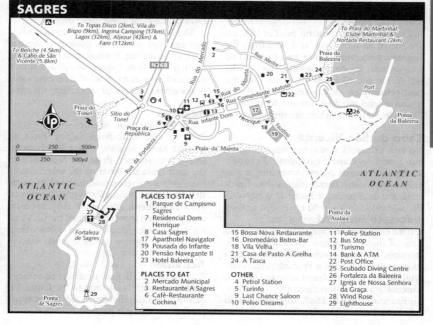

SAGRES

To Topas Disco (2km), Vila do Bispo (9km), Ingrina Camping (17km), Lagos (32km), Aljezur (42km) & Faro (112km)

To Beliche (4.5km) & Cabo de São Vicente (5.8km)

To Praia do Martinhal; Clube Martinhal & Nortada Restaurant (2km)

N268

Rua do Mercado

Rua Mestre

Praia da Baleeira

Rua do Moreta

Rua Comandante Matoso

Praia do Tonel

Sítio do Tonel

Rua Infante Dom Henrique

R Antonio Faustino

Port

Praça da República

Praia da Mareta

Ponta da Baleeira

ATLANTIC OCEAN

ATLANTIC OCEAN

Rua da Fortaleza

Ponta da Atalaia

Fortaleza de Sagres

Ponta de Sagres

0 · 250 · 500m
0 · 250 · 500yd

ALGARVE

PLACES TO STAY
1 Parque de Campismo Sagres
7 Residencial Dom Henrique
8 Casa Sagres
17 Aparthotel Navigator
19 Pousada do Infante
20 Pensão Navegante II
23 Hotel Baleeira

PLACES TO EAT
2 Mercado Municipal
3 Restaurante A Sagres
6 Café-Restaurante Cochina

15 Bossa Nova Restaurante
16 Dromedário Bistro-Bar
18 Vila Velha
21 Casa de Pasto A Grelha
24 A Tasca

OTHER
4 Petrol Station
5 Turinfo
9 Last Chance Saloon
10 Polvo Dreams

11 Police Station
12 Bus Stop
13 Turismo
14 Bank & ATM
22 Post Office
25 Scubado Diving Centre
26 Fortaleza da Baleeira
27 Igreja de Nossa Senhora da Graça
28 Wind Rose
29 Lighthouse

in the 18th century, it may have been made for Prince Henry. It seems unlikely that much else except the foundations dates from that time, though the oldest buildings, including a cistern tower to the east, a house and the small **Igreja da Nossa Senhora da Graça** to the west, and the remnants of a wall running part of the way across, may be recent replacements for what was there before. Many of the gaps between buildings are the result of a 1950s clearance of 17th- and 18th-century ruins to make way for a reconstruction (later aborted) to coincide with the 500th anniversary of Henry's death.

Today, there's little inside to warrant the massive entry fee ('no guided tours, no useful explanations, no signs, nothing!' complains one reader) apart from a big, ugly exhibition hall housing temporary exhibitions, and a café. Near the southern end of the promontory is a modern **lighthouse**. Death-defying anglers with huge rods perch atop the cliffs all around, hoping to land bream or sea bass.

Other Forts
Overlooking Sagres harbour are the ruins of the small **Fortaleza da Baleeira**, thought to have been built in the mid-16th century to protect the harbour.

The **Fortaleza do Beliche**, built in 1632 on the site of an older one, is 4.5km from the Sagres roundabout on the way to Cabo de São Vicente. Inside is a small chapel on the site of the ruined Igreja de Santa Catarina (and possibly an old convent), as well as a restaurant and two double rooms for rent (see Places to Stay later in this Sagres section).

Cabo de São Vicente
No visit to Sagres would be complete without a trip to Cape St Vincent, Europe's southwesternmost point. Awesome is the only word for this barren, throne-like headland, the last piece of home that nervous Portuguese sailors would have seen as they headed out into the unknown sea.

The cape – a revered place even in the time of the Phoenicians and known to the Romans as Promontorium Sacrum – takes its present name from a Spanish priest martyred by the Romans (see the boxed text 'St Vincent'). The old fortifications, trashed by Sir Francis Drake in 1587, were reduced to rubble by the 1755 earthquake.

St Vincent

St Vincent (São Vicente) was a Spanish preacher killed by the Romans in AD304 in Valencia. Legends say his body was either washed up at Cabo de São Vicente, or borne here on a boat accompanied by ravens (or perhaps carrion crows, like those still common in the area). A shrine to the saint, which Muslim chronicles refer to as the Crow Church, became an object of Christian pilgrimage, though it was apparently destroyed by Muslim fanatics in the 12th century.

Afonso Henriques, Portugal's first king, quick to see the saint's symbolic value, had the remains moved to Lisbon in 1173, again by ship and again supposedly accompanied by ravens. St Vincent was made Lisbon's patron saint (his remains now rest in the Igreja de São Vicente de Fora there) and there is a raven on the city's coat of arms.

At the end of the cape are a powerful lighthouse (hundreds of ocean-going ships round this point everyday) and a former convent. Some scholars place Henry the Navigator's house in a small castle to the right of the lighthouse grounds.

The best time to visit is at sunset, when you can almost hear the hissing as the sun settles into the sea. It would make a stunning clifftop walk from Sagres, though it's almost 6km each way in a stiff wind. There are cafés or restaurants at several spots along the road.

Beaches
There are four good beaches within a short drive or long walk from Sagres: **Praia da Mareta** just below the town; lovely, relatively undeveloped **Praia do Martinhal** to the east; **Praia do Tonel** on the other side of the Ponta de Sagres; and isolated **Praia de Beliche**, on the way to Cabo de São Vicente. **Praia da Baleeira**, adjacent to the harbour, is pretty polluted from all the boat traffic. Praia do Tonel is especially good for surfing, though local surfers are quite protective.

Activities
Turinfo (see earlier for details) can arrange **jeep tours** with Horizonte to the Costa Vicentina or into the Serra de Monchique (both trips €36 per person).

Praia do Martinhal is the focus for **windsurfing** (the water is wetsuit-cold). **Clube Martinhal aquatic sports centre** (☎ 282 624 333) offers sea-kayaking day trips, windsurfing, snorkelling and, in summer, scuba diving. Also organising **diving trips** (this is a great spot for shipwrecks between 12m and 30m) is the **Scubado Diving Centre** (☎ 282 624 594, 965 559 073; e scubado@clix.pt; Porto da Baleeira). Its introductory session costs €60, while the four-day PADI openwater course is €280.

Surfing is possible at all beaches except Praia do Martinhal. Baleeira is not suitable for swimmers or surfers.

Places to Stay

Sagres gets crowded in summer, though it's marginally easier to find accommodation here than in the rest of the Algarve during the high season, especially if you arrive before noon. Except at Pousada do Infante, all prices drop considerably outside summer; rates here are for July.

Camping Some 2km from town, just off the road to Cabo de São Vicente, **Parque de Campismo Sagres** (☎ 282 624 371, fax 282 624 445; adult/tent/car €4.10/3.30/3.50) is a well-maintained site.

Ingrina Camping (☎/fax 282 639 242; adult/tent/car €3.50/3.40/3) is about 17km northeast of Sagres, on the beach south of Raposeira.

Private Rooms & Pensões Every other house in Sagres seems to advertise private rooms or apartments. Doubles generally go for €25 and flats for €40 to €75 in high season.

Pensão Navegante II (☎ 282 624 442; e zelia-freitas@clix.pt; Sítio da Baleeira; doubles with breakfast €40) is old and run-down, but its rooms are huge and it's very easy-going.

Residencia Dom Henrique (☎ 282 620 003, fax 282 620 004; Praça da República; doubles with land/sea view €52.50/65) has plain but decent rooms (breakfast included).

Casa Sagres (☎ 282 624 358; doubles with breakfast €45) has a great location, with sea views and comfortable rooms.

Hotels Bagging the best eastern spot is **Hotel Baleeira** (☎ 282 624 212; e hotel .baleeira@mail.telepac.pt; Rua Comandante Matoso; doubles €98), with harbour views and spiffy rooms; rates include a buffet breakfast.

Aparthotel Navigator (☎ 282 624 354; e hotel.navigator@mail.telepac.pt; Rua Infante Dom Henrique; 2-person apartments €85) is a giant place with two swimming pools.

Pousada do Infante (☎ 282 624 222, fax 282 624 225; doubles Mon-Fri €135, Sat & Sun €148) provides the poshest doubles in town.

The little **fortaleza** (☎ 282 624 124, fax 282 624 225; doubles Mon-Fri €82, Sat & Sun €89), at Beliche, has just four rooms. You'll need to book well ahead in summer.

Places to Eat

Many of the following places close or operate shorter hours during the low season (November to April).

Restaurante A Sagres (☎ 282 624 171; Sítio do Tonel; dishes €6-10) is a popular first stop into Sagres. Try its fish soup for starters (€1.50).

Praça da República has several eateries, including **Café-Restaurante Cochina** (dishes from €4.50), with a large, cheap menu.

Casa de Pasto A Grelha (☎ 282 624 193; Rua Comandante Matoso; dishes from €4.80) does cheap, filling meals and great takeaway grilled chicken.

Nortada (☎ 282 624 147; Praia da Martinhal; dishes €6-10; open year-round), right on the beach, dishes up everything from pizzas to swordfish steak.

Casa Sagres (see Places to Stay; dishes around €8-12) is a smartish option, with tempting seafood dishes and a sea view.

Dromedário Bistro-Bar (☎ 282 624 219; Rua Infante Dom Henrique) serves up fresh juices and muesli for breakfast, pizzas and crepes during the day, and drinks till late in the summer season.

Bossa Nova Restaurante (☎ 282 624 566; dishes €4-10) has an attractive open-air dining area and good pizzas, salads and vegetarian dishes.

A Tasca (☎ 282 624 177; Porto da Baleeira; closed Sat Nov-Apr), overlooking the marina, has the best seaside views.

Vila Velha (☎ 282 624 788; Rua P António Faustino; fish dishes €10-16; open Tues-Sun) offers a refreshing change, including vegetarian dishes (€7.50 to €11.30).

ALGARVE

The *mercado municipal* provides great supplies for long days on the beaches.

Entertainment
A cheerful place for a drink with a sea view is the **Last Chance Saloon**, just down the hill from the square. **Polvo Dreams** is a bar-pub with satellite TV and video games, opposite the square. For nightly live music until dawn, head for **Topas Disco**, a couple of kilometres out of town, en route to Vila do Bispo.

Getting There & Around
Over a dozen buses daily run to/from Lagos (€2.40, 45 to 65 minutes) and five daily to/from Portimão (€3.60). A 'Rota do Infante' service from Portimão to Cabo de São Vicente, via Lagos and Sagres, runs once daily (€3.80, 1½ hours), twice daily from Praia da Rocha and three times daily from Sagres (€1, 10 minutes). Buy tickets from the newsagent kiosk on Praça da República. The bus stop is northeast of the turismo.

Through Turinfo you can hire a car, or rent mountain bikes (€9.50 per day).

NORTH OF SAGRES
Heading north along the Algarve's western coast you'll find some great beaches, largely free of development thanks to the Atlantic's cool, choppy, sometimes dangerous seas, and building restrictions imposed

to protect the Parque Natural do Sudoeste Alentejano e Costa Vicentina.

Carrapateira
Some 12km north of Vila do Bispo, this dozy village has two fine beaches: **Praia da Bordeira**, 2km off the road on the northern side of the village and backed by scrubby dunes, is popular with local fishermen; the sandier **Praia do Amado** is at the southern end of the village and attracts the surfing crowd. Contact **Algarve Surf Camp** (*☎/fax 282 639 479, 963 010 818;* e *wu.do.surf@mail.telepac.pt*), based at this beach, for surfing courses of one day (around €25) or longer.

Places to Stay & Eat A gem of a place, 100m from the road at the southern end of the village, is **Pensão das Dunas** (*☎/fax 282 973 118; Rua da Padaria 9; doubles €22.50, 1-/2-room apartments €35/47.50*), with rooms overlooking a pretty courtyard. The doubles have shared facilities. Meals are available here or next door at the tiny, no-frills **Restaurante Torres** (*☎ 282 973 222; Rua da Padaria 7; dishes €5-7*).

Casa Fajara (*☎ 282 973 123, 967 095 937;* e *casafajara@mail.telepac.pt; doubles €100; open Dec-Oct*), some 500m from the village or 1.2km from Praia da Bordeira, has rooms with shared kitchen, a swimming pool, tennis courts and horse-riding excursions for

Parque Natural do Sudoeste Alentejano e Costa Vicentina

The Southwest Alentejo & Costa Vicentina Natural Park is a strip of rugged, sparsely developed coastline with high cliffs and isolated beaches. Rarely more than 6km wide, it runs for about 120km from Burgau to Cabo de São Vicente and up nearly the entire western Algarve and Alentejo shore.

Established in 1995, the park was amalgamated from several protected areas in an effort to forestall development and protect an ecosystem rich and complex enough to have been designated a 'biogenetic reserve' by the Council of Europe. Here there are at least 48 plant species found only in Portugal, and a dozen or so found only within the park. Otters thrive in the river valleys, foxes roam in areas near the shore, and a few wild cats lurk in the deeper valleys. The most visible wildlife is birds: some 200 species enjoy the coastal wetlands, salt marshes and cliffs, including Portugal's last remaining ospreys. Storks nest on coastal outcrops. This is an important migratory stop in spring and autumn.

The N268/N120 road roller-coasters for long stretches along the inland edge of the pine-scented park, passing through hills deeply etched by rivers on their way to the sea. The most picturesque stretches are north and south of Carrapateira and between Rogil and Odeceixe.

The **park headquarters** (*☎ 283 322 735; Rua Serpa Pinto 32, Odemira*) is in Odemira, in the Alentejo. Colour brochures on the park are also available at Turinfo in Sagres (see that section). **Horizonte** (see under Salema) offers culturally sensitive, low-impact 4WD trips through the park for around €36 per person.

small groups of experienced riders (€30 per hour; €50 beach ride or €60 morning ride plus lunch). Discounts are available for longer stays; no children aged under six are allowed.

O Sítio do Rio (☎ 282 973 119; dishes €7-12), right on the scrubby dunes near Praia da Bordeira, is hugely popular with Portuguese at weekends. It offers two vegetarian dishes (€6.50 to €7.50) plus lots of mushroom sauces with its excellent grilled fish and meat dishes.

Restaurante do Cabrita (☎ 282 973 128; fish dishes €7-11, tourist menu €12), near the main N268, also specialises in grills; its tourist menu is good value.

Aljezur

Some 20km further north, this striking riverside village has two distinct halves: one Moorish, below a ruined 10th-century hilltop castle; the other, called Igreja Nova, a more modern settlement 600m up a steep hill to the east. Aljezur is close to some great surfing beaches, notably **Praia da Arrifana** (10km southwest, near a tourist development called Vale da Telha), a protected bay with some big northwest swells; and **Praia de Monte Clérigo**, about 8km northwest.

Orientation & Information Aljezur's turismo (☎ 282 998 229; open 9.30am-5.30pm Mon-Fri Sept-June; 9.30am-7pm daily July & Aug, closed lunch Sat & Sun), by a small covered market, is just before the bridge leading to the Lagos N120 road (Rua 25 de Abril). Banks with ATMs, a post office, shops and restaurants can all be found on Rua 25 de Abril.

Places to Stay The turismo in Aljezur has a list of accommodation in the area, including quartos.

Camping-Caravanning Vale da Telha (☎ 282 998 444; e vale.telha@clix.pt; adult/tent/car €2.20/2.20/2.30), about 2km south of Praia de Monte Clérigo, has a pool and tennis courts.

Parque de Campismo Serrão (☎ 282 990 220; e camping-serrao@clix.pt; adult/tent/car €3.70/3.40/2.50) is 4km north of Aljezur, then 800m down the road to Praia da Amoreira (the beach is 2.5km further). It has wheelchair access, a pool and apartments, plus bike rental and an Internet facility.

Residencial Dom Sancho II (☎ 282 998 119; e turimol@mail.telepac.pt; Igreja Nova; doubles €30), an unsigned establishment in Aljezur, next to the supermercados in Igreja Nova, has plain, poorly kept but spacious rooms.

Hospedaria São Sebastião (☎ 918 626 947; Rua 25 de Abril 150; doubles with breakfast €50; open July & Aug) has rooms with air-con.

Hospedaria O Palazim (☎ 282 998 249; doubles with breakfast around €40) is a modern, hill-top place 2km north of Aljezur on the Lisbon road.

In Praia da Arrifana are several quartos: try the small modern ones belonging to **Senhora Odete** (☎ 282 998 789; doubles €30), next to A Tasquinha café, on the road above the beach, just beyond Brisamar (see Places to Eat).

Hotel Residencial Vale da Telha (☎ 282 998 180, fax 282 998 176; doubles with breakfast €50) is 2.6km from the beach and feels rather isolated.

Places to Eat In Aljezur, two casual, popular places are **Restaurante Ruth** (☎ 282 998 534; Rua 25 de Abril 14; dishes €6-12, daily specials €5-6; open Sun-Fri) and **Primavera** (☎ 282 998 294; Rua 25 de Abril 67; dishes around €6), with an outdoor eating area.

Snack-Bar Tasca Matias (☎ 282 991 020) is a friendly café (run by English-speakers), opposite Residencial Dom Sancho II in Igreja Nova.

O Chefe Dimas (☎ 282 998 275; dishes €8-12; open Thur-Tues), next to Hospedaria O Palazim (see Places to Stay), is the best fish restaurant around, but it also offers various game, such as partridge (€20) or grilled rabbit (€6).

In Praia da Arrifana there's a string of seafood restaurants (packed with Portuguese at weekends) on the road above the beach, where you can expect to pay at least €7 for fish dishes. Options include **Brisamar** (☎ 282 998 436) and **O Pescador da Arrifana** (☎ 965 839 172).

At Praia da Amoreira check out **Restaurante Paraíso do Mar** (☎ 282 991 088; dishes from €7).

Odeceixe

Clinging to the southern side of the Ribeira de Seixe valley is tiny Odeceixe, right on the Algarve/Alentejo border. An almost exclusively German hang-out in high season, it has a gem of a beach, the small, lovely and very sheltered **Praia de Odeceixe**, 3.5km down the valley.

Places to Stay & Eat Located 1.5km north of Odeceixe, **Parque de Campismo São Miguel** (☎ *282 947 145, fax 282 947 245; adult/tent/car €4/4/3.50)* is well equipped, pine-shaded and wheelchair accessible.

There are plenty of well-advertised *quartos* in the village, especially along Rua Nova (en route to the beach). Expect to pay at least €27 a double.

Casa Verde (☎ *282 947 219, 919 697 299; e portico@ip.pt; Rua Nova 10; apartments €60-75)* also offers apartments.

Pensão Luar (☎ *282 947 194; Rua da Várzea 28; doubles €30)* is at the western edge of the village, en route to the beach.

Residência Parque (☎ *282 947 483; Rua dos Correiros; doubles with breakfast €40; open Apr-Oct)* is centrally located beside the post office.

There are several café-restaurants in the village, including **Restaurante Chaparro** *(dishes from €5)*, opposite the post office, and **Café O Retiro do Adelino** (☎ *282 947 352; Rua Nova 20; dishes €5-10)*, both serving simple, filling meals.

Getting There & Away Three to four buses daily run from Lagos to Odeceixe (€3, 80 minutes) via Aljezur (€2.40, 50 minutes). One bus daily connects Vila do Bispo with Aljezur (€2.80, 45 minutes) via Carrapateira on weekdays only. From Aljezur, where the bus stop is situated by the turismo, there's a twice-weekly service to Arrifana.

The Interior

MONCHIQUE
postcode 8550 • pop 7000 • elevation 410m
Up in the forested Serra de Monchique, 24km north of Portimão, this busy little town begins to feel like the real Portugal at last, the densely wooded hills surrounding it a welcome touch of wilderness after all the holiday villas further south. It makes a pleasant day trip together with Caldas de Monchique, or a longer stay if you want to take advantage of the area's biking, walking or horse-riding options.

Orientation & Information
Buses drop you in the central Largo dos Chorões, with its eye-catching water wheel, fountain and café. Here, too, is the **turismo** (☎ *282 911 189; open 10am-1pm & 1.30pm-4pm Mon-Fri Sept-May; to 4.30pm Mon-Fri, 9.30am-noon Sat June-Aug)*.

Old Town
A series of brown pedestrian signs starting near the bus station directs visitors up into the town's narrow old streets and major places of interest. The **igreja matriz** is the most notable piece of architecture, thanks to an extraordinary Manueline porch decorated with twisted columns looking like lengths of knotted rope.

Keep climbing and you'll eventually reach the ruined Franciscan monastery of **Nossa Senhora do Desterro**, which overlooks the town from its wooded hill top. Built in 1632, it's due to be redeveloped into a 24-room hotel.

Activities
All the following require advance reservations. German-run **Nature Walk** (☎ *282 911 041, 964 308 767)* organises one-day walking trips to nearby 773m Picota peak (adult/child €22.50/15) and full-moon walks during summer. **Alternativ Tour** (☎ *282 913 204, 965 004 337)* offers guided walking tours (€25, including 'Portuguese style' picnic) and bike tours for €33, including picnic (€15 on your own, with a map provided). Contact **Gunther** (☎ *282 913 657)* for guided horse-riding trips (€10 for first hour, plus €5 per subsequent hours). Advance notice is required; no beginners.

To soothe aching limbs after all this activity, call on **Nicole Joller** (☎ *282 913 522)* for a massage (€25 per hour).

Places to Stay
Residencial Estrela de Monchique (☎ *282 913 111; Rua do Porto Fundo 46; singles/doubles €17/25)*, near the bus station, provides good-value rooms.

Residencial Miradouro (☎ *282 912 163; Rua dos Combatentes do Ultramar; singles/doubles with breakfast €30/40)* is up steep Rua Engenheiro Duarte Pacheco (signposted to Portimão), near the bus station. This hilltop place offers breezy views and rooms with balcony.

Albergaria Bica-Boa (☎ 282 912 271; singles/doubles with breakfast €35/62.30), 1km out of town on the Lisbon road, is a cosy, Irish-run place overlooking a wooded valley, and has a little swimming pool in its garden. There's a decent restaurant here, too (with some vegetarian dishes).

Quinta de São Bento (☎/fax 282 912 143; doubles with breakfast €70), a former holiday home of the Portuguese royal family, is among upmarket places en route to Fóia. It also has a pool.

Places to Eat
There are several cheap café-restaurants around the bus station.

Restaurante Palmeirinha dos Chorões (☎ 282 912 588; Rua Serpa Pinto 23A; dishes €5-7), near the turismo, offers standard Portuguese fare.

A Charrete (☎ 282 912 142; Rua Dr Samora Gil 30-34; dishes €7-12, tourist menu €9.50) is the best upmarket option, where you can feast on specialities such as grilled boar steaks (€10) in a comfortable setting surrounded by cabinets of local pottery and other knick-knacks.

Monchique's Moonshine

You can find commercial brands of *medronho* (a locally made firewater) everywhere in Portugal, but according to those who have suffered enough hangovers to know, the best of all is the privately made brew from Monchique.

The Serra de Monchique is thick with *medronho*'s raw material – the arbutus, or strawberry tree. Its berries are collected in late autumn, fermented and then left for several months before being distilled in the kind of big copper stills you see for sale as souvenirs all over the Algarve.

Home-made *medronho* is usually clear and always drunk neat, like schnapps. It's strong, of course, but as long as you don't mix it with other drinks it doesn't give you a hangover (say the connoisseurs). Early spring (when distilling is underway) is the best time to track down some of this brew in Monchique: ask around.

Piri-Piri

All over the Algarve, especially in and around Monchique, are restaurants advertising *frango piri-piri*. What is it? A spicy condiment that made its way from Africa to Portuguese kitchens decades ago, piri-piri has since become a big hot hit when cooked with that all-time Portuguese favourite, roast chicken.

Getting There & Away
Nine weekday buses (five on weekends) make the run from Portimão to Monchique (€2.10, 45 minutes).

AROUND MONCHIQUE
Fóia
The 902m Fóia peak is the Algarve's highest point; it's 8km west of Monchique and accessible by a once-daily bus service from Monchique in summer only. Along the road, which climbs through eucalyptus and pines, is a string of restaurants specialising in piri-piri chicken (see the boxed text 'Piri-Piri'). The peak itself is a disappointment, bristling with ugly telecommunication towers, but its panoramic views make it a popular destination for tour buses. On clear days you can see out to the corners of the western Algarve – Cabo de São Vicente (near Sagres) to the southwest and Odeceixe to the northwest.

Caldas de Monchique
The snug hamlet of Caldas de Monchique, at the head of a delightful valley full of eucalyptus trees, acacias and pines, 6km south of Monchique, has been a popular spa for over two millennia. The Romans loved its 32°C, slightly sulphurous waters, which are said to be good for rheumatism, and respiratory and digestive ailments. Dom João II came here for years in an unsuccessful attempt to cure the dropsy that finally finished him off.

Disastrous floods in 1997 led to the closure of the spa hospital, followed by a major reconstruction of almost the entire place into an upmarket spa resort, its picturesque buildings repainted pastel pink, green and yellow.

Orientation & Information The hamlet is 500m below the main road. At reception (the first building on your left) you can

ALGARVE

book accommodation. Spa treatments and luxuries are available at the spa in the wooded valley below. There's an Internet facility at reception (€4 per hour).

Things to See & Do The most peaceful patch is a pretty, streamside garden above the hamlet's central square. Down the valley is the spa itself and below this is the huge bottling plant where the famous Caldas waters are bottled.

Just below the central square, in a small white building, you can taste the smelly, sulphurous water (beware – it's hot!).

Below, at the **spa** (☎ 282 910 913; open 9am-1pm & 3pm-7pm daily) you can indulge in everything from a hydromassage bath to a Vichy shower. The minimum available is a €20 'package', including sauna, Turkish bath and hydromassage (30% discount for hotel guests).

Places to Stay & Eat There are two private establishments: modern **Restaurante & Residencial Granifóia** (☎ 282 910 500, fax 282 912 218; singles/doubles with breakfast €30/37.50), 400m down the road from the turning to the hamlet, may not match the other smart hotels in looks, but it's friendly and excellent value (and there's a swimming pool).

Albergaria Lageado (☎ 282 912 616, fax 282 911 310; doubles with bathroom around €50; open year-round) is an attractive place in the hamlet itself, with a small pool surrounded by camellias.

The three other hotels located here all belong to **Termas de Monchique** (☎ 282 910 910; e spa@monchiquetermas.com): **Hotel Termal** (singles/doubles €53/60), next to the spa itself, is the cheapest and biggest; **Pensão Central** (singles/doubles €60/80), next to reception, has 13 beautifully furnished rooms; and **Estalagem Central** (singles/doubles €60/80, apartments €90), opposite reception, is the most luxurious of all.

The upmarket **Restaurante Dom João II** (dishes €8-22) is in the central square. It has pasta (€6.50) and vegetarian (€6 to €7) options, among other dishes.

Getting There & Away The Monchique to Portimão bus service (see under Monchique for details) goes via Caldas de Monchique (€1 from Monchique): the bus stop is on the road above the hamlet.

ALCOUTIM
postcode 8970 • pop 3700

As the N122 twists through coarse hills towards Alcoutim (ahl-ko-**teeng**), along the treeless valley of the Rio Guadiana (which forms the Algarve's entire eastern border), a fine hill-top stronghold comes into view. It's actually across the river in Alcoutim's mirror image, the Spanish village of Sanlúcar de Guadiana. It's hard to imagine that Alcoutim's lower, more humble fortress was ever a match for the Spanish one.

Like dozens of other fortified villages that face each other across the Rio Guadiana, these two castles are a reminder of centuries of mutual distrust. Forts have probably risen and decayed here ever since the Phoenicians made this village an important river port. Dom Fernando I of Portugal and Don Henrique II of Castile signed a tentative peace treaty here in the 14th century.

Within the Alcoutim area are eight *núcleos museológicos*, mini-museums that display everything from sacred art to traditional textiles and now neatly promoted as a cultural *roteiro* (tour); a €2.50 ticket gives admission to all of them. But it's easy to ignore such sightseeing in Alcoutim and simply wander the pretty, cobbled lanes, or ride a boat across (or along) the placid river.

Orientation & Information

The **turismo** (☎ 281 546 179; Rua 1 de Maio; open 9.30am-1pm & 2pm-5.30pm Fri-Mon, 9.30am-5.30pm Tues-Thur; to 7pm summer; sometimes closed Sat & Sun winter) is behind the central square, just a few steps from the river.

Casa dos Condes (☎ 281 546 104; open 9am-1pm & 2pm-5pm daily), opposite the turismo, has free Internet access plus a small display of local crafts. Another Internet facility is at **Café Vila Velha** (Rua da Misericordia; open around 8.30am-1am Mon-Sat), just off the central square, with access for €2.50 per hour.

Alcoutim has a new town development 500m north of the square across the Ribeira de Cadavais stream.

Castelo & Núcleo Museológico de Arqueologia

The original Portuguese castle (admission free; open 10am-1pm & 2pm-6pm daily) probably dates from pre-Moorish times;

what you see now is from the 14th century, with some grand river views from its battlements. Inside the castle grounds there's a small, excellent archaeological museum (*admission €1; open 10am-1pm & 2pm-6pm Tues-Sun*) displaying the remains of some medieval castle walls and other artefacts. An English text is available.

Activities
You can cross the river on a local boat (€1 one way; operating 9am to 1pm and 2pm to 6pm most days). Bikes (€7 per day) and canoes can be rented from the *pousada da juventude* (see Places to Stay).

Parque Mineiro Cova dos Mouros
Alcoutim's nearest 'theme park' is this prehistoric copper mine (*☎ 281 498 505; adult/child €5/4.20; open 10.30am-4.30pm daily Oct-Feb, 10.30am-6.30pm Mar-Sept*), 38km west near Vaqueiros. The site, which dates back to around 2500 BC, includes evidence of a Roman presence. You can follow a 1km walk past the old mine shafts and a reconstructed prehistoric house. For kids there are donkey rides and a nature trail. Swimming in the Rio Foupana is also possible.

Places to Stay & Eat
There are several private *quartos* available for around €25 a double; ask at the turismo for details. Recommended are those at **Loja das Prendas** (*☎ 281 546 221; Rua Dr João Dias 10A; singles/doubles €20/30*).

One kilometre north of the square, past the new town and fire station, is the fantastically situated **pousada da juventude** (*☎ 281 546 004;* [e] *alcoutim@movijovem.pt; dorm beds €12.50, doubles with bathroom €35, 4-/6-bed family rooms with bathroom €55/82.50; reception open 8am-noon & 6pm-midnight daily*), with a swimming pool and kitchen facilities, plus bikes and canoes for rent.

Estalagem do Guadiana (*☎ 281 540 120, fax 281 546 647; doubles with breakfast €74.30*), an upmarket place just below the *pousada da juventude*, also has its own pool and restaurant.

There are several café-restaurants around the square. **Snack Bar Restaurante O Soeiro** (*☎ 281 546 241; Rua do Município*) is the most tempting choice, with a few outdoor tables overlooking the river. This and **Casa de Pasto O Rogério** (*☎ 281 546 185; Praça da República*) serve great lunches (popular with locals, so go early) for under €7.

Getting There & Away
Alcoutim is at the end of a branch road off the N122 highway between Vila Real de Santo António and Beja in the Alentejo. A daily express bus to Lisbon (€11, five hours) starts from Vila Real and goes via Mértola and Beja, stopping 6km away from Alcoutim on the N122; a **taxi** (*☎ 281 546 173*) from Alcoutim to this bus stop costs around €4. Between July and September a second daily Lisbon express stops in Alcoutim itself, but you need to buy tickets a day ahead at Café Caçadora, opposite the turismo. On Monday and Friday there's an additional slower local service from Vila Real (€2.90, 70 minutes) to Beja (€6, two hours) via Mértola (€2.70, 50 minutes).

The Alentejo

Rolling plains and torrid summers characterise this vast southern province, one of the poorest and least populated parts of the country, stretching *alem Tejo* (beyond the Tejo) to cover almost a third of Portugal. You'll be struck by the emptiness and the austere, mesmerising nature of the land: mile after mile of huge agricultural estates freckled with cork and olive trees and awash with wheat. City folk may find it dull (and admittedly Baixo Alentejo, in the south, has few big attractions) but if you're looking for open spaces or for a Portugal steeped in rural traditions, here they are.

There's cultural history too, especially in the northern part of the province, the Alto Alentejo. The principal attraction is the delightful Renaissance city of Évora, of which the old centre is a Unesco World Heritage site. Nearby are the marble towns of Estremoz, Borba and Vila Viçosa, the heavily fortified frontier town of Elvas, and scores of prehistoric stone monuments.

It's the lure of the land, however, that makes the Alentejo special. Some of the country's finest rural architecture is found here, particularly in the medieval hill-top outposts of Monsaraz and Marvão. Alentejan folk dancers and singers are among the country's best and its cuisine one of the most distinctive (especially the inspired *carne de porco à Alentejana*, pork-and-clam stew). And the red table wines are famously punchy, the best from Borba and Reguengos de Monsaraz.

Coastal Alentejo, which includes part of the Parque Natural do Sudoeste Alentejano e Costa Vicentina (see the boxed text in the Algarve chapter), maintains a wild allure. If you like your swimming rough and refreshing, you'll love the beaches here. The popular but still low-key resort of Vila Nova de Milfontes is one of the best, with other smaller options nearby.

Transport between major towns is excellent, but in smaller places you're often down to a bus or two a day – which suits the pace of the province just fine.

History

The Alentejo's earliest residents left traces everywhere in the form of dolmens, menhirs

Highlights

- Visit the elegant, historic city of Évora, with its walled town and Roman temple
- Wander around the beautifully preserved hill-top villages of Monsaraz and Marvão
- Discover Neolithic standing stones in the wild countryside near Évora, Elvas and Castelo de Vide
- Survey Baixo Alentejo's dreamy, undulating landscape of wheat, cork and olive plains
- Spot storks and lesser kestrels in the culturally rich town of Mértola

and stone circles, making this one of the country's richest troves of prehistoric remains. But it was the Romans who had the greatest impact on the land, introducing vines, wheat and olives, building dams and irrigation schemes and, most significantly, founding huge estates called *latifúndios* (which still exist today) to make the most of the region's limited rivers and poor soil.

The Moors, arriving in the early 8th century, further developed the Romans' irrigation projects and introduced new crops such as citrus and rice. By 1279 they were on the run to southern Spain, or else were forced to live in special *mouraria* (segregated Moorish quarters) outside town walls. Many of their hill-top citadels were later reinforced by Dom Dinis, who forged a chain of

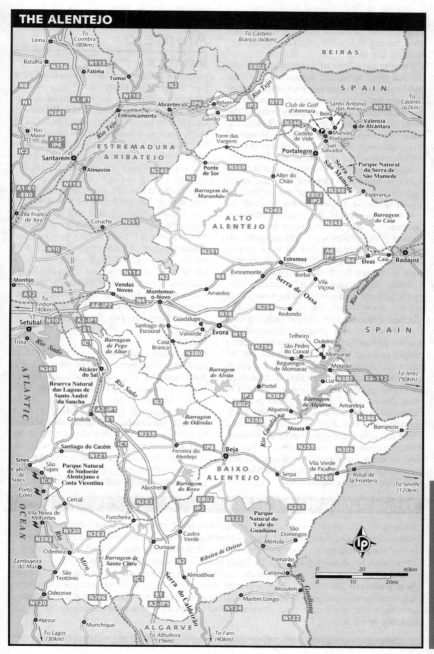

fortresses along the Spanish border. Rebuilt and reinforced countless times, they are now among the most spectacular strongholds in the land.

Despite the efforts of Romans and Moors, the Alentejo remained agriculturally poor and backward, increasingly so as the Age of Discoveries led to an explosive growth in maritime trade and as seaports became the focus of attention. Only Évora flourished, under the royal patronage of the House of Avis, although even this city declined once the Spanish seized the throne in 1580.

It was during the 1974 revolution that the Alentejo suddenly stepped into the limelight; landless rural workers who had laboured on the *latifúndios* for generations rose up in support of the communist rebellion and seized the land from its owners. Nearly 1000 estates were collectivised, although few succeeded and all were gradually reprivatised in the 1980s. Most are now back in the hands of their original owners.

Today the Alentejo remains among Europe's poorest and emptiest regions: Portugal's entry into the EU, increasing mechanisation meaning fewer jobs, successive droughts and greater opportunities elsewhere have all convinced many young people to head for the cities. In the last 40 years the Alentejo's population has nosedived by 45%, to just 255,000. Although its cork, olives, marble and granite are still in great demand, and the deep-water port and industrial zone of Sines is of national importance, this vast region contributes only a small fraction to the gross national product. Many are counting on the huge Alqueva dam to usher in a new era of agricultural prosperity (see the boxed text 'The Alqueva Dam' later in this chapter).

Coastal & Baixo Alentejo

MÉRTOLA

postcode 7750 • pop 1300 • elevation 70m
The delightfully flinty old village of Mértola is perched on a ridge between the serene Rio Guadiana and the Ribeira de Oeiras tributary. A picturesque cluster of little houses surrounding a Moorish castle, Mértola has huge historical and archaeological interest: the whole place is billed as a *vila museu* (open-air museum), with several *núcleos* (areas of historic interest).

It's also an increasingly popular tourist destination, famous for its visiting storks and rare lesser kestrels. But it still feels a long way from anywhere. The copper mines at São Domingos (15km to the east) once provided a source of local employment, but the site is now a ghost town. Agriculture has taken over: all around are grain fields and plantations of cork oaks, especially mesmerising on the road north towards Beja. Much of this is now part of the Parque Natural do Vale do Guadiana (see the boxed text).

History
Mértola goes back a long way. First to arrive were Phoenician traders, who sailed up the Guadiana. The Carthaginians followed. The settlement's strategic position – the northernmost port on the Guadiana, and the final destination for many Mediterranean routes – led the Romans to develop Mértola (naming it Myrtilis) as a major agricultural and mineral-exporting centre. Cereals and olive oil arrived from Beja, copper and other metals from Aljustrel and São Domingos. Many rich merchants settled here.

Parque Natural do Vale do Guadiana

Created in 1995, this 600-sq-km zone of hills, plains and deep valleys around Serpa and Mértola shelters the Rio Guadiana, one of Portugal's largest and most important rivers. Among its rich variety of flora and fauna are several rare or endangered species, including the black stork (most visible at Mértola), Bonelli's eagle, royal owl, grey kite, horned viper and Iberian toad.

The park also has a rich cultural heritage, especially the prehistoric remains around Mértola. **Park headquarters** (☎ 286 611 084; e pnvg@icn.pt; *Rua Dr Afonso Costa 40, Mértola*) has surprisingly little information (and none in English), though you can inquire here about park accommodation near the border town of Canavial, 20km southeast of Mértola, where there are two double rooms plus one house sleeping 12.

Later the Moors, who called it Martulah and made it a regional capital, further fortified Mértola and also built the mosque. Dom Sancho II and the Knights of the Order of Santiago captured the site in 1238. As commercial routes shifted to the Tejo, the Guadiana lost its commercial importance and Mértola declined. When the last steamboat service to Vila Real de Santo António ended and the copper mines of São Domingos (established by a British firm in 1857) closed in 1965, its role as a port finally ended.

Orientation

From the bus station in the new part of town, it's about 600m southwest to the historic old walled town. Old Mértola has few

right angles or horizontal surfaces, and driving into it is asking for trouble – even a donkey would struggle on its skewed, cobbled, narrow lanes.

Information

Just inside the walled town is the **turismo** (tourist office; ☎ 286 612 573; Rua Alonso Gomes 18; open 10am-1pm & 3pm-7pm daily June-Sept, 9am-12.30pm & 2pm-5.30pm daily Oct-May).

The **centro de saúde** (medical centre; ☎ 286 610 900) is just off Rua Dr Afonso Costa, along which are the **police station** (☎ 286 612 127), banks with ATMs and the **Parque Natural do Vale do Guadiana** headquarters (Rua Dr Afonso Costa 40). The post office is on Rua Alves Redol.

MÉRTOLA

PLACES TO STAY
1 Private Rooms (Café Campaniço)
2 Residencial San Remo
12 Pensão Oasis
13 Residencial Beira Rio
15 Casa Rosmaninho
22 Casa Janelas Verdes

PLACES TO EAT
3 Cegonha Branca
5 Restaurante Boa Viagem
14 Restaurante O Náutico

OTHER
4 Bus Station
6 Police Station
7 Parque Natural do Vale do Guadiana Headquarters
8 Bank & ATM
9 Centro de Saúde
10 Museu Paleocristão
11 Bank & ATM
16 Post Office
17 Oficina de Tecelagem
18 Tourist Office
19 Igreja Matriz
20 Castelo
21 Torre do Relógio
23 Museu Romano; Câmara Municipal
24 Alsafir
25 Al-Kazaf
26 Museu de Arte Sacra
27 Museu Islâmico
28 Torre do Rio

Largo Luís de Camões

This is the administrative heart of the old town, a tiny, picturesque square lined with orange trees, with the *câmara municipal* (town hall) at its western end. To reach the *largo* (small square), enter the old town and keep to the left at every fork in the road.

The cobbled lanes and sleepy atmosphere make strolling around this part of Mértola like entering a time warp. The **Torre do Relógio**, a little clock tower topped with a stork's nest and overlooking the Rio Guadiana, is northeast of the square.

Igreja Matriz

This striking parish church *(admission free; open variable hrs Tues-Sun)* – square, flat-faced and topped with little conical decorations – is best known for the fact that it was once a mosque, among the few to have survived the Reconquista. It was reconsecrated as a church in the 13th century. An unwhitewashed cavity in the wall on the right behind the altar is the former mosque's *mihrab* (prayer niche). Note also the goats, lions and other figures carved around the peculiar Gothic portal and the typically Moorish horse-shoe arch in the north door.

Castelo & Torre do Rio

Above the parish church looms Mértola's fortified castle *(admission free; open 24hr)*, most of which dates from the 13th century. It was built upon Moorish foundations next to an Islamic residential complex and *alcáçova* (citadel), which itself overlaid the Roman forum. For centuries the castle was considered western Iberia's most impregnable fortress. From its prominent **keep** (see Museums, following, for opening times and admission) you can look down on archaeological digs outside the castle on one side, and the old town and the river on the other.

At the river's edge, near its confluence with the Ribeira de Oeiras, is the ruined, Roman-era **Torre do Rio** (River Tower), which once guarded the vital port.

Museums

All of Mértola's museums, including the castle keep, have the same opening hours: 9am to 12.30pm and 2pm to 5.30pm Tuesday to Sunday October to May; 10am to 1pm and 3pm to 7pm Tuesday to Sunday June to

September. A single adult/student €3/1.50 admission fee covers all of the sights.

In the cellar of the *câmara municipal* is the modest but very good **Museu Romano** *(Roman Museum; Largo Luís de Camões)*. Its main attraction is the foundations of the Roman house upon which the building rests; it also contains a small collection of pots, sculpture and other artefacts.

At the southern end of the old town, the recently renovated **Museu Islâmico** (Islamic Museum) is a small but dramatic display (with atmospheric sound effects) of inscribed funerary stones, jewellery, pots and jugs from the 11th to 13th centuries.

The nearby **Museu de Arte Sacra** *(Museum of Ecclesiastical Art; Largo da Misericórdia)* exhibits religious statuettes from the 16th to 18th centuries and three impressive 16th-century retables, originally in the parish church, portraying the battle against the Moors.

North of the old town is the **Museu Paleocristão** *(Paleo-Christian Museum; Rossio do Carmo)*, which is perhaps the most impressive museum of all, with a partly reconstructed line of 6th-century Roman columns and poignant funerary stones, some beautifully carved with birds, hearts and wreaths. This was the site of a huge Paleo-Christian basilica, its adjacent cemetery used over the centuries by both Roman-era Christians and medieval Moors.

Convento de São Francisco

This former convent *(adult/student €1/0.50; open 10am-5pm daily May-Sept, 2pm-6pm Tues-Sun Oct-Apr)*, across the Ribeira de Oeiras, 500m southwest of Mértola along a rutted track, has been owned since 1980 by Dutch artist Geraldine Zwannikken and her family. They have transformed it into a rather bizarre nature reserve and art gallery: its grounds full of herbs, horses, rain temples and wild flowers; its former chapel exhibiting Geraldine's extraordinary art; and its riverside devoted to nesting storks and lesser kestrels. On offer are occasional workshops, as well as horse rides (by prior arrangement).

Places to Stay

Among several *quartos* (private rooms) are those belonging to Senhor Domingos at **Café Campaniço** *(☎ 286 612 285; Rua José Carlos Ary dos Santos; singles/doubles from €15/25)*.

Residencial San Remo (☎ 286 612 132, fax 286 611 139; Avenida Aureliano Mira Fernandes 8; doubles without bathroom €25) is a dingy option by the bus terminal.

Pensão Oasis (☎ 286 612 701; Rua Dr Afonso Costa; doubles €25), just below the old town and overlooking the river, is more attractively located (but often closed in low season).

Residencial Beira Rio (☎ 286 611 190; e beira.rio@mail.com; Rua Dr Afonso Costa 108; singles/doubles with air-con €35/38) is the best option of all. Several rooms boast large patios with river views. Reception opens at 4pm.

There are two beautifully converted Turihab properties: **Casa Rosmaninho** (☎ 286 612 005; Rua 25 de Abril 23; doubles €35) has superb rooms, including one with a Jacuzzi and another with a rooftop terrace; **Casa Janelas Verdes** (☎ 286 612 145; Rua Dr Manuel Francisco Gomes 38; doubles €35-40), in the old town, has traditional doubles, complete with a famously good breakfast.

Places to Eat

Mértola's specialities are *javali* (wild boar) and the regional dish *migas*, a filling but somewhat depressing sludge of pork and fried bread.

Restaurante Boa Viagem (☎ 286 612 483; Rua Dr Afonso Costa 1; dishes €5-8, daily specials from €4.50) is one of several modest restaurants near the bus station; its *pratos do dia* (daily specials) are guaranteed to fill you up.

Cegonha Branca (☎ 286 611 066; Avenida Aureliano Mira Fernandes 2C) is pricier and posher than Boa Viagem, with lampreys in season (around €20) and hearty *costeletas de javali* (wild boar cutlets; €7).

Restaurante O Náutico (☎ 286 612 596; Rua Serrão Martins 16; open Mon-Sat; dishes from €5), above the riverside Nautical Club, has a pleasant setting. Be brave and try the *migas à alentejano* (cornbread and fatty pork; €6).

Entertainment

There are a couple of bars in the old town, including **Alsafir** (☎ 286 618 049; Rua dos Combatentes da Grande Guerra 9; open 9pm-4am daily), which is at its most liveliest at weekends.

Shopping

Oficina de Tecelagen (admission free; open 9am-12.30pm & 2pm-5.30pm Tues-Sun Oct-May, 10am-1pm & 3pm-7pm June-Sept) is an appealing crafts centre that exhibits traditional wool weaving. It's located down some steps just before the old town entrance. **Al-Kazaf**, next to the Museu de Arte Sacra, is a workshop that produces finely painted ceramics in traditional styles.

Getting There & Away

There's a daily express bus (two daily from July to September) to Lisbon (€11, 4¼ hours) and Vila Real de Santo António (€6.80, 1½ hours); a slower local Vila Real service (€4.20, two hours) via Alcoutim (€2.70, 50 minutes) runs on Monday and Friday. Two ordinary services daily (€3.30, 1¼ hours) and one express (€7.60, 65 minutes) run to/from Beja.

Kestrel Haven

The kestrel that is commonly seen hovering alongside motorways all over Europe has a dainty Mediterranean cousin, the lesser kestrel, which nests in colonies and is much more specific in its habitat requirements. Unfortunately it is in serious decline, due mainly to changes in agricultural practices. In Spain the population has crashed from 100,000 pairs to less than 5000 in 30 years. It's estimated that there are fewer than 200 pairs left in Portugal.

Many of the remaining birds congregate around Mértola, where strenuous – and successful – efforts have been made to save them. Nest boxes have been placed under the Ribeira de Oeiras bridge, and in the Convento de São Francisco a specially designed nesting tower has been built. The lesser kestrel population is thriving here.

The best time to see this splendid falcon is between March and September. The castle ramparts make the best viewing spot.

Clive Viney

ALENTEJO

BEJA
postcode 7800 • pop 21,700
• elevation 240m
Baixo Alentejo's principal town – at the heart of what the tourist authorities call the Planície Dourada (Golden Plain) – is a hearty agricultural centre, with a historic and elegant old core. Good transport connections, accommodation and loads of great-value restaurants make this an attractive stopover between Évora and the Algarve. If you arrive on a Saturday there's the bonus of a very traditional market, spread around the castle.

History
The Romans founded Beja on the highest point of the surrounding plains. They called it Pax Julia, after Julius Caesar restored peace between the Romans and rebellious Lusitanians. It became an important agricultural centre, flourishing principally on trade in wheat and oil.

Little evidence remains of the 400 years of subsequent Moorish rule, except for some distinctive 16th-century *azulejos* (hand-painted tiles) in the Convento de Nossa Senhora da Conceição (now the Museu Regional). The town was recaptured from the Moors in 1162.

Beja's fame among the Portuguese rests on a series of scandalous 17th-century love letters allegedly written by one of the convent's nuns, Mariana Alcoforado, to a French cavalry officer, Count Chamilly. She was said to have had a love affair with the count while he was stationed in Beja during

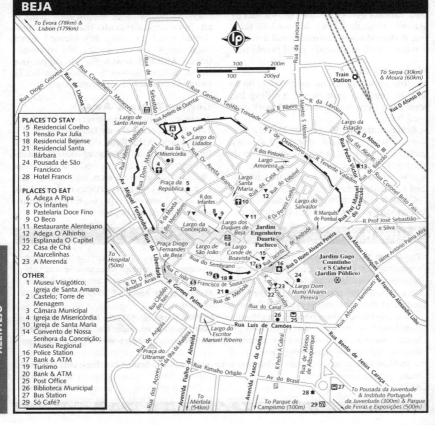

BEJA

To Évora (78km) &
Lisbon (179km)

To Serpa (30km)
& Moura (60km)

Train
Station

PLACES TO STAY
5 Residencial Coelho
13 Pensão Pax Julia
18 Residencial Bejense
21 Residencial Santa
    Bárbara
24 Pousada de São
    Francisco
28 Hotel Francis

PLACES TO EAT
6 Adega A Pipa
7 Os Infantes
8 Pastelaria Doce Fino
9 O Beco
11 Restaurante Alentejano
12 Adega O Alhinho
15 Esplanada O Capitel
22 Casa de Chá
    Marcelinhas
23 A Merenda

OTHER
1 Museu Visigótico;
   Igreja de Santa Amaro
2 Castelo; Torre de
   Menagem
3 Câmara Municipal
4 Igreja de Misericórdia
10 Igreja de Santa Maria
14 Convento de Nossa
    Senhora da Conceição;
    Museu Regional
16 Police Station
17 Bank & ATM
19 Turismo
20 Bank & ATM
25 Post Office
26 Biblioteca Municipal
27 Bus Station
29 Só Café?

the time of the Portuguese war with Spain. The passionate *Five Letters of a Portuguese Nun* first emerged in a French 'translation' in 1669 and later appeared in English. However, because the originals were never found, the letters' authenticity has been the subject of lively controversy ever since.

Orientation

Beja's historic core is circled by a ring road and surrounded by modern outskirts. The train station is about 500m northeast of the centre, the bus station 400m southeast. The main sights are all within an easy walk of each other. Drivers are advised to park near the bus station.

Information

The **turismo** (*☎/fax 284 311 9113;* **w** *www .rt-planiciedourada.pt; Rua Capitão João Francisco de Sousa 25; open 9am-7pm Mon-Sat June-Oct, 10am-1pm & 2pm-6pm Nov-May)* has colourful publications for sale, including the great multilingual *Tourist Guidebook to the Planicie Dourada* (€2.50) and *Nature Trails* (€1), both with suggested itineraries and maps.

Useful facilities include banks with ATMs near the turismo, a **police station** (*☎ 284 322 022; Largo Dom Nuno Álvares Pereira)* and a **hospital** (*☎ 284 310 200; Rua Dr António Covas Lima).* The **post office** (*Rua Luís de Camões; open 8.30am-6.30pm Mon-Fri)* has NetPost.

Free Internet access is available at the **Instituto Português da Juventude** (*IPJ; ☎ 284 325 458; Rua Acabado Janeiro; open Mon-Fri).* **Só Café?** (*☎ 284 327 541; Centro Comercial Pax Júlia, Loja 16; open 9am-midnight daily)* charges €1 per hour.

Praça da República

This attractive town square with a central *pelourinho* (stone pillory) and elegant Manueline arcade is the historic heart of the old city. Dominating the square is the 16th-century **Igreja de Misericórdia**, a hefty church with an immense porch that started life as a meat market – hence its suitably crude stonework. Incredibly, a mobile phone mast now sticks up right behind it.

Castelo

Dom Dinis built the castle (*admission free; open 10am-1pm & 2pm-6pm Tues-Sun May-*Oct, *9am-noon & 1pm-4pm Nov-Apr)* on Roman foundations in the late 13th century. There are grand views from the top of the very impressive 42m-high **Torre de Menagem** (*admission €1.20).* The ticket office has free bilingual leaflets on Beja's culture, arts and heritage.

Convento de Nossa Senhora da Conceição & Museu Regional

This former Franciscan convent (*Largo da Conceição; admission €0.50; open 9.30am-12.30pm & 2pm-5.15pm Tues-Sun),* founded in 1459, displays a mix of plain Gothic and fancy Manueline styles typical of the time. The interior is even more lavish than the exterior, especially the Rococo chapel dripping with 17th- and 18th-century gilded woodwork. The cloister has some splendid 16th- and 17th-century azulejos, although the earliest and most interesting examples are in the chapterhouse, which also sports an incredible painted ceiling and carved doorway.

The Museu Regional displays everything from Roman mosaics and stone tombs to 16th-century paintings, though it pales in comparison with the convent building itself. The admission fee includes entry to the Museu Visigótico.

Museu Visigótico

Found just beyond the castle, the Visigothic museum (*admission €0.50; open 9.30am-12.15pm & 2pm-5.15pm Tues-Sun)* is housed in the former Igreja de Santo Amaro, parts of which date from the early 6th century when it was a Visigothic church. This makes it one of Portugal's oldest standing buildings. Inside, some of the original columns display intriguing, beautiful carvings. The admission fee includes entry to the Museu Regional.

Special Events

Beja's biggest event is the Ovibeja agricultural fair in mid-March. Held in the Parque de Feiras e Exposições on the southeastern outskirts, it's grown from a livestock market to include an enthusiastic display of regional and national music, handicrafts and cuisine. Another attractive event, held in the same venue over a weekend in late November, is Expo Alentejo, showcasing regional handicrafts.

ALENTEJO

Places to Stay

Beja's municipal **parque de campismo** (camping ground; ☎ 284 311 911; Avenida Vasco da Gama; adult/tent/car €2/1.50/1.50) is part of a municipal sports area that includes a swimming pool and tennis courts.

The **pousada da juventude** (youth hostel; ☎ 284 325 458; Rua Prof Janeiro Acabado; e beja@movijovem.pt; dorm beds €9.50, doubles with/without bathroom €23/21) is next to the IPJ, 300m southeast of the bus station. It has laundry and kitchen facilities, plus bikes for rent (€5 per day).

Pensão Pax Julia (☎ 284 322 575; Rua Pedro Victor 8; doubles with/without bathroom €25/20) has musty, frilly rooms; those facing the road are noisy.

Residencial Coelho (☎ 284 324 031, fax 284 328 939; Praça da República 15; doubles €37.50) is rather shabby, though it does have some rooms overlooking the square.

Several notches higher are the welcoming **Residencial Bejense** (☎ 284 311 570, fax 284 311 579; Rua Capitão João Francisco de Sousa 57; doubles with breakfast €40), with an attractive lounge-bar with a log fire; and the briskly efficient **Residencial Santa Bárbara** (☎ 284 312 280, fax 284 312 289; Rua de Mértola 36; doubles with breakfast €37.50), offering spacious doubles. Both are in the pedestrianised town centre.

Hotel Francis (☎ 284 315 500; e hotel .francis@mail.telepac.pt; Praça Fernando Lopes Graça; doubles with breakfast €58) is a modern three-star place, boasting a well-equipped gym and easy parking.

Pousada de São Francisco (☎ 284 313 580, fax 284 329 143; Largo Dom Nuno Álvares Pereira; doubles with breakfast Mon-Fri €159, Sat & Sun €168) provides gorgeous luxury in the former 16th-century São Francisco Convent.

Places to Eat

There's no lack of fantastic places to eat here, including two very appealing adegas (wine taverns). **Adega A Pipa** (☎ 284 327 043; Rua da Moeda 8; meals under €6, half-portions from €4; open Mon-Sat), a typical Alentejan tavern, serves meals in a room as big as a barn. **Adega O Alhinho** (☎ 284 324 615; Rua da Casa Pia 28; open Mon-Sat), a little, unmarked place stacked with huge wine jars, is opposite the Red Cross headquarters. Choose your entrances carefully: the green door leads into a dark, seedy bar, while the red one leads into the tiny restaurant (go early to get a seat). The modestly priced dishes include delicious desserts.

O Beco (☎ 284 325 900; Rua dos Infantes; dishes €6) serves simple, standard fare.

Restaurante Alentejano (☎ 284 323 849; Largo dos Duques de Beja 6; dishes €5-6; open Sat-Thur), a popular local venue, serves generous helpings at great prices. Try the hearty cozido a Portuguesa (Portuguese-style meat stew) for €5.

Os Infantes (☎ 284 322 789; Rua dos Infantes 14; dishes from €9; open Thur-Tues), a classy place near O Beco, offers excellent Alentejan specialities.

For delicious regional pastries make a beeline for **Pastelaria Doce Fino** (Rua dos Infantes 29), or for the classier **Casa de Chá Marcelinhas** (☎ 284 321 500; Rua dos Açoutados 12), which serves typical doces conventuais (desserts traditionally made by nuns).

Esplanada O Capitel (☎ 284 325 708; Jardim Engenheiro Duarte Pacheco) is a relaxing open-air café serving snacks. **A Merenda** (☎ 284 327 726; Largo Dom Nuno Álvares Pereira 13B) is a plain, good-value café where lunch-time half-portions cost only €3.50 (leave room for the great puddings).

Getting There & Away

Bus From the bus terminal (☎ 284 313 620) six buses daily run to Évora (€7, 80 minutes); one express bus (€7.60, 65 minutes) and two local buses (€3.30, 1¼ hours) run to Mértola; and seven buses run to Serpa (€2.30, 45 minutes), five continuing to Moura (€3.50, 65 minutes). Around half this number operates on weekends. Three express buses run to Faro daily (€9.50, 3¼ hours) via Albufeira (€9, 2¼ hours), and six to Lisbon (€9.30, 3¼ hours).

Buses also run to the Spanish border town of Ficalho (€6.30, 65 minutes, two to three daily), and on Tuesday, Thursday and Saturday via Aracena (€9.30, 2½ hours) to Seville (€15.60, 3½ hours).

Train Beja is on the Lisbon to Funcheira (near Ourique) railway line. There are three direct intercidade (IC) services from Lisbon (€8.20, 2½ hours, including Tejo ferry crossing to Barreiro station) and three direct regional trains (€6.80, 3¼ hours).

Getting Around

Bikes are available for free use within the city from the *câmara municipal* (near Praça da República) or the turismo. Some form of ID (eg, passport) must be left as a deposit.

SERPA

postcode 7830 • pop 6400 • elevation 230m

If you approach Serpa from Beja (30km to the northwest) on a dusky summer's evening the striking outlines of the aqueduct and castle walls above the surrounding plains might lead you to believe you've arrived at an undiscovered medieval outpost (as long as you ignore the massive grain elevator on the outskirts!).

Inside the walls it's just as delightful, with an untouristed, laid-back atmosphere and narrow lanes, cobbled in patterns and lined with whitewashed houses. It makes a tempting place for a stop en route to Spain or the eastern Alentejo.

Orientation

Those arriving by car must brave tight gateways into the old town, blind corners and breathtakingly narrow streets.

The bus station, *mercado municipal* (municipal market) and *parque de campismo* are in the new town area, southwest of the old town. From the bus station, turn left and first right and keep walking till you see the walls.

Information

Right in the centre, the **turismo** (☎ 284 544 727; Largo Dom Jorge de Melo 2; open 9am-12.30pm & 2pm-5.30pm daily) sells a detailed, photocopy map of the old town and local handicrafts. There's a **bank** (Praça da República) around the corner from the turismo.

Internet access is available at **C@fe** (☎ 284 548 066; Rua Dr Eduardo Fernando de Oliveira 18; open 9am-1am Mon-Fri, 11am-4am Sat & Sun), a smoky dive 250m east of the *mercado municipal*. It charges €1/1.50 per 15/30 minutes.

On the fourth Tuesday of the month a huge country market sprawls beside Rua de Santo António on the northeastern outskirts of town.

Castelo

The courtyard of the surprisingly small castle (admission free; open 9am-12.30pm &

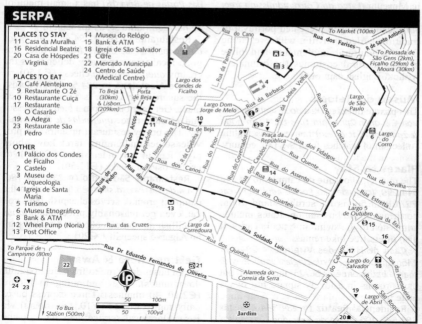

SERPA

PLACES TO STAY
11 Casa da Muralha
16 Residencial Beatriz
20 Casa de Hóspedes Virgínia

PLACES TO EAT
7 Café Alentejano
9 Restaurante O Zé
10 Restaurante Cuiça
17 Restaurante O Casarão
19 A Adega
23 Restaurante São Pedro

OTHER
1 Palácio dos Condes de Ficalho
2 Castelo
3 Museu de Arqueologia
4 Igreja de Santa Maria
5 Turismo
6 Museu Etnográfico
8 Bank & ATM
12 Wheel Pump (Noria)
13 Post Office
14 Museu do Relógio
15 Bank & ATM
18 Igreja de São Salvador
21 C@fe
22 Mercado Municipal
24 Centro de Saúde (Medical Centre)

2pm-5.30pm Tues-Sun) is entered beneath a precariously balanced bit of ruined wall. Inside is the small **Museu de Arqueologia** (admission free; open 9am-12.15pm & 2pm-5.15pm Tues-Sun), housing a small, poorly labelled collection of archaeological remnants that reveal bits of Serpa's history, which reaches back to the arrival of the Celts over 2000 years ago.

The castle's best feature is the view from its battlements, with close-ups of Serpa's aqueduct and cottage gardens and a panorama of undulating wheat fields.

Town Walls & Aqueduto

Walls still stand around most of the inner town. Along the west side (follow Rua dos Arcos) run the impressive remains of an 11th-century aqueduct. At the southern end is a huge 17th-century noria, or wheel pump, once used for pumping water along the aqueduct to the nearby **Palácio dos Condes de Ficalho** (still used by the de Ficalho family as a holiday home).

Museu Etnográfico

Serpa's beautifully maintained Ethnographic Museum (Largo do Corro; admission free; open 9am-12.30pm & 2pm-5.30pm Tues-Sun) features a well-presented portrayal of traditional Alentejan life, with everything from agricultural implements and olive presses to rural costumes (unfortunately without English captions).

Museu do Relógio

This private museum (Rua do Assento; admission €2; open 2pm-5pm Tues-Fri, 10am-noon & 2pm-5pm Sat & Sun) houses a fascinating collection of watches from the 18th century.

Places to Stay

The municipal **parque de campismo** (☎ 284 544 290; Largo de São Pedro; adult/tent/car €2/1.80/1.50) is on scrubby land 400m northeast of the bus station. Rates include admission to the swimming pool nearby. It also offers free bike rental.

Casa de Hóspedes Vírginia (☎ 284 549 145; Largo 25 de Abril; singles/doubles with shared bathroom €12.50/25) has spartan but clean rooms in a lovely square full of orange trees.

Residencial Beatriz (☎ 284 544 423, fax 284 543 100; Largo do Salvador 10; singles/ doubles with air-con & breakfast €26/37) is a comfortable place.

Casa da Muralha (☎/fax 284 543 150; Rua das Portas de Beja 43; doubles with breakfast €50), literally hugging the town walls, is a Turihab property, with five beautifully furnished rooms opening out onto an enchanting garden of bougainvillea and orange trees.

Pousada de São Gens (☎ 284 540 420, fax 284 544 337; doubles Mon-Fri €126, Sat & Sun €139) stands on a hill top 2km south of town, next to a dazzling white Moorish chapel. For a swimming pool and superb views, head for this isolated but accommodating place.

Places to Eat

Restaurante O Casarão (☎ 284 549 295; Largo do Salvador 20; dishes from €6) is a cheerful place that's popular with locals and offers generous servings.

A Adega (☎ 284 544 308, Rua do Rossio 76; pizzas €5-5.50), nearby, is a family-friendly pizzeria that also serves Portuguese fare (mostly €6 to €7.50).

Restaurante Cuiça (☎ 284 549 566; Rua das Portas de Beja 18) has a small menu of Alentejan specialities, including ensopada de borrego (lamb stew) for €6.50.

Restaurante O Zé (☎ 284 549 246; Praça da República 10; dishes from €4.30) has good local fare; especially delicious is the creamy queijo de Serpa cheese (€2.50).

Café Alentejano (☎ 284 544 189), across the square from O Zé, is a cool Art Deco place. Get your buzz from a bica (expresso) and a locally made queijadas de Serpa pastry. The pricey restaurant upstairs can provide some challenging fare: how about pigs' feet in coriander sauce (€6.30), or grilled ostrich steaks (€11.50)?

Restaurante São Pedro (☎ 284 543 186; Avenida da Paz; dishes €5.50-8), near the camping ground, serves cheapish fare; you can even get reasonably priced cataplanas (shellfish and ham cooked in a sealed pan, an Algarve speciality, €20).

Getting There & Away

Seven buses daily run to/from Beja (€2.30, 45 minutes), five continuing to Moura (€2.10, 40 minutes). Three express buses daily run to Lisbon (€10, four hours) via Beja. One local service goes daily to the

Spanish frontier at Ficalho (€2.10, 55 minutes). Far fewer services run at weekends.

MOURA

postcode 7860 • pop 8500 • elevation 180m

Surrounded by a soporific landscape of wheat fields and olive orchards, Moura feels a bit like a ghost town. Some 60km northeast of Beja, it was once a major agricultural and mining centre, patronised by the wealthy for its thermal spa (still in use). Now its quiet, broad streets and elegant houses seem oddly grandiose for such an out-of-the-way place.

The town's most dramatic historical moment has an element of fantasy, too. Legend says a Moorish woman, Moura Salúquiyya, opened the gates of the town to her betrothed only to find that a horde of Christians had murdered him and his escort, and dressed in their victims' clothes. They sacked the town, and Moura flung herself from a tower in despair. In fact, the Moors' 500-year occupation came to an end in 1232 with a rather less inspired takeover by Christian forces, though Moura's name lived on and her tower was incorporated into the town's coat of arms.

Today the town is gaining questionable fame as the nearest large town to the giant new dam at Alqueva, 15km to the north (see the boxed text 'The Alqueva Dam'). Already, new bridges span the empty landscape, much of which will be flooded by 2004, and a glaringly white new village has been built to rehouse the villagers of Luz, 28km north.

Meanwhile, Moura itself makes a pleasant excursion, if only to visit the immaculate Moorish quarter (it's one of the best preserved in Portugal).

Orientation

The bus station is by the defunct train station at the newer, southern end of town, around 500m from the old town and its central Praça Sacardo Cabral. All the main places of interest are within easy walking distance of the *praça* (town square).

Information

The **turismo** (☎ 285 251 375; Largo de Santa Clara; open 9am-1pm & 2pm-5pm Mon-Fri, 10am-1pm & 2.30pm-5.30pm Sat & Sun) is 400m downhill from the bus station; turn left into the first main street, Rua das Forças

Armadas, and right at the end. If you're driving from Serpa you'll pass it on your way into town. It has a colourful leaflet about Moura, but ask for the more useful photocopied map with street names.

There are banks on the *praça* and along Rua Serpa Pinto directly north of the turismo. The **post office** (Rua da República) is east of Rua Serpa Pinto.

Museu Municipal

This fine little museum (Rua da Romeira; admission free; open 9.30am-12.30pm & 2.30pm-6pm Tues-Fri, 10am-noon & 2.30pm-5pm Sat & Sun), off a residential lane about 200m east of the *praça*, contains local

The Alqueva Dam

The arid Alentejo is always gasping for water. One of Portugal's major agricultural regions, it employs a host of irrigation schemes and reservoirs to keep its soil from cracking. The most important source of water is the Rio Guadiana, which rises in Spain and flows through the Alentejo. Various agreements with Spain were meant to ensure that its waters were fairly shared.

Unfortunately, successive droughts have strained the arrangement. Spain is accused of using more water from the Guadiana than agreed, and it also has its own, incompatible water plans. After decades of delay the Portuguese finally took matters into their own hands and started work on a giant dam at Alqueva, near Moura, to guarantee both irrigation water and electricity for years to come.

The dam, completed in 2002, creates an 83km-long reservoir – Europe's largest, and big enough to substantially reduce the average temperature of the surrounding region. The economic benefits are also substantial: by feeding 15 other dams, it is expected to create 250 sq km of well-irrigated land by 2006, supposedly supporting lucrative crops of fruits, flowers, tomatoes and sugar beets. Tourism projects around the dam could also provide a major boost to the area.

There are serious environmental and social concerns, however (see Ecology & Environment in the Facts about Portugal chapter), and these are only likely to increase as the water rises.

ALENTEJO

prehistoric and Roman remains as well as Moorish funerary tablets.

Lagar de Varas do Fojo

The Oil Press of Varas de Fojo (*Rua João de Deus 20; admission free; open 9.30am-12.30pm & 2.30pm-5.30pm Tues-Sun*) recreates the oil-pressing factory that functioned here until 1941. The site is complete with giant wooden and stone-wheel presses.

Spa

The thermal spa (*open 8am-1pm & 3pm-6pm Tues-Sat*) is at the entrance to the shady Jardim Dr Santiago, at the eastern end of Praça Sacadura Cabral. For around €1 you can soak in a bath for 15 minutes. Bicarbonated calcium waters, said to be good for rheumatism, also burble from the richly marbled **Fonte das Três Bicas** (Fountain with Three Spouts) by the entrance to the *jardim*.

Igreja de São Baptista

Just outside the Jardim Dr Santiago you'll notice the Manueline portal of this 16th-century church. It's a flamboyant bit of decoration, with carvings of knotted ropes, crowns and armillary spheres on an otherwise dull facade. There's little of interest inside the church apart from some fine 17th-century Sevillian azulejos.

Mouraria

The old Moorish quarter (signposted 'Poço Árabe') lies at the western end of Praça Sacadura Cabral; it's a tight cluster of narrow, cobbled lanes and white terraced cottages sporting noticeably chunky or turreted chimneys. Dusk is an atmospheric time to wander here – people lean out of their stable doors for a chat and kids play hide-and-seek in the streets.

The **Núcleo Árabe** (*Travessa da Mouraria 11; admission free; variable opening hrs*) just off Largo da Mouraria is a small display of Moorish ceramics and an original 14th-century Arabic well. If the door's closed, knock at nearby Segunda Rua Mouraria 28.

Castelo

Above the old town is a ruined tower, the last remnant of a Moorish fortress. Rebuilt by Dom Dinis in the 13th century and again by Dom Manuel I in 1510, the castle itself was largely destroyed by the Spanish in the

18th century. There are plans to restore the entire area and make the tower accessible, but it'll probably take years.

Places to Stay

Residencial A Casa da Moura (*☎/fax 285 251 264; Largo Dr Rodrigues Acabado 47; doubles with breakfast €38*), in the heart of the old town near the museum, is a delightful 10-room place with a friendly ambience and tidy rooms.

Residencial Alentejana (*☎ 285 250 080; e pensaoalentejana@mail.telepac.pt; Largo José Maria dos Santos 40; doubles with aircon & breakfast €38*), close to the bus station, is very stylish. It's not signposted, so look for the green-shuttered house opposite the Galp petrol station.

Hotel de Moura (*☎ 285 251 090, fax 285 254 610; Praça Gago Coutinho; doubles with breakfast €45*) is a traditional hotel in an old mansion with a handsome tiled facade. It overlooks a very pretty square.

Places to Eat

There are plenty of budget café-restaurants around Praça Sacadura Cabral, where you'll also find the *mercado municipal* in a huge glass building.

Restaurante O Guadiana (*☎ 285 252 157; Rua da Latôa 1*), near the turismo, is one of the best choices in town for traditional Alentejan fare.

O Trilho (*285 254 261; Rua 5 de Outubro 5*), three streets east of Rua Serpa Pinto, is pricier than O Guardiana but is another local favourite.

Getting There & Away

Five buses daily (fewer at weekends) run to/from Beja (€3.50, 65 minutes) via Serpa (€2.10, 40 minutes). Rede Expressos has a once-daily run to Lisbon (€10.50, four hours) via Évora (€7, 1½ hours); the bus stop for this service is on the *praça*, near a small grocery store called Zelia, at No 36, where tickets are sold.

COASTAL ALENTEJO

The Alentejo's cool Atlantic coastline tends to get overlooked in favour of the warmer, better-known Algarve shores, but south of Sines (where the waters are polluted from the town's industries) you'll find some fantastic spots, many great for surfing. See, also, the

Algarve chapter for low-key resorts further south along the same coastline.

Vila Nova de Milfontes
postcode 6745 • pop 3000

This very pretty small port town at the mouth of the Rio Mira, 25km northwest of Odemira, is the Alentejo's most popular ocean resort. In August, when its population increases 10-fold, its charms are overwhelmed, but come any other time and you're in for a treat, with great seafood and a laid-back atmosphere. The best coastal beaches are on either side of the Rio Mira estuary, but watch out for very strong river currents. In summer, whenever enough passengers have arrived to fill it, a ferry crosses the estuary to the beaches on the other side.

Orientation & Information The main road into town from Odemira and Lisbon, Rua Custódio Bras Pacheco, is lined with restaurants, banks, shops and the post office. Vila Nova's **turismo** (☎ 283 996 599; *Rua António Mantas; open 10am-1pm & 2pm-6pm daily*) is off this road, opposite the **police station** (☎ 283 998 391), en route to the centre of town if you're driving. Buses stop a bit further along the same road.

Activities For guided walks and canoe trips contact **Stephane or Maëlle** (☎ 919 925 370); a three-hour, 8km walk costs €5 per person, and a one-day canoe trip €20. Canoe rental is available for €10 for two hours.

Scuba diving is organised by **Alentejo Divers** (☎ 939 145 368; *e gitte@netc.pt; Pousadas Velhas, Apt 129*), based near the Campiférios camping ground (see Places to Stay & Eat, following).

Places to Stay & Eat Note that prices are higher at all places in August.

Two camping grounds are nearby, both with swimming pools and restaurants:

Campiférias (☎ 283 996 409, fax 283 996 581; *Rua da Praça; adult/tent/car €2.60/2.20/1.90*), 500m northwest of the turismo, is shady and well-ordered.

Parque de Campismo Milfontes (☎ 283 996 140, fax 283 996 104; *adult/tent/car €2.90/2.30/2.40*), close by to Campiférias, is a better-equipped site.

Casa Amarela (☎ 283 996 632, 934 204 610; *e casa_amar@hotmail.com; Rua Dom*

Luis Castro e Almeida; doubles/quads with bathroom €35/50) is the best bargain *pensão* (guesthouse). It's a seven-room house north of the turismo, and the genial, well-travelled, English-speaking owner has filled it with eclectic art from around the world. There are two shared kitchens, plus a separate apartment with a kitchen (€37.50). Internet access costs €3 per hour, but is free to guests in low season.

Residencial Mil-Réis (☎ 283 998 233, fax 283 998 328; *Largo do Rossio 2; doubles with breakfast €37.50*) is a pretty house in the old town centre.

Pensão do Cais (☎ 283 996 268; *Rua do Cais 9; doubles/quads with breakfast €35/60*), on the road to the town pier, is a friendly, homely place with a popular, good-value restaurant.

Casa dos Arcos (☎ 283 996 264, fax 283 997 156; *Rua do Cais; doubles with breakfast €70*) is an attractive, mainstream hostelry boasting satellite TV and air-con in all rooms (some suitable for disabled patrons).

Quinta das Varandas (☎ 283 996 155, fax 283 998 102; *apartments with breakfast €60*) is a boring but convenient apartment complex about 700m west of the turismo.

Restaurante Miramar (☎ 283 996 136; *Largo Brito Pais*) offers good vibes, decent music and seafood stews.

A Fonte (☎ 283 996 265, *Rua Custódio Bras Pacheco 39; dishes €5-8*) has a select menu of traditional fare.

A Telha (☎ 283 996 138; *Rua do Pinhal 3*), two streets north of the turismo, is popular for its cheap and filling meals.

Getting There & Away Vila Nova has bus connections three times each weekday to/from Odemira (€2.10, 20 minutes). There are five to eight buses daily from Lisbon (€10.20, four hours) via Setúbal (€9.50, three hours) and one daily from Portimão (€8.30, two hours). The ticket office in Vila Nova is at Largo do Almada 1.

Zambujeira do Mar
Simpler, smaller and cheaper than Vila Nova de Milfontes, but almost as popular in summer, is Zambujeira do Mar, 30km southwest of Odemira. It has a fine Atlantic-facing beach, backed by black basalt cliffs, with cool, wind-chopped waters year-round. Several often-empty beaches lie

to the south, accessible by a thrilling clifftop walk.

There's a small **turismo** (☎ 283 961 144; open 9.30am-1pm & 2pm-5.30pm Tues-Sat, longer summer) on the main street leading to the beach.

Places to Stay & Eat In addition to the following places, there are *quartos* available; ask at the turismo.

Parque de Campismo Zambujeira (☎ 283 961 172, fax 283 961 320; adult/tent/car €2.60/2.80/2) is just 800m east of the village.

Residencial Mar-e-Sol (☎ 283 961 171, 283 961 193; Rua Miramar 17A; doubles €40-50), in Zambujeira's main street, has a super landlady, Dona Maria Fernanda (described by one reader as 'overwhelmingly charming'). Rooms are spic-and-span and all have a private (though not always en suite) bathroom; there's also a shared kitchen.

Taverna Ti Vítorio (Rua da Fonte), almost behind Residencial Mar-e-Sol, is a traditional *churrasqueira* (grill restaurant), the best place in Zambujeira for grilled dishes.

Cervejaria e Marisqueira (Rua Miramar 14; fish dishes €12-20, shellfish €16-36), opposite Residencial Mar-e-Sol, has a gigantic fish menu, featuring everything from barnacles to lobsters.

Getting There & Away In summer, Zambujeira has one to three daily connections with Vila Nova (€5.60, 40 minutes) and Lisbon (€11.20, 4¾ hours).

Alto Alentejo

ÉVORA
postcode 7000 • **pop 41,200**
• **elevation 250m**

Évora, Alentejo's capital and main agricultural marketplace, is also one of Portugal's most delightful towns, with a combination of historical elegance and a lived-in feel. Its well-preserved Moorish walled centre – a Unesco World Heritage site – contains ruins dating back to Roman times and a trove of other architectural and artistic treasures. Indeed, Évora boasts more official monuments and buildings of public interest than any Portuguese city, except Lisbon.

All this, plus good restaurants and a lively student atmosphere, make it an irresistible place to linger. You will need a couple of days to get the most out of it, but try to avoid Monday, when most tourist attractions are closed.

History
Évora's history is long and rich. The Celtic settlement of Ebora was here before the Romans arrived in 59 BC and made it a military outpost, and eventually an important centre of Roman-occupied Iberia called Ebora Liberalistas Julia.

After a depressing spell under the Visigoths, the town again flowered as a centre of trade under the Moors. In AD 1165 Évora's Muslim rulers were hoodwinked by a rogue Christian knight known as Giraldo Sem Pavor (Gerald the Fearless). According to one well-embellished story, Giraldo singlehandedly stormed one of the town's watchtowers by climbing up a ladder of spears driven into the walls. From there he distracted municipal sentries while his companions took the town with hardly a fight. The Moors took it back in 1192, holding on to it for another 20 years or so.

Évora's golden era came between the 14th and 16th centuries, when it was favoured by the Alentejo's own House of Avis, as well as by numerous scholars and artists. It was declared an archbishopric in 1540 and got its own Jesuit university in 1559.

When the cardinal-king Dom Henrique, last of the Avis line, died in 1580 and Spain seized the throne, the royal court left Évora and the town began wasting away. The Marquês de Pombal's closure of the university in 1759 was the last straw. French forces plundered the town and massacred its defenders in July 1808.

Ironically, it was this decline after the 16th century that helped to protect Évora's fine old centre from the destructive redevelopment that would have been inevitable in a more important town.

Orientation
Évora climbs a gentle hill above the Alentejo plain. Around the walled centre runs a ring road from which you can enter the town on one of several 'spoke' roads.

The town's focal point is Praça do Giraldo, 700m from the bus station to the southwest. The train station is outside the walls, 1km south of the square.

If you're driving, park outside the walls at one of the many signposted lots (eg, at the southern end of Rua da República). Except on Sunday, spaces inside the walls are extremely limited and/or metered; the better hotels provide spaces for guests.

Information

Tourist Offices The **turismo** (☎ 266 702 671, fax 266 702 950; Praça do Giraldo 73; open 9am-7pm Mon-Fri, 9.30am-12.30pm & 2pm-5.30pm Sat & Sun May-Sept; 9.30am-12.30pm & 2pm-5.30pm daily Oct-Apr) has a free town map with brief multilingual text, and the free *Historical Itineraries* leaflet (a pack of six other themed itineraries costs €1). The overpriced *Alentejo Guidebook* (€7.50) is cheaper at local newsagents and hotels!

For details of a *rota dos vinhos* (wine route) through the Alentejo with *adegas* (wineries) you can visit, go to the **Rota dos Vinhos headquarters** (☎ 766 746 498, fax 766 746 602; Praça Joaquim António de Aguiar 20).

There are several banks with ATMs on and around Praça do Giraldo.

Post & Communications Send your mail from the **main post office** (Rua de Olivença; open 9am-6.30pm Mon-Fri, 9am-noon Sat) or the **branch office** (Largo da Porta de Moura; open 9am-6.30pm Mon-Fri, 9am-noon Sat).

Free internet access is available at the **Instituto Português da Juventude** (IPJ; ☎ 266 737 300; e ipj.evora@mail.telepac.pt; Rua da República 119; open 9am-11pm Mon-Fri, 9am-3pm Sat). **Oficin@ Bar** (☎ 266 707 312; Rua da Moeda 27; open 8pm-2am Mon-Fri, 9pm-2am Sat) charges €0.50/2.50 for 10/60 minutes.

Travel Agencies Both **Policarpo** (☎ 266 746 970; e reservas.incoming.alentejo@ip.pt; Alcárcova de Baixo 43) and **Abreu** (☎ 266 769 180; Rua da Misericórdia 16) are competent agencies.

Bookshops Opposite the turismo, **Livraria Nazareth** (Praça do Giraldo 46) sells a few maps, including a detailed street map, *Planta de Évora*, and a few books in English. Well-stocked **Livraria Barata**, inside the university, gives you a good excuse to visit this handsome institution. **Tabacaria Central** (Rua do Raimundo 4) sells foreign newspapers and magazines and has phone booths.

Universities Outside the walls to the northeast is the Universidade de Évora, a descendent (reopened in the 1970s) of the original Jesuit institution founded in the 16th century. There are now some 6000 students at the university, which is well worth a visit for its beautiful azulejos and Italian Renaissance-style courtyards.

Laundry For one-day service visit **Lavandaria Olimpica** (☎ 266 705 293; Largo dos Mercadores 6; open 9am-1pm & 3.30pm-7pm Mon-Fri, 9am-1pm Sat). At the time of writing, the *pousada da juventude* (see Places to Stay) was planning to install a self-service laundry.

Medical Services & Emergency The **Évora District Hospital** (☎ 266 740 100; Rua do Valasco) is east of the centre. The PSP **police station** (☎ 266 746 977; Rua Francisco Soares Lusitano) is near the Templo Romano.

Praça do Giraldo & Around

This square has seen some potent moments in Portuguese history, including the 1483 execution of Fernando, Duke of Bragança; the public burning of victims of the Inquisition in the 16th century; and fiery debates on agrarian reform in the 1970s. Nowadays it hosts hordes of tourists and hungry pigeons.

The narrow lanes to the southwest once defined Évora's *judiaria* (Jewish quarter). To the southeast, Rua 5 de Outubro, climbing to the *sé* (cathedral), is lined with handsome townhouses flaunting wrought-iron balconies, while side alleys pass beneath Moorish-style arches.

Sé

Évora's richly endowed, fortress-like cathedral (admission free; open 9am-12.30pm & 2pm-5pm daily) was begun around 1186 – during the rule of Sancho I, Afonso Henriques' son – probably on the site of an earlier mosque. It was completed about 60 years later. The flags of Vasco da Gama's ships bound for India were blessed here in 1497.

You enter the cathedral through a portal flanked by 14th-century stone apostles, flanked in turn by massive, asymmetrical granite towers with 16th-century roofs. Stout and Romanesque at first glance, the cathedral gets more Gothic the closer you look. The chancel, remodelled when Évora became the seat of an archdiocese, represents the only significant stylistic change since the cathedral was completed.

Climb the steps in the south tower to reach the choir stalls and up to the **treasury** *(admission €2.50; open 9am-noon & 2pm-4.30pm Tues-Sun).* The latter has displays of sumptuous ecclesiastical gear, including vestments, statuary, chalices and paintings.

The cool **cloister** *(joint admission fee with treasury; same opening hrs)* is an early 14th-century addition. Downstairs are the stone tombs of Évora's last four archbishops. At each corner of the cloister a dark, circular staircase climbs to the top of the walls, from where there are good views.

Museu de Évora

Adjacent to the cathedral, in what used to be the archbishop's palace (built in the 16th century and frequently renovated), is the elegant Évora Museum *(adult/student or senior €1.50/0.80; open 9.30am-12.30pm & 2pm-6pm Tues-Sun).* Fragments of old Roman and Manueline statuary and facades line the courtyard, which has been excavated to reveal Visigothic, Roman and medieval remains. In polished rooms upstairs are former episcopal furnishings and a gallery of Flemish paintings. Most memorable is *Life of the Virgin*, a striking 13-panel series that was originally part of the cathedral's altarpiece, created by anonymous Flemish artists, most or all of them working in Portugal around 1500.

Templo Romano

Opposite the museum are the startling remains of a Roman temple dating from the 2nd or early 3rd century. It is the best-preserved Roman monument in Portugal, and probably on the Iberian Peninsula. Though it's commonly referred to as the Temple of Diana, there's no consensus about the deity to which it was dedicated. How did these 14 Corinthian columns, capped with Estremoz marble, manage to survive in such good shape for some 18 centuries? The temple was apparently walled up in the Middle Ages to form a small fortress, and was even used as the town slaughterhouse for a time. It was only rediscovered late in the 19th century.

Termas Romanas

Inside the entrance hall of the *câmara municipal* are more Roman vestiges, discovered in 1987. These Roman baths *(admission free; open 9am-5.30pm Mon-Fri),* which include a laconicum, a heated room for steam baths with a superbly preserved, 9m-diameter circular pool, would have been the largest public building in Roman Évora. The complex also includes an open-air swimming pool, discovered only in 1994.

Igreja de São João & Convento dos Lóios

The little Church of St John the Evangelist *(admission €2.50, including Salas de Exposição do Palácio €4.30; open 10am-12.30pm & 2pm-5pm Tues-Sun),* which faces the Templo Romano, was founded in 1485 by one Rodrigo Afonso de Melo, count of Olivença and the first governor of Portuguese Tangier, to serve as his family's pantheon. It is still privately owned, by the Duques de Cadaval.

Behind its elaborate Gothic portal is a nave lined with gorgeous floor-to-ceiling azulejos produced in 1711 by one of Portugal's best-known tile-makers, António de Oliveira Bernardes. Through grates in the floor you can see a Moorish cistern that predates the church, and an ossuary full of monks' bones. In the sacristy beyond are fragments of even earlier azulejos.

The former Convento dos Lóios to the right of the church has elegant Gothic clois-

Although the Roman walls have crumbled, the columns of Évora's Temple of Diana have withstood the test of time

ters topped by a Renaissance gallery. A national monument, the convent was converted in 1965 into a top-end *pousada* (upmarket inn). The management is clearly not thrilled to have tourists wandering around, so it's effectively out of bounds unless you can disguise yourself as a wealthy guest.

Palácio dos Duques de Cadaval & Salas de Exposição do Palácio

Northwest of the Igreja de São João is a 17th-century facade attached to a much older palace and castle, as revealed by the two powerful square towers that bracket it. The Palace of the Dukes of Cadaval was given to the governor of Évora, Martim Afonso de Melo, by Dom João I, and it also served from time to time as a royal residence. A section of the palace still serves as the private quarters of the de Melo family; the other main occupant is the city's highway department.

Some 1st-floor rooms have been transformed into the Salas de Exposição do Palácio *(admission €2.30; open 10am-12.30pm & 2pm-5pm Tues-Sun)*, a classy display of family portraits, early illustrated tomes and religious art dating from the 16th century. There are minimal explanations, however, and none in English.

Town Walls

About one-fifth of Évora's population lives within the town's old walls, some of which are built on top of 1st-century Roman fortifications. Over 3km of 14th-century walls enclose the northern part of the old town, while the bulwarks along the southern side, such as those running through the *jardim público* (public gardens), date from the 17th century.

Largo da Porta de Moura

The so-called Moor's Gate to the inner town stands beside busy Largo da Porta de Moura, just south of the cathedral. Among several elegant mansions around the square (and contemporary with the strange-looking, globular, 16th-century Renaissance fountain in the middle of it) is **Casa Cordovil**, built in Manueline-Moorish style. Across the road to the west, have a look at the extraordinary knotted stone doorway of the **Igreja do Carmo**.

Igreja de São Francisco & Capela dos Ossos

Évora's best-known church *(Praça 1 de Maio)* is a huge Manueline-Gothic structure, completed around 1510 and dedicated to St Francis. It's adorned with exuberant nautical motifs of the period. Legend has it that the Portuguese navigator Gil Vicente is buried here.

What draws the crowds, though, is the Capela dos Ossos *(Chapel of Bones; admission €0.50; open 9am-1pm & 2.30pm-5.30pm Mon-Fri, from 10am Sat & Sun)*, a small room behind the altar with walls and columns lined with the bones and skulls of some 5000 people. The bones were collected by 17th-century Franciscan monks from the overflowing graveyards of several dozen churches and monasteries. Adding to the ghoulish atmosphere are two desiccated corpses, including one of a child, off to the right. Portugal has other ossuary chapels but this one is the creepiest. An inscription over the entrance translates roughly as 'We bones await yours'.

The entrance is to the right of the main church entrance. It costs €0.30 extra to take photos.

Jardim Público & Palácio de Dom Manuel

Pleasant public gardens straddle the 17th-century fortifications south of the Igreja de São Francisco. Inside the walls is the so-called **Galeria das Damas** (Ladies' Gallery) of the 16th-century Palácio de Dom Manuel, built in a pastiche of Gothic, Manueline, neo-Moorish and Renaissance styles.

From the town walls you can see, a few blocks to the south, the crenellated, pointy-topped 'Arabian Gothic' profile of the **Ermida de São Brás** (Chapel of St Blaise), dating from about 1490. It's possibly an early project of Diogo de Boitac, considered to be the originator of the Manueline style; there's little of interest inside.

Igreja da Nossa Senhora da Graça

Located down an alley off Rua da República is one of Évora's more melancholy sights: the ungainly baroque facade of the Church of Our Lady of Grace, topped by four uncomfortable-looking stone giants. It's mainly of interest to art historians,

ÉVORA

To Arraiolos (22km)

To Estremoz (46km)

Porta de Avis

Aqueduto da Água de Prata

Avenida de Lisboa

Avenida D Manuel Trindade Salgueiro

Porta da Lagoa

Rua do Muro

Rua das Alcaçovas

Avenida de Lisboa

Rua de Santa Maria

Largo de Aviz

Rua dos Donelas

Rua Cândido dos Reis

Rua do Cano

Largo do Chão das Covas

Tv do Passarinho

Largo das Morenas

Rua das Fontes

Travessa do Amauris

To Bike Lab (400m)

Estrada de Malagueira

Rua do Carvalho

Travessa dos Lagares

Rua do Apóstolo

Largo Severim de Faria

Rua do Amério

1

2

3

Rua de Mostardeira

9

10

11

Rua do Aviz

Rua do Cano

Rua do Inferno

7

8

Rua da Mouraria

Largo Dr Evaristo Cutileiro

Largo dos Duques de Cadaval

Rua José Estêvão

Avenida de Lisboa

12

13

Praça Joaquim António de Aguiar

14

15

Rua Gabriel Victor Monte Pereira

Rua 31 de Janeiro

Rua José Elias Garcia

Rua R das Nobres

Rua do Menino Jesus

16

17

18

19

Jardim de Diana

20

21

22

Largo do Conde de Vila Flor

Rua da Cal Branca

Rua de Sta Catarina

Rua João de Deus

Salvador

Rua de Burgos

29

28

27

R das Casas Pintadas

26

25

Lg Alexandre Herculano

R de Olivença

R de Isabel

30

31

Tv da Milheira

33

32

34

Porta de Alconchel

Rua Serpo Pinto

Rua Serpo Pinto

Rua Nova

Rua de Cima

35

36

37

Lg Vasco da Gama

38

39

40

Largo da Porta de Moura

41

42

Lg do Marques de Marialva

Rua de Diogo Cão

Rua 5 de Outubro

To Bus Station (200m)

Avenida de São Sebastião

Rua da Moeda

52

51

48

50

49

57

56

53

54

Mercadores

47

46

45

44

43

60

61

63

64

65

R de Baixo

Praça do Giraldo

58

59

Valdevinos

66

Avenida D Nuno Álvares Pereira

Cemitério dos Remédios

Rua do Raimundo

55

Rua dos Touros

Rua Bernardo Matos

Rua do Lago dos Oramos

Tv do Cavalo

72

73

74

Largo da Misericórdia

Rua Miguel Bombarda

70

71

79

Tv da Graça

69

To Neolithic Monuments (16km), Gruta do Escoural & Anta Capela de São Brissos (25km) & Lisbon (130km)

Judiaria

Rua Romão

75

Praça 1 de Maio

77

78

Largo Dr Alves Branco

R Fria

Avenida Túlio Espanca

Porta do Raimundo

Rua do Raimundo

76

Jardim Público

Praça da República

80

Rua de Eborim

Rua da República

Parque Infantil

Avenida Marechal Carmona

81

Praça de Touros (Bullring)

Rua Gil Vicente

Rossio de São Brás

Avenida Dr Barahona

Av dos Combatentes da Grande Guerra

Avenida da

Gulbenkian

To Modelo Hypermarket (1.5km), Parque de Campismo (2km) & Alcáçovas (32km)

Avenida Dinis Miranda

82

83

Avenida Dinis Miranda

Rua Diana de Liz

To Train Station (500m)

To Monte da Serralheira (4km)

ALENTEJO

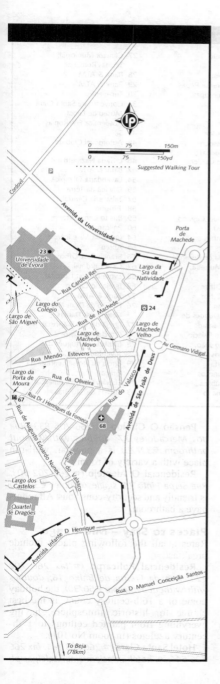

marking one of the first appearances (in the 17th-century cloister of the adjoining monastery) of the Renaissance style in Portugal.

Aqueduto da Água de Prata
Jutting into the town from the northwest is the Aqueduct of Silver Waters, designed by Francisco de Arruda (better known for Lisbon's Tower of Belém) to bring clean water to Évora, and completed in the 1530s. As you walk up Rua do Cano to the end of the aqueduct, the street drops and the aqueduct rises, with houses, shops and cafés built right into its perfect arches. The surrounding neighbourhood, plain and unbothered by tourism, has an almost village-like feel.

Organised Tours
Policarpo (☎ 266 746 970; e reservas.incoming.alentejo@ip.pt; Alcárcova de Baixo 43) organises numerous trips, including daily 2½-hour city tours by foot/minibus (€17.50/20 per person), half-day minibus tours to nearby megaliths (€24) and full-day trips to nearby towns such as Estremoz (€74.50, including lunch). A minimum of two is required. Guides speak English, French, German or Italian.

Mendes & Murteira (☎ 266 739 240; e m.murteira@mail.telepac.pt; Rua 31 de Janeiro 15A), operating out of the Barafunda boutique, offers personal, flexible tours (price negotiable) with knowledgeable guides.

TurAventur (☎ 266 743 134; e turaventur@mail.telepac.pt; Rua João de Deus 21) runs jeep tours to nearby megaliths and other attractions (adult/child under 12 €54/40 for a full day, including lunch, €30/20 half-day). It also runs adventurous hiking, biking and canoe tours.

Special Events
Évora's biggest annual bash, and one of the Alentejo's best country fairs, is the Feira de São João, held from 22 or 23 June to 1 or 2 July. The Friday before Palm Sunday features a sizable market fair called the Feira dos Ramos (Palm Fair).

Places to Stay
In high season it's essential to book ahead. We list July prices. If you're interested in long-term lets, check the student-oriented notices on the door of **Académica Fotocópias** (Rua Conde da Serra 8).

ALENTEJO

ÉVORA

PLACES TO STAY
22 Pousada dos Lóios
32 Hotel Santa Clara
34 Residencial O Alentejo
36 Residencial Riviera
39 Residencial Policarpo
44 Residencial Diana
56 Pensão O Giraldo
63 Solar Monfalim
70 Pousada da Juventude
73 Casa dos Teles
     (Private Rooms)
82 Hotel Dom Fernando

PLACES TO EAT
2 Katekero
4 O Portão
6 Manel dos Potes
7 Taberna Típica
    Quarta-Feira
8 Botequim da Mouraria
9 O Aqueduto
12 Restaurante Fialho
20 Jardim do Paço
31 O Antão
35 Café Arcada
37 Vasco da Gama
     Cafetaria
43 Pane & Vino
48 Cafetaria Cozinha de
     Santo Humberto
49 Snack-Bar Restaurante
     A Choupana
50 O Forcado
52 Restaurante Cozinha de
     Santo Humberto

53 Adega do Neto
62 O Jovem
71 Gelataria Zoka
74 Café Restaurante Repas
75 Mercado Municipal
81 La Gruta

BARS & CLUBS
3 Pub O Trovador
5 Bar Desassossego
10 Côdeas & Côdeas
11 Bar Amas do Cardeal
42 Bar UÉ
51 Oficin@ Bar
61 Kalmaria

OTHER
1 Silvano Manuel Cégado
    (Bike Rentals)
13 Rota dos Vinhos
     headquarters
14 Teatro Garcia de Resende
15 Mendes & Murteira;
     Barafunda
16 Telephone Office
17 Main Post Office
18 Police Station
19 Palácio dos Duques de
     Cadaval & Salas de
     Exposição do Palácio
21 Igreja de São João;
     Convento dos Lóios
23 Livraria Barata
24 Casa dos Bonecos
25 Biblioteca Pública
26 Templo Romano

27 Câmara Municipal;
     Termas Romanas
28 Bank & ATM
29 Bank & ATM
30 TurAventur
33 Convento de Santa Clara
38 Museu de Évora
40 Académica Fotocópias
41 Sé
45 Automóvel Club de
     Portugal
46 Livraria Nazareth
47 Bank & ATM
54 Lavandaria Olimpica
55 Oficina da Terra
57 Tabacaria Central
58 Turismo
59 Bus to Camp Site
60 Policarpo
64 Igreja da Misericórdia
65 Abreu
66 Branch Post Office
67 Casa Cordovil
68 Évora District Hospital
69 Igreja do Carmo
72 Bank & ATM
76 Palácio de Dom Manuel;
     Galeria das Damas
77 Igreja de São Francisco;
     Capela dos Ossos
78 Instituto Português da
     Juventude; IPJ Café-Bar
79 Igreja da Nossa Senhora da
     Graça
80 Eborim Centro Comercial
83 Ermida de São Brás

Places to Stay – Budget

Orbitur's well-equipped **parque de camp-ismo** (☎ *266 705 190, fax 266 709 830; adult/tent/car €3.60/2.90/3)* is 2km south-west of town. Urban Sitee bus No 5 or 8 from Praça do Giraldo, via Avenida de São Sebastião and the bus station, goes close by (€0.90).

The **pousada da juventude** (☎ *266 744 848;* e *evora@movijovem.pt; Rua Miguel Bombarda 40; dorm beds €12.50, doubles with toilet & shower €35)* is in a handsome former hotel, closed for renovations until late 2003.

Quartos are a good budget bet, costing around €30 a double with shared bathroom. **Casa dos Teles** (☎ *266 702 453;* e *casados teles@yahoo.com; Rua Romão Ramalho 27),* the best of the bunch, is run by a gentle-manly English speaker; attractive rooms at the back overlook a tiny courtyard. A small apartment with a kitchen costs €35.

Pensão O Giraldo (☎ *266 705 833; Rua dos Mercadores 27; doubles with/without bathroom €32/25)* is a popular, well-run place with a variety of rooms.

Residencial O Alentejo (☎ *266 702 903; Rua Serpa Pinto 74; singles/doubles €30/45)* is friendly and security-conscious. All rooms have a bathroom.

Places to Stay – Mid-Range

Rates at all the following places include breakfast.

Residencial Policarpo (☎/fax *266 702 424; Rua da Freiria de Baixo 16; doubles with/without bathroom €50/30),* the holiday home of a 16th-century count, is the best choice for historic atmosphere, having everything from painted ceilings to 17th-century azulejos (in room No 101).

Hotel Santa Clara (☎ *266 704 141, fax 266 706 544;* e *hotelsantaclara@mail.telelpac.pt;*

Travessa da Milheira 19; doubles €56) is a low-key establishment tucked away in a quiet location.

Residencial Diana *(☎ 266 702 008, fax 266 743 101;* e *residencialdiana@mail.telepac.pt; Rua de Diogo Cão 2; doubles with/without bathroom €49/40)* is a decent, very central choice.

Residencial Riviera *(☎ 266 703 304, fax 266 700 467; Rua 5 de Outubro 49)* is notably efficient. It was undergoing renovations at the time of writing.

On the plains around Évora are at least 10 converted *quintas* (estates), including **Monte da Serralheira** *(☎ 266 741 286;* e *monteserralheira@mail.telepac.pt; 2-/4-person apartments €45/80)*, 4km south, with charming self-catering apartments (some rather older than others), a swimming pool and horses and bikes to ride. The Dutch owner is a qualified local guide.

Places to Stay – Top End

Solar Monfalim *(☎ 266 750 000;* e *reservas@ monfalimtur.pt; Largo da Misericórdia 1; doubles with air-con & minibar €77.50)* is a delightful former 16th-century mansion with elegant rooms and a lovely patio overlooking the square. Car parking costs €3 per day.

Hotel Dom Fernando *(☎ 266 741 717;* e *domfernando@portugalmail.com; Avenida Dr Barahona 2; doubles €95)* is one of several modern hotels on the outer ring road – a convenient choice for car drivers.

Pousada dos Lóios *(☎ 266 704 051, fax 266 707 248; doubles Mon-Fri €177, Sat & Sun €195)*, occupying the former Convento dos Lóios opposite the Templo Romano, is in a luxury class of its own.

Places to Eat

Évora has some great restaurants, many of which take their Alentejan specialities so seriously that they devote a whole week (Semana Gastronómica) to the art of pork dishes (early March) and another to lamb (mid-April). The turismo has details of each restaurant's special offerings at this time.

Budget Great for solo travellers, with cheap counter meals (slightly pricier at tables), are **Adega do Neto** *(☎ 266 209 916; Rua dos Mercadores 46; dishes €4-6)* and **Snack-Bar Restaurante A Choupana** *(☎ 266 704 427; Rua dos Mercadores 16; dishes €6.50-8)*.

Café Restaurante Repas *(☎ 266 708 540; Praça 1 de Maio 19; dishes €5-6)* is rather touristy, serving so-so standard fare, but its location and outdoor seating are simply irresistible.

O Portão *(☎ 266 703 325; Rua do Cano 27; dishes from €4.50)*, right by the aqueduct, is popular with locals and tourists alike.

La Gruta *(☎ 266 708 186; Avenida General Humberto Delgado 2; half-portions from €4; open Sun-Fri)*, among several local eateries near the bullring, has hearty bargain fare.

Among cheap and cheerful cafés are the **IPJ Café-Bar** *(Rua da República 119; dishes from €3.50; open Mon-Sat)* and **Vasco da Gama Cafétaria** *(Rua de Vasco da Gama 10; dishes from €4.20)*.

Café Arcada *(Praça do Giraldo 10)*, busy and cavernous, has outdoor tables in the *praça* and serves reasonably priced daily specials. It's pricier if you sit outside.

Need a snack while trawling the bars? **Katekero** *(☎ 266 703 204; Largo Severim de Faria 1A; meals from €4.50)* is a genial snack-bar serving light meals.

Manel dos Potes *(Rua do Amauriz 9)* sports huge jars of wine. It's popular with students and very much a locals' hang-out.

Gelataria Zoka *(Largo de São Vicente 14, Rua Miguel Bombarda)* is heaven for ice-cream freaks.

Mid-Range The well-hidden but spacious **O Jovem** *(☎ 266 701 180; Páteo do Salema 9; dishes €6-9)* has decent traditional fare available.

Taberna Típica Quarta-Feira *(☎ 266 707 530; Rua do Inverno 16; dishes €9)* is a jovial spot in the heart of the Moorish quarter and is invariably packed out with locals.

O Aqueduto *(☎ 266 706 373; Rua do Cano 13A; open Tues-Sun; dishes €11)* will appeal if you're into game and other meaty specialities such as hare, partridge or pigs' feet. It also offers a good-value tourist menu (€18.30) and several lamb dishes.

O Forcado *(☎ 266 702 566; Rua dos Mercadores 26; dishes from €5.50, half-portions €4.30; open Mon-Sat)*, another traditional place, offers some unusual *bacalhau* (salt-cod) dishes.

Pane & Vino *(☎ 266 746 960; Páteo do Salema 22; pizzas or pasta from €5.50; open Tues-Sun)* is a busy, popular venue serving super Italian fare.

ALENTEJO

Top End The traditional, long-established **Restaurante Cozinha de Santo Humberto** (☎ 266 704 251; Rua da Moeda 39; open Fri-Wed) offers a big menu of regional fare (eg, *carne de porco com amêijoas*, a pork and clams dish, for €13.50). Its café on the *praça* serves cheaper versions of the dishes you'll find here.

O Antão (☎ 266 706 459; Rua João de Deus 5; dishes around €9; open Thur-Tues) is an award-winning, refreshingly modern venue; try its filling *sopa de cação* (fish soup; €9) or coriander *açorda* (bread-based soup; €9).

Restaurante Fialho (☎ 266 703 079; Travessa dos Mascarenhas 16; dishes €14-17, daily specials €12; open Tues-Sun) is a smart venue with a big menu of daily specials. Feeling wicked? Try the €62.50 grilled stonebass.

Jardim do Paço (☎ 266 744 300; dishes €10.50), beside Igreja de São João, has no rival for historic location; it's in the former garden of the Palácio dos Duques de Cadaval. On the menu are a mouth-watering €17.50 'regional buffet' and €6 lunch specials.

Botequim da Mouraria (☎ 266 746 775; Rua da Mouraria 16A; dishes €8.50-11; open lunch Mon-Sat) is quite another story: poke around the old Moorish quarter to find this 'snack bar', which serves some of Évora's finest food. You can't book ahead and there are no tables, just stools at the counter.

Self-Catering Pick up fruit and vegetables from the **mercado municipal** (Praça 1 de Maio; open Tues-Sun) and eat them in the adjacent *jardim público*.

There's a **Modelo** hypermarket just beyond the town limits on the road to the camping ground and Alcáçovas.

Entertainment

The town's cinema is in the **Eborim Centro Comercial** (Rua do Eborim).

Puppet Theatre Five actors from the municipal Teatro Garcia de Resende studied for several years with the only surviving master of a traditional rural puppetry style called *bonecos de Santo Aleixo* (Santo Aleixo puppets). Occasional performances of this and other styles take place, as well as hand-puppet shows for children, at a little theatre called **Casa dos Bonecos** (☎ 266 703 112) off Largo de Machede

Velho. For current performances, ask at the turismo. Tickets are around €3, children's matinees €2.

Bars Most bars open late and don't close until at least 2am (4am at weekends). Attracting all ages, friendly **Oficin@ Bar** (☎ 266 707 312; Rua da Moeda 27; open 8pm-2am Mon-Fri, 9pm-2am Sat) features relaxing jazz and blues.

Bar UÉ (☎ 266 706 612; Rua Diogo Cão 21), at the Associação de Estudantes da Universidade de Évora, is the main central student hang-out, with a great outdoor drinking area.

Most other bars are in the northwest of town: **Bar Desassossego** (☎ 266 706 475; Travessa do Janeiro 15) has dancing and late-night karaoke; the popular **Bar Amas do Cardeal** (☎ 266 701 133; Rua Amas do Cardeal 9A) attracts a mixed crowd for post-1am drinking and weekend dancing; and **Pub O Trovador** (☎ 266 707 370; Rua da Mostardeira 4) is a smarter venue for an older crowd. New at the time of writing, snazzy **Côdeas & Côdeas** (Rua do Cano) cranks it up as early as 4pm.

Kalmaria (☎ 266 707 505; Rua de Valdevinos) is the town's only central nightclub.

Spectator Sports

Évora has its own *praça de touros* (bull-ring), outside the southern walls near the *jardim público*. Three to four bullfights take place between May and October; the turismo has details.

Shopping

The lower end of Rua 5 de Outubro is a gauntlet of pricey *artesanatos* (handicrafts shops) with cork knick-knacks, hand-painted furniture and pottery. You'll find cheaper pottery on the shady side of the *mercado municipal*. There are more-upmarket shops along Rua Cândido dos Reis.

The imaginative and award-winning handicraft and clay-figure workshop-cum-gallery **Oficina da Terra** (☎ 266 746 049; Rua do Raimundo 51A; open 10am-7pm Mon-Fri, 10am-3pm Sat) is well worth a visit.

On the second Tuesday of each month a vast open-air market, with everything from shoes to sheep cheese ('a drama creating itself on the spot', says one reader), sprawls across the big Rossio de São Brás, just outside the walls on the road to the train station. On the second Sunday there's an **antique market** (open 8am-2pm) in Largo do Chão das Covas near the aqueduct.

Getting There & Away
Bus From the **bus station** (☎ 266 769 410) off Avenida de São Sebastião, there are six *alta qualidade* (fast deluxe) services daily to Lisbon (€9.20, 1¼ hours), plus half-a-dozen slower coaches. Three daily expresses go to Estremoz (€6.10, 45 minutes) and Elvas (€8, 1½ hours), four to Beja (€7, 1¾ hours), two to Portalegre (€8.20, 2½ hours) and two to Coimbra (€11.10, 4½ hours) via Santarém. There are two buses daily to Faro (€11.20, four to five hours).

Train The Évora station (☎ 266 702 125) is on a branch of the Lisbon–Funcheira (via Beja) railway line. There are three IC services daily to/from Lisbon (€6.90, 2½ hours, including Tejo ferry to Barreiro) with a change at Casa Branca.

Getting Around
Car & Bicycle If you want to rent a car get in touch with Abreu or Policarpo (see under Travel Agencies, earlier).

Évora has a branch of the **Automóvel Club de Portugal** (ACP; ☎ 266 707 533, fax 266 709 696; Alcárcova de Baixo 7).

You can rent a bike from **Bike Lab** (☎ 266 735 500; e bikelab@mail.telepac.pt, Centro Comercial da Vista Alegre, Lote 14), 800m northwest of the centre, for €7.50 to €15 per day (guided bike tours also available), or from **Silvano Manuel Cágado** (☎ 266 702 424; Rua Cândido dos Reis 66) for €7.50 per day.

Taxi If you want a **taxi** (☎ 266 734 734) you'll find them waiting in Praça do Giraldo and Largo da Porta de Moura. On a weekday you can expect to pay about €3 (or €4 with baggage) from the train station to the *praça*.

AROUND ÉVORA
The plains around Évora abound in prehistoric remains (see the boxed text 'Dolmens, Menhirs & Other Mysteries'). A sheet in the Évora turismo's *Historical Itineraries* details many of these. From the turismo you can also pick up the brief explanatory pamphlet,

Almendres (€0.50) or, for serious dolmen fans, the weighty *Paisagens Arqueologicas A Oeste de Évora* (€12.40), which has English summaries. An English-language video, *Megalithic Enclosures* (€10), is sold at the turismo and the Museu de Évora.

Cromeleque dos Almendres
From Guadalupe a dirt track winds through a beautiful landscape of olive and cork trees to the Almendres Cromlech. Considering that this is the Iberian Peninsula's most important megalithic group – a veritable Portuguese Stonehenge – it's been left amazingly uncommercialised.

The site consists of a huge oval of some 95 rounded granite monoliths – some of which are engraved with symbolic markings – spread down a rough slope. They were erected over different periods, probably for social gatherings, fertility rites or solar observations. Other sacred rituals may also have taken place here in honour of a religion that, according to one of the turismo leaflets, centred on 'a female super-divinity with huge sun-like eyes'.

Just off the dirt track en route to the *cromeleque* you can follow a short path to the solitary **Menir dos Almendres**, a single phallic stone.

Anta Grande do Zambujeiro
The Great Dolmen of Zambujeiro, a national monument, is Europe's largest dolmen. Under a huge sheet-metal shelter in a field of wild flowers and yellow broom are seven stones, each 6m high, forming a huge chamber. Archaeologists removed the capstone in the 1960s. Most of the site's relics – potsherds, beads, flint tools and so on – are in the Museu de Évora.

Anta Capela de São Brissos
This tiny, whitewashed chapel beside the Valverde–N2 road (just beyond the turn-off to São Brissos) was assembled in the 17th century from surviving stones of an *anta* (dolmen).

Gruta do Escoural
About 2km east of the village of Santiago do Escoural (25km from Évora) is a small, bat-filled cave (☎ 266 857 000; admission €1.50; open 9am-noon & 1.30pm-5.30pm Wed-Sun, 1.30pm-5.30pm Tues). It's adorned

ALENTEJO

Dolmens, Menhirs & Other Mysteries

You come across them all over the Alentejo plains: faintly engraved boulders, mysterious stone circles, towering fertility objects and cavelike stone tombs. They're part of a style of construction called megalithic (literally, 'large stone' in Greek) found all along the European Atlantic coast, and built some 5000 to 6000 years ago.

Nearly all are related to ritual worship of some kind. Dolmens (*antas* in Portuguese) were probably temples and/or tombs, covered with a large flat stone and usually built on hill tops or near water. Menhirs (individual standing stones) and cromlechs (stone circles) were also places of worship, and their construction represents a remarkable community effort.

The most outstanding examples are near Évora, Reguengos de Monsaraz, Elvas and Castelo de Vide; see under those towns for details.

NC

with Palaeolithic and Neolithic rock art, including a few faint ochre and black drawings of bison and engravings of horses, dating back 10,000 to 30,000 years.

Getting There & Away

There are no convenient buses to this area so your only option is to rent a car or bike (but note that about 5km of the route is rough and remote). Alternatively, you can take a guided trip (see Organised Tours under Évora earlier in this chapter).

With your own wheels, head west from Évora on the old Lisbon road (N114) for 10km, then turn south for 2.8km to Guadalupe. Follow the signs from here to the Cromeleque dos Almendres (4.3km).

Return to Guadalupe and head south for 5km to Valverde, home of the Universidade de Évora's school of agriculture and the 16th-century Convento de Bom Jesus. Following the signs to Anta Grande do Zambujeiro, turn into the school's farmyard and onto a badly pot-holed track. After 1km you'll see the Great Dolmen.

Continue west from Valverde for 12km. Before joining the N2, turn right for the cave at Santiago do Escoural.

MONSARAZ

postcode 7200 • pop 150 • elevation 190m

One of Portugal's most famous fortified hill-top villages, Monsaraz is visible for miles around, towering over a somnolent landscape of ploughed fields and wild meadows dotted with cork and olive trees and Neolithic monuments.

Settled long before the Moors arrived in the 8th century, Monsaraz was recaptured by the Christians under Giraldo Sem Pavor (Gerald the Fearless) in 1167, and subsequently given to the Knights Templar as a reward for their assistance. The castle was added in 1310. Now it's one of the most popular destinations in the Alentejo.

You only need half an hour to meander from one end of the immaculate village to the other, but it's worth considering an overnight stay; once the day-trippers have left, a magic, medieval aura descends on the place.

Orientation

Happily there's no room for coaches or cars inside the walled village, so your arrival at one of the four arched entrances will be as it should be – on foot. From the main parking lot, the Porta da Alcoba leads directly onto the central Praça Dom Nuno Álvares Pereira. The main entrance, Porta da Vila, is at the north end of town (the castle is at the other end) and leads into Rua São Tiago and the parallel Rua Direita, Monsaraz's two main streets.

Information

The **turismo** (☎ 266 557 136; *Praça Dom Nuno Álvares; open 10am-1pm & 2pm-6pm daily Sept-June, to 7pm July & Aug*) has various publications on the region, and bus timetables.

Igreja Matriz

The parish church (*open 9am-1pm & 2pm-6pm daily*), near the turismo, was rebuilt after the 1755 earthquake and again a century later. It has just one interesting feature, a 14th-century marble tomb carved with saints. An eye-catching 18th-century *pelourinho* topped by a Manueline globe stands outside. The **Igreja da Misericórdia** *(open 9am-1pm & 2pm-6pm daily)* is located opposite.

Museu de Arte Sacra
Housed in a fine Gothic building beside the parish church, the Museum of Sacred Art *(admission €1; open 10am-1pm & 2pm-6pm daily)* houses a small collection of 14th-century wooden religious figures and 18th-century vestments and silverware. Its most famous exhibit is a rare example of a 14th-century secular fresco, showing a good and a bad judge, the latter appropriately two-faced. Opening hours sometimes vary.

Castelo
The castle at the southwestern end of the village was one in the chain of Dom Dinis' defensive fortresses along the Spanish border. It's now converted into a small bullring, and its ramparts offer a fine panoramic view over the Alentejan plains.

Special Events
Monsaraz is packed out during its week-long Museu Aberto (Open Museum) music festival, held every July in even-numbered years, and on the second weekend of September when bullfights and processions feature in the Festa de Nossa Senhora dos Passos. Accommodation must be booked far in advance at these times. Bullfights also take place on Easter Sunday.

Places to Stay
Many villagers have converted their ancient cottages to guesthouses or self-catering apartments. Unless otherwise mentioned, all the following rates include breakfast. It's essential to book ahead in high season.

Casa Pinto *(☎ 266 557 388; Praça Dom Nuno Ávares Pereira 10; doubles €30)*, opposite the church, is a favourite and it has five cosy rooms.

Casa Dona Antónia *(☎ 266 557 142; Rua Direita 15; doubles with air-con €30, suite €90)* has four neat rooms. The suite is huge and includes a terrace.

Casa do Paço *(☎ 266 557 306; doubles €20-25, family room €42.40)*, nearby Dona Antónia, is a particularly attractive bargain, with three large rooms beautifully furnished in Alentejan style, and a kitchen and lounge downstairs. For more information, contact the owner at Rua Direita 2.

Casa Dom Nuno *(☎ 266 557 146, fax 266 557 400; Rua José Fernandes Caeiro 6; doubles €50)*, one of several fine Turihab properties, has eight elegant doubles and offers superb terrace views.

Estalagem de Monsaraz *(☎ 266 557 112; e estmonsaraz@hotmail.com; Largo São Bartolomeu 5; doubles €80)* is an attractive place just outside the walls. Breakfast is a steep €8.70.

There are several rural alternatives close by, including the gorgeous **Monte Alerta** *(☎ 266 550 150; e mail@montealerta.pt; doubles €75, 2-night minimum weekends)*, a beautifully converted *quinta* 2.5km away at Telheiro. It houses family antiques and eight spacious doubles, plus it has a pool and horses to ride.

Places to Eat
There's a handful of rather pricey restaurants, all offering traditional Alentejan dishes such as *borrego assado* (roast lamb) from around €8.50. All close by 9pm.

Café-Restaurante Lumumba *(☎ 266 557 121; Rua Direita 12; dishes €7-8.50)* is a popular place with a great ambience. Try the *ensopada de borrego* (lamb stew, €8.50).

A Casa do Forno *(☎ 266 557 190; Travessa da Sanabrosa; dishes €7-9)* bustles with visiting Portuguese at weekends; its desserts are irresistible.

Café Restaurante O Alcaide *(☎ 266 557 168; Rua São Tiago 15; dishes around €8)* has good grilled fish and lovely sunset views over the plains.

Restaurante São Tiago *(☎ 266 557 188; Rua São Tiago 3; dishes €7-9)*, nearby O Alcaide, is a lively venue with its own bar.

Self-catering options are limited to bread and cheese from a **grocery shop** *(Rua São Tiago)* at the Porta da Vila end of the street; wines from **Castas & Castiços**, next door; and pastries from **Pastelaria A Cisterna** *(Rua Direita)*, also at the Porta da Vila end.

Getting There & Away
Buses run to/from Reguengos de Monsaraz two to three times daily (three to five times during school time) during the week (€1.90,

ALENTEJO

35 minutes). The last bus back to Reguengos (where you can pick up connections to Évora) is at 5.20pm.

REGUENGOS DE MONSARAZ
postcode 7200 • pop 11,000
• elevation 200m

This modest market town, once famous for its sheep and wool production, is on the tourist trail because of its proximity to and connections with Monsaraz. It's also close to the pottery centre of São Pedro do Corval and an impressive half-dozen dolmens and menhirs (out of around 150 scattered across the surrounding plains). While you're here, enjoy some of the great local wine, Terras d'El Rei.

Orientation & Information
The bus station is 200m southwest of the central Praça da Liberdade. Just off the praça, is the turismo (☎ 266 503 315; Rua 1 de Maio; open 9am-12.30pm & 2pm-5.30pm Mon-Fri, from 10am Sat & Sun). Among publications available here is A Short Walk in the Alentejo (€6.20) by locally-based, award-winning novelist Robert Wilson, which has in-depth information on the region.

Espaço Internet (☎ 266 519 424; Rua do Conde de Monsaraz 32; open 10am-8pm Mon-Fri, 10am-1pm & 2pm-8pm Sat, 1pm-7pm Sun), about 100m northwest of the praça, offers free Internet access, mainly for local students.

Wineries
The Adega Cooperativa Agrícola de Reguengos de Monsaraz (☎ 266 509 310, fax 266 503 291), just outside town on the Monsaraz road, offers free group tours of its wine factory, and could probably be persuaded to take individuals who sound keen enough.

More geared to visitors is Herdade do Esporão (☎ 266 509 280; e esporao@mail .telepac.pt), a few kilometres south of town. Operating as a winery for seven centuries, with some lovely old wine cellars, it produces mostly red wines for the domestic market. It has a wine bar, restaurant and wine shop.

Megaliths
This area has some of the Alentejo's most striking ancient megaliths (see the boxed text 'Dolmens, Menhirs & Other Mysteries' earlier in this chapter), including the Menhir de Bulhoa, a phallic stone with intriguing carved circles and lines, 4km north of Monsaraz off the Telheiro–Outeiro road.

One of the most impressive groups is the 50-stone Cromleque do Xerez, which once stood 5km south of Monsaraz. It was moved in 2002, ahead of imminent flooding by the massive Alqueva dam near Moura (see the boxed text 'The Alqueva Dam' earlier in this chapter). Eventually the ensemble, including the striking seven-tonne phallic menhir at its centre, will form part of a new Museu de Arqueologia de Alqueva in Telheiro (1.5km north of Monsaraz near the Convento da Orada).

A sketch map of several other accessible megaliths is available at the turismo.

Places to Stay & Eat
Casa da Palmeira (☎ 266 502 362, fax 266 502 513; Praça de Santo António 1; singles/doubles €20/30) is a fantastic old mansion with old-world rooms, 200m northwest of the main square.

Pensão Fialho (☎ 266 519 266; Praça da Liberdade 17; singles/doubles with shower €12.50/25) is as spartan as it looks, with seven chilly rooms.

Pensão O Gato (☎/fax 266 502 353; singles/doubles with air-con €22.50/35), next door to Pensão Fialho, has bigger rooms but they're scruffy and overpriced. Its popular restaurant (dishes €6.30-7.30) offers several varieties of bacalhau.

Residencial Moira (☎ 962 854 745; Estrada de Alendroal; doubles with air-con €40-50) is a spanking new establishment 1.5km north of town, with seven brightly decorated rooms (five with big terraces) and its own rather pricey restaurant.

Restaurante Central (☎ 266 502 219; Praça da Liberdade; dishes €7-10) has good standard fare, and a tiny bar-café next door for cheaper snacks.

Restaurante Adega d'El Rei (☎ 266 503 879; Avenida Dr António de Almeida 18; dishes from €5.80; open Tues-Sun), around the corner from Restaurante Central and opposite the market, is a friendly, barnlike place serving local wine from huge jars.

Shopping
The town has a thriving handicrafts industry; mantas, hand-woven woollen blankets, are its speciality. You can see these, plus

ceramics, wickerware and hand-painted Alentejan furniture, being produced in a **workshop** (☎ 266 503 710, fax 266 501 104; open 10am-around 7pm daily) near the Adega de Cooperativa de Reguengos; you can also make purchases. The workshop-cum-showroom, converted from an old slaughterhouse, belongs to Tear (Loom), an association of young artisans founded to help preserve traditional local skills.

Fabrica Alentejana de Lanificios (☎ 266 502 179) is the last remaining hand-loom producer of *mantas Alentejanas*. If you're interested in hand-woven goods, check it out; it's on the Mourão road east of town.

Ceramics buffs should head for São Pedro do Corval, 5km east; the 32 workshops make it one of the largest (though perhaps not the highest-quality) pottery centres in Portugal. Traditional Alentejan wares made here include plates, pots and floor tiles.

For details of other handicrafts in the region, ask the turismo for its comprehensive list of local artisans.

Getting There & Away

On weekdays five to seven buses daily run to Évora (€2.40, 50 to 65 minutes; express €5.50, 35 minutes), with two continuing to Lisbon. There are also two direct Lisbon services (€10.80, 2½ to 3¼ hours).

ESTREMOZ

postcode 7100 • pop 7700 • elevation 420m

Dominated by its medieval hill-top castle, Estremoz (pronounced shtreh-**mozh**) is an elegant town of startling whiteness, thanks to the extensive use of marble in its construction. So plentiful is the supply of high-grade marble in this region that Estremoz and the neighbouring towns of Borba and Vila Viçosa are quite blasé about it, using it even for the doorsteps of its humblest cottages. But despite appearances, Estremoz is basically a simple market town, famous for its earthenware pottery, large Saturday markets, preserved plums and goat's cheese.

With a decent supply of restaurants and *pensões* it makes a good base for visiting the other marble towns, or a suitable stopover en route to Évora or Portalegre.

Orientation

The lower, newer part of town, enclosed by 17th-century ramparts, is arranged around a huge square, Rossio Marquês de Pombal (known simply as 'the Rossio'). Here you'll find most accommodation, restaurants and shops. A 10-minute climb west of the Rossio brings you to the medieval quarter, with its 13th-century castle (now a luxurious *pousada*) and keep.

The bus station is by the disused train station, 400m east of the Rossio.

Information

The **turismo** (☎ 268 333 541, fax 268 334 010; open 9.30am-12.30pm & 2pm-6pm daily) is tucked into the corner of Largo da República.

At the northern end of town is the **centro de saúde** (medical centre; ☎ 268 332 042; Avenida 9 de Abril). The **police station** (☎ 268 334 141) is in the *câmara municipal*. The **post office** (Rua 5 de Outubro; open 9am-6pm Mon-Fri) has NetPost.

Lower Town

On the fringes of the Rossio are several imposing old churches, former convents and, to the north, monastic buildings converted into cavalry barracks. Opposite these, by Largo General Graça, is a marble-edged water tank, called the **Lago do Gadanha** (Lake of the Scythe) after its scythe-wielding statue of Neptune. Some of the prettiest marble streets in town are south of the Rossio, off Largo da República.

Museu de Arte Sacra Overlooking the Rossio is the striking, bell-towered 17th-century Convento dos Congregados, which now houses the police station, *câmara municipal* and Museu de Arte Sacra (admission €1; open 10am-noon & 2.30pm-5.30pm Mon-Fri, 2pm-5.30pm Sat & Sun). The Museu de Arte Sacra features mostly 17th- to 18th-century ecclesiastical silverware and religious statues. You also get to see the restored marble church and, best of all, a rooftop view from the bell-towers themselves. The stairway to the top is lined with azulejos.

Museu Rural This delightful one-room museum (admission €1; open 9.30am-noon & 2pm-5.30pm Mon-Sat) portraying rural Alentejan life, much of it in cork and ceramic, is a lovingly displayed collection, and well worth a visit.

ALENTEJO

Museu Alfaia Agrícola A museum of old agricultural and household equipment (☎ 268 339 200; Rua Serpa Pinto; admission €1; open 8.30am-12.30pm & 2pm-4pm Tues-Fri, 2pm-5pm Sat & Sun) may not sound thrilling, but this cavernous old warehouse has some fascinating stuff displayed over its three floors: from old presses and threshers to huge brass pots and pans.

Upper Town
The easiest way to reach the upper town on foot is to follow narrow Rua da Frandina from Praça Luís de Camões and pass the inner castle walls through the Arco da Frandina.

Palace & Torre das Três Coroas At the top of the upper town is the stark, white former royal palace, now the Pousada de Santa Rainha Isabel. Dom Dinis built the palace in the 13th century for his new wife, Isabel of Aragon. After her death in 1336 (Dinis had died 11 years earlier) it was used as an ammunition dump. An inevitable explosion, in 1698, destroyed most of the palace and the surrounding castle, though in the 18th

century João V restored the palace for use as an armoury.

The 27m-high keep, the Torre das Três Coroas (Tower of the Three Crowns), survived and is still the dominant feature. It was supposedly built by three kings: Sancho II, Afonso III and Dinis.

Visitors are welcome to view the public areas of the *pousada* and climb the keep, which offers a panorama of the old town and surrounding plains. The holes at the keep's edges were intended for dumping boiling oil on invaders!

Capela de Santa Isabel This richly adorned chapel (admission free; open 9am-12.30pm & 3pm-6.30pm Tues-Sun May-Sept, 9am-12.30pm & 2pm-5.30pm Oct-Apr) behind the keep was built in 1659. The narrow stairway up to the chapel, and the chapel itself, are lined with 18th-century azulejos, most of them featuring scenes from the saintly queen's life.

Isabel was famously generous to the poor, despite her husband's disapproval. According to one legend the king once demanded to see what she was carrying in her

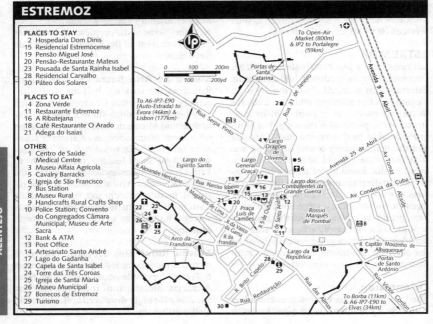

ESTREMOZ

PLACES TO STAY
2 Hospedaria Dom Dinis
15 Residencial Estremocense
19 Pensão Miguel José
20 Pensão-Restaurante Mateus
23 Pousada de Santa Rainha Isabel
28 Residencial Carvalho
30 Páteo dos Solares

PLACES TO EAT
4 Zona Verde
11 Restaurante Estremoz
16 A Ribatejana
18 Café Restaurante O Arado
21 Adega do Isaias

OTHER
1 Centro de Saúde
   Medical Centre
3 Museu Alfaia Agrícola
5 Cavalry Barracks
6 Igreja de São Francisco
7 Bus Station
8 Museu Rural
9 Handicrafts Rural Crafts Shop
10 Police Station; Convento
   do Congregados Câmara
   Municipal; Museu de Arte
   Sacra
12 Bank & ATM
13 Post Office
14 Artesanato Santo André
17 Lago do Gadanha
22 Capela de Santa Isabel
24 Torre das Três Coroas
25 Igreja de Santa Maria
26 Museu Municipal
27 Bonecos de Estremoz
29 Turismo

skirt; she let go of her apron and the bread she had hidden to donate to the poor was miraculously transformed into roses.

To visit the chapel, ask for the custodian at the Museu Municipal.

Museu Municipal This museum (☎ 268 339 200; admission €1; open 9am-12.30pm & 3pm-6.30pm Tues-Sun May-Sept, 9am-12.30pm & 2pm-5.30pm Oct-Apr) is in a former 17th-century almshouse near the *pousada*. It has an excellent display of beautifully carved spoons, cork and wooden figures (the rural scenes by Joaquim Velhinho are particularly engaging) by local artisans, plus a collection of typical 19th-century domestic Alentejan items. The highlight is the ground-floor display of Estremoz pottery figurines – some 500 pieces covering 200 years, including quaint ladies with huge floral headdresses.

Special Events
The town's biggest event is the Feira Internacional de Artesenato e Agro-Pecuária de Estremoz (Fiape), a huge handicrafts and agricultural event held for several days at the end of April in an open-air market area east of the bus station.

Places to Stay
Residencial Carvalho (☎ 268 339 370, fax 268 322 370; Largo da República 27; doubles with/without bathroom €30/22.50, with air-con €42.50) is appealingly old-fashioned. Rates include breakfast.

Residencial Estremocense (☎ 268 333 002; Travessa da Levada 19; doubles €30) has 12 neat, modern rooms.

Pensão Miguel José (☎ 268 322 326; Travessa da Levada 8; doubles with/without bathroom €30/25) is a warren of 13 tiny, plain rooms. Rates include breakfast.

Pensão-Restaurante Mateus (☎ 268 322 226, fax 268 324 224; Rua do Almeida 41; doubles with/without bathroom €40/30) is cheery and welcoming, with huge rooms in an old house and rates including breakfast.

Hospedaria Dom Dinis (☎ 268 332 717, fax 268 322 610; Rua 31 de Janeiro 46; singles/doubles €40/50), has well kitted-out rooms with a minibar and air-con.

Páteo dos Solares (☎ 268 338 400, fax 268 338 419; Rua Brito Capelo; doubles €172) is a converted bread factory, and is situated partly on the old city walls. There is a pricey but very good restaurant located here, as well.

Pousada de Santa Rainha Isabel (☎ 268 332 075, fax 268 332 079; doubles Mon-Fri €182, Sat & Sun €201) surpasses all for ambience, with its antique furnishings and fine tapestries.

There are several fine Turihab places near town, with doubles for about €50. The turismo has details.

Places to Eat
A Ribatejana (☎ 268 323 656; Largo General Graça 41; dishes €5-7) is a scruffy local favourite, famous for roast suckling pig.

Restaurante Estremoz (☎ 268 322 834; Rossio 14; dishes from €6.50), another popular rendezvous, especially on market Saturdays, offers hearty fare.

Pensão-Restaurante Mateus (Rua do Almeida 41; dishes €6.50-8.50) is a smart option with a good menu of regional fare, including *açorda alentejana com bacalhau* (€7.50).

Adega do Isaias (☎ 268 322 318; Rua do Almeida 21; open Mon-Sat) is an award-winning, rustic *tasca* (tavern). It has outdoor grills, communal bench tables and huge terracotta wine jars from which your wine is served. Grilled meat dishes (from €6.50) are a speciality.

Café Restaurante O Arado (☎ 268 333 471; Rua Narciso Ribeiro 7) is an easy-going place specialising in *frango no churrasco* (roast chicken).

Zona Verde (☎ 268 324 701; Largo Dragões de Olivença 86; dishes from €6; open Fri-Wed) has an attractive arched interior and serves good regional specialities.

Shopping
The weekly Saturday market along the southern fringe of the Rossio provides a great display of Alentejan goodies and Estremoz specialities, notably goat- and ewe-milk cheeses, and a unique style of unglazed, ochre-red pottery. There's also a small flea market, where a large crowd of Estremoz menfolk tend to loiter.

If you miss the Saturday market – or need horse tackle, cowbells or baskets – there's a great **handicraft and rural crafts shop** (☎ 268 323 130; Rua Victor Cordon 16) southeast of the Rossio. **Artesanato Santo**

André (*☎ 268 333 360; Rua da Misericórdia 2)* stocks a smaller selection of goods.

For contemporary, Estremoz-style ceramic figurines visit the **Bonecos de Estremoz** (*☎ 268 339 200)* workshop at the back of the Museu Municipal. Alternatively, pick up the leaflet from the turismo that has contact details for other local artisans.

Getting There & Away
The bus station is on the east side of town. Four local buses go to Évora (€3, 1½ hours) daily during the week, plus one express service (€6.10, one hour); five local buses go to Portalegre (€3.80, 1¼ hour), plus two express (€6.30, one hour). Five expresses go to Elvas daily (€5.60, 50 minutes), plus three to four local buses (€2.40, 1½ hours) via Borba (€1.50, 15 minutes) and Vila Viçosa (€1.90, 35 minutes). Five express buses daily head for Lisbon (€9.20, 2½ hours) and one to Faro (€12.40, six hours).

AROUND ESTREMOZ
The following places make great day trips or short stopovers from Estremoz.

Borba
Borba is the smallest of the three 'marble towns' (the other two are Estremoz and Vila Viçosa), and it is ringed by quarries and glows with marble whiteness. You can spend an agreeable few hours here, visiting its famous wineries and antique shops.

Borba's main square, Praça da República, with its ornate 18th-century marble fountain (Fonte das Bicas), is the focus of town. The **turismo** (*☎ 268 894 113; Rua do Convento das Servas)* is in the *câmara municipal*. The town comes to life once a year in early November, when it hosts a huge country fair.

Wineries The **Adega Cooperativa de Borba** (*☎ 268 894 264, fax 268 890 285; Rossio de Cima; open 9am-12.30pm & 2pm-5pm Mon-Fri)*, on the Estremoz road, is the largest of three *adegas* in town, all producing the famous Borba full-bodied red and white *maduro* (mature) wines. Opposite is **Sovibor** (*Sociedade de Vinhos de Borba; ☎ 268 894 210, fax 268 894 394; open 9am-12.30pm & 2pm-4.30pm Mon-Fri)*, of which the ornately carved portal is worth a look. Neither place is geared for tourists but will

accept visitors, and some readers have bought bargain wines here.

Getting There & Away Two to three buses daily connect Borba with Estremoz (€1.50, 15 minutes) and Vila Viçosa.

Vila Viçosa
Vila Viçosa is a palatial but relaxing place and the finest of the three marble towns; it has marbled streets, marble mansions, over 20 marble-adorned churches and a hill-top walled castle (alas, made only of stone). It's actually best known for its Paço Ducal, the palatial home of the Bragança dynasty, whose kings ruled Portugal until the republic was founded in 1910.

Orientation & Information The huge, sloping Praça da República is the attractive heart of town, with the *mercado municipal* and gardens 200m to the southeast. At the top of the *praça* is the 17th-century Igreja de São Bartolomeu; at the bottom is Avenida Bento de Jesus which lies at the foot of the castle. The ducal palace is 300m northwest of the *praça* (follow Rua Dr Couto Jardim).

Vila Viçosa has its own **turismo** (*☎ 268 881 101; Praça da República 34; open 9.30am-12.30pm & 2pm-5.30pm daily)*.

Paço Ducal The austere palace of the dukes of Bragança (*☎ 268 980 659; adult/child under 10 €5/free; open 9.30am-1pm & 2pm-5pm Tues-Sun Oct-Mar; 9.30am-1pm & 2.30pm-5.30pm Tues-Fri, to 6pm Sat & Sun Apr-Sept)* dates from the early 16th century when the fourth duke, Dom Jaime, decided to move out of his uncomfortable hill-top castle. The wealthy Bragança family, originally from Bragança in Trás-os-Montes, had settled in Vila Viçosa in the 15th century. After the eighth duke became king in 1640, he and his successors – especially the last of the line, Manuel I – continued to visit the palace, though it no longer hosted the banquets and festivities that took place during Dom Jaime's time.

The interior is now pretty dull – the best furniture went to Lisbon after the eighth duke ascended the throne, and some went on to Brazil after the royal family fled there in 1807. Even so, the private apartments hold a ghostly fascination – toiletries,

Skeletons in the Bragança Cupboard

The most illustrious member of the powerful Bragança family – descended from Dom João I's illegitimate son, Afonso – was the eighth duke, who in 1640 became a reluctant king, Dom João IV, sealing Portugal's liberation from Spanish rule. But there are murky corners in the dynastic history.

The third duke, Fernando, was executed in Évora in 1483 on the orders of his brother-in-law Dom João II, who deliberately struck at the family's immense power and wealth by accusing the duke of plotting against the monarchy.

By far the nastiest episode concerns the fourth duke, Dom Jaime, who murdered his young wife Leonor de Gusmão in a fit of jealous rage on 2 November 1512. Suspicious that his wife was having an affair, he caught a young pageboy climbing into the window of her quarters at the Paço Ducal in Vila Viçosa. Despite her pleas of innocence, the duke 'with five slashes ripped out her life'. Only later was it revealed that the pageboy was probably visiting one of the queen's ladies-in-waiting.

The most recent murderous event was the assassinations of Dom Carlos and his son in Lisbon on 1 February 1908. Two years later the monarchy was overthrown and the royal Bragança line came to an end. Today's leading Bragança noble, Dom Duarte, keeps a low, politically correct profile, supervising an experimental eco-farm in the north of the country.

knick-knacks and clothes of Dom Carlos and his wife, Marie-Amélia, are laid out as if the royal couple were about to return (Dom Carlos left one morning in 1908 and was assassinated in Lisbon that afternoon). A Portuguese-speaking guide leads the hour-long tours.

Other parts of the palace, including the 16th-century cloister, house additional museums containing specific collections (eg, porcelain, arms, coaches and so on). Last admission is one hour before closing time.

Castelo Dom Dinis' walled, hill-top castle was where the Bragança family lived before the palace was built. A few small houses (still inhabited), a 16th-century *pelourinho* and the 15th-century Igreja de Nossa Senhora da Conceição are all that remain of the town that once surrounded the castle.

The castle itself has been transformed into a **Museu de Caça e Arqueologia** (*Museum of Hunting & Archaeology; admission €2.50; open 9.30am-1pm & 2pm-5pm Tues-Sun Oct-Mar; 9.30am-1pm & 2.30pm-5.30pm Tues-Fri, to 6pm Sat & Sun Apr-Sept)*, stuffed with gruesome trophies, many snared by the dukes on their 20-sq-km hunting ground north of Vila Viçosa.

Places to Stay The *quartos* of elderly, genteel **Senora Maria de Conceição Paiseão** (*☎ 268 980 168; Rua Dr Couto Jardim 7; singles/doubles with shared bathroom*

€12.50/22.50) are beautifully kitted out with Alentejan painted furniture.

Hospedaria Dom Carlos (*☎/fax 268 980 318; Praça da República 25; singles/doubles €20/30)* is a mainstream place around the corner from Senora Maria de Conceição Paiseão.

Casa de Peixinhos (*☎ 268 980 472, fax 268 881 348; doubles with breakfast €92)*, a 17th-century manor house a few kilometres out on the Borba road, is the place for baronial ambience. Rooms are furnished with azulejos and antiques.

Pousada de Dom João IV (*☎ 268 980 742, fax 268 980 747; doubles Mon-Fri €159, Sat & Sun €168)*, a former royal convent that became the 'House of the Ladies of the Court', next to the ducal palace, offers the ultimate in palatial splendour.

Places to Eat The best of several café-restaurants found around Praça da República is **Café Restauração** (*☎ 268 980 256)*,which is just below the turismo, offering a decent menu of standard fare from around €6.40.

Os Cucos (*☎ 268 980 806; dishes €6.50-9)*, hidden in the gardens near the *mercado municipal*, is particularly recommended for grilled fish and meat dishes.

Getting There & Away There are three to four daily buses to/from Estremoz (€1.90, 35 minutes).

ELVAS

postcode 7350 • pop 15,100
• elevation 280m

This massively fortified frontier town, 15km west of Spanish Badajoz and 40km east of Estremoz, boasts 17th-century Europe's most sophisticated military architecture, with well-preserved moats, curtain walls, bastions, fortified gates and three forts. Astonishingly, there's poor information available and few tourist facilities. Indeed, inside the walls Elvas feels much like any other Alentejan market town, hosting Spanish day-trippers (busy shopping for cheap linen, china and candied plums) and coming to a complete standstill on Sunday afternoon.

Walkers will have a field day following the old aqueduct and town walls, or losing themselves in the warren of narrow streets.

History

Elvas only really charged into the history books in 1230, when it was recaptured from the Moors after 500 years of relatively peaceful occupation. The following centuries saw interminable attacks from Spain, interrupted by occasional peace treaties. The only successful attack was in 1580, allowing Felipe II of Spain (the future Felipe I of Portugal) to set up court here for a few months. The garrison's honour was redeemed during the Wars of Succession when, in 1644, it held out against a nine-day Spanish siege. In 1659, its numbers reduced to a mere 1000 men by an epidemic, the garrison withstood an attack by a 15,000-strong Spanish army.

The fortifications had their last period of glory in 1811 when the Duke of Wellington used the town as the base for an attack on Badajoz during the Peninsular War.

Orientation

The town centre is surprisingly compact considering the extent of the walls. Praça da República is the heart of the old town, with all major sights a short walk away. Those arriving by train will find themselves disembarking at Fontaínhas, 4km north of town off the Campo Maior road.

Drivers should park on the outskirts of town (or just inside Portas de Olivença) to avoid the narrow one-way streets in the centre.

Information

Tourist Offices The turismo (☎ 268 622 236; Praça da República; open 9am-6pm Mon-Fri, 10am-12.30pm & 2pm-5.30pm Sat & Sun May-Sept; to 5.30pm daily Oct-Apr) had no town map at the time of writing and only an outdated free Excursions around Elvas pamphlet.

Money In addition to many banks with ATMs around town, including **Banco Espirito Santo** (Praça da República), there's an exchange bureau, **Cota Câmbios** (Rua da Cadeia; open 8.30am-6.30pm Mon-Fri, 10am-2pm Sat).

Post & Communications The post office (open 8.30am-6pm Mon-Fri, 9am-12.30pm Sat) has NetPost. At **O Livreiro de Elvas** (☎/fax 268 620 882; Rua de Olivença 4A; open 9.30am-1pm & 3.30pm-5.15pm Mon-Fri, 10am-3pm Sat) you can surf the Internet for €1.50 per half-hour.

Medical Services & Emergency There's a **police station** (☎ 268 622 613; Rua Isabel Maria Picão). The **district hospital** (☎ 268 622 225) is opposite the Pousada de Santa Luzia.

Fortifications

Walls encircled Elvas as early as the 13th century, but it was in the 17th century that Flemish Jesuit engineer Cosmander designed the formidable defences you see today, adding moats, ramparts, bastions and fortified gates in the style of the famous French military architect, the Marquis de Vauban.

Also added was the Forte de Santa Luzia, just south of town. The Forte de Nossa Senhora da Graça, 3km north of town, was added in the following century; it's still in use as an army base and is closed to the public.

Castelo

One of the best views of the fortifications is from the castle walls (admission €1.30; open 9.30am-1pm & 2.30pm-5.30pm daily). The original castle was built by the Moors on a Roman site, and rebuilt by Dom Dinis in the 13th century, then again by Dom João II in the late 15th century. There's now a small café inside.

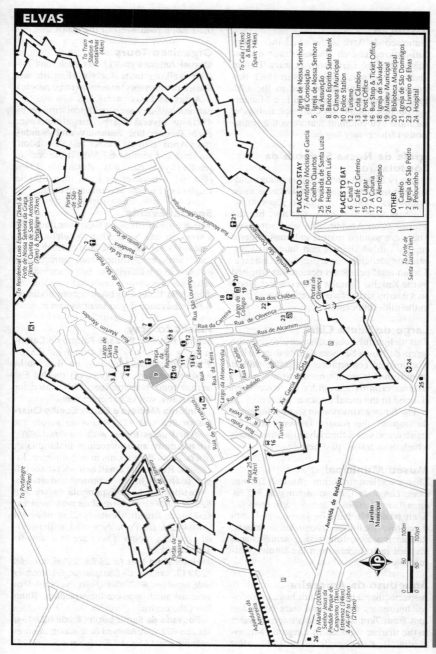

ELVAS

PLACES TO STAY
7 António Mocisso e Garcia
Coelho Quartos
25 Pousada de Santa Luzia
26 Hotel Dom Luís

PLACES TO EAT
6 Canal 7
11 Café O Grémio
15 O Lagar
17 A Coluna
22 O Alentejano

OTHER
1 Castelo
2 Igreja de São Pedro
3 Pelourinho
4 Igreja de Nossa Senhora
  da Consolação
5 Igreja de Nossa Senhora
  da Assunção
8 Banco Espírito Santo Bank
9 Câmara Municipal
10 Police Station
12 Turismo
13 Cota Câmbios
14 Post Office
16 Bus Stop & Ticket Office
18 Igreja de Salvador
19 Museu Municipal
20 Biblioteca Municipal
21 Igreja de São Domingos
23 O Livreiro de Elvas
24 Hospital

Igreja de Nossa Senhora da Assunção

Francisco de Arruda designed this rather dull-looking church (facing Praça da República) in the early 16th century. Before Elvas lost its episcopal status in 1882, this was the cathedral. Renovated in the 17th and 18th centuries, it retains a few Manueline touches, notably its south portal. Inside, the most eye-catching feature is the sumptuous 18th-century organ.

Igreja de Nossa Senhora da Consolação

It is very easy to overlook this plain building (admission free, donations welcome; open 9.30am-12.30pm & 2.30pm-6.30pm Tues-Sun May-Sept, to 5.30pm Oct-Apr) but the interior is an Aladdin's cave of surprises. There are painted marble columns under a cupola, gilded chapels and fantastic 17th-century azulejos covering every surface. The unusual octagonal design was inspired by the Knights Templar chapel, which stood on a nearby site before this church was built in the mid-16th century.

Largo de Santa Clara

This delightful cobbled square facing the Igreja de Nossa Senhora da Consolação has a whimsical centrepiece – a **polka-dotted pelourinho**. It wasn't meant to be fun, of course: criminals would once have been chained to the metal hooks at the top.

The fancy **archway** with its own loggia at the top of the square is pure Moorish artistry, and was a flourish in the town walls which once trailed past here.

Museu Municipal

This excellent museum (Museu Thomaz Pires; Largo do Colégio; admission €0.30; open 9am-12.30pm & 2pm-5.30pm Mon-Fri) is an incredible bargain, jam-packed with treasures, including Neolithic artefacts, Roman mosaics, folk crafts, azulejos and musical instruments from the former African colonies.

Aqueduto da Amoreira

A spectacular aqueduct with huge cylindrical buttresses and several tiers of arches runs from 7km west of town to bring water to the marble fountain in Largo da Misericórdia. It was completed in 1622, after about a century of work. It's best seen from the Lisbon road, west of the centre.

Organised Tours

Miguel Antunes (☎ 933 259 036) runs 2½-hour walking tours for €6 (English and French commentary; minimum three people).

Antas de Elvas (☎/fax 268 626 403) organises half-day archaeological circuits by 4WD to several nearby megaliths twice each Wednesday, Saturday and Sunday from April to mid-October (€15 per adult, students and seniors €7.50). At the castelo (castle) you can buy Antas de Elvas (€4.50), a booklet on local megaliths in English or French, and other material.

Special Events

The people of Elvas let their hair down for a week in late September to celebrate the Festas do Senhor da Piedade e de São Mateus, with everything from agricultural markets and bullfights to folk dancing and religious processions (especially on the last day). You'll need to book accommodation well in advance if you want to join in.

Places to Stay

Senhor Jesus da Piedade Parque de Campismo (☎ 268 623 772; adult/tent/car €2.50/2.50/2.80; open Apr-Nov), on the southwestern outskirts of Elvas, off the N4 Estremoz road, is rather basic. It's closed for the last two weeks in September.

António Mocisso e García Coelho Quartos (☎ 268 622 126; Rua Aires Varela 15; singles/doubles/triples with breakfast €20/30/40), down an inauspicious-looking lane, offers 20 modern rooms in two different locations. Rooms are small and poorly soundproofed but all have a bathroom and air-con.

Residencial Luso Espanhola (☎/fax 268 623 092; Rui de Melo; doubles with breakfast €38) is a friendly hostelry 2km north of town beside the Portalegre road, with smallish, modern rooms. There are two restaurants next door.

Hotel Dom Luís (☎ 268 622 756, fax 268 620 733; Avenida de Badajoz; singles/doubles with breakfast €57.50/63) is a lively modern establishment opposite the aqueduct, 700m from the centre.

Pousada de Santa Luzia (☎ 268 622 194, fax 268 622 127; Avenida de Badajoz; doubles with breakfast Mon-Fri €115, Sat & Sun €121) is a comfortable, mellow *pousada* dating from the 1940s.

Quinta de Santo António *(☎ 268 628 406, fax 268 625 050; Estrada de Barbacena; doubles with breakfast €68)*, a 30-room *estalagem* (smart inn) 7km northwest of Elvas, is an upmarket rural alternative, with pool, tennis courts and horses that you can ride.

Places to Eat

Café O Grémio *(☎ 268 622 711)*, right on the *praça*, has good-value dishes and attractive outdoor seating.

Canal 7 *(☎ 268 623 593; Rua dos Sapateiros 16; dishes from €3.70)* is a small, very simple *churrasqueira* with generous portions and take-away service.

O Alentejano *(☎ 268 621 925; Rua dos Chilões 29; dishes €5-7)* offers very reasonably priced Alentejan fare.

A Coluna *(☎ 268 623 728; Rua do Cabrito 11; dishes from €5)* is a cut above the rest, with azulejos on the walls and lots of *bacalhau* on the menu. Its two €9 set menus are good value.

O Lagar *(☎ 268 624 793; Rua Nova da Vedoria 7; dishes €6-8)* is a smartish new addition with regional cooking. *Espetada mista* (€7) is a mixed kebab of tasty morsels.

Shopping

Every Monday there's a big lively market around the aqueduct, just off the Lisbon road west of town.

Getting There & Around

The bus stop and **ticket office** *(☎ 268 622 875)* is in Praça 25 de Abril. On weekdays there are five express buses to Estremoz (€5.60, 50 minutes), two to Évora (€8, 1½ hours; with longer local services) and two to Portalegre (€3.80, 1¼ hours). Seven express coaches depart daily for Lisbon (€10.20, 3½ hours).

Twice-daily buses head for the frontier town of Caia (€1.30, 20 minutes), with connections to Badajoz in Spain.

One of the three daily Lisbon–Elvas trains (€9.10, 4½ hours; change at Abrantes and/or Entroncamento) continues to Badajoz (€0.90, 15 minutes).

Taxis *(☎ 268 623 526, 967 006 163)* charge around €3 from the train station at Fontaín into town.

PORTALEGRE

postcode 7300 • pop 15,200
• elevation 520m

Portalegre, Alto Alentejo's capital and commercial centre, is an appealingly untouristed place. Its small, walled centre has a 16th-century cathedral, some old and new azulejos adorning the streets, and a generous sprinkling of handsome 17th- and 18th-century mansions, thanks to a period of wealth from textile manufacturing. Tapestries made Portalegre famous in the 16th century, and silk in the 17th, but the bubble burst after the 1703 Treaty of Methuen led to an influx of English textiles.

For today's visitors, the town is a handy stopover en route to the Serra de São Mamede and its hill-top villages.

Orientation

Portalegre has an hourglass shape, with the new town found to the northeast and the old town spread across a hill top to the southwest. The waist is a traffic roundabout known as the Rossio, which is close to the bus station, from where it's about 400m to the old town via the pedestrianised Rua 5 de Outubro.

Information

The **turismo** *(☎ 245 331 359; open 10am-1pm & 3pm-7pm daily July & Aug, to 6pm Sept-June)* operates from the unsigned, green-shuttered Palácio Póvoas on the Rossio. It has an excellent town map with a suggested walking route. The **Região de Turismo de Sao Mamede** *(regional tourist office; ☎ 245 300 770; ⓦ www.rtsm.pt; Estrada de Santana 25)* is open during weekday business hours; enter through the back.

The headquarters of the **Parque Natural da Serra de São Mamede** *(☎ 245 203 631; ⓔ pnssm@icn.pt; Rua General Conde Jorge de Avilez 22)* has a free map and leaflet in English (also available at the turismo), plus leaflets with suggested walks (€0.50).

Among banks with ATMs is **Sotto Mayor** *(Rossio)* and **Caixa Geral de Déposítos** *(Rua 19 de Junho)* in the old town.

The **main post office** *(open 8.30am-6pm Mon-Fri, 9am-12.30pm Sat)* has NetPost. A **branch office** *(Rua Luís de Camões 39)* is in the old town. Free Internet access is available at the **Centro de Juventude**, where the *pousada da juventude* is also located (see

ALENTEJO

Places to Stay, later), from 9am to 7pm weekdays only.

The **police station** (☎ 245 300 620) is just outside Porta de Alegrete; the **hospital** (☎ 245 301 000) is 400m north of town.

Sé

In 1545 Portalegre became the seat of a new diocese and soon got its own cathedral. The sombre, twin-towered 18th-century facade, with a stork's nest and a broken clock, presides over the whitewashed Praça do Município. The sacristy contains an array of fine azulejos.

Castelo

Portalegre's castle *(admission €1; open 10am-noon & 2pm-5pm Tues-Sat, morning Sun)* dates from the time of Dom Dinis. There's little left but three restored towers.

Museu Municipal & Mansions

Beside the cathedral, in an 18th-century mansion and former seminary, is the modest town museum *(admission €1.80; open 9.30am-12.30pm & 2pm-6pm Wed-Mon)*, featuring obligatory period furnishings,

religious art – including a huge number of figures of Santo António – and some handsome Arraiolos carpets.

To the southeast, Rua 19 de Junho sports numerous faded 17th-century baroque townhouses and mansions.

Museu da Tapeçaria de Portalegre – Guy Fino

Opened in 2001, the splendid tapestry museum *(☎ 245 307 980; Rua da Figueira 9; admission €1.80; open 9.30am-1pm & 2.30pm-6pm Thur-Tues)*, named after the founder of the town's last remaining tapestry factory, displays some of that factory's brilliant creations from the mid- to late 20th century. It also displays old looms and a selection of the 5000 colours of thread used in tapestry production. Among the dazzling, often-huge creations are designs by some of the most famous names in Portuguese 20th-century art, including Almada Negreiros and Vieira de Silva. You'll need sharp eyes to spot the differences between two cockerels, one made at Aubuisson, the other at Portalegre, by French tapestry artist Jean Lurçat.

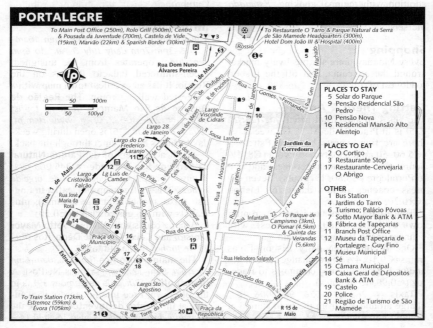

PORTALEGRE

To Main Post Office (250m), Rolo Grill (500m), Centro & Pousada da Juventude (700m), Castelo de Vide (15km), Marvão (22km) & Spanish Border (30km)

To Restaurante O Tarro & Parque Natural da Serra de São Mamede Headquarters (300m), Hotel Dom João III & Hospital (400m)

Rossio

Rua Dom Nuno Álvares Pereira

Rua de Maio

Rua 5 de Outubro

R. de Piacinha

Rua 31 de Janeiro

Gomes – Fernandes

Rua Cem Lacerça Machado

Rua dos Mizes

Largo Visconde de Cidrais

R. Sousa Larcher

Largo 28 de Janeiro

Largo do Dr Frederico Laranjo

R. dos Muros de Baxo

Rua Luis de Camões

Largo do Prão

R. Benvindo Cesa

Rua da Mouraria

Jardim da Corredoura

Rua de Olivença

Lg Luis de Camões

R. M. Albuquerque

Largo Cristovão Falcão

Rua 1 de Maio

Rua José Maria da Rosa

Rua do Comercio

Rua dos Arquiques

Rua de Elvas

Rua 31 de Janeiro

Jardim da Corredoura

Av. George Robinson

Infantaria 22

To Parque de Campismo (3km), O Pomar (4.5km) & Quinta das Verandas (5.6km)

Rua do Carmo

Praça do Município

Rua Achioul

Rua 19 de Junho

Rua Heliodoro Salgado

Estrada de Santana

R. do Arco

Largo Sto Agostino

Rua Nicolau Alves

Rua Garrett

Rua Cândido dos Reis

Rua Raimo Ferreira Rainho

To Train Station (12km), Estremoz (59km) & Évora (105km)

R. da Torre do Pesegueiro

Praça da República

R 15 de Maio

PLACES TO STAY
5 Solar do Parque
9 Pensão Residencial São Pedro
10 Pensão Nova
16 Residencial Mansão Alto Alentejo

PLACES TO EAT
2 O Cortiço
3 Restaurante Stop
17 Restaurante-Cervejaria O Abrigo

OTHER
1 Bus Station
4 Jardim do Tarro
6 Turismo; Palácio Póvoas
7 Sotto Mayor Bank & ATM
8 Fábrica de Tapeçarias
11 Branch Post Office
12 Museu da Tapeçaria de Portalegre - Guy Fino
13 Museu Municipal
14 Sé
15 Câmara Municipal
18 Caixa Geral de Dépositos Bank & ATM
19 Castelo
20 Police
21 Região de Turismo de São Mamede

ALENTEJO

The factory still operates, from a former Jesuit college on Rua Gomes Fernandes, just off the Rossio, producing specially commissioned works only.

Places to Stay

There's a good Orbitur **parque de campismo** (*☎/fax 245 202 848; adult/tent/car €3.20/2.60/3.30; open Apr-Oct*) at Quinta da Saúde, 3km northeast of town on the Estrada da Serra, high above town.

The **pousada da juventude** (*☎ 245 330 971; e portalegre@movijovem.pt; Estrada do Bonfim; dorm beds €9.50, doubles without bathroom €24; open 8am-10am & 7pm-midnight*), located 700m north of the Rossio in a big white building labelled 'Centro de Juventude', is fairly basic, although the adjacent Instituto Português da Juventude (IPJ), the town's main youth centre, is a lively rendezvous.

Pensão Nova (*☎ 245 331 212, fax 245 330 493; Rua 31 de Janeiro 26; doubles €22.50*) has pretty blue-and-white rooms. Under the same management is **Pensão Residencial São Pedro** (*☎ 245 331 212; Rua da Mouraria 14; doubles €22.50*), for which reception is at Pensão Nova.

Residencial Mansão Alto Alentejo (*☎ 245 202 290, fax 245 309 269; Rua 19 de Junho 59; singles/doubles/triples with air-con & breakfast €35/45/55*), the best choice in the old town, has completely renovated rooms with traditional painted furniture.

Hotel Dom João III (*☎ 245 330 192, fax 245 330 444; Avenida da Liberdade; doubles with breakfast €55*) is a modern three-star hotel with dull but comfortable rooms.

Solar do Parque (*Solar das Avencas; ☎ 245 201 028, 919 461 619; Parque Miguel Bombarda 11; doubles with breakfast €60*), an 18th-century manor house, is an atmospheric place to splash out at.

Some rural options along the Estrada da Serra, on spectacularly high, vineyard-clad hillsides within the Parque Natural da Serra de São Mamede, include the two-room, British-run **O Pomar** (*☎/fax 245 205 720; doubles with breakfast €60*), 1.5km beyond the Orbitur camp site; and the fabulously remote and peaceful three-roomed **Quinta das Verandas** (*☎/fax 245 208 883; doubles with breakfast €65*), about 2.6km beyond the camp site (there's a pool here, too).

Places to Eat

Budget choices near the bus station include **O Cortiço** (*☎ 245 202 176; Rua Dom Nuno Álvares Pereira 17; dishes from €5*); and the slightly nicer **Restaurante Stop** (*☎ 245 201 364; Rua Dom Nuno Álvares Pereira 13; dishes €5-6*).

Restaurante O Tarro (*☎ 245 309 254; dishes from €6.50*), at the top of Jardim do Tarro, has a chic indoor restaurant and pleasant outdoor café.

Restaurante-Cervejaria O Abrigo (*☎ 245 331 658; Rua de Elvas 74; dishes €6-7.50; open Wed-Mon*), inside the old town, is a welcoming, folksy venue.

Rolo Grill (*☎ 245 205 676; Avenida Pio XII, Lote 7; grills from €40*), incongruously located

---

Parque Natural da Serra de São Mamede

After the endless plains of Baixo Alentejo, the Serra de São Mamede comes as a refreshing change: four peaks (Fria, Marvão, Castelo de Vide and São Mamede) top off this 40km-long range running along the Spanish border near Portalegre. The park, stretching from Castelo de Vide south to just beyond Esperança, includes all four peaks.

A combination of Atlantic forest and Mediterranean bush provides ideal habitat for the rare trumpet narcissus and stonecrop, plus dozens of bird species – more than half of the species that breed in Portugal nest here. Keep an eye out especially for vultures, eagles, kites and black storks.

With your own transport you can delve right into the heart of the park, to traditional villages such as Alegrete and Esperança. Buses run from Portalegre to Castelo de Vide and Marvão.

At the park's **head office** (*☎ 245 203 631, fax 245 207 501; Rua General Conde Jorge de Avilez 22, Portalegre*) you can make reservations for park accommodation: four *casas de abrigo* (shelterhouses), each sleeping up to eight, cost €149 per day. Other information, including bilingual walking leaflets (€0.50), is available at the Marvão turismo and at the Centro de Interpretação in Castelo de Vide (see that section).

ALENTEJO

in an apartment block, is absolutely top-notch: the spread of desserts at the entrance is mind-blowing, the prices a little breathtaking. Grilled dishes are the speciality here: watch the chef at work while you wait.

Getting There & Around
From the **bus station** (☎ 245 330 723) three to four expresses daily run to Lisbon (€10.20, 4¼ hours). The twice-daily Braga to Faro express links Portalegre with various towns en route including Estremoz (€5.90, one hour) and Évora (€8.20, 1½ hours). Three buses daily go to Castelo Branco (€7.70, 1½ hours).

Trains from Lisbon run three times daily (€8.10, 3½ hours); change at Abrantes. The station is 12km south of town but shuttle buses (€1.20, 15 minutes) meet all trains.

For a taxi, call ☎ 245 202 375 or ☎ 966 772 947.

CASTELO DE VIDE
postcode 7320 • pop 3800 • elevation 570m
One of the Alentejo's most appealing fortified hill-top villages, Castelo de Vide, sits high above the surrounding olive plains at the northern tip of the Parque Natural da Serra de São Mamede, 15km north of Portalegre and just west of the Spanish border.

Despite some modern development outside the walls, this ancient spa town has maintained its traditional appearance and lifestyle, largely leaving the day-trippers to its smaller and more stunning neighbour, Marvão.

Castelo de Vide's own attractions include a 14th-century castle with some marvellous views and, below it, a medieval *judiaria*. To add to its seductive qualities, the town has a supply of famously good mineral water and plenty of decent accommodation.

Orientation
At the heart of town are two parallel squares backed by the Igreja de Santa Maria da Devesa. The turismo is in the upper 'pillory square', a wide area in Rua Bartolomeu Álvares da Santa with a *pelourinho* in the middle. Walk through the archway that is by the turismo to reach the southern square, Praça Dom Pedro V.

The castle, medieval quarter and *judiaria* lie to the northwest. Dive into the lanes

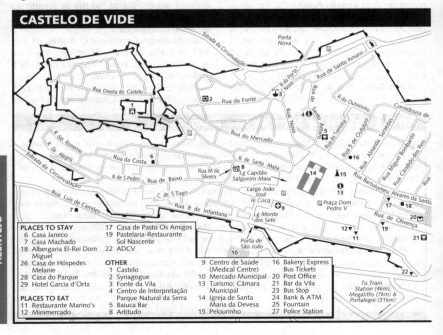

CASTELO DE VIDE

PLACES TO STAY
6 Casa Janeco
7 Casa Machado
18 Albergaria El-Rei Dom Miguel
26 Casa de Hóspedes Melanie
28 Casa do Parque
29 Hotel Garcia d'Orta

PLACES TO EAT
11 Restaurante Marino's
12 Minimercado

17 Casa de Pasto Os Amigos
19 Pastelaria-Restaurante Sol Nascente
22 ADCV

OTHER
1 Castelo
2 Synagogue
3 Fonte da Vila
4 Centro de Interpretação Parque Natural da Serra
5 Baiuca Bar
8 Artitudo

9 Centro de Saúde (Medical Centre)
10 Mercado Municipal
13 Turismo; Câmara Municipal
14 Igreja de Santa Maria da Devesa
15 Pelourinho

16 Bakery; Express Bus Tickets
20 Post Office
21 Bar da Vila
23 Bus Stop
24 Bank & ATM
25 Fountain
27 Police Station

ALENTEJO

behind the Igreja de Santa Maria da Devesa and follow the signs to Fonte da Vila (the old town fountain). From there it's a short, very steep climb to the synagogue and castle.

Buses stop at the fountain near the post office; the train station is 4km northwest of town.

Information

The **turismo** (☎ 245 901 361; e cm.castvide@ mail.telepac.pt; Rua Bartolomeu Álvares da Santa 81; open 9am-12.30pm & 2pm-7pm daily July & Aug, to 5.30pm Sept-June) is on the pillory square. There's also a Parque Natural da Serra de São Mamede **Centro de Interpretação** (☎ 245 905 299; Rua de Santo Amaro 27; open 9.30am-12.45pm & 2pm-5.45pm Mon-Fri).

Caixa Geral de Déposits bank is near the **post office** (Rua de Olivença; open 9am-6pm Mon-Fri). Internet access, at €3 per hour, is available at **Artitudo** (☎ 245 908 085; Rua Mouzinho da Silveira 14; open noon-2am daily), a classy café, art gallery and bookshop.

Emergency services include the **police station** (☎ 245 901 314; Avenida da Aramenha)

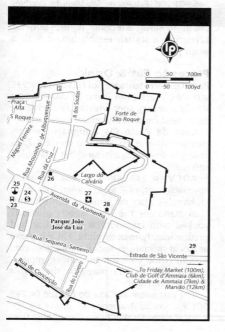

and **centro de saúde** (medical centre; ☎ 245 901 105; Praça Dom Pedro V).

An open-air market takes place every Friday (at its biggest on the last Friday of the month), 300m east of town near the municipal sports ground (it may eventually move to a new car park south of the centre).

Judiaria

The cluster of narrow lanes just below and southeast of the castle is Castelo de Vide's most atmospheric quarter – a medieval enclave of cobbled paths and dazzling white cottages with Gothic doorways and window frames adorned with flowers.

A sizable community of Jews settled here in the 13th century, attracted by the area's prosperity. The tiny **synagogue** (cnr Rua da Judiaria & Rua da Fonte; admission free; open 9am-5.30pm daily) – the oldest in Portugal – looks just like its neighbouring cottages. The bare interior shows little evidence of its former use, apart from a wooden tabernacle and a shelf where scriptures were placed.

Castelo

Originally Castelo de Vide's inhabitants lived within the castle's sturdy outer walls; even now there remain some inhabited cottages and a small church, the 17th-century Igreja da Nossa Senhora da Alegria.

Dom Dinis and his brother Dom Afonso built, within the inner walls, the castle itself (admission free; open 9am-7pm daily May-Sept, to 5pm Oct-Apr) between 1280 and 1365. Its most notable feature is a 12m-high brick tower, which probably predates the outer defences and may have been used as an armoury or lookout post. There are great views from the roof of the finely bricked and vaulted hall.

Fonte da Vila

In a pretty square just below and east of the judiaria is the well-worn 16th-century marble Fonte da Vila. This, along with several other fountains in the village, provides residents with the delicious mineral water for which Castelo de Vide is known.

Anta dos Coureleiros & Menhir da Meada

In the wild, boulder-strewn landscape around Castelo de Vide are dozens of ancient megaliths. The two most impressive

ALENTEJO

are the Anta dos Coureleiros, 5.3km north of town (with three other megaliths nearby making up what's called a Parque Megalítico), and the 7m-high Menhir da Meada, 8.5km further on – supposedly the tallest menhir in the Iberian Peninsula.

Both are easily accessible by car or on foot. Turismos here and in Marvão should have *Paisagens Megalíticas Norte Alentejana*, a free, glossy photographic map (English versions available) to help you track down these and other megaliths; follow the small wooden 'Antas' signs en route.

Cidade de Ammaia

Opened in 2001, this excellent little Roman museum (*São Salvador de Aramenha; admission €2; open 9am-1pm & 2pm-5pm Mon-Fri, 10am-1pm & 2pm-5pm Sat & Sun*) lies 7km east, en route to Marvão. From São Salvador head 700m south along the Portalegre road, then turn left following signs to Olhos d'Água restaurant.

In the 1st century AD this area was a huge Roman city called Ammaia, flourishing from the area's rich agricultural produce (especially oil, wine and cereals). Although evidence was found (and some destroyed) in the 19th century, it wasn't until 1994 that thorough digs began. Inside the museum you can see some of the finds – engraved lintels and tablets, jewellery, coins and some incredibly well-preserved glassware – however, you can also follow paths across the fields to where the forum and spa once stood and see several impressive columns and ongoing excavations.

Golf

The new **Club de Golf d'Ammaia** (*☎ 245 993 755*) golf course is 6km towards Marvão.

Special Events

Castelo de Vide's big bash is the four-day Easter festival, when hundreds of lambs are blessed and then slaughtered, and processions, folk dances, band music and much revelry occurs. Carnaval, too, is great fun, with everyone out to watch processions of fantastically costumed folk, including many in drag.

Places to Stay

Casa Janeco (*☎ 245 901 211; Rua da Costa 56A; doubles with shared bathroom €22.50*),

in the heart of the old town, is a humble abode with two small rooms. The elderly Senhora Janeco also has a room with a kitchen costing €25.

Casa Machado (*☎ 245 901 515; Rua Luís de Camões 33; doubles with bathroom €25-32*), on the western edge of town, is modern and great for families. The four rooms are spotless and there's a small, shared kitchen and outdoor patio.

There is a trio of more comfortable places on Largo do Paça Novo, where double-room prices range from €30 to €40 (with bathroom). **Casa de Hóspedes Melanie** (*☎ 245 901 632; Largo do Paça Novo 3; singles/doubles with air-con €25/35*), owned by English-speakers, is the best value. The five immaculate rooms are luxuriously spacious.

Casa do Parque (*☎ 245 901 250, fax 245 901 228;* [e] *vitor-guimaraes@mail.pt; Av da Aramenha 37; doubles with breakfast €45*) is in a peaceful spot overlooking the park.

Albergaria El-Rei Dom Miguel (*☎ 245 919 191, fax 245 901 592; Rua Bartolomeu Álvares da Santa; doubles with breakfast €50-60*) is a smart place on the main street.

Hotel Garcia d'Orta (*☎ 245 901 100, fax 245 901 200; Estrada de São Vicente; doubles with breakfast Mon-Fri €70, Sat & Sun €85*), 200m towards Marvão, is the golfers' favourite, a stylish establishment with a small pool.

Places to Eat & Drink

Pastelaria-Restaurante Sol Nascente (*☎ 245 901 789; Praça Dom Pedro V; dishes under €7*) is a cheery spot with wicked pastries, main meals and sunny outdoor seating.

Casa de Pasto Os Amigos (*Rua Bartolomeu Álvares da Santa; dishes €6-7*) is cramped and uncharismatic but has quick service.

ADCV (*☎ 245 905 125; Rua Alexandre Herculano; dishes €5-6*), known locally as 'Johnny's', after its genial patron (the initials stand for the local sports club), is packed with labourers at lunch time and predominantly men at night. On the menu are local specialities such as *molhinhos com tomata* (tripe with tomato sauce), supposedly a dish once favoured by the town's Jewish community.

The restaurant at **Casa do Parque** (*☎ 245 901 250; Av da Aramenha 37; dishes €6.50-7.50*) is considerably more respectable than most; it's a decent hotel restaurant that can get busy at lunch time with tour groups.

Restaurante Marino's (☎ 245 901 408; Praça Dom Pedro V, 6; dishes €9.50-17; closed Sun & lunch Mon) is posh and pricey, offering some unusual dishes (how about penne à vodka at €8?).

Bar da Vila (☎ 245 905 433; Rua de Olivença 11) is one of several popular bars. English-run **Baiuca Bar** (☎ 919 186 125; Rua Santo Amaro 6; open 7pm-2am Wed-Mon) also serves English-style teas on weekend afternoons.

Self-catering supplies are available at a **minimercado** (grocery shop; Praça Dom Pedro V).

Getting There & Away

Bus Three to four times each weekday, buses make the run to/from Portalegre (local €2, 35 minutes; express €4.50, 20 minutes). There are two daily express services to/from Lisbon (€11.50, 4¼ hours). Buy express tickets (and check timetables) at the bakery at Rua 5 de Outubro 6, just off the pillory square.

Train Two trains daily run between Lisbon and Castelo de Vide (€8.10, four hours; change at Abrantes and Torre das Vargens). The station is 4km northwest of town and there are no bus links. **Taxis** (☎ 245 901 271, 919 222 060), available from outside the turismo, charge around €4 to the station.

MARVÃO

postcode 7330 • pop 190 • elevation 862m

At its atmospheric best at dusk and dawn, this mountain-top eyrie is stunning. Enclosed within serpentine walls are bright white houses with vermilion-edged Manueline windows or Renaissance doorways, their lintels often graced by enchanting little stone faces.

Narrow cobbled streets wind up to an awesome castle rising from the rock, from where you can gaze out over a panorama of wild peaks and Spanish horizons. As with Portugal's other hill-top gems, summertime visitors often outnumber residents; to savour the best atmosphere, come during off-season or stay overnight.

History

Not surprisingly, considering its impregnable position and its proximity to the Spanish frontier 10km away, Marvão has long been a prized possession. Even before the walls and castle existed, there was a Roman settlement in the area, and Christian Visigoths were here when the Moors arrived in 715. It was probably the Moorish lord of Coimbra, Emir Maraun, who gave the place its present name; the Moors certainly had a hand in fortifying the village.

In 1160 Christians took control. In 1226 the town received a municipal charter, the walls were extended to encompass the whole summit, and the castle was rebuilt by Dom Dinis.

Marvão's importance in the defence against the Spanish Castilians was highlighted during the 17th-century War of Restoration, when further defences were added to the castle. Two centuries later it was briefly at the centre of the tug-of-war between the Liberals and Royalists; in 1833 the Liberals used a secret entrance to seize the town, the only time Marvão has ever been captured.

Orientation

Arriving by car or bus you'll approach Portas de Ródão, one of the four village gates, opening onto Rua de Cima, which has several shops and restaurants. Drivers can park outside or enter this gate and park in Largo de Olivença, just below Rua de Cima. The castle is up at the end of Rua do Espírito Santo.

Information

The **turismo** (☎ 245 993 886; e museu.mar vao@mail.telepac.pt; Largo de Santa Maria; open 9am-12.30pm & 2pm-5.30pm daily Sept-June, to 6pm July & Aug) is near the castle. Among brochures available here are walking leaflets (€0.50) describing walks and wildlife in the Parque Natural da Serra de São Mamede.

There's a bank and post office in nearby Rua do Espiríto Santo.

Castelo

The formidable castle (admission free; open 24hr), built into the rock at the western end of the village, dates from the end of the 13th century, but most of what you see today was built in the 17th century. The views from the battlements are staggering. Don't miss the huge vaulted cistern (still full of water) near the entrance. At the far end, the **Núcleo Museológico Militar** (Military Museum;

adult/student €1/0.80; open 10am-1pm & 1.30pm-5pm Tues-Sun) offers a fine little display of Marvão and its castle's history (in Portuguese only) as well as a flourish of 17th- to 18th-century muskets and bayonets.

Museu Municipal

Just east of the castle, the Igreja de Santa Maria houses this engaging little museum *(adult/student €1/0.80; open 9am-12.30pm & 2pm-5.30pm daily)*, with exhibits ranging from Roman remains and skeletons to gruesome old medical implements.

Megaliths

You can make a brilliant 30km round-trip via Santo António das Areias and Beirã, visiting some of the *antas* (megaliths) in the immediate vicinity; pick up the free *Paisagens Megalíticas Norte Alentejana* map from the turismo. Follow the wooden 'antas' signs through a fabulously quiet landscape of cork trees and stones, and where pigs rummage. Some of the megaliths are right by the roadside, others require a 300m to 500m walk. Be sure to bring refreshments: there's no village en route. You can continue north of Beirã to visit the megaliths in the Castelo de Vide area (see under Castelo de Vide for details). Ask at the turismo about bikes to rent.

Places to Stay

There are several *quartos* for €30 to €40 per double (try Bar-Restaurante Varanda do Alentejo – see Places to Eat) and an apartment with kitchen for €40 to €45; the turismo has details.

Casa Dom Dinis *(☎ 245 993 957, fax 245 993 959; Rua Dr Matos Magalhães 7; doubles with breakfast €50)* is a friendly place near the turismo.

Casa da Árvore *(☎/fax 245 993 854; Rua Dr Matos Magalhães 3; doubles with breakfast €60)* has five very pretty, individually furnished rooms and amazing adornments, including original Roman funerary stones and a João Tavares tapestry from the famous Portalegre factory. The breakfast room boasts a stunning view.

Casa das Portas de Ródão *(☎ 245 992 160; Largo da Silveirinha 2; doubles €50)*, a two-storey, three-bedroom house right by the entrance to town, with an outdoor terrace, could appeal to families, in particular.

Pousada de Santa Maria *(☎ 245 993 201, fax 245 993 440; Rua 24 de Janeiro; doubles Mon-Fri €126, Sat & Sun €139)* is the most elegant and intimate option.

Places to Eat

Restaurante Casa do Povo *(☎ 245 993 160; Rua de Cima; dishes €4.50-6)*, near the entrance, has a standard simple menu and a café with outdoor terrace below. The modest **Restaurante O Marcelino** *(☎ 245 903 138; Rua de Cima 3)* – its sign just says 'Bar' – offers home-style cooking that's been appreciated by several readers, one of whom wrote: 'just like having my grandmother cook for us'.

Bar-Restaurante Varanda do Alentejo *(☎ 245 993 272; Praça do Pelourinho 1; dishes €6-6.50)* has some earthy Alentejan specialities on its menu, including *sarapatel* (a type of blood sausage; €1.80).

Bar O Castelo *(☎ 245 993 957; snacks €1.30-3.50)*, opposite Casa Dom Dinis, serves great soups, local cheese and imaginative, humble fare such as scrambled egg with lettuce.

Getting There & Away

On weekdays only, two buses run daily between Portalegre and Marvão (€2, 45 minutes). There are two services (at 9am and 2pm) from Castelo de Vide, but the first requires a change of buses at Portagem (a major road junction 7.5km northeast). There are two buses daily leaving Marvão: the 7.10am to Castelo de Vide and Portalegre and the 1.10pm to Portalegre (change at Portagem for Castelo de Vide). Check the latest timetable at the turismo. Express buses run to Lisbon at 7.45am daily (€12.20, 4¾ hours), but you must tell the turismo the day before if you want to catch it or the bus won't detour here to pick you up.

The nearest train station, Marvão-Beirã, is 9km north of Marvão; it's worth a visit just to see its beautiful azulejo panels. Two trains daily run to/from Lisbon (€8.10, 4½ hours; change at Abrantes and Torre das Vargens). Taxis charge around €5.50 to the station.

The daily Lisbon–Madrid *Talgo Lusitânia* train stops here just before 1am, en route to Valência de Alcântara, and just before 5am on the journey to Lisbon (3¼ hours).

Taxis *(☎ 245 993 272; Praça do Pelourinho)* charge around €8 to Castelo de Vide.

Estremadura & Ribatejo

These two skinny provinces surrounding and stretching north of Lisbon are full of contrasts. They boast the country's most stunning architectural masterpieces: the monasteries of Mafra, Alcobaça and Batalha, and Tomar's Convento de Cristo. In Estremadura province (so called because it was the furthest land from the Douro – *extrema Durii* – when the Christians wrested it from the Moors) are the beautiful *parque natural* areas of Sintra-Cascais and Serras de Aire e Candeeiros, the last named hosting several famous caves. The coast is a brilliant destination for surfers and seafood-lovers, with lively resorts and a generous sprinkling of undeveloped beaches.

Although the Ribatejo is home to a large number of dull or heavily industrialised towns and factories (especially around Abrantes and Torres Novas), there's also plenty of fine countryside. The rich alluvial plains are important areas for growing wheat, olives and vegetables, and, most famously, for breeding bulls and horses. Santarém, host of the Feira Nacional da Agricultura (National Agricultural Fair), which celebrates the agricultural lifestyle of the province with gusto, is a notably attractive town. Also well worth visiting is Tomar, the relaxing former headquarters of the Knights Templar.

The Estoril coast, Setúbal Peninsula, Sintra, Mafra and Ericeira are all covered in the Around Lisbon chapter.

Highlights

- Marvel at the Gothic-Manueline Mosteiro de Santa Maria da Vitória and the 12th-century Cistercian Mosteiro de Santa Maria de Alcobaça, both Unesco World Heritage sites
- Visit delightful Tomar, former headquarters of the powerful Knights Templar
- Meander through the pretty walled village of Óbidos
- Sample superb seafood at Nazaré and Peniche

Estremadura

PENICHE
postcode 2520 • pop 16,000

Until recently Peniche was just a drab fishing port with a dark past, its huge and impressive 16th-century fort a notorious Salazar-era prison. Now it's smartened up its act considerably, with a brisk pedestrianised centre and new accommodation options. Its big attractions are bargain seafood and regular boat trips to the island Reserva Natural da Berlenga, 10km offshore. In addition, the surfing attractions of nearby Baleal are giving Peniche a cool new status, with surfing shops and bars proliferating.

Orientation

Peniche was once an island; it became joined to the mainland in the late 16th century when silt created a narrow isthmus. Driving into town, the main N114 turns left into Rua Alexandre Herculano, where the *turismo* (tourist office) is located, or continues straight on for 3km round the Peniche peninsula to Cabo Carvoeiro and its lighthouse. If you are arriving by bus, you willx be dropped at the market, about 20m northwest of the turismo. From the market it is a short walk south to the old town centre and fort, the harbour and Avenida do Mar, where most of the seafood restaurants are located. Passenger boats for Ilha Berlenga leave from the harbour (where there's also ample free car parking in Largo da Ribeira).

ESTREMADURA & RIBATEJO

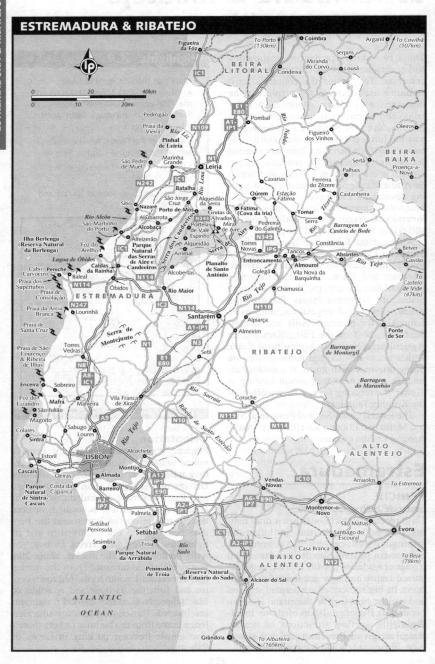

Information

The **turismo** (☎/fax 262 789 571; open 9am-8pm daily July & Aug, 10am-1pm & 2pm-5pm Sept-June) is in a shady public garden alongside Rua Alexandre Herculano. It has useful details of water-sports operators.

Among banks in town, **Caixa Geral de Dépositos** (Rua Alexandre Herculano 90) is opposite the turismo. **The police station** (☎ 262 789 555; Rua Heróis Ultramar) is about 400m west of the market; the **hospital** (☎ 262 780 900; Rua General Humberto Delgado) about 600m northwest.

Fortaleza

Dominating the southern end of the peninsula, Peniche's imposing 16th-century fortress (admission free; open 10.30am-12.30pm & 2pm-6pm Tues-Sun) was in military use as late as the 1970s, when it was converted into a temporary home for refugees from the newly independent African colonies. Twenty years earlier it had played a harsher role: it was one of Salazar's notorious jails for political prisoners. Right by the entrance, where prisoners once received visitors, is the **Núcleo-Resistência**, a grim display about these times, including prisoners' poignant letters to their children.

Housed in another part of the fort is the musty **Museu Municipal** (☎ 262 780 116; admission €1; open 10.30am-noon & 2pm-5.30pm Tues-Sun), the top floor of which reveals the even more chilling interrogation chambers and cells. Floors below this contain an extensive display on the town's lace-making tradition and its fishing and boat-building industries, plus a rather incongruous collection of paintings and personal belongings donated by the Peniche-born artist and politician, Paulino Montez.

Lace-Making Schools

Like another of Portugal's Atlantic fishing ports, Vila do Conde in the north, Peniche is famous for its bobbin lace. You can see it being made at **Escola de Rendas** (open 9.30am-12.30pm & 2pm-5.30pm Mon-Fri) in the turismo building and **Rendibilrosa** (Rua Alexandre Herculano 68; open 9am-12.30pm & 2pm-5.30pm Mon-Fri), nearby.

Baleal

About 4km to the northeast of Peniche is this tiny island village, connected to the mainland village of Casais do Baleal by a causeway. A fantastic sweep of sandy beach here offers some fine surfing.

Activities

Two surf camps in Baleal are **Maximum Surfcamp** (☎ 262 769 295) and **Baleal Surfcamp** (☎ 969 050 546; w www.balealsurfcamp.com), the latter offering packages that include accommodation. Surfboards can be rented from **Rip Curl Surf Shop** (☎ 262 787 206; Rua Alexandre Herculano 16) for €15 a day.

Scuba-diving operators include **Berlenga Sub** (☎ 966 788 160; e berlengasub@mail.telepac.pt; Largo da Ribeira 24) and **Mergulhão** (☎ 966 008 487), which can take you diving around the Peniche coast for about €15 or round Berlenga for €40.

For fishing trips, contact **Nautipesca** (☎ 917 588 358, fax 262 781 335), which has a kiosk at the harbour.

Centro Hípico A Coutada (Quinta das Tripas; ☎/fax 262 759 733; doubles €45), 5km east near Atouguia da Baleia, offers various activities, including horse riding, swimming and tennis.

Places to Stay

Camping The municipal **parque de campismo** (camp site; ☎ 262 789 529, fax 262 780 111; adult/tent/car €2/1.60/1.60) is 2km east of Peniche (opposite the BP station).

Peniche Praia (☎ 262 783 460, fax 262 789 447; adult/tent/car €2.80/2.80/2.40, doubles from €37) is on the high, windy north side of the peninsula, 1.7km from town and 2km from Cabo Carvoeiro. It also has a few bungalows and some rooms and bikes for rent.

Private Rooms The turismo has its own list of approved *quartos* (private rooms), costing about €25 a double, as well as apartments, though these are often booked out during August.

Pensões & Residenciais Unless otherwise stated, prices at all of the following places include breakfast.

Central Rua José Estevão has a string of *pensões* (guesthouses), including **Residencial Vasco da Gama** (☎ 262 781 902; Rua José Estevão 23; doubles €40), one of the older establishments, with smallish rooms; immaculate **Residencial Rima Vier** (☎ 262 789 459; Rua Castilho 6; doubles without *breakfast €30)* almost opposite; and **Residêncial Maciel** *(☎ 262 784 685; Rua José Estevão 38; doubles €50)*, the six rooms of which have huge bathrooms and polished, traditional decor (simpler rooms in a modern house nearby cost €40).

Pequena Baleia *(262 769 370; doubles €60)* is a pretty house in Baleal village, looking west across the sea to Peniche.

Casa das Marés *(☎ 262 769 371, 262 769 200; doubles around €65)*, at the northern end of Baleal, is an imposing house with sea views, which is actually three houses in one, owned by three sisters.

Places to Eat & Drink

Trawl Peniche's Avenida do Mar for seafood restaurants, including lively **Katekero I** *(☎ 262 781 480; Avenida do Mar 90)* and **Katekero II** *(☎ 262 787 107; Avenida do Mar 70)*.

Mira Mar *(☎ 262 781 666; Avenida do Mar 42)* also comes up with fabulous fishy goods – everything from sardines and squid to swordfish, salmon and shrimps. Expect to pay at least €6 per dish at all these places, or €20 for a delicious *arroz de tamboril* (monkfish rice).

Estelas *(☎ 262 782 435; Rua Arq Paulino Montez 19; dishes €10-14; open Thur-Tues)*, near the turismo, is a pricier seafood favourite.

Restaurante Meia Via *(☎ 262 782 283; Rua Ramiro de Matos Bilhau 8; dishes €6-7.50, half-portions €4.70)* is a cheaper option near the market.

In Baleal you'll find several restaurants right on the beach, including **Amigos do Baleal** *(☎ 262 769 865; Praia do Baleal; dishes €8.50)*.

Danau Bar *(☎ 262 709 818)* is a surfers' bar nearby, open all year and offering live music (and sometimes karaoke) at weekends. It's closed Monday in low season.

Getting There & Away

For buses out of Peniche you must go to the bus station, 400m northeast of the turismo (cross the Ponte Velha connecting the town to the isthmus). At least a dozen express buses daily run to/from Lisbon (€5.80, 1¾ hours) via Torres Vedras, plus four express buses to Coimbra (€9.50, 3½ hours) via Leiria (€8.40, 2¼ hours) and Caldas da Rainha (€5, 35 minutes). There are local

buses operating regularly to Caldas via Óbidos (€2.30, 45 minutes). Three buses daily (five in summer) connect Peniche to Baleal (€0.90, 15 minutes).

Getting Around

Bikes can be rented from **Micro-Moto** *(☎ 262 782 480; Rua António Conceição Bento 19A)*, beside the market, for €5 per day.

RESERVA NATURAL DA BERLENGA

Just 10km offshore from Peniche, the Berlenga archipelago consists of three tiny islands some 280 million years old, surrounded by clear waters full of shipwrecks. The largest island, Berlenga Grande, a treeless and desolate place with weird rock formations and caverns, is the only one accessible to visitors.

In the 16th century there was a monastery here, but now the most famous inhabitants are thousands of nesting seabirds (especially guillemots). The birds take priority over human visitors: the only development that has been allowed is houses for a small fishing community, a lighthouse, a shop and a restaurant-*pensão*. Paths are very clearly marked to stop day-trippers trespassing on the birds' domain.

Linked to the island by a narrow causeway is the squat 17th-century Forte de São João Baptista, now one of the country's most windswept and spartan hostels.

The reserve's **headquarters** *(☎ 262 787 910, fax 262 787 930; Porto da Areia Norte, Estrada Marginal)* are in Peniche.

Organised Tours

TurPesca *(☎/fax 262 789 960, 963 073 818)* and **Julius** *(☎ 918 619 311)* run privately organised cruises on demand throughout the year. Both need a minimum of six passengers, last four to five hours and cost €15 (children €10). There's usually a 10am trip, plus at least two more during the summer, at which time you may have to book at least two days ahead. Tickets and information are available at the operators' kiosks in Largo da Ribeira at the Peniche harbour.

Places to Stay & Eat

There's a small rocky area for **camping** *(2-person tent €5; open May-Sept)* near the harbour, but you have to book in advance at the Peniche turismo.

Forte de São João Baptista hostel (☎ 262 785 263; dorm beds €7.50) is dead basic: you need to bring your own sleeping bag and cooking equipment (though there is a small shop and a bar). To get a place during the summer you'll have to make reservations in May. Bring a torch (the island's generator goes off at midnight).

Pavilhão Mar e Sol (☎ 262 750 331; doubles with bathroom €75) offers the only decent accommodation, plus a pricey restaurant.

Getting There & Away

Viamar (☎ 262 785 646) does the 45-minute trip to the island between 15 May and 15 September (depending on the weather). During July and August there are two sailings, at 9.30am and 11.30am, returning at 4.30pm and 6.30pm. Tickets tend to sell out quickly during this period as only 300 visitors are allowed each day. In the low season there's only one run, at 10am, returning at 4.30pm.

If you're prone to seasickness, choose your day carefully – the crossing to Berlenga can be rough!

ÓBIDOS

postcode 2510 • pop 400 • elevation 80m
Fortified hill-top villages don't come much prettier than this immaculate little place, 6km south of Caldas da Rainha. Entirely enclosed by high medieval walls, Óbidos perches on a limestone ridge, overlooking a 16th-century aqueduct. Until the 15th century it overlooked the sea, but when the bay silted up, leaving only a lagoon, the town became landlocked.

In the half-dozen cobbled lanes, bright white houses are edged with jolly strips of blue or yellow and draped with bougainvillea or wisteria. No wonder Dom Dinis' wife, Dona Isabel, fell in love with the place when she visited in 1228. Her husband gave the village to her as a wedding gift, establishing a royal custom that continued until the 19th century.

Like the day-trippers who flock here in their thousands, you can see Óbidos in an hour if you are pressed, but by staying overnight you can still catch a hint of the town's medieval aura.

Orientation & Information

The town's fancy main gate, Porta da Vila, leads directly into the main street, Rua Direita. Buses stop on the main road just outside Porta da Vila, near a small local market. Here, too, in a kiosk, is the **turismo** (☎ 262 959 231; open 9.30am-7pm Mon-Fri, 10am-1pm & 2pm-7pm Sat & Sun May-Sept; to 6pm Oct-Apr).

Inside the town is the regional turismo headquarters, **Região de Turismo do Oeste** (☎ 262 955 060; e r.t.oeste@mail.telepac.pt; Rua Direita 45; open 10am-1pm & 2pm-6pm Mon-Fri).

Castelo

Although the walls date from the time of the Moors (and were later restored), the castle itself is one of Dom Dinis' 13th-century creations. It's a traditional, no-nonsense affair of towers, battlements and big gates. Converted into a palace in the 16th century, it's now enjoying another life as a deluxe *pousada* (upmarket inn).

Igreja de Santa Maria

The town's main church (Rua Direita; admission free; open 9.30am-12.30pm & 2.30pm-7pm daily May-Sept, to 5pm Oct-Apr), at the northern end of the street, was built on the site of a Visigothic temple that was later converted into a mosque. Restored several times since, it dates mostly from the Renaissance. It had its greatest moment of fame in 1444 when 10-year-old Afonso V married his eight-year-old cousin Isabel here.

Inside, it boasts a painted ceiling and 17th-century *azulejos* (hand-painted tiles). Take a look, too, at the fine 16th-century Renaissance tomb on the left, probably carved by the French sculptor Nicolas Chanterène, and the paintings by Josefa de Óbidos (see the boxed text later in this chapter) to the right of the altar.

Museu Municipal

The only real highlight in this dull museum of religious paintings (admission €1.50; open 10am-1pm & 2pm-6pm Tues-Sun May-Sept, 9.30am-1pm & 2pm-5.30pm Oct-Apr) is an outstanding portrait by Josefa de Óbidos, although it often tends to be on loan. The museum is next to the Igreja de Santa Maria.

Special Events

Óbidos holds an Easter-time Semana Santa with religious processions and re-enactments.

Josefa de Óbidos

Little known outside Portugal, Josefa de Óbidos produced some of the most accomplished Iberian paintings of the 17th century, enchanting for their personal, sympathetic interpretations of religious subjects and for their sense of innocence.

Born in 1630 in Seville (Spain) to a Portuguese painter (Baltazar Gomes Figueira), who later returned to Portugal, Josefa de Ayalla studied at the Augustine Convento de Santa Ana as a young girl. Although she later left the convent without taking the vows and settled in Óbidos (hence her nickname), she remained famously chaste and religious until her death in 1684.

One of the few female Portuguese painters to win lasting recognition, Josefa excelled in richly coloured still lifes and detailed religious works, delightfully ignoring established iconography.

Its annual festival of ancient music is usually held during the first week of October.

Places to Stay

There are several unofficial private rooms available. Most obvious are **Casa dos Castros** (☎ 262 959 328; Rua Direita 41; doubles with shared bathroom €25) with three, low-ceilinged old rooms; and the more spacious **Óbido Sol** (☎ 262 959 188; Rua Direita 40; doubles with shared bathroom €30) with a huge living room and views over the hills.

Casa do Relógio (☎/fax 262 959 282; Rua da Graça; doubles with breakfast €58, minimum 3-night stay) is one of several posher Turihab options, with eight splendid rooms.

Hospedaria Louro (☎ 262 955 100, fax 262 955 101; Casal da Canastra; doubles with breakfast €60), outside the walls 300m west of Porta da Vila, offers good, modern rooms, a small garden and swimming pool.

Pousada do Castelo (☎ 262 959 105, fax 262 959 148; doubles Mon-Fri €177, Sat & Sun €195) is the unrivalled choice if money's no problem. Its rooms are inevitably palatial.

Casa do Pinhão (☎/fax 262 959 078; Bairro Sra da Luz; doubles €70, 2-room suite €130, apartments €80-100, minimum 3-night stay) is a delightful rural alternative to

town accommodation. It's a large family home set in tranquil pinewoods 4km north (2.8km off the Caldas da Rainha road). There's plenty of space for kids to run about, plus a swimming pool.

Places to Eat

Sandwich Bar (☎ 262 959 872; open Tues-Sun), en route from the parking lot to Porta da Vila, is a bright new place offering self-service lunch-time meals for €4.80 (there's a bar downstairs).

In the village itself are several places with great locations and outdoor seating, including **Café-Restaurante 1 de Dezembro** (☎ 262 959 298; Largo de São Pedro; dishes €8, snacks €2.50-5; open Fri-Wed), next to the Igreja de São Pedro; and **Adega do Ramada** (☎ 262 959 462; Travessa Nossa Sra do Rosário; dishes €6.50-8.50; open Tues-Sun), in the adjacent lane, specialising in grills.

O Barco (☎ 262 950 925; Largo Dr João Lourenço; open Tues-Sun), hugging the eastern walls, near Adega do Ramada, is another highly recommended venue.

Bar Lagar da Mouraria (☎ 919 937 601; Rua da Mouraria; open noon-2am daily), north of Igreja de Santa Maria, is the best of several traditional bars in the village. It's housed in a former winery, with seats around a massive old winepress. You can snack on tapas, *chouriço* (spicy sausage) or sandwiches.

Getting There & Away

Buses run frequently to Caldas da Rainha (€0.90, 15 minutes) and Peniche (€2.30, 45 minutes). Change at Caldas for express runs to Lisbon (see Caldas da Rainha for details). Although Óbidos has a nearby train station, it's isolated, with infrequent services.

CALDAS DA RAINHA

postcode 2500 • pop 25,300 • elevation 90m
This quaint, old-fashioned town near Óbidos, famous for its spa and pottery, owes its existence – and its name – to *rainha* (queen) Dona Leonor, wife of Dom João II. As she passed by one day in the 1480s she noticed people bathing in the steaming sulphuric waters and decided to build a spa hospital, now Hospital Termal Rainha Dona Leonor. The *caldas* (hot springs) – said to be excellent for respiratory problems and rheumatism – once attracted a stream of nobility and royalty to

the town, its popularity reaching a peak in the 19th century.

Although the hospital is still going strong (open for long-term treatment only), today the town itself feels a bit dowdy. But thanks to Rafael Bordalo Pinheiro – the 19th-century potter who put the town on the map for his lovable clay figurines – and to several other famous artistic townsfolk, it's got a surprising number of museums and galleries to visit. This, plus loads of accommodation options and a great daily market, makes it a very enjoyable stopover.

Orientation

Ringed by sprawling new town development and highways, the central old town is compact in comparison. At its heart is the skinny market square, Praça da República, with the shady Parque Dom Carlos I a short walk away.

The best free car parking is nearby the hospital.

Information

There's a poorly signed **turismo** (☎ 262 839 700, fax 262 839 726; Praça 25 de Abril; open 9am-7pm Mon-Fri, 10am-1pm & 3pm-7pm Sat & Sun) next to the câmara municipal (town hall).

Among many banks in town is **Banco Comercial Portuguese** (Praça da República 110). Also on the praça is the **police station** (☎ 262 832 023). The **general hospital** (☎ 262 830 300) is nearby, off Rua Diário de Notícias.

CALDAS DA RAINHA

To Hotel Cristal Caldas (200m)
To Alcobaça (23km)

Train Station

Praça 25 de Abril

Avenida 1 de Maio

Rua da Estação
Rua da Algéria
Rua 15 de Agosto

Avenida da Independência Nacional

Rua Dr José Saudade e Silva

Rua Dr Miguel Bombarda

Rua Eng Duarte Pacheco

Rua Tenente Sangreman Henriques

Rua Coronel Soeiro de Brito

Rua Almirante Gago Coutinho

Rua da Praça de Touros

To Open-Air Market (300m)

Rua Alexandre Herculano

Rua Diário de Notícias

Rua Henrique Sales

Rua Heróis da Grande Guerra

Rua Coronel Andrade Mendoça

Tv da Cova da Onça

Rua Almirante Cândido dos Reis

Praça 5 de Outubro

Rua Sebastião de Lima

Rua General Queiroz

Rua do Rosário

Praça da República

Rua da Liberdade

Largo Dr José Barbosa

Largo do Conselheiro José Filipe

Rua de Camões

Largo do Conde de Fontalva

Avenida Dr Manuel Figueira Freire da Câmara

Largo da Rainha Dona Leonor

Largo João de Deus

Rua Maria Ernestina Martins Pereira

Rua Rafael Bordalo Pinheiro

Rua Visconde de Sacavém

Parque Dom Carlos I

To Foz do Arelho (8km)
To Supatra (700m), Óbidos (6km) & A8 to Lisbon (92km)

0   50   100m
0   50   100yd

PLACES TO STAY
5 Residencial Dona Leonor
11 Pensão Residencial Olhos Pretos
12 Pensão Residencial Central
18 Residencial Dom Carlos
20 Casa dos Plátanos

PLACES TO EAT
3 Copacabana
4 Sabores d'Italia
13 Pastelaria Baía
14 Tijuca
16 Restaurante Camões
17 Pastelaria Machado

OTHER
1 Câmara Municipal
2 Turismo
6 Post Office
7 Bus Station
8 General Hospital
9 Hospital Termal Rainha Dona Leonor
10 Police Station
15 Banco Comercial Portuguese & ATM
19 Louças e Artigos Regionais
21 Museu de José Malhoa
22 Faianças Artísticas Bordalo Pinheiro; Museu São Rafael; Restaurante Bar Museu São Rafael
23 Museu de Cerâmica

The **post office** *(Rua Eng Duarte Pacheco; open 8.30am-6.30pm Mon-Fri, 9am-12.30pm Sat)* has NetPost.

Museu de Cerâmica

The best out of the town's quartet of art museums, the Ceramics Museum *(admission €2, 10am-2pm Sun free; open 10am-12.30pm & 2pm-5pm Tues-Sun Oct-May, 10am-7pm June-Sept)* is in the former Palácio de Visconde de Sacavém, a delightful holiday mansion that the 19th-century viscount filled with beautiful azulejos from other palaces (even the exterior of the building is adorned with azulejos, as well as dragon and wild boar gargoyles). The viscount was a patron of the arts and something of an artist himself.

Inside, the rooms are largely devoted to Caldas da Rainha pottery, and particularly to the works of Rafael Bordalo Pinheiro who was inspired by flora and fauna. Most memorable works are the fabulous jars and bowls (by both Pinheiro and Manuel Mafra), encrusted with animals, lobsters and swirling snakes. The top floor is devoted to contemporary works, including some incredibly detailed Manueline-style carvings by José da Silva Pedro.

Museu de José Malhoa

This huge, impressive museum *(☎ 262 831 984; Parque Dom Carlos I; admission €2, 10am-2pm Sun free; open 10am-12.30pm & 2pm-5pm Tues-Sun)* was built in 1940 to house the works of the outstanding Caldas-born artist José Malhoa (1855–1933). It also contains works by other 19th- and 20th-century Portuguese artists, notably Sousa Lopes, Silva Porto (who painted lovely rural scenes) and Columbano Bordalo Pinheiro (whose massive *Last Interrogation of the Marquês de Pombal* is awesome). Among many fine sculptures, including those by Manuel Teixeira Lopes, is a set of towering historical figures by Francisco Franco. In the basement are ceramics and caricatures by Rafael Bordalo Pinheiro: the bust of Pinheiro at the entrance reveals just what a jovial fellow he must have been.

Faianças Artísticas Bordalo Pinheiro

The original ceramics factory *(☎ 262 839 380, fax 262 839 381; Rua Rafael Bordalo Pinheiro 53)*, founded in 1884 by Pinheiro, is still going strong. Although you can't wander round the production workshops you can visit the charming **Museu São Rafael** *(admission free; open 10am-noon & 2pm-4pm Mon-Fri)*, displaying some of the fantastically imaginative works created by Pinheiro and his factory craftsmen. Pinheiro was not only a ceramic artist but also a caricaturist and humourist (check out his caricatures in the Museu de José Malhoa) who transformed pottery into works of sculptural art, especially into amazing ceramic creatures.

Places to Stay

Residencial Dom Carlos *(☎ 262 832 551, fax 262 831 669; Rua de Camões 39A; doubles with breakfast €30)* is an old-fashioned, homely place.

Pensão Residencial Central *(☎ 262 831 914, fax 262 843 282; Largo Dr José Barbosa; doubles with/without bathroom €45/35, triples/quads with bathroom €70/80)* is a rambling establishment with various room options. Breakfast is €1.50 extra.

Pensão Residencial Olhos Pretos *(☎ 262 843 001, fax 262 842 452; Rua do Rosário 10; doubles/triples €40/45)* is probably the best budget choice, offering rooms with telephone, minibar and air-conditioning.

Residencial Dona Leonor *(☎ 262 838 430, fax 262 842 172; Hemiciclo João Paulo II 9; doubles with breakfast €43)* is quiet and well-run with decent rooms; garage parking is available (€2.50).

Casa dos Plátanos *(☎ 262 841 810, fax 262 843 417; Rua Rafael Bordalo Pinheiro 24; doubles with breakfast €70)*, a charming Turihab place, offers eight double rooms, each with beautifully carved beds.

Hotel Cristal Caldas *(☎ 262 840 260; e cristalcaldas@hoteiscristal.com; Rua António Sérgio 31; doubles €75)* is a big, modern, three-star hotel, with well-equipped rooms.

Places to Eat

Restaurante Camões *(☎ 262 836 856; Rua do Parque 56; dishes €8, half-portions from €4.70; open Tues-Sun, closed evening Sun)* is a modest eatery with good service.

Tijuca *(☎ 262 824 255; Rua de Camões 89; dishes €6, daily specials €5.50)* has a huge menu that caters to famished spa-goers.

Copacabana *(☎ 262 824 091; Rua Eng Duarte Pacheco 12; dishes €8-9, half-portions €4.50)* looks casual but it has upmarket

The Iberian Peninsula's most important Neolithic site is at Cromeleque dos Almendres, Évora

Hill-top Castelo de Vide

Pots from the Alto Alentejo, a region famous for its pottery

The ramparts of Marvão's formidable castle offer a panoramic view of the wild countryside

Pretty, but developing, seaside town of Ericeira

The 17th-century Aqueduto de Pegões, Tomar

Cobbled lanes and bright white houses in Óbidos

Step back in time at the 12th-century Cistercian Mosteiro de Santa Maria de Alcobaça

pretensions (ie, pricey nibbles, €2.30). It offers good-value half-portions (sometimes even featuring that rarity called vegetables!)

Sabores d'Italia (☎ 262 845 600; Rua Engenheiro Duarte Pacheco 17; pizzas from €7; open Tues-Sun) is an award-winning restaurant, serving great home-made pizzas and pastas. Try its special tagliatelle with seafood (€7).

Supatra (☎ 262 842 920; Rua General Amílcar Mota; dishes €7.50; open Tues-Sun), a Thai restaurant 700m south of the park, offers a fantastic Sunday buffet lunch (€12.50) that includes favourites such as satay and *tom yam kung* (spicy soup).

Restaurante Bar Museu São Rafael (☎ 262 839 380; Rua Rafael Bordalo Pinheiro 53; dishes €10) is a classy, relaxing venue next to the museum of ceramic works by Pinheiro. Naturally, it's adorned with ceramics.

Caldas is tough for dieters – its sweet *cavacas* (air-filled tarts covered with icing) are too good to miss. Try them at **Pastelaria Machado** (Rua de Camões 14) or **Pastelaria Baía** (Rua da Liberdade).

Shopping

The town's traditional daily **market** (Praça da República; open morning only) is one of the best in the region; tempting souvenirs include basketware and the famous local pottery (notably items shaped like cabbage leaves and tasteless phallic mugs). You can find more such tacky items, as well as amusing caricature figurines (from Fernando Pessoa to Woody Allen), in shops along Rua de Camões such as **Louças e Artigos Regionais** (Rua de Camões 23).

For the widest selection of ceramics, visit the shop at the **Faianças Artísticas Bordalo Pinheiro** (Rua Rafael Bordalo Pinheiro 53; open 10am-1pm & 2pm-7pm Mon-Fri, 10am-7pm Sat).

There's a big **open-air market** held every Monday some 300m east of the hospital.

Getting There & Away

There are six daily bus connections with Peniche (€2.30, 45 minutes) via Óbidos (€0.90, 15 minutes), and four daily to Leiria (€6.80, 80 minutes). On weekdays nine express buses run to Lisbon's Arco do Cego terminal (€5.50, 1¼ hours), including three superfast runs (50 minutes) using the A8 motorway (two on weekends).

Around seven regional trains daily run from Lisbon's suburban Cacém station (€4.90, 2 hours; connections from Lisbon's Rossio station) plus two *interregional* (IR) trains (€5.10, 80 minutes), continuing to Figueira da Foz (€5.10, 1½ hours) via Leiria (€2.80, 50 minutes).

FOZ DO ARELHO

The nearest beach to Caldas da Rainha (8km away) is the surprisingly undeveloped Foz do Arelho. It lies on the northern shore of a lagoon, Lagoa de Óbidos, that's popular for sailing and windsurfing. Along the seafront is a vast expanse of sand, and a promenade (Avenida do Mar) lined with cafés and bars. The village of Foz do Arelho is 1km inland.

Escola de Vela da Lagoa (☎ 262 978 592; e e.v.l.@mail.telepac.pt; Rua dos Reivais 40) rents windsurfers (€14 per hour) and sailing boats (€20 per hour for a Hobie-13) and also provides courses (15 hours, €85). Its base is 2.5km along Estrada do Nadadouro (from the village turn left towards the lagoon).

Places to Stay & Eat

A **parque de campismo** (☎ 262 978 683; adult/tent/car €3.30/2.70/3) is located 3km from the beach. It has bikes for rent.

Residencial Pendedo Furado (☎ 262 979 610; e penedo_furado@clix.pt; Rua dos Camarções 3; doubles with breakfast €60), in the village, is a smart, efficient *residencial* (guesthouse), and justifiably popular.

Quinta da Foz (☎ 262 979 369; Largo do Arraial; doubles €115, apartments €115) is the most romantic option. It's a Turihab place just 500m from the lagoon, with luxurious rooms in the main house plus separate apartments (minimum five-day stay).

Restaurante-Bar Atlântico (☎ 262 979 213), the oldest and scruffiest of the restaurants along Avenida do Mar, offers a yummy *caldeirada mista* (mixed-seafood casserole) costing €15 for two.

Cabana do Pescador (fish dishes €6.50-11), at the end of the *avenida*, is bigger and smarter than Atlântico, with a grand seaview terrace.

Restaurante Bar Adega Real (☎ 262 979 578; Largo do Arraial 1; dishes from €9, daily specials €7.50; open Wed-Mon) is the poshest choice in the village, with a separate bar sporting wide-screen TV.

Getting There & Away

At least six buses daily (fewer at weekends) connect Foz do Arelho with Caldas da Rainha (€1.10, 20 minutes).

SÃO MARTINHO DO PORTO

postcode 2465 • pop 4000

An almost perfectly enclosed bay ringed by a sandy beach has made this small seaside resort, 17km northwest of Caldas da Rainha, one of the most popular hang-outs south of Nazaré. The water here is calm and warm (a plus for families with kids). Sadly, the town itself is going the way of Nazaré, with villas and apartment blocks mushrooming on the surrounding hills and replacing the pretty old villas in the town.

Orientation & Information

The **turismo** (☎ 262 989 110; open 9am-1pm & 3pm-7pm Mon-Fri May-Sept, 10am-1pm & 2pm-6pm Sat & Sun year-round; closed Mon Oct-June) is at the northern end of the oceanside Avenida 25 de Abril (also called Avenida Marginal). The train station is about 700m to the southeast. Buses stop on Rua Conde de Avelar (a block inland), which leads to the N242.

Places to Stay

Colina do Sol (☎ 262 989 764, fax 262 989 763; adult/tent/car €2.90/2.50/2.40) is a well-equipped and friendly camp site 2km north of town.

The São Martinho **pousada da juventude** (☎ 262 999 506; e smartinho@movijovem.pt; dorm beds €9.50, doubles without bathroom €24) is actually about 4km inland at Alfeizerão, just off the main N8 highway (buses run about four times daily).

There are plenty of *quartos* (from around €25 a double) and apartments (from about €40); ask at the turismo or, if it's closed, at **Café Palmeira** (☎ 964 373 477) just behind.

Pensão Americana (☎ 262 989 170, fax 262 989 349; Rua Dom José Saldanha 2; doubles with breakfast €50), near the bus stop and about 300m southeast of the turismo, is the most popular budget *pensão*.

Pensão Carvalho (☎ 262 989 605; Rua Miguel Bombarda 6; doubles with breakfast €50), closer to the turismo than Americana, is a decent option.

Residencial Atlântica (☎ 262 980 151, fax 262 980 163; Rua Miguel Bombarda 6; doubles

with breakfast €50) is Carvalho's new three-star neighbour, and is also decent.

Two upmarket places run by the same management are **Residencial Concha** (☎ 262 985 010, fax 262 985 011; Largo Vitorino Fróis; doubles €80) and, opposite, **Albergaria São Pedro** (☎ 262 985 020, fax 262 985 011; Largo Vitorino Fróis; doubles €80). The Albergaria is open year-round, Concha (and the other *pensões*) only in summer.

Note that prices for all places soar in August.

Places to Eat

Restaurante Carvalho (Rua Miguel Bombarda 6), attached to Pensão Carvalho, offers a big menu of reasonably priced fare.

Snack-Bar A Cave (☎ 262 989 682; Rua Conde de Avelar 10; dishes €6.50, half-portions €4.30) is a budget place right by the bus stop.

Getting There & Away

Buses are the best option if coming from destinations other than Caldas da Rainha. Daily on weekdays at least five buses run to Nazaré (€1.40, 20 minutes), six to Alcobaça (€2.10, 35 minutes) and five to Lisbon (€6.80, 1½ hours).

Seven trains daily come here from Caldas da Rainha (€0.90, 10 minutes).

NAZARÉ

postcode 2450 • pop 15,000 • elevation 60m

Brash and bold, Nazaré has successfully shed its image as a charming little fishing village and has become a hard-selling Atlantic resort. Local fisherwomen, many dressed in traditional seven-petticoated skirts and colourful scarves, aggressively tout for customers for their private rooms or sell sweaters, dried fruits or pistachios on the beach.

Undeniably, Nazaré's sweeping beach is impressive, especially from the town's original cliff-top site on the Promontório do Sítio, but in summer it's packed (the sea itself is often too rough for swimming) and the streets are clogged with cars and tour buses. Come here for the sand and seafood by all means, but don't expect tradition or tranquillity.

Orientation

Until the 18th century the sea covered the present-day site of Nazaré; the locals lived inland at the hill-top Pederneira and the nearer Promontório do Sítio. Today, both places play second fiddle to Nazaré and its seafront Avenida da República, which is the main focus of activity. The former fisher-folk's quarter of narrow lanes now hosts restaurants and cafés.

Information

The **turismo** (☎ 262 561 194; *Avenida da República; open 10am-1pm & 3pm-7pm daily Apr–mid-June; to 8pm 15-30 June; 10am-10pm daily July & Aug; 10am-7pm Sept; 9.30am-1pm & 2.30pm-6pm daily other times)* has comprehensive information on rooms, transport and events.

The most convenient banks with ATMs are **Caixa Geral de Depósitos** *(Praça Sousa Oliveira 33)* and **BPI** *(Avenida Vieira Guimarães)*. The **post office** *(Avenida da Independência Nacional; open 9am-12.30pm & 2.30pm-6pm)* has NetPost.

Near the market is the **police station** *(☎ 262 551 268; Rua Sub-Vila)*. There's a **centro de saúde** *(medical centre; ☎ 262 551 647)* on the eastern edge of town; the **main hospital** *(☎ 262 561 140)* is in Sítio.

Promontório do Sítio

The Sítio cliff-top area, 110m above the beach, is popular for its tremendous views and, among Portuguese devotees, for its religious connections. According to legend it was here that the lost statue of the Virgin, known as Nossa Senhora da Nazaré and brought back from Nazareth in the 4th century, was finally found in the 18th century.

Even more famously, it is said that an apparition of the Virgin was seen here one foggy day in 1182. Local nobleman Dom Fuas Roupinho was out hunting a deer, when, with him in hot pursuit, the animal disappeared off the edge of the Sítio precipice. Dom Fuas cried out to the Virgin for help and his horse miraculously stopped just in time.

Dom Fuas built the small **Hermida da Memória** chapel on the edge of the belvedere to commemorate the event. It was later visited by a number of VIP pilgrims, including Vasco da Gama. The nearby 17th-century, baroque **Igreja de Nossa Senhora da Nazaré** replaced an earlier church, and is decorated with attractive Dutch azulejos.

From Rua do Elevador, north of the turismo, an *elevador* (funicular) climbs up the

hill to Sítio between 7am and 1am daily during summer (to midnight in winter); the fare is €0.60.

Special Events

The Nossa Senhora da Nazaré *romaria* (religious pilgrimage), held in Sítio on 8 September and the following weekend, is Nazaré's big religious festival, featuring sombre processions, folk dances and bullfights.

From July to mid-September, bullfights take place in the Sítio *praça de touros* (bullring) almost every weekend; check with the turismo for times and ticket availability.

Places to Stay

Room prices rocket in August (we list July prices here). In low season, most cheap places close. There are literally hundreds of *quartos* for rent in Nazaré. If the touts don't find you first, check the list at the turismo (though staff won't make bookings or recommendations). Expect to pay around €25 a double, and twice that during August.

Camping Orbitur's **Valado** *(☎ 262 561 111, fax 262 561 137; adult/tent/car €3.10/2.50/3)* camping site has good facilities and is 2km east of town, off the Alcobaça road.

Vale Paraíso *(☎ 262 561 546; e camping .vp.nz@mail.telepac.pt; adult/tent/car €3.40/2.90/2.90)* is 2km north off the N242 Leiria road. Well-equipped and security-conscious, it has bikes for hire and a pool. Both of these camping sites have bungalows for rent. Buses for Alcobaça and Leiria pass by.

Pensões & Residenciais The homely, six-room **Hospedaria Ideal** *(☎ 262 551 379; Rua Adrião Batalha 96; doubles €20, full-board €70)* gets lots of regular customers, so full-board is usually obligatory in August. The landlady speaks French.

Other cheap *pensões* (with shared bathroom) include **Residencial Marina** *(☎ 262 551 541, 262 552 098; Rua Mouzinho de Albuquerque 6; doubles around €25)* and **Pensão Nazarense** *(☎ 262 551 188; Rua Mouzinho de Albuquerque 48; doubles with breakfast from €25)*.

Vila Conde Fidalgo *(☎/fax 262 552 361, 262 085 090; Avenida de Independência 21A; doubles €30, 2/3/4-person apartments €50/60/75)* is a pretty little complex that is open year-round.

Residencial Beira Mar (☎ 262 561 358; Avenida da República 40; doubles with breakfast €45) is one of the best seafront deals and it is friendlier than most.

Residencial Ribamar (☎ 262 551 158, fax 262 562 224; Rua Gomes Freire 9; doubles with breakfast €50) is slicker than Beira Mar but, like it, is open year-round. Its sea-view rooms are more expensive.

Hotel Maré (☎ 262 561 122; e hotel .mare@mail.telepac.pt; Rua Mouzinho de Albuquerque 8; doubles with breakfast €93.40) is the most centrally located of Nazaré's three-star hotels.

Places to Eat & Drink

As well as the hotel restaurants there are dozens of other fancy tourist-oriented places

selling fantastic seafood. For something less pretentious, delve into the back lanes to find **Casa Marques** (☎ 262 551 680; Rua Gil Vicente 37; dishes €6) and **Oficina** (☎ 262 552 161; Rua das Flores 33; dishes €6). Both are tiny, former fishers' homes, brimming with character and run by typically Nazaréan women who dish up hearty meals. Oficina's door sign of a wine flagon reveals that locals like to drink here, too.

Cervejaria Sem-Nó (☎ 963 940 147; Rua Gomes Freire 54; snacks €4) is an appealing local drinking hole serving *petiscos* (snacks), including especially tasty cheeses and octopus salads.

Casa O Santo (Travessa do Elevador 11) is a rustic venue where you can start the evening with beer and *ameijoas* (clams).

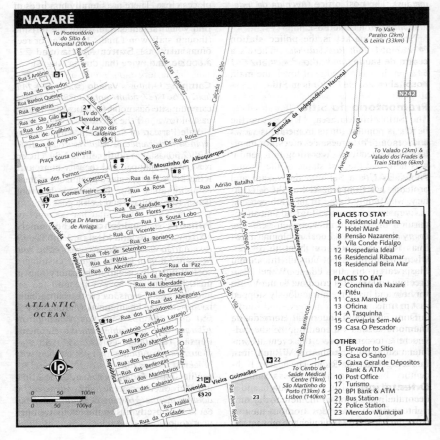

NAZARÉ

To Promontório do Sítio & Hospital (200m)

To Vale Paraíso (2km) & Leiria (33km)

Rua Casal das Figueiras

Calçada do Sítio

Avenida da Independência Nacional

N242

Rua M de Lima

Rua S António

Rua do Elevador

Rua Banhos Quentes

Rua Figueiras

Rua de Leiria

Tv do Elevador

Rua de São Gião

Rua do Juncal

Rua de Guilhim

Largo das Caldeiras

Rua do Amparo

Praça Sousa Oliveira

Rua Dr Rui Rosa

Rua Mouzinho de Albuquerque

Avenida de Oliveira

To Valado (2km) & Valado dos Frades & Train Station (6km)

Rua dos Fornos

B. Esperança

Rua da Fé

Rua Gomes Freire

Rua da Rosa

Rua Adrião Batalha

Rua da Saudade

Rua das Flores

Rua J B Sousa Lobo

Praça Dr Manuel de Arriaga

Rua Gil Vicente

Rua da Bonança

Rua Três de Setembro

Rua da Pátria

Rua do Alecrim

Rua da Paz

Tv do Açougue

Rua Mouzinho de Albuquerque

Rua da Regeneração

Rua da Liberdade

Rua da Graça

Rua das Abegorias

ATLANTIC OCEAN

Rua dos Lavradores

Avenida da República

Rua António Carvalho Laranjo

Rua dos Calafetes

Rua Irmão Manuel

Rua dos Pescadores

Rua das Berlengas

Rua dos Marinheiros

Rua das Cabanas

Rua Ocidental

Rua Sub Vila

Rua dos Barrancos

Avenida Vieira Guimarães

To Centro de Saúde Medical Centre (1km), São Martinho do Porto (13km) & Lisbon (140km)

Rua Aires Redol

Rua Atalaia

Rua da Caridade

0   50   100m
0   50   100yd

PLACES TO STAY
6 Residencial Marina
7 Hotel Maré
8 Pensão Nazarense
9 Vila Conde Fidalgo
12 Hospedaria Ideal
16 Residencial Ribamar
18 Residencial Beira Mar

PLACES TO EAT
2 Conchina da Nazaré
4 Pitéu
11 Casa Marques
13 Oficina
14 A Tasquinha
15 Cervejaria Sem-Nó
19 Casa O Pescador

OTHER
1 Elevador to Sítio
3 Casa O Santo
5 Caixa Geral de Depósitos Bank & ATM
10 Post Office
17 Turismo
20 BPI Bank & ATM
21 Bus Station
22 Police Station
23 Mercado Municipal

Conchina da Nazaré (☎ 262 561 597; Rua de Leiria 17D; dishes €5-6) is a dead simple place to eat, and a favourite with old locals.

More upmarket restaurants are the justifiably popular **A Tasquinha** (☎ 262 551 945; Rua Adrião Batalha 54; dishes €5-8); **Casa O Pescador** (☎ 262 553 326; Rua António Carvalho Laranjo 18A), which delivers a great *caldeirada* (fish stew) for around €7; and **Pitéu** (☎ 262 551 578; Largo das Caldeiras 8; fish dishes €6, shellfish €8), one of a clutch of places in this small square. Its huge fish menu includes awesome giant grilled shrimps for €52!

Getting There & Away

Bus At least five express buses daily (fewer at weekends) run to Lisbon's Arco do Cego terminal (€6.80, 1¾ hours) and Leiria (€5.60, 70 minutes). There are almost hourly runs to Caldas da Rainha (€4.50, 45 minutes) via São Martinho do Porto (€2.10, 25 minutes) and to Alcobaça (€1.20, 20 minutes). The turismo holds timetables.

Train The nearest train station is 6km inland at Valado dos Frades, which is connected to Nazaré by frequent buses. Two IR trains daily run to Lisbon's suburban Cacém station (€5.60, 1¾ hours) plus two to three regional services (€5.40, 2¾ hours). Cacém is regularly connected with Lisbon's Rossio station.

ALCOBAÇA

postcode 2460 ● pop 6200 ● elevation 60m
One of Portugal's greatest architectural masterpieces, and one of Europe's most significant medieval Cistercian monuments, dominates this low-key town, northeast of Caldas da Rainha. The 12th-century Cistercian monastery, Mosteiro de Santa Maria de Alcobaça is a Unesco World Heritage site and is worth going well out of your way for.

Apart from the monastery, and shops bursting with local pottery (blue-and-white ware is Alcobaça's speciality), the town offers little to detain you. It has few accommodation options and is best visited from Leiria or Caldas da Rainha.

Orientation

From the bus station in the new town, turn right along Avenida dos Combatentes to cross the Rio Alcôa and reach the monastery,

500m downhill. The turismo, restaurants and hotels are all near the monastery.

Information

The **turismo** (☎ 262 582 377; Praça 25 de Abril; open 10am-1pm & 3pm-7pm daily June, July & Sept, 9am-10pm Aug, 10am-1pm & 2pm-6pm Oct-May) is opposite the monastery. It has useful bus timetables.

The **post office** (open 8.30am-6pm Mon-Fri) is almost next door to the turismo and there are several banks with ATMs on the praça.

The **hospital** (☎ 262 590 400) is on the eastern edge of the new town, off Rua Afonso de Albuquerque. There's also a **police station** (☎ 262 595 400; Rua de Olivença) in town.

There have been frequent reports of theft from the car park by the abbey; be sure to keep your valuables with you.

Mosteiro de Santa Maria de Alcobaça

This monastery (adult/child or senior €3/1.50, church admission free; open 9am-7pm daily Apr-Sept, 9am-5pm Oct-Mar) was founded in 1153 by Dom Afonso Henriques to honour a vow he'd made to St Bernard after the capture of Santarém from the Moors in 1147. The king entrusted the construction of the monastery to the monks of the Cistercian order, also giving them a huge area around Alcobaça to develop and cultivate.

Building started in 1178 and by the time the monks actually moved in, some 40 years later, the abbey estate had become one of the richest and most powerful in the country. In those early days the monastery is said to have housed 999 monks, who held Mass nonstop in shifts.

Switching from farming to teaching in the 13th century, the monks used the estate's abundant rents to carry out further enlargements and changes to the monastery to suit the fashions of the day. Towards the 17th century, the monks turned their talents to pottery and the sculpting of figures in stone, wood and clay.

Revived agricultural efforts in the 18th century made the Alcobaça area one of the most productive in the land. However, it was the monks' growing decadence that became famous, thanks to the bitchy writings of 18th century travellers such as William

Beckford who, despite his own decadence, was shocked at the 'perpetual gormandising…the fat waddling monks and sleek friars with wanton eyes…'. It all came to an abrupt end in 1834 with the dissolution of the religious orders.

Church Modelled on the French Cistercian abbey of Clairvaux, the Alcobaça abbey church is more impressive inside than out. Much of the original facade was altered in the 17th and 18th centuries (including the addition of wings), leaving only the main doorway and rose window unchanged.

When you step inside the combination of Gothic simplicity and Cistercian austerity hits you immediately: the nave is a breathtaking 106m long but only 23m wide, with huge pillars and truncated columns.

Tombs of Dom Pedro & Dona Inês Occupying the south and north transepts are two intricately carved 14th-century tombs, the church's greatest possessions, which commemorate the tragic love story of Dom Pedro and his mistress (see the boxed text 'Love & Revenge').

Although the tombs themselves were badly damaged by rampaging French troops in search of treasure in 1811, they still show extraordinary detail and are embellished with a host of figures and scenes from the life of Christ. The Wheel of Fortune at the foot of Dom Pedro's tomb and the gruesome Last Judgment scene at the head of Inês' tomb are especially striking.

Kitchen & Refectory The grand kitchen, described by Beckford as 'the most distinguished temple of gluttony in all Europe', owes its immense size to alterations carried out in the 18th century, including a water channel built through the middle of the room so that a tributary of the Rio Alcôa could provide a constant source of fresh fish to the monastery.

Even now, it's not hard to imagine the scene when Beckford was led here by the abbey's grand priors ('hand in hand, all three together'). He saw 'pastry in vast abundance which a numerous tribe of lay brothers and their attendants were rolling out and puffing up into a hundred different shapes, singing all the while as blithely as larks in a corn field'.

The adjacent refectory, huge and vaulted, is where the monks ate in silence while the Bible was read to them from the pulpit. Opposite the entrance is a 14th-century *lavabo* (bathroom) embellished with a dainty hexagonal fountain.

Claustro do Silencio & Sala dos Reis The beautiful Cloister of Silence dates from two eras. Dom Dinis built the intricate lower storey, with its arches and traceried stone circles, in the 14th century. The upper storey, typically Manueline in style, was added in the 16th century.

Off the northwestern corner of the cloister is the 18th-century Sala dos Reis (Kings' Room), so called because statues of practically all the kings of Portugal line the walls. Below them are azulejo friezes depicting stories relevant to the abbey's construction, including the siege of Santarém and the life of St Bernard.

Museu Nacional do Vinho This museum (*admission €1.50; open 9am-12.30pm & 2pm-5.30pm Tues-Fri, 10am-12.30pm & 2pm-6pm Sat & Sun May-Sept; closed Sat-Mon Oct-Apr*), housed in a spacious old *adega* (winery) 1.2km east of town

---

Love & Revenge

Portugal's most famous love story revolves around Dom Pedro, the son of Dom Afonso IV, who fell in love with his wife's Galician lady-in-waiting, Dona Inês de Castro. Even after his wife's death his father forbade him to marry Inês because of her Spanish family's potential influence. Various suspicious nobles continued to pressure the king until he finally sanctioned her murder in 1355, unaware that the two lovers had already married in secret.

Two years later, when Pedro succeeded to the throne, he exacted his revenge by ripping out and eating the hearts of Inês' murderers. He then exhumed and crowned her body, and so the story goes he compelled the court to pay homage to his dead queen by kissing her decomposing hand.

On Pedro's orders, the lovers now lie foot to foot in the Mosteiro de Santa Maria de Alcobaça so that on the Day of Judgment they will see each other as soon as they rise.

on the Leiria road, provides an absorbing portrait of the region's famous wine-making history. You can also sample and buy wine.

Raul da Bernarda Museu

The oldest earthenware factory in Alcobaça (established in 1875) is also the only one geared to visitors. Its museum (☎ 262 590 610, fax 262 590 601; Ponte D Elias; admission free; open 10am-1pm & 3pm-7pm Mon-Fri, 10am-7pm Sat, 10am-12.30pm & 1.30pm-7pm Sun), on the northern edge of town, reveals the changing trends in the region's glazed earthenware, from traditional blue-and-white to today's multicoloured hues.

Places to Stay

The municipal **parque de campismo** (☎ 262 582 265; Avenida Professor Vieira Natividade; adult/tent/car €1.80/1/1) is a simple site 500m north of the bus station.

Hotel de Santa Maria (☎ 262 590 160, fax 262 590 161; Rua Dr Francisco Zagalo; doubles with breakfast €60) is the town's only decent hotel. Rates include garage parking.

Challet Fonte Nova (☎ 262 598 300, fax 262 596 839; Estrada Fonte Nova; doubles €75), a 19th-century mansion, has sumptuous doubles.

Places to Eat & Drink

Ti Fininho (☎ 262 596 506; Rua Frei António Brandão 34; dishes €5; open Thur-Tues) is our favourite budget nook, serving plain, honest fare.

Pensão Restaurante Corações Unidos (☎/fax 262 582 142; Rua Frei António Brandão 39; dishes €7), near Ti Fininho, has miserable, rundown rooms. However, it has a very agreeable traditional restaurant, famous for its hearty dishes, including the local speciality, frango a Alcobaça (€6), chicken cooked in a pucara (pot).

Celeiro dos Frades (☎ 262 582 281; Arco de Cister; dishes €6-7, grills €6.50; open Fri-Wed), under the arches near the north side of the monastery, is popular and has a lively bar.

Taverna dos Monges (☎ 262 58 22 74; Rua Dr Francisco Zagalo) is a zany bar and restaurant near Hotel de Santa Maria.

Getting There & Away

Bus Six express buses run daily to Lisbon's Arco do Cego terminal (€7.30, two hours). There are almost hourly local runs to

Nazaré (€1.30, 20 minutes), eight buses daily to Batalha (€2.10, 40 minutes) and Leiria (€2.40, 50 minutes) and four to Caldas da Rainha (€5.60, 30 minutes). Coming from Leiria you can easily see both Batalha and Alcobaça in a day trip (best in that order): the daily express back to Leiria (€5, 30 minutes) leaves at 4.25pm.

Train The nearest train station to Alcobaça is 5km northwest at Valado dos Frades, connected to Alcobaça by regular buses. See Getting There & Away under Nazaré earlier in this chapter for details of train services.

BATALHA
postcode 2440 • elevation 120m

The Gothic-Manueline Mosteiro de Santa Maria da Vitória – usually known as Mosteiro da Batalha (Battle Abbey) – is another architectural giant, rivalling those other national masterpieces, the Mosteiro dos Jerónimos at Belém (Lisbon) and the Mosteiro de Santa Maria de Alcobaça. Like them, Batalha boasts Unesco World Heritage status. You'd be hard pressed to choose the finest monument of the three, but Batalha wins for ornate decoration and mind-boggling flamboyance.

Orientation & Information

Buses stop in Largo 14 de Agosto, 200m east of the abbey. Facing the eastern end of the abbey, beside a modern complex of shops and restaurants, is the **turismo** (☎ 244 765 180; open 10am-1pm & 3pm-7pm daily June, July & Sept, 9am-10pm Aug, 10am-1pm & 2pm-6pm Oct-May).

Mosteiro de Santa Maria da Vitória

Like Alcobaça's monastery, this abbey (admission cloisters & Capelas Imperfeitas adult/child or senior €3/1.50, 9am-2pm Sun free; open 9am-6pm daily Apr-Sept, 9am-5pm Oct-Mar) was founded as the result of a battle vow, though the stakes at the 1385 Battle of Aljubarrota (fought 4km south of Batalha) were considerably higher than Alcobaça's Santarém battle. On one side was the 30,000-strong force under Juan I of Castile, who was claiming the Portuguese throne; on the other was the 6500-weak Portuguese army of rival claimant Dom João of Avis, commanded by Dom Nuno

Álvares Pereira and supported by a few hundred English soldiers.

Defeat for João meant Portugal would slip into Spanish hands. He called on the Virgin Mary for help and vowed to build a superb abbey in return for victory. He duly won the battle, and work on the Dominican abbey started three years later.

Most of the monument – the church, Claustro Real, Sala do Capítulo and Capela do Fundador – was completed by 1434 in flamboyant Gothic style, but the dominant theme is one of Manueline flamboyance, thanks to additions made in the 15th and 16th centuries. Work at Batalha only stopped in the mid-16th century when Dom João III turned his attention to expanding the Convento de Cristo in Tomar.

Exterior The ochre limestone monument is all pinnacles and parapets, flying buttresses and balustrades, carved windows in Gothic and flamboyant styles, as well as octagonal chapels and massive columns, after the English perpendicular style. The main western doorway features layers of arches packed with carvings of the Apostles, various angels, saints and prophets, and topped by Christ and the Evangelists.

Interior The vast vaulted Gothic interior is deceptively plain, long and high like Alcobaça's church, and warmed by light from modern stained-glass windows. To the right as you enter is the intricate **Capela do Fundador** (Founder's Chapel), a beautiful starvaulted square room, lit by an octagonal lantern. In the centre is the joint tomb of João I and his English wife, Philippa of Lancaster, whose marriage in 1387 established the special alliance that exists between Portugal and England to this day. The tombs of their four youngest sons line the south wall of the chapel, including that of Henry the Navigator (second from the right).

Claustro Real Afonso Domingues, the master of works at Batalha during the late 1380s, first built the Royal Cloisters in a restrained Gothic style, but it's the later Manueline embellishments by the great Diogo de Boitac that really take your breath away. Every arch is a tangle of detailed stone carvings of typically Manueline symbols, such as armillary spheres and crosses

of the Order of Christ, entwined with exotic flowers and marine motifs, such as ropes, pearls and shells. The overall effect is probably the finest marriage of Gothic and Manueline art in Portugal.

Claustro de Dom Afonso V The sober Dom Afonso V Cloister seems dull in comparison to the Royal Cloister. It's a plain Gothic affair and its main appeal lies in its austerity.

Sala do Capítulo To the east of the Claustro Real is the early 15th-century chapterhouse, containing a beautiful 16th-century stained-glass window. The huge unsupported 19-sq-m vault was considered so outrageously dangerous to build that only prisoners on death row were employed in its construction. The Sala do Capítulo contains the tomb of the unknown soldiers – one killed in Flanders in WWI, the other in Africa – now watched over by a constant guard of honour.

Capelas Imperfeitas The roofless Unfinished Chapels at the eastern end of the abbey are perhaps the most astonishing and tantalising part of Batalha. Only accessible from outside the abbey, the octagonal mausoleum with its seven chapels was commissioned by Dom Duarte (João I's eldest son) in 1437. However, the later Manueline additions by the architect Mateus Fernandes overshadow everything else, including the Renaissance upper balcony.

Although Fernandes' original plan for an upper octagon supported by buttresses was never completed, the staggering ornamentation gives a hint of what might have followed. Especially striking is the 15m-high doorway, a mass of stone-carved thistles, ivy, flowers, snails and all manner of 'scollops and twistifications', as William Beckford noted. Dom Duarte can enjoy it all for eternity; his tomb (and that of his wife) lies opposite the door.

Places to Stay & Eat
Restaurante Casa das Febras (☎ 244 765 825; Largo 14 de Agosto; rooms with shared bathroom €25; dishes €6.50) is a humble place with an extensive menu but less-impressive rooms.

Pensão Gladius (☎ 244 765 760; Praça Mouzinho de Albuquerque; doubles with *breakfast* €30) in the square by the abbey, is far better value, with clean modern rooms.

Restaurante Carlos (☎ 244 768 207; *Largo Goa Damão e Diu; dishes €6-7*), just off the square opposite the Centro Comercial, has a menu of standard fare.

Getting There & Away

There are six buses daily on weekdays to Alcobaça (€2.10, 40 minutes) and Leiria (€1.10, 20 minutes) and three buses daily to Fátima (€1.50).

LEIRIA

postcode 2400 • pop 42,700 • elevation 60m

Leiria (lay-ree-uh) is a low-key town beside the Rio Lis, with an eye-catching medieval hill-top castle and attractive old quarter. It was a good deal more important in medieval times: Dom Afonso III convened a *cortes* (parliament) here in 1254; Dom Dinis established his main residence in the castle in the 14th century; and in 1411 members of the town's sizable Jewish community built Portugal's first paper mill here.

Today its main attraction to travellers is as a convenient base for visiting Alcobaça, Batalha and Fátima, or the nearby beach of São Pedro de Muel, all easily accessible by bus. At the time of writing it was undergoing a massive ring road development, giving drivers nightmares.

Orientation

The old town is focused on Praça Rodrigues Lobo, with hotels and restaurants all nearby. The castle is perched on a wooded hill top a short walk to the north.

Leiria has a dastardly one-way system and limited car parking; head for the big free lot across the river in the northeast of town. The train station is 4km northwest of town, with frequent bus connections.

Information

The **turismo** (☎ 244 848 770; *open 10am-1pm & 3pm-7pm daily June-Sept, 10am-1pm & 2pm-6pm Oct-May*) is by Jardim Luís de Camões. You can buy an excellent town map here (€4.40). The headquarters for the **Região de Turismo Leiria-Fátima** (☎ 244 848 771; w *www.rt-leiriafatima.pt*) is upstairs, and is open during weekday business hours only.

Among many central banks with ATMs is **Sotto Mayor** (*Praça Rodrigues Lobo*).

The **post office** (*open 9am-6pm Mon-Fri*) has NetPost. Free Internet access is available at the **biblioteca municipal** (*town library;* ☎ 244 820 850; *Largo Cândido dos Reis*) and the **Instituto Português da Juventude** (*IPJ;* ☎ 244 813 421; *Avenida 25 de Abril; open 9am-9pm Mon-Fri*), 1km north of the centre. **Arquivo** (☎ 244 822 225, *Avenida Combatentes da Grande Guerra 53; open 9.30am-11pm Mon-Fri, 2.30pm-7.30pm Sat*), a bookshop-cum-gallery and café, offers access for €1.30 per half-hour.

The **St André District Hospital** (☎ 244 817 000) is about 1.5km east of town in the Olhalvas-Pousos district (follow the signs to the A1 motorway). The **police station** (☎ 249 813 799; *Largo Artilharia 4*) is by the castle.

Castelo

This long-inhabited hill-top site got its first castle in the time of the Moors. Captured by Afonso Henriques in 1135, it was transformed into a royal residence for Dom Dinis in the 14th century. Featuring a superb panoramic gallery (now frequently used for exhibitions), the castle (☎ 244 813 982; *admission €0.80; open 9am-6.30pm Mon-Fri, 10am-6.30pm Sat & Sun May-Sept; to 5.30pm Oct-Apr*) has been restored several times, most recently in the early 20th century by Swiss architect Ernesto Korrodi.

Also within the walls is the ruined but still lovely Gothic **Igreja de Nossa Senhora da Penha**, originally built in the 12th century and rebuilt by João I in the early 15th century.

In the castle keep, the new **Núcleo Museológic** (*open 10am-noon & 1pm-5pm Tues-Sun*) displays, on several floors, replicas of medieval weapons, spiky-nosed helmets and a few other pieces found in situ.

Special Events

Like many towns in Portugal, Leiria celebrates its cuisine with the annual Festival de Gastronomia. Leiria's festival lasts for nine days in early September. As well as stalls of mouth-watering food there's folk dancing in the *jardim* (garden), as well as other events.

Expect huge excitement in 2004 when the town hosts some matches of the European Football Championships in its 35,000-seat Estádio Municipal Dr Magalhães Pessoa. Leiria's own team is Unai o de Leiria.

ESTREMADURA & RIBATEJO

Places to Stay

The **pousada da juventude** (☎ 244 831 868; e leiria@movijovem.pt; Largo Cândido dos Reis 7D; dorm beds €10.50, doubles without bathroom €27) is in an attractive old house, and it has a kitchen.

Pensão Berlenga (☎ 244 823 846; Rua Miguel Bombarda 13; singles/doubles €15/30) has character if not comfort, with its low-ceilinged, wood-panelled rooms in an old house.

Pensão Residencial Alcôa (☎ 244 832 690; Rua Rodrigues Cordeiro 20; singles/doubles with breakfast €20/30) offers plain modern rooms, each with a telephone.

Residencial Dom Dinis (☎ 244 815 342, fax 244 823 552; Travessa de Tomar 2; doubles/triples with breakfast €35/40) is a well-run *residencial* that is only a short walk from the centre.

Pensão Residencial Leiriense (☎ 244 823 054, fax 244 823 073; Rua Afonso de Albuquerque 6; doubles with breakfast €40) has attractive doubles.

Hotel Eurosol (☎ 244 849 849, fax 244 849 840; e hoteleurosol@mail.telepac.pt; Rua Dom José Alves C da Silva; doubles with breakfast €82) is a big three-star hotel that provide the town's best accommodation.

Places to Eat & Drink

Along pedestrianised Rua Dr Correia Mateus are several traditional restaurants, including the family-friendly, no-nonsense **Restaurante Montecarlo** (☎ 244 825 406; Rua Dr Correia Mateus 32; dishes €6-8, half-portions

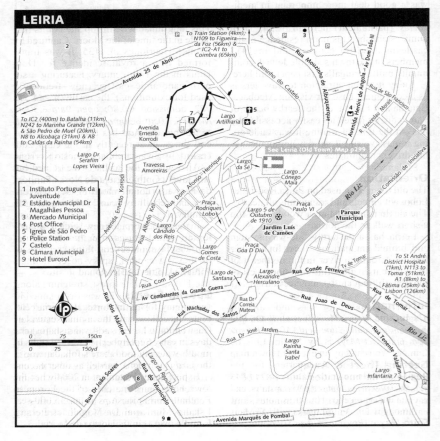

LEIRIA

To Train Station (4km); N109 to Figueira da Foz (56km) & IC2-A1 to Coimbra (65km)

Avenida 25 de Abril

Caminho do Castelo

Rua Mouinho de Albuquerque

Rua Dom João III

Av Dom João III

Avenida Herois de Angola

Rua de São Francisco

R Vencelau Morais

To IC2 (400m) to Batalha (11km), N242 to Marinha Grande (12km) & São Pedro de Muel (20km), N8 to Alcobaça (31km) & A8 to Caldas da Rainha (54km)

Avenida Ernesto Korrodi

Largo Artilharia

See Leiria (Old Town) Map p299

Largo Dr Serafim Lopes Vieira

Travessa Amoreiras

Largo da Sé

Largo Cónego Maia

Rua Comissão de Iniciativa

Rua Dom Afonso Henrique

Praça Rodrigues Lobo

Praça Paulo VI

Parque Municipal

Rio Liz

1 Instituto Português da Juventude
2 Estádio Municipal Dr Magalhães Pessoa
3 Mercado Municipal
4 Post Office
5 Igreja de São Pedro
6 Police Station
7 Castelo
8 Câmara Municipal
9 Hotel Eurosol

Rua Alfredo Keil

Largo Cândido dos Reis

Largo 5 de Outubro de 1910

Jardim Luís de Camões

Praça Goa D Diu

Largo Gomes de Costa

Rua Com João Belo

Largo de Santana

Largo Alexandre Herculano

Rua Conde Ferreira

Tv de Tomar

To St André District Hospital (1km), N113 to Tomar (51km), A1 (8km) to Fátima (25km) & Lisbon (126km)

Rua de Tomar

Av Combatentes da Grande Guerra

Rua Dr Correia Mateus

Rua Joao de Deus

Rio Liz

Rua dos Mártires

Rua Machados dos Santos

Rua Dr José Jardim

Largo Rainha Santa Isabel

Rua Tenente Valadim

0   75   150m
0   75   150yd

Rua Dr João Soares

Largo da República

Rua do Município

Largo Infantaria 7

Avenida Marquês de Pombal

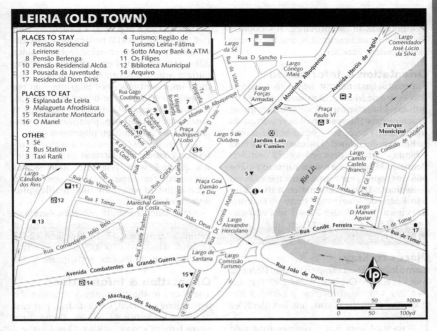

LEIRIA (OLD TOWN)

PLACES TO STAY
7 Pensão Residencial Leiriense
8 Pensão Berlenga
10 Pensão Residencial Alcôa
13 Pousada da Juventude
17 Residencial Dom Dinis

PLACES TO EAT
5 Esplanada de Leiria
9 Malagueta Afrodisiáca
15 Restaurante Montecarlo
16 O Manel

OTHER
1 Sé
2 Bus Station
3 Taxi Rank

4 Turismo; Região de Turismo Leiria-Fátima
6 Sotto Mayor Bank & ATM
11 Os Filipes
12 Biblioteca Municipal
14 Arquivo

---

from €3) and the more upmarket **O Manel** (☎ 244 832 132; Rua Dr Correia Mateus 50; dishes €7-9) as well, which boasts a huge fish menu.

Esplanada de Leiria (☎ 244 812 320), in the *jardim*, undergoing renovation at the time of writing, is popular and serves bargain weekday buffet lunches.

Malagueta Afrodisiáca (☎ 244 831 607; Rua Gago Coutinho 17; dishes €7-12; open noon-midnight Mon-Sat) is, as its name suggests, a deliberately provocative and stylish venue. In addition to aphrodisiac teas (€2.30) it also offers tititlating fare such as ostrich steaks (€11.30), plus vegetarian and children's meals (from €4.50).

There's a clutch of bars and cafés in Largo Cândido dos Reis, including **Os Filipes** (Largo Cândido dos Reis 1A; open 8pm-2am daily).

Getting There & Away

Bus From the bus station (☎ 244 811 507) at least 10 express buses daily run on weekdays to Coimbra (€6.10, 50 minutes) and Fátima (€4.50, 35 minutes), and around four run to Tomar (€6.30, 50 minutes).

Almost hourly express buses to Lisbon (€7.30, 1¼ hours).

Train Leiria is on the Cacém (a Lisbon suburb) to Figueira da Foz line. Two IR services run daily from Cacém (€6, 2¼ hours) to Leiria, plus a couple more regional services (€5.80, two to three hours), all continuing to Figueira da Foz (€2.80, 45 minutes). Cacém has frequent connections with Lisbon's Rossio station. Buses from the train station to town (15 minutes) cost €0.70.

PINHAL DE LEIRIA

The 110-sq-km pine forest, stretching along the coast west of Leiria, was first planted in the reign of Dom Afonso III, some 700 years ago. However, it was his successor, Dom Dinis, who expanded and shaped the forest (subsequently called the Pinhal do Rei or Royal Pine Forest) so that it would serve not only as a barrier against the encroaching sands but also as a supply of timber for the maritime industry – especially welcome during the Age of Discoveries.

Today the aromatic forest, stretching from Pedrógão in the north to São Pedro de

Muel in the south, is one of the most delightful areas in the province. It's popular for its picnic and camp sites, and for its several excellent beaches.

Orientation & Information
The nicest and nearest beach to Leiria is São Pedro de Muel (20km west), a low-key holiday-home resort. Two other popular beach resorts 16km north of here – Praia da Vieira and Pedrógão – have both become rather overdeveloped. The town of Marinha Grande, halfway between Leiria and São Pedro de Muel, has a useful **turismo** (☎ 244 566 644; open year-round) near the *câmara municipal*. There are smaller **turismos** in São Pedro de Muel (☎ 244 599 633), Praia da Vieira (☎ 244 695 230) and Pedrógão (☎ 244 695 411), all open from July to mid-September.

Places to Stay
Camping The best camp site at São Pedro de Muel is run by Orbitur (☎ 244 599 168, fax 244 599 148; adult/tent/car €3.80/3/3.30). It's 500m from the seaside and has plenty of facilities.

Praia da Vieira has a simpler road-side municipal **parque de campismo** (☎ 244 695 334; adult/tent/car €1.50/1.30/0.90; open June–mid-Sept).

The municipal **parque de campismo** (☎ 244 695 403, fax 244 695 447; adult/tent/car €1.60/1.60/1.60) in the forest at nearby Pedrógão is much better equipped.

Pensões & Residenciais In addition to some *quartos* (look for signs near the beach) there are a few hotels in São Pedro de Muel, including the seafront **Hotel Mar e Sol** (☎ 244 590 000, fax 244 590 019; Avenida da Liberdade 1; doubles €70).

Hotel Cristal (☎ 244 699 060; e cristalvieira@hoteiscristal.pt; Avenida Marginal; doubles with breakfast €80) is a 100-room hotel in Praia da Vieira. It's just 20m from the beach and has a swimming pool and health club.

Getting There & Away
From Leiria there are at least seven buses daily to Marinha Grande (€1.30, 15 minutes), from where you can pick up connections to São Pedro de Muel (€1.90), Praia da Vieira (€2.10) and Pedrógão (€2.30).

FÁTIMA
postcode 2495 • pop 7800 • elevation 320m
Before 13 May 1917 no-one paid any attention to this unremarkable little place 22km southeast of Leiria, but on that day Fátima was transformed into one of the most important places of pilgrimage in the Catholic world (see the boxed text 'Apparitions & Miracles' later in this chapter). It now rivals Lourdes in popularity and is visited by over four million pilgrims a year.

The town itself is more of a shrine to religious commercialism than to the Virgin: it's packed with boarding houses and restaurants for pilgrims, and shops selling every kind of souvenir imaginable, plus toys and handicrafts galore.

At the sanctuary itself, however, there's an extraordinary atmosphere, most dramatic at Fátima's key times, 12–13 May and 12–13 October, when up to 100,000 pilgrims arrive to commemorate the first apparitions.

Orientation & Information
The focus of the pilgrimages is where the apparitions occurred, Cova da Iria, just east of the A1 motorway. Where sheep once grazed there's now a vast 1km-long esplanade dominated by a huge white basilica.

Several major roads ring the area, including Avenida Dom José Alves Correia da Silva to the south, where the bus station is located. To reach the sanctuary turn right from the bus station and walk 300m, then left along Rua João Paulo II for 500m. The **turismo** (☎ 249 823 773; open 10am-1pm & 3pm-7pm daily June-Sept, 2pm-6pm Oct-May) is also on the *avenida* 300m beyond this turning.

Sanctuary
The 1953 **basilica** is the focus of intense devotion. Some supplicants even shuffle across the vast esplanade on padded knees. En route, they usually stop at the **Capela das Apariçoes** (Chapel of the Apparitions), the site where the Virgin appeared, which is always packed with devotees offering flowers and lighting candles.

Inside the basilica attention is focused on the tombs of Blessed Francisco (died 1919) and Blessed Jacinta (died 1920), both victims of a flu epidemic, who were beatified in 2000. Lúcia, the third witness of the apparition, entered a convent in Coimbra in 1928 and is still alive (aged 96 in 2003).

Eight masses are held daily in the basilica, and seven daily in the Capela das Apariços. (At least two masses daily are held in English; check at the information booth by the Capela for details.)

Places to Stay & Eat
There are dozens of reasonably priced restaurants, *pensões* and boarding houses, many geared for visiting groups of hundreds.

Hotel Coração de Fátima (☎ 249 531 433, fax 249 531 157; Rua Cônego Formigão; doubles with breakfast €47.50), next to the post office and not far from the turismo, offers brisk service.

Residencial Solar da Marta (☎ 249 531 152; e solar.damarta@ip.pt; Rua Francisco Marto 74; doubles with breakfast €37.50) is a homely place east of the basilica, in the thick of the shops.

Getting There & Away
Bus There are almost hourly buses daily to Leiria (€4.50, 25 minutes), three to Batalha (€1.50), nine to Coimbra (€7.50, 1½ hours) and 12 to Lisbon (€7, 1½ hours), three of them via Santarém (€5.70, one hour). Fátima is often referred to as Cova da Iria on bus timetables.

Train Fátima is on the Lisbon–Porto line but the station is 25km from town, with few bus connections. A better bet is to get off at Caxarias, two stops to the north, which has two IC (€7.50, 1¼ hours) and three IR direct services daily from Lisbon and the same number from Porto, plus numerous indirect services. A bus shuttles between Caxarias and Fátima (€2, 40 minutes) five times daily, twice at weekends.

PORTO DE MÓS
postcode 2480 • elevation 260m
At the northern tip of the Parque Natural das Serras de Aire e Candeeiros, 9km south of Batalha, Porto de Mós is a pleasant little town beside the Rio Lena, dominated by a 13th-century hill-top castle.

At the heart of a region once inhabited by dinosaurs (see the boxed text 'Dinosaur Footprints' later in this chapter), Porto de Mós became a major Roman settlement. The Romans used the Lena to ferry millstones hewn from a nearby quarry and, later, iron from a mine 10km south at Alqueidão da Serra, where you can still see a Roman road, fantastically cobbled and stretching up into the hills, offering a great 9km walk.

Today, the town serves as a jumping off point for visiting the nearby caves and scenically stunning park.

Orientation & Information
The town spreads out from a cluster of streets just below the castle to a newer area further south around the *mercado municipal* (municipal market) on Avenida Dr Francisco Sá Carneiro, where buses also stop.

Apparitions & Miracles

On 13 May 1917 three shepherd children from Fátima – Lúcia, Francisco and Jacinta – claimed to have seen an apparition of the Virgin. Only 10-year-old Lúcia could hear what the holy lady said, including her request that they return on the 13th of every subsequent month for the next six months. The word spread and by 13 October some 70,000 devotees had gathered. What happened then has been described as the Miracle of the Sun: intense lights shot from the sun, followed by the miraculous cure of the disabilities and illnesses suffered by some of the spectators.

What the Virgin apparently told Lúcia must have seemed especially potent in those WWI days; her messages described the hell that resulted from 'sins of the flesh' and implored the faithful to 'pray a great deal and make many sacrifices' to secure peace. Most controversially, the Virgin claimed that if her request were heeded, 'Russia *would* be converted and there *would* be peace'.

Until 2000 the third message remained secret, known only to successive popes. During an emotional ceremony that year, the visiting Pope John Paul II beatified Jacinta and Francisco, before a crowd of half a million, and revealed the third message, a prophetic vision written down by Lúcia: it predicted the attempt on the Pope's life in 1981. At the time of the attempt the Pope had insisted somewhat mysteriously that Our Lady of Fátima had saved his life; after he'd recovered, he had the bullet that wounded him welded into the crown of the Virgin's statue in Fátima.

Walk west from here towards the Rio Lena and you'll hit Alameda Dom Afonso Henriques, the main road through town.

The **turismo** (☎ 244 491 323; open 10am-1pm & 3pm-7pm Tues-Sun May-July & Sept, Mon-Sun Aug; 10am-1pm & 2pm-6pm Oct-Apr) is at the top of this road in the *jardim público* (public gardens).

Castelo

The distinctive green-towered castle *(admission free; open 10am-12.30pm & 2pm-6pm Tues-Sun May-Sept, to 5pm Oct-Apr)* was originally a Moorish possession, but was conquered in 1148 by Dom Afonso Henriques. It was rebuilt in 1450 and was undergoing another refurbishment at the time of writing. It hosts changing exhibitions.

Dinosaur Footprints

For years, a huge quarry 10km south of Fátima yielded nothing more interesting than chunks of limestone. When the quarry closed in 1994, however, a local archaeologist discovered huge footprints embedded in the sloping rock face. These the oldest and longest sauropod tracks in the world, some 175 million years old, plodding along for 147m.

The sauropods (they were those nice herbivorous dinosaurs with small heads and long necks and tails) would have been stepping through carbonated mud, later transformed into limestone. As you walk across the slope you can clearly see the large elliptical prints made by the feet *(pes)* and the smaller, half-moon prints made by the hands *(manus)*.

Another major dinosaur discovery – a partial skeleton of a flesh-eating *Allosaurus fragilis* – was made in April 1999 at nearby Pombal (26km northeast of Leiria). It proved to be the same species as fossils found in western USA, throwing into disarray the theory that the Atlantic Ocean opened only during the late Jurassic period.

Fátima's **Monumento Natural das Pegadas dos Dinossáurios** *(☎ 249 530 160, 244 848 770; adult/child 6-10 €1.50/0.50; open 10am-12.30pm & 2pm-8pm Tues-Sun 21 Mar-22 Sept, to 6pm 23 Sept-20 Mar)* is at Pedreira do Galinha, 9km east of the N360 running south of Fátima; follow the brown signs marked 'Pegadas da Serra de Aire'.

Museu Municipal

This little museum *(☎ 244 499 615; Travessa de São Pedro; admission free; open 10am-12.30pm & 2pm-5.30pm Tues-Sun)* is in a poorly signposted pink building beneath the *câmara municipal*, just off Largo Machado dos Santos, and contains a fabulous old-fashioned horde of treasures. Fading labels provide the briefest of details on extraordinary items such as fossils of turtles and dinosaur bones, Neolithic stones, Palaeolithic flints, Roman columns and ancient azulejo fragments. In addition, there are insects, butterflies, millstones, folk costumes, old typewriters, looms, books and spinning wheels. Great fun!

Places to Stay & Eat

Residencial O Filipe *(☎ 244 401 455; e rm filipe@iol.pt; Largo do Rossio 41; doubles/triples with breakfast €35/45)*, the only *pensão* in town, has been completely revamped and now offers 15 trim rooms, all with telephone and heating..

Quinta de Rio Alcaide *(☎ 244 402 124, 939 449 746; e rioalcaide@mail.telepac.pt; doubles with/without breakfast €43/35, per week high season €210, apartments 45.50/38, per week €225)*, 1km southeast of Porto de Mos, is a converted 18th-century paper mill with five small self-catering apartments, including one in a former windmill. There's a swimming pool here, too, filled with natural waters.

Restaurante O Miguel *(☎ 244 403 912; Av Dr Francisco Sá Carneiro 9B; dishes €6-7, half-portions from €3.50)* is one of several decent restaurants near the market.

Getting There & Away

One to two buses daily run to/from Leiria (€1.90, 45 minutes) via Batalha, plus three others which require a change at São Jorge Cruz, a junction on the N1 about 5km northwest of Porto de Mós. Five buses daily come from Alcobaça (€2.10, 35 minutes), also via São Jorge Cruz.

PARQUE NATURAL DAS SERRAS DE AIRE E CANDEEIROS

This park (PNSAC for short) stretches south from Porto de Mós, and occupies the most extensive and diversified limestone range in Portugal, from high plateaus and peaks to huge rocky depressions. The park is famous for its caves, but the landscape above is spectacular, too, in particular the high Planalto de Santo António (starting 2km south of the Grutas de Santo António). Sweeping hills covered in gorse and olive groves are divided by dry-stone walls and threaded by cattle trails, offering tempting walks.

Throughout the park there are over a dozen *parques de merendas* (picnic areas), along with several short *percursos pedestres* (walking trails), described in Portuguese-language pamphlets available from the park offices.

Information

The park has a **head office** (☎ 243 999 480, fax 243 999 488; Rua Dr Augusto César da Silva Ferreira) in Rio Maior, at the south of the park. There's also a Centro de Interpretação, called **Ecoteca** (☎ 244 491 904, fax 244 403 555; open 9.30am-12.30pm & 2pm-6pm Tues-Sun) in the public garden in Porto de Mós, where you can pick up information (mostly in Portuguese).

Mira de Aire

Portugal's largest, most popular **cave system** (☎ 244 440 322; adult/youth or senior/child under 12 €4/3/2.50; open 9.30am-8.30pm daily July & Aug, 9.30am-7pm June & Sept, 9.30am-6pm Apr & May, 9.30am-5.30pm Oct-Mar), at Mira de Aire, 14km southeast of Porto de Mós, was discovered in 1947 and opened to the public in 1971. The 45-minute guided tour leads you down through a series of colourfully lit caverns chock-full of stalactites and stalagmites. The last cavern, 110m down, contains a huge lake with a dramatic fountain display. Ticket sales stop 30 minutes before closing time.

There are three buses daily except Sunday from Porto de Mós to Mira de Aire (€2, 30 minutes) and two that return. Two buses daily on weekdays run from Nazaré (€3.60, 1½ hours) via Alcobaça (€2.80, 1¼ hours) and Porto de Mós. Other services may require a change at São Jorge; check the bus schedules carefully. Buses stop in Mira de Aire town, 1km from the caves.

Grutas de Alvados & Grutas de Santo António

Grutas de Alvados and Grutas de Santo António (☎ 244 440 787; open 9.30am-8.30pm daily July & Aug, 9.30am-7pm June & Sept,

9.30am-6pm Apr & May, 9.30am-5.30pm Oct-Mar) are about 15km southeast of Porto de Mós, and 2km and 3.5km, respectively, south of the N243 from Porto de Mós to Mira de Aire. They're smaller versions of the caves at Mira de Aire. Admission prices are the same as for Mira de Aire but you can also buy a combined ticket for these two caves only (€7.50/4.50 per adult/child aged under 12).

There are no direct buses to the Alvados and Santo António caves. Your best bet is to hop off the Porto de Mós-Mira de Aire bus and walk (steeply uphill!) from the N243. A **taxi** (☎ 244 491 351, 939 352 533) from Porto de Mós costs about €9 return, including an hour's wait at the caves.

Activities

Projecto Terra (☎ 919 118 619; e projecto.terra@vertigem-app.pt), based in Portela de Vale de Espinho, organises bird-watching from October to May, hiking, biking, caving and other activities.

Aire Tur (☎ 244 449 870; e airetur@hotmail.com; Rua 5 de Outubro 170, Mire de Aire) offers two-hour/half-day/full-day jeep tours for €20/30/50 per person. It can also arrange trips by donkey or bike.

Places to Stay

The park operates four *centros de acolhimento* (lodging centres) in its southern section, geared to groups of four to eight. The smallest, near Alcobertas, costs around €60 per night in high season. This accommodation must be booked at least a week in advance at the head office (☎ 244 449 700).

The **parque de campismo** (☎ 244 491 904, fax 244 405 555) at Arrimal, 17km south of Porto de Mós, operates in the summer only and is accessible by a bus that runs twice daily.

Ribatejo

SANTARÉM

postcode 2000 ● pop 28,800

Santarém (sang-tuh-**rayng**) is one of the most agreeable towns in the otherwise dull Ribatejo. This provincial capital is 'a book made of stone', wrote Portugal's famous 19th-century novelist, Almeida Garrett in *Travels in my Homeland*, 'in which the most interesting and most poetical part of our chronicles is written'.

As well as the churches and mansions to which Garrett refers, today's Santarém is famous for its bullfights and its various fairs and festivals, notably the agricultural fair held each June. Outside festival season its breezy panoramas, abundance of cafés and restaurants, and 5000-strong student population still make it a great one-day stopover (note that everything is closed on Monday).

History
The town's position in a fertile area high above the Rio Tejo made Santarém a prized possession even before the times of the Romans and Moors. Dom Afonso Henriques captured it in 1147, in one of the watershed

successes of the Reconquista; the king built the Mosteiro de Alcobaça on the strength of the victory.

Santarém subsequently became a favourite royal residence (partly because of its good hunting opportunities), and its palace served as the meeting place of the *cortes* during the 13th, 14th and 15th centuries. Royalty again favoured Santarém 400 years later, in 1833, when Dom Miguel used it as his base during his brief (and unsuccessful) war against his brother Pedro.

Orientation
Overlooking the Rio Tejo, Santarém commands some grand views of the Ribatejan plains. At the heart of the old town are the pedestrianised Rua Serpa Pinto and Rua

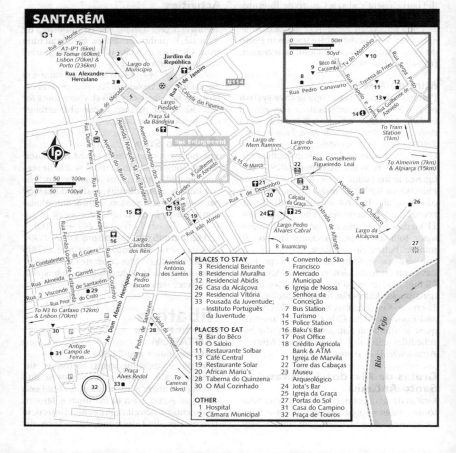

SANTARÉM

PLACES TO STAY
3 Residencial Beirante
8 Residencial Muralha
12 Residencial Abidis
26 Casa da Alcáçova
29 Residencial Vitória
33 Pousada da Juventude;
Instituto Português
da Juventude

PLACES TO EAT
9 Bar do Bêco
10 O Saloio
11 Restaurante Solbar
13 Café Central
19 Restaurante Solar
20 African Mariu's
28 Taberna do Quinzena
30 O Mal Cozinhado

OTHER
1 Hospital
2 Câmara Municipal
4 Convento de São
Francisco
5 Mercado
Municipal
6 Igreja de Nossa
Senhora da
Conceição
7 Bus Station
14 Turismo
15 Police Station
16 Baku's Bar
17 Post Office
18 Crédito Agrícola
Bank & ATM
21 Igreja de Marvila
22 Torre das Cabaças
23 Museu
Arqueológico
24 Jota's Bar
25 Igreja da Graça
27 Portas do Sol
31 Casa do Campino
32 Praça de Touros

Capelo e Ivens, where the turismo and most of the restaurants, shops and cheap accommodation are. Signposts to the Portas do Sol lookout lead visitors on a walk past most of the churches of interest.

The train station is way below town, 2.4km to the northeast, though there are regular buses to the centre. The bus station (*Avenida do Brasil*) is central.

Information

The **turismo** (☎ *243 304 437, fax 243 304 401; Rua Capelo e Ivens 63; open 9am-7pm Tues-Fri, 10am-12.30pm & 2.30pm-5.30pm Sat-Mon*) has a detailed town map with multilingual descriptive text. Not on display but available for €1 each are multilingual leaflets on the town's architectural riches.

The **hospital** (☎ *243 300 200*) is on the northern edge of town; the police station (☎ *243 322 022*) is on the northwestern side of Largo Cândido dos Reis. Among the many banks in town is **Crédito Agrícola** (*Rua Dr Teixeira Guedes 23*).

Free Internet access is available at the **Instituto Português da Juventude** (*IJP; ☎ 243 333 292; Avenida Grupo Forcados Amadores de Santarém*) from 9am to 8pm Monday to Friday. The **post office** (*Rua Dr Teixeira Guedes; open 8.30am-6.30pm Mon-Fri, 9am-12.30pm Sat*) has NetPost.

Igreja de Nossa Senhora da Conceição

This baroque, 17th-century Jesuit seminary church (*open 9am-12.30pm & 2pm-5.30pm Tues-Sun*), built on the site of the former royal palace, dominates the town's most impressive square, Praça Sá da Bandeira. Inside the church, which now serves as the town's cathedral, are the usual baroque frills, including a painted ceiling and gilded carved altars.

Igreja de Marvila

Dating from the 12th century but with 16th-century overlays, the most outstanding features of this endearing little church (*open 9am-12.30pm & 2pm-5.30pm Tues-Sun*) are its Manueline doorway and fantastic floor-to-ceiling, 17th-century azulejos.

Igreja da Graça

Just south of the Igreja de Marvila is Santarém's most impressive church (*open 9am-12.30pm & 2pm-5.30pm Tues-Sun*). It was built in the early 15th century and features a rose window. It houses the tombs of Pedro Álvares Cabral (the 'discoverer' of Brazil) and Dom Pedro de Menezes (the first governor of Ceuta, who died in 1437). Probably because the de Menezes family founded the church, Dom Pedro's tomb is considerably more ornate than that of the explorer.

The church often hosts exhibitions.

Museu Arqueológico

This is a neat, little archaeological museum (*admission €1; open 9am-12.30pm & 2pm-5.30pm Tues-Sun*), which is housed in the 12th-century Igreja de São João de Alporão. Among the stone carvings, azulejos, old chains and keys, and other dusty relics, the showpiece is undoubtedly the elaborately carved tomb of Dom Duarte de Menezes, who died in 1464 in a battle against the Moors in North Africa. The flamboyance of the tomb is in ironic contrast to the only bit of him that was apparently saved for burial – a single tooth.

Torre das Cabaças

This 15th-century belltower (*Torre do Relógio; admission €1; open 9am-12.30pm & 2pm-5.30pm Tues, Wed, Sat & Sun, 10am-12.30pm & 2pm-5.30pm Thur & Fri*), opposite the Museu Arqueológico, has been transformed into the Núcleo Museológico do Tempo or Museum of Time. Its imaginative display includes ancient stone sundials and 19th-century clock workings. There's a good view over the town from the glass-enclosed top floor.

Portas do Sol

The Gates of the Sun, on the site of the Moorish citadel at the southeastern edge of town, is the town's best panoramic viewpoint and picnic site. There is a garden with aviaries and a pond, and a fantastic view over the Rio Tejo and the plains beyond.

Special Events

Santarém's Feira Nacional da Agricultura (National Agriculture Fair) is famous nationwide for its horse races, bullfights and night-time bull-running in the streets. It lasts for 10 days from the first week in June and takes place 2km west of the town centre.

Gourmands should take note of the Festival Nacional de Gastronómia, held over a fortnight at the Casa do Campino at the end of October, which encourages you to eat as much traditional Portuguese fare as you can. Stalls sell regional specialities and some 25 restaurants from 18 different regions present their most sumptuous cuisine in massive dining rooms.

Places to Stay

Camping The nearest **parque de campismo** (☎ 243 557 040; adult/tent/car €2.70/2.70/2.70) is at Alpiarça, 15km to the east, close to a reservoir. It's reasonably well equipped.

Pensões & Residenciais There's a **pousada da juventude** (☎ 243 391 914; e santarem@movijovem.pt; Avenida Grupo Forcados Amadores de Santarém; dorm beds €9.50, doubles with bathroom €26.50). It's attached to the Instituto Português da Juventude in a grubby, graffiti-splattered building.

Residencial Abidis (☎ 243 322 017; Rua Guilherme de Azevedo 4; doubles with/without bathroom €35.40/30) an endearingly old-fashioned place, offers fading doubles from the 1950s (marvel at its antique telephone system on display downstairs). Rates include breakfast.

Residencial Muralha (☎ 243 322 399, fax 243 329 477; Rua Pedro Canavarro 12; doubles €30) has cheerful, pretty rooms right by the old town walls.

Residencial Beirante (☎ 243 322 547; Rua Alexandre Herculano 3; doubles with breakfast €35-40) is better than it looks from the outside. It's a big two-storey affair with decent, functional rooms.

Residencial Vitória (☎ 243 309 130, fax 243 328 202; Rua 2 Visconde de Santarém 21; doubles with breakfast €35-40), in a quiet residential area with relatively easy parking, is a homely place with spacious rooms run by grandmotherly Dona Vitória.

Casa da Alcáçova (☎ 243 304 030; e info@alcacova.com; Largo da Alcáçova; doubles with breakfast €125-150, minimum 2-night stay) is a 17th-century manor house with a swimming pool, superb views and eight luxury doubles.

Places to Eat

As you'd expect of an agricultural town that is packed with students, Santarém is chock-a-block with cheap restaurants.

Bar do Bêco (☎ 243 322 937; Bêco da Cacaimba; snacks €2.50-4) is a pleasant nook, serving snacks at lunch time.

Restaurante Solbar (☎ 243 322 271; Travessa do Froes 25; dishes €7) and **O Saloio** (☎ 243 327 656; Travessa do Montalvo 11; dishes €7.50; open Mon-Sat) are two traditional eateries that offer half-portions for around €5.

Restaurante Solar (☎ 243 322 239; Emilio Infante da Câmara 9; dishes €6-9) is popular for business lunches.

Café Central (☎ 243 322 303; Rua Guilherme de Azevedo 32), a stylish chrome and Art Deco venue, is an upmarket choice.

African Mariu's (☎ 243 326 517; Rua 1 de Dezembro 3; dishes €9.50) is an intimate venue. It has a particularly long meat menu but, despite its name, not much fare from Africa.

O Mal Cozinhado (☎ 243 323 584; Campo de Feiras; dishes around €7; open Tues-Sun), 700m south of town (near the bullring), is hugely popular and well worth finding; some half-portions are available.

Taberna do Quinzena (☎ 243 322 804; Rua Porto de Santarém 93; dishes €5-7; open Mon-Sat) is a typical Portuguese male-dominated taverna, the walls of which are plastered with bullfighting posters. At lunch time it serves only grilled fare and in the evening just one set dish.

There's a curious culinary speciality in this region called *fataça na telha* (mullet fish grilled on a tile), which occasionally appears on menus – depending on when the fish is available. The best place to try it is at **O Telheiro da Lúcia** (☎ 243 328 581), a simple riverside place in Caneiras, 5km south of town, where, as well as the famous fish, you can sample Lúcia's home-baked bread. Call ahead to check availability.

Entertainment

Baku's Bar (☎ 243 321 390; Rua Luiz Montez Mattoso 13) is a popular café-bar that is open to midnight on weekdays and to 2am on Saturday.

Jota's Bar (☎ 243 321 041), a modern place opposite Igreja da Graça, offers an unbeatable setting and upbeat music.

Getting There & Away

Bus There are a dozen buses daily to Lisbon's Arco do Cego terminal (€5.30, 1¼ hours) and three to Gare do Oriente. Two to four buses run daily to Caldas da Rainha (€3.80), Tomar (€6.10, one hour) and Fátima (€6.10, 1¼ hours).

Train Frequent *intercidade* (IC; €5.70) and IR (€3.70) trains go to Lisbon (45 minutes). Buses run between the town and train station nine times daily (€1, 12 minutes). **Taxis** (☎ 243 322 919) charge €3 for the trip.

CASTELO DE ALMOUROL

Ever since Gualdim Pais, Grand Master of the Order of the Knights Templar, built this castle on a rocky islet in the middle of the Rio Tejo in 1171, it has been imbued with romance and mystery. Its picturesque, isolated location on the site of an earlier Roman fort, and its striking fortifications – a rampart, 10 towers and a square keep – caught the attention of many poets and writers during the Age of Chivalry.

Places to Stay & Eat

Casa de **Pasto Aringa** (☎ 249 733 454; *Poligono de Tancos)*, 1.1km from the train station (near a military base), is a rough-and-ready café and the nearest option for a snack.

The best overnight choice is Constância (where poet Luís de Camões once lived), 5km east of Almourol. It has a pretty old town and riverside setting. **Casa João Chagas** (☎ 249 739 403; e vilapoema@mail .telepac.pt; *Rua João Chagas; singles/doubles Mon-Thur €37.40/42.40, Fri & Sat €39/45)* is an old house with modern trappings. The same management runs **O Café da Praça**, opposite; try the fantastic *queijinhos do Céu* (literally, 'sweets from heaven'), still made by local nuns.

Other restaurants can be found at Tancos, 2.5km west.

Getting There & Away

The tiny Almourol train station is 1km uphill from the castle. Four trains daily from Lisbon via Santarém (€1.90, 50 minutes), with a change at Entroncamento, stop here and at Praia do Ribatejo (€1.90, 55 minutes), the station serving Constância. For taxis, call ☎ 917 271 042.

A **ferry** (☎ 249 733 062, 914 506 562) takes visitors across to the island and back for €0.80 per person (€1.50 for a round-island trip).

Esplanada-Bar do Zézère (☎ 249 739 972; *Esplanada)* in Constância, rents bikes (€7.50 per day) and canoes.

TOMAR

postcode 2300 • pop 15,800 • elevation 70m
This attractive and historically outstanding town is an oasis of interest in the Ribatejo. It's home to the World Heritage–listed Convento de Cristo, former headquarters of the Knights Templar and one of the most significant architectural and religious monuments in the land.

The town itself, straddling the Rio Nabão, is brilliant for lazy wandering, with a delightful old quarter of cobbled lanes and the extensive Mata Nacional dos Sete Montes (Seven Hills National Forest) at the foot of the monastery walls. If you have your own transport, the town makes a perfect base for exploring the surrounding area, including the nearby Castelo de Bode reservoir, set in some very pretty countryside.

Orientation

The Rio Nabão neatly divides the town, with new developments largely concentrated on the east bank and the old town to the west. The monastery looks down on it all from a wooded hill top above the town to the west.

The bus and train station are close together, about 500m south of the turismo. Car drivers are advised to park in the large free lot by the bus station.

Information

The **turismo** (☎/fax 249 322 427; *Avenida Dr Cândido Madureira; open 10am-1pm & 2pm-6pm daily, longer July & Aug)* has a comprehensive town map and an accommodation list with prices. It also has a small 1:5000 map (with paths marked) of the national forest. For information about other places in the region, head for the **regional turismo** (☎ 249 329 000, fax 249 324 322; *Rua Serpa Pinto 1; open Mon-Fri)*.

If both are closed, try **Alma Rústica** (☎ 249 314 237; *Rua do Teatro 28; open 10am-7pm Tues-Sun)*, a wonderful 'ethnographic' shop, with multilingual owners who have lots of useful tips (plus Portuguese arts and crafts, CDs and books for sale).

The **post office** (*Avenida Marquês de Tomar; open 8.30am-6pm Mon-Fri, 9am-12.30pm*

ESTREMADURA & RIBATEJO

Sat) has NetPost. Free Internet access is available at the **biblioteca municipal** *(town library;* ☎ *249 329 800; Rua Gualdim Pais; open 10am-7pm Mon-Sat).* **Residencial Luz** *(Rua Serpa Pinto 144)* charges €1.50 per half-hour.

There's a new **district hospital** *(*☎ *249 320 100; Via da Cintura)* 1km east of town and a central **police station** *(*☎ *249 313 444; Rua Dr Sousa).* Among the numerous banks with an ATM is **Caixa Geral de Depósitos** *(Rua Serpa Pinto 97).*

Convento de Cristo

Set on wooded slopes above the town and enclosed within 12th-century walls, the former headquarters of the Knights Templar (see the boxed text 'The Order of the

Knights Templar') reflects perfectly the power and mystique that this religious military order held between the 12th and 16th centuries.

The monastery *(*☎ *249 313 481; adult/ youth or student €3/1.50, 9am-noon Sun free; open 9am-6.30pm daily July-Sept, 9am-5.30pm Oct-June; last admission 30min before closing)* was founded in 1160 by Gualdim Pais, Grand Master of the Templars. It has a number of various chapels, cloisters and chapterhouses, added over the centuries by successive kings and Grand Masters, which reveal the changing architectural styles in spectacular fashion. You can choose to follow a short route (30 to 45 minutes) or take a more comprehensive 90-minute tour.

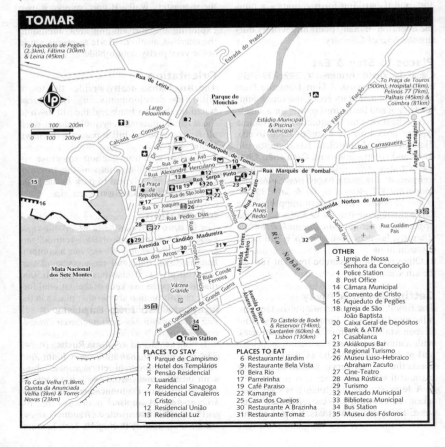

TOMAR

To Aqueduto de Pegões (2.3km), Fátima (30km) & Leiria (45km)

Estrada do Prado

Rua de Leiria

To Praça de Touros (500m), Hospital (1km), Pelinos 77 (35km), Palhais (45km) & Coimbra (81km)

Largo Pelourinho

Parque do Mouchão

Estádio Municipal & Piscina Municipal

Calçada do Convento

Avenida Marquês de Tomar

Rua Fábrica de Fiação

Rua Carrasqueira

Avenida Angela Tamagnini

Rua Dr Sousa

Rua de Gil de Avô

Rua Alexandre Herculano

Rua Serpa Pinto

Rua Marquês de Pombal

Praça da República

Rua de São João

Rua Dr Joaquim Jacinto

Rua dos Moinhos

Rua Everard

Praça Alves Redol

Avenida Norton de Matos

Rua Santa Iria

Rua Gualdim Pais

Rua Pedro Dias

Avenida Dr Cândido Madureira

Rua dos Arcos

Coronel L A Aparicio

Rua Conde Ferreira

Avenida Torres Pinheiro

Rio Nabão

Mata Nacional dos Sete Montes

Várzea Grande

Av dos Combatentes da Grande Guerra

Avenida D Nuno Alvares Pereira

To Castelo de Bode & Reservoir (14km), Santarém (60km) & Lisbon (130km)

Train Station

To Casa Velha (1.8km), Quinta da Anunciada Velha (3km) & Torres Novas (23km)

PLACES TO STAY
1 Parque de Campismo
2 Hotel dos Templários
5 Pensão Residencial Luanda
7 Residencial Sinagoga
11 Residencial Cavaleiros Cristo
12 Residencial União
13 Residencial Luz

PLACES TO EAT
6 Restaurante Jardim
9 Restaurante Bela Vista
10 Beira Rio
17 Parreirinha
19 Café Paraíso
22 Kamanga
25 Casa dos Queijos
30 Restaurante A Brazinha
31 Restaurante Tomaz

OTHER
3 Igreja de Nossa Senhora da Conceição
4 Police Station
8 Post Office
14 Câmara Municipal
15 Convento de Cristo
16 Aqueduto de Pegões
18 Igreja de São João Baptista
20 Caixa Geral de Depósitos Bank & ATM
21 Casablanca
23 Akiákopus Bar
24 Regional Turismo
26 Museu Luso-Hebraico Abraham Zacuto
27 Cine-Teatro
28 Alma Rústica
29 Turismo
32 Mercado Municipal
33 Biblioteca Municipal
34 Bus Station
35 Museu dos Fósforos

Charola This extraordinary 16-sided Templar church dominates the monastery. Built in the late 12th century, its round design is based on that of the Church of the Holy Sepulchre in Jerusalem. It's said that the Knights Templar arrived here on horseback for Mass. The aisle is circular, with a high altar enclosed within a central octagon. Restored wall paintings date from the early 16th century. A huge funnel to the left is an ancient organ pipe (the organ itself no longer exists).

Dom Manuel was responsible for tacking the nave on to the west side of the Charola and for commissioning the architect Diogo de Arruda to build a chapterhouse with a *coro alto* (choir) above it. The main western doorway into the nave – a splendid example of Spanish plateresque style (named after the ornate work of silversmiths) – is the work of Spanish architect João de Castilho, who later repeated his success at Belém's Mosteiro dos Jerónimos.

Claustro do Cemitério & Claustro da Lavagem These two beautifully serene, azulejo-decorated cloisters to the east of the Charola were built during the time when Prince Henry the Navigator was Grand Master of the order in the 15th century. The Claustro do Cemitério (Burial-Ground Cloisters) contains two 16th-century tombs, while the water tanks of the two-storey Claustro da Lavagem (Ablutions Cloisters) is now full of plants.

Chapterhouse The most famous feature of the entire monastery – reproduced on countless postcards – is the 'window' (actually built onto a wall) on the west side of the chapterhouse, best seen from the roof of the adjacent Claustro de Santa Bárbara (follow signs to the *janela*). Although now covered in lichen and in dire need of restoration, it's still obviously a stupendous expression of Manueline art, which the confidence of the seafaring Age of Discoveries made tangible in stone.

Designed around 1510 by the master of Manueline flamboyance, Diogo de Arruda (he and his brother were also responsible for Lisbon's Torre de Belém), it's an exuberant celebration of tangled ropes, seaweed, coral and cork floats, topped by the Cross of the Order of Christ and the royal arms and armillary spheres of Dom Manuel. Frustratingly obscured by the Claustro Principal is an almost equally fantastic window on the southern side of the chapterhouse.

Claustro Principal The elegant Renaissance Great Cloisters stand in striking contrast to the flamboyance of the monastery's Manueline architecture. Commissioned during the reign of João III, they were probably designed by the Spaniard Diogo de Torralva but were completed in 1587 by an Italian, Filippo Terzi. These foreign architects were among several responsible for introducing a delayed Renaissance style into Portugal. The Claustro Principal is arguably the country's finest expression of that style: a sober ensemble of Greek columns and Tuscan pillars, gentle arches and sinuous, spiralling staircases.

The outlines of a second chapterhouse, commissioned by João III but never finished, can be seen from the cloisters' southwestern corner.

Aqueduto de Pegões
This immensely impressive aqueduct, striding towards the monastery from the northwest, was built in the early 17th century to supply water to the monastery. It features 180 arches and was allegedly designed by Italian Filippo Terzi. It's best seen just off the Leiria road, 2.3km from town.

Igreja de Nossa Senhora da Conceição
Downhill from the monastery sits this little Renaissance basilica, striking in its simplicity. It was probably built by Francisco de Hollanda, one of Dom João III's favourite architects, in the middle of the 16th century. At the time of writing it was closed for extensive restoration.

Igreja de São João Baptista
The old town's most striking church (*admission free; open 9.30am-noon & 3.30pm-7pm daily*) faces Praça da República, itself an eye-catching ensemble of 17th-century buildings. The newly restored church, now blindingly white, dates mostly from the late 15th century. It has an octagonal spire and richly ornamented Manueline doorways on its northern and western sides. Gregório Lopes, one of the finest of Portugal's 16th-century

The Order of the Knights Templar

This religious military order was founded in about 1119 by French knights, who vowed to protect pilgrims visiting the Holy Land from bands of marauding Muslims. King Baldwin of Jerusalem housed them in a part of his palace that was once a Jewish temple – hence the name of the order.

It soon became a strictly organised, semireligious affair headed by a Grand Master. Each Templar took vows of poverty and chastity, and to emphasise their religious vows, the knights wore white coats emblazoned with a red cross. By 1139 they were directly under the pope's authority and soon became the leading defenders of the Christian crusader states in the Holy Land. In Portugal their main role was to help to expel the Moors from the country.

Rewarded with land, castles and titles, the order quickly grew very rich, with properties all over Europe, the Mediterranean and the Holy Land. This network, and their military strength, gave them another influential role: that of bankers to kings and pilgrims alike.

By the mid-13th century, however, Christians had recaptured all of Portugal and by 1300 the Knights Templar were left without a role.

There was talk of merging the order with their age-old rivals, the Hospitallers (another military religious order), but in France things began to turn ugly when King Philip IV – either eager for the order's wealth or afraid of its power – initiated an era of persecution (supported by the French pope Clement V). He arrested all of the knights, accusing many of heresy and seizing their property. In 1314, the order's last Grand Master was burned at the stake.

In Portugal, things didn't go nearly so badly for the order. Dom Dinis did follow the trend by dissolving the order in 1314, but a few years later he cannily re-established it as the Order of Christ, under the control of the throne. It was largely thanks to the wealth of the order that Prince Henry the Navigator (Grand Master from 1417 to 1460) was able to fund the launch of the Age of Discoveries. Dom João III took the order into a humbler phase, shifting it towards monastic duties. From the 17th century its power diminished and in 1834, together with all of the other religious orders, it finally broke up.

artists, painted the six panels hanging inside the especially for the church.

Museu Luso-Hebraico Abraham Zacuto

On a charming cobbled lane in the old town, you'll find the country's best-preserved medieval synagogue *(Rua Dr Joaquim Jacinto 73; admission free; open 10am-1pm & 2pm-6pm daily)*. Built between 1430 and 1460, it was used as a Jewish house of worship and meeting for only a few years, until Dom Manuel's edict of 1496 forced the Jews of Portugal to convert to Christianity or leave the country. The synagogue subsequently served as a prison, chapel, hay loft and warehouse until it was classified as a national monument in 1921.

Largely thanks to the efforts of Luís Vasco (who comes from one of two Jewish families left in Tomar), the small, plain building now serves as a Luso-Hebraic museum. It's named after the 15th-century Jewish mathematician and royal astrologer, who helped Vasco da Gama plan his voyages.

Inside are various tombstones engraved with 13th- and 14th-century Hebraic inscriptions, as well as many gifts from Jewish visitors from around the world. The upturned jars high in the wall served to improve the acoustics of the room.

Museu dos Fósforos

Housed in the Convento de São Francisco is a mind-boggling collection – the largest in Europe – of matchboxes *(admission free; open 11am-5pm daily)*. It was amassed by Aquiles da Mota Lima from the 1950s onwards.

Activities

Tomar has a generous supply of adventure-sports organisations that offer walking, biking and canoeing trips, rock-climbing and even parachuting. Most are geared to groups, but (with advance notice) may be able to accommodate individuals, especially **Via Aventura** *(☎/fax 249 324 054; e via@ aventura.web.pt)*, which organises regular Saturday afternoon canoeing jaunts on the Rio Nabão in town and rents out canoes and bikes. Other major players include 1000 Léguas (☎ 249 324 807, 919 802 184; e cor reio@1000leguas.com) and Templar (☎ 249 323 493, fax 249 321 720).

The biggest water-sports operator in the area is **Centro Náutico do Zêzere** (☎ 274 809 745; e aquaventura@mail.telepac.pt). It rents out jet skis, yachts, water-skis, canoes and kayaks on the Rio Zêzere (which feeds into the Castelo de Bode reservoir) from its centre in Palhais, 45km northeast of Tomar.

For horse riding contact **Centro Equestre da Quinta da Atouguia** (☎ 249 345 587) or **Coudelaria Ruy Escudeiro** (☎ 249 314 371), both about 3km from town.

Special Events
Tomar's most famous event is the Festa dos Tabuleiros (see the boxed text).

Another important religious festival is the Nossa Senhora da Piedade candle procession held on the first Sunday in September, when floats decorated with paper flowers are paraded through the streets.

Places to Stay
Camping Tomar's municipal **parque de campismo** (☎ 249 329 824, fax 249 322 608; adult/tent/car €2.30/1.40/2.10) is next to the football stadium and municipal swimming pool.

Pelinos 77 (☎ 249 301 814; adult/tent/car €3/2.50/1.50) 7km northeast at Pelinos, has a pool but otherwise simple facilities; bus connections are poor.

Pensões & Residenciais Unless otherwise stated, all the following rates include breakfast.

Residencial Luz (☎ 249 312 317; e info@ residencialluz.com; Rua Serpa Pinto 144; singles/doubles €25/32.50) is threadbare but homely (no breakfast offered).

Residencial União (☎ 249 323 161, fax 249 321 299; Rua Serpa Pinto 94; singles/ doubles €25/35) is smarter than Luz and on the same pedestrianised road.

Pensão Residencial Luanda (☎ 249 323 200, fax 249 322 145; Avenida Marquês de Tomar 15; singles €25-27, doubles €42-45, triples €50) has a jovial owner and a two-room suite perfect for families (€70).

Two posher places that offer singles/ doubles for around €33/48 are **Residencial Cavaleiros Cristo** (☎ 249 321 203, fax 249

321 192; Rua Alexandre Herculano 7) and **Residencial Sinagoga** (☎ 249 323 083; e residencial.sinagoga@clix.pt; Rua de Gil de Avô 31) in a quiet residential area.

Hotel dos Templários (☎ 249 321 730; e hoteltemplarios@mail.telepac.pt; Largo Cândido dos Reis 1; doubles €95-104), a huge river-view property, has a swimming pool, health club and rooms with all the frills.

Quinta da Anunciada Velha (☎ 249 345 218, fax 249 345 469; doubles €65, apartment €80), among several lovely Turihab properties in the area, is the nearest to Tomar, and is located 3km southwest of town at Cem Soldos.

Places to Eat
There are loads of good-value restaurants in town. Among the cheapest, all offering half-portions from around €3.50, are **Kamanga** (☎ 249 316 424; Rua São João 51; dishes €5.50), a tiny, tourist-friendly, family-run place; and **Restaurante Jardim** (☎ 249 312 034; Rua Silva Magalhães 39; dishes €6.50),

---

Festa dos Tabuleiros

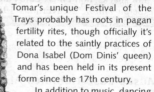

Tomar's unique Festival of the Trays probably has roots in pagan fertility rites, though officially it's related to the saintly practices of Dona Isabel (Dom Dinis' queen) and has been held in its present form since the 17th century.

In addition to music, dancing and fireworks, the highlight of the festival is a procession of about 400 young white-clad women (traditionally virgins!) bearing headdresses of trays stacked enormously tall with loaves, decorated with colourful paper flowers and topped with a white paper dove. Young male attendants (not apparently required to be virgins), dressed in black and white, help the girls balance the load, which can weigh up to 15kg. The following day, bread and wine are blessed by the priest and handed out to local families.

The festival is held every four years; the next one is in 2003.

NC

at which the list of local wines is almost as long as the menu.

Parreirinha (☎ 917 673 051; Rua Pé da Costa de Baixo 28; dishes €6; open Sun-Fri) has a saloon-door entrance and offers rustic ambience.

Beira Rio (☎ 249 312 806; Rua Alexandre Herculano 1; dishes €6-7) is a mid-range option with a cosy, traditional feel.

Restaurante Tomaz (☎ 249 312 552; Rua dos Arcos 31; dishes €6-7; open Mon-Sat) is a popular, bright option near the bus station.

Restaurante Bela Vista (☎ 249 312 870; Rua Fonte do Choupo 6; dishes €6-9; open Tues-Sun) wins the prize for looks and location; its outdoor tables are shaded by wisteria and overlook the river.

Restaurante A Brazinha (☎ 249 313 020; Rua dos Arcos 55; dishes €9-10; open Sun-Fri) is a pricier option (though it too offers half-portions for €6).

Casa Velha (☎ 249 324 277; Casal dos Aromas, Algarvias; dishes €9.50-12), 1.8km southwest of town (look for the blue signs 1.1km from the turismo), is an agreeable out-of-town venue with terrace dining in summer.

For snacks, don't miss **Café Paraiso** (Rua de Serpa Pinto), a cavernous 1950s-style

venue, and **Casa dos Queijos** (Rua Everaro 105), a deli selling all kinds of regional fare, including *chouriço* (spicy sausage) and the best regional cheeses.

Entertainment
Akiákopus Bar (Rua de São João 28) is usually open from 9.30pm daily. **Casablanca** (Rua de São João 85) opens from 10pm Wednesday to Saturday and has happy hour Wednesday and Thursday. Both places stay open until 2am (4am Friday and Saturday).

Fatias de Cá (☎ 249 314 161; e fatiasdeca@ oneinet.pt) is a Tomar-based theatre company. It presents highly unusual and entertaining performances, often in amazing locations (eg, castles, distilleries or old palaces) and with audience participation. Tickets cost around €15 to €25.

Getting There & Away
From the **bus terminal** (☎ 249 312 738) there are seven express buses daily to Lisbon (€6.10, two hours) and around three each to Fátima (€5.30, 40 minutes) and Leiria (€6.30, 70 minutes). Weekday train services run almost hourly to/from Lisbon (€5.40, two hours).

The Beiras

At the heart of Portugal lies the Beira region, and at the heart of the Beira is the country's highest mountain range and main geophysical landmark, the austerely beautiful Serra da Estrela. This and the region's lesser ranges help to define the three Beira provinces – *litoral* (coastal), *alta* (upper) and *baixa* (lower) – that mirror Portugal's own multiple personalities.

Atlantic air masses tumble against these granite ranges, spilling their moisture and giving birth to several major river systems which have laid down a rich subsoil in and west of the mountains. Unlike most of Portugal's better-known rivers, which have their headwaters in Spain, the Rio Mondego rises in the Serra da Estrela and is the longest exclusively Portuguese river.

Beira Litoral's fine coastline has so far escaped serious development; the only major resort is at Figueira da Foz. Aveiro presides over a complex estuary at the mouth of the Rio Vouga, and there's an important wildlife refuge at São Jacinto. From the coast a fertile, sometimes boggy plain stretches inland to the Gralheira, Caramulo and Buçaco hills and, to the south, into the foothills of the Serra da Estrela.

Coimbra is the Beiras' biggest town and, with Lisbon and Porto, one of Portugal's historic capitals and a major centre of culture and learning. Around it lie the spa town of Luso, the holy forest of Buçaco and, at Conimbriga, Portugal's finest Roman ruins. Arcing southeast and east are the Serra de Lousã and Serra de Açor, some of the loveliest and least visited ranges in the land.

Beira Alta, hemmed in by mountains, was the heartland of the Lusitani, who, under the legendary Viriato – Portugal's original national hero – so stubbornly resisted the Romans. Its dour people see few visitors other than those who stumble upon Viseu or the provincial capital, Guarda. Most travellers head, via Seia or Gouveia, straight into the Serra da Estrela. Robbed of rain, the eastern parts of this high-elevation province are sparsely populated and thinly cultivated.

Beira Baixa, though hilly in the north, is much like the Alentejo, with good-natured people, ferocious summer weather and

Highlights

- Roam the back lanes of the ancient, *fado*-loving university town of Coimbra
- Gaze upon the country's finest Roman ruins, at Conimbriga
- Walk all day in the hallowed forest of Buçaco and unwind at the spa at nearby Luso
- Survey the high peaks and traditional settlements of the Parque Natural da Serra da Estrela

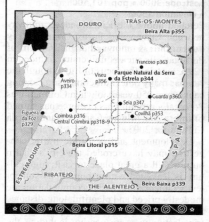

hypnotically flat landscapes of cork oaks, olive groves and giant agricultural estates. It's of minimal interest, except to lovers of vast, quiet, open spaces. Conspicuous exceptions are the proud hill-top towns of Monsanto and Sortelha.

Activities

The Beiras probably offer more ways to let go in the outdoors than any part of Portugal, with everything from surfing to mountain climbing. Outfits with programmes that focus on this region include:

Capitão Dureza (☎ 233 427 772, 919 079 852, 914 929 407, **w** www.capitaodureza.com) Apartado 247, 3081-801 Figueira da Foz; rafting and kayaking on the Rio Paiva (year-round) and Rio Minho (summer), canyoning, walking, bungee jumping

Cumes do Açor (☎ 235 205 959, 965 546 782, e cumes.acor@clix.pt) Avenida das Forças Armadas, 3300-011 Arganil; sea and river kayaking, off-road cycling, walking, canyoning, climbing, riding

Trans Serrano (☎/fax 235 778 938, ☎ 966 217 787, W www.transserrano.com) Rua Forno 6, 3330-325 Góis; accompanied kayak trips on the Rio Alva and other rivers of the Beira Litoral, walking, climbing, off-road cycling

Beira Litoral

COIMBRA
postcode 3000 • pop 101,100
• elevation 150m

Perched above the Rio Mondego midway between Lisbon and Porto, Coimbra (say **queem**-bra) is renowned as the 'Oxford of Portugal'. Its ancient university, founded in 1290, remains the focus of life although the city has many other attractions, some dating back some 850 years to when Coimbra was Portugal's capital. This pedigree has earned Coimbra the title of Capital Nacional da Cultura for 2003.

Development and desperate traffic congestion may have eroded the city's charm but it's still a great place to visit: high culture is leavened with a bumptious student temperament, food and accommodation are modestly priced and plentiful, long-distance transport is good, and some appealing daytrip destinations are nearby, including the country's finest Roman ruins at Conímbriga.

If you're here in May, throw yourself into the spirit of Coimbra's huge, boozy student bash, Queima das Fitas (see under Special Events later in this section).

Beware Mondays, when most museums are closed.

History
The Romans founded a major settlement at nearby Conímbriga, and the Moors settled in Coimbra itself until Christians booted them out in the 12th century. Afonso Henriques made the city his new capital in 1145 but, just over a century later, Afonso III moved the capital to Lisbon. The Universidade de Coimbra, Portugal's first university (and among the first in Europe), was actually founded in Lisbon by Dom Dinis in 1290 but settled here in 1537, attracting a steady stream of teachers, artists and intellectuals from across Europe.

The 16th century was a particularly heady time for Coimbra thanks to Nicolas Chanterène, Jean de Rouen (João de Ruão) and other French sculptors who helped to create here a school of sculpture that was to influence styles all over Portugal.

Today Coimbra's university has fewer students than Lisbon's but remains the country's most prestigious academic establishment. The city's prosperity in modern times, however, has come from its three Ts: tanning, textiles (although Asian competition has many textile firms on the skids) and tourism.

Orientation
Compact Coimbra is best toured on foot, though you can't do it without some climbing. Crowning its hill top is the university, with the old town in a tangle of lanes around and below it.

The new town, locally called 'Baixa', sprawls at the foot of the hill and along the Rio Mondego. Hubs of activity down below include the *mercado municipal* (municipal market) to the north, the pedestrianised shopping axis of Rua Ferreira Borges and Rua Visconde da Luz (traditionally known as the Calçada) to the west, and Praça da República down a huge stairway to the east.

Sights of interest across the river are accessible on foot via the Ponte de Santa Clara. The Ponte Europa, a new bridge 1.4km upstream, due for completion in time for the 2004 European Football Championships (Euro2004), will divert traffic around the town centre to Coimbra's new stadium complex.

From the main bus station on Avenida Fernão de Magalhães it's about 1.2km to the old centre. There are three train stations: Coimbra B (also called *estação velha*, or old station) 2km northwest of the centre; central Coimbra A (also called *estação nova*, or new station, and on timetables called just 'Coimbra'); and Coimbra Parque, south of the centre. Coimbra A and B are linked by a rail shuttle, free for those with an inbound or outbound long-distance ticket.

If you come by car, be ready for traffic jams and scarce parking. One place to leave your vehicle for a day hike around town is across the river on Avenida de Conímbriga.

Information

Tourist Offices Coimbra has two **municipal turismos** *(tourist offices; ☎ 239 832 591; Largo Dom Dinis; open 9am-6pm Mon-Fri, 9am-12.30pm & 2pm-5.30pm Sat & Sun ● ☎ 239 833 202; Praça da República; open 10am-6.30pm Mon-Fri, 10am-1pm & 2.30pm-6.30pm Sat & Sun).*

There's also a **regional turismo** *(☎ 239 855 930; e rtc-coimbra@turismo-centro.pt; Largo da Portagem; open 9am-7pm Mon-Fri mid-June–Sept, 9am-6pm Oct–mid-June; 10am-1pm & 2.30pm-5.30pm Sat & Sun year-round).*

A good town map as well as a very detailed bi-monthly cultural agenda, *Coimbra Viva*, are both available from all three tourist offices.

Money There are numerous banks with ATMs along Avenida Fernão de Magalhães, Avenida Emídio Navarro and Rua Ferreira Borges.

Post & Communications The main post office *(☎ 239 850 700; Avenida Fernão de Magalhães 223, postcode 3000; open 8.30am-6.30pm Mon-Fri)* is best for poste restante. The two **branch post offices** *(Rua Olímpio Nicolau Rui Fernandes; open 8.30am-6.30pm Mon-Fri & 9am-12.30pm Sat ● Praça da República; open 9am-6pm Mon-Fri)* are more convenient.

Three places offering free Internet access for up to 30 minutes are the municipal **Esp@ço Internet** *(37 Praça 8 de Maio; open 10am-8pm Mon-Fri, 10am-10pm Sat & Sun);*

BEIRAS

the **Centro de Juventude** (☎ *239 790 600; Rua Pedro Monteiro 73; open 9am-12.30pm & 2pm-5.30pm Mon-Fri*); and, next door, at the public library in the **Casa Municipal da Cultura** (☎ *239 702 630; Rua Pedro Monteiro; open 10am-12.30pm & 2pm-6.30pm Mon-Fri, 2pm-6pm Sat*), where you must first obtain a free library card.

Internet cafés include **Centralmodem** (*Rua Quebra Costas; open 11am-4am Mon-Fri, 3pm-4am Sat & Sun*) at €0.60 per 15 minutes, and **Coimbra Digital** (*96 Avenida Sá da Bandeira; open 9am-1pm & 2pm-7pm Mon-Fri*) at €0.80 per 15 minutes.

Travel Agencies For student cards and youth travel discounts go to **Usit Tagus** (☎ *239 836 205; Associação Académica de Coimbra, Rua Padre António Vieira*). Other reliable agencies include **Intervisa** (☎ *239 828 904; Avenida Fernão de Magalhães 11*) and **Top Tours** (☎ *239 855 970; Avenida Sá da Bandeira 62*).

Bookshops There's a cluster of bookshops on Rua Ferreira Borges, including **Coimbra Editora** (*Rua Ferreira Borges 75*), which stocks mainly Portuguese-language titles, and the more useful **Livraria Bertrand** (*Rua Ferreira Borges 11*).

Universities The historic Velha Universidade (Old University) is the heart of the university campus and its most interesting part. The **AAC** (*Associação Académica de Coimbra; Rua Padre António Vieira*), the stu-

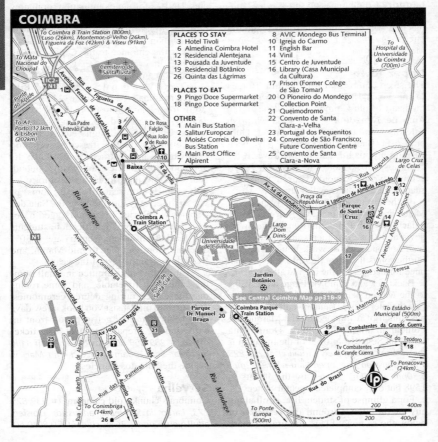

COIMBRA

To Coimbra B Train Station (800m),
Luso (26km), Montemor-o-Velho (26km),
Figueira da Foz (42km) & Viseu (91km)

To Mata
Nacional do
Choupal

To A1,
Porto (123km)
& Lisbon
(202km)

Rua Padre
Estevão Cabral

Cemitério de
Santa Justa

PLACES TO STAY
3 Hotel Tivoli
6 Almedina Coimbra Hotel
12 Residencial Alentejana
13 Pousada da Juventude
19 Residencial Botânico
26 Quinta das Lágrimas

PLACES TO EAT
9 Pingo Doce Supermarket
18 Pingo Doce Supermarket

OTHER
1 Main Bus Station
2 Salitur/Europcar
4 Moisés Correia de Oliveira
   Bus Station
5 Main Post Office
7 Alpirent

8 AVIC Mondego Bus Terminal
10 Igreja do Carmo
11 English Bar
14 Vinil
15 Centro de Juventude
16 Library (Casa Municipal
   da Cultura)
17 Prison (Former Colege
   de São Tomar)
20 O Pioneiro do Mondego
   Collection Point
21 Queimodromo
22 Convento de Santa
   Clara-a-Velha
23 Portugal dos Pequenitos
24 Convento de São Francisco;
   Future Convention Centre
25 Convento de Santa
   Clara-a-Nova

To
Hospital da
Universidade
da Coimbra
(700m)

Largo Cruz
de Celas

Praça da
República

Parque
de Santa
Cruz

Coimbra A
Train Station

Universidade
de Coimbra

Largo
Dom
Dinis

Jardim
Botânico

See Central Coimbra Map pp318-9

Parque
Dr Manuel
Braga

Coimbra Parque
Train Station

Rua Santa Teresa

To Estádio
Municipal (500m)

Rua Combatentes da Grande Guerra

Tv Combatentes
da Grande Guerra

To Teodoro

To Penacova
(24km)

To Conimbriga
(14km)

Rio Mondego

To Ponte
Europa
(500m)

0   200   400m
0   200   400yd

dent union, has a sweaty canteen and some student-oriented shops.

Cultural Centres Catch up with British newspapers at the library of the **British Council** (☎ 239 823 549; Rua de Tomar 4; open 2pm-6pm Mon, 2pm-8pm Tues-Thur, 10am-8pm Fri, 10am-12.30pm & 2.30pm-5pm Sat; closed Aug).

Medical Services & Emergency The **Hospital da Universidade da Coimbra** (☎ 239 400 400; Largo Professor Mota Pinto) is 1.5km northeast of the centre. Two **police stations** (☎ 239 822 022; Rua Olímpio Nicolau Rui Fernandes ● ☎ 239 824 045; Rua Venâncio Rodrigues 25-31) are near the centre.

Laundry Coimbra has no self-service laundrettes but you can leave your laundry to be machine-washed and dried at **Lavandaria Lucira** (Avenida Sá da Bandeira 86; open Mon-Fri, morning Sat).

Upper Town

The steep climb from Rua Ferreira Borges to the Velha Universidade takes you into the heart of old Coimbra. Pass beneath the **Arco de Almedina** – the city's Moorish gateway – and up the stairs known as Quebra Costa (Backbreaker). People have been gasping up this hill and falling down it for centuries; a local story says it was the 19th-century writer Almeida Garrett who persuaded the mayor to install stairs.

To the left up Rua Sub Ripas is the grand Manueline doorway of the early-16th-century **Palácio de Sub Ripas**; its Renaissance windows and stone ornaments are the work of Jean de Rouen, whose workshop was nearby. Further on is the **Torre de Anto**, a tower that once formed part of the town walls.

Backtrack and climb via Largo da Sé Velha to the Museu Nacional Machado de Castro (see the later section) and the dull 'new' campus, much of it founded by the Marquês de Pombal in the 18th century. Dominating Largo da Sé Nova in front of the museum is the severe **sé nova** (new cathedral; ☎ 239 823 138; admission free; open 9am-noon & 2pm-5.30pm Mon-Fri), started by the Jesuits in 1598 but only completed a century later.

For a glimpse of student life, stroll along any of the alleys around the sé velha or below the sé nova. Flags and graffiti mark

the cramped houses known as repúblicas, each housing a dozen or so students from the same region or faculty.

Velha Universidade

The Old University, packed with cultural treasures from the 16th to 18th centuries, is set around a wide square, the **Patio das Escolas**. Here a **statue of João III** turns his back on a fine view of the city and the river (it was he who re-established the university in Coimbra in 1537 and invited renowned scholars to teach here). The square's most prominent feature is a much-photographed 18th-century **clock tower**, nicknamed a cabra (the goat) by students.

From the courtyard gate take the stairway on the right to the **Sala dos Capelos** (Graduates' Hall), a former examination room now used for degree ceremonies. Beyond dull portraits of Portugal's kings is a catwalk with brilliant city views. Below the clock tower is the entrance to the **Capela de São Miguel**, an ornate chapel with a gilded baroque organ.

But everything pales before the **Biblioteca Joanina** (João V Library) next door. A gift from João V himself in the early 18th century, its rosewood, ebony and jacaranda tables, Chinoiserie designs etched in gilt, and ceilings with fine frescoes seem too extravagant and distracting for study. Its 300,000 books, ancient and leather-bound, deal with law, philosophy and theology.

It costs €4 to visit all these rooms, or €2.50 to see only the library or the Sala dos Capelos (half-price for visitors aged 65 or over). With suitable identification, students and teachers from any country get a 30% discount from October to mid-March, and free admission the rest of the year.

Visitors are only admitted in small numbers and on a timetable, and some rooms may be closed during degree ceremonies. The turismo may insist you book a few days ahead, but you may get in if you front up early and are prepared to wait. The **ticket office** (☎ 239 859 800; visits 9am-7pm daily mid-Mar–Sept, 10am-5pm Oct–mid-Mar) is beside the Sala dos Capelos.

Sé Velha

Coimbra's chunky old cathedral (☎ 239 825 273; Largo da Sé Velha; admission cloisters adult/youth under 26 or student €0.80/0.50;

BEIRAS

open 10am-6pm daily, closed afternoon Fri) looks more like a fortress, and deliberately so, since it was built in the late 12th century when the Moors were still a threat.

Little has been done to it since then; even the 16th-century Renaissance doorway in the northern wall is so eroded you hardly notice it. Otherwise, what you see is pure, austere Romanesque, one of the finest Portuguese cathedrals of its time. The interior is equally simple, with the exception of a 16th-century gilded altarpiece.

Museu Nacional Machado de Castro

Housed in a former Bishop's Palace, with a 16th-century loggia overlooking the sé velha and the old town, this museum (☎ 239

823 727; w www.ipmuseus.pt; Largo Dr José Rodrigues) houses one of Portugal's most important collections of 14th- to 16th-century sculpture. Alas, this gem closed in 2003 for renovations, with no firm reopening date at the time of writing. Ask at the turismo for an update.

Igreja de Santa Cruz

From the trendy shops out on Praça 8 de Maio, the 16th-century Santa Cruz Church (☎ 239 822 941; admission cloister €1; open 9am-noon & 2pm-5.45pm Mon-Sat, 4pm-6pm Sun) plunges you back to Manueline and Renaissance times. Step through the Renaissance porch and flamboyant 18th-century arch to find some of the Coimbra School's finest work, including an ornate

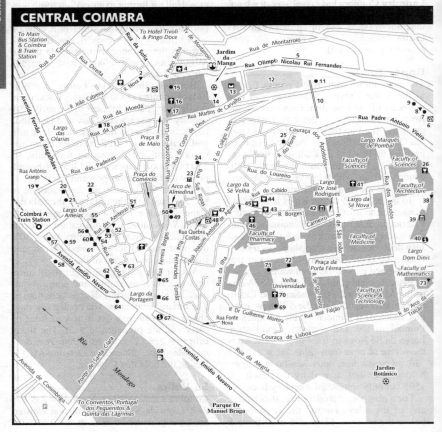

CENTRAL COIMBRA

pulpit and the elaborate tombs – probably carved by Nicolas Chanterène – of Portugal's first kings, Afonso Henriques and Sancho I. The most striking Manueline work is in the restrained 1524 cloister.

At the rear of the church are the **Jardim da Manga** – once part of the cloister – and its curious fountain.

Edifício Chiado

This lovely building on Rua Ferreira Borges, a sunlit confection in wrought iron, opened in 1910 as a commercial emporium. Inside, a branch of the **Museu da Cidade** (☎ *239 840 754; adult/student or senior €1.50/1; open 11am-7pm Tues-Sun*) now hosts exhibitions and a permanent collection of paintings, sculpture, ceramics, furniture and splendid silverware donated by local collector José Carlos Telo de Morais.

Casa Museu Bissaya Barreto

Bissaya Barreto was a local surgeon, scholar and collector whose handsome late-19th-century mansion has been turned into a museum (☎ *239 853 800; Rua da Infantária 23; admission €2.50; open 3pm-6pm Tues-Sun Easter-Oct, 3pm-6pm Tues-Fri Nov-Easter*), full of Portuguese sculpture and painting, Chinese porcelain, old *azulejos* (hand-painted tiles) and period furniture.

Azulejos

Coimbra is adorned with some grand azulejos, the finest of them in the former university hospital, now home to the otherwise staid

BEIRAS

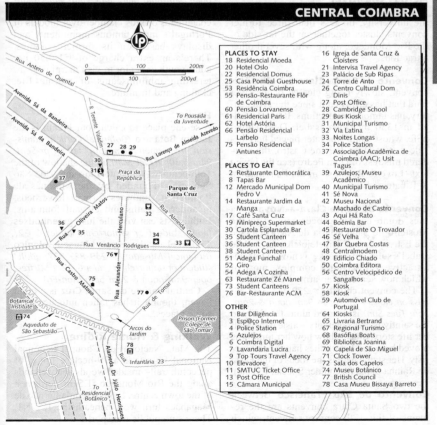

CENTRAL COIMBRA

PLACES TO STAY
18 Residencial Moeda
20 Hotel Oslo
22 Residencial Domus
25 Casa Pombal Guesthouse
53 Residência Coimbra
55 Pensão-Restaurante Flôr de Coimbra
60 Pensão Lorvanense
61 Residencial Paris
62 Hotel Astória
66 Pensão Residencial Larbelo
75 Pensão Residencial Antunes

PLACES TO EAT
2 Restaurante Democrática
8 Tapas Bar
12 Mercado Municipal Dom Pedro V
14 Restaurante Jardim da Manga
17 Café Santa Cruz
19 Minipreço Supermarket
30 Cartola Esplanada Bar
35 Student Canteen
36 Student Canteen
38 Student Canteen
51 Adega Funchal
52 Giro
54 Adega A Cozinha
63 Restaurante Zé Manel
73 Student Canteens
76 Bar-Restaurante ACM

OTHER
1 Bar Diligência
3 Esp@ço Internet
4 Police Station
5 Azulejos
6 Coimbra Digital
7 Lavandaria Lucira
9 Top Tours Travel Agency
10 Elevadore
11 SMTUC Ticket Office
13 Post Office
15 Câmara Municipal
16 Igreja de Santa Cruz & Cloisters
21 Intervisa Travel Agency
23 Palácio de Sub Ripas
24 Torre de Anto
26 Centro Cultural Dom Dinis
27 Post Office
28 Cambridge School
29 Bus Kiosk
31 Municipal Turismo
32 Via Latina
33 Noites Longas
34 Police Station
37 Associação Acadêmica de Coimbra (AAC); Usit Tagus
39 Azulejos; Museu Acadêmico
40 Municipal Turismo
41 Sé Nova
42 Museu Nacional Machado de Castro
43 Aqui Há Rato
44 Boémia Bar
45 Restaurante O Trovador
46 Sé Velha
47 Bar Quebra Costas
48 Centralmodem
49 Edifício Chiado
50 Coimbra Editora
56 Centro Velocipédico de Sangalhos
57 Kiosk
58 Kiosk
59 Automóvel Club de Portugal
64 Kiosks
65 Livraria Bertrand
67 Regional Turismo
68 Basófias Boats
69 Biblioteca Joanina
70 Capela de São Miguel
71 Clock Tower
72 Sala dos Capelos
74 Museu Botânico
77 British Council
78 Casa Museu Bissaya Barreto

and stuffy **Museu Acadêmico** (☎ 239 827 396; Colégio de São Jerónimo; adult/student or senior €1/0.50; open 10am-12.30pm & 2pm-5pm Mon-Fri), around the corner from the municipal turismo on Largo Dom Dinis.

Big outdoor panels opposite the market depict Coimbra's old buildings in their prime.

Prison

The turismo fails to mention one of Coimbra's largest landmarks. When João III moved the university here in the 16th century he also founded several preparatory schools, including the Colege de São Tomar, south of Praça da República. After religious orders were abolished in 1834 this was converted to a prison, which it still is.

Across the River

In a kind of ecclesiastical counterweight to the university, no less than three former convents cluster together on the far side of the Rio Mondego, along with several other attractions.

Convento de Santa Clara-a-Velha This convent, slowly being cleared of the river mud that has drowned it since the 17th century, has famous connections. It was founded in 1330 by Dona Isabel, Dom Dinis' wife, whose tomb was later placed here beside that of Dona Inês de Castro, the murdered mistress of Dom Pedro (see the boxed text 'Love & Revenge' in the Estremadura & Ribatejo chapter).

Convento de Santa Clara-a-Nova Dona Inês' tomb has since been moved to the Mosteiro de Santa Maria de Alcobaça (see the Estremadura & Ribatejo chapter), while Isabel's solid-silver casket is now in this unattractive 17th-century complex, most of which now serves as an army barracks.

The convent **church** (☎ 239 441 674; admission cloister €1; open 9am-noon & 2pm-5pm Tues-Sun) is devoted almost entirely to the saintly Isabel's memory – aisle panels tell her life story, others show how her tomb was moved here and her clothes hang in the sacristy. Her statue here is the focus of the Festa de Rainha Santa (see under Special Events).

Convento de São Francisco Between the two Santa Clara convents are the remains of this 18th-century convent, which did duty as a soap factory in the post-Pombal era. It has now been absorbed into a convention centre that has been under construction, though mired in local politics, for years.

Quinta das Lágrimas Legend says Dona Inês was killed in the gardens of this private estate. It has now been opened as a deluxe hotel (see Places to Stay), although you can visit the **gardens** (admission €0.80; open 9am-5pm daily), including the Fonte dos Amores (Lovers' Fountain), where the dastardly deed is said to have been done.

Portugal dos Pequenitos At this overrated theme park (☎ 239 441 225; adult/youth 5-13 or senior/child under 5 €4/2/free; open 9am-8pm daily June–mid-Sept, 10am-5pm mid-Sept–Feb, 10am-7pm Mar-May), coachloads of kids clamber over models of Portugal's most famous monuments and displays based on its former colonies. There's an extra charge of €1/0.50 per adult/youth or senior to visit marginally interesting minimuseums of marine life, clothing and furniture.

Parks

A serene place to catch your breath is the **Jardim Botânico** (Botanical Garden; admission free; open 9am-8pm daily Apr-Sept, 9am-5.30pm Oct-Mar), in the shadow of the 16th-century Aqueduto (aqueduct) de São Sebastião. Founded by the Marquês de Pombal, it combines formal flowerbeds, meandering paths and elegant fountains. Enthusiasts can visit the lush **greenhouses** (adult/student or senior/child under 6 €2/1.50/free) and the adjacent **Museu Botânico** (Botanical Museum; ☎ 239 822 897; adult/student or senior/child under 6 €2/1.50/free; open 9am-noon & 2pm-5pm Mon-Fri).

Central **Parque de Santa Cruz** is a quiet haven, though it has fallen into decay in some places.

Walking & Horse Riding

The Mata Nacional do Choupal (Choupal National Forest) is a 79-hectare finger of peaceful, trail-threaded woods and wetlands along the Rio Mondego, 1.5km northwest of the town centre. From Avenida Fernão de Magahães turn west beneath the IC2/N1. There's no public transport.

Extravagant Palace Hotel do Buçaco, near Luso

Feeding the pigeons in the back streets, Coimbra   Ruins of the Roman bath house of Conimbriga

With its clear air and amazing scenery Parque Natural da Serra da Estrela is an ideal place for walking

The entry hall of São Bento station, Porto, doubles as an *azulejo* display, with works by Jorge Colaço

It's a wonderland of outdoor cafés at night in Porto's Unesco-listed Ribeira area

Terraced vineyards and orchards in the scenic Douro valley

To trot on horseback around the area contact the **Centro de Hípico de Coimbra** (Coimbra Riding Centre; ☎ 239 837 695) there.

River Trips

Basófias (☎/fax 239 491 900, ☎ 966 040 695) runs boat trips (€8.20, 1¼ hours) on the Rio Mondego, daily except Monday year-round. Departures, from beside Parque Dr Manuel Braga, are at 3pm, 4.30pm and 6pm Tuesday to Sunday, plus 11am and 7.30pm on weekends.

Daily from June to September, **O Pioneiro do Mondego** (☎/fax 239 478 385; call 8am-10am, 1pm-3pm & 8pm-10pm daily) rents kayaks for paddling the Rio Mondego from Penacova to Coimbra, a 25km, four-hour trip costing €15; a shorter version to Torres de Mondego, with transport back to Coimbra, costs the same. A minibus takes you to Penacova from the eastern corner of Coimbra's Parque Dr Manuel Braga at 10am.

Trans Serrano (☎/fax 235 778 938, ☎ 966 217 787; w www.transserrano.com; Rua Forno 6, 3330-325 Góis) organises guided descents of the same stretch for about €15 per person plus lunch. Trips go year-round if there are enough participants; try to call a few days ahead.

Special Events

Queima das Fitas During the Burning of the Ribbons festival, starting on the first Thursday in May, Coimbra's students celebrate the end of the academic year with impressive gusto. The calendar includes a midnight *fado* (Portuguese-style blues)

Glug, Glug, Glug

Queima das Fitas surely rivals Munich's Oktoberfest for European beer-consumption records. The parade features some 100 floats, each with about 30 people on it. In their rush to sponsor individual floats, Portuguese breweries provide a free case of beer for just about every one of those people, to be consumed or given away before the parade ends. Relations between students and police are amazingly friendly, but the strain on local hospitals is heavy, with a strong emphasis on stomach-pumping; and there is a tendency for students to fall into the river.

---

concert in front of the *sé velha*; a week of concerts at the so-called Queimodromo, across the Ponte de Santa Clara; and a massive parade (see the boxed text 'Glug, Glug, Glug') from the hill top down to Portagem, with everyone in their black gowns and coloured top hats.

Festa da Rainha Santa Held around 4 July in even-numbered years, this important festival commemorates the queen-saint Isabel with a procession that takes her statue from the Convento de Santa Clara-a-Nova to Igreja do Carmo and back. Events during the festival (which coincides with the Festa da Cidade, or Town Festival) include folk music, dancing and fireworks.

Other Events Among other annual events in Coimbra are international festivals of music in July and of magic in mid-September (Coimbra is the home of Luís de Matus, Portugal's most famous magician). Encontros de Fotografia, a photography show held throughout November in even-numbered years, is a major European event.

There's folk music and dancing in Praça 8 de Maio and open-air fado at the Arco de Almedina and along Rua Quebra Costas from late June to mid-September, usually on Tuesday and Thursday.

There are sure to be events and exhibitions around town during 2003 in connection with Coimbra's designation as Capital Nacional da Cultura, although there were few details at the time of writing.

Places to Stay – Budget

Camping & Hostels Coimbra's municipal camp site has closed to make way for Euro2004 redevelopment, with no replacement in sight. The next nearest camp sites are two near Penacova, some 25km northeast on the N110.

Coimbra's pleasant **pousada da juventude** (youth hostel; ☎ 239 822 955; e coimbra@ movijovem.pt; Rua Dr António Henriques Seco 12-14; dorm beds €10.50, doubles with toilet €29) is located 500m northeast of Praça da República. From Coimbra A station take northbound bus No 46.

Pensões & Residenciais The neighbouring **Residencial Paris** (☎/fax 239 822 732; Rua da Sota 41; twins with/without bathroom

BEIRAS

from €30/25) and **Pensão Lorvanense** (☎ 239 823 481; *Rua da Sota 27; doubles or twins €25)* have little personality but they do have big, clean rooms and offer good value for this neighbourhood around Coimbra A.

Residencial Domus (☎ 239 828 584; e *resi dencialdomus@sapo.pt; Rua Adelino Veiga 62; doubles/triples from €35/43)*, a family-run place in a shopping zone near Coimbra A, has plain, quiet rooms, including some cheaper ones with shared toilet.

Pensão Residencial Larbelo (☎ 239 829 092, fax 239 829 094; *Largo da Portagem 33; doubles/triples €32.50/42.50)* lacks personality but is bang in the centre, and the rather grand rooms are surprisingly cheap.

Residencial Moeda (☎ 239 824 784, fax 239 834 398; *Rua da Moeda 81; twins/doubles €30/35)*, recently opened near the Igreja de Santa Cruz, has plain, functional rooms with air-con.

Places to Stay – Mid-Range

Rooms at the following places each have a TV, private toilet and shower/bathroom except as noted.

Pensão-Restaurante Flôr de Coimbra (☎ 239 823 865, fax 239 821 545; *Rua do Poço 5; doubles with shower & shared/private toilet May-Sept €25/30, Oct-Apr €20/25)* is a congenial, well-tended place near Coimbra A. Its restaurant is popular with locals, and a buffet breakfast (€2.50) is available from May to September.

Casa Pombal Guesthouse (☎ 239 835 175, fax 239 821 548; *Rua das Flores 18; doubles with/without bathroom from €44/38; closed mid-Dec–mid-Jan)* has everything from bathless cubicles to eyries with huge views. Food options in the neighbourhood are limited, but the room rate includes a superb buffet breakfast. Book ahead if possible.

Residencial Botânico (☎ 239 714 824, fax 239 405 124; *Bairro de São Jose 15; doubles/triples with breakfast €45/58)*, at the bottom of Alameda Dr Júlio Henriques, has big air-con rooms, including family suites. Rates include a good breakfast.

Residencial Alentejana (☎ 239 825 903; e *residencialalentejana@hotmail.com; Rua António Henriques Seco 1; doubles/triples with breakfast €45/60)* offers a mix of handsome old and new rooms.

Residência Coimbra (☎ 239 837 996, fax 239 838 124; *Rua das Azeiteiras 55; twins*

€45), in a street full of modest cafés and restaurants, offers small, quiet twins.

Pensão Residencial Antunes (☎ 239 854 720, fax 239 854 729; *Rua Castro Matoso 8; doubles with breakfast €47.50)* has creaky doubles and that Coimbra rarity – abundant street parking.

Hotel Oslo (☎ 239 829 071/2/3, fax 239 820 614; *Avenida Fernão de Magalhães 25; doubles €60)* combines modest rooms with free parking.

Almedina Coimbra Hotel (☎ 239 855 500; e *geral@residencial-almedina.pt; Avenida Fernão de Magalhães 199; doubles €60)* offers big, plain rooms with double-glazed windows to keep out traffic noise.

Places to Stay – Top End

Rooms in this range each have a private bathroom, air-con and TV.

Hotel Astória (☎ 239 853 020; e astoria@ almeidahotels.com; *Avenida Emídio Navarro 21; doubles with breakfast €95)*, its Art Deco face contemplating the river and Largo da Portagem, has more character than warmth but its rooms (with double-glazed windows) are quiet and plush.

Hotel Tivoli (☎ 239 858 300; e htcoimbra@ mail.telepac.pt; *Rua João Machado; doubles with breakfast €135)* is central Coimbra's 'business-class' hotel, with a pool, sauna and some off-street parking, though surrounding streets are choked with traffic.

Quinta das Lágrimas (☎ 239 802 380, fax 239 441 695; *doubles/twins with breakfast from €110/134)* is the nearest Turihab property, and pretty splendid. Some of its doubles look out on the garden where Dona Inês de Castro is said to have met her tragic end.

Places to Eat

Coimbra dines late, with few restaurants opening for the evening meal before 7pm; those that serve food all day are noted here. Especially at weekends, some of the mid-range places get heavily booked by student groups, making it hard to get in and hard to have a quiet time if you do.

West of the University The dining room at **Pensão-Restaurante Flôr de Coimbra** (☎ 239 823 865; *Rua do Poço 5; mains from €5; open noon-2pm & 7.30pm-9.30pm Mon-Sat)* offers immense helpings, with lots of green vegetables, at honest prices. In addition to meat and fish options, there's always a proper vegetarian main dish or two.

Restaurante Zé Manel *(☎ 239 823 790; Beco do Forno 12; mains from €9; open noon-3pm Mon-Sat, 6.30pm-10pm Mon-Fri)* is tiny, eccentric (papered with knick-knacks and scribbled poems) and popular, so come early or be ready to wait. Try the good *feijoada á leitão* (beans and suckling pig).

Restaurante Democrática *(☎ 239 823 784; Rua Nova; mains from €5; open Mon-Sat)*, family-friendly and multilingual, has good-value standards in a no-frills setting.

A concentration of good-value eateries is in the lanes west of Rua Ferreira Borges, especially along Rua das Azeiteiras.

Giro *(☎ 239 833 020; Rua das Azeiteiras 39; mains about €7; open Mon-Sat)* is a quick-service, good-value *churrasqueira* (grill restaurant); it's open all day.

Adega Funchal *(☎ 239 824 137; Rua das Azeiteiras 18; mains about €7; open Sun-Fri night)* is proud of its *chanfana carne de cabra* (goat stewed in red wine), but offers modest *pratos do dia* (daily specials), too.

Adega A Cozinha *(☎ 239 827 115; Rua das Azeiteiras 65; mains about €8; open Thur-Tues)*, cheerful and locally popular, has meaty half-portion specials under €6 and good shrimp kebabs for €11.

Restaurante Jardim da Manga *(☎ 239 829 156; dishes around €5; open 7am-9.30pm Sun-Fri)*, a student-friendly self-service place at the back of the Jardim da Manga, behind the Igreja de Santa Cruz, has a small menu of meaty dishes tailored to tight budgets.

Around Praça da República At four plain **student canteens**, anyone with a student ID card can queue for a meal for as little as €2 during school-term time. Downstairs behind the Centro de Juventude (see Post & Communications, earlier), a **canteen** *(mains from €3; open 9am-9.30pm Mon-Fri)* features salads and simple meals, though its staff might ask to see student ID.

Bar-Restaurante ACM *(☎ 239 823 633; Rua Alexandre Herculano 21A; half-/full-portions about €3.50/5; open noon-2.30pm & 7pm-9.30pm Mon-Fri, noon-2.30pm Sun)* offers plain fare and quick service. ACM is Portugal's YMCA.

Tapas Bar *(☎ 239 826 048; Avenida Sá da Bandeiras 80; open 10am-4am daily)* is recommended as much for the relaxed late-night scene as for the all-hours food – snacks from 10am, light fish and meat dishes (around €6) from 8pm into the night, and a cheerful bar until the wee hours.

Cafés Top among Coimbra's cafés is **Café Santa Cruz**, a vaulted annexe of the Igreja de Santa Cruz. Sit on creased leather chairs inside or at tables outside.

Cartola Esplanada Bar *(Praça da República)* offers overpriced light meals but is good for student-watching and taking the sun.

Self-Catering The newly modernised town market is **Mercado Municipal Dom Pedro V** *(Rua Olímpio Nicolau Rui Fernandes; open Mon-Sat)*; it is busiest on Saturday. In Rua das Azeiteiras are several small **fruit-and-vegetable shops**, open during the day, at least on weekdays. Supermarkets include **Pingo Doce** *(Rua João de Ruão)* in the Baixa, with another branch *(Travessa Combatentes de Grande Guerra)* southeast of the centre, and **Minipreço** *(Rua António Granjo 6C)*.

Entertainment

Fado Coimbra-style fado is more cerebral than the Lisbon variety, and its adherents staunchly protective. A fracas erupted in Coimbra in 1996 when a woman named Manuela Bravo decided to record a CD of Coimbra fado, which is traditionally sung only by men.

You can listen to it in several *casas de fado* (fado houses) on just about any late Friday or Saturday evening: try **Bar Diligência** *(☎ 239 827 667; Rua Nova 30)*, where the music is usually live; **Boémia Bar** *(☎ 239 834 547; Rua do Cabido 6)*; or **Restaurante O Trovador** *(☎ 239 825 475; Largo da Sé Velha 15-17)*. *Casas de fado* are often restaurants too, usually with a minimum charge equivalent to a small meal or several pricey drinks.

The AAC (student union) sponsors weekly fado performances in the Café Santa Cruz during March, and there's open-air fado at the Arco de Almedina and along Rua Quebra Costas in summer (see Special Events).

Bars & Clubs Bars around Arco de Almedina favour more traditional sounds or easy listening; those nearer Praça da República lean towards disco. Most are open from Monday to Saturday.

BEIRAS

In the former category are **Aqui Há Rato** (☎ *239 824 804; Largo da Sé Velha 20)*, with a dance floor, and **Bar Quebra Costas** (☎ *239 821 661; Rua Quebra Costas 45-49)*. In the latter category are **Noites Longas** *(Rua Almeida Garrett 9)* and the cavernous bar at **Centro Cultural Dom Dinis** (☎ *239 838 593; Largo Marquês de Pombal)*, with live music on Friday and Saturday (though you may be asked for student ID).

The **English Bar** *(Rua Lourenço de Almeida Azevedo 24)* has light meals downstairs and a bar with draught Murphy's upstairs. Another agreeable night stop is the **Tapas Bar** *(see Places to Eat)*.

Popular discos include **Via Latina** (☎ *239 820 293; Rua Almeida Garrett 1; open Mon-Sat)* and **Vinil** (☎ *239 404 047; Avenida Afonso Henriques 43; open Tues-Sat)*.

Spectator Sports

Académica is the name of Coimbra's second-division football team and its first-division rugby team, both of which play at the **Estádio Municipal** (☎ *239 701 605)*, 1.5km east of the centre (take bus No 7T from Coimbra A, or No 5, 7, 11 or 24 from Praça da República). The stadium is being enlarged for Euro2004, and the surrounding neighbourhood heavily redeveloped.

Getting There & Away

Bus From the main bus station *(Avenida Fernão de Magalhães)*, **RBL/Rede Expressos** (☎ *239 827 081)* caters for most major destinations. At least a dozen buses each go daily to Lisbon (€9, 2½ hours) and to Porto (€8.40, 1½ hours), and there are frequent express services to Braga (€9.50, 2½ hours), Évora (€11.70, 4¼ hours) and Faro (€17, 7½ hours). RBL also goes to Luso (see Luso & the Mata Nacional do Buçaco later in this chapter). In winter there are frequent services to Seia (€8.20, 1¾ hours), Guarda (€9, three hours) and also to other points around the Parque Natural da Serra da Estrela.

AVIC Mondego (☎ *239 820 141; Rua João de Ruão 18; open Mon-Sat)* and RBL run buses to Condeixa and Conimbriga (see the Conimbriga section). **Moisés Correia de Oliveira** (☎ *239 828 263; Rua Dr Rosa Falção 10; open Mon-Fri)* and Rede Expressos have multiple daily services to Figueira da Foz (€2.90, 1½ hours).

Train A few fast international trains stop only at Coimbra B, but most trains call at both Coimbra A (called just 'Coimbra' on timetables) and Coimbra B. International bookings must be made at Coimbra A. There's no left-luggage office at either station.

Coimbra is linked by seven daily *intercidade* (IC) trains to Lisbon (€10.30, 2¼ hours) and four to Porto (€7.20, 1¼ hours). Additional *interregional* (IR) services take 30 minutes longer and cost about €2 less. IR trains also run to Luso/Buçaco and to Figueira da Foz.

Car The local branch of the **Automóvel Club de Portugal** *(ACP; ☎ 239 852 020; Avenida Emídio Navarro 6)* is by Coimbra A.

Car-rental agencies include **Avis** (☎ *239 834 786; Coimbra A station)*, **Salitur/Europcar** (☎ *239 838 983; Edifício Tricana, Rua Padre Estevão Cabral)* and **Alpirent** (☎ *239 821 999; Avenida Fernão de Magalhães 234)*. All of these companies will drop off the rental car at your hotel.

Getting Around

Bus Green, university-operated Ecovia minibuses run about every 10 minutes on weekdays and Saturday morning, on two routes – one from the bus station via Avenida Sá da Bandeira and Rua Padre António Vieira to Largo Dom Dinis and on to the stadium, and the other from the hospital via Praça da República to the bus station. Tickets (purchased on board) cost €1.50/2.50 for two/four trips.

The only municipal line serving the university is the No 1 from Largo da Portagem and Coimbra A, via the Baixa. Nos 3, 8 and 29 go from Coimbra A to Praça da República. Multiuse tickets (two/five/10 trips for €0.90/2.10/4) – also usable on the *elevadore* (see the next section) – are available at the **SMTUC office** (☎ *239 824 175; Largo do Mercado; open 7.30am-7.30pm Mon-Fri, 8am-1pm Sat)* at the foot of the *elevadore*, at official kiosks such as the one on Praça da República and at also some *tabacarias* (tobacconist/newsagent). Tickets bought on board cost €1.20 per trip.

Elevadore do Mercado The *elevadore* *(7.30am-11.30pm Mon-Sat, 9am-11.30pm Sun)* – a combination of elevator, walkway and funicular between the market and the university – can save you a tedious walk, though it's slow and fickle. See the earlier Bus section about where to buy tickets, which you punch once for each ascent or descent. You can't buy tickets at the top.

Bicycle For mountain-bike rental, **Centro Velocipédico de Sangalhos** (☎ 239 824 646; Rua da Sota 23; open 9am-7pm Mon-Fri) charges €7.50 per day.

AROUND COIMBRA
Conimbriga
The Roman ruins at Conimbriga, 16km southwest of Coimbra, are the finest you'll see in Portugal and among the best preserved in the Iberian Peninsula. The Conimbriga site actually dates back to Celtic times (*briga* is a Celtic term for a defended area) but when the Romans settled here in the 1st century AD they developed it into a major city on the route from Lisbon (Olisipo) to Braga (Bracara Augusta).

In the 3rd century the townsfolk, threatened by invading tribes, built a huge defensive wall right through the town centre, abandoning the residential area. This wasn't enough to stop the Suevi seizing the town in 468, and the inhabitants fled to nearby Aeminius (Coimbra) – thereby saving Conimbriga from destruction.

Museum It's worth visiting the small museum (☎ 239 941 177; admission including ruins €3; open 10am-1pm & 2pm-8pm Tues-Sun mid-Mar–mid-Sept, to 6pm mid-Sept–mid-Mar) first, to get a grip on Conimbriga's history and layout. There are no English labels in the museum but the displays are excellent, presenting every aspect of Roman life from hairbands to hoes. Murals, mosaics and temple medallions, statues and tombstones are also on display. There's a café-restaurant at the back.

Ruins The defensive wall slices like a scar through the site (admission including museum €3; open 9am-1pm & 2pm-8pm daily mid-Mar–mid-Sept, to 6pm mid-Sept–mid-Mar). Outside the wall is the so-called Casa dos Repuxos (House of Fountains); though partly destroyed during the wall's construction, the layout of ponds and rooms is obvious. There are some striking mosaic floors showing the four seasons and various hunting scenes.

The site's most important villa, on the other side of the wall, is said to have belonged to one Cantaber, whose wife and children were seized by the Suevi in an attack in 465. It's a palace of a place, with baths, pools and a sophisticated underground heating system.

Excavations continue in the outer areas. Eye-catching features include the remains of a 3km-long aqueduct, which led up to a hill-top bathing complex, and a forum, once surrounded by covered porticoes.

Getting There & Away You can catch a bus from Coimbra directly to the site (€1.50, 30 minutes) with **AVIC Mondego** (☎ 239 820 141) at 9.05am or 9.35am (only 9.35am at weekends). Buses depart for the return trip at 1pm and 6pm (only 6pm at weekends).

There's also a service to Condeixa (€1.40) with AVIC Mondego about every half-hour (less often at weekends) and less often with **RBL** (☎ 239 827 081). But from Condeixa to the site it's an uphill, poorly signposted 2km walk, some of it along the hard shoulder of a high-speed road.

Luso & the Mata Nacional do Buçaco
The 105-hectare Buçaco (or Bussaco) National Forest, on the slopes of the Serra do Buçaco 24km northeast of Coimbra, is no ordinary forest. For centuries it's been a religious haven, a place of sanctity and peace, surrounded by a high stone wall. Even today, overrun by weekend picnickers and summer tourists, it retains its mystical (and botanical) appeal. There are an astounding 700 different tree species, including huge Mexican cedars, giant ferns and ginkgos.

For decades Portuguese tourists have also been coming to the prim spa town of Luso (population about 2000) just to the west, to soak in its waters, a balm for everything from gout to asthma. The forest and spa make an easy day trip from Coimbra. If you want to linger here, Luso has a handful of *residenciais* (guesthouses). Travellers with the dosh can stay at an astonishing neo-Manueline palace right in the forest.

History The area was probably used as a refuge by 2nd-century Christians, although the earliest known hermitage was founded

BEIRAS

in the 6th century by Benedictine monks. In 1628 this was sold to Carmelite monks, who embarked on an extensive programme of forestation, introducing exotic species, marking out cobbled paths and enclosing the forest within walls. It grew so famous that in 1643 Pope Urban VIII decreed that anyone damaging the trees would be excommunicated.

The peace was briefly shattered on a September morning in 1810, during the Peninsular War, when Napoleon's forces under Masséna were soundly beaten by the Anglo-Portuguese army of the future Duke of Wellington (the battle is re-enacted as part of a local fair here every 27 September). In 1834, when religious orders throughout Portugal were abolished, the forest became state property and further tree species were introduced.

Orientation & Information From Luso-Buçaco train station it's a 15-minute walk downhill (east) via Rua Dr António Granjo to the turismo and spa in the centre of Luso. Buses stop on Rua Emídio Navarro, near the turismo. By road the Portas das Ameias, the nearest gate into the forest, is 900m east of the turismo. From May to October there's a charge of €5 per car entering the forest, though walkers go in free.

The **turismo** (☎ 231 939 133; e jtlb@ oninet.pt; Rua Emídio Navarro; open 9am-7pm Mon-Fri June-Sept, 9.30am-12.30pm & 2pm-6pm Oct-May; 10am-1pm & 3pm-5pm Sat-Sun year-round) has accommodation information, town and forest maps, and leaflets (in English) detailing flora and points of historical interest.

Forest The aromatic forest is threaded with trails, dotted with crumbling chapels and graced with ponds and fountains. Some popular trails lead to areas of great beauty, such as the Vale dos Fetos (Valley of Ferns), but you can get enjoyably lost on more overgrown routes. Among several fine viewpoints is 545m **Cruz Alta**, reached by a path called the Via Sacra.

What most visitors come to see is the **Palace Hotel do Buçaco**. This over-the-top wedding cake of a building – all turrets and spires, neo-Manueline carving and azulejos with scenes from *Os Lusíados* – was built in 1907 as a royal summer residence, on the

site of a 17th-century Carmelite monastery. Three years later the monarchy was abolished, so the royals hardly got a look-in. It's now a deluxe hotel (see Places to Stay), though staff are surprisingly tolerant of all the gawpers. By road the hotel is 2.1km from the Portas das Ameias.

All that remains of the monastery, the Convento Santa Cruz do Buçaco, is a tiny **church** (admission €0.50; open 9am-12.30pm & 2pm-5.30pm Tues-Sat), in the shadow of the Palace Hotel. Inside are a few cork-lined cells (in one of which Wellington spent the night before the 1810 battle) and a frieze of azulejos depicting the battle.

Museu Militar Those interested in the Battle of Buçaco will find maps, weapons and other paraphernalia in a small military museum (adult/child under 10 or senior €1/free; open 10am-noon & 2pm-5pm Tues-Sun), just outside the northeastern Portas da Rainha.

Spa The **Termas de Luso** (☎ 231 937 444; open 8am-noon & 4pm-7pm daily) welcomes drop-in visitors only from May to October, and prefers that they visit only in the afternoon. The main 'therapies' available to day visitors are general massage (€13) – just the ticket after a long walk in the forest – and a kind of high-velocity shower called duche de Vichy plus massage (€14).

Other Attractions You can fill your bottle with spa water at the **Fonte de São João** (fountain), a block east of the turismo. Beside the fountain is Luso's **former casino**, now a venue for exhibitions, folk dancing and fado. There's a municipal **swimming pool** west of the centre in Parque do Largo.

Places to Stay Occupying a small site, **Orbitur camping ground** (☎ 231 930 916, fax 231 930 917; Bairro do Comendador Melo Pimenta; adult/tent/car €3.20/2.60/3.30; open year-round) is 1.3km south of the turismo. Bungalows are also available.

Luso has plenty of quartos (private rooms); look for the signs or check the turismo's good list. Doubles cost €15 to €20.

Modestly priced pensões (guesthouses) include the **Central** (☎ 231 939 254; Rua Emídio Navarro; doubles with breakfast from €40), and the **Astória** (☎ 231 939 182; Rua

Emídio Navarro; doubles €38), beside the turismo.

Pensão Alegre (☎ 231 930 256; *Rua Emídio Navarro; doubles with breakfast from €35*) is a 19th-century townhouse with swimming pool and large doubles.

Palace Hotel do Buçaco (☎ 231 937 970; e *bussaco-palace@clix.pt; doubles from €170*) will put you in a royal mood.

Places to Eat The Art Deco **Salão de chá** (tearoom), by the Fonte de São João, perfectly capturing the spa-town atmosphere, is the place for tea and cakes.

Most *pensões* have reasonable restaurants of their own.

Varanda do Lago (☎ 231 930 888; *Parque do Largo; meals about €10; open Tues-Sun*), 350m west of the turismo and overlooking the municipal park's pleasant lake, is the budgeteer's choice. Omelettes and snacks are also available.

Restaurante Lourenços (☎ 231 939 474; *Rua Emídio Navarro; mains from €6; open Thur-Tues*), a block east of the turismo, offers regional specialities – including the ubiquitous *leitão a bairrada* (roast suckling pig) – in a dignified setting.

Palace Hotel do Buçaco (see Places to Stay) offers a blowout meal for about €40 per person plus drinks.

Getting There & Away Buses are the most convenient for a day trip. RBL has three leaving by 1pm from Coimbra's main bus station (€2.30, 50 minutes) on weekdays, two Saturday and one Sunday, all continuing to the Palace Hotel do Buçaco. The last bus back leaves from the Palace Hotel at about 6.25pm (4.25pm Sunday).

The only trains of any use depart from Coimbra A at about 7.40am and 11.45am (€1.20, 30 minutes). The last train back departs from Luso-Buçaco station at about 6pm.

The train schedules change, so check with the turismo or station for current times.

Reserva Natural do Paúl de Arzila

Bird-watchers and other nature fans may wish to detour to the 535-hectare Arzila Marsh Natural Reserve, home to some 120 species of resident and migratory birds, as well as otters. There is an **on-site centre** (☎ 239 980 500), from where you can take a two-hour interpretive walk. For further information, contact the **main office** (☎ 239 499 020) in the Mata Nacional do Choupal, Coimbra.

PIÓDÃO
postcode 6285 • pop 60 • elevation 690m

Arcing up into the Serra da Estrela from the southwest is a beautiful, surprisingly remote range of vertiginous ridges, deeply cut valleys, frisky rivers and virgin woodland called the Serra de Açor (Goshawk Mountains). Until the 1970s many of its settlements were reachable only by pavement, and even now a walk here is like slipping through a time warp.

Clinging to the side of a terraced valley in the upper range, with the peaks of the Serra da Estrela peeping over the top, is the village of Piódão (say **pyoh**-dow(n) or **pyoh**-do(m)e), a serene, curiously picturesque composition in grey slate. Until 1972 the nearest roadhead was 12km away. So remote was the village that a 19th-century Robin Hood figure called João Brandão made it his hide-out.

Diogo Lopes Pacheco, one of Inês de Castro's assassins (see the boxed text 'Love & Revenge' in the Estremadura & Ribatejo chapter), is said to have quietly returned from Spain and settled here.

But Piódão has been wrenched from isolation with its designation as one of 10 Aldeias Históricas (Historic Villages) de Portugal in the Serra da Estrela region (others include Monsanto, Sortelha, Almeida and Idanha-a-Velha). Money is flowing in for the restoration of its trademark schist-walled, slate-roofed houses, many of which now sport shiny brass fittings, electricity meters, and doors and window frames of sky-blue (in support of a local story that the old village store only sold one colour).

Cafés and handicrafts shops are sprouting around the little square. Looming over everything is a mammoth *'pousada'* built by Inatel, a Portuguese workers' organisation with a network of hotels, camp sites and leisure programmes, and co-sponsor (with the EU's European Fund for Local Development) of the Historic Villages scheme. Some people worry that Piódão may go the way of some of its more lifeless fellow Historic Villages; however, it's a lovely place for a visit, and the gorgeous hills beg to be explored.

BEIRAS

Orientation & Information

Houses and adjacent fields descend in terraces to Largo Cónego Manuel Fernandes Nogueira – smaller than its name – and the fairy-tale parish church, the Igreja Nossa Senhora Conceição. The village **turismo** (☎ 235 732 787; open 10am-noon & 1pm-6pm Sat-Wed June-Sept, 9am-noon & 1pm-5pm Wed-Sun Oct-May) is just to the right of the church.

Things to See & Do

The village itself is the main attraction; note the many doorways with crosses over them, said to offer protection against curses and thunderstorms. Alternatively, head northeast to the equally vertical and almost equally picturesque hamlets of **Foz d'Égua**, on a path that gently drops about 200m in 2.8km, or **Chãs d'Égua**, a fairly level 4km away. The turismo has a village map, and a free English-language booklet on these and other local walks, with some usable topographic maps.

Two adventure companies with **walking** and **cycling** programmes in the area, as well as descents of the Rio Alva which marks the northern edge of the Serra de Açor, are Trans Serrano and Cumes do Açor; see Activities in the introduction to this chapter for details.

Special Events

The area's patron saint, São Pedro do Açor, is honoured with a Mass, procession and ball, and a handicrafts fair, during the Santos Populares no Piódão on the last weekend in June.

Places to Stay

Parque de Campismo de Côja (☎ 235 729 666; e fpcampismo.pt; Côja; adult/tent/car €2.50/2/1.90; open mid-Mar–mid-Oct), a well-equipped facility 21km west on the Rio Alva, is open to Camping Card International (CCI) holders (see Visas & Documents in the Facts for the Visitor chapter).

Campismo de Ponte de Trés Entradas (☎ 238 670 050; e ponte3entradas@mail .telepac.pt; adult/tent/car €2.80/2.50/2.40; open Dec-Oct), a riverside place 30km from Piódão near Avô, also has bungalows.

Parque de Campismo de Arganil (☎ 235 205 706; Sarzedo; adult/tent/car €3.20/2.60/ 3.30; open year-round) is an Orbitur site, 33km from Piódão near Arganil.

Parque de Campismo da Bica (☎ 235 731 382; person/site €1.90/2.70; open mid-June–mid-Sept) is a spartan option, 39km from Piódão at Pomares.

There are *quartos* everywhere, of uneven quality and seriously overpriced at about €25 per person.

Casas de Aldeia (☎ 235 731 424; doubles €25, with toilet/bathroom €40/65) is a private house just beyond the centre, kitted out with help from the village-improvement committee. The rooms have kitchenettes.

Casa da Padaria (☎ 235 732 773), **Casa do Algar** (☎ 235 746 720) and **Casa do Malhadinho** (☎ 235 746 720) are village Turihab properties with doubles from €35 to €40 (breakfast included).

The oversized caricature of a Piódão house, under construction on a ridge above the village, is set to become the **Estalagem do Piódão** (☎ 235 730 100, fax 235 730 104), a hotel with en-suite rooms and a restaurant, run by Inatel.

Places to Eat

Two simple cafés on the *largo* (small square), **Pacheco** and **A Gruta**, serve pastries and toasted sandwiches.

Restaurante O Fontinha (☎ 235 731 151; mains about €6; open daily), one lane back from the *largo*, was the village's only restaurant at the time of writing; it's gloomy and uninspiring.

Getting There & Away

The only transport other than car or bicycle is a bus from Arganil that stops in the *largo* on Monday and Thursday and goes right back, rendering it useless for either a day or an overnight trip.

The area's breathtaking views, narrow roads and sheer drops are a lethal combination for drivers, who should also note that side roads marked '4WD' are axle-breakers for ordinary cars.

FIGUEIRA DA FOZ
pop 27,700 • postcode 3080

Once beloved by Spanish beach-seekers, the old-fashioned resort and fishing port of Figueira da Foz (fi-**guy**-ra da **fosh**) still has a faithful, mostly Portuguese following. Some come for the casino, some for the surf (this is a regular championship venue) and some just to loll on its vast beach. There's plenty of accommodation, restaurants and bars, though high prices may come as a surprise after Coimbra, and cheap rooms are hard to find in midsummer.

Orientation

The town is 45km west of Coimbra at the mouth *(foz)* of the Rio Mondego. Just inland from the beach and the 16th-century Forte de Santa Catarina is a knot of streets with the turismo, most of the accommodation and restaurants, and the casino. Seafront development continues clear to Buarcos, a former fishing village 3km to the north.

The train station is 1.5km east of the beach (for local transport see Getting Around later in this section); the bus station is slightly closer. High-season parking is a headache, even in the evenings, thanks to the casino.

Information

The **turismo** (☎ *233 422 610;* **e** *turismofigue ira@mail.telepac.pt; Avenida 25 de Abril; open 9am-midnight daily June-Sept; 9am-12.30pm & 2pm-5.30pm Mon-Fri, 10am-12.30pm & 2.30pm-6.30pm Sat & Sun Oct- May)* faces

the beach. During renovations (expected to last at least until summer 2003) the turismo is temporarily located about a block to the north.

Banks on Avenida Foz do Mondego and Praça 8 de Maio all have ATMs. The **main post office** *(Passeio Infante Dom Henrique; open 8.30am-6.30pm Mon-Fri, 9am-12.30pm Sat)* faces the *jardim municipal* (town garden), and there's a **branch** *(Rua Miguel Bombarda 76; open 9am-12.30 & 2pm-6pm Mon-Fri)* near the turismo.

A newsagent called **Press Center** *(Rua Bernardo Lopes 113)* stocks a few foreign newspapers.

Beaches

Figueira's beach is immense and shadeless, and packed and scorching in August.

For more character and more surf, head north to Buarcos. Alfredo Farreca Rodrigues runs buses from the train station via the mercado municipal and the turismo to Buarcos (€0.70) every half-hour on weekdays and at least hourly at weekends, with additional services (Teimoso) from 7am to 9am weekdays.

FIGUEIRA DA FOZ

PLACES TO STAY
18 Pensão Residencial Bela Figueira
21 Hotel Wellington
23 Pensão Central
25 Hotel Hispânia
29 Pensão Residencial Moderna
30 Pensão Sãozinha

PLACES TO EAT
12 Pastelaria Restaurante Acrópole
17 Cervejaria Bergano; Emanha
20 Restaurante Caçarola II
27 Mercado Municipal

OTHER
1 Bus Station
2 Museu Municipal do Dr Santos Rocha
3 Praça de Toros
4 AFGA Travel Agency; Buses to Porto
5 Bergantim
6 Saltwater Pool
7 Temporary Turismo
8 Post Office
9 Dom Copo
10 Cocktail
11 Estúdio 24
13 Press Center
14 Viagens Marcos
15 AVIC Buses to Lisbon
16 Turismo
19 Perfumaria Pub
22 Casino da Figueira
24 Dona Bárbara
26 Rolls Bar
28 Main Post Office
31 Câmara Municipal

To Buarcos & Restaurante Dory Negro (1.5km), Serra de Boa Viagem (4km) & Praia de Quiaios (10km)

To Parque Municipal de Campismo (1.6km)

Praia da Figueira da Foz

Forte de Santa Catarina

To Train Station (450m), IC1 (1.3km), Praia de Cabadelo (3km), Foz do Mondego & Orbitur Camping Grounds (3.5km), Praia de Gala (4km), Montemor-o-Velho (16km), Praia de Mira via IC1 (42km), Coimbra (45km) & Aveiro (64km)

Rio Mondego

BEIRAS

For more seclusion, continue on around the Cabo Mondego headland to **Praia de Quiaios**, about 10km north of Figueira da Foz. AVIC services run from the bus station to Quiaios (€1.10) seven times daily (less often on weekends).

South across the mouth of the Rio Mondego is **Praia de Cabedelo**, another prime surfing venue; a little further on (4km from Figueira) is **Praia de Gala**. Alfredo Farreca Rodrigues buses to Cova run from the train station via the mercado municipal to Cabedelo and Gala (both €0.70) every half-hour on weekdays (less often at weekends).

Saltwater Pool

The Atlantic Ocean notwithstanding, you'd be surprised at the number of visitors who prefer to take their seawater in a pool. There's an open-air saltwater pool *(open 9am–around 7pm daily June–at least Sept)* a block north of the turismo.

Museu Municipal do Dr Santos Rocha

This modern museum *(☎ 233 402 840; Rua Calouste Gulbenkian; adult/child under 12 €1.30/free; open 9.30am-5.15pm Tues-Sun, 9.30am-2.15pm Sat & Sun Oct-May)*, beside Parque das Abadias, houses a surprisingly rich archaeological collection and a less impressive fine-arts section.

Serra de Boa Viagem

For those with wheels, this headland, found 4km north of Figueira and carpeted in pines, eucalyptus and acacias, is a fine place for panoramas, picnics and cool walks. Take the coastal road to Buarcos, turn right at the lighthouse and follow the signs to Boa Viagem.

Special Events

The Festas da Cidade, or Town Festival, carries on for two weeks at the end of June, with folk music, parades and concerts at the *praça de toros* (bullring).

The town is mobbed for about a week in late July or August in most years for the Mundialito de Futebol de Praia (World Beach-Football Championships).

Figueira has hosted its own **Festival Internacional de Cinema** *(☎ 218 126 231)* for more than 25 years; it takes place in the casino during the first 10 days of September.

Places to Stay

The turismo has details of a few *quartos* for €20 to €25 per double. Touts may approach you at the bus or train station with their own offers.

Camping Parque Municipal de Campismo *(☎ 233 402 810, fax 233 402 818; Estrada de Tavarede; adult/tent/car €2/1.50/1.50; open year-round)*, northeast of the centre, is 2km from the beach but there's a pool nearby. Take a Casal de Areia bus (€0.70, six to 10 daily) from the train station, mercado municipal or Parque Abadias.

Foz do Mondego *(☎ 233 402 740, fax 233 402 749; e info@fpcampismo.pt; Praia de Cabedelo; adult/tent/car €2.60/2.10/1.90; open mid-Jan–mid-Nov)* requires a CCI (see Visas & Documents in the Facts for the Visitor chapter).

Orbitur *(☎ 233 431 492; e info@orbitur.pt; Praia de Gala; adult/tent/car €3.80/3/3.30; open year-round)*, south of Foz do Mondego, is 1km from the nearest bus stop.

Parque de Campismo de Quiaios *(☎ 233 910 499, fax 233 910 260; Praia de Quiaios; adult/tent/car €2/1.80/1.80; open year-round)* is by the seaside, 8km north of Figueira.

For transport details to Cabedelo and Quiaios, see Beaches earlier in this chapter.

Pensões & Residenciais Figueira brims with accommodation. Prices ratchet up in July and rise even further in August, but off-season rates can drop by half. The following places have private showers or bathrooms unless noted.

Residencial Sãozinha *(☎ 233 425 243; Ladeira do Monte 43; twins/doubles €30/35)* is a plain, quiet place near the train station. The rooms have a shared shower and toilet.

Pensão Residencial Moderna *(☎ 233 422 701; Praça 8 de Maio 61; doubles with breakfast from €40)* has a whiff of faded elegance about it, with a rear garden and handsome, high-ceilinged rooms (with bathroom). It has free off-street parking.

Pensão Central *(☎ 233 422 308; e pensaocentral@figueira.net; Rua Bernardo Lopes 36; doubles with breakfast €40)* has immense, fully equipped doubles.

Pensão Residencial Bela Figueira *(☎ 233 422 728, fax 233 429 960; Rua Miguel Bombarda 13; doubles with/without bathroom from €48/39)*, around the block from the turismo, has plain, sunny rooms; breakfast is included.

Hotels A dignified throwback to earlier days, **Hotel Hispânia** (☎ 233 422 164, fax 233 429 664; Rua Dr Francisco António Dinis 61; doubles/triples with breakfast €40/50) has threadbare but good-value rooms, each with a bathroom. Rates include off-street parking.

Hotel **Wellington** (☎ 233 426 767/8; e hotelwellington@mail.telepac.pt; Rua Dr Calado 23-27; doubles with breakfast €80), in the town centre, is good value; its rooms have air-con and cable TV. Off-street parking is available.

Places to Eat
Younger visitors sun themselves at **Cervejaria Bergano** and an ice-cream shop called **Emanha 2** on Esplanada Silva Guimarães.

Indian-Portuguese fare in the restaurant at **Pensão Residencial Bela Figueira** (restaurant open June-Sept; meals around €11) – see Places to Stay – makes a welcome change.

Pastelaria Restaurante Acrópole (☎ 233 428 948; Rua Bernardo Lopes 76; open all day Wed-Mon) has half a dozen tables at the back where you can order pretty good burgers and omelettes (about €5) in an atmosphere devoid of pretension – a good budget choice.

Restaurante Caçarola II (☎ 233 426 930; Rua Bernardo Lopes 85; mains from €9; open 9am-2am Mon-Thur, 9am-4am Fri & Sat) is a popular, hectic *marisqueira* (seafood restaurant) dishing up good-value fish dishes; or you can have a slap-up seafood dinner for about €15 plus drinks.

Seafood is cheaper in Buarcos. The huge menu at **Restaurante Dory Negro** (☎ 233 421 333; Largo Caras Direitas 16, Buarcos; open Wed-Mon) includes crab, lobster, shrimps, clams and deep-sea fish, and you can eat well for as little as €10 plus drinks. Its scrumptious *arroz de marisco*, a rich stew of seafood and rice, must be booked at least a day ahead.

The **mercado municipal** (Passeio Infante Dom Henrique; open daily Apr-Oct) is opposite the *jardim municipal*.

Entertainment
Casinos The **Casino da Figueira** (☎ 233 408 400; Rua Bernardo Lopes; open 3pm-3am daily) has roulette (€4 admission) and slot machines, plus a cinema (€4), piano bar, disco (Kastigo) and live entertainment after

11pm most nights. You're not welcome at night in beach attire, flip-flops (thongs) or sports shoes.

Bars & Clubs Figueira's best bars are **Estúdio 24** (☎ 233 420 674; Rua Dr Calado 24), **Dona Bárbara** (☎ 233 426 060; Rua Acadêmico Zagalo 7) and **Rolls** (☎ 233 426 157; Rua Poeta Acácio Antunes 1E). Others worth a try are **Dom Copo** (☎ 233 426 817; Rua de São Lourenço 13), **Cocktail** (☎ 233 420 446; 1a Travessa de São Lourenço 4) and **Perfumaria Pub** (☎ 233 426 442; Rua Dr Calado 37).

Flashen (☎ 233 910 377), in Praia de Quiaios, is tops among the local discos. Others are **Bergantim** (☎ 233 423 885; Rua Dr A Lopes Guimarães), and **Kastigo** (☎ 233 408 400) in the casino.

Getting There & Away
Bus Figueira is served by three long-distance companies located at the main terminal: **Moisés Correia de Oliveira** (☎ 233 426 703), **AVIC Mondego** (☎ 233 422 648) and **RBL/Rede Expressos** (☎ 233 423 095). Oliveira runs multiple daily services via Montemor-o-Velho (see the Around Figueira da Foz section) to Coimbra (€2.90, 1½ hours). Useful AVIC routes are to Mira (see Praia de Mira) and up to five buses daily to Aveiro (€6.70, 1½ hours). Services thin out at weekends.

Rede Expressos also has Mira and Aveiro connections, plus daily express trains to Lisbon (€9.20, three hours). An AVIC express bus from Buarcos to Lisbon stops near the turismo at 7am each weekday and 6.30pm Sunday; buy tickets on board or book ahead at **Viagens Marcos** (☎ 233 425 113; Rua Maestro David de Sousa 103). An express bus runs to Porto each weekday from the **AFGA travel agency** (☎ 233 402 222; Avenida Miguel Bombarda 79).

For details on transport to local beaches, see Beaches earlier in this section.

Train Two daily services link Figueira da Foz with Lisbon via Caldas da Rainha and Leiria. Trains to/from Coimbra (€1.50, one hour) are superior to buses, with connections every hour or two all day long.

Getting Around
Local buses of **Alfredo Farreca Rodrigues** (☎ 233 422 828) run from the train station

BEIRAS

past the mercado municipal (€0.50) and turismo (€0.70) to Buarcos every half-hour on weekdays and at least hourly on weekends.

AROUND FIGUEIRA DA FOZ
Montemor-o-Velho
A stunning hill-top **castle** *(admission free; open 10am-12.30pm & 2pm-5pm Tues-Sun)* rises like a brooding ghost above marshy fields 16km east of Figueira da Foz, on the N111 to Coimbra. Montemor-o-Velho served both the Romans and the Moors. The rulers of the new kingdom of Portugal made it a royal retreat, though no sizable town ever grew around it.

The place begs for a bit of pageantry; it's a letdown inside, except for a few restored towers and a charming **Mozarab chapel** *(admission €0.50)*, Romanesque in outline. The lawns and flower beds are less photogenic than the views across the landscape, and the main drama is derived from watching kids climbing on the unfenced battlements.

There are several restaurants and lots of bus parking in the village beneath the castle's southern and eastern walls, though little in the way of accommodation.

Trains between Coimbra (€1, 45 minutes) and Figueira da Foz (€1.10, 30 minutes) stop here every hour or two. Moisés Correia de Oliveira buses between Coimbra (€2.30, 55 minutes) and Figueira (€1.70, 30 minutes) stop 10 to 15 times daily (but just twice on Sunday).

PRAIA DE MIRA
In the 50km of mostly deserted coastline between Figueira da Foz and Aveiro are two major access points to the sea, Praia da Tocha and Praia de Mira. If you're looking for a few days of sunny, windblown torpor, you couldn't ask for a better stretch of the Atlantic. If you also fancy seafood, beer and indoor plumbing, go to Praia de Mira.

The small, plain village sits between the sea and a canal-fed lagoon. The beach is long and clean, and – aside from the candy-striped Igreja da Nossa Senhora Conceição on the beachfront – there are no important museums or monuments to feel guilty about not visiting. You may still glimpse local fishermen hauling in their colourful *xavega* boats in summer, though they're a vanishing species.

You won't have Praia de Mira to yourself, though – it's packed out in July and August and prices climb unmercifully with demand.

Orientation & Information
Praia de Mira is 7km west of Mira on the N109, itself 35km north of Figueira da Foz.

Praia de Mira's axis is Avenida Cidade de Coimbra, the Mira road (N342). The **turismo** *(☎ 231 472 566, fax 231 458 185; Avenida da Barrinha; open 9am-12.30pm & 2pm-5.30pm Wed-Sun)*, 450m south of Avenida Cidade de Coimbra beside the lagoon, shares a wooden house with a little ethnographic exhibition.

Places to Stay
Parque de Campismo Municipal *(☎ 231 472 173, fax 231 458 185; adult/tent/car €2/2/2; open May-Sept)*, 250m south of the turismo, is the town's downmarket facility. Hot showers cost €0.80 extra.

Orbitur *(☎ 231 471 234; e info@orbitur .pt; adult/tent/car €3.60/2.80/3.30; open Feb-Nov)*, about 500m past the municipal camp site, is a good choice, with bungalows available too.

Camping Vila Caia *(☎ 231 451 524; e vl caia@portugalmail.com; Lagoas; adult/tent/car €3.30/2.80/2.50)*, a well-equipped, lakeside place 4km inland on the N342, also has bungalows.

Parque Campismo Praia da Tocha *(☎ 231 442 343; Rua dos Pescadores; adult/tent/car €1.50/1.50/1.60; open year-round)* is the next nearest camp site, a functional place near the sea, 28km south at Praia da Tocha. Hot showers cost €0.90.

The **pousada da juventude** has both **hostel accommodation** *(☎ 231 471 199; e mira@ movijovem.pt; dorm beds €9.50, doubles with toilet €26.50; open year-round)* and **camping** *(☎ 231 471 275; open mid-June–mid-Sept)*, although the latter was under renovation at the time of writing, to reopen in 2004. Rates at the hostel include breakfast; other meals and bar service are available from mid-June to mid-September. To get here, turn left opposite the Orbitur camp site.

Rates given here are for the high season (mid-July to August). At other times the rates may drop by 30% or more, though even then they're seriously overpriced. A what-you-see-is-what-you-get attitude seems to prevail. Many places close down outside high season.

The town abounds in *quartos*, typically €25 to €40 per double. Watch for signs, or ask at the turismo.

Residencial Canadian Star *(☎ 231 471 516; Avenida da Barrinha; doubles with breakfast €45)*, facing the lagoon instead of the sea, has more modest rates; rooms have bathroom and those with a lagoon view cost €5 more.

Residencial do Mar *(☎ 231 471 144; e resi dencialmar@hotmail.com; Avenida do Mar; doubles with breakfast €67.50; closed Jan)* is well-kept and hospitable; all rooms have a bathroom and face the sea, and most have balconies.

English is spoken at both places.

Places to Eat
In summer there are more snack bars and cafés than you can shake a stick at.

Restaurante Canas *(☎ 231 471 296; Avenida da Barrinha; mains €6-8; open Mon-Sat)*, opposite the turismo, offers mainly fish dishes in a no-frills setting.

Restaurante Caçanito *(Restaurante Ilhabar; ☎ 231 472 678; Avenida do Mar; mains from €10; open Tues-Sun)* is literally *on* the beach, with unpretentious decor and 270-degree sea views. That's what you pay for, but the food is pretty good too: *caldeirada* (fish stew) is a speciality, and budgeteers should also try the good *lulas grelhadas* (grilled squid).

Entertainment
Sixties Bar *(Travessa Arrais Manuel Patrão)*, an Irish-flavoured pub on the first street back from the seafront, is tops for atmosphere. The **Country Bar** *(Rua Padre Manuel Domingues)*, a block south, has country-and-western tunes on the box. **New Captain** *(Avenida da Barrinha)*, facing the lagoon, is a popular dance bar.

Contrabaixo *(Rua Cidade de Viseu 28; closed Mon low season)*, beside the canal, is Praia de Mira's jazz headquarters.

In summer most of these places are open nightly, and still going strong at 4am.

Getting There & Away
Aveirense *(☎ 234 423 513)* runs direct Praia de Mira buses from Aveiro's train station (€2.60, three to four daily).

Most coastal transport stops inland only at Mira. AVIC Mondego comes from Aveiro

(€2.10, 50 minutes, 11 daily), Figueira da Foz (€2.40, one hour, six daily) and Coimbra, with more limited weekend services; most of these have easy onward connections (€1) to Praia de Mira. Rede Expressos stops at Mira twice daily en route between Figueira da Foz and Aveiro.

If you need a taxi, call ☎ 231 471 257 (Praia de Mira) or ☎ 231 451 165 (Mira).

AVEIRO
pop 55,300 • postcode 3800
Aveiro (uh-**vye**-roo) sits at the mouth of the Rio Vouga and the edge of a marshy lagoon known as the Ria, part of an extraordinary network of wetlands paralleling the seafront for 50km. Canals and humpback bridges give the town a vaguely genteel Dutch feel, and pastel-painted houses border the canals around the busy fish market. Attractions include several nearby beaches, a world-class bird reserve at São Jacinto and a good museum.

History
Aveiro prospered as a seaport in the early 16th century thanks to its saltpans, fishing fleet and the growing trade in *bacalhau* (salted cod). But a ferocious storm in the 1570s closed the river mouth, creating fever-breeding marshes, which contributed to a 75% drop in Aveiro's population in the following two centuries.

In 1808 the Barra Canal forged a passage back to the sea, the marshes were drained to form salt lagoons and within a century Aveiro was back as a fishing and industrial centre, its prosperity reflected in a spate of Art Nouveau houses and azulejo friezes around town.

Salt remains an economic mainstay. Once the harvesting of *molico* (seaweed) from the estuary (for use as fertiliser) was too, but this is on the decline. Many of the beautifully painted, high-prowed *moliceiro* boats moored along the canals now only carry tourists through the Ria.

Euro2004 will give Aveiro another boost, with a brand new stadium, upper-end hotels and infrastructure improvements.

Orientation
From the azulejo-clad train station it's about 1km southwest down the main street, Avenida Dr Lourenço Peixinho and Rua

BEIRAS

AVEIRO

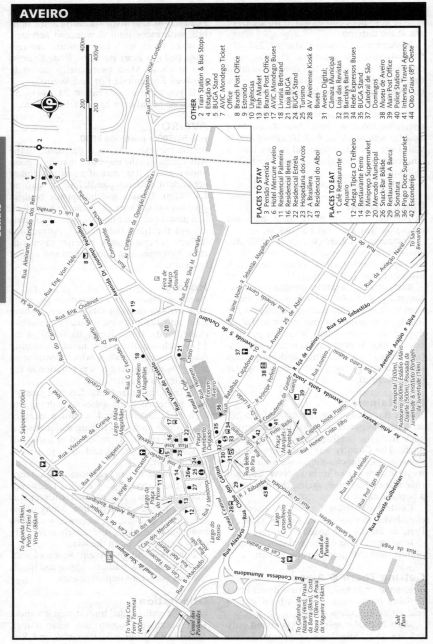

OTHER
2 Train Station & Bus Stops
4 Estação 90
5 BUGA Stand
7 AVIC Mondego Ticket Office
8 Branch Post Office
9 Estrondo
10 Urgências
13 Fish Market
15 Branch Post Office
17 AVIC Mondego Buses
18 Livraria Bertrand
21 Loja BUGA
24 BUGA Stand
25 Turismo
28 AV Aveirense Kiosk & Buses
31 Aveiro Digital; Câmara Municipal
32 Loja das Revistas
33 Barclays Bank
34 Rede Expressos Buses
35 BUGA Stand
37 Catedral de São Domingos
38 Museu de Aveiro
39 Main Post Office
40 Police Station
41 Intervisa Travel Agency
44 Oito Graus (8°) Oeste

PLACES TO STAY
3 Pensão Avenida
6 Hotel Mercure Aveiro
11 Residencial Palmeira
16 Residencial Beira
22 Residencial Estrela
23 Hospedaria dos Arcos
27 A Brasileira
43 Residencial do Alboi

PLACES TO EAT
1 Café Restaurante O Aquario
12 Adega Tipica O Telheiro
14 Restaurante Ferro
19 Minipreço Supermarket
20 Mercado Municipal
26 Snack-Bar Bólide
29 Restaurante A Barca
30 Sonatura
36 Pingo Doce Supermarket
42 Esconderijo

Viana do Castelo (together called Avenida by all) to Praça Humberto Delgado (straddling the Canal Central). Nearby are the turismo and a pedestrianised centre dominated by the trendy Forum Aveiro shopping mall.

Parking is dire, and getting worse. Fight your way into the centre, past the turismo to the Largo do Rossio car park, and leave your car there for the duration.

Information

Tourist Offices The good regional turismo (*☎ 234 423 680; e aveiro.rotadaluz@inovanet.pt; Rua João Mendonça 8; open 9am-8pm daily June-Sept; 9am-7pm Mon-Fri, 9am-1pm & 2.30pm-5.30pm Sat Oct-May*) is in Art Nouveau headquarters beside the Canal Central.

Money There are banks with ATMs all along the Avenida, and a Barclays across the canal from the turismo.

Post & Communications The main post office (*Praça Marquês de Pombal; open 8.30am-6.30pm Mon-Fri, 9am-12.30pm Sat*) is the place for poste restante, but there are handier **branches** (*Rua José Estevão 17 • Avenida Dr Lourenço Peixinho 171; both open 9am-6pm Mon-Fri*).

In 2000 Aveiro pioneered municipally sponsored Internet access in Portugal, offering a big menu of free services in a scheme called **Aveiro Digital** (*☎ 234 371 666; e gab-tecnico@aveiro-digital.pt; open 10am-8.30pm Mon-Sat*), from a room at the rear of the câmara municipal (town hall). Sign in for at least half an hour online as soon as a computer is available.

The **Instituto Português da Juventude** (*☎ 234 381 935; Rua das Pombas 182*), about 1km from the centre, has free Internet access during weekday business hours.

Travel Agencies A reliable mainstream agency is **Intervisa** (*☎ 234 386 764; Rua Gustavo Ferreira Pinto Basto 29*).

Bookshops The most useful bookshop is **Livraria Bertrand** (*☎ 234 428 280; Avenida Dr Lourenço Peixinho 87C*).

Medical Services & Emergency The hospital (*☎ 234 378 300; Avenida Artur Ravada*) is about 1.2km south of the town centre.

The **police station** (*☎ 234 422 022; Praça Marquês de Pombal*) is a few blocks south of the Canal Central.

Museu de Aveiro

This fine, if somewhat single-minded, museum (*☎ 234 423 297; Avenida Santa Joana Princesa; adult/youth 14-25 or senior/child €1.50/0.80/free, free 10am-2pm Sun; open 10am-5.30pm Tues-Sun*), in the former Mosteiro de Jesus, opposite the Catedral de São Domingos, owes its finest treasures to Princesa (later beatified as Santa) Joana, daughter of Afonso V.

In 1472, 11 years after the convent was founded, Joana 'retired' here and, though forbidden to take full vows, stayed until her death in 1490. Her tomb, a 17th-century masterpiece of marble mosaic, sits in an equally lavish baroque chancel decorated with azulejos depicting her life. The museum's paintings include a late-15th-century portrait of her, attributed to Nuno Gonçalves.

Reserva Natural das Dunas de São Jacinto

Stretching north from São Jacinto to Ovar, between the sea and the N327, is a 6.7-sq-km wooded nature reserve, equipped with trails and bird-watching hides. Entry is via an **interpretive centre** (*☎ 234 331 282; e rnpa.santosmf@icn.pt*) on the N327. To minimise the impact on wildlife, you can only enter between 9am and 9.30am or between 1.30pm and 2pm, for a maximum stay of 2½ hours. There's usually a guide on hand to give a free tour, or materials available to help you make the best of a visit on your own. Book ahead if you can.

To get here, take a Forte da Barra bus from the **AV Aveirense kiosk** (*☎ 234 423 513; Rua Clube dos Galitos*) to the end of the line (€1.40), from where a small passenger ferry (€0.70 for adults) crosses to the port of São Jacinto. Ferries (€1.30 for adults) also run from Vera Cruz, on the Canal das Pirâmides beyond the IP5 bridge, a 10-minute walk from the turismo. Children aged four to 10 and seniors go for half-price on both ferries, and bikes can be taken free. Ask at the turismo for current timetables.

From São Jacinto port the reserve entrance is 1.3km down the Torreira road. Note that by road the entrance is 50km from Aveiro!

BEIRAS

Beaches

Though not the Costa de Prata's finest beaches, the surfing venues of Praia da Barra and Costa Nova, located 13km west of Aveiro, are good for a day's outing. The prettier **Costa Nova** has a beachside street lined with cafés, tacky gift shops and candy-striped cottages.

AV Aveirense buses go via Gafanha da Nazaré to Costa Nova (€1.50) about hourly from the kiosk on Rua Clube dos Galitos; the last bus back departs at about 8.15pm in summer and 6.55pm in winter.

Wilder and more remote is **Praia de São Jacinto**, on the northern side of the lagoon. The vast beach of sand dunes is a 1.5km walk from São Jacinto port (see the Reserva Natural das Dunas de São Jacinto section for details), through a residential area at the back of town.

Activities

Aveirosub (☎ 234 367 555; W www.aveirosub .co.pt; Avenida José Estevão 724, Gafanha da Nazaré) offers **scuba-diving** classes (36 sessions of 50 minutes, about half of them in the sea, for €350).

From mid-June to mid-September the turismo organises daily, three-hour **motor-launch trips** across the Ria to Costa Nova, with a half-hour pause there. They depart at 10am and at 2.30pm from the Canal Central in front of the turismo, provided there are enough passengers (at least eight). The trips cost €8/5/free per adult/child aged eight to 12/child under 12.

One-hour private **moliceiros trips** (€7) around the Ria are available subject to passenger numbers; tickets are available at the turismo. Two-hour *moliceiros* trips to São Jacinto may also be on offer in the summer months; ask at the turismo.

Special Events

The Feira de Março (March Fair), from late March to late April, dates back 5½ centuries. Nowadays it features everything from folk music to rock concerts.

The Festas do Município sees two weeks of merrymaking around 12 May in honour of Santa Joana (see the earlier Museu de Aveiro section, earlier).

Aveiro celebrates its canals and *moliceiros* at the Festa da Ria, from mid-July to the end of August. Highlights include folk dancing and a *moliceiros* race. Another *moliceiros* race features in the Festas do São Paio in Murtosa (on the northern side of the lagoon) in the first week of September.

Places to Stay

Summer accommodation is even tighter than parking here; consider booking a week or so ahead in peak season.

Camping & Hostels At least six camp sites are within reach of Aveiro. Nearest and cheapest is Aveiro's **Parque Municipal de Campismo** (☎/fax 234 331 220; adult/tent/ car €1.80/0.90/0.60; open Mar-Nov) at São Jacinto, 2.5km from the pier along the Torreira road. **Orbitur** (☎ 234 838 284; e info@orbitur.pt; adult/tent/car €3.20/2.60/ 3.30; open Feb-Nov) is 2.5km further on. There's no bus service along this road; see the earlier Reserva Natural das Dunas de São Jacinto section for transport details.

Parque Municipal de Campismo de Ílhavo (☎ 234 369 425; e camarilhavo@mail .telepac.pt; Praia da Barra; adult/tent/car €2/1.80/3; open Jan-Nov) and **Parque de Campismo da Gafanha da Nazaré** (☎ 234 366 565, fax 234 365 789; adult/tent/car €1.10/1/1.90; open year-round), southeast of Gafanha da Nazaré, are other budget options. For public transport options, see the earlier Beaches section.

Southward are Parque de Campismo da Costa Nova (☎ 234 369 822; e inovacess@ mail.telepac.pt; Costa Nova; adult/tent/car €2.80/2.50/2.50; open year-round) and Parque de Campismo da Vagueira (☎ 234 797 526, fax 234 797 093; Vagueira; adult/tent/car €3.30/3/2.50; open year-round).

The **pousada da juventude** (☎ 234 420 536; e aveiro@movijovem.pt; Rua das Pombas 182; dorm beds €9.50, doubles with toilet €26.50), Aveiro's youth hostel, is 1.5km south of the centre.

Private Rooms Near the fish market, **Restaurante Ferro** (☎ 234 385 428; Rua Tenente Resende 30; doubles €17.50) has noisy, downmarket rooms (with shared facilities).

A Brasiliera (☎ 234 428 634; Rua Tenente Resende 47; doubles with basin €25, with toilet & shower €30) is a dark warren of a boarding house, however, it's clean and well run.

Pensões & Residenciais A bargain near the train station is **Pensão Avenida** (☎ 234 423 366; Avenida Dr Lourenço Peixinho 259; singles/doubles/triples without shower from €15/25/30, doubles/triples with shower from €25/35), with high ceilings and a calm atmosphere. Rooms have shared toilet.

Two neighbouring townhouses converted into residenciais, bang in the centre, are the laid-back **Residential Estrela** (☎ 234 423 818; Rua José Estevão 4; doubles with/without shower from €35/20) and no-nonsense **Residential Beira** (☎ 234 424 297; Rua José Estevão 18; doubles from €45).

Hospedaria dos Arcos (☎ 234 383 130; Rua José Estevão 47; doubles €37.50), with a just-like-home atmosphere, spotless, quiet rooms and a generous breakfast, makes a superb retreat, though it's not a place that would welcome the kids.

Residencial Palmeira (☎ 234 422 521; e residencial.palmeira@netc.pt; Rua da Palmeira 7; singles/doubles with breakfast €30/40) is another quiet, well-run choice.

Residencial do Alboi (☎ 234 380 390; e alboi@residencial-alboi.com; Rua da Arrochela 6; doubles with/without bathroom €53/49), in a lane south of the canal, has quiet rooms and an air of dignity; breakfast is included.

Hotels Best known as the old Paloma Blanca is **Hotel Mercure Aveiro** (☎ 234 404 400; e h2934@accor-hotels.com; Rua Luís Gomes de Carvalho 23; singles/doubles with breakfast €70/85). It occupies a handsome 1930s mansion near the train station. Off-street parking costs €3 per night.

Places to Eat

Snack-Bar Bólide (☎ 234 424 796; Rua Domingos Carrancho 11; meat/fish dishes from €4/5; open Sun-Fri) is a modest little shop with a few good, simple meals, plus burgers, francesinha (a toasted sandwich of beef, ham, sausage and cheese) and other 'fast food'.

Sonatura (☎ 234 424 474; Rua Clube dos Galitos 6; set meals €3.80, €4.30 & €5; open noon-6.30pm Mon-Fri) offers a few wholesome, carefully prepared vegetarian dishes in a no-frills, self-service setting. Even non-vegetarians will love seeing so many vegetables on a Portuguese plate, and at earthy prices.

Adega Típica O Telheiro (☎ 234 429 473; Largo Praça do Peixe 20-21; mains around €10; open Sun-Fri) dishes up grilled seafood at fair prices. Star of the 'starters' menu is the €1.50 sopa de mer, a great warming chowder. The adega (wine tavern) atmosphere – hams hanging from the ceiling, huge rounds of bread, red wine by the jug – is half the fun.

Esconderijo (☎ 234 422 754; Rua Luís Cipriano 23; mains around €6.50; open 10am-10pm Sun-Fri), a plain churrasqueira behind the câmara municipal, has a dozen half-/full-portion lunch specials at about €4/6 or enough arroz de marisco for two for €8 – great value.

Restaurante Ferro (☎ 234 385 428; Rua Tenente Resende 30; dishes around €8) is the proverbial clean, well-lit place, noisy and popular, with lots of fish and meat dishes, plus omelettes.

Restaurante A Barca (☎ 234 426 024; Rua José Rabumba 5A; dishes around €10; open lunch Mon-Sat, dinner Mon-Fri) has a casual atmosphere and good grilled fish.

There's little to recommend near the train station, though **Café Restaurante O Aquário** (☎ 234 425 014; Rua Almirante Cândido dos Reis 139; open Mon-Sat) is at least clean and cheerful.

Self-caterers can choose from the **mercado municipal** (open Mon-Sat) and supermarkets, including **Pingo Doce** in the Forum Aveiro mall and **Minipreço** on the Avenida.

Entertainment

There are three good bars along the Canal de São Roque beyond the fish market: **Estrondo** (☎ 234 383 366; Cais de São Roque 74), **Urgências** (☎ 234 428 082), on the adjacent corner, and **Salpoente** (☎ 234 382 674), at No 83.

Autocarro (☎ 234 425 309) is a bar fashioned from an old bus, near the pousada da juventude.

Oito Graus (8°) Oeste (☎ 234 383 169; Cais do Paraíso 19) is both a popular club and a restaurant.

Spectator Sports

Aveiro's good second-division team, SC Beira Mar, currently plays at **Estádio Mário Duarte**, just beyond the hospital. The city is building a 30,000-seat stadium at Tabueira, 5km northeast of the town centre, for Euro2004.

BEIRAS

Getting There & Away

Bus Few long-distance buses actually terminate here; there isn't even a bus station.

Rede Expressos has two to three daily services to/from Lisbon (€10.80, four hours); get tickets and timetables at the **Loja das Revistas** newsagent *(Praça Humberto Delgado)* and catch the bus around the corner, or book it at Intervisa (see Travel Agencies earlier in this section).

AVIC Mondego *(☎ 234 423 747; tickets at Rua Comandante Rocha e Cunha 55)* goes up to five times a day to Figueira da Foz (€6.70, two hours) from Rua Viana do Castelo and the train station. AV Aveirense's direct Praia de Mira services (€2.60, three to four daily) and Joalto buses for Viseu (€5.60, 1½ hours, twice daily) leave from the train station.

Train Aveiro is actually within Porto's *suburbano* network, which means there are hourly commuter trains to/from Porto (€1.70, 1½ hours); there are also four IC trains a day (€5.70, 55 minutes). Other IC links include Coimbra (€5.70, 35 minutes, four daily) and Lisbon (€11.50, three hours, four daily), plus additional Alfa and IR services.

Getting Around

Local bus routes converge on the Avenida and the train station. A *bilet de cidade* (city ticket) from a kiosk or *tabacaria* costs €0.90 for two journeys; from the driver they're €2 for one trip. The ticket source closest to the train station is a *pastelaria* (pastry or cake shop) called **Estação 90** *(Avenida Dr Lourenço Peixinho 352)*.

Aveiro runs a pioneering free-bike scheme, Bicicleta de Utilização Gratuita de Aveiro (BUGA). At any blue-and-white 'Parque BUGA' stand you insert a €0.50 coin, take a bike and ride it as long as you like within designated town limits, return it to any station and get a coin back. If there are no bikes anywhere else, go to **Loja BUGA** *(☎ 967 050 441; open 10am-12.30pm & 1.30pm-6pm Mon-Fri, 9am-7pm Sat & Sun)*, a souvenir kiosk beside the Canal do Cojo.

Beira Baixa

CASTELO BRANCO
postcode 6000 • pop 30,500
• **elevation 360m**

The provincial capital of Beira Baixa is pretty, prosperous and friendly, but surprisingly dull. Its alibi is its proximity to the frontier, 20km to the south, which has made it the target of so many attacks over the centuries – including a vicious one by the French in 1807 – that few historic monuments remain.

Its value for travellers is as a base for visiting the fortress village of Monsanto and the curious hamlet of Idanha-a-Velha (see later in this chapter), though its excellent city museum is a worthy stop.

Orientation & Information

From the bus station, turn right down Rua do Saibreiro to central Alameda da Liberdade. From the train station the Alameda is 500m north on Avenida Nuno Álvares. In a pedestrian area beside the Alameda is the **turismo** *(☎ 272 330 339;* e *cmcb@mail.telepac.pt;*

Colchas

Colchas – silk-embroidered linen bedspreads or coverlets – trace their luxurious origins to India and China, where early Portuguese explorers commissioned the first versions in the 16th and 17th centuries. Back in Portugal they became a Castelo Branco speciality, a sign of prestige and wealth. Once woven for every rich girl's bridal trousseau, their designs of exotic flora and fauna abound in symbolism (two birds symbolise lovers, trees represent families and so on) and still include Oriental features.

On weekdays you can watch them being made in the Museu de Francisco Tavares Proença Júnior or at the **Loja da Villa** *(☎ 272 341 576, 933 498 155; Rua da Misericórdia 37)*, a workshop in the old town. Choose from a portfolio of dozens of designs, their meanings patiently explained. You may have to wait up to a year for your own. Prices range from €925 for a small item to €7500 for a bedspread-sized colcha. Not bad, considering that the one on display in the museum's workshop (which took 596 days to make) is on offer for €27,500!

open 9.30am-7.30pm Mon-Fri, 9.30am-1pm & 2.30pm-6pm Sat & Sun). Everything of interest is an easy walk from here.

The headquarters for the **Parque Natural do Tejo Internacional** (☎ 272 321 445; e pnti .silveiras@icn.pt; Rua Senhora da Piedade 4A) is two blocks southeast of the turismo.

The **post office** (Rua da Sé; open 8.30am-6.30pm Mon-Fri, 9am-12.30pm Sat) has Net-Post. The **Instituto Português da Juventude** (☎ 272 326 910; Rua Dr Francisco José Palmeiro), 1km northwest of the centre, has free Internet access from 9am to 6.30pm weekdays.

Palácio Episcopal

The Palácio Episcopal (Bishop's Palace), in the north of town, is a sober 18th-century affair housing the **Museu de Francisco Tavares Proença Júnior** (☎ 272 344 277; e mftpj@ ipmuseus.pt; Rua Frei Bartolomeu da Costa; adult/student/child under 14 €2/1/free; open 10am-12.30pm & 2pm-5.30pm Tues-Sun). The museum was named after a prominent 19th-century archaeologist who donated his collection to the museum and became its first director.

The museum concentrates on the history of the episcopacy, with fine 16th-century religious paintings and 18th-century portraits of various popes, kings and cardinals. Best of all is an exhibition of Castelo

Branco's famous *colchas* (see the boxed text), including several 17th-century versions made in India and China, complete with English captions.

Beside the museum is the **Jardim Episcopal** (Bishop's Garden; admission €0.50; open 9am-8pm daily Apr-Sept, 9am-5pm Oct-Mar), a baroque whimsy of clipped box hedges and little granite statues. Notice that the statues of the Spanish kings Felipe I and II are smaller than those of the Portuguese monarchs!

Castelo

There's little left of the castle, built by the Knights Templar in the 13th century and extended by Dom Dinis. The Miradouro de São Gens garden, which has supplanted the walls, offers grand views over town and countryside. The old lanes that lead back down to the town centre are very picturesque.

Places to Stay

At the time of research, the **Parque Municipal de Campismo** was closed for much-needed improvements.

The **pousada da juventude** (☎ 272 323 838; Rua Dr Francisco José Palmeiro; dorm beds €9.50, doubles with toilet €26.50) is beside the Instituto Português da Juventude (see Information).

Budget *pensões* include the friendly **Pensão Império** (☎ 272 341 720, fax 272 343 567;

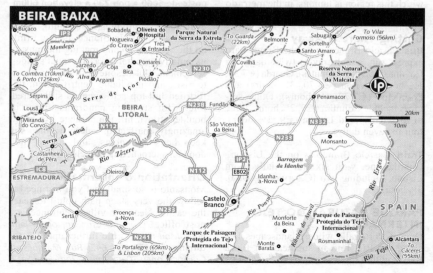

BEIRA BAIXA

BEIRAS

Rua Prazeres 20; singles/doubles with break-fast €20/32.50) in a backstreet near the post office; and the businesslike **Pensão Residencial Arraiana** (☎ 272 341 634; Avenida 1 de Maio 18; singles/doubles with breakfast €20/40), on a busy main road. Both offer rooms with air-con.

Hotel Rainha D Amélia (☎ 272 326 315; e hrdamelia@mail.telepac.pt; Rua Santiago 15; singles/doubles €59.40/72.40), around the corner from the Arraiana, is a Best Western franchise with all the frills.

Places to Eat
Café Restaurante Central (☎ 272 344 636; Rua Tavares Proença Júnior 14; dishes under €7), near Pensão Império, provides generous servings.

Upmarket choices include **Restaurante Zé dos Cachopos** (☎ 272 345 537; Rua Emilia Oliveira Pinto 13; dishes €6-9; open Wed-Mon), with a big meat menu and a comfortable ambience; **Praça Velha** (☎ 272 328 640; Largo Luís de Camões; dishes €12.50, fondue for 2 people €25; open Tues-Sun) in a former Knights Templar abode in the old town; and **Frei Papinhas** (☎ 272 323 090; Rua dos Prazeres 31; dishes €8.50-11.50), which specialises in grills (start with a choice of four different local cheeses!).

Self-caterers can find supplies, including the *queijo de ovelha* (sheep's cheese) for which this region is famous, in the **mercado municipal** (Avenida 1 de Maio).

Getting There & Away
Bus Castelo Branco is on the Braga–Faro express run, which travels twice daily via Covilhã (€5.50, 50 minutes), Guarda (€7.30, 1½ hours), Viseu (€8.70, 3½ hours) and Portalegre (€7.70, 1½ hours). Other services include Coimbra (€9, 2¼ hours, three to four daily) and Lisbon (€9, 3½ hours, four to seven daily).

Train Castelo Branco is on the Lisbon–Guarda line, with six trains daily from Lisbon, including two IC services (€9.80, 3½ hours).

PARQUE NATURAL DO TEJO INTERNACIONAL
One of Portugal's wildest landscapes lies along the Rio Tejo in southeastern Beira Baixa, within the watersheds of three of its tributaries, the Rio Ponsul, Ribeira do Aravil and Rio Erges. Residents include some of the country's rarest animal species: black stork, Bonelli's eagle, royal eagle, Egyptian vulture, black vulture and griffon vulture. In June 2000, following a major public education effort by the private environmental organisation Quercus (see Ecology & Environment in the Facts about Portugal chapter for details), a 230-sq-km *parque natural* was established here.

Information
Park headquarters is in Castelo Branco (see that section for details), though the best source of park information is the Castelo Branco office of the private environmental organisation **Quercus** (☎ 272 324 272; e quercusc.branco@mail.telepac.pt; Travessa do Espirito Santo 54, Castelo Branco).

At Castelo Branco's turismo you can buy Quercus' 250-page *Guia de Percursos Tejo Internacional*, a guide (in Portuguese) to regional geology, climate, flora and fauna, villages, trails and transport.

Quercus is setting up biking, walking and other programmes. Basic accommodation is available at Rosmaninhal and Monte Barata; for details contact **Paulo Monteiro** (☎ 277 477 463) at Quercus.

MONSANTO
postcode 6060 • pop 200 • elevation 600m
Once the least visited of Portugal's medieval fortress villages, Monsanto, 48km northeast of Castelo Branco, is now firmly on the tourist map and making the most of its putative reputation as Portugal's oldest settlement. But despite a steady stream of tourists, and inevitable gentrification, this fortified hill-top settlement is still incredible, with stunning panoramas from its boulder-strewn hill top. Village life seems amazingly unaffected; elderly women still keep hens and goats, and sit on their doorsteps, crocheting and chatting.

Orientation & Information
Monsanto is so small that you just need to follow the very steep path uphill to reach the castle. Near the village entrance is a **post office** (Largo do Cruzeiro; open 9am-noon Mon-Fri). A little further uphill is the **turismo** (☎ 277 314 642; Rua Marquês da Graçioça; open 10am-1pm & 2pm-6pm Sat &

Sun); it may possibly be open longer hours in summer.

Village

Houses near the village entrance are surprisingly grand, some sporting Manueline doorways and stone crests. Since Monsanto won a 1939 award as 'Portugal's most traditional village', building restrictions have kept a lid on creeping modernisation. Along the twisting upward path, cottages and animal sheds are built in among the boulders that are often topped by stone crosses. Halfway to the castle you'll come across the **gruta**, a chilly cavern apparently once used as a drinking den!

Castelo

There was probably a fortress here before the Romans came, but after Dom Sancho I booted out the Moors in the 12th century it was beefed up. Dom Dinis refortified it but after centuries of attacks from across the border it finally fell into ruin.

Today it's a hauntingly beautiful site, populated by lizards and wildflowers. Immense vistas (marred only by the inevitable mobile-phone masts) include Spain to the east and the Barragem da Idanha lake to the southwest. But it's the village below that offers a glimpse of medieval Portugal at its toughest and truest.

Just below the castle entrance is a plaza used for folk dances at festival time. To the right is a ruined Renaissance church and bell tower, and five stone tombs carved into the rock.

Special Events

On 3 May Monsanto celebrates the Festa das Cruzes, commemorating a medieval siege. The story goes that starving villagers threw their last calf over the walls, as if they had them to spare; this so disheartened their attackers that the siege was abandoned. These days, young girls throw baskets of flowers instead, after which there's dancing and singing beside the castle walls.

Places to Stay & Eat

The only easily available *quartos* are at **Adega Típica O Cruzeiro** (☎ 277 314 528; *Rua Fernando Namora 4; doubles €40*). Near the village entrance is the modest, comfortable **Pousada de Monsanto** (☎ 277 314 471,

fax 277 314 481; doubles Mon-Fri €89, Sat & Sun €94).

Adega Tipica O Cruzeiro *(see earlier; daily specials around €6-7)*, near the village entrance, has rustic decor and decent daily specials. Similarly priced is the new (still-unsignposted) **Lapa da Moura** (☎ 966 150 424; *Rua do Castelo 15)*, near the *gruta*. Neither place goes in for menus; just ask what's available.

For snacks and sandwiches, there's simple **Café Monsantinho** (☎ 277 314 493; *Rua de Nossa Senhora do Castelo)*. There are also souvenir shops selling home-made honey cakes, some laced with *aguardente* (alcoholic 'firewater')!

Getting There & Away

On weekdays two buses run daily from Castelo Branco (€3.90, 1¾ hours); the first requires a change at Idanha-a-Nova. The return service leaves only at 6.20am (4.50pm on Sunday).

IDANHA-A-VELHA

Idanha-a-Velha, a remote 15km southwest of Monsanto, is an extraordinary place with an even more extraordinary history. Once a sizable Roman city called Igaeditânia, it was rebuilt by the Visigoths (who erected a cathedral here), occupied by the Moors and then taken over by the Knights Templar.

So why did this much-desired enclave, once rich with gold deposits, suddenly fade into obscurity? Rats. Or some say ants. A plague of one or the other apparently drove the inhabitants out, leaving Roman and Visigothic ruins everywhere.

Today it's basically a simple farming hamlet, but it has been designated one of the region's 10 Aldeias Históricas, and conservation money is on the way. Unfortunately, the most obvious results so far are an ugly iron walkway on top of the Roman walls and a morguelike display gallery by the cathedral, housing Roman funerary and other inscribed stones. But just walking around the hamlet is undeniably worthwhile, an eerily memorable experience.

Information

The **turismo** (☎ 277 914 280; *Rua do Castelo; open 10am-1pm & 2pm-6pm daily)* may not always be open if staff members are on guided visits.

BEIRAS

Things to See

From the turismo it's a short walk to the 6th-century Visigothic **cathedral**, under restoration at the time of research but accessible with turismo staff. The nearby **Lagar de Varas** *(admission free; open 10.30am-11.30am & 3pm-5pm daily by request at turismo)* shows the workings of a traditional olive-oil press.

The only evidence of the Knights Templar is the **Torre des Templários**, made of massive chunks of stone and now surrounded by clucking hens. Wander round the back of the village to see the Roman bridge and walls.

After all this history it's a delight to come across the **Forno Comunitário** *(communal bakery; Rua do Castelo)* and discover villagers sliding trays of biscuits into the huge stone oven.

Places to Eat

Café Lafiv *(Rua da Amoreira)*, near the turismo, is the village's only café, serving little more than sandwiches and smoked sausage.

Getting There & Away

On weekdays during term-time only, there's one bus daily from Idanha-a-Nova (40 minutes). Two to three buses daily run to Idanha-a-Nova from Castelo Branco (€2.60, 55 minutes).

SORTELHA

postcode 6320 • pop 800 • elevation 760m
Sortelha is the oldest of a string of rock fortresses guarding the frontier east of Guarda and Covilhã. It's also one of the loveliest, a 12th-century walled village with Moorish origins, built into a boulder-strewn hillside. Although it's less dramatic and less well known than Monsanto, it boasts similarly fine views over a wild landscape.

Since it was designated one of the region's 10 Aldeias Históricas, most of old Sortelha's stout granite cottages have been finely restored, and many converted to bars, restaurants or upmarket tourist accommodation. But in the process it has been transformed into a kind of medieval-Beiras diorama, cleansed of atmosphere and life. The restored part of the village within the ancient walls now has about half a dozen permanent residents! You will just have to use your imagination.

Orientation & Information

'New' Sortelha lines the Santo Amaro–Sabugal road, along which are two restaurants and several Turihab properties. The medieval hill-top fortress is a short drive, or a 10-minute walk, up one of two lanes signposted 'castelo'.

The Liga dos Amigos de Sortelha runs an unofficial 'turismo' and handicrafts shop a block uphill from the castle ruins, but its opening hours are unpredictable.

Old Village

The entrance to the fortified village is a grand, stone Gothic **gate**. From Largo do Corro, just inside the gate, a cobbled lane leads up to the heart of the village – a *pelourinho* (stone pillory) in front of the remains of a small **castle** to the left and the parish **church** to the right. Higher still is the **bell tower**. Climb right up to the bells for a view of the entire village (but a sign begs visitors not to ring the bells), or tackle the ramparts around the village (but beware of some very precarious sections).

Reserva Natural da Serra da Malcata

The 218-sq-km Serra da Malcata Nature Reserve sprawls across rounded, scrubby hills on the border with the Spanish province of Extremadura. Oak woodland and dense stands of alder, willow and ash in the valleys of the Rio Côa and its tributaries are habitat for the Iberian lynx (Lynx pardinus). Thanks to poaching, the march of pine and eucalyptus plantations, and a declining population of hares and wild rabbits, this solitary, nocturnal cat is Europe's most endangered carnivore and the world's most endangered wild cat.

The reserve was created in 1981 specifically to save the lynx, but at the time of writing there was said to be just one left. For more information contact the reserve's **main office** (☎ 277 394 467; e rnsm@icn.pt; Rua dos Bombeiros Voluntários, 6090 Penamacor).

Places to Stay

Sortelha boasts several atmospheric Turihab properties, complete with kitchens, thick stone walls and imperfect heating. Calling a week or two ahead is essential in high season.

Casa da Cerca (*☎/fax 271 388 113; e aja marques@clix.pt; double €56*), on the main road, is a 17th-century house sleeping two people. Next door and under the same management is **Casa do Páteo** (*2/4 people €60/75*). Within the village walls the same owners have a cottage, **Casa da Vila** (*Rua Direita; 2-7 people from €40-126*) accommodating two to seven guests.

Casas do Campanário (*☎ 271 388 198; Rua da Mesquita; double €60*) has a house for two people and another for up to six; ask at Bar Campanário, at the top of the village beyond the turismo.

Casa Árabe (*☎ 271 388 129*) and **Casa do Palheiro** (*☎ 271 388 182*) are two other double-bedroom places within the walls.

Places to Eat

Café Restaurante Palmeiras (*☎ 271 388 260*), on the main road at the northern end of the village, has zero atmosphere but lots of cheer, a few pots on the stove and a short list of specials for around €4.

Restaurante O Celta (*☎ 271 388 291; open Wed-Mon*), Sortelha's wedding-parties-and-evenings-out venue, at the rear of a café of the same name on the main road, offers a bigger menu and a bit of atmosphere for marginally higher prices.

Restaurante Típico Alboroque (*☎ 271 388 129; Rua da Mesquita; dishes €6-12*), in the walled village, has the trappings of a medieval inn and a menu to match, with lots of wild boar and kid.

Restaurante Dom Sancho I (*☎ 271 388 267; Largo do Corro*), just inside the gate, has an atmospheric bar downstairs and stratospheric food prices upstairs, though the food is first-rate.

Getting There & Away

Getting here by public transport is hard work. A daily bus from Sabugal only runs during the school term. Regional trains on the Covilhã–Guarda line (three daily) stop at Belmonte-Manteigas station, 12km to the northwest, from where the local **taxi** (*☎ 271 388 182*) will collect you for about €9.

Parque Natural da Serra da Estrela

The glacially scoured plateau called the Serra da Estrela – mainland Portugal's highest mountain range, topping out at the 1993m Torre (Tower) – forms a conspicuous natural boundary between north and south. At higher elevations it's decidedly alpine, with rounded peaks, boulder-strewn meadows and icy lakes. Lower down, the land furrows into stock trails, terraced fields defined with dry-stone walls, and pine plantations.

Two rivers rise here and embrace the range on either side: the Mondego (the longest river rising within Portugal) to the north and the Zêzere (a tributary of the Tejo) to the south.

Mountain people – some still living in traditional one-room, stone *casais* (huts) thatched with rye straw, but now mostly concentrated in valley hamlets – raise sheep (for wool, meat and milk), grow potatoes, other vegetables and rye, and increasingly depend on touristic variants of their traditional activities, such as the selling of woollen goods and *queijo da serra* (mountain cheese), and renting out rooms.

The Parque Natural da Serra da Estrela (PNSE; Serra da Estrela Natural Park) was founded in 1976 to preserve not merely habitats and landscapes but the plateau's rural character and cultural identity. Its 1011 sq km – Portugal's largest protected area – straddles Beira Alta and Beira Baixa provinces, with more than half of it above an altitude of 700m. Crisp air and immense vistas make this a fine place for walking,

> ## Cuisine of the Beiras
>
> Coimbra likes its roast suckling pig and Aveiro its fried eels, but the cuisine of the Beiras is most strongly defined by the hearty, warming food of the mountains: roast lamb, roast kid and grilled trout; smoked ham, sausages and bacon; roast chestnuts and several varieties of *feijoacas* (little beans); rye bread and stout yellow corn bread; and the strong, semisoft cheese of the Serra da Estrela. Finish your meal with a local *aguardente* made from honey or juniper berries.

aided by a system of marked trails and maps to go with them.

Enough snow falls in winter to allow skiing, and there are modest facilities at Torre. Every weekend (and all week in July and August) Portuguese families come up by car and bus in the thousands, creating massive traffic jams around Torre. Sabugeiro and a few other formerly quiet villages now bristle with *pensões* and souvenir shops. But for the rest of the week, and off the road at almost anytime, the mountains do indeed seem empty.

The weather constantly goes to extremes: scorching summer days give way to freezing nights, and chilling rainstorms blow through with little warning. Mist is a big hazard because it obscures walking routes and landmarks, and because it can stealthily chill you to the point of hypothermia. You may set out on a warm, cloudless morning and by noon find yourself fogged in and shivering, so always pack for the cold and the wet, too.

Wildflowers bloom in late April, though the finest walking is from May to October. Winter is harsh, with snow at the higher elevations from November or December to April or May.

Information

There are park offices at Manteigas (headquarters), Seia, Gouveia and Guarda, though not all staff speak English. Turismos at Seia, Gouveia, Manteigas, Covilhã, Torre and Guarda also have park information.

PARQUE NATURAL DA SERRA DA ESTRELA

Specially Protected Area
Rentable Shelter-houses
Main Walking Route
Variations on Main Walking Route

If you're serious about exploring the park, the 1:50,000 topographic map *Carta Turística: Parque Natural da Serra da Estrela* (€5.50) includes paths, shelters and camp sites. A useful English-language booklet, *Discovering the Region of the Serra da Estrela* (€4.30), has trail profiles, walking times, historical notes and flora and fauna basics.

Flora and fauna details are in the booklet *Estrela: A Natural Approach* (€3.30). The handsome *Guia Geológico e Geomorfológico do PNSE* (€5; English version in preparation) tells you what's under your feet. There are other brochures (Portuguese only) on medicinal plants (€5) and archaeology (€6.20). All are available at park offices and some turismos.

Flora & Fauna

Endangered or vulnerable animal species in the Parque Natural da Serra da Estrela include the black stork *(Ciconia negra)*, Montagu's harrier *(Circus pygargus)*, raven *(Corvus corax)*, chough *(Pyrrhocorax pyrrhocorax)*, turtle dove *(Streptopelia turtur)* and 10 species of bats.

Animals in the park that are considered 'rare' are the mountain gecko *(Lacerta monticola)* and a long list of birds, including the peregrine falcon *(Falco peregrinus)*, eagle owl *(Bubo bubo)*, black-shouldered kite *(Elanus caeruleus)*, alpine swift *(Apus melba)*, bullfinch *(Pyrrhula pyrrhula)*, redstart *(Phoenicurus phoenicurus)* and fieldfare thrush *(Turdus pilaris)*.

Their popularity as medicinal remedies have put several PNSE plants in the list of endangered or vulnerable species, including mountain thrift *(Armeria transmontana;*

endemic to Portugal), great yellow gentian *(Gentiana lutea)* and juniper *(Juniperus communis)*.

Walking

Serra da Estrela is the only *parque natural* with a system of well-marked and mapped trails. But surprisingly few people use them, even in summer, and walkers may get the wonderful impression that they have the park to themselves.

There are three main 'official' routes, plus branches and alternative trails. T1 runs the length of the park (about 90km), taking in every kind of terrain, including the summit of Torre. T2 and T3 (both around 80km) run respectively along the western and eastern slopes. All of them pass through towns and villages, making for easy access and wide choice of accommodation. Many of the finest walks start around Manteigas (see Manteigas later in this chapter).

Within a zone of special protection (almost everything above 1200m altitude) camping and fires are strictly prohibited, except at designated sites, all of them on the main trails. Cutting trees and picking plants are also prohibited in this zone.

Skiing

The ski season typically runs from January to March, with the best conditions in February. For a rundown on what's available for skiers, see Torre later in this chapter.

Places to Stay

Useful bases include Seia, Gouveia, Manteigas, Covilhã and Guarda. Whereas camp sites drop their rates or close in winter, many hotels, *pensões* and *residenciais* actually

BEIRAS

The Estrela Mountain Dog

The shaggy, handsome *cão da Serra da Estrela* is perfectly suited to its mountain environment: strong, fierce (thanks to wolf ancestry) and able to endure the cold, though not all are long-haired. They're all pretty big; an adult can weigh up to 50kg.

Traditionally used by farmers to protect their flocks from wild animals, the breed was, until recently, in danger of dying out. Now several breeding kennels in the area work to preserve the pedigree. You may also see pups for sale along the roadside in Sabugeiro, though these probably aren't pure-bred.

BEIRAS

raise their rates, typically from January to around April.

There are hostels at Penhas da Saúde and Guarda, and at least eight camp sites near the centre of the park. Turismo Habitação properties, concentrated on the western slopes, can be booked through turismos or Adruse (see under Gouveia later in this chapter).

Shopping
Souvenir shops in Serra towns sell *queijo da serra* (see the boxed text), loaves of heavy *pão de centeio* (rye bread) and *pão de milho* (corn bread), honey, smoked hams and sausages. Nonedible items for sale include woollen hats, slippers, rugs, coats and waistcoats, as well as baskets and miniature wine barrels and tubs.

Getting There & Around
Express buses run daily from Coimbra to Seia, Guarda and Covilhã, and from Aveiro, Porto and Lisbon to Guarda and Covilhã.

Serra da Estrela Cheese
Creamy, semisoft *queijo da serra* is made, usually in 1kg to 2kg rounds, during the cold, humid months from November to April. Curing takes about 40 days. A healthy by-product is curd cheese, made from the liquid drained during cheese production.

Most Serra da Estrela farming families make their own cheese, though the process is becoming industrialised, with certified cheese factories (offering tours and sales) on the increase. Towns with cheese factories include Algodres, Arcozelo, Cadafaz, Carrapichana, Celorico da Beira, Folgosinho, Linhares, São Romão and Vale de Azares.

Cheese-centred regional markets are held from November to mid-April, including at Carrapichana (Monday), Fornos de Algodres (every second Monday) and Celorico da Beira (every second Friday). But go early: they're usually in full swing by sunrise and all over by 9am. Good *queijo da serra* costs €12 to €13 per kilogram, though certified pure sheep's-milk cheeses go for €18 to €24 or more.

Big cheese fairs are also a feature of Carnaval weekend (February or March) in Seia (Saturday), Gouveia (Sunday) and Manteigas (Monday).

There are daily IC trains from Lisbon and Coimbra to Guarda (plus IR services calling at Gouveia) and from Lisbon to Covilhã (with IR services on to Guarda) – see town listings for details.

There are regular, though infrequent, bus services around the edges of the park but none directly across it.

Driving can be hairy, thanks to mist and wet or icy roads at high elevations, and stiff winds. The Gouveia–Manteigas N232 road is one of the most tortuous in Portugal. Be ready for traffic jams around Torre on weekends.

SEIA
postcode 6270 • pop 5,700 • elevation 532m
Seia (**sye**-ah), 2km from the N17/IC6 and equipped with big shops and adequate accommodation, is a useful base for weekenders seeking an easy taste of the Serra da Estrela. There is little other reason to stop here though.

Orientation & Information
From the bus station, it's 700m up Avenida Dr Afonso Costa to the **post office** (*Avenida 1 de Maio; open 8.30am-12.30pm & 2pm-6pm Mon-Fri*), the mercado municipal, and the **turismo** (*☎ 238 317 762, fax 238 317 764; open 9am-6pm Mon-Fri, 9am-12.30pm & 2pm-5pm Sat-Sun*).

At the top of Rua Dr Simões Pereira is Praça da República (which, despite the name, is just a street). Here you'll find the small **Parque Natural da Serra da Estrela office** (*☎ 238 310 440, fax 238 310 441; Praça da República 28; open 9am-12.30pm & 2pm-5.30pm Mon-Fri*).

Espaço Internet (*☎ 238 315 601; open 10am-7pm Mon-Fri, 2pm-5pm Sat*) is a municipal facility offering free Internet access. You can get here from Avenida dos Combatentes de Grande Guerra (stairs beside the Junta de Freguesia office) or Avenida Luís Vaz de Camões (stairs at left side of Cinema Teatro Jardim).

Places to Stay
Residencial Jardim (*☎ 238 311 414, fax 238 310 091; Edifício Jardim II, Avenida Luís Vaz de Camões; doubles €35*) is a sparsely furnished, squeaky-clean place in a shopping complex.

Hotel Camelo (*☎ 238 310 100; e hotelcamelo@mail.telepac.pt; Avenida 1 de Maio 16; doubles Jan-Apr & Sat & Sun year-round €67,*

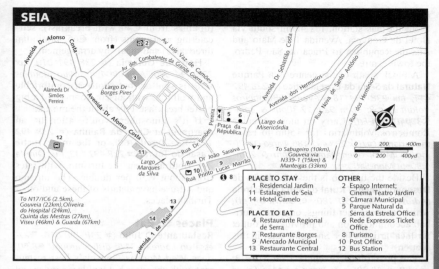

SEIA

PLACE TO STAY	OTHER
1 Residencial Jardim	2 Espaço Internet;
11 Estalagem de Seia	Cinema Teatro Jardim
14 Hotel Camelo	3 Câmara Municipal
	5 Parque Natural da
PLACE TO EAT	Serra da Estrela Office
4 Restaurante Regional	6 Rede Expressos Ticket
de Serra	Office
7 Restaurante Borges	8 Turismo
9 Mercado Municipal	10 Post Office
13 Restaurante Central	12 Bus Station

Mon-Fri July–mid-Sept €55, Mon-Fri other times €45) is a luxurious alternative with a pool, tennis court and free off-street parking. All rooms face away from the street and most have views. Breakfast is included in the rates.

Estalagem de Seia (☎ 238 315 866, fax 238 315 538; Avenida Dr Afonso Costa; doubles €58) offers elegant rooms with antique furniture, in the town's oldest building.

Quinta das Mestras (☎ 238 602 988, fax 238 602 989; w www.pandaline.pt/qtames tras; N510 Nogueira do Cravo–Bobadela road; doubles with/without shower & toilet €45/40, cabanas with shared facilities €34) is a renovated farmhouse and stables, 27km west of Oliveira do Hospital. It has peaceful private rooms, two isolated cabanas, and a small kitchen (€10 extra). Breakfast is included in the rates. Visitors without cars can take a taxi from Seia (about €9) or a Lisbon-bound bus from Gouveia (€6.50, four daily) to Oliveira, where your hosts can collect you.

Places to Eat
Restaurante Central (☎ 238 314 433; Avenida 1 de Maio 12B; mains €7.50, daily specials €6; open daily), near Hotel Carmelo, offers modest prices and quick service.

Restaurante Regional de Serra (☎ 238 312 717; Avenida dos Combatentes da Grande Guerra 14; specialities around €9; open daily) is well known for hearty regional specialities, including chanfana á serrana (highland goat), plus pricey seafood.

Restaurante Borges (☎ 238 313 010; 1st floor, Travessa do Funchal 7; daily specials €5-10; open Fri-Wed) offers good-value food; try its arroz de feijão (a stew of beans and rice).

Getting There & Away
The main long-distance carriers are **Rede Expressos** (☎ 238 313 102) and **Marques** (☎ 238 312 858). Each goes to Gouveia (€1.60, 25 minutes), and Marques continues to Guarda (€7.70, two hours), five times each weekday. Rede Expressos runs daily from Sunday to Friday via Guarda (€6.70, 1¼ hours) to Covilhã (€8.50, two hours), and daily to Coimbra (€8.20, 2¼ hours). Marques goes six times daily to Viseu (€3, 1½ hours), less often at weekends.

Rede Expressos also has a central **ticket office** (Rua da República 52).

GOUVEIA
postcode 6290 • pop 3800 • elevation 650m
Dozy Gouveia (goo-**vye**-ah), located 5km from the N17, has just about enough information, accommodation, food and transport to be a base for exploring the western side of the parque natural. Its sole attraction is the charming Abel Manta Museu de Art Moderna.

Orientation & Information

From the bus station, it's 450m south via Hotel de Gouveia, Avenida 1 de Maio and Rua da República to Praça de São Pedro, the town centre.

A block south of the centre is a **Parque Natural da Serra da Estrela office** (☎ 238 492 411, fax 238 494 183; Avenida Bombeiros Voluntários 8; open 9am-12.30pm & 2pm-5.30pm Mon-Fri). Carry on along Avenida Bombeiros Voluntários for 150m to reach the **turismo** (☎/fax 238 492 185; Largo Dr Alípio de Melo; open 9am-12.30pm & 2pm-5.30pm Mon-Sat).

Beside the turismo is the **Associação de Desenvolvimento Rural da Serra da Estrela** (Adruse; ☎ 238 490 180; e adruse@ip.pt), which, among other things, organises Turihab accommodation and provides an outlet for local artisans (see Shopping later in this section).

The **post office** (Avenida 1 de Maio 3; open 9am-12.30pm & 2pm-6pm Mon-Fri) is between Praça de São Pedro and the Hotel de Gouveia. Free Internet access is available at the **municipal library** (☎ 238 490 230; Praça de São Pedro 5; open 10am-12.30pm & 2pm-6pm Mon-Fri).

Abel Manta Museu de Arte Moderna

Gouveia's favourite son, Abel Manta (1888–1982), was a painter whose round-faced portraits now fill the former manor house of the Condes de Vinhós (☎ 238 493 648; Rua Direita 45; admission free; open 9.30am-12.30pm & 2pm-6pm Tues-Sun), south off Praça de São Pedro. But it's his son João Abel Manta who steals the show with an amazing breadth of style, from haunting portraits to cartoons.

Places to Stay

Curral do Negro (☎ 238 491 008; e info@fp campismo; adult/tent/car €2.40/1.90/1.90; open Mar-Nov), 3km east on the Folgosinho road, is open to holders of the CCI (see Visas & Documents in the Facts for the Visitor chapter).

Quinta das Cegonhas (☎ 238 745 886, 964 887 641; e cegonhas@cegonhas.com; Nabainhos; adult/car €3/2.20, tent €2.50-3.30; open year-round), 6km northeast of Gouveia, is a restored 17th-century quinta (farmhouse) with a pool, tent sites with grand views, caravans (from €26), rooms (doubles from €40 with breakfast), self-catering apartments (from €65, minimum three days) and meals by arrangement.

Hotel de Gouveia (☎ 238 491 010, fax 239 494 370; Avenida 1 de Maio; doubles €38) is soulless but spotless, comfortable and well run, with air-con rooms and a big buffet breakfast. Pity about the muzak.

If it's atmosphere you're after, try an apartment at **Casa da Rainha** (☎ 238 492 132; Rua Direita 68), or the more rustic **Casas do Toural** (☎ 238 492 132; Rua Direita 74). Both are near the turismo, with rates from about €50 per double. The turismo and Adruse have details of these and other Turihab places.

Places to Eat

Restaurante O Júlio (☎ 238 498 016; Travessa do Loureiro 11A; dishes around €8.50; open Wed-Mon) is Gouveia's best restaurant, with cheerless but faultless service and regional specialities such as cabrito à serrana (mountain kid). Even the cheapest feijoada (pork-and-bean casserole) is made with care, and helpings are generous.

Bar Impérium (☎ 238 492 142; Travessa do Loureiro 1; light meals from €4.50; open Tues-Sun), across the path from O Júlio, offers cheaper lunches from the same kitchen.

Self-caterers will find the **mercado municipal** (open Mon-Fri & morning Sat), opposite the turismo, at its best on Thursday.

Shopping

O Mundo Rural (Largo Dr Alípio de Melo; open 10am-12.30pm & 2.30pm-6.30pm Mon-Sat, 10am-3pm Sun) is housed at Adruse (see Orientation & Information) and serves as an outlet for regional artisans. Products include ceramics, fabrics and food – quiejo de serra, Dão wines, vinegar, honey – and prices are lower than at some of the park's private outlets.

Cabaz Beirão (☎ 238 491 225; Rua da Cadeia Velha 2), around the block from the library, is a small grocery shop that's savvy about Serra cheese and other local products and sells them at nontourist prices.

Getting There & Away

Long-distance coaches stop at the bus station (Rua Cidade da Guarda) and in the centre. The main operators are **Rede Expressos**

(☎ *238 493 675)* and **Marques** *(☎ 238 312 858)*. Each runs to Seia (€1.60, 25 minutes) five times per weekday, with Rede Expressos continuing to Coimbra (€8.70, 2¼ hours) and Lisbon. A Marques bus goes daily to Guarda (€2.40, 1½ hours).

Gouveia is on the Beira Alta line from Lisbon to Guarda (the station is 14km north near Ribamondego) – regional trains stop five times a day between Coimbra and Guarda. A taxi between Gouveia and the station will cost around €10.

SABUGEIRO
postcode 6270 • pop 700 • elevation 1050m
Sabugeiro, 12km southeast of Seia on the N339 to Torre, is at heart a typical Serra da Estrela mountain village, with chickens on the paths and sturdy farmer-shepherd families living in stone houses with slate roofs. But it also happens to be Portugal's highest village, and has therefore become a tourist magnet. The main road is a gauntlet of *pensões* and souvenir shops.

There is still an 'old' Sabugeiro too, centred on a small granite church; you can even stay in a renovated village house. Accommodation is pricey in winter but great value the rest of the year, and on summer weekdays the village is positively somnolent.

Sabugeiro is also a good place to pick up *queijo da serra*, smoked ham, rye bread, juniper-berry firewater, and fleecy slippers of Serra sheep's wool.

Places to Stay & Eat
Casa do Serrinho *(☎ 238 314 304; Largo Nossa Senhora de Fátima; doubles summer/ winter about €25/35)*, at the top of the village, has four rooms and a shared kitchen.

Abrigo da Montanha *(☎/fax 238 315 262; doubles summer/winter €35/43)*, across the road from Casa do Serrinho, has rooms with private shower; breakfast is included. This and other places along the road also have restaurants.

You can get closer to local life in one of several dozen restored village houses that are equipped with fireplace, kitchenette and bathroom. Rates per day for two/four people start at €45/70 in midsummer (higher in winter). They fill up fast on weekends and in winter. Book through **Casas do Cruzeiro** *(☎ 238 315 872; e quintadocrestelo@quinta docrestelo.pt)*; to get there from the main

road near the bottom of the hill, follow 'Turismo de Aldeia' (Village Tourism) signs to the old centre.

Getting There & Away
The only public transport is a single bus to/from Seia each Wednesday (Seia's market day), departing Sabugeiro about 8am and returning from Seia about noon. A taxi from Seia would cost around €7.50.

MANTEIGAS
postcode 6260 • pop 4050 • elevation 720m
Manteigas is the best base for exploring the Serra da Estrela: centrally located, with a park office, adequate supplies, decent food and comfortable accommodation. Set in a valley at the 700m-high confluence of the Rio Zêzere and several tributaries, it's also one of the most picturesque towns in the range. All around are dizzily steep, terraced hillsides clad in pine and dotted with stone *casais*, beehives and little meadows. The cathedral-like Vale do Zêzere ascends from here to the foot of Torre, and there are good walks in every direction.

There has been a settlement here since at least Moorish times, perhaps because of the hot springs around which the nearby spa of Caldas de Manteigas has grown (open only to those with a medical reference, sadly). Manteigas' once-thriving cloth industry has fallen on hard times, but the area has received a boost from the SkiParque down the road (see this section later in the chapter).

Orientation & Information
From Seia or Gouveia you approach Manteigas down a near vertical switchback road, the N232. The bus from Covilhã or Guarda sets you down at the **turismo** *(☎/fax 275 981 129; Rua Dr Esteves de Carvalho; open 9.30am-noon & 2pm-6pm Tues-Fri, to 8pm Sat)* on the N232.

The headquarters for the **Parque Natural da Serra da Estrela** *(☎ 275 980 060, fax 275 980 069; e pnse@icn.pt; Rua 1 de Maio 2; open 9am-12.30pm & 2pm-5.30pm Mon-Fri)* is across the intersection from the turismo.

The town has no real centre; there's an ATM opposite the Galp station and several banks with currency exchanges on Rua 1 de Maio (turn left as you approach the park office). The police station is about 200m east of the turismo.

BEIRAS

Walking

You could spend weeks looping in and out of Manteigas. Following are the outlines of a few modest walks. For details, and more walks, ask at the turismo or pick up *Discovering the Region of the Serra da Estrela* from the park office. Don't go without a decent topographical map, rain protection and water.

Poço do Inferno A 7km, tree-shaded climb takes you to Poço do Inferno (Hell's Well), a waterfall in the craggy gorge of the Ribeira de Leandres. From the turismo go 500m down the N232, turn right and walk for 1km to bridges. Take the right-hand one across the Rio Zêzere and head downstream. About 200m along, turn right on a forestry track. From here it's 1½ to two hours up to the waterfall, with an elevation change of 400m and fine views northeast.

Return the same way, or head back towards Manteigas down a roughly paved road for about 2.5km, to a pine plantation. To the right of the plantation gate, drop down a few steps past a former forestry post, descend to houses by the river, cross the bridge and climb back to Manteigas, for a total walk of about 3½ hours.

Alternatively, carry on past the plantation for a further 3.5km to Caldas de Manteigas, plus 3km along the road back to Manteigas (total 4½ hours).

Penhas Douradas & Vale do Rossim A more demanding walk goes to Penhas Douradas, a collection of windblown holiday houses. The track climbs northwest out of town via Rua Dr Afonso Costa to join a sealed, switchback forestry road and, briefly, a wide loop of the Seia-bound N232. Branch left off the N232 almost immediately, on another forestry road to the Meteorological Observatory. From there it's a short, gentle ascent to Penhas Douradas.

You're about 700m above Manteigas here, and you mustn't miss the stunning view from a stub of rock called Fragão de Covão; just follow the signs. (You can also drive up the N232 just for the view: about 18km from Manteigas, then left at the first turning after the one marked *observatório*, and 1km to the sign for Fragão de Covão; save your oil-pan and walk the rest of the way.)

Walking back the same way makes for a return trip of about 5½ hours. Alternatively,

carry on for 3.4km to the Vale do Rossim reservoir and camp site (see Places to Stay).

Vale do Zêzere A long day-walk or a lingering two-day trip takes you through this magnificent, glacier-scoured valley at the foot of Torre. Its only drawback: the trail is shadeless, and baking in clear summer weather.

Follow the N338 for about 3km to Caldas de Manteigas, leaving the road just below the spa, for the track up the valley. En route are typical stone *casais*. About 9km from Manteigas at Covões (where there's a shelter), a bridge takes you over the Rio Zêzere. Where the huts end, climb up to the N338; a few hundred metres along the road is a crystalline spring. About 3km along the road at a hairpin turn is the Covão da Ametade camp site (see Places to Stay), about 3½ hours from Manteigas.

SkiParque

SkiParque (☎ 275 982 870; e skiparque@iol .pt; N232; open 10am-6pm Sun-Thur, 10am-10pm Fri & Sat) is a big dry-ski run 7.5km east of Manteigas, with a lift, gear rental, café and camp site (see Places to Stay). Manteigas hoteliers love it, as their bookings are no longer cancelled when there's no snow. Prices for weekday/weekend/night-time skiing start at €10/12/14.50 for two hours, and group lessons are available.

Places to Stay

Camping Two park-run camp sites that are, surprisingly, free of charge are **Covão da Ametade**, a popular tents-only site 13km from Manteigas at the head of the Vale do Zêzere, and **Covão da Ponte**, 5.4km up the N232 and 6km along an access road to the Rio Mondego. Toilets, a snack bar and (at Covão da Ponte) showers are open, and park staff on hand, in July and August; the rest of the year, campers are asked to notify the park office at Manteigas in advance.

Vale do Rossim (☎ 275 334 933), beside a reservoir 23km from Manteigas, has hot showers, a café-restaurant, small shop and limited shade. At the time of writing, rates and seasons were uncertain due to a change in management; contact the park office at Manteigas for an update.

Relva da Reboleira (☎ 275 982 870; e skiparque@iol.pt; adult/tent/car €1.50/

1.50/1.30; open year-round) is a treeless, functional facility at the foot of SkiParque. Hot showers cost an extra €0.50.

Rossio de Valhelhas (☎ 275 487 160; e *jfvalhelhas@clix.pt; Valhelhas; adult/tent/car €1.60/1.40/1.50; open May-Sept)* is a flat, grassy and shady municipal facility by the N232, about 15km from Manteigas.

Quinta do Covão de Santa Maria (☎ 275 982 359; *tent sites per person about €2.50)* has space for pitching a small tent.

Pensões & Residenciais With newly renovated rooms, **Pensão Serradalto** (☎ 275 981 151; *Rua 1 de Maio 15; doubles with bathroom & breakfast €35)* offers fine valley views. It also has a café and restaurant. To get here, turn left (south) at the park office.

Residencial Estrela (☎ 275 981 288; *Rua Dr Sobral 5; doubles with breakfast €45)* provides comfortable doubles, with full bathroom. Relax, the church bells across the road go quiet from 10pm to 7am. To get here, bear right (north) at the park office.

Quinta do Covão de Santa Maria (☎ 275 982 359; *doubles €30)* is a solitary farm, the owners of which farm organically, mill their own rye flour and make *queijo de cabra* (goat cheese). You can prepare your own meals in their kitchen, or they'll feed you for an extra charge. English and French are spoken. Each of the two rooms has a private bathroom. It's beside the Rio Mondego, 3km down a bad road opposite the Pousada de São Lourenço (see later in this section), from where the owners can collect you. Book ahead.

Pousadas & Turihab A welcoming and surprisingly good-value Turihab house is **Casa de São Roque** (☎ 275 981 125, Oct-May Lisbon ☎ 218 871 993; *Rua de Santo António 51; doubles Apr-May & Oct-Nov about €40, rest of year about €45)*, with antique furnishings and with complimentary breakfast served on the patio. From the turismo take the second left beyond Pensão Serradalto.

Quinta de Leandres (*inquire at Casa de São Roque; twins with bathroom or doubles with shower Apr-May & Oct-Nov about €40, rest of year about €45)* is a restored farmhouse east of town, with a swimming pool, a play frame for the kids and apple orchards.

Pousada de São Lourenço (☎ 275 982 450, fax 275 982 453; *doubles €117)* is

13km above and north of town on the N232, with stupendous views up the Vale do Zêzere and, on a clear day, into Spain.

Places to Eat
Cervejaria Central (☎ 275 982 787; *grilled dishes €6-7; open Mon-Sat)*, a block back from the park office, has a cheap and cheerful dining space with a short list of decent lunchtime and evening grills.

Residencial Estrela (see Places to Stay) has higher aspirations and prices than Cervejaria Central, with a member of the Académie de Gastronomie Brillat-Savarin in the kitchen. But at the time of writing the restaurant was undergoing an energetic renovation, and there were few clues about future prices.

Clube de Compras (*Rua 1 de Maio; open around 8am-8pm daily)* is a well-stocked grocery store opposite Pensão Serradalto. **Bar-Bar** (☎ 275 982 540; *Rua 1 de Maio; open 8.30am-late daily)*, the corner café-bar just north of the grocery store, has munchies when everything else is closed.

Getting There & Away
Joalto/RBI buses leave from Guarda for Manteigas at around 11.30am and 5pm daily, returning from Manteigas at about 7am and 12.45pm.

To reach Manteigas from Covilhã, catch an 8.20am Guarda-bound bus and change at Vale Formoso; returning from Manteigas, catch the 7am Guarda-bound bus and change at Vale de Amoreira. During school-term time there's also a direct Covilhã–Manteigas service. All trips cost about €3.30 and take about 1½ hours; none run on weekends or holidays.

TORRE
Mainland Portugal's highest point is rather disappointing – flat, featureless and occupied by several ageing radar domes. The official elevation is 1993m, though an obelisk at the roadhead reaches up to 2000m. Skiers will find three lifts, beginner-grade slopes, a sweaty shopping arcade smelling of cheese and smoke, and (throughout the winter and on every weekend) a gleeful sea of Portuguese and their cars and coaches.

A **regional turismo** (☎ 275 314 551; *open 9.30am-1pm & 2pm-5.30pm Fri-Tues year-round)* shivers in the arcade. **Ski-gear rental**

BEIRAS

(open 9am-5pm daily during ski season), is available from a building a few hundred metres down the Seia road, and includes skis, poles and boots (€18 per day), snowboards (€15 per day) or sledges (€8/10 per 30/60 minutes). The receipt for your refundable deposit is also your lift ticket.

There are no bus services to Torre. A taxi costs about €20 from Covilhã, €30 from Seia, or €16 from Manteigas.

PENHAS DA SAÚDE

Penhas, about 10km from Covilhã on the N339, isn't a town but a weather-beaten collection of private chalets at an elevation of about 1500m. It's located uphill from a burned-out tuberculosis sanatorium (slated for renovation as a Pousada de Portugal) and downhill from the Barragem do Viriato dam. Supplies are limited; if you're planning to go walking, do your shopping in Covilhã.

Places to Stay & Eat

Pousada da juventude *(☎ 275 335 375;* **e** *pe nhas@movijovem.pt; dorm beds summer/ winter €8.50/12.50, doubles with bathroom €24/35, without bathroom €20.50/30; open year-round)* is Penhas' first-rate hostel.

Pensão O Pastor *(☎ 275 322 810, fax 275 314 035; doubles summer/winter about €40/ 50)* has uninspiring rooms and a gift shop; breakfast is included.

Hotel Serra da Estrela *(☎ 275 310 300;* **e** *hse@turistrela.pt; doubles mid-Apr–Nov €70, Dec–mid-Apr €107)* is the top place to stay at Penhas – posh and professional, with handsome rooms as well as six-bed chalets. The same owners run the 'resort' at Torre.

There are several cafés along the N339.

Getting There & Away

At weekends from around mid-July to mid-September, and daily during August, local **Transcovilhã** *(☎ 275 336 017)* buses (€1.30) climb to Penhas from the kiosk on Rua António Augusto d'Aguiar in Covilhã, departing at about 8am and 2pm. Otherwise, you must take a taxi (about €15), hitch, cycle or walk.

COVILHÃ

postcode 6200 • pop 35,100
• elevation 700m

This dour university town is the urban centre closest to the heart of the Parque Natural da Serra da Estrela, with modestly priced accommodation and a convenient regional turismo. It's of minor interest in itself aside, from a good museum of the old local mainstay, wool-making.

Though Covilhã is actually in Beira Baixa, we have put it here because of its essential connection to the mountains and the park.

Orientation

Covilhã seems pinned to the side of the Serra da Estrela foothills. From train and long-distance bus stations (both on a road called Eixo TCT) it's a punishing 1.5km climb to Praça do Município, the town centre – for local transport options see Getting Around later in this section.

Street parking is dire; drivers should park well away from the centre, or use the parking garage on Rua Visconde da Coriscada.

Information

The **regional turismo** *(☎ 275 319 560;* **e** *turismo.estrela@mail.telepac.pt; Avenida Frei Heitor Pinto; open 9am-12.30pm & 2pm-5.30pm Mon-Sat)*, by the *jardim público* (public gardens), dispenses information, bank-like, from behind a glass window.

On Praça do Município are several banks with ATMs, and the **post office** *(open 8.30am-6.30pm Mon-Fri, 9am-12.30pm Sat)*. **PostNet** *(Rua Comendador Campos Melo 27; open 9am-7.30pm Mon-Fri, 9am-1pm Sat)* is a franchise stationery shop offering Internet access for €0.80 per 15 minutes, plus stamps and other postal services; don't confuse it with the post office's NetPost.

Pêro de Covilhã

Covilhã is the birthplace of one Pêro de Covilhã, a young Arabic-speaking Portuguese who went east in search of spice markets, and perhaps to find the legendary Christian priest-king Prester John, on behalf of Dom João II. Disguised as a Muslim trader he journeyed through Egypt, India and even to the holy cities of Mecca and Medina. He was finally detained by a Coptic Christian king in what is now Ethiopia, where he married and lived out his days. His is the statue in Praça do Comércio, and the pavement beside it bears a huge map showing his travels.

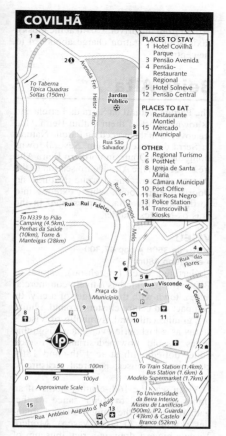

COVILHÃ

PLACES TO STAY
1 Hotel Covilhã Parque
3 Pensão Avenida
4 Pensão-Restaurante Regional
5 Hotel Solneve
12 Pensão Central

PLACES TO EAT
7 Restaurante Montiel
15 Mercado Municipal

OTHER
2 Regional Turismo
6 PostNet
8 Igreja de Santa Maria
9 Câmara Municipal
10 Post Office
11 Bar Rosa Negro
13 Police Station
14 Transcovilhã Kiosks

To Taberna Típica Quadras Soltas (150m)

Jardim Público

Avenida Frei Heitor Pinto

Rua São Salvador

Rua C Campos

Rua Rui Faleiro

To N339 to Pião Camping (4.5km), Penhas da Saúde (10km), Torre & Manteigas (28km)

Rua Melo

Rua das Flores

Rua Visconde da Coriscada

Praça do Município

0   50   100m
0   50   100yd
Approximate Scale

To Train Station (1.4km), Bus Station (1.6km) & Modelo Supermarket (1.7km)

To Universidade da Beira Interior, Museu de Lanifícios (500m), IP2, Guarda (43km) & Castelo Branco (52km)

Rua António Augusto d'Aguiar

BEIRAS

The **police station** (☎ 275 320 922; Rua António Augusto d'Aguiar) is just south of Praça do Município.

The regional university, the Universidade da Beira Interior, is situated well south of the centre. Few of its 5000 students seem to venture into town.

Things to See

There's little to look at, although the narrow, winding streets west of Praça do Município have a plain, quiet charm. In the midst of them is the **Igreja de Santa Maria**, with a startling facade covered in azulejos.

Covilhã, the centre of what used to be one of Europe's biggest wool-producing areas, has fallen on hard times thanks to Salazarera neglect and then Asian competition. On

the site of the former Real Fábrica de Panos (Royal Textile Factory; founded in 1764 by the Marquês de Pombal), and now within the university, is the **Museu de Lanifícios** (*Museum of Wool-Making; ☎ 275 319 700, ext 3131; adult/youth 15-25/child under 15 €2/1/free; open 9.30am-noon & 2.30pm-6pm Tues-Sun*), which looks back at this vanishing local industry. The centrepiece is a phalanx of huge dyeing vats.

Places to Stay

Camping Some 4km up the N339 towards Penhas da Saúde, **Pião Camping** (*☎ 275 314 312; nonmembers per adult/car €2/1.60, tent €2-2.50; open year-round*) is a snug but wooded facility run by the Clube de Campismo e Caravanismo de Covilhã. Bungalows are also available, at €30 per double.

Pensões & Residenciais Quiet **Pensão-Restaurante Regional** (*☎/fax 275 322 596; Rua das Flores 4; doubles with breakfast €25*) has threadbare rooms with a shared toilet, and a good-value restaurant.

Pensão Central (*☎ 275 322 727; Rua Nuno Álvares Pereira 14; rooms per person €10*) is an ancient place with old-fashioned, spotless rooms (no TV); insist on a room at the back, with fine views and no street noise. It's good value, despite the dreary exterior and seriously sloping floors.

Pensão Avenida (*☎ 275 322 140; Rua São Salvador; doubles €23-25, Sat Jan-Mar €30*), facing the *jardim público*, has sunny, high-ceilinged old rooms with a shared shower and toilet; some rooms sleep up to five people at better rates.

Hotels Briskly run and as central as you can get, **Hotel Solneve** (*☎ 275 323 001/2, fax 275 314 773; Rua Visconde da Coriscada 126; doubles with breakfast €43, Fri & Sat Nov-Mar €65*) has many rooms with super views. All have a full bathroom, and there is free off-street parking.

Hotel Covilhã Parque (*☎ 275 327 518; e imb@mail.telepac.pt; Avenida Frei Heitor Pinto; doubles/triples €46/63, Fri & Sat Nov-Apr €58/82*), in the high-rise building by the turismo, is newly renovated and big enough to have space even in peak season. Rooms have air-con and the upper ones have splendid views. Rates include a generous buffet breakfast.

Places to Eat

Pensão-Restaurante Regional (*see Places to Stay; specials under €5, mains €6-7; open Mon-Sat, morning Sun*) offers a meaty menu of good-value local dishes, plus burgers and omelettes.

Restaurante Montiel (*☎ 275 322 086; Praça do Município 33-37; daily specials around €8; open daily*) is a friendly venue for a caffeine hit, with good pastries. The upstairs dining room is OK if a bit pricey, with regional cooking and *pratos do dia*.

Restaurante Solneve (*mains from €6, specials under €5; open Mon-Sat, morning Sun*), below the hotel of the same name (see Places to Stay), serves lunch specials plus interesting local and international dishes. Hotel guests pay 10% less.

Self-caterers will find abundant fruit and vegetables available most mornings at the **mercado municipal** (*Rua António Augusto d'Aguiar*). There's a big **Modelo** supermarket a block south of the bus station (both on Eixo TCT).

Entertainment

Taberna Típica Quadras Soltas (*☎ 275 313 683; Avenida de Santarém 39*), well above the town centre, is a cheerful café-bar that sometimes has late-night fado on an unpredictable schedule (typically on Friday or Saturday).

Bar Rosa Negro (*Praça do Município; open Mon-Sat*), near the post office, is a popular central nightspot.

Getting There & Away

All long-distance buses run from the **main bus station** (*☎ 275 336 700*). Joalto and Rede Expressos go jointly to Guarda (€3.80, 45 minutes), and via Castelo Branco (€5.50, one hour) to Lisbon, each about three times a day. Each has multiple daily services to Viseu (€8, 2¼ hours) and to Porto (€10.20, 4½ to 5½ hours). Rede Expressos also goes via Guarda to Seia (€8.50, two hours) once daily Sunday to Friday.

One daily IR (€10.20, 5½ hours) and two IC (€11, 4½ hours) trains run direct from Lisbon, with Porto connections.

Getting Around

Bus No 2 (Rodrigo) runs about every 30 minutes from the bus and train stations, to

the Transcovilhã kiosk by the police station (€0.80 from the driver, €0.40 at the kiosk). Taxis at either station charge about €4 to the centre.

Beira Alta

The Parque Natural da Serra da Estrela and its towns, most of them within Beira Alta, are covered in the preceding Parque Natural da Serra da Estrela section. Several towns along the Rio Douro in northern Beira Alta are covered in the Alto Douro section of the Douro chapter. The Parque Natural do Douro Internacional, which extends into northeast Beira Alta, is presented in the Trás-os-Montes chapter.

VISEU

postcode 3500 • pop 47,300
• elevation 480m

Underrated Viseu (vi-**zeh**-oo), capital of Beira Alta province, is a lively commercial hub, a town with the swagger of a city. Its compact old centre clusters around a hulking granite cathedral, symbolic of Viseu's status as a bishopric ever since Visigothic times. Its old, now-pedestrianised market zone, dotted with stoic 17th- and 18th-century townhouses, is a real pleasure to squeeze through.

Viseu was the 16th-century home of an important school of Renaissance art that gathered around the painter Vasco Fernandes (known as O Grão Vasco). Modern Viseu's biggest draw is a rich museum of his work and that of his friends and students. Although it's presently closed for renovations, some of the finest works are on view elsewhere in town.

Much of the town's modern wealth comes from the excellent wines of the adjacent Dão region (see the boxed text).

You could do Viseu justice in under a day (you'll find that accommodation is tight and a bit pricey), but an overnight stop lets you while away an evening in one of several good restaurants and the wee hours in a cheerful pub.

History

Legend says Viriato, chief of the Lusitani tribe (see History in the Facts about Portugal chapter), took refuge in a cave here before being hunted down in 139 BC by the Romans, though there's scant evidence for this and no sign of a cave.

The Romans did build a fortified camp just across the Rio Pavia from Viseu, and some well-preserved segments of their roads survive nearby (see Roman & Other Remains later in this section). The town, conquered and reconquered in the struggles between Christians and Moors, was finally taken by Dom Fernando I in 1057.

Afonso V completed Viseu's sturdy walls in about 1472. The town soon spread beyond them, grown large and wealthy from agriculture and trade. An annual 'free fair' declared by João III in 1510 carries on today as one of the region's biggest agricultural and handicrafts expositions.

Orientation

Viseu sits beside the Rio Pavia, a tributary of the Mondego. In the middle of town is Praça da República, known to all as O Rossio. From here the shopping district stretches east along Rua Formosa and Rua da Paz, and then north into the historic centre along Rua do Comércio and Rua Direita.

At the town's highest point and historical heart is the cathedral.

The bus station is 500m northwest of the Rossio along Avenida Dr António José de Almeida. Drivers should avoid the old town, with its harrowing one-way lanes.

Information

The **regional turismo** (☎ 232 420 950; e *turismo@rt-dao-lafoes.com; Avenida Calouste Gulbenkian; open 9am-12.30pm & 2.30pm-6pm Mon-Fri, 10am-12.30pm & 2.30pm-5.30pm Sat, 9.30am-12.30pm Sun May-Oct*) can help you get oriented.

Banks with ATMs line Rua Formosa, and the **main post office** (*Rua dos Combatentes da Grande Guerra; open 8.30am-6.30pm Mon-Fri, 9am-12.30pm Sat*) is nearby. The local **Instituto Português da Juventude** (*IPJ;* ☎ 232 483 410; *Portal do Fontelo*) has free Internet access for half-hour intervals from around 9am to 6pm weekdays.

Emergency services include the district **São Teotónio Hospital** (☎ 232 420 500; *Avenida Dom Duarte*), south of the centre; and the **police station** (☎ 232 480 380; *Rua Alves Martins*).

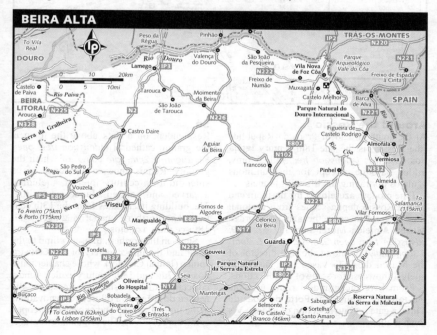

BEIRA ALTA

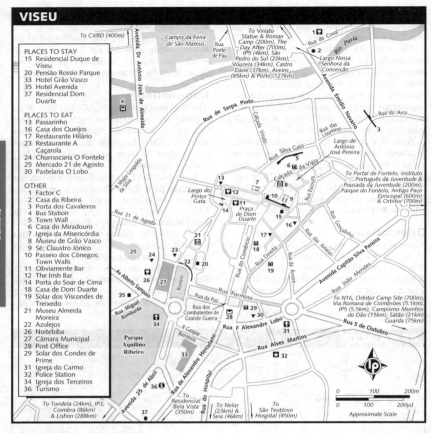

VISEU

PLACES TO STAY
15 Residencial Duque de Viseu
20 Pensão Rossio Parque
33 Hotel Grão Vasco
35 Hotel Avenida
37 Residencial Dom Duarte

PLACES TO EAT
13 Passarinho
16 Casa dos Queijos
17 Restaurante Hilário
23 Restaurante A Caçarola
24 Churrascaria O Fontelo
25 Mercado 21 de Agosto
30 Pastelaria O Lobo

OTHER
1 Factor C
2 Casa da Ribeira
3 Porta dos Cavaleiros
4 Bus Station
5 Town Wall
6 Casa do Miradouro
7 Igreja da Misericórdia
8 Museu de Grão Vasco
9 Sé; Claustro Jónico
10 Passeio dos Cónegos; Town Walls
11 Obviamente Bar
12 The Irish Bar
14 Porta do Soar de Cima
18 Casa de Dom Duarte
19 Solar dos Viscondes de Treixedo
21 Museu Almeida Moreira
22 Azulejos
26 Noitebiba
27 Câmara Municipal
28 Post Office
29 Solar dos Condes de Prime
31 Igreja do Carmo
32 Police Station
34 Igreja dos Terceiros
36 Turismo

Around the Rossio

At the southern end of Praça da República (the Rossio) is the late-18th-century **Igreja dos Terceiros** (admission free), all gloomy, gilded baroque, except for the luminous azulejos portraying the life of St Francis.

Fine modern **azulejos** at the northern end of the Rossio depict scenes from regional life. Beyond these is the azulejo-adorned **Museu Almeida Moreira** (☎ 232 423 769; admission free; open 9am-12.30pm & 2pm-5.30pm daily), home of the first director of the Museu de Grão Vasco (see later) and lately a showcase for some of its collections.

From here the grandest route into the old town is through the **Porta do Soar de Cima**, a gate set into a section of Afonso V's town walls.

Sé

Resplendent on a rock above the town is the granite cathedral (admission free; open 8am-noon & 2pm-7pm daily), of which the gloomy Renaissance facade conceals a splendid 16th-century interior, including a carved and painted Manueline ceiling. The building itself dates from the 13th century. The northern chapel is graced with 18th-century azulejos.

Stairs in the northern transept climb to the choir and the upper gallery of the **Claustro Jónico** (Ionian Cloister), whose chapterhouse boasts 17th- and 18th-century azulejos and a collection of ecclesiastical treasures, the **Museu do Arte Sacra** (closed for renovations at the time of writing and expected to reopen some time in 2003). The original, lower level of the cloister is one of Portugal's earliest Italian Renaissance structures. Returning to the church you pass through a Romanesque-Gothic portal, rediscovered during restoration work in 1918.

Facing the cathedral is the 1775 **Igreja da Misericórdia** – rococo, symmetrical and blindingly white outside, and neoclassical, severe and rather dull inside. At the time of writing some of the finest works from the Museu de Grão Vasco were on temporary display *(admission €1.50, 10am-12.30pm Sun free; open 2pm-6pm Tues, 10am-6pm Wed-Sun)* in rooms at the right side of this church.

Museu de Grão Vasco

Adjoining the cathedral is a great, square granite box, the Paço de Três Escalões (Palace of Three Steps), probably a contemporary of the cathedral and originally built as the Bishop's Palace. In 1916 it reopened as a museum (☎ *232 422 049;* e *mgv@ipmuseus.pt)* for the works of Viseu's own Vasco Fernandes, one of Portugal's seminal Renaissance painters (see the boxed text 'Grão Vasco & the Viseu School'), and of others in the so-called Viseu School.

Unfortunately, this fine collection is closed for renovations until at least 2004, though the most famous of Grão Vasco's works are on display at the Igreja da Misericórdia (see earlier).

Around the Sé

North of the cathedral along Rua Silva Gaio is the longest remaining stretch of the old **town walls**. At the bottom, across Avenida Emídio Navarro, is another old town gate, the **Porta dos Cavaleiros**.

South of the cathedral beneath the Passeio dos Cônegos (Curates Walk, on part of the old wall) is **Praça de Dom Duarte**, named after the Portuguese monarch (brother of Prince Henry the Navigator) who was born in Viseu. Several of the square's old mansions show off their wrought-iron balconies and genteel contours. Southward is **Casa de Dom Duarte** *(Rua Dom Duarte; closed to public)*, a house with a beautiful Manueline window and traditionally regarded as the king's birthplace.

Rua Augusto Hilário runs southeast through Viseu's former **judiaria** (14th- to 16th-century Jewish quarter). **Rua Direita**, Viseu's most appealing street and once the most direct route to the hill top, is now a lively melee of shops, souvenir stands, restaurants and old townhouses.

Mansions

The most handsome of Viseu's many old townhouses is the 18th-century **Solar dos Condes de Prime** *(Rua dos Andrades)*, also called Casa de Cimo de Vila, currently in use as a music conservatory. Among other stately homes are the 18th-century **Solar dos Viscondes de Treixedo** *(Rua Direita)*, now a bank, and the 16th-century **Casa do Miradouro** *(Calçada da Vigia)*, just off Largo de António José Pereira. None of these homes are open to the public.

Parque do Fontelo

In Viseu's biggest green area, beyond the Portal do Fontelo, are the 16th-century Antigo Paço Episcopal (former Bishop's Palace), being refurbished as a Solar do Dão (see the boxed text 'Wines of the Dão Region'), the once-lovely Renaissance gardens, a stadium and recreation complex.

Roman & Other Sites

On an embankment north of the centre is a **statue of Viriato**, chief of the Lusitani. Behind it is the site of a **Roman military camp**, though there's little to see.

Grão Vasco & the Viseu School

Viseu and Lisbon were the main centres of a uniquely Portuguese style of Renaissance art in the 16th century. The brightest lights in the so-called Viseu School of painting were Vasco Fernandes – known as O Grão Vasco, 'the Great Vasco' (1480–1543) – and his colleague and collaborator Gaspar Vaz.

Grão Vasco's work, heavily influenced by the Flemish masters, includes a range of direct, luminous, extra-realistic compositions painted for the cathedral and other churches. Most of them are now at home in the Museu de Grão Vasco.

Wines of the Dão Region

The velvety red wines of the Dão region (an area demarcated in 1907, roughly within the watershed of the Rio Mondego and tributary Rio Dão, south and east of Viseu) have enjoyed a solid reputation since the 16th century, and are today among Portugal's best. Vines have been cultivated here for over 2000 years and possibly longer, though serious wine production only began with the Romans.

Some three-dozen Dão vineyards and producers offer multilingual cellar tours and tastings of these 'Burgundies of Portugal'. The Viseu turismo has a brochure, *Rota do Vinho do Dão*, listing them all. They prefer advance bookings, but one vineyard open to drop-in visitors is **Casa da Ínsua** (☎ 232 642 222; Penalva do Castelo), 30km east of Viseu on the IP5 and N329-1.

Coordinating them all, marketing their wines and maintaining standards is the **Comissão Vitivinicola Regional do Dão** (CVRD; ☎ 232 410 060; e cvrdao@mail.telepac.pt; Avenida Capitão Homem Ribeiro 10, Viseu). The CVRD owns the 16th-century Antigo Paço Episcopal (see Parque do Fontelo) and is ever so slowly converting it into a Solar do Dão, where you can sample a range of Dão wines. Meanwhile the CVRD offers its own tastings and sales, by appointment during week-day business hours.

White Dão wines are also available, though the full-bodied reds are the best (and strongest). Another local speciality is the sparkling white wines of the separate, small Lafões region, northwest of Viseu.

About 5km southeast of the town centre, off the N16, is the **Via Romana de Coimbrões**, a well-preserved stretch of Roman road. The turismo has a good free booklet with information on this and numerous other regional sites of archaeological interest, from the Stone Age to the 19th century.

Special Events

Viseu's biggest annual event is the Feira de São Mateus (St Matthew's Fair), a jamboree of agriculture and handicrafts, which carries on from mid-August to mid-September, augmented by folk music, traditional food, amusements and fireworks. This direct descendant of the town's old 'free fair' still takes place on the Campo da Feira de São Mateus, set aside for the event by João III in 1510.

Places to Stay

Camping About 1.5km east of the Rossio on the N16, adjacent to the Parque do Fontelo, **Orbitur** (☎ 232 436 146; e info@ orbitur.pt; adult/tent/car €3.20/2.60/3.30; open Apr-Sept) operates a shady, well-equipped camp site.

Campismo Moinhos do Dão (☎ 232 610 586; w www.portugal-aktief.com; c/o Café Pinheiro, Tibaldinho, 3530 Mangualde; adult/ small tent €2.50/2.50; open May-Oct) offers something a little different – a no-electricity, no-frills rural camp site, weedy and relaxed,

and built by Dutch dropouts around several restored water-mills on the Rio Dão, 15km southeast of Viseu. In addition to riverside tent sites there are 'gypsy' wagons and bungalows (available per week), a simple restaurant with vegie and nonvegie dishes at dinner, and breakfast and lunch supplies. To get here, follow the blue camping signs for 6km from exit 19 on the IP5, east of Viseu.

Other camp sites are located at São Pedro do Sul, 23km northwest of Viseu; Sátão, 21km northeast; Tondela, 24km southwest; Vouzela, 34km west; and Castro Daire, 37km north.

Hostels Beside the IPJ at Portal do Fontelo is **Pousada da juventude** (☎ 232 420 620; e viseu@movijovem.pt; dorm beds €9.50, doubles with toilet €26.50). There is also another **pousada da juventude** (☎ 232 724 543; e spedrosul@movijovem.pt; dorm beds €12.50, doubles with toilet €35), 22km northwest at the spa centre of São Pedro do Sul.

Pensões & Residenciais Breakfast is included in the rates of all the following places.

Residencial Duque de Viseu (☎/fax 232 421 286, ☎ 965 811 569; Rua das Ameias 22; singles/doubles €20/30) is the best middle-bracket bet, a snug place right below the cathedral with sunny, quiet air-con rooms at the back, and big bathtubs.

BEIRAS

Pensão Rossio Parque (☎ 232 422 085; Rua Soar de Cima 55; doubles with/without bathroom from €35/30), as central as you can get, is a lethargic but well-kept old place overlooking the Rossio.

Residencial Dom Duarte (☎ 232 421 980, fax 232 424 825; Rua de Alexandre Herculano 214; doubles from €25) and the plainer but more efficiently run **Residencial Bela Vista** (☎ 232 422 026, fax 232 428 472; Rua de Alexandre Herculano 510; doubles €45), south of the centre, have big, air-con rooms; the Bela Vista has free off-street parking and does not accept credit cards.

Hotels The **Hotel Avenida** (☎ 232 423 432; w www.turism.net/avenida; Avenida Alberto Sampaio 1; doubles/triples €43/50), within sight of the Rossio, has fussy but good-value rooms, with a generous breakfast included.

Hotel Grão Vasco (☎ 232 423 511, fax 232 426 444; e meliagraovasco@mail.telepac.pt; Rua Gaspar Barreiros; doubles €82.50) is top of the scale in central Viseu. Its rooms have air-con, and the rates include a big breakfast and free off-street parking.

Places to Eat
Viseu is awash in good food for any budget.

Pastelaria O Lobo (Rua Francisco Alexandre Lobo 37; open 8am-8pm daily) is the place for a hit of coffee, pastry and uptown atmosphere.

Passarinho (☎ 232 422 851; Rua Silva Gaio 16; daily specials €3.50; open daily), a threadbare casa de pasto (casual eatery) near the Igreja da Misericórdia, is good for a simple meal if your budget's tight.

Churrascaria O Fontelo (☎ 232 424 221; Rua Conselheiro Afonso de Melo 45; open daily), plain and cheery, has great grilled chicken (€8 for two) and fish (around €6).

Restaurante A Caçarola (☎ 232 421 007; Travessa Major Teles 3; half-/full-portion specials under €5/7; open daily) – clean, bright and popular – offers brisk service and lots of meaty specials.

Casa dos Queijos (☎ 232 422 643; Travessa das Escadinhas da Sé 7; pratos do dia from €4.50, mains €6; open Mon-Sat) gets top marks for carefully prepared cozidos (stews) and grilled salmon, as well as lunch-time pratos do dia – but you could blow your budget on the cheeses and good

maduro (mature) wines, which are on sale at the shop downstairs.

Restaurante O Hilário (☎ 232 436 587; Rua Augusto Hilário 35; half-/full-portions €4/6; open 7pm-9.30pm Mon-Sat) has a menu of imaginative meaty dishes, plus righteous prices and attentive service.

Self-caterers will find fruit, vegetables and other goodies at the **Mercado 21 de Agosto** (Rua 21 de Agosto; open Mon-Sat).

Entertainment
Popular central bars include **Obviamente OK** (☎ 232 426 635; Largo do Pintor Gata 26; open 8.30pm-4.30am Mon-Sat), with good food right into the night; **The Irish Bar** (☎ 232 436 135; Largo Pintor Gata 8; open 9am-2am Mon-Sat), with occasional live Irish music; and **Factor C** (☎ 232 415 808; Largo Nossa Senhora da Conceição 39-43; open 11pm-4am Mon-Sat).

Noitebiba (Rua Conselhero Afonso de Melo 32; open midnight-7am Tues, Fri & Sat) is a dance bar behind the câmara municipal.

The Day After (☎ 232 450 645; open 11pm-7am Tues-Sun), found on the N16 west of the Cava de Viriato, is possibly Portugal's biggest disco, with its 10 dance halls as well as tenpin bowling, go-karts, a restaurant and more.

Shopping
Handicrafts here are noticeably cheaper than in more touristy towns; local specialities include basketware and lace.

Casa da Ribeira (Largo Nossa Senhora da Conceição; open 9am-12.30pm & 2pm-5.30pm Mon-Sat) is a municipal space for local artisans to work and sell their products, including fabrics, basketware, black pottery, wrought iron and glassware. The quality here is good, and prices reasonable. Also look for small handicrafts shops around Rua Direita.

Getting There & Away
Operators at the bus station include the companies **RBL/Rede Expressos** (☎ 232 422 822), **Marques** (☎ 232 423 766) and **Joalto** (☎ 232 426 093).

The best connections – two or more buses each day – are to Coimbra (€6.30, 1½ hours) and Lisbon (€9.80, four hours) with RBL; Aveiro (€5.60, 1½ hours) and Porto (€6.70, two hours) with Marques or

Joalto; Braga (€9, three hours) with Joalto or RBL; and Guarda (€6.10, 1¼ hours) and Covilhã (€8, 2¼ hours) with Joalto.

Rede Expressos and Joalto each have a daily bus via Trancoso and Vila Nova de Foz Côa to Bragança (€10, 3½ hours).

GUARDA
postcode 6300 • pop 26,000
• elevation 1056m
This district capital and bishopric, founded in 1199 to guard the frontier, doesn't have much trouble living up to its traditional description: *fria, farta, forte e feia* (cold, rich, strong and ugly). Even in summer sunlight it is granite-grey, dour and distant, and being at an altitude of over 1000m – it is Portugal's highest fully fledged city – it's nearly always cold. And yet on weekends and holidays it overflows with visitors and accommodation can be tight.

What's the attraction? Perhaps the looming cathedral, the vaguely melancholy lanes of the old Jewish quarter or, for some Spanish tourists, the shops. Guarda is also the base for exploring the untouristy northeastern corner of the Parque Natural da Serra da Estrela, a rugged frontier zone dotted with medieval fortified towns.

Just bring your jumper and woolly hat.

Orientation
Old Guarda is perched on a steep hill, a rambling climb from the IP5 or the spanking new train station; the latter is 5km northeast of the old centre, linked by a shuttle bus.

From the bus station on Rua Dom Nuno Álvares Pereira, it's 800m northwest to Praça Luís de Camões (also called Praça Velha), heart of the old town. Most accommodation, restaurants and places of interest are near the *praça*.

Information
The **municipal turismo** (☎ 271 205 530, fax 271 205 533; e postodeturismo@hotmail .com; Praça Luís de Camões; open 9am-12.30pm & 2pm-6.30pm Mon-Sat, to 5.30pm Oct-May) is in the *câmara municipal*. There's also a small **Parque Natural da Serra da Estrela office** (☎/fax 271 225 454; Rua Dom Sancho I 3; open 9am-12.30pm & 2pm-5.30pm Mon-Fri).

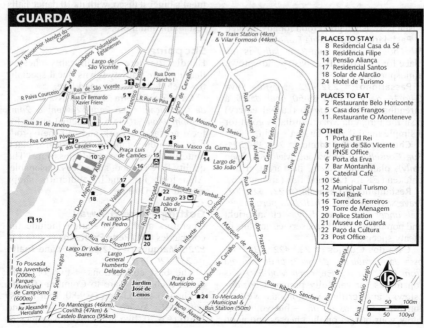

GUARDA

PLACES TO STAY
8 Residencial Casa da Sé
13 Residência Filipe
14 Pensão Aliança
17 Residencial Santos
18 Solar de Alarcão
24 Hotel de Turismo

PLACES TO EAT
2 Restaurante Belo Horizonte
5 Casa dos Frangos
11 Restaurante O Monteneve

OTHER
1 Porta d'El Rei
3 Igreja de São Vicente
4 PNSE Office
6 Porta da Erva
7 Bar Montanha
9 Catedral Café
10 Sé
12 Municipal Turismo
15 Taxi Rank
16 Torre dos Ferreiros
17 Torre de Menagem
20 Police Station
21 Museu de Guarda
22 Paço da Cultura
23 Post Office

There are banks with ATMs all around the centre. The **post office** (Largo João de Deus; open 8.30am-6pm Mon-Fri, 9am-12.30pm Sat) is southeast of the centre. **Mediateca VIII Centenário** (☎ 271 205 531; Praça Luís de Camões; open 9.30am-12.30 & 2pm-5.30pm Mon-Fri), above the turismo, is a municipal Internet shop, offering free Internet access.

For emergencies contact the **police station** (☎ 271 222 022; Rua Alves Roçadas 15).

Sé

This sober Gothic fortress of a cathedral (Praça Luís de Camões; open 9am-noon & 2pm-5pm Tues-Sat) looks less daunting now that it's had a good face-lift. The earliest bits date from 1390 but as it took 150 years to finish; it's dotted with Manueline doors and windows and Renaissance ornamentation.

The most striking feature in the immense, cold, granite interior is a four-storey Renaissance altarpiece attributed to Jean de Rouen (João de Ruão), one of a team of 16th-century French artists who founded an influential school of sculpture at Coimbra. Notice the 'twisted' Manueline columns at each transept.

Restoration work is ongoing, and the tower was closed at the time of writing.

Old Town

With its 16th- to 18th-century **mansions**, Praça Luís de Camões is the most attractive spot in town. A **statue** of Dom Sancho I looks down from the centre of the square.

Little remains of Guarda's 13th-century castle except the simple **Torre de Menagem** (castle keep; closed to public), on a hill top above the cathedral. Of the old walls and gates, the stalwart **Torre dos Ferreiros** (Blacksmiths' Tower; Rua Tenente Valadim) is still in good condition. Two other surviving gates are the **Porta d'El Rei**, the ancient steps of which you can still climb, and the **Porta da Erva**.

Some medieval atmosphere survives in the cobbled lanes and huddled houses north of the cathedral. At the heart of this area, around Rua de São Vicente, is the city's former **judiaria** (Jewish quarter). Sharp-eyed visitors will notice crosses and other symbols scratched into a few 16th-century vaulted doorframes – eg, in Rua Rui de Pina and Rua Dom Sancho I – to identify the homes of marranos or 'New Christians'

during the Inquisition (see History and Religion in the Facts about Portugal chapter).

Museu de Guarda

The Guarda Museum (☎ 271 213 460; Rua Alves Roçadas 30; admission €2, 9am-12.30pm Sun free; open 9am-12.30pm & 2pm-5.30pm Tues-Sun) occupies the severe 17th-century Episcopal Seminary, adjacent to the old Bishop's Palace. The museum's collection runs from Bronze Age swords to Roman coins, from Renaissance art to armaments of the 17th to 20th centuries.

The adjacent **Paço da Cultura** (admission free; open 2pm-8pm daily) features changing art exhibitions.

Special Events

Guarda hosts a jazz festival called Ciclo de Jazz de Guarda, with several performances each week from March to mid-April.

Places to Stay

We found summer accommodation tight, so booking ahead might be in order. There's no winter high-price season here, though Guarda is almost as close to the snow as the park's other main towns.

Camping & Hostels Southwest of the town centre is **Parque Municipal de Campismo** (☎ 271 221 200, fax 271 210 025; Rua do Estádio Municipal; adult/tent/car €1.50/ 1.50/1; open year-round), Guarda's own basic camp site.

The **pousada da juventude** (☎ 271 224 482; e guarda@movijovem.pt; Avenida Alexandre Herculano; dorm beds summer/winter €7.50/10.50, doubles with toilet €21/29), Guarda's youth hostel, is near the camp site.

Private Rooms Casa dos Frangos (doubles €15) has a few very basic rooms with shared facilities, above the restaurant of the same name (see Places to Eat). Other quartos are advertised around the town.

Pensões & Residenciais All rooms have a private bathroom, and rates include breakfast, except as noted.

Pensão Aliança (☎ 271 222 235, fax 271 221 451; Rua Vasco da Gama 8A; doubles from €25) is short on style but hospitable, with dowdy rooms and a pretty good restaurant. Off-street parking is available.

Residencial Casa da Sé *(☎ 271 212 501; e reservas@casa-da-se.com; Rua Augusto Gil 17; doubles with/without shower & toilet €42/33)*, with attractive, woody decor and azulejos in the hallways, is within sight of the cathedral. Breakfast costs extra here.

Residência Filipe *(☎ 271 223 658, fax 271 221 402; Rua Vasco da Gama 9; doubles/triples €35/45)* has pretty rooms, brisk service and a central location.

Residencial Santos *(☎ 271 205 400, fax 271 212 931; Rua Tenente Valadim 14; doubles/twins €40/45)* stands out with its ultramodern interior. The rooms are very comfortable and it's efficiently run.

Hotels & Turihab The **Hotel de Turismo** *(☎ 271 223 366; e sales@hotelguarda.com; Praça do Município; doubles €55)*, a Best Western franchise, has boringly deluxe doubles – worth a try if nobody else has room.

Solar de Alarcão *(☎/fax 271 214 392; Rua Dom Miguel de Alarcão 25-27; doubles €70)* is a 17th-century granite mansion with its own courtyard and loggia, and three gorgeous rooms stuffed with antique furniture.

Places to Eat

Casa dos Frangos *(☎ 271 212 704; Rua Francisco de Passos 47; dishes under €5; open all day Mon-Sat)* is nothing to write home about but it's cheap and open long hours, including for breakfast.

Pensão Aliança *(see Places to Stay; specials around €6, mains from €8; open daily)* has a locally popular restaurant with quick service and lunch-time specials.

Restaurante Belo Horizonte *(☎ 271 211 454; Largo de São Vicente 1; specialities from €7; open Sun-Fri)* packs them in for lunch and dinner, with regional specialities such as *chouriçado* (a spicy sausage dish) and *cabrito grelhado* (grilled kid).

Restaurante O Monteneve *(☎ 271 212 799; Praça Luís de Camões 24; daily specials around €7, mains from about €8; open Tues-Sun)*, with bright, chrome-and-brick decor, has excellent daily fish (and some meat) specials.

Self-caterers can head to the *mercado municipal* near the bus station.

Entertainment

Guarda has about a dozen bars and dance-bars. Two popular, central ones are **Catedral** **Café** *(Rua dos Cavaleiros 18)*, with frequent DJ gigs, and **Bar Montanha** *(Rua Dr Bernardo Xavier Friere 13)*.

Getting There & Away

Bus The joint company **Joalto/RBI/Rede Expressos** *(☎ 271 221 515)* runs services around three times daily via Covilhã (€3.80, 45 minutes) to Castelo Branco (€7.30, 1¾ hours) and Lisbon; and several times daily to Viseu (€6.10, 1½ hours), Porto and Coimbra.

Marques *(☎ 238 312 858)* goes daily via Gouveia (€2.40, 1½ hours) to Seia (€7.70, two hours). Rede Expressos goes to Seia (€6.70, 1¼ hours) once daily Sunday to Friday.

Train Guarda's **train station** *(☎ 271 211 565)* is served by two lines from Lisbon. The Beira Alta line, via Coimbra, has three IC trains daily from Lisbon (€12.60, 4¼ hours); from Porto, change at Pampilhosa. Trains on the Beira Baixa line via Castelo Branco take an hour longer and require a change at Covilhã.

Six local trains trundle the 40km (€2.10, 50 minutes) between Guarda and the border at Vilar Formoso each day.

Getting Around

Shuttle buses run between the train station and the bus station (€0.60), with a stop at Rua Marquês de Pombal, every half-hour during the day. For a taxi call ☎ 271 221 863, or board one at the rank on Rua Alves Roçadas.

TRANCOSO

postcode 6420 • pop 4500 • elevation 870m
This peaceful hill-top town 43km north of Guarda offers a window onto many ages, from prehistory to the Peninsular War. Most visible is its medieval personality, especially within Dom Dinis' 13th-century walls. Dinis underscored the importance of this border fortress by marrying the saintly Dona Isabel of Aragon here in 1282.

The cobbled streets of the old centre sport ornamented arcades, wrought-iron balconies and handsome granite porches. Like many northern towns, Trancoso acquired a sizable Jewish community following the expulsion of Jews from Spain at the end of the 15th century, and much evidence remains of this period.

The town's favourite legend is that of Bandarra, a 15th-century shoemaker and fortune-teller who put official noses out of joint by predicting the end of the monarchy. In 1558, shortly after Bandarra's death, the young Dom Sebastião died, heirless, in the disastrous Battle of Alcácer-Quibir in Morocco. Soon afterward Portugal fell under Spanish rule.

Orientation & Information

Buses stop near the **turismo** (☎ 271 811 147; **e** geral@cm-trancoso.pt; open 9am-12.30pm & 2pm-5.30pm Mon-Fri, 10am-12.30pm & 2pm-5.30pm Sat & Sun), just outside the Portas d'El Rei gate.

The main square is Largo Padre Francisco Ferreira (also called Largo do Pelourinho, or Largo Dom Dinis), anchored by an octagonal **pelourinho** dating from 1510.

The **post office** (Estrada de Lamego; open 9am-12.30pm & 2pm-6pm Mon-Fri) is outside the Portas do Prado gate. The **police station** (☎ 271 811 212) is right behind the Igreja São Pedro.

Things to See

The **Portas d'El Rei** (King's Gate), named after Dom Dinis and surmounted by the town's ancient coat of arms, has always been the town's main entrance. A guillotine-like door sealed out unwelcome visitors. The **town walls** run intact for over 1km around the medieval core.

The old **judiaria** covered roughly the southeastern third of the walled town.

BEIRAS

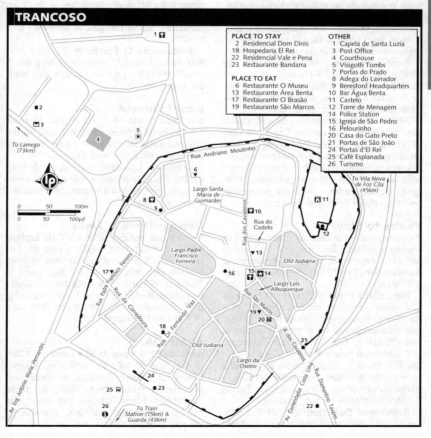

TRANCOSO

PLACE TO STAY
2 Residencial Dom Dinis
18 Hospedaria El Rei
22 Residencial Vale e Pena
23 Restaurante Bandarra

PLACE TO EAT
6 Restaurante O Museu
13 Restaurante Área Benta
17 Restaurante O Brasão
19 Restaurante São Marcos

OTHER
1 Capela de Santa Luzia
3 Post Office
4 Courthouse
5 Visigoth Tombs
7 Portas do Prado
8 Adega do Lavrador
9 Beresford Headquarters
10 Bar Água Benta
11 Castelo
12 Torre de Menagem
14 Police Station
15 Igreja de São Pedro
16 Pelourinho
20 Casa do Gato Preto
21 Portas de São João
24 Portas d'El Rei
25 Café Esplanada
26 Turismo

To Lamego (73km)

Rua Andriano Moutinho

0   50   100m
0   50   100yd

Largo Santa Maria de Guimarães

Rua dos Cavaleiros

Rua do Castelo

To Vila Nova de Foz Côa (45km)

Largo Padre Francisco Ferreira

Rua Padre Francisco Ferreira

Rua da Corredoura

Old Judiaria

Rua São Marcos

Largo Luís Albuquerque

Rua Dr Fernando Vaz

Old Judiaria

Largo da Oseiro

IR dos Cavaleiros

Av Eng António Maria Hernandes

Av Comendador Costa Lima

Rua Diamantino Tavares

To Train Station (15km) & Guarda (43km)

Among dignified reminders of that time is a former rabbinical residence called the **Casa do Gato Preto** *(House of the Black Cat; Largo Luís Albuquerque)*, decorated with the gates of Jerusalem and other Jewish images.

On a hill in the northeastern corner is the **castelo** (castle; 10th to 13th centuries), with crenellated towers, and the squat, Moorish **Torre de Menagem**, with sloping walls. Kids and dogs hurtle around the otherwise empty courtyard. The concrete bulge near the keep is a relatively modern water cistern.

To the west is a **14th-century house** typical of the time, with a big door into a storage area or shop, and a columned porch leading to living quarters (or in some cases a smaller ground-floor door opening onto interior stairs). This particular house – now sadly neglected – served as regional *quartel-general* (headquarters) for Viscount William Beresford during the Peninsular War. Restaurante O Museu (see Places to Eat) occupies a similar house around the corner.

Across the road from the Portas do Prado, beside the courthouse, is an untended rock outcrop carved with eerie, body-shaped cavities, thought to be **Visigoth tombs** of the 7th or 8th century.

About 150m northward is Trancoso's prettiest church, the 13th-century **Capela de Santa Luzia**, with heavy Romanesque door arches and unadorned dry-stone construction. Trancoso abounds with other churches heavy with baroque make-up, most prominently the **Igreja de São Pedro**, behind the *pelourinho* on Largo Padre Francisco Ferreira.

Places to Stay

Trancoso has some *quartos*, most rented to students outside summer and university holidays. One place to ask is **Restaurante Bandarra** *(☎ 271 812 241)*, beside the Portas d'El Rei.

Hospedaria El Rei *(☎ 271 811 411; Rua da Corredoura; singles or doubles about €18)*, a traditional stout granite house full of lovely old furniture, may be the best bargain in town. You may find it closed until evening.

Residencial Vale e Pena *(☎ 271 811 219, fax 271 828 027; Largo Senhora da Calçada; rooms with breakfast per person €15)* is a plain, cheery place just outside the Portas de São João; rates include parking.

Residencial Dom Dinis *(☎ 271 811 525, fax 271 811 396; Estrada de Lamego; doubles/*

twins with breakfast €27/29), located behind the post office, has stylish, upmarket rooms.

Places to Eat

Restaurante Área Benta *(☎ 271 817 180; Rua dos Cavaleiros 30; mains €7.50-9.50; open Tues-Sun)* offers very good traditional fare in a handsome, modern setting. Specialities include *ensopada de borrego* (lamb stew) and *camarões* (prawns), and the half-portion *prato do dia* (€5) is good value. Book ahead or prepare to wait.

Restaurante São Marcos *(☎ 271 811 326; Largo Luís Albuquerque; daily specials under €6; open Mon-Sat)* has good *feijoada* and an efficient, get-it-on-the-table atmosphere.

Restaurante O Museu *(☎ 271 811 810; Largo Santa Maria de Guimarães; dishes from about €8)* has a similar range of Portuguese standards, as well as pricier seafood (€15 to €40).

Restaurante O Brasão *(☎ 271 811 767; Rua Padre Francisco Ferreira; mains €6-7; open Sun-Fri)* is a popular place, with a modest, meaty menu.

Entertainment

Bar Água Benta *(☎ 271 812 390; Rua dos Cavaleiros 36A; open daily)* is a café in the afternoon and the old town's best bar in the evening, with occasional live music.

Adega do Lavrador *(open daily)*, behind the Beresford headquarters, is a plain *cervejaria* (beer house), with recorded music and a young clientele.

Getting There & Away

Catch buses and buy tickets at **Café Esplanada** *(☎ 271 811 188)*, which is near the turismo. Joalto has a weekday bus to/from Guarda (€5.80). An EAVT bus goes to Lamego (€8.40) each weekday, to Joalto less often. Rede Expressos buses stop daily in Trancoso en route between Bragança (€7.60) and Viseu (€5.80).

ALMEIDA

postcode 6350 • pop 1600 • elevation 760m
In the time of João IV, following Spain's loss of control over Portugal, the three most important fortified towns along the tense border were Elvas, Almeida and Valença do Minho. Almeida's compact, star-shaped fortress – completed in 1641 on the site of

its medieval predecessor, 15km from Spain
– is the least famous but perhaps hand-
somest of the three.

When its military functions ceased in
1927, Almeida settled into rural obscurity.
But the fortress and its old village, already
a designated national monument, have recently been anointed one of 10 Aldeias
Históricas in the Serra da Estrela region.
Conservation money is flowing in and
things are being tidied and refashioned for
tourism (a Pousada de Portugal has been
here since 1987).

Neither here nor yet there, Almeida has
the disquieting calm of a museum, but
enough history and muscular grandeur to
make up for it.

Orientation & Information
The fortress is on the northern side of 'new'
Almeida. Most visitors arrive via the handsome Portas de São Francisco, consisting of
two long tunnel-gates. Drivers are better off
parking outside the town and negotiating
the inner town on foot. A separate gate was
cut through the walls for the *pousada*.

Much has been spent on a posh **turismo**
(☎ 271 570 020, fax 271 570 021; open 9am-
12.30pm & 2pm-5.30pm daily, from 10am
Sat & Sun) in an old guard-chamber within
the Portas de São Francisco. Here you can
get a map of the fortress.

A bank with an ATM is across Praça da
República from the turismo. The **post office**
(Rua Comendador Cardoso 2; open 9am-
12.30pm & 2pm-5pm Mon-Fri) is 150m
northwest of the turismo.

Things to See
The long arcaded building just inside the
Portas de São Francisco is the 18th-century
Quartel das Estradas (Infantry Barracks).

In a bastion 300m northeast of the turismo are the **casamatas** (casemates or
bunkers; open 9am-12.30pm & 2pm-5.30pm
Mon-Fri, from 10am Sat & Sun), a warren of
20 underground rooms used for storage,
barracks and shelter in times of siege, and
in the 18th century as a prison.

The fort's **castle**, and much more, was
destroyed during a French siege in 1810,
when ammunition supplies blew up. You

can still see the foundations, 300m northwest of the turismo, from an ugly catwalk.
Below the ruins is a riding school, in the
former Royal Riding Academy.

In Praça da Liberdade, on the way back,
is the **Paços do Concelho** (council hall), in
the former artillery barracks.

Places to Stay
Pensão-Restaurante A Muralha (☎/fax 271
574 357; Bairro de São Pedro; doubles/triples
with breakfast €35/45), 300m outside the
Portas de São Francisco on the Vilar Formoso road, has functional, quiet rooms.

Casa Pátio da Figueira (☎ 919 469 170,
914 697 803; Rua Direita 48; doubles €70) at
the northern end of the village is a restored
18th-century townhouse, now with a swimming pool, garden and four elegant double
rooms. This road is signed 'Rua dos Combatentes Mortos Pela Patria' but nobody
uses the name.

Pousada Nossa Senhora das Neves (☎ 271
574 290, fax 271 574 320; doubles with breakfast €115), on the site of former cavalry
quarters near the north bastion, is a deluxe,
rather out-of-place *pousada*.

Places to Eat
There are half a dozen snack-bars and café-
bars inside the walls, and a dismal *casa de
pasto* on Praça Matias. Of these, the closest
thing to a restaurant is **Snack Bar 1810**
(☎ 271 571 093; Rua Direita). Also agreeable
is **4 Esquinas Bar** (☎ 271 574 314; Travessa
da Pereira 7).

Restaurante O Granitos (☎ 271 574 834;
Largo 25 de Abril; daily specials around €6;
open daily), just outside the Portas de São
Francisco, has ho-hum, overpriced fare.

Pensão-Restaurante A Muralha (see
Places to Stay; dishes under €5.50) has an
adequate restaurant serving standard Portuguese fare.

Getting There & Away
RBI/Rede Expressos has two Guarda-
Almeida buses (about €3, 1¼ to two hours)
each weekday, though the timing gives you
little time to see the fortress without spending the night. The bus stop is by the BPI
bank outside the Portas de São Francisco.

BEIRAS

The Douro

Douro province is dominated by Portugal's second-largest city, Porto, and by its best-known river, the Douro. Rising in Spain, the Rio Douro (River of Gold) defines the Spain-Portugal border from north of Miranda do Douro (Trás-os-Montes) down to Barca de Alva (Beira Alta), then runs west for 200km to Porto. It's in the region called the Alto Douro, from the Spanish border to Peso da Régua, that Portugal's illustrious port-wine grapes are grown, on steep terraced hillsides of schist that trap the region's intense summer heat.

The Douro valley is today one of Portugal's most popular tourist destinations. The river, tamed by five dams in the 1980s, is navigable all the way to Barca de Alva, allowing passenger cruises to slip through dramatic gorges into the heart of the port-wine country.

The Douro railway, which opened in 1887 and runs from Porto to Pocinho (Beira Alta), is another fine way to travel. Three narrow-gauge lines climb out of the valley from the main line, offering slow, enchanting diversions: the Linha da Tâmega from Livração to Amarante, the Linha da Corgo from Peso da Régua to Vila Real, and the Linha da Tua from Tua to Mirandela (for details see respectively the Amarante, Peso da Régua and Alto Douro sections in this chapter; for some background see the boxed text 'Narrow-Gauge Railways' in the Getting Around chapter).

Porto, naturally, makes a fine base for exploring this region. The beaches immediately north and south of Porto are some of Portugal's filthiest, but Vila do Conde's fine seaside is within easy reach.

This chapter includes towns from both the Beira Alta and Trás-os-Montes, which lie along the Rio Douro. The Parque Natural do Douro Internacional, on the Douro's upper canyon, is introduced in the Trás-os-Montes chapter.

PORTO
postcode 4000 • pop 263,100
• elevation 80m

Portugal's second-largest city is a vibrant contrast to Lisbon: while the capital revels in its elegance, Porto is brawny and hard

Highlights

- Soak up the atmosphere of Porto's World Heritage–listed Ribeira district, and take bird's-eye photos from the Ponte de Dom Luís I

- Enjoy the light in Porto's fine modern art showcase, the Museu de Arte Contemporânea

- Titillate your taste buds with a glass or two of port wine at the lodges of Vila Nova de Gaia

- Take a slow train up the vineyard-terraced Douro valley, or the narrow-gauge Linha da Tua to Mirandela

- Gaze on Stone Age art, scratched into the rocks of the Vale do Côa tens of thousands of years ago

working, its people down-to-earth and welcoming. Proud Portoenses recite an old saying: 'Coimbra sings, Braga prays, Lisbon shows off and Porto works.' Traditionally mocked by Lisboêtas as *tripeiros* (tripe-eaters), they refer to the southerners in turn as *alfacinhas* (lettuce-eaters).

Porto – only foreigners call it Oporto (The Port) – is the country's most important manufacturing and commercial centre, but its sleeves-up reputation belies its considerable charm. Built on granite bluffs above the Rio Douro, its heart is a 19th-century tangle of lanes tumbling down to the river.

The riverside is a beguiling blend of fishing quarter and tourist trap.

Straddling the river are six dramatic bridges to Porto's 'other half', Vila Nova de Gaia, historic home of the port-wine lodges and the city's biggest tourist draw.

Perhaps to Porto's own surprise, its grimy old centre was in 1996 designated a Unesco World Heritage site, and the area has bristled with gantries ever since. An underground railway system is under construction too, adding to the maddening chaos in the city's narrow streets. To top it off, Porto is building a new stadium and renovating another for the 2004 European Football Championships.

You'll need a minimum of two days to soak up the atmosphere and the port wine. This is also a natural place from which to explore not only the beautiful Douro valley but a host of attractive towns in the Minho, all easily accessible by train or bus.

History

Porto is the 'Portu' in 'Portugal'. In Roman times a Lusitanian settlement called Cale, on the south bank of the Douro near the river's mouth, became an important crossing on the Lisbon–Braga road. Another settlement, Portus (Harbour), soon grew up on the other side. Portus-Cale subsequently became the capital of the county of Portucale, lying between the Rio Minho and Rio Douro. This was the land given to Henri of Burgundy on his marriage to the daughter of the king of León in 1095. From here Henri's son Afonso Henriques launched the Reconquista, ultimately founding the independent kingdom of Portugal.

Porto's status grew with the building of a cathedral in 1111 and was confirmed with subsequent royal favours. In 1387 Dom João I married his English queen, Philippa of Lancaster, here and in 1394 their most famous son, Henry the Navigator, was born here. While Henry's explorers were groping around Africa for a sea route to India, British traders found a foothold in Porto with their trade in port wine.

Over the following centuries Porto acquired a reputation for rebelliousness. In 1628 a mob of women attacked the minister responsible for a tax on linen. In 1757 a 'tipplers' riot' against the Marquês de Pombal's regulation of the port-wine trade was savagely put down. In 1808 Porto citizens arrested the French governor and set up their own junta. The French army, which took the city back the following year, was finally given the boot by the British under the future Duke of Wellington, but Porto radicals soon turned against British 'control', demanded a new liberal constitution and in 1822 got one.

Porto stood by its principles and Miguel's constitutionalist brother Pedro when the absolutist Miguel I usurped the throne in 1828. Miguel's forces laid siege to the city in 1832 after Pedro arrived from Brazil, but the liberal cause won through in the following year when Miguel's fleet was captured off Cabo São Vicente.

Demonstrations continued to erupt in Porto in support of liberals throughout the 19th century. Portugal's first republican deputy was elected from Porto in 1878.

Orientation

'Old' Porto clambers up the gorge 9km from the mouth of the Douro; 'new' Porto runs out to the polluted seashore at Foz do Douro. Though it's a separate town, Vila Nova de Gaia, the port-wine centre across the river, has played such a large role in Porto's history that it's treated as part of the city.

The city's axis is Avenida dos Aliados (called 'Aliados' by all), a handsome avenue/ square carved out as part of a civic renovation programme started in 1915 during a period of general infatuation with the French Art Nouveau style. At its northern end are the *câmara municipal* (town hall), the main city *turismo* (tourist office), the main post office, banks and currency exchanges.

Central hubs for city and regional buses are at Praça da Liberdade, Praça Almeida Garrett (by São Bento station) and Largo dos Lóios (known as just Lóios) at the southern end of Aliados, and at Jardim da Cordoaria (or Cordoaria, but called Jardim de João Chagas on some maps) about 400m west of Aliados. South of Aliados the city extends down to the riverside Ribeira district.

A lively shopping district surrounds the Mercado do Bolhão (Bolhão Market), northeast of Aliados. Another big commercial zone is Boavista, around the giant Praça de Mouzinho de Albuquerque roundabout. Here architect Rem Koolhaas' Casa da Música (Music Hall), meant to become the city's cultural flagship, is under interminable construction.

DOURO

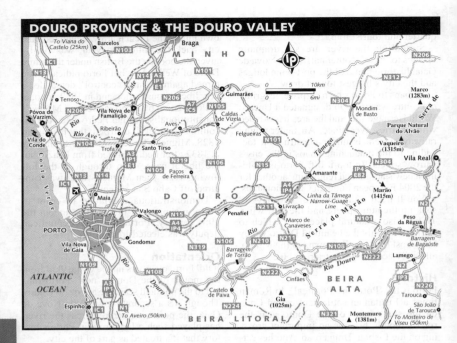

DOURO PROVINCE & THE DOURO VALLEY

Porto's Francisco Sá Carneiro airport is 19km northwest of the city centre. There are two train stations: Campanhã, 2km east of the centre, and central São Bento. Trindade station, just north of Aliados, is being renovated as the hub of Porto's future metro system. Bus terminals are scattered all over the city; see the Getting There & Away section for more information.

The demarcated World Heritage zone reaches from the Torre dos Clérigos, São Bento station and the cathedral down to the Cais da Ribeira. Also included are the Ponte de Dom Luís I and the Mosteiro da Serra do Pilar in Vila Nova de Gaia. A wider protective zone, where any new development is prohibited, takes in Cordoaria, Aliados, upstream and downstream riverfront areas and the amphitheatre of port-wine lodges at Vila Nova de Gaia.

Information
Tourist Offices The **main city turismo** (☎ 223 393 470, fax 223 323 303; e *turismo .central@mail.telepac.pt; Rua Clube dos Fenianos 25; open 9am-7pm Mon-Fri July-Sept, 9am-5.30pm Mon-Fri Oct-June; 9.30am-*

4.30pm Sat, Sun & holidays year-round) is opposite the *câmara municipal*. There's a smaller **turismo** (☎ 222 009 770; *Rua Infante Dom Henrique 63; open 9am-5.30pm Mon-Fri)* in the Ribeira.

Both offer a detailed city map, the *Agenda do Porto* cultural calendar, the *Tourist Guide*, which bulges with practical information, and the *Museum Guide* – all free – and a map-brochure with neighbourhood, city and regional maps and information (€0.80). Both turismos also sell the Passe Porto, a one-/two-day tourist pass (€4/5.50) that is good for free bus and tram travel, reduced museum admission and some other discounts, but not great value unless you plan to go everywhere by bus and see every museum in the city.

The main turismo's **Loja da Mobilidade** (e *loja.mobilidade@cm-porto.pt*) desk dispenses a handy brochure, *Guia de Transportes*, and can provide details on everything from bus timetables to parking lots to future metro stations.

For countrywide queries visit the national **ICEP turismo** (☎ 222 057 514; *Praça Dom João I 43; open 9am-7.30pm daily July &*

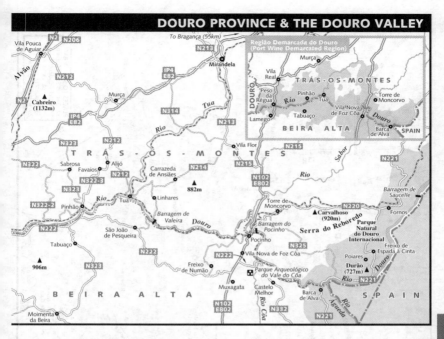

DOURO PROVINCE & THE DOURO VALLEY

Aug; 9am-7.30pm Mon-Fri, 9.30am-3.30pm Sat & Sun Sept & Apr-June; 9am-7pm Mon-Fri, 9.30am-3.30pm Sat & Sun Nov-Mar). There's another office (open 8am-11.30pm daily Apr-Christmas, 8am-11pm daily Christmas-Mar) at the airport.

Money ATMs are plentiful all along Aliados and in every shopping area.

The best rates for travellers cheques are at private exchange bureaus, such as **Portocâmbios** (Rua Rodrigues Sampaio 193; open Mon-Fri, morning Sat) and **Intercontinental** (Rua de Ramalho Ortigão 8; open Mon-Fri, morning Sat). American Express (AmEx) travellers cheques can be cashed at Top Tours (see under Travel Agencies).

There is a 24-hour currency exchange, as well as a **bank** (open 8.30am-3pm Mon-Fri) and an ATM, beside the ICEP turismo in the airport arrivals hall.

Post & Communications The **main post office** (Avenida dos Aliados; open 8am-9pm Mon-Fri, 9am-6pm Sat & Sun), which includes poste restante, is opposite the main city turismo. There are also smaller **post offices** (Rua Ferreira Borges 67, Ribeira ● Praça da Batalha; both open 8.30am-6pm Mon-Fri). AmEx card and travellers cheque customers can have mail and faxes sent to Top Tours (see Travel Agencies).

The handiest place for long-distance calls, using either cardphones or pay-afterward *cabines*, is the **Portugal Telecom office** (Praça da Liberdade 62; open 10am-10pm Mon-Sat, 2pm-9pm Sun). This and the post office, plus many kiosks and newsagents, also sell Portugal Telecom (PT) phonecards.

International and domestic faxes can be sent from the post office, and domestic faxes from the PT office.

Two libraries with free Internet access are the **Biblioteca Municipal Almeida Garrett** (Jardim do Palácio de Cristal; open 10am-6pm Mon-Sat), which has one-hour slots and long waits, and the main **biblioteca municipal** (Rua Dom João IV; open 9am-7.30pm Mon-Fri, 10am-6pm Sat), which has 30-minute slots.

Portweb (☎ 222 005 922; Praça General Humberto Delgado 291; open 10am-2am Mon-Sat, 3pm-2am Sun) charges €0.50 per hour until 4pm and €1.20 after that.

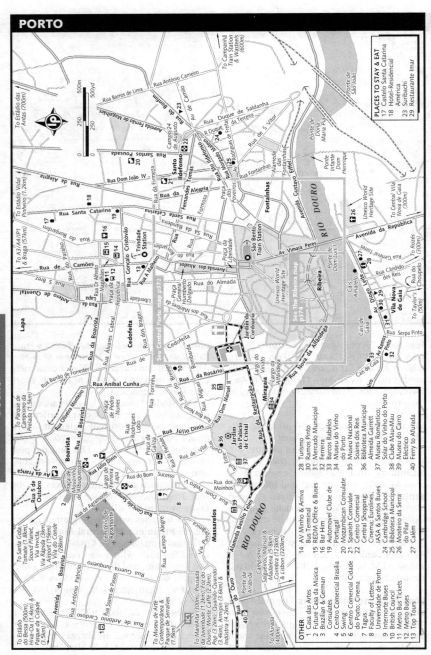

PORTO

To Estádio das
Antas (700m)

500m
500yd

250
250

0
0

Rua António Carneiro

Rua Barros de Lima

Rua de Camilo

To Campanhã
Train Station
& Bus Wastells
(600m)

Ponte de
São João

Rua do Bonfim

Av de Camilo

Av. Duque de Terceira

Rua Duque de Saldanha

Campo 24
de Agosto

Avenida Fernão de Magalhães

R. Duque
de Bragança

Rua de Freitas da Terceira

Rua de S Vítor

Ponte de
Dona
Maria Pia

Rua Santos Pousada

22

Santo
Ildefonso

Rua Fernandes Tomás

Rua Morais

5

Rua Rodrigues de Freitas

Alameda
das
Fontainhas

Ponte
Infante
Dom
Henrique

To Estádio Vidal
Pinheiro (1.2km)

Rua Dom João IV

Rua da Firmeza

Praça
Poveiros

Rua Fontainhas

Rua de
Fernandes
Alegria

Fontainhas

Avenida Gustavo Eiffel

RIO
DOURO

To A3/A4/IP1
& Braga (57km)

Rua da Alegria

18

Rua Santa Catarina

19

Rua da
Alegria

Rua Santa Catarina

Rua Sá da Bandeira

Praça da
Formosa

São Bento
Train Station

Av. Vimara Peres

To Central Vila
Nova de Gaia
(300m)

Unesco World
Heritage Site

26

Avenida da República

To Rozés
(300m)

17

Rua do Bonjardim

16

15

14

Trindade
Station

Rua Gonçalo Cristóvão

13

Rua do Aleixo

Praça da
Liberdade

Ribeira

Ponte de
Dom Luís I

See the Ribeira map p374

Rua Cândido
dos Reis

To Rozés
(300m)

Rua de
Camões

Rua Dr Alfredo

11

12

Rua A Malheiro

Praça
Gen Humberto
Delgado

Rua do Almada

Cais
Amarelo

AV DOURO LEITE

27

Vila Nova
de Gaia

30 29

31

To Taylor's
(50m)

To A3/A4km
& Vila do Conde

Antero de Quental

Lapa

Rua da Boavista

Praça da
República

Cedofeita

Rua dos Bragas

Jardim da
Cordoaria

Cais de
Gaia

AV Ramos
Pinto

33

32

To Afurada
(400m)

To Parque de
Campismo da
Prelada (1.5km)

Boavista

Rua da Boavista

Rua Álvares Cabral

Cedofeita

Rua de

Bombarda

10

Rua da Rosário

35

Largo da
Alfândega

Miragaia

Rua Nova da Alfândega

Cais de Gaia

Rua Serpa Pinto

Rua Oliveira Monteiro

Rua Barão de Forrester

Rua Aníbal Cunha

Praça de
Pedro
Nunes

Rua Tormila

Rua Miguel Bombarda

Rua Dom Manuel II

Largo do
Viriato

34

Rua Júlio Dinis

Rua Rodrigues Lobo

Praça da
Galiza

36

Jardim do
Palácio
de Cristal

Rua da

37

To MareAlta (300m),
Pousada
da Juventude (1.2km); Foz do
Douro, Monte Caffè (2.2km),
Pop (3.2km), Quando-Quando
(3.4km), Armijm (3.6km) &
Industria (4.2km)

Boavista

5

Rua Júlio Dinis

Largo de
Ferreira
Lapa

6

Rua do Bom
Sucesso

9

Rua de Vilar

Entre Quintas

To Estádio
do Bessa (500m),
Hiva-Oa (1.4km) &
Parque da Cidade
(3.5km)

Avenida da Boavista

Av da
França

Praça de
Mouzinho de
Albuquerque

2

Boavista

3

4

Rua 5 de
Outubro

Rua Gonçalo Sampaio

Rua Dom Pedro V

Rua dos
Moinhos

7

8

38

39

Massarelos

Cemitério de
Agramonte

Rua de Agramonte

Rua Campo Alegre

Alameda Basílio Teles

RIO DOURO

To Santa Gota,
Tomate (1.8km),
Sound Planet,
Via Invicta,
Via Rápida (3km),
Airport (28km)

To Centro Comercial Brasília

To Museu de Arte
Contemporânea &
Parque de Serralves
(1.5km)

Avenida da Boavista

1

Rua de António Patrício

Rua Cardoso

Rua Soares de Passos

Rua Guerra Junqueiro

Via Panorâmica

Via Rápida

To Campismo
Salgueiros, Marisol &
Madalena (5-8km),
Coimbra (123km)
& Lisbon (320km)

Rua do Ouro

Ponte da
Arrábida

40

To Afurada
(400m)

PLACES TO STAY & EAT
17 Castelo Santa Catarina
18 Hotel-Residencial
    América
23 Suribachi
29 Restaurante Imar

OTHER
1   Casa das Artes
2   Future Casa da Música
3   Brazilian & German
    Consulates
4   Centro Comercial Brasília
5   Swing
6   Centro Comercial Cidade
    do Porto; Cinema
7   Tagus
8   Faculty of Letters,
    Universidade de Porto
9   Internorte Buses
10 British Council
11 Metro Bus Tickets
12 Metro Buses
13 Top Tours

14 AV Minho & Arriva
    Bus Terminal
15 REDM Office & Buses
16 Bar Him
19 Automóvel Clube de
    Portugal
20 Mozambican Consulate
21 Spanish Consulate
22 Centro Comercial
    Central Shopping;
    Cinema; Eurolines;
    IASA & Santos Buses
24 Cambridge School
25 Biblioteca Municipal
26 Mosteiro da Serra
    do Pilar
27 Calém

28 Turismo
30 Ramos Pinto
31 Mercado Municipal
32 Ferreira
33 Barcos Rabelos
34 Museu do Vinho
    do Porto
35 Museu Nacional
    Soares dos Reis
36 Biblioteca Municipal
    Almeida Garrett
37 Museu Romântico;
    Solar do Vinho do Porto
38 Clube Mau-Mau
39 Museu do Carro
    Eléctrico
40 Ferry to Afurada

DOURO

The **PT office** *(Praça da Liberdade 62)* has pricey, phonecard-operated terminals with Internet access for €2 per hour, and post offices offer NetPost service (see under Post & Communications in the Facts for the Visitor chapter) at €2.40 per hour.

Travel Agencies Two youth-oriented agencies that sell discounted plane, train and coach tickets, rail passes and international youth and student cards are **Tagus** *(☎ 226 094 141; Rua Campo Alegre 261)*; and **Wasteels** *(☎ 225 194 230; Rua Pinto Bessa 27-29)*, located opposite Campanhã train station.

Top Tours *(☎ 222 074 020, fax 222 074 039; Rua Alferes Malheiro 96)* is Porto's AmEx representative. AmEx card or travellers cheque holders can exchange currency (commission-free, except 1% on euro-denominated cheques) and have mail and faxes held or forwarded here.

A reliable general travel agency is **Intervisa** *(☎ 222 079 200; Praça Dona Filipa de Lencastre 1)*.

Bookshops Reference bookshop **Livraria Porto Editora** *(☎ 222 007 681; Praça Dona Filipa de Lencastre 42)* stocks 1:25,000 military topographic maps covering Portugal (€5.90 per sheet), and many other maps.

There are lots of other shops selling new and second-hand books in the streets south of here. **Livraria Bertrand** *(Rua 31 de Janeiro 65 • Centro Comercial via Catarina, Rua Santa Catarina)*, with other branches in Porto's bigger shopping centres, has a selection of travel books and maps.

Even if you're not after books, don't miss **Livraria Lello** *(Rua das Carmelitas 144)*, an Art Deco confection stacked to the rafters with new, second-hand and antique books, in lavish quarters more suited to a gentlemen's club.

Porto has surprisingly few newsagents selling foreign-language newspapers. One that does is **Lotarias Atlânticos** *(Rua Sampaio Bruno; open Mon-Fri, morning Sat)*, just off Aliados.

Universities Faculties of the Universidade de Porto are scattered across the city, with the majority in north-central Porto. Closest to the centre is the Faculty of Letters, south of Boavista.

Cultural Centres The **British Council** *(☎ 222 073 060; Rua do Breiner 155; open 2pm-8.30pm Mon & Wed, 10am-1pm & 2pm-8.30pm Tues & Thur, 2pm-7.30pm Fri, irregular hrs Sat mid-Sept–mid-June; 2pm-5.30pm Mon, Wed & Fri, 10am-1pm & 2pm-5.30pm Tues & Thur mid-June–mid-Sept; closed Aug)* has a library full of English-language books and newspapers.

Laundry Porto's cheapest laundry is the municipal **Lavandaria São Nicolau** *(☎ 222 084 621; Rua Infante Dom Henrique, Ribeira; open 8.30am-7.30pm Mon-Fri, 8.30am-4pm Sat & Sun)*, in an underground complex that also includes showers. It'll cost you €4.50 to wash and dry a 6kg load.

Medical Services There are some English-speaking staff at **Hospital Geral de Santo António** *(☎ 222 077 500; Rua Vicente José Carvalho)*.

Emergency The place to go for police help or inquiries is the multilingual **tourism police** *(☎ 222 081 833; Rua Clube dos Fenianos 11; open 8am-2am daily)* beside the main city turismo. There's another **police station** *(☎ 222 006 821; Rua Augusto Rosa)* south of Praça da Batalha.

Dangers & Annoyances Porto has plenty of dimly lit alleys best avoided after dark, in particular in riverside areas off Rua Nova da Alfândega and Avenida Gustavo Eiffel. Even the most central parks and squares, such as Praça Gomes Teixeira and Praça da Batalha, have their share of weirdos, drunks and oddballs, and solo women travellers may feel uncomfortable taking a lunch-time picnic. São Bento train station and the Ribeira district are other areas where you might not want to be alone late at night.

Stay away from the appallingly filthy beach at Foz do Douro. You won't find a really clean beach until you reach Vila do Conde (26km to the north) or Ovar (40km to the south).

Torre & Igreja dos Clérigos

One of the best places to get your bearings and your photographs of the city is Torre dos Clérigos *(Rua dos Clérigos; admission €1; open 10am-1pm & 2pm-8pm daily Aug, 9.30am-1pm & 2pm-7pm daily Apr-July &*

DOURO

Sept-Oct, 10am-noon & 2pm-5pm daily Nov-Mar), a 76m-high baroque tower. The Italian architect Nicolau Nasoni designed the 225-step tower and the adjoining oval-shaped Igreja dos Clérigos in the mid-18th century.

Sé

This fortress of a cathedral *(☎ 222 059 028; admission cloister €2; cathedral open 8.45am-12.30pm & 2.30pm-7pm daily; cloister open 9am-12.15pm & 2.30pm-6pm Mon-Sat, 2.30pm-6pm Sun; both close 1hr earlier Nov-Mar)* dominates central Porto from its highest hill. It was founded in the 12th century but rebuilt a century later and extensively altered in the 18th century.

Only a Romanesque rose window and the 14th-century Gothic cloister remain from earlier incarnations. Much of the rest, inside and out, bears the baroque stamp of Nicolau Nasoni. Best of all is the upper storey of the cloister (reached via a Nasoni-designed stairway), decorated with 18th-century *azulejos* (hand-painted tiles) and affording some fine views.

Other Churches

The plain-faced Gothic **Igreja de São Francisco** *(☎ 222 062 100; Rua Infante Dom Henrique; admission €2.50; open 9am-6pm daily)* houses one of Portugal's most dazzling displays of baroque and over-the-top rococo gilt decoration, with nearly 100kg of gold leaf adorning altars, pillars and ceiling. Such earthly extravagance may only have driven thoughts of heaven away, for the

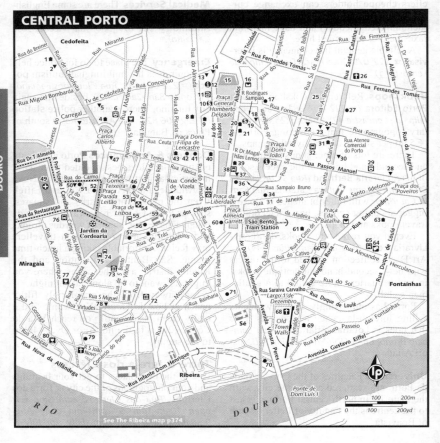

CENTRAL PORTO

church no longer holds services and is packed instead with tour groups.

A ho-hum museum in its catacombs contains furnishings from a Franciscan monastery that once stood here, and a pit full of 19th-century human bones (there are creepier ossuary chapels in Évora and Faro).

The **Igreja de Santa Clara** *(Largo 1 de Dezembro; open 9.30am-11.30am & 3pm-7pm Mon-Fri)*, east of the cathedral, was part of another Franciscan convent. Gothic in shape, with a fine Renaissance portal, its interior is also dense with carved, gilded woodwork.

Behind the rococo facade of the **Igreja da Misericórdia** *(☎ 222 074 710; Rua das Flores 15; admission €1.50; open 9.30am-noon & 2pm-5.30pm Mon-Fri)* – now a museum – is the superb, anonymous Renaissance painting known as *Fons Vitae* (Fountain of Life), showing Dom Manuel I and his family around a fountain of blood from the crucified Christ.

The 17th-century **Igreja de São Lourenço** *(Igreja dos Grilos; Largo Dr Pedro Vitorino, Ribeira; open 10am-noon & 2pm-5pm Tues-Sat)*, west of the cathedral, is of interest only for its baroque facade and its prominence in any view of Porto from across the river.

Palácio da Bolsa

The neoclassical Bolsa *(Stock Exchange; ☎ 223 399 000; Rua Ferreira Borges, Ribeira; open 9am-7pm Apr-Oct, 9am-1pm & 2pm-6pm Nov-Mar)* is a splendidly pompous monument to Porto's past-and-present money merchants. It took 68 years to build (1842–1910) and is now the headquarters of the city's Commercial Association.

Just past the entrance hall is the glass-domed **Pátio das Nações** (Hall of Nations), wallpapered with international coats of arms, where the exchange once operated. But this pales beside other rooms deeper inside, and to visit these you must join one of the €5 guided tours that set off every 20 to 30 minutes. You can usually join any group; tours are given in any two of Portuguese, English and French.

CENTRAL PORTO

PLACES TO STAY
1 Pensão-Residencial Estoril
4 Pensão São Marino
8 Pensão Porto Rico
9 Residencial Pão de Açucar
20 Residencial Paulista
21 Pensão Chique
31 Grande Hotel do Porto
35 Hotel Peninsular
39 Residencial Universal
40 Residencial dos Aliados
43 Hotel Infante de Sagres
45 Residencial Porto Chique
61 Pensão Mondariz
63 Pensão Aviz
69 Pensão Astória

PLACES TO EAT
2 Confeitaria Rian
3 Adega do Carregal
5 Pão de Ló Margaridense
13 Minipreço
14 Café Metro da Trindade
18 Pedro dos Frangos
22 Confeitaria do Bolhão
23 Confeitaria do Bolhão Shop
24 A Pérola do Bolhão
25 Mercado do Bolhão
28 Pingo Doce
30 Café Majestic
37 Café Embaixador
47 Restaurante Romão

50 Restaurante A Tasquinha
78 Restaurante O Oriente no Porto

OTHER
6 Auditório Nacional Carlos Alberto
7 Moinho de Vento
10 Intercontinental
11 Portweb
12 Main City Turismo; Tourism Police
15 Câmara Municipal
16 Main Post Office
17 Casa Januário
19 Portocâmbios
26 Capela das Almas
27 Centro Comercial Via Catarina; Livraria Bertrand; Modelo
29 Coliseu do Porto
32 Rodonorte Bus Terminal
33 ICEP Turismo
34 Livraria Bertrand
36 Lotarias Atlânticos
38 AeroBus Terminus
41 Intervisa
42 Livraria Porto Editora
44 Portugal Telecom Office
46 Livraria Lello
48 Igreja do Carmo

49 Hospital Geral de Santo António
51 Garrafeira do Carmo
52 Café Ancôra Douro
53 Bus Nos 56 & 76
54 Centro Comercial Clérigos Shopping
55 Bus No 50
56 Torre dos Clérigos
57 Casa Oriental
58 Artesanato dos Clérigos
59 Igreja dos Clérigos
60 STCP Service Point
62 Post Office
64 Angolan Consulate
65 Paragem Atlântico Terminal; Rede Expressos & RBL Buses
66 Teatro Nacional de São João
67 Police Station
68 Igreja de Santa Clara
70 Ribeira Negra Mural
71 Mercado de São Sebastião
72 Igreja da Misericórdia
73 Centro Português de Fotografia
74 Bus Nos 93 & 96
75 Bus Nos 24, 41 & 56
76 Renex Buses
77 Boys 'R' Us
79 Restaurante O Fado
80 Arcadas Pub

The highlight is a stupendous ballroom called the **Salão Árabe** (Arabian Hall), with gilded stucco (18kg of gold was used) and Arabic inscriptions glorifying Dona Maria II, who commissioned the building.

Ribeira

The riverside Ribeira district is the most alluring part of Porto, a window onto the past with shadowed lanes, grimy cobbled passages and boats at the quayside (now mostly for show, advertising or tourist jaunts). Despite the trendy restaurants and flocks of tourists it remains easy-going and surprisingly ungentrified. This is also the traditional centre of the city's nightlife.

Henry the Navigator is said to have been born (in 1394) in the handsomely renovated **Casa do Infante** (☎ 222 056 025; Rua Alfândega 10, Ribeira; admission free; open 8.30am-5pm Mon-Fri), which later served as Porto's first customs house and now houses its historical archives.

Museums

Unless otherwise noted, children from four to 12 years old, students and seniors get 40% to 50% off the admission price, and children up to age four get in free.

Museu de Arte Contemporânea Porto's fine Museum of Contemporary Art (☎ 226 156 500; Rua Dom João de Castro 210; admission museum & park €4; open 10am-7pm Tues, Wed & Fri-Sun, 10am-10pm Thur Oct-Mar; 10am-7pm Tues, Wed & Fri, 10am-10pm Thur, 10am-8pm Sat & Sun Apr-Sept) is the descendant of an art and architectural design collection belonging to the nonprofit Fundação de Serralves, founded in 1989 to stimulate public interest in contemporary art and the environment.

The collection, featuring works from the late 1960s to the present, is housed in a striking museum and cultural centre designed by the eminent Portuguese architect (and Porto native) Álvaro Siza Vieira. Of interest as much for the building as for its contents, it features Siza Vieira's trademark minimalist style, full of vast whitewashed spaces and natural light. Nearby is Casa de Serralves, a pink 1930s Art Deco mansion that served as the original museum and is now an exhibition space.

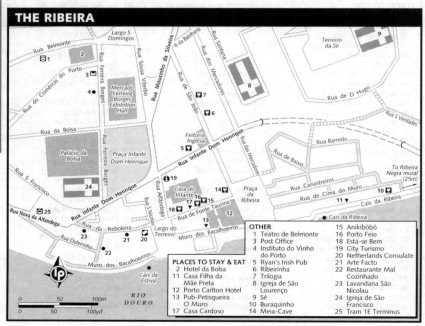

THE RIBEIRA

DOURO

Surrounding it all is the foundation's 18-hectare estate, **Parque de Serralves** (admission €2.50; open 10am-7pm Tues-Sun Oct-Mar; 10am-7pm Tues-Fri, 10am-8pm Sat & Sun Apr-Sept). These handsome modernist gardens – now a national landmark – are worth a visit in their own right. Estate and museum are 4km west of the city centre; take bus No 78 from Praça da Liberdade.

Museu Nacional Soares dos Reis

Porto's other important art museum (☎ 223 393 770; Rua Dom Manuel II 44; admission €3; open 2pm-6pm Tues, 10am-6pm Wed-Sun) occupies the staid neoclassical Palácio das Carrancas. During the Peninsular War Marshal Soult, the French commander, made his headquarters here but was evicted so suddenly by the future Duke of Wellington that he left an unfinished banquet behind.

Transformed into a museum of fine and decorative arts in 1940, its best works are from the 19th century, including sculpture by António Soares dos Reis (see especially his famous O Desterrado, The Exile) and António Teixeira Lopes, and the naturalistic paintings of Henrique Pousão and António Silva Porto.

Centro Português de Fotografia

The massive former prison (1796) facing Cordoaria is now home to the Portuguese Photography Centre (☎ 226 061 170; Campo Mártires da Pátria; admission free; open 9am-noon & 2pm-5.30pm Mon-Fri). Multiple exhibitions offer a portrait of Porto and Portugal in the age of photography, but they don't even begin to occupy this muscular space, with its massive walls and iron doors. Indeed this is more of an architectural monument than a gallery, and it's free. Don't miss it.

The gloomy, rundown lanes south of Cordoaria were once part of Porto's *judiaria* (Jewish quarter).

Museu do Vinho do Porto

At the time of writing a long-overdue Port Wine Museum (☎ 222 053 644; Rua do Monchique 45-52; adult/student or senior Tues-Sat €0.80/free, admission Sun free; open 10am-12.30pm & 2pm-5.30pm Tues-Sat, 2pm-5.30pm Sun) was to start showcasing the history of Porto's most famous tipple.

Museu do Carro Eléctrico

The Tram Museum (☎ 226 158 185; Alameda Basílio Teles 51; admission €2.50; open 10am-12.30pm & 2.30pm-6pm Tues-Fri, 3pm-7pm Sat & Sun), a cavernous former switching-house with dozens of beautifully restored old trams, is right beside the STCP (municipal transport agency) building.

See Getting Around for information on Porto's surviving tram lines.

Museu Romântico

Beside the Jardim do Palácio de Cristal (see following) is the Quinta da Macieirinha, where the abdicated king of Sardinia, Carlos Alberto, spent his final days in 1843. It's now a marginally interesting 'Romantic Museum' (☎ 226 057 033; Rua Entre-Quintas 220; admission Tues-Fri €0.80, Sat & Sun free; open 10am-12.30pm & 2pm-5.30pm Tues-Sat, 2pm-5.30pm Sun) featuring the king's belongings among dainty period furnishings.

Jardim do Palácio de Cristal

This modest, leafy park (main entrance Rua Dom Manuel II; open 8am-9pm Apr-Sept, 8am-7pm Oct-Mar), named after a long-gone 19th-century crystal palace, is home to a sports pavilion, gardens and a pond, roving peacocks and a reasonable self-service restaurant. But pride of place goes to the new, high-tech **Biblioteca Municipal Almeida Garrett** (open 10am-6pm Mon-Fri) and adjacent **Palácio Gallery** (open 10am-6pm Mon-Fri).

Azulejos

Porto sports some dramatic tilework. Largest and most intricate is Silvestre Silvestri's panel illustrating the legend of the founding of the Carmelite order, covering an outer wall of the **Igreja do Carmo** (Praça Gomes Teixeira). Another church covered in blue tiles – in traditional style but dating from the early 20th century and undertaken by Eduardo Leite – is the **Capela das Almas** (Rua Santa Catarina). Five 18th-century panels by Vital Rifarto decorate the Gothic cloisters of the **cathedral**.

In the entrance hall of **São Bento train station** several huge works by Jorge Colaço (1930) depict scenes ranging from daily life to historic battles (other train stations serving as azulejo art galleries are at Aveiro and Pinhão).

DOURO

Newest of the lot, though no patch on the other azulejos, is a multicoloured mural called **Ribeira Negra** by Júlio Resende (1987), featuring life in the old Ribeira district. It's in central Porto beside the tunnel to the lower deck of the Ponte de Dom Luís I.

Pontes

Some of Porto's most distinctive landmarks are its *pontes* (bridges) across the Rio Douro. From west to east they are: the modern Ponte da Arrábida linking Porto to the A1/IC1 Lisbon highway; the immense, two-level Ponte de Dom Luís I to Vila Nova de Gaia; the new Ponte do Infante Dom Henrique, nearing completion at the time of writing; two railway bridges, the Ponte de Dona Maria Pia (designed by Gustav Eiffel in 1876) and adjacent Ponte de São João; and the uninspiring Ponte do Freixo, linking to the A3/E1.

A walk to Vila Nova de Gaia across the vertiginous upper deck of the Ponte de Dom Luís I is a Porto highlight, offering truly stupendous views. This deck's vehicle traffic, between central Porto and central Gaia, will eventually be displaced by the new metro line and shifted to the Ponte Infante Dom Henrique.

River Cruises

Several outfits offer cruises in ersatz *barcos rabelos*, the colourful boats once used to transport port wine from the vineyards. Cruises last 45 to 55 minutes and depart at least hourly on summer days. Board at Porto's Cais da Ribeira or Cais da Estiva, or Vila Nova de Gaia's Cais de Gaia or Cais Amarelo. Shop around – tickets cost €8 to €10 and kids usually go for half-price.

These outfits and other companies also have longer Douro trips; see under Peso da Régua later in this chapter.

Bus Tours

The company **Diana Tours** *(Porto Visão;* ☎ *223 771 230;* e *dianatours@dianatours.pt)* runs a daily hop-on-hop-off city tour (€12.50, half-price for children aged seven to 12) that includes a visit to a port-wine lodge. You can start at any of the chosen sights (eg, Aliados), linger at others and then just catch the next of its buses, which run hourly except at lunch time. You can buy tickets on the bus, at travel agencies or upper-end hotels. A range of thematic tours is also on offer.

Special Events

Porto's biggest bash is the Festa de São João (St John's Festival, also called the Festa da Cidade) from 23 to 24 June, when the city erupts into merrymaking. But there's a stream of cultural events throughout the year (ask at the main city turismo); among the long-standing ones worth catching are:

February/March
  Fantasporto (international fantasy film festival)
March
  Super Bock Super Rock (a fortnight of rock concerts in Porto and Lisbon)
March/April
  Festival Intercéltico do Porto (festival of Celtic music)
Early May
  Queima das Fitas (student week)
Late May
  Festival Internacional de Teatro para a Infância e Juventude (international children's theatre festival)
June
  Festa de São João (St John's Festival)
June/July
  Ritmos (rhythms; festival of ethnic music)
Late July
  Festival Internacional de Folclore (international folk festival)
Late August
  Noites Ritual Rock (festival of Portuguese rock)
Mid-September
  Desfile de Carros Eléctricos (tram parade)
October
  Grande Noite do Fado (gala evening of *fado*)
October/November
  Festival de Jazz do Porto (jazz festival)
Early December
  Festival de Marionetas (international puppet festival)

Places to Stay

Unless otherwise noted, rooms in establishments listed here have a private toilet and bath or shower.

Places to Stay – Budget

Porto's year-round municipal facility, **Parque de Campismo da Prelada** *(*☎ *228 312 616; Rua Monte dos Burgos; adult/car €3.10/ 2.60, tent €2.60-4.90)*, is 4km northwest of the city centre. To get here take bus No 6 from Praça da Liberdade or bus No 50 from Jardim da Cordoaria.

Three seaside places across the river, all open year-round, are linked by a road from the Ponte da Arrábida: basic **Campismo Salgueiros** (☎ 227 810 500, fax 227 810 136; Praia de Salgueiros; adult/car €1.50/0.80, tent €1.50-2), **Campismo Marisol** (☎ 227 135 942, fax 227 126 351; Praia de Canide; adult/car €1.50/2.30, tent 2.50-4.80) and Orbitur's **Campismo Madalena** (☎ 227 122 520; e info@orbitur.pt; Praia da Madalena; adult/car €3.80/3.30, tent €3-4). Bus No 57 runs to all three from Praça Almeida Garrett. Note that the sea at these places is far too polluted for swimming.

Porto's fine **pousada da juventude** (youth hostel; ☎ 226 177 257; e porto@movijovem .pt; Rua Paulo da Gama 551; dorm beds/doubles €15/42; open 24hr) is 4km west of the centre. Reservations are essential. Take bus No 35 from Praça da Liberdade; bus No 1 from Praça Almeida Garrett also runs nearby.

Pensão Mondariz (☎ 222 005 600; Rua do Cimo de Vila 139; doubles with/without toilet & shower €20/15), a tatty, old place in the upper Ribeira, is a good option with big, TV-less rooms and traces of Art Nouveau.

Residencial Porto Chique (☎ 222 080 069; Rua Conde de Vizela 26; doubles with/without bathroom €25/15) has basic rooms and a central location.

Pensão Astória (☎ 222 008 175; Rua Arnaldo Gama 56; singles/doubles with shared bathroom from €19/30) is a hidden gem at the edge of the Unesco zone. Some of the handsome old rooms (no TV) have great river views; rates include breakfast. Book well in advance.

Pensão Porto Rico (☎ 223 394 690, fax 223 394 699; Rua do Almada 237; singles/doubles/triples/quads with breakfast €20/30/35/40) is a budget-friendly place near Aliados, with plain rooms and an affable, English-speaking owner.

Places to Stay – Mid-Range
Breakfast is included in the price at all places in this section.

Aliados Centrally located **Hotel Peninsular** (☎ 222 003 012; e hotel.peninsular@clix.pt; Rua Sá da Bandeira 21; doubles with/without bathroom from €32/25) is a surprise bargain – all polished wood, ancient lifts and faultless service – though rooms are a trifle damp. Try for a quieter room at the rear.

Other places with honest rates, full attached bathroom and turn-of-the-century charm are plain **Residencial Paulista** (☎ 222 054 692, fax 222 005 730; Avenida dos Aliados 214; doubles €35), comfortable **Pensão Chique** (☎ 222 009 011, fax 223 322 963; Avenida dos Aliados 206; doubles €42.50), with small rooms, and smart **Residencial Universal** (☎ 222 006 758, fax 222 001 055; Avenida dos Aliados 38; doubles €49.50), with a good buffet breakfast. All these places have some back rooms free from street noise.

Residencial Pão de Açucar (☎ 222 002 425, fax 222 050 239; Rua do Almada 262; doubles from €50), richly Art Nouveau inside, has handsome rooms with satellite TV, some (costing €75) opening onto a top-floor terrace; reservations are essential.

Residencial dos Aliados (☎ 222 004 853, fax 222 002 710; Rua Elísio de Melo 27; doubles with/without air-con from €70/60), a well-run, helpful place in one of Aliados' trademark Art Nouveau buildings, is good value, though street-facing rooms are noisy.

Around Cordoaria Cheerful, family-run **Pensão-Residencial Estoril** (☎ 222 002 751, fax 222 082 468; Rua de Cedofeita 193; doubles/triples €37/54) also has cheaper rooms with shared facilities.

Pensão São Marino (☎ 223 325 499; e residencial_s.marino@clix.pt; Praça Carlos Alberto 59; singles/doubles €32/38) has prim, quiet rooms, which are good value in an otherwise droopy neighbourhood.

Praça da Batalha The only place worth noting in this neighbourhood is brisk, group-friendly **Pensão Aviz** (☎ 223 320 722, fax 223 320 747; Avenida Rodrigues de Freitas 451; singles/doubles €31.50/42.50), with a bar and plain, functional rooms.

North of Aliados The cheerful **Hotel-Residencial América** (☎ 223 392 930, fax 222 083 862; Rua Santa Catarina 1018; doubles €53) has hygienically clean rooms, a winter garden, generous buffet breakfast and free off-street parking. It doesn't take block bookings so there's usually space even at the peak of the season.

Castelo Santa Catarina (☎ 225 095 599, fax 225 506 613; Rua Santa Catarina 1347; doubles €60) is a late-19th-century pseudo-Gothic castle, an over-the-top hideaway in a palm-shaded garden. Doubles in the castle are small and gloomy but there are others in a modern annexe. Off-street parking is free. Don't confuse this with Residencial Santa Catarina, nearer to the centre on the same road.

Places to Stay – Top End

Buffet breakfast is part of the package at the following establishments.

Hotel da Bolsa (☎ 222 026 768; e hotelda bolsa@mail.telepac.pt; Rua Ferreira Borges 101; singles/doubles with air-con & cable TV €63/76), well-run and centrally located in the Ribeira, has a few rooms with river views for an additional €14.

Grande Hotel do Porto (☎ 222 076 690; e reservas@grandehotelporto.com; Rua Santa Catarina 197; singles/doubles with air-con & cable TV €95/105), built in 1880, is a lovely place with surprisingly plain rooms, complete with full bathroom.

Hotel Infante de Sagres (☎ 223 398 500, fax 223 398 599; e his.sales@mail.telepac.pt; Praça Dona Filipa de Lencastre 62; singles/ doubles from €180/200) is a splendid time warp of a place with liveried doorman, crystal chandeliers, stained glass, antique furnishings and marble baths.

Porto Carlton Hotel (☎ 223 402 300; e porto.carlton@mail.telepac.pt; Praça da Ribeira 1; singles/doubles with air-con & satellite TV from €108/122) has the choicest spot on the Ribeira waterfront, and plush executive rooms, many with an up-close river view.

Places to Eat

Many restaurants are closed on Sunday, but seem to change their minds about it frequently, so call ahead to be sure.

Aliados Nothing in the neighbourhood approaches **Café Embaixador** (☎ 222 054 182; Rua Sampaio Bruno 5; open 6.30am-10pm daily) for value, with table service downstairs and, during the day, cheaper, pay-by-weight self-service on the mezzanine. Assemble a respectable meal from grilled meat, fish and a gorgeous salad bar for under €5.

Café Metro da Trindade (Rua Dr Ricardo Jorge; dishes from €3.30; open Mon-Sat), around the corner from the main city turismo, offers good, cheap lunch fare and quick service.

Pedro dos Frangos (Rua do Bonjardim 219; open Wed-Mon) is a tiny place that

---

A Load of Tripe

It's not what most of us look for on the menu, but many Porto folk can think of nothing finer than a rich stew of tripe (cow's stomach). This affection, so the story goes, dates back to 1415 when Henry the Navigator was preparing to sail for Ceuta in Morocco. Porto's loyal citizens donated their best meat, keeping the offal for themselves and earning the nickname *tripeiros* (tripe-eaters).

---

draws the crowds for good *frango no espeto* (spit-roasted chicken) and other cheap grills; a whole chicken (€7.30) is enough for two.

Around Cordoaria Cheerfully downmarket **Restaurante Romão** (Casa Viúva; ☎ 222 005 639; Praça Carlos Alberto 100; open Mon-Sat) has a long list of northern specialities, including €4.50 half-portions of *rojões à Transmontanho* (crispy pork) and *feijoada* (pork-and-bean casserole).

Confeitaria Rian (Rua de Cedofeita 185; open daily) is a plain café with lovely pastries and delicious *lulas grelhadas* (grilled squid).

Restaurante A Tasquinha (☎ 223 322 145; Rua do Carmo 23; mains €6-10; open daily) has good, well-prepared regional dishes for lunch and dinner, and almost as many desserts as wines.

Adega do Carregal (Taberna do Carregal; ☎ 222 081 200; Travessa do Carregal; dishes €11-16; open Mon-Sat) offers cask wines, garlicky appetisers and good though very pricey northern specialities.

Ribeira Of the Ribeira's many touristy riverfront restaurants, **Casa Filha da Mãe Preta** (☎ 222 055 515; Cais da Ribeira 39; half-portions under €7; open Mon-Sat) is the most congenial. Go early to bag an upstairs front table for views of the Rio Douro. Don't confuse this place with the old taverna of the same name, one street back.

Pub-Petisqueira O Muro (☎ 222 083 426; Muro dos Bacalhoeiros 88; dishes under €9; open Mon-Sat), on the upper riverfront walkway, is recommended as much for its cheerful atmosphere and quirky decor as for the well-prepared local dishes. It stays open all day for meals.

Casa Cardoso (☎ 222 058 644; Rua de Fonte Taurina 58; half-portions under €6; open Mon-Sat) is a small, airy, locally popular place, with a few dishes under €5 and lots of half-portions.

Vegetarian Not surprisingly in a city famous for tripe, vegetarians are poorly catered for – though you could do very well with the vegetables on offer at the Café Embaixador (see earlier entry).

Suribachi (☎ 225 106 700; Rua do Bonfim 134-140; dishes under €6; open 9am-10pm daily), a squeaky clean macrobiotic restaurant, cheerful and contemplative, offers relief from meat and urban stress. It serves food all day and into the evening.

Restaurante O Oriente no Porto (☎ 222 007 223; Rua São Miguel 19; lunch plate €4.50; open 12.30pm-3pm Mon-Sat), in the dreary neighbourhood south of Cordoaria, serves a peaceful macrobiotic set lunch in a centre for alternative therapies.

Cafés & Confeitarias Porto's best-known tea shop, **Café Majestic** (☎ 222 003 887; Rua Santa Catarina 112; open Mon-Sat), has prancing cherubs, gilded woodwork and gold-braided waiters who'll serve you a €14 set breakfast or €7.50 afternoon tea.

Confeitaria do Bolhão (☎ 222 009 291; Rua Formosa 339), an airy place with a relaxed ambience, has lunch-time specials and a big selection of local sweets, including a sponge cake called *pão de ló*. If you like *pão de ló* you can stock up at a lovely old bakery and confectionery called **Pão de Ló Margaridense** (Travessa de Cedofeita 20B).

Café Ancôra Douro (Praça de Parada Leitão 55; open Mon-Sat), near Cordoaria, is a downmarket counterpoint to Porto's posher cafés. It's a cavernous, casual place where students nurse coffees for hours and fill their tummies with crepes, hot dogs or light meals.

Self-Catering Porto's municipal market, the **Mercado do Bolhão** (open 8am-5pm Mon-Fri, 8am-1pm Sat), brings you cheese, olives, fresh bread, strawberries and more. It's at its liveliest in the morning.

Two handsome shops across from the market – a branch of the **Confeitaria do Bolhão** (Rua Formosa 305) and the Art Deco **A Pérola do Bolhão** (Rua Formosa 279) – have nuts, dried fruit and other quality groceries.

Central supermercados include **Minipreço** (Rua Conceição), **Pingo Doce** (Rua Passos Manuel 213) and **Modelo** (Centro Comercial Via Catarina, Rua Santa Catarina).

Entertainment

Porto is a lively place day and night, with a busy cultural calendar. You'll find *Agenda do Porto*, a monthly cultural events brochure, at city turismos and there are similar listings in the *Jornal de Notícias* and *Público* newspapers.

Bars & Clubs – Ribeira Here's where you'll find Porto's good older bars. Take bus No 57 or 91 from Praça Almeida Garrett to the Ribeira stop, except as noted.

Anikibóbó (☎ 223 324 619; Rua Fonte Taurina 36-38; admission €5; open 10pm-4am Mon-Sat) offers vanguard music, an artsy crowd, Thursday exhibitions and theatre.

Arcadas Pub (☎ 222 002 965; Rua Miragaia 167; admission free; open 10pm-2am Mon-Sat) has fado (sometimes live) and other music for a middle-aged crowd. To get here catch bus No 1 from Praça Almeida Garrett to the Alfândega stop.

Buraquinho (Cais da Ribeira 50; admission free; open 11am-4am daily) is a congenial café-bar with commercial tunes.

Está-se Bem (☎ 222 004 249; Rua Fonte Taurina 70-72; admission free; open 8pm-4am Mon-Sat) is a low-key bar-café with cheap drinks for an artsy clientele.

Fado

Porto has no *fado* tradition of its own, but you can enjoy the Lisbon or Coimbra version of 'Portugal blues' into the wee hours (except Sunday) at **Restaurante O Fado** (☎ 222 026 937; Largo de São João Novo 16) or **Restaurante Mal Cozinhado** (☎ 222 081 319; Rua Outerinho 11, Ribeira). The food isn't the main attraction – and in any case is grossly overpriced – but there's a minimum charge, equivalent to a light meal or several drinks.

A bar offering occasional live fado is the **Arcadas Pub** (☎ 222 002 965; Rua Miragaia 167; admission free; open 10pm-2am Mon-Sat). Porto has its own fado festival in October (see Special Events earlier).

Solar do Vinho do Porto

The finest place in Porto to drink port wine is the **Solar do Vinho do Porto** (☎ 226 097 793; *Rua Entre-Quintas 220; open 2pm-midnight Mon-Sat, closed holidays*), a posh bar with a river view terrace beside the Jardim do Palácio de Cristal. Waiters will help you choose from hundreds of varieties, from around €0.80 per glass.

Meia-Cave (☎ 223 323 214, *Praça da Ribeira 6; admission €7.50; open 10pm-4am daily*) is a venerable place with a dance floor. It offers occasional live rock, an irreverent atmosphere and a summertime pavement café.

Porto Feio (☎ 222 054 485; *Rua Fonte Taurina 52-54; admission free; open 10pm-2am Mon-Sat*) is a bar-cum-art gallery with background music.

Ribeirinha (☎ 223 322 572; *Rua de São João 70-72; admission €3; open 11pm-2am daily*), the Ribeira's oldest bar, is student-friendly, with all kinds of music.

Ryan's Irish Pub (☎ 222 005 366; *Rua Infante Dom Henrique 18; admission €3.50; open 5pm-2am daily*) is a café-bar serving up Guinness, Irish whisky and Irish tunes.

Trilogia (☎ 222 051 159; *Rua de São João 48-50; admission Sat €5, Sun-Fri free; open 3pm-4am daily*), a dance bar with Latin/Brazilian sounds, is popular with students.

Bars & Clubs – Massarelos & Rua do Ouro

Massarelos, the riverside strip near the Jardim do Palácio de Cristal, and its westward extension, Rua do Ouro, is Porto's newest nightlife zone. Take bus No 1 from Praça Almeida Garrett; the last bus back passes by at about 1.30am.

Clube Mau-Mau (☎ 226 076 660; *Rua do Outeiro 4; bus stop Massarelos; admission €15; club open 11pm-4am Wed, Fri & Sat, restaurant 8.30pm-2am Tues-Sat*) has a trendy crowd, house music with guest DJs, and late-night food.

Maré Alta (☎ 226 091 010; *Rua do Ouro; bus stop Gás; admission Wed-Sat €5, Sun €7.50; open 10pm-2am Wed & Thur, 10pm-4am Fri & Sat, 8pm-4am Sun*) offers all kinds of music, and is located on a boat with a dance floor.

Bars & Clubs – Foz do Douro

There's a brisk night scene out at the mouth of the Douro, near the beach; take bus No 1 from Praça Almeida Garrett.

Armipin (☎ 226 181 810; *Rua da Agra 86; bus stop Gondarem; admission €5; open 10pm-2am daily*) has DJs spinning oldies, commercial and Latin nightly.

Monte Caffé (☎ 938 305 820; *Rua da Beneditina 213C; bus stop Pilotos; admission free; open 9.30pm-2am daily*) has a good atmosphere, cheap drinks and a wide range of music, plus karaoke Tuesday and Latin Thursday.

Quando-Quando (☎ 226 102 797; *Avenida do Brasil 60; bus stop Fonte Luz; admission €3.50; open 10.30pm-5am daily*) is a beachfront bar at Praia dos Ingleses, with good pop, rock and vanguard music.

Indústria (☎ 226 176 806, *Avenida do Brasil 843; bus stop Molhe; admission €7.50; open 11.30pm-4am Fri & Sat*), a beachside club with soul, funk and house, has a good atmosphere.

Pop (☎ 226 183 959; *Rua Padre Luís Cabral 1090; bus stop Castelo Foz; admission €7.50; open 9pm-4am Thur-Sat*) offers vanguard, commercial and house music for the Beautiful People.

Bars & Clubs – Boavista to Ramalde

For something a bit different, try **Hiva-Oa** (☎ 226 179 663; *Avenida Boavista 2514; admission free; open 6pm-2am daily*), a Polynesian bar. To get here, take bus No 3 from Praça da Liberdade, or No 24 from Cordoaria, to the Pinheiro Manso stop.

Ramalde is an industrial area 2km to 3km northwest of Boavista. Clubs noted here open from midnight to 6am and charge €7.50, except as noted.

Santa Gota (☎ 226 163 220; *Rua Manuel Pinto de Azevedo 2; open Fri-Sat*) plays commercial, house and techno for a very young crowd. To get here, take bus No 52 from Praça da Liberdade to the Manuel P Azevedo stop.

Sound Planet (☎ 226 107 232; *Avenida Fontes Pereira de Melo 449; open Thur-Sat*) has commercial and house music, and occasional guest DJs. Take bus No 76 from Praça da Liberdade or Cordoaria to the Fontes P Melo stop.

Swing (☎ 226 090 019; *Praceta Engenheiro Amáro da Costa 766; open daily*) is Porto's oldest disco, playing '80s, commercial and house music. Catch bus No 3, 52 or 78 from Praça da Liberdade to the Bom Sucesso stop.

Tomate (☎ 226 162 487; Rua Manuel Pinto de Azevedo 15; open Wed, Fri & Sat) has commercial and house music, and features guest DJs. To get here, take bus No 41 from Praça da Liberdade or Cordoaria to the Manuel P Azevedo stop.

Via Invicta (☎ 226 108 172; Rua Delfim Ferreira 564; admission €5-10; open Fri-Sun) – Porto's favourite venue for live Brazilian music. Take bus No 52 from Praça da Liberdade to the Bairro Ramalde stop.

Via Rápida (☎ 226 109 427; unit 5, Rua Manuel Pinto de Azevedo 567; admission €10; open midnight-7am Fri & Sat) plays house music. Catch bus No 3 from Praça da Liberdade to Manuel P Azevedo stop.

Gay & Lesbian Nightclubs Clubs welcoming gay men and gay women include:

Boys 'R' Us (Portofolio; ☎ 917 746 271) Rua Dr Barbosa de Castro 63; open 10pm to 4am Wednesday and Friday to Sunday

Moinho de Vento (☎ 222 056 883) Rua Sá Noronha 78; open 10.30pm to 4am daily

Bar Him (☎ 222 084 383) Rua do Bonjardim 836; open 10pm to 4am Tuesday to Sunday

Swing (see under Bars & Clubs – Boavista to Ramalde) is also gay-friendly.

Theatres & Concert Halls Traditional venues for classical music and drama are the **Auditório Nacional Carlos Alberto** (☎ 223 395 050; Rua das Oliveiras 43) and **Casa das Artes** (☎ 226 006 153; Rua de António Cardoso 175).

The **Teatro Nacional de São João** (☎ 222 086 634; Praça da Batalha) is Porto's prime preforming-arts venue, though it has no drama company of its own.

The **Coliseu do Porto** (☎ 223 394 947; Rua Passos Manuel 137) hosts larger-scale dance, rock and other performances.

The **Teatro de Belmonte** (☎ 222 083 341; Rua Belmonte 57) is the place to go for puppet shows.

Cinemas Porto has a generous supply of cinemas, often featuring subtitled English-language films. There are multiscreen cinemas at the large **Centro Comercial Central**

Shopping (☎ 225 102 785; Rua Santos Pousada 290) and at **Centro Comercial Cidade do Porto** (☎ 226 009 164; Rua Gonçalo Sampaio 350, Boavista).

Spectator Sports

Porto's favourite football (soccer) team and frequent national champion is FC Porto. You can watch the team play at **Estádio das Antas**, northeast of the centre on Avenida Fernão de Magalhães (bus No 6 or 78 from Praça da Liberdade). A 50,000-seat stadium under construction next door will host the opening ceremonies and first game of the 2004 European Football Championships, and will be FC Porto's new home.

But the heroes in the 2001–02 season were Porto's own underfunded Boavista FC, who broke a half-century-plus grip by the big three (FC Porto and Lisbon's Sporting Clube de Portugal and SL Benfica) to seize the championship. Boavista FC plays at **Estádio do Bessa**, west of the centre on Avenida da Boavista (take bus No 3 from Praça da Liberdade), which was under renovation for Euro2004 at the time of research.

The city's second-division team is Salgueiros. Although not a Euro2004 venue, its **Estádio Vidal Pinheiro** (Rua Augusto Lessa; bus No 6 from Rua Sá da Bandeira or No 79 from Aliados) is also slated for replacement.

Check with the city turismo or the local edition of *Público* or *Jornal de Notícias* for upcoming fixtures.

Shopping

Even if you don't buy a thing, Porto is a great place to shop: establishments range from funky to chic, and there are entire streets specialising in particular items (try Rua Galeria de Paris for fine art or Rua da Fábrica for bookshops).

Modern *centros comerciales* (shopping centres) are multiplying. Big centres include **Via Catarina** (Rua Santa Catarina), underground **Clérigos Shopping** (Rua das Carmelitas), **Central Shopping** (Campo 24 de Agosto), **Cidade do Porto** (Rua Gonçalo Sampaio) and **Brasília** (Boavista).

Port & Other Wines Port is an obvious purchase, and you needn't go to Vila Nova de Gaia for it. **Garrafeira do Carmo** (Rua do Carmo 17) specialises in vintage port and high-quality wines, at reasonable prices.

DOURO

Other good sources are **Casa Januário** *(Rua do Bonjardim 352)* and the photogenic **Casa Oriental** *(Campo dos Mártires da Pátria 111)*.

Handicrafts Appealing handmade textiles, puppets, toys, glass and pottery can be found at **Arte Facto** *(Rua da Reboleira 37, Ribeira; open 10am-noon & 1pm-6pm Tues-Fri, 1pm-7pm Sat & Sun)*, the sales outlet for the **Centro Regional de Artes Tradicionais** *(CRAT; ☎ 223 320 201)*. Arte Facto also has exhibitions on handicrafts production.

A modest shop with simple pottery, tiles, embroidery, copper and pewter work, plus key chains, postcards and novelties, is **Artesanato dos Clérigos** *(Rua Assunção 33)*, behind the Torre dos Clérigos. Stalls in the **Mercado do Bolhão** sell basketry and ceramics.

Shoes Porto has some great shoe bargains. You'll find *sapatarias* (shoe shops) everywhere, especially along Rua Mouzinho da Silveira, Rua 31 de Janeiro and Rua de Cedofeita.

Markets See Places to Eat, earlier, for information on good food markets.

The most rewarding of Porto's many flea markets runs from 6am to noon on Saturday at Alameda das Fontaínhas, southeast of Praça da Batalha. A touristy market along the Cais da Ribeira is good for T-shirts, woolly jumpers and traditional toys. A scrawny flea market occupies Calçada da Vandoma, north of the cathedral, daily.

Getting There & Away

Air International and domestic flights use **Francisco Sá Carneiro airport** *(flight information ☎ 229 412 141)*, 20km northwest of the city centre. It's in the throes of a major expansion for Euro2004.

Portugália and TAP have multiple daily flights to/from Lisbon. Direct international connections include one or more flights on most days to London, Madrid, Paris, Frankfurt, Amsterdam and Brussels; see the Getting There & Away chapter for details.

There's no left-luggage facility at the airport.

Bus – International There are **Eurolines** *(☎ 225 189 299; Centro Comercial Central Shopping, Rua Santos Pousada 200; bus No 6 from Praça da Liberdade)* services to/from cities all over Europe.

IASA *(☎ 225 373 205; Centro Comercial Central Shopping, Rua Santos Pousada 200)* has three buses a week to/from Paris via Viseu and Guarda.

Northern Portugal's own international carrier is **Internorte** *(☎ 226 052 420; Praça da Galiza 96; bus No 3 or 52 from Praça da Liberdade)*.

Most travel agencies can book outbound buses with any of these operators. See under Bus in the Getting There & Away chapter for details.

Bus – Domestic There are at least five places where you can catch long-distance buses to points within Portugal.

Renex *(☎ 222 003 395; Campo dos Mártires da Pátria 37; open 24hr)* is the choice for Lisbon (€12.50, 3½ hours), with the most direct routes and eight to 12 departures daily, including one continuing to the Algarve. Renex also goes about as often to Braga (€4.50, 1¼ hours).

Rede Expressos *(☎ 222 006 954)* departs many times a day for just about anywhere from the smoggy **Paragem Atlântico terminal** *(Rua Alexandre Herculano 370)*. Its affiliate Rodoviária da Beira Litoral (RBL) runs from here to Coimbra (€8.40, 1½ hours) and other points in the Beiras.

For fast Minho connections, mainly on weekdays, three lines run from around Praceta Régulo Magauanha, off Rua Dr Alfredo Magalhães. **REDM** *(☎ 222 003 152)* runs chiefly to Braga (€3.60, one hour). **AV Minho** *(☎ 222 006 121)* goes mainly via Vila do Conde (€2.10, 55 minutes) to Viana do Castelo (€6, 1¼ hours). **Arriva** *(☎ 222 051 383)* serves Guimarães (€3.60, 50 minutes).

Rodonorte *(☎ 222 005 637; Rua Ateneu Comercial do Porto 19)* has multiple daily departures (fewer on Saturday) for Amarante (€4.30, one hour), Vila Real (€5.30, 1½ hours) and Bragança (€8, 3½ hours).

Santos *(☎ 225 104 915; Centro Comercial Central Shopping, Rua Santos Pousada 200; bus No 6 from Praça da Liberdade)* buses run to Lisbon (€11.50), Coimbra (€7.50), Vila Real (€5.30) and Bragança (€8).

Train Porto is a rail hub for northern Portugal. Long-distance (most international and all *intercidade* – IC) services start at

Campanhã station, 2km east of the centre. Most *suburbano*, regional and *interregional* (IR) trains start from São Bento station, though all these lines also pass through Campanhã.

For destinations on the Braga, Guimarães or Aveiro lines, or up the Douro valley as far as Marco de Canaveses, take one of the frequent *suburbano* trains (use the green ticket machines or window 7, 8 or 9 at São Bento); don't spend extra money on IR or IC trains to these destinations (eg, Porto–Braga costs €1.70 by *suburbano* but €5.70 by IC train). São Bento will eventually be the sole terminal for *suburbano* trains.

Sample 2nd-class IR/IC fares and times for direct journeys from Porto are Viana do Castelo (IR €4.80, 1½ hours, two daily; no direct IC), Coimbra (IR €5.40, 1½ hours, two daily; IC €7.20, 1¼ hours, four daily) and Lisbon (IR €11, 4½ hours, two daily; IC €14.10, 3½ hours, four daily).

At São Bento you can book tickets for journeys departing from either station. Any ticket bought at São Bento for a journey starting from Campanhã entitles you to a free ride between the stations (five minutes) via *suburbano* train.

There are information offices at both **São Bento** (open 8.30am-8pm daily) and **Campanhã** (open 9am-7pm daily). For telephone information call Caminhos de Ferro Portugueses' (CP) local-rates number, ☎ 808 208 208.

Car Drivers can get information from the **Automovel Clube de Portugal** (☎ 222 056 732; Rua Gonçalo Cristóvão 2/6).

The lowest unlimited-mileage rental rates we found were at **Budget/AA Castanheira** (☎ 808 252 627). Other agencies with low rates are **Auto Jardim** (☎ 800 200 613), **Sixt** (☎ 229 485 813) and **Auro** (☎ 229 440 111). International agencies include **Europcar** (☎ 808 204 050), **National/Alamo** (☎ 800 201 078), **Avis** (☎ 800 201 002) and **Hertz** (☎ 800 238 238). All these companies have desks at the airport.

Getting Around
To/From the Airport A flexible bus service is **AeroBus** (☎ 808 200 166), which runs between Aliados and the airport via Boavista every half-hour from 7am to 6.30pm. The trip takes 25 minutes in favourable traffic.

The €2.50 ticket, purchased on the bus, also serves as a free bus pass until midnight of the day you buy it. Arriving TAP passengers who present their boarding pass get this ticket free.

The bus will drop passengers at any train station, the Parque de Campismo da Prelada, the *pousada da juventude* or any of about three-dozen major hotels. If you're staying at one of these, it will also collect you if you call ☎ 225 071 054 by 10pm the preceding day.

Bus No 56 runs between Cordoaria and the airport (€1.70) about every half-hour from 6.30am to 8.30pm. In the evening it continues to Praça da Liberdade.

A taxi costs around €20 to/from Praça da Liberdade. Taxis authorised to run *from* the airport are labelled 'Maia' and/or 'Vila Nova de Telha'; the rank is just outside the arrivals hall. Porto city taxis can take passengers *to* the airport but cannot bring any back (some do anyway, and a few overcharge).

During peak traffic time, you should allow an hour or more between the city centre and the airport.

Bus Porto's municipal transport agency is **STCP** (*Sociedade de Transportes Colectivos do Porto; information ☎ 808 200 166*). It operates an extensive bus system, which has central hubs at Praça da Liberdade, Praça Almeida Garrett (São Bento train station) and Cordoaria.

Maps and timetables for day and night routes are available from the city turismos and from an **STCP office** (open 8am-7.30pm Mon-Fri, 8am-1pm Sat) opposite São Bento station.

Tickets are the cheapest if bought in advance – from the STCP office and from many newsagents and *tabacarias*. Trips within Porto city limits cost €0.50, those to outlying areas (including Vila Nova de Gaia) cost €0.70 and longer trips (including the airport) cost €1.70, this last fare is also valid for a return journey. Tickets are sold singly or in discounted *cadernetas* (booklets) of 10. A ticket that is bought on the bus (one way to anywhere in the STCP system) costs €1.

Also available is a €2 *bilhete diário* (day pass) valid for unlimited trips within the city on buses and the tram. The city sells its own more general tourist pass, the Passe Porto, through city turismos.

Metro Work has started on Porto's underground system, the hub for which will be Trindade station, a few blocks north of the *câmara municipal*. The network is eventually to reach north to the city limits, east to Campanhã, south to Vila Nova de Gaia (via the upper deck of the Ponte Dom Luís I), west through the suburb of Matosinhos and northwest up the coast all the way to Vila do Conde and Póvoa de Varzim.

The Matosinhos line is scheduled for completion in 2002 or 2003, the rest by 2004. Meanwhile the metro authority is running buses along selected parts of the network, including Póvoa, from Praça da República (tickets are available at the temporary cabin at Praça da República or on board the buses).

Tram Porto's trams used to be one of its delights, but only two are left. The No 1E trundles from near the Igreja de São Francisco (Ribeira), via the Tram Museum (see the earlier Museums section) at Massarelos, out to Foz do Douro (a 25-minute trip); when the metro and other work is completed it will continue along the seafront. The No 18 goes from near the Igreja do Carmo down to Massarelos. Both run every half-hour from about 8.15am to 7.30pm daily. The fare is €0.50, or you can use a day pass.

Taxi You will find taxis at ranks around the centre, or you can call a **radio taxi** (☎ *225 073 900)*. Figure on paying around €3 across the city centre during the day. An extra charge is levied if you leave the city limits, which includes crossing the bridge to Vila Nova de Gaia. For a customised city tour (at higher rates) you can hire a Mercedes **'turismo' taxi** (☎ *228 312 986)*.

AROUND PORTO
Afurada

Afurada is a quiet fishing village west of Vila Nova de Gaia, its houses decked with azulejos and its cafés known locally for their *caldeirada* (a hearty seafood stew).

From Jardim da Cordoaria, bus Nos 93 and 96 cross the Ponte da Arrábida to Centro Comercial Arrábida Shopping, a 10-minute walk from the village. A more relaxing alternative is to take the tram from the Ribeira, bus No 1 from Praça Almeida Garrett or bus No 24 from Cordoaria to the Gás stop, just west of the Ponte da Arrábida. There you can catch a small daily commuter ferry (about €0.50) across the river to the village. It departs about every 10 minutes from 6am to midnight.

VILA NOVA DE GAIA
postcode 4400 • pop 178,300
• elevation 100m

Porto's best-known attraction, an enclave of historic port-wine 'lodges', isn't even in Porto but lies across the river in Vila Nova de Gaia. Above and beyond these the town of Vila Nova de Gaia goes about its own business.

Since the mid-18th century port-wine bottlers and exporters have been obliged to maintain their lodges – basically dressed-up warehouses for pre-export storage and maturing – here. The lodges, now numbering around 60, are crammed cheek by jowl from the waterfront to the top of the steep slope, the oldest and biggest of them sporting huge signs. Most are open to visitors and many offer tours and tastings. The lodges and the very Mediterranean view of Porto from this side are really the only reasons to go over to Vila Nova de Gaia.

Port-wine types and vintages are discussed in the special section on port in this chapter.

Orientation & Information

Staff at the riverfront **turismo** (☎/*fax 223 751 902; Avenida Diogo Leite; open 10am-7pm Mon-Sat, 2pm-7pm Sun July & Aug; 10am-6pm Mon-Sat Sept-June)* dispense a good town map and a brochure listing the lodges open for tours. In any case you need only say the name of a lodge and local people will point you to it.

Wine Tasting & Tours

About two-dozen lodges are open for tours and tastings on weekdays and Saturday. In high season (June to mid-September) the larger ones run visitors through like clockwork and you'll wait no more than 15 minutes to join a tour. At other times they can accommodate you more or less on the spot.

[Continued on page 388]

PICARD & Cie PARIS

Title page: Stained-glass window of nymph and satyr (courtesy of Adriano Ramos Pinto)

Top: Ramos Pinto poster (courtesy of Adriano Ramos Pinto)

Bottom: Anyone for a drink? Bottles of port, Douro valley

Vinho do Porto (port) is Portugal's most famous export, a wine made exclusively from grapes grown in a demarcated region of the Douro valley, fortified with grape brandy and matured in casks or large oak vats. It was traditionally stored at Vila Nova de Gaia, across the Rio Douro from Porto, the city that gave port its name.

History

The first British traders to set up in Porto in the 13th century had no interest in wine. Their compatriots in Viana do Castelo dabbled with a local brew dubbed 'red Portugal', but it was olive oil, fruit and cork they wanted, in trade for wheat and woollen cloth from England and dried cod from Newfoundland.

But in 1667 Louis XIV's protectionist minister Colbert forbade the import of English cloth into France. Charles II retaliated with a ban on French wines in England. English merchants in Viana and Porto saw an opening, and shipped as much 'red Portugal' to England as they could lay hands on.

Demand grew for finer stuff. Two sons of a Liverpool wine merchant, visiting the upper Douro valley in 1678, are said to have found what they wanted – a sweet brew known as 'priest's port' – in a Lamego monastery, and shipped gallons of it home via Porto. They may have added brandy to help it travel better, thereby 'inventing' port as we know it today. (The addition of brandy to arrest fermentation, retain sweetness and raise the alcohol level was actually not standard practice until 1850, and happened only gradually in response to demand.)

By the early 1700s the Viana wine merchants were on the Douro trail. Among the first to establish a Porto base and regularly make the hazardous journey up the Douro were the founders of today's Taylor Fladgate & Yeatman, Croft's and Warre's. Thanks to a 1654 treaty, the English already enjoyed enormous commercial privileges in Portugal, and English and Scots traders were soon the most powerful wine merchants in Porto. The 1703 Methuen Treaty secured further profits by reducing British duty on Portuguese wines to a third less than that on French wines.

By the 18th century port was quite indispensable among proper Englishmen ('claret is the liquor for boys; port for men,' proclaimed Dr Johnson). But when supply trailed demand, growers resorted to various malpractices such as mixing port with elderberry juice or sweet Spanish wine. By 1755 the English traders refused to buy the wine unless the adulteration stopped.

The fracas gave the powerful Marquês de Pombal an opportunity to loosen the English grip. He founded a state monopoly (the Companhia Geral da Agricultura dos Vinhos do Alto Douro, nicknamed the Companhia Velha, or Old Company) with control over standards and prices. It was decreed that only port from a specific region in the Alto Douro – the world's first demarcated wine region – could be exported.

The English were outraged, but the resulting improvement in quality won the day. By the late 18th century English merchants had settled back down to a business that remained steadily profitable right up until

WWII. In 1926 Vila Nova de Gaia was designated as the place for storage, maturing and bottling prior to shipment overseas.

When port returned to the market after the war, it found stiff competition from sherry and cheap 'British wines' (mixtures of imported wine and grape juice). Many Porto firms sold up or amalgamated. Others, notably Sandeman, decided the future lay in advertising under their own name (Sandeman's logo, a black-hatted Spanish don, was a startling innovation).

The market has changed dramatically in three centuries. The French are now the biggest per-capita consumers of port, drinking three times as much as the English – though the English get through more vintage stuff than anyone else.

In 2001 Unesco gave a nod to the demarcated port-wine region's historical importance by declaring it a World Heritage site (for details see the website **w** www.unesco.org).

Transportation of Port

Port wine is stored, fortified and fine-tuned in huge vats or 25,000L oak casks in the port lodges' cool, dark *armazéns* (warehouses). It's then matured in the cask or in black glass bottles, depending on the quality of the harvest.

For centuries young port wine was brought by river from the wine estates – in February and March, following the autumn harvest – via

JOHN KING

Left: Casks of tawny port in the cellar of Taylor Fladgate & Yeatman port-wine lodge, Vila Nova de Gaia, Porto

Peso da Régua to Vila Nova de Gaia. It came in barrels stacked on the decks of *barcos rabelos*, which are handsome, flat-bottomed boats with billowing square sails. But progress, initially in the form of a railway line up the valley, caught up. The last commercial journey by a *barco rabelo* was in 1956, and tanker trucks now speed the wine down the valley.

Every summer the most river-worthy of the old boats, navigated by company officials, compete in a race at Vila Nova de Gaia. Aside from that they just serve as floating advertisements for the lodges, adding colour to the quays.

Since 1986 it has been legal to store and age port in the upper Douro valley. Some *quinta* (estate) owners now market their own 'estate-bottled' products. Though the big bottling and shipping firms still like to project a family-owned image, many have gobbled one another up or are in multinational hands.

The **Instituto do Vinho do Porto** (☎ 222 071 600; e ivp@mail.ivp .pt; Rua Ferreira Borges, Porto) is a private organisation dedicated to maintaining port-wine quality and the appellation's reputation. You're unlikely to get past the front desk but there are informative glossy booklets for those curious enough to visit. The institute also has an office in Peso da Régua.

Types of Port

Cheapest and sweetest are ruby and red ports, made from a blend of lesser wines, bottled early and drunk young (after about three years). Also blended are semisweet or sweet tawny ports, named after the mahogany colour they gain after years in oaken casks, and popular as an aperitif. The older they are, the better. Vintage character port is a cheap, blended version of a single-harvest port, aged for about four years.

Single-harvest ports range from *colheita*, a tawny port made from high-quality wines and aged for at least seven years before bottling, to late-bottled vintage (LBV) ports, produced from an excellent harvest and aged four to six years before bottling. Most sublime (and expensive) of all is vintage port, produced from a single harvest of outstanding quality, bottled within two years and aged for up to two decades, sometimes more. This is the ultimate after-dinner drink, always served from a decanter (not for show but because there's always sediment in the bottle).

Little known outside Portugal but worth trying are white ports, ranging from dry to rich and sweet. The dry variety is served chilled with a twist of lemon.

Price of Port

The main difference in price and quality is between blended ports (from several different harvests) and vintage port (from a single high-quality harvest). All genuine ports carry the Instituto do Vinho do Porto seal.

You needn't shell out for a whole bottle just to try port (though a cheap white or ruby only costs about €4): any café, bar or restaurant will serve you a glass for about €1. Vintage ports cost at least €13 a bottle; superior vintage port starts at about €4 a glass or €20 a bottle.

[Continued from page 384]

Of the old English-run lodges, **Taylor's** *(Taylor Fladgate & Yeatman; ☎ 223 719 999; Rua do Choupelo 250)* has the best tour and a taste of top-of-the-range (late-bottled vintage) wine. At **Ramos Pinto** *(☎ 223 707 000; Avenida Ramos Pinto 380)* a €2 tour includes the historic old company offices. Portuguese-run **Ferreira** *(☎ 223 745 292; Rua da Carvalhosa 19)* also has a good tour. Small, independent lodges include **Calém** *(☎ 223 746 660; Avenida Diogo Leite 26)* and **Rozés** *(☎ 223 771 680; Rua Cândido dos Reis 526)*.

If you can't be bothered to cross the river, you can taste all the lodges' port at the Solar do Vinho do Porto, a posh 'pub' in Porto; see the boxed text under Entertainment in the Porto section.

Barco Rabelos

At a boatyard on Cais de Gaia at the western end of the waterfront, you can watch *barcos rabelos* being built – on a touristic scale but using traditional methods.

Mosteiro da Serra do Pilar

Gaia's one architectural monument is this severe 16th-century monastery on a crowning hill beside the Ponte de Dom Luís I. The future Duke of Wellington made his headquarters here – probably because of the view of Porto – before crossing the river and chasing the French out of Porto in 1809.

Much of the monastery, including a striking circular cloister, now belongs to the army. At the time of writing the rest was closed for renovations (except during Sunday services).

Places to Eat

Restaurante Imar *(☎ 223 792 705; Avenida Diogo Leite 56; half-portions under €5; open Tues-Sun)*, 200m west of the turismo, offers regional dishes at reasonable prices, and smart service. A clutch of cheery, overpriced cafés and *adegas* (wine bars) near the *mercado municipal* (municipal market) do snacks and light meals (€3 to €4).

Several lodges, including Taylor's, serve lunch in their own posh, pricey restaurants.

Getting There & Away

Bus Nos 32, 57 and 91 run between Praça Almeida Garrett in Porto and Gaia's turismo, via the lower deck of the bridge.

For the Mosteiro da Serra do Pilar, take bus No 82 or 84 from Praça Almeida Garrett or No 33 or 83 from Aliados. These stop far above the lodges, although you can work your way down through narrow lanes to the riverfront.

VILA DO CONDE
postcode 4480 • pop 25,700

Once a ship-building port, and famous for its lace, Vila do Conde is now a popular seaside resort and handicrafts centre. Its beaches are some of the best north of Porto, and transport is easy enough to make a day trip feasible.

The town remains peaceful and charmingly unaffected by the activity at the beach, and offers a less touristy atmosphere than at the overdeveloped resort of Póvoa de Varzim, 4km to the north. Looming over everything is the immense hill-top Mosteiro de Santa Clara, which, along with surviving segments of a long-legged aqueduct, lends the town an air of unexpected monumentality.

Orientation & Information

Vila do Conde sits on the north side of the Rio Ave where it empties into the sea. Buses stop at the station on the N13 (Rua 5 de Outubro), in the shadow of the monastery. From the train station it's an 800m walk west to the N13 and north to the bus station.

Vila do Conde has two **turismos** *(☎ 252 248 473, fax 252 248 422; Rua 25 de Abril 103 • Rua 5 de Outubro 207; both open 9am-7pm Mon-Fri, 10am-6pm Sat & Sun)*, just 150m apart. When one is closed for lunch, the other is open. The one opposite the bus station shares a space with a small handicrafts gallery.

The town's beach, appreciated by surfers and sun-worshippers alike, stretches north for 3km from the mouth of the river. From the turismos it's 1.2km west along Avenida 25 de Abril, Avenida Dr João Canavarro and Avenida Sacadura Cabral to the beachfront road, Avenida Brasil.

The quietest accommodation, and a rank of cheerful cafés and bars, is around Praça da República, two blocks south of the bus station and a stone's throw from the little harbour.

Mosteiro de Santa Clara

The Mosteiro de Santa Clara was founded in 1318 by Dom Afonso Sanches. Only the fortified church outside the main complex retained its severe Gothic style following major reconstruction in the 18th century. At one time over 100 nuns lived here, but after the 1834 decree abolishing religious orders only a few were allowed to stay; the last died in 1893. Since 1944 the building has been a reformatory for teenage boys.

Nuns' tombstones line the path to the church. Inside are the carved tombs of Dom Afonso and his family, and the remains of a fine 18th-century cloister. Ring the bell for a free guided tour, possibly by one of the reformatory boys.

The massive aqueduct – used to bring water to the convent from Terroso, 7km away – once had 999 arches. The church and aqueduct are now national monuments.

Other Churches

The Manueline **igreja matriz** (parish church; Rua 25 de Abril; open irregular hrs) dates from the early 16th century, excpting its 17th-century belfry. It has an ornate doorway that was carved by Basque artist João de Castilho. Outside is a *pelourinho* (stone pillory) topped by the sword-wielding arm of Justice. Inside is the **Museu de Arte Sacra** (☎ 252 631 424; admission free; open 10am-noon & 2pm-4pm daily June-Sept, 2pm-4pm Oct-May), a modest collection of ecclesiastical art.

The 17th-century **Capela da Nossa Senhora de Socorro** (Largo da Alfândega; open daily), west of Praça da República, stands out with its mosque-like, whitewashed dome. The interior is covered in azulejos as old as the church itself.

School & Museum of Lace-Making

It's no accident that seafaring fingers, so deft at making nets, should also be good at lace-making. Long famous for its lace, Vila do Conde is one of the few places in Portugal with an active school of the art, founded in 1918. Children as young as four or five years old come to learn from local experts.

The school, in a typical 18th-century townhouse, includes a **Museu das Rendas de Bilros** (Museum of Bobbin Lace; ☎ 252 248 470; ⓦ www.mrbvc.net; Rua São Bento 70; admission free; open 9am-noon & 2pm-6pm Mon-Fri), with eye-popping examples of work from around the world. To visit the school itself (weekdays only), inquire at the turismo.

Another coastal town known for its lace is Peniche (see the Estremadura & Ribatejo chapter).

Museu da Construção Naval

Shipbuilding and seaborne trade have been in Vila do Conde's bones since at least the 13th century; many of the stoutest ships of the Age of Discoveries were made here.

Homage is paid to this side of the town's history at the Museum of Shipbuilding (☎ 252 240 740; Largo da Alfândega; admission free; open 10am-6pm Tues-Sun) in the restored Royal Customs House, just west of Praça da República. The building, fitted out with an entire ship's prow, is of more interest than the earnest but uninspiring exhibits on import/export taxation.

At a small **shipyard** (open Mon-Fri summer) across the river, a *nau* (a sort of pot-bellied caravel used in the old days for cargo and naval operations) is being lovingly hand-built using traditional methods, alongside the more routine construction of fishing boats. When finished it will join the exhibits at the Museum of Shipbuilding.

Seafront

The two best beaches, broad Praia da Forno and Praia de Nossa Senhora da Guia, have calm seas suitable for young children. Buses marked 'Vila do Conde' from Póvoa de Varzim stop at the station and then continue out to the beach, about every half-hour all day.

At the river mouth is the 17th-century **Castelo de São João Baptista**, once a castle but now a small, deluxe and very expensive hotel. A knot of snack bars and cafés is across the road from the *castelo*.

Special Events

A major handicrafts fair, the Feira Nacional de Artesanato, takes place here in the last week of July and first week of August.

The biggest religious event is the Festa de São João, held 23 June, when a candle-light procession winds through the streets to the beach.

Places to Stay

The turismo has a list of *quartos* (private rooms), which get snapped up quickly in summer (most owners prefer long-stay guests).

DOURO

Camping There are two seaside camp sites south of town, both open year-round and equipped with a *minimercado* (grocery shop), café-restaurant and bar. **Parque de Campismo da Árvore** *(☎ 252 633 225, fax 252 643 593; Rua do Cabreiro, Árvore; adult €4.10, tent €4.40-5)* is 3km away near Praia da Árvore beach and **Parque de Campismo Vila Chã** *(☎ 229 283 163, fax 229 280 632; Rua do Sol 150, Vila Chã; adult/car €2.70/1.90, tent €2.90-4.90)* is 4km further from town.

Pensões, Residenciais & Hotels There are quiet rooms with shower and toilet at **Residencial O Manco d'Areia** *(☎/fax 252 631 748; Praça da República 84; singles/doubles from €35/45)*, plus triples with shared facilities. Breakfast costs €1.50; credit cards are not accepted.

Restaurante Le Villageois *(see Places to Eat; doubles with bathroom €30)* has a few comfortable rooms, though breakfast isn't included; book well ahead in summer.

Pensão Patarata *(☎ 252 631 894; Cais das Lavandeiras 18; doubles/twins €35/40)*, off the southwest corner of the square, has prim en-suite rooms and a cheerful café.

Estalagem do Brasão *(☎ 252 642 016; e estalagembrazao@mail.telepac.pt; Avenida Dr João Canavarro; doubles with breakfast €78)*, 200m west of the Rua 25 de Abril turismo (the one opposite the bus station), is a central place with all the comforts.

Places to Eat
Adega Beira Rio *(☎ 252 633 012; Cais das Lavandeiras 4; half-portions under €5)* serves good half-portions at lunch time, and has canaries competing with the TV. Another local favourite is the café at **Pensão Patarata** *(see Places to Stay; half-portions around €6; open daily)*.

Restaurante Le Villageois *(☎/fax 252 631 119; Praça da República 94; open Tues-Sun; mains from €9)* has a huge menu of well-prepared French and Portuguese dishes. Come early or be prepared to wait.

Shopping
The **Centro de Artesanato** *(Rua 5 de Outubro 207)*, sharing space with the turismo opposite the bus station, is a good place for pottery, wooden toys, basketry, embroidered linen and, of course, lace. Local lacemakers sometimes work here too.

An excellent general market materialises opposite the other turismo every Friday.

Getting There & Away
Vila do Conde is 33km away from Porto, a straight shot on the IC1 highway.

It will also be a stop on Porto's metro line to Póvoa de Varzim when that's completed in 2004. Meanwhile the **metro authority** *(☎ 808 200 166)* runs buses (€1.10, 1¼ hours, two per hour Monday to Saturday morning, hourly Saturday afternoon and Sunday) from Porto's Praça da República.

AV Minho express buses stop a dozen times daily (fewer at weekends) en route between Porto (€2.10, 55 minutes) and Viana do Castelo (€4.20, one hour). AVIC also has two or three daily services.

AMARANTE
postcode 4600 • pop 11,700
• elevation 150m
This gracious town, straddling the Rio Tâmega, is worth visiting just for the setting. The river is dotted with geese and rowing boats, the banks lined with willows. Balconied houses rise in tiers up the steep banks. At one side at the end of the handsome, old stone bridge are a church and monastery dedicated to the town's patron saint, Gonçalo. Not surprisingly, they crawl with tourists on holidays and all summer.

Amarante is famous for its eggy pastries – and not just the phallic cakes that appear during the cheerful festivals of São Gonçalo.

The most appealing way to get here is on the narrow-gauge Linha da Tâmega railway (see Getting There & Away later in this section).

History
The town may date back as far as the 4th century BC. Gonçalo, a 13th-century hermit, is credited with everything from the founding of the town to the construction of its first bridge. His hermitage grew into the trademark church by the old bridge.

Amarante's strategic position on the Rio Tâmega and on the roads to Porto, Braga and Trás-os-Montes was nearly its undoing in 1809, when the French lost their brief grip on Portugal. Marshal Soult's troops retreated to the northeast after abandoning Porto, plundering as they went. On 18 April a detachment under General Loison arrived here in search of a river crossing, but plucky citizens and troops led by General Francisco da Silveira (the future Conde do Amarante) held them off, allowing residents to escape to the far bank, and bringing the French to a standstill.

The French retaliated by burning much of the upper town to the ground, but it was two weeks before they managed to bluff their way across. Loison withdrew from the area about a week later and the French were soon in full retreat across the Minho and Trás-os-Montes.

Amarante has also suffered frequent natural invasions by the Tâmega. Little *cheia* (high-water level) plaques in Rua 31 de Janeiro and Largo Conselheiro António Cândido tell the harrowing story. The last big flood was in 1962.

Orientation

The Tâmega flows through the middle of town, spanned by the old Ponte de São Gonçalo and a modern highway bridge. On the northwest bank is Amarante's drawcard, the Igreja (and Mosteiro) de São Gonçalo. In the former cloisters, the *câmara municipal*

and the turismo face the market square, Alameda Teixeira de Pascoaes.

From the little train station it's an 800m walk southeast to the Ponte de São Gonçalo. Nearly all coaches stop in Largo Conselheiro António Cândido, just across the river.

Information

The **turismo** (☎ 255 420 246, fax 255 420 203; Alameda Teixeira de Pascoaes; open 9am-12.30pm & 2pm-7pm daily July–mid-Sept, 9am-12.30pm & 2pm-5.30pm mid-Sept–June) is in the former cloisters of São Gonçalo.

Banks with ATMs are plentiful along Rua 5 de Outubro and Rua António Carneiro. The **post office** (Rua João Pinto Ribeiro; open 8.30am-6pm Mon-Fri) is near the train station. The **Calouste Gulbenkian Library** (open 9am-12.30pm & 2pm-5.30pm Mon-Fri), on the ground floor of the Museu Amadeo de Souza-Cardoso (see later), has free Internet access.

Livraria O Professor (Rua António Carneiro; open Mon-Sat) is a bookshop with some foreign-language magazines and newspapers.

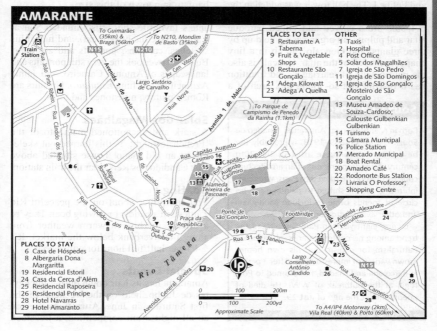

AMARANTE

PLACES TO STAY
6 Casa de Hóspedes
8 Albergaria Dona Margaritta
19 Residencial Estoril
24 Casa da Cerca d'Além
25 Residencial Raposeira
26 Residencial Príncipe
28 Hotel Navarras
29 Hotel Amaranto

PLACES TO EAT
3 Restaurante A Taberna
9 Fruit & Vegetable Shops
10 Restaurante São Gonçalo
21 Adega Kilowatt
23 Adega A Quelha

OTHER
1 Taxis
2 Hospital
4 Post Office
5 Solar dos Magalhães
7 Igreja de São Pedro
11 Igreja de São Domingos
12 Igreja de São Gonçalo; Mosteiro de São Gonçalo
13 Museu Amadeo de Souza-Cardoso; Calouste Gulbenkian Gulbenkian
14 Turismo
15 Câmara Municipal
16 Police Station
17 Mercado Municipal
18 Boat Rental
20 Amadeo Café
22 Rodonorte Bus Station
27 Livraria O Professor; Shopping Centre

DOURO

The **hospital** (☎ 255 410 500; Largo Sertório de Carvalho) is north of the centre. The **police station** (☎ 255 432 015; Rua Capitão Augusto Casimiro) is near the turismo.

Ponte de São Gonçalo

The granite São Gonçalo bridge is Amarante's visual centrepiece and historical symbol (the defence against the French is marked by a plaque at the southeastern end). It also offers one of the best views of town. The original bridge, allegedly built at Gonçalo's urging in the 13th century, collapsed in a flood in 1763; this one was completed in 1790.

Igreja de São Gonçalo & Mosteiro de São Gonçalo

The monastery of São Gonçalo and its dour church (admission free; open 8am-6pm daily) were founded in 1540 by João III, though the buildings weren't finished until 1620. Beside the church's multitiered, Italian Renaissance side portal is an arcaded gallery with 17th-century statues of Dom João and the other kings who ruled while the monastery was under construction: Sebastião, Henrique and Felipe I. The bell tower was added in the 18th century.

Inside are a carved and gilded baroque altar and pulpits, an organ casing held up by three giants, and Gonçalo's tomb in a tiny chapel to the left of the altar. Gonçalo is also the patron saint of marriages, and tradition has it that the not-so-young in search of a mate will have their wish granted within a year if they touch the statue on the outside of the tomb. Its limestone toes, fingers and face have been all but rubbed away.

Through the north portal is a peaceful Renaissance cloister – two cloisters actually, one still attached to the church and the other now occupied by the town hall.

Other Churches

Up the switchback path and steps beside São Gonçalo is the round, 18th-century Igreja de São Domingos, with a little museum of church furnishings that never seems to be open. Up on Rua Miguel Bombarda, the baroque-fronted Igreja de São Pedro has a nave decorated with 17th-century blue and yellow azulejos.

Museu Amadeo de Souza-Cardoso

In one of the monastery's cloisters is a delightful, eclectic collection of contemporary art (☎ 255 420 233; Alameda Teixeira de Pascoaes; adult/student under 26 or senior/child under 15 €1/0.50/free; open 10am-12.30pm & 2pm-5.30pm Tues-Sun), a surprise and a bargain in a town of this size.

It's named after and dominated by Amarante's favourite son, artist Amadeo Souza-Cardoso (see the boxed text), and full of his sketches, cartoons, portraits and abstracts. But don't overlook the very still portraits and landscapes of António Carneiro, and Jaime Azinheira's touching Escultura. Upstairs are Roman pottery, millstones and tools.

Solar dos Magalhães

A stark and uncaptioned memento of the 'French fortnight' is this burned-out skeleton of an old manor house situated above Rua Cândido dos Reis, near the train station.

Boating

You can potter about on the peaceful Rio Tâmega in a paddle or rowing boat. They're available for hire in warm weather from along the riverbank below the market. It's €4/7 per half/full hour for either boat.

Special Events

Amarante lets its hair down during the Festas de Junho, held on the weekend of the first Saturday in June. Attractions include an all-night drum competition, a livestock

Souza-Cardoso

Born in Manhufe, near Amarante, Amadeo de Souza-Cardoso (1889–1918) is probably the best-known Portuguese artist of the 20th century. After dropping out of an architecture course in Lisbon he moved to Paris, where his interest gradually shifted to painting and his circle of friends came to include Modigliani and other avant-garde artists.

During eight years in Paris, he bucked the trend among his contemporaries, abandoning naturalism for cubism and his own home-grown variety of impressionism. After a period in Barcelona and Madrid, he returned to Portugal at the outbreak of WWI. He died of pneumonia at the age of just 29.

fair, a children's parade, a handicrafts market, bullfights and fireworks – all rounded off with a procession from the Igreja de São Gonçalo, since this is also a *romaria* (pilgrimage festival) in honour of the town's patron saint. Not surprisingly, accommodation is hard to find at this time.

During the Festas de Junho (and on São Gonçalo's day, 13 January) unmarried men and women swap little phallic pastry cakes called *falus de Gonçalo* or *bolos de Gonçalo*, a delightfully frank tradition that probably descends from a pre-Christian fertility rite. Gonçalo is the patron saint of marriages, and this is the time to pray for a partner.

Places to Stay
Except during the Festas de Junho there's plenty of accommodation; however, most of it is overpriced. Rooms each have a private bathroom except as noted. There's little to recommend near the train station.

Camping & Hostels About 1.5km upstream from the town centre is **Parque de Campismo de Penedo da Rainha** (☎ 255 437 630, fax 255 437 353; Lugar de Fridão; adult/car €3.40/1.70, tent €1.80-2.70; open Feb-Nov), a big, shady site descending to the river and equipped with hot showers, a *minimercado*, bar and pool. CCI holders (see Visas & Documents in the Facts for the Visitor chapter) get 10% off (25% from October to April).

Casa de Hóspedes (☎ 255 423 327; 1st floor, Rua Cândido dos Reis 288; singles/doubles/twins €18/25/33), the closest thing to a youth hostel here, has spartan rooms with shared facilities.

Residenciais A few doors from the bus station, **Residencial Raposeira** (☎ 255 432 221; 1st floor, Largo Conselheiro António Cândido 41; doubles with/without shower & toilet €30/25) has clean, bright rooms and a plain, somewhat overpriced restaurant.

Residencial Príncipe (☎ 255 432 956; Largo Conselheiro António Cândido 78), across the way from Raposeira, has older rooms with a bit of personality for the same price, and a café. Neither place is very welcoming, though breakfast (extra at both places) is more cheerful at the Príncipe.

Residencial Estoril (☎ 255 431 291; e res taurante.estoril@oninet.pt; Rua 31 de Janeiro

49; doubles facing street/river €30/40, with balcony €45) offers location, location and location. The best of its modern, uncluttered rooms overlook the river, and two of these have lovely balconies.

Casa da Cerca d'Além (☎ 255 431 449; Avenida Alexandre Herculano, Madalena; suite singles/doubles with breakfast €50/55), a few blocks from the bus station, is one of several fine manor houses around Amarante. Ask the turismo for details of this and others.

Hotels A handsome townhouse with antique furnishings and polite service, **Albergaria Dona Margaritta** (☎ 255 432 110, fax 255 437 977; Rua Cândido dos Reis 53; doubles with air-con & breakfast €45) is Amarante's best bargain in its price range. If you can, bag one of the splendid (and always heavily booked) riverside rooms.

Hotel Navarras (☎ 255 431 036, fax 255 432 991; Rua António Carneiro; doubles with air-con & breakfast €63) has uninspiring but comfortable rooms and a swimming pool.

Hotel Amaranto (☎ 255 410 840; e ho telamaranto@mail.telepac.pt; doubles with breakfast €55) is equally luxurious as Navarras but subject to some traffic noise. Off-street parking is available.

Places to Eat
Restaurante São Gonçalo (☎ 255 422 707; Praça da República; open daily) is the place for coffee and pastries. You're paying for location – under the eye of Gonçalo – but the atmosphere is nice on a sunny day.

Adega A Quelha (☎ 255 425 786; Rua de Olivença; half-portions €4-9; open daily, closed evening Mon) invites you to wash down local cheese and smoked ham with a mug of red wine at the bar, or sit down to some of the Douro's best – and best-value – food, including abundant vegetables.

Restaurante A Taberna (☎ 255 431 670; Rua Nova; mains with wine around €5; open Tues-Sun) is plainer than Adega A Quelha, but the welcome is warm and the food is worth the climb through the old town.

Adega Kilowatt (☎ 255 433 159; Rua 31 de Janeiro 104) serves ham sandwiches and local wine until 9pm, though it's too photogenic for its own good.

Many *residenciais* have their own restaurants. The best of these is at the **Residencial**

Estoril (mains €6-7; open daily), with a balcony option in warm weather.

There are several fruit-and-vegetable shops on lower Rua 5 de Outubro. The biggest days at the *mercado municipal*, east of the turismo, are Wednesday and Saturday.

Entertainment

Among the here-today-gone-tomorrow bar-clubs along Avenida General Silveira, one that has lasted is the **Amadeo Café**. In summer, bars open along the riverside here.

Getting There & Away

Bus At the busy **Rodonorte bus station** (☎ 255 422 194; Largo Conselheiro António Cândido), buses stop at least five times daily from Porto (€4.30, one hour) en route via Vila Real (€4.30, 40 minutes) to Bragança (€8, 2¾ hours). Rodonorte also runs daily to Braga (€5.30, 2½ hours), Coimbra (€8.50, 2¾ hours) and Lisbon (€13, 5½ hours).

Train The journey on the narrow-gauge Linha da Tâmega, which runs from the Douro mainline at Livração up to Amarante, takes 25 minutes and costs €0.90 (buy tickets on board). There are seven to nine trains a day, most with good mainline connections. The full journey between Porto and Amarante (€3.70, five or six trains a day) takes two hours.

LAMEGO

postcode 5100 • pop 8800 • elevation 550m
Lamego, 12km south of the Rio Douro, is a prosperous, handsome town surrounded by hills terraced with vineyards and orchards. Though formally in the Beira Alta, in tradition it belongs to the Douro: the snaking road and the bridge linking it with Peso da Régua were built by the Marquês de Pombal in the 18th century, specifically so Lamego's famously fragrant wine could be shipped to Porto. Nowadays that road and bridge lie in the shadow of a giant IP3 highway bridge and bypass.

Today Lamego's Raposeira sparkling wine (the best of Portugal's few such wines) gives the town unique status among connoisseurs. And the astonishing baroque stairway of the Igreja de Nossa Senhora dos Remédios puts it on the cultural map. Well worth a digression from the Rio Douro trail, Lamego is also a natural base for exploring the half-ruined monasteries and medieval chapels in its environs.

History

Lamego was considered to be an important centre even in the time of the Suevi, who made it a bishopric, a status that was re-established in 1071. In 1143 Portugal's first *cortes* (parliament) was convened here, in order to confirm Afonso Henriques as king of Portugal.

The town's wealth grew from its position on east-west trading routes and from its wines, already famous in the 16th century. Some of its most elegant mansions were built at this time; others date from the 18th century, when Lamego's wine production took off commercially.

Orientation

The town's main axis is Avenida Visconde Guedes Teixeira (known as Jardim and shaded by lime trees) and Avenida Dr Alfredo de Sousa (called Avenida and shaded by chestnut trees), the central islands of which are well-used miniparks. Drivers take note: parking is free around the Avenida but not around the Jardim.

At the far end of the Avenida an immense stairway ascends to the Igreja de Nossa Senhora dos Remédios, on top of one of the two hills overlooking the town. Northwards, atop the other hill, stand the ruins of a 12th-century castle.

Information

The **regional turismo** (☎ 254 612 005, fax 254 614 014; e douro.turismo@mail.telepac .pt; Avenida Visconde Guedes Teixeira; open 10am-12.30pm & 2pm-7pm Mon-Fri, 10am-12.30pm & 2pm-5pm Sat & Sun July-Sept; 10am-12.30pm & 2pm-6pm Mon-Fri, 10am-12.30pm Sat Oct-June) has plenty of information on Lamego and the region.

Other services include several banks with ATMs along the Jardim/Avenida and Avenida 5 de Outubro, and the **post office** (Avenida Dr Alfredo de Sousa; open 8.30am-6pm Mon-Fri). Free Internet access is available in 30-minute chunks at the **library** (☎ 254 614 013; Rua de Almacave 9; open 10am-12.30pm & 2pm-6.30pm Mon-Fri).

The **hospital** (☎ 254 609 980) and **police station** (☎ 254 612 022) are opposite one another on Rua António Osorio Mota.

Igreja de Nossa Senhora dos Remédios

This 18th-century church (*admission free; open 7.30am-8pm daily, 7.30am-6pm winter*) is a major pilgrimage site, especially during the Festas de Nossa Senhora dos Remédios (see Special Events later in this section) when devotees arrive in their thousands. The marginally interesting church is quite overshadowed by the fantastic stairway, decorated with azulejos, urns, fountains and statues, which zigzags up the hill to it.

If you can't face stairs, the church is 3km by road (turn off 1km out on the Viseu road).

Sé

Lamego's cathedral (☎ 254 612 766; admission free; open 8am-1pm & 3pm-7pm daily) is older than Portugal itself, though there's little left of the 12th-century original except the base of its square belfry. The rest, including the brilliantly carved Flamboyant Gothic triple portal, dates mostly from the 16th and 18th centuries. The luminous ceiling frescoes (of biblical tales) and high choir stalls are the work of the 18th-century Italian architect Nicolau Nasoni, also responsible for much that's lovely about Porto's cathedral.

With luck you'll find the door open to the peaceful 16th-century cloisters, around the corner.

Igreja Santa Maria de Almacave

This little church (☎ 254 612 460; open 7.30am-noon & 4pm-7.30pm daily) is Lamego's oldest surviving building, its oldest

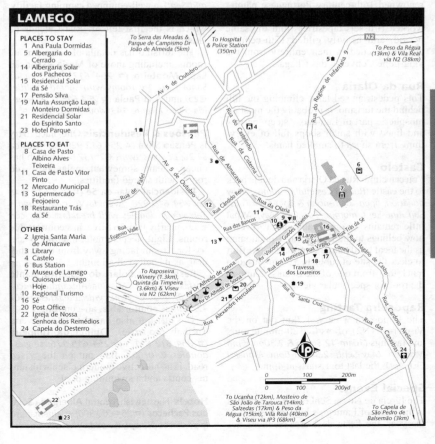

LAMEGO

PLACES TO STAY
1 Ana Paula Dormidas
5 Albergaria do Cerrado
14 Albergaria Solar dos Pachecos
15 Residencial Solar da Sé
17 Pensão Silva
19 Maria Assunção Lapa Monteiro Dormidas
21 Residencial Solar do Espírito Santo
23 Hotel Parque

PLACES TO EAT
8 Casa de Pasto Albino Alves Teixeira
11 Casa de Pasto Vitor Pinto
12 Mercado Municipal
13 Supermercado Feojoeiro
18 Restaurante Trás da Sé

OTHER
2 Igreja Santa Maria de Almacave
3 Library
4 Castelo
6 Bus Station
7 Museu de Lamego
9 Quiosque Lamego Hoje
10 Regional Turismo
16 Sé
20 Post Office
22 Igreja de Nossa Senhora dos Remédios
24 Capela do Desterro

To Serra das Meadas & Parque de Campismo Dr João de Almeida (5km)

To Hospital & Police Station (350m)

To Peso da Régua (13km) & Vila Real via N2 (38km)

Av 5 de Outubro

Rua do Castelinho

Rua do Regime de Infantaria 9

Rua de Almacave

Rua de Fafel

Rua de Cisterna

Rua Cândido Reis

Rua da Olaria

Rua dos Bancos

Rua Eugenio Valle

Rua Visconde Guedes Teixeira

Largo da Sé

Rua Trás da Sé

Rua Magalino de Castro

Rua Virgílio Correia

Travessa dos Loureiros

Av dos Loureiros

Av Visconde Guedes Teixeira

To Raposeira Winery (1.3km); Quinta da Timpeira (3.6km) & Viseu via N2 (62km)

Av Dr Alfredo de Sousa

Av Alexandre Herculano

Rua da Santa Cruz

Rua das Canastras

Rua Cardoso Avelino

0   100   200m
0   100   200yd

To Ucanha (12km), Mosteiro de São João de Tarouca (14km), Salzedas (17km) & Peso da Régua (15km), Vila Real (40km) & Viseu via IP3 (68km)

To Capela de São Pedro de Balsemão (3km)

DOURO

bits dating from the 12th century. The church occupies the site of a Moorish cemetery, some of its grave markers now in the Museu de Lamego (see the following section). On the south side is a lovely Romanesque portal.

It's thought that an early version of the *cortes*, Portugal's proto-democratic assembly of nobles and clergy, met here from 1142 to 1144.

Museu de Lamego

Housed in the grand, 18th-century former episcopal palace is one of Portugal's finest regional museums (☎ 254 600 230; admission €2, 10am-12.30pm Sun free; open 10am-12.30pm & 2pm-5pm Tues-Sun). The collection features some remarkable pieces, including a series of five works by the renowned 16th-century Portuguese painter Vasco Fernandes (Grão Vasco), richly worked Brussels tapestries from the same period, and heavily gilded 17th-century chapels rescued in their entirety from the long-gone Convento das Chagas.

Rua da Olaria

This pedestrianised lane, climbing the hill behind the turismo, is probably the most atmospheric part of Lamego – steep, narrow and lined with small shops full of everything from shoes to smoked hams.

Castelo

You can climb Rua da Olaria and double back to the castle (Rua do Castelinho; admission by donation; open 10am-noon & 3pm-6pm Tues-Sun June-Sept, morning Sun Oct-May). What little remains – some walls and a tower – now belongs to the Boy Scouts, functioning as the local headquarters since a 1970s effort to clear the site of rubbish. You might get a quick tour from one of the Scouts. Climb to the roof for spectacular views.

Raposeira Tasting

The Raposeira winery, 1.7km out on the Viseu road (N2), offers free 20-minute tours and tastings (10am-12.30pm & 2.30pm-5pm Mon-Fri May-Sept; 2.30pm-5pm Mon-Fri Oct-Apr); the last tour starts at 4pm.

Special Events

The Igreja de Nossa Senhora dos Remédios is the focus of Lamego's biggest festival of the year, the Festa de Nossa Senhora dos Remédios, which carries on for several weeks from late August to mid-September. The highlight is a procession on the afternoon of 8 September, when ox-drawn carts carrying religious *tableaux vivants* parade through the streets and devotees climb the stairway on bended knee.

Less-religious events in the days leading up to the festival include rock concerts, folk dancing, car racing, parades and an all-night party. The turismo has details.

Places to Stay

Camping & Private Rooms Some 5km west of town is **Parque de Campismo Dr João de Almeida** (☎ 254 613 918; ⓔ naturi mont@mail.telepac.pt; Serra das Meadas; adult/car €2/1.80, tent €2-2.80; open June–mid-Sept), a well-equipped camping facility. To get here take the Estrada Florestal, which is the first left off Rua Calçada da Guerra.

The turismo has details of some private rooms, including those of **Maria Assunção Lapa Monteiro** (☎ 254 612 556; Rua da Santa Cruz 15; rooms with shared facilities €25) and **Ana Paula** (☎ 254 613 022; Avenida 5 de Outubro 143; doubles €30).

Pensões & Residenciais One place to try is **Pensão Silva** (☎ 254 612 929; Rua Trás da Sé 26; doubles/twins €25/37.50), which has cheap, clean, somewhat melancholy old rooms with shared facilities.

Residencial Solar da Sé (☎ 254 612 060, fax 254 615 928; Avenida Visconde Guedes Teixeira 7; doubles with breakfast & air-con €39), nearby Pensão Silva, has comfortable rooms. Light sleepers note: in either place, try for a room facing away from the cathedral, as its bells toll all night.

Residencial Solar do Espírito Santo (☎/fax 254 655 060; Rua Alexandre Herculano 8; doubles/twins with breakfast €40/42.50) has comfortable, air-con rooms.

The turismo also has details of several Turihab properties. **Quinta da Timpeira** (☎ 254 612 811, fax 254 615 176; singles/doubles €40/60), 4km out on the Viseu road, is an attractive modern place with tennis courts and a swimming pool.

Hotels The newish, central **Albergaria Solar dos Pachecos** (☎ 254 600 300; ⓔ albergariaso larpachecos@clix.pt; Avenida Visconde Guedes

Teixeira 27; singles/doubles with air-con €35/60) has elegantly spare rooms, and a generous buffet breakfast included in the price.

Hotel Parque (☎ 254 609 140, fax 254 615 203; singles/doubles €35/50) has an unrivalled location in a wooded park by the Igreja de Nossa Senhora dos Remédios. Rates include a buffet breakfast. The turn-off for the hotel is 1km out on the Viseu road (N2).

Albergaria do Cerrado (☎ 254 613 164, fax 254 615 464; Rua do Regime de Infantaria 9; singles/doubles €43/53) offers similar over-the-top luxury but without the view.

Places to Eat

If you're after a sugar-and-caffeine hit, Lamego is awash with cafés. There's an easy-going evening café scene under the Avenida's trees, and this is also a nice venue for a sunny breakfast.

For cheap local dishes at lunch time you're spoilt for choice. **Casa de Pasto Albino Alves Teixeira** (Rua da Olaria 1; dishes under €5; open daily) packs diners into barren upstairs rooms; **Casa de Pasto Vitor Pinto** (Rua da Olaria 61; dishes under €4; open daily), up the hill, is slightly cheaper and quite adequate.

Restaurante Trás da Sé (☎ 254 614 075; Rua Virgílio Correia 12; half-portions €4-5, evening dishes from €5; open daily) is unabashedly touristy but the adega-style atmosphere is friendly, the menu short and simple, the food good and the vinho maduro (wine matured for more than a year) list long.

Several grocery shops on Rua da Olaria sell Lamego's famous hams and wines –perfect picnic food. Try **Supermercado Feojoeiro** (Avenida 5 de Outubro 11) or the **mercado municipal** (open Mon-Fri, morning Sat) for other supplies.

Getting There & Away

The most appealing route to Lamego from anywhere in the Douro valley is by train to Peso da Régua (see the later Peso da Régua section for details) and by bus or taxi from there. A **taxi** (☎ 254 321 366) from Régua costs about €10.

Three companies use Lamego's bus station. **Joalto** (☎ 254 612 116) goes about hourly to Peso da Régua (€1.40, 20 minutes) and daily to Viseu (€3.90, 1¼ hours).

Guedes (☎ 254 612 604) has multiple daily services to Peso da Régua and Viseu, and goes twice daily via Coimbra (€8, three hours) to Lisbon (€12, 5¾ hours).

Rodonorte buses also stop here at least twice each weekday en route from Chaves (€7.90, 2¼ hours) and Vila Real (€4.50, 55 minutes) to Lisbon. Rede Expressos stops twice daily en route between Vila Real and Viseu. Quiosque Lamego Hoje, a newsagent beside the turismo, sells tickets for these services.

AROUND LAMEGO
Capela de São Pedro de Balsemão

This lovely 7th- to 10th-century chapel (☎ 254 655 656; admission free; open 10am-12.30pm & 2pm-6pm Wed-Sun, 2pm-6pm Tues, closed 3rd weekend of month) is one of Portugal's finer examples of Visigothic architecture, with Corinthian columns, round arches and numerous whimsical/mysterious symbols scratched into the walls. Most of its ornate 14th-century additions were commissioned by the Bishop of Porto, Afonso Pires, who's buried under a slab in the floor. An ancient casket supported by lions, with the Last Supper engraved on one side, dominates the otherwise simple interior.

The chapel is tucked away in the hamlet of Balsemão, 3km southeast of Lamego above the Rio Balsemão. It's a pleasant walk from Lamego: from the 17th-century Capela do Desterro at the end of Rua da Santa Cruz, head southeast over the river and follow the road to the left. Most of the time there's a Portuguese-speaking guide on hand .

Mosteiro de São João de Tarouca

In the wooded Barosa valley below the Serra de Leomil, 15km southeast of Lamego, are the remains of Portugal's first Cistercian monastery (☎ 254 678 766; admission free; open 10am-12.30pm & 2pm-6pm Wed-Sun, 2pm-6pm Tues), founded in 1124. It fell into ruin after religious orders were abolished in 1834.

Only the church, considerably altered in the 17th century, stands intact among the eerie ruins of the monks' quarters. Its treasures include the imposing 14th-century tomb of the Conde de Barcelos (Dom Dinis' illegitimate son), carved with scenes from a

DOURO

boar hunt; gilded choir stalls; and 18th-century azulejos. The church's pride and joy is a luminous *São Pedro* painted by Gaspar Vaz, contemporary and colleague of Grão Vasco (see the boxed text 'Grão Vasco & the Viseu School' in the Beiras chapter).

From Lamego, Joalto/EAVT has eight services each weekday (fewer at weekends) to São João de Tarouca (€1.40).

Ponte de Ucanha

Ucanha is an unremarkable village about 12km south of Lamego, off the N226 just north of Tarouca. The lane leads down to its 12th-century fortified bridge, Ponte de Ucanha, over the Rio Barosa. The chunky tower was added by the Abbot of Salzedas in the 15th century, probably as a tollgate. Stonemasons' initials are visible on almost every block. The medieval stone washing enclosures under the bridge are no longer used, though village women still hang their laundry under the bridge.

There are three Joalto/EAVT buses travelling each weekday between Lamego and Ucanha (€1.80).

Mosteiro de Salzedas

About 3km further up the Barosa valley from Ucanha are the ruins of another Cistercian monastery, the Mosteiro de Salzedas (☎ 254 670 627; admission free; open 10am-12.30pm & 2pm-6pm daily). This was one of the grandest monasteries in the land when it was built in 1168 with funds from Teresa Afonso, governess of Dom Afonso Henriques' five children. The church, extensively remodelled in the 18th century, dominates the humble village around it. Black with decay, it seems past hope of restoration, though students beaver away each summer, bringing it back to life.

From Lamego, Joalto/EAVT runs three buses each weekday to Salzedas (€1.80).

PESO DA RÉGUA

postcode 5050 ● pop 9400 ● elevation 125m

Régua (as it's usually called), at the western edge of the demarcated port-wine region, is Lamego's businesslike alter ego. As the largest regional centre with river access, it grew in the 18th century into a major port-wine entrepot, though the unofficial title of 'capital of the trade' has now shifted 25km upstream to Pinhão.

Régua today is a colourless town and transport junction offering little beyond learning about (and tasting) port wine. Its only appealing side is the one facing the river, with a waterside promenade and a few photogenically placed *barcos rabelos*. Nevertheless, it suffices as a base for visiting the port-wine country, cruising the Rio Douro and riding the Corgo railway line to Vila Real.

Orientation & Information

From the train station or adjacent bus stops bear right at Residencial Império into Rua dos Camilos to find the post office and a few restaurants. Carry on via Rua da Terreirinha to reach the **turismo** (☎ 254 223 846, fax 254 322 271; Rua da Terreirinha 505; open 9am-12.30pm & 2pm-7pm daily July–mid-Sept, 9am-12.30pm & 2pm-5.30pm Mon-Fri mid-Sept–June), about 1km west of the station. Old Régua is a steep climb above these streets. For the *cais fluvial* (river terminal) bear left at the Residencial Império and continue for about 600m.

Those with an interest in port-wine production can collect an armful of brochures from the **Instituto do Vinho do Porto** (☎ 254 320 130; Rua dos Camilos 90; open 9am-12.30pm & 2pm-5.30pm Mon-Fri), though the staff is not thrilled about casual visitors.

Quinta do Castelinho

This port-wine lodge (☎ 254 320 262; open 9am-7pm daily May-Sept, 9am-6pm daily Feb-Apr & Oct-Dec, closed Jan) is the nearest to Régua and the easiest to visit, and offers free tours and tasting. It also has a good **restaurant** (open Tues-Sat, morning Sun). To reach it from the train station, go 600m east on the Vila Real road, turn left and continue for 400m.

Train Trips & River Cruises

Several companies market identical journeys along various stretches of the Rio Douro, all from or via Peso da Régua. The main choices are:

Porto–Barca de Alva–Porto weekend; boat, train and hotel (47 hours, from €230)
Porto–Pinhão–Porto Saturday or Sunday; boat and train (11 hours, from €80)
Porto–Régua–Porto Saturday or Sunday; boat and train (11 hours, from €75)

DOURO

Porto–Régua–Porto weekend; boat, train and hotel (32 hours, from €170)
Régua–Pinhão–Régua Saturday or Sunday; boat (four hours, with/without lunch about €45/30)
Régua–Porto Sunday; boat (nine hours, €75)

The big operators are:

DouroAcima (☎ 222 006 418,
   w www.douroacima.pt)
Douro Azul (☎ 223 402 500,
   w www.douroazul.com)
Rota do Douro (☎ 223 759 042,
   w www.rotadodouro.com)

Also on offer, if there are enough passengers booked, are Saturday-only journeys in restored steam trains along the beautiful Linha do Douro line.

Most trips run only between about mid-April and mid-October. Telephone reservations are recommended.

Places to Stay
Residenciais with bland but comfortable, air-con rooms (breakfast included) and free parking include the **Residencial Império** (☎ 254 320 120, fax 254 321 457; Rua José Vasques Osório 8; doubles €38), in the high-rise just west of the train station, and the **Don Quixote** (☎ 254 321 151, fax 254 322 802; 1st floor, Avenida Sacadura Cabral 1; doubles €32.50), 800m west of the turismo.

Places to Eat
Restaurante O Maleiro (☎ 254 313 684; Rua dos Camilos; mains €6-7.50; open daily), opposite the post office, offers friendly service, a good atmosphere and meaty Portuguese standards prepared with style.

   Restaurante Cacho d'Oiro (☎ 254 321 455; Rua Branca Martinho; mains around €10; open daily), 150m west of the turismo, offers a wider choice and a more upmarket atmosphere than Maleiro. Splurge on cabrito no churrasco (grilled kid) for €12.

Getting There & Away
Joalto buses run hourly to/from Lamego (€1.40, 20 minutes); Guedes also makes the run several times a day. AV Tâmega runs to Vila Real (€2.10, 40 minutes) about hourly on weekdays and three times daily at weekends, and Rodonorte goes four times each weekday.

There are 12 trains daily from Porto (€5.10, 2½ hours); eight go up the valley to Pinhão and Tua (see the following Alto Douro section). Five trains depart daily heading to Vila Real (€1.40, 55 minutes) on the narrow-gauge Corgo line.

THE ALTO DOURO
Though not actually part of Douro province, the Douro valley east of Peso da Régua – defining the border between Trás-os-Montes and Beira Alta – is included here because it's an integral part of the region and because the easiest way to get here is from Porto.

The Alto Douro (upper Douro) is a harsh, hot landscape refashioned by human activity, namely two millennia of wine production. Terraced vineyards wrap around every precipitous, crew-cut hillside, and whitewashed port-wine quintas (estates) dot the valley. Villages are small, and architectural monuments rare. Come here for the panoramas, the port wine or just the train ride. If you're in doubt, take it from Unesco, which in 2001 designated the entire Alto Douro wine-growing region a World Heritage site.

Wine isn't the only local product on offer: signs at every second gate advertise olives and honey, cheaper and better than at

---

Blossoms by Rail

When the almond trees are in bloom (late February to mid-March), the upper Douro valley is lovelier than ever. **Caminhos de Ferro Portugueses** (☎ 808 208 208) will take you up for a look, by special train plus coach, on a long-weekend day trip from Porto's São Bento station.

   Trains chug to Freixo de Numão or Pocinho, coaches shuttle you around southern Trás-os-Montes and/or northern Beira Alta (there are four itineraries to choose from) and you return by train. Trains have restaurant and bar service, and lunch is included, though the 16-hour journeys offer little chance to stretch your legs. A 1st-/2nd-class ticket costs €29/21 (€25/17 for kids aged four to 12).

   All depends, of course, on the timely arrival of the blossoms. Tickets are sold at São Bento station from the last week in January. For more information contact CP.

any tourist shop. Port-wine *quintas* offer some of Portugal's finest rural accommodation, though it gets scarce in late September and early October during the *vindima* (grape harvest).

Daily trains run from Porto, with a change at Régua, up to Pinhão, Tua and Pocinho. Travellers with their own set of wheels can take the river-hugging N222 from Régua to Pinhão, beyond which the roads climb in and out of the valley. For information on river cruises, see under Peso da Régua.

Pinhão
postcode 5085 • elevation 120m

Unassuming little Pinhão, 25km upriver from Peso da Régua, is today considered the world centre of quality port-wine production. It's surrounded by vineyards and dominated by the large signs of several port-wine lodges; even the train station has azulejos depicting the wine harvest. The town itself is of little interest, though you can chill out in one of the area's splendid *quintas*.

If you're feeling active, there are several fine day-trip possibilities by train (see Train Trips, following). If you have your own wheels, a 12km digression northeast up the N322-3 to Favaios will reward you with the discovery of a little-known muscatel wine, one of only two produced in Portugal (the other comes from Setúbal).

Orientation & Information The **turismo** (☎ 254 732 883; *Largo do Estação; open 10am-noon & 2pm-7pm Mon-Fri, 10am-1pm Sat & Sun May-Oct*) is at the right-hand end of the **train station** (☎ 254 732 391), which also serves as the main bus stop. Also on the *largo* (small square) is a bank with an ATM. There's also a **post office** (*Rua António Manuel Saraiva*).

Train Trips The most beautiful of Portugal's narrow-gauge lines is the Linha da Tua, running from the sun-blasted backwater of Tua (13km upriver) for 52km up the Tua valley to the market town of Mirandela (see the Trás-os-Montes chapter). The two-hour Pinhão–Mirandela journey (€6.40 return, change at Tua) is feasible as a day trip, departing about 10.30am and leaving Mirandela about 6pm.

Alternatively, you could take the same mainline train and stay on for the one-hour

trip, past dams and vineyards, to the end of the line at Pocinho (€3.80 return), visiting the Pocinho dam and returning the same day (depart Pocinho about 7pm), or taking a taxi on up to Vila Nova de Foz Côa (see that entry following).

Check with the turismo about precise train times.

Places to Stay & Eat A cheerful place opposite the train station, **Residencial Douro** (☎/fax 254 732 404; *Largo do Estação; doubles with air-con €50*) has some large rooms facing a quiet rear courtyard and a sunny restaurant (the price includes a generous breakfast).

Quinta de la Rosa (☎ 254 732 254; e *mail@quintadelarosa.com; doubles from €68*), a small *quinta* above the river 2km west of Pinhão, has a few lovely rooms and a swimming pool. Book well ahead for July or August, though drop-ins might find a vacancy at other times.

There are dozens of Turihab properties in the area, many marketed by **Quintas do Douro** (☎/fax 254 322 788; *Enoteca Regional do Granjão, 5040 Mesão Frio*), with high-season doubles from €50 to €100.

Pousada de Barão de Forrester (☎ 259 959 215, fax 259 959 304; *doubles Mon-Fri €126, Sat & Sun €132*) is a Pousada de Portugal property at Alijó, 15km northeast of Pinhão.

Within a few blocks of the station you can choose from **Restaurante Casa Branca** (☎ 254 731 194; *Rua António Manuel Saraiva; mains €6-10; open daily, closed evening Sun*) or several modest cafés. Nearby is a small *supermercado*, and on Wednesday there's a food market in the town centre.

Getting There & Away Regional trains run from Peso da Régua (€1.20, 25 minutes, nine daily). From Porto you must change at Régua; the quickest links (€5.60, 2½ hours, four daily) are by IC train as far as Régua. There are limited bus services from Régua.

VILA NOVA DE FOZ CÔA
postcode 5150 • pop 2800 • elevation 420m

In the 13th century refugees escaping attacks by the king of León founded Vila Nova de Foz Côa (meaning 'new town by the mouth of the river Côa') in the *terra quente* (hot country) of the upper Douro.

Ever mindful of his frontiers, Dom Dinis chartered the place in 1299.

Once remote, the town has been put firmly on the map with the discovery in the 1990s of thousands of Palaeolithic rock engravings in the nearby Rio Côa valley. A *parque arqueológico* was founded to protect them and the valley was designated as a Unesco World Heritage site.

The region also has some lesser archaeological attractions, and the town a few Manueline highlights. It feels like Spain in the way that Miranda do Douro (in Trás-os-Montes) does: clean, whitewashed, brisk and orderly. The climate is startlingly Mediterranean if you've just come from the mountains, and the surrounding hillsides sport the highest density of almond trees in Portugal. The town seems to have the country's highest density of teenagers, who come here for school from surrounding villages.

Orientation

Long-distance coaches stop at the bus station, from where it's 150m south to a petrol station at Avenida Gago Coutinho. From here the town stretches eastwards for about 1km along Avenida Gago Coutinho,

Rock Art in the Vale do Côa

In the rugged valley of the Rio Côa (a tributary of the Douro), 15km from the Spanish frontier, is an extraordinary Stone Age art gallery, with thousands of rock engravings dating back tens of thousands of years. Fifteen years ago nobody knew they were there.

Initial discoveries were made in 1989 in the course of environmental studies for Electricidade de Portugal (EDP), which had proposed building a hydroelectric dam that would have flooded the valley. Surveys revealed an array of ancient sites, including four rock shelters with prehistoric paintings. Nevertheless, the dam proposal was approved.

It wasn't until 1992, after construction was underway, that the real discoveries began. Clusters of petroglyphs (rock engravings), mostly dating from the Upper Palaeolithic period (approximately 10,000 to 40,000 years ago), were found by 'rescue archaeologists' at the site now called Canada do Inferno. Once these finds were publicised, local people cooperated in the search for other sites, and the inventory quickly grew.

Battle commenced between EDP and archaeologists who insisted the engravings were of worldwide importance.

Rocha 3, Quinta da Barca

Only after an international campaign was launched and the Socialist Party came to power in 1995 was the half-built dam formally abandoned and the site given official protection as a national monument. The Parque Arqueológico Vale do Côa (Côa Valley Archaeological Park) was launched in 1996, and in 1998 those stubborn archaeologists got their ultimate reward when the valley was designated a Unesco World Heritage site.

Today the park encompasses the largest known array of open-air Palaeolithic art in the world. Several thousand engravings are scattered for 17km along the Côa and tributary valleys. Horses, aurochs (ancestors of domesticated cattle) and long-horned ibex (a once-common wild goat that appears in petroglyphs from many parts of the world) figure prominently; some petroglyphs also depict human figures. Since 1995 surveys have been underway to locate Palaeolithic habitation sites as well.

The discovery has challenged existing theories about humankind's earliest art. Smaller open-air sites have been found in France, Spain and elsewhere in Portugal, but nothing of this scale or covering such a time span. It was probably the valley's resistant schist bedrock and Mediterranean microclimate that saved this site from Ice Age destruction.

pedestrianised Rua Dr Juiz Moutinho de Andrade and Rua Dr Júlio de Moura to the old town's centre, Praça do Município. The train station is at Pocinho, 7km north on the N102.

Information
The **municipal turismo** (☎ *279 765 243; open 9am-12.30pm & 2pm-5.30pm daily)* is a long trek without transport; from the town centre go 1.2km southwest on the N102 to a roundabout with a giant Vila Nova de Foz Côa sign, then left for 600m.

Staff at the **Parque Arqueológico office** (☎ *279 768 260;* w *www.ipa.min-cultura.pt /coa; Avenida Gago Coutinho 19A; open 9am-12.30pm & 2pm-5.30pm daily)* is kept busy shuttling visitors out to the rock engravings but they do have telephone numbers for some local accommodation.

There are ATMs outside the park office and below Residencial Marina (see Places to Stay). The **post office** *(Avenida Dr Artur de Aguilar 6; open 9am-12.30pm & 2pm-6pm Mon-Fri)*, three blocks north of the park office via Largo do Rossio, has NetPost Internet access; the *pousada da juventude* (see Places to Stay) offers access for €1.50/2.50 per 15/60 minutes.

The **police station** (☎ *279 762 316; Rua Dr José Augusto Saraiva de Aguilar)* is a block behind the park office.

Parque Arqueológico Vale do Côa
See the boxed text 'Rock Art in the Vale do Côa' for information about the site and the archaeological park.

Although the park is an active research zone, three sites may be visited – Canada do Inferno from the **park office** *(open daily, trips Tues-Sun)* in Vila Nova de Foz Côa, Ribeira de Piscos from the **Muxagata visitor centre** (☎ *279 764 298; open Tues-Sun)* on the western side of the valley, and Penascosa from the **Castelo Melhor visitor centre** (☎ *279 713 344; open Tues-Sun)* on the eastern side.

There is also a private site (owned by the Ramos Pinto port-wine lodge) at Quinta da Ervamoira, with vineyards, wine tasting and a museum featuring Roman and medieval artefacts. This can be included in some tours.

Visitors can front up at one of the visitor centres, from where they're taken, eight at a time in the park's own 4WDs, for a guided tour of one of the sites (two hours at Canada

do Inferno and Penascosa, three hours at Ribeira de Piscos). Visitors with mountain bikes may go on their bicycles (with a guide on a bicycle) in similar-sized groups. The price in either case is €5 per person.

You have little hope of seeing these sites without a booking, at least a few weeks ahead and preferably longer for bicycle trips. For information or bookings, contact the park office (see under Information). Several private tour operators include park trips in their own programmes; local operators include **Ravinas do Côa** (☎ *966 484 288;* w *www.ravinasdocoa.lda.pt; Rua de Moçambique 28, Vila Nova de Foz Côa)* and **Impactus** (☎ *962 838 261;* w *www.impactus .pt; Rua da Igreja 2, Castelo Melhor)*.

Old Town
Since you've come all this way, walk down to Praça do Município and have a look at the granite *pelourinho* topped by an armillary sphere, and the Manueline-style parish church, with its elaborately carved portal and painted ceiling. Just east off the square is the tiny Capela de Santa Quitéria, a chapel that was once the town's synagogue.

Other Attractions
The region around Freixo de Numão, 12km west of Vila Nova de Foz Côa, has yielded a surprising range of archaeological finds from the Stone Age to the 18th century. A modest collection can be viewed at Freixo de Numão, in the **Museu da Casa Grande** (☎ *279 789 117, fax 279 789 573; adult/child under 12 €1.50/0.75; open 9am-noon & 2pm-6pm Tues-Sun)*, a baroque townhouse with Roman foundations. The collection includes Bronze Age tools, furnishings from several Roman villas, medieval jewellery and more. Some English and French are spoken here.

A free brochure provides for a **self-guided archaeological tour** of the region. On sale are Portuguese-language booklets (€1 each) on the museum, and on the rich Neolithic/Roman/medieval site at Prazo, about 3km west of Freixo de Numão. Guided tours are available by arrangement with the museum.

Places to Stay & Eat
The **pousada da juventude** (☎ *279 768 190;* e *fozcoa@movijovem.pt; Caminho Vicinal, Currauteles No 5; dorm beds €12.50, doubles*

with toilet €35) is an 800m walk north from the town centre, or 1.4km by road.

A few homes and cafés in the area around Largo do Tabulado advertise *quartos*.

Two neighbouring *residenciais* near the petrol station are the snug but gracious **Marina** (☎ 279 762 112; Avenida Gago Coutinho 2-4; doubles €25) and the brusque **Avenida** (☎/fax 279 762 175; Avenida Gago Coutinho 10; doubles €30). Rooms at both have a shower and toilet; neither offers breakfast.

Residencial O Retiro (☎ 279 762 159; doubles/twins with shower €20/25) is 500m north of the bus station on the N102.

The choice of places to eat is generally dreary, though several *pastelarias* (pastry or cake shops) along Rua Dr Juiz Moutinho de Andrade open by 8am for breakfast.

Restaurante Avenida (☎ 279 764 393; Avenida Gago Coutinho 23; daily specials from €5; open Mon-Sat), a few doors from the park office, has light lunches and dinners in a plain dining room at the back.

Snack Bar-Restaurante A Marisqueira (☎ 279 762 187; Rua Dr Juiz Moutinho de Andrade; daily specials under €5; open daily) has a small menu of daily specials, but despite the name there isn't much seafood.

There are several well-stocked fruit-and-vegetable shops on the little squares at either end of Rua Dr Juiz Moutinho de Andrade, and a **minimercado** (Rua Dr Juiz Montinho 11).

Getting There & Away

Rede Expressos and Joalto buses each visit daily from Bragança (€5.80, 1¾ hours). Rede Expressos buses come once daily from Miranda (€5.80, 2½ hours) and four times daily via Trancoso from Viseu (€8, 1¾ hours).

Four daily trains run to Pocinho, at the end of the Douro valley line, from Porto (€6.50, four hours) and Peso da Régua (€3.30). A taxi between Pocinho and Vila Nova de Foz Côa costs about €5.

The Minho

Portugal's northwestern corner, tucked under the hem of Spanish Galicia, is traditional, conservative, lush and lovely. The inland mountains attract plentiful rain, and rich soil encourages intensive farming, mostly smallholdings of maize and vegetables outlined by low stone walls. Despite EU money, rural life remains stubbornly poor and old-fashioned, with many farmers still relying on lyre-horned oxen to pull their carts and plough their fields.

The Minho clings to its traditions. Here you'll find some of Portugal's most vibrant country markets, and there are dozens of festivals and *romarias* (religious pilgrimages) on the calendar commemorating local saints. Religion holds an important place in daily life, and Easter in Braga, Portugal's ecclesiastical capital, is an extraordinary combination of fervour and merrymaking.

Minhotos have reason to be proud of their history, too, for this is where Portugal was born. Guimarães is the birthplace of Portugal's first king, Afonso Henriques, and the place from which he launched the main thrust of the Reconquista against the Moors in 1139. In almost the same place over a millennium earlier, Celtiberians maintained their last strongholds against the Romans. It's no accident that Unesco has added Guimarães to its list of World Heritage sites.

Braga, Barcelos and Guimarães lie within easy reach of one another in southern Minho. Lashed by the Atlantic, the coastal region – sometimes called the Costa Verde (Green Coast) – has fewer attractions, though the seafront north of the cultured resort of Viana do Castelo has good beaches and offers plenty of solitude.

The Minho's real pull is inland, along the Rio Minho, which forms the frontier with Spain, and the dreamy Rio Lima. Here is Portugal's highest concentration of Turihab properties, offering accommodation in anything from converted farmhouses to mansions. Further inland is the Parque Nacional da Peneda-Gerês, with a cornucopia of outdoor sports and several outfits ready to show you around. Although the park extends into Trás-os-Montes, we have included it, and several associated Trás-os-Montes towns, entirely within this chapter.

Highlights

- Navigate rugged hill-top roads and explore borderland villages in the Parque Nacional da Peneda-Gerês
- Immerse yourself in architectural history at the cathedral in Braga, Portugal's spiritual capital, and climb heavenwards at nearby Bom Jesus do Monte
- Meander through Barcelos' huge and famous weekly market
- Enjoy good cheer and festivals at the seaside resort of Viana do Castelo
- Turn back the time at the Celtic hill settlement of Citânia de Briteiros

It would be hard to rush through the Minho; the pace of the region is nearly always slow and its distractions are numerous – not least the local *vinho verde*, a young, slightly sparkling white or red wine that is among Portugal's most addictive, and features as the house wine in many restaurants.

Southern Minho

BRAGA
postcode 4700 • pop 109,500
• elevation 200m
Braga is one of Portugal's oldest settlements, with genuine Celtic roots. More importantly to the Portuguese, Braga is their religious

capital, with a Christian pedigree dating from the 6th century. From the 11th to the 18th centuries this was the seat of the archbishop, considered Primate of All Spain, or at any rate Primate of Portugal (these days the archbishop ministers as far south as Coimbra).

Braga overflows with churches, having at least 35; bells toll all day long, though thankfully not at night. However, only Braga's ancient cathedral merits much attention, having survived the wholesale baroque renovations that smothered the other churches in the 18th century.

The city's best-known attraction, Bom Jesus do Monte, isn't actually in the city at all but just to the east (see Around Braga later in this chapter). Nevertheless, the centre of Braga is relaxing and attractive, and the

students of the Universidade do Minho add youthful leavening to an otherwise proud, pious, somewhat dour city. Braga will soon get a strong dose of the outside world, as it's one of the venues for the 2004 European Football Championships (Euro2004).

History
It is believed that a Celtiberian tribe, the Bracari, may have founded Braga. In about 250 BC the Romans moved in, named it Bracara Augusta and made it the administrative centre of Gallaecia (present-day Douro, Minho and Spanish Galicia). Braga's position at the intersection of five Roman roads turned it into a major trading centre.

Braga fell to the Suevi around AD 410, and was sacked by the Visigoths 60 years

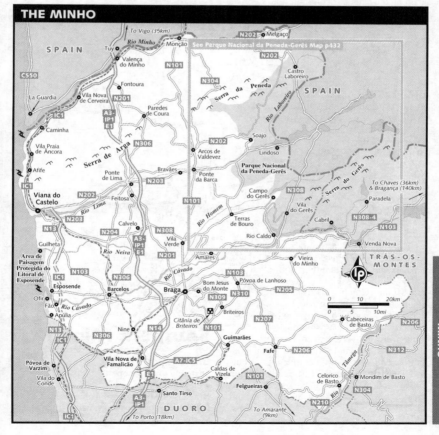

THE MINHO

later. The Visigoths' conversion to Christianity and the founding of an archbishopric in the following century put the town atop the Iberian Peninsula's ecclesiastical pecking order. The Moors moved in around 715, but the Reconquista was already under way in northern Spain and in 740 Braga fell again to Christian forces.

The Moors took Braga back in 985 but were finally dislodged in 1040 by Fernando I, the king of Castile and León. Fernando's son Alfonso VI called for help from European crusaders, and to one of them, Henri of Burgundy (Dom Henrique to the Portuguese), he later gave his daughter Teresa in marriage, throwing in Braga as dowry. From this marriage came Afonso Henriques, the first king of Portugal.

The archbishopric was restored in 1070, though prelates bickered with their Spanish counterparts for the next five centuries over who was Primate of All Spain. The pope finally ruled in Braga's favour. The sturdy elegance of the city's churches and palaces reflects its subsequent power and prosperity, only curtailed when a separate Lisbon archdiocese was created in the 18th century.

It was from conservative Braga that the 1926 coup was launched, putting António de Oliveira Salazar in power and introducing Portugal to half a century of dictatorship.

Orientation

Praça da República is a 500m walk south of the bus station, or 1.1km east from the train station. The *praça*, with its big fountain, and

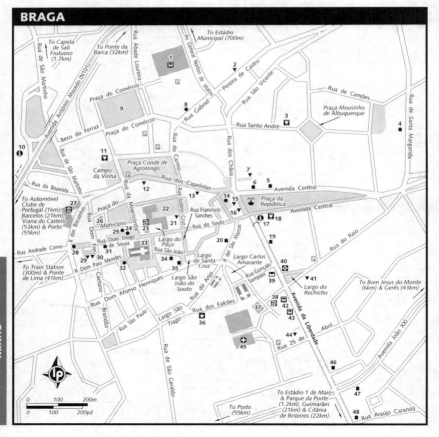

the park stretching eastwards from it form the heart of Braga. The park and the road that passes on its two long sides are together usually called Avenida Central (the road is sometimes called by its older name, Avenida dos Combatentes). Through traffic has been cleverly routed underground here, though this hardly alters central Braga's desperate parking situation.

Information

Tourist Offices Braga's good **turismo** (☎ 253 262 550; W www.cm-braga.pt; Praça da República; open 9am-7pm Mon-Fri, 9am-12.30pm & 2pm-5.30pm Sat year-round; also Sun Aug) is in an Art Deco–style building facing the fountain. Here you'll find a free monthly what's-on brochure, Braga Cultural.

The headquarters of **Parque Nacional da Peneda-Gerês** (☎ 253 203 480; e pnpg@icn .pt; Quinta das Parretas; open 9am-12.50pm & 2pm-5.30pm Mon-Fri) is 800m west of the town centre and reached via a tunnel under busy Avenida António Macedo.

Money There are banks with currency exchange desks and ATMs all along Avenida da Liberdade, Rua dos Capelistas and elsewhere in the centre.

Post & Communications The post office (Rua Gonçalo Sampaio; open 8.30am-6pm Mon-Fri, 9am-12.30pm Sat) is just off Avenida da Liberdade.

Free 30-minute access to the Internet is available at a video archive called **Videoteca Municipal** (Rua do Raio; open 9.30am-12.30pm & 2pm-6pm Mon-Sat), at the biblioteca municipal (town library) in the Antigo Paço Episcopal (see the later section on this) and at **Casa da Juventude** (Instituto Português da Juventude; ☎ 253 204 250; Rua de Santa Margarida; open 9am-7.30pm Mon-Fri), at the southern end of the pousada da juventude (youth hostel; see Places to Stay). **Café James Dean** (Rua Santo André 85; open 8am-2am Mon-Sat, 10am-midnight Sun) charges €2.30 per hour.

Travel Agencies The agency **Usit Tagus** (☎ 253 215 144; Praça do Município 7; open Mon-Fri) makes budget hotel and transport bookings, sells ISIC cards and organises Portugal and Spain trips. **AVIC** (☎ 253 270 302; Rua Gabriel Pereira de Castro; open Mon-Fri) is a bus line and travel agency.

Bookshops A limited selection of maps, guides and English-language material is on display at **Livraria Bertrand** (Rua Dom Diogo de Sousa 129-133). Many tabacarias (eg, by Café Vianna and outside the cathedral's west portal) stock foreign-language periodicals.

Universities The Universidade do Minho, founded here in 1973, operates from part of the Antigo Paço Episcopal on Largo do

BRAGA

PLACES TO STAY
4 Pousada da Juventude; Casa da Juventude
5 Hotel Residencial CC Bragashopping; Braga Shopping
6 Hotel Francfort
19 Grande Residência Avenida
20 Residencial São Marcos
34 Casa Santa Zita
35 Hotel-Residencial Dona Sofia
46 Hotel Turismo
47 Hotel Carandá
48 Hotel João XXI

PLACES TO EAT
2 Retiro da Primavera
7 Pingo Doce Supermarket
9 Mercado Municipal
12 Lareira do Conde

13 Pastelaria Ferreira Capa
15 Café Astória
16 Café Vianna
21 Salão de Chã Lusitana
29 Casa de Pasto Pregão
30 Taberna do Felix
41 Restaurante A Ceia
44 Pingo Doce Supermarket

OTHER
1 Bus Station
3 Café James Dean
8 AVIC
10 Parque Nacional da Peneda-Gerês Headquarters
11 Populum
14 Torre de Menagem
17 Turismo
18 Barbieri Café
22 Jardim de Santa Bárbara

23 Antigo Paço Episcopal; Municipal Library
24 Livraria Bertrand
25 Usit Tagus
26 Câmara Municipal
27 Museu dos Biscaínhos
28 Arco da Porta Nova
31 Lavandaria Confiança
32 Tabacaria
33 Sé
36 Police Station
37 Casa do Raio
38 Videoteca Municipal
39 Post Office
40 Centro Comercial Galeries do Bingo
42 Buses to Bom Jesus do Monte
43 Buses to Parque da Ponte
45 Hospital de São Marcos

MINHO

Paço. Various faculties are located along Rua do Castelo and Rua Abade Loureira.

Laundry For dry cleaning and laundry services visit **Lavandaria Confiança** *(Rua Dom Diogo de Sousa 46; open Mon-Sat)* or **Lavandaria 5 á Sec** *(Largo de Santa Cruz 35; open Mon-Sat).*

Medical Services & Emergency The **Hospital de São Marcos** *(☎ 253 209 000; São Lazaro)* is a block west of Avenida da Liberdade. The **police station** *(☎ 253 200 420; Rua dos Falcões)* is around the left side of the Governo Civil building.

Praça da República
This broad plaza, containing a computer-controlled fountain is a good place to start or finish your day. On the western side are two of Portugal's best venues for coffee and people-watching, Café Vianna and Café Astória, both still exuding a faint *fin-de-siècle* atmosphere (the Vianna does light meals).

The square, crenellated tower behind the cafés is the **Torre de Menagem** *(castle keep; Largo Terreiro do Castelo)*, which is all that survives of a fortified palace built in 1738. It's used for occasional art exhibitions.

Sé
Braga's cathedral *(admission free; open 8.30am-6.30pm daily May-Oct, 8.30am-5.30pm Nov-Apr)* is the oldest in Portugal, begun after the restoration of the archdiocese in 1070 and completed in the following century. It is a rambling complex of chapels and little rooms in a jumble of architectural styles. You could spend half a day probing its corners and distinguishing the Romanesque bits from the Gothic attachments and baroque ornamentation.

The original Romanesque style survives in the overall shape; in the Porta do Sol entrance on the south side; and in the marvellous west portal, carved with scenes from the medieval legend of Reynard the Fox (and now sheltered inside a Gothic porch). The cathedral's most appealing exterior feature is its filigree Manueline towers and roof. In a niche on the east wall is the lovely *Nossa Senhora do Leite* (The Virgin Suckling the Christ Child), thought to be by the 16th-century, expatriate French sculptor Nicolas Chanteréne.

You can enter the cathedral through the west portal, or via a courtyard and cloister lined with Gothic chapels on the north side. Highlights inside the church include a fine Manueline carved altarpiece, a tall chapel with *azulejos* (hand-painted tiles) depicting scenes from the life of Braga's first bishop and fantastic twin baroque organs.

Upstairs are more **chapels** and the two-storey **treasury** *(admission choir, chapels & treasury adult/child under 12 €2/free)*. In the Capela dos Reis (Kings' Chapel) are the tombs of Henri of Burgundy and Dona Teresa, parents of the first king of Portugal, Afonso Henriques. Not surprisingly for a cathedral of this stature, the treasury is a trove of ecclesiastical booty, including a 10th-century ivory casket in Arabic-Hispanic style and a plain iron cross that was used in 1500 to celebrate the first Mass in Brazil.

This is the only church in town of any real interest, and everybody else will be heading for it too, so get here early.

Antigo Paço Episcopal & Around
Opposite the cathedral is the severe, sprawling former Archbishop's Palace *(admission free; open 9am-12.30pm & 2pm-7.30pm Mon-Fri)*. Begun in the 14th century and enlarged in the 17th and 18th centuries, it's now home to university offices and part of the municipal library. A handsome carved, painted and gilded ceiling looks down on the library's computer room; this and the azulejos lining the main stairway are well worth a look.

Outside the spiky-topped north wing is the **Jardim de Santa Bárbara**, which dates, like this wing of the palace, from the 17th century. Adjacent, the pedestrianised Rua Justino Cruz and Rua Francisco Sanches fill, on sunny days, with buskers and café tables.

At the western end of neighbouring Praça do Município, Braga's **câmara municipal** (town hall) sports one of Portugal's finest baroque facades, designed by André Soares da Silva. A more extrovert Soares work is the **Casa do Raio** *(Casa do Mexicano; Rua do Raio)*, its rococo face covered in azulejos.

Arco da Porta Nova
This weedy 18th-century arch, west of the old centre, was for some time the city's main gate. It bears the ostentatious coat of arms of the archbishop who commissioned it, Dom José de Bragança.

Museu dos Biscaínhos

An 18th-century aristocrat's palace is now home to the municipal museum (☎ 253 217 675; Rua dos Biscaínhos; adult/youth 14-25 or senior €2/1, 10am-2pm Sun free; open 10am-12.15pm & 2pm-5.30pm Tues-Sun), with an attractive collection of Roman relics and 17th- to 19th-century pottery and furnishings.

More intresting is the building itself, an attractive mansion with painted and chestnut-panelled ceilings, and 18th-century azulejos featuring hunting scenes. The ground floor is paved with ribbed stones on which carriages would have once driven through to the stables.

Special Events

Braga may no longer be Portugal's religious capital, but it's still the capital of religious festivals. Easter Week here is a serious and splendid affair. The city blazes with lights and features altars representing the Stations of the Cross, and the churches are bedecked with banners. Most amazing is the torch-lit Senhor Ecce Homo procession of barefoot, black-hooded penitents. Held on Maundy Thursday evening, it starts and ends at the cathedral.

The Festas de São João, held on 23 and 24 June (continuing into the wee hours of the 25th), is a pre-Christian solstice bash dressed up to look like holy days, but it's still full of pagan energy. It features medieval folk plays, processions, dancing, bonfires and illuminations. A funfair is held in the city park and mysterious little pots of basil appear everywhere.

Places to Stay

Accommodation tends to be pricey here, and private rooms are rare. Bom Jesus do Monte has additional upper-end hotels (see Around Braga).

Camping About 1.5km south of the centre is **Parque da Ponte** (☎ 253 273 355; adult/tent/car €1.90/2.20/1.60; open year-round), a weedy municipal camp site that's little more than a clutch of caravan patches. From the second of four bus stands on Avenida da Liberdade there are about four services (€1.10) hourly (bus Nos 9, 18 and 56) that stop at the camp site; fewer services at weekends.

Hostels Braga's **pousada da juventude** (☎ 253 616 163; e braga@movijovem.pt; Rua de Santa Margarida 6; dorm beds €9.50, doubles with toilet €26.50) is a 700m walk from the turismo.

Casa Santa Zita (☎ 253 618 331; Rua São João 20; doubles with shared bathroom €25) is a quiet hostel with spartan rooms geared mainly for pilgrims. It's unmarked but for a small tile plaque reading 'Sta Zita'.

Pensões & Residenciais Rooms in the following places each have a private bathroom except where noted.

Hotel Francfort (☎ 253 262 648; Avenida Central 7; doubles with/without shower €35/25) is a bargain, its big, creaky old rooms tended by ladies of a similar vintage. It fills up in summer, so calling a few days ahead is recommended.

Grande Residência Avenida (☎ 253 609 020, fax 253 609 028; 2nd floor, Avenida da Liberdade 738; doubles with/without bathroom €45/33) is a well-run place with big rooms (quiet at the back) and helpful staff. Breakfast is included and English is spoken.

Residencial São Marcos (☎ 253 277 187, fax 253 277 177; Rua de São Marcos 80; doubles with air-con €50) has big, carpeted and rather pricey doubles. It has a welcoming atmosphere.

Hotel Residencial CC Avenida Bragashopping (☎ 253 275 722, fax 253 616 363; Avenida Central 27-37; doubles/triples with breakfast from €37/40) has sterile, air-con rooms and one self-catering apartment (€60). To reach the residencial, take the lift inside the Braga Shopping centre.

Hotel-Residencial Dona Sofia (☎ 253 263 160, fax 253 611 245; Largo São João do Souto 131; doubles €60) proudly offers English breakfast with its prim, spotless rooms.

Hotel Turismo (☎ 253 206 000; e htb@hotelturismobraga.com; Praceta João XXI; doubles Fri & Sat €65, Sun-Thur €73) is one of several big, business-friendly hotels found south of the centre. It has large, fully equipped rooms and buffet breakfast is included in its rates.

Hotel João XXI (☎ 253 616 630, fax 253 616 631; Avenida João XXI) and **Hotel Carandá** (☎ 253 614 500, fax 253 614 550; Avenida da Liberdade 96) are nearby options that have similar rates.

MINHO

Places to Eat

Restaurante A Ceia (☎ 253 263 932; *Largo do Rechicho 331; half-/full-portions about €5/8; open Tues-Sun*) is a spacious, easy-going *adega* (wine tavern), with standard Portuguese dishes and a few Minho specialities, such as *alheira*, a light, garlicky sausage of poultry or game – great with salad and a jug of red *vinho verde*.

Taberna do Felix (☎ 253 617 701; *Praça Velha 17; dishes from €6; open dinner Mon-Sat*), near the Arco da Porta Nova, prepares simple and interesting Franco-Portuguese dishes; try the tapas (€4.50) or delicious *pataniscas* (fish fritters; €6.80).

Casa de Pasto Pregão (☎ 27 72 49; *Praça Velha 18; dishes €7; open Mon-Sat*), next door to Taberna, has a plainer menu of standard Portuguese fare, with generous helpings and a generous atmosphere.

Lareira do Conde (☎ 253 611 340; *Praça Conde de Agrolongo 56; half-portions from €4; open Thur-Tues*) is a no-frills, no-smiles but better-than-average *churrasqueira* (grill restaurant).

Retiro da Primavera (☎ 253 272 482; *Rua Gabriel Pereira de Castro 100; half-portions under €5; open Sun-Fri*) is an unpretentious, good-value place near the bus station, with lots of meat and fish dishes.

Two good venues for a coffee-and-pastry break are **Pastelaria Ferreira Capa** (*Rua dos Capelistas 38-50; open 7am-8pm Mon-Sat year-round, also morning Sun May-Sept*) and **Salão de Chã Lusitana** (*Rua Justino Cruz 119; open Tues-Sun*).

The **mercado municipal** (*municipal market; Praça do Comércio*) buzzes on weekdays and on Saturday morning. There are Pingo Doce supermarkets in the Braga Shopping centre (enter from Rua dos Chãos) and on Avenida da Liberdade. Several fruit-and-vegetable shops are open during the day along Rua São Marcos.

Entertainment

Recommended café-bars near the centre are **Barbieri Café** (*Avenida Central 42-44; open midnight-5am Fri & Sat*) and the newish **Café James Dean** (*Rua Santo André 85; open 8am-2am Mon-Sat, 10am-midnight Sun*) – no prizes for guessing what the decor features.

Two popular discos are **Populum** (☎ 253 610 966; *Campo da Vinha 115; open 10pm-5am Thur-Sat*), with two dance halls (on Friday one is for Latin music, the other ballroom dancing!) and one upstairs from **Café Astória** (*Praça da República; open midnight-5am Fri & Sat*), a genteel café on the plaza.

Spectator Sports

Braga's first-division football team, Sporting Clube de Braga, plays at **Estádio 1 de Maio** in the municipal park south of the centre; you can buy match tickets at the team shop in the Centro Comercial Galeries do Bingo. The team is to move to the new 30,000-seat **Estádio Municipal**, under construction north of the town centre for Euro2004.

Getting There & Away

Bus The following bus lines are represented at the bus station:

AMI & Rodonorte	☎ 253 278 354
Arriva	☎ 253 264 693
AVIC, Joalto & Linhares	☎ 253 262 623
Empresa Hoteleira do Gerês	☎ 253 262 033
REDM & Rede Expressos	☎ 253 616 080
Salvador & Renex	☎ 253 263 453

Empresa Hoteleira do Gerês runs all day to Rio Caldo and Vila do Gerês (see Parque Nacional da Peneda-Gerês, later in this chapter, for details). Other destinations with multiple daily departures from Braga include the following:

destination	company	duration	fare (€)
Arcos de Valdevez	Salvador	1¼ hrs	2.60
Barcelos	Linhares	50 mins	1.60
Coimbra	Rede Expressos Renex	3 hrs	9.50
Guimarães	Arriva Rede Expressos	40 mins	2.10
Lisbon	Rede Expressos Renex	5 hrs	14
Monção	Salvador	2 hrs	5.30
Ponte de Lima	Rede Expressos	30 mins	2.40
Porto	Rede Expressos Renex	1½ hrs	3.60
Viana do Castelo	Rede Expressos	1¾ hrs	3

Train Braga is at the end of a branch line from Nine, and within Porto's *suburbano* network, which means commuter trains travel every hour or two from Porto (€1.70, 1¾ hours); don't waste €5.70 on an *intercidade* (IC) train. Useful IC links include Coimbra (€10, three hours, one daily) and Lisbon (€14.90, five hours, one daily).

Car & Motorcycle Braga has a branch of the **Automóvel Clube de Portugal** (*ACP;* ☎ *253 217 051; Avenida Conde Dom Henrique 72*). **AVIC** (☎ *253 270 302; Rua Gabriel Pereira de Castro; open Mon-Fri*) is an agent for Hertz car rentals.

The A3/IP1 motorway makes Braga an easy day trip from Porto. However, the N101 from Braga to Guimarães must be one of Portugal's most tortuous, congested and poorly signposted roads.

AROUND BRAGA
Bom Jesus do Monte
Bom Jesus, 5km east of central Braga on the N103, is the goal of legions of pilgrims every year. This sober neoclassical church, completed in 1811, stands atop a forested hill that offers grand sunset views across Braga, and at the head of an extraordinary, and considerably more famous, baroque staircase, **Escadaria do Bom Jesus**.

Escadaria do Bom Jesus is actually several staircases, from several decades of the 18th century. The lowest is lined with chapels representing the Stations of the Cross, and startlingly lifelike terracotta figurines. The Stairway of the Five Senses features allegorical fountains and over-the-top Old Testament figures. Highest is the Stairway of the Three Virtues, with chapels and fountains representing Faith, Hope and Charity.

You can ascend the hill by the stairs, as all pilgrims do (though you needn't go on your knees, as some do); ride the adjacent, gravity-driven **funicular** (*operating 9am-8pm daily*), the first on the Iberian Peninsula and in service since 1882; or drive up the twisting road.

The area around the church has become something of a resort, with sumptuous hotels, flower gardens, tennis courts, woodland paths and a little lake with boats for hire. It's choked with tourists on summer weekends.

Places to Stay & Eat Accommodation here is splendid, pricey and usually full.

Hotel do Elevador (☎ *253 603 400;* e *hbj@ hoteisbomjesus.web.pt; doubles with air-con*

& *satellite TV €87.50)* and the adjacent, turn-of-the-century **Hotel do Parque** (☎ *253 603 470)* have the same management and room prices (which include a grand buffet breakfast). The Hotel do Elevador and its restaurant have the best views.

Two peaceful Turihab properties within a five-minute walk are **Casa dos Lagos** (☎ *253 676 738, fax 253 679 207; doubles with breakfast €75)*, with a pool and fine views, and **Castelo de Bom Jesus** (☎ *253 676 566, fax 253 677 691; doubles with breakfast €100)*.

Getting There & Away City bus No 2 runs to Bom Jesus (€1.10, 15 minutes) every half-hour all day (hourly Sunday) from the topmost of four bus stops on Braga's Avenida da Liberdade.

BARCELOS
postcode 4750 • pop 20,600 • elevation 98m
The Minho is known for its traditional markets, geared to the agricultural community, and none is more famous than the one in this ancient town on the banks of the Rio Cávado, 22km west of Braga. Indeed the Feira de Barcelos, held every Thursday, has become so famous that tourists now arrive by the busload, and cheap rooms can be hard to find on Wednesday and Thursday nights.

Even if you don't come on a Thursday you'll find Barcelos an open-hearted town, with two good museums, several major festivals and a thriving pottery tradition.

Orientation
From the train station it's an 850m walk southwest to the heart of town, Campo da República (also called Campo da Feira), an immense shady square where the market is held. Various bus companies have terminals northeast and south of the Campo. The medieval town is on the slopes above the river, southwest of the Campo.

Information
The **turismo** (☎ *253 811 882;* e *turismo-barcelos@clix.pt; Largo da Porta Nova; open 10am-6pm Mon-Fri, 10am-12.30pm & 2.30pm-5.30pm Sat, 2.30pm-5.30pm Sun Mar-Oct; 9.30am-5.30pm Mon-Fri, 10am-12.30pm & 2.30pm-5.30pm Sat Nov-Feb)* is located in the Torre de Menagem (the former castle keep), along with a big handicrafts and souvenir shop.

MINHO

The **post office** (*Avenida Dr Sidónio Pais; open 8.30am-6.30pm Mon-Fri, 9am-12.30pm Sat*) and **police station** (☎ 253 802 570) face the south side of the Campo. **Hospital Santa Maria Maior** (☎ 253 809 200) is just east of the Campo.

Casa do Pedro (*Avenida da Liberdade 12*) is a newsagency that stocks some foreign periodicals.

Feira de Barcelos

Despite tourist attention, the market (held on the Campo da República) remains a local, rural affair. Villagers hawk everything from scrawny chickens to hand-embroidered linen, and Romia (Gypsy) women bellow for business in the clothes section. Snack on sausages and home-made bread as you wander among the cow bells, hand-woven baskets and carved ox yokes.

Pottery is what outsiders come to see, especially the distinctive, yellow-dotted *louça de Barcelos* ware and the gaudy figurines á la Rosa Ramalho, a local potter who put Barcelos on the map for its ceramics in the 1950s. The trademark Barcelos cockerel (see the boxed text) is everywhere – on tea towels, key rings and bottle openers, and in pottery form in every size.

Tour buses arrive by mid-morning Thursday and the whole scene winds down after midday, so get there early.

The Barcelos Cockerel

The cockerel motif that you see all over Portugal – especially in pottery form – has its origins in a 16th-century (some say 14th-century) 'miracle'. According to the story (which also crops up in Spain) a Galician pilgrim on his way to Santiago de Compostela was wrongfully accused of theft while passing through Barcelos. Though pleading his innocence, he was condemned to hang.

In his last appearance at the judge's house the pilgrim declared that the roast cockerel on the judge's dinner table would stand up and crow to affirm his innocence. The miracle occurred, the pilgrim was saved and the cockerel gradually became the most popular folk-art motif in the country, akin to a national icon.

Museu Arqueológico & Around

On a ledge above Barcelos' 14th-century bridge over the Rio Cávado are the roofless ruins of the former palace of the counts of Barcelos and dukes of Bragança. Practically obliterated by the 1755 earthquake, it now serves as an alfresco archaeological museum (*admission free; open 9am-5.30pm daily*).

Among the mysterious phallic stones, Roman columns, medieval caskets and bits of azulejos, the most famous item is a

---

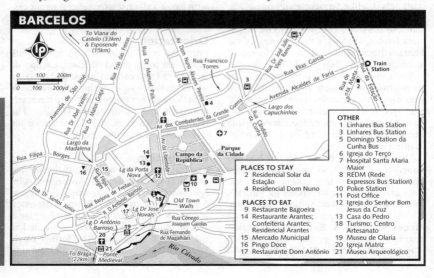

BARCELOS

To Viana do Castelo (33km) & Esposende (15km)

Rua Trás das Freitas
Av. Dom Nuno Álvares Pereira
Rua Dr Manuel Pais
Rua Francisco Torres
Av. de José Júlio Vieira Ramos
Rua Elias Garcia
Train Station
Avenida Alcaides de Faria
Rua de Santa Marta
Rua da Estação
Largo dos Capuchinhos
Rua do Clérigo da Cunha
Avenida de São José
Rua Dr Abel Varzim
Rua Dr Matos Graça
Av. dos Combatentes da Grande Guerra
Largo da Madalena
Rua Filipa Borges
Campo da República
Parque da Cidade
Av. da Liberdade
Lg da Porta Nova
Rua Dr Santos Júnior
Rua Barjona de Freitas
Rua Filipa Borges
R D António Barroso
Lg Dr José Novais
Old Town Walls
Rua Cónego Joaquim Gaiolas
Lg D António Barroso
Rua Fernando de Magalhães
To Braga (22km)
Ponte Medieval
Rio Cávado

0   100   200m
0   100   200yd

OTHER
1 Linhares Bus Station
3 Linhares Bus Station
5 Domingo Station da Cunha Bus
6 Igreja do Terço
7 Hospital Santa Maria Maior
8 REDM (Rede Expressos Bus Station)
10 Police Station
11 Post Office
12 Igreja do Senhor Bom Jesus da Cruz
13 Casa do Pedro
18 Turismo; Centro Artesanato
19 Museu de Olaria
20 Igreja Matriz
21 Museu Arqueológico

PLACES TO STAY
2 Residencial Solar da Estação
4 Residencial Dom Nuno

PLACES TO EAT
9 Restaurante Bagoeira
14 Restaurante Arantes; Confeitaria Arantes; Residencial Arantes
15 Mercado Municipal
16 Pingo Doce
17 Restaurante Dom António

MINHO

14th-century stone cross, the Crucifix O Senhor do Galo, depicting the Gentleman of the Cockerel story and said to have been commissioned by the lucky pilgrim himself. Near the entrance is a late Gothic *pelourinho* (stone pillory) topped by a granite lantern.

Eastwards along the bluffs is a stretch of the medieval **town walls**.

Peek inside the **igreja matriz**, the stocky Gothic parish church behind the museum, to see its 18th-century azulejos and gilded baroque chapels.

Museu de Olaria

This good pottery museum (☎ 253 824 741; *Rua Cónego Joaquim Gaiolas; adult/youth under 26 or senior/child under 14 €1.40/0.70/ free, morning Sun free; open 10am-6pm Tues-Sun)* features ceramics in many of Portugal's regional styles, from Azores pots to Barcelos, Estremoz and Miranda do Corvo figurines, and some striking pewter grey ware.

Igreja do Senhor Bom Jesus da Cruz

On the corner of the Campo is this arresting octagonal church *(Templo do Bom Jesus; admission free; open 8.30am-12.30pm & 2pm-5.30pm daily)*, built in 1704 and overlooking a garden of obelisks. João Antunes designed the church, and was also responsible for Lisbon's Igreja da Santa Engrácia. Its baroque interior includes some bright azulejos and a grand gilded altarpiece.

Igreja do Terço

Inside this deceptively plain church *(admission free; open 10am-noon & 2pm-5pm daily)*, once part of a Benedictine monastery, are handsome azulejos on the life of St Benedict by the 18th-century master, António de Oliveira Bernardes. Competing for attention are a carved, gilded pulpit and a ceiling painted with more scenes from the saint's life.

Special Events

For one week surrounding 3 May, the Festas das Cruzes (Festival of the Crosses) turns Barcelos into a fairground of coloured lights, flags and flowers, and the city parties.

The Festival de Folclore, a celebration of traditional folk song and dance, is held on the last Saturday of July.

Places to Stay

Residencial Solar da Estação (☎ 253 811 741; *Largo Marechal Gomes da Costa 1; doubles with bathroom & breakfast €30)*, opposite the train station, has basic, renovated rooms behind its shabby pink exterior.

Residencial Arantes (☎ 253 811 326, fax 253 821 360; *Avenida da Liberdade 35; doubles with/without bathroom €42.50/27.50)*, beside the Arantes Restaurante (see Places to Eat), has spacious, homely doubles and rates including breakfast.

Residencial Dom Nuno (Don Nuno; ☎ 253 812 810, fax 253 816 336; *Rua Francisco Torres 141; doubles with breakfast from €42.50)* offers unexceptional modern rooms with bathroom.

Places to Eat

Restaurante Dom António (☎ 253 812 285; *Rua Dom António Barroso 85; mains around €8; open daily)* is a local favourite with lots of good daily half-portions for under €5. House specialities include roast kid and grilled game meat, including wild boar and deer.

Restaurante Arantes (☎ 253 811 645; *Avenida da Liberdade 33; open Wed-Mon)* offers speedy service and regional specialities such as *rojões á moda do Minho* (a casserole of marinated pork) for around €8. The modest *confeitaria* of the same name next door makes its own mouth-watering pastries; try a custard-filled *sonho* (dream) drenched in syrup or sugar.

Restaurante Bagoeira (☎ 253 811 236; *Avenida Dr Sidónio Pais 495; dishes from €9; open daily)* copes with the jovial chaos of market day, serving up good but overpriced regional items.

Two stops for self-caterers are the **mercado municipal** (Largo da Madalena; closed afternoon Sat, Sun) and a nearby **Pingo Doce** (Rua Filipa Borges) supermarket.

Getting There & Away

Bus Services of REDM/Rede Expressos (☎ 253 814 310; *Avenida Dr Sidónio Pais 445)* go to/from Braga (€1.60, 50 minutes) at least hourly, and to/from Porto (€3.60, two hours) five times each weekday.

Linhares (☎ 253 811 571; *Praça do Almada 41)* has services every hour or two to Braga and Porto (€3.10, two hours) daily, and to Viana do Castelo (€2.30, 50 minutes) on weekdays. Linhares buses stop at Largo dos Capuchinhos.

Domingos da Cunha (☎ 253 815 843; Avenida Dom Nuno Álvares Pereira 203) buses go to Ponte de Lima (€2.30, 55 minutes) four to six times a day.

All bus services are less frequent at the weekend.

Train Barcelos is on the Porto–Valença line. There are at least seven direct trains a day from Porto (€2.80, one hour) or, with a change at Nine, from Braga (€1.40, 45 minutes).

AROUND BARCELOS
Área de Paisagem Protegida do Litoral de Esposende

The Esposende Littoral Protected Landscape Area covers the Braga district's entire 18km of seashore, including the mouth of the Rio Cávado, for an average 250m inland. It was set aside in 1987 for the protection of its unstable sand dunes, the delicate vegetation that holds them together and the remnants of an ancient way of life – symbolised by the Minho's photogenic, decrepit coastal windmills – that's being nibbled away by the sea on one side and by human activity on the other. The partnership of land and sea, which probably goes back to Celtic and Roman times, is illustrated by the area's unique agricultural fields, sited immediately behind the dunes, watered by ocean spray and fertilised with algae and crustaceans harvested from the sea.

Attempts are being made to stabilise the dunes with fencing and plants, and access is largely restricted to elevated walkways. For more information on the programme contact the **area office** (☎ 253 965 830; e apple@icn.pt; Rua 1 de Dezembro 65, 4740-226 Esposende).

Places to Stay Basic accommodation is available at Esposende, some 15km west of Barcelos, and at Ofir and Apúlia.

At Fão, 3km south of Esposende, there's a basic **camp site** (☎ 253 815 383; e cccb@ esoterica .pt; Rua São João de Deus; adult/car €2.80/2, tent €2.50-3; open year-round) that's open to holders of the Camping Card International (CCI; see Visas & Documents in the Facts for the Visitor chapter); and also a **pousada da juventude** (☎ 253 981

790; e fozcavado@movijovem.pt; Alameda Bom Jesus; dorm beds €10.50, doubles with toilet €29).

Getting There & Away AV Minho and AVIC buses stop at Esposende three or four times daily en route between Viana do Castelo and Porto.

GUIMARÃES
postcode 4810 • pop 52,200
• elevation 400m

Guimarães is chock-a-block with history. Afonso Henriques was born here in 1110 and some 30 years later he launched the main thrust of the Reconquista against the Moors from here. Although he was to move the capital of his new kingdom to Coimbra, Guimarães' locals justifiably consider their town the cradle of the nation.

Despite industrial development on the outskirts, the city's large historic core is an exceptionally well-preserved, and still very much lived in, enclave of medieval monuments, important enough to be named a Unesco World Heritage site in 2001.

But Guimarães knows how to party too. This is a university town, and its lively atmosphere explodes into full-scale merrymaking during the annual Festas Gualterianas (see under Special Events, later). Guimarães is also one of the venues for Euro2004.

There's enough to warrant a full day's sightseeing in Guimarães, with a base either here or in Braga. For those with euros to spare, Guimarães' two Pousadas de Portugal are among the country's finest.

History

Guimarães caught the royal eye as early as AD 840 when Alfonso II of León convened a council of bishops here, but it only started to grow in the 10th century after the powerful Countess Mumadona Dias, widowed aunt of another king of León, gave it her attention, founding a monastery and building a castle built to protect it. Henri of Burgundy chose Guimarães for his court, as did his son Afonso Henriques until he shifted the capital to Coimbra in 1143.

Orientation

Old Guimarães is in the northeast of the modern city. Most points of interest lie within a demarcated tourism zone stretching south from the castle to an arc of public gardens at Alameda de São Dâmaso. Guimarães' commercial heart is Largo do Toural.

The main turismo is a 600m walk north up Avenida Dom Afonso Henriques from the train station. It is a 1km slog up Avenida Conde de Margaride from the main bus station, which is beneath the Centro Comercial Guimarães Shopping.

Information

The **main turismo** (☎ 253 412 450; Alameda de São Dâmaso 86; open 9.30am-7pm daily July-Sept, 9.30am-12.30pm & 2pm-6.30pm Mon-Fri Oct-June) can help with most inquiries, but there's a more central and enthusiastic **branch turismo** (☎ 253 518 790; Praça de Santiago; open 9.30am-7pm daily July-Sept; 9.30am-6.30pm Mon-Fri, 10am-6pm Sat, 10am-1pm Sun Oct-June) in the old centre.

Numerous banks with ATMs line Largo do Toural and Rua Gil Vicente. The **post office** (Largo Navarros de Andrade 27; open 8.30am-6.30pm Mon-Fri, 9am-12.30pm Sat) is north of Largo do Toural. The **biblioteca municipal** (municipal library; Largo Conego José M Gomez; open 2pm-7pm Mon & Thur,

10am-12.30pm, 2pm-6pm & 9pm-11pm Tues, 10am-6pm Wed & Fri) has free Internet access. The best bookshop is **Livraria Ideal** (Rua da Rainha 34; open Mon-Sat).

Emergency services include the **hospital** (☎ 253 512 612; Rua dos Cotileros, Creixomil), opposite the bus station, and the **police station** (☎ 253 513 334; Avenida Dr Alfredo Pimenta).

An engineering branch of Universidade do Minho is located north of the centre.

Paço dos Duques

Recognisable by its forest of brick chimneys, the Paço dos Duques (Ducal Palace; ☎ 253 412 273; adult/youth under 26 or senior/child under 14 €3/1.50/free, morning Sun free; open 9.30am-5pm daily July-Sept, 9.30am-12.30pm & 2pm-5pm Oct-June) has pushed its way into the foreground on Guimarães' hill top. Built in 1401 by a later and equally famous Afonso (the future first Duke of Bragança), it fell into ruin after the family moved to Vila Viçosa in the Alentejo. Tastelessly restored under Salazar, it has since become a museum. The only items of interest on a tedious tour are some Flemish tapestries

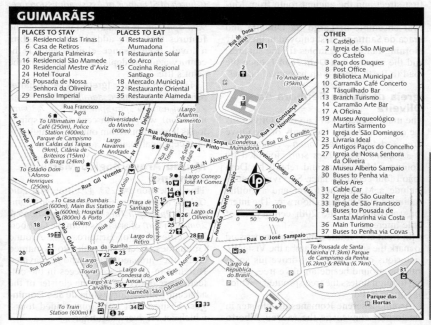

GUIMARÃES

PLACES TO STAY	PLACES TO EAT	OTHER
5 Residencial das Trinas	4 Restaurante Mumadona	1 Castelo
6 Casa de Retiros	11 Restaurante Solar do Arco	2 Igreja de São Miguel do Castelo
7 Albergaria Palmeiras	15 Cozinha Regional Santiago	3 Paço dos Duques
16 Residencial São Mamede	18 Mercado Municipal	6 Post Office
20 Residencial Mestre d'Aviz	22 Restaurante Oriental	9 Biblioteca Municipal
24 Hotel Toural	35 Restaurante Alameda	10 Carramão Café Concerto
26 Pousada de Nossa Senhora da Oliveira		12 Tásquilhado Bar
29 Pensão Imperial		13 Branch Turismo
		14 Carramão Arte Bar
		17 A Oficina
		19 Museu Arqueológico Martins Sarmento
		21 Igreja de São Domingos
		23 Livraria Ideal
		25 Antigos Paços do Concelho
		27 Igreja de Nossa Senhora da Oliveira
		28 Museu Alberto Sampaio
		30 Buses to Penha via Belos Ares
		31 Cable Car
		32 Igreja de São Gualter
		33 Igreja de São Francisco
		34 Buses to Pousada de Santa Marinha via Costa
		36 Main Turismo
		37 Buses to Penha via Covas

and two paintings attributed to Josefa de Óbidos (see the boxed text 'Josefa de Óbidos' in the Estremadura & Ribatejo chapter).

Castelo & Igreja de São Miguel do Castelo

The seven-towered castle (admission castle keep adult/youth under 26 or senior/child under 14 €1.30/0.70/free, morning Sun free; open 9.30am-5pm daily July-Sept, 9.30am-12.30pm & 2pm-5pm Oct-June), built by Henri of Burgundy in about 1100 and still in fine shape, is considered the birthplace of Afonso Henriques. A claustrophobic climb to the top of Countess Mumadona's keep rewards you with bird's-eye views.

Sandwiched between the palace and castle is the little Romanesque Church of St Michael of the Castle (admission free; open same hrs as castle) where Afonso Henriques was probably baptised. Under its floor rest many of Afonso Henriques' companions-at-arms.

Ancient Squares & Streets

Among Guimarães' most picturesque and important areas are Rua Santa Maria, its first street and the ancient route from Mumadona's monastery to the castle; the medieval ensemble of Largo da Oliveira and Praça de Santiago, best enjoyed in the early morning before café tables fill the squares; and the narrow Rua Dom João I, once the road to Porto, lined with balconied houses.

Igreja de Nossa Senhora da Oliveira

The main attraction in Largo da Oliveira is the convent-church, Our Lady of the Olive Tree (admission free; open 7.15am-noon & 3.30pm-7.30pm Tues-Sun), founded by Countess Mumadona and rebuilt by Dom João I four centuries later. Surviving details include a Manueline tower and a Gothic pediment over the main doorway. The interior, renovated in the 20th century, is of little interest.

In front is a Gothic canopy and cross said to mark the spot where Wamba the Visigoth, victorious over the Suevi, drove his spear into the ground beside an olive tree, refusing to reign unless the tree sprouted – which of course it did.

Around a serene Romanesque cloister in the former convent is the Museu Alberto Sampaio (☎ 253 423 910; adult/youth under 26 or senior/child under 14 €2/1/free, morning Sun free; open 10am-12.30pm & 2pm-5.30pm Tues-Sun), an excellent collection of ecclesiastical art and wealth. Highlights include a 14th-century silver gilded triptych, the tunic said to have been worn by João I at the Battle of Aljubarrota and a 16th-century silver Manueline cross. English-language notes are available in each room. Attendants hover, enforcing the no photos rule, although part of the cloister can be photographed from the street.

Antigos Paços do Concelho

The building on 'legs' facing Largo da Oliveira is Guimarães' 14th-century town hall, the finest feature of which is its painted wooden ceiling. At the time of writing it was closed for renovations; previously it had been home to the uninspiring Museu de Arte Primativa Moderna (Museum of Modern Primitive Art; ☎ 253 414 186; admission free).

Other Churches

The 13th-century Igreja de São Francisco (Church of St Francis of Assisi; admission free; open 9am-noon & 2.30pm-5pm Mon-Sat, 9am-1pm Sun) is primarily of interest for the features that were added later, including a lovely Renaissance cloister and 18th-century azulejos depicting scenes from the saint's life.

The 18th-century Igreja de São Gualter (Church of St Walter; admission free; open 7.30am-noon & 3pm-5pm Mon-Sat, 7.30am-noon Sun), with its 19th-century twin spires, looks harmonious from outside, though it is unexceptional inside.

Museu Arqueológico Martins Sarmento

This collection (☎ 253 415 969; Rua Paio Galvão; adult/senior €1.50/free; open 10am-noon & 2pm-5pm Tues-Sat, 10.30am-noon & 2pm-5pm Sun) of artefacts from the Celtiberian settlements of Briteiros (see Around Guimarães, later) and Sabroso is named after the archaeologist who excavated Briteiros in 1875. Larger pieces in the collection are dotted around the cloister of the adjacent 14th-century Igreja de São Domingos. Visitors can only join guided tours, which set off every half hour.

The banks of the high-flowing Rio Homem in the Parque Nacional da Peneda-Gerês, the Minho

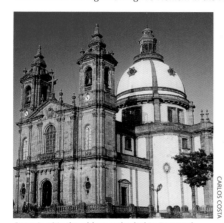

Braga's sé is the oldest cathedral in Portugal

Stairway to Bom Jesus do Monte, near Braga

Folk dancing in the handsome market town of Ponte de Lima, the Minho

Three wooden-masked boys celebrating the Festa dos Rapazes, 'Festival of the Lads', Vinhais

Castle in citadel of Bragança

Church front, Rio de Onor, Parque Natural de Montesinho

The Roman bridge in Chaves, Trás-os-Montes, is still open for traffic after 1900 years

Penha & the Mosteiro de Santa Marinha da Costa

Some 7km south-east up a twisting, cobbled road is the wooded summit of Penha, overlooking Guimarães and, at 617m, the highest point in the Serra de Santa Catarina. It makes a fine escape from the city.

The Mosteiro de Santa Marinha da Costa, about 1.5km from the town centre on the lower slopes of the hill, dates from 1154 when Dona Mafalda, wife of Afonso Henriques, commissioned it for the Augustinians, honouring a vow to Santa Marinha, patron saint of pregnant women. Almost entirely rebuilt in the 18th century, it reopened in 1985 as a flagship Pousada de Portugal (see Places to Stay). Nonguests can visit the chapel and extensive gardens.

The easiest route to the monastery is on municipal bus No 51 or 52 to São Roque (€0.90, every half-hour Monday to Saturday, hourly Sunday), which departs from the south side of the public gardens; get off at Costa.

For the summit you can take a Mondinense bus via Covas from opposite the main turismo (€1.30, every half-hour Monday to Saturday, hourly Sunday), or less often via Belos Ares from Largo da República do Brasil (€1). But the finest way to the top is on the **Teleférico da Penha** (cable car; one-way/return €1.50/2.50; operating 11am-7pm Mon-Fri, 10am-8pm Sat, Sun & holidays May-Sept; 11am-6pm Fri, 10am-7pm Sat, Sun & holidays Oct-Apr), which starts from Parque das Hortas, 600m east of the old centre.

Special Events

The Festas de Cidade e Gualterianas, held on the first weekend of August, is marked by a free fair (held in Guimarães since 1452), plus folk dancing, rock concerts, bullfights, and, on the Monday, a float parade. São Gualter is the town's patron saint.

Encontros de Primavera is a series of classical and early music concerts held at historical venues in late May and June. Guimarães hosts a jazz festival all through November.

Places to Stay

Camping Near the top of Penha, **Parque de Campismo da Penha** (☎ 253 515 912; adult/car €1.80/1.60, tent €1.60-2.60; open Apr-Sept) is a well-equipped and densely

wooded municipal camp site. There are few camp sites in Portugal so lofty. See Penha & the Mosteiro de Santa Marinha da Costa, earlier, for transport options.

Parque de Campismo das Caldas das Taipas (☎ 253 576 274; Largo das Termas, Taipas; adult/car €2.10/1.60, tent 1.60-2.30; open June-Sept) is a dismal, weedy patch by the Rio Ave, 9km northwest of Caldas das Taipas. Take any Braga-bound bus.

Hostels For good value at the budget end try **Casa de Retiros** (☎ 253 511 515, fax 253 511 517; Rua Francisco Agra 163; singles/doubles/triples €18/32/42), a plain, peaceful, Catholic missionary hostel. You must pay on arrival, stay out until 6pm and be in by 11.30pm, but at these prices (including breakfast) the hardship is bearable.

Pensões & Residenciais Don't get your hopes up. Guimarães has few budget choices, and even its mid-range options may leave you cold, though prices are negotiable outside high season. Breakfast is included except where noted.

Pensão Imperial (☎ 253 415 163; Alameda São Dâmaso 111; doubles with/without shower €30/22.50), a warren of dark staircases and ancient, overpriced rooms, is probably a firetrap but it's central. Breakfast is not included.

Residencial São Mamede (☎ 253 513 092, fax 253 513 863; Rua São Gonçalo; doubles €35) has cable TV, which helps drown out the traffic noise, and it's air-conditioned.

Albergaria Palmeiras (☎ 253 410 324, fax 253 417 261; 4th floor, Centro Comercial Palmeiras, Rua Gil Vicente; doubles €35) is similarly free of atmosphere but is quiet. Enter through the shopping centre's side entrance on Travessa dos Bimbais.

Residencial Mestre d'Aviz (☎ 253 422 770, fax 253 422 771; Rua Dom João I 40; doubles €37.50) looks like the best mid-range bargain. It has a few tastefully modern rooms, a small bar and minimal street traffic.

Residencial das Trinas (☎ 253 517 358, fax 253 517 362; Rua das Trinas 29; doubles €40) has chintzy but comfortable rooms with double-glazing in a restored building in the historical zone. It will be good value once the owners learn to smile.

Hotel Toural (☎ 253 517 184; e hoteltoural @netc.pt; Largo AL Carvalho; singles/doubles

MINHO

with *air-con* €58/75), pride of the town, business-friendly and recently renovated, offers big, uncluttered rooms with full bathroom and buffet breakfast. Older, noisier rooms face Praça Toural.

Casa das Pombais (☎ 253 412 917; *Avenida de Londres; doubles €75)* is a 17th-century manor house that has peacocks in the garden and incongruously surrounded by housing estates. It has just two rooms available.

At the top end of the market Guimarães has two Pousadas de Portugal:

Pousada de Nossa Senhora da Oliveira (☎ 253 514 157, fax 253 514 204; Rua de Santa Maria; doubles Mon-Fri from €126, Sat & Sun from €132) is a 16th-century house in the heart of the old town. It is lovely except for the sound of late-night revelry at weekends.

Pousada de Santa Marinha (☎ 253 511 249, fax 253 514 459; doubles Mon-Fri from €159, Sat & Sun from €176) is a restored former monastery on the slopes of Penha. Guests may wander around the cloister past azulejos by the 18th-century master Policarpo de Oliveira Bernardes, and sleep in converted monks' cells.

Places to Eat
Restaurante Oriental (☎ 253 414 048; *1st floor, Largo do Toural 11; open to 2am daily)* is no great shakes but is cheap, friendly and has long opening hours.

Restaurante Mumadona (☎ 253 414 971; Rua Serpa Pinto 268; dishes €7-10, half-portions €4-6; open Mon-Sat), a snug and family-friendly place, has a menu rather heavy on pork and *bacalhau* (dried salted cod), but lunch-time half-portions are good value for Guimarães.

Cozinha Regional Santiago (☎ 253 516 669, Praça de Santiago 16; mains €7-10, half-portions around €6; open daily) is a modest place with modest prices, considering its location, and the food is good. Try their *feijoada*, a rough-and-ready pork-and-bean casserole.

Restaurante Solar do Arco (☎ 253 513 072; Rua de Santa Maria 50; dishes around €12-17; open Mon-Sat) is the place for a seafood splurge.

Self-caterers will like the **mercado municipal** (Rua Paio Galvão; open morning Mon-Sat).

Entertainment
Carramão Café Concerto (☎ 253 413 815; Largo Cónego José Maria Gomes 39; open to 4am Sat) and its sibling **Carramão Arte Bar** (☎ 253 413 815; Praça de Santiago; open to 2am daily) have pop and rock on the box.

Tásquilhado Bar (☎ 253 515 197; Rua de Santa Maria 42) plays alternative sounds until 2am nightly.

Ultimatum Jazz Café (☎ 253 415 294; Rua Rei do Pegú; open to 4am) has classical, jazz and piano-bar sounds, including live music on Thursday and Friday and disco from 1am Friday and Saturday nights.

Spectator Sports
Estádio Dom Afonso Henriques, northwest of the centre, is home to Guimarães' first-division football team, Vitória SC Guimarães. At the time of writing, the stadium was under heavy renovation for Euro2004.

Shopping
Today, as in medieval times, Guimarães is known for its linen. Other crafts contributing to its prosperity are goldsmithing and silversmithing, embroidery and pottery. For good-quality work by Guimarães artisans, visit the municipal outlet **A Oficina** (☎ 253 515 250; Rua Paio Galvão 11; open Mon-Sat).

A big flea market takes over Praça de Santiago and Largo da Oliveira on the first Saturday of each month.

Getting There & Away
Bus Every half to two hours **REDM/Rede Expressos** (☎ 253 516 229) has links to Braga (€2.10, 40 minutes). **Arriva** (253 423 501) goes to Braga less often; it goes to Porto (€3.60, 50 minutes) about hourly on weekdays but less often at weekends, and to Lisbon (€13.50, five hours) daily. **Rodonorte** (☎ 253 412 646) heads for Amarante (€4.30, 50 minutes), Vila Real (€5.50, 1½ hours) and Bragança (€9.50, four hours) two or three times daily Sunday to Friday.

Train Guimarães is the terminus of a branch of Porto's wide *suburbano* network, though the line was being rebuilt at the time of writing. When it's finished in 2003, commuter trains will potter out to Guimarães from Porto (€1.70, 1½ hours) about eight times a day; meanwhile they run as far as Trofa, with CP buses available from there.

AROUND GUIMARÃES
Citânia de Briteiros
Scattered around the Minho are the remains of Celtic hill settlements, called *citânias*, dating back at least 2500 years. One of the best-preserved and most spectacular sites is at Briteiros, 15km north of Guimarães.

The 3.8-hectare site *(admission free; open 24hr)*, inhabited from about 300 BC to AD 300, may have been the Celtiberians' last stronghold against the invading Romans. When archaeologist Dr Martins Sarmento excavated it in 1875 he discovered the foundations and ruins of more than 150 rectangular, circular and elliptical stone huts, linked by paved paths and a water distribution system, and surrounded by multiple protective walls. He spent years clearing away the debris, reconstructed two huts and created one of the country's most evocative archaeological sites.

The most interesting artefacts are on display in the Museu Martins Sarmento in Guimarães, but there's a small **exhibit** *(adult/child €1.50/0.75; open 9am-6pm daily June-Sept, 9am-5.30pm Oct-May)* and shop at the site entrance. A detailed plan, keyed to markers around the site, is available here.

Getting There & Away From Guimarães, Arriva buses go to within about 1km of the site (€1.50, 30 minutes); get off between Briteiros town and Santa Leocádia. Useful departures (weekdays only) are at 7.30am, 10.45am, 1.30pm and 2.30pm, with buses passing by on the return journey about 12.55pm, 2.05pm, 3.05pm, 5.05pm and 6.35pm. Check with the Arriva or Guimarães turismo for current timetables.

From Braga, bus connections involve a change at Taipas and then awkwardly timed local buses from there. By car it's a scenic 15km journey via Bom Jesus do Monte.

Coastal & Northern Minho

VIANA DO CASTELO
postcode 4990 • pop 36,100
Viana, on the northern bank of the Rio Lima estuary, is the Minho's largest, liveliest resort, an elegant town of Manueline and Renaissance houses and rococo palaces. It also stands out for its multitude of good festivals (see Special Events, later). This is an agreeable base for exploring the lower Lima valley, or for just unwinding, with fine beaches right across the river and up the coast.

History
On Monte de Santa Luzia, above the town, are the remains of a Celtiberian settlement, though there's little evidence of the Romans, Suevi, Visigoths and Moors who followed. The Romans called their town Diana, which over the years became Viana.

Dom Afonso III, who wanted an urban and fishing centre at the mouth of the Rio Lima, charted the town in 1258. Manueline mansions and monasteries attest to Viana's 16th-century prosperity, thanks to its sailors who fished for cod off Newfoundland. By the mid-17th century this was northern Portugal's biggest port, its merchants trading as far afield as Russia. At the same time expatriate British cloth merchants here were beginning to export large quantities of local 'red Portugal' wine to England (see the special section on port wine in the Douro chapter).

More money arrived in the 18th century with the Brazilian sugar and gold trade. But with Brazil's independence and the rise of Porto as a wine-exporting port, Viana fell into decline. It has since revived as a deep-sea-fishing and industrial centre and an increasingly popular tourist destination.

Orientation
From the train station at the foot of Monte de Santa Luzia, the main axis down to the river is Avenida dos Combatentes da Grande Guerra (called Avenida dos Combatentes, or just 'Avenida'). East of the Avenida dos Combatentes is the old town, centred on Praça da República. West lies the old fishing quarter.

From the bus station it's a 2km trek along Avenida Capitão Gaspar de Castro to the centre, though many regional buses stop at the station and beside Viana's riverside park, the Jardim Marginal.

Information
Tourist Offices The **regional turismo** (☎ 258 822 620, fax 258 827 873; Rua Hospital Velho; open 9am-12.30pm & 2.30pm-6pm Mon-Sat Feb-Oct, to 5.30pm Mon-Sat Nov-Jan; morning Sun year-round) is in a building

that opened in 1468 as, appropriately, a shelter for travellers. Here you can get a town map and a free what's-on monthly, *Agenda Cultural*.

Money There are banks with ATMs on Avenida dos Combatentes and Praça da República.

Post & Communications The post office *(open 8.30am-6pm Mon-Fri, 9am-12.30pm Sat)* is located at the top of Avenida dos Combatentes.

There is free Internet access at the **Instituto Português da Juventude** *(☎ 258 808 800; Rua do Poço 16-26; open 9am-12.30pm & 2pm-5.30pm Mon-Fri)* and a single terminal at the **biblioteca municipal** *(☎ 258 809 302; Rua Cândido dos Reis; open 9.30am-12.30pm & 1pm-9pm Mon-Fri, 9.30am-12.30pm Sat)*.

The **pousada da juventude** *(☎ 258 800 260; Rua da Argaçosa; open 8am-midnight)* has access for €2.50 per hour.

Bookshops The most useful bookshop in town is **Livraria Bertrand** *(Rua de Sacadura Cabral 32)*. Foreign-language newspapers

are available at many of the *tabacarias* around the centre.

Laundry The self-service **Lavandaria Automática Viana** *(LAV; Rua do Marquês 17; open 9am-10pm daily)* is in the fishing quarter. There's an unnamed **lavandaria** *(Rua Grande 106; open Mon-Sat)* near the centre.

Medical Services & Emergency The **hospital** *(☎ 258 829 081; Estrada de Santa Luzia)* is north of the train station. The **police station** *(☎ 258 822 022)* is on Rua de Aveiro.

Praça da República

This well-preserved zone of mansions and monuments is the heart of the old town, and is Viana's most picturesque quarter. Its centrepiece is the **Chafariz**, a Renaissance fountain built in 1554 by João Lopes the Elder. It's topped with the familiar Manueline motifs of an armillary sphere and the cross of the Order of Christ. The fortresslike **Antigos Paços do Concelho** is the old town hall and another 16th-century creation.

At right angles to this is the striking former **Misericórdia** almshouse, designed in 1589 by

VIANA DO CASTELO

PLACES TO STAY
8 Residencial Laranjeira
18 Residencial Viana Mar
20 Residencial Magalhães
24 Pensão Restaurante Dolce Vita
31 Casa de Hóspedes Guerreiro
32 Residencial Jardim

PLACES TO EAT
12 Mercado Municipal
21 Restaurante Laranjeira
25 A Gruta Snack Bar
26 Restaurante Os Três Arcos
33 Restaurante O Garfo

OTHER
1 Hospital
2 Funicular
3 Scandal Surf
4 Police Station
5 Glamour
6 Biblioteca Municipal
7 Post Office
9 Misericórdia
10 Antigos Paços do Concelho
11 Capela das Malheiras
13 Indian Bar
14 AV Cura/Transcolvia Buses
15 Igreja Matriz
16 Chafariz
17 AVIC Travel Agency
19 AV Minho Office
22 Livraria Bertrand
23 Instituto Português da Juventude
27 Lavandaria
28 Regional Turismo
29 AVIC/Transcoinha Office
30 AV Cura TransGunha
34 Museu Municipal Transcolvia Office
35 Lavandaria Automática Viana
36 Gil Eannes
37 Ferry Pier

João Lopes the Younger, its loggias supported by monster caryatids. The adjoining **Igreja de Misericórdia** *(admission free; open 10am-12.30pm & 2pm-5pm Mon-Fri Aug, 11am-12.30pm Sun year-round)* was rebuilt in 1714 and is adorned with some of Portugal's finest azulejos, by the master António de Oliveira Bernardes and his son Policarpo.

Igreja Matriz

This parish church *(admission free; Rua da Aurora do Lima; open 9am-11.30am & 3pm-5.30pm Mon-Fri)* – also known as the *sé* – dates from the 15th century, though it has since had several reincarnations. Its finest features are its sculpted Romanesque towers and a Gothic doorway carved with figures of Christ and the Evangelists.

Museu Municipal

The 18th-century Palacete Barbosa Maciel is home to a very fine collection *(☎ 258 820 377; Largo de São Domingos; admission €0.90; open 9am-noon & 2pm-5pm Tues-Sun)* of 17th- and 18th-century ceramics (especially blue Portuguese china), azulejos and furniture.

Castelo de São Tiago da Barra

The grandiose castle at the river mouth began its life in the 15th century as a small-ish fort. It was integrated into a larger fort, commissioned by Felipe II of Spain (Felipe I of Portugal) in 1592, to guard the prosperous port from pirates. The buildings inside have now been converted to office space.

Monte de Santa Luzia

There are two good reasons to visit Viana's 228m, eucalyptus-clad hill. One of them, everyone agrees, is the god's-eye **view** down the coast and up the Lima valley.

Not everyone agrees about the other reason, the hill's over-the-top, 20th-century neo-Byzantine **Templo do Sagrado Coração de Jesus** *(Temple of the Sacred Heart of Jesus; ☎ 258 823 173; admission free; open 8am-7pm daily Apr-Sept, 8am-5pm Oct-Mar)*. You can, however, get a little closer to heaven on its roof, via a claustrophobic stairway (€0.50; take the entrance marked *zimbório*) or the lift (€0.70).

Predictably there's a Pousada de Portugal (see Places to Stay) up here, too, behind and above the basilica. Behind that is another

attraction, the poorly maintained ruins of a Celtiberian **citânia** from around the 4th century BC. From an ugly gangway you can make out the remains of walls and circular stone huts. You can also make the short walk onwards to the summit.

You can get up the mountain by car or taxi (3.5km) or on foot, a 2km climb of about fourteen zillion steps – only for the penitent. The road starts by the hospital, and the steps begin about 200m up the road. At the time of writing, an old funicular to the top was growing rusty from disuse.

Gil Eannes

From its home port of Viana, the naval hospital ship *Gil Eannes* (pronounced zheel **yan**-ish) provided on-the-job care for those fishing off the coast of Newfoundland. Recently restored, the ship *(adult/child under 6 €1.50/free; open 2pm-7pm Mon-Fri July-Sept, 9am-noon & 2pm-7pm Sat, Sun & holidays Apr-Sept, 9am-noon & 2pm-5.30pm Sat, Sun & holidays Oct-Mar)*, which is moored near Largo 5 de Outubro, is now open to the public.

Beaches

Viana's big beach, Praia do Cabedelo, is one of the Minho's best, with little development beyond a couple of dockside cafés. It's across the river from town, and one way to get there is by **passenger ferry** *(☎ 968 022 348)* from the pier south of Largo 5 de Outubro. The five-minute trip costs €0.80 one way, and the ferry goes about hourly between 8.45am and 8pm daily May to September, and to midnight between mid-July and mid-August.

TransCunha *(☎ 258 829 711; Avenida dos Combatentes 127)* buses go to Cabedelo (€0.60) from Largo 5 de Outubro at 7.35am, 10.15am and 12.50pm weekdays (plus weekends from July to September); the last bus back departs Cabedelo at 5.10pm. Inquire with TransCunha for the current timetable.

There's a string of fine beaches north of Viana for 25km to Caminha, including good surfing venues at Afife and Moledo and a low-key resort at Vila Praia de Âncora. AV Cura/Transcolvia buses (see Getting There & Away) depart at least hourly every day for Caminha (€1.50), with a stop by the Jardim Marginal. At least eight daily regional and *interregional* (IR) trains (€1.20) also make their way up the coast, though not all stop at Afife.

River Trips
If there are enough passengers, boats run up and down the Rio Lima daily in summer, from the pier south of Largo 5 de Outubro. Trips range from 20 minutes (about €2.50) to three hours (about €13, with lunch). For details call **Portela & Folhos** (☎ 258 842 290, 968 022 348) or check at the pier.

Special Events
Viana has acquired a reputation for celebrations. The Romaria de Nossa Senhora d'Agonia is the region's biggest annual bash (see the boxed text 'Who's Sorry Now?'), and Carnaval festivities here are considered northern Portugal's best.

Other annual events include Encontros de Viana, a cinema festival in the first week of May; Festival Maio, a national folk-dance extravaganza at the end of May; Canto Luso, a gathering of singing groups from around the Portuguese-speaking world, which is held during the second week of July; Jazz na Praça da Erva, a jazz festival held during the first week of August; and Simply Blues, a blues festival in the third week of November. The town's **cultural activities office** (☎ 258 809 350; e dac@nortenet.pt) has details.

The town also goes a little nuts in mid-May during Semana Académica (or Queima das Fitas), a week of end-of-term madness similar to Coimbra's.

Places to Stay
Accommodation may be tight in summer but bargains are plentiful outside high season. The turismo keeps a list of trustworthy *quartos* (private rooms); expect to pay at least €25 for a double in summer. It also has details of several nearby cottages and manor houses, though most are hard to reach without a car. Expect to pay €60 to €80 for a double.

Camping Within walking distance of the ferry pier on the Cabedelo side is the **Orbitur** (☎ 258 322 167; e info@orbitur.pt; Praia do Cabedelo; adult/car €3.80/3.30, tent 3-5.30; open mid-Jan–Nov) camp site, which also has bungalows for rent. It gets packed out in the summer. Next nearest are two facilities at Vila Praia de Âncora, 16km to the north.

Who's Sorry Now?
Viana's Romaria de Nossa Senhora d'Agonia (Our Lady of Sorrows) is one of the most spectacular of the Minho festivals, featuring everything from sombre processions to parades and fireworks. In the main procession, statues from the Igreja de Nossa Senhora da Agonia are carried around the streets. The streets themselves are decorated with coloured sawdust, the women come out in their traditional finery and the men drink like there's no tomorrow.

The festival takes place for three or four days around 20 August. Accommodation is very tight at this time, so you'll need to book well ahead.

Hostels The town's newish **pousada da juventude** (☎ 258 800 260; e vianacastelo@movijovem.pt; Rua da Argaçosa; dorm beds €12.50, doubles with toilet €35) is about 1km east of the town centre.

Pensões & Residenciais Prices given here are for high season, and include breakfast except where noted.

Casa de Hóspedes Guerreiro (☎ 258 822 099; Rua Grande 14; singles/doubles with shared facilities €19/25), a boarding house with tatty but clean rooms, is good value at the bottom of the market (no breakfast).

Pensão-Restaurante Dolce Vita (☎ 258 824 860; Rua do Poço 44; rooms per person €15) has a few small rooms, each with shower and toilet but no TV. Breakfast is not included, but Dolce Vita is good value for being in the town centre.

Residencial Viana Mar (☎/fax 258 828 962; Avenida dos Combatentes 215; double with bathroom €35-45) is a congenial place with a small bar. There are also some rooms with shared facilities and no TV. Breakfast is pricey at €3.80.

Residencial Laranjeira (☎ 258 822 261, fax 258 821 902; Rua General Luís do Rego 45; doubles with bathroom €40-50) is a well-run place with modest, comfortable rooms, and a good restaurant around the block (see Places to Eat). Off-street parking is €2.50 per day.

Residencial Magalhães (☎ 258 823 293, fax 258 828 962; Rua Manuel Espregueira 62;

doubles with/without bathroom from €43/ 38) is central but conspicuously quiet. Carpeted and wood-panelled, this *residencial* is a bargain in its range.

Residencial Jardim *(☎ 258 828 915, fax 258 828 917; Largo 5 de Outubro 68; doubles €50)* offers a bit of pampering. Some rooms have river views.

Pousada do Monte de Santa Luzia *(Pousada de Viana do Castelo; ☎ 258 828 889, fax 258 828 892; doubles with/without sea view Mon-Fri from €145/135, Sat & Sun from €159/148)*, atop Monte de Santa Luzia, surely outdoes the other Pousadas de Portugal for grand views.

Places to Eat

Most mid-range *pensões* (guesthouses) have restaurants that welcome nonguests and offer reasonable food and prices.

Restaurante Laranjeira *(☎ 258 822 258; Rua Manuel Espregueira 24; daily special €5.50; open Sun-Fri)* is a very agreeable spot to meet and eat, with brisk service, a bright setting, good Portuguese standard fare and a view of the spotless kitchen. Sunday brings traditional dishes such as *sarrabulho*, a rich pork stew.

Pensão-Restaurante Dolce Vita *(☎ 258 824 860; Rua do Poço 44; most dishes under €5; open daily)* is popular, with a big menu of pasta dishes and pizza.

A Gruta Snack Bar *(☎ 258 820 214; Rua Grande 87; mains €4-8; open Mon-Sat)* has a lunch menu with good salads for under €3, a few specials at €4 and well-prepared local dishes.

Restaurante O Garfo *(☎ 258 829 415; Largo 5 de Outubro 28; mains €8; open Sun-Fri)* is an unpretentious eatery offering lots of fresh fish.

Restaurante Os Três Arcos *(☎ 258 824 014; Largo João Tomás da Costa 25; open Tues-Sun)* has freshwater-fish dishes for around €8 and seafood for more; the adjoining bar does half-portions.

Viana's Restaurante *(☎ 258 824 797; Rua Frei Bartolomeu dos Mártires 179; dishes €12- 14, half-portions €7-8; open afternoon Tues-Sun)* is a modest place in the fishing quarter where you can choose from several varieties of the *bacalhau* for which it's famous.

The **mercado municipal** *(Rua Martim Velho; open morning Mon-Sat)* is just east of the centre. Rua Grande and its eastward

extension have numerous small fruit-and-vegetable shops.

Entertainment

Glamour *(☎ 258 822 963; Rua da Bandeira 179-185)* is tops among bar/clubs near the centre, with occasional live music and other events. Another popular venue is **Kathedral Caffe** *(☎ 258 828 794; Rua Nova de São Bento 131)*.

Shopping

A huge open-air market sprawls across the area beside the Castelo de São Tiago da Barra every Friday. A handy surf shop is **Scandal Surf** *(Rua Santo António 100; open Mon-Sat)*.

Getting There & Away

Bus Several long-distance bus companies operate from the bus station, though most of these also sell tickets at their town-centre offices, including: **AV Cura/Transcolvia** *(☎ 258 829 348; Avenida dos Combatentes 81)*; **AV Minho** *(☎ 258 800 340; Avenida dos Combatentes 181)*; **AVIC** *(☎ 258 800 364; Avenida dos Combatentes 206)*. **REDM/Rede Expressos** *(☎ 258 825 047)* operates from the station.

AV Cura/Transcolvia runs up the Lima valley to Ponte de Lima (€2.10, 50 minutes), Ponte da Barca (€2.70, 1½ hours) and Arcos de Valdevez (€2.90, 1½ hours) at least hourly every day; you can also board these services by the Jardim Marginal. Tickets are 10% cheaper from the office. Rede Expressos has multiple weekday services to Braga (€3, 1¼ hours).

AV Cura coastal express buses go north to Valença (€3.20, 1¼ hours) and Monção (€4, 1½ hours) several times daily; AV Minho goes less often.

AV Minho goes south to Porto (€6, two hours) three or four times daily. AVIC and Rede Expressos each have daily expresses to Porto (€5/6.10), Lisbon (€14/13.50, 5½ hours) and to the south.

Regional services are limited at the weekend.

Train Daily direct services from Porto include four IR/international trains (€4.10, 1½ hours) and five regional services. For Braga (€2.80, from 1¼ hours, 12 daily), change at Nine.

VALENÇA DO MINHO
postcode 4930 • pop about 5000
• elevation 60m

From its hill-top position, the citadel of Valença do Minho (usually called just Valença) overlooks the Rio Minho frontier with Spanish Galicia.

The earliest recorded fortifications were built here in the 13th century by Afonso III, to safeguard Portugal's northern frontier. At that time Valença was called Contrasta and the fortress across the river at Tuy provided its counterpart. Today's muscular, well-preserved *fortaleza* (fortress) dates from the 16th century, its design inspired – as were several others in northern Portugal – by the French military architect Vauban.

Nowadays Spanish day-trippers troop across from Tuy in the hundreds to buy cheap linen and towels from the shops along the fortress' cobbled streets. Once they go home, the silence seeps up from the river bank and the fortress regains a sense of tranquil isolation.

Orientation & Information

A dull new town sprawls at the foot of the fortress. From the bus station it's an 800m walk north via Avenida Miguel Dantas (the N13) and the Largo da Trapicheira round-about (also called Largo da Esplanada) to the **turismo** (*☎/fax 251 823 374; Avenida de Espanha; open 9.30am-12.30pm Mon-Sat year-round, 2.30pm-6pm daily Apr-Sept, 2pm-5.30pm daily Oct-Mar*). The train station is just east of Avenida Miguel Dantas.

From the turismo you can climb for 400m to enter the fortress through the Portas do Sol. Coming from Viana or from Spain on the N13, turn west at Largo da Trapicheira and enter through the southern gateway, the Portas da Coroada. An interchange from the A3/IP1 motorway also leads to the Portas da Coroada.

The fortress has its own **post office** (*open 9am-12.30pm & 2pm-5.30pm Mon-Fri*). There are numerous banks with ATMs in the lower town, and one off Rua Mousinho de Albuquerque in the north fortress.

Fortaleza

There are actually two fortresses, bristling with bastions, watchtowers, massive gateways and defensive bulwarks, and joined by a single bridge. The old churches and Manueline mansions inside testify to how successful the fortifications were against several sieges as late as the 19th century.

Much of the fortress is now given over to commercialism, a kind of Vaubanesque shopping centre, with restaurants and tacky shops cheek by jowl along its cobbled lanes. But press on through the towel merchants to the far end of the larger northern fortress, which incorporates Dom Afonso's original stronghold and contains almost everything that's of interest.

From Praça da República bear right, then left, into Rua Guilherme José da Silva. On the left, opposite the post office, is the **Casa da Eira**, with a handsome Manueline window. The 14th-century **Igreja de Santo Estevão**, with its Renaissance facade, is at the end of the street. Nearby is a 1st-century **Roman milestone** from the Braga–Astorga road where it crossed the Rio Minho.

From the milestone continue northwards to the end of Rua José Rodrigues and the Romanesque parish church, the **Igreja de Santa Maria dos Anjos** (St Mary of the Angels) dating from 1276. At the back is a tiny **chapel** with leering carved faces and Romano-Gothic inscriptions on the outside, though this is in a state of serious disrepair and closed to the public.

To the left of the parish church is the **Capela da Misericórdia** and beyond it the Pousada São Teotónio (see Places to Stay). Turn right and descend to one of Dom Afonso's **original gates**.

Places to Stay

Some private rooms are available, and campers sometimes pitch tents below the northwestern ramparts. There are only two official places to stay inside the fortress, both at the northern end and with fantastic views into Spanish Galicia, and both decidedly top-end.

Pousada de São Teotónio (*☎ 251 800 260, fax 251 824 397; Rua de Baluarte do Socorro; doubles €115*) has prime views, of course.

Casa do Poço (*☎ 251 825 235; w www .casadopoco.fr.fm; Travessa da Gaviarra 4; suites €100*) is a gorgeously restored 18th-century house that once lodged the sick from the Misericórdia hospital. It now cares for the wealthy, with contemporary European art, a library, billiard room and six silk-wallpapered suites.

The rest of us sleep outside the walls, on the road to the Portas do Coroada. Prices listed are for the local high season, July to mid-September; outside this period they're at least a third less.

Val Flores (☎ 251 824 106, fax 251 824 129; Centro Comercial Val Flores; doubles with bathroom €40) is a fairly boring residencial, though the price includes breakfast.

São Gião (☎ 251 823 797, fax 251 823 703; 1st floor, Centro Comercial Alvarinho; doubles with bathroom €40) is less appealing than Val Flores, and here breakfast isn't included.

Hotel Lara (☎ 251 824 348, fax 251 824 358; doubles with bathroom €60) is just uphill and breakfast is included in the room rate.

Places to Eat
Eating in the fort with Spanish tour groups isn't as bad as it sounds if you like a jolly atmosphere. Nothing's cheap, but you can keep the bill down by just ordering a few starters.

Restaurante Monumental (☎ 251 823 557; mains about €8; open daily), built into the Portas da Coroada, is one of the few places around with personality.

A Gruta (☎ 251 822 270; dishes €7-10; open daily June-Aug, Tues-Sun Sept-May) is a snappy little bar-restaurant built into the portal between the two fortresses.

Outside the fort there are several mediocre mid-range restaurants, along the same strip as the residenciais.

Getting There & Away
Bus There are **AV Cura/Transcolvia** (☎ 251 809 581) services to Monção (€1.60, 20 minutes) about hourly on weekdays (less often at the weekend), and via Viana do Castelo (€3.20, 1¼ hours) to Porto daily. AVIC and **AV Minho** (☎ 251 824 175) have similar but less frequent services.

Train There are three IR/international trains running daily to Valença from Porto (€5.60, 2¼ hours), which continue on as far as Vigo in Spain.

MONÇÃO
postcode 4950 • pop 2600 • elevation 60m
Modest Monção (pronounced mohng-**sawng**), 17km up the Rio Minho from Valença, is popular with Portuguese tourists for its spa (unfortunately not open for casual

visitors). Sizable chunks of a sturdy, irregular fortress remain intact around a small, atmospheric old town centre, and there's plenty of good food and wine.

History
Dom Dinis completed Monção's fortress in 1306.

The town's most famous daughter is one Deu-la-Deu Martins, who, according to local legend, tricked a force of Castilians into calling off a siege in 1368. She scrabbled together enough flour from starving citizens to make a few loaves of bread, and in a brazen show of plenty tossed them to the Castilians with the message, 'if you need any more, just let us know'. The disheartened force withdrew.

Three centuries later, as Portugal was shaking off Spanish rule, another woman brought another siege to an end. Mariana de Lencastre, Countess of Castelo Melhor, surrendered to Spanish besiegers on condition that they end the siege and honour those inside. This they did, raising their flags to the 236 defenders, the only survivors of a force of over 2000.

Orientation & Information
From the newish bus station it's 600m east to the defunct train station, then two blocks north up Rua General Pimenta de Castro to the first of the town's two main squares, Praça da República. Praça Deu-la-Deu and the heart of the old town lie a block further.

The **turismo** (☎ 251 652 757, fax 251 652 751; open 9am-7pm Mon-Fri, 9am-12.30pm & 2pm-6pm Sat, 9.30am-12.30pm & 3pm-6pm Sun) is upstairs in the restored Casa do Curro, along with a permanent exhibit on local Alvarinho wines. Enter the building from Praça Deu-la-Deu or Praça da República.

The **post office** (open 9am-12.30pm & 2pm-5.30pm Mon-Fri) is on the north side of Praça da República. Free Internet access is available at the **biblioteca** (Casa do Curro; open 9am-7pm Mon-Fri, 9am-12.30pm & 2pm-6pm Sat, 9.30am-12.30pm & 3pm-6pm Sun), in the rooms adjacent to the turismo.

Old Monção
In chestnut-shaded Praça Deu-la-Deu, a statue of its namesake tops a **fountain**. The Senhora da Vista bastion at the north end offers a gentle view across the Rio Minho into

Spain, a stone's throw away. The **Capela da Misericórdia** at the square's southern end has a coffered ceiling painted with cherubs.

East of the square is the snug, cobbled old quarter. Two blocks along Rua da Glória is the Romanesque **igreja matriz**, where Deu-la-Deu is buried.

Wine Tasting
Alvarinho is a variety of white *vinho verde* produced around Monção and neighbouring Melgaço. If you'd like a tasting, contact the **Adega Cooperativa de Monção** (☎ 251 652 167) a few days in advance. It's 1.8km south of Monção on the N101 to Arcos de Valdevez and Braga.

Special Events
The town's biggest party is the Festa de Corpo de Deus, on Corpus Christi (the ninth Thursday after Easter). Events include a religious procession and a medieval fair, with a re-enactment of the mythical battle between St George and the Dragon.

Another big celebration is the five-day Festa da Nossa Senhora das Dores (Our Lady of Sorrows), which surrounds a big procession on the next-to-last Sunday in August.

Places to Stay
The nearest camp site is the basic **Termas de Peso** (☎ 251 403 282, fax 251 402 647; adult/car €2.40/1.90, tent €2.20-4.10; open year-round), 20km east on the N202.

Dormidas O Abrigo (☎ 251 652 329; Rua Bispo de Lemos 2 • Rua 11 de Dezembro 5; doubles €20) has two houses, with well-kept rooms, in the old centre.

Croissanteria Raiano (☎ 251 653 534; Praça Deu-la-Deu 34; doubles with shower & toilet €30) offers spotless, overfurnished rooms, some with views across to Spain.

Residencial Esteves (☎ 251 652 386; Rua General Pimenta de Castro; doubles from €30) offers good-value rooms and a friendly welcome.

Albergaria Atlântico (☎ 251 652 355, fax 251 652 356; Rua General Pimenta de Castro 15; doubles with air-con €60) and the more modest **Pensão Residencial Mané** (☎ 251 652 355, fax 251 652 356; Rua General Pimenta de Castro 5; doubles with air-con €45) next door are under the same uncheerful management.

For Turihab properties, ask the turismo. Closest to town are two manor houses located on estates producing Alvarinho wine grapes:

Casa de Rodas (☎ 251 652 105; Lugar de Rodas; doubles €75) is 1km south of the town centre.

Solar de Serrade (☎ 251 654 008, fax 251 654 041; Mazedo; doubles €60-75) is a few kilometres further on from Casa de Rodas.

Places to Eat
Local specialities here include shad, salmon and trout from the Rio Minho, and lamprey eels (in season from January to March). Wash your meal down with a pitcher of Alvarinho wine.

Café A Regional (Largo Alfândega; lunch €4; open Mon-Sat), a tiny, busy place in an alley just west off Praça da República, is good value for money with half a dozen choices of honest local fare.

Café-Restaurante Central (☎ 251 652 805; Praça Deu-la-Deu; dishes from €5; open Mon-Sat) has lots of grilled meat and fish dishes for under €8; enter through the café or at the back.

Croissanteria Raiano (☎ 251 653 534; Praça Deu-la-Deu 34; lunch about €5; open Mon-Fri), a few doors from the turismo, has a few modest lunch-time specials (with vegetables, hurray!) and snacks into the evening.

Restaurante Cabral (☎ 251 651 755; Rua 1 de Dezembro; dishes €6-10; open daily) is a good place for fish and seafood.

Getting There & Away
From Monção, **Salvador/Renex** (☎ 251 653 881) goes to Arcos de Valdevez (€2.60, 45 minutes) and Braga (€5.30, two hours) three to six times daily. **AV Cura/Transcolvia** (☎ 251 652 801) goes to Valença (€1.60, 20 minutes) hourly on weekdays and less often at weekends, and to Viana (€4, 1½ hours) and Porto several times daily. **AV Minho** (☎ 251 403 051) travels this route less often.

PONTE DE LIMA
postcode 4990 • pop 2740
This dignified, handsomely restored and photogenic market town by the Rio Lima comes alive every other Monday, when a vast market sprawls along the river bank, offering everything from farm tools and wine barrels to fresh fruit, cheese and bread.

MINHO

When the Romans first passed through here, the soldiers were convinced that the Rio Lima was the River Lethe – the mythical 'river of oblivion' – and that if they crossed it they'd forget everything. It was only after their leader, Decimus Junius Brutus, plunged ahead and shouted back his legionaries' names that they braved the waters. The Ponte Romana (Roman Bridge) after which the town is named – part of the Roman road from Braga to Astorga in Spain – supposedly marks the very spot.

If it's not market day when you visit, you too may find yourself slipping into forgetful slumber here…either that or the annoying street muzak may drive you away. You can do the town justice in a day, and it's expensive to linger here if you're on a budget. The heartland of Turismo de Habitação (see Accommodation in the Facts for the Visitor chapter), the Ponte de Lima area has more Turihab properties than anywhere else in Portugal.

Orientation

The bus station is 800m uphill from the town centre, though all long-distance buses loop down to within a block of the turismo, on Praça da República. Most things of interest are in the two-block strip between the turismo and the river bank. The local shopping zone is Rua do Souto. Downriver, the Ponte de Nossa Senhora da Guia carries the Braga–Valença N201.

Information

The well-organised **turismo** (☎ 258 942 335, fax 258 942 308; Praça da República; open 9am-12.30pm & 2pm-6pm daily June-Aug, 9.30am-12.30pm & 2.30pm-6pm Sept-May) shares a space with a small handicrafts gallery.

There are at least three banks with ATMs on Rua Inácio Perestrelo. The **post office** (open 8.30am-5.30pm Mon-Fri) is opposite the turismo. Free Internet access is available at the **biblioteca municipal** (Largo da Matriz; open 2pm-6.30pm Mon, 10am-12.30pm & 2pm-8pm Tues & Thur, 10am-12.30pm & 2pm-6.30pm Wed & Fri, 10am-12.30pm Sat).

The **hospital** (☎ 258 909 500; Rua Conde de Bertiandos) and the **police station** (☎ 258 941 113; Rua Dr Luís da Cunha Nogueira) are to the east of the turismo.

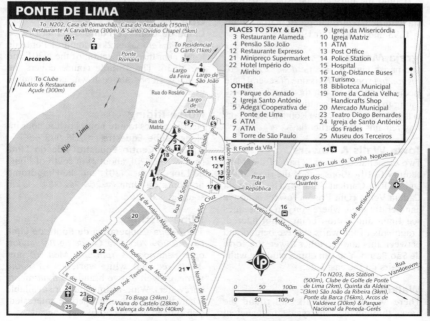

PONTE DE LIMA

PLACES TO STAY & EAT
3 Restaurante Alameda
4 Pensão São João
12 Restaurante Expresso
21 Minipreço Supermarket
22 Hotel Império do Minho

OTHER
1 Parque do Arnado
2 Igreja Santo António
5 Adega Cooperativa de Ponte de Lima
6 ATM
7 ATM
8 Torre de São Paulo
9 Igreja da Misericórdia
10 Igreja Matriz
11 ATM
13 Post Office
14 Police Station
15 Hospital
16 Long-Distance Buses
17 Turismo
18 Biblioteca Municipal
19 Torre da Cadeia Velha; Handicrafts Shop
20 Mercado Municipal
23 Teatro Diogo Bernardes
24 Igreja de Santo António dos Frades
25 Museu dos Terceiros

Ponte Romana & Arcozelo

The 31-arched bridge (Ponte Romana) across the Rio Lima actually dates from the 14th century, when the original Roman bridge was rebuilt and extended. Apart from the road surface, the segment on the north bank by the village of Arcozelo is original Roman work. The bridge is now pedestrian only.

In down-at-heel Arcozelo are the little **Igreja Santo António** and **Parque do Arnado**, the latter a peaceful, architecturally themed park and pavilion created by landscape designer Caldeira Cabral. At the Ponte de Lima end is **Largo de Camões**, a tranquil spot at sunset, with a fountain resembling a giant bonbon dish.

Museu dos Terceiros

Downriver, the 18th-century Igreja de São Francisco dos Terceiros is now a rambling museum of ecclesiastical and folk treasures (☎ 258 942 563; admission €1; open 10am-noon & 2pm-6pm Wed-Mon), although the highlight is the church itself, with its gilded baroque interior. The Renaissance-style **Igreja de Santo António dos Frades**, once a convent church, is adjacent to the museum.

Behind the museum, on Rua Agostinho José Taveira, stands Ponte de Lima's pride, the galleried Teatro Diogo Bernardes, built in 1893 and restored in 1999.

Igreja Matriz

The parish church (Rua Cardeal Saraiva; admission free; open daily) is one of several staid medieval monuments in the neighbourhood, dating from the 15th century and remodelled in the 18th century. A fine Romanesque doorway remains from earlier days.

Town Walls & Towers

Two crenellated towers – part of the 14th-century fortifications – face the river at the end of Rua Cardeal Saraiva. The **Torre da Cadeia Velha** (Old Prison Tower) is now a handicrafts shop, where you can sometimes see linen and cotton being embroidered. Fragments of the walls survive behind and between this and the other tower, the **Torre de São Paulo**. You can climb onto the walls via stairs on the east side.

Walking

There are charming walks all round the area – through the countryside, past ancient monuments, along cobbled lanes trellised with vines. The turismo has produced *Trilhos Alto Minho*, a free folio of five walks ranging from 5km to 14km, though the maps and text are not 100% reliable. Take a picnic; cafés and restaurants are rare.

A steep climb up a hill just north of Arcozelo (the turismo's folio has details) will reward you with panoramic views, 15km or more up and down the Lima valley. At the summit, about 5km from Ponte de Lima, is an irregularly opening, tiny and bizarre **chapel** dedicated to Santo Ovídio, patron saint of ears. The interior is covered with votive wax ears, offered in hopes of, or in thanks for, the cure of an ear affliction. You can also drive up; the turning off the N202 is about 2.5km upstream of the N201 bridge.

Boating

The **Clube Náutico** (☎ 258 944 499; open 10am-1pm & 4pm-7pm daily July-Sept, Sat & Sun Oct-June), across the river and 400m downstream by the N201 bridge (walk via Arcozelo or drive over the highway bridge), rents canoes and plastic kayaks for tootling around on the river, for €3 per 1½ hours.

Golf

Clube de Golfe de Ponte de Lima (☎ 258 743 414; Feitosa) is 2km south of Ponte de Lima near the intersection of the N201 and the N536. The 18-hole course covers the wooded slopes above town, commanding grand views.

Horse Riding

Nearby places to hire horses by the hour include **Clube Equestre** (☎ 258 942 466) in Arcozelo; **Centro Equestre Vale do Lima** (☎ 258 743 620), about 1km south of Ponte de Lima off the N201; and the **Hípodromo de Ponte de Lima** (☎ 258 762 784), 12km south at Calvelo.

Wine Tasting

The **Adega Cooperativa de Ponte de Lima** (☎ 258 909 700; Rua Conde de Bertiandos; open 8am-noon & 1pm-5pm Mon-Fri) produces red and white varieties of *vinho verde*, as well as two brands of *aguardente* (firewater). Wine-tasting tours are available when there are enough people interested; you'll need to book a few days ahead.

MINHO

Special Events

One of Portugal's most ancient ongoing events, the Feiras Novas (New Fairs), has been held here since 1125, when Dona Teresa, wife of Henri of Burgundy, granted the town a royal charter. Stretching over three days in mid-September and held on the riverfront beside the Ponte Romana, Feiras Novas is a combined market and fair, featuring folk dances, fireworks, brass bands and lots of merrymaking. It's a great show. You'll need to book accommodation well ahead.

Another centuries-old tradition is the Vaca das Cordas, a form of bull-running in which young men goad a hapless bull (restrained by a long rope) as it runs through the town. During the more pious Festa do Corpo de Deus, held the following day, patterns of flowers carpet the streets. The festival is held annually around Corpus Christi, the ninth Thursday after Easter.

Places to Stay

The turismo keeps a list of approved private rooms on hand.

Pensão São João (☎ 258 941 288; Largo de São João; doubles with/without toilet & shower €35/25) is the best lower-end choice, with plain, bright but serviceable rooms (no TV, no breakfast) that get some street noise.

Residencial O Garfo (☎/fax 258 743 147; Rua do Arrabalde; doubles/twins with breakfast €35/39) has plain rooms in a quiet setting 1.3km northeast of the centre.

Hotel Império do Minho (☎ 258 741 510, fax 258 942 567; Avenida dos Plátanos; doubles with bathroom & breakfast €60), bathed in the surrounding shopping-centre's muzak, has sterile, air-con rooms, each with a balcony and satellite TV. It has an outdoor pool.

There are about 40 Turihab properties in the Ponte de Lima area, from farmhouses to mansions. You can book them through the turismo or (sometimes more cheaply) directly with the owners. Many of them close in winter.

Quinta da Aldeia (☎ 258 741 355; São João da Ribeira; cottage-apartments from €60) is a child-friendly, Turihab manor house about 3km northeast on the N203.

Two Turihab options in Arcozelo are: **Casa de Pomarchão** (☎ 258 741 742; double apartments from €68), and a restored 1770 manor house, **Casa do Arrabalde** (☎ 258 742 442; double apartments €75).

Places to Eat

Restaurante Alameda (☎ 258 941 630; Largo da Feira; dishes under €8; open Tues-Sun) heaves with happy customers at lunch time. Half-portions (under €4.50) of meaty regional specialities are a very good bargain, and the upstairs room is nonsmoking and non-TV.

Restaurante Expresso (☎ 258 942 849; Rua Inácio Perestrelo; mains under €9; open Sun-Fri) offers well-prepared Portuguese standard dishes, including a few green vegetables, though the unsmiling service takes the edge off. Some half-portions are available.

Restaurante A Carvalheira (☎ 258 742 316; N202; mains €10-13; open Tues-Sun), on the N202 at the north end of Arcozelo, is generally agreed to serve the area's best food, and won't let you down if you fancy a splurge. Booking ahead is essential.

Restaurante Açude (☎ 258 944 158; Arcozelo; mains around €10; open Wed-Mon), beside the Clube Náutico, has lots of knotty pine, big windows onto the river, and pretty good food.

Self-caterers can try the **Minipreço supermarket** (Rua General Norton de Matos). The venerable mercado municipal was being completely rebuilt at the time of writing.

Getting There & Away

Long-distance buses can be boarded on Avenida António Feijó (buy tickets on board) or at the bus station. All services thin out on Sunday.

AV Cura (☎ 258 829 348) goes down to Viana do Castelo (€2.10, 50 minutes, about hourly), jointly with AV Minho, and up to Ponte da Barca (€2, 40 minutes, five daily) and Arcos de Valdevez (€2.10, 50 minutes, nine daily). **Domingos da Cunha** has less frequent Lima valley services, and goes to Barcelos (€2.30, 55 minutes, six daily). **REDM/Rede Expressos** (☎ 258 942 870) runs to Braga (€2.50, 30 minutes, three daily) and via Barcelos to Porto (€4.30, two hours, four daily).

PONTE DA BARCA

postcode 4980 • pop 2000

Ponte da Barca, named after the barca (barge) that once ferried pilgrims and others across the Rio Lima, has a dreamy riverfront park, a handsome 16th-century bridge, a tiny old centre and some appealing local walks. It's also the home of the best single source of information on the Parque Nacional de Peneda-Gerês.

The town springs to life every other Wednesday (alternating with Arcos de Valdevez), when a huge market spreads along the riverside.

Orientation

The old town, just east of the bridge, is packed into narrow lanes on both sides of the main road, Rua Conselheiro Rocha Peixoto. Uphill and away from the river, where the main road becomes Rua António José Pereira and Rua Dr Joaquim Moreira de Barros (and eventually the N101 to Braga), is the unappealing new town.

Information

The **turismo** (*☎/fax 258 452 899; Rua Conselheiro Rocha Peixoto; open 9.30am-12.30pm & 2.30pm-6pm Mon-Sat June-Sept; 9.30am-12.30pm & 2.30pm-5.30pm Mon-Fri, 9.30am-12.30pm Sat Oct-May)*, about 200m east of the bridge, has a town map and accommodation information.

Upstairs from the turismo is **Adere-PG**, the Peneda-Gerês Regional Development Association. (See under Information in the Parque Nacional da Peneda-Gerês section later in this chapter for details on park information available here.)

There are no banks with ATMs in the old town but plenty along Rua António José Pereira in the new town. In the same neighbourhood you'll find the **post office** (*Rua das Fontaínhas; open 9am-12.30pm & 2pm-5.30pm Mon-Fri*).

Ponte & Jardim dos Poetas

The lovely 10-arched bridge across the Rio Lima dates from 1543, though it has been rebuilt several times since then. Beside it is the former arcaded marketplace and a little garden, Jardim dos Poetas, which is dedicated to two 16th-century poet brothers, Diogo Bernardes and Agostinho da Cruz, born in Ponte da Barca.

Walking

The turismo and Adere-PG can suggest some fine long hikes in the area, punctuated with ancient sites.

You could take a simple stroll westwards for 3.5km to Bravães, a village famous for

its lovely, small Romanesque **Igreja de São Salvador**, once part of a Benedictine monastery. Its west portal is adorned with intricate carved animals, birds and human figures; its interior adorned with simple frescoes of the Virgin and of the Crucifixion.

Special Events

The Festa de São Bartolomeu, held from 19 to 24 August, is the occasion for folk music and dancing, parades and fireworks, in addition to a procession on the final day.

Places to Stay

Parque de Campismo de Entre Ambos-os-Rios (*☎ 258 588 361, fax 258 452 450; Entre Ambos-os-Rios; person/car €2/2.20; open mid-May–Sept)* is a basic riverside camp site, 9km upriver from town. It's run by the national park but can be booked through Adere-PG. Take any Lindoso-bound bus to reach it (see Lindoso under Parque Nacional da Peneda-Gerês later in this chapter).

Pensão Restaurant Gomes (*☎ 258 452 288, 258 454 016; Rua Conselheiro Rocha Peixoto 13; doubles with shared facilities around €20)* has homely old doubles at bargain rates; rooms and the rooftop terrace offer views of the river and bridge.

Residencial San Fernando (*☎ 258 452 580; Rua Herois da India; double/twin/triple with breakfast €24/25/32)*, 700m from the turismo, at the top of the new town, has little atmosphere but is fair value at this price.

Casa Nobre do Correio-Mor (*☎/fax 258 452 129; e laceme@mail.telepac.pt; Rua Trás do Forno 1; doubles €60-100)* is a beautifully restored, 17th-century Turihab manor house across the road from the turismo (behind the arched town hall).

There are four more Turismo Rural properties within 5km of town, including **Quinta da Prova** (*☎ 258 452 163; 2-/4-bed suites €60/100)* across the river. These, and others nearer the national park, can be booked through Adere-PG.

Places to Eat

Restaurante O Emigrante (*☎ 258 452 248; Rua António José Pereira 26; half-portions under €4; open daily)* offers meaty main dishes, cheery service and good value.

Pensão Restaurant Gomes (*☎ 258 452 288; Rua Conselheiro Rocha Peixoto 13; mains about €7-12)* offers lethargic service but decent regional fare, including *truta á Rio Lima* (river trout).

Entertainment
Bar Del Rio (☎ 933 959 509; *Margin do Lima; open daily June-Sept, Fri & Sat Oct-May*), a riverside café-bar during the day, operates indoors as a bar-club until the wee hours, with occasional live local music.

Getting There & Away
Arcos de Valdevez and Braga buses stop beside Restaurante Gomes in the old town, and up in the new town. Buses to/from Ponte de Lima and Viana do Castelo stop just west of the bridge on Rua Diogo Bernardes (N203).

AV Cura and Domingos da Cunha each run to Arcos de Valdevez (€0.70, 10 minutes), Ponte de Lima (€2, 40 minutes) and Viana do Castelo (€2.90, 1½ hours) four to five times daily. Renex/Salvador passes through Ponte da Barca about hourly, travelling between Braga (€2.50, one hour) and Arcos de Valdevez.

ARCOS DE VALDEVEZ
postcode 4970 • pop 2200 • elevation 200m
Arcos has two old churches and several stately homes in a small, almost tourist-free old centre. It has a pleasant setting on the west bank of the Rio Vez, a tributary of the Lima. It doesn't merit a special trip, but it's a handy gateway to the northern Parque Nacional da Peneda-Gerês.

Orientation & Information
The town centre is around Praça Municipal, a block uphill (west) from the turismo; the commercial centre is Largo da Lapa, two blocks on. Every other Wednesday is market day, alternating with Ponte da Barca.

The bus station is almost 1km north of the town centre, but regional buses will stop on request in front of the **turismo** (☎ 258 516 001, fax 258 516 007; *Campo do Transladário; open 9.30am-12.30pm & 2.30pm-6pm Mon-Sat April-Oct, 9am-12.30pm & 2.30pm-5.30pm Nov-Mar*), which is on the N101 just north of where it crosses the river.

An unhelpful **national park office** (☎ 258 515 338, fax 258 522 707; *Rua Tomás de Figueiredo; open 9am-12.30pm & 2pm-5.30pm Mon-Fri*) is two blocks west of the riverfront fountain.

Churches
To reach the churches from the turismo climb Rua AB Cerqueira for a block beyond Praça Municipal. Around to the right is the tiny, Romano-Gothic **Capela da Nossa Senhora da Conceição** (*Capela da Praça; Rua da Praça*), dating from the late 14th or early 15th century. Inside are bas-relief grave markers and a surviving fragment of once-rich frescoes. If it's closed, the Café Regional, opposite, has the key.

Carry on up to the oval, oddly pretty baroque **Igreja da Nossa Senhora da Lapa** (*Largo da Lapa*), as whitewashed in as it is out.

Places to Stay & Eat
Pensão Flôr do Minho (☎ 258 515 216; *Rua da Valeta 106-108; doubles with shared facilities around €30*) is the best budget option and is down behind Praça Municipal; take the lane along the left side of the Capela da Nossa Senhora da Conceição.

Residencial Tavares (☎ 258 516 253; *Largo da Lapa; doubles with bathroom & breakfast €37.50*), opposite the Igreja da Nossa Senhora da Lapa, is a tightly run place with well-kept rooms.

Residencial Dona Isabel (☎ 258 520 380, fax 258 520 389; *Rua Mário Júlio Almeida Costa; doubles/twins with breakfast €40/45*), on the roundabout opposite the N101 bridge, has modern rooms, spare and attractive.

Restaurante Floresta (☎ 258 515 163; *Rua Mário Júlio Almeida Costa; half-portions around €4; open daily*), a popular, no-frills place feeding the crowds at a frantic pace, has just a couple of daily specials and no menu. Go early or be ready to wait. It's beside the Residencial Dona Isabel.

Getting There & Away
Leaving town you can flag out-bound buses by the turismo and buy a ticket on board.

AV Cura (☎ 258 515 236) has at least eight daily services to Viana do Castelo (€2.90) via Ponte de Lima, with half of them going via Ponte da Barca, too. **Domingos da Cunha** (☎ 258 815 843) runs at least four times daily to Ponte da Barca (€0.70, 10 minutes) and Ponte de Lima (€2.10, 50 minutes). **Renex/Salvador** (☎ 258 521 504) runs via Ponte da Barca to Braga (€2.60, 1¼ hours) about hourly, and to Monção (€2.60, 45 minutes) six times daily. All services are reduced on weekends.

MINHO

Parque Nacional da Peneda-Gerês

The 703-sq-km Peneda-Gerês National Park was Portugal's first protected area, established in 1971 to safeguard not only natural riches but a rural way of life. The crescent-shaped park takes in four granite massifs: the Serra da Peneda, Serra do Soajo, Serra Amarela and Serra do Gerês. These cover northeastern Minho and a bit of Trás-os-Montes.

It's crossed by the Rio Lima (which rises in Spain) and almost dissected by the Rio Homem (which rises high in the park). Two other rivers help define its boundaries: the Laboreiro, between the Serra da Peneda and

Spain, and the Cávado, along the entire southeastern edge of the park. Five hydroelectric dams form reservoirs within the park, three of them on the Cávado.

In the outer part of the crescent are some 115 villages, totalling 15,000 people. The heights close to the Spanish border, especially in the Serra do Gerês where several peaks rise over 1500m, are almost free of human activity, other than the shifting of livestock to high pastures in summer. The park shares 80km of frontier with Spain's Orense province and embraces a corresponding Spanish reserve, Parque Natural Serra do Xures.

Peneda-Gerês, especially the accessible southern Serra do Gerês, offers good hiking as well as other sports, some attractive rural

accommodation and a window on a vanishing rural way of life. The main base is the spa town of Vila do Gerês (also called Caldas do Gerês – *caldas* means hot springs – but usually just Gerês). Portuguese day-trippers swarm up here on summer weekends, though they tend to stick to the main camping areas.

Information

Adere-PG *(Parque Nacional da Peneda-Gerês Regional Development Association;* ☎ *258 452 250;* w *www.adere-pg.org; Largo da Miserico \'rdia 10, Ponte da Barca; open 9am-12.30pm & 2.30pm-6pm Mon-Fri)*, an EU-assisted consultancy involved in culturally sensitive development in the region, is the best resource on the park. Materials available (all free at the time of writing, most in English and French translations) include pamphlets on the park's natural, architectural and human landscapes; brochures detailing village-to-village walks on marked trails; *Roteiro de Artesanato*, a guide-map to the region's artisans; and a booklet on park accommodation. Adere-PG is also the booking agent for a range of camp sites, shelters and rural houses in the park, and for a range of Turihab and Turihab-like programmes in the five *concelhos* (municipalities) covering the park. Don't confuse this with a similar but independent programme called Adere-Soajo (see under Soajo, later).

The next most useful are the municipal turismos at Gerês, Arcos de Valdevez and Ponte da Barca.

Least useful and user-friendly are the park information centres at Braga headquarters and Arcos de Valdevez, Gerês and Montalegre (see under those towns for details), and the **interpretive centres** *(open Mon-Fri)* at Lamas de Mouro and Mezio. These centres do, however, dispense free brochures on the park and on its reptiles, a multilingual park map (€2.60) indicating many roads and tracks but no trails, and Portuguese-language booklets detailing interpretive trails at Pitões das Júnias (€1.50) and Preguiça (free).

If you want topographical maps it's best to buy them in your home country or in Porto or Lisbon (see under Information for those cities in the relevant chapters), although the Cerdeira camp site at Campo do Gerês has a few maps (see under Campo do Gerês, later).

Flora & Fauna

The park has a striking diversity of climate, habitat and landscape, nourished by heavy rainfall (the Serra da Peneda gets more rain than anywhere else in Portugal). Sheltered valleys hold stands of white oak, arbutus, laurel and cork oak. Forests of black oak, English oak and holly give way at higher elevations to birch, yew and Scots pine, and in alpine areas to juniper and sandwort. In a small patch of the Serra do Gerês grows the Gerês iris, found nowhere else in the world. The upper reaches are blanketed in yellow gorse and purple heather in April and May.

In the more remote areas there are wolves, wild boar, foxes, badgers, polecats and otters, as well as roe deer and a few wild ponies. Closer to the ground are grass snakes and the occasional venomous black viper. Birds found here include red kites, buzzards, goshawks, golden eagles and several species of owl.

The park's best-known domestic animals are long-horned cattle (the mahogany-coloured *barrosã* and darker *cachena*), goats and sheep, and the sturdy Castro Laboreiro sheepdog.

Protected Areas

Peneda-Gerês can call itself a national park because it meets certain conditions of the World Conservation Union (IUCN), particularly the presence of valuable and reasonably undisturbed ecosystems, which the government has taken steps to protect.

The park has a high-elevation inner zone, partly set aside for research and closed to the public, and an outer buffer zone, where development is strictly controlled. Most villages, roads, tracks and trails are in the latter area.

The most assiduously protected area is a virgin oak, chestnut and mistletoe forest called the Mata de Albergaria, north of Gerês. Ironically, it's crossed by the N308 highway, which, because it serves an EU-appointed border crossing, cannot simply be closed. Satisfying both the IUCN and the EU keeps park officials awake at night.

On a 6km stretch of road above Gerês, from the 862m Portela de Leonte pass to the border at 757m Portela do Homem, motorised traffic is tolerated but forbidden to linger. At checkpoints at either end, drivers get time-stamped tickets and have 15 minutes

MINHO

to turn them in at the other end. This stretch is patrolled daily from July to September and at weekends the rest of the year. Two side roads are also no-go areas for vehicles: southwest down the Rio Homem valley (except for residents) and east from Portela do Homem into the high Serra do Gerês.

Rules on camping – essentially that you can only use designated sites – are strictly enforced in trafficked areas, and park rangers are more like police than the cheerful helpers you might expect. Limits on walking are tied to those on camping: if you can't get to a designated camp site you're expected to come back out.

There are also restrictions on boats in the park's *albufeiras* (reservoirs): motorised boats are allowed on the Caniçada; only electric motors on the Lindoso; only non-motorised boats on the Salamonde; and no boats at all on the Vilarinho das Furnas and Paradela. Even swimming is prohibited in the Vilarinho das Furnas.

Traditional Culture

Many of the park's oldest villages remain in a time warp, with oxen trundled down cobbled streets by black-clad old women, and horses shod in smoky blacksmith shops. The practice of moving livestock, and even entire villages, to high pasture for up to five months still goes on in the Serra da Peneda and Serra do Gerês.

Despite the founding of the park, and other government and private efforts, this rustic scene is fading away as young people head for the cities. Village populations are shrinking, and an astonishing 75% of local people are over 65. The road between Cabril and Paradela, for example, reveals a deeply ironic picture – a string of sparsely populated, decaying villages, surrounded by grand scenery, fertile soil, pristine air and clean water.

Tourism may turn out to be a friend of tradition, with entrepreneurs restoring old buildings as rustic accommodation (see Places to Stay, later in this section). But it's an uphill battle: the spruced-up village of Sirvozelo near Paradela, for example, has less than a dozen permanent residents left.

Megaliths

There are Stone Age dolmens and *antas* (megaliths) on the high plateaus of the Serra da Peneda and Serra do Gerês, near Castro

Laboreiro, Mezio, Paradela, Pitões das Júnias and Tourém. For details see Adere-PG's free *Megalith* brochure. For more on Portugal's ancient stone monuments see the boxed text 'Dolmens, Menhirs & Other Mysteries' in The Alentejo chapter.

Activities

Local outfits long involved in the park's outdoor activities are:

AML (Água Montanha Lazer; ☎ 253 391 779, 968 021 142, **W** www.aguamontanha.com) Lugar de Paredes, 4845-024 Rio Caldo
PlanAlto (☎ 253 351 005, 917 540 903, **e** rafaelima@clix.pt) Parque de Campismo de Cerdeira, Campo do Gerês, 4840-030 Terras de Bouro
Trote-Gerês (☎/fax 253 659 860, 253 659 930, **e** trote_geres@hotmail.com) Parque de Campismo Outeiro Alto, Eiredo, 5470-013 Cabril

Scenery, crisp air and the rural panorama make **walking** a pleasure in Peneda-Gerês. Although the park administration has abandoned plans to establish a network of long trails, Adere-PG has pioneered several fine, marked loop trails from 4km to 9km, described in free brochures available at its Ponte da Barca office.

Day walks around Vila do Gerês are popular but crowded; see that section, later, for details. PlanAlto has marked some good loop trails in the Campo do Gerês area and produced maps for them (see under Campo do Gerês), and organises interpretive walks. Trote-Gerês offers guided walks for €20/ 12.50 per person per day with/without lunch.

Elsewhere in the park there's a certain amount of dead reckoning involved, although tracks of some kind (animal or vehicle) are everywhere in the populated buffer zone, nearly all within a half-day's walk of a settlement or a main road.

Two useful books setting out routes in the park are *Walking in Portugal* and *Landscapes of Portugal*; see Books in the Facts for the Visitor chapter.

If you're keen on **mountain biking**, bikes can be hired from PlanAlto for €7.50/12.50 per half/full day.

The only places for **water sports** are the park's reservoirs. Rio Caldo, 8km south of Gerês, is the base for the Albufeira da Caniçada; AML rents out single/double kayaks for €3.50/6 for the first hour, plus pedal boats, rowboats and small motor boats. They'll also take you water-skiing.

For paddling the Albufeira de Salamonde, Trote-Gerês rents two-/three-person canoes for €6/7 per hour or €30/37.50 per day.

For **horse riding**, Trote-Gerês offers hire (€12.50 per hour, €50 per day) and lessons (€22.50 per hour), and can organise excursions. The park operates riding facilities beside the Vidoeiro camp site near Gerês.

Places to Stay

Camp sites include basic park-run sites at Entre Ambos-os-Rios and Vidoeiro (open at least from mid-May to September) and private sites at Campo do Gerês and Cabril. Campo do Gerês has a youth hostel. For private rooms, ask at 'gateway' turismos.

You can book a restored house in Soajo or Lindoso (see those sections) under a programme called Turismo de Aldeia (Village Tourism); or around Arcos de Valdevez or Ponte da Barca under Adere-PG's Casas Antigas e Rústicas (Traditional & Rural Houses) programme. Prices for two start at about €40. Adere-PG manages 10 rustic, self-catering *casas de abrigo* (shelter-houses) with four doubles in each. They're great value at €65 per night, but as these must be rented in full they're impractical for individuals.

Gerês has many *pensões*, though they tend to fill up quickly in summer; booking ahead is a good idea. These and other options are noted under individual towns in this section.

Shopping

Local honey is on sale everywhere. The best – unpasteurised, unadulterated and with a faint piney taste – is from small dealers; look for signs on private homes.

Getting There & Around

Bus From Braga there are daily buses to Rio Caldo, Vila do Gerês, Campo do Gerês and, via Arcos de Valdevez, to Soajo and Lindoso. A few run on weekdays to Paradela from Montalegre in Trás-os-Montes. See the respective towns for details.

No public buses operate within the park, though **Agência no Gerês** (☎ 253 391 141; *Hotel Universal, Gerês*) organises 2¼ to 5¼ hour minibus park tours for €5 to €10 per person (minimum eight people).

Car & Motorcycle There are entry roads at Lamas de Mouro (from Monção), Mezio (from Arcos de Valdevez), Entre Ambos-os-Rios (from Ponte de Lima and Ponte da Barca), Covide, Rio Caldo and Salamonde (from Braga), and Sezelhe, Paradela and Vila Nova (from Montalegre). Four roads cross the (unstaffed) border from Spain. There's no practical way to travel between the Peneda and Gerês sections of the park, except from outside of it – most conveniently via Spain.

Note: the back roads can be axle-breakers, even when maps suggest otherwise.

SOAJO

postcode 4970 • pop 500 • elevation 300m

Sturdy, remote Soajo (pronounced soo-**ahzh**-oo), high above the upper Rio Lima, is best known for its photogenic *espigueiros*, or stone granaries (see the boxed text). Thanks to village enterprise and the Turismo de Aldeia programme, you can stay in one of Soajo's restored stone houses and look out onto a vanishing way of life. Indeed the programme has succeeded so well that the place is overrun with visitors in July and August.

Orientation & Information

Soajo is 21km northeast of Ponte da Barca on the N203 and N530, or the same distance

Espigueiros

These huge slatted-granite caskets on stilts were used in the 18th and 19th centuries for storing maize or winnowed grain and protecting it from rats – and many are still in use. In clusters above their villages, grizzled with moss and topped with little crosses, they look like miniature cathedrals, or giants' tombs. The brass-belled, long-horned cows grazing around them, and the washing lines tied to them, do little to dispel their eerie appearance.

MINHO

from Arcos via the scenic N202 and N304. Buses stop by Restaurante Videira at the intersection of these two roads. A few hundred metres down the N530 towards Lindoso are Soajo's trademark *espigueiros*.

The **Turismo de Aldeia office** *(Adere-Soajo; ☎/fax 258 576 427;* e *turismo.adere-soajo@ sapo.pt; Larga da Cardeira, Bairros; open 9am-noon & 2pm-7pm Mon-Fri, 9am-1pm Sat)* is the village's de facto turismo; follow the signs west from the bus stop for 150m. Here you can book a room (see Places to Stay), get tips on good walks and pick up a schematic map of the region.

Adere-PG (no relation to Adere-Soajo; see Information at the start of this Parque Nacional da Peneda-Gerês section) has its own detailed free booklet on every aspect of visiting Soajo and Lindoso.

Soajo's small main square, Largo do Eiró – with a *pelourinho* topped by what can only be an ancient smiley face – is down a lane in the opposite direction from the bus stop. There's a bank with an ATM below the parish council office, off the far side of the square.

Walking

Soajo is filled with the sound of rushing water, a resource painstakingly managed over the centuries. A steep walk above the village provides a glimpse of how important these streams once were.

On the N304, 250m north of the bus stop, is a roofed pool for communal laundry. At a 'T' on the track directly behind it, turn left and immediately right. A path paved with immense stones and grooved by centuries of oxcart traffic climbs though a landscape intensely shaped by agriculture, past granite houses, *espigueiros* and superb views. Further up are three derelict **water mills** – probably abandoned within the lives of Soajo's older citizens – for grinding corn; stone channels that once funnelled the stream from one mill to the next; and the reservoir that fed them. This much takes half an hour.

Above here a network of paths, easy to lose and often overgrown, leads to more mills and the abandoned **Branda da Portelinha**. (A *branda* was a settlement of summer houses for villagers, who drove their livestock to high pastures and lived with them all summer.) Ask at the Turismo de Aldeia office for advice.

Another walk, a steep two-hour round-trip, takes you down to the **Ponte da Ladeira**, a simple medieval bridge. The path drops down to the right from the Lindoso road, about 150m down from the *espigueiros*; then fork to the right further down.

Places to Stay

Eleven **village houses** *(for 2/8 people €40/160)* are available for tourist accommodation under the Turismo de Aldeia scheme. Each has a fireplace or stove (with firewood in winter) and a kitchen stocked with breakfast food, including fresh bread on the doorstep each morning. Stays of more than one night are preferred at the weekend. These houses are best booked here at Soajo, though you can also book through Adere-PG in Ponte da Barca.

Another available house, not in the scheme, is **Casa do Adro** *(☎/fax 258 576 327; rooms with bathroom & breakfast €42, minimum 3-night stay July & Aug)*, off Largo do Eiró by the parish church.

Places to Eat

There are two good restaurants, both on the pricey side.

Restaurante Videira *(☎ 258 576 205; mains €7-10; open lunch Thur-Tues)*, by the bus stop, has the cheerier setting and more authentic regional snacks such as ham, sausage and *pataiscas* (fish fritters).

Restaurante Espigueiro de Soajo *(☎ 258 576 136; mains €8-10, half-portions from €5; open Tues-Sun)*, north of the centre on the N304, has taciturn service but good food.

Soajo also has several cafés and a *mini-mercado* (grocery shop), all found near the bus stop.

Getting There & Away

Salvador buses to Soajo (€1.80, 45 minutes) depart from Arcos de Valdevez at 5.45pm weekdays, plus 12.20pm Monday and Friday. They return at 7.40am weekdays, plus 1.20pm Monday and Friday. A taxi from Arcos costs about €13; for a Soajo taxi, ring ☎ 933 235 360.

LINDOSO

postcode 4980 • pop 525 • elevation 380m
Lindoso (pronounced leen-**doze**-oo), across the Rio Minho from Soajo, offers a peek at what Soajo may have looked like before the

tourist money rolled in – more lived-in and less prosperous, with chickens pecking on the paths, houses in an unsteady equilibrium between repair and decay, and cows tethered at their doors. People still keep warm at night by living upstairs from their animals.

The village, and a cluster of *espigueiros*, sit at the foot of a small, restored **castle** *(adult/child €2/free; open at least 10am-noon & 2.30pm-5pm Tues-Sun, closes 30-60min earlier Oct-Mar)* founded in the 13th century by Afonso III. Beefed up by Dom Dinis, it was occupied by the Spanish in 1662–64 and used as a military garrison until 1895. Now it's 'garrisoned' by the national park, with an overpriced, poorly captioned exhibit on the castle and the village, and unreliable hours.

Places to Stay & Eat
Lindoso has at least half a dozen restored village houses, with prices similar to those in Soajo. These must be booked through Adere-PG in Ponte da Barca.

Restaurante Lindoverde *(☎ 258 578 010; open daily)*, on the N304-1 about 900m east of the turning to the village, also does duty as a café-bar and disco. Several cafés lurk at the village turning.

Getting There & Away
Salvador buses run to Lindoso on weekdays from Arcos (€2.30, one hour, departing about noon and 6.15pm) via Ponte da Barca (€2.20, departing five to 10 minutes later), and returning from Lindoso about 7.30am and 1.20pm.

VILA DO GERÊS
postcode 4845 • pop 800 • elevation 350m
If the Gerês end of the national park has a 'centre', it's the somnolent spa town of Vila do Gerês (also known as Caldas do Gerês, though usually just called Gerês and pronounced zh-**resh**), wedged into the valley of the Rio Gerês. The spa and many, but not all, *pensões* close from October to April.

Orientation & Information
The town is built on an elongated, one-way loop of road, with the *balneário* (spa centre) in the pink buildings in the middle. The original hot spring, some baths and the turismo are in the staid colonnade at the northern end. Buses stop on Avenida Manuel F

Costa, just south of the *balneário*, opposite the Universal and Termas hotels.

The **turismo** *(☎ 253 391 133, fax 253 391 282; open 9.30am-12.30pm & 2.30pm-6pm Mon-Fri, 9.30am-12.30pm Sat year-round; also afternoon Sat, morning Sun July & Aug)* is in the colonnade. A block uphill is the **park office** *(☎ 253 390 110; open 9am-1pm & 2pm-6pm Mon-Fri)*.

The **post office** *(open 9am-12.30pm & 2pm-5.30pm Mon-Fri)* is by the roundabout at the southern end of the village. There are two banks with ATMs on Avenida Manuel F Costa.

Walking
Miradouro Walk About 1km up the N308 is a picnic site, which is the start of a short, popular stroll with good views to the south.

Gerês Valley A park-maintained loop trail, the **Trilho da Preguiça**, starts on the N308 about 3km above Gerês, by a lone white house, the Casa da Preguiça. For 5km it rollercoasters through the valley's oak forests. A free, Portuguese-language brochure about the walk can be obtained from the park office. You can also carry on – or hitch or take a taxi up the N308 – to the **Portela de Leonte**, 6km from Gerês.

Further on, where the Rio Homem crosses the road (10km above Gerês), a walk east up the river takes you to a picturesque **waterfall**.

Next Exit Vilarinho das Furnas

A 320km Roman military road once ran up the valley of the Rio Homem and over the mountains here, between Braga and Astorga (in Spain). A 2km stretch – now with World Heritage status – is still visible along the southern side of the Albufeira de Vilarinho das Furnas. The park publishes a detailed, somewhat technical Portuguese-language booklet (€4.50) on this stretch.

Milestones – each inscribed with its position and the name of the emperor during whose rule it was erected – remain at miles XXIX, XXX and XXXI; the nearest one to Campo do Gerês is about 1km above the camp site there. Others have been haphazardly collected at the Portela do Homem border post, 13km from Gerês.

❀ ◉ ◎ ◉ ❀ ◉ ◎ ◉ ❀ ◉ ◎ ◉ ❀ ◉ ◎ ◉ ❀

MINHO

(See under Protected Areas, earlier in this section, for driving and parking restrictions in the Mata de Albergaria.)

An 8km walk goes southwest from the Mata de Albergaria along the Rio Homem and the Albufeira de Vilarinho das Furnas to Campo do Gerês. This route takes you along part of an ancient **Roman road** (see the boxed text 'Next Exit Vilarinho das Furnas'). Swimming is not permitted in the reservoir.

Trilho da Calcedónia A narrow, sealed road snakes over the ridge from Vila do Gerês to Campo do Gerês, offering short but spectacular, high-elevation walks from just about anywhere along its upper reaches. One of these walks is an easy, Adere-PG–signposted, 3km (two-hour) loop that climbs a 912m **viewpoint** called the Cabeço Calcedónia, with views to knock your socks off.

The road is easy to find from Campo but trickier from Gerês; the turning is about 700m up the old Portelo do Homem road from Pensão Adelaide.

Ermida & Fafião From the picnic site above Gerês (see the preceding Miradouro Walk) a dirt road runs 11km southeast to Ermida, a village of smallholdings and sturdy stone houses that cling to the steep hillsides. **Casa do Criado** (*☎ 253 391 390; Ermida; doubles with breakfast €25, half-board €40*) has plain rooms (book ahead) and a simple restaurant. The village also has **private rooms** (*around €20*), several cafés and a *minimercado*. Walkers can also continue east for 6km to Fafião village, which has rooms and a café or two.

From Fafião it's a steep 5km south on a sealed road across the Salamonde dam and up to the N103, where nearby Salamonde village is a stop for Braga–Chaves buses. A **taxi** (*in Salamonde ☎ 253 658 281*) between Fafião and Salamonde costs about €4.

You can drive to Ermida on a 7km sealed road from the N308 at Vilar de Veiga, and to Fafião from Salamonde, but the Ermida–Fafião road is *not* suitable for cars.

Balneário
At the spa (*open 8am-noon & 3.20pm-6pm Mon-Sat*) you can drink the water, or soak in it at various temperatures. Tourists are welcome for one-off visits; buy a ticket at the entrance to the *balneário*, 150m south of

the turismo. A sauna or steam bath costs about €6, a full massage €18.

Places to Stay
Private rooms are available in summer for around €25 per double; owners often approach travellers at the bus stop or around town. Gerês also has plenty of *pensões*, though in summer you may find some block-booked for spa patients. Others may fill up a month or more ahead, so advance reservations are wise. Outside July and August, on the other hand, prices drop and bargaining is in order.

Camping About 1km north of Gerês is **Parque de Campismo de Vidoeiro** (*☎ 253 391 289; e aderepg@mail.telepac.pt; Vidoeiro; person/car €2/2.20; open mid-May–mid-Oct*), a spartan but comfortable park-run facility. You can book ahead through Adere-PG.

Pensões & Residenciais By the park office you'll find **Pensão Baltazar** (*☎ 253 392 058, fax 253 392 057; N308; doubles from €50*), a sober, family-run place, with newly renovated rooms and a popular restaurant.

Pensão da Ponte (*☎ 253 391 121; Rua da Boa Vista; doubles with/without bathroom €40/30*) is the only place with personality, complete with erratic plumbing, sloping floors and a faintly *Addams Family* atmosphere. Its very plain rooms, many overlooking the roaring river, are fairly good value.

Along Rua da Arnassó there are another half-dozen places, all with TV, private bathroom, breakfast, parking and something passing for a restaurant. Not all stay open year-round.

Residencial Carvalho Araújo (*☎ 253 391 185, fax 253 391 225; doubles €57; open year-round*), a welcoming place near the bottom, wins for decor with its bright, attractive rooms.

Pensão Adelaide (*☎ 253 390 020, fax 253 390 029; doubles from €40; open year-round*), the big place at the top, wins for value and has a pretty decent restaurant.

There are more *pensões* at the lower (southern) end of town.

At the **Hotel Universal** (*☎ 253 391 141/3/4, fax 253 391 102; Avenida Manuel F Costa*) and the stodgier **Termas** (*☎ 253 391 141/3/4, fax 253 391 102*) next door, deluxe doubles cost €72.50 in August. For this you also get to use the swimming pool, tennis courts and snooker hall.

Places to Eat

It may come as a surprise in Portugal to find restaurants already crowded at 11.30am and again at 6.30pm, with customers washing down huge meals with water. Don't worry, they're all spa patients, on a spa regimen.

Pensão Baltazar (N308; mains €7-10, half-portions €5-6; open daily) has Gerês' best-value restaurant. This family-run place is always busy, and its small menu always includes one daily regional special. The fare is meaty, and bland enough to keep the spa patients happy, but with *lots* of vegetables. The helpings are huge, even on the half-portions.

Most other *pensões* do equally hearty, equally unadventurous meals, which are also available to nonguests. The restaurant at **Pensão Adelaide** (mains €8-11; open daily) pulls the biggest crowds.

Restaurante Lurdes Capela (☎ 253 391 208; Avenida Manuel F Costa; dishes €5-9; open daily), a modest, family-run eatery at the bottom of the village, offers good-value regional fare.

Getting There & Away

Empresa Hoteleira do Gerês (☎ 253 391 141) operates 10 buses a day (fewer at weekends) from Braga to Gerês (€2.90, 1½ hours).

CAMPO DO GERÊS

postcode 4840 • pop 150 • elevation 690m

Campo do Gerês (called São João do Campo on some maps, and just Campo by nearly everybody) is barely more than a hamlet, near the Albufeira de Vilarinho das Furnas. The youth hostel and camp site here make excellent hiking bases.

Orientation & Information

The Braga bus stops by the Museu Etno-gráfico, on the main road, then continues 1.5km on to the village centre. The youth hostel is 1km up a side road from the museum. About 200m before the town centre, the road to the dam branches right, with the camp site about 700m along it.

Vilarinho das Furnas & Museu Etnográfico

Vilarinho das Furnas was a remarkable democratic community, with a well-organised communal life, shared property and decisions made by consensus. Even under Salazar it maintained its principled, independent way of life. But the village was submerged when the reservoir was created in 1972, and its people were relocated. In summer when the reservoir level falls, the empty village walls rise like spectres from the water and the near shore.

In anticipation of the end of their old way of life, villagers donated many articles for a proposed memorial. These have been fashioned into a rather touching ethnographic museum (☎ 253 351 888; adult/child under 16 €0.60/free; open 8.30am-noon & 2pm-5pm Tues-Fri, 10am-noon & 2pm-5pm Sat & Sun), where the Campo road forks to the youth hostel. Unfortunately the many quotations about the lost village from Portuguese writers of the day are only in Portuguese.

This is a recommended stop before you visit the spooky remains of the village, about 2.5km beyond the dam, which is a comfortable three-hour return hike from Campo or the camp site.

Other Attractions

PlanAlto, based at the Parque Campismo de Cerdeira, has marked three loop trails around Campo do Gerês, lasting from two to five hours, and printed its own walking/orienteering maps (€1.50); also on hand are a few military topo sheets (€7.50). Among its activities are interpretive walks (including the collection of medicinal plants), tree plantings, traditional games, a mountain-fitness circuit and orienteering competitions. The camp site itself has programmes linked to local festivals, such as Desfolhada Minhota (the harvest festival) in October and Matança do Porco (a communal pork meal and other events) in January.

Places to Stay & Eat

Parque Campismo de Cerdeira (☎ 253 351 005; e parque.cerdeira@portugalmail.pt; adult/car €4/3.50, tent €3-4.50, 2-/4-person bungalows with kitchenette €53/73; open year-round) has oak-shaded sites, a laundry, minimercado and a good restaurant. You might be asked for a CCI in July or August; this camping card is good for a 10% discount in July and August, 15% the rest of the year. Booking ahead is definitely recommended.

MINHO

Restaurante Cerdeira (☎ *253 357 065; open daily; mains €6-10)*, the camp site's good restaurant, offers carefully prepared local specialities such *bersame* (a pork-and-vegetable stew) at mid-range prices, plus salads, omelettes, burgers and snacks.

Pousada da Juventude de Vilarinho das Furnas (☎ *253 351 339;* e *vilarinho@movijovem.pt; dorm beds €9.50, doubles with/without toilet €26.50/24)*, Campo's sprawling hostel, began life as a dam workers' camp. Book ahead if you can.

The road to Cerdeira is lined with signs advertising **houses** *(for 4 people €40-50)* and rooms for rent.

Albergaria Stop (☎ *253 350 040, fax 253 350 047; doubles with bathroom & breakfast €50)*, smart and renovated, and with a pool and tennis court, is near the turn-off for the camp site.

Getting There & Away
From Braga, **REDM** (☎ *253 616 080)* has seven daily buses (€2.80, 1½ hours; fewer at weekends), stopping at the museum crossroad and the village centre.

RIO CALDO
postcode 4845 • pop 1000 • elevation 160m
Just inside the park on the Albufeira de Caniçada, Rio Caldo is little more than a base for water sports on the reservoir.

English-run **AML** *(Água Montanha Lazer;* ☎ *253 391 779, 968 021 142;* w *www.aguamontanha.com; Lugar de Paredes)* is the place to go for boat activities and rental. The shop is 100m from the N304 roundabout, but at weekends and most summer days you're more likely to find them by the water on the other side of the bridge to Gerês. AML also has several local **houses** *(for 4/9 people €55/110)* for rent.

EASTERN PENEDA-GERÊS
Cabril, on the eastern limb of the national park, and Montalegre, just outside it, are actually in Trás-os-Montes, but are included here for continuity. You're unlikely to visit unless you're coming in or out of the park.

Cabril
postcode 5470 • pop 700 • elevation 400m
Though it hardly looks the part, peaceful Cabril – set with its outlying hamlets in a wide, fertile bowl – is the administrative

centre of Portugal's biggest *freguesia* (parish), stretching from Fafião to Lapela and up to the Spanish border.

What to do? Chill out, ride a horse, paddle a canoe or walk – all courtesy of **Trote-Gerês** (☎/fax *253 659 860, 253 659 930,* e *trote_geres@hotmail.com)* at Cabril's Outeiro Alto camp site.

Orientation & Information The reference point is Largo do Cruzeiro, with its old *pelourinho*. To one side is the little Igreja de São Lourenço, said to have been moved five centuries ago, brick by brick, by villagers of nearby São Lourenço in search of a more propitious locale. Some 400m southwest is a bridge over an arm of the Albufeira de Salamonde.

Places to Stay & Eat Over the bridge and 800m up the Pincães road is **Parque de Campismo Outeiro Alto** (☎/fax *253 659 860; Eiredo; person/small tent €2.50/2.50; open year-round)*. This woodland facility has 45 small tent sites and a patch for caravans, hot showers, a café-bar and an adjacent riding centre. Try to book a few weeks ahead in summer.

There are some rooms available in the village: **Café Águia Real** (☎ *253 659 752)* is 300m up the Paradela road and has doubles without/with bathroom for €15/20 and a two-bed apartment with kitchenette for €40. The café does light meals and carries on in the evening as a bar.

Trote-Gerês manages two **stone houses** *(bookings* ☎ *276 566 165, fax 253 659 930; €45)*, each with a double bed, kitchen, fireplace and firewood, in the restored village of Sirvozelo, 15km northeast of Cabril. It also manages the **Pousadinha de Paradela** *(doubles with/without bathroom €30/25)*, a cottage 3.5km further on at Paradela (breakfast included; other meals by arrangement).

Restaurante Ponte Nova (☎ *253 659 882; half-portions €3-4; open daily)*, by the bridge, does trout, *cabrito* (kid), *vitela assada* (roast veal) and other specials, from a verbal menu.

Getting There & Away There are no buses to Cabril. The best option if you're not driving is to get off any Braga–Montalegre or Braga–Chaves bus at Salamonde and take a **taxi** (☎ *253 658 281, or ask at Restaurante*

MINHO

Retiro da Cabreira), which will cost about €13. Drivers can cross into the park from the N103 via the Salamonde dam; a longer but more scenic route is via the Venda Nova dam, 14km east of Salamonde at Cambedo.

Montalegre
postcode 5470 • pop 1822
• elevation 1000m

You're unlikely to visit Montalegre unless you're en route between Chaves and the national park. Presiding over the town and the surrounding plains is a small, partially restored castle, part of Dom Dinis' 14th-century necklace of frontier outposts. The future Duke of Wellington rested in the castle after chasing the French from Porto.

This is *terra fria* (the cold country), with wide seasonal contrasts and long, harsh winters.

Orientation & Information
From the bus station it's 500m west on Rua General Humberto Delgado to a five-way roundabout, beside which you'll find the town hall and the **turismo** (☎ 276 511 010, fax 276 510 201; open 9am-12.30pm & 2pm-5.30pm daily June-Sept, 9am-12.30pm & 2pm-5.30pm Mon-Fri Oct-May).

There's a gruff **park information office** (☎ 276 512 281; Rua do Reigoso 17; open 9am-12.30pm & 2pm-5.30pm Mon-Fri) two blocks north beyond the town hall on Rua Direita, then right at the *pelourinho*.

Several banks around the *câmara municipal* have ATMs. The **post office** (open 9am-12.30pm & 2pm-5.30pm Mon-Fri) is 400m northeast of the roundabout down Avenida Dom Nuno Álvares Pereira.

Places to Stay & Eat
On the Braga road, 300m south of the roundabout, **Residencial Fidalgo** (☎ 276 512 462; Rua da Corujeira 34; doubles €30) is not generous with the heating but has big and comfortable rooms. Insist on one facing away from the traffic.

Quality Inn Montalegre (☎ 276 510 220; e reservas@quality.pt; Rua do Avelar 2; doubles with breakfast €65), just southwest of the roundabout, has air-con rooms, each with satellite TV. It also has a swimming pool.

Restaurante Floresta (☎ 276 512 420; Rua da Corujeira 42; mains €5-7; open Sun-Fri), an earnest, friendly eatery 500m up the Braga road, does good Portuguese standard fare.

Opposite the park office is the unexceptional **Café-Restaurante Ricotero** (☎ 276 512 122; Rua do Reigoso; mains €5; open daily). Across the road is **Pizzaria Cantinho** (☎ 276 511 095; open daily).

Getting There & Away
There are **REDM/AV Tâmega** (☎ 276 512 131) services stopping at Montalegre en route between Braga (€4.60, 2¼ hours) and Chaves (€3.60, 1¼ hours) six times each weekday, and less often at weekends. Change at Chaves for Bragança, Vila Real or Porto.

Trás-os-Montes

Portugal's northeastern province is largely ignored, even by Portuguese travellers, who consider it too far, too uncomfortable, too backward, perhaps even too pagan. Trás-os-Montes (pronounced trahsh-oosh-**montsh**) means 'beyond the mountains', and indeed the Gerês, Alvão and Marão mountain ranges make it feel more walled out than walled in.

The name implies more than geographical isolation. Here the climate tends to extremes too: the north is a *terra fria* (cold land) where winter temperatures may drop to freezing for months at a time, and the south, towards the Alto Douro, is a *terra quente* (hot land) where searing summers ripen olives, almonds, chestnuts, fruit, rye and the port-wine grapes of the Douro and Tua valleys.

Isolation and harsh conditions have bred a culture of rock-solid self-reliance, laced with mysterious practices and beliefs (eg, see the boxed text 'Devils in Disguise' in the Eastern Trás-os-Montes section). In this vast province – almost twice the size of the Minho but with less than half the population – there are still villages that European Union (EU) funds have failed to find and where farmers struggle to make ends meet, plough their fields with oxen and live with their hens, pigs and donkeys in the humblest of granite cottages. Few places in Europe offer such a sense of remoteness.

Getting to the major cities of Vila Real, Chaves, Bragança, and Miranda do Douro is no longer a problem, thanks to the IP4/E82 motorway, long-haul bus services and even trains: from the Douro valley the narrow-gauge Linha da Corgo runs to Vila Real and the Linha da Tua to Mirandela. But while these cities make useful bases and have a few unique attractions, it's the smaller villages that will stick in your memory. To reach these you'll need time and patience – local bus services often disappear entirely at weekends and outside school terms – or your own transport.

And beyond rural Trás-os-Montes you can glimpse some near-wilderness. The Parque Natural do Douro Internacional, safeguarding the deep canyon of the upper Rio Douro where it defines the border with

Highlights

- Stroll across Chaves' Roman bridge, still taking traffic after 1900 years
- Cool off in a tunnel of trees behind the Vila Real mansion pictured on the label of Mateus rosé wine
- Let your imagination go in Bragança's lofty *cidadela*, and ponder why pigs were once honoured with statues
- Ride a bike over the gentle, faraway hills of the Parque Natural de Montesinho
- Spend a few peaceful hours in Rio de Onor – half-Portuguese, half-Spanish, but in a world of its own

Spain, is Portugal's second-largest protected area (after Serra da Estrela) and probably the best place in the country to see large birds of prey.

Walkers will like the province's two other *parques naturais* – Alvão, near Vila Real, and Montesinho, near Bragança. Neither has as many facilities or trails as Peneda-Gerês, but neither sees any crowds either. If serious walking is on your mind, talk to staff at park offices in Vila Real and Bragança first.

A few of the province's middle Douro valley towns are covered in the Douro chapter. Montalegre and some villages within the Parque Nacional da Peneda-Gerês are included in the Minho chapter.

Western Trás-os-Montes

VILA REAL

postcode 5000 • pop 24,500
• elevation 445m

Above the confluence of the Rio Corgo and Rio Cabril sits the district capital, Vila Real, a university and industrial town with a population that swells by 40% during the academic year. Cultural attractions are few aside from the Palácio de Mateus. But this is a transport hub, and a springboard into the underrated hills of the Serra do Marão and Serra de Alvão, with parts of the latter comprising the Parque Natural do Alvão.

Orientation

Accommodation and food options cluster around the axis of Avenida Carvalho Araújo. To the turismo it's about 1km across the Rio Corgo from the train station, about 400m from the bus stand for AV Tâmega, Rede Expressos and Santos buses, and 300m from the Rodonorte bus station on Rua Dom Pedro de Castro.

Information

The **regional turismo** (☎ 259 322 819; [e] *turismarao@mail.telepac.pt*; *Avenida Carvalho Araújo 94*; open 9.30am-12.30pm & 2pm-5pm Mon-Sat Oct-Mar; to 7pm Mon-Fri, to 6pm Sat & Sun Apr-Sept*) is in a Manueline-designed headquarters in the town centre.

The **Parque Natural do Alvão office** (☎ 259 302 830; [e] *pnal@icn.pt*; *Largo dos Freitas*; open 9am-12.30pm & 2pm-5.30pm Mon-Fri*) is just behind the *câmara municipal* (town hall).

ATMs are numerous in the centre; one is near the turismo. The **post office** (*Avenida Carvalho Araújo*; open 8.30am-6pm Mon-Fri, 9am-12.30pm Sat*) is opposite the turismo.

The **Instituto Português da Juventude** (☎ 259 309 640; *Rua Dr Manuel Cardona*; open Mon-Fri*), upstairs from the *pousada da juventude* (youth hostel; see Places to Stay), has free Internet access; enter at the back of the building. There's also an Internet café behind it, the **Triplé Café** (*Rua Poeta Alberto Miranda 17*; open Mon-Sat*)

The **Hospital de São Pedro** (☎ 259 300 500; *Lordelo*) is 2km northwest of the centre. The **police station** (☎ 259 322 022; *Largo*

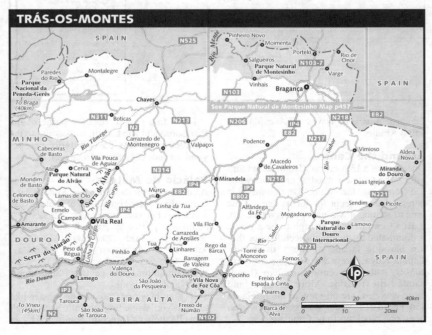

TRÁS-OS-MONTES

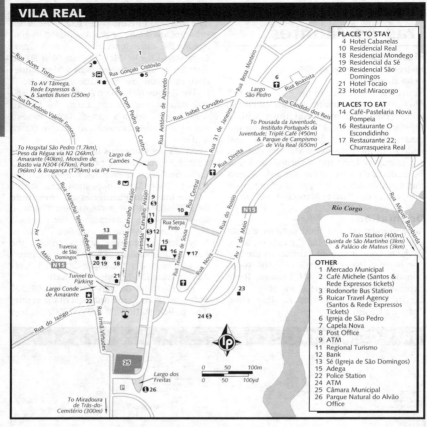

VILA REAL

Conde de Amarante) is west off Avenida Carvalho Araújo.

Around the Centre

Once part of a 15th-century Dominican monastery, the Gothic cathedral or **sé** *(Igreja de São Domingos; Travessa de São Domingos)* is unremarkable except for for its age. At the time of writing it was undergoing a face-lift.

Rua Central, wide enough to be a plaza, is dominated by the magnificently over-the-top baroque facade of the 17th-century **Capela Nova** *(Igreja dos Clérigos; closed to public)*, with 18th-century *azulejos* (hand-painted tiles) inside. More baroque, and more azulejos, are on view at the **Igreja de São Pedro** *(Largo de São Pedro; admission free)*, one block north of Capela Nova.

For a fine view across the gorge of the Rio Corgo and Rio Cabril, walk south to the **Miradouro de Trás-do-Cemitério**, just beyond a small cemetery and chapel.

Palácio de Mateus

Also known as the Solar de Mateus, and famously depicted on bottles of Mateus rosé wine, this baroque creation *(☎ 259 323 121; admission palace & gardens €6, gardens €3.50; open 9am-7.30pm daily June-Sept, 9am-1pm & 2pm-6pm Oct & Mar-May, 10am-1pm & 2pm-5pm Nov-Feb)* is the work of the ubiquitous 18th-century Italian architect Nicolau Nasoni.

Its granite wings ('advancing lobster-like towards you' wrote English critic Sacheverell Sitwell) shelter a forecourt dominated by an ornate balustraded stairway and overlooked by rooftop statues. Behind the palace is an Alice-in-Wonderland garden of tiny box hedges, prim statues and a fragrant cypress tunnel. Inside you can visit just a few rooms, heavy with velvet drapes and fussy period furnishings, though the price is exorbitant.

The palace is 3.8km east of the town centre. Useful Santos buses (€0.70, 30 minutes) leave at 9am, 10.45am, noon, 12.30pm, 1pm and 1.30pm weekdays from the bus stand on Rua Dr António Valente Fonseca; ask at the turismo for the latest timetable. If you ask for 'Mateus' the bus will set you down about 250m from the palace (if you don't ask, it may not stop).

As for the rosé, it's made in Porto now, but the palace does produce its own range of jams and wines, which are sold in a shop on the premises.

Special Events
The Festa de São Pedro on 28–29 June is one of the town's liveliest events, with a huge market in the streets east of the turismo – a good occasion to shop for the region's unusual black pottery and other handicrafts.

Places to Stay
Camping Located 1.2km northeast of the centre, **Parque de Campismo de Vila Real** (☎ 259 325 625, 259 324 724; Rua Dr Manuel Cardona; adult/car €2.80/1.80, tent 1.80-2.30; open mid-Jan–mid-Dec), a simple, shady hillside camp site above the Rio Corgo, has free hot showers and a small restaurant. A Camping Card International (CCI; see Visas & Documents in the Facts for the Visitor chapter) gets you a 10% discount.

Hostels The **pousada da juventude** (☎ 259 373 193; e vilareal@movijovem.pt; Rua Dr Manuel Cardona; dorm beds €9.50, doubles with toilet €26.50) is at the rear of a yellow building 200m before the camp site (see earlier). No meals are available but you can use the kitchen, and the dreary, high-rise residential neighbourhood has a few cafés.

Pensões & Residenciais The two guesthouses **Residencial Mondego** (☎/fax 259 322 039; Travessa de São Domingos 11; rooms €23) and **Residencial São Domingos** (Travessa de São Domingos 33; rooms €23) have the same owner, rates and ropey, last-resort

rooms (poor value for solo travellers as there's no single rate).

Residencial da Sé (☎ 259 324 575; Travessa de São Domingos 19-23; doubles with breakfast from €30) is a better bet, with modest, well-kept old rooms.

Residencial Real (☎ 259 325 879, fax 259 324 613; Rua Central 5; doubles with breakfast €32.50) is in the middle of a pedestrian zone, so its tidy rooms are the quietest choice at night.

Hotels Leaky old **Hotel Tocaio** (☎ 259 323 106, fax 259 325 905; Avenida Carvalho Araújo 45; doubles €35) is the sort of place apt to be renovated any day now. Meanwhile its threadbare, traffic-noisy rooms are fair value, and the price includes a small buffet breakfast.

Proper luxury (and a generous breakfast) are on offer at **Hotel Cabanelas** (☎ 259 323 153, fax 259 374 181; Rua Dom Pedro de Castro 17; doubles €45) and **Hotel Miracorgo** (☎ 259 325 001; e miracorgo@mail.telepac .pt; Avenida 1 de Maio 78; doubles €64).

Turihab The Turihab property **Quinta de São Martinho** (☎ 259 323 986; e quinta.s .martinho@clix.pt; Lugar de São Martinho, Mateus; doubles €65), on the way to the Palácio de Mateus, is is a comfortable former country house, also known for its good restaurant.

Some handsome rural properties in the region are better deals than the town's hotels; the turismo has information about them all.

Places to Eat & Drink
Café-Pastelaria Nova Pompeia (Rua Carvalho Araújo 82; meals under €5; open Mon-Sat), the best of a gaggle of cafés and confeitarias (pastisserie or confectionary shop) opposite the cathedral, has toasted sandwiches and burgers for under €3, plus light meals.

Churrasqueira Real (☎ 259 322 078; Rua Teixeira de Sousa 14; mains under €5; open Mon-Sat) has takeaway food plus basic sitdown service; soup and a quarter-chicken (€3.50) will fill you up.

Restaurante O Escondidinho (☎ 259 325 535; Rua Teixeira de Sousa 7; dishes under €7.50; open daily) is a modest place with regional dishes and good pasta, and is one of the few central restaurants open on Sunday evening.

Restaurante 22 (☎ 259 321 296; 1st floor, Rua Teixeira de Sousa 16; mains under €8; open Mon-Sat) takes care with its excellent fish and meat dishes (some half-portions) and has a few lunch-time pratos do dia (daily specials) for under €4.

Self-caterers are able to stock up on rural produce at the mercado municipal (municipal market; Rua de Santa Sofia; open Tues, morning Fri).

A dusty old adega (wine tavern; Rua António de Azevedo 20) near the cathedral offers a certain seedy charm and a cheap slug of the local vintage.

Getting There & Away

Bus There are several bus lines serving Vila Real, including:

AV Tâmega (☎ 259 322 674) corner Rua Dr António Valente Fonseca and Avenida Cidade de Ourense

Rodonorte (☎ 259 340 719) Rua Dom Pedro de Castro 19

Santos & Rede Expressos – boarding on the corner of Rua Dr António Valente Fonseca and Avenida Cidade de Ourense; tickets available on the bus or from Ruicar travel agency (☎ 259 324 761) Rua Gonçalo Cristóvão 16 – open Monday to Sunday morning, or from Café Michele (☎ 259 375 894) Rua Dom Pedro de Castro 31 – open Monday to Saturday

Trás-os-Montes destinations include Chaves (€5.30, 1¼ hours) with Rodonorte or AV Tâmega; and Bragança (€7.30, two hours) with Rodonorte, Rede Expressos or Santos, all departing several times daily.

For the Minho, Rede Expressos goes to Braga (€6.30, 2¾ hours) three times daily except Saturday; and Rodonorte goes to Guimarães (€5.50, 1½ hours) several times a day.

Douro valley points include Porto (€5.30, 1½ hours, every few hours) on board AV Tâmega, Rodonorte, Rede Expressos or Santos; Amarante (€4.30, 40 minutes, five daily) with Rodonorte; and Lamego (€4.50, 55 minutes, twice daily) with Rede Expressos.

Weekend services tend to be less frequent or nonexistent.

Train Vila Real is at the end of the narrow-gauge Linha da Corgo from Peso da Régua (€1.40, 55 minutes), with three to four daily departures from Porto (€5.60, 3½ to

four hours). A taxi between the train station and town centre costs about €3.

PARQUE NATURAL DO ALVÃO

This 72-sq-km natural park – Portugal's smallest – straddles the 1300m-plus central ridgeline of the Serra de Alvão, between Vila Real and Mondim de Basto. In a transition zone between humid coast and dry interior, the park has diverse flora and fauna, but it's the harsh natural and human landscape at higher elevations that is most striking.

The Rio Ôlo, a tributary of the Rio Tâmega, rises in the park's broad granite basin. A 300m drop above Ermelo gives rise to the spectacular Fisgas de Ermelo waterfalls, the park's major tourist attraction.

Exploring the park on your own is not simple, as maps and public transport are limited. Before setting out on foot, pay a visit to one of the park offices.

Information

There are park information centres in Vila Real (see that section) and Mondim de Basto (see that section). Both sell leaflets, with English-language inserts, on local products (including linen cloth and smoked sausages), handicrafts, land use, flora and fauna. Mondim de Basto's turismo is another good source of park information.

Ermelo & Fisgas de Ermelo

The 800-year-old village of Ermelo includes many traditional slate-roofed houses and espigueiros (stone granaries), an ancient chapel, a granite pelourinho (pillory) and the Ponte de Várzea, a Roman bridge rebuilt in medieval times.

Half a dozen local linen weavers have joined in a park-sponsored project to open their workshops to the public. Inquire at the Vila Real park office about visiting them.

The Ermelo turn-off is about 16km south of Mondim de Basto on the N304; you can get there from Mondim on a local Transcovizela bus (see the Mondim de Basto section). From the turnoff it is about half a kilometre to the nearest parts of the village, though the village continues along the track for at least 1km.

About 1.3km closer to Mondim de Basto on the N304 is a turn-off to the dramatic Fisgas de Ermelo waterfalls. It is a shadeless 4km climb to the falls; take water and snacks. To do this as a day trip you must catch the 7am bus from Mondim de Basto. The last bus back to Mondim passes by about 6.40pm on weekdays (there's nothing late enough on weekends). Check current times at Mondim de Basto's turismo.

Other Attractions

Notes on a three-hour hike around **Arnal** in the southern part of the park, plus information on flora, fauna and traditional farming, are in *Guia do Percurso Pedestre* (€0.40), a park leaflet with an English-language insert. The route offers views east beyond Vila Real to the Serra do Marão.

A restored slate-roofed house at Arnal, the **Núcleo das Técnicas Tradicionais** (Centre for Traditional Techniques), has handicraft displays and information on mountain agriculture and animal husbandry, but at the time of writing it was only open by arrangement with the park office in Vila Real.

Another worthwhile destination is **Lamas de Ôlo**, with its ancient mill and thatched houses, in the heart of the park at an altitude of about 1000m.

Some other walks, ranging from 2.5km to 11.5km, are outlined in a Portuguese-language booklet, *Percurso Pedestre: Mondim de Basto/Parque Natural do Alvão* (€0.60), with a rough, 1:50,000 trail map. No other maps are available at park offices.

Activities

A local outfit arranging **walks, mountaineering** and **mountain-biking** (and bike rental) – and, outside summer season, **river trips** – with English or French-speaking guides is **Basto Radical** (☎ 255 382 637, 966 628 543; **w** *www.basto-radical.pt*).

Places to Stay & Eat

There's a park-managed, gloriously isolated 12-bed **cottage** *(per person with/without own sleeping bag €10/15)* near Arnal, for a minimum of four people. Bookings must be made in advance through the park office in Vila Real.

Restaurante A Cabana *(☎ 259 341 745; Lamas de Ôlo)* is known for its trout dishes, and has one double room for rent.

Ermelo has three **cafés**, where you can also inquire about private rooms. For more accommodation options, see the Mondim de Basto section.

An alternative base is at Campeã, 12km west of Vila Real. **Casa do Mineiro** *(☎ 259 979 720;* **e** *casadacruz@mail.telepac.pt; Lugar de Trás do Vale, Campeã; double €50)* and **Casa da Cruz** *(☎ 259 979 720; cottages per 2/4/6 people €50/90/120)* are self-catering traditional-style rural cottages.

Basto Radical (see earlier) also has advice on local accommodation.

Getting There & Away

Transcovizela and Rodonorte jointly run buses between Vila Real and Mondim de Basto (see that section), skirting the park near Ermelo. Additional villages have bus services during school term; ask at the park offices or the turismos in Vila Real or Mondim.

There are no buses to Lamas de Ôlo. A **taxi** *(Mondim ☎ 255 381 259)* costs about €20 from Mondim or €10 from Vila Real; taxis are also available at Lamas de Ôlo.

MONDIM DE BASTO
**postcode 4880 • pop about 6000
• elevation 200m**

This plain mountain town found near the intersection of the Douro, Minho and Trás-os-Montes provinces (around 30km northeast of Amarante, 50km northwest of Vila Real) is redeemed by its surroundings, its friendly people and a strong wine for which the Terras de Basto region is known. It's of interest chiefly as a base from which to explore the Parque Natural do Alvão.

Orientation & Information

Buses stop behind the *mercado municipal*, from where it's 150m west to the **turismo** *(☎ 255 381 479; Praça 9 de Abril; open 9am-9pm daily July–mid-Sept, 9am-12.30pm & 2pm-5.30pm Mon-Fri mid-Sept–June)*, and what remains of the old town.

About 500m west of the turismo is a **Parque Natural do Alvão office** *(☎/fax 255 381 209;* **e** *pna@icn.pt; Lugar do Barrio; open 9am-12.30pm & 2pm-5.30pm Mon-Fri)*.

Walking

A popular walk from Mondim finishes at the Capela de Senhora da Graça on the summit of pine-clad Monte Farinha, two to three hours up. The path starts east of town on the N312 (the turismo has a rough map). At the top you can reward yourself with a restaurant lunch (see Places to Eat later in this section).

TRÁS-OS-MONTES *(side tab)*

By car, turn off the N312 3.5km from Mondim in the direction of Cerva; from there it's a twisting 9.5km to the top.

Swimming
At Senhora da Ponte, 2km south of town on the N304, is a rocky swimming spot by a disused water mill on the Rio Cabril. Follow signs to the Parque de Campismo de Mondim de Basto and then take the track to the right.

Wine Tasting
The nearest 'Basto' *vinho verde* (semi-sparkling young wine) is produced at Quinta do Fundo (see Places to Stay). Other labels come from **Quinta da Veiga** (☎ 255 361 212) in Gagos, west across the Rio Tâmega, and **Quinta d'Onega** (☎ 255 386 195) in Ate, 15km north of Mondim. Ask at the turismo for details.

Places to Stay
Camping One kilometre south of town beside the Rio Cabril is the **Parque de Campismo de Mondim de Basto** (☎/fax 255 381 650; adult/car €2.50/1.90, tent €2-3.30), a plain facility open to CCI holders.

Pensões & Residenciais Two adequate places on Avenida Dr Augusto Brito, west of the turismo, are **Residencial Carvalho** (☎ 255 381 057; singles/doubles with breakfast €15/25), by the petrol station, and **Residencial Arcádia** (☎ 255 381 410; singles/doubles with breakfast €17.50/30), which is further south.

Turihab Near the turismo is **Casa das Mourôas** (☎ 255 381 394; Rua José Carvalho Camões; doubles from €43), a converted 19th-century hayloft.

Quinta do Fundo (☎ 255 381 291, fax 255 382 017; Vilar de Viando; doubles/suites with breakfast €45/70) is a handsome property located 2km south on the N304, which has a tennis court and swimming pool, horses and bikes for hire, and also produces its own *vinho verde*.

Quinta da Barreiro de Cima (☎ 255 386 491, fax 255 386 106; Parada de Atei; doubles €65, apartment €100), found about 5km to the north of Mondim has double rooms, one self-catering apartment and a swimming pool.

Places to Eat
Adega Sete Condes (☎ 255 382 342; Rua Velha; half-portions around €5; closed Mon night), behind the turismo, has a small menu of well-prepared traditional dishes, including *bacalhau* (dried, salted cod) and a very tasty *feijoada* (pork and bean casserole); a half-portion is plenty.

Adega Santiago (☎ 255 386 957; Rua Velha; open Mon-Sat), near Adega Sete Condes, is similarly priced and equally homely.

Restaurante Alto da Senhora da Graça (☎ 255 386 960), atop Monte Farinha, has unexceptional food at steep prices, but unmatched views (see Walking, earlier).

Getting There & Away
Rodonorte (☎ 259 340 719) and **Transcovizela** (☎ 255 381 296) run a coordinated service from Vila Real (€2.40, one hour) three times each weekday and once on Saturday, with a change at Avecção do Cabo.

Transcovizela runs to Mondim from Amarante train station (€3.15, 1½ hours) three times on weekdays and twice on Saturday, with a change at Fermil.

CHAVES
postcode 5400 • pop 17,500
• elevation 369m

This unassuming, rather attractive spa town straddles the Rio Tâmega just 10km south of the Spanish frontier. The name (meaning 'keys') hints at its historical importance as a frontier gateway: Romans, Suevi, Visigoths, Moors, French and Spanish have all squabbled over it. The Romans, who founded the town in AD 78, called it Aquae Flaviae after the healthy waters and their emperor, Flavio Vespasianus. Even today the Roman 16-arched bridge is a major traffic-bearing feature of the town.

Chaves (**shahv**-sh) is best known to Portuguese for its warm springs and for its delicious smoked *presunto* (ham) and sausages. It also has enough worth seeing – a modest medieval quarter, a 14th-century castle keep and a muscular fortress – to make it worth a detour, though you'd be smart to book accommodation at least a few days ahead in summer.

Orientation
The town centre is a 700m walk southwest of the AV Tâmega bus station, or a few

blocks northeast of the Rodonorte bus stop on Rua Joaquim Delgado. The backbone of the old town is Rua de Santo António.

Information

The **regional turismo** (☎ 276 340 661; e rtur ismoatb@mail.telepac.pt; Terreiro de Cavalaria; open 9.30am-12.30pm & 2pm-6pm daily June-Sept, Mon-Sat Oct-May), north of the old town, is at the end of Rua de Santo António.

Banks with ATMs dot Rua de Santo António, Rua Direita and Largo do Arrabalde. The **post office** (open 8.30am-6pm Mon-Fri, 9am-12.30pm Sat) is on Largo General Silveira.

The **district hospital** (☎ 276 300 900; Avenida Francisco Sá Carneiro) is northwest of the centre. The **police station** (☎ 276 322

169; Avenida Bombeiros Voluntários) is near the turismo.

Lavandaria Popular (Rua do Tabolado; open 9am-1pm & 3pm-7pm Mon-Fri) will cheerfully do your wash the same or next day.

Ponte Romana

Chaves' handsome bridge was completed in AD 104 by Emperor Trajan (hence its other name, Ponte Trajano). It probably served as a link on the important road between Braga and Astorga (Spain). In the middle are two engraved Roman milestones.

Spa

The warm, salty waters of the Balneário das Caldas de Chaves are said to be good for rheumatism, liver complaints, digestive dis-

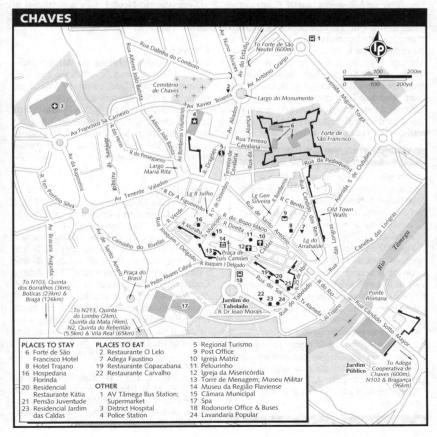

PLACES TO STAY	PLACES TO EAT	5 Regional Turismo
6 Forte de São Francisco Hotel	2 Restaurante O Lelo	9 Post Office
8 Hotel Trajano	7 Adega Faustino	10 Igreja Matriz
16 Hospedaria Florinda	19 Restaurante Copacabana	11 Pelourinho
20 Residencial Restaurante Kátia	22 Restaurante Carvalho	12 Igreja da Misericórdia
21 Pensão Juventude	OTHER	13 Torre de Menagem; Museu Militar
23 Residencial Jardim das Caldas	1 AV Tâmega Bus Station; Supermarket	14 Museu da Região Flaviense
	3 District Hospital	15 Câmara Municipal
	4 Police Station	17 Spa
		18 Rodonorte Office & Buses
		24 Lavandaria Popular

orders, and high blood pressure; local *residenciais* (guesthouses) are full of elderly patients on extended courses of treatment. The only thing available to casual visitors is a drink of the stuff, which tastes pretty awful.

Museu da Região Flaviense

This regional archaeological-ethnographic collection *(Praça de Luís Camões; admission including Museu Militar adult/child under 18 €0.50/free; open 9am-12.30pm & 2pm-5.30pm Tues-Fri, 2pm-5.30pm Sat & Sun)* naturally has lots of Roman artefacts, but the most interesting items are stone menhirs and carvings, some dating back over 2500 years.

Torre de Menagem & Museu Militar

The Torre de Menagem (castle keep) is the only major remnant of a castle built by Dom Dinis in the 14th century. After Dom João triumphed at Aljubarrota in 1385 he gave the castle to his loyal constable, Dom Nun' Álvares Pereira. It was inherited by the House of Bragança when Nun' Álvares' daughter married the Count of Barcelos, the future Duke of Bragança.

Around the Torre de Menagem are manicured gardens and a stretch of old defensive walls, with views over town and country-side (other less visible walls run beside Rua Cândido dos Reis and Rua do Sol). The Torre now houses a dull military museum *(admission including Museu da Região Flaviense €0.50; open same hrs)*.

Forte de São Neutel & Forte de São Francisco

The style of these two 17th-century forts, like the one at Valença do Minho, was inspired by the work of the French military architect Vauban.

Forte de São Francisco was completed in 1658, around a Franciscan convent founded in the previous century. It's now a top-end hotel (see Places to Stay, later), though nobody minds if you snoop around outside or climb on the walls.

Forte de São Neutel, 1.2km northeast of the centre, is open only as the venue for occasional summertime concerts.

Churches

The 17th-century **Igreja da Misericórdia** *(Praça de Luís Camões)* catches the eye with its exterior porch and columns. Inside are some huge 18th-century azulejos.

Also on the square is the **igreja matriz** (parish church), Romanesque in form but thoroughly remodelled in the 16th century – though the doorway and belfry retain some original features. There's little of interest inside.

Activities

You can take **horse-riding** lessons or hire a horse at **Quinta dos Borralhos** *(☎ 936 194 199; Curalha)*, 4km southwest of town.

If you fancy some **wine tasting**, modest local wines include São Neutel (reds and sparkling whites), Flavius (sturdy reds and whites) and Vespasiano reds. The **Adega Cooperativa de Chaves** *(☎ 276 322 183; Avenida Duarte)*, 1km southeast of the centre, is open during weekday business hours for tours and tastings. For something a little out of the mainstream, see the boxed text 'Wine of the Dead'.

Special Events

The weeklong Feira de Todos Santos (All Saints Fair) is Chaves' annual bash. The biggest days are 31 October and 1 November, with folk music, brass bands and market stalls in the streets.

Wine of the Dead

From the otherwise unremarkable town of Boticas, 23km southwest of Chaves, comes the bizarrely named *vinho dos mortos* (wine of the dead), a rough red brew generously described by tourist literature as 'famous, tasty clarets'.

In 1809, so the story goes, villagers hid their bottled wine from the invading French by burying it underground. Discovering afterwards that the taste had noticeably improved – thanks, presumably, to darkness and constant temperature rather than anything supernatural – they continue to this day to bury wine in deep cellars for up to a year.

This earthy product is mostly for private consumption, though you can sample it at **Café Armindo** *(Rua de Sanguinhedo, Boticas)* and other local spots. Ask about it at the Boticas **turismo** *(☎ 276 410 200; Rua 5 de Outubro)*.

Dia de Cidade (City Day) on 8 July features bands, parades, fireworks and laser shows.

Places to Stay
Camping Just off the N2 6km southwest of Chaves, **Quinta do Rebentão** (☎/fax 276 322 733; Vila Nova de Veiga; adult/car €2.50/ 2.50, tent €2-4; open Jan-Nov) is a grassy, partly shaded, suburban facility with hot showers and basic supplies.

Pensões & Residenciais In summer, when Chaves' better accommodation gets booked out by spa patients, booking ahead is a good idea. Rooms have private bathroom except as noted.

Pensão Juventude (☎ 276 326 713; Rua do Sol 8; doubles €25) has eight clean, spartan rooms (with shared bathroom) above a café.

Hospedaria Florinda (☎ 276 333 392, fax 276 326 577; Rua dos Açougues; singles/ doubles with breakfast €25/35), close to the centre, has spotless, pretty rooms.

Residencial Restaurante Kátia (☎ 276 324 446; Rua do Sol 28; doubles with breakfast about €35), backed up against the old town walls, has low-profile service and well-kept rooms.

Residencial Jardim das Caldas (☎ 276 331 189; e jardimdascaldas@mail.telepac.pt; Jardim do Tabolado 5; doubles with breakfast €40), facing Chaves' riverside park, has squeaky-clean, serviceable rooms with full bathroom.

Hotels You need to book well ahead for **Hotel Trajano** (☎ 276 301 640; e info@ hoteltrajano.com; Travessa Cândido dos Reis; doubles with breakfast from €45), a courteous old place with a recent face-lift and big, simply furnished rooms with air-con.

Forte de São Francisco Hotel (☎ 276 333 700; e webmaster@forte-s-francisco-hoteis .pt; doubles Sun-Thur €125, Fri & Sat €140), an extraordinary blend of four-star hotel and restored national monument, has faultless rooms, swimming pool, tennis courts, sauna – and its own church.

Turihab If you've got wheels and the wherewithal (about €60 for a double), ask at the turismo about **Quinta do Lombo** (☎/fax 276 321 404; Lombo), 2.5km southeast off

the N213, with a swimming pool; or **Quinta da Mata** (☎ 276 340 030; Solares de Portugal e info@turihab.pt; Nantes), a 17th-century manor house 2km further out the N213, with tennis courts and sauna.

Places to Eat
Most residenciais and many restaurants serve big helpings of unexceptional fare at reasonable prices.

Restaurante O Lelo (☎ 276 327 033; Largo do Monumento; local specialities around €5; open lunch Sun-Fri) is a humble eatery that offers the town's best lunch-time bargain; a €4 half-portion of feijoada will feed two.

Adega Faustino (☎ 276 322 142; Travessa Cândido dos Reis; dishes €3-5; open Mon-Sat) is one of the most agreeable eateries we found in Portugal – a cavernous ex-winery now filled with light and birdsong, with a big list of carefully prepared light meals, from salpicão (small rounds of smoked ham) to pig's ear in vinaigrette sauce.

Restaurante Copacabana (☎ 276 323 570; Rua do Sol 38; dishes under €7; open daily) is a proud little place with a family atmosphere, a short, meaty menu and good food for the price (half-portions available).

Restaurante Carvalho (☎ 276 321 727; Jardim do Tabolado; dishes around €8; open Fri-Wed), a sober place in a street full of boisterous parkside cafés, is too posh to put a menu outside, but the regional dishes are top-notch.

Self-caterers must settle for the **supermarket** upstairs from the AV Tâmega bus station.

Getting There & Away
From the bus station **REDM/AV Tâmega** (☎ 276 332 384) has services via Montalegre (€3.60, 80 minutes) to Braga (€5.50, 3½ hours) five times daily; to Vila Real (€5.30, 1¼ hours) three times daily; to Mirandela (€3.30) three times each weekday; via Porto (€9, 2½ hours) to Coimbra daily; and to Bragança (€7.40, 2¼ hours) twice daily.

Rodonorte (☎ 276 333 491; Rua Joaquim Delgado) goes via Vila Real and Amarante (€7.40, two hours) to Porto eight times per weekday, less often at the weekend.

AV Tâmega also has four local services each weekday to the border at Feces de Abaixo, where you can pick up Spanish buses to Orense.

Eastern Trás-os-Montes

BRAGANÇA

postcode 5300 • pop 20,300
• elevation 650m

The name Bragança has rung down through Portuguese history since the 15th century, when Dom João I created a duchy here as a reminder to the Spanish that this remote corner was part of the Portuguese kingdom. Though the dukes of Bragança came to prefer their vast holdings in the south (see the Vila Viçosa section in the Alentejo chapter), their hometown's isolation remained a symbol of national determination – especially after they ascended the throne in 1640 (to rule until the fall of the monarchy in 1910).

Thanks to mountains, bad roads and poor communications, the isolation continued right into the late 20th century. But in the early 1990s the IP4/E82 motorway rather suddenly brought Bragança to within a few hours of Porto and Madrid, and in summer its sober streets now fill with Portuguese and Spanish tourists.

But despite an air of self-importance – and a walled citadel that presents, from afar, one of the most stirring views in northern Portugal – the town is surprisingly modest in scale, a backwater at heart.

Why come all this way? Bragança still has a dollop of medieval atmosphere and one of the country's best regional museums, and it's the obvious base for a look at the underrated Parque Natural de Montesinho. If you're driving or cycling, a route to Bragança through the upper Douro valley and Eastern Trás-os-Montes reveals some of Portugal's loveliest and least-seen landscapes.

History

The town has Celtic roots, as Brigantia or Brigantio. The Romans fortified it and called it Juliobriga. Trashed during repeated Christian and Moorish campaigns, it was rebuilt in the early 12th century by Fernão Mendes, an in-law of Afonso Henriques, as the capital of a semi-independent fiefdom. Afonso's son Sancho I granted Bragança its first charter in 1187.

In 1442 Dom João I, determined to keep a grip on the region, assumed direct control, created the duchy of Bragança – a thumb in

the eye for Castile and León – and declared his bastard son Afonso the first Duke of Bragança. The House of Bragança soon became one of the country's wealthiest and most powerful families. In 1640, following 60 years of Spanish rule, the eighth Duke of Bragança reluctantly took the Portuguese throne as João IV.

During the Peninsular War Bragança and other Trás-os-Montes towns were besieged for a time before being bailed out by Portuguese and English troops. Shortly afterwards Bragança scored an ecclesiastical coup when the bishopric was transferred here from Miranda do Douro.

Orientation

Bragança sits just by the southern edge of the Parque Natural de Montesinho. Beside

---

Devils in Disguise

In contrast to the mix of cheer and piety characteristic of the Minho's festivals, some in Trás-os-Montes have a vaguely licentious side to them, a tilt towards earthier, pre-Christian traditions.

Carnaval seems to bring these to the surface. Most of Portugal's Carnaval celebrations feature Rio-style parades and parties, but up north there's an echo of ancient rites of passage, a whiff of mischief. Witness the antics of the Caretos of Podence (near Macedo de Cavaleiros) – gangs of young men in leering masks (*caretos*) and vivid, candy-cane costumes who invade the town centre, bent on cheerfully humiliating everyone in sight. Prime targets, naturally, are young women, at whom they thrust their hips and wave the cowbells hanging from their belts. Similar figures are to be seen in Varge, in the Parque Natural de Montesinho.

Saturnalian high jinks also take place in many villages around Christmas or Twelfth Night during the so-called Festa dos Rapazes ('Festival of the Lads'), when unmarried boys over 16 light all-night bonfires and rampage around in robes of rags and masks of brass or wood.

Festas, Feiras e Romarias is an annual rundown of Eastern Trás-os-Montes festivals and fairs, published by the Nordeste Transmontanho regional tourist office and often available at local turismos.

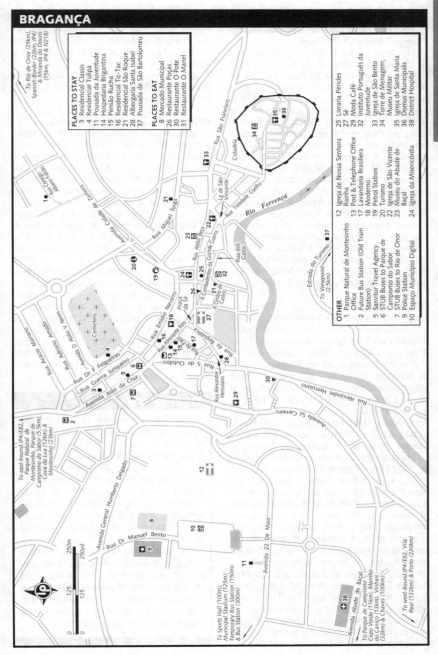

BRAGANÇA

PLACES TO STAY
3 Residencial Classis
4 Residencial Tulipa
11 Pousada da Juventude
14 Hospedaria Brigantina
15 Pensão Rucha
16 Residencial Tic-Tac
21 Residencial São Roque
28 Albergaria Santa Isabel
37 Pousada de São Bartolomeu

PLACES TO EAT
8 Mercado Municipal
26 Restaurante Poças
30 Restaurante O Pote
31 Restaurante O Manel

OTHER
1 Parque Natural de Montesinho Office
2 Future Bus Station (Old Train Station)
5 Sanvitur Travel Agency
6 STUB Buses to Parque de Campismo do Sabor
7 STUB Buses to Rio de Onor
9 Police Station
10 Espaço Município Digital
12 Igreja de Nossa Senhora Rainha
13 Post & Telephone Office
17 Lavandaria Brasileira
18 Moderno
19 Petrol Station
20 Turismo
22 Igreja de São Vicente
23 Museu do Abade de Bacal
24 Igreja da Misericórdia
25 Livraria Péricles
27 Sé
29 Moda Café
32 Instituto Português da Juventude
33 Igreja de São Bento
34 Torre de Menagem; Museu Militar
35 Igreja de Santa Maria
36 Domus Municipalis
38 District Hospital

it runs the Rio Fervença, a tributary of the Rio Sabor, which runs right across Eastern Trás-os-Montes to the Douro.

The town centre is Praça da Sé, in front of the old cathedral: from here one road runs to the citadel, one to Spain and one to the rest of Portugal. The main axis is Avenida João da Cruz, Rua Almirante Reis and Rua Combatentes da Grande Guerra (the latter is commonly called Rua Direita).

At the time of writing, central Bragança was suffering several large public works, including a highway tunnel, a municipal theatre and redevelopment of the area across the river, with completion dates expected to be in 2003. After that the defunct train station at the northern end of Avenida João da Cruz will become the central bus station; meanwhile, long-distance buses set you down over 1km west near the municipal sports ground. The youth hostel is a stone's throw from there, but for anything else you must take a taxi or local bus into the centre (see Getting Around, later).

Information

Help is on hand at the **turismo** (☎ 273 381 273, fax 273 304 298; e turismocmb@sapo.pt; Avenida Cidade de Zamora; open 9am-12.30pm & 2pm-5pm Mon-Fri, 10am-12.30pm Sat).

The headquarters of the **Parque Natural de Montesinho** (☎ 273 381 444; e pnm@ icn.pt; Rua Cónego Albano Falcão 5; open 9am-12.30pm & 2pm-5.30pm Mon-Fri) is northeast of the turismo; a free schematic park map is available, and some good publications (all in Portuguese) on the park's human and natural resources are for sale.

There are banks with currency exchange and ATMs throughout the town centre.

The **post office** (open 8.30am-5.30pm Mon-Fri, 9am-12.30pm Sat) is at the top of Rua Almirante Reis, behind a bronze statue of a postman. The post office doubles as a telephone office. Free Internet access is available at the **Instituto Português da Juventude** (Rua da Oróbio de Castro 76; open 9am-12.30pm & 2pm-5.30pm Mon-Fri) for up to 30 minutes, and at the **Espaço Município Digital** (open 9am-12.30pm, 2pm-5.30pm & 8pm-11pm Mon-Fri), behind the câmara municipal, for up to an hour.

Livraria Péricles (Rua Combatentes de Grande Guerra 182) stocks a few English classics and English-language magazines.

The **district hospital** (☎ 273 310 800; Avenida Abade de Baçal) is west of the centre. The **police station** (☎ 273 303 400; Rua Dr Manuel Bento) is just north of the câmara municipal.

Leave your dirty socks at **Lavandaria Brasiliera** (Rua do Paço 22; open Mon-Sat), which has a next-day service.

Museu do Abade de Baçal

This museum of archaeology, ethnography and art (☎ 273 331 595; Rua Abílio Beça; adult/child under 14 €2/free, morning Sun free; open 10am-5pm Tues-Fri, 10am-6pm Sat & Sun), in the 16th-century Paço Episcopal (Bishop's Palace), is one of Portugal's best regional museums. Inside you will find a wide-ranging, high-minded collection based on that of its namesake, the Abbot of Baçal, Francisco Manuel Alves (1865–1947), a dedicated scholar of regional history and architecture.

Displays downstairs include ancient pottery and tools, mysterious stone pigs called berrões (see the boxed text 'Pig Mysteries') and other animal totems, and Roman funeral stones. Upstairs are remnants of the palace's own chapels, luminous wooden church statues and other furnishings. A garden at the back is dotted with more tombstones and stone animals. Unfortunately there's no information in English.

Pig Mysteries

Scattered around remoter parts of Trás-os-Montes and the Zamora region of Spain are hundreds of crudely carved granite pigs or boars known as berrões (singular: berrão). Some date back over 2000 years, others to the 2nd or 3rd century AD. No-one knows what they were for, though there are plenty of theories: they may be fertility or prosperity symbols, grave guardians, offerings to, or representations of, Iron Age gods – or simply property markers.

You can take a close look at these mysterious pigs in museums in Bragança, Chaves and Miranda do Douro, or in situ in Bragança's citadel, where there's one pierced through its middle by a pillory. A large, well-preserved one sits on a pedestal in a square in tiny Murça, 30km northeast of Vila Real.

Sé

Don't get your hopes up. This old but forgettable church *(admission free; open 10.15am-5.30pm Mon-Fri)*, which started out in 1545 as the Igreja de São João Baptista, was declared a cathedral in 1770 when the bishopric was moved here from Miranda do Douro. Bragança's modern cathedral, which is also called the Igreja de Nossa Senhora Rainha, is just west of the centre.

Other Churches

Facing little Largo de São Vicente (also commonly called Largo do Principal) is the **Igreja de São Vicente**, Romanesque in origin but rebuilt in the 17th century. Tradition has it that the future Dom Pedro I secretly married Inês de Castro here around 1354 (see the boxed text 'Love & Revenge' about this star-crossed, ultimately grisly affair, in the Estremadura & Ribatejo chapter).

Bragança's most attractive church is a block eastward on Rua São Francisco: the **Igreja de São Bento**, with a Renaissance stone portal, a wonderful trompe l'oeil ceiling over the nave and an Arabic-style inlaid ceiling over the chancel.

Cidadela

From Largo de São Vicente you can climb up to the walled and amazingly well-preserved 13th-century *cidadela* (citadel). People still live in its narrow lanes, sharing them these days with abundant handicrafts shops and posh restaurants.

Within the walls is what remains of the original castle, beefed up in the 15th century by João I for the dukes of Bragança. The stout **Torre de Menagem** served as a residence too (note the Gothic window upstairs), and was garrisoned in the 19th and early 20th centuries. It now houses a marginally interesting **Museu Militar** *(Military Museum; ☎ 273 322 378; adult/child under 10 €1.50/free, morning Sun free; open 9am-11.45am & 2pm-4.45pm Fri-Wed)*. In front of the Torre is an extraordinary, primitive *pelourinho*, atop a granite boar similar to the *berrões* found around the province.

At the rear of the citadel is an odd, severe, five-sided building known as the **Domus Municipalis** *(Town House; admission free; open 9am-11.45am & 2pm-4.45pm Fri-Wed)*, the oldest town hall in Portugal – although its precise age is a matter of scholarly

disagreement – and one of the few examples of civil (nonchurch) Romanesque architecture on the Iberian Peninsula. Upstairs in an arcaded room, Bragança's medieval town council met to settle land or water disputes; below was the citadel's precious cistern.

Beside the Domus Municipalis is the early-16th-century **Igreja de Santa Maria**, with a portal covered in carved vines, and a deteriorating 18th-century trompe l'oeil ceiling depicting the Assumption.

A fine view of the citadel is from a hilltop viewpoint near the old Mosteiro de São Bartolomeu; from the town centre cross the river on Rua Alexandre Herculano and take the first left.

Market

A flea market takes over the area around the municipal stadium on Avenida Abade de Baçal, west of the centre, on the 3rd, 12th and 21st of each month (or the following Monday when any of these falls on the weekend).

Special Events

The Feira das Cantarinhas is Bragança's biggest market of the year: a huge street fair of traditional handicrafts held every 2–4 May. (A *cantarinha* is a small terracotta pitcher.)

Places to Stay

Camping There are two camp sites in the nearby Parque Natural de Montesinho – the Parque de Campismo do Sabor and Parque de Campismo do Cepo Verde (see that section for details).

Hostels The **pousada da juventude** *(☎ 273 304 600; e bragança@movijovem.pt; Avenida 22 de Maio; dorm beds €12.50, doubles with toilet €35)*, Bragança's newish hostel, is about 900m west of the town centre. A four-bed apartment with kitchenette (€60) and a six-bed family room (€82.50) are also available.

Private Rooms Under the same management, **Restaurante Poças** *(☎ 273 331 428; Rua Combatentes de Grande Guerra 200)* and the truly bare-bones **Hospedaria Brigantina** *(☎ 273 324 321; Rua Almirante Reis 48)* both have plain rooms with shared facilities for €10 per person.

TRÁS-OS-MONTES

Pensões & Residenciais Top value at the budget end is **Pensão Rucha** (☎ 273 331 672; Rua Almirante Reis 42; doubles €25), a well-kept place with a sunny, peaceful atmosphere, in a genteel old building. Rooms have shared facilities.

Rooms at the following places have private bathroom, and rates include breakfast.

Three neighbouring *residenciais* with plain, comfortable air-con rooms are the **Residencial Tulipa** (☎ 273 331 675, fax 273 327 814; Rua Dr Francisco Felgueiras 8-10; doubles €42.50), which is the best value for money (credit cards are not accepted); **Residencial Tic-Tac** (☎ 273 331 373, fax 273 331 673; Rua Emídio Navarro 85; doubles €45); and **Residencial Classis** (☎ 273 331 631, fax 273 323 458; Avenida João da Cruz 102; doubles €47.50).

Residencial São Roque (☎ 273 381 481, fax 273 326 937; Rua Miguel Torga; doubles €40), in a high-rise near the turismo, has large, comfortable rooms and views into the Parque Natural de Montesinho.

Albergaria Santa Isabel (☎ 273 331 427, fax 273 326 937; Rua Alexandre Herculano 67; doubles with air-con €45), newly renovated, has views of the citadel from the top floor, though rooms facing Rua Alexandre Herculano are quieter.

Turihab & Pousadas A converted water mill 13km west of Bragança on the N103, **Moinho do Caniço** (☎ 273 323 577; Castrelos; doubles about €65) is one of several appealing Turihab properties the turismo can tell you about. It has two rooms (with bathroom), kitchen and fireplace.

Pousada de São Bartolomeu (☎ 273 331 493, fax 273 323 453; Estrada do Turismo; doubles Mon-Fri €126, Sat & Sun €132) sits alone, 1.5km southeast of the centre, with every comfort and, of course, fine views across to the citadel.

Places to Eat

Restaurants at the *residenciais* **Tulipa** and **Tic-Tac** (see Places to Stay) serve undistinguished, and rather overpriced Portuguese standards as well as some Trás-os-Montes specialities.

Restaurante Poças (☎ 273 331 428; Rua Combatentes de Grande Guerra 200; dishes €6-8; open daily) is an enjoyable place to tuck in, with loads of well-prepared fish and meat dishes (some half-portions too) and polite, relaxed service.

Restaurante O Pote (☎ 273 333 710; Rua Alexandre Herculano 186; dishes €6-10; open Mon-Sat), with a café-bar downstairs and an over-formal restaurant upstairs, specialises in regional dishes.

Adega Mourisca (☎ 273 333 471; Rua Combatentes de Grande Guerra 52; dishes from about €8) has one daily special and other regional dishes made from local, organically raised meat and vegetables – pricey but delicious.

Restaurante O Manel (☎ 273 322 480; Rua Oróbio de Castro 27-29; dishes €9-11; open Mon-Sat) offers excellent food, especially fish and seafood (including €7 half-portion *pratos do dia*), in a calm, bright, simple setting.

Self-caterers will find numerous **mini-mercados** (grocery shops) in the backstreets. It's a long walk to the new **mercado municipal**, behind the *câmara municipal*.

Entertainment

Popular disco/clubs include **Moderno** (Rua Almirante Reis) and **Moda Café** (Avenida Sá Carneiro).

Getting There & Away

Rede Expressos and AV Tâmega bus tickets are sold by the **Sanvitur travel agency** (☎ 273 331 826; Avenida João da Cruz 38; open business hrs Mon-Fri, Sat morning Apr-Oct). Sanvitur, **Rodonorte** (☎ 273 300 183) and **Santos** (☎ 273 326 552) have ticket offices at the bus station, though these tend to open only around arrival or departure times.

Bragança–Miranda do Douro connections are by Santos (€5.30, one each weekday) and Rodonorte (€4.70, three each week-day), the latter from Avenida João da Cruz rather than the bus station. Rede Expressos and Joalto (no Bragança office) each have a daily service via Vila Nova de Foz Côa and Trancoso to Viseu (€10, 3½ hours).

Between them Rede Expressos, Rodonorte and Santos have over a dozen buses daily via Vila Real (€7.30, two hours) to Porto (€8, 3½ hours); Rede Expressos also has some nonstop Porto services. Rodonorte goes via Guimarães to Braga (€9.50, four hours, two to three daily).

Most of the weekend services are less frequent.

Getting Around

STUB (the municipal bus company) has regular connections between the temporary bus station and the town centre. Bus No U2 passes the station ('Zona Desportiva' stop) about 35 minutes past each hour heading to Praça da Sé (€0.80, 30 minutes). To go back, get on at Avenida João da Cruz about 25 minutes past the hour, and off at the station 15 minutes later. A taxi costs about €2.60.

PARQUE NATURAL DE MONTESINHO

Montesinho Natural Park, sticking into Spain in what looks like an annex of Trás-os-Montes, is a modest and quite lived-in protected area with 88 small, lean villages sprinkled across 750 sq km of undulating grassland and deciduous forest. The park embraces two slatey massifs – the lush, wet Serra da Corôa in the west and the Serra de Montesinho in the east.

There have been settlements here for thousands of years; Iron Age foundations, adapted by the Romans, have been found in several places. Many villages bear distinctly Germanic names, conferred by Visigothic settlers. In order to create a sustainable fabric of life in this harsh, remote *terra fria*, early Portuguese rulers established a system of collective land tenure, and communal practices persist today.

The overall population is about 8000, an average of less than 90 souls per village. The park was founded in part to protect and revitalise this fragile social structure, but remote villages continue to be deserted by their young. The main exception is the biggest one, Moimenta, a stepping-stone for many and therefore growing healthily.

Many villages shelter in deep valleys, peaceful gems easily overlooked by the casual visitor. To counter the spread of modern stucco and red-tile construction, government help is offered to those who will restore traditional slate-roofed stone houses, churches, forges, mills and the conspicuous, charming *pombals* (dovecotes). Villages that have successfully retained at least some traditional character include Pinheiro Novo, Sernande, Edroso, Santalha and Moimenta in the west, and Donai, Varge, Rio de Onor and Guadramil in the east.

The natural base from which to explore the park is Bragança. There's some accommodation at Vinhais and villages within the park, though public transport is very limited.

Information

There are park information offices at Bragança (see the Bragança section) and **Vinhais** (☎ 273 771 416; Casa do Povo, Rua Dr Álvaro Leite; open 9am-12.30pm & 2pm-5.30pm Mon-Fri). A free schematic park

PARQUE NATURAL DE MONTESINHO

map is available from both offices. Brochures on flora, archaeology and handicrafts, and a booklet on park walks, are in Portuguese although staff at Bragança are very willing to answer questions.

Flora & Fauna
In vast forests of Iberian oak and chestnut, and among riverside alders, willows, poplars and hazel, there are roe deer, otter and wild boar; in the grasslands are partridge, kite and kestrel. Above 900m the otherwise barren ground is carpeted in heather and broom in spring. And stands of birch grow at the highest elevations of the Serra de Montesinho.

Although huge state plantations of pine mar the park's eastern limb, this and the Serra de Montesinho host the richest diversity of animals. The northeastern corner, along with the adjoining Reserva Nacional de Sierra Culebra on the Spanish side, is the last major refuge for the endangered Iberian wolf (for more on this wolf, see under Flora & Fauna in the Facts about Portugal chapter). Other threatened species found here are the royal eagle and the black stork.

Walking & Mountain Biking
Spring and summer are usually the best times for walking and mountain biking, though visually the park is at its best in the chilly autumn.

There are no trails specifically for self-propelled visitors, though a network of roads and dirt tracks pushes out to the furthest villages. The prettiest areas with the fewest paved roads are the watersheds of the Rio Sabor north of Soutelo and França, and the Rio Tuela between Dine and Moimenta. The park operates some basic shelters in these areas (see Places to Stay & Eat).

The park's own schematic map shows villages, roads and tracks, camp sites and rural accommodation, but not trails. Serious walkers and bikers should talk with staff at the park offices. There are some two dozen military topographic maps that cover the park at 1:25,000, though you can only buy these in Porto or Lisbon (see under Information for those cities).

Park offices also sell a fairly detailed booklet (€2.50) covering a 35km bicycle route in the Moimenta area, and leaflets (€0.50) on two short biking tracks. The

Abrigo do Montanha da Senhora da Hera (see Places to Stay & Eat) has a few bikes for rent (€5/7 per day for guests/nonguests).

Rio de Onor
postcode 5300 • pop 70 • elevation 730m
Little Rio de Onor, 25km northeast of Bragança on the border with the Spanish province of Castilla y León, is one of the park's most interesting villages, not only for its well-preserved stone buildings but also because it has held staunchly to the independent-minded communal lifestyle once typical of the region. Many people still speak an ancient dialect called *mirandês*, descended almost directly from Latin (and in 1999 officially recognised as Portugal's second language).

The border runs through the middle of the village and the Rio Onor trickles along perpendicular to it. The road from Bragança branches left to cross the border and right to cross the river on an old stone bridge, to the prettiest part of the village.

There is no reliable tourist accommodation, nor cafés or restaurants, in the village.

STUB bus No 5A (€1) departs from Avenida João da Cruz in Bragança at about 5.50pm on weekdays but comes right back, so you'd have to stay the night. On schooldays an additional bus departs at about 2pm, which would give you two hours here. A taxi from Bragança costs €17 one way or double that for a return trip with an hour's wait.

Places to Stay & Eat
Camping Found 6km north of Bragança by the Rio Sabor, **Parque de Campismo do Sabor** (☎ 273 331 535; N103-7 Estrada de Rabal; adult/car €1.50/2, tent €1.90-2.50; open May-Sept) is Bragança's flat, featureless but shady and quiet municipal camp site. Facilities include showers, a café and a *minimercado*. You can get there on STUB bus No 7 ('Meixedo'; €1, 17 minutes), departing from Avenida João da Cruz in Bragança about 12.30pm and 1.25pm weekdays and 5.50pm Monday to Saturday. At 2pm and 6pm on school days you can also catch Rodonorte's Bragança–Portelo bus (€1) from the bus station.

Parque de Campismo Cepo Verde (☎ 273 999 371; adult/tent/car €3/1.80/1.80; open Apr-Sept), 12km west of Bragança near Gondesende village, is a medium-sized rural facility with café, pool and lots of shade. Rodonorte's Bragança–Vinhais bus, departing from Bragança's bus station at noon and 5pm on weekdays (€1.30, 20 minutes), stops about 500m away on the N103. Villagers, if asked, may also allow free camping on common land.

Private Rooms & Houses There are a few private rooms, notably at Montesinho (population about 35), 23km from Bragança. In July and August these rooms get booked out but from October to May you needn't book at all. Contact **Dona Maria Rita** (☎ *273 919 229*), **Dona Constância** (☎ *273 919 227*) or **Senhor Antero Pires** (☎ *273 919 248*). A taxi from Bragança to Montesinho costs about €15.

Other places that usually have private rooms include **Café Turismo** (☎ *273 919 163; França*), **Snack Bar O Careto** (☎ *273 919 112; Varge*) and **Restaurante Fraga dos Três Reinos** (☎ *273 649 174; Moimenta*). There's also a house to rent in Rio de Onor (see that section, earlier).

The park operates several basic **casas de retiro** (retreat houses), open year-round and equipped with sheets, blankets and towels, hot water, kitchens, fireplaces and firewood. The four smallest ones are excellent value for money: **Estúdio de Moimenta** (*Moimenta; double €30*); **Casa das Escadas** (*Montouto; twin plus sofa €45*); **Abrigo de Montesinho** (*Montesinho; double or twin €60*); and **Abrigo de Lama Grande** (*twin €40*), northwest of Montesinho. Book well in advance at either park office, with a 50% deposit.

Abrigo de Montanha da Senhora da Hera (☎ *273 999 414; Cova da Lua; doubles/triples €45/60; open Feb-Dec*) is a rambling country house with rooms of all sizes (breakfast included; other meals by arrangement), a pool, and a few bikes for rent – good value and popular, so try to book ahead. It also has a **restaurant** (*meals about €8; open lunch & dinner daily*) with one or two good, home-style dishes; from September to June, book a day ahead. It's 12km from Bragança on the N308. Rodonorte's Mofreita-bound bus stops here (€1.40), departing twice daily from Bragança's bus station.

Getting Around
Exploring the park is hard without a car, bike or sturdy feet. Most tracks marked on

the park map are fire roads, sometimes dicey in bad weather; unsealed 'scenic' routes are marginally better. If you plan to drive on any of them, ask at the park office about current conditions.

Public buses are scarce within the park, especially on weekends, and most don't return the same day. Many school-term services disappear during summer. STUB, Bragança's municipal bus company, has routes close to Bragança; and Rodonorte covers most of the park.

MIRANDELA
postcode 5370 • pop 10,700
• elevation 270m

Mirandela is a down-to-business market town and transport junction, quite literally at the centre of Trás-os-Montes' vast agricultural heartland (cereals, grapes, cherries and vegetables). Historical monuments are few, and tourist development refreshingly minimal, but this is a good place to take the pulse of the province. On the 3rd, 14th or 25th day of the month, the region's hardy farmers stream in to market.

As a tourist you're most likely to pass through en route to/from the Alto Douro via the lovely, narrow-gauge Linha da Tua (see under Pinhão in the Douro chapter for more on this railway line). You can walk the few steps between train and bus stations without seeing Mirandela, but if you've an hour to spare it's worth strolling beside the Rio Tua and having a look at the proud buildings in the old town centre.

Orientation & Information
Rua Dom Afonso III runs in front of the neighbouring train and bus stations. Take it to the right, then right again (north) along the river, to the town's medieval bridge and an adjacent new one. By the old bridge you can either carry on along Rua da República to the turismo and market (about 800m from the train station), or turn right and uphill on Rua Dom Manuel I to the *câmara municipal* and the old town.

The **turismo** (☎ *278 200 272; Jardim do Mercado; open 9.30am-12.30pm & 2pm-6pm Mon-Fri, 10.30am-12.30pm & 2pm-3.30pm Sat*) is at the western end of the *mercado municipal*.

Banks with ATMs are along Rua da República. The **post office** (*Rua Dom Manuel I;*

open 8.30am-12.30pm & 1.30pm-6pm Mon-Fri) is just below the *câmara municipal*.

The **district hospital** (☎ 278 260 500; *Avenida Nossa Senhora do Amparo*) is just across the old bridge, while the **police station** (☎ 278 265 416; *Praça 5 de Outubro*) is four blocks north of the post office.

Things to See & Do

The medieval **Ponte Românica** (Romanesque bridge; 15th century) with 20 arches, each one different, has been put out to pasture as Portugal's most elegant footbridge.

Dom Dinis built a castle and town walls in the 13th century, though all that remains is the **Porta de Santo António**, a low arch of mortared schist a block north of the post office.

Old Mirandela is centred on the *câmara municipal*, in the splendiferous **Palácio dos Távoras** (*Praça do Município*), built in the 17th century for António Luiz de Távora, patron of one of northeast Portugal's powerful aristocratic families. From the same period, but looking pretty down-at-heel, is the **Palácio dos Condes de Vinhais** (*Praça 5 de Outubro*), with its admiral's-hat pediment.

Places to Stay

Parque de Campismo des Três Rios (☎ 278 263 177; *Maravilha*; adult/tent/car €2.80/2.30/2.30, 2-/4-person bungalows €50/65; open year-round), 3km north of the centre on the N15, is a flat, shady, riverside camp site that has a restaurant, *minimercado* and swimming pool.

Pensão Praia (☎ 278 262 497; *Largo 1 de Janeiro 6*; doubles from €25), a creaky old place with small, clean rooms (with shared bathroom) around a skylit atrium, is good value at the budget end.

Pensão O Lagar (☎ 278 262 712; *Rua da República 120*; doubles with breakfast €30) has sparsely furnished rooms (with full bathroom) and a homely, boarding-house atmosphere.

Hotel Mira-Tua (☎ 278 200 140, fax 278 200 143; *Rua da República 38*; doubles with breakfast €45) offers comfortable, nondescript mid-range rooms, but there's traffic noise at the front.

Hotel Dom Dinis (☎ 278 260 100; *Avenida Nossa Senhora do Amparo*; doubles €80), located across the river and between the two bridges, is Mirandela's top-end address.

Places to Eat

There's little to choose from around the *mercado municipal* and the central riverfront. Keep an eye out for fish from the Rio Tua, or the local speciality, *alheira de Mirandela*, a light, garlicky sausage of poultry or game.

Café-Restaurante Jardim (☎ 278 265 720; *Jardim do Mercado*; dishes under €6; open Mon-Sun, closed night Sun), a few steps from the turismo, is popular and frantic at lunch time, and does cheap grills.

Restaurante O Lagar (☎ 278 261 001; *Rua da República 118*; half-portions €4-7) is a small, plain place below the *pensão* of the same name, and has ho-hum regional dishes on offer.

The **mercado municipal** hums along every morning except Sunday, trailing off into the afternoon.

Getting There & Away

Bus REDM/Rede Expressos (☎ 278 265 805), Rodonorte (☎ 278 262 541) and AV Tâmega (☎ 278 265 791) all have multiple daily buses to Bragança (€5.30, 1¼ hours) and to Vila Real (€5, one hour), with Rede Expressos and AV Tâmega continuing on to Porto (€7.60, 2½ hours).

Other weekday services include AV Tâmega to Chaves (€3.30) and Santos (☎ 278 265 471) to Bragança and Miranda do Douro (€6.30).

Train From Mirandela two daily trains take the slow and scenic, narrow-gauge Linha da Tua down to Tua (€2.80, 1½ hours, departing 8.35am and 6.08pm) in the Douro valley; check at the turismo or the **station** (☎ 278 262 517) for current times. The bright green carriages of Mirandela's suburban train, the Metro, were in use on this line at the time of writing, in place of more photogenic but ageing stock. CP also runs a daily bus to Tua, departing around 2.30pm.

The train journey to Porto (€7.10, five to six hours, twice daily) requires a change of trains at both Tua and Peso da Régua.

MIRANDA DO DOURO

postcode 5210 • pop 1960 • elevation 560m

This sleepy town, facing Spain across the Rio Douro gorge in the furthest corner of Trás-os-Montes, is one of Europe's smallest cities – for despite its small population, a 'city' is what history made it. That history is one of Miranda's few present claims to fame.

This is the most easterly town of any size in Portugal, more accessible from Spain than from Portugal, and seemingly populated at any given time by more Spaniards than Portuguese. People here speak the ancient dialect of *mirandês*, as they do across the river in rural Castilla y León.

What is there to see? Views of the Douro canyon, the scattered ruins of a medieval castle, a cathedral without a diocese and a charmingly eclectic ethnographic museum. The cobbled streets of the old town, lined with blindingly whitewashed 15th- and 16th-century houses, echo with the chatter of Spanish tour groups in summer and at the weekends. The region's famous *pauliteiros* (stick-dancers; see the boxed text) are hard to catch.

This town would make a pleasant day trip if it were closer to anywhere else in Portugal. It's possible to see everything in a couple of hours, but the vagaries of public transport make it almost essential for non-drivers to stay longer. Don't come on Monday, when the museum and cathedral are closed.

History
Miranda was an important bulwark during Portugal's first two centuries of independence, and the Castilians had to be chucked out at least twice: in the early days by Dom João I, and in 1710 during the Wars of the Spanish Succession. In 1545, perhaps as a snub to the increasingly powerful House of Bragança, a diocese was created here, an oversized cathedral was built and the town was declared a *cidade* (city).

During a siege by French and Spanish troops in 1762 the castle's powder magazine blew up, pulverising most of the castle, killing 400 people and leaving almost nothing to besiege. Twenty years later, shattered Miranda lost its diocese to Bragança. No-one saw fit to rebuild the castle, and nobody paid much attention to Miranda again until the Barragem de Miranda (dam) was built in the 1950s.

Orientation
Buses stop at Largo da Moagem, a roundabout on the N218. The new town – with handicrafts shops, *pensões*, restaurants and

---

The Pauliteiros

The most high-profile representatives of Trás-os-Montes folk customs are the *Pauliteiros* (stick dancers) of the Miranda do Douro region, who look and dance very much like Britain's Morris dancers – and, say some travellers, like groups as far afield as Peru and Nepal. Local men dress in linen kilts and smocks, black waistcoats, bright flapping shawls, and black hats covered in flowers and ribbons, and do a rhythmic dance to the complex clacking of short wooden sticks (*paulitos*). It looks a bit like a sword dance, from which it may well have descended in Celtic times.

In fact there are at least 10 *Pauliteiros* groups, from villages around Miranda and Sendim. They've gone big time, appearing at major festivals around the region and all over Portugal, and are rarely seen in their home-towns except at local festivals. The best time to catch them in Miranda is during the Festas de Santa Bárbara (also called Festas da Cidade, or City Festival) on the third weekend in August.

---

the *mercado municipal* – is down to the left (northeast).

Uphill (southwest) from the roundabout, past the old walls and castle ruins, are the old town and what was once the citadel. The axis is Rua da Alfândega (also called Rua Mouzinho da Albuquerque), and halfway along is central Praça de Dom João III. On Largo da Sé at the end is the cathedral.

Information
The **turismo** (☎ 273 431 132; *Largo da Moagem; open 9am-12.30pm & 2pm-5.30pm Mon-Sat*) is right on the N218. There are banks with ATMs near the turismo; beside the **post office** (*Largo da Sé; open 9am-12.30pm & 2pm-5.30pm Mon-Fri*) is another.

A **Parque Natural do Douro Internacional office** (☎/fax 273 431 457; *Palácio da Justiça, Rua do Convento; open 9.30am-12.30pm & 2pm-5.30pm Mon-Fri*) is around the block from the cathedral.

Museu de Terra de Miranda
This municipal ethnographic museum (☎ 273 431 164; *Praça de Dom João III; adult/youth 14-25 or senior €1.30/0.70, to 2pm Sun free; open 9.30am-12.30pm & 2pm-6pm Wed-Sun,*

2pm-6pm Tues Apr-Oct; 9am-12.30pm & 2pm-5.40pm Wed-Sun, 2pm-5.40pm Tues Nov-Mar) offers a miscellany of the region's past, laid out with the guilelessness of a school project. Highlights include a *berrão*, 14th- and 15th-century stones with Hebrew inscriptions, rough woollen *mirandês* clothing, and Portuguese and Spanish regional pottery. Best of all is a musty collection of musical instruments, masks and ceremonial costumes.

Old Town
The backstreets in the old town all look alike, save for a few unwhitewashed but dignified 15th-century **facades** on Rua da Costanilha (which runs west off Praça Dom João III) and a **Gothic gate** at the end of it.

The severe **sé** *(cathedral; admission free; open same hrs as Museu de Terra de Miranda)*, dating from the founding of the bishopric in the 16th century, is unremarkable except for its size. Inside is a grand, gilded altarpiece. In a case in one transept stands the arresting Menino Jesus da Cartolinha, a Christ child in a top hat whose wardrobe is bigger than Imelda Marcos', thanks to local devotees.

Behind the cathedral are the roofless remains of the former **Bishop's Palace**, which burned down in the 18th century.

Barragem de Miranda
A road crawls across this 80m-high dam about 1km east of town, and on to Zamora, 55km away in Spain. Even dammed, the gorge is dramatic.

You can take a one-hour boat trip through the gorge (€12) at 4pm daily (plus 11am on weekends) from the **Parque Náutico** (☎ 273 432 396), beside the dam on the Portuguese side.

This is one of five dams on the Rio Douro along the Spanish border, the upper three for use by Portugal. About 20km southwest from here on the N221 is the Barragem de Picote, and 35km away is the Barragem da Bemposta, the latter also a border crossing.

Places to Stay
Parque de Campismo de Santa Luzia *(☎ 273 431 273;* e *mirdouro@mail.telepac.pt; adult/ car €0.50/1, tent €1-1.50; open June-Sept)* is a modest municipal camp site at the end of a residential street, 1.8km west of Largo da

Moagem across the Rio Fresno. Houses nearby advertise **private rooms**.

Rooms at the following are uniformly tidy, spotless and equipped with shower and toilet; all rates include breakfast.

Pensão Vista Bela *(☎/fax 273 431 054; Rua do Mercado 63; big doubles from €35)*, in the new town, is worth the price just to gawp at the view across the gorge. **Hospedaria Flôr do Douro** *(☎ 273 431 186; Rua do Mercado 7)*, up the street from Pensão Vista Bela, has similar rates and views.

Residencial do Planalto Mirandês *(☎ 273 431 362;* e *planalto@esoterica.pt; Rua 1 de Maio 25; doubles €35)*, around the corner from Flôr do Douro, is a bright, functional place; all rooms have balconies.

Pensão Santa Cruz *(☎ 273 431 374, fax 273 431 341; Rua Abade de Baçal 61; doubles €30)*, in the old town off the *largo* by the castle ruins, has pretty rooms and a welcoming atmosphere.

Pousada de Santa Catarina *(☎ 273 431 005, fax 273 431 065; doubles Mon-Fri from €82, Sat & Sun from €89)* practically falls into the gorge from its prime perch, offering unimpeded views and every comfort.

Places to Eat
Most *pensões* have a restaurant of some description, open at lunch and dinner.

Restaurante-Pizzeria O Moinho *(☎ 273 431 116; Rua do Mercado 47D; dishes under €8; open daily)*, one of many new-town spots with Douro views, has salads, pizzas (€4) and Portuguese standards.

Restaurante Balbina *(☎ 273 432 394; Travessa da Misericórdia 5; dishes under €7.50)* is a popular, no-frills place with a good-value lunch-time *ementa turística* (tourist menu) for €6.50, and a good *arroz de marisco* (rich seafood and rice stew).

Restaurante Buteko *(☎ 273 431 231; Rua da Trindade 55; open Mon-Sat)*, upstairs from its ice-cream parlour on Praça de Dom João III, is another good choice.

Getting There & Away
Santos *(☎ 273 432 667)* buses stop beside the turismo; **Rodonorte** *(☎ 273 432 444)* also stops there and at its ticket office on Praça de Dom João III.

Santos' weekday Bragança (€4.65, 1¼ hours) services include one from Miranda via Mogadouro (€5.25, 50 minutes) and one from Vila Nova de Foz Côa (€5.75, 2¼ hours) via the train station at Pocinho (€5.50, two hours) in the Alto Douro. Santos also goes via Mogadouro, Mirandela (€6.25, 2½ hours) and Vila Real (€8, 3¼ hours) to Porto daily except Saturday.

Rodonorte has three buses to Bragança and one via Vila Real to Porto, daily except Saturday.

By car, the quickest road from Bragança is the N218 and N218-2, a winding 80km trip. The 80km route (N216/N221) from Macedo de Cavaleiros via Mogadouro is one of the loveliest – and wiggliest – in Portugal. It crosses a *planalto* (high plain) dotted with olive, almond and chestnut groves, with a dramatic descent into the Rio Sabor Valley.

MOGADOURO
postcode 5200 • pop about 5000
• elevation 750m

This rough-and-ready, sun-bleached agricultural town is on the map because it's home to the headquarters of the Parque Natural do Douro Internacional (see later in this chapter). Little remains of its Celtic and Moorish past, but it's a handy base for visiting the park.

Orientation & Information
Buses stop at the central Largo Trindade Coelho.

The headquarters of the **Park Natural do Douro Internacional** (*☎ 279 340 030;* e *pn di@icn.pt; Rua de Santa Marinha 4*) is at the southwestern end of the *largo*. Also on the *largo* is the **post office** (*open 9am-12.30pm & 2pm-5.30pm Mon-Fri*).

Mogadouro's **turismo** (*☎ 279 343 756; Largo de Santo Cristo; open 9am-12.30pm & 2pm-6pm Mon-Fri*) is on a rise about 600m northeast of the park headquarters. There are several banks with ATMs along Avenida Nossa Senhora do Caminho, on the way to the turismo.

Things to See & Do
The Knights Templar (see the boxed text about this military-religious order, under Tomar in the Estremadura & Ribatejo chapter) built a castle here in the 12th century, part of the effort to drive the Moors out. All that's left are the photogenic remains of a **tower** (*admission free; open daily*) on a hill southwest of the park headquarters.

In the square to the south is a **pelourinho**, probably dating back to the 12th century. To the north is the **igreja matriz**, parts of which date from the 16th century.

Places to Stay & Eat
Restaurante-Residencial A Lareira (*☎ 279 342 363; Avenida Nossa Senhora do Caminho 58*) and **Pensão-Restaurante Russo** (*☎ 279 342 134; Rua 15 de Outubro 10*), between the park headquarters and the turismo, both offer doubles for around €20 to €25, including breakfast.

Hotel Trindade Coelho (*☎ 279 340 010;* e *hotelcoelho@nerba.pt; Largo Trindade Coelho; doubles €43*) offers spacious, spotless rooms with full bathroom and breakfast; some rooms have balconies and big views to the north.

Café-Restaurante Europeu (*☎ 279 343 891; 1st floor, Avenida do Sabor; half-portions from about €3; open daily*), about 200m northeast of the turismo, is the obvious local favourite, a madhouse of hungry regulars eating from a small verbal menu of daily specials.

Getting There & Away
Santos (*☎ 279 342 537; Largo Trindade Coelho*) is Trás-os-Montes' busiest local operator, with mostly weekday buses to Bragança (€5.30, 1½ hours), Miranda do Douro (€2.90, 50 minutes), Vila Nova de Foz Côa (€4.50, 1¾ hours), and via Mirandela (€6.30, 1½ hours) and Vila Real (€7.30, 2½ hours) to Porto (€9.30, 3¾ hours).

From a kiosk at the other end of the Largo Trindade Coelho, Rodonorte has similar services to Miranda do Douro, Mirandela, Vila Real and Porto, and Joalto goes to Vila Nova de Foz Côa once daily except Saturday.

PARQUE NATURAL DO DOURO INTERNACIONAL
Portugal's second-largest protected area (after the Parque Natural da Serra da Estrela) is the 852-sq-km Parque Natural do Douro Internacional, founded in 1998 to protect the monumental geological landscape of the upper Rio Douro where it defines the Portugal-Spain border, and the fragile human landscape of remote Eastern Trás-os-Montes.

In 2002 Spain inaugurated its own 106-sq-km Parque Natural de Arribes del Duero on the other side. Together these two parks line the Douro Canyon (dammed here into a series of silent lakes), and part of the tributary Rio Águeda in the south, for over 120km. The park also includes an EU-designated Special Protection Area (SPA).

The Douro's towering, granitic cliffs are habitat for several threatened bird species, in particular black storks and a host of raptors (birds of prey), including Egyptian vultures, griffon vultures, peregrine falcons, golden eagles and Bonelli's eagles. Indeed this is probably the best place in Portugal to observe large birds of prey. Other breeding species of interest are short-toed eagles, booted eagles, eagle owls, alpine swifts and choughs. Resident mammals include wolves, wild cats and roe deer.

Southward the valley opens and rounds out into a microclimatic zone known as *terra quente*, with mild winters and parching summers – ideal for growing grapes. In fact the park overlaps the Douro Superior zone of Portugal's demarcated port-wine region.

Some 17,000 people live in 46 communities within the park. Their ancestors include convicts banished here in medieval times, and Jews who fled the Spanish and Portuguese Inquisitions. Portugal's now-official 'second language', the ancient dialect of *mirandês*, is still widely spoken in the northern parts of the park.

Orientation & Information

The park's headquarters is in Mogadouro (see earlier in this chapter), with smaller park offices in Miranda do Douro, **Figueira de Castelo Rodrigo** (*☎/fax 271 313 382; Rua Artur Costa 1*) and **Freixo de Espada à Cinta** (*☎/fax 279 658 130; Largo do Outeiro*).

Miranda do Douro and Mogadouro are the easiest places from which to visit the park.

The park headquarters and offices sell a Portuguese-language booklet about the park, a 1:1,500,000 park map (€1), four leaflets (€0.50) on nature trails within the park, a Portuguese-language booklet (€2.50) on the Egyptian vulture (the park's symbol), and *Entre Duas Margens* (Between Two Riverbanks; €30), a handsome hardback packed with information (in Portuguese) on the region's flora, fauna, festivals, food, buildings and language.

Things to See & Do

The finest places to look into this yawning, green 'Grand Canyon of Portugal' – echoing with birdsong and occasionally shadowed by the flights of vultures – are sturdy **viewing platforms** at (north to south, with the nearest village in parentheses): São João das Arribas (Aldeia Nova), Fraga do Puio (Picote), Carrascalinho (Fornos), Penedo Durão (Poiares) and Santo André (Almofala).

You can do **day-walks** to the canyon's edge via these and other villages off the N221 (which runs almost the entire length of the park). In addition there are five marked trails within the park, ranging from 8km to 62km, starting from near Miranda do Douro; Duas Igrejas/Freixo de Espada à Cinta; Lamoso; Poiares/Barca de Alva; and Almofala/Vermiosa. At the time of writing, park leaflets were available for all but the Lamoso walk.

Getting There & Around

The bus company with the most local services to the park's towns and villages is **Santos** (*Freixo de Espada à Cinta ☎ 279 652 188; ⓦ www.santosviagensturismo.pt*).

Language

Nearly all *turismo* (tourist office) staff speak some English. In Lisbon, Porto, most of the Algarve and other big tourist destinations it's fairly easy to find English-speakers, especially among younger people. Some in the service industry (eg, waiters) may insist on showing off their English skills, despite your attempts to stick to Portuguese. Among older folk, and in the countryside, English speakers are rare. In the Minho and other areas where their emigrant workers have spent time abroad, you may find people able to speak French or German.

Using a few Portuguese words and phrases – greetings, the essentials of getting a room and ordering a meal, bus and train timetable basics, plus 'please', 'thank you', 'yes' and 'no' – can transform people's willingness to welcome and help you.

PORTUGUESE

Like French, Italian, Romanian and Spanish, Portuguese is a Romance language, derived from Latin. It's spoken by 10 million Portuguese and 130 million Brazilians, and is the official language of five African nations (Angola, Cape Verde, Guinea-Bissau, Mozambique and São Tomé e Príncipe). In Asia you'll hear it in the former Portuguese territories of Macau and East Timor, and in enclaves around Malaka, Goa, Damão and Diu.

Foreigners are often struck by the strangeness of the spoken language, but those who understand French or Spanish will see how similar written Portuguese is to the other Romance languages.

The pre-Roman inhabitants of the Iberian Peninsula are responsible for the most striking traits of the Portuguese language. The vulgar Latin of Roman soldiers and merchants gradually took over indigenous languages and a strong neo-Latin character evolved.

After the Arab invasion in AD 711, Arabic became the prestige cultural language in the Iberian Peninsula. Its influence on the Portuguese language ended with the expulsion of the Moors in 1249.

During the Middle Ages, Portuguese underwent several changes, mostly influenced by French and Provençal (another Romance language). In the 16th and 17th centuries, Italian and Spanish were responsible for innovations in vocabulary.

For a more detailed practical guide, get a copy of the new edition of Lonely Planet's *Portuguese phrasebook*.

Pronunciation

Pronunciation of Portuguese is difficult; as with English, vowels and consonants have more than one possible sound depending on position and stress. The following list should give you a rough idea of pronunciation, but listening to how local people speak will be your best guide.

Vowels

a	short, as the 'u' in 'cut'; long, as the 'e' in 'her'
e	short, as in 'bet'; longer, as the 'air' in Scottish *laird*; silent at the end of a word and in unstressed syllables
é	short, as in 'bet'
ê	long, as the 'a' in 'gate'
i	long, as in 'marine'; short, as in 'ring'
o	short, as in 'off'; long, as in 'note', or as the 'oo' in 'good'
ô	long, as in 'note'
u	as the 'oo' in 'good'

Nasal Vowels

Nasalisation is represented by **n** or **m** after a vowel, or by a tilde over it (eg, **ã**). The nasal **i** exists only approximately in English, such as the 'ing' in 'sing'. Try to pronounce nasal vowels with your nasal passages open, creating a similar sound to when you hold your nose.

Diphthongs

au	as the 'ow' in 'now'
ai	as the 'ie' in 'pie'
ei	as the 'ay' in 'day'
eu	pronounced together
oi	similar to the 'oy' in 'boy'

Nasal Diphthongs

Try the same technique as for nasal vowels. To say *não*, pronounce 'now' through your nose.

LANGUAGE

ão   nasal 'now' (owng)
ãe   nasal 'day' (eing)
õe   nasal 'boy' (oing)
ui   similar to the 'uing' in 'ensuing'

Consonants

c   before **a**, **o** or **u**, hard as in 'cat'; before **e** or **i**, soft as in 'cell'
ç   as in 'cell'
ch   as the 'sh' in 'ship' (variable)
g   before **a**, **o** or **u**, hard as in 'game'; before **e** or **i**, soft as the 's' in 'treasure'
h   never pronounced at the beginning of a word
nh   as the 'ni' in 'onion'
lh   as the 'll' in 'million'
j   as the 's' in 'treasure'
m, n   not pronounced when word-final; it simply nasalises the previous vowel
qu   before **a** or **o**, as the 'qu' in 'quad' before **e** or **i**, as the 'k' in 'key'
r   at the beginning of a word (or **rr** in the middle of a word) a harsh, guttural sound similar to the 'ch' in Scottish *loch*. In some areas of Portugal it's strongly rolled rather than guttural; in the middle or at the end of a word it's a rolled sound stronger than English 'r'
s   at the beginning of a word, as in 'see'; between vowels, as the 'z' in 'zeal'; before another consonant or at the end of a word, as the 'sh' in 'ship'
ss   as in 'see' (in the middle of a word)
x   as the 'sh' in 'ship', the 'z' in 'zeal', or the 'ks' sound in 'taxi'
z   as the 's' in 'treasure' (before another consonant, or at the end of a word)

Word Stress

Word stress is important in Portuguese, as it can change the meaning of the word. In Portuguese words with a written accent, the stress always falls on the accented syllable.

Gender

In Portuguese, things (as well as people) can be either masculine or feminine, with most masculine nouns ending in **-o** and most feminine ones ending in **-a**. This applies also to words or phrases about a person, with the ending agreeing with the person's gender – for example, *Obrigado/a* (Thank you), or *É casado/a?* (Are you married?).

The only single numbers with gender are 'one' or 'a' (*um* is masculine, *uma* feminine) and 'two' (*dois* is masculine, *duas* feminine).

Endings denoted as **-o/a** in the following sections indicate a choice based on the gender of the speaker or subject.

Basics

Yes/No.	*Sim/Não.*
Maybe.	*Talvez.*
Please.	*Se faz favor/Por favor.*
Thank you.	*Obrigado/a.*
That's fine/ You're welcome.	*De nada.*
Excuse me.	*Desculpe/Com licença.*
Sorry/Forgive me.	*Desculpe.*

Greetings

Hello.	*Bom dia.*
Hi. (informal, among friends)	*Olá/Chao.*
Good morning.	*Bom dia.*
Good evening.	*Boa tarde.*
Goodbye.	*Adeus.*
Bye. (informal)	*Chao.*
See you later.	*Até logo.*

Small Talk

How are you?	*Como está?*
I'm fine, thanks.	*Bem, obrigado/a.*
What's your name?	*Como se chama?*
My name is ...	*Chamo-me ...*
Where are you from?	*De onde é?*

I'm from ...	*Sou de ...*
Australia	*Austrália*
Japan	*Japão*
the UK	*o Reino Unido*
the USA	*os Estados Unidos*

How old are you?	*Quantos anos tem?*
I'm ... years old.	*Tenho ... anos.*
Are you married?	*É casado/a?*
Not yet.	*Aindo não.*
How many children do you have?	*Quantos filhos tem?*
daughter	*filha*
son	*filho*

Useful Adjectives & Adverbs

angry	*zangado*
beautiful	*belo*
better	*melhor*

delicious	*delicioso*
excellent	*excelente*
good	*bom/boa*
happy	*feliz*
hungry	*faminto*
ill	*doente*
lovely	*lindo*
married	*casado/a*
next (in time)	*seguinte or próximo*
one more/another	*mais um(a)*

Language Difficulties

I understand.	*Percebo/Entendo.*
I don't understand.	*Não percebo/entendo.*
Do you speak English?	*Fala inglês?*
Could you please write it down?	*Pode escrever isso, por favor?*

Getting Around

What time does ... leave/arrive?	*A que horas parte/ chega ...?*
the boat	*o barco*
the bus (city)	*o autocarro*
the bus (intercity)	*a camioneta*
the metro	*o metro*
the train	*o combóio*
the tram	*o eléctrico*

Where is the ...?	*Onde é a ...?*
bus stop	*paragem de autocarro*
metro station	*estação de metro*
train station	*estação ferroviária*
tram stop	*paragem de eléctrico*

I want to go to ...	*Quero ir a ...*
How long does it take?	*Quanto tempo leva isso?*
Is this the bus/train to ...?	*E este o autocarro/ combóio para ...?*

I'd like a ... ticket.	*Queria um bilhete ...*
one-way	*simples/de ida*
return	*de ida e volta*
1st class	*de primeira classe*
2nd class	*de segunda classe*

left-luggage office	*o depósito de bagagem*
platform	*cais*
timetable	*horário*

I'd like to hire ...	*Queria alugar ...*
a bicycle	*uma bicicleta*
a car	*um carro*
a motorcycle	*uma motocicleta*
a tour guide	*uma guia intérprete*

Signs

Entrada	**Entrance**
Saída	**Exit**
Empurre/Puxe	**Push/Pull**
Entrada Gratis	**Free Entry**
Turismo	**Tourist Office**
Quartos Livres	**Rooms Available**
Informações	**Information**
Aberto	**Open**
Fechado/ Encerrado	**Closed**
Não Fumadores	**No Smoking**
Posto Da Polícia	**Police Station**
Proíbido	**Prohibited**
Lavabos/WC	**Toilets**
Homens (H)	**Men**
Senhoras (S)	**Women**

Fill it up, please. (ie, the tank)	*Encha a déposito, por favor.*

Directions

How do I get to ...?	*Como vou para ...?*
Is it near/far?	*É perto/longe?*
Go straight ahead.	*Siga sempre a direito/ sempre em frente.*

Turn left ...	*Vire à esquerda ...*
Turn right ...	*Vire à direita ...*
at the traffic lights	*no semáforo/nos sinais de trânsito*
at the next corner	*na próxima esquina*

What ... is this?	*O que ... é isto/ista?*
street/road	*rua/estrada*
suburb	*subúrbia*
town	*cidade/vila*

north	*norte*
south	*sul*
east	*leste/este*
west	*oeste*

Around Town

Where is (a/the) ...?	*Onde é ...?*
(nearest) bank	*o banco (mais próximo)*
city centre	*o centro da cidade/ da baixa*
... embassy	*a embaixada de ...*
exchange office	*um câmbio*
hospital	*o hospital*
hotel	*um hotel*
market	*o mercado*

police station	*o posto da polícia*
post office	*os correios*
public toilet	*os sanitários*
telephone office	*a central de telefones*
toilet	*os lavabos*
tourist office	*o turismo*
What time does it open/close?	*A que horas abre/ fecha?*
I'd like to make a telephone call.	*Quero usar o telefone.*
I'd like to change ...	*Queria trocar ...*
some money	*dinheiro*
travellers cheques	*uns cheques de viagem*

Accommodation

I'm looking for ...	*Procuro ...*
a camp site	*um parque de campismo*
a youth hostel	*uma pousada da juventude*
a guesthouse	*uma pensão (pl pensões)*
a hotel	*uma hotel (pl hotéis)*
Do you have any rooms available?	*Tem quartos livres?*
I'd like to book ...	*Quero fazer una reserva para ...*
a bed	*uma cama*
a cheap room	*um quarto barato*
a single room	*um quarto individual*
a double room	*um quarto de casal/ um quarto de matrimonial*
a twin-bed room	*um quarto de duplo*
a room with a bathroom	*um quarto com casa de banho*
a dormitory bed	*cama de dormitório*
for one night	*para uma noite*
for two nights	*para duas noites*
How much is it ...?	*Quanto é ...?*
per night	*por noite*
per person	*por pessoa*
Is breakfast included?	*O pequeno almoço está incluído?*
Can I see the room?	*Posso ver o quarto?*
Where is the toilet?	*Onde ficam os lavabos (as casas de banho)?*

It's very dirty/ noisy/expensive.	*É muito sujo/ ruidoso/caro.*

Shopping

How much is it?	*Quanto custa?*
Can I look at it?	*Posso ver?*
It's too expensive.	*É muito caro.*
bookshop	*livraria*
chemist/pharmacy	*farmácia*
clothing store	*boutique/confecções*
department store	*magazine*
laundrette	*lavandaria*
market	*mercado*
newsagents	*papelaria*
open/closed (shop or office)	*aberto/encerrado*

Health

Where is ...?	*Onde é ...?*
a hospital	*um hospital*
medical clinic	*um centro de saúde*
I'm ...	*Sou ...*
diabetic	*diabético/a*
epileptic	*epiléptico/a*
asthmatic	*asmático/a*
I'm allergic to ...	*Sou alérgico/a a ...*
antibiotics	*antibióticos*
penicillin	*penicilina*
I need a doctor.	*Preciso um médico.*
I'm pregnant.	*Estou grávida.*
antiseptic	*antiséptico*
aspirin	*aspirina*
condoms	*preservativo*
constipation	*constpaçao*
contraceptive	*anticoncepcional*
diarrhoea	*diarreia*
dizzy	*vertiginoso*
medicine	*remédio/medicamento*
nausea	*náusea*
sanitary napkins	*pensos higiénicos*
tampons	*tampões*

Time & Dates

What time is it?	*Que horas são?*
At what time?	*A que horas?*
When?	*Quando?*
today	*hoje*
tonight	*hoje à noite*
tomorrow	*amanhã*
yesterday	*ontem*
morning/afternoon	*manhã/tarde*

Emergencies

Help!	*Socorro!*
Call a doctor!	*Chame um médico!*
Call the police!	*Chame a polícia!*
Go away!	*Deixe-me em paz!/*
	Vai-te embora! (inf)
I've been raped!	*Fui violada!/*
	Violarem-me!
I've been robbed.	*Fui roubado/a.*
I'm lost.	*Estou perdido/a.*

Monday	*segunda-feira*
Tuesday	*terça-feira*
Wednesday	*quarta-feira*
Thursday	*quinta-feira*
Friday	*sexta-feira*
Saturday	*sábado*
Sunday	*domingo*

Numbers

1	*um/uma*
2	*dois/duas*
3	*três*
4	*quatro*
5	*cinco*
6	*seis*
7	*sete*
8	*oito*
9	*nove*
10	*dez*
11	*onze*
12	*doze*
13	*treze*
14	*catorze*
15	*quinze*
16	*dezasseis*
17	*dezassete*
18	*dezoito*
19	*dezanove*
20	*vint*
21	*vint e um*
22	*vint e dois*
30	*trinta*
40	*quarenta*
50	*cinquenta*
60	*sessenta*
70	*setenta*
80	*oitenta*
90	*noventa*
100	*cem*
101	*cento e um*
123	*cento e vinte e três*

200	*duzentos*
300	*trezentos*
1000	*mil*
2000	*dois mil*
one million	*um milhão (de)*

FOOD

I'm looking for ...	*Ando à procura ...*
food stall	*quiosque de comida/*
	bancada
grocery	*mercearia/*
	minimercado
market	*mercado*
restaurant	*restaurante*
supermarket	*supermercado*
Is service included	*O serviço está incluído*
in the bill?	*na conta?*
I'm a vegetarian.	*Sou vegeteriano/a.*
lunch	*almoço*
counter in bar	*balcão*
or cafe	
bill (check)	*conta*
cover charge for	*couvert*
service	
menu	*ementa*
tourist menu	*ementa turística*
evening dinner	*jantar*
half-portion of a	*meia dose*
dish	
breakfast	*pequeno almoço*
daily special	*prato do dia*

Places to Eat

casa/salão de chá – teahouse
casa de pasto – a casual eatery with cheap, simple meals
cervejaria – (lit: a beer house); also serves food
churrasqueira – (lit: a barbecue or grill); usually a restaurant serving grilled foods
marisqueira – seafood restaurant
pastelaria – pastry and cake shop
tasca – simple tavern, often with rustic decor

Entradas (Starters)

cocktail de gambas	prawn cocktail
salada de atum	tuna salad
omeleta de ...	... omelette
marisco	shellfish
presunto	smoked ham
cogumelos	mushroom

Sopa (Soup)

caldo verde	potato and shredded-cabbage broth
gazpacho	refreshing cold vegetable soup
canja de galinha	chicken broth and rice
sopa à alentejana	bread soup with garlic and poached egg
sopa de legumes	vegetable soup
sopa de feijão verde	green-bean soup

Peixe/Mariscos (Fish/Shellfish)

ameijoas	clams
atum	tuna
bacalhau	dried, salted cod
camarões	shrimp
carapau	mackerel
chocos	cuttlefish
enguia	eel
espadarte	swordfish
gambas	prawns
lagostins	crayfish
lampreia	lamprey (like eel)
linguada	sole
lulas	squid
pargo	sea bream
peixe espada	scabbard fish
pescada	hake
polvo	octopus
robalo	sea bass
salmão	salmon
sardinhas	sardines
savel	shad
truta	trout

arroz de marisco – rich seafood and rice stew
caldeirada – fish stew with onions, potatoes and tomatoes
cataplana – a combination of shellfish and ham cooked in a sealed wok-style pan and typical of the Algarve region

Carne e Aves (Meat & Poultry)

borrego	lamb
bife	steak (not always beef)
cabrito	kid
carne de vaca (assada)	(roast) beef
carneiro	mutton
chouriço	spicy sausage
coelho	rabbit
costeleta	chop
entrecosto	rump steak
fiambre	ham
fígado	liver
frango	young chicken
galinha	chicken
javadi	wild boar
leitão	suckling pig
lombo	fillet of pork
pato	duck
perú	turkey
presunto	smoked ham
salsicha	sausage
tripas	tripe
vaca	beef
vitela	veal

Legumes (Vegetables)

alface	lettuce
alho	garlic
arroz	rice
batatas	potatoes
cebolas	onions
cenouras	carrots
cogumelos	mushrooms
couve	cabbage
couve-flor	cauliflower
ervilhas	green peas
espargos	asparagus
espinafres	spinach
favas	broad beans
feijão	beans
lentilhas	lentils
pepino	cucumber
pimentos	peppers
salada	salad
salada mista	mixed salad

Ovos (Eggs)

cozido	hard boiled
escalfado	poached
estrelado	fried
mexido	scrambled
omeleta	omelette
quente	boiled

Frutas (Fruit)

alperces	apricots
ameixas	plums
amêndoas	almonds
ananás	pineapple
bananas	bananas
figos	figs
framboesas	raspberries
laranjas	oranges
limões	lemons
maças	apples
melões	melons

morangos	strawberries
pêras	pears
pêssegos	peaches
uvas	grapes

Condiments, Sauces & Appetisers

azeite	olive oil
azeitonas	olives
manteiga	butter
pimenta	pepper
piri-piri	chilli sauce
sal	salt

Snacks & Supplements

batatas fritas	French fries
gelado	ice cream
pão	bread
pão integral	wholemeal bread
queijo	cheese
sandes	sandwiches
uma torrada	an order (two pieces) of toast

Cooking Methods

| *assado* | roasted |
| *cozido* | boiled |

ensopada de ...	stew of ...
estufado	stewed
frito	fried
grelhado	grilled
na brasa	braised
no carvão	on coals (charcoal grilled)
no espeto	on the spit
no forno	in the oven (baked)

Drinks

água mineral	mineral water
(com gás)	(sparkling)
(sem gás)	(still)
aguardente	firewater
café	coffee
chá	tea
(com leite)	(with milk)
(com limão)	(with lemon)
sumo de fruta	fruit juice
vinho da casa	house wine
(branco)	(white)
(tinto)	(red)
vinho verde	semi-sparkling young wine

Glossary

See the Food section at the end of the Language chapter for a listing of culinary terms.

aberto – open
abrigo – shelter or shelter-house
adega – cellar, usually wine cellar; also may denote a winery; also a traditional bar or bar-restaurant serving wine from the barrel
Age of Discoveries – the period during the 15th and 16th centuries when Portuguese sailors explored the coast of Africa and finally charted a sea route to India
aguardente – strongly alcoholic 'firewater'
albergaria – upmarket inn
albufeira – reservoir, lagoon
aldeia – village
almoço – lunch
alta or **alto** – upper
alta qualidade – fast deluxe bus
aluga-se quartos – rooms for rent
anta – see *dolmen*
arco – arch
armazém – warehouse
armillary sphere – celestial sphere used by early astronomers and navigators to chart the stars; a common decorative motif used in Manueline architecture and atop *pelourinhos*
arrabalde – outskirts, environs
arraial, arraiais (pl) – street party
artesanato – handicrafts shop
ATM – automated teller machine
avenida – avenue
aviação – airline
azulejo – hand-painted tile, typically blue and white, used to decorate buildings

bagagem – left-luggage office
bairro – town district
baixa or **baixo** – lower
balcão – counter in a bar or café
balneário – health resort, spa
barcos rabelos – colourful boats once used to transport port wine from vineyards
barragem – dam
beco – cul de sac
berrão, berrões (pl) – ancient stone monument shaped like a pig, found mainly in Trás-os-Montes and the adjacent part of Spain
biblioteca – library

bicyclete tudo terrano (BTT) – mountain bike
bilhete diário – day pass

câmara municipal – city or town hall
caderneta – booklet of tickets (train)
Carnaval – Carnival; festival that takes place just before Lent
cartão telefónico – plastic card used in Credifone telephones
casa de abrigo – shelter house (eg, for staff and/or the public in a national/natural park)
casa de banho – toilet (literally bathroom)
casa de fado – fado house; a place (usually a café or restaurant) where people gather to hear *fado* music
casa de hóspedes – boarding house, usually with shared showers and toilets
casa de pasto – casual, cheap eatery
casa de povo – village common house
castelo – castle
castro – fortified hill town
CCI – Camping Card International
Celtiberians – descendants of Celts who arrived in the Iberian Peninsula around 600 BC
centro de acolhimento – lodging centre
centro de comércio – shopping centre
centro de saúde – state-administered medical centre
chegada – arrival (of bus, train etc)
cidade – town or city
citânia – Celtic fortified village
claustro – cloisters
concelho – municipality, council
confeitaria – patisserie or confectionary shop
conta – bill (in a restaurant)
coro alto – choir stalls overlooking the nave in a church
correios – post office
cortes – Portugal's early parliament
couvert – cover charge added to restaurant bill to pay for sundries
CP – Caminhos de Ferro Portugueses (the Portuguese state railway company)
Credifone – card-operated public telephone
cromlech – circle of prehistoric standing stones
cruz – cross

direita – right; abbreviated as D, dir or Dta
distrito – district
dolmen – Neolithic stone tomb (*anta* in Portuguese)
Dom, Dona – honorific titles (like Sir, Madam) given to royalty, nobility and landowners; now used more generally as a very polite form of address
dormidas – sign indicating a rooming house
duplo – room with twin beds

elevador – lift (elevator), funicular
ementa – menu
ementa turística – tourist menu
encerrada or **encerrado** – closed or shut down (eg, for repairs)
entrada – entree/starter or entrance
espigueiros – traditional stone granaries
esplanada – terrace, seafront promenade
esquerda – left; abbreviated as E, esq or Esqa
estação – station (usually train station)
estação de rodoviária – bus station
estacionamento – parking
estalagem – inn; more expensive than an *albergaria*

fado – traditional, melancholy Portuguese style of singing
farmácia – pharmacy
fechada or **fechado** – closed (eg, for the day/weekend or holiday)
feira – fair
férias – holidays, vacation
festa – festival
FICC – Fédération Internationale de Camping et de Caravanning (International Camping and Caravanning Federation)
fortaleza – fortress
FPCC – Federação Portuguesa de Campismo e Caravanismo (Portuguese Camping and Caravanning Federation)
freguesia – parish

gelado – ice cream
GNR – Guarda Nacional Republicana, the national guard (the acting police force in rural towns without PSP police)
gruta – cave

hipermercado – hypermarket
horários – timetables
hospedaria – see *casa de hóspedes*

IC (intercidade) – express intercity train
ICEP – Investimentos, Comércio e Turismo de Portugal, the government's umbrella organisation for tourism
IDD – International Direct Dial
igreja – church
igreja matriz – parish church
ilha – island
infantário – children's daycare centre
IR (interregional) – fairly fast train without too many stops
IVA – Imposto sobre Valor Acrescentado, or VAT (value-added tax)

jantar – evening meal
jardim – garden
jardim municipal – town garden or park
jardim público – public garden or park
judiaria – quarter in a town where Jews were once segregated
junta de turismo – see *turismo*

largo – small square
latifúndios – Roman system of large farming estates
lavabo – toilet
lavandaria – laundry
litoral – coastal
lista – see *ementa*
livraria – bookshop
loggia – covered area or porch on the side of a building
lugar – neighbourhood, place

Manueline – elaborate Gothic/Renaissance style of art and architecture that emerged during the reign of Dom Manuel I in the 16th century
meia dose – half-portion (food)
menir – menhir, a standing stone monument typical of the late Neolithic Age
mercado municipal – municipal market
mesa – table
MFA – Movimento das Forças Armadas, the military group that led the Revolution of the Carnations in 1974
minimercado – grocery shop or small supermarket
miradouro – lookout
Misericórdia – from Santa Casa da Misericórdia (Holy House of Mercy), a charitable institution founded in the 15th century to care for the poor and the sick; usually designates an old building founded by this organisation

moliceiro – high-prowed, shallow-draft boats traditionally used for harvesting seaweed in the estuaries of the Beira Litoral
mosteiro – monastery
mouraria – the quarter where Moors were segregated during and after the Christian *Reconquista*
mudéjar – originally meant a Muslim under Christian rule; also used as an adjective to describe the art and architecture of the mudéjars
museu – museum

obras – repairs

paço – palace
parque de campismo – camp site
parque de merenda – picnic area
parque infantil or **recreio infantil** – playground
partida – departure (of bus, train etc)
pastelaria – pastry or cake shop
Pauliteiro – traditional 'stick dancers' of Trás-os-Montes
pelourinho – stone pillory, often ornately carved; erected in the 13th to 18th centuries as symbols of justice and sometimes as places where criminals were punished
pensão, pensões (pl) – guesthouse, the Portuguese equivalent of a bed and breakfast (B&B), though breakfast is not always served
pequeno almoço – breakfast, traditionally just coffee and a bread roll
percurso pedestre – walking route
planalto – high plain
pombal – dovecote, a structure for housing pigeons
portagem – toll road
posto de turismo – see *turismo*
pousada or **Pousada de Portugal** – government-run scheme of upmarket inns, often in converted castles, convents or palaces
pousada da juventude – youth hostel; usually with kitchen, common rooms and sometimes rooms with private bath
praça – square
praça de touros – bullring
praia – beach
prato do dia – daily special, dish of the day

pré-pagamento – prepayment required (as in some café-restaurants)
PSP – Polícia de Segurança Pública, the local police force

quarto de casal – room with a double bed
quarto individual – single room
quarto particular or just **quarto** – room in a private house
quinta – country estate or villa; in the Douro wine-growing region it often refers to a wine lodge's property

R (regional) – slow train
Reconquista – Christian reconquest of Portugal (718–1249)
rés do chão – ground floor (abbreviated as R/C)
residencial, residenciais (pl) – guesthouse; slightly more expensive than a *pensão* and usually serving breakfast
ribeiro – stream
rio – river
romaria – religious pilgrimage
rua – street

sanitários – public toilets
sapataria – shoe shop
sé – cathedral
selos – stamps
sem chumbo – unleaded (petrol)
serra – mountain, mountain range
solar – manor house
supermercado – supermarket

tabacaria – tobacconist-cum-newsagent
talha dourada – gilded woodwork
termas – spa
torre de menagem – castle tower, keep
tourada – bullfight
troco – change (money)
Turihab – short for Turismo Habitação, a scheme for marketing private accommodation (particularly in northern Portugal) in cottages, historic buildings and manor houses
turismo – tourist office

vila – town
vindima – grape harvest
vinho da casa – house wine
vinho verde – semisparkling young wine

Thanks

Many thanks to the travellers who used the last edition and wrote to us with helpful hints, useful advice and interesting anecdotes:

Sonia Afonso, Marisa Alexandra, Kate Anderson, Lori Anderson, Christian Appel, Jeff Ardis, Laurence Auffret, Ian Barnard, Thomas Baumeister, Amir Bergman, Mauricio Bergstein, Olav Bol, Juliet Bothams, Barbara Brown, Geoff Brown, Dr Olivier Brunel, Silvia Bruno, Ian Buchanan, David Carnegie, Louise Carnegie, Luigi Ceccarini, Andrew Chick, Jason Christie, Yossi Cohen, Jennifer Comerford, Lucy Cooper, Kim Dorin, Lynn Davies, Ben De Pauw, Susan Del Gobbo, Colleen Densmore, J Dietschi, Peter Drake, Catherine Early, Ana Sofia e Guilherme, Michael Feil, Jorge Andres Ferrando, Teodor Flonta, Ines Fontes, Lorenza Fonzari, Liz Foulis, Joao fraga, Marcelo Gameiro de Moura, Elizabeth Garber, John Gillett, Sabrina Giudici, Clara Gomes, Fransisco Goncalves, Joost Groen, Jean Graupman, Paul Grayhurst, Mike Gwyther, Fleur Hadden, Jeremy Han, Karina Hansen, Mike Harries, J Harris, Jennifer Harry, Richard Harvey, Bruce Hawker, Christine Henderson, David Hoare, Lars Christian-Holmsen, Dorte Hvidemose, Mary Jennision, Nick Kanellias, Emilio Kapodistrias, Vlasta Kappus, Ravi Kapur, Caroline Van Kessel, Christoph Kessel, Omar Khan, Eva Korcz, Mihaly Kovacs, Mats Kullstedt, Mark Lambert, Eva Lefevere, Ethan Lincoln, Andez Macleod, Bruce MacRae, Sean Maher, Edith Maker, Fay Mander-Jones, Frauke Manninga, 'Alfredo Marques, Roy Marques, Irene Martin, Steve Martin, Dalia Mateus, Michelle Matsui, Karsten Matzen, Frank McClintock, David & Valerie McKay, Jon Mckenzie, Karen Mealer, Loyal Mealer, Jordan Medenthall, Vibecke Mehn-Andersen, Connie Menting, Lucia Miele, Marina Mogli, Al Morrison, Tim Mueller, Tess Ng, Maria Mejer Nielsen, Petr Necas, Beryl Nicholson, Ed O'Brian, Ricardo Oliveira, Desiree O'Neill, Gustavo Orlanda-Zon, Ros Osbourne, Roger Peake, Tammy Pearce, LaMont Powell, Millie Powell, Barry & Liz Preston, Helen Proudley, Suzy Provost, Thomas Rau, Graham Rinzai, Sue Roddick, Andrea Rogge, Bjarne Rosted, Andreas Ruefenacht, Julie Sanders, Sandra Santos, Luis Antonio Santos, Nelly Schipper, Friedhelm Schuetter, Oliver Selwyn, Jack Semple, Brigado Serrano, Darren Sharma, Byron Sharp, Rita Simoes, Saso Skalic, Margot Smith, Boone Spooner, Michael Stringer, Philip Stynen, Emanuela Tasinato, Joao Read Teixeira Beato, Susanne Thurnay, Jill Toft-Hansen, Heidi Tsao, Margreet van der Ham, Mary Lou Van Handle, Tom Van Steenbrugge, Koen Van Treeck, Patrick Vandermeulen, J D R Vernon, Marjo Vepsa, Willy Visser, Fotis Vlachos, Isabel Walker, Svenja Walther, Anne Ward, R Watts, Viktor Weisshaeupl, Peter Wheeler, Jorgen Wide, Claus Winterscheid, John Wood, Karven Wong, Alan Wright, Clare Wright, Joachim Wuttke, Wendy Young, Manon Ziech

LONELY PLANET

Guides by Region

Lonely Planet is known worldwide for publishing practical, reliable and no-nonsense travel information in our guides and on our Web site. The Lonely Planet list covers just about every accessible part of the world. Currently there are 16 series: Travel guides, Shoestring guides, Condensed guides, Phrasebooks, Read This First, Healthy Travel, Walking guides, Cycling guides, Watching Wildlife guides, Pisces Diving & Snorkeling guides, City Maps, Road Atlases, Out to Eat, World Food, Journeys travel literature and Pictorials.

AFRICA Africa on a shoestring • Botswana • Cairo • Cairo City Map • Cape Town • Cape Town City Map • East Africa • Egypt • Egyptian Arabic phrasebook • Ethiopia, Eritrea & Djibouti • Ethiopian Amharic phrasebook • The Gambia & Senegal • Healthy Travel Africa • Kenya • Malawi • Morocco • Moroccan Arabic phrasebook • Mozambique • Namibia • Read This First: Africa • South Africa, Lesotho & Swaziland • Southern Africa • Southern Africa Road Atlas • Swahili phrasebook • Tanzania, Zanzibar & Pemba • Trekking in East Africa • Tunisia • Watching Wildlife East Africa • Watching Wildlife Southern Africa • West Africa • World Food Morocco • Zambia • Zimbabwe, Botswana & Namibia
Travel Literature: Mali Blues: Traveling to an African Beat • The Rainbird: A Central African Journey • Songs to an African Sunset: A Zimbabwean Story

AUSTRALIA & THE PACIFIC Aboriginal Australia & the Torres Strait Islands •Auckland • Australia • Australian phrasebook • Australia Road Atlas • Cycling Australia • Cycling New Zealand • Fiji • Fijian phrasebook • Healthy Travel Australia, NZ & the Pacific • Islands of Australia's Great Barrier Reef • Melbourne • Melbourne City Map • Micronesia • New Caledonia • New South Wales • New Zealand • Northern Territory • Outback Australia • Out to Eat – Melbourne • Out to Eat – Sydney • Papua New Guinea • Pidgin phrasebook • Queensland • Rarotonga & the Cook Islands • Samoa • Solomon Islands • South Australia • South Pacific • South Pacific phrasebook • Sydney • Sydney City Map • Sydney Condensed • Tahiti & French Polynesia • Tasmania • Tonga • Tramping in New Zealand • Vanuatu • Victoria • Walking in Australia • Watching Wildlife Australia • Western Australia
Travel Literature: Islands in the Clouds: Travels in the Highlands of New Guinea • Kiwi Tracks: A New Zealand Journey • Sean & David's Long Drive

CENTRAL AMERICA & THE CARIBBEAN Bahamas, Turks & Caicos • Baja California • Belize, Guatemala & Yucatán • Bermuda • Central America on a shoestring • Costa Rica • Costa Rica Spanish phrasebook • Cuba • Cycling Cuba • Dominican Republic & Haiti • Eastern Caribbean • Guatemala • Havana • Healthy Travel Central & South America • Jamaica • Mexico • Mexico City • Panama • Puerto Rico • Read This First: Central & South America • Virgin Islands • World Food Caribbean • World Food Mexico • Yucatán
Travel Literature: Green Dreams: Travels in Central America

EUROPE Amsterdam • Amsterdam City Map • Amsterdam Condensed • Andalucía • Athens • Austria • Baltic States phrasebook • Barcelona • Barcelona City Map • Belgium & Luxembourg • Berlin • Berlin City Map • Britain • British phrasebook • Brussels, Bruges & Antwerp • Brussels City Map • Budapest • Budapest City Map • Canary Islands • Catalunya & the Costa Brava • Central Europe • Central Europe phrasebook • Copenhagen • Corfu & the Ionians • Corsica • Crete • Crete Condensed • Croatia • Cycling Britain • Cycling France • Cyprus • Czech & Slovak Republics • Czech phrasebook • Denmark • Dublin • Dublin City Map • Dublin Condensed • Eastern Europe • Eastern Europe phrasebook • Edinburgh • Edinburgh City Map • England • Estonia, Latvia & Lithuania • Europe on a shoestring • Europe phrasebook • Finland • Florence • Florence City Map • France • Frankfurt City Map • Frankfurt Condensed • French phrasebook • Georgia, Armenia & Azerbaijan • Germany • German phrasebook • Greece • Greek Islands • Greek phrasebook • Hungary • Iceland, Greenland & the Faroe Islands • Ireland • Italian phrasebook • Italy • Kraków • Lisbon • The Loire • London • London City Map • London Condensed • Madrid • Madrid City Map • Malta • Mediterranean Europe • Milan, Turin & Genoa • Moscow • Munich • Netherlands • Normandy • Norway • Out to Eat – London • Out to Eat – Paris • Paris • Paris City Map • Paris Condensed • Poland • Polish phrasebook • Portugal • Portuguese phrasebook • Prague • Prague City Map • Provence & the Côte d'Azur • Read This First: Europe • Rhodes & the Dodecanese • Romania & Moldova • Rome • Rome City Map • Rome Condensed • Russia, Ukraine & Belarus • Russian phrasebook • Scandinavian & Baltic Europe • Scandinavian phrasebook • Scotland • Sicily • Slovenia • South-West France • Spain • Spanish phrasebook • Stockholm • St Petersburg • St Petersburg City Map • Sweden • Switzerland • Tuscany • Ukrainian phrasebook • Venice • Vienna • Wales • Walking in Britain • Walking in France • Walking in Ireland • Walking in Italy • Walking in Scotland • Walking in Spain • Walking in Switzerland • Western Europe • World Food France • World Food Greece • World Food Ireland • World Food Italy • World Food Spain **Travel Literature:** After Yugoslavia • Love and War in the Apennines • The Olive Grove: Travels in Greece • On the Shores of the Mediterranean • Round Ireland in Low Gear • A Small Place in Italy

LONELY PLANET

You already know that Lonely Planet produces more than this one guidebook, but you might not be aware of the other products we have on this region. Here is a selection of titles that you may want to check out as well:

Portugese phrasebook
ISBN 1 86450 225 8
US$7.95 • UK£4.50

Europe phrasebook
ISBN 1 86450 224 X
US$$8.99 • UK£4.99

Spain
ISBN 1 74059 337 5
US$17.99 • UK£12.99

Lisbon
ISBN 1 86450 127 8
US$14.99 • UK£8.99

World Food Portugal
ISBN 1 86450 111 1
US$13.99 • UK£8.99

Western Europe
ISBN 1 74059 313 8
US$27.99 • UK£16.99

Mediterranean Europe
ISBN 1 74059 302 2
US$27.99 • UK£16.99

Europe on a shoestring
ISBN 1 74059 314 6
US$24.99 • UK£14.99

Available wherever books are sold

Index

Bold indicates maps.

Bold indicates maps.

Boxed Text

Bold indicates maps.

MAP LEGEND

CITY ROUTES

Freeway	Freeway
Highway	Primary Road
Road	Secondary Road
Street	Street
Lane	Lane
	On/Off Ramp

	Unsealed Road
	One Way Street
	Pedestrian Street
	Stepped Street
	Tunnel
	Footbridge

REGIONAL ROUTES

	Tollway, Freeway
	Primary Road

	Secondary Road
	Unsealed Road

BOUNDARIES

	International
	Autonomous Community
	Province
	Fortified Wall

TRANSPORT ROUTES & STATIONS

	Local Railway
	Underground Rlwy
	Subway, Station
	Lightrail Tram

	Cable Car, Chairlift
	Ferry
	Walking Tour
	Path

HYDROGRAPHY

	River, Creek
	Lake
	Spring; Rapids
	Waterfalls

AREA FEATURES

	Building
	Park, Gardens
	Market
	Sports Ground
	Beach
	Cemetery
	Plaza
	Swamp

POPULATION SYMBOLS

◎ CAPITAL	National Capital	● City	City
◉ CAPITAL	Provincial Capital	● Town	Town

● Village	Village		Urban Area

MAP SYMBOLS

♠	Place to Stay
▼	Place to Eat
●	Point of Interest

✈ Airport		Fado House		Museum		Stately Home
⊖ Bank		Fountain		Parking		Shopping Centre
Bus Terminal		Golf Course	)(	Pass		Swimming Pool
Cable Car, Funicular	✚	Hospital		Police Station		Telephone
Church		Internet Cafe		Post Office		Theatre
Cinema		Lookout		Pub or Bar	●	Tourist Information
Embassy, Consulate	▲	Monument		Ruins		Zoo

Note: not all symbols displayed above appear in this book

LONELY PLANET OFFICES

Australia
Locked Bag 1, Footscray, Victoria 3011
☎ 03 8379 8000 fax 03 8379 8111
email: talk2us@lonelyplanet.com.au

UK
10a Spring Place, London NW5 3BH
☎ 020 7428 4800 fax 020 7428 4828
email: go@lonelyplanet.co.uk

USA
150 Linden St, Oakland, CA 94607
☎ 510 893 8555 TOLL FREE: 800 275 8555
fax 510 893 8572
email: info@lonelyplanet.com

France
1 rue du Dahomey, 75011 Paris
☎ 01 55 25 33 00 fax 01 55 25 33 01
email: bip@lonelyplanet.fr
www.lonelyplanet.fr

World Wide Web: www.lonelyplanet.com *or* AOL keyword: lp
Lonely Planet Images: www.lonelyplanetimages.com